VILLAGE ON THE EUPHRATES

A. M. T. Moore
G. C. Hillman
A. J. Legge

With contributions by
J. Huxtable, M. Le Mière, T. I. Molleson, D. de Moulins,
S. L. Olsen, D. I. Olszewski,
V. Roitel, P. A. Rowley-Conwy, & G. Willcox

OXFORD
UNIVERSITY PRESS

2000

OXFORD
UNIVERSITY PRESS

Oxford New York
Athens Auckland Bangkok Bogotá Buenos Aires Calcutta
Cape Town Chennai Dar es Salaam Delhi Florence Hong Kong Istanbul
Karachi Kuala Lumpur Madrid Melbourne Mexico City Mumbai
Nairobi Paris São Paulo Shanghai Singapore Taipei Tokyo Toronto Warsaw

and associated companies in
Berlin Ibadan

Published by Oxford University Press, Inc.
198 Madison Avenue, New York, New York 10016

Library of Congress Cataloging-in-Publication Data
Moore, A. M. T. (Andrew M. T.)
Village on the Euphrates : from foraging to farming at Abu Hureyra /
A. M. T. Moore, G. C. Hillman, A. J. Legge : with
contributions by J. Huxtable . . . [et al.].
p. cm.
Includes bibliographical references and index.
ISBN 0-19-510806-X ; 0-19-510807-8
1. Abu Hureyra, Tell (Syria) 2. Neolithic period—Syria.
3. Excavations (Archaeology)—Syria. 4. Syria—Antiquities.
I. Hillman, Gordon C. II. Legge, A. J. (Anthony J.) III. Title.
GN776.32.S95M66 1998
939'.43—dc21 98-2893

9 8 7 6 5 4 3 2 1

Printed in the United States of America
on acid-free paper

Preface

Abu Hureyra is one of the few archaeological sites in the world to have revealed the remains of a settlement of hunters and gatherers that developed into a village of early farmers. That, together with the great size and excellent preservation of the site, and its location in a region where agriculture began earlier than anywhere else, gives it extraordinary significance. This book is an account of the excavation of Abu Hureyra and of the results of our research on its remains. Our main interest throughout has been the sequence of cultural development of the two settlements at Abu Hureyra, and what the site has to tell us about the transition from foraging to farming.

The project began as a salvage excavation, since Abu Hureyra was to be flooded by the construction of a dam across the Euphrates River. The site was so important, however, that from the beginning we conceived of the excavation as an exercise in research that should be conducted to the highest prevailing standards. We devised an excavation plan, beginning a year in advance of the dig itself, that encompassed not only the placing of our trenches but also appropriate methods of systematic recovery of artifacts and organic remains. We assembled our team of specialists and prepared an outline plan for the subsequent study of the site and preliminary publication of our results well before starting fieldwork. Our principal objectives in the excavation were to determine the sequence of occupation and to reconstruct the economy of the site. We established the outline of the cultural sequence during our first season of excavation and continued to fill in the details in subsequent analysis. This outline provided the framework for all our subsequent research, yet once achieved it ceased to be the principal focus of our attention. We found that the enormous quantities of organic remains and artifacts we had recovered enabled us to investigate economic, social, and environmental changes at Abu Hureyra in unprecedented detail. We could trace them through the entire span of occupation thanks to tight control of the exemplary stratification of the site and an unusually precise chronology determined through radiocarbon dating.

Wherever possible, we have tried to reach beyond considerations of cultural sequences and economy to reconstruct the lives of the people themselves, the regularities of their seasonal round, and something of their life histories. We have tried to remember always that our task should be to explore the world of the people who lived at Abu Hureyra.

We have brought our observations and interpretations of the stratification, artifacts, economy, human remains, and environment together in this book to construct an integrated account of the development of Abu Hureyra. Our aim is to present a comprehensive statement that not only describes what we found but also explains our view of the meaning and significance of the site and of the momentous changes that took place there. Such an encompassing statement of one site and its place in prehistory is rare in modern archaeology. It is our hope that this account will stand as a definitive interpretation for some time to come, but it cannot be the final word on the subject. Our studies on the abundant record of the excavation and its material remains continue, as do those of others. Thus, we anticipate that more analyses of the evidence will be published in the years ahead.

The sheer quantity of material we recovered required lengthy study, but its importance and quality called for special attention. Accordingly, we began a series of research projects on it that are now sufficiently far advanced for us to bring the results together in this book. Looking back, it has all taken a long time to accomplish, but there were several special factors that slowed progress. One was the advances in analytical techniques that enabled us to explore questions thought to be beyond our grasp at the beginning, and another was our growing realization that each element of the remains was intimately related to the others. We had to undertake a detailed investigation of those connections in order to construct a comprehensive account of the development of the site and of the transformation in the way of life of its inhabitants.

These aims have determined the structure of the book. In part I we introduce our subject by describing the circumstances of the project and the nature of the site; we discuss the theoretical considerations that underlay the research, and we explain how we dug Abu Hureyra. In chapter 3 we describe in detail the setting of the site, present and past, giving special attention to changes in climate, flora, and fauna, since an understanding of these factors is essential for interpreting the record of the excavation. Part II begins with a brief chapter describing the methods of excavation and interpretation that we used at Abu Hureyra, continuing with a description of the village of Abu Hureyra 1, an analysis of the artifacts we recovered from it, and a discussion of its chronology. Chapter 7 concludes with a review of the culture of this settlement and its place in the region's prehistory. In part III we discuss the village of Abu Hureyra 2, its excavation and chronology, the nature of its buildings, and the layout of the settlement. Chapters 10 and 11 are devoted to a discussion of the burials, inferences about the ideology of the inhabitants that may be derived from them, and the study and interpretation of the human skeletons.

Our analysis of the plant and animal remains, and the information to be obtained from them concerning the economy, is contained in part IV. It is here that we consider in detail the transformation of Abu Hureyra from a settlement of hunter-gatherers to a village of farmer-herders. We analyze the extraordinary evidence that suggests this fundamental transformation in human existence took place earlier there than anywhere else so far recorded. Here, as in several other chapters, we have kept description of the methods of analysis we have used to a minimum in order not to burden the text, preferring to give references to the standard accounts of them available elsewhere.

The book concludes in part V with two chapters that draw the preceding discussions together to present our comprehensive, integrated interpretation of Abu Hureyra. Chapter 14 concentrates on the site itself and elucidates its sequence of habitation and the changes in the way of life of the people who lived there. It is in this chapter that we have gathered much of what we wish to say about our understanding of how Abu Hureyra developed. The final chapter places Abu Hureyra in its regional setting and links the changes there to the transition from hunting and gathering to farming across Western Asia.

The book is the result of a close collaboration among the three of us that began more than a quarter of a century ago, in 1971. It reflects our considered views, matured over many years, as we have explored, and sometimes rejected, a variety of possible interpretations of the evidence. Several colleagues have carried out analyses of different categories of material that have become an essential part of our understanding of the site, and their accounts are included here. We have composed the book in such a way, however, that it may be read as a continuous narrative from beginning to end. We have included summaries of sections of the text and individual chapters in order to provide markers to guide our readers. Throughout, we have endeavored to use a direct prose style and have kept technical terms to a minimum. In this way we have tried to construct a straightforward account that may be understood by the widest possible readership.

Together, we have written part I, chapter 4 in part II, and part V. Moore has composed chapters 5 and 7–9, and chapter 10 with T. I. Molleson. In chapter 6, D. I. Olszewski discusses the chipped stone and S. L. Olsen describes the bone artifacts. T. I. Molleson has written chapter 11 and also appendix D. Hillman has composed chapter 12, with a section by D. de Moulins on the plant remains from Abu Hureyra 2. Legge and P. A. Rowley-Conwy have written chapter 13. J. Huxtable has prepared the note on thermoluminescence dating of sherds in appendix A, and M. Le Mière discusses her analyses of pottery and plaster in appendix C. Finally, in appendix E, V. Roitel and G. Willcox present their studies of charcoal from Abu Hureyra 1.

Our analyses have produced a large body of primary information about the site and its contents that we have drawn upon to write this book. These data—principally tables of levels and inventories of artifacts, burials, and organic remains—form a considerable archive that will be of limited interest to many of our readers and would be expensive and burdensome to publish as appendices to this book. That information needs to be made available, however, to students of the subjects explored here who may wish to verify our conclusions and to perform their own analyses. We have chosen to compile an archive of such data using electronic means of storage that may be readily opened and downloaded from anywhere in the world by anyone who has access to a computer and a modem (the electronic address is http://www.rit.edu/abuhureyra). To ensure that these records will always be available, we shall place printed copies of them in the archives of the Syrian antiquities authorities and the major institutions that have supported the project.

The book contains an account of virtually everything that we found in Abu Hureyra 1, and selected studies of Abu Hureyra 2. We expect to publish more information about Abu Hureyra 2 in due course. Research continues on the artifacts, human remains, animal bones, and seeds, while we anticipate that new chronological problems will arise as we pursue fresh questions about the site. As more information becomes available, the circle of those engaged on research into the record from Abu Hureyra will widen.

But we have kept our readers waiting long enough. Abu Hureyra contained a remarkable record of human life spanning several millennia and one of the fundamental transformations in human existence. It has been our privilege to dig the site and to analyze its remains. We have tried to present a true record of what we found, and to interpret it honestly in order to arrive at a proper understanding of its significance. We continue to be astonished at the richness of the evidence we were able to recover. It is thus with a poignant sense of loss that we reflect on the now inaccessible information contained within the vast bulk of the site covered by the waters of the new lake in the Euphrates Valley.

Advent 1998

Andrew Moore
Gordon Hillman
Anthony Legge

Acknowledgments

We express our deep gratitude to the staff of the Directorate General of Antiquities and Museums of the Syrian Arab Republic for their invitation to excavate Abu Hureyra and their continued support during the subsequent lengthy period of analysis and publication. Particular thanks are due to Dr. Adnan Bounni, Director of Excavations, who invited us to go the Euphrates Valley to choose a site and gave his personal support to the project thereafter, and to the then Director General, Dr. Afif Bahnassi, for his continued interest. We thank the successive directors of the National Museum in Aleppo for their help: Mr. Mahmud Hreitani, Mr. Shawki Shaath, and Dr. Wahid Khayata. The representatives of the Directorate General who accompanied us into the field, Radwan Sharaf, Majid Musli, and Mohammed Muslim, gave us every assistance.

Our success in the field owed much to the devoted and skilled labor of our workers from the village of Abu Hureyra. We express our particular thanks to our teams of students and specialists in both excavation seasons:

1972: Barbara Moore, assistant director and conservator, Thomas Holland; Suzanne Howe; Leon Marfoe; Peter Parr; Ann Stedman, registrar; Donald Whitcomb; David Williams.

1973: Barbara Moore, assistant director and conservator; Anthony Allen, photographer; Alison Betts; Benjamin Branch; Catherine Brooks; Thomas Davidson; Clifford Denham; Elizabeth Downie; John Kilvington; Susan Leppard; Dianna Leslie; Photini McGeorge; Neil Roberts; Charles Sachs; Deborah Sachs; Colin Taylor, surveyor; Valerie Thomas.

We are obliged to the Warrington Museum for releasing Colin Taylor from his duties to join the excavation as our surveyor.

The institutional sponsors of the excavation were the Pitt Rivers Museum of the University of Oxford and, in the first season, the Oriental Institute of the University of Chicago. In addition to the sponsors, the following contributed the funds that enabled us to dig the site: the Birmingham City Museum and Art Gallery; Bolton Museum and Art Gallery; the British Academy; British

Museum; City of Liverpool Museum; Manchester University Museum; Royal Ontario Museum, Toronto; the Russell Trust; the Ashmolean Museum, Wainwright Fund, Meyerstein Fund, and University College, University of Oxford; Miss A. C. Western, and several anonymous donors. We are most grateful to them all.

In the years since the conclusion of the excavation, numerous public and private institutions, foundations, and individuals have contributed further, often substantial, funds to the project. They include the National Endowment for the Humanities, Washington, D.C.; the British Government's Natural Environment Research Council, and Science and Engineering Research Council; the Gwynn-Vaughan Trust; the Leverhulme Trust; the University of Arizona; Yale University; the Archaeological Associates of Greenwich, Connecticut; the Cotsen Family Foundation; Dr. Ernestine Elster; Mrs. Gertrude Howland; and a number of anonymous donors.

The project has benefited much over the years from the strong support of numerous institutions across the world. We acknowledge here, in addition to those mentioned above, the following: the British Institute of Archaeology at Ankara; the Research Laboratory of the British Museum; L'Institut Français de Beyrouth, its sometime director, the late Professor Daniel Schlumberger, and Mme Schlumberger, and its former secretary, the late M. Henri Abdelnour; L'Institut Français d'Etudes Arabes, Damascus, and especially its director at the time of the excavation, Professor André Raymond, and Mme Raymond; the International Center for Agricultural Research in the Dry Areas (ICARDA), Aleppo; La Maison Orientale, Lyon; the Natural History Museum, London; the University of Cambridge; the University of London, especially the Centre for Extra-Mural Studies, Birkbeck College, and the Institute of Archaeology, University College; and at the University of Oxford, the Donald Baden Powell Quaternary Research Centre, and its head, Dr. Derek Roe, the Research Laboratory for Archaeology and the History of Art and its staff, especially Dr. Robert Hedges, Dr. Rupert Housley, and Dr. Paul Pettitt, and Wolfson College.

It is with a special sense of gratitude that we honor two people here who gave the project their strong backing in the crucial initial stages, the late Bernard Fagg, curator of the Pitt Rivers Museum, and the late Dame Kathleen Kenyon, principal of St. Hugh's College, Oxford. We thank M. Henri de Contenson for introducing Moore to Syrian prehistory, and our many friends in Aleppo who offered unlimited hospitality and friendship, especially the late Mr. Krikor Mazloumian, Mrs. Sally Mazloumian, and their family.

Numerous other friends and colleagues in Syria, Britain, and North America have provided us with significant assistance and advice, too many to mention individually. We do, however, wish to record the particular help of Dr. Susan Colledge, archaeobotany; Dr. Afif Dakermanji of ICARDA for cooperation in botanical field studies; Jeanne Ferris, editing; Dr. David Hill for assistance with matters of surveying and draftsmanship; Elizabeth Lattanzi, secretarial help; Thomas Moore, editing; Dr. Frederick Pough, stone and mineral identifications; and students of the Centre for Extra-Mural Studies, University of London, especially Phoebe and John Williams, Patricia Stevens, and Myrtle Kyllo, for aid in sorting human and animal bones.

Most of the photographs were taken by Anthony Allen; Richard Anderson took the aerial photograph of Abu Hureyra; Rupert Cook drew the frontispiece and reconstructions of dwellings in the villages of Abu Hureyra 1 and 2; Lorraine

Copeland drew the flints; Ivan Crowe drew the reconstructions of plant processing; Armand Morgan drew the animal vignettes; Brigid Sullivan drew many of the artifacts; Colin Threadgall drew the illustration of injuries incurred using a saddle quern; Douglas Williamson drew several of the maps; and Barbara Moore drew most of the sections and plans.

We extend our profound thanks to all those mentioned here.

Contents

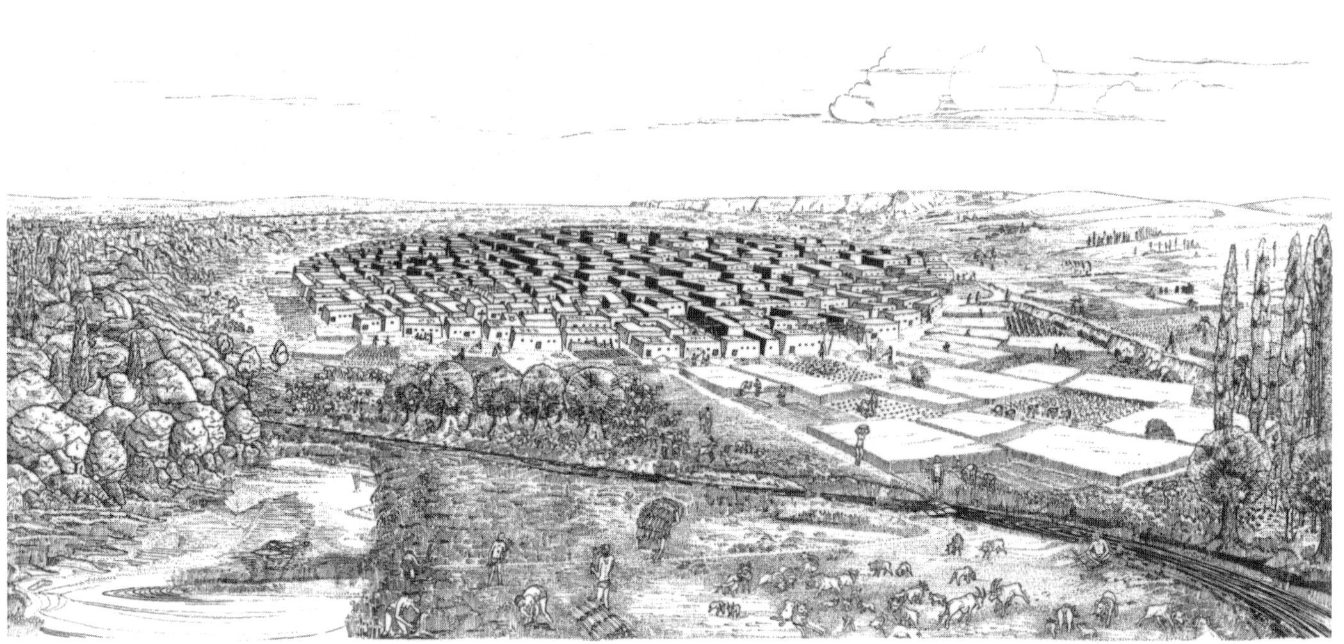

Part I THE INCEPTION OF THE EXCAVATION

1 The Themes of the Research

THE POTENTIAL OF THE SITE

The Euphrates River rises in the mountains of eastern Asia Minor and flows southwestward through high, rugged hills to within two hundred kilometers of the Mediterranean. The river, now broad and swift, turns south toward open country and, at the ancient crossing point of Meskene, bends sharply eastward across the plains of inner Syria, to sweep on through the length of Mesopotamia to the Persian Gulf. It was there, at the great bend in the middle course of the Euphrates, that the prehistoric village of Abu Hureyra was founded 11,500 years ago (figure 1.1).

The site was located on the south side of the Euphrates valley, at a point where a low terrace jutted out into the floodplain. The place was carefully chosen; it was close to the river, yet above flood level and free of the mosquitoes that bred on the damp valley floor. Two contrasting environmental zones met there: the steppe to the south and the lush valley bottom to the north. Our investigations have shown that, in this favored place, two villages were established in succession. The remains of these two superimposed settlements made up the ancient mound of Abu Hureyra, a huge archaeological site 11.5 ha (28.5 acres) in extent, with habitation deposits as much as 8 m deep. The inhabitants of the first village, Abu Hureyra 1, were specialized hunters and gatherers who supported themselves by systematically extracting sustenance from the wild plants and animals they found in the vicinity of the site season by season. After a few centuries, they developed agriculture. They were thus among the first people anywhere in the world to embark on this new way of life. There followed an intermediate episode of occupation, and then a second village, Abu Hureyra 2, was formed there; its occupants were farmers who continued to collect some wild plants and to hunt game. Later, they became wholly dependent on their crops and domesticated animals. This community of farmers rapidly increased in numbers, and the village expanded to accom-

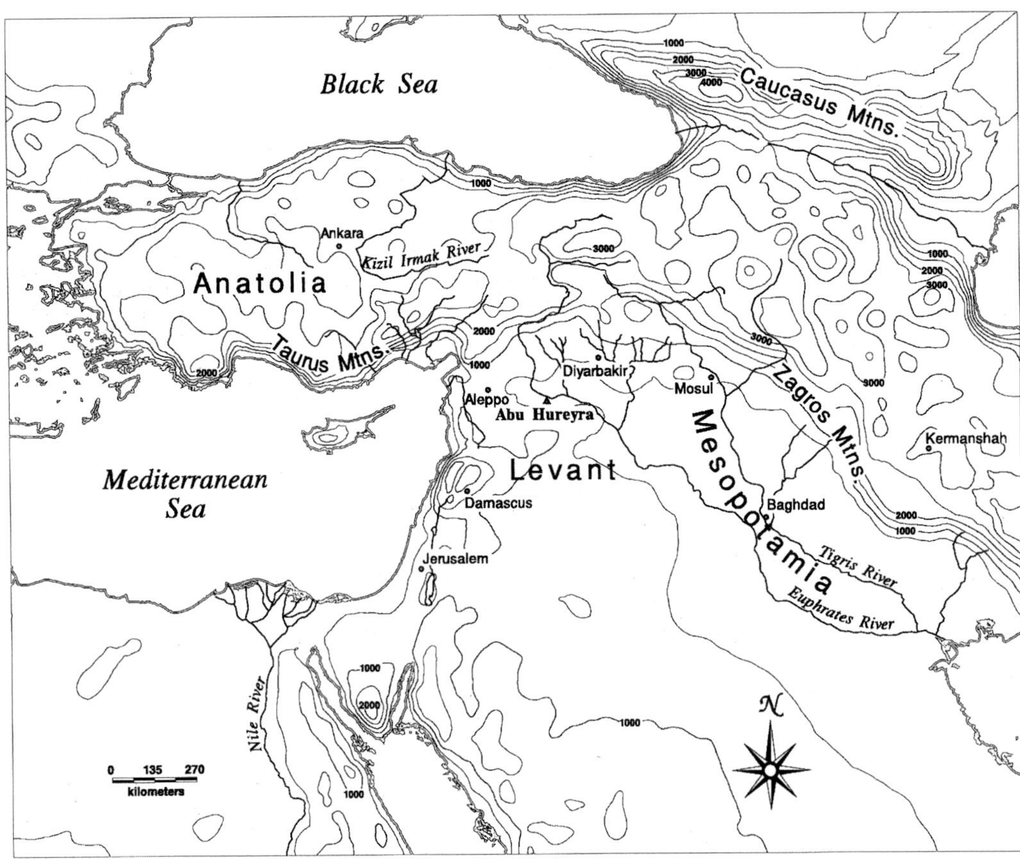

Figure 1.1 Physical map of Southwest Asia, with geographical regions (Anatolia, Mesopotamia, Levant), main towns, and Abu Hureyra.

modate them until it exceeded in size almost all other contemporary sites in Southwest Asia (figure 1.2). It was to endure for over two thousand years.

The potential of Abu Hureyra for archaeological investigation was great. First, the site was occupied for an unusually long period of time through a crucial period of economic and cultural change in Southwest Asia. This was the transformation from hunting and gathering to farming, and the coeval transition from the Mesolithic or Epipalaeolithic period to the Neolithic. Abu Hureyra afforded a rare opportunity to compare these two ways of life on a single site in the same environmental setting. Moreover, since occupation at Abu Hureyra spanned the period of agricultural development in Southwest Asia, we could study how this fundamental transformation in human existence came about in one place and determine what factors in the lives of the inhabitants themselves contributed to it. There were abundant animal bones and charred plant remains in all levels of the site that we could recover using special techniques and use to document directly the transformation from foraging to farming at Abu Hureyra. Second, Abu Hureyra was settled as the Pleistocene was coming to an end and was finally abandoned when the Holocene was well advanced. The site thus spanned a major episode of environmental change that we could study through our plant and animal remains to see how it affected the economic transformation that was taking place. Third, the remains of the site and its contents—huts, mudbrick houses, tools of flint, stone, and bone—were unusually well preserved, permitting close study of cultural change. Furthermore, Abu Hureyra 2 contained numerous burials of humans that could tell us much about the people themselves and the impact of agriculture on their lives. Abu Hureyra had the potential, therefore, to provide unprecedented

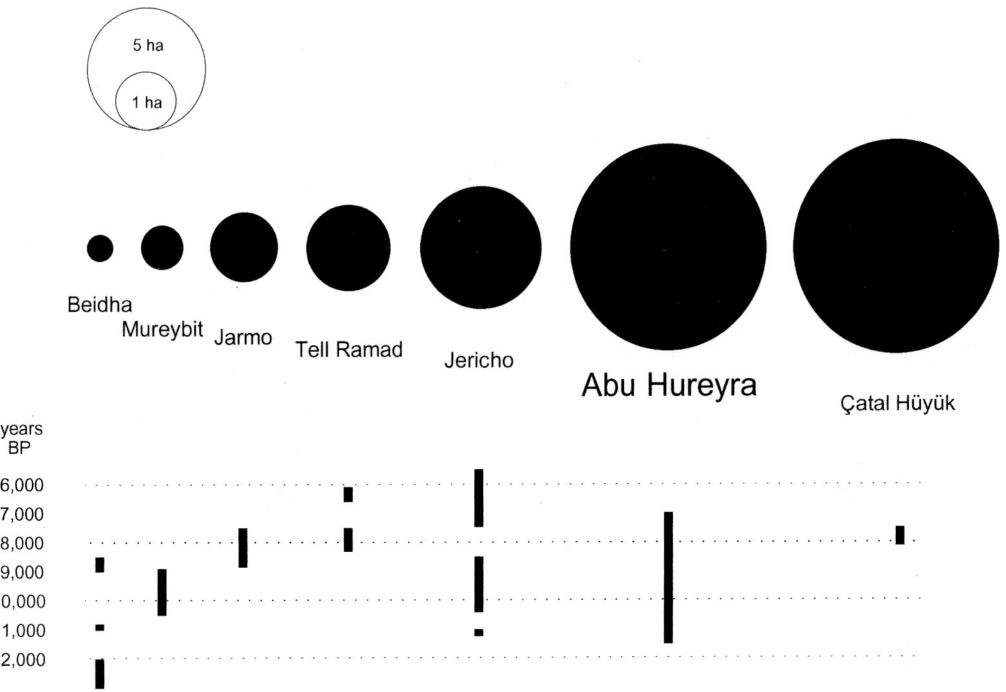

Figure 1.2 Comparisons of the size and duration of occupation of several well-known Neolithic sites in Southwest Asia. Abu Hureyra was much larger and was occupied for far longer than almost all other sites.

insights into the whole process of agricultural development and its impact on the people who undertook it.

The opportunity to investigate Abu Hureyra arose in 1971. The government of the Syrian Arab Republic was constructing a dam across the Euphrates at Tabqa, now Medinat el Thawra, 40 km upstream from Raqqa. The Directorate General of Antiquities and Museums in Syria had organized an international program of surveys and excavations to recover as much information as possible about past human settlement in the stretch of the Euphrates that would be flooded following completion of the dam. The Directorate General invited us to participate in the program of salvage archaeology by excavating a prehistoric site. We chose Abu Hureyra. There was irony in this: the site was discovered because of the salvage program, but the investigation of it would have to conclude by the end of 1973 when the dam would be finished and the valley flooded. This was the only opportunity there would ever be to excavate the site, and we would have to work under severe pressure of time in, as it turned out, field conditions of exceptional rigor.

This book is the record of that excavation and our analysis of the material that was recovered in it. Our aim throughout has been to conduct an integrated investigation of economic and cultural change at Abu Hureyra. The results have profound implications for our understanding of a series of major problems in the prehistory of Southwest Asia. These arise, above all, from the transformations that took place there from 12,000 to 7,000 years ago.

The cultural changes were striking enough. During the Epipalaeolithic most people lived on small campsites in groups of from one to five families that moved frequently. Much of Southwestern Asia was sparsely settled or even unoccupied during this period. The Neolithic pattern of settlement was quite different: people lived in large, nucleated (that is, tightly clustered) villages of mudbrick houses that endured for centuries. They developed a range of crafts—the manufacture of stone and pottery vessels, stone axes, and textiles—that denoted a new stage of cultural achievement. The population increased, and villages were founded over much of the rain-fed landscape of Southwest Asia. What factors were responsible for such dramatic cultural changes? How were these innovations carried through? What effects did they have on the societies that undertook them?

The economic transformation was even more far-reaching because its effects spread well beyond Southwest Asia. Epipalaeolithic hunters and gatherers depended on wild plants and animals for food. By contrast, Neolithic farmers subsisted on plants and animals that they themselves controlled. This required the domestication of the species concerned: wheat, barley, legumes, sheep, goats, cattle, and pigs, whose wild ancestors were all indigenous to Southwest Asia. The oldest domesticated remains of these species have been recovered from archaeological sites in the region, and this suggests that people domesticated them there. Farming was a quite different way of life from hunting and gathering. Hunters and gatherers went out almost every day to search for food, although the quest might leave them considerable leisure time. Every few days or weeks they would move to a new campsite. Farmers in Southwest Asia and adjacent regions, on the other hand, lived in permanent villages. Their year was divided into episodes of heavy agricultural work and of relative ease. They had to invest for the future by preparing land for cultivation, making animal pens, and constructing buildings and containers in which to store food. What circumstances led to such a fundamental change in the economy? How did the process of domestication proceed, and what was its impact?

The climate of Southwest Asia about 18,000 years ago, when the glaciers in higher latitudes were at their maximum extent, was cool and dry (Bottema and van Zeist 1981, p. 129). Toward the end of the Pleistocene the temperature rose and, for a time, rainfall increased. Thereafter, in the mid-Holocene, the climate became warmer and drier, approaching that of the present day. The pattern of these changes was complex, and it varied from one locality to another. The most important fact to note is that the Pleistocene-Holocene transition in Southwest Asia was a time of marked environmental change. We know that the climatic fluctuations caused the contraction and expansion of vegetation zones, sometimes over thousands of square kilometers. This altered the distribution of the wild plants and animals, the potential domesticates among them, on which hunters and gatherers depended for food. What impact did this have on patterns of subsistence? How did it affect the shift from dependence on wild resources to cultivation and herding?

We thought it likely that the changes in culture, economy, and environment were related. The excavation of Abu Hureyra provided an opportunity to explore those links and thereby to contribute to fuller understanding of one of the major transformations in human prehistory. The site itself raised other questions. Here was one of the oldest villages in the world that grew unprecedentedly large and flourished over several thousand years. Why was it founded in that place, and what factors contributed to its success over so long a period? Its great size marked it out for investigation, but did it really stand alone or was it one of many such sites in Syria?

THE ARCHAEOLOGICAL CONTEXT

The thrust of our research will become clearer if we examine its context more closely. The transition from Epipalaeolithic to Neolithic was a time of fundamental change throughout Southwest Asia. The region with the most detailed cultural record was the Levant, where Abu Hureyra was situated. The Levant borders the eastern Mediterranean and extends from Sinai in the south to the Taurus Mountains in the north; its eastern boundary is the North Arabian desert. Most archaeological research had been conducted in the southern Levant, especially Palestine, but little was known about the later prehistory of Syria in the north. This was especially regrettable because this area was the geographical link between the Levant and the rest of Southwest Asia, and thus a potential path for the diffusion of cultural and economic innovations. We expected that the excavation of Abu Hureyra would help to fill this gap in knowledge.

The Epipalaeolithic stage in the Levant may be divided into two stages (figure 1.3): Epipalaeolithic 1, lasting from c. 20,000 to 12,500 before present (BP), and Epipalaeolithic 2, from c. 12,500 to 10,000 BP (Moore 1985, p. 12). Epipalaeolithic 1 may be further subdivided into an early phase, called the Kebaran in Palestine, and a later one, the Geometric Kebaran (Bar-Yosef 1981, figure 1). The Epipalaeolithic is characterized by flint tool industries with high proportions of microliths; differences in the composition of these assemblages distinguish the phases.

Epipalaeolithic 1 sites were extremely small, usually less than 100 m^2 in area, and consisted of no more than thin scatters of debris. There were remains of huts at En Gev (Bar-Yosef 1970, figures 89, 90, 102), but most of the sites had no structures. A few ground stone pestles, mortars, and bowls have been found at some of them, but almost the only other artifacts to survive were flint tools. Epipalaeolithic 1 sites were apparently used by small groups of hunters and gatherers who camped on them for just a few days or weeks while they foraged for wild foods in the vicinity. Human groups were thinly but widely distributed along the Mediterranean coast and up to 200 km inland during this period. In the Geometric Kebaran there was an expansion of settlement southward into northern Sinai (Bar-Yosef 1981, figure 6) and around El Kum (M.-C. Cauvin 1981a, p. 384) that coincided with an increase in temperature and in rainfall.

The next stage, Epipalaeolithic 2, is of great importance in the story of cultural development. Sites of this period were first excavated in Palestine in the 1920s, where they were ascribed to the Natufian culture (Garrod 1957, p. 212). That term has recently been applied to contemporary sites found on the Middle Euphrates (M.-C. Cauvin 1980, p. 18), but this begs several questions that we shall consider in the light of the evidence from Abu Hureyra. Most Epipalaeolithic 2 sites in the Levant were still small camps, hardly altered from those of

Stages	Years Before Present
	7,000
Neolithic 3	
	8,000
Neolithic 2	
	9,600
Neolithic 1	
	10,000
Epipalaeolithic 2	
	12,500
Epipalaeolithic 1	
	20,000

Figure 1.3 The successive stages of the Epipalaeolithic and Neolithic in the Levant.

Epipalaeolithic 1. A few were substantially larger and different in form. These settlements were from 800 to 2,000 m^2 in area, and one or two may have been even more extensive. The most impressive sites were clustered around Mount Carmel, in the Judean hills, and in the Jordan valley. It is here, in the Natufian heartland, that the most striking cultural changes have been documented. One settlement, Ain Mallaha (figure 1.4), was composed of circular huts, sufficient in number for the site to be called a village (Redman 1978, p. 73). Others, Mugharet el Wad, Jericho, and Nahal Oren among them, had walls built of stones, paved areas, and pits. Several of these sites yielded rich assemblages of bone tools—sickle hafts, pins, needles, and borers—and a much greater array of ground stone tools, especially bowls, pestles, large mortars, querns, and rubbers. Some of the bone and stone tools were carved to resemble animals, and others were engraved with abstract ornament. Fine human and animal figurines in stone expanded the canon of naturalistic art. The other notable innovation was the practice of burying the dead within the settlement. Several skeletons at Mugharet el Wad were decked with headdresses of dentalium shells and necklaces of bone beads (Garrod and Bate 1937, pp. 18–19), while a burial of a woman at Ain Mallaha was accompanied by a puppy, presumably a pet (Valla 1975–1977, p. 288).

The relatively rich remains of the larger Natufian sites, especially the distinctive art and indications of ceremonial burial, have attracted much attention, and part of the traditional significance of the culture stems from this. It has been suggested that such sites were permanently inhabited "base camps" (Bar-Yosef 1981, p. 401), although this has yet to be confirmed. It is only recently that relevant evidence for this interpretation has been considered (for example, S.J.M. Davis 1983). Garrod thought that the reaping equipment found on these sites indicated that the Natufians had begun to farm, and she called their culture "Mesolithic with agriculture" (Garrod 1957, pp. 216, 226). This gave the Natufian even greater significance, but it proved to be a controversial interpretation. It was challenged first by Perrot (1968, cols. 382–383), who pointed out that there was no incontestable evidence to prove that the Natufians had domesticated any wild species. He preferred to interpret their achievement as a final flourish of the traditional Palaeolithic hunting and gathering way of life in a rich environment. More recent excavations of Natufian sites, using modern methods to recover organic material, have failed to find many plant remains. This is usually attributed to poor preservation (Bar-Yosef 1981, p. 403), but it has led to the suggestion that wild cereals and legumes may have played only a minor role in the diet of these Epipalaeolithic 2 people (Legge 1986, p. 20).

The development of new forms of settlement in the Natufian implies that an important change was taking place in social organization, but this has never been seriously examined. The principal Natufian sites were all situated in the Mediterranean forest zone of Palestine. Many other Epipalaeolithic 2 sites have been found in the steppe zone of Transjordan and Syria, but none of them has the full range of artifacts found in the classic Natufian, and their relationship to Natufian sites remains to be determined. We know that they shared in some of the cultural changes, in particular the development of microlithic flint industries with lunates. The rest of the cultural evidence makes it clear, however, that there were considerable differences between the Epipalaeolithic 2 groups in the Mediterranean and the steppe zones, and we might reasonably expect that this would extend to their subsistence. The fundamental questions of how these different Epipalaeolithic 2 groups obtained their food and whether

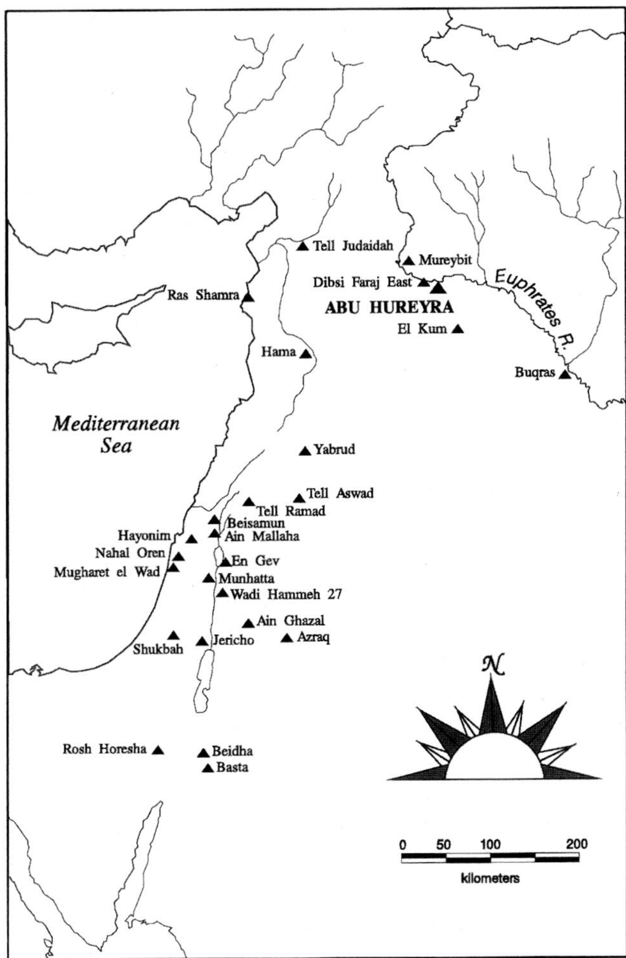

Figure 1.4 Map of the Levant showing the location of key prehistoric sites.

they had begun to domesticate plants and animals have never been satisfactorily answered. Abu Hureyra is the first site to produce plant and animal food remains in quantities sufficient to address such questions, and it is here that the site has one of its most important contributions to make.

There was one further change in Epipalaeolithic 2 of significance for economy and culture. A comparative study of the distribution and nature of sites in both Epipalaeolithic 1 and 2 has indicated that the population increased substantially from one stage to the next (Moore 1983, p. 94). This trend began toward the end of Epipalaeolithic 1 and continued into the succeeding stage. The reasons for the growth in population are not fully understood, but it appears to have coincided with the improvement in environment that we have already noted. The move toward a more sedentary pattern of existence in Epipalaeolithic 2 would have reinforced it. This trend should have markedly affected those alterations in culture just outlined, but precisely how remains to be established. It would have been closely linked with whatever was happening to the economy, and we shall consider this issue in the light of the evidence from Abu Hureyra.

The Neolithic began within a few centuries of 10,000 BP throughout the Levant. The earlier Neolithic may be divided into two stages: Neolithic 1 to c. 9,600 BP, and Neolithic 2, which lasted until about 8,000 BP. These stages have been called the Pre-Pottery Neolithic A and B at the key site of Jericho. There were immediate changes in the pattern of settlement. Most Neolithic sites were large villages of closely spaced mudbrick houses. Several Neolithic 1 sites covered a few thousand square meters, while two, Tell Aswad (a maximum of 2.7 ha) and Jericho (4 ha), were substantially larger than any earlier settlement (figure 1.2). Sites increased in size still more in Neolithic 2. Archaeologists have found some villages 1–2 ha in size, but several were very much bigger than this. Three of the best known are Jericho (4 ha), Ras Shamra (8 ha), and, of course, Abu Hureyra itself (11.5 ha). Relatively few sites were occupied in Neolithic 1, suggesting that the population regrouped. In Neolithic 2 the number of sites vastly increased, indicating that the population rose sharply during this stage (Moore 1983, p. 98). These radical changes in settlement form and population density suggest that a major restructuring of society took place as well. Precisely what the new configurations were remains difficult to determine, but we can make some suggestions based on the Abu Hureyra evidence.

It has always seemed likely that these changes were connected with the advent of agriculture, but views on this question have differed sharply. Kenyon (1979, pp. 27–28) published evidence that indicated the inhabitants of the first Neolithic village at Jericho were farmers, but others (Perrot 1968, col. 389; Redman 1978, p. 80) insisted that they were still hunters and gatherers. The problem arose from the fact that so little direct evidence in the form of plant remains and animal bones had been recovered from Epipalaeolithic and Neolithic sites. Plant remains from Tell Aswad in the Damascus Basin confirmed that agriculture had already begun in Neolithic 1 (van Zeist and Bakker-Heeres 1979), but the few animal bones that had been studied from Jericho, Nahal Oren, and other sites suggested that meat was still being obtained from wild animals (Clutton-Brock 1979; Noy, Legge, and Higgs 1973).

The changes in artifact technology are better known, but much of our evidence has come from a small group of sites in Palestine and the Damascus Basin. This hinted at some regional variation but the results of the Abu Hureyra excavation will permit us to examine this question much more thoroughly. One of the most striking developments was a new house-building industry, requiring the manufacture of mudbricks and plaster on a considerable scale. The flint industry changed from the production of microliths to large blade tools like arrowheads and sickle blades. Heavy cutting tools, axes and adzes mainly, were made from both flint and hard stones. Querns, rubbing stones, and other ground stone artifacts were common finds on early Neolithic sites, and some of the Neolithic 2 stone bowls and dishes were exceedingly fine. A wide range of beads and other objects of adornment was manufactured from bone, shell, and carefully chosen colored stones. All of this indicates that there were technological advances and much elaboration of material culture during the earlier Neolithic. It should be noted, too, that a small but regular percentage of the raw materials used to make these artifacts was imported from localities several hundred kilometers distant. There had been some local exchange of shells and stones used for grinding tools in the Epipalaeolithic, but this practice grew considerably in the Neolithic. Regular long-distance exchange of obsidian for cutting tools and colored stones for beads was apparently a Neolithic innovation. All these new elements were abundantly represented in the second settlement at Abu Hureyra. We can thus add much to our understanding of Neolithic culture from an area about which little was known before the site was excavated.

Cultural description is most valuable when it permits deeper understanding of the way of life of an extinct society, and why it functioned in the way it did. It has been demonstrated that the culture of Neolithic peoples in the Levant developed from Epipalaeolithic antecedents (Moore 1982a, pp. 4–8). Much has still to be learned about the nature and rate of this change. Was the emergence of a new culture a wholly indigenous process, or did developments elsewhere in Southwest Asia influence the outcome? What were the links between the innovations in culture and the development of an agricultural economy?

THE PROBLEM OF AGRICULTURAL GENESIS

We have sought greater understanding of the development of agriculture from the outset of our research because of the intrinsic importance of the process, and the exceptionally favorable opportunity to investigate it at Abu Hureyra. It has long been thought that Southwest Asia was one of the most significant centers of agricultural development in the Old World because plants and animals of economic importance worldwide were domesticated there. This economic revolution initiated far-reaching cultural changes that, several millennia later, led to the development of the first civilizations anywhere in the world, the city-states of Sumer and their counterparts elsewhere in Mesopotamia and the Levant. Southwest Asia is the only region in the world where we can trace these developments directly, from the initial domestication of plants and animals by hunters and gatherers to the crystallization of urban societies. The agricultural economy that developed there was based on the cultivation of wheat, barley, and legumes and on the raising of ovicaprines, cattle, and pigs. Later, it spread to Africa, where it became an essential element in the development of Egyptian civilization and a contributor to cultural change well beyond the Nile valley. It was transmitted to Europe, where in modified form it provided the subsistence system that underlay all later cultural development in that continent, from the Neolithic to the present. Elements of the Southwest Asian agricultural economy passed eastward, too, beyond the Caspian and to the Indus Valley, contributing to the development of higher cultures in South Asia. The domesticates themselves have proved of enduring economic value, and they are still key elements in many contemporary agricultural systems. Indeed, the domestic wheat that originated in Southwest Asia is the world's principal source of carbohydrate today.

The concept of domestication was central to our investigation. Domestication may be defined in several ways (for example, Bökönyi 1989), but the essence of it is that humans usually influence the breeding of the species concerned. They also own the animals and the fields in which the plants grow. Recent hunters and gatherers have manipulated wild species to encourage them to produce more abundantly. The /Xam Bushmen replanted the shoots of roots, while the Kumeyaay (Kamia) of southern California sowed grass seeds and tree nuts (Bleek 1936; Shipek 1989). The Paiute of the Owens Valley in eastern California flooded land to increase the productivity of wild grasses and roots (Steward 1938). Hunters and gatherers have even engaged in landscape management, frequently using fire to burn off scrub to promote the growth of grasses and other annuals. Such practices were common among the Native Americans of California, the Australian aborigines, and many others (Lewis 1973; Hallam 1979, p. 15). These activities brought humans into close contact with particular species of plants and animals and could result in intensive management and harvesting of wild foods, but they stopped short of systematic selection and propagation of those species. Only when that step was taken could domestication and the change to food production occur. We wanted to study the impact of domestication on the people of Abu Hureyra. When and in what circumstances were domesticated populations of plants and animals introduced to the economy of the site? Did the people of Abu Hureyra themselves actually domesticate any plants or animals? How rapidly were domesticates adopted, and what effects did they have on the lives of the inhabitants?

Our understanding of agricultural development within Southwest Asia itself has remained remarkably thin and uneven, despite the general significance of the process. The location and timing of the domestication of each species within Southwest Asia are still uncertain. The conventional view had it that the cereals and pulses could have been domesticated in a large arc, from Palestine around the fringe of the Fertile Crescent to the Persian Gulf, the ovicaprines probably in the Zagros foothills, and the cattle and pigs almost anywhere within the region (Renfrew 1973; Bökönyi 1976). The best archaeological evidence for this was found in two areas, in the southern Levant at sites like Jericho and Beidha, and in the foothills of the Zagros at Jarmo. The discovery of a flourishing Neolithic culture at the huge site of Çatal Hüyük (figure 1.2) on the Anatolian plateau during the 1960s suggested that this might be a third area of indigenous agricultural development. Early Neolithic sites do exist there, but they are only now being excavated, so the possibility remains to be confirmed. The place of Syria within this scheme was unknown. It spanned three major environmental zones, the Mediterranean woodland of the coast and hinterland, a broad expanse of steppe farther east, and the desert of North Arabia. Several of the progenitors of the plant and animal domesticates were native to the forest and steppe. The evidence from Abu Hureyra will indicate that certain favored parts of the steppic interior of Syria were indeed a focus of agricultural development within Southwest Asia.

A major impediment to greater understanding of the development of agriculture was the dearth of direct evidence for economic change. Animal bones had survived quite well on some Epipalaeolithic and Neolithic sites and had been recovered in sufficient quantities for the main species of economic importance to have been identified. The samples were usually inadequate, however, for faunal analysts to determine how they had been exploited. Our understanding of the use of plants on these prehistoric sites was even more sketchy, because plant remains had rarely been found on prehistoric sites. The total number of charred seeds recovered from Epipalaeolithic and Neolithic sites in the Levant would scarcely have filled a whisky tumbler. With samples as modest as these, it was hardly surprising that so little could be said about domestication and the course of economic change. New methods had to be employed to obtain larger samples of animal bones and seeds for study.

These uncertainties made tackling other problems difficult. It was of great importance to know how each step in the process of economic transformation was related to the successive stages of cultural evolution and episodes of population growth. Here the patchy nature of the sequences that had already been constructed made it difficult to fit even existing knowledge into a tight cultural framework. Did the changes take place together, or at least in a coordinated manner? Could we discern relationships of cause and effect? Or were there more subtle interactions that close study of changes in culture, and the use of animals and plants, in a single, long sequence might reveal?

The development of agriculture in Southwest Asia was complex because the agricultural economy that developed there combined both domesticated plants and animals. Their wild progenitors had particular requirements that were influenced strongly by the climatic contrasts between winter and summer. The herds of ungulates in the steppe had to migrate to find pasture in successive seasons. Any hunter-gatherer group that depended heavily on such animals for food would have had to pursue a mobile way of life if it wanted to obtain fresh meat year-round. This rule still governs the lives of nomadic herders of domesticated stock throughout Southwest Asia today. The species of plants of interest to hunters and gatherers were each abundant for a short period in different seasons of the year. It would therefore have been necessary to move through the landscape seasonally to profit from local occurrences of plants as they fruited. A cycle of movement based on a seasonal succession of plants would be different from one constructed around the movements of animals. How did Epipalaeolithic hunters and gatherers cope with these conflicting needs? How, in such circumstances, were plants and animals domesticated, and how were they ultimately combined in one system of sedentary farming, as the available archaeological evidence suggested?

There were further intriguing questions that arose from the kinds of species that were selected for domestication. The animal bones indicated that Epipalaeolithic groups in the Levant killed large quantities of a few species of game, gazelle at many sites in Palestine, fallow deer and goats at Ksar Akil (Hooijer 1961) at the foot of the Mountains of Lebanon, and both ibex and bezoar goats at Wadi Madamagh and Beidha (Perkins 1966, p. 67) in southern Transjordan. Only one of these species, the bezoar goat *Capra aegagrus*, was among the domesticates found in later Neolithic villages. Ovicaprines were evidently hunted by Epipalaeolithic groups in the Zagros, one reason why they were thought to have been domesticated there, but there was little indication that cattle and pigs were exploited by those people until after they had been domesticated. What factors, then, governed the choice of animals by Epipalaeolithic groups, and why were particular species, often of little prior economic importance, selected for domestication? The same questions needed to be asked about the plants. Why were particular species of cereals and pulses chosen in preference to other plants? What was the place of these species in the diet of Epipalaeolithic hunters and gatherers before they were domesticated? An important contribution of the evidence recovered from Abu Hureyra is that it provides answers to these questions.

The agricultural way of life that developed in Southwest Asia was based on sedentary villages, that is, settlements occupied throughout the year. Sedentism was a corollary of the full-time cultivation of cereals and pulses, and several archaeologists believed that it was an essential precursor to agriculture (for example, Flannery 1969; Harris 1977). The switch from a mobile to a sedentary existence based on farming is thought to have stimulated population growth as birth spacing decreased (Lee 1979, p. 442). Sedentism had other implications that were of great importance for the subsequent development of more complex societies in Southwest Asia. Large-scale craft production—of pottery, stone vessels, mudbrick, and plaster, for example—could take place only in sedentary communities. The adoption of sedentary village life required new forms of social organization that would maintain harmony in communities of many families who lived close together all the time. Such communities needed to regulate the use of land around their villages and to resolve disputes between their members. It was from such arrangements that more advanced political systems developed, of the kind that would eventually control affairs in the first city-states.

There could be no doubt of the importance of sedentism in the development of agriculture, but when were settlements first occupied year-round? Most Epipalaeolithic 1 sites looked as though they had been occupied briefly, whereas later Neolithic villages seemed to have been inhabited for many years. The first significant alteration in the form of settlements took place during Epipalaeolithic 2 with the foundation of the larger Natufian sites. Some concluded that they had been inhabited year-round (Perrot 1968, col. 383; Henry 1981), but there was no confirmation of this hypothesis. The trouble was that the argument rested on the appearance of the settlements: sites that lacked structures were presumed to have been temporary camps, and those with solid buildings permanently occupied. The ethnographic record provided plenty of examples of an inverse relationship, as Higgs and Vita-Finzi (1972, p. 29), among others, pointed out. Although arguments based on the form of settlements would always be indecisive, unequivocal evidence for or against permanent occupation was hard to come by. What was needed was some definite indication that humans had remained on a site throughout the year. Bones of mice and sparrows had been found at the Natufian site of Hayonim, and it was thought that those species depended so on humans that they could have lived at the site only if it was permanently inhabited (Bar-Yosef and Tchernov 1966, p. 125). Similar arguments have been used to show that the early Neolithic site of Ganj Dareh in the Zagros Mountains was inhabited year-round (Hesse 1979). These inferences may be correct, but they are still open to doubt (Byrd 1989, p. 183; Edwards 1989b, p. 29). A more certain approach is to examine the plant and animal food remains from the site to determine at what seasons of the year they were collected and, therefore, when the site was occupied. This is what we have done at Abu Hureyra.

THEORIES OF AGRICULTURAL DEVELOPMENT

Archaeologists and others have often tried to explain how agriculture developed in Southwest Asia, and some have linked this process with the wider phenomenon of the inception of agriculture in centers across the world beginning about 10,000 years ago. Several writers have concentrated on defining stages of economic and cultural development in order to establish a framework that would permit a description of what happened. One of the first was Braidwood, who set up a sequence for the Zagros and adjacent areas (Braidwood and Howe 1960, chapter X). His scheme was developed further by Hole and Flannery (1967; Hole 1977). Vaux (1966) and Perrot (1968) presented sequences of development for Palestine, while Kenyon (1979, pp. 19–65) published another that was derived mainly from the record at Jericho. The most comprehensive description was by Mellaart (1975), who reviewed the cultural development of the whole of Southwest Asia from the Epipalaeolithic to the end of the Neolithic. This was a necessary step before investigation of processes of economic and cultural change could proceed very far, but these schemes served only as partial frameworks because there were substantial gaps in the record, from area to area and through time. Enough was known to see that the pattern of economic and cultural development varied from one part of Southwest Asia to another, and that there were considerable differences in environment and in the resources available to humans that might account for some of these variations, but more fieldwork was required to fill the gaps in the record.

The question of the locations in which agriculture may have developed prompted further debate. Childe had suggested (1928, p. 42), in an early discussion of the genesis of agriculture, that the climate became arid at the end of the Pleistocene. Consequently, people and the potential domesticates were forced into close association near rivers and oases. In these circumstances of environmental stress, they domesticated plants and animals in order to assure a continued supply of food. Thus, according to Childe's hypothesis, agriculture developed in the fertile, but dry, lowlands. The theory eventually fell out of favor because little evidence was found to support it. Kenyon's discovery in the 1950s of a very early Neolithic farming settlement at Jericho beside a spring in an arid section of the Jordan valley gave new life to Childe's ideas, but Braidwood had already directed the attention of archaeologists to a "nuclear zone" in which the wild progenitors of the main plant and animal domesticates are found today. This was in the "hilly flanks of the Fertile Crescent" (Braidwood and Howe 1960, p. 3) that stretched from Palestine and Lebanon around to the foothills of the Zagros in the east. Braidwood's data suggested that the environment had reached its present form before domestication occurred (Braidwood and Howe 1960, p. 163), and thus that the boundaries of his "nuclear zone" were much the same in the past as in the present. More recent studies of pollen and geomorphology have shown that there have been marked changes in the climate in the last 18,000 years that have altered the extent of vegetation zones. Were the wooded foothills of the "hilly flanks" the only area where the wild ancestors of the domesticates flourished? Might not some of the wild grasses and animals like cattle and sheep also have been at home on the steppe, so enlarging the potential area of domestication considerably? Had the plants and animals been domesticated everywhere in this vast area of wooded hills and open steppe, or in only a few locations within it? The answers to these questions were beyond the scope of a single project, but excavation of a site with well-preserved organic remains on the steppe would contribute to their resolution.

There were widely divergent views on when agriculture began. Garrod, as we have seen, believed that the Natufians were the first cultivators in Southwest Asia, and Kenyon (1979, p. 20) accepted that this was likely. Perrot, on the other hand, concluded that agriculture in Palestine began much later. There was no conclusive evidence of farming at his Natufian site of Ain Mallaha, and studies by Ducos (1968) of animal bones found on Neolithic sites excavated by Perrot implied that domesticated animals were not kept in Palestine until late in the Neolithic. Some even thought that the inhabitants of Neolithic villages like Suberde in Anatolia lived mainly by hunting wild animals, in this case sheep, supplemented by plant gathering (Bordaz 1973, p. 283) long after farming had begun in other areas, although this view has been widely criticized. So when were plants and animals domesticated? Did agriculture develop rapidly, or over several millennia? These sharply differing views raised in acute form the question of the link between economic and cultural change. Yet the information we had on the timing of economic change was so limited that no consensus could be reached.

The reasons why agriculture began in Southwest Asia have proved even more difficult to determine. Binford (1968), in a wide-ranging survey of changes in adaptation at the close of the Pleistocene, was inclined to favor population pressure as the key factor (p. 328). He thought that some groups in the Levant established sedentary settlements in the more favored areas and that this caused the population there to increase. Some groups migrated out to areas with fewer people but less abundant wild foods. This placed an excessive demand on wild resources, obliging some groups to begin farming. No evidence has been found to substantiate the pattern of migration that Binford proposed, but the notion that agriculture developed in response to increases in population density has found support.

For Boserup (1965, p. 11) population growth was an independent variable that has influenced the course of economic development in simple farming societies today. She described a succession of more intensive stages of farming that a society would pass through under the pressure of increasing numbers. These ideas were taken up by archaeologists, and Smith and Young (1972, 1983) applied them directly to the development of agriculture and early civilization in the Zagros and Mesopotamia. They argued that the population of the Zagros valleys increased during and after the Epipalaeolithic, and they suggested that this led to the development of agriculture there (Smith and Young 1983, pp. 145–146). It has proved difficult, however, to validate such a general hypothesis on the evidence from individual sites and localities.

Flannery's model placed the development of agriculture in the context of long-term changes in economy and culture. He thought that before 20,000 years ago there was an adjustment in the economy of Southwest Asian hunters and gatherers, who began to forage for small game, fish, and wild grass seeds for the first time (Flannery 1969, p. 77). This "broad-spectrum revolution" was accompanied by the development of several cultural "preadaptations" for agriculture, in particular grinding stones and storage pits. Like Binford, he invoked population pressure to account for economic changes, both the "broad-spectrum revolution" and the development of cereal cultivation (Flannery 1969, pp. 79, 81). People would be obliged to increase their supply of food and so turn to agriculture as the density of population increased. This would happen first in marginal areas where Flannery considered wild foods would be less abundant. These ideas were intriguing, but they needed testing. The idea of a "broad-spectrum revolution" could only be investigated if large samples of organic remains were recovered systematically from Upper Palaeolithic and Epipalaeolithic sites. It was also necessary to determine if plants and animals were first domesticated in the steppe, as both Binford and Flannery thought, and if so whether it was really as "marginal" a zone as they imagined.

It has always seemed a powerful coincidence that the development of agriculture in Southwest Asia, and, indeed, in several other centers across the world, occurred about the time of the Pleistocene-Holocene transition. One could infer from this that climatic change contributed in some way to the transformation in human existence. Childe's theory of agricultural development was based on the idea that the climate became arid in the early Holocene. Later writers were inclined to minimize the importance of environmental change as a factor because they saw little evidence for it in Southwest Asia. The notion has found more support in recent years as it has become clear that there were, after all, significant changes in climate and vegetation in Southwest Asia, as elsewhere in the world, from the late Pleistocene on. It now seems likely that the changes in climate and vegetation during the Pleistocene-Holocene transition could have influenced the adoption of agriculture and sedentary life in Southwest Asia itself (Moore and Hillman 1992, p. 491).

The British Academy Major Research Project in the Early History of Agriculture was a unique attempt to investigate the development of agriculture in Southwest Asia and Europe by one team. The British Academy project was significant for two reasons: it deliberately placed investigation of the economy itself at the center of its research, and it developed new field methods for recovering economic data from archaeological sites. Its members stressed the importance of the symbiosis between humans and certain wild species of plants and animals over long periods of time (Higgs and Jarman 1969, p. 38). For them the domestication of plants and animals was simply a more intimate version of modes of exploitation that had a long prior history. These ideas were investigated by recovering large samples of animal bones and plant remains from a series of current excavations through the systematic use of novel methods of collection, mainly sieving and froth flotation. The British Academy project was of great value in bringing fresh thinking to the problem of agricultural genesis, although its approach played down the significance of the consequences of agriculture seen throughout Southwest Asia. Its members had already made considerable progress in their research by the time we decided to dig Abu Hureyra, and their work was an important influence on our excavation plans. One of us (AJL) was a member of the British Academy project when work at Abu Hureyra commenced, and another (GCH) was engaged in associated research at the British Institute of Archaeology at Ankara.

There have been several more recent contributions to the debate concerning the development of agriculture in which the significance of different factors has been stressed. Barbara Bender (1978, p. 206) has emphasized the importance of social pressures in stimulating economic change, and this view has found an echo in the writings of Jacques Cauvin. He has argued that a series of cultural factors influenced the decision to develop agriculture in Southwest Asia, and that this had nothing to do with ecological imperatives (J. Cauvin 1977, pp. 42–45). More recently, Cauvin has claimed that changes in social psychology and belief systems led to the development of a farming way of life (J. Cauvin 1994, p. 92). Another author has tried to bring the whole discussion back to basic biological principles by stressing the underlying processes of evolution that would have governed such a major change in the way of life of our species (Rindos 1984). This approach has obvious theoretical strengths, but it is so far removed from the actual archaeological evidence that it does not provide much assistance in determining what actually happened in Southwest Asia.

We started work against this background of so much uncertainty concerning the advent of agriculture. The locations within Southwest Asia where agriculture might have begun could be described in only the most general manner, the timing of agricultural development was the subject of serious disagreement, and the processes of domestication were unknown. It looked as though major changes in culture, economy, and environment took place over the same period of time, but the connections between these factors remained to be determined. There were general theories that offered insights on how agricultural development might have occurred, but they were difficult to relate to the archaeological evidence from individual sites. This gap was a large one to close, but we suspected that part of the difficulty was that these theories relied on just one or two determining factors. The process of agricultural development was more complex than this.

At Abu Hureyra we intended to excavate a site in an area, not yet investigated, that was potentially of great importance for the genesis of agriculture. The site had a long sequence of occupation that would span a significant portion of the period during which agriculture became the basis of life. We would obtain substantial evidence of the cultural changes that took place and would endeavor to date them closely. We intended to use new methods to recover substantial quantities of plant and animal remains that should make it possible to state how people lived, season by season, during the year. This, in turn, would enable us to determine what changes took place in the economy of the site while it was inhabited, and to establish the links between cultural and economic change at Abu Hureyra. Evidence of this kind would help us to sort out some of the more general questions, at least for the Middle Euphrates: the nature and timing of the early stages of agricultural development, its impact on the societies concerned, and its relation to cultural and environmental change.

2 Beginning Work

THE SALVAGE CAMPAIGN

From Carchemish on the Turkish frontier the Euphrates flows through a gorge down to Rumeileh (figure 2.1). The valley widens there, and in the 40 km stretch from Jebel Aruda to Qal'at Jabar it is 5–7 km across (figure 2.2). At Tabqa it narrows once more to a width of 2.5 km between bluffs of Eocene chalk and limestone (Heinzelin 1967, p. 22). Here the government of the Syrian Arab Republic decided to build a dam across the river (figure 2.3) that would create a lake extending 80 km upstream, as far as Yusef Pasha in the Euphrates gorge. The dam would provide water for irrigation projects and generate electricity for much of Syria, but the lake would drown not only the modern villages but also the remains of many ancient settlements in the valley. It was important that the threatened archaeological sites should be investigated before they disappeared. The Directorate General of Antiquities and Museums in Syria responded to this emergency by launching an international campaign of salvage excavations under the patronage of UNESCO in 1963.

The campaign proceeded in three stages (Bounni 1973, pp. 4–5). First, two surveys were carried out to assess the archaeological potential of the region (Rihaoui 1965; van Loon 1967). In the second stage, studies were made of how to preserve outstanding historic monuments in the valley, and excavations began at several sites, among them the prehistoric mound of Mureybit. The third stage of most intense activity lasted from 1971 to 1973, during which several historic buildings were saved and over a score of sites of all periods from the prehistoric to the Islamic were excavated. It was early in the third stage, during the spring of 1971, that the Directorate General invited Moore to choose a prehistoric site to dig. The offer provided an unprecedented opportunity to learn more about the Neolithic in northern Syria and the role of this region in the development of agriculture. Moore accepted the invitation, paid an immediate brief visit to the Euphrates Valley, and followed this with a more extended survey in June.

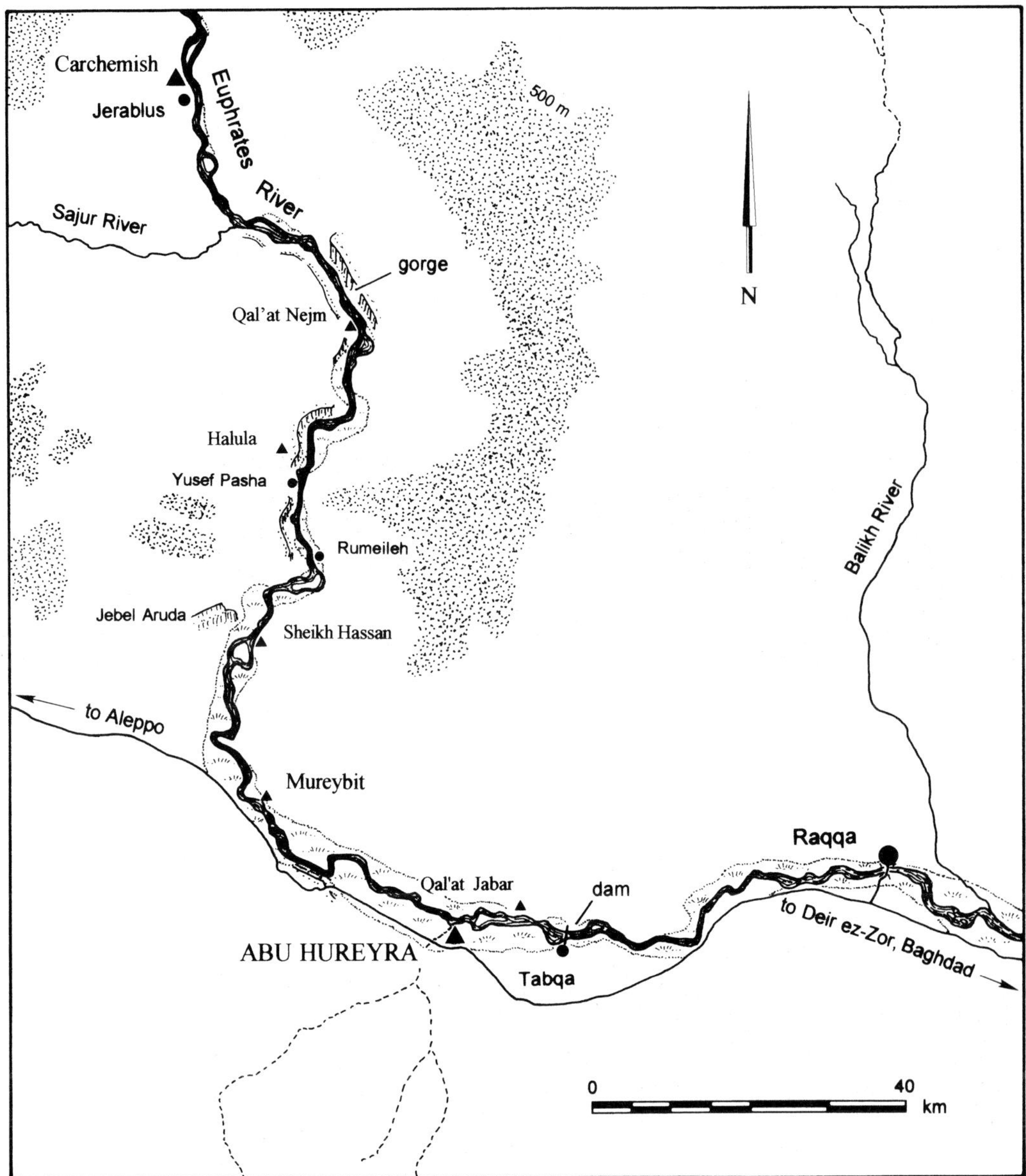

Figure 2.1 Middle Euphrates from Jerablus (Carchemish) to Raqqa, showing the location of Abu Hureyra.

The Euphrates River has connected Mesopotamia with Syria, Asia Minor, and the Mediterranean world since the beginning of civilization. The inhabitants of the city-states of Sumer in the third millennium BC came up the Euphrates to obtain timber, stone, and metals from the Amanus mountains and Anatolia (Bottéro 1971, p. 324). Echoes of those journeys are found in the *Epic of Gilgamesh* (Kovacs 1989, pp. 41, 47). The trade routes from the Mediterranean to southern Mesopotamia and beyond met the Euphrates at Meskene or farther downstream near its confluence with the Khabur. The road from Assyria to the Mediterranean crossed the Euphrates in the vicinity of Carchemish. The movements of goods and people along these routes brought much traffic to the river valley in the historic period and, perhaps, in earlier times.

The Euphrates has been a frontier since at least the first millennium BC. For the Assyrian kings it marked the western limit of the territory they regularly controlled (Grayson 1982, p. 260). Later, the Euphrates became the effective

Figure 2.2 The Euphrates Valley, looking downriver to the east from the Dibsi Heights to Abu Hureyra and Tabqa.

Figure 2.3 The Tabqa Dam under construction in 1971.

eastern frontier of the Roman Empire as it expanded into Asia, separating it from the Parthians. The Middle Euphrates remained a frontier region between the Byzantine and Islamic empires. One of the most important battles in early Islamic history, the battle of Siffin, took place near Abu Hureyra itself in AD 657 (AH 35). The battle was of great significance for Moslems because it led to the loss of the caliphate by Ali, and the rise of the Umayyad dynasty. Later, in Abbasid times, a small settlement grew up nearby, known as Old Abu Hureyra. The unusual circular mudbrick minaret of its mosque was carefully removed during the salvage campaign and re-erected at Tabqa. Trade along the river resumed during the early Islamic period, giving shipping points like Meskene renewed significance. It was then that the Abbasid caliphs developed Raqqa as an important political and cultural center, famous for its buildings and the production of fine pottery.

Settlement in the Euphrates Valley was disrupted by the Mongol invasions of the thirteenth century AD, and thereafter the region declined in importance until the advent of more secure conditions and the introduction of modern agricultural techniques after the First World War. Trade continued to pass along the valley, and the Euphrates attracted fresh interest as the European powers expanded their influence in Asia during the eighteenth and nineteenth centuries. Britain considered using it as an alternative route to India and sponsored an expedition by Chesney from 1835 to 1837 to explore the possibility (Chesney 1868, p. v). He launched two steam-driven vessels at Birecik, one of which later sank in a storm; the other succeeded in reaching the Persian Gulf, proving that such a Euphrates route was feasible. The river was difficult to navigate, however, and there were political difficulties that hindered regular traffic, so the plan was abandoned.

This much was known about the historical importance of the Middle Euphrates, but little archaeological research had been carried out there, and none in the stretch of the valley that would be inundated by the dam. Passemard and Pervès had collected flint artifacts from the terraces of the Euphrates early in the twentieth century that indicated humans had used the valley during the Lower and Middle Palaeolithic (Passemard 1926, p. 367; Pervès 1946–1948, p. 111). Excavations at Carchemish (Woolley 1921; Woolley and Barnett 1952) and Tell Ahmar (Thureau-Dangin and Dunand 1936) had provided some information about the archaeological sequence from the end of the Neolithic to Hellenistic times. Contenson and van Liere (1966) had recently excavated Buqras, a Neolithic site farther down the Euphrates, below its confluence with the Khabur, that dated from about 8,000 BP. This excavation was important because it indicated that there had been settlements along the Middle Euphrates during the Neolithic. But that was the extent of our knowledge of the prehistory of the region before the salvage campaign commenced.

There were still large gaps in our knowledge of the later prehistory of Syria when we started to dig. Excavations at Hama (Thuesen 1988) and in the Amuq basin (Braidwood and Braidwood 1960) before the Second World War had provided an outline sequence for the later Neolithic from 8,000 to 7,000 BP. This was the earliest period in which simple pottery was made, some of it of the kind known as "dark-faced burnished ware" (Braidwood and Braidwood 1960, p. 49). Those discoveries were augmented by the excavation of deep soundings at Ras Shamra (Schaeffer 1962, pp. 152–153) that carried the sequence back into the earlier Neolithic of the ninth millennium BP, before pottery came into use. Several more sites of shorter duration had been excavated: Tabbat el Hammam on the coast (Braidwood 1940, p. 196), Tell Ramad near Damascus (Contenson 1971), and Buqras in the Euphrates Valley (Contenson 1985), that dated from the eighth to the mid ninth millennium BP. The remainder of the early Neolithic, perhaps extending back to 10,000 BP, was virtually unknown. The only early Neolithic settlement that had been found was Mureybit. Van Loon's excavation of this site suggested that it was a permanently occupied village whose inhabitants were still supporting themselves by hunting and gathering animals and wild plants (van Loon 1968, p. 280). It seemed to confirm the models that suggested agriculture began relatively late in the Levant.

The Neolithic cultural sequence was thus incomplete in Syria. The sequence for the later Neolithic after 8,000 BP had been outlined, but too few sites had been excavated for us to discern variations in culture from one area to another. Most of the known sites were on the coast, or around Damascus in the central Levant, while much of the rest of Syria had still not been surveyed for Neolithic sites. Little was known about the earlier Neolithic. As far as the Euphrates was concerned, Buqras and Mureybit were far apart in time, so the sequence there, as elsewhere, was incomplete. Furthermore, the economic status of both sites was uncertain.

The stage preceding the Neolithic, the Epipalaeolithic, was hardly known at all. The only substantial Epipalaeolithic site discovered in Syria was at Yabrud on the eastern flank of the Anti-Lebanon Mountains (Rust 1950, pp. 107–121). No other Epipalaeolithic sites had been found farther north or east. This meant that nothing was known of the antecedents of either Neolithic culture or an agricultural way of life in the northern Levant.

SELECTION OF ABU HUREYRA

Once the surveys had been carried out, it became clear that the Middle Euphrates had considerable potential for prehistoric research. The initial excavation in 1965 of the small early Neolithic mound of Mureybit (van Loon 1968, table 1) showed that the valley had been inhabited when agriculture and settled life began, and thus that there was a good chance of learning more about this crucial transformation. The surveys located two other Neolithic sites, Tell Sheikh Hassan, a small prehistoric mound overlain by settlements of historic date (Rihaoui 1965, p. 107; van Loon 1967, p. 15), and Abu Hureyra itself, discovered by van Loon (1967, p. 7). During the reconnaissance of June 1971, Moore visited both and also attempted to find new prehistoric sites that might have been missed in the published surveys. It soon became clear that, although there were other Neolithic surface sites, Sheikh Hassan and Abu Hureyra were the only mounds with significant Neolithic deposits on them. The choice, then, was between these two.

Sheikh Hassan stood on the east bank of the Euphrates. Neolithic deposits could be seen on the river side of the mound where the terrace underneath was eroding away. The few flints collected there were similar to those from Mureybit, indicating that the two sites had been occupied at about the same time. Ashy layers and animal bones were washing out of the site, so organic preservation appeared to be quite good, but the mound was small and seemed to have been but briefly inhabited. It would not, therefore, yield the long Neolithic sequence of occupation that was one of our principal objects. Furthermore, the prehistoric deposits were almost completely buried by later remains. This made it a poor choice for an excavation that would have to be completed rapidly.

Abu Hureyra was a different kind of site. It lay 130 km east of Aleppo and 35 km downstream from Meskene (35° 52' N, 38° 24' E), on the north side of the modern village of Abu Hureyra (figure 2.4). The village bestrode the old valley road from Aleppo to Deir ez-Zor, and on to Baghdad. The lowest terrace projected out into the floodplain here, and it was on this prominent point that the prehistoric settlement was sited. On a clear day it commanded an uninterrupted view 60 km upriver as far as Jebel Aruda and 16 km downstream

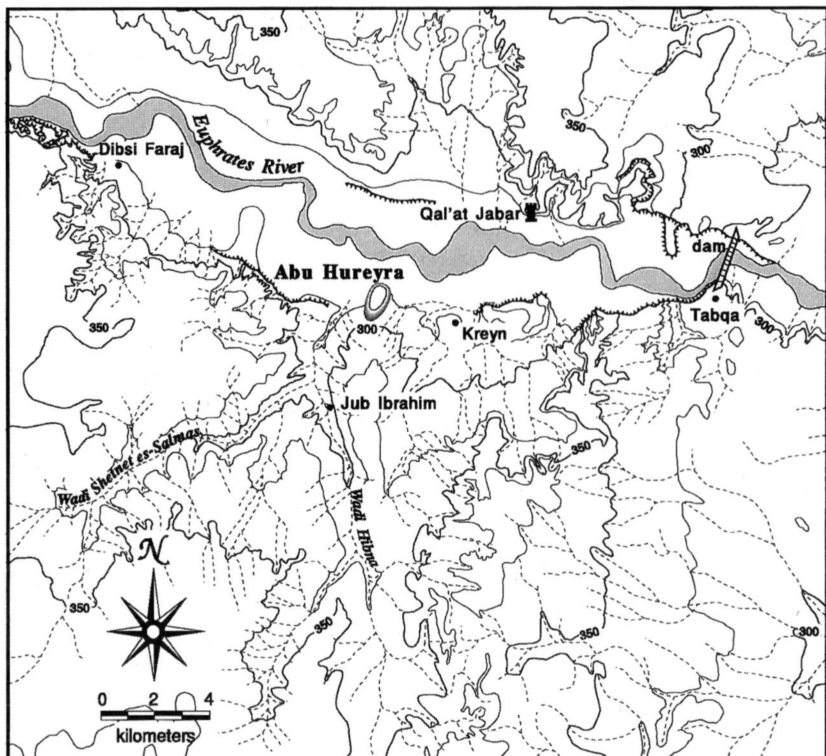

Figure 2.4 The Euphrates Valley from Dibsi to Tabqa and the immediate environs of Abu Hureyra.

to Tabqa (figures 2.5, 2.6). The prehistoric settlement was a very large, trapezoidal mound. The west side sloped steeply up from the edge of the floodplain to a ridge running from north to south, the main axis of the site (figure 2.7). The mound sloped more gently down to the floodplain on its northern side and fell away gradually to the east and south to merge with the terrace. Erosion had cut two gullies in the steep western slope, while on the north side modern fields covered a low projection of the ancient site onto the floodplain (figure 2.8). The mound was so large that it formed a significant feature in the landscape, particularly when viewed from the west, but it had eroded so much that at first glance it looked like a natural hill. Only when we walked over the mound did we become aware of its real nature, as the dense scatter of flints on the surface crunched beneath our feet.

The cemetery of the modern village of Abu Hureyra covered part of the eastern sector of the site (figure 2.9). There was one modern mudbrick house and traces of mudbrick police buildings dating from the French Mandate on the ridge of the mound, and several Byzantine graves were also visible at the northern end of the site, but the rest of its surface was clear. Van Loon (1967, p. 7) had collected a few sherds and flints that he compared to material from Buqras. We found no sherds but large quantities of flints scattered all over the surface of the mound as well as fragments of obsidian and basalt tools. The flints clearly resembled those from Buqras, and the scarcity of pottery indicated that the bulk of the deposits on the site must date from the aceramic, or early, Neolithic. The absence of any later material on the surface indicated that the settlement had not been inhabited since prehistoric times.

The site, then, had obviously been occupied for a long period during the early Neolithic. Its long cultural sequence should span much of the early history of agricultural development in north Syria. The mound was sufficiently

Figure 2.5 The Euphrates Valley looking west from Trench D on the Abu Hureyra mound. An oxbow lake, a relic of a recent meander of the Euphrates, lies at the foot of the mound. Several people are returning to the village bringing water from the river in cans strapped to their donkeys.

Figure 2.6 The Euphrates Valley looking east from the mound of Abu Hureyra to the Tabqa Heights. The dam lies on the horizon to the left of the heights. Note the sharp transition from the floodplain to the first terrace of the river on which Abu Hureyra sits and the steppe beyond.

Figure 2.7 The mound of Abu Hureyra seen at a distance from the northwest.

Figure 2.8 The Abu Hureyra mound from the northeast, viewed from the floodplain. The modern village lies to the south of the site on the left of the photograph.

Figure 2.9 Aerial photograph of the Abu Hureyra mound, from the northeast, taken from a kite. The sunlit area illuminates much of the surface of the prehistoric site. The northern end of the site extends into the present floodplain as far as the irrigation ditch that runs parallel with it diagonally across the photograph. Compare with Figure 2.14.

massive to conceal even older material that would leave no trace on the surface of the site. Furthermore, we could see that there were plenty of ashy deposits and quantities of animal bones on the site, so the chances of recovering good economic evidence were high. The absence of any later material, most unusual in itself, meant that excavation could begin at once in Neolithic levels. These advantages were so great that we applied to the Directorate General to excavate Abu Hureyra. Permission was readily granted, but it took a year to raise the money for the first season of excavation, so work did not begin until the summer of 1972.

The Syrian authorities had modified their Antiquities Law to accommodate the special circumstance of the salvage campaign. The Directorate General monitored all excavations, but excavators of sites in the dam area were permitted to retain half the artifacts they recovered for distribution to the institutions supporting their work. The other half was to be deposited in the Aleppo Museum. This dispensation made it easier for museums and other research institutions abroad to contribute money to the Abu Hureyra excavation, since they would receive well-documented material from the site to add to their collections (see appendix 7 for locations of artifacts). The Syrian authorities demonstrated great understanding in allowing us to export all our samples of organic remains for analysis once the excavation was over.

It was clear from the beginning that the excavation of Abu Hureyra should concentrate as much on questions of economy as on traditional cultural concerns. Scientists with interests in archaeobotany and faunal analysis should be invited to join the project team at the earliest possible moment, to contribute to the planning of the excavation before fieldwork began. Gordon Hillman was approached in Ankara at the conclusion of the initial surveys in 1971 and at once agreed to participate. Moore visited the University of Cambridge in February 1972 to consult the members of the British Academy Major Research Project on methods for recovering organic remains. During those discussions Anthony Legge offered to carry out the analysis of the faunal remains from Abu Hureyra. Thus, an archaeobotanist and archaeozoologist were full members of the team from the outset, and Hillman was able to join the excavation in the field during both seasons.

The advice of scientists in several other institutions was sought before the excavation started, and later as excavation and analysis proceeded. The collaboration with the Research Laboratory for Archaeology and the History of Art of the University of Oxford has been especially useful and has continued down to the present. We agreed initially to try to recover for them samples for archaeomagnetic dating, and asked for their help in obtaining thermoluminescence dates on potsherds. More recently, they have dated samples from Abu Hureyra in one of the most extensive programs of accelerator mass spectrometry (AMS) dating yet undertaken. One of the distinctive features of the Abu Hureyra project has been the long-term commitment of individual scientists and their institutions to the research.

LOCATION OF ABU HUREYRA

Abu Hureyra was sited on the lowest of the Euphrates terraces, called the "Mureibit Formation" by Heinzelin (1967, p. 24). The terrace drained easily and so the ground on which the settlement was built was dry and firm, in contrast to the floodplain, which was moist, often waterlogged, and occasionally flooded.

Abu Hureyra receives a little over 200 mm of rain a year today and so is just within the zone where dry farming may be carried on. The local climate of the valley is more temperate than that of the surrounding steppe. It is relatively humid there at all seasons of the year, and from autumn to spring mist forms in the early morning. In winter the temperature is a little higher and the winds less keen than on the adjacent plateau. These more clement conditions attract some beduin into the valley to escape the worst of the cold and to seek grazing near the river (figure 2.10). In summer a strong breeze from the west is funneled down the valley. Abu Hureyra is sufficiently elevated and juts far enough out into the valley to benefit from the breeze's refreshing effects.

The Euphrates dominates the environs of Abu Hureyra (figure 2.11). In its middle reaches it is a mature river that meanders across a broad floodplain. The course of the river changes frequently as the meanders migrate downstream. Thus, at the time of the Franco-British map survey in 1943, water still flowed in an old meander that ran along the western side of Abu Hureyra. This channel had been cut off many years before we came to excavate there, forming an oxbow lake. Because the Euphrates is wide, fast flowing, and relatively difficult to cross, it divides the floodplain into two halves. When the river flows on the far side of the floodplain, a large area of bottomland is accessible to the inhabitants of a settlement on the hither terrace. At other times, when the river approaches the terrace, the available land is sharply reduced.

There are no springs in the vicinity of Abu Hureyra today, so the inhabitants of the prehistoric site may have obtained their water from the Euphrates,

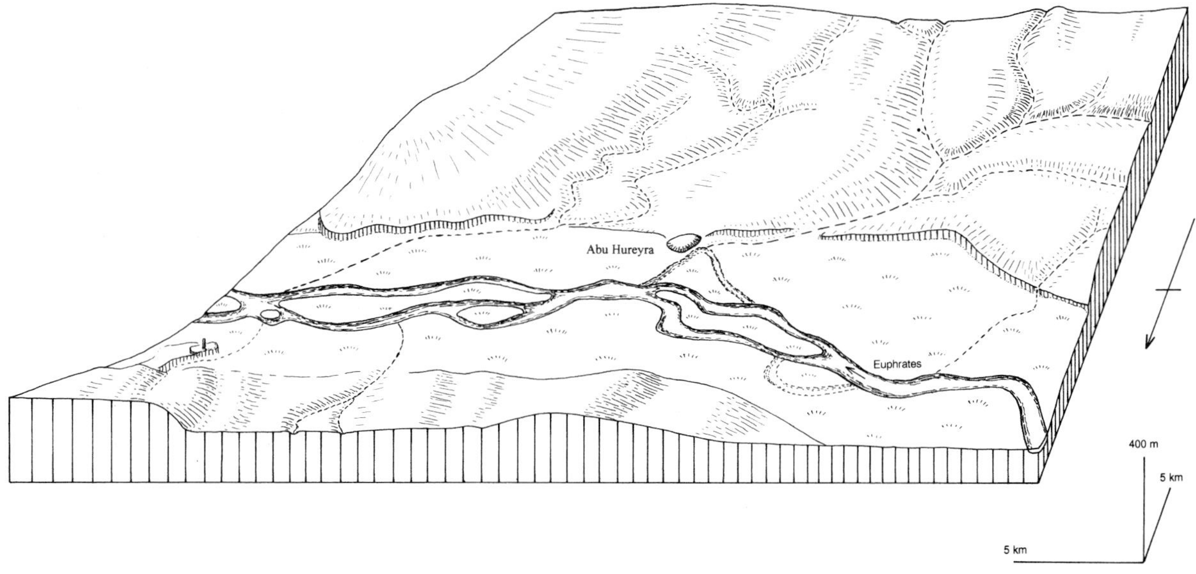

Figure 2.10 *(top)* A beduin encampment on the southern slopes of the mound, photographed in November 1973.

Figure 2.11 *(bottom)* Block diagram of Abu Hureyra and its environs, viewed from the northwest. Note the location of the site at the junction of the broad valley of the Euphrates and the gently dissected steppe country to the south.

like the people of the modern village. The evidence of the plant remains from Abu Hureyra indicates that much use was made of the floodplain, which in turn suggests that the river was often some distance away when the site was inhabited. Thus, some members of each family may have spent hours each day walking to and from the river to fetch water. It seems more likely, however, that there was another source of water close at hand in the valley formed by the confluence of the Wadi Shetnet es-Salmas and the Wadi Hibna.

The Wadi Shetnet es-Salmas and the Wadi Hibna together drain 2,500 km² of the steppe southwest of Abu Hureyra, a huge catchment that extends as far as the hills 80 km distant, the main ridge of which is formed by the Jebel Abu Rujmein (figure 2.12). The single wadi formed by their confluence debouches onto the floodplain 1 km west of Abu Hureyra. It is dry for much of the year today, but given the moister climate that prevailed 11,500 years ago and the extensive area of the wadi's catchment, it probably had a perennial stream then. There are springs in the wadi system, and the nearest of these, Jub Ibrahim, is 8 km up the Wadi Hibna from Abu Hureyra. This spring was dry when we saw it in the autumn of 1973 but was surrounded by tufa, indicating that it had flowed in the past. At the time the site was occupied, the wadi may have coursed eastward along the low scarp at the edge of the floodplain to join the Euphrates, bringing a source of water almost to the foot of the site. The wadi still had a relatively high water table, and the alluvial bottomlands in its lower reaches were being cultivated at the time of our excavation. The farmers of prehistoric Abu Hureyra, too, could have used this excellent arable land. The stream would have raised the moisture content of the soil and have watered an extensive area near the site, both in the wadi and on the adjacent floodplain.

The location of Abu Hureyra at the junction of the floodplain and the steppe was particularly advantageous for the inhabitants since it gave them ready access to the resources of both zones. Each has its own type of soil and distinct suite of plants and animals. The floodplain is covered with moist alluvium and marshes, with beds of reeds in old meanders and other damp places. These backswamps are edged with extensive patches of salt. The steppe to the south, on the other hand, is open, dry, undulating country. It has a thin cover of soil and is well drained, since much of the rainfall runs rapidly off the surface and the remainder is rapidly absorbed by the permeable underlying rocks. Both the floodplain and the steppe are heavily degraded today because much of their vegetation has been removed by humans and their livestock.

Our site catchment analysis of the vicinity of Abu Hureyra (figure 2.13) showed that the inhabitants of the modern village exploited the floodplain and steppe in different but complementary ways. The principal occupation of most villagers was arable farming, although they kept a few sheep, goats, cattle, and fowls as well. Until the middle years of this century the main crops grown in the valley had been wheat, barley, sorghum, and legumes, a traditional crop base that had its beginnings in the Neolithic. In recent decades these had largely been replaced by cotton, grown with official encouragement as a cash crop for export. The cotton was cultivated on the floodplain with the aid of pump irrigation. Because the floodplain remained moist for several months after the spring floods, the crop was irrigated only from the late summer until the harvest in mid autumn. Camels were rented from the beduin at harvest time to help bring in the huge sacks of cotton from the fields because the ground was too soft and uneven for vehicles to perform the task. The villagers still grew some wheat, barley, bitter vetch, peas, and chickpeas on the floodplain, and sorghum as a summer crop in hollows which remained damp through the

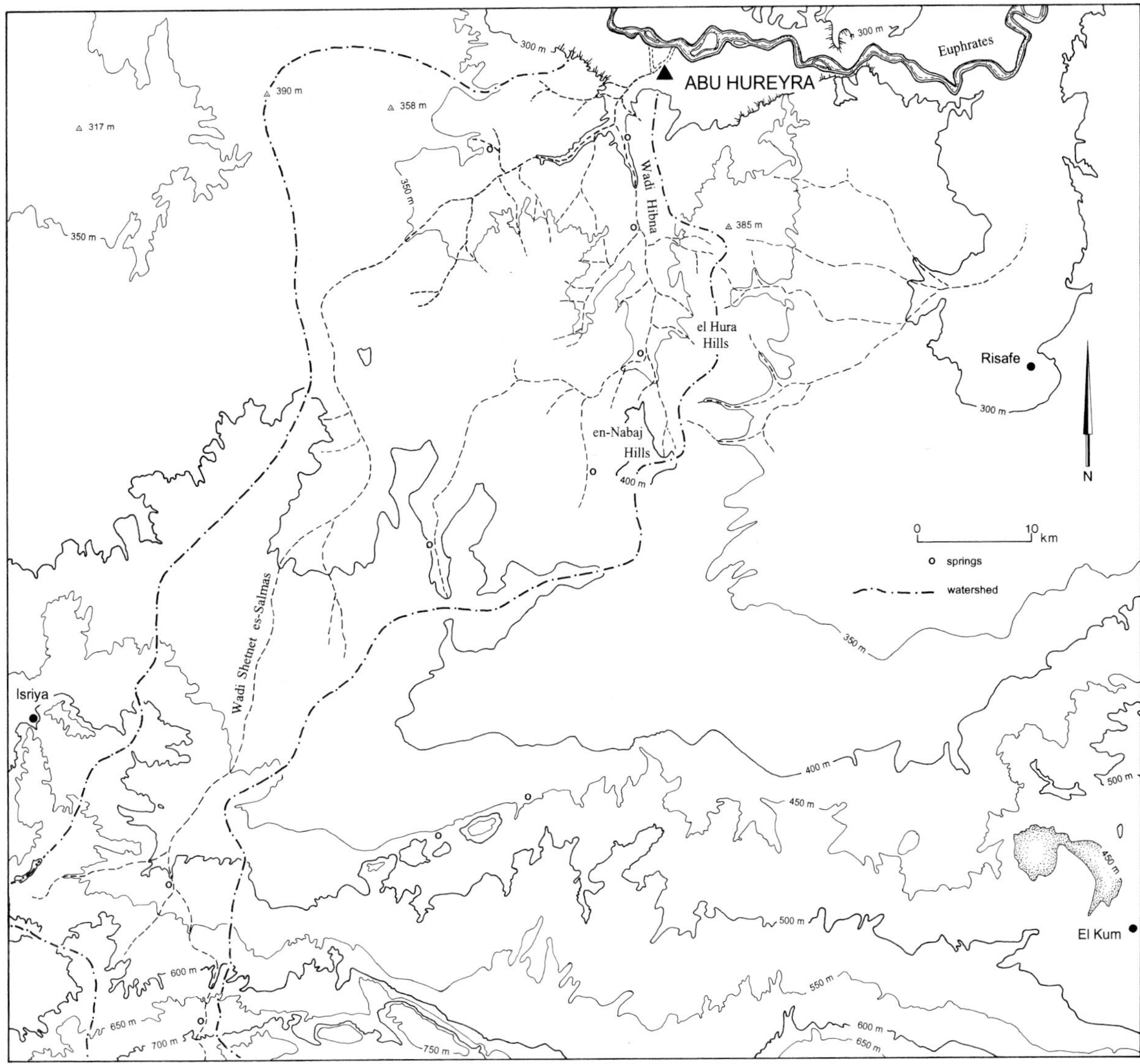

Figure 2.12 The Wadi Shetnet es-Salmas and Wadi Hibna drainage systems. Their combined catchment area is 2,500 km^2.

hotter months. To these were added tomatoes, aubergines, onions, and other vegetables. These crops were grown mainly for local consumption.

Some crops were planted on the steppe, mainly in hollows and lower slopes of the wadis where the moisture content of the soil was higher. Those crops would yield a significant return only in years of above-average rainfall. Thus, in 1972 wheat was grown on the steppe, and we even observed a few plantings of cotton in particularly damp hollows and, more extensively, below the break of long slopes. The next winter was unusually dry, such that all crops planted on the steppe in the spring of 1973 failed.

The villagers of modern Abu Hureyra used the steppe mainly as grazing for sheep and goats. The animals were kept in the village and would be taken out early each morning by the herdsmen or boys. Because of many years of overgrazing, they sometimes had to travel so far from the village to find plants on which to feed that they did not return until late at night. There was some other permanent grazing on the floodplain along the saline, silted-up meanders of the river and the south bank of the Euphrates. Following the harvest in May

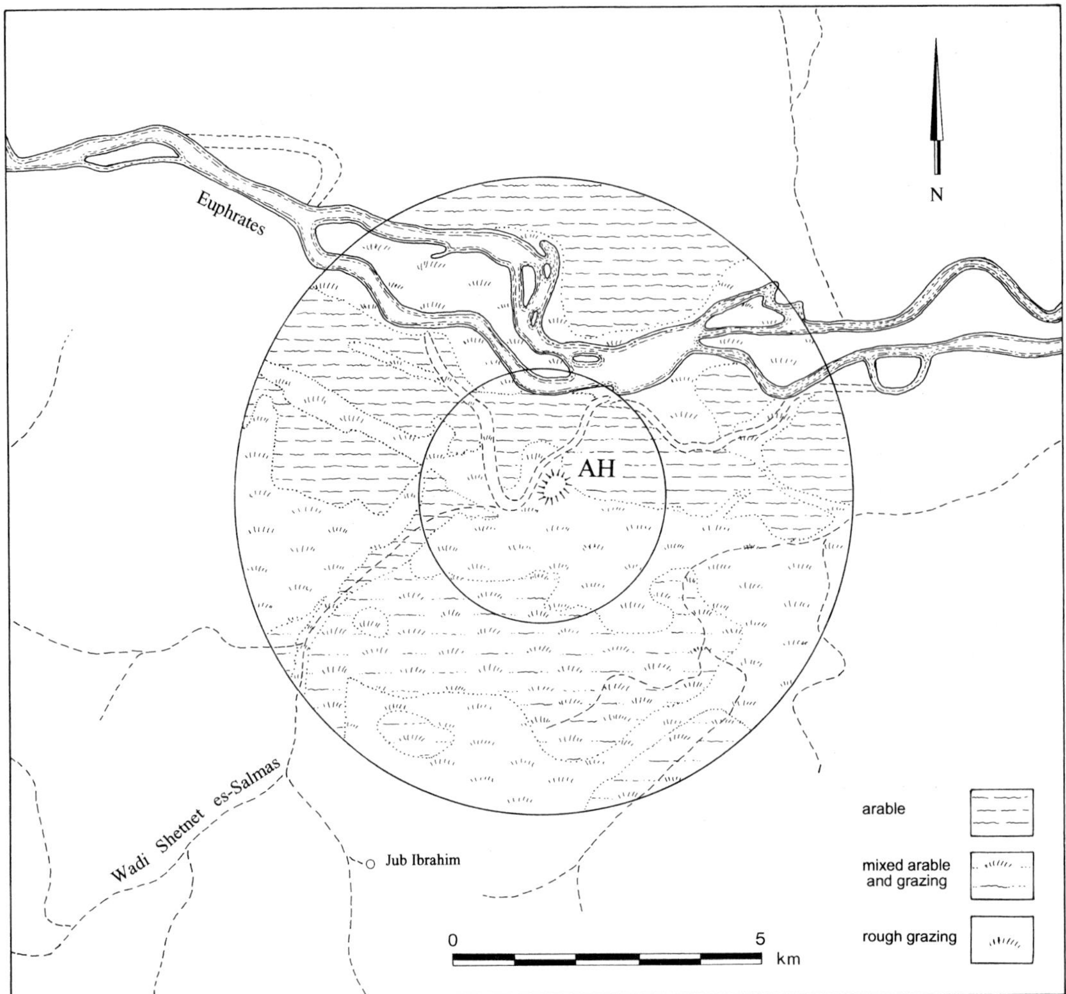

Figure 2.13 Modern land use in the Abu Hureyra site catchment. The map shows the distribution of the different types of land at distances of 2 and 5 km from the site. About half the catchment today consists of good quality arable. The other half is composed of mixed arable and grazing land and rough pasture. Much of the steppe south of the site would have afforded good arable land during the time the site was inhabited, so the proportion of arable to grazing land would have been significantly higher then.

and June, the fields of wheat and barley stubble on the floodplain were opened up for grazing. As the level of the river fell in the late summer, the flats and islands provided more pasture. This additional grazing was important because it provided new feeding grounds at a time of the year when the spring vegetation of the steppe had withered.

The modern villagers exploited the steppe and floodplain in contrasting ways, yet our understanding of the environment during the prehistoric occupation of Abu Hureyra suggests that a different balance would have been more appropriate in the past. The steppe and floodplain would have supported a much richer vegetation, while the soils on the steppe would have been more productive. Furthermore, the effective rainfall was higher during the prehistoric occupation, further enhancing the potential of the steppe.

The immediate environs of the site provided inorganic raw materials that were of use to the prehistoric inhabitants of Abu Hureyra. The gravels along the banks of the Euphrates were composed of a variety of rocks, many of them hard, igneous pebbles that were foreign to the local geological succession. These stones had been carried downriver from the mountains of eastern Turkey. Many of the stone axes, chisels, weights, hammers, and other heavy stone tools at Abu Hureyra were shaped from these pebbles. Nodules of flint on the surfaces of the lower Euphrates terraces and in nearby wadis derived from eroded surface conglomerate, some of which still survived on the Dibsi heights 20 km to the west. This was the flint from which many of the implements at Abu Hureyra were made. The Eocene chalk of the valley sides contained beds of fresh, finer-grained flint of better quality than the terrace material. We think this was probably the source of the flint used to make many of the blade tools at Abu Hureyra. The harder chalk itself was used to make palettes, platters, and other artifacts.

There was some limestone available a few kilometers away that was used for grinding stones, but the inhabitants of Abu Hureyra 2 had to travel farther to obtain the great quantities of gypsum they needed for plaster. The nearest out-crops were in the Risafe Basin, the center of which lay 40 km to the east southeast. It is possible that the fine, colored limestones used to make small bowls and dishes came from this area, but we have not identified their sources. The inhabitants of both settlements used basalt for grinding stones. The nearest sources were lava flows at Khanasir, 80 km to the west, and Halebiye, 130 km down the Euphrates. The people of Abu Hureyra 2 lined their baskets and mats with bitumen and used it to haft some of their flint tools. Chesney (1833, p. 46) reported that there was said to be a seep of bitumen across the river at Qal'at Jabar, a statement we have been unable to confirm. There are numerous seeps of bitumen above Deir ez-Zor (Ainsworth 1888, I, p. 332), 160 km downstream from Abu Hureyra, so the substance may also have been collected from there. Thus, raw materials that were used in considerable quantities in both settlements at Abu Hureyra were obtained not only from the immediate vicinity of the site but also from sources that were a day or two's walk away, while the most prolific bitumen seeps were four to five days distant (see figure 7.1).

EXCAVATION STRATEGY

Our lack of knowledge of the earlier stages of the Neolithic in Syria was the most important consideration that influenced our plans to excavate Abu Hureyra. We thought it essential, first, to obtain from the site as long and complete a sequence of occupation as possible. To achieve this, we dug a series of deep trenches across the site from the surface of the mound to the natural subsoil beneath (figure 2.14). The trenches were spaced wide apart in order to establish the sequence of occupation in all sectors of the mound. Four of them, Trenches A, B, C, and E, were dug along the main north-south axis of the site, because we expected that the deepest deposits with the most complete sequences would be found there. Trenches A, B, and C were placed near the summits of the three highest points along the ridge, avoiding the remains of the modern buildings on each (figure 2.15). Trench D was placed as far down the western slope of the site as possible, to find out if there had ever been terrace walls on that side, or a perimeter wall around the settlement, as at Jericho. Trench E was sited on a level platform at a lower elevation that formed the northern end of the mound. In the second season we excavated Trenches F and G in the eastern half of the site, where the deposits were shallower, to learn more about the history of expansion and contraction of the settlement. All the trenches, except Trench A, were excavated to the natural subsoil. We learned from them that there had been two settlements at Abu Hureyra. The remains of the earliest, Abu Hureyra 1, a settlement of Mesolithic or Epipalaeolithic affinities, were

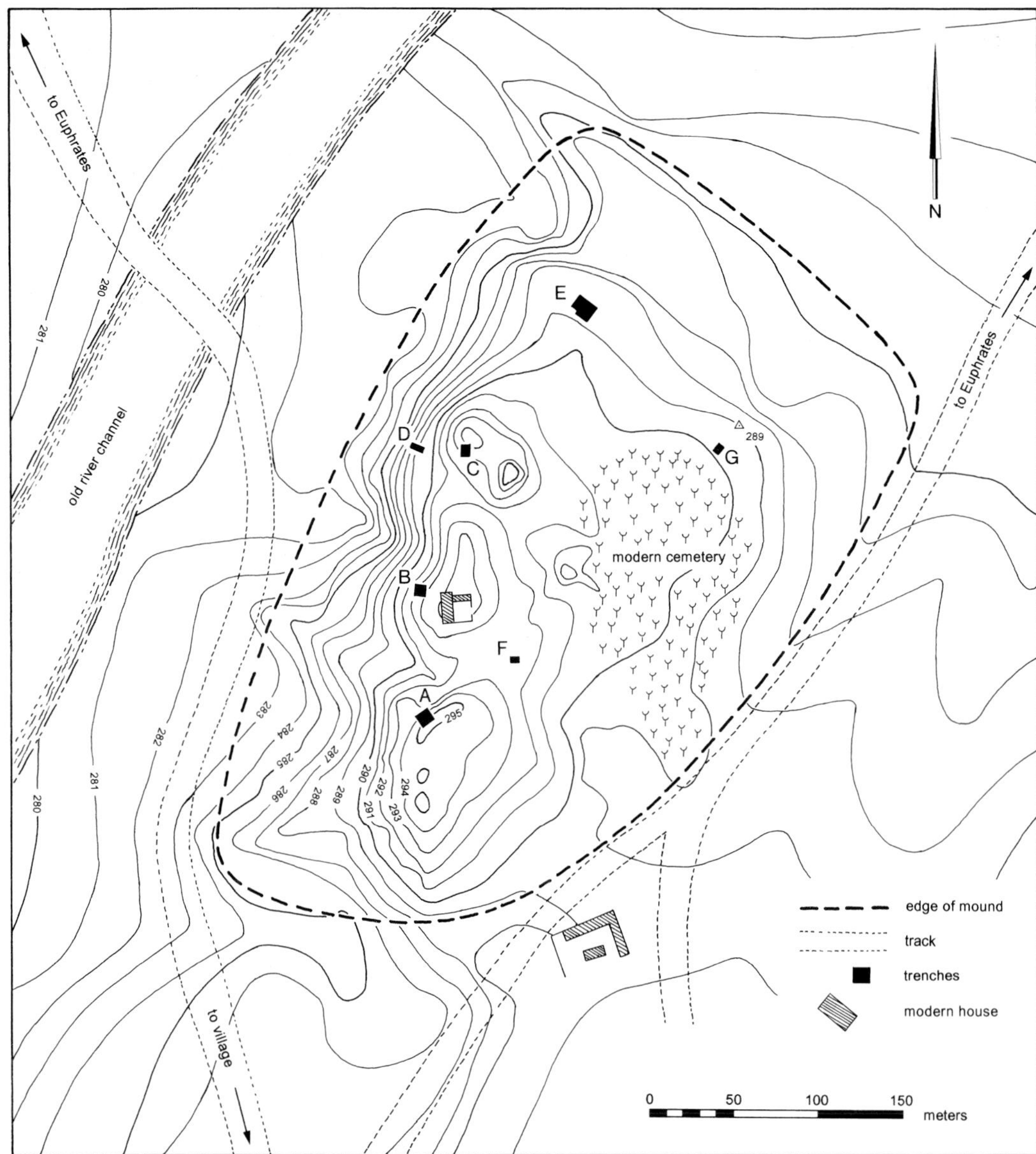

Figure 2.14 Contour plan of the mound of Abu Hureyra showing the extent of the site and the location of the trenches. Compare with Figure 2.9.

found only in Trench E, so we concluded that this settlement had been confined to the northwest corner of the site. The deposits of the second, the early Neolithic village of Abu Hureyra 2, made up the bulk of the mound and covered completely the remains of Abu Hureyra 1 (figure 2.16).

Our second aim was to examine the layout of these settlements and to recover plans of individual buildings. To accomplish this, Trenches A, B, C, and E were enlarged in the second season of excavation. That enabled us to determine the orientation and form of the houses of Abu Hureyra 2 and the plans of several of them. In Trench E we were able to excavate structures of the underlying Abu Hureyra 1 settlement.

Our third aim was to obtain as complete a sample of artifacts and organic remains as possible from the trenches, in order to reconstruct the culture and economy of the inhabitants of each settlement. The most informative categories of economic evidence were expected to be animal bones and carbonized

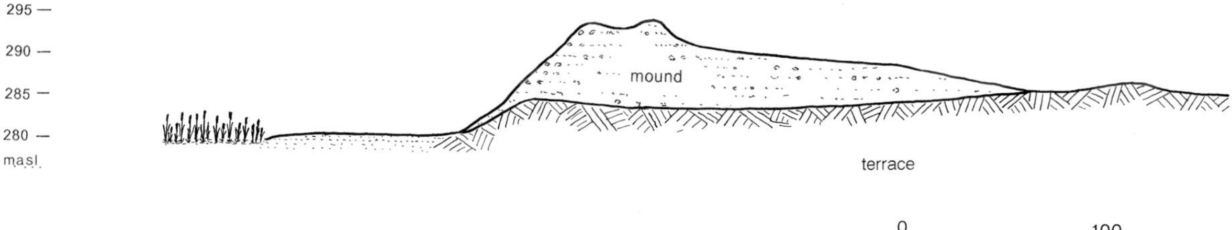

seeds, most of which were remains of food. The artifacts and bones were collected as the trenches were dug and from dry sieving all the excavated soil. Large samples of soil were then passed through froth flotation machines to extract the seeds. These methods had been pioneered at Nahal Oren (Noy, Legge, and Higgs 1973, p. 75) and a few other recently excavated sites in Southwest Asia, but this was the first time they had been used systematically in the excavation of a big site. The systematic application of these methods of recovery enabled us to collect nearly all the artifacts, bones, and seeds present in the soil we excavated.

Figure 2.15 (*top*) The west slope of the mound from the southwest, showing Trenches, A, B, and C under excavation.

Figure 2.16 (*bottom*) Section across the mound from northwest to southeast in the vicinity of Trench C. The drawing shows how the natural terrace beneath the mound dips down toward the floodplain.

The fact that we were excavating Abu Hureyra as part of a salvage program set limits to what we could achieve. The chief constraint was shortness of time, since we would have to complete the excavation in two years. The strategy for the excavation had to be decided at the outset and adhered to as far as was possible. We had to concentrate on the main goals of our project and achieve them as fast as we could. The two most important were to determine the sequence of occupation and to recover evidence for the economy. Yet we were excavating a prehistoric site where care would be required to recover evidence of structures, artifacts, and, often fragile, organic material. We decided, therefore, to conduct the excavation as a research project and to aim for the highest standards of fieldwork that we could reach. We would try to excavate as much of the site as we could and to recover the largest possible samples of artifacts and organic remains in the time available. The analysis of most of those remains would have to be postponed until after the dig was finished.

We planned two seasons of work. The first was a campaign two months long, from 23 September to 28 November 1972. The site itself was so extraordinary, and its sequence potentially so significant, that we had to establish an outline of the history of its development in this first season. The excavation of Trenches A, B, C, D, and E began at once, and before the season was over, we reached the natural subsoil in Trenches D and E. Late in the season in Trench E we reached the deposits of Abu Hureyra 1, beneath the remains of Abu Hureyra 2. This unexpected discovery added greatly to the significance of the site because it gave us an opportunity of investigating two superimposed settlements, one probably of hunters and gatherers and the other of early farmers. The excavation of Trench E also suggested that there was a gap in the sequence of occupation between the end of Abu Hureyra 1 and the foundation of Abu Hureyra 2. From Trenches A, B, C, and E we learned something of the nature of the later phases of Abu Hureyra 2, while Trench D provided information about its early years.

We started to recover the organic samples we needed immediately. All soil was dry sieved from the outset, and samples were processed in a flotation machine. Hillman visited the excavation in October 1972 to give advice on recovery methods and to study the local vegetation. He examined some of the flotation samples and was able to confirm at once that Abu Hureyra 2 was an early agricultural settlement.

The results of the first season of excavation made it imperative that the work be conducted on a larger scale in the second season, planned for the following year. The campaign was extended to four months, the digging itself lasting from 20 August to 2 December 1973. Trench E demanded special attention because of the discovery of the settlement of Abu Hureyra 1 there. This trench was expanded greatly to examine the two superimposed settlements over as large an area as possible. It was vital that organic remains continued to be recovered systematically from every trench and that a special effort be made to recover all seeds and bones from Abu Hureyra 1.

The circumstances of the project demanded that we concentrate on Abu Hureyra itself, but we could not fully interpret the cultural and economic data from the excavation unless we knew something of the setting of the site. To obtain the necessary basic information about the nature of the immediate environment and present use of the land, we carried out a site catchment analysis of the vicinity of Abu Hureyra (Moore 1975, p. 66). This was complemented by a survey of other prehistoric sites nearby, to relate Abu Hureyra to contemporary patterns of settlement.

The size of the site and the short time available in which to excavate it compelled us to work on a larger scale than usual when digging a prehistoric site in Southwest Asia. We took a team of 10 people into the field in 1972 and 20 in 1973. Many of them had worked on prehistoric sites in Britain and elsewhere. Most acted as site supervisors but others were engaged in the cleaning, registration, and drawing of finds. As was customary on excavations in Syria, we employed people from the village of Abu Hureyra to dig the site and man the flotation machines, an average of 25 in 1972 and a maximum of 50 in 1973.

The modern village of Abu Hureyra, like many of the villages along the Middle Euphrates both ancient and modern, was strung out along the edge of the low terrace beside the floodplain. Most of its inhabitants were farmers, members of several ethnic groups who had moved to the Euphrates Valley shortly after the foundation of the independent state of Syria in 1946. We lived in the village close to the site, in tents and mudbrick houses. Living conditions were simple; there was neither electricity nor running water. Women brought up water from the Euphrates 1 km away for their own households in cans strapped to donkeys, an activity that could occupy a third of their day. There were two watermen who carried water from the river in large, mule-drawn carts, from whom we obtained water for washing and flotation.

In the second season the excavation began well, and we made substantial progress in the first few weeks. Then on 6 October we learned that war had broken out. The war at once became the main concern of our Syrian hosts, and it placed us in a delicate position as their guests. Would they prefer us to continue working or to depart? The well-being of our team and the needs of our project were our two other principal concerns. We had enlarged our trenches but had not yet excavated them to the necessary depth. Although we were making good progress in Trench E, we could not hope to excavate the underlying settlement of Abu Hureyra 1 until early November. Our organic samples were already substantial, but they were still almost all from the upper levels of the site. The archaeological case for continuing to dig was strong, and we knew that if we left we could not return to finish our task before the site was flooded. The few other foreign teams still at work in Syria were nearing the end of their campaigns that year, and they soon departed. The staff of the Directorate General of Antiquities and Museums declared that they wished us to finish our excavation as we had planned. It was clear that we were in no danger because we were working far away from the front line. We decided to continue.

The remainder of the season was a difficult time for us all. Supplies of fuel for cooking and vehicles ran out. This loss restricted travel and made it difficult to provide hot food for our team as winter advanced. The young men of the village were conscripted, and some of them were killed. The memory of the funeral ceremonies for them in the village and the expressions of grief of their families is with us still. Through all this our Syrian colleagues and friends offered reassurance and did all they could to support us. Our team responded by giving their best. It was through their determination and fortitude, leavened with good humor, that the task we set ourselves was accomplished.

In such circumstances, it was essential to maintain the routine of the excavation and to concentrate on the most important objectives. The survey was curtailed and resources were conserved for excavation and flotation. The excavation itself was continued on the largest possible scale, but we concentrated on reaching the natural subsoil in all the trenches and on examining the Abu Hureyra 1 settlement. In the end, we achieved almost all that we had intended.

By the end of the second season we had confirmed the sequence of occupation across the site. Remains of Abu Hureyra 1 were found in Trench E alone. In all the other trenches we encountered substantial deposits of the second settlement, Abu Hureyra 2. This settlement was obviously very large and long-lived. Scant traces of an intermediate phase of occupation were found in our excavations so it appeared that there had been an interruption in occupation between these two settlements. Several of the trenches were expanded to investigate the use of space across the site. These exposures were sufficient to give us a general idea of the layout of Abu Hureyra 2 and some information about how individual buildings had been used. We were also able to determine the nature and disposition of some of the structures of Abu Hureyra 1. It was not possible in the time we had available to open up large areas of the site to examine in detail the plans of the two settlements.

At the conclusion of the excavation we had recovered systematically several metric tons of flints and 4,000 registered objects. We had excavated the remains of about 150 humans from Abu Hureyra 2, and others from more recent burials in the surface of the mound, a sample of about 200 individuals in all. We had saved all the available charcoal for radiocarbon dating and had plaster, minerals, and other materials for analysis. There were samples of soil for insect and pollen analysis, more soil to provide a check on the efficacy of the flotation system, as well as mudbricks for archaeobotanic study of their temper.

The sieving and flotation had yielded unprecedented quantities of faunal remains and carbonized seeds. We had collected animal bones from almost every level in each trench, the whole sample amounting to more than two metric tons in weight. There were also small quantities of shells. The flotation program had yielded well over 500 liters of plant remains, recovered from every trench. We were unable to process all the flotation soil samples from the last few weeks of the excavation because of difficulties caused by the war. Notwithstanding, we took away from the site several complete sequences of plant remains from Abu Hureyra 2, as well as substantial quantities of material from each phase of occupation of Abu Hureyra 1.

We departed from Abu Hureyra on 6 December 1973. In March of the following year the sluice gates of the new dam were closed and the valley behind began to fill with water. Abu Hureyra disappeared one week later (figure 2.17). It was time to begin to analyze the records we had made and the materials we had recovered, to reconstruct the culture and economy of the ancient inhabitants of the site.

ANALYSIS OF THE RESULTS

Our next task was to carry out an initial study of the material and to publish a preliminary account of the results of the excavation. That report (Moore 1975) described the setting of the site, outlined its sequence of occupation, and illustrated some of the characteristic finds. It also gave a general indication of the place of Abu Hureyra in Levantine prehistory. We provided information about the plants and animals used in the two settlements, pointed out some of the differences in their economies, and proposed some initial hypotheses by way of explanation.

We knew that Abu Hureyra was an extraordinary site, but it became clear to us that the record of human activity there had much greater potential than we had realized for investigation of the development of cultivation and herding in Southwest Asia. This was possible because of the quality of the material we had recovered and its quantity. That itself posed problems: the mass of material awaiting study was so daunting that several years passed before we could make much headway with it. The scope of the project had to be ex-

Figure 2.17 The remains of the modern village of Abu Hureyra seen in November 1974, with the old Aleppo to Baghdad road in the center. The prehistoric mound lies behind the ruins of the village under the waters of the new lake.

panded, and large-scale studies of the plant remains and fauna carried out, in addition to the work already planned on the cultural record. After years of steady but slow progress, beginning in 1981 Hillman and Legge mounted separate research projects to study these remains, funded by the British Science and Engineering Research Council and conducted at the University of London. Two more scientists were recruited to help, Susan Colledge for the plants and Peter Rowley-Conwy for the animal bones.

Studies of the rest of the Abu Hureyra material have since been carried out. Theya Molleson, of the Natural History Museum in London, is analyzing the substantial collection of human remains from the site. The initial results of her work are presented here, and further analyses are in progress to complete this research project. Other archaeologists have analyzed the artifacts. Deborah Olszewski has studied the entire collection of flints from the Abu Hureyra 1 settlement, and the results of her work are published here in full. Lawrence Keeley (1983), Emily Moss (1983), and Patricia Anderson-Gerfaud (1983) have examined the traces of microwear on flint tools from both settlements. The results have been encouraging, and there is clearly scope for much more research of this kind in the future. Sandra Olsen has analyzed all the bone tools from Abu Hureyra, and the results of part of her work are published in this book. Marie Le Mière has analyzed some of the plaster, plaster vessels, and pottery from the site to determine the nature of the materials from which they were made and the manner of their manufacture. Recently, Valerie Roitel and George Willcox have analyzed samples of charcoal that have expanded our understanding of the ecology of the region during Abu Hureyra 1 times.

A program of radiocarbon dating has established the dates of the two settlements at Abu Hureyra. The initial series of dates was obtained by the British Museum (Burleigh, Matthews, and Ambers 1982; Burleigh, Ambers, and Matthews 1982). These were of great value in providing an outline chronology for the site, but the dates themselves raised several questions, and the need for a more detailed chronology of the site and its contents grew as the analysis proceeded. The new technique of accelerator dating has provided the means of resolving the outstanding chronological problems. The large number of accelerator dates obtained by the Radiocarbon Accelerator Unit of the Oxford Research Laboratory has had a profound impact on our interpretation of Abu Hureyra (Moore 1992).

There has been more fieldwork, too. The abrupt end of the modest survey we had intended to carry out around Abu Hureyra seemed all the more regrettable as we came to appreciate better the implications of the nature and location of the site. Legge, Hillman, and their colleagues have carried out further field studies in north Syria and adjacent regions to obtain more information about the ecological potential of the environs of Abu Hureyra. Those studies have taken on special significance since they have led us to reconsider many of the traditional ecological assumptions on which earlier work in those domains has been based. Moore, too, has been back to the Euphrates Valley, in 1976, 1977, 1984, and in 1992 to look for other sites contemporary with Abu Hureyra. He has attempted to fill in the details of the cultural landscape in order to understand the relationship of Abu Hureyra to other sites. This would allow us to answer the question of whether Abu Hureyra was a unique site or simply one of several that flourished in the Euphrates Valley. The results of some of this work have already been published (Sanlaville 1985), and a brief answer to the question may be given here. There are very few Epipalaeolithic and early Neolithic sites contemporary with Abu Hureyra in the entire stretch of the Euphrates Valley from Jerablus down to the Halabiye narrows, above Deir ez-Zor. Nearly all those sites that have been found are in the salvage area. No other site of the scale of Abu Hureyra has been discovered anywhere else in the Euphrates Valley, though two other large Neolithic sites, Mollah Assaad and Halula (Molist Montaña 1996), have been found west of the river above Yusef Pasha. It thus appears that the section from Meskene to Tabqa was the most favorable location in the valley for settlement at the time of the Pleistocene-Holocene transition, and that only at Abu Hureyra did the right conditions exist for a very large, long-lived village to develop.

The excavators of any archaeological site incur an obligation to publish a description of the results in full, and in as objective a manner as possible. That obligation is especially strong when the site itself is of more than local importance and is subsequently destroyed. We intend to go further in this book, to bring together the results of the cultural and economic studies to present an integrated interpretation of the development of Abu Hureyra. We hope thereby to make a contribution to understanding the development of farming and sedentary life far beyond the Euphrates Valley. To make the basis of our interpretations clear, we shall present many of the data from which they are derived to permit the reader to check our results. To facilitate this, we have tried throughout to separate the presentation of data from our discussions of their implications. We recognize, nonetheless, that any publication of data is itself necessarily a subjective exercise.

This book is intended to be a definitive statement of our results. It will be followed, in time, by further detailed studies of particular issues that arise from our conclusions. There will be more analyses of trenches A, C, and F not discussed here, the economic data, the human remains, and the artifacts. The record recovered from Abu Hureyra has the capacity to answer many more questions than the ones we have thought to ask so far. Methods of analysis developed since the conclusion of the excavation, of which accelerator dating is an excellent example, have already made it possible to address issues we thought were beyond our reach even a few years ago. That will happen again in the future.

3 The Setting

THE GEOGRAPHICAL BACKGROUND

Syria lies at the heart of Southwest Asia, contiguous with Asia Minor, Mesopotamia, and the southern Levant. The Taurus and Anti-Taurus Mountains on the northern horizon separate the Syrian plains from the high Anatolian plateau. To the west Syria confronts the Mediterranean. Immediately inland from the coast lies the Jebel Ansariye (Alawiye) that rises to 1,500 m (figure 3.1). It is part of a chain of mountains that stretches the length of the Levant from the Amanus south to the Mountains of Lebanon and the Judean Hills. A line of massive faults on the inland side of these coastal mountains, the northernmost extension of the African Rift Valley, marks the western edge of the Arabian plate. The faults define a series of deep trenches in which flow the Orontes, Litani, and Jordan rivers. Beyond lies the interior of Syria, a plateau that slopes gently down to the east. This plateau is separated from the Mediterranean zone by the Jebel Ansariye but is open southward and eastward to Arabia and Mesopotamia. Its climate is thus continental in character.

Lines of hills stretch northeastward across the plateau from the Anti-Lebanon Mountains to the Jebel Sinjar. The rest of the Syrian plateau is open, rolling country of vast horizons. The surface rocks of this region consist of limestone, chalk, marls, and gypsum (Wolfert 1967, p. 282). Volcanic activity right across Syria, from Jebel Druze in the southwest to Hasseke and the Tigris in the northeast, has left extensive fields of basalt on the surface. Much of this vulcanism took place during the Pleistocene, and some even in the Holocene.

The structural geology of Syria has dictated the pattern of surface drainage. The Euphrates dominates the drainage system of the interior, and its course follows the tilt of the plateau toward Mesopotamia. Two modest tributaries, the Balikh and the Khabur, join the Middle Euphrates from the north, and one, the Sajur, from the west, but these rivers contribute little to its flow. Much of the rest of the interior is drained by an extensive series of wadis that runs

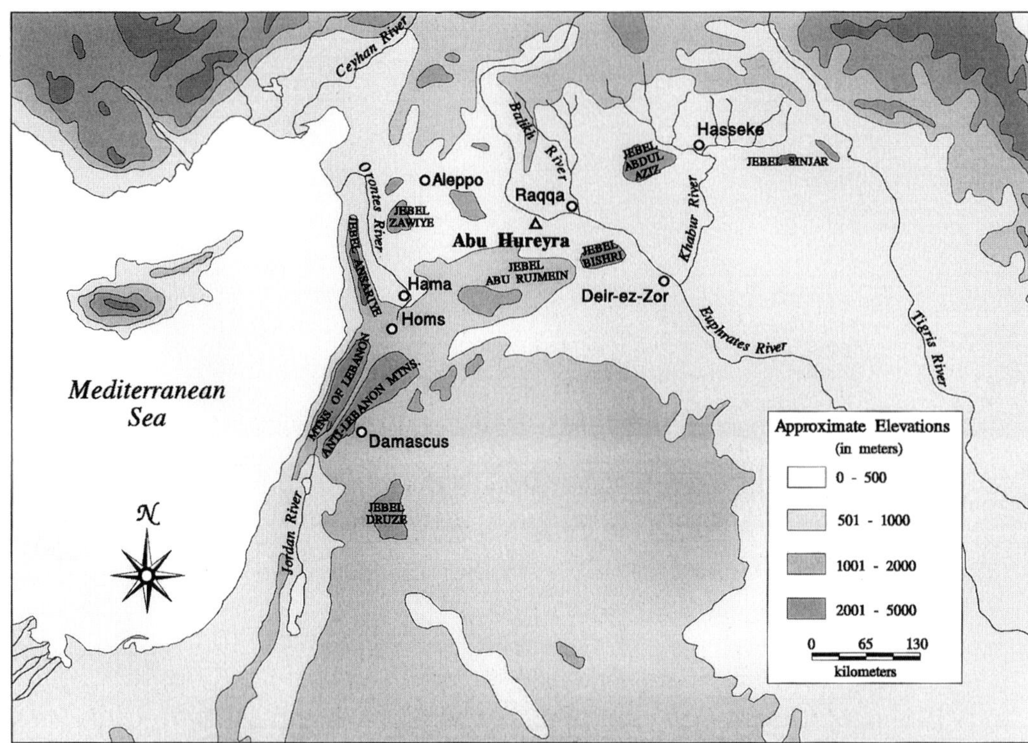

Figure 3.1 Physical map of Syria.

into the Euphrates from the west. These wadis are very large but carry little water today. This suggests that they were created long ago, perhaps in the early Quaternary, during periods of much higher rainfall (Fisher 1978, p. 39). Surface water from those few areas of the plateau that lie outside the Euphrates catchment runs into interior basins.

The Euphrates is deeply incised into the plateau, a distinctive characteristic attributed to tectonic changes and a greater flow of water in the past (van Liere 1960–1961, p. 8). The left bank slopes gently down to the floodplain, but the right or south bank of the river has cliffs all along its middle course. This is because the river is slowly shifting southwestward across the plateau (Wilkinson 1978, p. 225). It appears that the Euphrates is going through a phase of downcutting, leaving a series of terraces at higher levels that were created during the Pleistocene. Evidence from Abu Hureyra has provided indications of a contrary trend, aggradation of the floodplain of the river, in the last 10,000 years. We found that the natural surface underlying the Abu Hureyra 1 settlement in Trench E was at about the same elevation as the present level of the floodplain. If we assume that this early village was comfortably above flood level when it was inhabited, then several meters of alluvium have accumulated on the valley floor since.

The Euphrates receives most of its water from winter snow and rain in the mountains of eastern Anatolia. This gives the river a distinctive seasonal pattern of rise and fall (Ionides 1937, chapter 4). The middle course of the river is at its lowest in September (figure 3.2). There is a slight rise in October and November as evaporation declines and the winter rains begin. Heavier precipitation from December onward leads to a marked increase in its level. Rains and then melting snow cause the Euphrates to rise steadily thereafter, until it reaches a peak in April. The level stays high through May and then declines rapidly. For much of the year the surface of the river is well below the level of

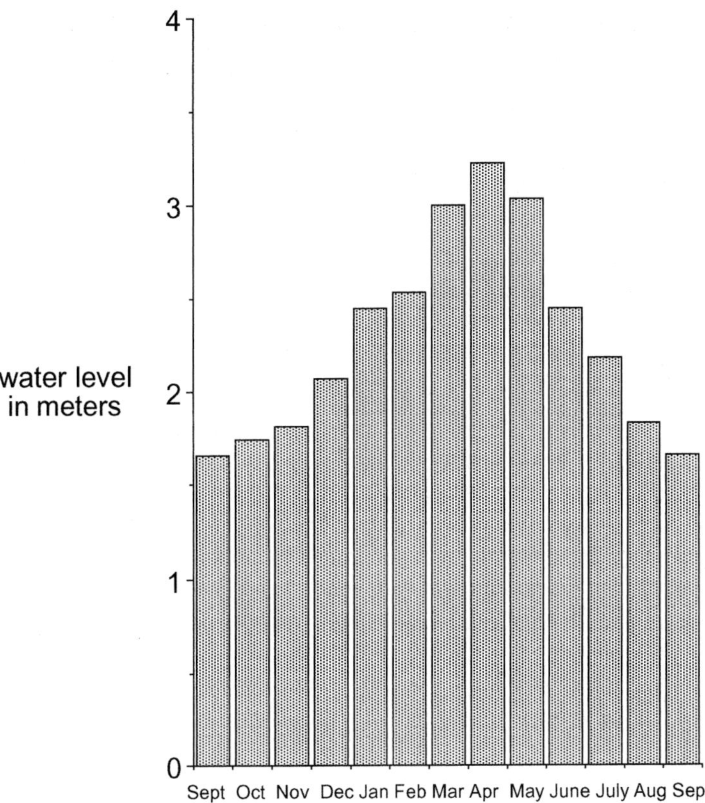

Figure 3.2 Graph of the mean rise and fall of the Euphrates at Jerablus 1930–1932 (after Ionides 1937, table 18). The water level was measured from an arbitrary datum.

the floodplain. The rise in water level comes too late in the growing season to be of much use for irrigating crops. Before the advent of water wheels and mechanical pumps, its waters could be used for irrigation only by digging massive canals, several kilometers in length. This was beyond the capacity, or needs, of the inhabitants of early villages. We think, therefore, that the people of Abu Hureyra made little use of the Euphrates to irrigate their fields.

The climate of Syria is determined by regional patterns of pressure, precipitation, and temperature, but these are strongly modified by the local topography. We know that the climate has fluctuated significantly over the last 20,000 years, yet many of the same controlling factors have remained important throughout. Moreover, it has always been marked by strong seasonal contrasts. We need, therefore, to understand the nature of the climate of the present if we are to determine in what ways it was different in the past.

The coastal mountains separate Syria into two climatic zones: the Mediterranean coast and the arid interior. The winds over Syria at all seasons of the year are predominantly from the west. During the summer, an area of low pressure over Arabia draws in air from the continental interior of Asia to the northeast. A subsidiary low over Cyprus turns these air currents such that they reach Syria from the southwest (Fisher 1978, p. 46). This air carries little moisture, so no rain falls during the summer months. Air circulation in the winter is dominated by the buildup of a massive high pressure zone over Asia, with sometimes a subsidiary high in Anatolia. This draws in air from the west from October to May. Sometimes depressions from the Atlantic travel the length of the Mediterranean to reach Syria but, more often, smaller depressions form in the eastern Mediterranean. It is from these that the Levant receives much of its rain today (Fisher 1978, p. 48). The depressions continue on across Syria, turn southeast into Mesopotamia, and eventually reach the Persian Gulf. The effect of relief on the distribution of rainfall is strong. The coast is relatively moist, but the Jebel Ansariye and the Mountains of Lebanon create a rain-shadow, so the plateau is arid even though its western edge is only 70 km inland (figure 3.3). On the plateau itself the isohyets are widely spaced, especially in the latitude of Abu Hureyra. This means that a slight rise or fall in rainfall can move them many kilometers and have an equally pronounced effect on the boundaries of vegetation zones.

The general patterns of circulation are interrupted by incursions of air from other directions that can have a profound effect on the local weather. Air from the frigid interior of Asia may reach the Levant from the northeast in the autumn and early winter. This leads to anticyclonic conditions with bright, dry, cool days. Then, in the late winter, raw, moist air from eastern Europe may come in behind a depression, bringing distinctly unpleasant, wet weather. During the spring and autumn the depressions may draw in hot, dry air from the Arabian interior. The effects of this can be sudden and severe. The wind turns southerly or southwesterly and increase to gale force, often bringing with it a massive load of dust. The humidity drops sharply, and temperatures can rise between 15° and 20°C in a few hours. These desert storms, or *khamsins*, are especially common in the spring, when they can cause severe damage to crops. One such *khamsin* sank the steamer *Tigris* on Chesney's Euphrates Expedition in 1836 (Chesney 1868, p. 252).

The summers in Syria are dry with cloudless skies, while nearly all the rain falls in the winter, often in sudden, short-lived storms. A little rain may fall as

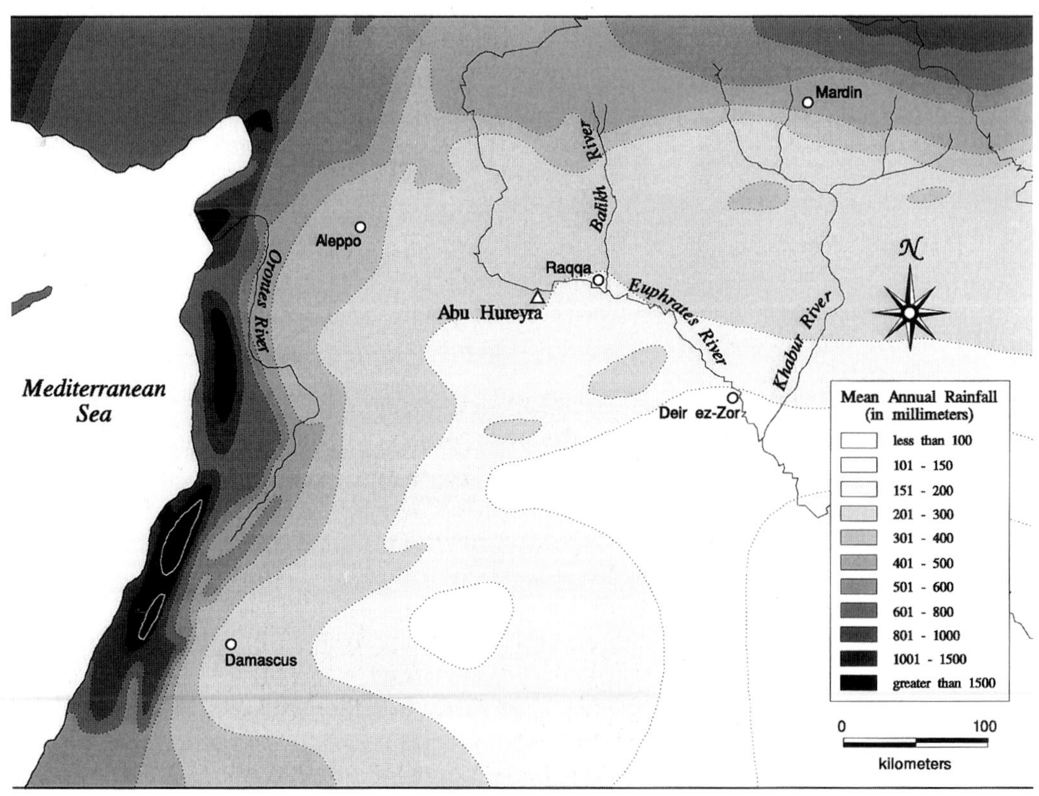

Figure 3.3 Map of mean annual rainfall in Syria and adjacent regions today. *Sources*: Haude (1963); International Center for Agricultural Research in the Dry Areas (ICARDA); Syrian Arab Republic, Central Bureau of Statistics (1947–1997); U.S Department of Commerce (1966); and local knowledge.

early as September, but the beginning of the rainy season comes in October (figure 3.4). Fair spells may be quite frequent thereafter until early December. The wettest months are December, January, and February, but rainstorms can occur as late as June. The most important point to note about the rainfall is that it varies greatly in amount from year to year and from decade to decade (figure 3.5; Haude 1963, p. 282). These wide variations considerably increase the risks of farming in the drier regions of Syria. Several years of drought can have a catastrophic effect on both agriculture and stockraising and disrupt patterns of settlement. The vegetation cover of the arid interior is now so thin that, after a few dry years, disturbance of the surface by humans can lead to serious erosion by wind and rainstorms.

The range of temperatures experienced in the interior of Syria is wide, both diurnally and annually. The continentality of the area, the scarcity of vegetation, and generally clear skies all accentuate these effects. Mean monthly temperatures at Aleppo range from 6°C in January to 29°C in August, and at Deir ez-Zor from 7.5°C in January to 33°C in July (figure 3.6). Because of its relatively high elevation, temperatures in winter on the interior plateau are often quite low for the latitude. Frosts are frequent from November to March, and snow falls occasionally on the plains. By contrast, the summers are hot, with a high evaporation rate. Abu Hureyra experiences these extremes as strongly as the rest the interior, although the Euphrates Valley moderates them slightly.

The surface geology and the climate are the main factors that have determined the nature of the soils in Syria. These soils may be divided into three main groups (Muir 1951, p. 166): soils of the Mediterranean zone, the steppe, and desert. All of them are low in humus, and highly calcareous because of the prevalence of limestone and chalk. The most characteristic soil of the Mediterranean zone is terra rossa, a fertile clay loam containing a relatively high amount of ferric oxide (Reifenberg 1952, p. 78), which accounts for its distinctive red color. A brown clay soil is formed on basalt flows in the same climatic zone. The surface of the steppe zone (receiving 400–200 mm rainfall annually,

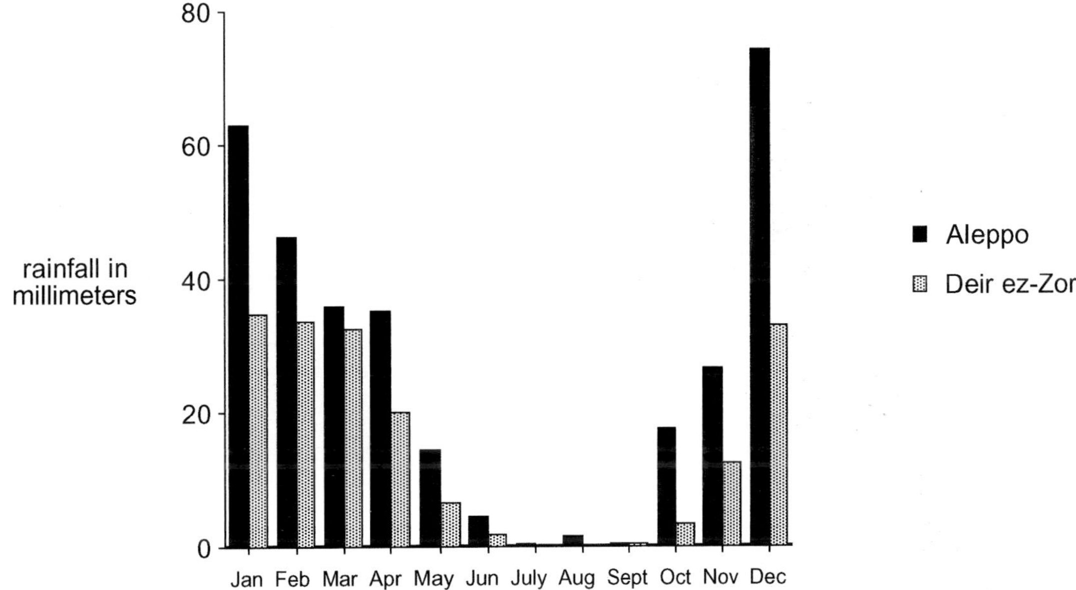

Figure 3.4 Mean monthly rainfall at Aleppo and Deir ez-Zor from 1951 to 1960 (U.S. Department of Commerce 1966, pp. 442, 444).

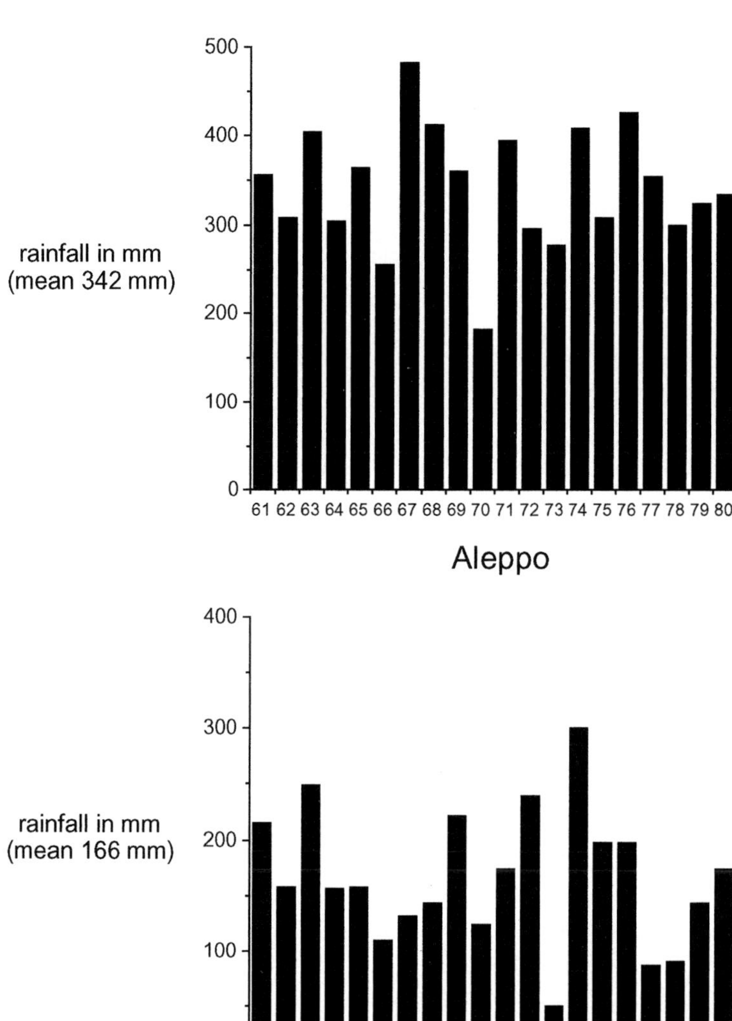

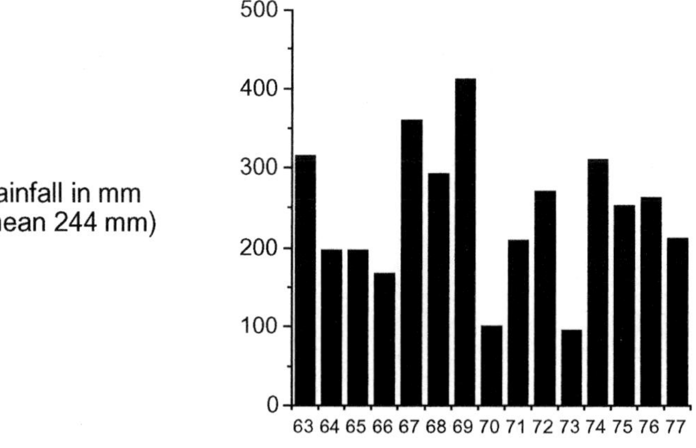

Figure 3.5 Mean annual rainfall at Aleppo and Deir ez-Zor from 1961 to 1980, and at Raqqa, the nearest town to Abu Hureyra, from 1963 to 1977. Note the great variation in the amount of rainfall from year to year (Syrian Arab Republic, Central Bureau of Statistics 1964–1978). The rainfall at Raqqa was unusually high during this period compared with earlier decades in this century, for which only partial records exist.

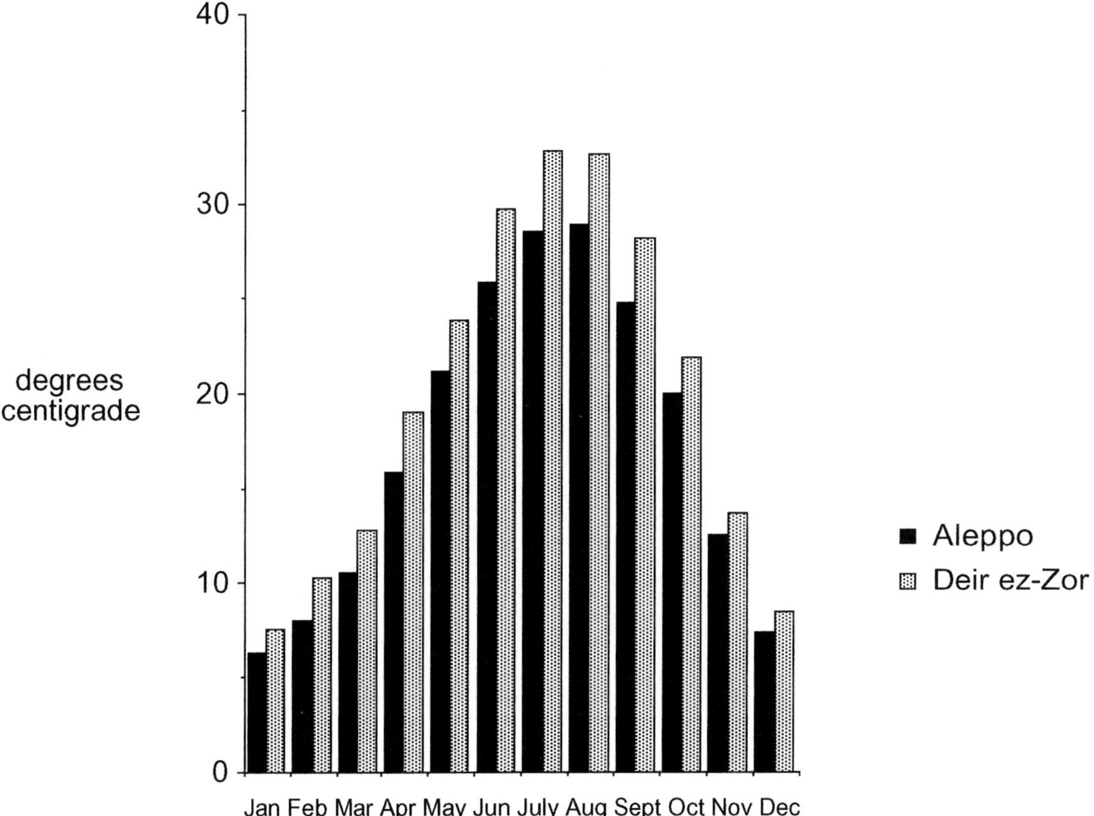

Figure 3.6 Mean monthly temperature at Aleppo and Deir ez-Zor from 1951 to 1960 (U.S. Department of Commerce 1966, pp. 442, 444).

according to the soil scientists) is frequently covered with red-brown or gray steppe soils with a soft crumb structure (Muir 1951, p. 171). These are the typical soils of the dry-farming zone of northern and western Syria. The desert proper is often carpeted with wind-polished flints, under which there is a shallow layer of poorly developed brown soil (Muir 1951, p. 167) or marl. The surfaces of these desert soils are continually being removed by wind erosion. The steppe south of Abu Hureyra today lies at the junction of the red-brown steppe type and the desert soils, a distinction that is determined mainly by the amount of rainfall each zone receives. Desert soils are characteristic of the Raqqa district and the region south of the Euphrates to Palmyra and beyond. The red-brown steppe soils are the main soil type between the Euphrates and Aleppo.

THE POTENTIAL VEGETATION UNDER MODERN CLIMATIC CONDITIONS

The vegetation of modern Syria and adjacent territories can be divided into seven zones. The map (figure 3.7) indicates the types of vegetation that each zone would probably support under present-day climatic conditions in the absence of deforestation, cultivation, and heavy grazing by domestic animals, and shows the potential natural limits of each zone. The map is based on a number of years of ecological fieldwork in the region by Hillman and his colleagues, much of it undertaken as background research for the Abu Hureyra project.[1]

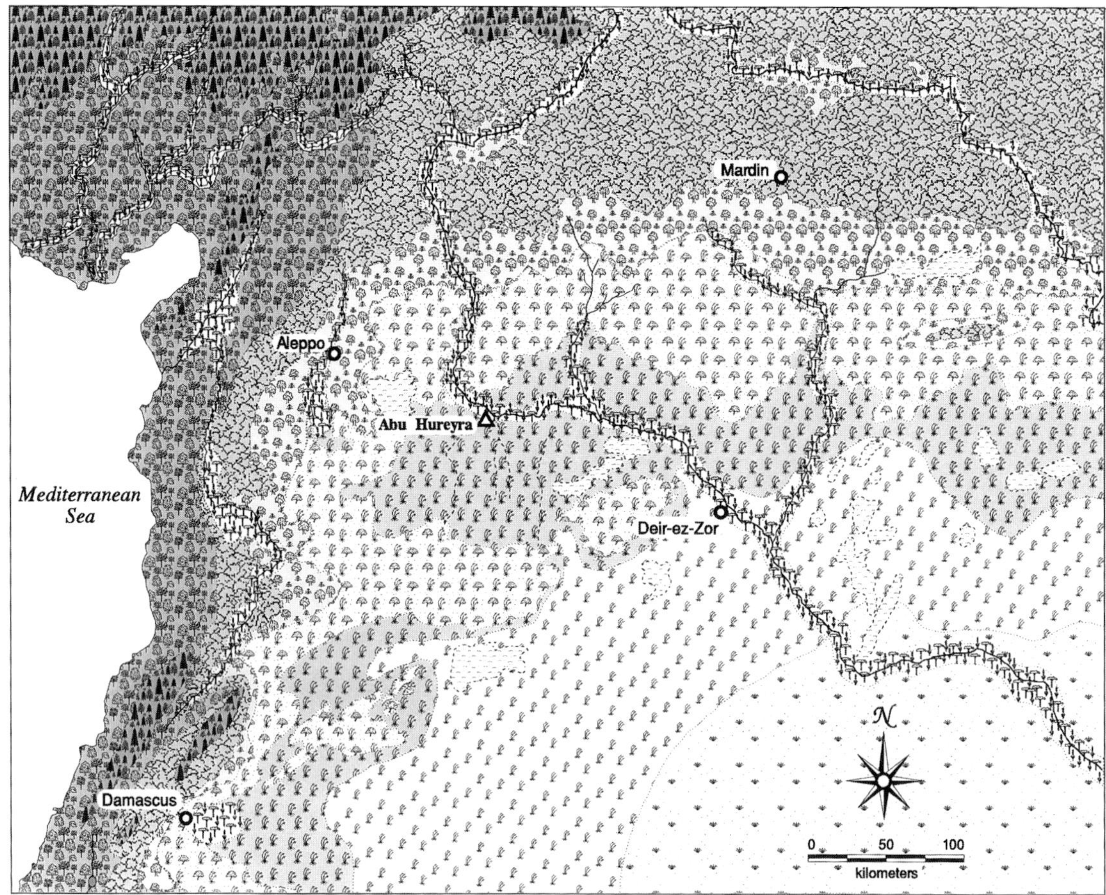

Figure 3.7 Distribution of potential vegetation on the Middle Euphrates under modern climatic conditions, but in the absence of deforestation, grazing, or cultivation.

In delimiting the zones we have used the following information: (1) studies of present-day vegetation, particularly in areas protected from intense grazing, noting marker species diagnostic of former, less-degraded states of the vegetation; (2) rainfall levels, especially those recorded at specified localities for a span of years, rather than isohyet contour maps, which are often innacurate; (3) insolation and temperature levels, where available; (4) altitude and topography, especially the effect of aspect; (5) solid geology and soil type, and the general rockiness of the surface, inasmuch as this would allow trees to extend deeper into arid zones than would otherwise be the case; (6) the relative density of settled villages and farmsteads on large-scale topographical maps predating the widespread availability of irrigation pumps, as an approximate index of the intensity of arable farming and thence of soil moisture availability; (7) patterns of concentration of less ephemeral wadis as indicated on the topographical maps; and (8) the accounts of early travelers.

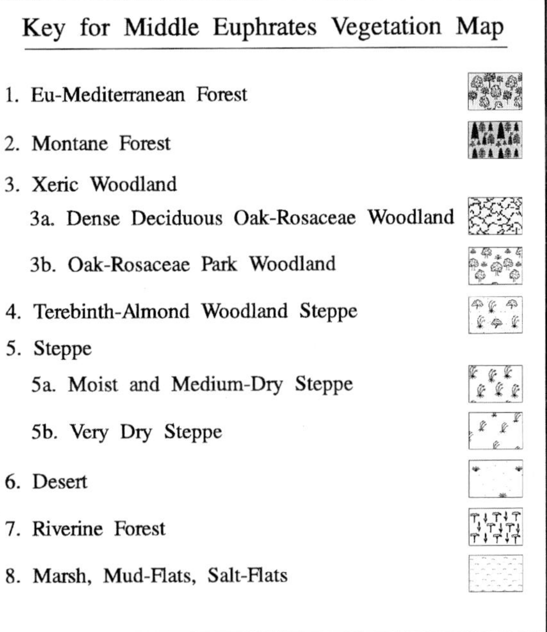

The purpose of this reconstruction of potential modern vegetation is to provide an explicitly defined starting point for modeling ancient patterns of plant food availability at Abu Hureyra from pollen, wood charcoal, and other palaeoenvironmental data. Such modeling is clearly central to any understanding of the Epipalaeolithic economy when the inhabitants were heavily dependent on food resources occurring naturally. However, in using a reconstruction of potential modern vegetation as the first step in modeling ancient vegetal resources, we cannot assume that the structures of plant communities in the Epipalaeolithic were the same as those of recent times. Rapid migration of plants during the Late Pleistocene severely dislocated previous patterns of plant association (M. Davis 1983; Huntley 1991; Huntley and Webb 1989; Webb 1986), and we have therefore had to model the migration and colonization of the major food plants such as wild ryes and wild einkorn wheat separately from, for example, the deciduous oaks with whose fringes these wild cereals are associated today.[2]

Next, in translating this reconstruction of potential modern vegetation into assessments of potential resource availability, we have had to make measurements in each major source habitat of the harvestable yields of each of the food plants likely to have served as major caloric staples. However, when these ecological models of past patterns of resource availability are used to interpret ancient remains of plants foods in terms of past human subsistence, they have to be combined with ethnographic models of probable past patterns of resource preference and resource scheduling based, in turn, on cross-cultural common denominators extracted from observations of a broad spectrum of hunter-gatherers occupying analogous resource environments in recent times.[3]

In the ensuing section we outline our conclusions as they relate to modern vegetation, both actual and potential, in the northern Levant and the eastern part of the northern Fertile Crescent. For each zone, we summarize first what is traditionally regarded as the "natural" vegetation type, and then the vegetation that survives today. For four of the zones that most concern Abu Hureyra (zones 3, 4, 5, and 7), we then return to a much more detailed consideration of the vegetation that could potentially exist today in the absence of deforestation, cultivation, and heavy grazing.

Zone 1

The first zone (figure 3.7) is *eu-Mediterranean woodland* (the "primary maquis" of Polunin and Walters 1985). This zone enjoys moderate rainfall ranging from an annual mean of 600 mm to over 1,500 mm that falls mainly between early autumn and late spring. Potentially, the zone would be dominated by dense evergreen woodland with an often thick understory of shrubs. The native trees and shrubs of this zone include several oaks, especially the holly-leaved oak, *Quercus calliprinos*; the Valonia oak, *Q. ithaburensis*; the Turkey oak, *Q. cerris*; the Lebanon oak, *Q. libani*; areas of Calabrian pine, *Pinus brutia*, and Aleppo pine, *P. halepensis*, which, despite its name, grows nowhere near Aleppo except where planted artificially (M. Zohary 1973, figure 134); the terebinth shrub, *Pistacia palaestina*; the storax shrub, *Styrax officinalis*, source of the gum storax used in incense; and down on the coast the carob tree, Judas tree, and mastic shrubs. There would be a mosaic of glades where the soil is thin, allowing a dense growth of low shrublets such as the red-flowered, thorny burnet, *Sarcopoterium spinosum*; rock roses, *Cistus* spp., with their huge flowers ranging from white to pinks and mauves; and an array of aromatic members of the thyme and sage family, the Lamiaceae (formerly the Labiatae).

Today, the land is cultivated throughout this zone wherever the terrain allows. Cultivation here includes not only arable fields, but also vineyards, olive groves, and a rich variety of orchards, which often produce good yields, thanks to relatively high winter rainfall. Combined with pastoralism, this has allowed quite high population densities. Deforestation in this zone has been correspondingly intense from the Neolithic onward.[4] However, the rainfall in this particular zone is high enough to have allowed relatively rapid regeneration, and it was probably only in the last millennium that deforestation accelerated to the point where it massively outstripped regeneration rates and primary forest disappeared almost completely. Today, most of the forest is either secondary maquis exhibiting various degrees of degradation, replaced by garigue (a formation dominated by low and dwarf shrubs and herbaceous perennials [M. Zohary 1973, p. 532]), still further reduced to *batha* dominated by dwarf-prostrate species of shrublets and herbaceous perennials, or lost altogether to fields, orchards, vineyards, and olive groves.

Zone 2

Zone 2 combines various types of *montane forest*.[5] In the northern Levant they are mostly coniferous and potentially dominated by firs; cedar; black pine; junipers, particularly *Juniperus excelsa*, with rather fewer trees of the viciously sharp-leaved *J. drupacea*; and also some Lebanon oak. However, this zone is of only peripheral importance in reconstructing the plant components of the ancient resource base available at Abu Hureyra.

Zone 3

Zone 3 is *xeric woodland* dominated in the most moist areas by high oak forest (zone 3a on figure 3.7), and in drier areas by open park-woodland vegetation with a mosaic of grassland and oak-Rosaceae-terebinth woodland (zone 3b).[6] In contrast to zone 1, most of the trees and shrubs of xeric woodland are winter deciduous, a trait that adapts them not only to cold winters, but also in some circumstances to extremely dry summers (Blumler 1991). Hillman suggests that, even under modern climatic conditions, the combined xeric woodlands of zone 3 could potentially occupy a very broad swathe of country separating the Levantine eu-Mediterranean woodland of zone 1 from the moist steppe of zone 5. Within the Levant, the spatial limits of this proposed swathe coincide approximately with those of Pabot's (1957) *zone syrienne* or "Fertile Crescent" zone. However, Hillman's argument that the northeastern Levant potentially would support this broad sweep of oak-dominated xeric woodland differs radically from the complete absence of potential xeric woodland in the northern Levant indicated in van Zeist and Bottema (1991, map 4 and p. 30) and in Zohary (1985, map D), and goes a good deal further than Sankary (1982) and van Zeist and Bakker-Heeres (1982, p. 169), who do at least suggest that much of the area would potentially be dominated by terebinth-almond woodland-steppe, our zone 4, which Sankary's map appropriately extends almost to the Middle Euphrates bend.

Hillman's two subzones of zone 3 xeric woodland also extend northeastward around the hilly flanks of the Anti-Taurus and Zagros mountains. They would separate the montane forest from the woodland steppe in those regions, just as the depauperate remnants of these subzones do today. There they would embrace an extended version of Zohary's "Kurdo-Zagrosian xerophilous deciduous steppe-forest" zone (see M. Zohary 1973, map 7).

Today, the Levantine limb of zone 3, that is, the western part of zone 3 south of the modern Syro-Turkish border, is largely treeless. Zohary (1973, map 7) classifies much of the drier, eastern half of it as straight steppe, which we find surprising, and the moister, western part of it as "sub-Levantine semi-steppe *batha*" ("*Ballotetalia undulatae*" in Zohary's phytosociological classification). The latter is a largely treeless division of his "Mediterranean steppe-*maquis*" zone, dominated by low and dwarf shrubs and herbaceous perennials with a "pronounced concentration of annuals."[7] Pabot (1957), in contrast, is concerned primarily with forage plants, and the diagnostic features he lists for his equivalent *partie ouest de la zone syrienne* are an abundance of legumes of the vetch and clover tribes, and of *Scorpiurus* and *Hymenocarpus*, also legumes, but an absence of spiny tragacanths, *Astragalus* spp. (cushion-shrub legumes).

However, Pabot adds a further *partie est de la zone syrienne* that extends almost to the Middle Euphrates bend and that he again regards as distinct from true steppe. He suggests that it is characterized by, for example, various spiny tragacanths, *Astragalus* spp.; yellow-flowered yarrow, *Achillea santolina*; the prickly wild lettuce, *Lactuca orientalis*; a ferociously spiny borage, *Onosma aleppica*; and fewer vetches and members of the clover group than in his western subzone—with the exception of the wild relatives of fenugreek, the *Trigonella* spp., which are here more abundant.

Hillman's own fieldwork in the region, like Pabot's, supports the designation of the entirety of the area we have called zone 3 as essentially nonsteppic, even in its present-day degraded state, and indicates that it is potentially capable of supporting xeric oak-dominated woodland. At best, the vegetation of some drier areas could be regarded as *secondary* steppe. In the field, the four markers that Hillman advocates as the most convenient for distinguishing this zone from genuine, primary steppe (and from areas capable of supporting woodland-steppe) are as follows: (a) the frequent occurrence of the great white asphodel, *Asphodelus microcarpus*, which is essentially Mediterranean and sub-Mediterranean (Polunin and Walters 1985; M. Zohary 1973, pp. 138, 527) and has even had a sub-Mediterranean *batha* association named after it, "*Asphodeletum microcarpi*" (M. Zohary 1973, p. 541); (b) the relative rarity of harmal, *Peganum harmala* (source of the psychotropic harmaline, a beta-carboline not dissimilar to ayahausca of Central America), which abounds primarily in overgrazed primary steppe and in the degraded remnants of terebinth-almond woodland-steppe; (c) the preponderance of fertile red-brown soils, tending toward gray-brown in the drier fringes; and (d) intensive rain-fed arable farming subject to relatively infrequent crop failure. This last feature is also stressed by Pabot (1957).

We can now consider in more detail the potential distribution of the two subzones of zone 3, 3a and 3b, in the absence of deforestation, cultivation, and heavy grazing by domestic animals. Clearly, the distribution of potential vegetation can be correlated only very crudely with mean annual rainfall; equally critical covariables include the seasonal distributions of that rainfall, particularly the amount of rain falling during the spring growing season, insolation, temperature, aspect, soil type, and solid geology. There are, in any case, radical discrepancies in the published mean annual rainfall data for several of the areas which support remnants of oak park-woodland and terebinth woodland-steppe. As a result, our data on the levels of aridity tolerated by these types of vegetation on given soil types remain approximate.

Nevertheless, field studies in these and equivalent areas of Southwest Asia, combined with the types of evidence listed in the caption to figure 3.7, lead us to suggest that those areas of the Levant with rainfall above about 400 mm could potentially support fairly dense forest. On the vegetation map, therefore, we have suggested that high forest dominated by deciduous oaks (which constitutes our zone 3a) could potentially extend from the 600 mm limit of eu-Mediterranean vegetation down to the 400 mm isohyet, albeit with adjustments to take account of the boundary of Pabot's present-day *Astragalus*-free zone. Southwest Asian examples of dense forest surviving close to the 400 mm limit include Beynam Forest southeast of Ankara.

Field studies further suggest that areas with annual rainfall of between 400 mm and 300 mm, and with reasonably water-retentive soils, could generally support a more open form of oak-dominated woodland, generally termed *park-woodland*, and it is this which characterizes our zone 3b on the vegetation map. We have, however, adjusted the 300 mm (inner) boundary to take some account of the eastern limits of Zohary's "Mediterranean steppe-*maquis* (*Ballotetalia undulatae*)," Pabot's *partie ouest de la zone syrienne*, Sankary's *Quercus calliprinos* zone, and our own observations of occurrences of the four indicators proposed above for distinguishing areas of potential xeric oak-woodland from areas of potential woodland-steppe and steppe.

Nevertheless, it must be stressed that, even between these isohyets, and in areas free from human impact, oaks will often fail to establish on deep, fine-grained soils (Blumler 1993, pp. 291–293; Naveh 1967), this despite the presence of typical herbaceous commensals of deciduous oak park-woodland such as the wild wheats. This apparently reflects the greater availability of moisture in coarse-textured soils and around rocks, and the failure of rainwater to penetrate fine-grained soils beyond the upper layers exploited by the herbs (Noy-Meir 1973). However, this pattern is not universal. For example, on the Jebel Abdul Aziz, factors such as the rocky terrain and rainfall averaging in excess of 300 mm would, on this basis, be expected to favor the establishment of oak park-woodland. But, in fact, there are not only no oak trees, but also only transient traces of the more moisture-loving herbaceous components of park-woodland such as the wild wheats. Whatever is reducing soil-water availability during the growing season is also reflected in the very low concentration of farming villages south and west of the Jebel, and the apparent ephemerality of all the wadis flowing south from the Jebel toward the Euphrates seen on large-scale maps of the region.

The Plants of Zone 3a

We can now consider the vegetal composition of the two subzones of zone 3 in more detail, concentrating on the northern Levant east to Hasseke. In the fairly dense forest of zone 3a the vegetation would be dominated by oaks such as the Turkey oak, Boissier's oak (often mistaken for *Q. infectoria*), the holly-leaved oak, and, at higher elevations, at least, some trees of the Lebanon oak. The rose/plum family Rosaceae would abound, particularly hawthorns such as the yellow-fruited *Crataegus aronia* and the tastier, red-fruited *C. azarolus*; the Syrian pear *Pyrus syriaca*; a wild relative of the domestic almond, *Amygdalus communis* subsp. *microphylla*, which can grow as a small tree, and in the forest glades shrub almonds such as the sessile-leaved *A. trichamygdalus*; together with shrubs of the succulent-berried *Amelanchier integrifolia*; the mahaleb cherry, *Cerasus mahaleb*, the cyanogenic kernels of which are today used to de-louse hair, and its almost fleshless-fruited cousin the dwarf cherry, *C. microcarpa*. Other trees and shrubs would include the great terebinth, *Pistacia atlantica*, the terebinth bush, *P. palaestina*; the dryland hackberry tree, *Celtis tournefortii*, with small sweet fruits that ripen from yellow to pale brown; junipers such as the scale-leaved *Juniperus excelsa* and the shrubby, needle-leaved *J. oxycedrus*; dryland maples such as *Acer obtusifolium* subsp. *syriacum*; and buckthorn shrubs such as *Rhamnus palaestinus*, source of an intense yellow dye. It should be noted that the two *Pistacia* species involved here, the great terebinth tree and the terebinth bush, are not the nut-bearing pistachio species, *P. vera*, which is a native of central Asia. The fruits of the terebinths are small, rounded "nutlets" that contain no real nut meat but are added to food merely as a flavoring and preservative; in recent times, they were also a source of turpentine.

The Plants of Zone 3b

Farther east in the Levant and south from the Anti-Taurus Mountains, the fairly dense forest of zone 3a would thin out to form *open park-woodland* of zone 3b with a mosaic of oak-dominated areas interspersed with grassland, not dissimilar to the vegetation in figure 3.8, albeit without the signs of pollarding and overgrazing apparent in the first three of these photographs. The dominant oak would again be Boissier's oak with probably a small admixture of the holly-leaved oak, certain forms of which exhibit marked drought tolerance, for example, in southern Transjordan (M. Zohary 1973, pp. 356–357). That Boissier's oak would, indeed, be the dominant oak of this subzone right up to its arid eastern border, abutting on terebinth-almond woodland-steppe, is apparent from its distribution on the Tur Abdin Plateau east of Mardin in southeast Asia Minor. Here, Mark Nesbitt informs us, Boissier's oak grows with another drought-resistant oak, Brandt's oak, *Q. brandtii*, right down to the present-day forest-to-steppe ecotone. In the present-day Levant, however, Brandt's oak would probably not itself be a major component of the zone 3 forest because, although it dominates the xeric woodland zone throughout the Anti-Taurus and Zagros ranges, it extends west only as far as the northeastern Amanus, and south as far as Kilis, 50 km north of Aleppo (Browicz 1982; Zohary 1973, figure 147).

Associated with these oaks would be many of the same rosaceous trees as those listed above for zone 3a, particularly the wild relative of the domestic almond, *Amygdalus communis* subsp. *microphylla*; some of the shrub almonds; the yellow-fruited hawthorn; and the wild pear. Equally abundant would be the great terebinth, the dryland hackberry, and the dryland maple. Shrubs would abound here around the edge of the myriad patches of woodland, particularly the amelanchier; the mahaleb cherry; the dwarf cherry; buckthorns such as *Rhamnus palaestinus*; xeric shrub-honeysuckles, *Lonicera* spp.; the needle-leaved, red-fruited juniper; and the meter-high sumac, *Rhus coriaria*, whose heads of purple-red fruitlets yield flaky husks that are today used to give soups a delicious lemon flavor.

The open areas of the park-woodland mosaic would be dominated by grasses and legumes. The grasses would include both annuals and perennials, but up to early summer it is the annuals that would be the most conspicuous. Promi-

a

b

c

d

e

Figure 3.8 (a–e, facing page) Oak park-woodland surviving in the present day. a, Park-woodland dominated by Brandt's oak, *Quercus brandtii*, and Boissier's oak, *Q. boissieri*, growing in the foothills of the Anti-Taurus Mountains close to the site of Hallan Çemi. Note the increased density of vegetation at breaks of slope, particularly at the foot of the mountain. b, A closer view of the same park-woodland. Despite pollarding of the trees to provide fuel, and heavy grazing of the herb layer, the woodland appears to retain much of its original character. c, Equivalent park-woodland in the Muş area of eastern Asia Minor, here subject to less intense grazing and showing dense areas of grassland dominated by annuals between the bushy islands of coppiced oak and low shrubs. d, Park-woodland comprising two species of American oak with ground cover dominated by grasses on low foothills surrounding the Sonoita Plateau, southern Arizona, 1987. e, General view of the same oak park-woodland, showing it being replaced by grassland-steppe as the slopes level out onto the Sonoita Plateau and the oaks fail to establish on the deeper, finer-grained soils.

nent among the annuals would be a range of bromes such as *Bromus danthoniae*; oat-grasses, among them *Avena barbata* and *A. wiestii*; barley-grasses such as *Hordeum geniculatum*, and members of the *H. murinum* group; and goat-face grasses, close relatives of the wheats, including *Aegilops speltoides*, *Ae. triuncialis*, and *Ae. columnaris*.

Wild cereals would probably be plentiful in many of the drier parts of this zone, particularly the two wild einkorns, *Triticum urartu* and *T. boeoticum*; wild oats, *Avena sterilis*; and wild annual rye, *Secale cereale* subsp. *vavilovii*, which is the immediate ancestor of domestic rye. Stands of the wild einkorns would have included a minor admixture of wild emmer, *T. dicoccoides*, just as they do today around the entirety of the Fertile Crescent (D. Zohary and Hopf 1993, map 3). With the exception of the wild oats, each of these wild cereals would form dense, extensive stands under appropriate conditions (figure 3.9). Potentially, these stands of wild cereals would become more extensive in the drier parts of the potential park-woodland zone, where other, less drought-tolerant grasses would compete less effectively. Wild barley, *Hordeum spontaneum*, would also be present but would probably achieve its greatest abundance in only the driest of these areas, and even more conspicuously in parts of zone 4.

The perennial grasses would primarily be tussock or bunchgrass species such as wild mountain-rye, *Secale montanum*; bulbous barley-grass, *Hordeum bulbosum*; cocksfoot, *Dactylis glomerata*; the hairy *Hyparrhenia hirta*; and, in partially shaded glades, a large-grained rice-grass, *Oryzopsis holciformis*. However, the tall culms of spreading rhizomatious species of couch-grass, *Agropyron*, and of the bulb canarygrass, *Phalaris tuberosa*, would also be conspicuous in many areas, especially around patches of scrub.

The legumes of the open areas would include spiny-shrub restharrows, *Ononis* spp., together with a broad spectrum of clovers, *Trifolium* spp.; medics, *Medicago* spp.; vetches, *Vicia* and *Lathyrus* spp.; bird's-foot trefoils, *Lotus* spp.; and some of the wild relatives of fenugreek, *Trigonella* spp., although Pabot's observations (1957, p. 69) would suggest that most of the *Trigonella* spp. would increase eastward toward zone 4 in parallel with a decrease in some of the many species of clover, medic, and vetch. In many of the glades we would probably also find one of the wild lentils, *Lens orientalis*, especially where partial shade reduces competition, together with a wild pea, *Pisum sativum* subsp. *humile*. Both are ancestors of "founder crops" of Southwest Asian agriculture (D. Zohary 1989).

Together with these plants, which are so typical of the glades of park-woodland, we would almost certainly also find some of the plants that are characteristic primarily of woodland-steppe and the most moist zone of steppe, for example, perennial feather-grasses like *Stipa lagascae* and *S. parviflora*, shrublets of the steppe wormwood, *Artemisia herba-alba*, and chenopods such as occasional camphor plants, *Camphorosma monspeliaca*. However, these would occur in much smaller numbers than in the steppe and woodland-steppe to the east and south.

We noted above that on deep fine-grained soils oaks and other trees fail to establish in areas with seemingly adequate rainfall. In these circumstances, the herbaceous ground cover typical of oak-Rosaceae park-woodland, including the wild cereals, can extend significantly beyond the limits of oak trees. Indeed, it is here that we often find the densest stands of cereals such as einkorn, particularly at breaks of slope and north-facing aspects around wadi systems, albeit not up to the wadi banks themselves, where scrub dominates. These ex-

Figure 3.9 Wild cereals growing in primary habitats in Southwest Asia. *(Top)* A dense population of wild einkorn growing between patches of scrub oak on a basaltic slope in the Munzur Mountains, eastern Asia Minor, 1971. *(Middle)* Equally dense populations of wild annual rye growing on the lower slopes of Mount Ararat (Büyük Ağri Dağ) in eastern Asia Minor, one of its last refugia, with Thilaka Hillman serving as scale, 1992. Virtually all the pale areas were dominated by the wild rye, and the stands stretched for kilometers across the flanks of the mountain. *(Bottom)* Small part of a dense, extensive stand of wild barley, *Hordeum spontaneum*, growing on a steep, north-facing slope of the Jebel Abdul Aziz in northeast Syria, April 1983. Despite relatively low grazing pressure in the area, barley was the only wild cereal growing in this remote outpost of the terebinth-almond woodland-steppe zone. There was no trace of either the wild wheats or ryes.

tensions of the herbaceous vegetation of zone 3b beyond the limits of the oaks occupy too narrow a band, however, to be separately represented on the map (figure 3.7).

Zone 4

At its eastern and southern edge, the xeric park-woodland of zone 3b would give way to the more arid *terebinth-almond woodland-steppe* of zone 4. Here, rainfall is too low to support forest trees such as oaks, but it is still sufficient to support a thin scatter of drought-tolerant trees such as the great terebinths, shrubby almonds, dwarf cherries, and the occasional hawthorn and Syrian pear. Woodland-steppe also differs from the park-woodland of zone 3b in the much lower density of trees and the absence of all the more moisture-demanding herbs, and in the greater abundance of many of the plants of true steppe, most conspicuously the wormwoods, *Artemisia* spp., and feather-grasses, such as *Stipa lagascae*. This zone thus represents a transition between xeric woodland and true, arid, treeless steppe.

Today, relict terebinth-almond woodland-steppe survives only as isolated islands on ranges of hills deep in the steppe such as Jebel Abu Rujmein, Jebel Abyad, Jebel Bishri, and Jebel Abdul Aziz (figure 3.10), and, until recently, as a thin fringe of trees at the edge of park-woodland on mountains such as Karadağ in Anatolia. The islands of woodland-steppe are separated from each other and from the edge of the oak-dominated park-woodland by great expanses of cultivation and degraded steppe-like rangelands. Potentially, however, terebinth-almond woodland-steppe could grow throughout many of these areas to form a very broad zone extending from the edge of the oak-dominated park-woodland, as indicated in figure 3.7. This woodland-steppe would probably be largely continuous except in certain low-lying areas where the reduced water availability in deep, fine-grained soils is sufficient to limit the growth of even these drought-resistant trees (Blumler 1993, pp. 291–293; Naveh 1967; Noy-Meir 1973).[8] At the ecotone with open steppe, it would form a more obvious mosaic, with the trees restricted to hilltops and moister, north-facing slopes.

Hillman's field studies of four of the relict islands of woodland-steppe and of the Karadağ fringes indicate that this form of vegetation can thrive in areas with annual rainfall of between 300 and 200 mm, depending on soil type and geology, and this permits us to suggest the approximate potential limits of zone 4 indicated on the map.[9] However, in some areas with rainfall seemingly sufficient for terebinth woodland-steppe, we have drawn the limits well within the 200 mm isohyet, for example, on the plateau sloping south from the Jebel Abdul Aziz, where there is evidence of reduced availability of soil water. In other cases such as the region around Jebel Abu Rujmein and Jebel Bishri, we have extended woodland steppe well beyond the 200 mm isohyet in response to our observations of terebinth trees in this area in locations with rainfall of probably no more than 180 mm.

It is clear that certain components of terebinth woodland-steppe can also penetrate far beyond the 200 mm isohyet in wadis or in other habitats where soil water is locally enhanced through features such as breaks in slope. A key example exists in Transjordan, where the great terebinth grows in wadis penetrating not only into the steppe but also, at least in the aptly named Wadi Butum,[10] right through the steppe zone and 30 km into the black desert gravel

Figure 3.10 *Top,* An example of terebinth-almond woodland-steppe of zone 4: view over north-facing slope of the Jebel Abdul Aziz in northeast Syria, dominated by two species of the great terebinth, *Pistacia atlantica* and *P. khinjuk*, April 1983. *Middle,* The yellow-fruited hawthorn, *Crataegus aronia*, growing with the terebinths of figure 3.10a. *Bottom,* The great terebinth, *Pistacia atlantica*, here penetrating deep into the black desert reg of the Azraq Basin along the banks of the Wadi Butum, far beyond the limits of woodland-steppe, June 1986.

or reg of the Azraq Desert Basin, where mean annual rainfall is a paltry 100 mm (figure 3.10c).

The tree and large shrub flora of the woodland-steppe is dominated, as indicated above, by the great terebinths or turpentine trees, *Pistacia atlantica* and *P. khinjuk*; wild almonds such as the small-leaved, drought resistant relative of the domestic almond, *Amygdalus communis* subsp. *microphylla*, which can grow as a shrub or small tree, the shrubby sessile-leaved almond, *A. trichamygdalus*, the furry-leaved oriental shrub almond, *A. orientalis*, the broom-almond, *A. scoparia*, and the Arab almond, *A. arabica*, the latter usually on wadi banks; the yellow-fruited hawthorn; and even some wild pear trees, whose small fruits are packed with stone-cells and offer culinary delights akin to those of eating gravel. However, these pear fruits become almost edible once bletted, that is, allowed partially to rot. We also find quite a lot of smaller shrubs in this zone, and of these, the most prominent are the buckthorns, particularly *Rhamnus palaestinus*; the dwarf cherry; spiny wolf-berries, *Lycium* spp.; and the capers, *Capparis spinosa* and *C. ovata*, both armed with recurved barbs and source of the pickled flower buds.

All of these woody plants grow in fairly open formations together with a rich herbaceous ground cover (figure 3.10a, 10b), although in especially favorable areas the trees can grow close together, as described by English merchants (1707, pp. 137–138) traveling from Aleppo to Palmyra in 1678 and passing Jebel Abu Rujmein, which, they recalled, was "cover'd on both sides with turpentine trees . . . very thick and shady . . . several of them loaded with a vast abundance of a small round nut, the chief use of which is to make oil, though some eat them . . . ." A similar observation comes from Peters (1897), who observed "a considerable forest" covering these ranges. Khaled Assad of the Palmyra Museum has told us that his grandfather described the terebinth woodland on Jebel Abyad and adjacent ranges as having been too dense to pass through with a camel. A scatter of terebinth trees still survived on Jebel Abu Rujmein when we camped nearby in 1983, but on Jebel Abyad we found only their low-cut stumps.

In the islands of terebinth-almond woodland-steppe surviving today, ground cover includes many of the same grasses and other herbs as in the open areas of zone 3b, but with the addition of a range of plants that characterize the open steppe of zone 5, particularly the wormwood, chenopod shrublets such as the camphor plant, *Camphorosma monspeliaca*, the tall, felted, and shamelessly malodorous *Krascheninnikovia*, the gray-green *Kochia prostrata*, patches of the furry annual chenopod *Chenolea arabica*, and most conspicuously of all, the most moisture-loving of the perennial feather-grasses, the tall *Stipa lagascae* and sometimes *S. barbata*.

Hillman has observed that the wild wheats and wild annual rye are largely absent from these islands, as is the large-grained rice-grass. The exception is Jebel Abdul Aziz, which is located only 90 km from the present edge of the oak-woodland zone and where Mouterde (1966) records finding at least a few plants of one of the wild einkorns. However, on a visit there in 1983 Hillman could find no trace of either of the wild einkorns, although there were vast, dense stands of wild barley on the steepest of the north-facing slopes.

However, if we accept that woodland-steppe could potentially occupy an almost continuous broad swathe extending from the edge of the oak-dominated park-woodland of zone 3b, as proposed in figure 3.7, then we can expect that the wild wheats and wild annual rye could potentially grow in vast stands in the moistest parts of this extensive zone 4, especially in areas close to the fringe of oak-dominated park-woodland. These dense stands of wild wheats would therefore be continuous with those of zone 3b, including any areas at the edge where deep, fine-grained soils would limit the establishment of oaks. Indeed, it is these relatively tree-free areas of 3b and the proximal parts of zone 4 where stands of wild einkorn and wild rye probably achieved their greatest density.

A bit farther out into drier parts of zone 4, however, stands of wild wheats and ryes would have been limited to moisture-enriched areas such as north-facing inclines, breaks of slope, and networks of small wadi beds.[11] In the most water-stressed of these stands, it is probably the less familiar species of einkorn, *Triticum urartu*, that would predominate, rather than the more widespread *T. boeoticum*. By contrast, wild barley, *Hordeum spontaneum*, grows more extensively and in denser stands in this woodland-steppe zone than in perhaps any other vegetal formation (figure 3.9c). In favorable habitats, it could potentially extend well into some drier parts of the zone.

In light of the distribution of the wild wheats and ryes, the predominant cereals found in the village of Abu Hureyra 1, therefore, zone 4 can be split into two subzones. The first, a relatively narrow zone 4a abutting the edge of park-woodland, would potentially support extensive stands of wild wheats and ryes; the second, zone 4b, would encompass the remaining, drier terrain that is incapable of supporting dense extensive stands of these cereals, although stands of wild barley would flourish in favorable locations. However, zone 4a is too narrow to represent separately in figure 3.7, although we have plotted it in the large-scale map of vegetation around Abu Hureyra 1 in figure 12.1.

Today, the surviving patches of zone 4 vegetation also support an abundance of wild lentil, particularly at breaks in slope, along with prolific producers of potentially edible seeds such as the medics and the many wild relatives of fenugreek, *Trigonella* spp. Geophytes, that is, herbaceous perennials with underground storage organs, many of which are edible, are particularly common. Examples include the pale cranesbill, *Biebersteinia multifida*; various salsifys, *Scorzonera* spp.; and the blue-flowered Tartar lily, *Ixiolirion tataricum*.

Where woodland-steppe successfully penetrates along wadi systems through the steppe and into the desert, as in Wadi Butum in Transjordan, there is generally little more than a line of trees, many of them very large, in a narrow strip of wadi-bank vegetation bounded on either side by bare, black, desert reg. Such vegetation also includes shrubs such as the bitter oriental almond, the desert almond, the caper bush, the occasional wolf-berry, the inevitable tamarisk scrub, and grasses such as annual beard-grass, *Polypogon monspeliensis*, and Bermuda grass, *Cynodon dactylon*.

Zone 5

The ragged eastern and southern frontiers of terebinth-almond woodland-steppe eventually give way to *arid steppe*, zone 5 (figure 3.7). Today, the steppe of Southwestern Asia is generally referred to as "*Artemisia*-Chenopodiaceae steppe," reflecting the fact that it is dominated by wormwoods, principally *Artemisia herba-alba*, together with various perennial members of the chenopod family Chenopodiaceae. The chenopods involved here are not the familiar annuals such as fat hen or goosefoot, but instead perennial shrublets, mostly with green, sometimes fleshy, stems and succulent or reduced leaves. Despite their shrubby and often succulent habit, some of these perennial chenopods die back to ground level after they have shed their seed. It was perhaps shrubs of this sort that were observed by Plaisted (1750, published 1929), who describes the steppe two days north of Taibe, and presumably not far from Abu Hureyra, as "abounding with shrubs."

The term "*Artemisia*-Chenopodiaceae steppe" is misleading, however, when considering the potential "climax" form of steppe vegetation. Even today, low-growing grasses are codominant with the perennial shrublets in all moist subzones of steppe, and they often form an almost continuous, dense sward. Indeed, in Transjordan, this dense grass sward extends eastward right through the driest zone of steppe and abuts the black desert gravel of the Azraq Basin. Furthermore, in the absence of heavy grazing by domestic animals, there would be many taller grasses that can thrive in even the driest subzones of steppe, which would make this codominance more obvious. This point is also stressed by van Zeist and Bottema (1991, p. 31), who refer to the "grass steppe" of central Anatolia, for example. A more appropriate title for Southwest Asian steppe is therefore "*Artemisia*-Chenopodiaceae-Poaceae steppe."[12]

The principal sward-grasses of many forms of steppe vegetation are perennial poas such as *Poa bulbosa* and *P. sinaica* whose wiry, glaucous leaves are only 2–5 cm high, often forming a natural, gray-green lawn, and whose mass of fibrous roots are responsible for the stability of many present-day steppic soils. Their flowering heads reach 20–30 cm in height and bear viviparous florets; that is, instead of setting seed, they produce miniature grass plants that, once shed, have a head start in the short growing seasons. In addition to the perennial poas, there are a number of low-growing *annual* grasses that also contribute to the steppic sward in the early part of the year. Wherever water lies during the winter, these grassy swards are invaded by the dwarf dryland sedge, *Carex stenophylla*, forming conspicuous patches of pale yellow-green (see figure 3.12b).

In the absence of heavy grazing by domestic animals, however, the Syrian steppe would also carry a rich growth of tall grasses, particularly the perennial, tussocked, feather-grasses such as *Stipa lagascae*, mainly in the most moist zones of steppe, and, throughout a broader range, *S. barbata*, *S. hohenackeriana*, and *S. parviflora* (figure 3.11). Their flowering heads can reach a meter or more and produce long silky plumes (modified awns), which glisten silvery in the sunlight, and blow in billows across the rolling steppe. Similar steppe in Central Asia inspired the novelist and poet Boris Pasternak to evocative descriptions of the "sighing" of the feather-grass steppe that blew in waves and was "boundless . . . as a seascape."[13] On thinner soils a similar effect is produced by the lower-growing *Stipagrostis* species, each bearing scores of three-plumed feathery florets.

Our evidence for this form of "climax" grassland comes from areas of steppe from which grazing animals have been excluded, whether in nature reserves, reservoir enclosures, or military training grounds. The rich and rapid regrowth of perennial species of *Stipa* in such exclosures is reported by Birand (1970; see in particular his photograph, figure 5), Louis (1939), Sankary (1977), and Walter (1956; see his figure 6). Hillman has also studied regenerated feather-grass steppes in both central Anatolia and Syria. The Anatolian example was in moist steppe on a tank training-range near Karapinar in Konya Province that, sadly, could not be photographed. There the hitherto degraded, moist, wormwood-sage-chenopod steppe, represented here by *Artemisia fragrans*, *Salvia cryptantha*, and *Noaea mucronata*, respectively, was thick with tussocks of silvery-headed *Stipa lagascae* growing chest-high, rendering the rest of the vegetation invisible. It was perhaps grassland of this sort that Campbell (1907, p. 131) encoun-

Figure 3.11 Dense stands of one of the perennial, tussocked feather-grasses, *Stipa lagascae* (= *S. holosericea*), here in an area of the eastern Anatolian Plateau where local legislation has recently reduced grazing. Feather-grasses were formerly codominants throughout much of the Southwest Asian steppe and woodland-steppe.

tered in 1669 when traveling between Aleppo and Baghdad: "in ye wilderness of Arrabia, is grasse in most places up to ye belly, but no rode but wtt ye deer make or wyld beasts."

Even in the much drier and drastically overgrazed steppe at Halebiye, northwest of Deir ez-Zor on the Euphrates, we found prostrate, miniaturized tussocks of both feather-grasses, *Stipa* spp., and dwarf feather-grasses, *Stipagrostis* spp., scattered across most of the close-cropped sward. Examples from Transjordan further reveal that Southwest Asian steppe could potentially support an abundance of feather-grasses in even its driest subzones, right down to the boundary with desert, albeit with much lower densities of the large-grained species. Thus, in the western Azraq Basin, although the steppe abutting the desert is grazed close to extinction, Hillman has studied islands of what is essentially steppe vegetation far out in the black, magnesium-varnished desert gravels, too distant from the boundary of continuous steppe to be worth grazing regularly. Here he found an abundance of the feather-grasses *Stipa barbata*, *S. hohenackeriana*, and occasionally *S. parviflora*, in all cases accompanied by the annual *S. tortilis*. If they can grow there with annual rainfall of about 100 mm, the same species of feather-grasses could surely grow even better in the slightly moister conditions of the proximal zone of dry steppe, just as they do in exclosures in the moister zones of steppe described earlier.

The vegetation of the steppe comes in many forms, but the wormwood, *Artemisia herba-alba*, component is common to most of them, with the notable exception of the central Anatolian steppe where this particular wormwood is replaced by another species, *A. fragrans*, or less commonly, *A. scoparia*. The various types of steppe generally reflect different rainfall regimes and soil types and can be classified on the basis of the identity of the codominant shrublets, whether these are perennial chenopods, plants such as the hummock sage, *Salvia cryptantha*, or the cushion thyme, *Thymus squarrosus*. The latter two characterize two different types of very moist steppe studied by Hillman in central Anatolia, as, in other areas, do perennial chenopods such as the spiny *Noaea mucronata*, the camphor shrublet, *Camphorosma odorata*, and the meter-tall, furry-white *Krascheninnikovia ceratoides,* which rejoices in a fragrance successfully combining the smell of unwashed human bodies and rotten fish.

Moving to slightly drier forms of steppe—the expanse stretching southward from present-day Abu Hureyra, for example—we encounter quite different types of chenopod shrublets, albeit again growing as codominants with wormwood. Here they include *Hammada eigii* and *Anabasis syriaca*, which are often accompanied by three *annual* chenopods: *Salsola vermiculata*, *Chenolea arabica*, and *Aellenia autrani* (figure 3.12a). In still drier steppe we find more *Anabasis syriaca*, but here with the spiny *Salsola spinosa* and *Hammada scoparia*, both perennial shrublets again. In spring, in the steppe around the El Kum oasis, these three chenopod shrublets, together with the *Artemisia*, stand in a thick carpet of the white-and-mauve flowered crucifer *Erucaria bornmulleriana* (figure 3.12b). In yet drier steppe, for example, in the southeast of present-day Syria, quite different perennial chenopods codominate, namely, the spiny *Cornulaca setifera* and *Hammada salicornica*, sometimes with another perennial chenopod, the dwarf shrublet, *Halogeton alopecuroides*.

Throughout the steppe, the wormwoods, shrubby chenopods, and perennial tussock-grasses are invariably accompanied by other shrublets such as the joint pine, *Ephedra alata*, a source of the medicine ephedrine, now recognized as hallucinogenic, and a kaleidoscope of knapweeds, including the mauve-flowered *Centaurea damascena*. In the wadis there are also two other common shrubs, the spiny dwarf oriental mesquite, *Prosopis farcta* (Arabic "shauk"), and capers, *Capparis spinosa* and *C. ovata*. The oriental mesquite grows knee-high, with gray foliage and brown-purple, dry-pithed, liquorice-flavored fruits that are edible if picked young. Capers often reach a meter or more, with tenacious recurved spines, great white flowers, and pendulous green fruits that offer a flash of color once they have ripened and split to reveal their edible, but pip-infested, crimson flesh.

For the traveler, however, it is the herbaceous plants that catch the eye and that, even today, turn the steppe into a blaze of color in the spring. This is particularly the case in the most moist zones of steppe, for example, around Wadi el-Adhib, west of the remote outpost of Isriya. Here, after a wet winter, we witnessed herbaceous flora of a type that was probably approaching its potential "climax," a state achieved through our host, Sheikh Zaharan, who maintained very low grazing pressures by discouraging the flocks of other shepherds with the judicious use of his armory of Kalashnikov rifles, kept ready beneath rugs in his black goat-hair tent.

Here, the annuals included a dazzling array of scarlet and crimson poppies, *Papaver* spp.; orange-horned poppies, *Glaucium* spp.; purple *Roemeria* spp.; a generous scatter of yellow-flowered *Hypecoum* spp. with their segmented, pendulous fruits; a sea of cream-flowered and mauve-flowered members of the mustard family such as *Torularia torulosa*, together with their white- and pink-flowered relatives, the *Matthiola* spp.; red-, orange-, and yellow-flowered pheasant's eyes, *Adonis* spp.; iridescent blue- and purple-flowered delphiniums, *Delphinium* and *Consolida* spp.; golden buttercups; pink-striped sainfoins, *Onobrychis* spp.; clovers and medics of every color; and so the list goes on. Then we had the herbaceous perennials, including the bluish purple-flowered Tartar lilies; the purple-and-white-flowered *Gladiolus allepicus*; blue and mauve grape hyacinths, *Muscari* and *Bellevalia* spp.; yellow gageas; and carpets of sky-blue, white, cream, and purple species of *Iris* (figure 3.13a). Even in steppe that was probably less efficiently protected from heavy grazing, Parsons (1808, p. 86), traveling from Aleppo to Taibe, observed "clover as high as the horses knees."

Figure 3.12 Examples of overgrazed absinthe-chenopod steppe representing different degrees of aridity and with various perennial chenopods as codominants. In each case, however, the feather grasses have been largely grazed out. *Top,* Steppe south of the Euphrates between Raqqa and Abu Hureyra, September 1972, here dominated by the usual absinthe, a shrubby perennial chenopod, *Hamada eigii,* and a close sward of the bulbous poas, *Poa bulbosa* and *P. sinaica. Bottom,* Steppe southeast of El Kum, April 1985, dominated by the same absinthe with three perennial chenopods, *Salsola spinosa, Anabasis syriaca,* and some *Hamada scoparia*; together with the bulbous poas; a dwarf sedge, *Carex stenophylla*; and, at this time of year, a carpet of *Erucaria bornmulleriana*—a white-and-mauve flowered annual of the mustard family.

Grasses also abounded in the luxuriant Wadi el-Adhib steppe, including two of the feather-grasses, *Stipa lagascae* and *S. barbata*, described above, although it was only in exclosures established locally by Mohammed Sankary of Aleppo University that grazing pressures were sufficiently reduced to allow these perennial *Stipa* species to start regenerating in quantity (Sankary 1977). However, in the wadi bottoms and other depressions, the grasses grew so densely that the vegetation resembled lush hay meadows studded with scarlet poppies (figure 3.13b). These formations were dominated by the barley-grasses, *Hordeum*

Figure 3.13 The steppe west of Isriya after a moist early spring, April 1983. *Top,* The steppe in flower north of the Wadi el-Adhib, near the encampment of Sheik Zaharan. Although the sheik ensured that grazing pressures were relatively low, they were still sufficient to limit reestablishment of the feather-grasses, which were making a comeback only in areas that were largely free of grazing. *Bottom,* Lush vegetation in the shallow valley of the Wadi el-Adhib. The vegetation is dominated by barley-grasses, *Hordeum murinum* aggregate, growing thigh-high and studded with scarlet poppies. Susan Colledge provides a scale.

leporinum, and its allies, here growing knee-high, with occasional dense patches of a low-growing relative of couch-grass, *Eremopyron bonaepartis*. In areas of natural disturbance in some of the wadis, we also found small amounts of wild barley. However, it was only in wadis in the drier zones of steppe that we found two other wild cereal relatives, both of them goat-face grasses, *Aegilops crassa* and, more notably, *Ae. squarrosa*, which is one of the parents of the bread-wheat line. This find represents its most southwesterly recorded present-day occurrence (compare D. Zohary and Hopf 1993, map 4).

In the drier zones of steppe, the potential climax herbaceous flora would be less luxuriant than in this most moist subzone, but it would nevertheless be vastly richer than that which survives there today. The example from Wadi el-Adhib, like those from exclosures in Anatolia, thus provides a useful glimpse of just how much richer the steppe floras potentially can be, compared with those commonly surviving in the present-day, and how much richer they could have been during early phases of the Epipalaeolithic.

Zone 6

Zone 6 is *desert*. The details of this zone are of limited interest to Abu Hureyra and so are omitted here. It should nevertheless be noted that the feature Hillman uses in distinguishing desert from steppe, and which has applied in drawing figure 3.7, is that in steppe the root growth of the vegetation is sufficient to allow the development of a continuous true soil cover, even if a very thin one, wherever rocks do not break the surface. In deserts, by contrast, soil formation, if it occurs at all, is patchy and discontinuous. In eastern Transjordan the soil of the driest zone of steppe is generated by a range of low-growing plants, but particularly by *Poa sinaica*, as explained above. Moving southeast through this driest zone of steppe, soil moisture levels eventually drop so low that these soil-building plants can no longer grow. That is where the desert begins.

In the desert there is generally no wormwood, except in the steppic "islands" described above, and we are left with a sparse cover of shrubby, perennial chenopods, mostly different ones from those of the steppe. In the deserts of eastern Transjordan, the key chenopod is *Anabasis articulata,* which in November produces flowers ranging from rose-red through rust-brown to lemon-yellow. This is often accompanied by *Halocnemum strobilaceum*; in many of the wadis and flushes, the prostrate *Anabasis setifera*, patches of *Hammada salicornica*, and yet more *Anabasis syriaca*; and often, huge populations of meter-tall shrubs of *Siedlizia rosmarinus*, each bush of which yields cupfulls of edible, oil-rich seed.

Zone 7

Zone 7 is *riverine forest,* which would potentially form the dominant vegetation of the valley-bottom alluvium of the major rivers dissecting the region, particularly the Euphrates. Today, no high riverine forest survives in Southwest Asia, and the "climax" vegetation here proposed for the Euphrates is based on Hillman's studies of, first, a 2 km stretch of near-pristine riverine forest in the Kelkitçay Valley in Asia Minor, which has since been felled; second, a much more disturbed example in the Tedzhen Valley in southeastern Turkmenistan that has since dried out; and, third, small isolated patches elsewhere in the Euphrates and Tigris catchments.

In the Kelkitçay Valley, the riverine forest was dominated by the oriental plane, *Platanus orientalis*. For some distance across the valley floor from the valley sides, the trees were fairly well spaced but grew to a great height, and the trunks, many of which were close to a meter in diameter, grew straight and smooth until they reached the crown. The canopy, all of 30 m aloft at some points, was dense and allowed in only an occasional slender shaft of sunlight, while the flat alluvial forest floor, cracked and flaking after flushing by spring floods, was correspondingly dark and bereft of ground vegetation. This high canopy was supplemented by a thick trellis of lianas, mainly wild vines, *Vitis sylvestris* subsp. *sylvestris*, with bunches of small purple grapes occasionally visible, dangling through the sea of leaves (figure 3.14), but also some *Smilax* with its spiny stems and shiny, heart-shaped leaves. The overall effect was of standing in a tall, empty, dimly lit cathedral with colonnades of huge, smooth, living columns, complete with multiple echoes. Any sense of tranquility quickly

Figure 3.14 Wild grapes, *Vitis vinifera* subsp. *sylvestris*, trailing from ash trees in riverine woodland in the narrow gorge of the Çemisgezek Suyu, a tributary of the Murat branch of the upper Euphrates in eastern Asia Minor.

evaporated, however: there on the forest floor were fresh, unmistakable prints of wild boar, adults with their young, classic inhabitants of valley-bottom ecosystems, and likely to be unenthusiastic about the arrival of an uninvited human.

Closer to the river the planes gave way to poplars and ash trees, which grew shorter and closer, and still nearer the river there was an impenetrable tangle of willows and dense thickets of tamarisk, *Tamarix*. Finally, on the river gravels, were isolated thickets of the chaste plant, *Vitex pseudo-negundo*, mauve-flowered and growing to two or so meters, its fruits like those of its close cousin, *V. agnus-castus*, the source of a condiment reputed to have helped dampen the carnal desires, doubtless ever-resurgent, of monks of another age (Polunin and Huxley 1967, p. 155). A short way upstream, however, were backwaters dominated by reeds, mostly the common reed, *Phragmites australis*, but in some areas solid stands of the cattail or reedmace, *Typha domingensis* and *T. latifolia*, and in some of the muddy shallows dense populations of the sea club-rush, *Scirpus maritimus*.

Potentially, most of the valley floor of the Middle Euphrates could support similar dense forest dominated by tall trees, certainly the Euphrates poplar, *Populus euphratica*, together with ash, *Fraxinus rotundifolius*, and, at the valley's edge, occasional elms, *Ulmus* spp. However, it is possible that the great oriental plane could also grow there. Zohary (M. 1973, p. 377) reports that the southern limit of the oriental plane in the eastern Mediterranean lies on the latitude of Jerusalem. Perhaps, therefore, it could potentially form a codominant with the poplar, and produce high forest analogous to that on the Kelkitçay.

However, the considerable width of the Euphrates Valley at Abu Hureyra would also allow a mass of back-swamps not seen in such abundance on the

Kelkitçay, and these can reasonably be expected to support extensive stands of not only the common reed and perhaps the reputedly hallucinogenic great reed, *Aundo donax*, but also the cattail or reedmace; the true bulrush, *Schoenoplectus* spp.; and, in shallower water and on mud flats, the sea club-rush, and the purple nut-grass, *Cyperus rotundus*. Certainly, all these wetland plants grow in the Euphrates Valley today, and with no drainage or cultivation of the valley floor, there would be many areas where each of them could form extensive stands. Even in 1972, the Euphrates Valley near Raqqa had kilometers of back-swamps with several areas of open water, in this case supporting large populations of sea club-rush, although by 1983 the swamps had been extensively drained, and the salty soil was sown with barley, which was instantly infested with equal numbers of club-rush plants (figure 3.15).

Nevertheless, not all areas of exposed mud would be immediately colonized by these wetland plants. It is probable that a number of other elements of the valley-bottom flora typical of this area would gain a foothold. Examples characteristic of saline areas include grasses such as dwarf mud-grass, *Aeluropus littoralis*; the prostrate desert timothys, *Crypsis* spp.; in less saline areas, the lovegrasses, *Eragrostis* spp. (relatives of the small-grained domestic cereal of Ethiopia called teff); and a range of grasses of the millet subfamily (Panicoideae), although these would probably have achieved their greatest abundance in flushed flats where wadis entered the main valley. Another conspicuous member of the valley-bottom flora would be the dwarf knotgrass, *Polygonum corrigioloides*, which, even in the early 1970s, formed extensive, pink-tinged swards in the Euphrates Valley below Abu Hureyra on the saline mud surrounding backwaters formed by the previous spring's overbank flooding. All these plants produce human foods, and we shall meet them again later in this book.

Areas of dried-out mud not yet colonized by tamarisk would quickly be dominated by the finger-headed Bermuda grass; succulent-leaved shrubby chenopods, such as the seablites *Suaeda* spp.; spiny annual chenopods such as sodaweed or saltwort, *Salsola kali*, a tumbleweed that in 1972 was still being burnt by the villagers of modern Abu Hureyra to provide caustic ash for soapmaking (figure 3.16); and the omnipresent, spiny, knee-high oriental mesquite, with its chocolate brown, nodular-spheroidal, pithy, liquorice-flavored pods.

At the edge of the valley, where the ground starts to rise above the alluvial floor and its riverine vegetation, we would encounter a narrow band of transitional, shrubby vegetation with an often impenetrable tangle of caper and wolf-berries, interwoven with the three common lianas, wild grape-vine, *Smilax*, and the yellow-flowered oriental clematis, *Clematis orientalis*, all scrambling up through the nearest trees and into the crowns of the high riverine-forest canopy. This forest-edge tangle would also include occasional bushes of the low shrub form of wild fig, *Ficus carica* subsp. *rupestris* (M. Zohary 1973, p. 630). Figs would also grow on rocky outcrops on the valley sides and around seeps on steep slopes, especially where the valley-side faces north or east, and they can still be found in such habitats today in the Euphrates Valley farther to the north (figure 3.17). In such locations figs tend to form low, semiprostrate bushes bearing almost undivided, hirsute leaves and small, sweet, deep-purple fruits with many times the purgative potential of their cultivated cousins. At the center of many such seeps we would find a thick growth of the wild sugar cane, *Saccharum officinale*, and around the edge of the seeps, extensive stands of the bulbous barley-grass, just as we do today.

Where wadis fuse to form flushed flats before entering the main valley as, for example, at the northern end of the Risafe Basin, we would encounter scrub

Figure 3.15 Populations of sea club-rush, *Scirpus maritimus*, in a back-swamp of the Euphrates Valley below Raqqa in 1972 *(top)* and in 1983, after partial drainage *(bottom)*.

vegetation dominated by tamarisk and the chaste plant, spiny caper shrubs, and swathes of the equally spiny oriental mesquite, pink-flowered camel-thorns, and sodaweeds with, in more saline hollows, shrublets of the succulent-leaved, edible-seeded seablites. On wadi banks we would also find the shrubby Arab almond, and, in flushed, gravely wadi bottoms, abundant scatters of the wild, bitter-fleshed watermelon, *Citrullus colocynthus*. Finally, many slightly raised areas would be thick with grasses, particularly the soft-headed lovegrasses and wild members of the millet subfamily such as torpedo grass, *Panicum repens*;

Figure 3.16 Boys dragging dry shrubs of soda-weed, *Salsoli kali*, gathered from valley-bottom scrub into the modern village of Abu Hureyra. The shrubs were burned and the alkali ashes used to make soap.

red finger-grass, *Digitaria sanguinalis*; and in drier areas barnyard millet, *Echinochloa crus-galli*; and yellow bristle-grass, *Setaria glauca*. Indeed, it is here that they would probably form their densest and most extensive stands.

ENVIRONMENT IN THE LATE PLEISTOCENE AND EARLY HOLOCENE

We have long known that the Quaternary was a time of major climatic fluctuations but have had little information about how these might have affected Southwest Asia. Geomorphological and palynological studies carried out in recent years have shown that changes in climate during this period had a marked effect on the landscape there (see reports in Bintliffe and van Zeist 1982; Brice 1982). It has also become clear that these climatic fluctuations could hap-

Figure 3.17 Wild fig growing on a cliff beside the Murat branch of the upper Euphrates in eastern Anatolia.

pen rapidly, in just a few human generations. We have long accepted that the climatic amelioration that accompanied the transition from Pleistocene to Holocene in Europe and North America led to major alterations in the modes of life of hunters and gatherers in those continents, but the same was probably true of the inhabitants of semi-arid regions such as the interior of Syria. Abu Hureyra itself was occupied during this transition and after, long enough for its inhabitants to have experienced local alterations in their natural environment brought about by climatic change. We must assess, therefore, the effects of climatic and environmental change in north Syria at the time when the site was occupied.

Oxygen-isotope studies of deep-sea cores in the Atlantic and Pacific oceans have established that there have been numerous, regular cycles of warm and cold climate throughout the Quaternary, whose effects have been felt worldwide (Shackleton and Opdyke 1976; Emiliani 1978). The cold phases were the Ice Ages. The validity of these cycles has been confirmed by comparisons between the climatic record from deep-sea cores and terrestrial sources, notably long sequences of loess accumulation (Kukla 1977), and the few pollen curves that extend back 100,000 years or more, like those from Grand Pile in France (Woillard and Mook 1982) and Tenaghi Philippon in northern Greece (Wijmstra 1969).

The oxygen-isotope curves show that during the last cold phase of the Pleistocene (oxygen-isotope stage 2) the temperature reached a minimum about 18,000 BP. Mean annual temperatures in the latitudes spanning Southwest Asia would have been at least 4°C below present levels (Crowley and North 1991, p. 79). Sea levels dropped more than 100 m, substantially reducing the volume of the Mediterranean. The coastal plain of the Levant increased in width by at least 5 km from Lattakia south to Mt. Carmel, and by 15 km along the coast of Palestine. The Persian Gulf was reduced to less than half its present extent, and the Red Sea decreased in width. The water temperature of the eastern Mediterranean dropped sharply because of inflows of meltwater from the rivers of southern Russia via the Black Sea (Thunell 1979).

The fall in temperature in stage 2 lowered the snowline by at least 1,000 m in the mountains surrounding the Anatolian plateau, the Mountains of Lebanon, and Mt. Hermon (Kaiser 1961; Messerli 1966, p. 61; 1967). Glaciers formed in the Taurus Mountains, and probably in the Mountains of Lebanon also. The most important effect of the drop in temperature would have been to reduce evaporation rates in Southwest Asia. It was this, rather than increases in rainfall, that allowed lakes in Southwest Asia to rise to higher levels than today. The most striking example of this phenomenon was Lake Lisan (Neev and Emery 1967, p. 26), a body of water some 220 km long that formed in the Rift Valley now occupied by its successor, the much smaller Dead Sea, and the valley of the Jordan River.

Changes in precipitation during the last cold phase caused a marked contraction of forest vegetation throughout Southwest Asia. One of the reasons for this was a reduction in rainfall during the summer growing season (El-Moslimany 1990, p. 349). The impact on the vegetation of the Levant can be seen clearly in two pollen cores, one from the Huleh Basin in the upper Jordan Valley (Baruch and Bottema 1991) and the other from the Ghab section of the Orontes River (Niklewski and van Zeist 1970). These conditions persisted until c. 15,000 BP, when precipitation began to rise again during the spring and summer.

The air temperature started to increase at the end of oxygen-isotope stage 2, causing sea levels to rise worldwide from about 15,000 BP (Bard et al. 1990, p. 405). The temperature reached a maximum as recently as 5,000 BP, before declining two or three degrees in recent millennia. Pollen records from Southwest Asia and Europe make it clear that this rise in temperature was anything but smooth.

The percentage of carbon dioxide (CO_2) in the atmosphere also increased markedly between 15,000 and 12,000 BP (Sage 1995, p. 95), stimulating plant growth and productivity. Sage (1995) has argued that this would have created more favorable conditions for the development of farming, a hypothesis that accords strongly with the evidence from the Levant.

The most significant return to cooler conditions was the sharp climatic reversal known as the Younger Dryas. During this episode, lasting from c. 11,000 to 10,000 BP (Berger 1990, p. 219), the climate returned to near-glacial conditions as the temperature dropped sharply. This had profound effects on the environment, causing glaciers to expand once more and the boundaries of vegetation zones to move many kilometers. The onset of the Younger Dryas was often accompanied by increased aridity that had its own marked environmental impact.

The Younger Dryas cooling episode was first recognized in Europe (Iversen 1954), the continent that has yielded the most detailed evidence of its effects, but its impact has since been recognized across the world. The Younger Dryas was sufficiently sharp and prolonged to be evident in ice cores from Greenland (Dansgaard and Oeschger 1989, pp. 296–298) and in oxygen-isotope records from the ocean floor of the Pacific (Shackleton and Opdyke 1973, figure 6). Bond and colleagues (1993, figure 3) have recently established a firm correlation for the Younger Dryas between sedimentary records from the North Atlantic and a new ice core from Greenland. Records published in the last few years from a lake in western Tibet, the Sulu Sea in the Philippines archipelago, and the Franz Josef Glacier in New Zealand confirm the worldwide impact of this event (Gasse et al. 1991; Kudrass et al. 1991; Denton and Hendy 1994).

Recent research has shown that the Younger Dryas had a considerable impact on climate and environment in Southwest Asia (Moore and Hillman 1992). This can be seen very clearly in the well-dated pollen core from Lake Huleh (Baruch and Bottema 1991, figure 3), where the cooler conditions and a steep drop in precipitation during the spring and summer growing seasons caused a marked reduction in tree cover. Similar trends can be seen in other pollen cores across Southwest Asia: the Ghab, Lake Zeribar in the Zagros Mountains, a core from western Anatolia, and, particularly clearly, from Tenaghi Philippon in Macedonia (Wijmstra 1969, p. 520). The decline in precipitation associated with the onset of the Younger Dryas also caused a sharp drop in the level of the Dead Sea (Yechieli et al. 1993, p. 65). We have found that the Younger Dryas climatic reversal altered the vegetation around the village of Abu Hureyra 1 (see chapter 12) and thus affected the way of life of its hunter-gatherer inhabitants. The implications of these findings are of considerable importance since they suggest that the Younger Dryas episode was a significant factor in the transition from foraging to farming at Abu Hureyra and, we believe, elsewhere in Southwest Asia.

Climatic and environmental conditions ameliorated after 10,000 BP in the early Holocene; the temperature rose but it seems that moisture levels increased at the same time, especially during the summer (El-Moslimany 1994), allowing vegetation to flourish and lakes to fill. The volume of water in the Dead Sea increased and the lake held more water than today for much of the earlier Holocene (Yechieli et al. 1993, p. 65). The level of the lake in the Damascus Basin rose and then fluctuated up and down for several millennia (Kaiser et al. 1973).

The higher level of this lake was caused partly by an increase in discharge of the Barada River (van Liere 1960–1961, p. 54). Eventually, the Damascus Basin lake shrank and split into its present remnants, the Hijjane and Ateibe lakes. The late Pleistocene in the rest of Syria was sufficiently arid to prevent the filling of other inland drainage basins (van Liere 1960–1961, p. 10). The lakes on the Anatolian plateau, however, still stood at relatively high levels at the end of the Pleistocene and into the early Holocene (Erol 1978, figure 6).

During the Late Glacial the westerly air stream lay farther south than today (Lamb and Woodroffe 1970, pp. 49–51; Kutzbach et al. 1993). It is thought that as the temperature rose these winds strengthened, letting rain reach the Levant more frequently. Winter rainfall would have been greater than at present, and the rainy season may have lasted longer. That is why the Levant enjoyed a period of moister climate at the same time as the temperature was rising. The Younger Dryas would have caused a millennium-long reversal of these trends. Then early in the Holocene the pattern of circulation altered once more. The North American ice sheet was still shrinking, but the Scandinavian one had almost gone, while the differences between land and sea temperatures increased. This stimulated a more vigorous wind system and caused the Atlantic westerlies to follow a more northeasterly course, so the amount of moist air that could reach the Levant was reduced. The strongest contrasts in seasonality of rainfall occurred around 10,000–9,000 BP (Byrne 1987; COHMAP Members 1988) and declined thereafter, while the continued rise in temperature would have increased evaporation. Consequently, in the mid Holocene the Levant became more arid.

Vegetation Following the Glacial Maximum, c. 18,000–11,000 BP

During the cool, relatively dry conditions of the Glacial Maximum and the ensuing three millennia, high forest remained restricted to the Black Sea coastal zone, with open woodland surviving in the western Levant, western Asia Minor, the southern Taurus Mountains, and possibly in more restricted form in a few small refugia in the Anti-Taurus and Zagros mountains. The rest, namely, the entirety of the interior, was steppe, desert-steppe, and true desert. The general pattern is conveniently summarized in the map-model of van Zeist and Bottema (1991, figure 42).[14]

The woodland of the Levantine refuge was probably open rather than dense forest, as shown in the transect reconstructions of Niklewski and van Zeist (1970, figure 4). Down on the coast trees were probably unable to survive, and there the vegetation would have been dominated by low shrublets such as the spiny burnet and aromatic members of the sage and lavender family. But a short distance inland there would have been a scatter of evergreen oaks, lentisc, and carobs. As the terrain rose into the mountains, these would have given way to deciduous oaks, terebinths, various members of the rose family (Rosaceae), junipers, pines, and cedars. However, on lower slopes farther inland, deciduous oak-dominated mixed woodland very quickly thinned to the much sparser scatter of trees of the woodland-steppe: great terebinths, probably accompanied by almonds and hawthorns, and beyond this narrow band, nothing but boundless steppe stretching all the way to the Hindu Kush, itself giving way to desert farther south.

The composition of the ground cover in the different tree zones is difficult to suggest. This is because, first, many of the herbaceous plants are insect pollinated, so their pollen is never dispersed to pollen-coring sites, unlike wind-pollinated species. Second, the pollen of plants such as the grasses cannot be identified beyond the level of family. Third, the patterns of association among plants familiar to us in present-day plant communities will have been dislocated during the periods of rapid plant migration characterizing much of the terminal Pleistocene.[15] Nevertheless, it is inevitable that annual grasses, including the wild cereals, would have been a conspicuous component of the open oak-dominated woodland, and it is probable that the wild cereals formed their densest and most extensive stands in the drier fringes of this zone and for a short distance into the adjacent woodland-steppe zone (see map, figure 12.1).

In the pollen record for this period, steppe is, as usual, indicated by wormwoods and chenopods, the latter almost certainly dominated by perennial shrublets. But, as we have already indicated for present-day steppe, perennial tussock grasses (bunch-grasses) will have been codominant, and the most conspicuous of these will doubtless have been the feather-grasses, *Stipa* and *Stipagrostis* spp.

The Jordan Valley was probably just within the Levantine woodland refuge or at its eastern edge, although it is shown largely outside in van Zeist and Bottema's map (1991, figure 38). Certainly, the remains of plant foods identified by Kislev from the site of Ohalo II, dating to the Glacial Maximum and sitting on the shore of the Sea of Galilee, suggest that the occupants had access to much the same resources as those available in and around lower sections of the Jordan Valley today, even if the source plants were somewhat differently assorted and the tree cover was much sparser. They gathered a wide range of plant foods including acorns from the oaks that were presumably located along the rims of valleys nearby, wild emmer, wild barley, wild lentils, and fruits and seeds from salt scrub and salt-marsh in the valley bottom (Kislev, Nadel, and Carmi 1992).

From 15,000 BP increasing levels of atmospheric CO_2 (Sage 1995) combined with the increasingly warm and moist conditions allowed the woodland of the Levantine refuge to develop into full forest and to start to spread inland from the subcoastal refugia, invading the proximal parts of the steppe. Most notably, woodland spread around the Fertile Crescent—first across the foothills of the Anti-Taurus Mountains and then down the Zagros. Evidence for the later stages of this spread comes from pollen studies at Lakes Zeribar and Mirabad in the Zagros, Urmia in northwest Iran, and Van in eastern Asia Minor.[16]

The possible state of spread at c. 12,000–11,000 BP is presented in map form in van Zeist and Bottema (1991, figure 43). However, our own reconstruction of potential vegetation of the present day (figure 3.7), combined with evidence from plant remains from the earliest Epipalaeolithic levels at Abu Hureyra, indicates that park-woodland and woodland-steppe actually penetrated much farther east from the Levantine refuge than indicated in van Zeist and Bottema's map, and would have invaded an altogether much broader swathe of the northern Fertile Crescent.

Hillman (1996) has modeled the pattern and rates of spread in some detail. He argues that the spread was spearheaded by a thin scatter of trees such as terebinth, probably together with some wild almonds, hawthorns, and shrubs such as buckthorn and Christ's-thorn. These were closely followed by a bow wave of annual grasses including wild einkorn, wild barley, and probably wild annual rye. The wild einkorn stands probably also included some wild emmer, just as they do today around the northern Fertile Crescent (D. Zohary and Hopf 1993, map 3). Stands of these wild cereals can produce yields matching their domestic derivatives under traditional cultivation (Harlan 1967; Zohary 1989, p. 369), and in many areas the advancing army of wild cereals probably resembled nothing so much as a limitless, if patchy, field with a sparse scatter of terebinth and almond trees. Following in the wake of the wild cereals, albeit increasingly left behind, were the first deciduous oaks and other trees that would eventually form oak-Rosaceae park-woodland. This easterly pattern of spread from woodland refugia in the northern Levant and across the northern Fertile Crescent (engulfing Abu Hureyra) is summarized in the four maps in figure 3.18.[17]

These changes had a profound effect on the plant food resource-base available to local hunter-gatherers. The amelioration of conditions starting around 15,000 BP had already stimulated higher yields from plant foods indigenous to the then steppe, particularly from the perennial feather-grasses and from plants with edible roots such as the salsifys, Tartar lilies, and the pale cranesbill. With the invasion of annual grasses, particularly the wild cereals, yields of foods capable of serving as caloric staples were vastly increased, and the simultaneous spread of the trees such as wild almonds added to this abundance. This had far-reaching effects on patterns of storage and mobility practiced by the steppic hunter-gatherers, and in some cases, is likely to have led to the eventual cultivation of some of these same cereals (Hillman 1996).

Within two millennia of the 15,000 BP start of woodland expansion from the western Levant, the sparse scatter of trees such as terebinth probably extended almost to Abu Hureyra. They were closely followed by the first bow wave of invasive annual grasses, including the wild cereals, and together they would probably have formed something resembling a grassy woodland-steppe. Oaks and some of the other trees characteristic of the present-day zone 3b entered the area quite a bit later, and as conditions became progressively moister dur-

Figure 3.18 Models of the distribution of forest, park-woodland, wild cereals, woodland-steppe, and steppe in the northern Fertile Crescent during the spread of vegetation from the northern Levant after 15,000 BP. a, The spread of vegetation at c. 13,000 BP, two thousand years after the beginning of the expansion of woodland-steppe and annual grasses . b, The pattern of vegetation at c. 11,000 BP after four thousand years of expansion, when the onset of the dry, cold conditions of the Younger Dryas would have interrupted the continued spread of woodland-steppe and annual grasses. c, *(opposite top)* The pattern at c. 10,5000 BP after the cold conditions of the Younger Dryas had not only arrested the eastward spread of vegetation by preventing flowering, fruiting, and germination of trees such as oaks throughout the drier areas, but had also caused whole-sale dieback of these trees. Trees and cereals in all the areas colonized during the preceding 4,500 years would have survived only in isolated pockets such as moist hollows and breaks on steep north-facing slopes, where the soils remained sufficiently moist (see the small circles on the map). Across the rest of the dry dieback zones scatters of dead trees would have littered the landscape. The small pockets of survivors in most of the drier fringes such as the Abu Hureyra area would eventually have died out. Nevertheless, drought-resistant trees such as the great terebinth would probably have continued to grow along some wadis, as in figure 3.10c. d, *(bottom)* The vegetation at c. 9,000 BP after the return of moister, warmer conditions had allowed trees and wild cereals to spread out from the surviving pockets, to fill many of the gaps in their former distribution, and to continue their eastward expansion. However, the reexpansion was only partial, and the trees and cereals never again recolonized the area around Abu Hureyra and equivalent areas along the dry, inner flanks of the Fertile Crescent, as they had at c. 11,500 BP. In the continuation of their eastward expansion, the trees and cereals now followed a narrower trajectory restricted to higher elevations.

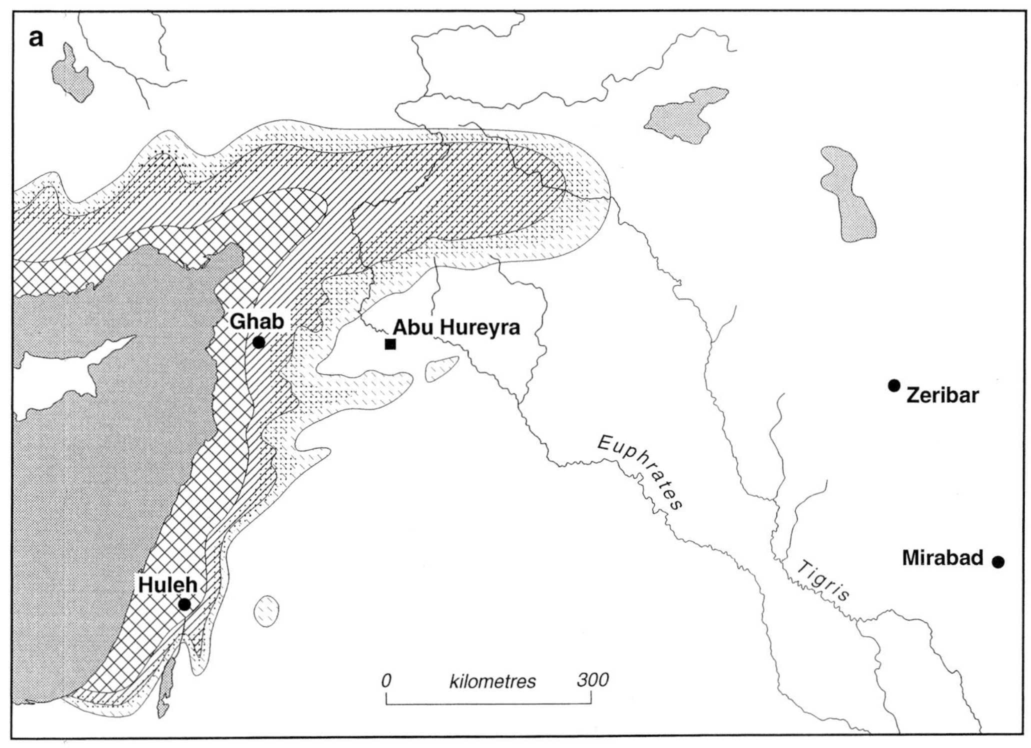
a
Ghab
Abu Hureyra
Zeribar
Euphrates
Mirabad
Tigris
Huleh
0 kilometres 300

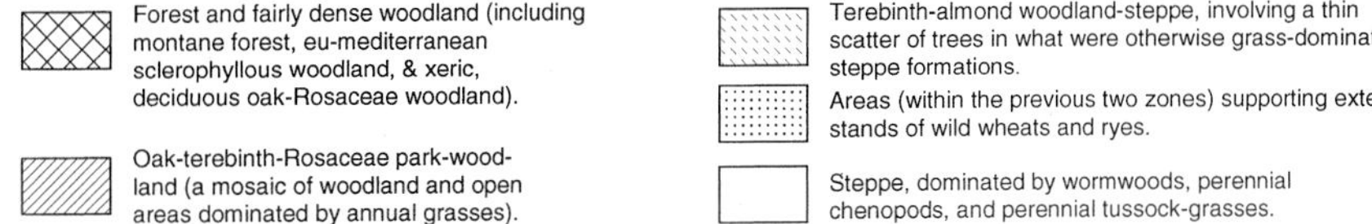
Forest and fairly dense woodland (including montane forest, eu-mediterranean sclerophyllous woodland, & xeric, deciduous oak-Rosaceae woodland).
Oak-terebinth-Rosaceae park-woodland (a mosaic of woodland and open areas dominated by annual grasses).
Terebinth-almond woodland-steppe, involving a thin scatter of trees in what were otherwise grass-dominated steppe formations.
Areas (within the previous two zones) supporting extensive stands of wild wheats and ryes.
Steppe, dominated by wormwoods, perennial chenopods, and perennial tussock-grasses.

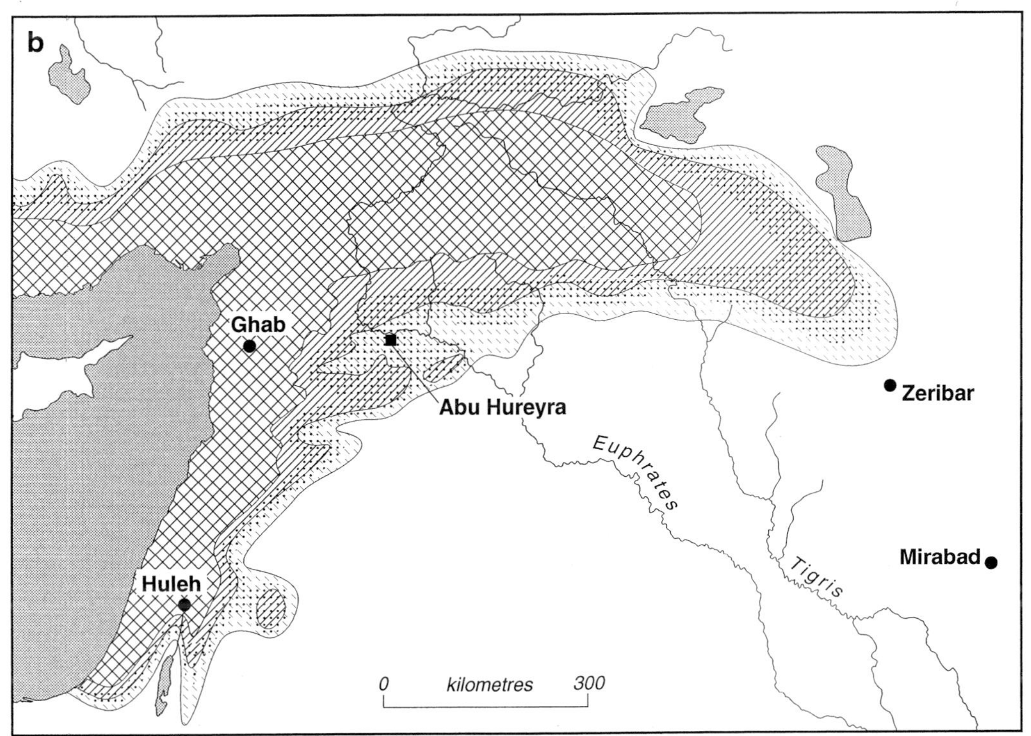
b
Ghab
Abu Hureyra
Zeribar
Euphrates
Mirabad
Tigris
Huleh
0 kilometres 300

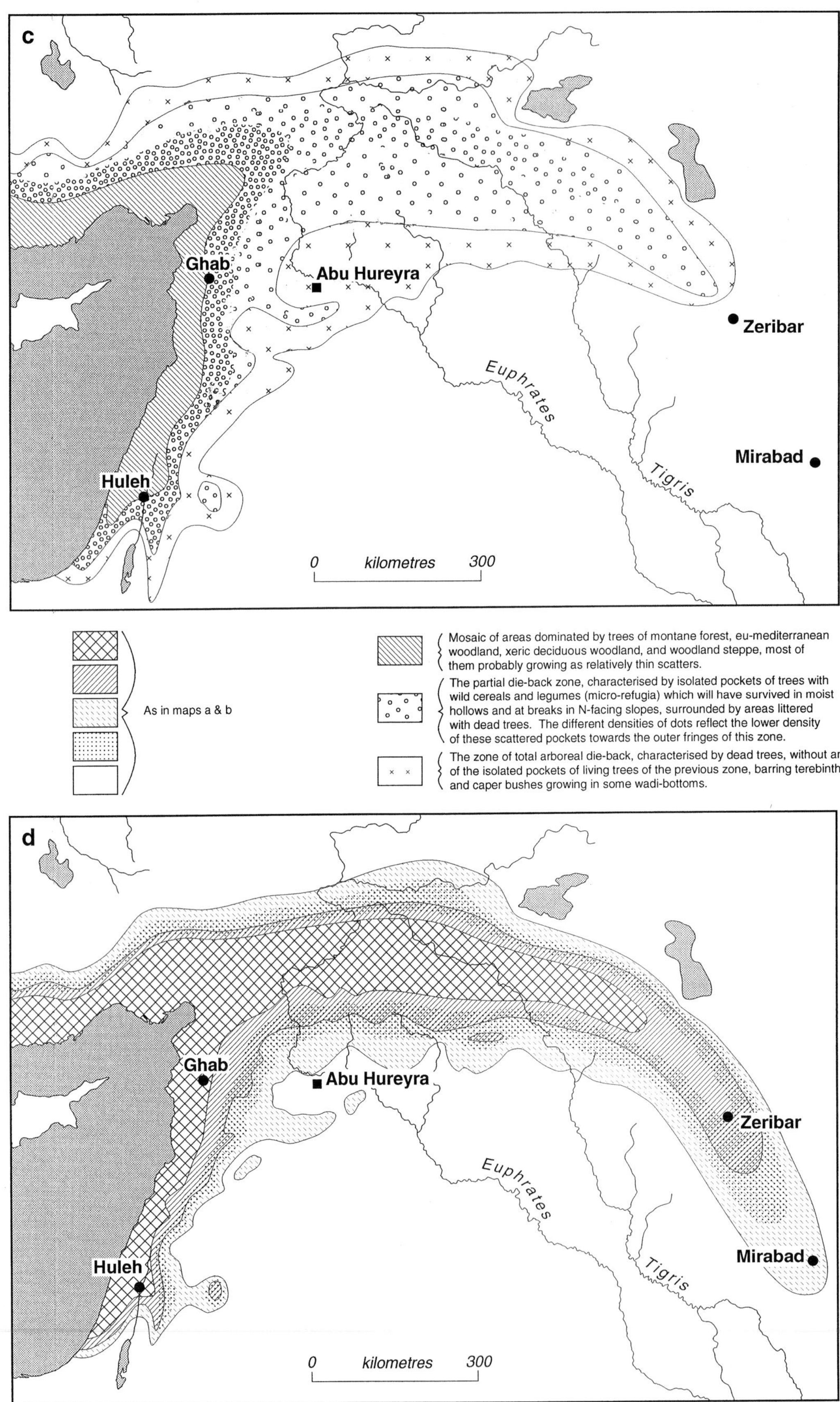
c
Ghab
Abu Hureyra
Zeribar
Euphrates
Mirabad
Tigris
Huleh
0 kilometres 300
As in maps a & b
Mosaic of areas dominated by trees of montane forest, eu-mediterranean woodland, xeric deciduous woodland, and woodland steppe, most of them probably growing as relatively thin scatters.
The partial die-back zone, characterised by isolated pockets of trees with wild cereals and legumes (micro-refugia) which will have survived in moist hollows and at breaks in N-facing slopes, surrounded by areas littered with dead trees. The different densities of dots reflect the lower density of these scattered pockets towards the outer fringes of this zone.
The zone of total arboreal die-back, characterised by dead trees, without any of the isolated pockets of living trees of the previous zone, barring terebinths and caper bushes growing in some wadi-bottoms.
d
Ghab
Abu Hureyra
Zeribar
Euphrates
Mirabad
Tigris
Huleh
0 kilometres 300

ing the ensuing two millennia they slowly increased in number to form the beginnings of oak-Rosaceae park-woodland. By 12,000 BP, half a millennium before the start of Epipalaeolithic settlement, the Abu Hureyra area probably offered an array of rich resource zones.

Some form of park-woodland could have established itself in areas extending to within 10–15 km of what was to become the site of Abu Hureyra, with smaller scatters of oak trees probably growing considerably closer. Terebinth-almond woodland-steppe would have extended far beyond Abu Hureyra to the east. Dense stands of wild cereals would have become established not only in the drier subzone (3b.ii in figure 12.1) of park-woodland, but also in favored habitats within the moister subzone (4a) of the woodland-steppe zone, with the closest stands probably growing within sight of what was to become the site of Abu Hureyra.

Changes in Vegetation between c. 11,000 and 10,000 BP

The very sharp retreat in woodland and forest beginning about 11,500 BP in the pollen sequences from Lake Huleh in the southern Levant (Baruch and Bottema 1991) and, according to Yasouda, the Ghab in the northern Levant clearly demonstrates a decrease in soil moisture during the spring and summer growing period.[18] As we have noted above, there are indications of related retreats at Tenaghi Philippon in Greece, and at Karamik Batakliği and Söğüt Gölü in southwest Asia Minor at about the same time or a few centuries later. The equally dramatic woodland retreat seen in Niklewski and van Zeist's (1971) earlier core from the Ghab also appears to fit these events perfectly—given adjustment of the single, suspect date (see n.14). The synchronous changes in steppe flora around Lake Zeribar at this point (van Zeist and Bottema 1977) again reveal sharply increased aridity.

The onset of drier conditions at all these pollen-coring sites coincided closely with the start of the Younger Dryas. Because the Younger Dryas was a global phenomenon, it is hardly surprising that the remains of food plants from Abu Hureyra 1 indicate a forest retreat and progressive increase in aridity synchronous with those reflected in the pollen. Indeed, the closely dated sequence of changes at Abu Hureyra provides what is currently the most detailed record available of the impact of the Younger Dryas on local vegetation and local subsistence.

As at Lake Huleh, the initial retreat did not remove woodland resources from the Abu Hureyra area altogether. The Huleh diagram shows that at 11,000 BP, after 500 years of retreat, the local woodland was still occupying a greatly expanded territory. So, too, the people of Abu Hureyra during phase 1 of the occupation, between c. 11,500 and 11,000 BP, continued using some park-woodland resources, reflecting maintenance of at least some long-distance access (figure 12.1). Indeed, the occasional fragments of oak charcoal suggest that oak park-woodland, or at least thinner scatters of oak trees, grew quite close to the site (appendix E). Likewise, the wild cereals, which would have achieved their highest concentrations in the ecotone between park-woodland and woodland-steppe, were still accessible to a degree that seemingly allowed their heavy and undiminished use.

Plant foods of the drier subzone of woodland-steppe (zone 4b in figure 12.1) were also apparently readily available during phase 1. Certainly, the use of terebinth fruitlets continued unabated, and there was increasingly heavy exploitation of feather-grass grains during this period. But this apparently increased use of feather-grass may, in fact, indicate the first phase of vegetal retreat. At 11,500 BP woodland-steppe would have extended well beyond Abu Hureyra into drier areas to the east and southeast (figure 3.18b), and the highest concentrations of feather-grass would have been found to the east, in the drier subzone of woodland-steppe (zone 4b) and in the more distant moist subzone of steppe (zone 5a). It is therefore only with a partial retreat of these zones back toward the northern Levant that high densities of feather-grass would have become locally available across really huge areas, possibly prompting increased use of the sort we see here. The supply of terebinth fruitlets, by contrast, would have stayed the same, precisely as indicated by the charred remains.

However, at the beginning of phase 2, around 11,000 BP, we see a systematic change in the use of plant foods, indicating reduced local access to, or reduced productivity of, all the more moisture-demanding of the food plants represented in the remains. This, in turn, presumably reflects a progressive reduction in soil moisture during the spring and summer growing season. The Younger Dryas was beginning to "bite."

First, foods of park-woodland were seemingly no longer collected, although, appropriately, the gathering of seeds, and perhaps the edible roots, too, from the slightly more drought-tolerant asphodel continued for a fraction longer than those from the trees. Second, there was a dramatic slump in the use of the wild cereals just after the start of phase 2, around 10,900 BP (see chapter 12). This suggests that the inhabitants were losing their nearest stands, with concomitant increases in transport costs that would have eroded net caloric returns from these wild cereals. A similar decline also seems to have affected the use of wild relatives of the moisture-demanding millets, which, because they were probably gathered primarily from open scrub formations of the lower wadi systems and fans, would have been hit by reduced wadi discharge.

The use of the grain of feather-grasses peaked at about this point and then held steady before finally starting to decline later in phase 2. This decline suggests that, after woodland-steppe (zone 4b) was replaced by moist steppe (zone 5a), it in turn was rapidly replaced toward the end of phase 2 by dry steppe (zone 5b). The combined species of feather-grasses, particularly the large-grained species, grow at significantly lower densities in dry steppe. Today, the Abu Hureyra hinterland supports what is potentially moist steppe, while dry steppe gets no closer than El Kum (figure 3.7, zone 5b). The decline in use of feather-grass grain therefore accords with the pollen evidence, which suggests that, at the peak of the Younger Dryas, conditions were drier than those of the present day. It also fits with the suggestion of Byrne (1987) and others that maximum seasonality coincided with the end of the Pleistocene and produced dry hot summers that probably began earlier in the growing season than they do even today. This would have sharply reduced the grain production of the late-flowering perennial feather-grasses.

It might be imagined that any decline in the use of terebinth fruitlets would have occurred slightly before the decline in feather-grass grains in phase 2. In fact, terebinth fruitlets declined only in phase 3. This accords precisely with our expectation. As a nonstaple used mainly as a flavoring or preservative, the pungent terebinth fruitlets would have been gathered in only small quantities, and the needs of the whole population could readily have been met from relatively few trees. Even when the area was dominated by dry steppe, plenty of terebinth trees would have survived on the banks of local wadis, just as they do today along the Wadi Butum in Transjordan (figure 3.10c).

Eventually, around 10,000 BP, we see a decline in the use of two of the apparent staples of the valley bottom flora, the nutlets of club-rush and knotgrass (see chapter 12). This presumably reflects reduced overbank flooding during the spring spate. That the decline in use of these two valley-bottom foods was delayed relative to that of other plant foods probably reflects the fact that the Euphrates flood water at Abu Hureyra derived from the headwaters of the river high on the east Anatolian Plateau where spring discharge was largely a product of snow melt; changes in the regime of the river there apparently followed a different chronology.

All these changes in use of food plants thus accord closely with expectations based on the pollen evidence of climate change at this time and on studies of present-day vegetal ecology. However, this evidence for progressive desiccation might appear to conflict with the continued presence of occasional fragments of oak charcoal right through phases 2 and 3 of Abu Hureyra 1 (appendix 6). There is, once again, a simple explanation. With progressive desiccation, trees such as oak firstly stop producing flowers and fruit, and so cease to appear in pollen spectra and in the seed record; the majority of the trees will then eventually die. In an arid climate such as that of Southwest Asia during the Younger Dryas, these dead trees could remain standing (or, eventually, lying) for centuries, rather like many of the bristle-cone pines in the White Mountains of California that have been dead for thousands of years. In other words, their dead wood would have remained available for the rest of the Younger Dryas. In the case of oak, the wood becomes more suitable for burning once it is dead, and the fallen branches are easier to gather, too, so we might actually anticipate a temporary *increase* in the use of their wood for fuel once they started to die off. We would therefore expect to encounter occasional fragments of oak charcoal throughout the Epipalaeolithic—well after the point when all evidence for the gathering of fruits of park-woodland ceased.

Following the sharp reductions in the archaeological record of nearly all the food plants discussed above, their frequency thereafter continued at the same reduced level. There are two possible explanations for this continued reduction. First, although the Lake Huleh pollen record indicates that the forest reexpansion toward the end of the Younger Dryas was complete by about 10,000 BP, the reestablishment of growing-season precipitation may have been less marked in the interior. Second, the need to utilize fully these wild starch staples may have been obviated by the cultivation of one or more cereals that started just as the effects of the Younger Dryas drought began to be felt by the inhabitants of Abu Hureyra 1, as we shall explain in chapter 12.

Correspondingly, the modest *increases* in the frequency of a complex of small-seeded wild legumes and small-grained wild grasses from the start of phase 2 of the Abu Hureyra 1 village are best explained as their flourishing as weeds of early cultivation and the preservation of their seeds by charring through the disposal onto the fire of waste fractions separated during the cleaning of the cultivated grain, just as they often are today.

Changes in Vegetation between c. 10,000 and 6,000 BP

All the pollen spectra cited above show a substantial reexpansion of woodland or forest at the end of the Younger Dryas (figure 3.18d). As the temperature was rising throughout this period, the initial expansion of woodland and forest necessitated a great increase in the availability of soil moisture during the spring and early summer growing periods. Following the expansion, the west Anatolian and southeastern European spectra show that this extended forest cover continued well into the Holocene, albeit with a sharp but brief recession at Söğüt Gölü and at Tenaghi Philippon. By contrast, the Lake Huleh sequences suggest that the reexpansion was followed by a slow retreat in woodland and forest cover, and this trend was arguably even more pronounced at the Ghab.

After the spread of agriculture in the ninth millennium BP, it is difficult to distinguish climatic and anthropogenic effects, although van Zeist and Bottema (1977, 1982) tentatively identify the start of forest clearance around 4,500 BP at the Ghab and a fraction later at Lake Zeribar. In dry areas where the period of active growth is limited to spring and early summer and where regeneration is correspondingly slow, it is probable that agrarian communities had some effect on tree cover quite early. However, in areas of moderate rainfall, rapid regeneration probably ensured that extensive tree cover generally continued well into our era and that any changes in forest composition would be largely undetectable in pollen spectra. It was primarily in areas that were then park-woodland, woodland-steppe, and moist steppe that Neolithic farmers had the most significant impact.

These climatic and vegetation changes may be summarized as follows. About 18,000 BP the Levant was cool with dry summers. From c. 15,000 BP the temperature began to rise, CO_2 levels rose dramatically, and rainfall increased, especially during the growing season, in part because of changes in the patterns of circulation of the winds. Not only did the rainy season last longer, but evaporation rates, though rising, were still lower than today, so the discharge of rivers was greater than at present. The woodland and woodland-steppe zones expanded eastward to the vicinity of Abu Hureyra. The vegetation record from the site indicates that the country south of Abu Hureyra consisted of rich grassland with scattered trees and shrubs, and park-woodland beyond no more than a couple of hours' walk away. The moister climate would have increased the humic content of soils over much of the Syrian interior and have altered their distribution. The terra rossa zone probably extended farther east than at present, approaching Abu Hureyra, while the soils around Abu Hureyra itself are likely to have been the fertile, red-brown steppe type that is so suitable for dry farming. The climate was still one of marked differences between winter and summer, with pronounced continental effects in the interior. The summers would have been a few degrees cooler than today with more moisture during the spring growing season, and the winters a little sharper with more frosts, but the Middle Euphrates would always have been semi-arid. These are the conditions that prevailed in north Syria at the time that Abu Hureyra was first settled. The environment was more favorable for human settlement than it was to become during the mid Holocene, but it was still delicately balanced. Modest fluctuations in temperature or rainfall would have had profound effects on vegetation, soils, and available moisture.

The onset of the Younger Dryas c. 11,000 BP, 500 years after the founding of Abu Hureyra 1, brought a swift return to the cooler, drier climate of the full glacial. Those conditions persisted until near the end of Abu Hureyra 1. By the time the village of Abu Hureyra 2 began to grow the climate had resumed its warming trend, and for a time moisture levels increased. Then the rise in temperature, combined with shifts in the wind systems, led to the onset of more arid conditions.

THE PRESENCE IN HISTORICAL TIMES OF THE LARGE VERTEBRATES FOUND AT ABU HUREYRA

Most of the vertebrate species found at Abu Hureyra survived in Syria into recent times, and something of their former distribution and abundance can be recovered from the journals of travelers in the region during the recent past. This discussion focuses on species of economic importance at Abu Hureyra, either because the animal is abundant in the bone remains, or because historical accounts show that it was commonly eaten within the region. Some species not so far identified among the bones from Abu Hureyra, but which were recorded in the vicinity of the site, are included.

Gazelles are the most prominent species at Abu Hureyra. The taxonomy of the modern gazelles is complex, with many species and subspecies recognized in the area of their natural distribution (Groves and Harrison 1967; Harrison 1968; Harrison and Bates 1991; Groves 1969, 1983). It is doubtful that the prehistoric distribution of species and subspecies can now be fully reconstructed from the very limited samples of recent specimens that have been collected. At the simplest level, three species of gazelles are recognized in Southwest Asia:

(a) the Palestine or Mountain gazelle, *Gazella gazella*
(b) the Dorcas gazelle, *Gazella dorcas*
(c) the Persian or Goitred gazelle, *Gazella subgutturosa*

Each of these has subspecies, but as these are seldom defined on osteological criteria they have little relevance to this work. The most comprehensive recent survey of the distribution of gazelle species in this region is that of Harrison (1968, pp. 349–365), which shows that they are, to a significant degree, sympatric.

The present-day distributions are summarized briefly as follows:

> The Palestine gazelle, *Gazella gazella*: This species now occupies the uplands of the coastal regions of the Arabian peninsula, including the coasts of the Mediterranean and Red seas and the Persian Gulf.
>
> The Dorcas gazelle, *Gazella dorcas*: This most desert adapted of the gazelles in Southwest Asia is distributed in the more arid regions of the interior of the Arabian peninsula. Subspecies are found in the Egyptian deserts inland from the western coast of the Red Sea.
>
> The Persian gazelle, *Gazella subgutturosa* (figure 3.19): This species is widespread in the Arabian peninsula, and its distribution extends far to the east through Mesopotamia and Iran, northward around the Caspian Sea, in Turkmenia, and on to central Asia. It is primarily the gazelle of steppe conditions, and it has a more gregarious habit than other species.

Gazelles were commonly seen by travelers, often in considerable abundance. Russell (1758), who was resident in Aleppo, recorded that the country "abounded with antelopes," noting that these were of two sorts: the "mountain antelope," described as having a dark brown back and neck, and the "plains antelope," of a lighter color. Although Russell's description is too vague for certain identification, it is likely that two species were indeed seen in the vicinity of the city, probably the Palestine gazelle as the "mountain antelope" and the Persian gazelle as the "plains antelope." It must be remembered that the rainfall at Aleppo is somewhat higher than at Abu Hureyra, and that the city is situated within a different environmental zone, the xeric woodland (zone 3b). It does not follow that both species would commonly be present on the steppe near Abu Hureyra, though there is some evidence for the occasional presence of a second small species of gazelle at the site.

Further evidence of the gazelle species found recently in the steppe regions of Syria comes from Upton (1881, p. 252). Traveling westward from Damascus in what he records as the spring, gazelles "sweep across our path in strings at a gallop," running with lowered heads. Vesey-Fitzgerald (1952) describes this as the characteristic flight posture of the Persian gazelle.

The onager, *Equus hemionus* (figure 3.20), was already comparatively rare by the eighteenth century AD and was seen by few travelers in recent times. The species was, however, much more common when the Persian expedition described by Xenophon, c. 375–370 BC, crossed the Euphrates from the west to the east bank at Thapsacus, near the modern town of Tabqa. This was apparently during late summer. From there, and for about 170 km to the south, onagers as well as ostrich and gazelles were described as abundant (Xenophon 1972).

Apart from such early historical records, the onager was seen in large groups only by travelers in the sixteenth and seventeenth centuries AD. Eldred (1583, published 1927) traveled north from Baghdad to Aleppo, crossing the Euphrates at Hit. Although the exact location of his observations is not given, he noted "wild asses all white, roebucks (by which he must mean gazelles), wolves, leopards, foxes and many hares" (pp. 327–328). A virtually identical description is given by Cartwright (1611); so similar is the wording that the two accounts cannot be unconnected.

Teixeira (1604) saw onagers a little to the south of Taibe; the translation gives "many hares and great herds of wild asses" (p. 99). Layard (1853) recorded that the onager was rare by the mid nineteenth century, and the live specimens that he obtained as foals soon died. Blunt (1879) saw an onager foal in the spring that was kept as a semi-tame pet at Raqqa. The species was almost unknown to the west of the Euphrates from the early nineteenth century.

Travelers commonly observed wild pigs, *Sus scrofa* (figure 3.21),in the vicinity of the thick cover of the Euphrates Valley and adjacent to other areas of refuge inhabited by this species. During the rainy season these animals would often move considerable distances from cover to forage for roots and tubers. Blunt (1879) commonly saw wild boar along the Euphrates, and she recorded that the land a little to the south of Abu Hureyra was of "wide grassy plains interspersed with tamarisk bushes . . . acres of land furrowed up as if by the plough, but in reality by wild boars" (I, p. 90). Irby and Mangles (1844) also noted that land to the northwest of Palmyra had the appearance of being plowed due to the activities of wild boars. Helfer (1878) even recorded wild boar feeding on bulbs in the open steppe south of Aleppo, near to Sfira, the ground appearing to be "literally ploughed up."

This latter is the area around the Jabbul Lake to which English merchants resident in Aleppo would go to hunt. Goodyear (1707) called this "antelope or hog hunting, according to the season" (p. 158), and Teonge (1675–1679, published 1928) and Drummond (1754) also recorded such activity. Neale (1851) described an occasion on which "one European gentleman . . . shocked his brother sportsmen of the Moslem faith by introducing into the field a young wild boar . . . [which] hunted as well and as orderly as any of his canine companions" (II, p. 268). It is possible that the sportsman was inspired by the ex-

ample of a domestic pig known as "Slut" (Zeuner 1963, p. 266), which was famed for the same skills in eighteenth century England.

The fallow deer, *Dama mesopotamica,* is well known from the late Palaeolithic sites of the Mount Carmel region, especially from the work of Bate (1937). The species declined sharply in abundance through the postglacial, and although it has been found in most sites of the period, it seldom comprises more than a few percent of the mammal remains. Although it is known widely from archaeological sites bordering the eastern Mediterranean, records of fallow deer are rare farther to the east. It was evidently not seen along the Euphrates Valley in historical times. The species survives to the east of the Tigris River, and it is recorded by Harrison (1968) as a recent extinction in the mountain areas of the eastern Mediterranean. A single fallow deer was seen by Tristram (1889) near the Sea of Galilee. It is primarily an animal of woodland and can only have been locally abundant in Southwest Asia.

Figure 3.19 *(left)*
A male Persian gazelle.

Figure 3.20 *(top right)*
The onager.

Figure 3.21 *(bottom right)*
Wild pig.

Even less common is the roe deer, *Capreolus capreolus*. Travelers' accounts occasionally refer to sightings of "roebuck," though usually in desert areas where this species is highly unlikely to be found. It is virtually certain that these are examples of a familiar English name being incorrectly applied to gazelles. The species survives now in Asia Minor, in northern Mesopotamia around the upper tributaries of the Tigris River, and possibly in northern Syria (Harrison 1968). Although occasionally found at Abu Hureyra, the species has not been recorded in the wooded valley of the Euphrates in the historic past, and it can never have been other than rare in that environment.

Although bones of the camel, *Camelus camelus,* have been recognized from Mousterian sites on Mount Carmel in Palestine (Garrard and Payne 1983), from the Douara Cave in Syria (Payne 1983, p. 57), and from the Negev Desert (Grigson 1983), it is exceedingly rare on later Palaeolithic or Epipalaeolithic sites. A single camel bone from Abu Hureyra (a lateral malleolus) is from a comparatively superficial context and may be intrusive.

The hare, *Lepus capensis,* is mentioned so often in the journals of travelers that a detailed account of these here would be superfluous. Plaisted's (1750, published 1929) instructions to travelers on this overland journey are typical: "Onions should never be forgot, because you will meet with hares almost every day, and these are all the fresh meat that you must expect" (p. 66). It may be noted that Plaisted also advised that travelers should take the desert route to Basra in the winter (as was the established practice), for the advantage of more abundant water and lower temperatures. This probably accounts for the fact that gazelles were seldom seen in the northern deserts, as the historical evidence shows that they would have departed on their southward migration by that time (see chapter 13).

The method of taking hares described by Plaisted was simple: the camel drivers would throw their sticks at each hare put up, that is rose from cover, with a sufficient rate of successful hits for this to be the most common meat used by the caravans. Parsons (1808) recorded that "the Arabs easily knock them down with their sticks" (p. 82) when traveling south of Aleppo, and Beawes (1745, published 1929) also describes the capture of hares in this manner, in sufficient number to feed the whole caravan with which he was traveling. There are occasional records of hares being taken by coursing with dogs or hawks (Musil 1928a, 1928b), but this appears to have been an activity pursued as a recreation rather than as a regular food supply.

The usual method of cooking hares was by means of a small earth oven (Russell 1758). A small pit was fired with the available dry vegetation, and when it was heated the hare was placed whole in the pit and covered with earth. Beawes (1745, published 1929) found the flesh to be "exceedingly disagreeable," while Carré (1672–1674, published 1948) found it to be "delicious."

The presence of the beaver, *Castor fiber,* in the Euphrates River in ancient times has been discussed elsewhere (Legge and Rowley-Conwy 1986a), and it is uncertain if this species was seen during the historical period, though, as Kumerloeve has old us, it certainly survived in Asia Minor at least until recently (see also Kumerloeve 1967). One bone and one tooth, unquestionably of beaver, were found at Abu Hureyra. The species was at its southern limits in the Middle Euphrates and must have always been rare there.

The hedgehog, *Hemiechinus auritus*, is common now in Syria. It was described as "very tasty" by Musil (1928b); Burckhardt (1830) noted that it was generally eaten, and Blunt (1879) included the hedgehog among the animals eaten by the Sleyb hunters.

Wolves, *Canis lupus*, were seldom seen in the recent past; Blunt (1879) saw two near Raqqa. The wolf survives now in Syria, and a cub was seen by Legge and Hillman in the possession of beduin at Isriya southwest of Abu Hureyra in 1983. The large quantity of partly digested bones at Abu Hureyra (chapter 13) suggests that the dog was present from the time of the first settlement (figure 3.22). The distinction between the dog and the wolf at an early stage of domestication of this species is problematic, as this rests more on a particular state of mind in the tame animal than on the morphology of its body. As with other species of *Carnivora*, the wolf is rare among the bones from Abu Hureyra.

The jackal, *Canis aureus*, was a common animal of the Euphrates down to the present and was often seen in considerable numbers. Blunt (1879) noted

Figure 3.22 Domestic dog.

that jackals were abundant in the "jungles" of the Euphrates Valley near to Abu Hureyra. Ainsworth (1888) was chased by packs both when on horseback and when on foot. We saw several in the vicinity of Abu Hureyra during the excavation. Despite the recent abundance of the species, and their tendency to enter human habitations in search of food (Kinglake 1898), the species is rare in the faunal remains from Abu Hureyra.

The fox, *Vulpes vulpes*, survives widely in the deserts of Syria now. Musil (1928b) recorded that the animal was occasionally eaten by desert people, and he described the species being taken by coursing with dogs. Although common in the Pre-Pottery Neolithic of Jericho (Clutton-Brock 1979), the species is rare at Abu Hureyra.

The brown bear, *Ursus arctos syriacus,* is now known only from the mountains of Anatolia and, Bruce Schroeder informs us, perhaps the Anti-Lebanon Mountains; it possibly survives, too, in the mountain woodlands of north Syria. A single bone from Abu Hureyra is attributed to the brown bear.

The leopard, *Panthera pardus,* was occasionally seen by earlier travelers (Ainsworth 1888), and other middle-sized felids like the lynx, *Felis lynx,* are also recorded (Russell 1758), although the exact species is often difficult to determine. The bones of felids are again uncommon at Abu Hureyra.

SPECIES OF THE REGION APPARENTLY ABSENT FROM ABU HUREYRA

We referred one upper molar to the oryx, *Oryx leucoryx,* in an earlier report on the mammals from Abu Hureyra (Legge 1975). We withdraw this tentative identification here, and it seems improbable that this highly desert-adapted antelope would be found as far north as Abu Hureyra.

Few records exist of the historical survival of the other large antelopes that have been occasionally recorded in Southwest Asia, the hartebeest, *Alcelaphus buselaphus*, and the addax, *Addax nasomaculatus*. The hartebeest was possibly seen near to Kerak in Jordan by Hill (1901, p. 226), who recorded a "white cow . . . a kind of antelope," and the addax was seen at some distance and identified by its horn shape by Tristram (1889) in the northern Wadi Araba, near the southern end of the Dead Sea. It was probably this species that was shot at Fars in Iran by Porter, who described its "fine spiral black horns" (Porter 1855, I, p. 468). These species of large antelopes have not been recognized among the bones identified from Abu Hureyra.

The ostrich, *Struthio camelus syriacus*, a large terrestrial bird well adapted to existence in very arid lands, is absent from the bones identified from Abu Hureyra. There is no reason to expect that it would occur other than as a rare vagrant as far to the north as Abu Hureyra. The species was seen, however, not far to the south.

Parsons (1774, published 1808) was traveling southeast from Aleppo on the desert route to Basra. Five days south of Aleppo, and while still some distance to the north of Taibe, one of the caravan found 15 ostrich eggs that contained developed chicks. A little to the south of this Coote (1780, published 1860) found an ostrich egg near "el Koom" (El Kum) about 15 km north of Taibe, and Irwin (1780) found an ostrich nest while traveling from the ancient city of Palmyra eastward to the Euphrates. In Taibe, both Coote (1780/1860) and Griffiths (1805) observed that the interior of the mosque was decorated with ostrich eggs. Olivier (1797, published 1809) saw ostrich south of Deir ez-Zor, at about latitude 35° N. Other travelers saw the ostrich quite commonly in these deserts, for example, Teixeira (1604), Taylor (1789), Plaisted (1750/1929), and Burckhardt (1830). Apparently the Syrian ostrich was perfectly tamable, as Parsons (1808, p. 148) saw 20 tame ostriches in a beduin camp, each wearing a red collar ornamented with bells, and they could be fed from the hand "as gently as a trained spaniel."

It is notable that references to the ostrich in the area around and north of Palmyra occur mainly before AD 1800, and that it was uncommon after that time. Burckhardt (1830) said that a few persisted in the Hauran, and "every year a few are taken even within 2 days journey of Damascus" (p. 217). To the south this species persisted in the Arabian peninsula until recent times. This suggests that the ostrich was at about its northernmost distribution in the El Kum and Taibe region, and it was locally hunted to extinction soon after that time.

Killing ostriches was difficult before firearms, and the animals were occasionally taken by stalking or with the help of fast dogs. Among undated rock engravings seen by the writers about 100 km east of Amman in Jordan is a scene of ostriches in which humans with dogs are depicted as driving them toward bowmen.

Hunting lions, *Felis leo*, is well known from Assyrian art (for example, Layard 1849, II, p. 77), and the species is commonly recorded in travelers' journals usually, as may be expected, in dramatic circumstances. The unfortunate Abbé Carré (1672–1674/1948) attempted to travel by horse from Aleppo to Hit on the Euphrates, only to have the animal die in the desert to the south of Taibe. He arrived at the Euphrates on foot, robbed of all his possessions and most of his clothing, and was forced to hide among bushes while lions came close and "roared in a terrifying manner." Later, and lower on the Euphrates, he saw more lions and ultimately shot two of them. Lions were recorded on the Middle Euphrates by Coote (1780/1860) and Blunt (1879), who stated that the government was paying a bounty for lion skins at that time. A little to the south of Abu Hureyra she met a group of water buffalo herders who lived in the tamarisk scrub of the valley bottom and whose buffalo they claimed would attack lions. Ponafidine (1911), writing of the later nineteenth century, says that lions by then were rare, although the species survived in the Tigris-Euphrates region into the twentieth century (Harrison 1968). Despite the widespread distribution of the lion in historic times, it has not been found at Abu Hureyra.

Most recorded travels on the caravan route from Aleppo to Baghdad and Basra took place at a time when the Euphrates Valley was depopulated due to political circumstance, and habitation was mainly by herding people who were to some degree nomadic. The wild fauna therefore survived under a rather low level of hunting pressure, and this provides evidence for its possible earlier distribution and abundance. The larger vertebrates found in the archaeological levels of Abu Hureyra, with only minor exceptions, could live in the region now, and in consequence the fauna is not indicative of major, climatically induced, environmental change.

European travelers in the historic past were, of course, prone to notice the more threatening animals, such as the lion, leopard, wolf, and jackal, which may give an enhanced impression of their former abundance. However, it is notable that such species are uncommon or not represented at all in the fauna from Abu Hureyra. It is possible that sustained hunting on the part of the early villagers rapidly reduced these species to a low level and, if this did indeed occur, immigration would be slow, as only the narrow Euphrates corridor offers a suitable route in a landscape that is otherwise seasonally arid. It is equally possible that the carcasses of such species would not be carried back to the site, though, as in the case of the beaver described above, it might be expected that some smaller bones would be brought back with the skin.

Part II THE SETTLEMENT OF ABU HUREYRA 1

4 Methods of Excavation at Abu Hureyra

NATURE OF THE DEPOSITS

The mound of Abu Hureyra was composed of the materials used to build the two prehistoric settlements and the detritus accumulated by their inhabitants. Abu Hureyra 1 consisted of humic debris from the decay of its structures, a little clay from floors, some soil, and much organic waste from the human occupation. The Abu Hureyra 2 settlement was densely packed with mudbrick houses, and their remains composed much of the mound. Once the houses were built, they started to decay, a process accelerated by rain each winter. Thus, a considerable amount of mud washed from the walls of the houses into the spaces between them. Plenty of organic residues were deposited outside and, to a lesser extent, within the houses from the intense human activity in the settlement.

The site had been abandoned so long ago that its surface had weathered through the action of wind and rain. Its contours were gently rounded on all but the western side, where the river had cut into the site, creating a steep slope down to the valley floor. Evidently, a great deal of material had eroded away since Abu Hureyra was abandoned. The top 20 cm of deposit in each trench contained a dense layer of flints from this deflation. Thus, much of the evidence for the later centuries of prehistoric occupation had disappeared.

The vast accumulation of debris in the mound, as much as 8 m in Trench B, compacted the deposits. This compressed and sometimes buckled individual levels, and it caused walls to lean a few degrees from the vertical. These forces and the composition of the levels affected the preservation of the remains contained within them. Some of the bones of humans and animals were crushed, and other fragile materials were damaged. Artifacts and bones were weakened further through the action of salts. The mud of the valley floor contained sodium chloride, and more came from human excretions. The subsoil of the site and some of the material brought onto it contained gypsum and other salts.

Sodium chloride and selenite crystals formed on and within bones and other materials, causing them to crack.

The annual cycle of winter rain and summer drought, insects, bacteria, and other agents of decay had ensured the disappearance of almost all wooden artifacts, textiles, basketry, and matting. Only occasional impressions in soil and bitumen attested that the ancient inhabitants of Abu Hureyra had used such items. Many other categories of artifacts and organic remains had survived well. Considering their great antiquity, the overall state of preservation of the excavated remains was quite good. The animal bones, for example, though affected by salts, were present in great quantity. Not only were the bones of larger ruminants preserved, but also the small bones of infantile gazelle and fish vertebrae. Bone tools, likewise, were found in good condition, although many of them were small and fragile.

We encountered some evidence of disturbance in the deposits. Successive generations of inhabitants had dug into the accumulating debris to obtain building material and to bury waste. The top meter of the mound was severely disturbed by graves of recent date. Furthermore, gerbils and other rodents had burrowed deeply into the site since its inception. Their burrows were particularly noticeable in Abu Hureyra 1. We feared that these sources of disturbance might have caused significant displacement of debris and artifacts, but this proved not to be the case. A glance at one of the Abu Hureyra 2 section drawings, the east face of Trench B, for instance figure 8.2, will show that most of the levels were effectively sealed by those above and have suffered little from disturbance. The problem was more evident in Abu Hureyra 1, but even here human digging and rodent burrowing had not seriously displaced most of the artifacts and organic remains.

EXCAVATION AND RECORDING

Each trench was excavated by a group of about five workmen with a site supervisor. During the second season several such teams were combined to excavate Trench E because of the large scale of the work there. Most of the digging was done with small hand picks, shovels, and rubber baskets—tools with which our workmen were familiar. We used trowels where appropriate, but the mudbrick and mud wash deposits of Abu Hureyra 2, in particular, were often too stiff for these tools to be effective. We proceeded slowly during the first week of each season to accustom the men to the nature of archaeological excavation. They proved to be adept and careful workers who, in time, could be entrusted with the most delicate tasks, notably the excavation of skeletons with dental tools and brushes.

We excavated Abu Hureyra stratigraphically. We distinguished the successive levels of soil in each trench from each other by their texture and color, and we dug them separately. A level could be a floor of trodden soil or plaster, a deposit of occupation debris, the filling of a pit, or the wall of a building. Study of the stratification has permitted us to work out the entire sequence of occupation in each trench: the series of thin surfaces in the settlement of Abu Hureyra 1; the construction, modification, and abandonment of individual buildings in Abu Hureyra 2; and the superimposed levels of debris in the open spaces between the structures. It is this stratigraphic sequence of levels that has provided the framework for interpreting the history of the site.

We gave each level an individual number, using two series of level numbers in trenches A, B, C, and D, one for each of the 1972 and 1973 seasons. We also used separate series of level numbers in each of the four subdivisions of Trench E. These series have been replaced by a single, continuous sequence of level numbers for trenches B, D, and E. Collections of artifacts and organic remains deposited in museums are identified by the original field level numbers only.[1]

Five main categories of material were identified, recovered, and recorded separately as digging progressed: flints, animal bones, small finds, samples, and plant remains. The flints and bones comprised by far the greatest quantity of remains and were given separate series of flint (F) and bone (B) bag numbers. Small finds (SF) were artifacts, including retouched flint tools, and human skeletons. The position of each small find recognized in a trench was recorded in three dimensions. In addition, any particular grouping or association of artifacts and animal bones was noted and recorded. Materials that might require analysis later were saved as samples—for example, fragments of floor plaster, pieces of ochre and bitumen, and shells. Samples of charcoal were collected for radiocarbon dating, and some sherds with the soil in which they were embedded were saved for thermoluminescence determinations.

We took care to recover these remains directly from the trenches, but all the soil we excavated was dry sieved to recover as high a proportion as possible of the artifacts and animal bones remaining in it. We used industrial screens with circular holes 1 cm in diameter (figure 4.1). These screens gave excellent rates of recovery for the excavation of Abu Hureyra 2 without clogging up, even though the deposits were sticky and contained some stones. The earth from Abu Hureyra 1 was passed through two screens in succession, with holes 1 cm and 3 mm in diameter, to recover as many microliths as possible.

We separated the plant remains systematically from the excavated soil using a flotation system. We conducted the flotation on as large a scale as we

Figure 4.1 A workman sieving soil from the excavation of the Abu Hureyra 2 village.

could manage in order to recover the largest possible sample of these remains. After some experiment, we decided to process a regular amount of soil from all the levels excavated in the main trenches—A, B, C, D, and E—and a few potentially interesting samples from F and G. In this way we hoped to recover the full range of plant remains that survived at Abu Hureyra, to establish several sequences of plant use through time, and to sample the many different contexts in which plant remains occurred across the site. A maximum of four wheelbarrow loads (approximately 200 liters) of sieved soil from each level was saved for flotation, but most levels contained less than this. In a few substantial levels with low frequencies of plant remains or in others with especially great scientific value, for example those from Abu Hureyra 1, we processed very much larger amounts of soil, as many as 2,000–3,000 liters in some instances.

We employed the froth flotation system developed by Legge and others at the University of Cambridge (Jarman, Legge, and Charles 1972). This had a high recovery rate, was easy to transport, and was sparing in its use of water. Thus, a flotation machine could be set up on the site and water brought to it in a mule cart. One machine was used in 1972 and two in 1973 (figure 4.2); they were run by a site supervisor assisted by several workmen. The system worked by separating the plant remains from the soil in a cylinder of water, to which frothing agent and kerosene (paraffin) were added to aid flotation. The water was agitated by a stream of air bubbles to assist in breaking up the soil as it was poured in (figure 4.3). The plant remains were collected in a granulometry sieve of 1 mm mesh size, although fragments considerably smaller than this were also caught (figure 4.4). We air-dried these samples in the shade and then packed them in polythene bags for transport to the laboratory. The residue of soil was wet-sieved through another screen with holes 3 mm in diameter to separate out other remains (figure 4.5). This residue was dried, and then sorted by hand most effectively for us by three women from the village (figure 4.6). It con-

Figure 4.2 Filling a flotation machine with water. Two buckets of soil awaiting flotation stand beside the settling tank.

Figure 4.3 The operator pours sieved soil into the flotation machine.

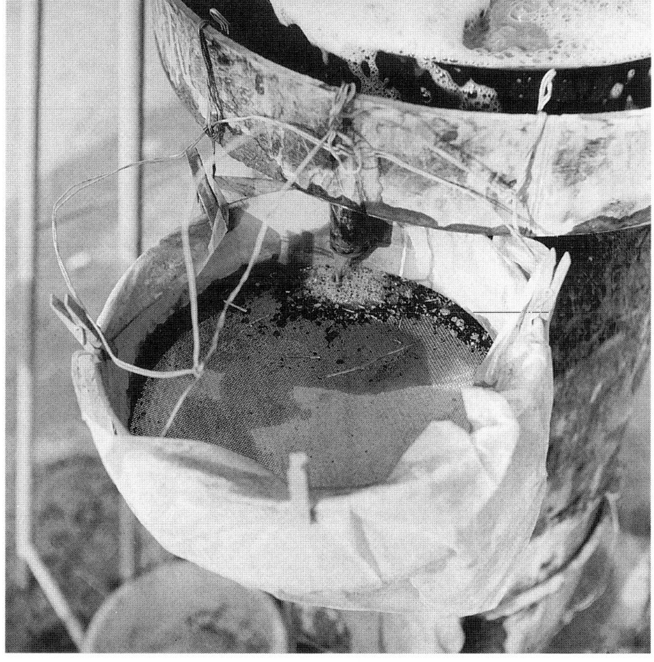

Figure 4.4 Plant remains and charcoal are collected in the granulometry sieve.

tained beads, microliths, other artifacts, mollusca, and tiny bones, often of fish and rodents. We retained a few two-liter soil samples to examine later in the laboratory as a check on the efficiency of the flotation system. Careful examination of the residues in the field and of the soil samples has shown that almost all the macroscopic plant remains were recovered in flotation.

Mudbricks often preserve impressions of straw and other vegetable matter and so can be useful additional sources of information about the use people made of plants. We saved samples of mudbricks, many of which Hillman ex-

Figure 4.5 The soil residue is washed in the retaining sieve.

Figure 4.6 The clean residue is sorted by hand to recover small artifacts and bones.

amined on the spot. He broke the lumps into successively smaller fragments, each time inspecting the fracture surfaces for plant imprints. We took bricks with identifiable impressions back to the laboratory where we made latex casts of the imprints for further study.

We attempted to obtain additional information about the environment and economy of the site through study of two other categories of remains, insects and pollen. A series of stratified soil samples was taken for insect analysis, following the advice of G. R. Coope and P. J. Osborne of the University of Birmingham. Examination of these samples in their laboratory indicated that no insect remains had been preserved. A few soil samples were also collected for pollen analysis, in collaboration with G. W. Dimbleby of the University of London, to see if they would yield data complementary to the plant remains from flotation. Very few pollen grains could be separated from these samples in the laboratory; those that could be identified were from oak trees (*Quercus* sp.) and grasses (*Poaceae* sp.).

We were equipped to carry out basic field conservation of the artifacts and other materials we recovered. The aims of our conservation program, organized by assistant director Barbara Moore, who is herself a conservator, were to ensure the careful recovery of all fragile materials from the soil, their stabilization, and their safe transport to the museum or laboratory for later study. In addition, artifacts that had deteriorated in the soil or were broken were consolidated and repaired.

The main conservation problem was the delicate state of the human and animal bones. The structure of these had decayed so much that they were very weak, even when from the exterior they appeared to be complete. Furthermore, they were usually damp and often crumbled when touched. This posed a large-scale conservation problem, because most of the bones were too fragile in their natural state to survive transport to the laboratory.

Every effort was made to lift bones intact from the soil whenever possible so that the maximum scientific value could be realized from their later study. Some delicate bones deemed to be potentially the most informative, usually from human skeletons, were treated before removal from the soil in the standard manner with polyvinyl acetate (PVA) emulsion (Vinamul 6525), the solvent for which is acetone. The bones were brushed with PVA emulsion and strengthened with bandages when necessary. Once they had dried, which often took many hours, they were lifted and transported back to the dig house for further treatment and packing. Because of the time-consuming nature of the process, only a small proportion of the most fragile bones could be treated in this way. All the other bones were recovered as carefully as possible and taken to the dig house for treatment. There they were washed in dilute PVA emulsion, laid on mats to dry, and then bagged for transport. The use of this technique ensured the safe removal from the site of most of the bone, which was later sent to England by rail.

A problem has arisen in subsequent laboratory examination of some of the human and animal bones. It has proved exceedingly difficult to remove the bandages that were strengthened in this manner without causing further damage to the bones themselves. This is because the solvent that removes the bandages also softens the PVA in the bones, which revert to their original exceedingly fragile state. In other instances the PVA emulsion has cross-linked and so become insoluble. Because of recent developments in the science of polymers, other consolidants are now available that are thought to provide better long-term stabilization of bone from archaeological sites (Sease 1987, pp. 14–15).

Information about the excavation of each trench was recorded in a trench notebook. We kept a daily account of each level removed, including its nature, contents, and stratigraphic position. Descriptions of the various buildings, hearths, and other features were entered in the notebooks as they were excavated. We recorded the small finds, flints, bones, and other material recovered in each level day by day. An index was prepared for each of these categories of information in the notebooks, and the indices have provided an invaluable means of checking and correcting errors made in recording. The artifacts and other remains were brought back to the dig house at the end of each day to be cleaned, conserved when necessary, and then listed and described in the excavation registers. At this stage we gave all small finds an absolute site number (for example, 72.359, 73.2064) that was written on each object as well as on its accompanying labels. A representative series of registered artifacts was presented to the Syrian authorities at the end of each season, in accordance with their regulations.

We made a visual record of the progress of the excavation in plans, sections (profiles), and photographs. Most of the plans and sections were drawn at a scale of 1:10 to record small features satisfactorily. We noted the location of every structure and many of the artifacts on the plans. Sections were drawn for each side of every trench and across some walls and other significant features. Two sets of sections were prepared. The trench supervisor drew a running section of levels excavated as work progressed, and then the Moores drew a final section to record every significant detail of the stratification. These final sections were drawn on transparent film so that they could be laid over the running sections for comparison. The system has made it possible to prepare section drawings for this book that combine an exact record of the stratification of each trench with information about how the levels were dug.

Black-and-white photographs were taken of the trenches at every stage of excavation to document almost all structural features, burials, and assemblages of artifacts. We also took color photographs of many of these subjects. These site photographs were all made using twin-lens reflex cameras of 6 cm × 6 cm (2¼" × 2¼") format. Many of the small finds were photographed with a 35 mm camera and drawn in the field.

INTERPRETATION

The stratigraphic information from Abu Hureyra is of central importance because it provides the framework on which our discussions of culture and economy depend. A detailed description is given here of the stratigraphic sequence in four of the seven excavated trenches—B, D, E, and G—that together establish the sequence of occupation on the mound. The stratigraphy of Abu Hureyra 1, found only in the lower levels of Trench E, is presented in part II of this book, and that for Abu Hureyra 2 in part III; the format is the same in each. A brief description is given of the successive phases of occupation in each trench, and their main features. Each phase represents a new episode of building or major change in the organization of the space within each trench and comprises a number of levels. Thus, in Abu Hureyra 1 the successive phases mark the new configurations of structures that occurred as the subsoil was covered over with occupation debris, while in Abu Hureyra 2, a phase usually begins with the rebuilding of a house. The description of a particular level in the text has a reference to its number in brackets.

The phase descriptions are accompanied by illustrations and tables that are intended to provide full information about the sequence of deposits in each trench. The section drawings give the essential information about the stratification. The plans illustrate the disposition and layout of most of the structures that we found in many of the phases. Plans and maps in this book are oriented to true north unless otherwise indicated. Important features are illustrated further by photographs and reconstruction drawings. The sections present as much information about individual levels as can reasonably be shown in drawings published at a greatly reduced scale. Complete information about the nature of each level and its stratigraphic position is given in the level tables and level diagrams that accompany the phase descriptions.[2] Level diagrams have come into general use in archaeology since the publication of Harris's (1975) matrix system, after we had completed the excavation of Abu Hureyra. We have found it helpful to compose them for our own stratigraphic analysis because they provide a fuller understanding of the stratification than can be obtained from a section drawing alone. The reconstruction drawings are intended to provide as accurate an illustration as possible of the original appearance of some of the major structures we excavated. They are based on careful study of all the archaeological evidence. Most of the details in the drawings can be corroborated by the data we recovered.

We found remains of the Abu Hureyra 2 settlement in all the trenches excavated, so the final step in the stratigraphic analysis has been to link the sequences of phases in each of these trenches. That task has been difficult because the history of occupation was not necessarily the same in each part of the site. Our trenches were spaced as much as 100 m apart, so we can rarely establish stratigraphic correlations between these sequences based on shared building episodes. We have preferred to rely on stratigraphic evidence whenever possible to link the trench sequences, but we have supplemented this with other information. The two most important additional kinds of evidence are the radiometric dates and the sequences of changes in use of animals and plants in each trench. For example, an abrupt shift from gazelle hunting to shepherding during the occupation of Abu Hureyra 2 has provided a significant stratigraphic marker across the site. Finally, we have taken account of changes in the occurrence of artifacts from trench to trench and through time. This has enabled us, in part III, first to correlate the sequences of phases in the four trenches considered here, and then to group them in periods that represent the major episodes of occupation of the Abu Hureyra 2 settlement.

CHRONOLOGY

Two series of radiocarbon dates have been obtained for the sequence of occupation at Abu Hureyra, one by the British Museum Research Laboratory using the conventional method, and the other by the Radiocarbon Accelerator Unit of the Research Laboratory for Archaeology and the History of Art at the University of Oxford with accelerator mass spectrometry (AMS). The Oxford laboratory has, in addition, obtained three thermoluminescence (TL) dates from samples of pottery, in order to date the later episodes of activity at Abu Hureyra that could not readily be dated by other methods. A complete list of the dates is given in appendix 1. The dating of the sequences of occupation in Abu Hureyra 1 and 2 is discussed at appropriate places in the text.

We collected samples of wood charcoal for radiocarbon dating during the excavation. The British Museum laboratory dated two series of these samples (Burleigh, Matthews, and Ambers 1982; Burleigh, Ambers, and Matthews 1982), a total of 13 determinations in all. The laboratory has recently found it necessary to revise its calculations for the second series of determinations (Bowman, Ambers, and Leese 1990). The figures for the corrected dates are little altered, but their standard deviations have increased. These revised dates are used here, with the letter R added to their laboratory numbers as suggested by the British Museum laboratory.

The British Museum dates confirmed the great antiquity of the successive settlements, in itself most valuable information, but did not tell us precisely how long each had been inhabited. There appeared to have been a lapse of time of as much as 1,400 years between the two settlements of Abu Hureyra 1 and 2, suggesting that the site had been abandoned for a long intervening period. As our study of the remains from the site proceeded, it became imperative to obtain a more detailed chronology to resolve problems concerning not only the duration of the phases of occupation at Abu Hureyra, but also the domestication of plants and animals and the precise age of the human remains.

For a long time it seemed impossible to obtain a more detailed series of dates because wood charcoal was scarce in the deposits at Abu Hureyra, and all the samples large enough to be dated had been used by the British Museum laboratory. Furthermore, so little collagen survived in the bones that they could not be used as a substitute material for conventional radiocarbon dating. The advent of accelerator dating has enabled us to resume the dating program, to fix the age of the site with unusual precision, and to resolve the other chronological problems that have arisen during our analyses (Moore et al. 1986; Moore 1992). The principal advantage of the accelerator method is that it can date directly exceedingly small quantities of organic material. This has enabled us to determine the age of individual bones and charred seeds of significance for the changing economy of the site, and to confirm that they are indeed of the antiquity that their stratigraphic position would suggest. The method can achieve such great precision that problems of dating may be resolved in sequences of occupation lasting just a few centuries. More than fifty accelerator dates have been obtained so far for Abu Hureyra,[3] and these have transformed our understanding of the duration of the two settlements and the pace of economic change.

One of the most important results of this dating program concerns the duration of occupation at Abu Hureyra. Enough dates have now been obtained from the site to confirm that it was occupied continuously from its foundation c. 11,500 years ago to its desertion sometime after 7,000 BP. Habitation seems to have been less intense during the tenth millennium BP than both earlier and later, but the site continued to be occupied throughout.

We should explain the conventions we use when discussing the radiocarbon, thermoluminescence, and other dates in the text of this book. We have attempted throughout to be consistent, and to conform to current international practice. All radiocarbon dates are calculated on the 5568 year half-life for ^{14}C and are quoted uncalibrated in years BP before AD 1950. Dates are sometimes converted to calendar years for purposes of comparison, using the calibration curves published in *Radiocarbon* (Stuiver and Kra 1986; Stuiver 1993). These calibrated dates are given as Cal BP or, exceptionally, Cal AD or Cal BC. We follow here the recommendations of the 12th International Radiocarbon Conference (Mook 1986). Dates based on thermoluminescence determinations are given as "years ago," because we recognize these are calculated on a different basis from radiocarbon dates. Historical dates are given as AD years or years BC (for example, AD 1066, 55 BC).

5 The Excavation of Abu Hureyra 1

A. M. T. Moore

EXCAVATION OF TRENCH E

Trench E was excavated to determine the sequence of occupation at the northern end of the site. We dug a 4 × 4 m trench on a low platform in the northwest corner of the mound in 1972 (figures 5.1, 5.2) that revealed two superimposed settlements. The later one, Abu Hureyra 2, had mudbrick structures and a flint assemblage similar to those found elsewhere on the mound. The earlier settlement, Abu Hureyra 1, consisted of a deposit of dark occupation soil over 1 m thick that covered the natural subsoil. It contained a microlithic flint assemblage. This settlement was quite different from that of Abu Hureyra 2 and represented a significantly earlier stage of development. Consequently, it required detailed examination over as large an area as possible in the 1973 season. Trench E was expanded to 112 m^2 in 1973 for the excavation of the Abu Hureyra 2 remains (figure 5.3). We had hoped to excavate the underlying Abu Hureyra 1 settlement over this entire area, but shortage of time prevented us from doing so. In the last three weeks of excavation the trench was reduced to a square of 7 × 7 m, and this area was then dug down to the natural surface (figure 5.4).

The Abu Hureyra 1 settlement was so different from that of Abu Hureyra 2 that we considered it necessary to modify our digging techniques in order to excavate it. The first season's excavation had shown that occupation here had been intense; there were numerous, superimposed, thin floor surfaces that were exceedingly difficult to see and to separate. Although the deposit was quite shallow, it probably represented many centuries of habitation. Furthermore, it contained great quantities of animal bones and carbonized plant remains, as well as chipped stone artifacts, among them many microliths. We had to dig in a manner that would separate the levels as finely as possible from top to bottom and also allow for variations in the horizontal distribution of features and other remains. Our methods of recovery of artifacts and organic material

Figure 5.1 The location of Trench E at the northern end of the mound, seen from Trench C. The photograph shows the 4 × 4 m sounding that was excavated in 1972. A workman is operating a sieve just to the right of the trench.

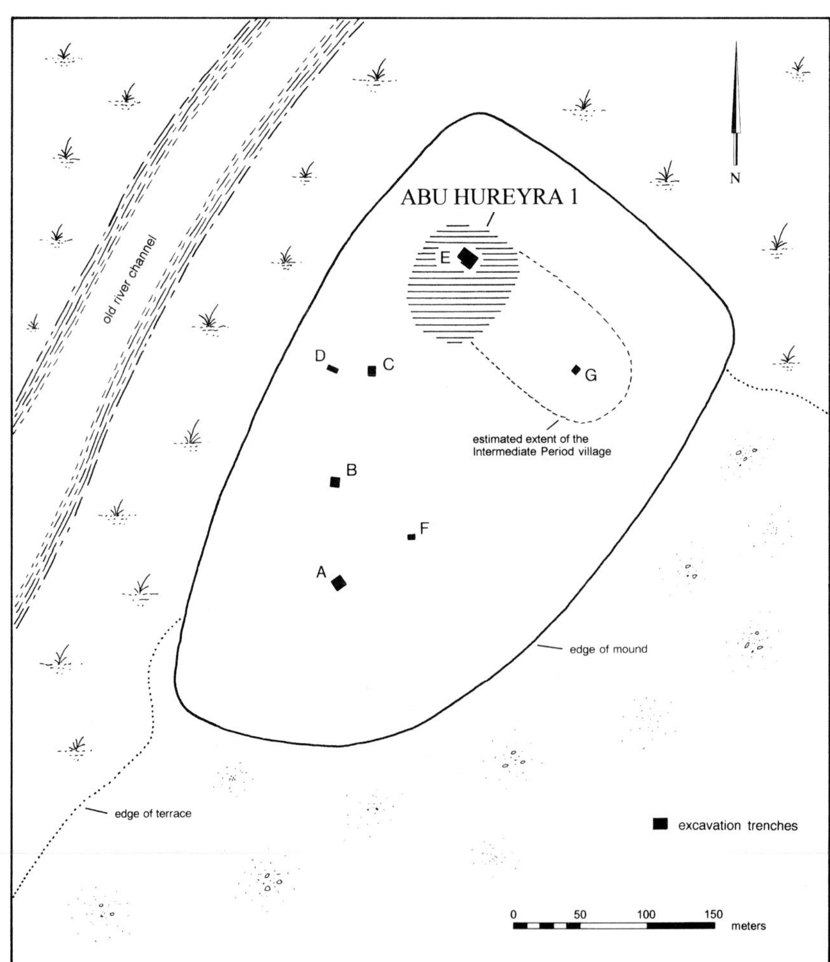

Figure 5.2 The location of the settlement of Abu Hureyra 1 at the northwest corner of the mound.

Trench E

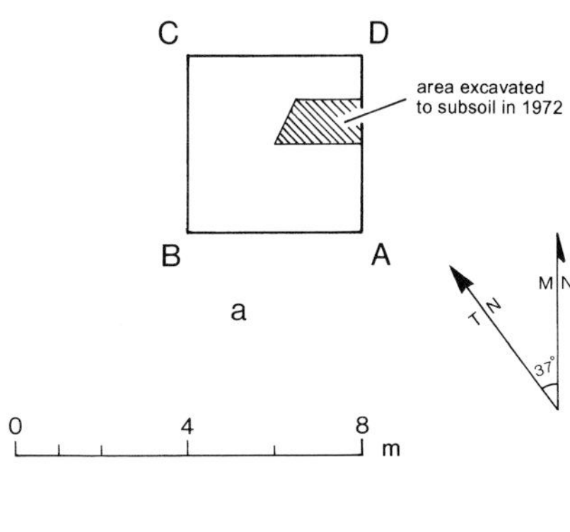

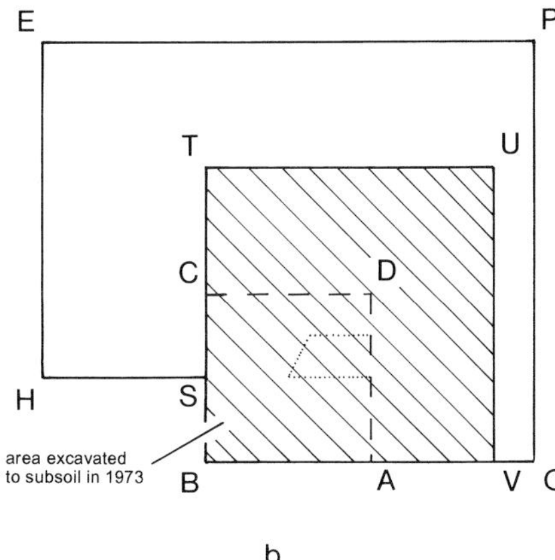

Figure 5.3 The excavation of Trench E in 1972 (a) and in 1973(b). The magnetic declination at Abu Hureyra during the excavation was approximately 37° east of true North.

Figure 5.4 The superimposed settlements of Abu Hureyra 1 and 2 in Trench E at the conclusion of the excavation, from the southeast. A mudbrick house of the overlying Abu Hureyra 2 settlement has been partly removed to expose the underlying deposits of Abu Hureyra 1. Abu Hureyra 1 has been excavated down to the natural subsoil, exposing a series of shallow pits and associated postholes with, to the left, a level bench and a low bank. The stratigraphic break between Abu Hureyra 1 and 2 may be seen in the three visible sections as a horizontal line 50 cm to 1 m above the subsoil. Compare with figures 5.12 and 8.45. Scale, 1 m.

had to be modified to ensure that we saved as many of the small flints, bones, and seeds as we could. The greatest constraint was time: the season was far advanced and little time remained in which to complete the task.

Our solution was to excavate thin spits about 5–8 cm thick, which we called levels (figures 5.5–8). Every effort was made to adjust the slope of these spits to the natural stratification of the site. Some layers in phases 1 and 2 sloped slightly down to the northwest corner, and we made allowances for this as we proceeded. We continued to dig for the most part with hand picks, using trowels to excavate specific features. The first four levels were excavated across the whole 7 × 7 m trench. This area was then divided into quarters to provide smaller horizontal divisions (figure 5.9). As the excavation proceeded downward and a subsoil bank became visible, we adjusted the horizontal divisions of the trench. Few features could be seen in the deposits until near the bottom, but when firepits, hearths, areas of heavy burning, and pits were detected, they were excavated separately and given their own level numbers. These methods have enabled us to make fine stratigraphic distinctions (figure 5.10) and to detect changes through time in the plant remains and chipped stone. They have also made it possible to date the sequence of developments in unprecedented detail by means of conventional and AMS radiocarbon dating.

We continued to dry-sieve all the soil we excavated, exercizing particular care. We used sieves with 1-cm-diameter holes and supplemented them as

Figure 5.5 *(top)* Trench E, Section T-U, showing the levels as excavated (compare with figure 8.46).

Figure 5.6 *(bottom)* Trench E, Section U-V, showing the levels as excavated (compare with figure 8.47).

Trench E

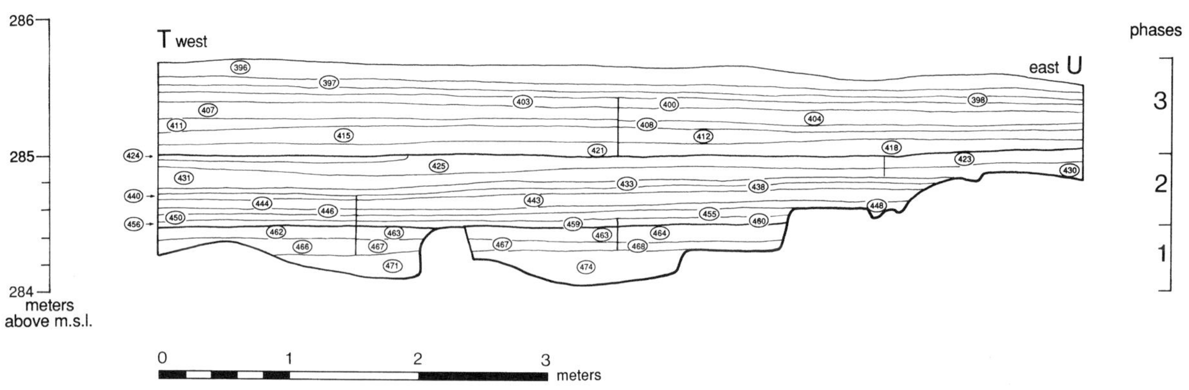

Trench E

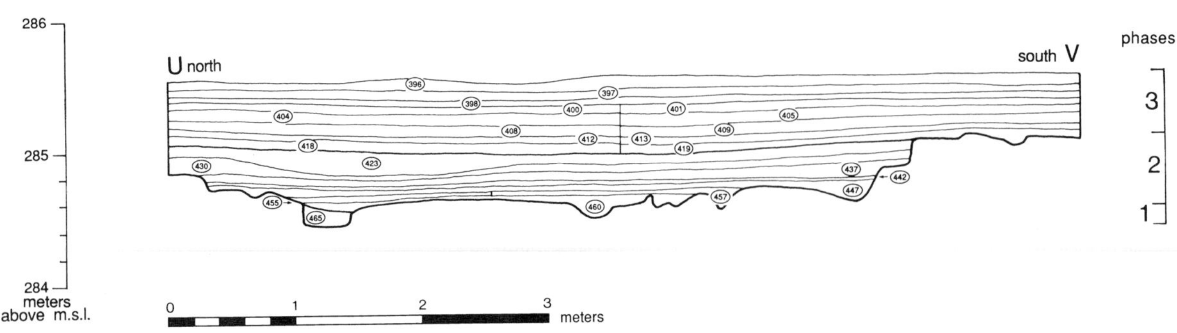

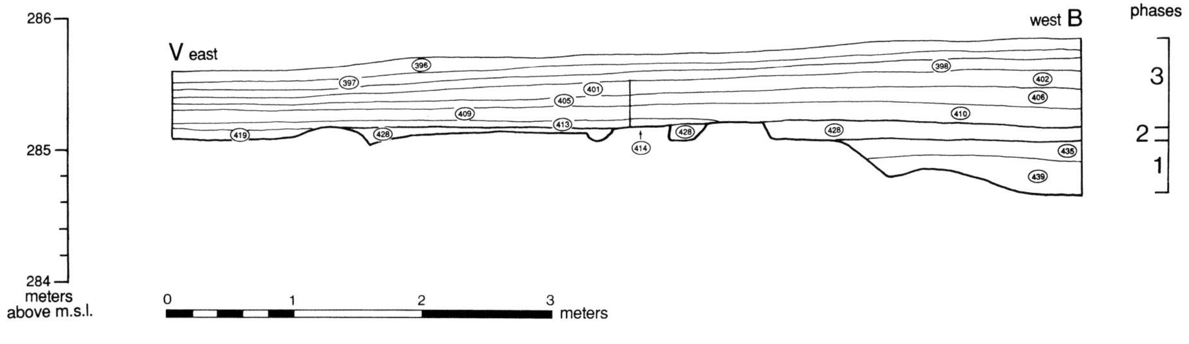

Figure 5.7 *Top*, Trench E, Section V-B, showing the levels as excavated (compare with figure 8.43).

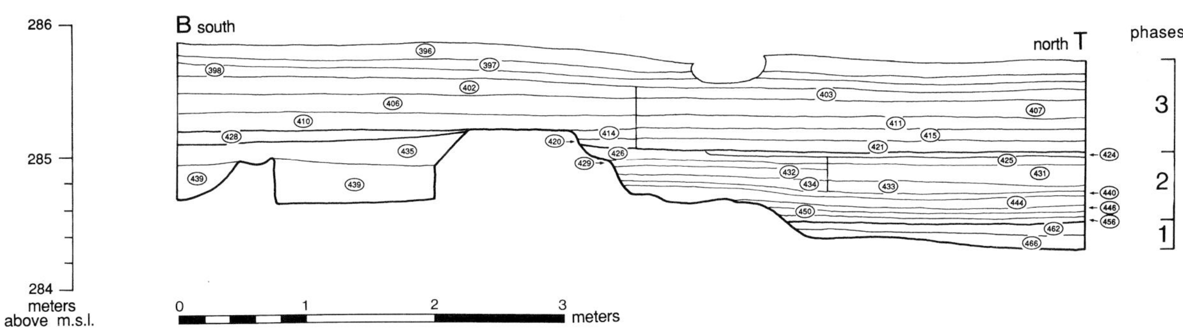

Figure 5.8 *Bottom*, Trench E, Section B-T, showing the levels as excavated (compare with figure 8.45).

much as possible with sieves whose holes were 3 mm in diameter. We knew that this would recover nearly all the flints and other artifacts, and most of the animal bones. Because these deposits were so special, and the quality of preservation of organic material so good, we decided to attempt to pass all the excavated soil through the two flotation machines. In this way we would achieve near-total recovery of seeds, bones, and artifacts. This aim proved impossible to achieve because of shortage of time and the difficulties of supply occasioned by the war. We succeeded in floating much or all of the soil from 39 out of the 85 levels excavated, or 46% of the total. This represented about 24 m^3 out of an estimated volume of 53 m^3 of soil removed from the Abu Hureyra 1 settlement, a prodigious amount nonetheless.

The deposits of Abu Hureyra 1 had suffered some disturbance, so the effects of this have to be considered. The inhabitants of the overlying Abu Hureyra 2 settlement not only leveled the surface of Abu Hureyra 1 to build their mudbrick houses, but also dug firepits and other holes in the upper levels of the site. A firepit (417) just below the surface of Abu Hureyra 1 was found to contain Neolithic artifacts and so was clearly intrusive. Burrowing rodents were another source of disturbance. Their tunnels ran throughout the deposits, causing further mixing of the soil. In consequence, a few Abu Hureyra 2 flint artifacts

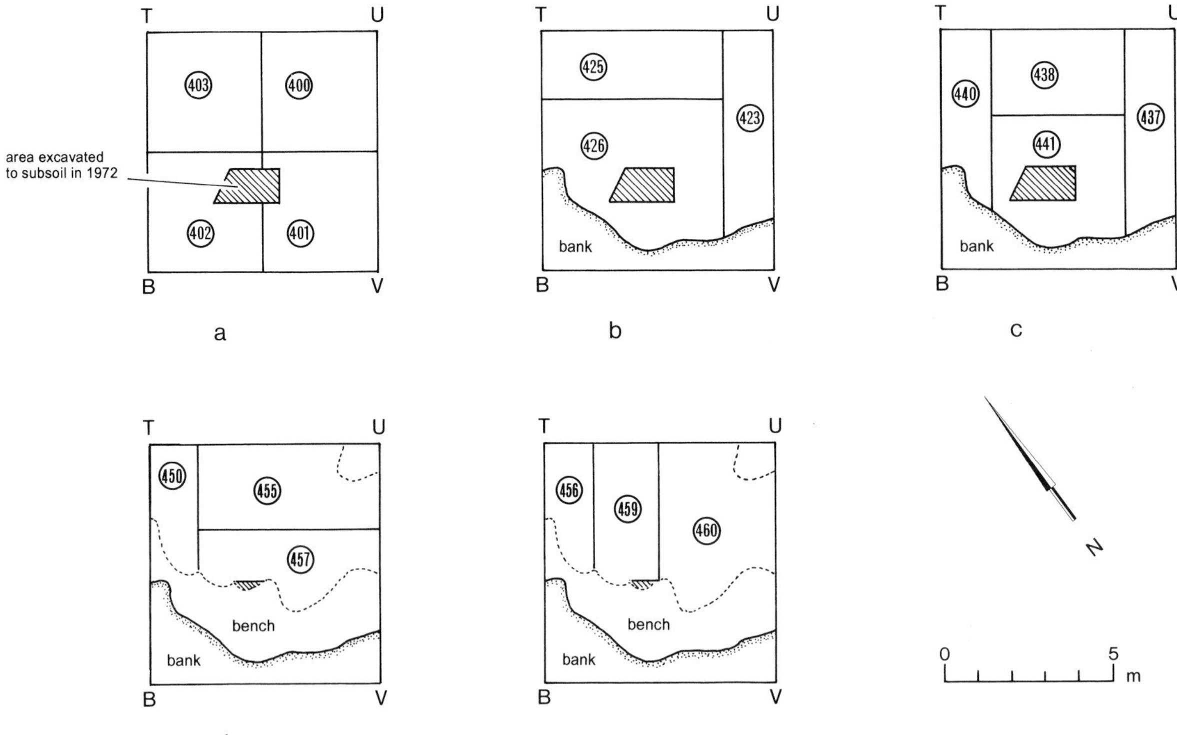

Figure 5.9 The horizontal division of levels used in the excavation of Abu Hureyra 1: a, phase 3; b–e, phase 2.

that had been carried down from the settlement above were found throughout the Abu Hureyra 1 deposits. These artifacts could readily be separated out because of their different forms and technology.

What were the effects of these disturbances on our organic samples and radiocarbon dates? A few of the samples used for both the conventional and AMS radiocarbon dates were obviously intrusive or out of stratigraphic order because of the disturbances to the deposits, but the effects were less marked than we might have expected. Other samples of seeds and bones that we have dated have proved to be of the age of the deposits in which they were found. This leads us to suggest that, while there has been significant mixing of the Abu Hureyra 1 deposits, the soil, artifacts, and organic remains have moved rather little, and the effects of this can largely be allowed for in analysis.

The one outstanding conundrum is the presence of 42 pieces of obsidian in the Abu Hureyra 1 settlement. Does this indicate that exchange of obsidian was already underway at this early stage, or did these pieces filter down from the overlying Abu Hureyra 2 deposits? The quantity of obsidian is not very great, and Olszewski points out in chapter 6 that some of the pieces were chipped using techniques similar to those employed in Abu Hureyra 2. On the other hand, these artifacts had already been partly prepared before they arrived at the site, so the cores, at least, were fashioned elsewhere. Furthermore, the obsidian occurred throughout the Abu Hureyra 1 sequence. It seems likely, therefore, that most of these pieces belong in the levels in which they were found, indicating that exchange of obsidian was already taking place in the Levant. Obsidian has been found at the nearby site of Mureybit in phases IA

Trench E levels
Abu Hureyra 1

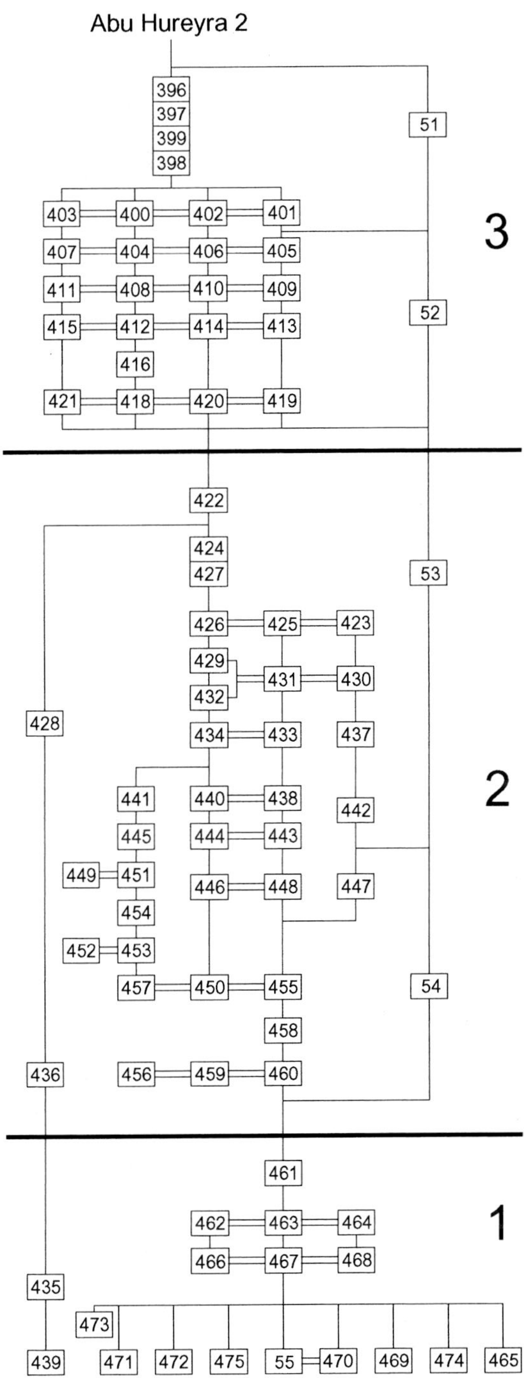

1 phases

324 levels

Figure 5.10 Trench E, level diagram for phases 1–3 (Periods 1A–1C).

and IB (J. Cauvin 1977, pp. 21, 23) and at El Kum 1 (M.-C. Cauvin 1981a, p. 384), although both these deposits were also overlain by a Neolithic settlement from which the obsidian could have filtered down. All three sites are much closer to the obsidian sources in Anatolia than Natufian sites in Palestine, yet obsidian has also been found in unequivocal contexts at one of these, Ain Mallaha (Valla 1975a, p. 74). It would appear, therefore, that exchange of obsidian did begin in the Levant a thousand years earlier than is usually supposed. The traffic in obsidian in the Zagros is even older, since it began there during the Upper Palaeolithic and continued through the Epipalaeolithic (Renfrew, Dixon, and Cann 1966, pp. 40–43).

THE SEQUENCE OF OCCUPATION

Abu Hureyra 1 was situated at the extreme northern point of the terrace underlying the settlement where it jutted well out into the Euphrates floodplain. That was the closest to the river the inhabitants could live while still being above flood level. The Euphrates was probably their main source of water, but they may also have had recourse to the stream in the Wadi Shetnet es-Salmas. Two other neighboring sites of approximately the same age were similarly located on the terrace edge, Mureybit and Dibsi Faraj East (van Loon 1968; Wilkinson and Moore 1978). Abu Hureyra stood at precisely the point where the steppe to the south met the dense vegetation of the valley bottom. That "jungle" may have been thick enough to have obscured the otherwise extensive view the site commanded of the river valley to the west and east.

We excavated 49 m^2 of Abu Hureyra 1, but it was evident that the settlement was much larger than this. The significant depth of deposit on all four sides of the trench, as much as 1.4 m in the northwest corner, indicated that the settlement spread a considerable distance in all directions. Even if the deposits began to thin out just beyond the boundaries of our excavation, the settlement would have been at least 20 m in diameter. In fact, there is good reason to suppose from the faunal and botanical evidence that the settlement was home to a substantial population and so was much bigger. It probably covered an area of several thousand square meters. Deposits of the Abu Hureyra 1 settlement were found only in Trench E. The two nearest trenches were C and G, but these were each over 100 m away. They provide a generous upper limit for the size of Abu Hureyra 1. It should be noted that soil from Abu Hureyra 1 was used as fill outside an early Abu Hureyra 2 house in Trench C. This suggests that the surface of part or all of Abu Hureyra 1 was still exposed at the time of that event and that it was also quite close to Trench C. This reinforces our view that the Abu Hureyra 1 settlement was relatively large. A few lunates and other microliths were found in mudbricks and occupation debris from Abu Hureyra 2 levels in most of the other trenches, indicating that a little of the Abu Hureyra 1 deposit, perhaps from surface leveling, was spread widely across the site in later building activities.

Phase 1

The surface of the subsoil in Trench E lay at about the present level of the Euphrates floodplain, indicating that the alluvium on the valley floor has risen considerably since Abu Hureyra 1 was inhabited. This surface sloped gently down from south to north toward the Euphrates (see figures 8.44, 8.45). The subsoil consisted of a calcareous sandstone with a high clay content and inclusions of chalk and pebbles. It was exceedingly soft and crumbly when wet but turned hard as it dried out. Gerbils and other rodents had burrowed through the overlying Abu Hureyra 2 settlement into the Abu Hureyra 1 deposits. Their tunnels penetrated a few centimeters into the subsoil, and these, together with the numerous features cut by the inhabitants, gave the natural surface the appearance of Gruyère cheese.

The first inhabitants of the site cleaned the surface of the subsoil of all vegetation and soil and then cut a series of features in it that separated the excavated area into three zones (figures 5.11, 5.12). On the south side was a low bank, and north of it was a level bench. The third zone, which occupied half of the trench, consisted of several large pits dug into the subsoil (figure 5.13). Cutmarks on the sides of the larger pits suggested that the work was done with flint or stone tools when the subsoil was moist. It is possible that some of the heavy flint tools identified by Olszewski were used for this purpose.

The top of the bank was 50 cm above the surface of the bench, providing some protection for the settlement in its lee from southwest and west winds. A complex of large pits (439) was cut into the bank in the southwest corner of the trench, with several small pits (436) close by. The bench had been enlarged by cutting the bank back to a near-vertical curved edge. The bench itself was covered with debris from many fires that had burned the surface of the subsoil red. The area of reddened subsoil extended down the southeast side of pit 469, indicating that the inhabitants lit fires here from early in phase 1, but the bench continued to be used as a zone for hearths well into phase 2.

Figure 5.11 The settlement of phase 1 (Period 1A) established on the natural subsoil, from the south. In the foreground is a bank defined by a steep cut edge. Pit complexes and their associated postholes extend over much of the northern half of the trench. Between the bank and the pit complexes is a level bench. Note that the surface of the bench has been darkened by the many fires lit there. Compare with figure 5.12. Scale, 1 m.

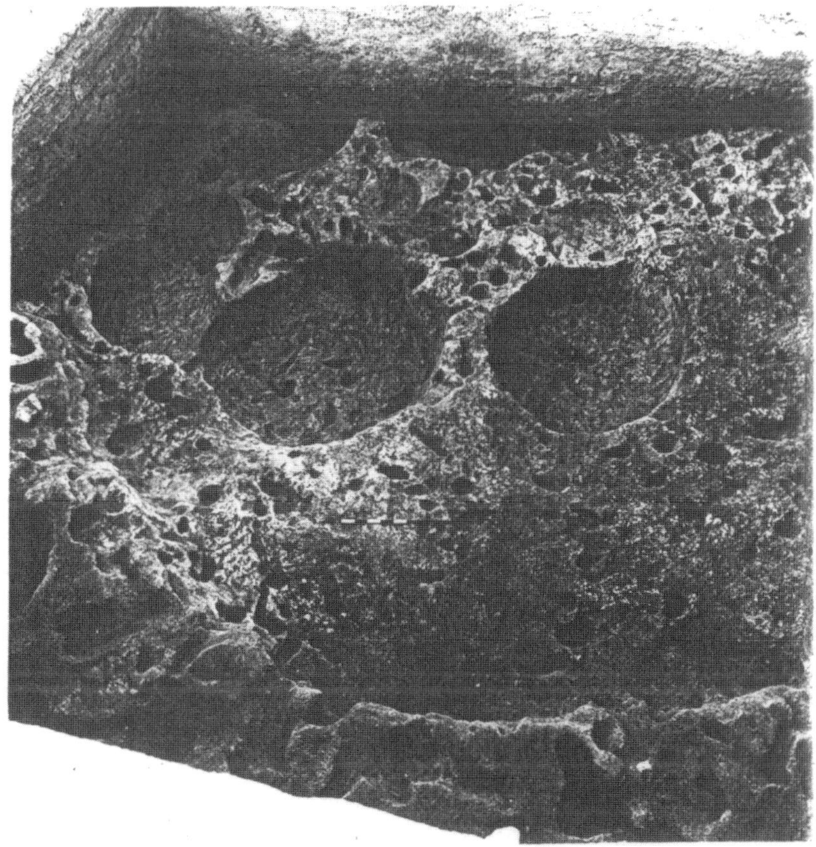

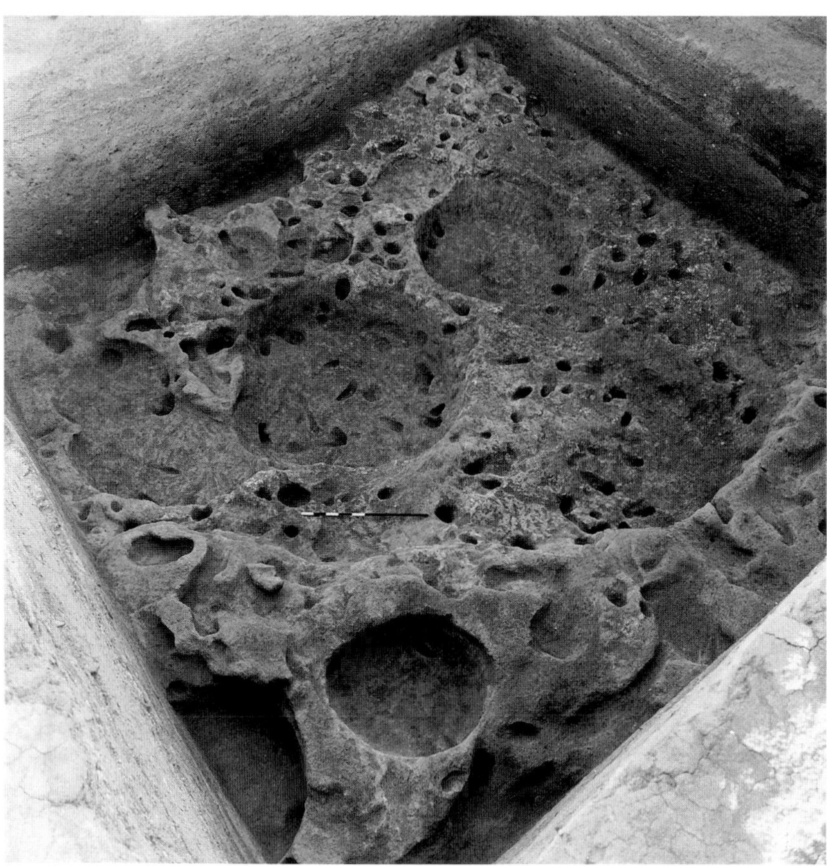

Figure 5.12 The settlement of phase 1 (Period 1A) from the southwest. The pits of complex 3 are in the foreground, while those of complexes 2 and 1 are in the top half of the photograph. Scale, 1 m.

The larger pits were usually subcircular in plan, often 2–2.5 m in diameter, and up to 70 cm deep. The southern one (439) was probably much bigger, even, than that. The pits were joined together in three complexes, 1, 2, and 3 (figure 5.14), that we interpret as family dwellings. The large pits may not all have been cut at the same time, but those in each complex were linked together and functioned as a unit (figure 5.15). Associated with these were smaller pits, no more than 1 m across, a few of which—for instance, the shallow 473 group—may have been cut later than the others. The other conspicuous features in the pit zone were vertical cylinders or postholes cut into the subsoil. The postholes were of two sizes, about 5 cm and 10 cm in diameter, and usually about 20 cm deep. Their regular form distinguished them from the oblique, irregular gerbil burrows. The larger postholes were in and adjacent to the clusters of pits, suggesting that their functions were related. They probably supported roofs over the pits, while some of the smaller ones held up the walls. Many of the small postholes were in the northeast corner, where they supported other lightweight structures. There were hardly any postholes in the bank or bench.

Several of the pits contained tools of ground stone, for example, a pestle (73.3233) and rubbing stone (73.3234) in pit 439, and another rubbing stone (73.3419) in pit 465. The most conspicuous examples were two large querns (73.3424, 73.3425) in pit 470 of complex 2 (figure 5.16). Both appeared to lie close to where they were last used. They had traces of red ochre on them but were presumably used with the rubbing stones mainly for grinding plant foods. The pits contained substantial quantities of animal bones and carbonized ed-

Trench E

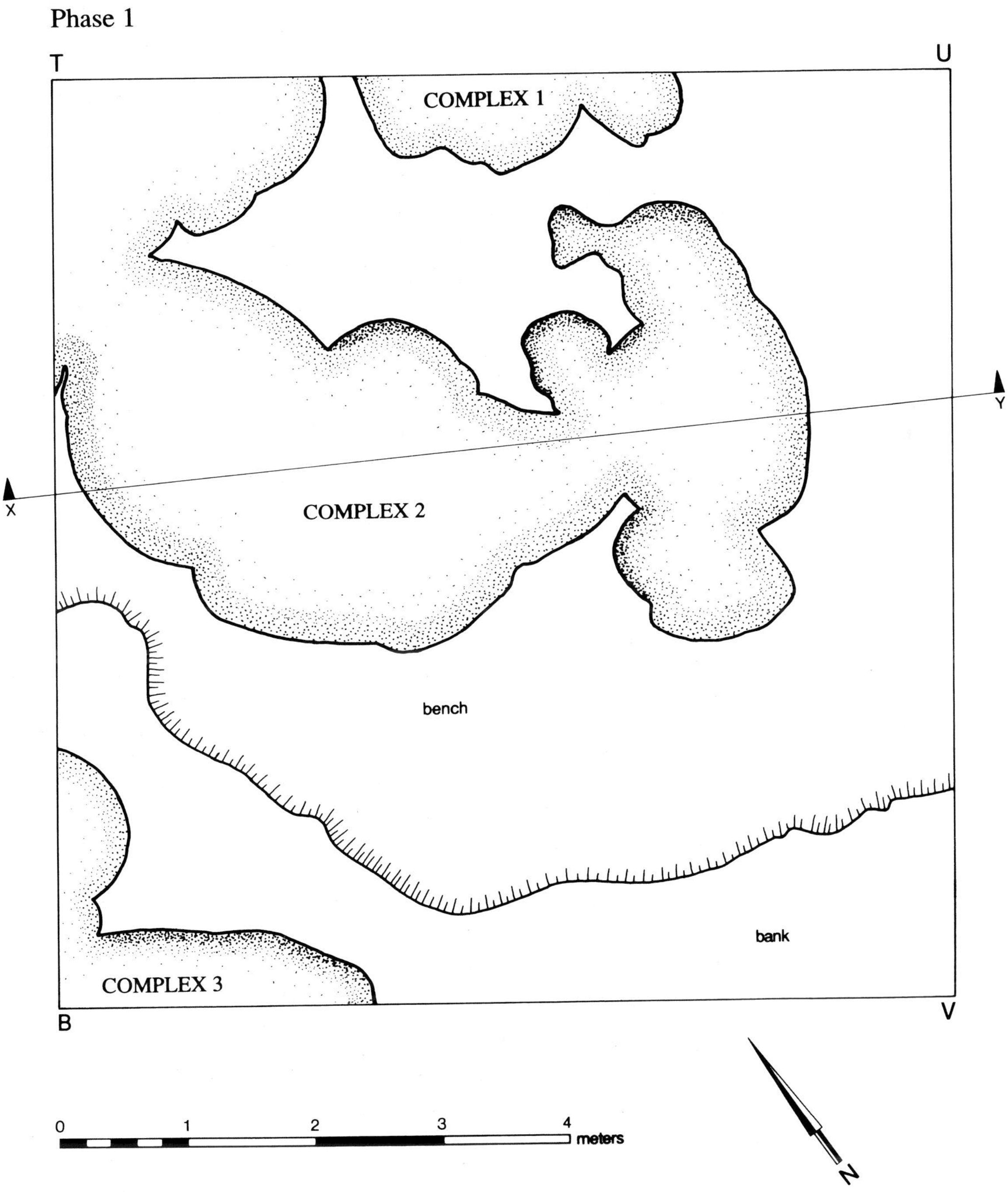

Figure 5.13 Plan of the settlement in phase 1 (Period 1A). See appendix 3.

Trench E

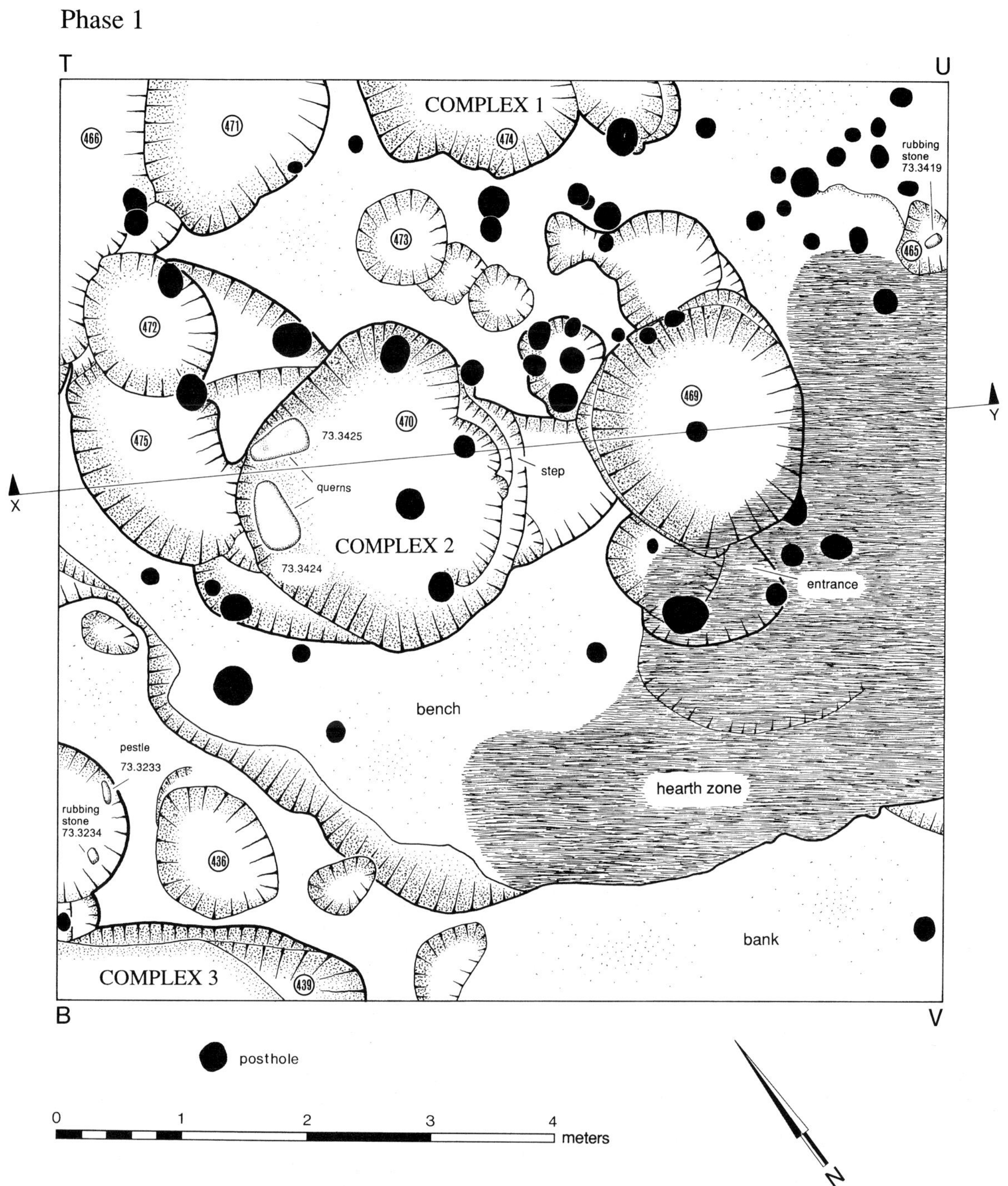

Figure 5.14 The pit complexes in phase 1 (Period 1A).

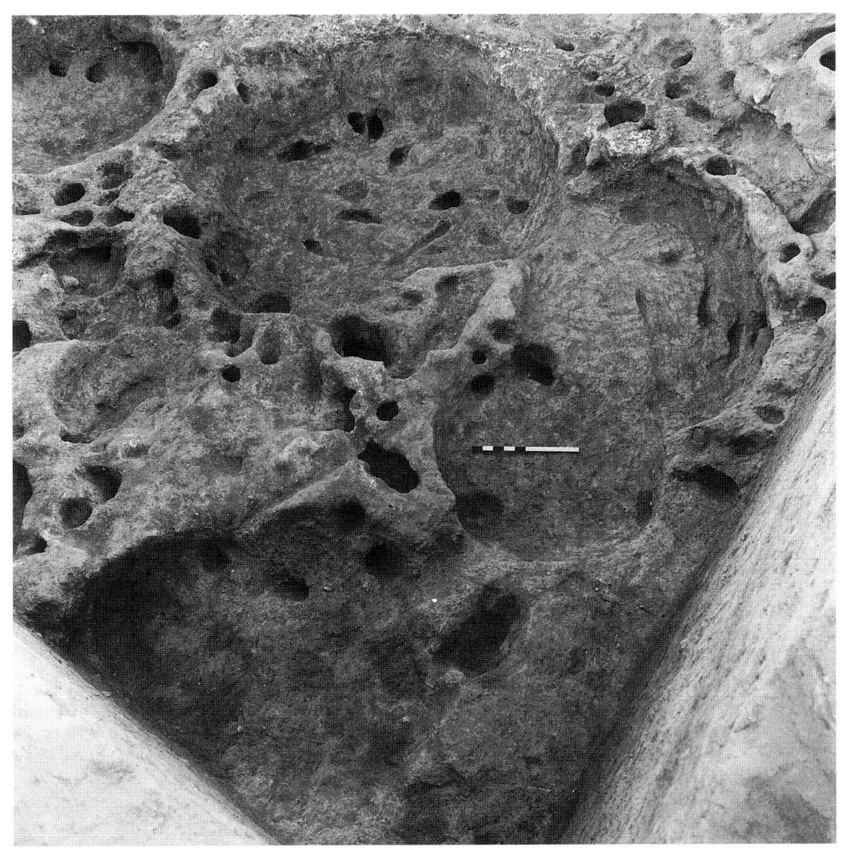

Figure 5.15 Part of pit complex 2 and its associated postholes, from the north. Note the marks left in the sides and bottoms of the pits from the tools used to dig them out. Scale, 50 cm.

Figure 5.16 Two basalt querns (73.3424 and 73.3425) in pit 470 of pit complex 2, from the southeast. Scale, 20 cm.

ible seeds as well as the grinding stones. This strongly suggests that the three complexes of large pits were used as dwellings. The small pits nearby may have been used for storage, with suitable basketry linings. The pits and postholes gradually filled up with dark brown and black occupation soil which contained much chipped stone. In time, the pits were covered completely and passed out of use.

Close inspection of the features cut into the subsoil tells us much about their functions. A great deal of care and effort went into creating the bank, bench, and pits. Several of the heavy grinding tools found in them appeared to be permanent fixtures. These facts imply that the settlement was intended for regular use over a long period. The faunal and floral remains suggest, moreover, that throughout its existence this substantial village was inhabited in all seasons of the year.

The pits in the three main complexes were apparently in use at the same time. Complex 2 illustrates this most clearly. The curve of its southern edge followed that of the bank, although it swung away from it. This suggests that pits 425, 470, and 469, at least, were used as a group and, incidentally, that there was a relationship between them and the bank. Within the complex there were definite links between pits. A sill 50 cm high separated pits 469 and 470, the top of which was cut 10 cm down from the level of the surrounding ground. This sill had two steps cut into its west side in pit 470 to ease passage from one pit to the other (figures 5.13, 5.15, 5.17). Pits 466, 471, and 472 not only were joined together in an extension of complex 2, but also opened out in the northwest corner to a larger area beyond the trench where the deepest deposits occurred. The location of several of the postholes also strongly suggests that the pits were linked because several of them were at points where the edges of pits intersected with each other. Pit 472 had two such postholes, one of them at the join with pit 425. There was another posthole between the two pits of complex 3.

Complex 2 had an entrance through the south side of pit 469. The subsoil of the bench had been cut away here to provide a low step in and out of the pit. From there one could step west into the other pits of the complex. This

Figure 5.17 Trench E, Section X-Y across pit complex 2.

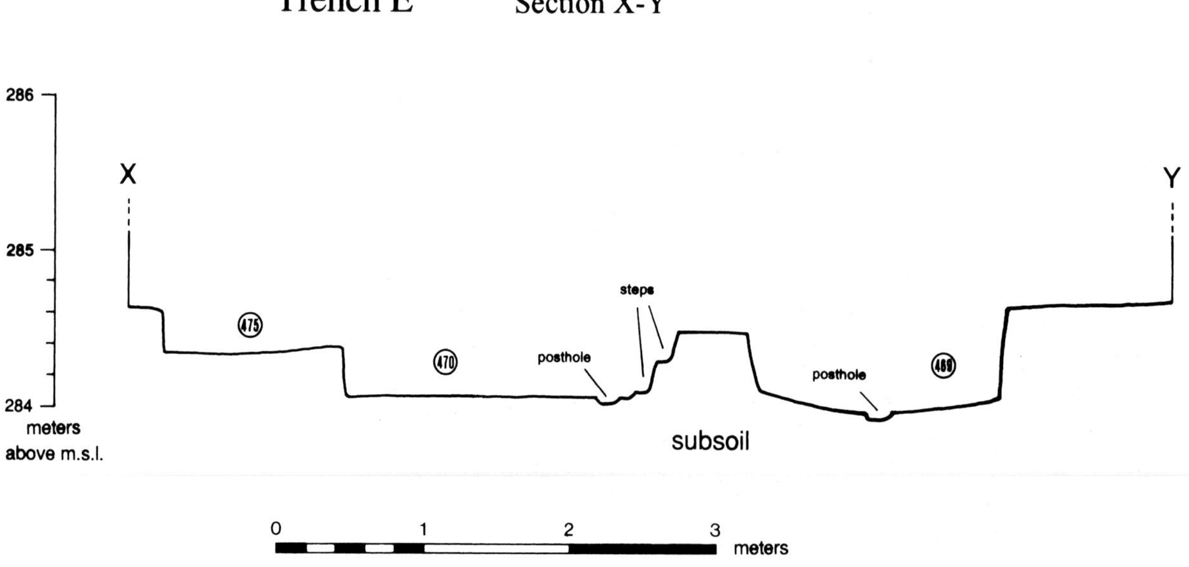

was the only convenient way in from this side since the southern edges of the other pits were too high to step over comfortably. The entrance opened out to the burned area of the bench, suggesting that it was often the inhabitants of complex 2 who lit fires there for cooking, warmth, and other purposes (figure 5.18). The location of these fires southeast of dwelling complexes 1 and 2 may indicate that the wind was in the northwest quarter more often than today. The presence of two large querns in pit 470, but not in adjacent ones, suggests that each pit in a complex had a different function.

The next question to consider is how the three complexes of dwelling pits were roofed, since the close association of pits and postholes suggests that they were protected from the weather. The principal needs during much of the year would have been shade from the sun during the day and shelter from the wind. Protection from winter weather, cooler than at present, would also have been desirable. The pits themselves would have moderated both summer heat and winter chill. The materials available to construct shelters over them would have come mostly from the valley bottom: poplar poles, tamarisk brush, and reeds, with the addition of grasses from the steppe. The pit complexes were probably thatched with the common reed, *Phragmites australis*. All these species are attested in the plant remains. The inhabitants may also have used skins of gazelle and onagers to cover their dwellings, like recent nomadic gazelle hunters who used gazelle skins for their clothing and tents (Blunt 1879, 2, pp. 110–111).

Figure 5.18 View of pit complex 2, the bench and bank, from the east. The entrance to pit 469 is on the left.

The covering could have been formed in several ways. The larger postholes were spaced at quite wide intervals around the outside of complexes 1 and 2. Pits 469 and 470 had centerposts, and additional postholes on opposite sides of the bottom or sides. There were more posts on the shelves around each complex. The larger postholes would have supported a strong framework of vertical poplar poles. The walls might then have been completed with bunches of reeds or reed mats, and the roofs, likewise, covered with reeds or brush. The southwest edge of complex 2 was so close to the bank that the base of the wall may have rested on it there. The form of the roof is uncertain, but two possibilities suggest themselves. Each large pit or group of pits may have had a conical roof (figure 5.19). The difficulties with this reconstruction are that there were few center postholes and very few small postholes around the edge of the pits to support the walls. Alternatively, the roof may have sloped down from ridge poles in the manner of a beduin tent (figure 5.20), a reconstruction that better fits the arrangement of the postholes, and which we therefore prefer. A third possibility might be that a framework of light poles was erected and then pulled together to form a domed cover for the pits, in the manner of pygmy and !Kung Bushmen huts. This seems less likely because the postholes were vertical, substantial, and widely spaced. Each of the two reconstructions we propose would have provided excellent shelter for these dwellings from the spring to the autumn, and some protection during the winter months. They would also have ensured a degree of separation and privacy for the families that we presume inhabited them.

The irregular outline of the pit dwellings was a consequence of the way they were composed, as one pit or room was added to another. Furthermore, the pits communicated with each other internally. Thus, the inhabitants were constructing quite complex dwellings that foreshadowed the multiroomed houses of the first stage of the Neolithic, the Pre-Pottery Neolithic A, found at Jericho (Kenyon 1981, p. 277) and Mureybit (Aurenche 1980) over a millennium

Figure 5.19 A reconstruction of the pit dwellings in phase 1 (Period 1A): version 1.

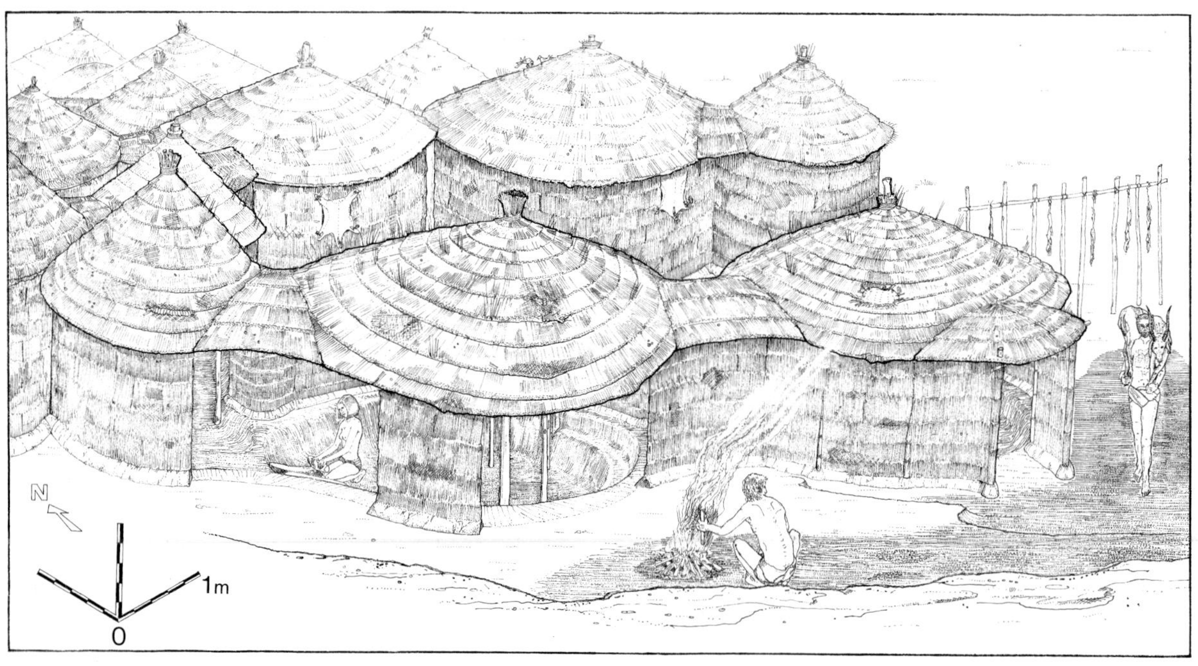

Figure 5.20 A reconstruction of the pit dwellings in phase 1 (Period 1A): version 2. It is probable that the pit complexes were roofed in this manner.

later. It is likely that the dwellings of the Abu Hureyra 1 settlement as a whole were arranged in a pattern, dictated by the nature of the location, climatic factors, and social constraints, but these cannot be determined from the area we excavated.

The structures of phase 1, the dwelling pits, small pits, and cut edge of the bank, were all subcircular or curvilinear in form. Round structures were built on other Levantine sites during the second stage of the Epipalaeolithic, so the Abu Hureyra ones fall within a widespread tradition. The best known is a village of circular huts excavated at Ain Mallaha in Palestine (Perrot 1966). These huts were often dug partly into the hillside, but they had low exterior walls of stone. The roof of at least one large hut was supported inside by a row of posts that followed the curve of the exterior wall (Perrot 1974, plate 1). A few of the Ain Mallaha huts were similar in size to the Abu Hureyra dwellings, but most were substantially bigger, up to 8 m in diameter (Valla 1981a, p. 412). Smaller pits were also found there, often 1 m in diameter but some up to 1.8 m across (Valla 1981a, figure 4). They were not dwellings but are thought to have been used for storage and other purposes, like the smaller ones at Abu Hureyra. Some of the little Ain Mallaha pits were used for burials (Perrot 1966, p. 460), but that was not the case at our site. Oval huts with low walls of stone have also been found at Nahal Oren (Stekelis and Yizraely 1963, p. 11), and farther south at Rosh Zin in the Negev (Henry 1976, p. 318). The Rosh Zin examples were from 2.5 to 3 m across, comparable in size, though not in form, to the Abu Hureyra dwellings. A large, round hut sunk partly into the ground and several circular firepits full of burned debris were found at Mureybit (J. Cauvin 1977, pp. 21, 23). They, too, fall within the round structure tradition but they were otherwise unlike anything found at Abu Hureyra.

This review of other sites of approximately the same age indicates that the pit dwellings of Abu Hureyra were unique; nothing precisely like them can be identified in the ethnographic records we have consulted. Pits similar to the smaller ones in phase 1 at Abu Hureyra do, however, seem to have been used at other sites. Likewise, there are no close Levantine analogies for our settlement during phases 2 and 3, although the nature of the deposits is reminiscent of those of the Proto-Neolithic settlement found in Trench M at Jericho (Kenyon 1981, p. 224). Abu Hureyra 1 was probably still inhabited when this settlement at Jericho was established.

Phases 2 and 3

The form of the Abu Hureyra settlement changed in phase 2 (figure 5.21). The subsoil bank and level bench on the southern side of the excavated area were still visible, and subsoil protruded from occupation deposits in the northeast corner of the trench. However, no more large pits were dug, and the space where they had been gradually filled up with dark occupation soil in which could be seen many thin, trodden floor surfaces. Some of these floors had been patched with clay. One almost complete clay floor (442) was rectangular in shape.

The bench, still defined on its southern side by the curved edge cut into the bank and somewhat sheltered from the wind, continued to be used as a hearth area. A deposit of heavily burned soil accumulated here in which could be seen many individual ash patches, the remains of numerous small fires (figures 5.21, 5.22). This hearth area was more extensive than in phase 1, spreading toward the center of the trench to cover the zone where pits 469 and 470 had been.

We recovered large quantities of chipped stone artifacts and food debris from these deposits, indicating that human occupation of the excavated area continued to be intense throughout phase 2. The presence of numerous floor surfaces suggests that the inhabitants constructed their dwellings directly on the surface of the ground. A few small pits in the bank were used during this phase, and we found a couple of pestles (73.3230, 73.3231) with a quern fragment (73.3229) in place in one of them (figure 5.23). Another cluster of ground stone objects—a mortar (73.3259), a rubbing stone (73.3261), and a grinding dish fragment (73.3260)—was found on the surface of the subsoil in the northeast corner.

Continued intense occupation led to a gradual accumulation of soil that covered the bench and the subsoil in the northeast corner. Eventually, the ground surface built up to the top of the bank, the subsoil was no longer visible, and the occupation surface consisted of a level expanse of ground. This marked the transition to phase 3. The nature of the settlement changed little in this phase, but the absence of the subsoil protrusions meant that there were no longer natural features present to influence the location of human activities. Thus, traces of floors with clay patches and hearths were found all over the excavated area (figures 5.24, 5.25), although the soil was less heavily burned. The floors were virtually all that remained of the light dwellings that were probably built over much of the settlement. In the upper levels of phase 3 we found a few postholes that may have been used for such structures. We detected fewer floors in phase 3 than in phase 2, though hearths were as numerous as ever. The upper levels of the Abu Hureyra 1 settlement were so severely weathered that such slight traces of structures were particularly difficult to see, but it seems that dwellings were more widely spaced in this phase. The upper levels were somewhat affected, too, by disturbance from the overlying Abu Hureyra 2 settlement. A firepit (417) had been dug into these levels from above and a few flint artifacts were found that were obviously intrusive.

Most of the hearths consisted of small pits or patches of ash with tiny scraps of charcoal. One of them, 416, was a more substantial affair. It was circular and

Trench E

Phase 2

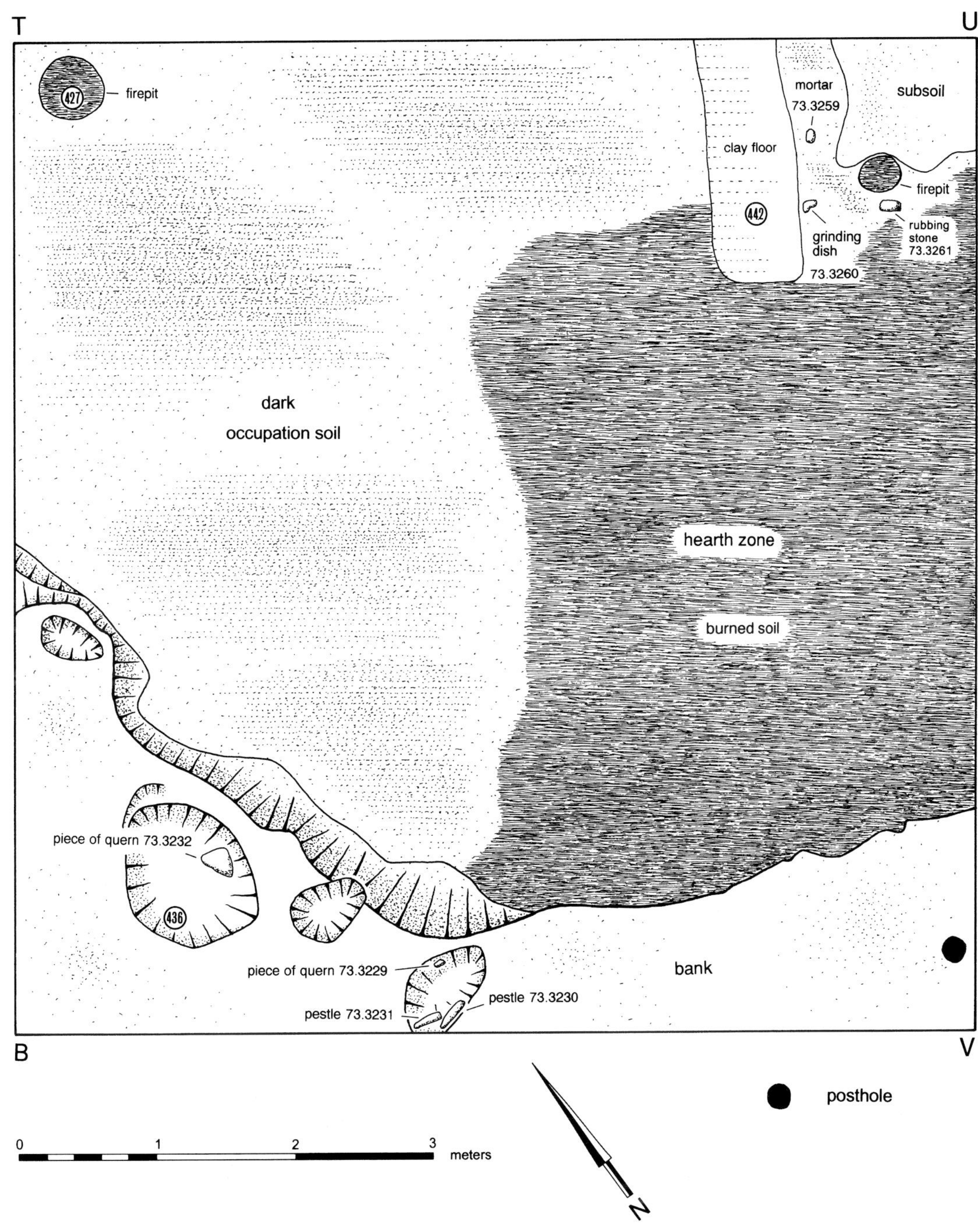

Figure 5.21 Plan of the settlement in phase 2 (Period 1B).

Figure 5.22 The phase 2 (Period 1B) settlement, from the southeast. The bench is still visible on the left side. The small excavation in the top center of the photograph is the bottom of the sounding dug here in the 1972 season. Scale, 1 m.

Figure 5.23 Two basalt pestles (73.3230, 73.3231) and a quern fragment (73.3229) in a pit. Scale, 20 cm.

Trench E

Phase 3

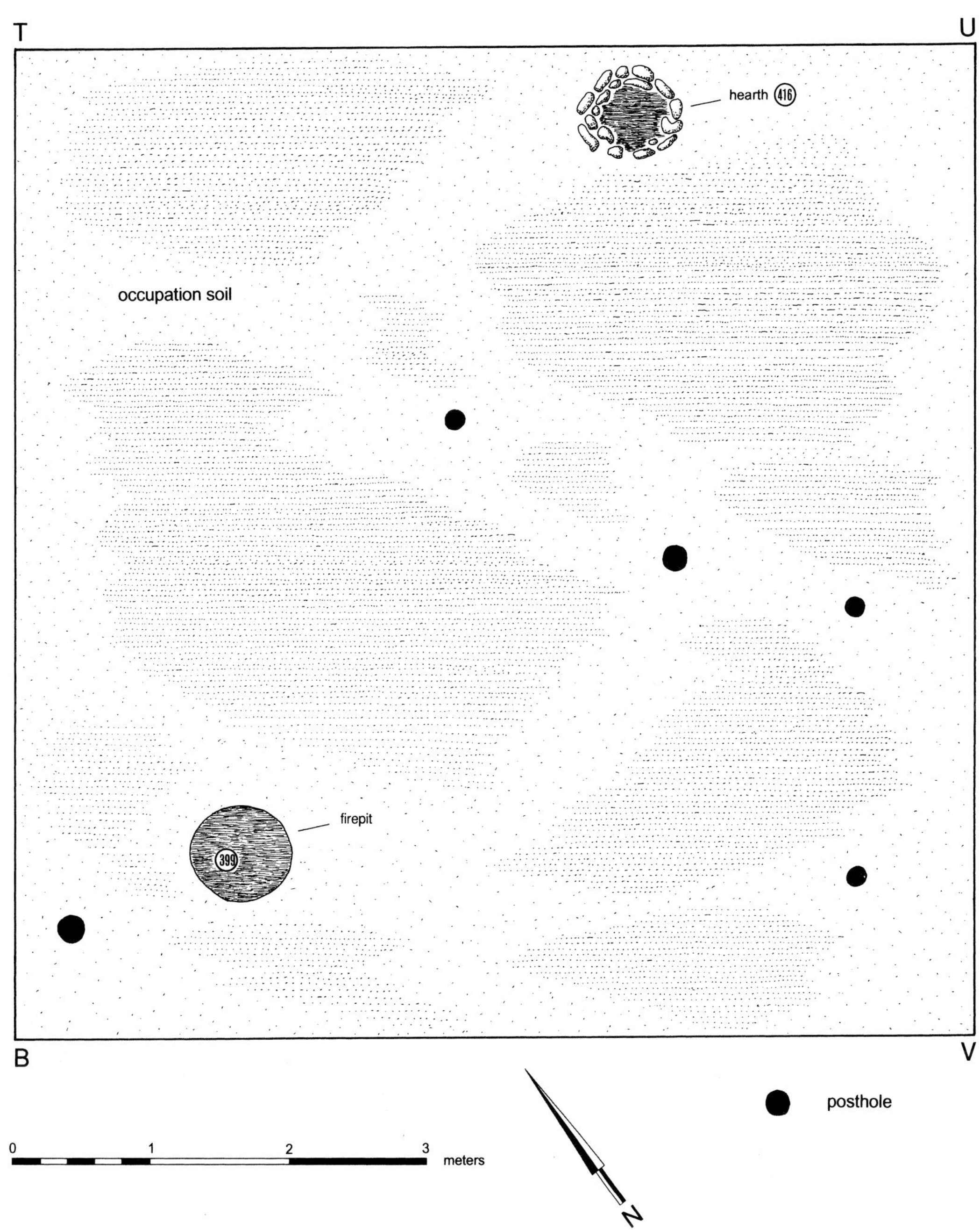

Figure 5.24 Plan of the settlement in phase 3 (Period 1C).

Figure 5.25 The northeastern sector of the trench in phase 3 (Period 1C) showing the location of hearth 416, from the southwest. Scale, 50 cm.

almost 80 cm in diameter, with a double ring of pebbles around it (figure 5.26). Some of the pebbles were different from the usual range from the banks of the Euphrates: there were several of a green, sedimentary rock and others of conglomerate. They had apparently been selected because of their curious appearance.

In phases 2 and 3 the inhabitants started to build their dwellings directly on the surface of the ground. These were probably huts constructed of light materials from the valley bottom—reeds and branches over a framework of poplar poles and skins. The shape of floor 442 indicates that the idea of building structures on rectilinear principles was beginning to take hold. It looks as though the settlement was relatively large, with dense clustering of activities.

The top of the phase 3 settlement was removed when this area was leveled by the inhabitants of Abu Hureyra 2 to build their houses. Thus, Abu Hureyra 1 was occupied for significantly longer than indicated by the deposits we excavated. Following the occupation of Abu Hureyra 1 its surface lay exposed for several centuries. The consequent weathering leached some of the color out of the upper levels, turning them a gray-brown, in contrast with the dark brown and black of levels nearer the bottom.

THE CHRONOLOGY OF ABU HUREYRA 1

The first radiocarbon date obtained for Abu Hureyra 1 was 10,792 ± 82 BP (BM-1121; Burleigh, Matthews, and Ambers 1982, p. 253). The amount of char-

Figure 5.26 Phase 3 (Period 1C). Hearth 416, from the southwest. Scale, 10 cm.

coal available was so small that the laboratory combined six samples from phases 2 and 3 to obtain the date. It could provide an approximate age only for the settlement. The British Museum laboratory obtained two more dates (see appendix 1, table A.1), one of which, 11,140 ± 140 BP (BM-1718R) for a level early in phase 2, indicated that the settlement had been founded before 11,000 BP (Bowman, Ambers, and Leese 1990, p. 77). The other (BM-1719R) for a level near the top of phase 3 gave a result suggesting that the charcoal from which it was obtained had intruded from the overlying Abu Hureyra 2 settlement.

The Oxford laboratory has obtained 26 accelerator mass spectometry (AMS) dates for samples from Abu Hureyra 1 levels (Moore et al. 1986; Gowlett et al. 1987, pp. 133–134), together with several more of a purely experimental nature. They form a tight series, most of which fall between 11,500 and 10,000 BP (table A.1). They indicate that the settlement was occupied for an unusually long period of time for a site of this age and culture. Nine of the determinations are derived from humic fractions, which the laboratory considers to give a less reliable result for the samples concerned. Those determinations are listed in table A.1 but have not been used in the discussion that follows. One sample, a piece of *Bos* bone from phase 1 (OxA-387, OxA-468), has yielded two dates of the same age. Two other dates look out of place. OxA-882 is later than any occupation deposit we found at Abu Hureyra, though of similar age to an Ubaid sherd we found in a surface level in Trench B. OxA-475 from the top level of phase 3 derives from a bone that has clearly intruded from the Abu Hureyra 2 settlement above and, significantly, is close to BM-1719R.

Twelve dates call for special comment. In sorting the flotation residues Hillman and Susan Colledge isolated a large number of cereal grains, mostly of the wild type. Among these, Hillman identified 40 grains of domestic cereals, and several more that are probably domestic, from Abu Hureyra 1 levels (see chapter 12). Almost all of the grains come from phases 2 and 3. These grains potentially provide direct evidence for cereal cultivation at Abu Hureyra as much as a millennium before the earliest dates for farming elsewhere in Southwest Asia. This would set the beginning of agriculture in the late Epipalaeolithic rather than the early Neolithic. The immediate question that we had to address was, were these grains of the age of the deposits in which they had been found, or were they intrusive and later in date. The only way to determine this was to date the grains directly by AMS.

In consultation with the Oxford laboratory we were able to isolate twelve of these domestic grains that had the necessary characteristics for dating. They included one grain of hulled six-rowed barley, three grains of free-threshing wheats, three of domestic einkorn, and five of domestic rye. We give the results in appendix 1. The five domestic rye grains provided a sequence of dates. The oldest grain gave a date of 11,140 ± 100 BP (OxA-8718). The second from level 455 was dated to 10,930 ± 120 BP (OxA-6685); on comparison with dates from adjacent levels, it was clearly of the same age as the Epipalaeolithic deposit in which it was found. The third rye grain dated to 10,610 ± 100 BP (OxA-8719). The fourth grain gave a date of 9,860 ± 220 BP (OxA-6996). This grain could have derived from the upper levels of Abu Hureyra 1 that had been removed when the inhabitants of Abu Hureyra 2 leveled this part of the mound, or from the intermediate episode of occupation that followed. The fifth rye grain was dated to 8,275 ± 75 BP (OxA-5843); this grain must have come from the overlying Abu Hureyra 2 deposits in Trench E. All five of these rye grains exhibited the same domestic morphology. The dates confirm that agriculture began with the cultivation of rye at the beginning of phase 2 of Abu Hureyra 1 and continued through into Abu Hureyra 2 times. Thus, it was the hunter-gatherer inhabitants of Abu Hureyra 1 who were the first at this site to adopt the new way of life.

The dates for six of the other seven grains clustered between 8,290 and 8,115 BP, with one somewhat earlier date of 8,700 ± 240 BP (OxA-6995) for an einkorn grain. These seeds, like one of the rye grains (OxA-5843), presumably came from the Abu Hureyra 2 deposits above.

We have a total of 16 conventional and AMS dates from which to ascertain the age of Abu Hureyra 1. They are shown in both chronological and stratigraphic order in figures 5.27 and 5.28. The dates form a good stratigraphic sequence in which only five appear to be somewhat out of order. OxA-473 seems a little late for its stratigraphic position at the top of phase 2, and both OxA-386 and OxA-170 look a little early, even though they come from levels well down in phase 3. And OxA-8718 is significantly earlier than its stratigraphic position would suggest. These apparent discrepancies are the result of movement caused by humans and rodents of the parent samples within the deposits of Abu Hureyra 1. BM-1718R was obtained from wood charcoal, which may give an earlier date for a level than an AMS date for organic material such as animal bone from short-lived species.

The dates suggest that Abu Hureyra 1 was founded about 11,500 BP. This estimate is derived in part from the earliest date in the series, 11,450 ± 300 BP (OxA-883), which has a larger than average standard error but is given some support by OxA-387/468, OxA-8718, and BM-1718R. On a more conservative

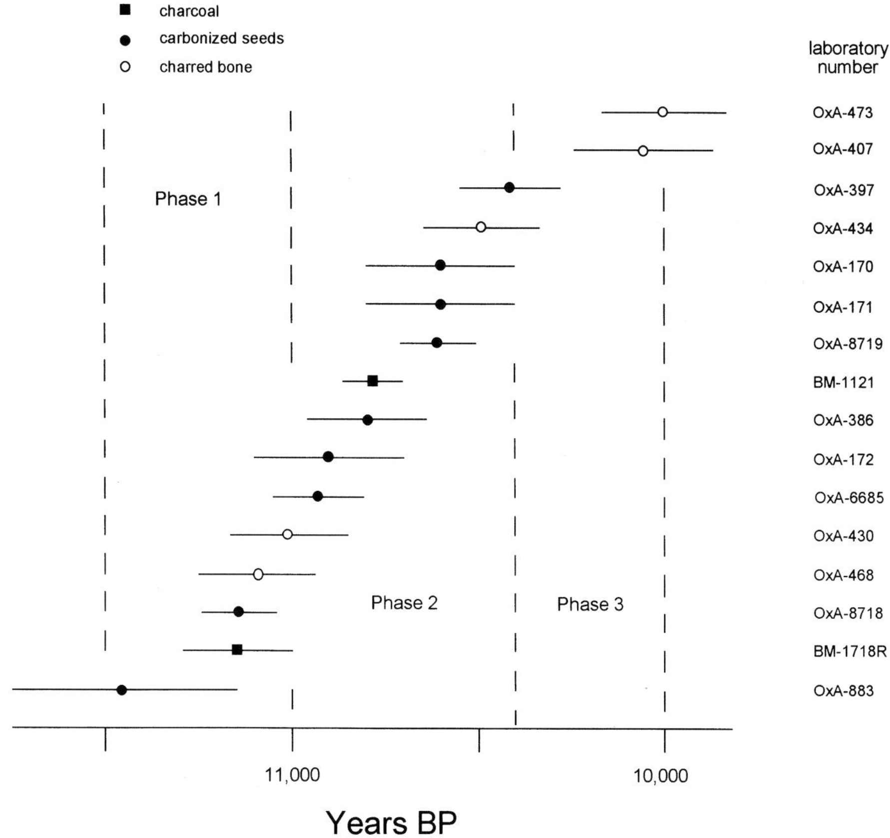

Figure 5.27 Radiocarbon dates for Abu Hureyra 1 plotted in chronological order.

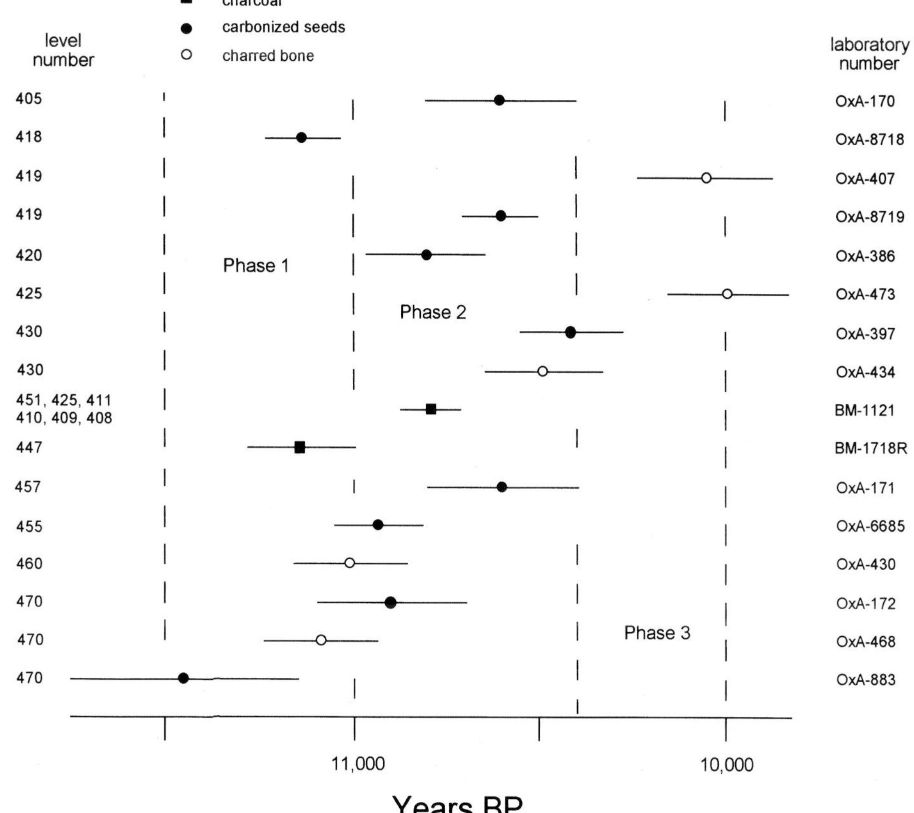

Figure 5.28 Radiocarbon dates for Abu Hureyra 1 plotted in stratigraphic order.

reading of the dates, the settlement could have been established a couple of centuries later, but an even earlier date is also possible.

Abu Hureyra 1 continued to be inhabited until at least 10,000 BP. This is suggested by both OxA-473 from phase 2 and OxA-407 from phase 3, which have yielded comparable dates. OxA-407 comes from a sample of bone that was found at the bottom of the phase 3 deposits, themselves over 60 cm deep, and so should be significantly older than the upper levels of this phase. Furthermore, it should be remembered that the surface levels of the Abu Hureyra 1 settlement were removed by the inhabitants of Abu Hureyra 2. Two inferences may be made from these observations: that the figure of 10,000 BP is a conservative one for the age of the upper levels of Abu Hureyra 1 that survived to be excavated by us, and that the settlement continued to be inhabited somewhat later than this date.

It is possible to suggest approximately how long each phase of Abu Hureyra 1 lasted, taking into account both the radiocarbon dates and the stratigraphic position of their parent samples. The date of the transition from phase 1 to phase 2 is given by OxA-468, OxA-430, OxA-6685, and OxA-172. All four dates are close together and indicate that the transition occurred about 11,000 BP.

The date of the transition from phase 2 to phase 3 is more problematic. The latest date in phase 2 for a sample in unequivocal stratigraphic position is 10,420 ± 150 BP, OxA-397. OxA-473 comes from a slightly higher level, but it seems a little late for its stratigraphic position when compared with the dates for phase 3. OxA-386 and OxA-170, on the other hand, look rather early for the location of their samples in the phase 3 stratigraphic sequence. We suggest, with due caution, that the transition may have occurred about 10,400 BP, but recognize that it could have taken place a century or two earlier. It seems less likely to us that it took place much later than this date.

The settlement of Abu Hureyra 1 represents the first period of occupation at Abu Hureyra, and so may be designated Period 1. The period may be subdivided to take account of the sequence of phases; thus, Period 1A is equivalent to phase 1, Period 1B to phase 2, and Period 1C to phase 3. These terms may seem a complication in the context of Abu Hureyra 1 alone, but they are necessary to maintain consistency with the terminology used to describe the evolution of the later settlements at Abu Hureyra.

Figure 5.29 gives the proposed chronology for Abu Hureyra 1 in summary form. The dates suggested can only be approximations and are subject to some uncertainty. The most important facts to note are that the settlement appears to have been inhabited for at least a millennium and a half in radiocarbon years, and that it probably continued to be occupied for some time after the date of 10,000 BP given here.

Periods	Phases	Years BP
		10,000
1C	3	
		10,400
1B	2	
		11,000
1A	1	
		11,500

Figure 5.29 Proposed chronology of the Abu Hureyra 1 settlement.

The publication of calibration curves extending back to 13,300 BP (Stuiver et al. 1986, figure 7) allows us to make a tentative estimate of the age of the Abu Hureyra 1 settlement in absolute years. The estimated calibrated date for the founding of the settlement is 12,700 Cal BP, and for the transition to the Intermediate Period 11,100 Cal BP. Thus, the age of the settlement is a full 1,000 years earlier in real time, but the span of occupation is increased only slightly. The calibration data published most recently suggest that the real dates may be somewhat older than these estimates (Bard et al. 1993).

6 The Chipped Stone and Bone Artifacts

The Chipped Stone

D. I. OLSZEWSKI

The characteristics of the chipped stone artifacts and the radiocarbon dates indicate that the assemblage from Abu Hureyra 1 belongs within the Levantine late Epipalaeolithic period (Epipalaeolithic 2).[1] This assemblage from Abu Hureyra 1 is of great significance for several reasons. The excavation of the Abu Hureyra 1 settlement (Trench E, levels 396–475) yielded 99,357 chipped stone pieces, making this one of the largest late Epipalaeolithic collections to be studied systematically. In addition, the careful recovery of both large and small artifacts means that the proportions of the various tool and debitage classes accurately represent the chipped stone present in Trench E. This is in contrast with early excavations in the Levant that often produced a biased picture of the chipped stone assemblage (Olszewski and Barton 1990).

The radiocarbon dates from Abu Hureyra 1 suggest that the settlement was inhabited for a millennium and a half. Since the levels are in good stratigraphic order, it is possible to examine long-term cultural change as reflected in the manufacture and use of chipped stone artifacts. Additionally, changes in the chipped stone assemblage can potentially be correlated with the sequences of plant and animal remains.

Prior to the early 1970s, our knowledge of the late Epipalaeolithic in the Levant was, with few exceptions, limited to the many sites from the Palestinian region that are classified as Natufian (for example, Garrod 1932; Garrod and Bate 1937; Neuville 1951; Bar-Yosef 1970). The materials from Abu Hureyra 1 represent one of only two extensive collections from this time period from excavations in northern Syria, the other being that from phase Ia at Mureybit (J. Cauvin 1972, 1974). Thus, the chipped stone assemblage from Abu Hureyra 1 provides an excellent opportunity to examine late Epipalaeolithic adaptations in an area other than the Natufian core region of Palestine.

My analysis and interpretation of the chipped stone assemblage from Abu Hureyra 1 have three main aims. The first is to provide a detailed description of the assemblage from each level, an essential guide to comparative analyses. My second aim is to use the information generated to examine chronological relationships in the levels of Abu Hureyra 1 and to determine if changes occurred in the types of tools and in the assemblage as a whole over the span of occupation. The time depth of the Abu Hureyra 1 settlement and the recovery methods used make this site one of the few late Epipalaeolithic occupations for which such methodology is possible. This is because the majority of the stratified Natufian sites with considerable time depth were excavated when excavation techniques were less rigorous, although recent excavations at Ain Mallaha (Valla 1984) and the reexcavation at Mugharet el Wad (Valla et al. 1986) have clarified the sequence for the Natufian region. My third aim is to compare and contrast the Abu Hureyra 1 assemblage with those of other contemporary northern Levantine sites and of the Natufian area of the southern Levant. In this way we may test the validity of referring to all Levantine late Epipalaeolithic assemblage as Natufian (M.-C. Cauvin 1980), and see if the northern Levantine assemblages reflect the generalized late Epipalaeolithic patterns of adaptation that are common in the southern Levant.

DESCRIPTION OF THE CHIPPED STONE ASSEMBLAGE

In this section I shall describe the varieties of tool and debitage types present in the Abu Hureyra 1 assemblage, based on the typological distinctions previously defined in Olszewski (1984, 1986a). A complete typological listing of the assemblage by level can be found in the electronic archive (see appendix 8).

Tools

Of the chipped stone assemblage recovered from Abu Hureyra 1, 5.6% or 5,587 artifacts are tools. These can be conveniently divided into the following categories: scrapers, burins, perforators and borers, backed pieces, notches and denticulates, truncations, nongeometric microliths, geometric microliths, heavy tools, multiple tools, retouched pieces, and varia.

Scrapers on flakes are the most characteristic scraper type in the Abu Hureyra 1 assemblage. These are usually made by retouching the distal end of the flake, but the retouch can also extend onto the lateral edges (figure 6.1a–d). Scrapers are fashioned on cortical or primarily cortical blanks throughout the Abu Hureyra 1 sequence. Denticulated scrapers are fairly common (figure 6.1e), with the denticulation being of the coarse or large variety, rather than the fine serration that is exemplified by the Ksar Akil scraper type (Besançon et al. 1975–1977, p. 37, figure 5.9). Another less common scraper is the carinated or core-like variety (figure 6.2a). Rare forms of scrapers include endscrapers on blades, nosed and shouldered types, and double scrapers. Finally, we also find occasional examples of scraper-planes (figure 6.2b).

The burin, or graver, class can be divided into five main types. These are burins struck from the striking platform (which can be considered a specialized burin on natural edge), burins struck from a natural or unbroken and unmodified edge, dihedral burins, burins made on broken edges, and burins struck from truncations (figure 6.3a–e). All other types of burins, including multiple burins and transverse burins, are rare in the Abu Hureyra 1 collections.

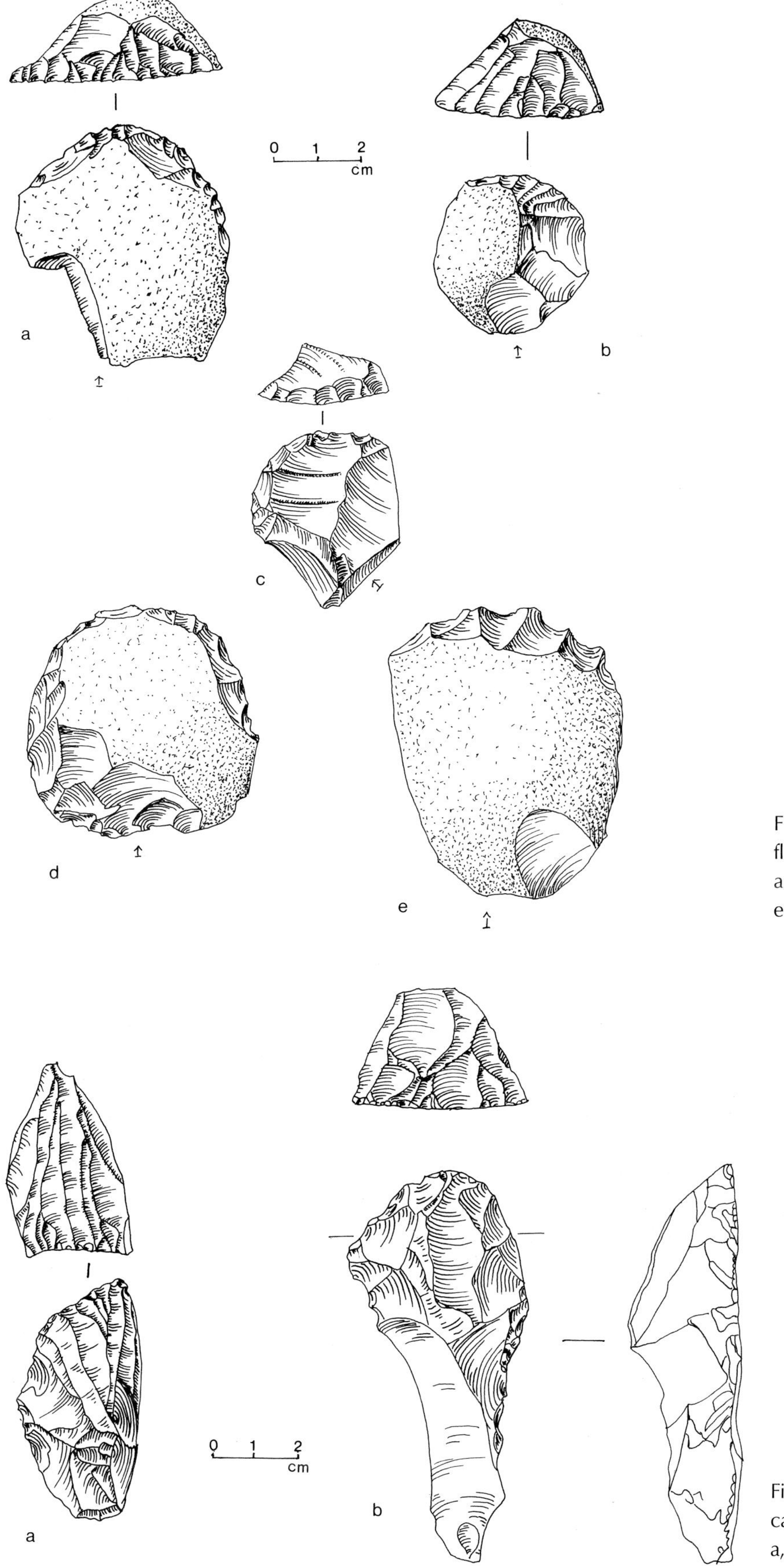

Figure 6.1 Abu Hureyra 1: flake and denticulated scrapers. a–d, scrapers on flakes; e, denticulated scraper.

Figure 6.2 Abu Hureyra 1: carinated and plane scrapers. a, carinated (core-like) scraper; b, scraper-plane.

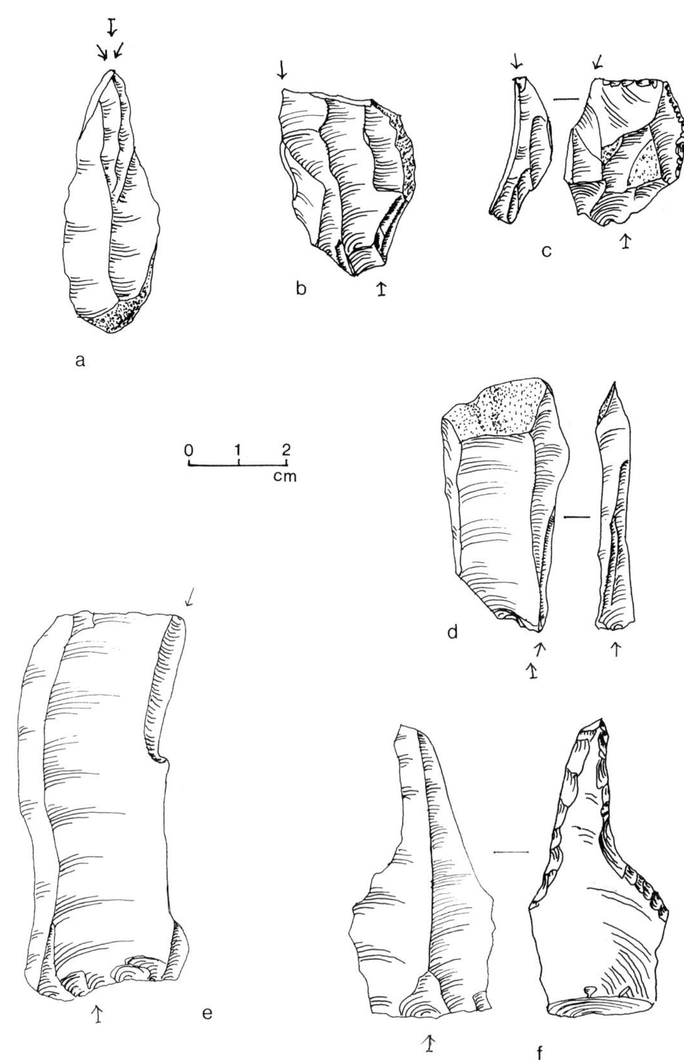

Figure 6.3 Abu Hureyra 1: burins and borer. a, straight dihedral burin; b, burin on break; c, burin off truncation; d, burin off striking platform; e, burin on natural edge; f, large borer.

Perforators are characterized as having a small, pointed projection, while borers have thick, stubby noses. Single perforators are the most common type in this tool class, followed by single borers of both large and small varieties (figures 6.3f, 6.4a,b,k). Double perforators and borers are rare, as are perforators made on backed bladelets. Small numbers of a distinctive type of perforator, sometimes with a curved or hooked form, known from the excavations at Mureybit (M.-C. Cauvin 1980, p. 13, figure 2.8, 11), are also present (figure 6.4c,d).

The tool class of backed pieces includes both backed flakes and backed blades of various types. Within this category, the most common artifacts are backed flakes (figure 6.4e). Backed blades make up a smaller portion of this class, with the more characteristic forms being blades that are partially backed and others with convex backs, straight backs or distal ends that are convex backed (figure 6.4f–h). We also find several miscellaneous backed pieces of irregular form.

Notches and denticulates are well represented in the Abu Hureyra 1 assemblage. Notched flakes dominate, followed by denticulated flakes (figure 6.4i,j). Both notched and denticulated blades and bladelets are present, but they are not numerous.

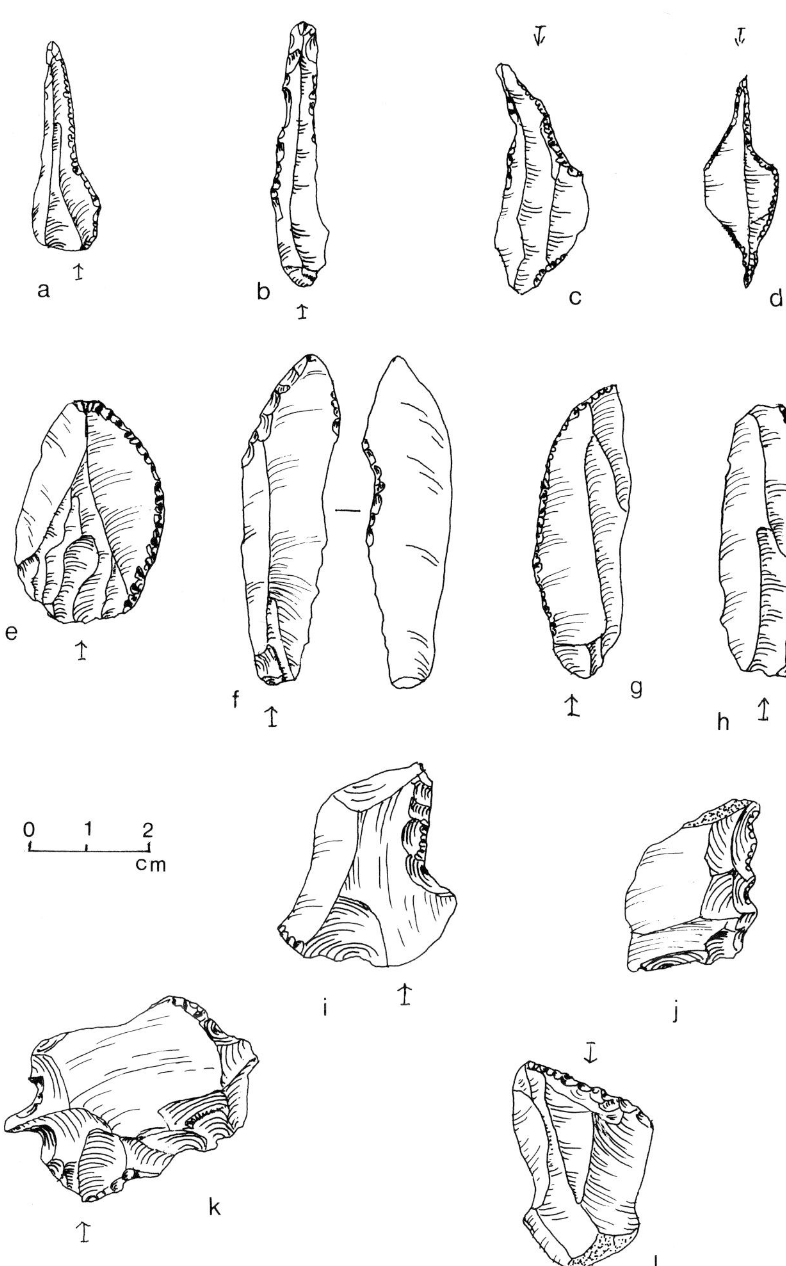

Figure 6.4 Abu Hureyra 1: perforators, backed pieces, notches, and truncation. a, c, d, and k, simple perforators; b, borer; e, backed flake; f, partially backed blade; g, curved-backed blade; h, straight-backed blade with blunt end; i, notched flake; j, denticulated flake; l, truncation.

The truncated class comprises flake and blade blanks. Truncated bladelets are counted with the nongeometric microlith tool class, as is the case in many typologies. The majority of the truncations in this category are of the straight, oblique variety (figure 6.4l). Concave and convex truncations are extremely rare.

The most common nongeometric microlith form at Abu Hureyra 1 is the straight-backed and pointed bladelet (figure 6.5a). Other, less common types are partially backed bladelets and those with distal ends that are convex backed (figure 6.5b). Rare types include convex-backed bladelets (figure 6.5c), backed bladelets with an obtuse or blunt distal end, truncated bladelets, backed-and-truncated bladelets, double-backed bladelets, and backed bladelets that have an undulating or irregular backed edge.

The geometric microlith tool class at Abu Hureyra 1 is overwhelmingly dominated by lunates (figure 6.5f–s). The majority of these are backed using semi-abrupt and abrupt retouch. There are also numerous examples of bipolar backing retouch, but no Helwan (or oblique, bifacial) backing retouch. A few other geometric forms occur, but they are not abundant (figure 6.5d,e). These include scalene triangles, isosceles triangles, and trapezes. It is probable that the small numbers of these other geometric forms are the result of lunate microlith production in which the typical lunate form was not achieved, as pointed out by Moore (1975, p. 58).

Heavy tools represent a small but important portion of the assemblage from Abu Hureyra 1. Three forms in particular deserve special mention: gouges, axes,

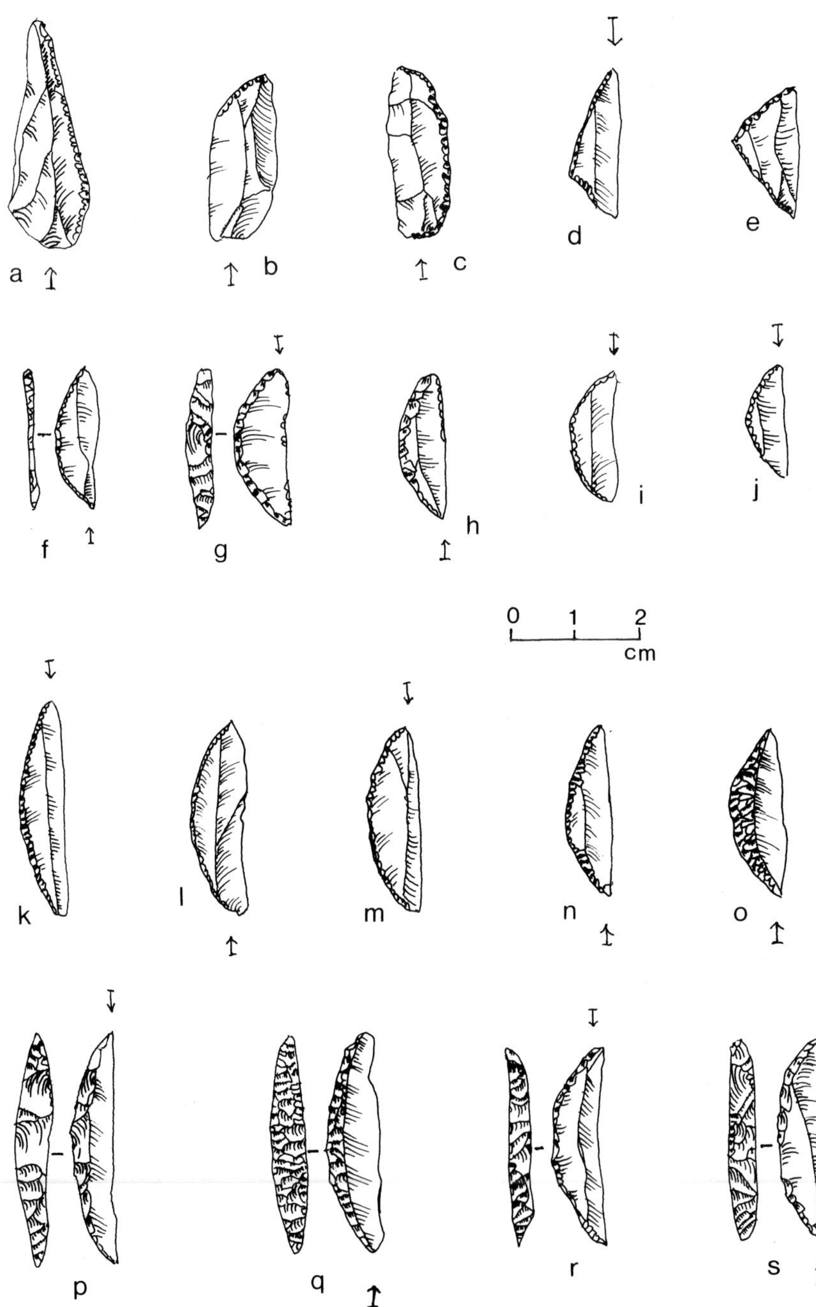

Figure 6.5 Abu Hureyra 1: nongeometric and geometric microliths. a, straight-backed bladelet; b, curved-backed end bladelet; c, curved-backed bladelet; d and e, triangles; f–s, lunates.

and blunted implements. The gouge is a tool fashioned on a complete nodule of chert. In general, the piece is worked on all sides, excepting the butt end on some examples (figure 6.6). The lateral edges of the gouge usually have a battered appearance. The "working" end of the tool has a shallow concave area produced by the removal of a flake parallel to the long axis, while the edge on the reverse of the concave portion often has the appearance of a scraper, with many retouch scars parallel to the long axis of the piece (Olszewski 1986a, p. 189). The axe, like the gouge, is manufactured on a complete nodule, has battering on the lateral edges, and occasionally has an unworked butt end (figure 6.7). However, the "working" edge of the tool is much thinner in appearance and is manufactured by the removal of tranchet-like flakes from both sides of the edge (Olszewski 1986a, p. 189). Such tools are also known from the Epipalaeolithic site of Nahr el-Homr (Boerma and Roodenberg 1977, p. 12, figure 3.9) and have been reported from a mixed Epipalaeolithic/Neolithic context at J10, a site near the ancient lake of Bahret el Mallaha in southwestern Syria (M.-C. Cauvin et al. 1982, p. 281, figure 6.3). Blunted implements, as with the gouges and axes, are made on complete chert nodules and have battered lateral edges (figure 6.8). The distinguishing characteristic of these tools is that their "working" edges have a blunted appearance (Olszewski 1986a, p. 189). This suggests that this tool form may represent the exhausted remains of gouges or axes, especially as my close examination of a few of the blunted implements from Abu Hureyra 1 has revealed the remnants of formerly large flake removals, like those seen on gouges and axes. There is some similarity in overall form to "picks" and "choppers" reported from the Neolithic settlement at Beidha (Kirkbride 1966, p. 45, figure 16.1; p. 46, figure 17.1). Finally, the heavy tool class also includes choppers, bifacial pieces, and an occasional battered piece.

Combination tools, or multiple tools, on the same piece are unusual in the Abu Hureyra 1 assemblage. Scraper-burins and scraper-denticulates are the most frequently encountered ones (figure 6.9a,h). Very rare types include scraper-perforators, burin-perforators, burin-notches, and sidescraper-notches, as well as a few others.

Retouched flakes are the most numerous implements in the retouched piece class (figure 6.9d). We find very few retouched blades and bladelets.

The varia tool class at Abu Hureyra 1 is composed mainly of sidescrapers (figure 6.9e,g). I have placed sidescrapers in the varia category because they

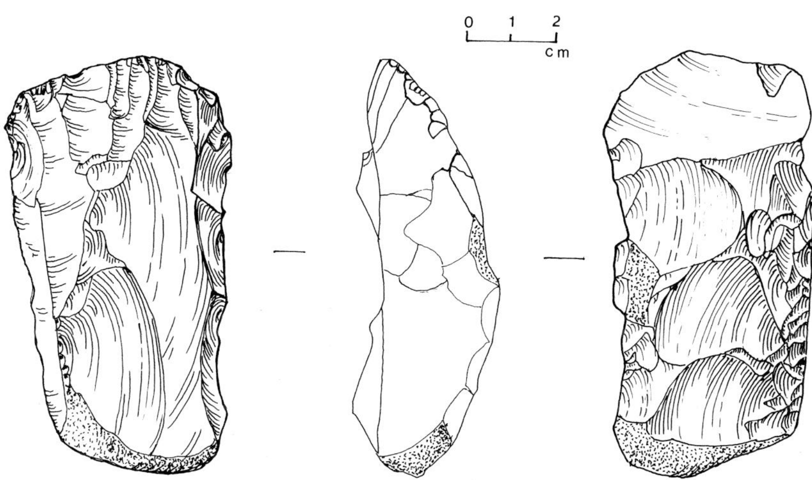

Figure 6.6 Abu Hureyra 1: gouge heavy tool.

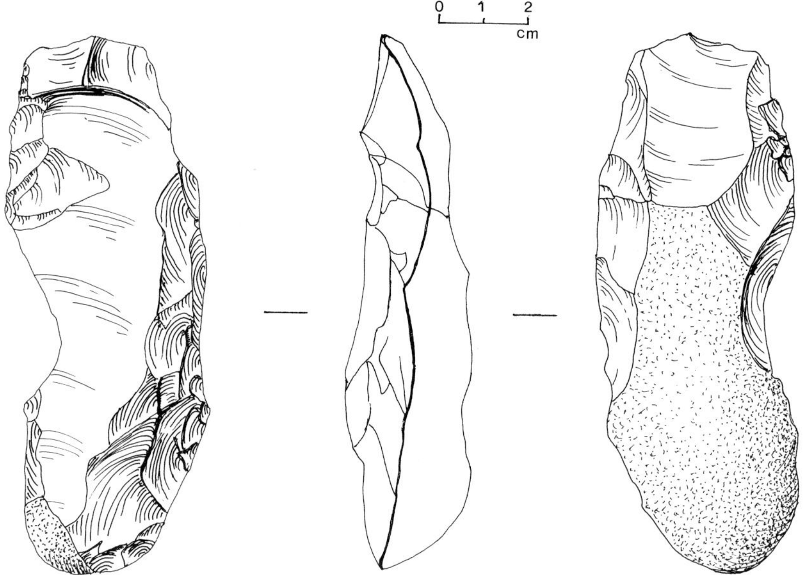

Figure 6.7 Abu Hureyra 1: axe heavy tool.

are not generally counted as components of the scraper class in most typologies. If the sidescrapers were included with the scrapers at Abu Hureyra, they would not be directly comparable to the scraper classes at other late Epipalaeolithic sites. The varia class includes a few naturally backed knives (figure 6.9f) and three sickle blades. The sickle blades are defined by the presence of sickle gloss and have abrupt retouch backing. The other forms are too diverse to enumerate here but consist of oddly shaped and retouched pieces that cannot be assigned by definition to any of the established tool classes and types.

Debitage

The debitage category comprises the majority of the chipped stone artifacts present at Abu Hureyra 1, 93,770 (94.4%) of the 99,357 total artifacts. Included in this grouping are cores, hammerstones, pieces with nibbling, microburins, burin spalls, flakes, blades, bladelets, and debris.

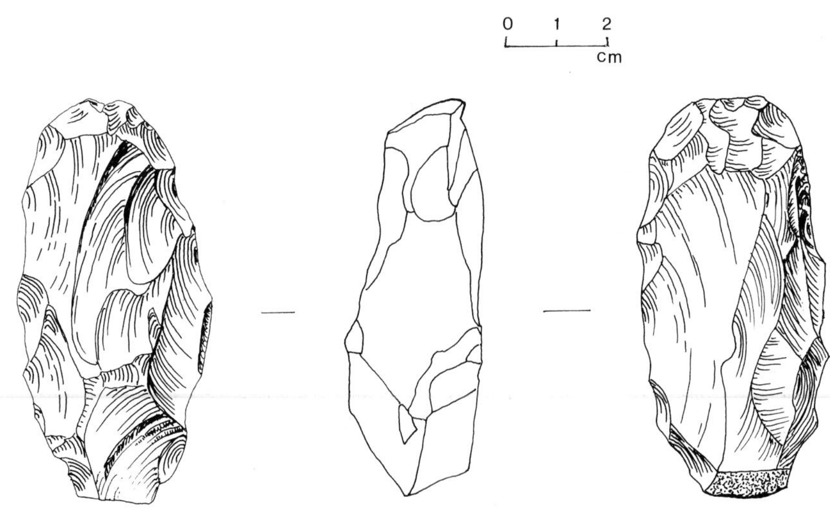

Figure 6.8 Abu Hureyra 1: blunted heavy tool.

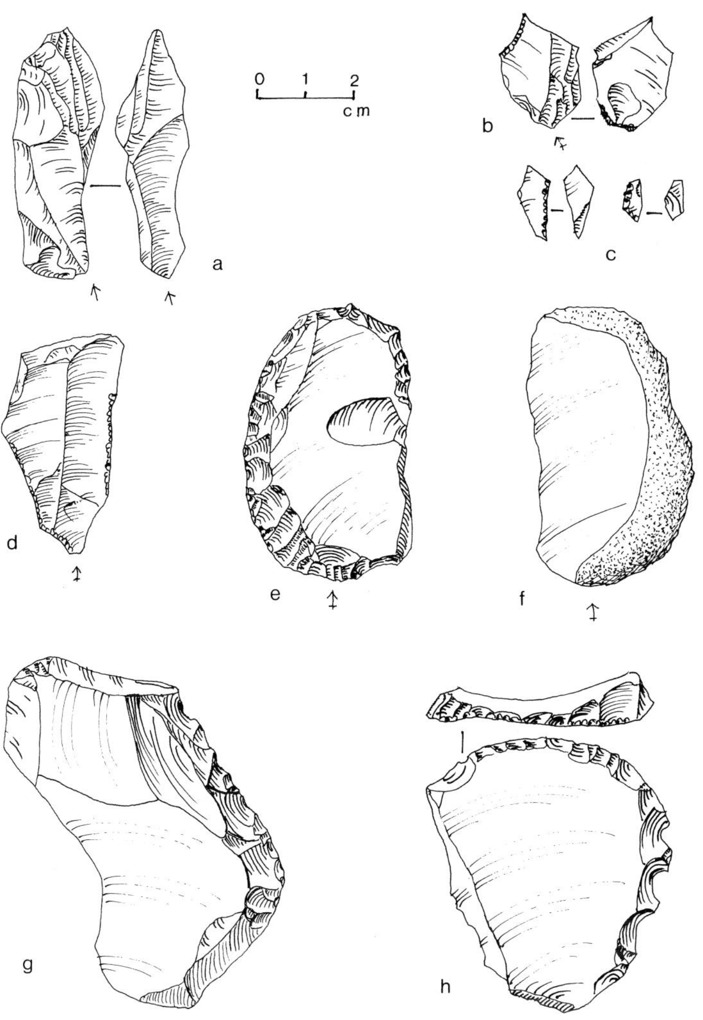

Figure 6.9 Abu Hureyra 1: multiple tools, retouched piece, varia, and microburins. a, endscraper-burin; b, true microburin; c, Krukowski microburins; d, retouched blade-like flake; e and g, sidescrapers; f, naturally backed knife; h, scraper-denticulate.

The most common cores are simple single-platform and multiple-platform types, although a variety of others was used (figure 6.10). In this assemblage, cores for the production of flakes greatly outnumber those for the manufacture of blades and bladelets. The cores used to obtain flakes are most often either simple single-platform or multiple-platform types. Occasionally, flakes are also detached from specialized single-platform cores such as the subpyramidal core, and from double-platform cores like the opposing- and opposed-platform varieties, as well as the 90° core.

Blades and bladelets are generally manufactured from simple single-platform cores. However, they are also obtained from opposed- and opposing-platform cores and subpyramidal cores. The use of the other core varieties to produce blades and bladelets is rarer.

Hammerstones have battering marks caused by striking blanks from cores. Of the pieces used as hammerstones at Abu Hureyra 1, about half are unmodified nodules, while the others are former cores of various types.

Pieces with nibbling are listed under debitage since, at present, it is not possible to determine if the nibbling, or irregular, small removals, along the edges of blanks indicates their use as tools. Most pieces with nibbling are flakes, although some are blades, bladelets, and debris.

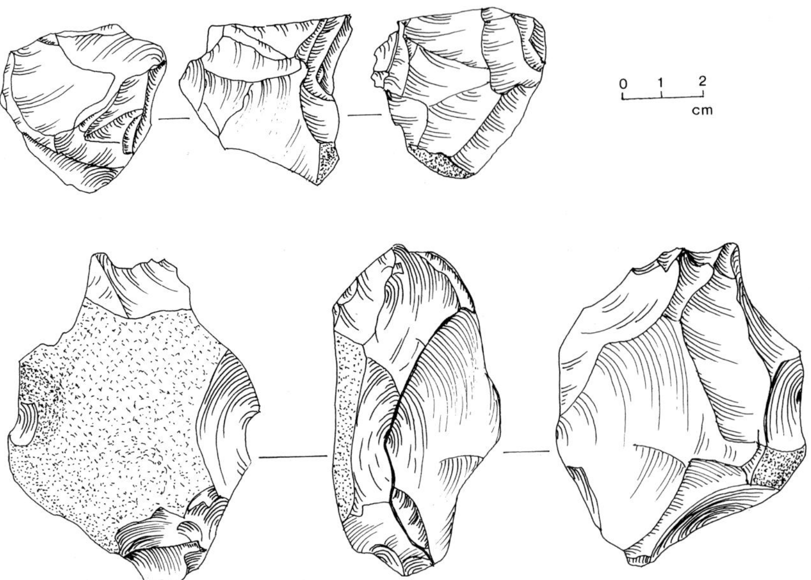

Figure 6.10 Abu Hureyra 1: multiple platform cores.

Three types of microburins are present at Abu Hureyra 1. These are true microburins, Krukowski microburins, and trihedral microburins (*microburin trihèdre*) (figure 6.9b,c). These types represent different techniques of snapping a larger blade into segments. The smaller segments can then be made into various microlithic tools. However, the low numbers of microburins overall suggest that the microburin technique, both that using true microburins and that using Krukowski microburins, as for example in the Mushabian industry of the Sinai Desert (Phillips and Mintz 1977, p. 164), was not commonly employed as a method to manufacture microliths at Abu Hureyra 1. Of the three types of microburins, those of the Krukowski variety are the most frequent, followed by the true microburin.

Burin spalls are occasionally found in the chipped stone assemblage from Abu Hureyra 1. These are the by-products of manufacturing the bit edge of a burin.

Flakes are the most numerous blank types at Abu Hureyra 1. They represent all stages in the reduction of cores and include the following types: cortical flakes (> 90% cortex); flakes with some cortex (10–90% cortex); noncortical flakes (<10% cortex); core-rejuvenation or preparation flakes; and microflakes, probably the products of shaping and resharpening tools.

Blades and bladelets are less common than flake blanks. They include several varieties from stages in the process of reduction of blade/bladelet cores, such as blade/bladelets with one exterior ridge and with multiple exterior ridges, as well as blade/bladelets struck off to rejuvenate the core. Among these are a few examples of crested blade/bladelets.

The debris category includes chips, chunks, and pieces that some archaeologists have called shatter. Debris probably represents breakage due to flaws in the parent materials used as cores. Pieces of debris are rarely used as blanks to manufacture tools.

TEMPORAL CHANGES IN CHIPPED STONE

The chipped stone tool and debitage classes in Abu Hureyra 1 form a homogeneous assemblage in terms of technology and typology. However, it is possible to subdivide the assemblage into three chronological units, based on changes in the frequencies of certain tool classes, and following the stratigraphic sequence outlined in chapter 5.

First, I combined the chipped stone counts from each level into units corresponding to the three phases of occupation of Abu Hureyra 1. I then reduced the chipped stone tool data into a more manageable set by condensing the various tool types into their respective tool classes for each unit (table 6.1). This reduction into fewer categories did not alter the interpretive potential of the data, since the types of tools being made and used at Abu Hureyra 1 were consistent throughout the various levels.

Although there are twelve tool classes present at Abu Hureyra 1, I use only nine of these initially for the purpose of examining percentage changes in chipped stone tool classes through the sequence of phases. From this analysis I have excluded heavy tools, multiple tools, and varia because, first, they represent very small percentages of the total number of tools and are absent from over half of the levels, and second, the varia and the multiple tool classes consist, by definition, of a number of perhaps unrelated tools and therefore do not, as a category, reveal useful information. The frequency counts discussed below do, however, show that we can make some observations related to temporal changes using the sidescrapers from the varia class and three of the heavy tool types.

In phase 1, representing the lowest levels of the Abu Hureyra 1 occupation, we find moderately high percentages of notches, scrapers, and geometric microliths, and low numbers of retouched pieces, nongeometric microliths, burins, backed pieces, truncations, and perforators. In phase 2 the percentages of notches, scrapers, and geometric microliths, as well as nongeometric microliths and retouched pieces, are moderately high. Other tool classes, backed pieces, perforators, burins, and truncations, occur less frequently. The tool classes in phase 3 show an emphasis on notches, retouched pieces, and geometric and nongeometric microliths. Other tool classes, including scrapers, backed pieces, truncations, perforators, and burins, are present in lesser frequencies.

CHIPPED STONE TOOL FREQUENCIES: CHANGES AND INTERPRETATIONS

Tool Classes

The data presented in table 6.1 facilitate an examination of the patterns of change and stability in certain tool classes through time. Most of the tool classes

Table 6.1 Changes in the Abu Hureyra 1 chipped stone tool assemblage from phase 1 through 3

	Phase 1		Phase 2		Phase 3	
Tool classes	N	%	N	%	N	%
Scrapers	96	21.8	326	16.6	334	10.9
Burins	35	7.9	118	6	180	5.9
Perforators	28	6.4	109	5.6	170	5.5
Backed pieces	31	7	162	8.2	277	9
Notches	113	25.7	396	20.2	621	20.3
Truncations	21	4.8	114	5.8	198	6.5
Nongeometrics	39	8.9	214	10.9	399	13
Geometrics	44	10	286	14.6	387	12.6
Retouched pieces	33	7.5	238	12.1	496	16.2
TOTAL	440		1963		3062	

show temporal change, with the strongest directional shift seen in the scrapers, retouched pieces, and nongeometric microliths. The percentages of burins, perforators, backed pieces, notches, and truncations also change. Finally, geometric microliths increase from phase 1 to phase 2 but then show a subsequent decline in relative frequency.

There is a steady decrease through time in the percentages of scrapers, but retouched pieces occur more often. Additional information obtained from changes in the percentages of sidescrapers (a member of the varia class) are also useful here. As seen in table 6.2, although sample size is small, sidescrapers increase from phase 2 to 3. While we cannot make definitive assessments concerning the meaning of such changes without extensive microwear analyses, which may suggest the actual uses to which chipped stone tools have been put, we can place at least two possible interpretations on these changes in frequencies.

The first is that the activities for which scrapers were used at Abu Hureyra 1 decreased in importance through time, while the activities represented by the production of retouched pieces and sidescrapers became more significant. According to this hypothesis, scrapers, retouched pieces, and sidescrapers would represent different sets of activities. We could also look at these trends as evidence of a change in the preference for a certain tool class or classes used to perform a particular set of activities. Thus, from this perspective retouched pieces and sidescrapers replace scrapers as the preferred tools for a given set of activities.

These two alternatives have quite different implications for the interpretation of the human behaviors that occurred at Abu Hureyra 1. The first suggests that the functions of the site that are reflected in the chipped stone tools changed through time. The second implies that functions may not have changed, but that the prehistoric inhabitants chose to perform certain activities with a set of tools that were more ad hoc in appearance (that is, the tools did not exhibit standardized forms or patterns of retouch as defined in archaeological typologies) and with tools that represented a "specialized" form of scraper. We can determine our preferred interpretation only with the aid of information from other studies, of the faunal and plant remains, for example, as well as the use of microwear analyses. However, since the chipped stone technologies at Abu Hureyra 1 were slow to change through time, and since new types of tools are not usually substituted for existing ones unless there is a change in activity orientation, it is likely that at least a partial change in site function occurred, as indicated by the plant remains (see chapter 12).

Within the microlithic tool class, there appears to be a general trend toward the production of more nongeometric microliths through time, while geometric microlith percentages fluctuate, increasing from phase 1 to 2 but decreasing from phase 2 to 3. One of the interesting features here, though, is the comparison between the two classes of microliths in each phase. Thus, in phases 1 and 2 geometric microliths are more prevalent than nongeometric microliths. However, in phase 3 both geometric and nongeometric microlith classes ex-

Table 6.2 Changes in the frequencies of sidescrapers from phase 1 to 3

	Phase 1	Phase 2	Phase 3
Total number of sidescrapers	8	35	76
Total number of tools	465	1981	3144
Percentage of sidescrapers to all tools	1.7	1.8	2.4

hibit virtually identical frequencies. Again, it is difficult to state with certainty what this pattern means in terms of prehistoric behavior, but it may relate to the use of microliths in general as components of arrowheads, since geometric forms are often thought to be the barbs and tips of arrows, as Anderson-Gerfaud (1983, pp. 81–84) has demonstrated for some of the Abu Hureyra 1 examples. Nongeometric forms, on the other hand, may be associated with the processing of plant foods (Byrd 1987, pp. 295–296).

Although the percentage changes through time for the tool classes of burins, perforators, notches, backed pieces, and truncations are relatively small, the directional changes have potentially interesting implications for behavioral changes at Abu Hureyra 1. Tool classes such as scrapers, burins, perforators, and notches are commonly thought to be associated with the processing of animal products. Scrapers could be used to work hides, perforators to punch holes in hides, notches to cut sinew and tendons, and burins to scrape bone (Büller 1983). At Abu Hureyra 1, all of these classes decrease through time. This may suggest a lessening emphasis on animal processing. Both backed pieces and truncations increase slightly throughout the sequence, but the association of these tools with particular activities is less clear.

Pit Structures

The phase 1 settlement is particularly interesting because of the presence of several pit structures in the area of the bank and bench, and in the subsoil at the bottom of Trench E. I have examined the chipped stone artifacts from these areas to ascertain the extent to which differences or similarities existed among the various pit structures themselves, and among the three pit complexes.

A comparison of the tool data from each pit structure does not reveal easily discernible differences (table 6.3). This is probably due in part to the small sample of tools from each pit structure, the range being from 15 to 68. For this particular table, levels 435 and 439 were combined since 435 overlies 439, and so were levels 472 and 475 because they were adjacent, interlocking pits that may have been part of the same structure. Pit level 473 was not included since it contained only two tools. Of the tool types not included in table 6.3, but which may be of some relevance, two sidescrapers were found in pit structure 435/439 of complex 3, and one axe and one gouge were identified from pit structure 469 of complex 2.

Table 6.3 The frequencies of tool classes from the pit structures of phase 1 at Abu Hureyra 1

	Levels 435, 439		Levels 472, 475		Level 469		Level 470		Level 471		Level 474	
Tool classes	N	%	N	%	N	%	N	%	N	%	N	%
Scrapers	9	18.4	4	19	15	39.5	13	19.1	1	6.7	3	20
Burins	3	6.1	1	4.8	0	0	6	8.8	3	20	1	6.7
Perforators	3	6.1	1	4.8	3	7.9	6	8.8	2	13.3	0	0
Backed pieces	2	4.1	2	9.5	2	5.3	6	8.8	0	0	1	6.7
Notches	15	30.6	8	38.1	9	23.7	16	23.5	5	33.3	4	26.6
Truncations	3	6.1	0	0	1	2.6	4	5.9	0	0	1	6.7
Nongeometrics	4	8.2	1	4.8	2	5.3	6	8.8	1	6.7	1	6.7
Geometrics	7	14.3	1	4.8	2	5.3	10	14.7	2	13.3	0	0
Retouched pieces	3	6.1	3	14.2	4	10.5	1	1.5	1	6.7	4	26.6
TOTAL	49		21		38		68		15		15	

Table 6.4 The frequencies of tool classes in pit complexes 1, 2, and 3

	Complex 1 Level 474		Complex 2 Levels 466, 469–473, 475		Complex 3 Levels 435, 439	
Tool classes	N	%	N	%	N	%
Scrapers	3	20	38	24.7	9	18.4
Burins	1	6.7	12	7.8	3	6.1
Perforators	0	0	12	7.8	3	6.1
Backed pieces	1	6.7	12	7.8	2	4.1
Notches	4	26.6	40	25.9	15	30.6
Truncations	1	6.7	5	3.2	3	6.1
Nongeometrics	1	6.7	11	7.1	4	8.2
Geometrics	0	0	14	9.1	7	14.3
Retouched pieces	4	26.6	10	6.5	3	6.1
TOTAL	15		154		49	

When we consider the pit complexes, we find several differences in the frequencies of the tool classes in complex 3 as opposed to those from complexes 1 and 2 (table 6.4). The pits in complexes 1 and 2 have a somewhat higher frequency of scrapers and fewer geometric microliths than the pit structure from complex 3. Overall, the pit structure from complex 3 is characterized by large numbers of notches, followed by scrapers and geometrics, while the complex 1 and 2 pit structures are represented by almost equal numbers of notches and scrapers, followed by geometric and nongeometric microliths.

Gouges, Axes, and Blunted Implements

The site contained very few heavy tool types of gouges, axes, and blunted implements overall, and therefore the sample sizes within each of the three phases are small. Despite this, we can see a shift through time in the frequencies of these types (table 6.5).

In phase 1, the earliest occupation, the number of these heavy tools is too small to assess. In phase 2, gouges are the most common of these heavy tools, followed by axes. Blunted implements are rare. By phase 3, axes have become the most common heavy tool, followed by blunted implements, but gouges are relatively few in number.

One possible explanation for this shift in the manufacture of these particular types of heavy tools is related to the use of the Euphrates River floodplain during the Epipalaeolithic period. The evidence from the macrobotanical analy-

Table 6.5 The frequencies of gouges, axes, and blunted implements from phase 1 to 3

	Phase 1		Phase 2		Phase 3	
Heavy tools	N	%	N	%	N	%
Axes	2	50.0	7	18.9	12	44.4
Gouges	2	50.0	15	40.5	4	14.8
Blunted implements	0	0	4	10.8	8	29.6
Fragments	0	0	11	29.7	3	11.1
TOTAL	4		37		27	

ses suggests that many of the floodplain plant food resources found in the Abu Hureyra 1 levels are ones that would have benefited from some clearance of the riverine forest. In addition, forest species in the riverine area were a fuel source. Thus, the increase in numbers of the axes through time may be tied to more intensive clearance of the valley floor. The forest species themselves may have been felled by other means, such as ringing or burning, with the axes perhaps used for trimming. In this context, the blunted implements may potentially be interpreted as exhausted or discarded axes that increased in frequency through time as the inhabitants of the village cleared more of the vegetation on the valley floor.

The decrease in the gouges through time may relate to the covering up of the subsoil bank and bench areas. Moore suggests in chapter 5 that some of these heavy tools (perhaps the gouge type) may have been used to dig the pits in the subsoil. As the cultural deposits gradually filled the pits and eventually covered the bank and bench, the need for these types of tools would have declined.

The morphology of the axes and the blunted implements suggests links to later Neolithic forms. The axes from Abu Hureyra 1 are similar to Neolithic chipped stone axes at Beidha (Kirkbride 1966, p. 37, figures 10.9, 10.10), for example. In addition, these chipped stone axes are probably related to some types of Neolithic polished stone axes, since only the manufacture of the bit end differs as, for example, at Mureybit (M.-C. Cauvin 1974, p. 62, figure 1.4).

The blunted implements from Abu Hureyra 1 share some similarities with the pick tool type, a rare form at Natufian Epipalaeolithic sites in the southern Levant, for example, at Mugharet el Wad (Garrod and Bate 1937, plates VIII: 3, X: 6), but also found in the Neolithic period, as at Beidha (Kirkbride 1966, p. 45, figure 16.1). However, the blunted implements from Abu Hureyra 1 have a bit that is characteristically less pointed than the picks from the Natufian Epipalaeolithic and from the Neolithic.

The gouge tool type at Abu Hureyra 1 is also reported from the early Natufian site of Wadi Hammeh 27 in Transjordan (information from Edwards; see also Edwards 1988, p. 313). My earlier suggestion (Olszewski 1984, p. 255–260; 1986a, p. 189) that the gouge might be analogous to the well-defined *erminette* from Mureybit (J. Cauvin 1972, p. 112, figure 2) no longer seems warranted. This is because the gouge usually has a distinct concavity on the bit end, while the *erminette* is flat for most of one surface and has a flared end.

Lunate Geometric Microliths

Lunates are the most frequent form of geometric microlith at Abu Hureyra 1. One attribute of lunates with temporal significance is the measurement of average lunate length (Bar-Yosef and Valla 1979; Valla 1981b, 1984). The lunates in the assemblages from each of the three phases of Abu Hureyra 1 follow the same chronological trend from longer to shorter average length through time, as at late Epipalaeolithic Natufian sites in the southern Levant. Table 6.6 summarizes the descriptive statistics relating to the lunates from each phase at Abu Hureyra 1. It shows that lunates from phases 1 and 2 are virtually identical, while those from phase 3 are significantly shorter.

Even though lunates on average become shorter through time at Abu Hureyra 1, the lunates from phase 3 are still considerably longer than those from contemporary Final Natufian sites in the southern Levant (25.4 vs. 13.2 mm). The

Table 6.6 Descriptive statistics of the lunates from Abu Hureyra 1

	Phase 1	Phase 2	Phase 3
N	21	143	155
Mean length (mm)	28.2	28.0	25.4
Variance	28.3	24.2	36.8
Standard deviation	5.32	4.92	6.06

Two-sample t-test for equality of Phase 2 and Phase 3 Means: p-value < .0001

Table 6.7 The number of lustered pieces from Abu Hureyra 1

Tool	Phase 1	Phase 2	Phase 3	Total
Complete lunates	2	9	8	19
Sickle blades	1	2	0	3
TOTAL	3	11	8	22

likeliest explanation for this persistence of long lunates relates to the manner in which animals were exploited at Abu Hureyra 1.

Anderson-Gerfaud's (1983, pp. 81–85) microwear analyses of lunates from Abu Hureyra 1 and Mureybit have suggested that long lunates were employed as transverse arrowheads while short ones served as arrow barbs or as arrowheads with one tip of the lunate as the arrow tip. If this is correct, then the lunate data from Abu Hureyra 1 indicate that transverse arrowheads were probably used most frequently, although lunate tip arrowheads were also made. Burin-like scars on the tips of some lunates support this interpretation. Experimental archaeology has shown that such scars can be produced by flint arrowhead breakage upon impact (Bergman and Newcomer 1983). On complete lunates from Abu Hureyra 1, the frequency of burin-like scars increases through time, occurring on 4.8% of the phase 1 lunates, on 14.7% of the phase 2 lunates, and on 16.8% of the phase 3 lunates.

Further support for a relatively conservative tradition in the techniques used to fashion arrows at Abu Hureyra 1 is found in the faunal evidence. The primary animal hunted at Abu Hureyra 1 was the gazelle. There are no indications that this changed significantly through time. Thus, with little if any change in the hunting pattern, it is reasonable that the actual tools used underwent few changes.

Lunates were probably infrequently mounted in composite knives to cut plants high in silica content, such as reeds, since only 19 (5.9%) of 319 complete lunates from Abu Hureyra 1 had traces of a visible polish (table 6.7). This represents a minimum figure, because only complete lunates were closely examined for gloss, and it was not possible to examine all the broken lunates in detail. The gloss on these lunates does not approach the high polish found on Epipalaeolithic and Neolithic sickle blades, so they cannot have been used for very long.

Obsidian Artifacts

The levels at Abu Hureyra 1 contained a few chipped stone artifacts of obsidian. Table 6.8 shows the distribution of these by phase. The obsidian was most

Table 6.8 The number of obsidian artifacts from Abu Hureyra 1

	Phase 1	Phase 2	Phase 3	Total
Obsidian pieces	1	10	31	42
Total assemblage	8,351	35,510	55,496	99,357
Percentage of obsidian in total assemblage	0.01	0.02	0.05	0.04

common in phase 3 and occurred at lower percentages in the two earlier phases. There are two possible explanations for the presence of the obsidian in Abu Hureyra 1 levels.

One interpretation would be that the obsidian was intrusive from the overlying Abu Hureyra 2 levels. Obsidian use during the Neolithic period in the Levant is well documented, and obsidian was imported by the people of Abu Hureyra 2. Some of the obsidian artifacts in the Abu Hureyra 1 levels were struck using manufacturing techniques characteristic of later periods, for example, pressure flaking to make blades. Others, however, are more ambiguous in technique and form. The percentages of obsidian in the three phases (table 6.8) are quite low, and phase 3, immediately below the Abu Hureyra 2 levels, is precisely that which has the largest frequency of obsidian.

We could also suggest that the obsidian found in the Abu Hureyra 1 levels, except for a few pieces that may be intrusive from Abu Hureyra 2, is potential evidence for the earliest known use of obsidian in the Levant. The north Syrian area where Abu Hureyra 1 is located is closer than most of the other Levantine Epipalaeolithic sites to the obsidian sources in the Konya Plain and the Lake Van region of Anatolia. It might be expected, therefore, that some of the earliest use of obsidian would be found in this region. The increase through time of obsidian at Abu Hureyra 1 may reflect increased contact with Anatolia as the transition to the Neolithic way of life took place.

ABU HUREYRA 1 AND THE MIDDLE EUPHRATES

The chipped stone assemblage information of Abu Hureyra 1 can best be compared to the data from the Epipalaeolithic occupations of Mureybit phase Ia; Nahr el-Homr Test C, Levels 2–4; and Dibsi Faraj East. All four sites share in common a location along the Euphrates River.

The excavations at Mureybit (J. Cauvin 1972, 1974, 1978) revealed a late Epipalaeolithic occupation in phase Ia. Radiocarbon dates from this context place phase Ia at about 10,250 BP or slightly later (M.-C. Cauvin 1980, p. 17). Thus, phase Ia appears to be contemporary with phase 3 at Abu Hureyra 1. Similar tool classes are found at both sites, but we cannot yet make complete descriptive statistical comparisons, since only preliminary data on the tools from Mureybit have been reported.

One of the major similarities between Abu Hureyra 1 phase 3 and Mureybit phase Ia is the dominance of the lunate microlith in the geometric microlith class. However, unlike the relatively long lunates from Abu Hureyra 1, those from Mureybit average 15 mm in length (M.-C. Cauvin 1980, p. 13). It is not clear if this average length is representative, since sample size is very small, with only 26 lunates reported for phase Ia by Calley (1986, p. 372). Other tools common to both sites are perforators, burins, retouched pieces, denticulated pieces, and scrapers. Mureybit is also noted for the presence of drills of the *mèche de foret* type, *erminettes*, microperforators—although Calley's data (1986, p. 372) would indicate that these are few in number—rare sickle blades, and a few picks.

From the partial tool data presented by Calley (1986, p. 372), we can contrast a few tool classes from Mureybit phase Ia and Abu Hureyra phase 3. The total number of tools from Mureybit is 215, from Abu Hureyra 3,240. Geometric microliths are similar in frequency from both sites, with 12% at Mureybit and 11.9% at Abu Hureyra. The percentages of microperforators are also similar, with 2.7% at Mureybit and 1.7% at Abu Hureyra. Flake scrapers are more common at Abu Hureyra (9.2%) than at Mureybit (3.7%). The largest difference is in the comparison of the nongeometric microlith class. At Mureybit these account for 39% of the tools, while at Abu Hureyra they comprise only 12.3%. Thus, it does appear that some different sorts of activities occurred at the two sites. The presence of numerous nongeometric microliths at Mureybit might indicate a greater emphasis on plant food processing. The small average size of the lunates from Mureybit suggests that different forms of arrows were manufactured at the two sites, with perhaps a lesser emphasis on transverse arrowheads at Mureybit. This may be related to differences in faunal exploitation at the two sites, with onager a major species at Mureybit (J. Cauvin 1972, p. 108) and gazelle at Abu Hureyra.

Another site that has yielded deposits that may be contemporary with Mureybit and Abu Hureyra 1 phase 3 is Nahr el-Homr. The chipped stone tools from Levels 2–4 in Test Pit C at Nahr el-Homr have been likened to those from Mureybit phase Ib (Boerma and Roodenberg 1977, p. 16). Like their contemporaries at Mureybit, the inhabitants of Nahr el-Homr preferred to hunt onager (Clason and Buitenhuis 1978, p. 82).

The chipped stone assemblage from Nahr el-Homr Test C has some similarities with that of Abu Hureyra 1 phase 3. Both sites have yielded relatively low percentages of scrapers, burins, perforators, and backed pieces and relatively high frequencies of retouched pieces, notches (denticulates), and nongeometric microliths (Boerma and Roodenberg 1977, p. 15, figure 6). However, there are three distinct differences: the presence of peduncular points, Helwan lunates, and a very low percentage of geometric microliths at Nahr el-Homr.

Peduncular points are found in Mureybit phase Ib (J. Cauvin 1974, p. 47), and this may indicate that the Nahr el-Homr Epipalaeolithic assemblage from Test C is slightly later in date than phase 3 at Abu Hureyra 1. Further support for a date very late in the Epipalaeolithic sequence for Nahr el-Homr comes from the fact that both scrapers and geometric microliths occur in lower frequencies here than in Abu Hureyra 1 phase 3. That would be a continuation of the temporal trend of fewer scrapers and an increased ratio of nongeometric to geometric microliths through time that occurs at Abu Hureyra 1.

The only puzzling contradiction for placing Nahr el-Homr late in the Epipalaeolithic, or as a transitional industry leading to the early Neolithic, is the presence of a few Helwan lunates. The Helwan style of backing retouch is a well-known marker for Epipalaeolithic assemblages dating to the twelfth millennium BP in the southern Levant (Bar-Yosef and Valla 1979). The character of the Nahr el-Homr assemblage does not suggest that these Helwan lunates are twelfth millennium in date. Therefore, either they are intrusive or Helwan retouch does not have the same temporal significance in the northern Levant as it does farther south. Helwan retouch is not found at Mureybit, Abu Hureyra 1, or Dibsi Faraj East, although it has been reported from undated late Epipalaeolithic contexts in central and southern Syria (figure 6.11), for example, at El Kum

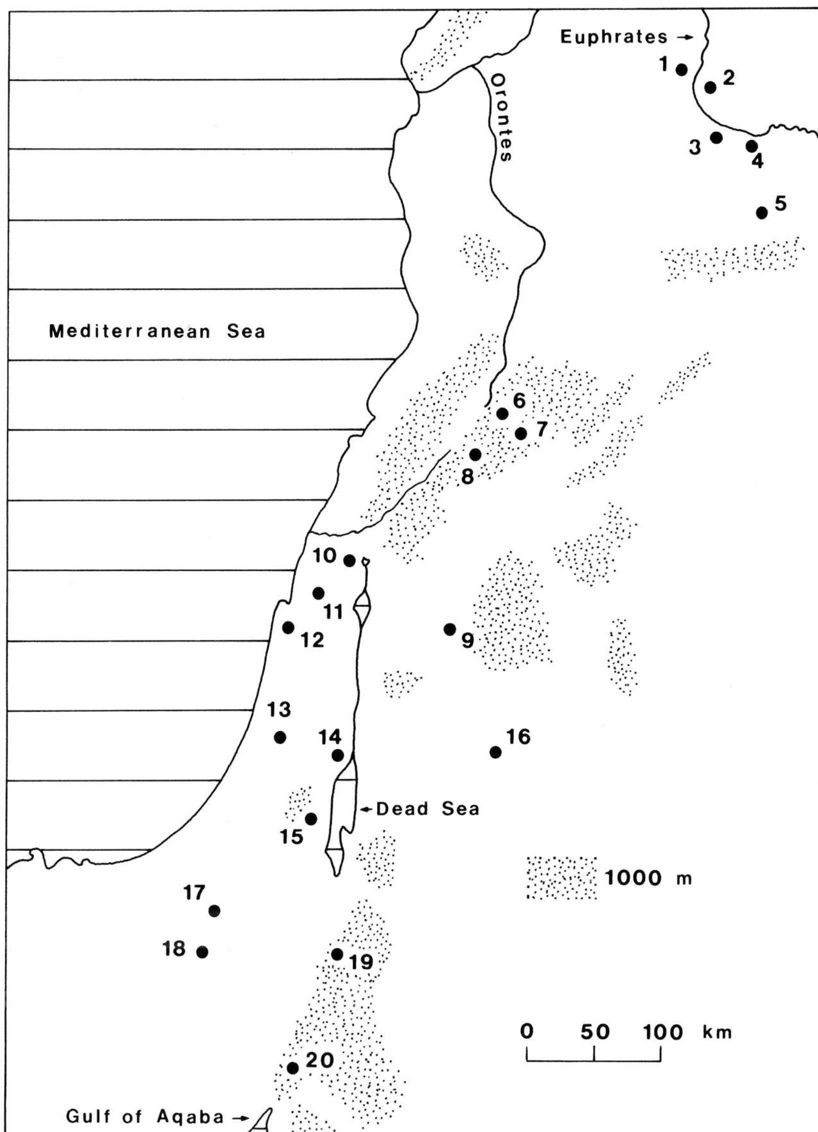

Figure 6.11 Selected Levantine Late Epipalaeolithic sites. 1, Nahr el-Homr; 2, Mureybit; 3, Dibsi Faraj East; 4, Abu Hureyra; 5, El Kum area; 6, Yabrud; 7, Bahret el Mallaha area; 8, Qornet Rharra; 9, Taibe; 10, Ain Mallaha; 11, Hayonim Cave, Hayonim Terrace; 12, Nahal Oren, Mugharet el-Wad, Kebara; 13, Shukbah; 14, Jericho; 15, El Khiam; 16, Black Desert 14/7; 17, Rosh Zin; 18, Rosh Horesha; 19, Beidha, 20, Wadi Judayid J2, Wadi Humeima J406a.

(J. Cauvin et al. 1979; M.-C. Cauvin 1981a), Yabrud III (Rust 1950), Qornet Rharra (Contenson 1966), Taibe (M.-C. Cauvin 1973), and along the shores of the ancient lake of Bahret el Mallaha (M.-C. Cauvin et al. 1982).

The final Euphrates River site with late Epipalaeolithic remains is Dibsi Faraj East, where Wilkinson and Moore collected chipped stone artifacts from the surface. The assemblage from this site bears a close resemblance to that from Abu Hureyra 1, both in types of tools and in the technology of blank production (Wilkinson and Moore 1978, pp. 29–36; Olszewski 1986a, pp. 215–218). The character of the Dibsi Faraj East assemblage and the presence of very long lunates (average 30.3 mm) suggest that the occupation here was probably earlier than those of Nahr el-Homr, Mureybit phases Ia and b, and phase 3 at Abu Hureyra 1. The percentage of scrapers at Dibsi Faraj East (12.8%) is similar to that of phase 3 at Abu Hureyra 1 (10.9%), and retouched pieces are likewise relatively frequent at both sites. However, Dibsi Faraj East has an elevated percentage of geometric microliths (25.6%) that is not paralleled at Abu Hureyra 1. This may be because surface collectors notice long lunate microliths easily.

The late Epipalaeolithic northern Levantine sites of Abu Hureyra 1, Mureybit phase Ia, Nahr el-Homr, and Dibsi Faraj East share a similar range of chipped stone tools. The differences noted among these sites seem to be largely chronological and may reflect changed emphases in site activities through time. Some of the differences may also be related to specific tasks—for example, the high frequency of nongeometric microliths at Mureybit—or forms of tools related to the animals characteristic of each location, perhaps the use of transverse arrowheads at Abu Hureyra 1 and other forms of arrowheads at Mureybit.

The chronological sequence of these four sites appears at present to be the following: phases 1 and 2 at Abu Hureyra 1, with the occupation at Dibsi Faraj East occurring not later than phase 2 at Abu Hureyra 1; phase 3 at Abu Hureyra 1, which may be partially contemporary with phase Ia at Mureybit; and finally the occupations at Nahr el-Homr and Mureybit phase Ib. This means that phases 1 and 2 at Abu Hureyra 1 are, to date, our only extensive record of the earlier portion of the late Epipalaeolithic sequence of settlement along the Euphrates River.

ABU HUREYRA 1 AND THE LEVANT

One way to assess the assemblage from Abu Hureyra 1 is to see to what extent it represents generalized patterns of chipped stone tool use common in the Levant during the late Epipalaeolithic period. A second is to consider the specific differences that separate it from other Levantine late Epipalaeolithic collections.

Previous analyses using major tool classes, such as scrapers, burins, perforators, and the like, all of which are present at the sites used in the studies, have discerned some correlations between particular tool groups and either environment (Henry 1973, 1977) or environment and locational context (Olszewski 1986a, 1988). These associations seem valid for both southern and northern Levantine sites.

These correlations may be briefly summarized as follows. Open air steppic sites, such as Abu Hureyra 1, Rosh Zin (Henry 1976), Black Desert 14/7 (Betts 1982), and others (figure 6.11), are characterized by high frequencies of notches (denticulates), perforators (borers), and in some cases geometric microliths (Byrd 1987). Sites in the Mediterranean forest, for example, Nahal Oren (Valla 1975b) and Hayonim Terrace (Henry and Leroi-Gourhan 1976), are distinguished by high percentages of nongeometric microliths. Mugharet el Wad (Garrod and Bate 1937) and Shukbah (Garrod 1942) also probably have high counts of nongeometric microliths, since recent reanalysis by Valla and colleagues (1986) and Olszewski and Barton (1990) have corrected the earlier perception that geometric microliths were common at these two sites. Scrapers and burins appear, at present, to be markers of specialized activity sites in both the steppe and Mediterranean forest, as at Hayonim Cave (Bar-Yosef and Tchernov 1966) and El Khiam (Gonzalez-Echegaray 1966).

Lunates also exhibit trends characteristic of the entire Levantine region during this period. Studies of lunate length and retouch type in assemblages from the Natufian core area in the southern Levant have shown these to be valuable indicators of the place in time (Garrod 1932, p. 261; Bar-Yosef and Valla 1979; Valla 1981b, 1984; Valla et al. 1986) and environmental setting (Olszewski 1986b) of the sites concerned. The research at Abu Hureyra 1 and elsewhere has shown that decrease in average lunate length through time is also typical of the northern Levant, although it is not possible to use Helwan retouch as a time marker here, since this technique has not been recorded from radiocarbon-dated contexts in this region.

These generalized patterns of chipped stone tool use in the Levant between about 12,500 and 10,000 BP suggest that the hunting, gathering, and collecting strategies appropriate to particular environmental settings and site locations were widespread in the Levant. It is not, however, necessarily appropriate to regard these generalized patterns as symptomatic of a correspondingly widespread chipped stone industrial complex, or of the presence of a "homogeneous" Natufian culture, as is sometimes claimed (M.-C. Cauvin 1980; Henry 1983, p. 150). This is because when we examine the technology of manufacture and the tool blank types in chipped stone assemblages from the southern and northern Levant, we find several important features that separate the industries of these two areas. Perhaps the most significant of these is the utilization of a core reduction strategy centered on the production of flakes in the northern Levant, and on the manufacture of blade/bladelets in the southern Levant (Olszewski 1988). This carries over into the types of blanks selected for tools, with tools on blade/bladelets far more frequent in the southern Levant, as at Beidha (Byrd 1988), Rosh Zin (Henry 1976), and Rosh Horesha (Marks and Larson 1977), and tools on flakes more common in the northern Levant, as at Abu Hureyra 1. Extensive debitage studies that have only recently become available contribute much to our understanding of these processes in both the northern and the southern Levant (Calley, 1984, 1986; Valla 1984).

We can also find smaller, but perhaps no less significant, differences in certain tool types and temporal trends. The presence of gouge, axe, and blunted heavy tools in the northern Levant and of *lames à machure*, picks, and massive scrapers, denticulates, and notches in the southern Levant (Henry 1981, pp. 422–423) suggests that some different activities occurred in these two regions.

Furthermore, despite the temporal trend toward shorter lunate lengths at Abu Hureyra 1, lunates in phase 3 are considerably longer (table 6.6) than lunates from contemporary Final Natufian assemblages in both the forest/coastal and the steppic areas of the southern Levant (see data in Valla 1981b, table 7; Olszewski 1986b). While the lunates reported from Mureybit by M.-C. Cauvin (1980, p. 13) are not as long as those from Abu Hureyra 1 phase 3, they are longer than their southern Levantine counterparts.

Thus, from this second perspective of the differences between chipped stone assemblages from the Natufian area of the southern Levant and the Middle Euphrates region in the north, we may consider these two regions to be different interaction spheres. This is not to ignore, however, the possibility that cultural contact also occurred between groups in the northern and southern Levant. It is unfortunate that comparable data of this time period from Anatolia immediately to the north and upper Mesopotamia to the east of the Middle Euphrates are at present lacking, since there may have been communication and contact among sites in all three regions. It is clear, however, that we must regard the northern Levant as a distinct region during the late Epipalaeolithic period, one which cannot be labeled Natufian.

SUMMARY

The chipped stone assemblage from Abu Hureyra 1 spans a millennium and a half during the period generally known as the late Epipalaeolithic. This assemblage documents several changes in the types of chipped stone tools used that probably relate both to changes in activites over time and to shifts in the preferences for certain tools to perform the same sorts of tasks. As the only stratified site in the northern Levant with such a considerable time depth, Abu Hureyra 1 is our sole record of the processes of change leading to the development of Neolithic forms of stone tools, as well as other attributes related to changes in food procurement activities and social organization.

The prehistoric people who occupied Abu Hureyra 1 during this period shared certain generalized patterns of chipped stone tool use with the inhabitants of sites in the southern Levant. However, differences in the technology of tool blank production and in certain types and temporal trends of stone tools suggest that the northern and southern Levant were distinct regions during this period. The chipped stone industry of Abu Hureyra 1 may have been more closely allied to others in Anatolia or upper Mesopotamia, or they may reflect a localized Middle Euphrates grouping that included Nahr el-Homr, Mureybit, and Dibsi Faraj East.

The Bone Artifacts

S. L. OLSEN

There are 453 pieces of worked bone from the Epipalaeolithic and Neolithic levels at Abu Hureyra. Of these, 96 are from Abu Hureyra 1 and the remainder are from Abu Hureyra 2 (table 6.9). This is the third largest collection of prehistoric bone artifacts from Southwest Asia, after Jarmo (Watson 1983) and Jericho (Marshall 1982). The results from the analysis of the Abu Hureyra bone artifacts are generally similar to those obtained from other sites in the Levant during these time periods. There is remarkable consistency in the composition of the collection through time, with most of the common types occurring throughout the deposits. The only distinct difference between the Abu Hureyra 1 and 2 assemblages is the complete disappearance of bone bipoints at the close of Abu Hureyra 1. This matches the findings from other sites in the Levant. Other minor differences in the presence or absence of types between Abu Hureyra 1 and 2 may be partly due to the smaller size of the sample from Abu Hureyra 1, where rare types may simply fail to be represented.

The Abu Hureyra collection of worked bone provides an excellent basis for comparisons with other Epipalaeolithic and Neolithic assemblages from the Levant. It is important to accumulate substantial information from such larger settlements so that we can reliably compare smaller samples from other sites and establish significant differences between time periods and geographic areas.

The Abu Hureyra artifact surfaces are extremely well preserved considering their age, a consequence of the relative aridity of the region in recent millennia. Taphonomic processes such as root etching, animal gnawing, and weathering have had little effect on the interpretation of microscopic manufacturing and use-wear traces. Despite excellent surface preservation, the bone artifacts are very fragile, and some have been damaged in the soil, hampering quantitative analysis and classification in many cases.

METHODS

I analyzed the bone artifacts from Abu Hureyra in a number of ways to glean as much information as possible from the material. I examined micro- and

Table 6.9 The bone artifacts from Abu Hureyra 1 by type and taxon (total 96)

Bone tool types	*Aves*	Mammal	Ruminant	*Gazella*	*Ovis/Capra*	*Bos/Equus*	*Equus*
Bipoint		14					
Flat implement						1	
Utilized splinter		1		2			
Needle		2					
Needle or pin		7					
Awl fragments		37	2				
Splinter awl	1	5					
Plain-based awl			1				
Awl with articular base			10	5			1
Tooth pendant		1					
Miscellaneous worked bone		2					
Debitage				3	1		
TOTAL	1	69	13	10	1	1	1

macroscopic traces on their surfaces, conducted experiments to replicate the artifacts, and analyzed their distribution. Then I combined the information gained with studies of the forms of the artifacts to reconstruct their techniques of manufacture and to decipher their function wherever possible.

For each artifact, I measured its length and width; described its form and drew it; recorded zoological information such as the taxon, element, and portion of element used; described cultural modifications such as manufacturing traces, use wear, and burning; and noted taphonomic alterations. I examined each artifact with a stereomicroscope, and I then studied examples of particular surface traces with a scanning electron microscope.

The predominance of long, narrow, pointed objects in most bone artifact collections obliges the analyst to establish quantitative, as well as qualitative, means of distinguishing between the different types. Many factors make it difficult to define the shape of the functional end of a tool with a concise set of measurements. Tips may range in cross section from triangular to round, ovate, lenticular, concavo-convex, rectangular, or irregular. The cross section changes as one progresses from the tip upward along the shaft, so where the measurement is taken is very important. A combination of factors, such as the bone selected for raw material, the method and amount of manufacturing employed, the tool function, and the amount of use and resharpening may contribute to the final form in a manner that renders each implement unique.

I established a method of standardizing the tip measurements by using a small metric board with an upright piece at one end, against which the tip of an artifact could be abutted. Tip width and thickness measurements were taken from the plane that passed through the object transversely 5 mm from the end. The widest part of the tip was first measured with sliding calipers, and the artifact was then turned 90° so the thickness measurement could be taken.

The metric analysis I conducted on the Abu Hureyra specimens showed general trends among the tool types but did not distinguish groups solely on proportions or absolute size. While I used size, cross section, and general morphology to distinguish tool types, no single group of measurements established distinct classes of objects. Use-wear traces often helped me to assign a function to a particular artifact, but there were still a few objects that were marginal and difficult to place under a single typological heading, particularly if they were fragmentary.

MANUFACTURING TECHNIQUES FOR THE BONE ARTIFACTS

All of the manufacturing techniques used at Abu Hureyra were known in Southwest Asia by the Upper Palaeolithic and were fully represented in the Abu Hureyra 1 collection. The most basic manufacturing technique employed at the site consisted of simply shattering bone with a hammerstone and collecting long, narrow splinters for use without further modification. Utilized splinters are recognizable as artifacts because of the wear at one end, rather than by any evidence of manufacture.

The inhabitants did use more sophisticated techniques, especially annular and longitudinal grooving and snapping. The groove-and-snap technique (Olsen 1984) is the most efficient means of cutting out a blank of precise size and shape with minimum waste and effort. The groove is begun by making a scratch along the surface that is gradually deepened and widened by repeated strokes back and forth (figure 6.12). Experiments have shown that a flint borer rather than a burin or blade is the most effective tool for grooving. Within the groove, the walls are marred by fine, parallel striations created by irregularities in the stone tool's cutting edge. When the groove is of sufficient depth (usually three quarters through the thickness of the bone) to ensure that the blank will be snapped free along the designated outline, force is applied and a crack is opened within the groove. The products of this technique are the artifact blank and the debitage, or offcuts, which are usually discarded. Artifacts from Abu Hureyra 1 showing traces of this technique include awls and flat implements. The bipoints, needles, and pins were probably also begun with the groove-and-snap technique, although the characteristic marks would have been obliterated by final scraping. Unfinished grooved pieces and bone manufacturing debitage discarded after grooving and snapping were recovered from Abu Hureyra 1.

Incising was used in a minor way on awl handles, either as a simple form of decoration or to improve the user's grip. It was probably done in the same manner as grooving, except that the incised lines are narrower and shallower than grooves that were to be snapped in making a tool.

The most prominent manufacturing traces on finished artifacts were those created by scraping with a flint implement. Over half of the tool types and the majority of actual artifacts displayed some traces of scraping. The edges and tips of awls and the entire surfaces of the bipoints, needles, and pins were scraped. Scraping may be performed with flint flakes or scrapers, but experi-

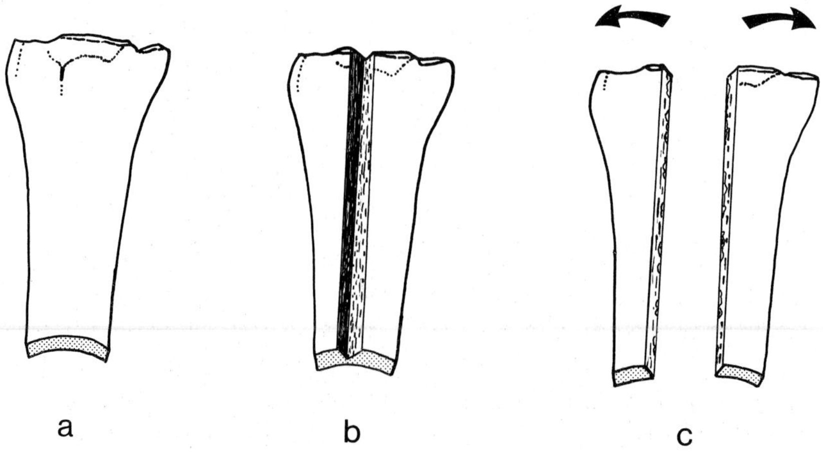

Figure 6.12 The groove and snap technique. a, the clean bone at the start of work. b, a longitudinal groove is cut into the bone with a flint piercer. c, the bone is split in two parts along the groove.

ments show that the edge of a burin is far more effective in removing material. By using a burin to scrape modern bone to replicate artifacts, I succeeded in recreating striae similar to those seen on bone artifacts from Abu Hureyra (figure 6.13). The characteristic traces consist of wavy, parallel striations with accompanying transverse ripples or chattermarks.

A few artifacts displayed traces of grinding or abrading that were applied during manufacture. Specimens bearing the characteristic striations associated with abrading include the base of a needle and bases of some of the awls.

Figure 6.13 Scanning electron microscope photographs of wear traces on bone artifacts. a, awl tip showing surface scraping; b, modern bone experimentally scraped with a flint tool.

Drilling was used to make an eye in the base of a needle and a perforation in the tooth pendant. Biconical drilling with a flint drill was employed in both cases.

The eye of another needle was made by carefully gouging a longitudinal trough on both flat surfaces of the base until the centers of the gouge marks met to form a small perforation. There may be many reasons why this technique seems to have been preferred over drilling. To drill a very small perforation biconically on a narrow surface requires considerable skill and patience. On an unfinished needle from Abu Hureyra 2, the hole was drilled too close to one edge, so as it was deepened, the perforation expanded over to the margin of the needle and broke through. With gouging, which is a slow, gradual process, it is easier to control the centering of the perforation. The most obvious advantage of gouging a perforation is that a trough is formed on either side of the perforation, similar to the eye of a modern needle. When the hole is drilled rather than gouged, the thread has to make a sharp bend as it emerges from the eye. This causes the thread to drag through the cloth during sewing and break some of its fibers. The trough formed by gouging, on the other hand, accommodates the thread so that it can lie next to the needle and avoid catching on the cloth.

THE BONE ARTIFACT TYPES

The bone artifacts from Abu Hureyra 1 are listed by type and taxon in table 6.9. All of these types, except bipoints, also occur in the Abu Hureyra 2 levels.

The bipoints from Abu Hureyra 1 demonstrate great continuity with the Upper Palaeolithic, as witnessed in the fine array of bone and antler points from Ksar Akil (Newcomer 1974). At Abu Hureyra the points are made of bone rather than antler. Like those made on bone at Ksar Akil, the points at Abu Hureyra are round in cross section rather than lenticular or flattened. Unfortunately, breakage of one or both ends has made measuring and determination of form very difficult, but it seems that most of the artifacts are either bipoints or at least have a tapered base. Some are so finely pointed at both ends that it is difficult to distinguish between the base and tip (figure 6.14b), but on three of the specimens the tapered base has a small truncation formed by the failure to completely sharpen it during manufacture. The largest and one of the best preserved examples still bears traces of annular grooving and snapping at the base (figure 6.14c).

Only four of the points are complete enough to allow a range of measurements to be taken. The location of the maximum width on the shaft tends to be near the midpoint, since both ends are tapered. The tips of the bipoints are round in cross section and are similar in dimensions, measuring between 3 and 3.5 mm in diameter.

All of the points exhibit striations and often chattermarks, typical of tools shaped by longitudinal scraping, over their entire surface. How their blanks were formed is not clear because of the lack of unfinished pieces and other manufacturing traces on completed specimens. The maximum diameter is large enough to indicate that the thick cortical walls of the diaphyses of long bones from cattle, equids, or equally large mammals were used.

The absence of antler points at Abu Hureyra is quite significant. Antler, especially when presoaked, is easier to work than dense bone. Experiments have shown that antler is more resilient and therefore less likely to break on impact

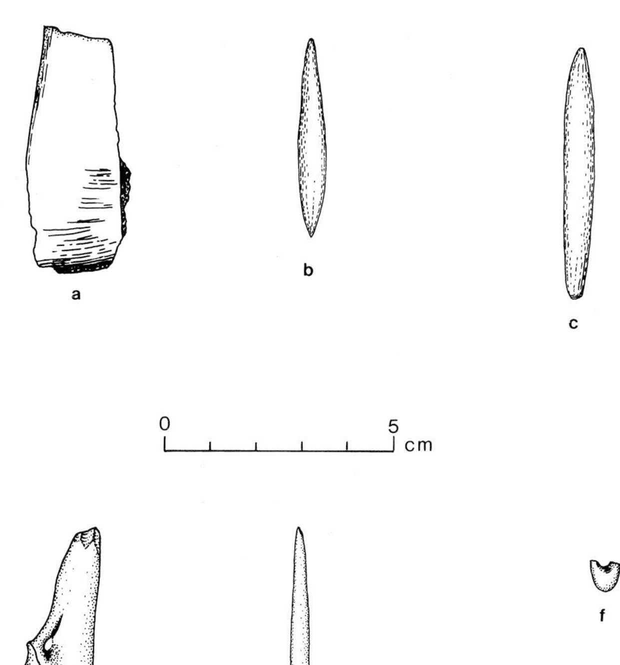

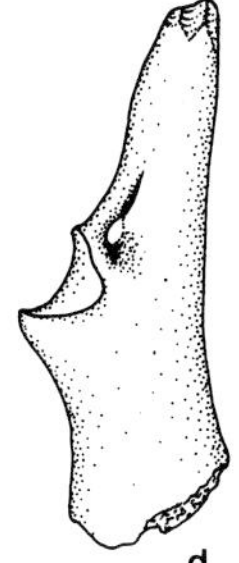

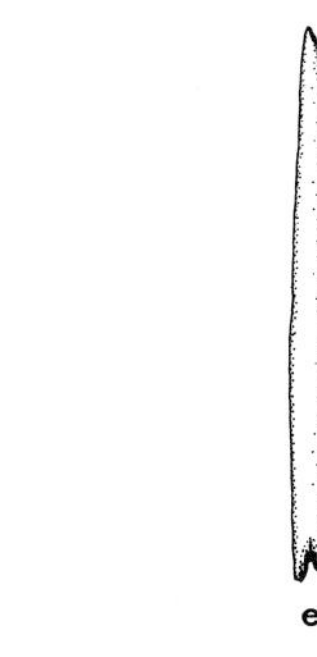

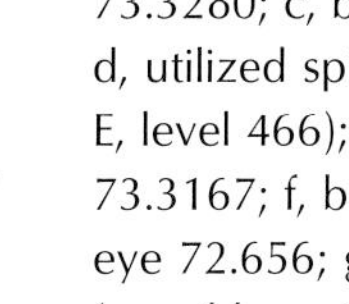

Figure 6.14 Examples of bone artifacts. a, flat implement fragment (Trench E, level 419); b, bipoint 73.3280; c, bipoint with truncated base 73.3284; d, utilized splinter made on a gazelle ulna (Trench E, level 466); e, needle with eye made by gouging 73.3167; f, basal fragment of a needle with drilled eye 72.656; g, root of a drilled tooth pendant (possibly a pig or wild boar incisor) 73.3446.

(Albrecht 1977; MacGregor and Currey 1983). The fact that there are relatively few pieces of worked antler in the site and that all projectile points are made of postcranial bone is probably related to availability. Unworked deer bone and antler are not common at Abu Hureyra, and it appears that populations of gazelles, sheep, cattle, and small equids were much more plentiful than any of the cervids in the vicinity of the site (chapter 13).

Seven of the points have damage at their tips that may have been caused by use. This consists of slight inward crushing of the tip in one case and the removal of a narrow flake from the tip to between 2 and 5 mm up the shaft in the remaining six. Experiments shooting bone- and antler-tipped arrows into a sheep carcass and a lamb shoulder demonstrate that breakage of this kind may occur during impact with a resistant surface (Olsen 1984; Arndt and Newcomer 1986). Although there is no indication whether the ancient breakage happened when the point hit its intended target or the ground, the high incidence of this pattern in the small collection from Abu Hureyra 1 supports the argument that bipoints were used as tips of projectiles. The small size of the points would imply that they were used to tip arrows rather than spears.

Bipoints are well documented at numerous Natufian sites, including Kebara and Mugharet el Wad on Mount Carmel, Erq el Ahmar in Judea, Hayonim and Ain Mallaha in Galilee, and at Mureybit near Abu Hureyra (Stordeur 1979).

Flat implements are far more plentiful in Abu Hureyra 2, but their complete morphology and function are still poorly understood. They are generally made on split ribs or long-bone diaphyses of large animals like cattle or asses. Their thin edges are often smoothed by grinding or scraping. Use wear consists of a light polishing along the edges. The high frequency of charring (50%) of these knife-like tools from Abu Hureyra 2 levels may indicate that they were used in cooking.

Only one example of a flat implement (figure 6.14a) was found in Abu Hureyra 1. This consists of a section of rib from *Bos taurus* or *Equus* sp. that had been grooved and snapped transversely at one end but was broken at the other. Light use polish could be seen along the edge near the broken end.

Some tools were made simply by breaking a bone with a hammerstone and removing an appropriate splinter. What distinguishes these utilized splinters as tools is the concentration of polish and transverse striations at one end. The distribution of polish primarily on the outer convex surface suggests that these tools were used to burnish, smooth, or flatten soft materials like plant fibers or animal hides.

Two splinters, one from a large mammal long bone and one from a gazelle metatarsal, bore traces of polish and light transverse striations on the convex outer bone surface at one end. A gazelle ulna (figure 6.14d) also bore polish at the broken end of the shaft and partially up its edges, suggesting that it was used briefly. The olecranon process at the proximal end would have served as the handle.

The shafts or tips of seven needles or pins, all made on mammalian bone, were collected from Abu Hureyra 1 levels. A nearly complete needle shaft (figure 6.14e), missing only the tip and a portion of the base above the eye, was also recovered. This fine specimen was shaped by longitudinal scraping, and the perforation was made by means of bifacial gouging. The basal end of a fairly large needle (figure 6.14f) had part of a biconically drilled eye with a diameter of about 3 mm.

There are three basic kinds of awls from Abu Hureyra, differentiated on the basis of their form and technique of manufacture rather than differences in function. These are splinter awls, plain-based awls, and awls with articular ends as bases. The most important variation among them seems to be the amount of time and effort allotted to their manufacture. There is a range of sizes of tips within each of the three categories of awls, but no significant difference among the groups. The predominant form of tip in each case is round in cross section and measures between 1 and 3.5 mm in diameter.

Awls may serve as piercing instruments in a variety of tasks. The most common ethnographic uses are for perforating hides and for weaving coiled baskets. Despite the difficulty of proving that hides were sewn at Abu Hureyra, the large number of animal bones from the site indicates they were readily available. Woven materials have been indirectly preserved through impressions in bitumen and plaster, while wear marks on the teeth of individuals from the Abu Hureyra 2 settlement show they made baskets (Molleson 1994, p. 74).

Since the tips of awls were sharpened by scraping, the most consistent traces at the working ends are longitudinal striations and chattermarks formed during manufacture. Frequently, the manufacturing marks are partially obliterated from the end of the tip to a distance of a few millimeters up the shaft by use polish. In experiments this polish has been recreated on tools used in both basket weaving and hide piercing. In a few cases from Abu Hureyra, excessive attrition has caused a sharp reduction in the diameter of the tip, forming a shoulder between the shaft and the point. The length of the tip below the shoulder is thus likely to give a good indication of the depth of penetration of the awl during use. Occasionally, a series of concentric striations appears around the tip that suggests the awl was rotated as it bored into a material. The microcutting of the fine scratches in the tip's surface may have been caused by particles in the substance on which the awl was used, or simply by loose grit.

That breakage was common during use is evident from the fact that some of the awls from Abu Hureyra have considerable polish overlying fractured surfaces. Two kinds of fractures are represented with high frequency. The first, a clean transverse break occurring at right angles to the implement's upper and lower surfaces, is found on all types of tools and at various locations on their shafts. Straight transverse breaks often occurred after the artifacts were discarded because much of the organic matrix of the bone became denatured or dehydrated. These do not show evidence of reuse on their fracture surfaces.

The second kind of breakage pattern I define as "impact fracture" because it happens when the tip of an awl meets a resistant body with sufficient force to drive a flake off the end. Although this may include accidents, such as dropping the awl with the point downward, as well as use, it is less likely that impact fractures will occur once the tool has been incorporated in archaeological deposits. It is on this type of fracture that use polish is sometimes found.

Six awls were made on fortuitous splinters, one from a bird bone and the others from mammalian long bones (figure 6.15a). These were modified simply by scraping the tip to a point. The faces and edges of the shafts are unaltered.

Only one shaped awl (73.3351) from Abu Hureyra 1 had a plain base without an articular surface. This specimen, made on a ruminant metapodial, was unfortunately broken into five pieces, but the rounded base and delicate tip are both intact. The tool was made by longitudinal grooving-and-snapping and scraping. The base was probably shaped by grinding. Plain-based awls differ from splinter awls in having edges that were shaped by the groove-and-snap technique, scraping, or abrading.

Fourteen awls were made on small ruminant metapodials that were split sagittally but retained the proximal articular end as the base (figure 6.15c). Three of these (73.3192; two from Trench E level 441) have deeply incised lines on the shaft near the basal end, perhaps to improve the grip by roughening the surface or, in the case of 73.3192, as decoration. Incidentally, the point end of 73.3192 had been chewed by a carnivore, presumably one of the dogs kept by the inhabitants. Another awl retained the whole distal condyle as the base (figure 6.15d). However, the deepening of the nutrient sulcus by grooving indicates that the metatarsal was originally meant to be split sagittally. Two extremely short awls were manufactured on ruminant metapodials split sagittally so that one half of the distal condyle served as the base (figure 6.15e). One was clearly used and resharpened until it became so short that it could no longer be of service. The last awl that kept an articular end at its base was made on a vestigial second or fourth metapodial of an equid (figure 6.15b). Because the shafts of equid metapodial splints are naturally tapered, they may be used after only minimal sharpening of the distal end.

A small fragment of the base of a pendant (figure 6.14g) demonstrates the use of large teeth for ornamentation. Only the root of this tooth pendant survives, but its base was ground until smoothly rounded and a biconically drilled perforation was made 1 cm from the basal end. Immediately adjacent to the perforation on one side is a pit where drilling was abandoned before completion. The first attempt at drilling the tooth was apparently too near the margin, so work was interrupted; another perforation was started close to the center and far enough from the other edge to prevent it from breaking through. Visible on the upper edge of the perforation's wall is a light polish that suggests

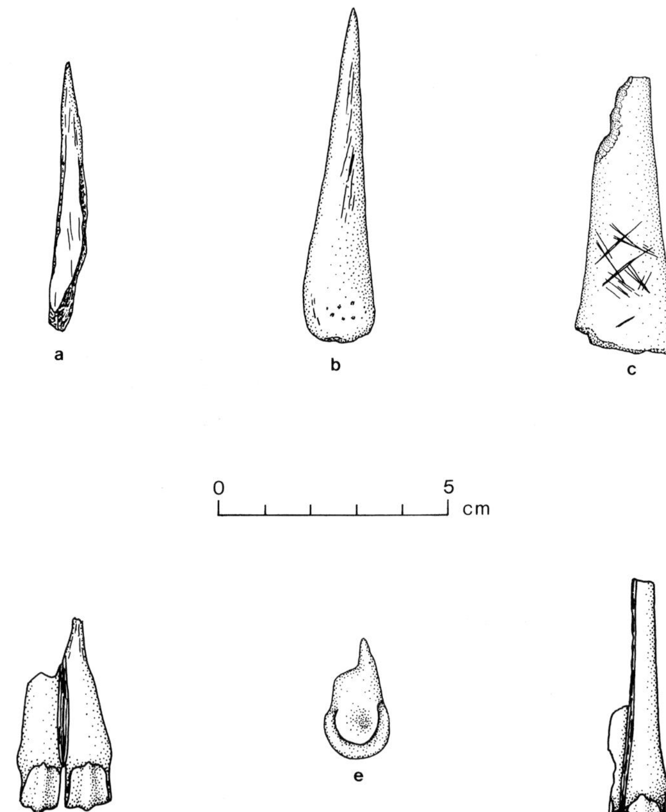

Figure 6.15 Examples of bone artifacts. a, splinter awl 73.3287; b, awl 73.3421 with an articular end as the base, made on the metapodial splint of *Equus* sp.; c, incised awl 73.3192 made on a ruminant metapodial, retaining the proximal end as the base; d, awl retaining the whole distal condyle of a sheep metapodial as the base (Trench E, level 455); e, awl made on a gazelle metapodial, retaining hal of the distal condyle as the base (Trench E, level 439); f, manufacturing debitage (gazelle metacarpal), probably discarded during awl making (Trench E, level 447).

that the pendant had actually been strung and worn. The diameter of the hole is 1.5 mm. I made numerous attempts to compare this fragmentary tooth root with teeth of mammalian species from the Abu Hureyra area but could not identify its taxon.

During the Natufian at Hayonim, canine teeth of foxes and hyenas were drilled through the root, presumably for stringing as pendants (Bar-Yosef and Tchernov 1970, p. 145). Stordeur (1982, p.15) records the presence of a drilled boar's canine at Ramad. It is interesting to note that two completed biconical perforations are visible on the Ramad specimen, but in this case the holes are aligned one below the other instead of side by side.

Two pieces of medium mammal long bones bear traces of longitudinal scraping on their outer surfaces, but they provide no further indication of their original form or function.

Three metapodials of small ruminants were grooved and snapped sagittally and abandoned as either unfinished pieces or the offcuts left behind during the manufacture of awls. A distal end of a gazelle metacarpal (figure 6.15f) had been partially grooved sagittally on both faces but was discarded before being snapped into two equal parts.

CONCLUSIONS

The collection of worked bone from Abu Hureyra 1 is one of the largest assemblages of its kind from the Epipalaeolithic of the Levant. It demonstrates considerable continuity throughout the occupation of the site into Neolithic times. The most significant change is the disappearance of bone bipoints in Abu Hureyra 2. The absence of antler artifacts, especially bipoints, is in keeping with the paucity of cervid remains in the faunal assemblages. Most of the artifacts were made on the bones of small ruminants, including gazelle and sheep. The bones of cattle and small equids were also employed.

We may present some general remarks about the temporal development of bone artifacts in the Levant, although definitive conclusions would be premature at this stage of our knowledge. During the Palaeolithic there were just two major types of bone and antler artifacts: points and awls. These were well made and occasionally even had ornamentation in the form of incising, but it was during the Epipalaeolithic that a great expansion of types and styles of bone artifacts took place. It was then, too, that craftsmanship and artistic expression reached a climax. The Neolithic brought no drastic alterations in methods of manufacture or variety, although some individual types disappeared as others arose.

One of the larger Upper Palaeolithic collections of bone tools was collected at Ksar Akil. Projectile points and awls made on splinters constituted the major types there (Newcomer 1974). Antler, which in later times declined in quantity in the Levant, was used in the manufacture of large, symmetrical points with lenticular cross sections. The bone bipoints with round cross sections from Ksar Akil differed little except in their greater dimensions from those found in Abu Hureyra 1. Splinter awls, worked mainly at the tip by longitudinal scraping, closely resembled those from Abu Hureyra. Two awls were marked with groups of transverse incisions. The most elaborately incised specimen was an awl made on a metatarsal of a small ruminant marked with five rows of more than thirty lines each (Tixier 1974).

There was little change in the Kebaran, since plain and incised awls continued to be made, such as those from Jiita, near Ksar Akil (Copeland and Hours 1977).

By the Natufian a variety of bone implements and ornaments were being used at Hayonim Cave (Bar-Yosef and Tchernov 1970), including drilled canine and globular bone pendants, tubular beads, bipoints and gorgets, awls, choppers, spatulas, sickle hafts, and numerous pieces exhibiting punctuated or incised designs. Natufian levels at Mugharet el Wad (Garrod and Bate 1937) also produced a wide range of highly developed artifact types, such as barbed points, "lissoirs," sickle hafts, beads and pendants of various designs, a shaft-straightener (Campana 1979), and the usual awls with articular ends as bases. Kebara yielded several fine examples of sculptured bone sickle hafts, as well as fishhooks, weaving combs, barbed points, and awls. Three of the sickle hafts had a carved animal head at one end.

It is thus during the Epipalaeolithic that the people of the Levant developed a wide range of bone tool types. They used a variety of techniques, drilling, carving, and other methods, to produce these tools and to finish some of them with elaborate designs. They began to use abrasives and polishing with some frequency on certain artifacts such as beads and pendants. Regional variation was expressed in ornaments, but awls, in particular, remained consistent through time and space from the Upper Palaeolithic onward in the Levant.

The Abu Hureyra 1 excavations provide a large sample of Epipalaeolithic worked bone that is primarily utilitarian rather than ornamental in function. The well-preserved nature of the material has allowed us to make detailed reconstructions of manufacturing processes. Furthermore, we can suggest how some of the tools were used, based on their form and wear traces, for example, as projectile tips, for making baskets and piercing hides, and as ornaments.

7 Stone and Other Artifacts

A. M. T. Moore

We found 149 artifacts made of materials other than flint and bone in the Abu Hureyra 1 deposits. Almost all of them were fashioned from several kinds of stones, and only two from shell. We also recovered a variety of unworked shells that the inhabitants of the village had obtained from the Euphrates River and the Mediterranean Sea.

RAW MATERIALS

The people of the village made most of the stone objects of river pebbles from the Euphrates and from imported basalt; they also used several other rocks, nearly all of which occurred locally. The most common raw material was basalt, used for almost half (72) of the stone artifacts. Many of these were grinding dishes made of fine-grained basalt, or rubbing stones and querns with a slightly coarser grain. The inhabitants probably obtained the stone for these from a source like that at Khanasir (figure 7.1). They made some of the rubbing stones and pestles from basalt river pebbles. They used stones from the river for over 40 other artifacts, many of them distinctive, flat, notched pebbles. The pebbles included a variety of sedimentary and metamorphic rocks, the latter originating from parent material in the mountains to the north. They used two other rocks to make significant quantities of artifacts, limestone (ten objects) and chalk (eight objects), and obtained both locally. The raw materials for the few small beads of jadeite and a rod of slate (73.3194) that we found probably came from far to the north. The source of several pieces of limonite is, however, unknown. River snails were used to make two shell beads.

TYPES OF ARTIFACTS

The artifacts are described here according to type. My aim is to group artifacts that look similar and seem to have been made and used in the same way. I have

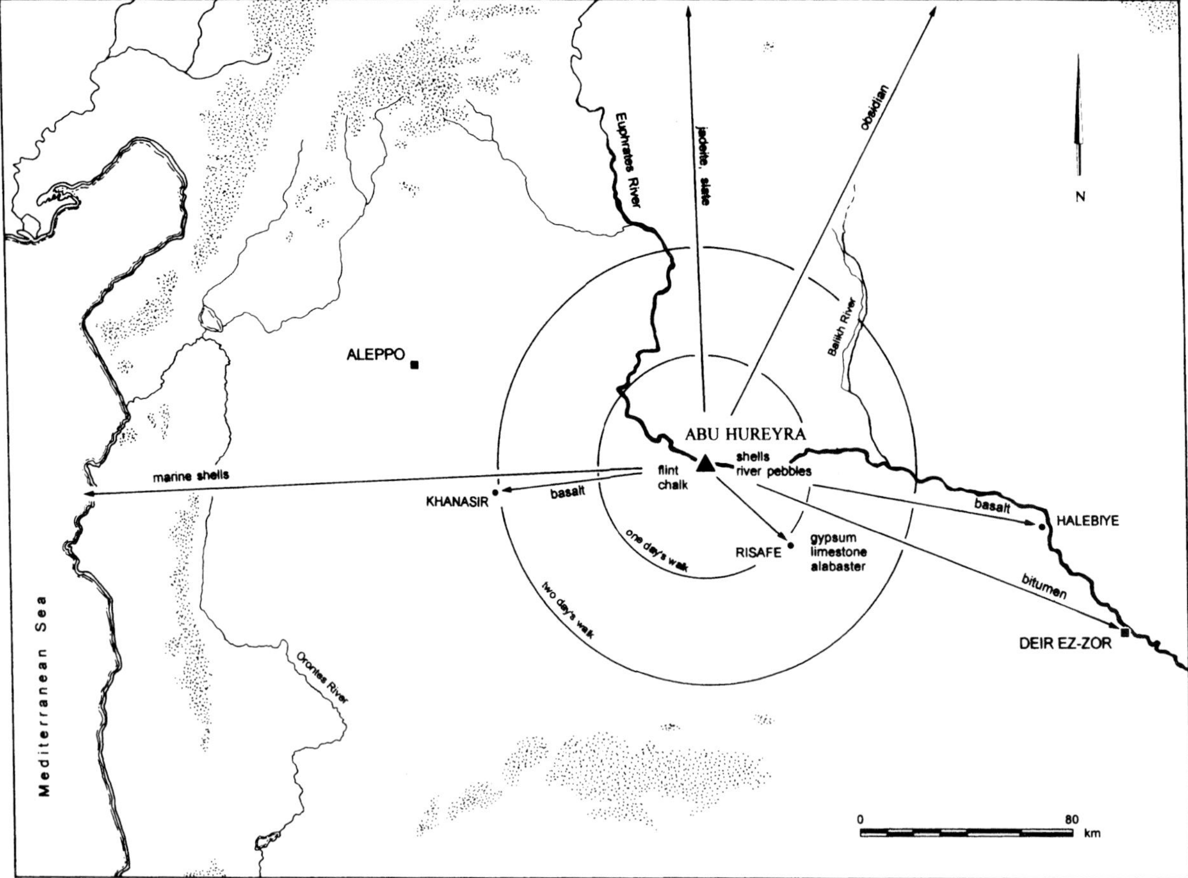

Figure 7.1 The sources of the raw materials used by the villagers of Abu Hureyra.

attempted to keep the number of types to a minimum, recognizing that there may be considerable variations in shape among the artifacts in each type. Most of the artifacts fall into a few categories: grinding dishes and querns, rubbing stones and pestles, and notched pebbles. There are very few artifacts of other types. A complete inventory with details of each object is provided in the Abu Hureyra electronic archive (see appendix 8).

The grinding dishes (figures 7.2, 7.3) are oval or subcircular in plan and slightly concave in section. Some have a smooth, rounded rim and are finely finished by careful hammering. None was found complete, so their dimensions are hard to determine accurately, but 73.3232, a quite large example (figure 7.2), was apparently about 35 cm long, 25 cm wide, and only 2 cm thick. The bottoms of most of the dishes are equally thin, varying from 1.5 to 3 cm in thickness. Fragment 73.3232 weighs 1.34 kg, so the complete dish would have been about 3.4 kg originally. They were thus relatively light and portable.

Most of the grinding dishes are made on fine, evenly grained basalt, carefully chosen for the purpose. Almost all were found as small fragments, so apparently the pieces continued to be used even after the original artifact was broken. It is likely that they were valued highly because the basalt came from a quite distant source and was particularly well suited for the functions of the dishes. Many of the fragments were burned, either accidentally or because they had been heated for a particular task. The burning seems to have shattered several dishes into small fragments.

Nearly all the grinding dish pieces have a series of linear striations on one or both surfaces, clearly visible with a hand lens. These striations are usually

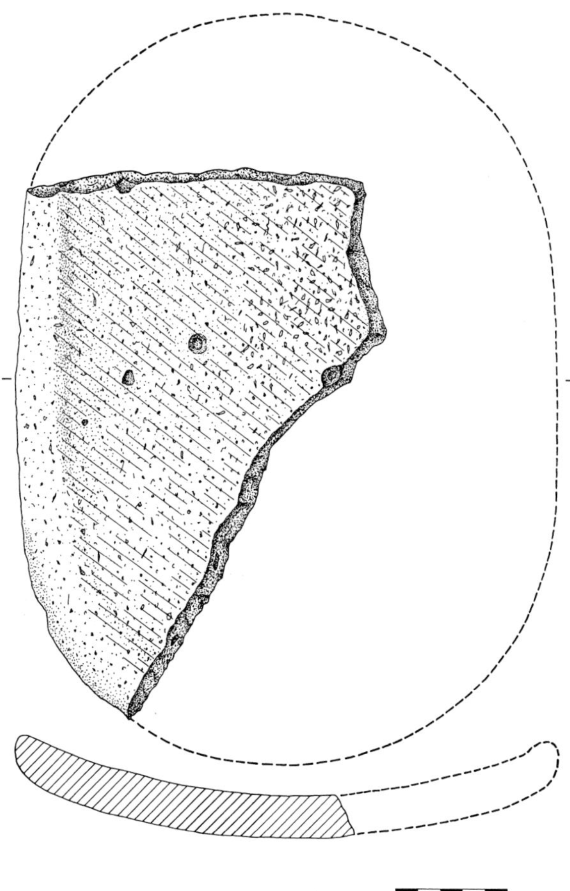

Figure 7.2 A basalt grinding dish 73.3232. The surface of the dish was stained with red ochre, indicated by cross hatching. Scale is in centimeters.

aligned with the long axis of the dishes. Some dishes have additional linear striations at an angle of between 40° and 90° to the long axis. On a few examples the striations are curvilinear, following the curved edge of the dish. The striations suggest that a rubbing stone was pushed back and forth along the length of the dish when grinding. Movement of the dish itself on the ground added additional striations to the bottom.

Many of the grinding dishes have patches of red ochre on their upper surfaces. Some also have it on the bottom, presumably from spillage. Spectrographic analysis of the red ochre on a grinding dish (73.3415) and a rubbing stone (73.3275) by the laboratory of the Natural History Museum in London has confirmed that it is ferric oxide. The red ochre that was reduced to powder on the grinding dishes was presumably used as coloring matter and for other purposes. Red ochre has been noticed on ground stone artifacts from contemporary sites in Palestine, for example, at Ain Mallaha (Perrot 1966, p. 466). We may note in passing that the grinding tools from Ain Mallaha, like those from Abu Hureyra, are of excellent workmanship.

Seeds and other plant foods were almost certainly also processed on the dishes. Similar small grinding dishes were commonly employed for this purpose by many of the aboriginal peoples of North America, for example, the Paiute,[1] and of Australia (Gould 1969, p. 93). Many of the dishes found in ethnographic museum collections were burned, indicating that they were regularly heated during use. One of their functions was to parch grain or seeds, like dishes traditionally used for this purpose in the Orkney Islands (Fenton 1978, p. 375).

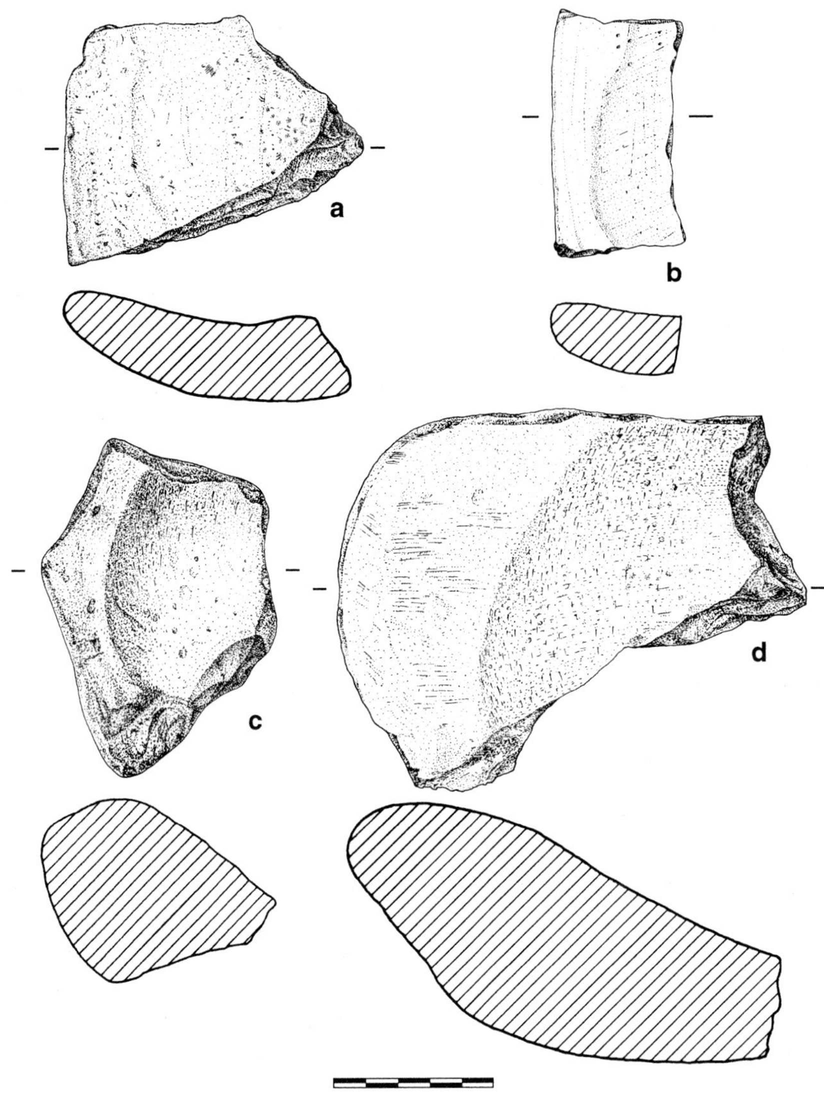

Figure 7.3 Basalt grinding dishes. a, 73.3326; b, 73.3361; c, 73.3352; d, 73.3336. Scale is in centimeters.

It is probable that the grinding dishes from Abu Hureyra 1 were also used in this way.

Over half of the grinding dish fragments were found in four levels in phase 2. Four of them (73.3170, 73.3172, 73.3174, 73.3177) were found with four rubbing stones and a stone ball in level 429, and five more (73.3324, 73.3326, 73.3327, 73.3329, 73.3330) with a single rubbing stone in level 455. Pieces of no fewer than 11 grinding dishes (73.3336, 73.3337, 73.3339, 73.3342–73.3347) with one rubbing stone were found in level 459. Fragments of another four dishes, a quern, a mortar, and a rubbing stone in the adjacent level 460 (73.3352–73.3358) were clustered together around a firepit. The groupings of grinding dishes and ground stone artifacts attest to heavy activity in these levels of floors, hearths, and spreads of burned material.

The querns are of a different shape and of greater size and weight than the grinding dishes. They are made of a coarser-grained basalt, the slabs of which were carefully chosen for their approximation to the required shape. The final form of the querns was achieved by hammering, although the sides and bases were never fully smoothed off. Two complete ones (73.3424, 73.3425) were found in pit 470 of pit complex 2 in phase 1 (figure 7.4; see also figures 5.11, 5.14), apparently where they were used. They are trapezoidal in shape, with a narrow butt that probably touched the operator's knees during use. The largest one is 55 cm long, 31 cm wide, over 7 cm thick, and weighs 13 kg. The upper, slightly dished, surfaces of these querns have linear striations aligned with their long axes. This suggests that the surfaces of each were ground with a rubbing stone in a back-and-forth motion.

The two complete querns have traces of red ochre on them, indicating that, like the grinding dishes, they were used for crushing this mineral. It is probable, however, that their main purpose was to grind plant foods. The querns are so heavy that they would have been used on the ground. Chocked with small stones, they would have remained firmly in place during many hours of vigorous labor. This would have made them ideal tools for prolonged grinding of seeds or other vegetable foods.

The rubbing stones (figure 7.5) are usually oblong, are oval or plano-convex in cross section, and often have squared-off ends. A few are subrectangular in shape. They range from 9 to 22 cm in length, probably reflecting some differences in use. Most are made from river pebbles of fine-grained basalt or greenstone. Several have been carefully finished with hammering and pecking to achieve a regular shape. They frequently have heavy wear on one or both of their flatter sides, with striations at right angles to the long axis. This indicates that they were held at each end and rubbed back and forth. Some of the rubbing stones have pitting on the ends from use as hammers, and a few have traces of red ochre on them. Most of these tools appear to have been used with the grinding dishes and querns.

The mortars (figure 7.6) have a deeper depression than the grinding dishes and querns. Materials were apparently pounded in them with a pestle, rather than ground out with a rubbing stone. One (73.3094) is flaked from a flint nodule and is very small. There are too few mortars to offer further observations.

The pestles (figure 7.7) are usually in the shape of tapered cylinders as much as 21 cm long, and circular or subcircular in cross section. They are carefully finished to achieve a balanced tool with a smooth surface, like many of the other

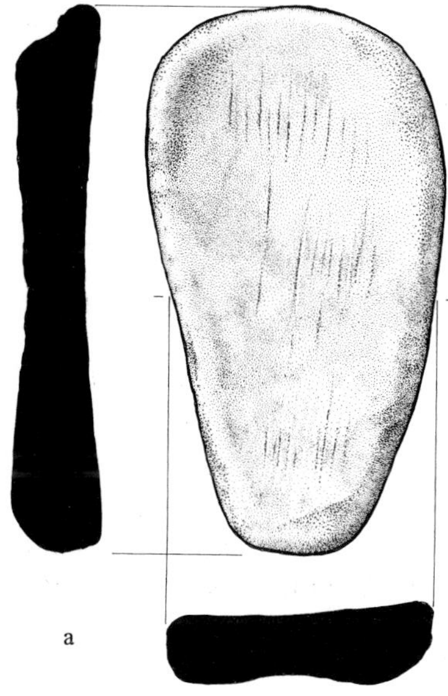

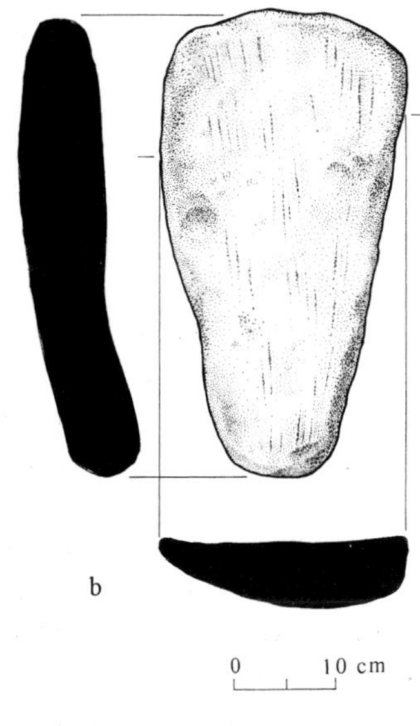

Figure 7.4 The two large querns from phase 1 that were found in pit 470 of complex 2. a, 73.3424; b, 73.3425 (compare figure 5.16).

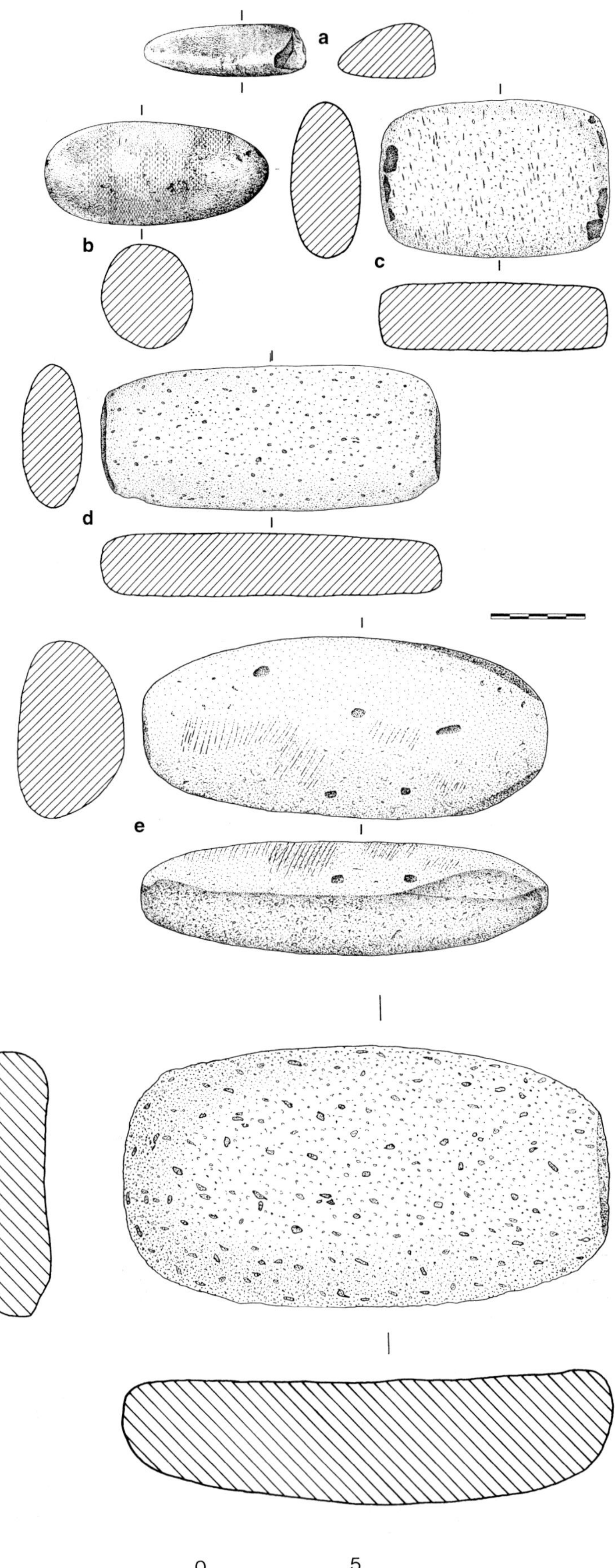

Figure 7.5 Basalt rubbing stones. a, 73.3173; b, 73.3180; c, 73.3419; d, 73.3137, e, 73.3136. Scale is in centimeters.

Figure 7.6 A basalt mortar 73.3259

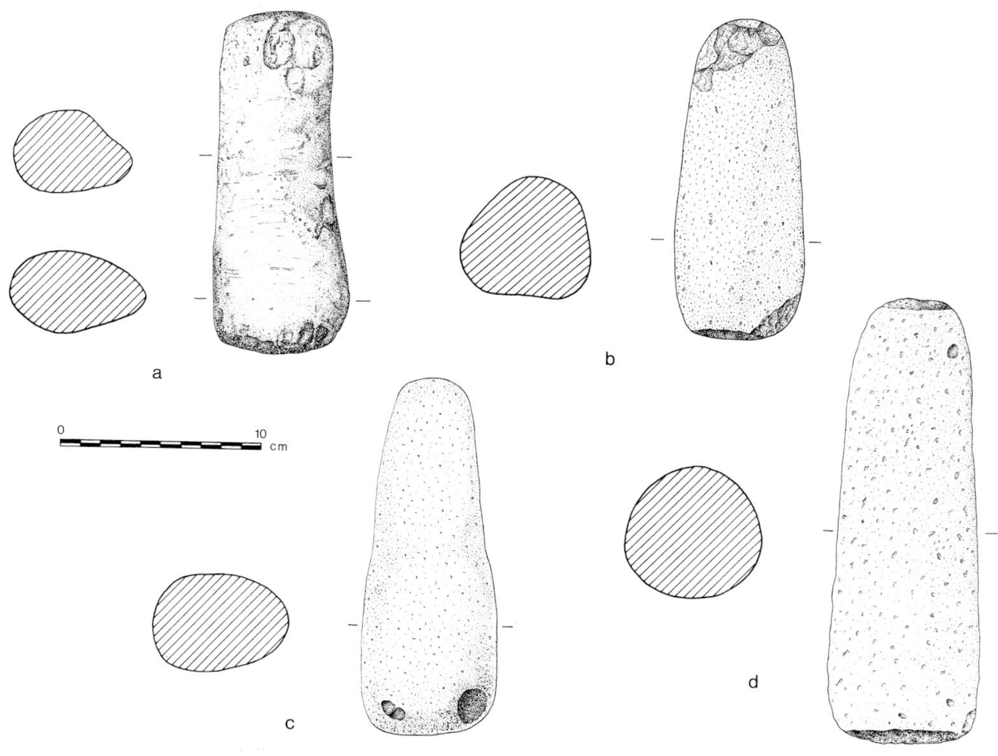

Figure 7.7 Basalt pestles. a, 73.3290; b, 73.3175; c, 73.3231; d, 73.3230.

grinding tools. Several are heavily battered at one or both ends, showing how they were normally used. A few have striations on the surface of the body of the artifact, so the pestles were sometimes used as rubbing stones.

Traces of red ochre on 73.3290 and chalk on 73.3211 suggest that the pestles were used for pounding these minerals. Red ochre was also found on basalt pestles at Mugharet el Wad (Garrod and Bate 1937, p. 41). It is probable, however, that the main function of the pestles was to prepare plants for food and other purposes. Their shape made them ideal for pounding these substances in the stone mortars we found. Stone mortars were scarce in Abu Hureyra 1, so it may be that the pestles were mainly used in wooden mortars. The combination of stone pestle and wooden mortar was frequently employed to pound foods by North American aboriginal groups, for example, the people of the Eastern Woodlands and the Paiute (Conkey, Boissevain, and Goddard 1978, figure 6; Fowler and Liljeblad 1986, figure 6). The inhabitants of Abu Hureyra 1 may have used the pestles and other pounding and grinding tools, not only to process plant foods, but also to crush small animals to pulp in order to eat them. Studies of stone tools from archaeological sites in California have shown that some were used for precisely this purpose (Yohe, Newman, and Schneider 1991), a practice well attested ethnographically.

Most of the hammers (figure 7.8a) are made on river pebbles. Some have been little modified and are thus elongated in shape with battered ends. Others have been pecked to a squat cylindrical shape close to that of the stone balls and then battered in use. They are a varied group of tools that may have been used to retouch flint, but also to perform a wide range of other tasks.

The hammer-chopper (figure 7.9) from Abu Hureyra 1 is a unique artifact made from a large, heavy, basalt rubbing stone. One end has been pecked out

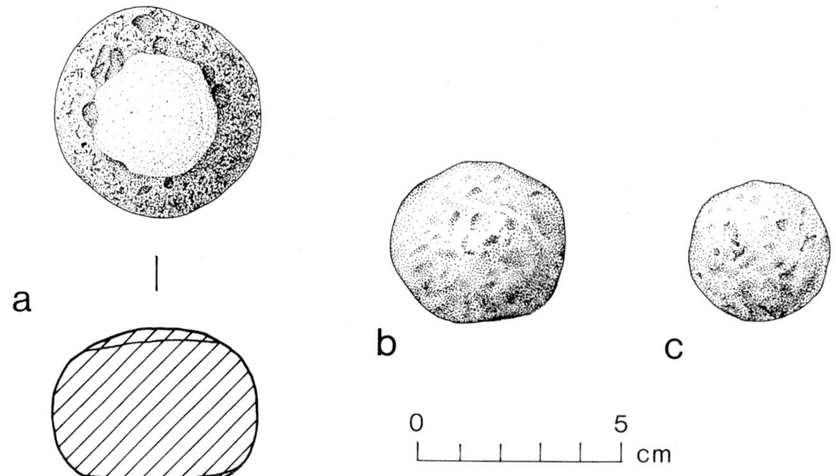

Figure 7.8 a, a limestone hammer 73.3120. b and c, stone balls 73.3169, 73.3108.

as a handle of trapezoidal cross section. One side of the other end has been flaked to make an edge which has been used for hammering and chopping.

The stone balls (figure 7.8b,c) are spherical, or nearly so, and usually 4 cm or less in diameter. These small artifacts have been pecked out with care to a quite smooth and regular finish. Some retain a little of the original surface of the stone from which they were made; in almost every case it appears that they were fashioned from river pebbles. On a visit to the excavation of the early village site of Hallan Çemi (c. 10,600–10,000 BP) in southeastern Turkey in 1993, I watched one of the young Kurdish workmen peck out a stone ball from a

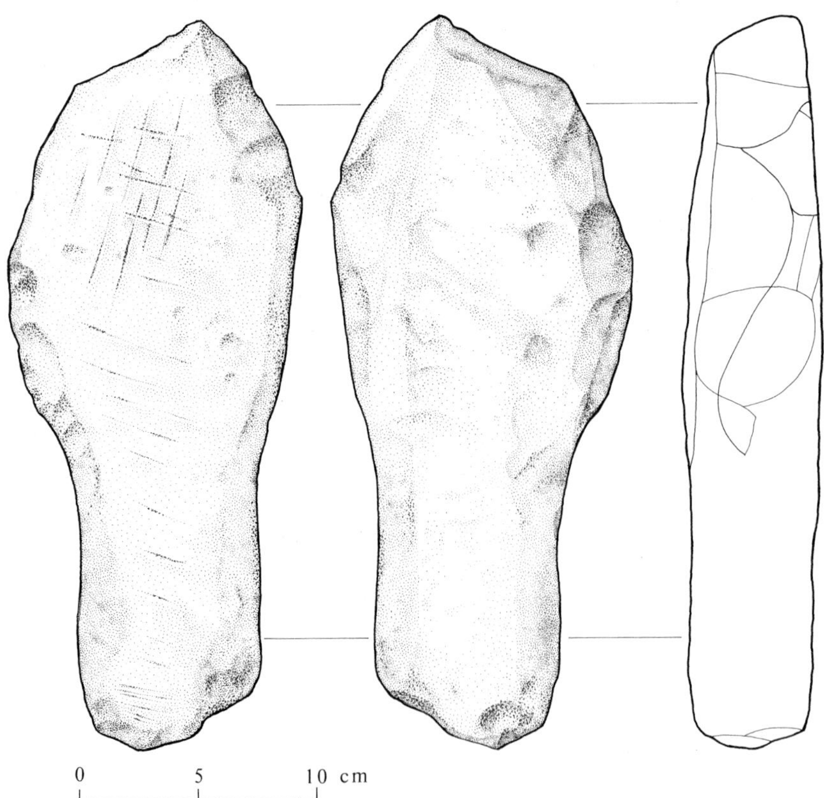

Figure 7.9 The hammer-chopper 73.3092.

river pebble in less than an hour using another pebble as a hammer. The stone balls he made were identical to those from Abu Hureyra.

We have weighed the stone balls, with intriguing results. It appears that they are of three sizes, and that several in each group are of almost the same weight (figure 7.10). The smallest ones are about 40 gm, those of middling size from 71 to 80 gm, and the largest two are 101 gm each. The sample size is small, but these figures suggest that their makers were trying to manufacture stone balls of regular weights. We have noticed that many of the stone balls from Abu Hureyra 2 also seem to have been made in standard weights.

The function of the stone balls is, nonetheless, uncertain. Among the possibilities that come to mind are the following. The regularities in their shape and size suggest that they may have served as units of measurement, tokens, or as pieces in a game; 73.3122, found placed in a large shell (figure 7.11), hints at something of the kind. They may have been used as weights in composite artifacts, perhaps nets or bolases. They might even have been used as sling bullets, a use for which their regular shape would have made them particularly suitable. The main objection to this is that their owners may have been reluctant to risk losing them in such an activity. Or they may have served as small pounders, though most seem too small for this. On balance, we are inclined to think they were used as weights, perhaps to determine small quantities of plant substances, medicines, or the like.

The stone vessels (figure 7.12) are a small, miscellaneous group of containers. Two, 73.3381 and 73.3438, are pieces of well-made vessels carved from carefully chosen, fine-grained basalt. Fragment 73.3381 is part of a deep bowl, heavily decorated with incised designs on the outside. Much of the design appears to have been cut out with flint blades. The piece has two holes at the top, probably close to the original rim; these holes were, presumably, for suspension. There are traces of burning at the bottom, suggesting that the bowl was used to heat substances over a fire.

One river pebble has a patch of red ochre on its flat side and may have been used as a palette.

The single bitumen smearer (figure 7.13a) is a short, tapering bar of chalk with oval cross section. It was carved with flint blades, leaving characteristic grooves on the surface. There are smears of bitumen along its length and a trace on the wider end. Both ends are broken, but the presence of bitumen on one of them indicates that the tool continued to be used in its truncated state. The tool was presumably employed to apply bitumen to other artifacts such as baskets. A number of such tools were found in Abu Hureyra 2.

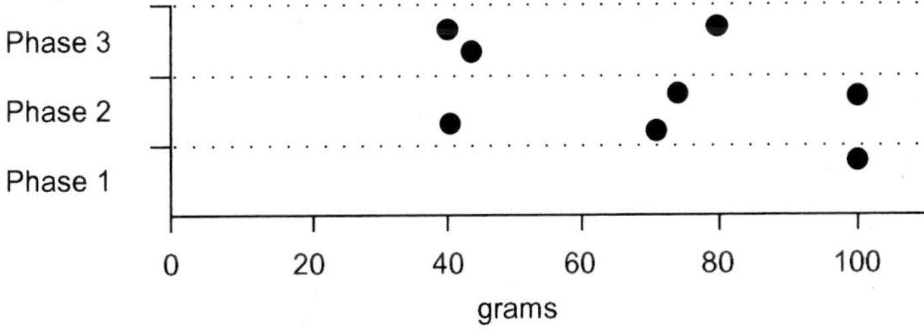

Figure 7.10 The stone balls plotted by weight and in approximate stratigraphic position. Note that they fall into three clusters by weight.

Figure 7.11 This stone ball, 73.3122, was found in a large shell.

The discs (figure 7.13b–e) are a varied group of tools that may have had a similar function. All are circular in shape with a central hole and appear to be quite carefully balanced. This suggests that they served as weights of some kind. Four are thin, pierced, flat discs of chalk, and the fifth is a retouched, chunky, flint nodule. The smaller ones could have been used as spindle whorls.

The notched pebbles (figure 7.14) are of various sizes but consistent in form. They are made on wide, thin river pebbles that are frequently pointed at one end. Each pebble has two notches, one flaked on each side. The notches are often ground down to remove the sharp edges of the flake scars. These features suggest that the pebbles were tied with cord around the middle; a few (for example, 73.3266) had additional notches so they could also be tied along the long axis. Some of the pebbles were used long enough for the surface to become a little polished. It seems that the precise mass of the artifacts was less important than their form, since the weight of the pebbles varies greatly.

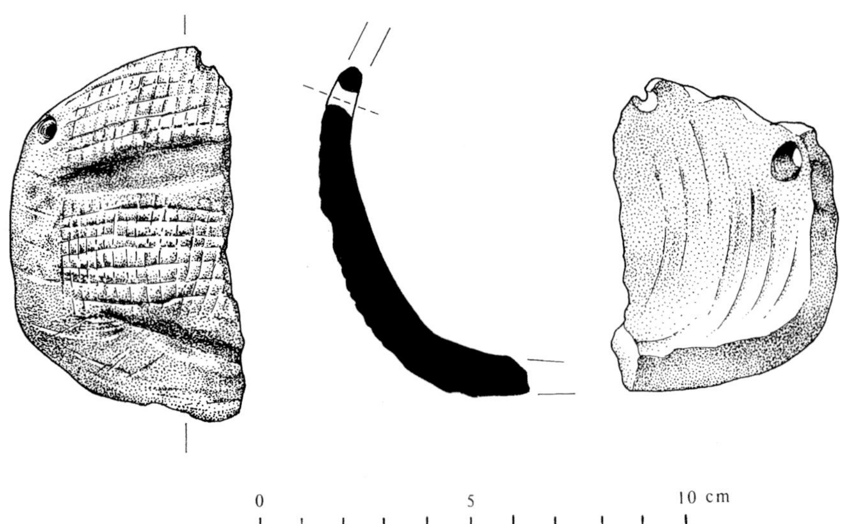

Figure 7.12 A basalt vessel with incised designs, 73.3381.

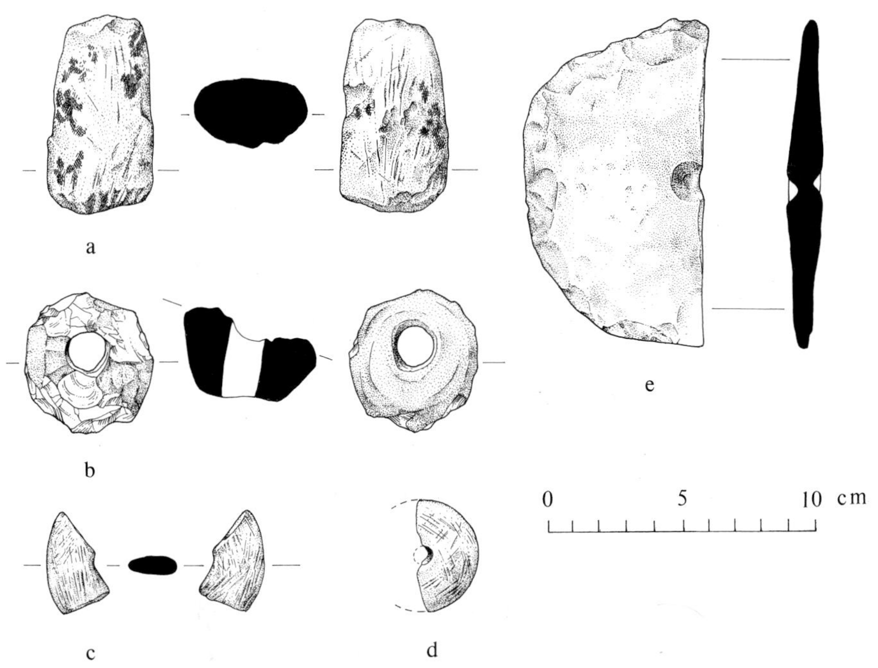

Figure 7.13 a, a bitumen smearer 73.3216. b–e, stone discs 73.3286, 73.3148, 73.3185, 72.589.

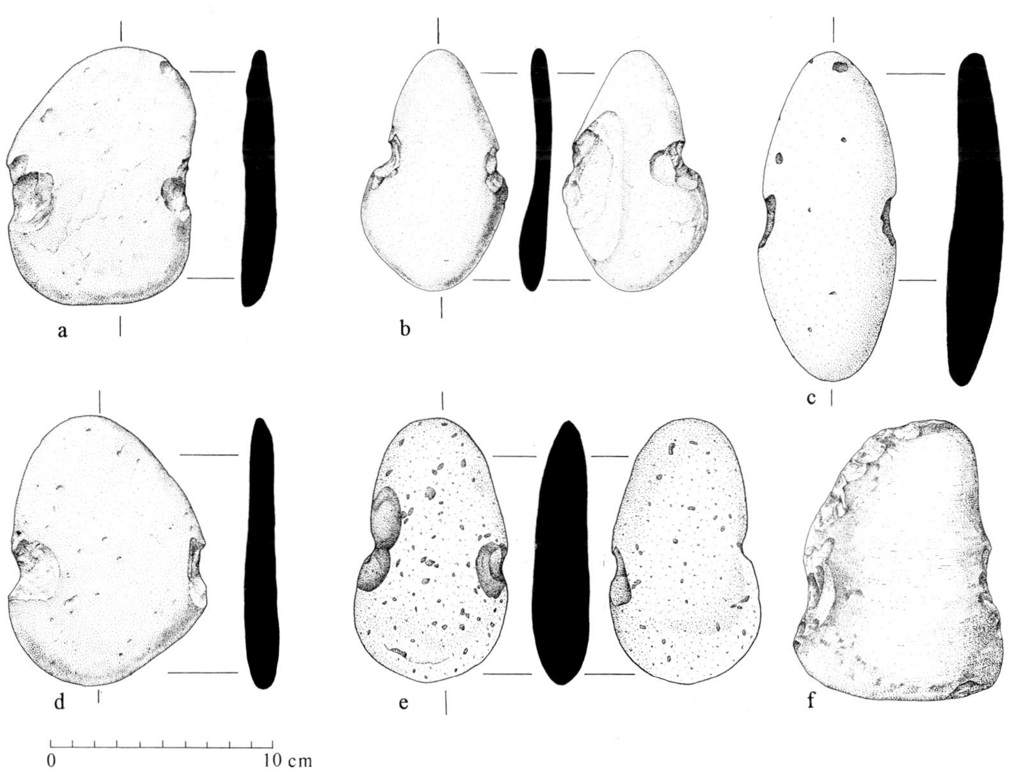

Figure 7.14 Notched pebbles. a, 73.3164; b, 73.3183; c, 73.3111; d, 73.3222; e, 73.3227; f, 73.3190.

These simple tools appear to have been used as weights. The notched pebbles were probably mainly used as sinkers on lines or nets for fishing in the Euphrates. Similar artifacts were found at the lakeside settlement of Ain Mallaha (Perrot 1966, figure 20, 1–4) but have rarely been remarked at other contemporary Levantine sites. Notched pebbles were made by the Indians of the Northwest Coast of America and others as sinkers to weight fishing lines and nets (Rau 1884, p. 156). They continued to be used widely in North America and in northwest Europe until recent times; the Pitt Rivers Museum has specimens of similar line sinkers from the west coast of Ireland (figure 7.15).

Almost half the notched pebbles were found in three levels in phase 2. Pebbles 73.3188–73.3191 were clustered together in level 434 as if ready for use, perhaps as part of the same artifact. Pebbles 73.3266, 73.3269, and 73.3276 were all in level 445. Level 438 had two clusters of notched pebbles that were apparently in the process of being manufactured. Pebbles 73.3218 and 73.3219 were unfinished examples; 73.3222 and another unfinished one, 73.3223, were found with an unworked pebble, 73.3439, selected because it was of the correct shape for a notched pebble weight. Two other notched pebbles (73.3213, 73.3214) were also recovered from this level.

There is one small, oval, indented pebble with notches chipped at each end that was almost certainly used as a weight at first (figure 7.16c). The form of this artifact was subsequently changed: the ends were ground down to a bevel

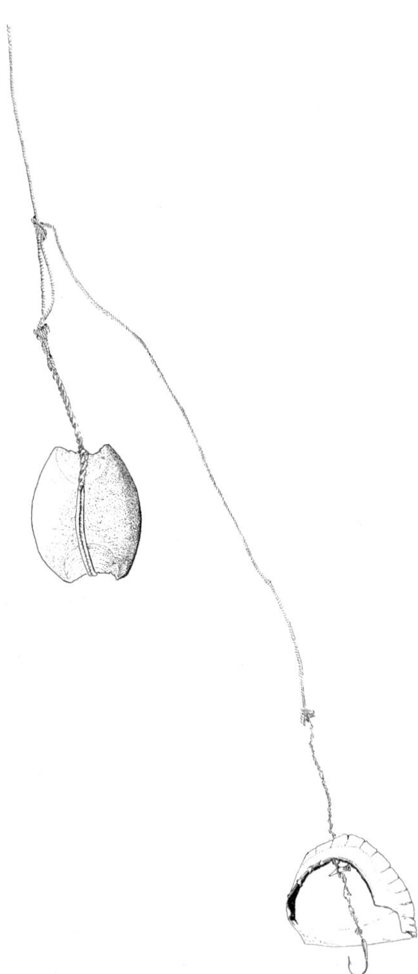

Figure 7.15 A fishing line with a notched pebble sinker that was used to catch wrasse in beds of seaweed off the west coast of Ireland. Pitt Rivers Museum, University of Oxford, #2273 and #2274.

on both sides, removing much of the notches, and two hollows had been scratched out with a flint tool on each face of the pebble. The function of the final form of this artifact is uncertain.

Chipped pebbles are elongated, flat pebbles with flakes removed from one end, perhaps through accidental breakage during use. There are lengthwise striations on a couple of them, suggesting they were used for rubbing.

A small pecked pebble is in the shape of an ellipsoid or rugby ball. It may have served as a weight or missile. Another tiny pebble has many facets ground on its surface. The rest of this faceted pebble is highly polished.

Of the two incised pebbles (figure 7.16b,d), 73.3149 is an elongated object of chalk with a design scratched on it. The design is schematic but may have been intended to represent a human being. The other, 73.3228, is a small disc with a design of radial lines scratched on both sides and a line cut around its circumference. This pebble may have been used as a gaming piece. Similarly decorated bones, fruit stones, and pebbles were used in dice games by most North American aboriginal tribes (Culin 1907, pp. 44–49).

The incised chalk piece is a fragment (73.3423) with a grid design scratched on one face (figure 7.16e).

The beads (figure 7.16g) are all very small and are made either from colored stones or from river shells. The stones are exotic and most probably Anatolian in origin, but a few may have been collected from the Euphrates gravels near the site. A single pebble pendant found in Abu Hureyra 1 (figure 7.16f) has a hole for suspension.

The slate rod, 73.3194, is a unique piece of uncertain, perhaps symbolic, function (figure 7.16a). The slate from which it is made is not found locally and so came from some distance away, probably Asia Minor. The rod bears some resemblance to an artifact found in a somewhat later context at Mureybit (J. Cauvin 1977, figure 18).

The few limonite nodules may have been picked up and brought to the site because of their great densities and curious shapes. They seem to have been handled a good deal, giving a polish to the surface, but may have served no practical purpose. Many additional unpolished pieces were found during the excavation.

COMMENTARY

The most numerous categories of stone and shell artifacts that have survived in the Abu Hureyra 1 deposits are grinding stones and notched pebble weights. The principal function of these objects seems to have been to obtain and process food; thus, a concern with subsistence was apparently the main reason for manufacturing these tools. Ten percent of the artifacts are mainly ornamental or symbolic in nature, among them the beads, the incised pebbles, and the slate rod. We should note, too, that many of the grinding dishes, and even some of the rubbing stones and pestles, were finely made, with embellishments that went beyond the purely utilitarian. The most notable example of this combination of functional and symbolic traits is the decorated basalt bowl 73.3381.

We see from this evidence that the inhabitants of Abu Hureyra 1 were prepared to spend a considerable amount of time in making artifacts that were aesthetically pleasing as well as functionally efficient. These stone artifacts embodied concepts of both form and design that were obviously important to their makers. The distinctive nature of some of the stone artifacts and the care

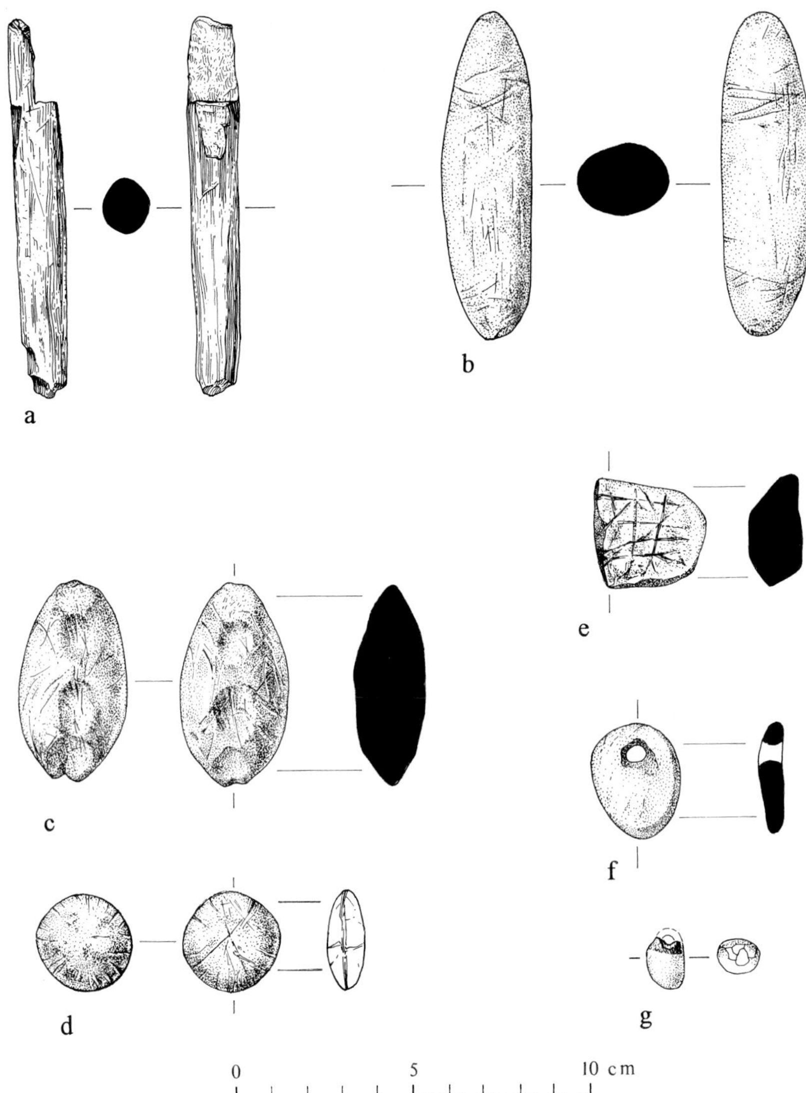

Figure 7.16 a, slate rod 73.3194; b, incised chalk pebble 73.3149; c, indented pebble 73.3184; d, incised pebble 73.3228; e, incised chalk piece 73.3423; f, pebble pendant 73.3151; g, jadeite bead 73.3145.

taken in their manufacture hint at another dimension: that the objects were of ideological significance to the people of Abu Hureyra 1.

The distribution of the stone and shell artifacts varied greatly from phase to phase (table 7.1). Seventy percent of the objects recovered were from phase 2, and over 80 % from phases 1 and 2 together, even though these phases contained less than half the volume of deposit excavated. It appears from these figures that the manufacture of such artifacts reached a peak in phase 2, then sharply declined in phase 3. The volume of deposit excavated increased from phase 1 to 3, while each phase was of slightly different duration, so it is important to consider changes in the proportion of artifacts from one phase to another in relation to these factors. The figures are somewhat different from the simple percentage of objects found in each phase, but the general trend is similar. Phase 2 held double the number of objects than the mean for the deposits as a whole, both by volume of deposit and by century; phase 3 accounted for fewer objects than average.

Our total sample of artifacts is not large, and the duration of each phase can only be approximately determined; nonetheless, the changes in the quantity

Table 7.1 The number and percentage of stone and shell artifacts in each phase, per volume of deposit, and by radiocarbon century

Phase	Number of objects per phase	Percentage of objects per phase	Volume of deposit in m^3	Number of objects to each m^3 of deposit (mean 2.81 per m^3)	Timespan in ^{14}C years	Number of objects per ^{14}c century (mean 9.93)
3	27	18.1	30	0.9	400	6.75
2	104	69.8	17	6.1	600	17.33
1	18	12.1	6	3	500	3.6
TOTAL	149	100	53		1500	

of artifacts recovered from phase to phase are so striking that they call for explanation. Part of the answer concerns the contexts from which the artifacts came. One of the most conspicuous features in phase 2 was the area of heavy burning over the bench in the east and southeast sectors of the trench. This consisted of individual hearths and the ashes from them. Many of the densest concentrations of broken pieces of grinding dishes, rubbing stones, and notched pebbles in phase 2 were in these burned levels. It appears that occupation was particularly intense here, and artifacts, both complete and broken, were dropped near the hearths. Thus, one of the reasons why phase 2 had so many artifacts was because it contained this hearth area that seems to have been the focus of much activity.

Consideration of context provides only part of the explanation, however. The variations in the proportions of artifacts from phase to phase are so marked that we need to look at other factors, in particular changes in the nature of the settlement and in the functions of the tools themselves. The settlement changed significantly in phase 3; it probably expanded, and there were no longer the constraints on use of space imposed by the subsoil bank and pit dwellings. It is possible, therefore, that some of the activities for which we found evidence in the earlier phases were performed elsewhere in phase 3, leaving fewer stone tools for us to recover in the area we excavated. This hypothesis is not supported, however, by the chipped stone data. Olszweski has found that the quantity of both flint tools and waste increased from phases 1 to 3 (see tables 6.1, 6.8). The density of chipped stone per volume of deposit excavated does not vary greatly from phase to phase, but the number of pieces per century increased sharply through time. Thus, the changes in the occurrence of chipped stone do not reinforce the notion that alterations in the nature of the settlement markedly influenced the decline in the deposition of the other stone tools.

The grinding stones, dishes, querns, rubbing stones, mortars, and pestles made up the bulk of the stone tools. Seventy-two of these artifacts came from phases 1 and 2 and only six from phase 3. We have already concluded that these were probably used mainly to process plant foods, in particular to parch, dehusk, and grind seeds. The seeds were probably those of wild cereals, especially einkorn and millets, and some other wild grasses, in particular *Stipa* spp. The seeds of the sea club-rush and the dwarf knotgrass may also have been roasted and ground using these tools. Acorns and almonds could have been prepared with some of the stone tools, while terebinth fruits may have been pounded with pestles in mortars to make a paste for preserving meat. It is significant, therefore, that Hillman has found the greatest concentration of these plant remains in the earlier levels and a sharp reduction in their occurrence later on. The decrease in einkorn, grasses, small-seeded plants from the valley bottom, and terebinth fruits began early in phase 2, and it was then that the incidence of grinding stones also started to decline. It thus appears that the occurrence of grinding stones correlates with that of the seed plants from the valley bottom, the wild cereals, feather-grasses, and terebinth fruits, and that a decrease in the use of those foods was matched by a reduction in the manufacture and use of the artifacts necessary to process them.

THE CULTURE OF ABU HUREYRA 1

The settlement of Abu Hureyra 1 lasted for about 1,500 radiocarbon years, apparently without interruption. It was thus extraordinarily long-lived. Only two other Levantine late Epipalaeolithic sites, Mugharet el Wad and Ain Mallaha, may have been occupied for as long as this, but neither has a sufficient spread of radiocarbon dates for us to be sure. The dwellings in the Abu Hureyra 1 settlement were built of perishable materials—wooden posts, reeds, brush, and perhaps skins—that formed a very compact deposit as they decayed. Thus, the debris representing a millennium and a half of habitation accumulated slowly, to a maximum depth of 1.6 m against the north section T-U. The depth of deposit would have been somewhat greater originally before the removal of the surface deposits of Abu Hureyra 1 by the inhabitants of Abu Hureyra 2.

Abu Hureyra 1 changed markedly in form during its life. The characteristic structures of Period 1A (phase 1) were the pit dwellings. Once these had filled up, they were replaced in Period 1B (phase 2) by dwellings built on level ground, but enough of the subsoil still protruded to influence the location of the new structures. These constraints no longer existed in Period 1C (phase 3), so dwellings could be built wherever convenience and social norms suggested. The huts of Period 1C seem to have been of the same type as those of Period 1B. The main change in the form of the settlement was therefore in the transition from Period 1A to 1B. We think it probable that the settlement expanded in Periods 1B and 1C.

The dwellings of Period 1A were already complex, multichambered structures, presaging the houses with several rooms characteristic of early Neolithic Levantine settlements. We were unable to determine the precise form of the dwellings in Periods 1B and 1C; we know only that they were constructed on the ground with a frame of poles, and that they had trodden earth or clay floors. We found areas of hearths and the remains of numerous individual fires in all three periods of the settlement. The presence of hearth areas outside the dwellings and the use of the bank and bench in Period 1A indicate that the inhabitants maintained a sense of discrete use of space across the settlement. The form of the pit complexes and the presence of the querns in pit 470 suggest that this also applied within the dwellings.

We did not find any formal burials in the Abu Hureyra 1 deposits, but we did recover a few human bones (see chapter 10). This suggests, indirectly, that humans were buried in the settlement and that some of their bones were subsequently scattered through the deposits as a result of disturbance.

Abu Hureyra 1 yielded a wide range of artifacts, a greater variety, indeed, than most contemporary sites. The variety of artifacts recovered from the admittedly modest area excavated of phase I at Mureybit, for example, seems to have been quite limited (J. Cauvin 1977, pp. 21–25). Assemblages of artifacts of equivalent or greater range and quality have been found on only a few Natufian sites, principally Mugharet el Wad, Hayonim, and Ain Mallaha in

Palestine (Garrod and Bate 1937; Bar-Yosef and Goren 1973; Perrot 1966), and Wadi Hammeh 27 in Transjordan (Edwards 1991). The manufacture of such a wide range of artifacts and the care taken in finishing them were new phenomena in human society in the Levant. Despite this variety, we must always be mindful that we can examine only those objects, principally of flint, stone, and bone, that have survived. We might reasonably expect the inhabitants of a riverine site such as Abu Hureyra 1 to have made clothing for themselves from skins or fibers and to have used a wide range of wooden tools, baskets, mats, and cordage, as well as ornamental and ritual artifacts of organic materials, all of which have disappeared.

The functions of the flint tools can be discussed only in general terms, pending further study. Anderson-Gerfaud's (1983, pp. 82–85) microwear analysis of a few of the lunates, combined with Olszewski's examination of lunate breakage patterns (chapter 6), indicates that many of them were used to arm arrows. Olsen's work (chapter 6) suggests that the bone bipoints were also arrowheads. Thus, the inhabitants of Abu Hureyra 1 regularly used the bow, presumably in the hunt. Other lunates seem to have been mounted in knives, some of which were used for reaping. Some of the backed pieces with luster were also hafted as sickles for harvesting grasses (Anderson-Gerfaud 1983, p. 96).

The many scrapers among the flint tools were probably used, among other things, in butchery and for preparing skins. It is quite clear from the faunal evidence that large numbers of gazelles, as well as onagers and other animals, were killed for food. The butchery of these animals would have yielded a regular and ample supply of skins, sinew, and other products, as well as meat.

The other numerous class of flint tools was the notched pieces. The functions of these artifacts are less certain, but they and the burins may have been used to work wood, reeds, and bone. Thus, these tools were probably employed in crafts, as well as to obtain food and to make weapons.

The evidence of the stone tools is similar: most of them seem to have been made to obtain and prepare food, but a small proportion were probably used for crafts. The discs, interpreted as spindle whorls, suggest that the inhabitants twisted yarn and wove, while the bone needles indicate that they sewed with fine fiber or thread. They may have used some of the bone awls to prepare rawhide and leather goods. The care they took over the manufacture of the grinding dishes, rubbing stones, and pestles is another good indication of artisan activity.

The form and finish of some of the artifacts attest to the aesthetic and symbolic concerns of the inhabitants, while the presence of beads, pendants, and other items indicates they were preoccupied to some extent with personal adornment. The possibility that the stone balls may have been used as weights implies that a system of measurement may have been in use. These indications, and the hints in the material record of the practice of crafts, suggest that the inhabitants had developed a range of activities that required a considerable investment of time, the acquisition of skills, and access to supplies of appropriate raw materials. Such activities are most likely to have flourished where there was stability of settlement. They should be seen, therefore, as corollaries of the year-round occupation of Abu Hureyra 1 indicated by the plant and animal remains.

Most of the raw materials used for artifacts—the flint, river pebbles, limestone, chalk, and bone—were obtained from the vicinity of the site, but small quantities of other materials were brought from farther away. The basalt used for the grinding dishes came from flows that were at least 80 km distant. The people of Abu Hureyra may have walked there themselves or obtained the basalt through exchange with others. There was no basalt waste in the Abu Hureyra 1 deposits, which implies that the basalt artifacts were shaped where the raw material was quarried. The source of the small quantities of bitumen we recovered is less certain; it may have been in the vicinity of Abu Hureyra or farther down river near Deir ez-Zor.

There are a few other materials that reached the site from time to time, several *Dentalium* sp. shells from the Mediterranean, jadeite, slate, and the obsidian from Anatolia. Visual examination of the obsidian suggests that it came from the Cappadocian and east Anatolian sources. The quantities of marine shells and obsidian are very small, but they are a sign that exchange of some kind was taking place with the inhabitants of the coast 250 km to the west and with central and eastern Anatolia 500 km away. The latter implies, in the absence of contemporary archaeological evidence from Cappadocia, Bingöl, and Lake Van, that there were people living near the obsidian sources 10,000–11,000 years ago.

Abu Hureyra 1 was occupied for so long that we might expect that there would have been significant changes in the artifacts over time. In fact, the most abundant category, the chipped stone, showed remarkable stability. The only noticeable trends were a gradual decrease in scrapers, an increase in retouched pieces, and a reduction in lunate length. This extraordinary continuity matches that of the exploitation of animals. The bone tools exhibited much the same stability of incidence and form, given their small sample size. The stone tools, on the other hand, changed markedly over time. Most of them were concentrated in Period 1B, followed by a sharp decrease in Period 1C. The trend was most striking for the grinding tools, nearly all of which were found in Period 1A and the first half of Period 1B, precisely those parts of the sequence in which the incidence of wild cereals, wild grasses, and small-seeded plants from the valley bottom was highest. Thus, the occurrence of grinding tools, at least, correlated with those plants.

The culture of Abu Hureyra 1 was distinctive and contrasted strongly with that of the settlement that succeeded it only a few centuries later, Abu Hureyra 2. The structures were quite different in the two settlements: pit dwellings followed by huts built of perishable materials in Abu Hureyra 1; multiroomed, rectilinear, mudbrick houses in Abu Hureyra 2. The chipped stone industries also looked different. In Abu Hureyra 1 there was an emphasis on the production of flakes, flake tools, and microliths, while in Abu Hureyra 2, although flakes and flake tools were still a significant element in the assemblage, most of the tools were made on blades, and some of them were new types such as tanged arrowheads. The artifacts would seem to suggest that an almost complete cultural transformation took place in the transition from Abu Hureyra 1 to 2. Yet some elements of the material culture of Abu Hureyra 1 were found in Abu Hureyra 2, indicating that there was a degree of cultural continuity. The bone tools of Abu Hureyra 1 and their methods of manufacture were similar to those of Abu Hureyra 2, with the addition of a few new types. Several kinds of stone tools were found in both Abu Hureyra 1 and 2: the stone balls, hammers, and the distinctive chalk bitumen smearers. The rubbing stones of Abu Hureyra 1 were similar to those of Abu Hureyra 2, although the grinding dishes, already greatly diminished by Period 1C, were replaced by new shapes of grinding slabs. Just as significant were the similarities in the patterns of exchange of raw materials. The range of exotic raw materials was greater in Abu Hureyra 2, but their origin hardly changed. Most of them came from the same sources in a radius of about 150 km, while obsidian and other stones continued to reach Abu Hureyra from Anatolia, and some marine shells from the coast. The only novelty was the appearance of a few rare materials such as turquoise from the southern Levant.

There are still very few contemporary sites known in the Euphrates Valley or elsewhere in central and northern Syria with which to compare the culture of Abu Hureyra 1. Of the three other sites found above the Euphrates dam during the salvage campaign, Dibsi Faraj East and Mureybit (Wilkinson and Moore 1978; J. Cauvin 1977), like Abu Hureyra, were on terraces overlooking the floodplain. Dibsi Faraj East was only 16 km upstream from Abu Hureyra and was visible from it. It was probably once a substantial site which, judging by the similarities in the chipped stone collected from the surface, was occupied about the same time as Abu Hureyra 1 by people with a similar culture. Nahr el Homr (Boerma and Roodenberg 1977) was quite a small site in a side valley 2 km back from the river. It seems to have been inhabited intermittently in Epipalaeolithic 1, late in Epipalaeolithic 2, and early in the Neolithic, on the evidence of the flint tools excavated there. Neither of these sites yielded other artifacts or structures that would allow us to reconstruct their culture more fully.

Mureybit was first inhabited toward the close of the Epipalaeolithic. Only the first phase of occupation here, phase IA, contained artifacts characteristic of this stage. The radiocarbon dates from phase IA indicate that it was contemporary with Period 1C of Abu Hureyra 1 (J. Cauvin 1977, p. 47). Phase IB at Mureybit was clearly transitional in culture between Epipalaeolithic and Neolithic, and phase II was Neolithic. The structures of phase IA were of two kinds, clay floors, presumably of dwellings, and hearths, three of which were pits filled with pebbles and burned debris. The clay floors are reminiscent of Abu Hureyra 1, but the hearths were different.

The artifacts from Mureybit IA consisted of a flint assemblage dominated by microliths; two grinding stones; bone tools, among which bipoints were conspicuous; and several ornaments of polished stone and shell (J. Cauvin 1977, pp. 21–23). This inventory is generally similar to that of Abu Hureyra 1, but there are important differences. The lunates from Mureybit were quite short, and there were small drills in the assemblage of a kind rare at Abu Hureyra. Three of the four grinding stones from both phases I and II were mortars, and only one a quern (Nierlé 1982, p. 197), again a significant departure from Abu Hureyra 1, even allowing for the small sample size. It would appear that the culture of these two sites, only 36 km apart, had many differences in detail. The sites lay on opposite sides of the river, and this seems to have presented a significant obstacle to close cultural interaction.

There are at least two Epipalaeolithic 2 sites in the El Kum basin (Cauvin, Cauvin, and Stordeur 1979, p. 92). Their cultural affiliations are potentially of much interest, given their location on the major route south from Abu Hureyra that passes between the Jebel Abu Rujmein and the Jebel Bishri. Not enough is known about their contents for us to determine the similarities and differences between the culture of these sites and Abu Hureyra 1.

Farther afield there are other Epipalaeolithic 2 sites that have some cultural affinities with Abu Hureyra 2. At Khazne on the north slopes of the Jebel Abdul Aziz, 200 km to the east northeast we found in 1984 a late Epipalaeolithic site with a microlithic assemblage that included lunates. The site is of interest mainly because this is the farthest east that a site of the Levantine late Epipalaeolithic has yet been located. There are general similarities, too, between the flint assemblages of Abu Hureyra 1 and the Epipalaeolithic sites of Beldibi

(Bostanci 1959, p. 146) and Belbaşi (Bostanci 1962, pp. 254–255), 700 km to the west on the south coast of Anatolia near Antalya. In Syria itself there is contemporary material from Yabrud, 250 km to the southwest (Rust 1950, p. 119), and from recently discovered sites in the Jayrud basin nearby (Cauvin et al. 1982).

The best-known comparable contemporary culture is the Natufian of Palestine, the heartland of which lies 500 km to the southwest of the Middle Euphrates. The Natufian was first discovered and then defined by Garrod (1957), who listed a number of features that were characteristic of the more substantial Natufian sites: a microlithic flint industry with plentiful lunates; ground stone tools, among which mortars and pestles were conspicuous; a rich bone industry; fine carvings in bone and stone of humans and animals; and burials of humans on dwelling sites, often accompanied by strings of beads, headdresses, and other decorative elements. She noted, too, that several of the main sites had structures: walls, pavements, and, we may now add, circular huts. Most of these features have been found at the larger Natufian sites, Mugharet el Wad, Erq el Ahmar, Ain Mallaha, Hayonim, and Wadi Hammeh 27 (Garrod and Bate 1937, pp. 9–13; Neuville 1951, pp. 109, 117–118; Perrot 1966; Bar-Yosef and Goren 1973; Edwards 1991).

How similar is the culture of Abu Hureyra 1 to that of the Natufian, so far from the Euphrates? The question is important because the Natufian has yielded such remarkable material remains and has been the subject of intense study by archaeologists for seventy years. We gave an initial answer to the question in our preliminary report published soon after the conclusion of the excavation. It seemed to us that while Abu Hureyra 1, other late Epipalaeolithic sites in the region, and the Natufian shared certain general similarities, there were so many differences in detail between the culture of Abu Hureyra 1 and the Natufian that they should be regarded as distinct (Moore 1975, p. 68). The question has taken on additional significance because some other archaeologists have chosen to link the Epipalaeolithic 2 sites on the Euphrates with the Natufian, and so to extend and effectively alter the definition of this culture (M.-C. Cauvin 1980; Bar-Yosef and Belfer-Cohen 1989, p. 467). Now that we have completed our analysis of the Abu Hureyra 1 remains we can give a more considered response. The structures at Abu Hureyra are quite different from those found on Natufian sites. The chipped stone industry, too, is significantly different in both technology and typology, as Olszewski has shown in her analysis. There are ground stone tools at Abu Hureyra of a quality similar to that at Ain Mallaha and Mugharet el Wad, but the most numerous objects are the grinding dishes, a type rare on Natufian sites where mortars and pestles predominated. The bone tools at Abu Hureyra seem more restricted in range than on Natufian sites, and there are no fine naturalistic carvings in bone or stone. These differences are sufficiently marked to confirm our view that the culture of Abu Hureyra 1 should be distinguished from the Natufian (Moore 1991, pp. 286–291). It has its own special characteristics that give it independent standing as a regional late Epipalaeolithic culture.

The heartland of the Natufian lay in the zone of Mediterranean forest, and both its culture and economy reflect this. The attempt by some to assimilate the Euphrates sites with the Natufian, even allowing for some regional nuances (M.-C. Cauvin 1981b, p. 440), not only distorts the classic definition of the Natufian but also obscures the real ecological and cultural differences between these two groups of sites. Abu Hureyra 1 was in the steppe zone yet lay in the

Euphrates Valley, and its closest relations were with other sites in the immediate vicinity along the right bank of the river. Both its culture and economy were conditioned by its location. It had distinctive structures and a settlement history that developed over a long period of time. Its artifacts reflect the way of life of its inhabitants, the intensive use of the bow, and grinding tools for processing seeds, for example. The significance of these features can only be understood properly when they are considered on their own terms.

SUMMARY

The location of Abu Hureyra 1 was carefully chosen to take advantage of the resources of both the river valley and the steppe. The place was so favorable for human occupation that it permitted successive generations of inhabitants to remain there for an unprecedented 1,500 years. Abu Hureyra 1 is the only site of its age in Southwest Asia where such a lengthy span of occupation has been conclusively demonstrated, and one of only two or three contemporary sites in the entire Levant that may have been occupied for comparable lengths of time. During at least the previous 10,000 years sites were occupied intermittently for a few years at most, so the establishment of this new kind of long-lived settlement in a few highly favorable locations represented a revolution in the prevailing pattern of settlement.

The structures used in the settlement did change through time, most strikingly in the transition from Period 1A to 1B with the replacement of the pit dwellings with above-ground huts. This shows that cultural change could occur rapidly in the settlement. Yet the shifts in the use of the excavated area were more gradual: the hearth area on the east side remained in use for several hundred years, and the entire space seems to have been used for domestic activities throughout. In the absence of any evidence for temporary desertions of the site, it appears that occupation was extraordinarily intense throughout the life of the settlement in the area we excavated.

The slight changes in the chipped stone and bone tool assemblages over the life of the settlement also attest to remarkable cultural stability. The stone tools did drop sharply in number from Period 1B to 1C, largely because of a decrease in the manufacture of grinding tools. This appears to have been linked to the decrease in the use of seeds and nuts noted by Hillman, as the Mediterranean forest moved farther away from the Euphrates Valley. While most artifacts seem to have been used primarily in subsistence pursuits, we have seen that the inhabitants practiced crafts, activities that accord well with the evidence for long-term occupation. This, and the care with which some types of artifacts were made, is evidence for some elaboration of culture. There are indications, too, that the people of Abu Hureyra 1 had symbolic as well as aesthetic concerns.

We should note that the most complete assemblages of artifacts were found in Periods 1A and 1B and that there was little subsequent change in the form of individual types. This implies that the culture typical of the earlier centuries of Abu Hureyra 1 had already been developed elsewhere in the region by the ancestors of those who founded the settlement. Settlements typical of this putative stage of cultural development have yet to be found.

The inhabitants obtained nearly all the raw materials they needed from the environs of Abu Hureyra 1, but they were prepared to seek farther on occasion to obtain basalt for their grinding tools and other prized materials they particularly wanted. This wider zone had a maximum radius of about 150 km. The modest evidence for exchange of shells and exotic stones from much more distant sources does indicate that they were in touch infrequently with other groups over a much wider area of the northern Levant and central Anatolia. Nonetheless, the cultural evidence clearly indicates that, for most of the inhabitants, their world extended no more than a day or two's march from the site.

Part III THE VILLAGE OF ABU HUREYRA 2

8 The Excavation of Abu Hureyra 2

A. M. T. Moore

TRENCH B

Excavation of the Trench

Trench B was one of four trenches that we excavated along the north-south axis of Abu Hureyra to obtain a complete stratigraphic sequence of occupation for the site (figure 2.14). A modern house stood on a high point astride this axis towards the center of the mound. A little level ground lay between the house and the steep western slope of the mound. We laid Trench B out there.

We opened a trench 4 by 5 m in size in the 1972 season (figure 8.1). Once the phase 9 building was exposed in 1973, it became necessary to enlarge the trench to clear more of this structure. The east and west sides were extended by 1 m and the north side by 2 m, creating a 6 × 7 m trench. After the phase 8 house was excavated we had to reduce the area of the trench to a 4 × 4 m square to speed the work. The trench was further reduced to a 4 × 1.5 m rectangle for the excavation of phases 6 to 1 down to the natural subsoil. The stratification and phasing of the levels we excavated are shown in figures 8.2–7.

The Stratigraphic Sequence

In phase 1 the hard, pebbly subsoil was leveled off and a building was constructed on it (figures 8.2, 8.3). This building had a black plaster floor laid directly on the subsoil (221). The plaster floor ran up to a wall that cut across the northwest corner of the trench (figure 8.8). The floor was replaced twice in this phase; each time, its surface was covered with a layer of clay and new black plaster was laid on top.

This building was the first of a series to be built on this part of the site (figure 8.2). We think they were all houses because of the general similarity of their

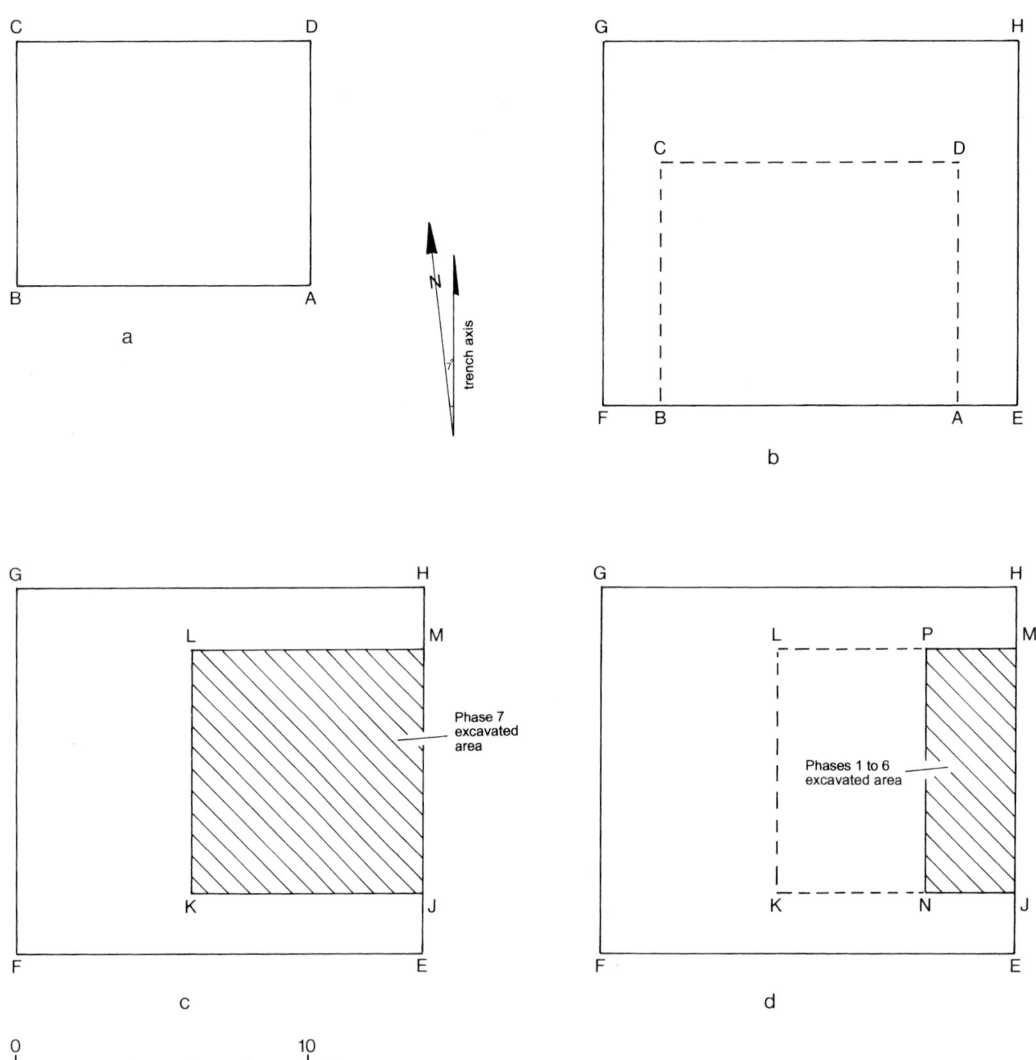

Figure 8.1 The excavation of Trench B in 1972(a) and in 1973, phases 8-11(b), phase 7 (c), and 1–6(d).

form, construction, and contents. Only part of one room was excavated in the small area exposed in the bottom of the trench, but the structure was presumably a multiroomed house like its successors. It was on the same general northwest-to-southeast alignment as all the later houses superimposed on it.

The phase 1 house was remodeled in phase 2. A mudbrick wall was built across the northeast corner of the trench. A black plaster floor was laid on the floor of the room to the south and later renewed three times (220 and 219). The uppermost floor had a firepit at the north end of the trench (218). Then this room was deliberately filled with clay (216). Occupation debris accumulated on this fill (215).

In phase 3 a new building was erected on the site of the phase 2 house (figures 8.2, 8.8). The surface was partly covered with clay (214) and then a series

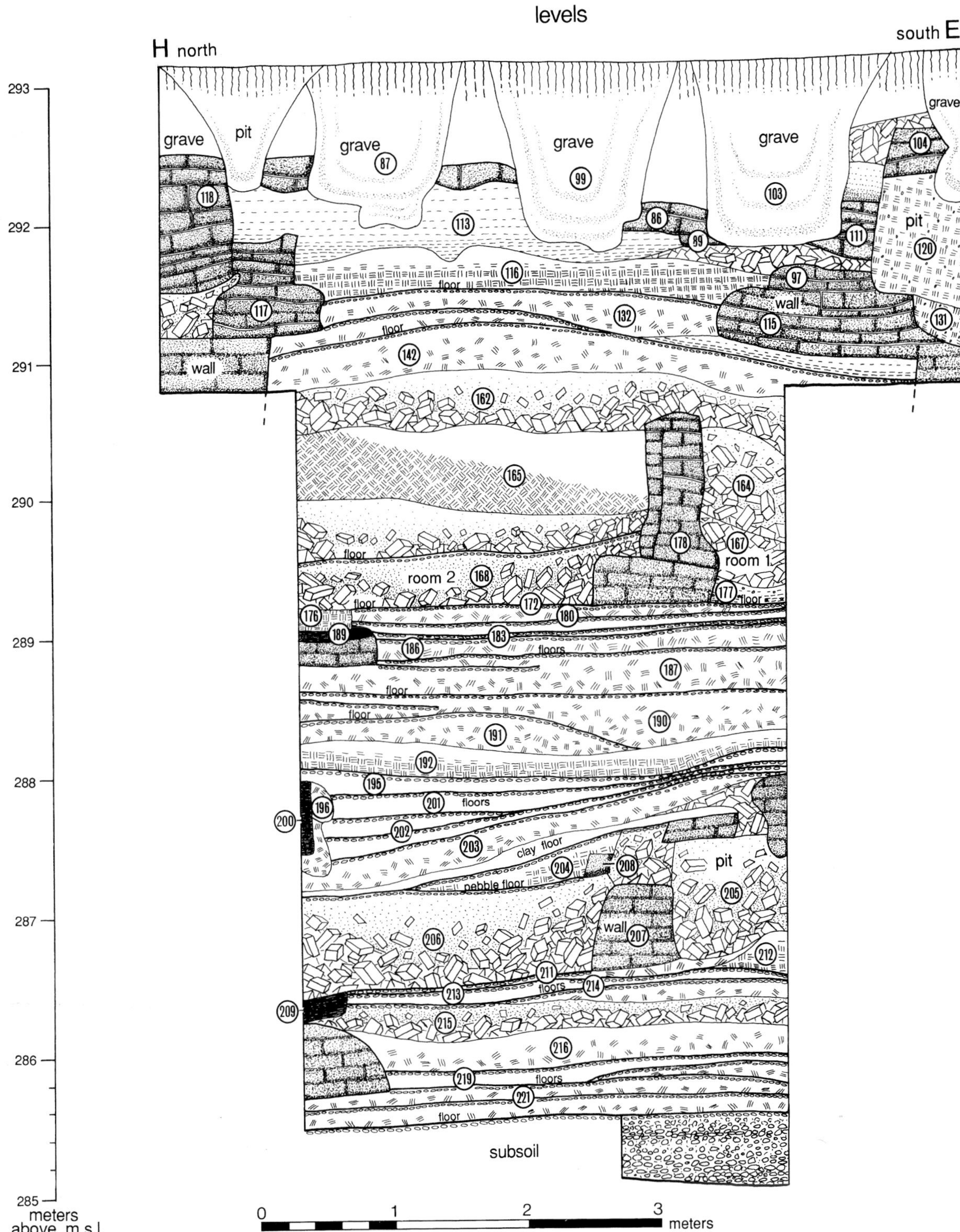

Figure 8.2 Trench B, Section H-E, levels. See appendix 3.

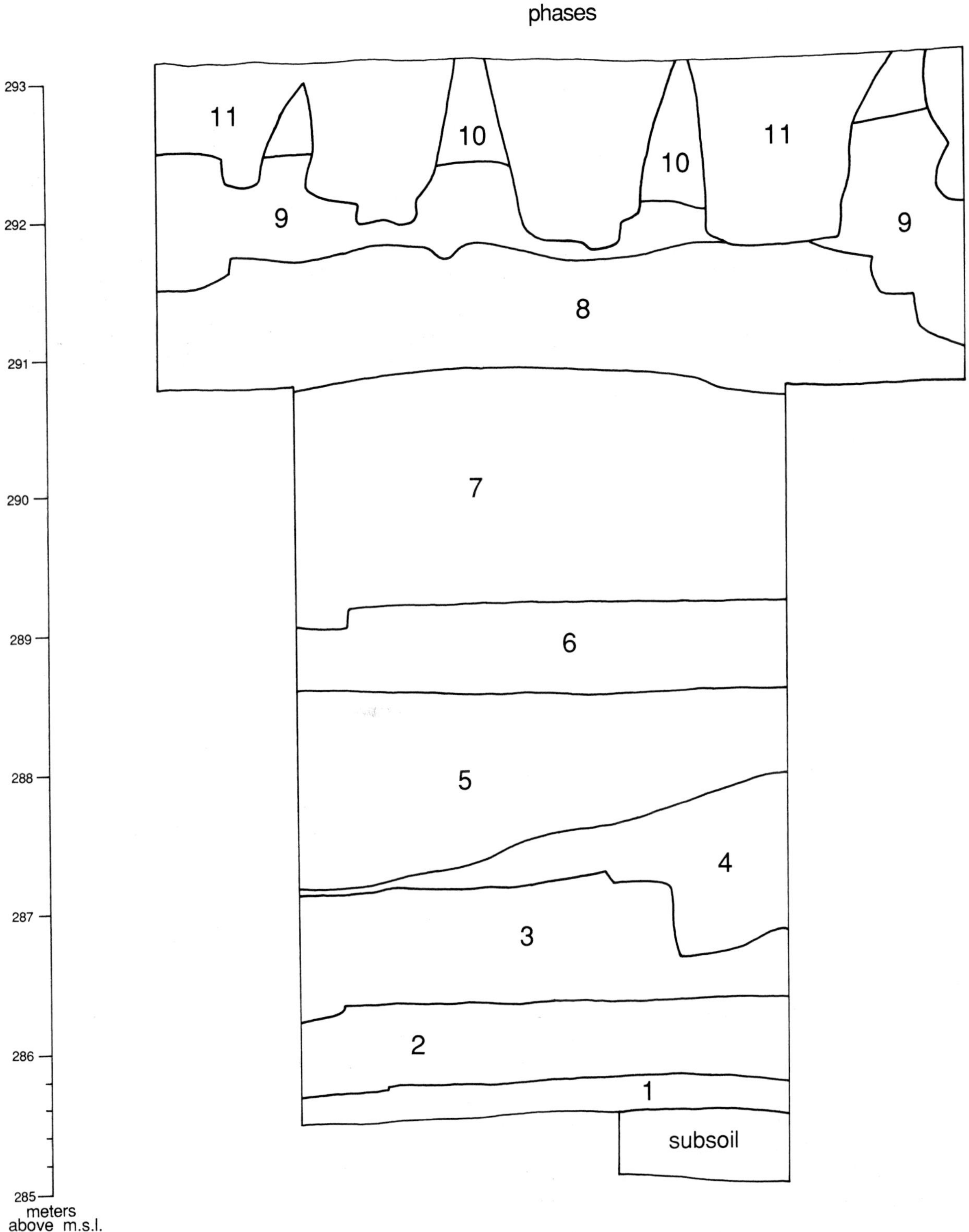

Figure 8.3 Trench B, Section H-E, phases.

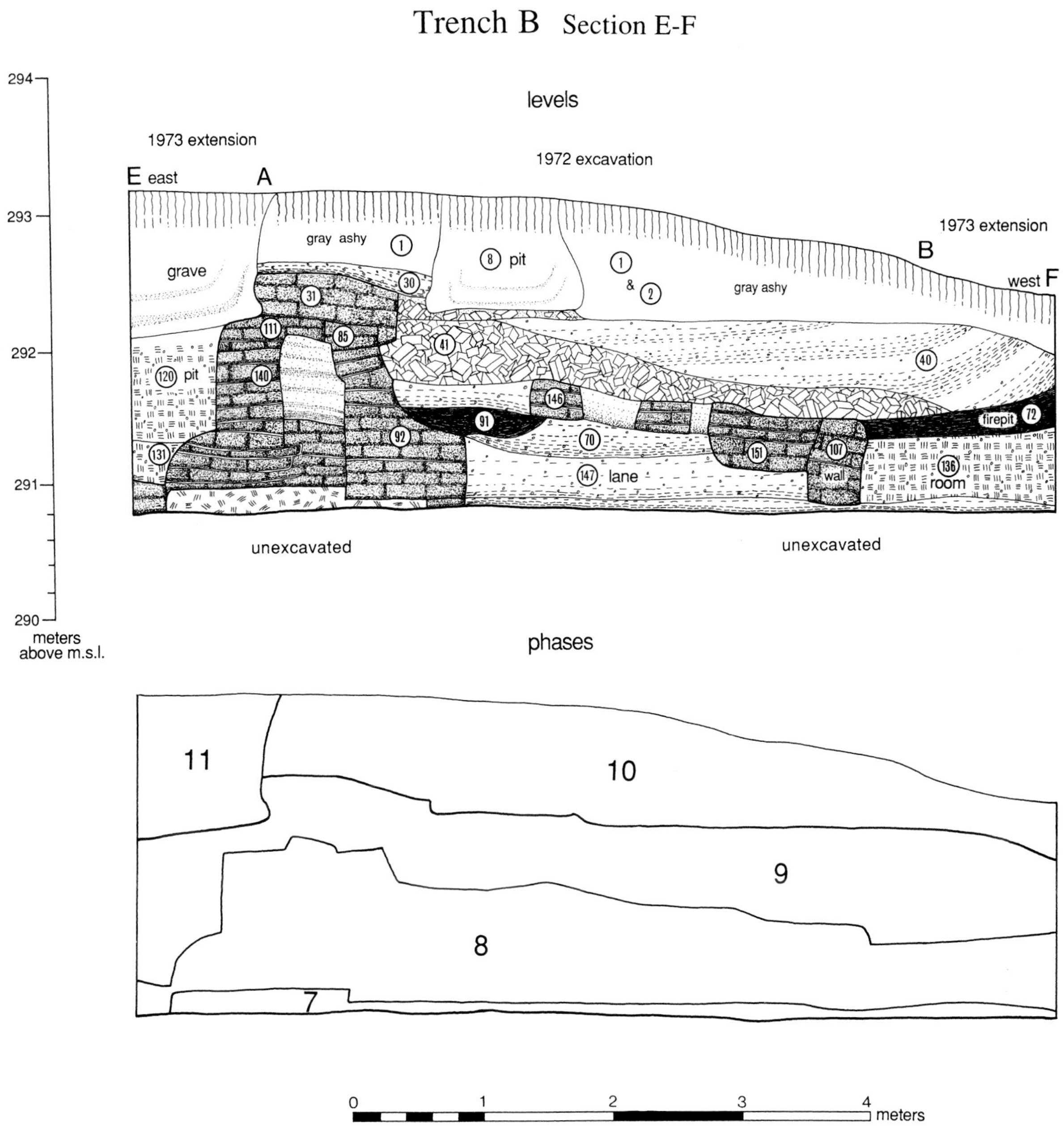

Figure 8.4 Trench B, Section E-F, levels and phases.

of plaster floors was laid on top (213, 211). These all ran up to a firepit in the northeast corner of the trench (209). The occupants of the houses in phases 5, 6, and 7 constructed a hearth in almost exactly the same place. Late in phase 3 a wall (207) was built on the uppermost plaster floor (211) to divide the room into two. The building then went out of use, and mudbrick debris and occupation material (206) accumulated on the north side of wall 207.

In phase 4 a mudbrick wall (208) was built on the site of the phase 3 house that curved away to the northwest. This wall followed approximately the line of wall 207 of phase 3. A pebble floor was laid down on the north side of wall 208. A pit (205) was dug on the south side of this wall that damaged it and penetrated the phase 3 building. Later in phase 4, wall 208 collapsed. There were traces of other structures on top and then the building was replaced altogether.

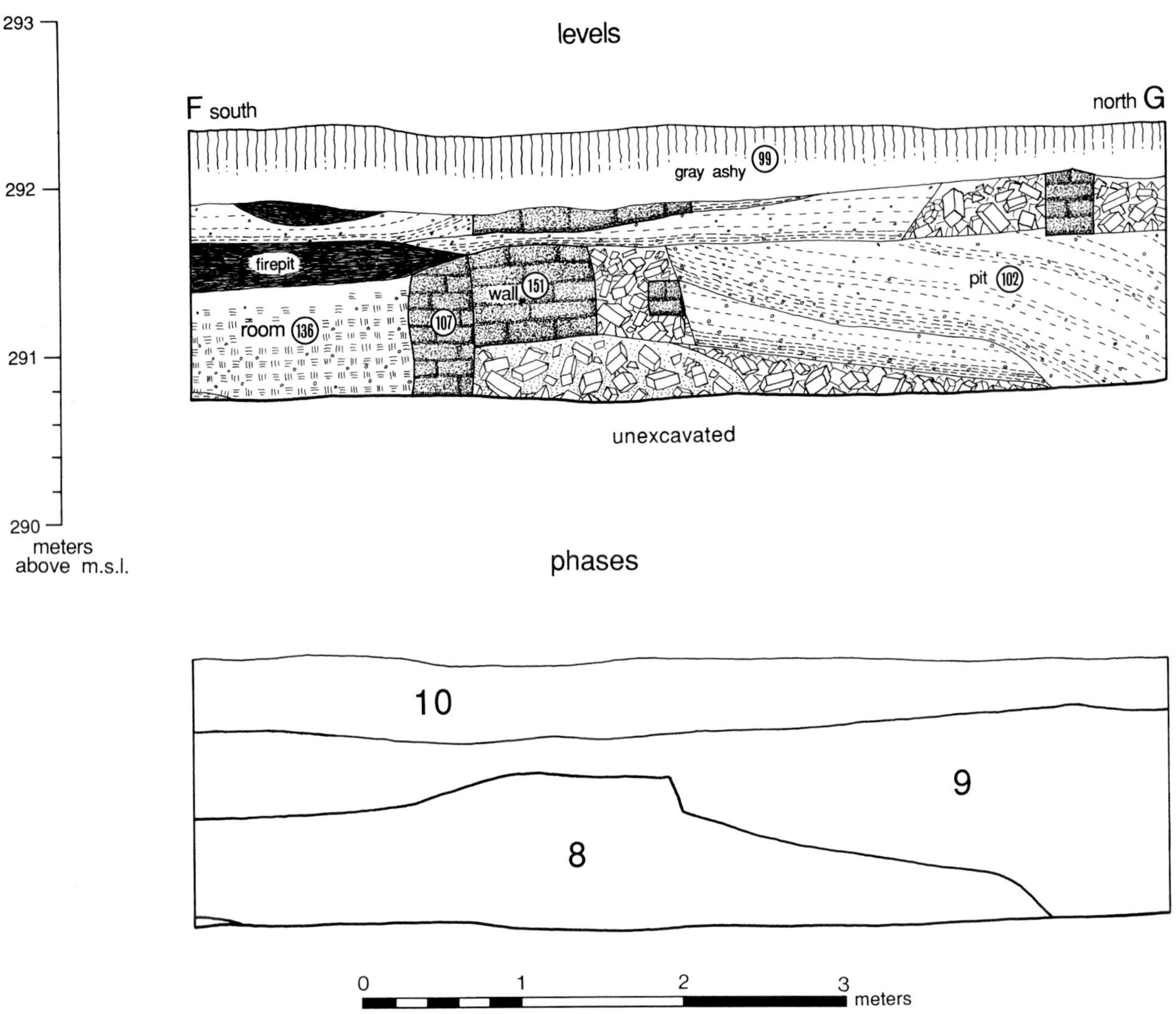

Figure 8.5 Trench B, Section F-G, levels and phases.

A layer of red clay (203) was laid down in phase 5 in which there were traces of floor surfaces, and then a new building was constructed over the phase 4 structure. The trench cut through part of one room of this building (figures 8.2, 8.9). This room had a series of ten black plaster floors (202, 201, 199, 197, 195, 193), each laid on a bed of red clay and pebbles. The nine lower floors all had a hearth in the northeast corner of the trench (200) and another at the southern end (198). The uppermost floor (193) had a square hearth toward the middle of the trench.

One of these floors (197) had a design painted on it in red at the southern end of the trench (figure 8.9) that resembled a child's drawing of a sun. There were faint traces of other painting in red to the north on the same floor. The sun design was relatively well preserved because it had been covered by a low, black plaster platform that had been constructed over it in the southwest cor-

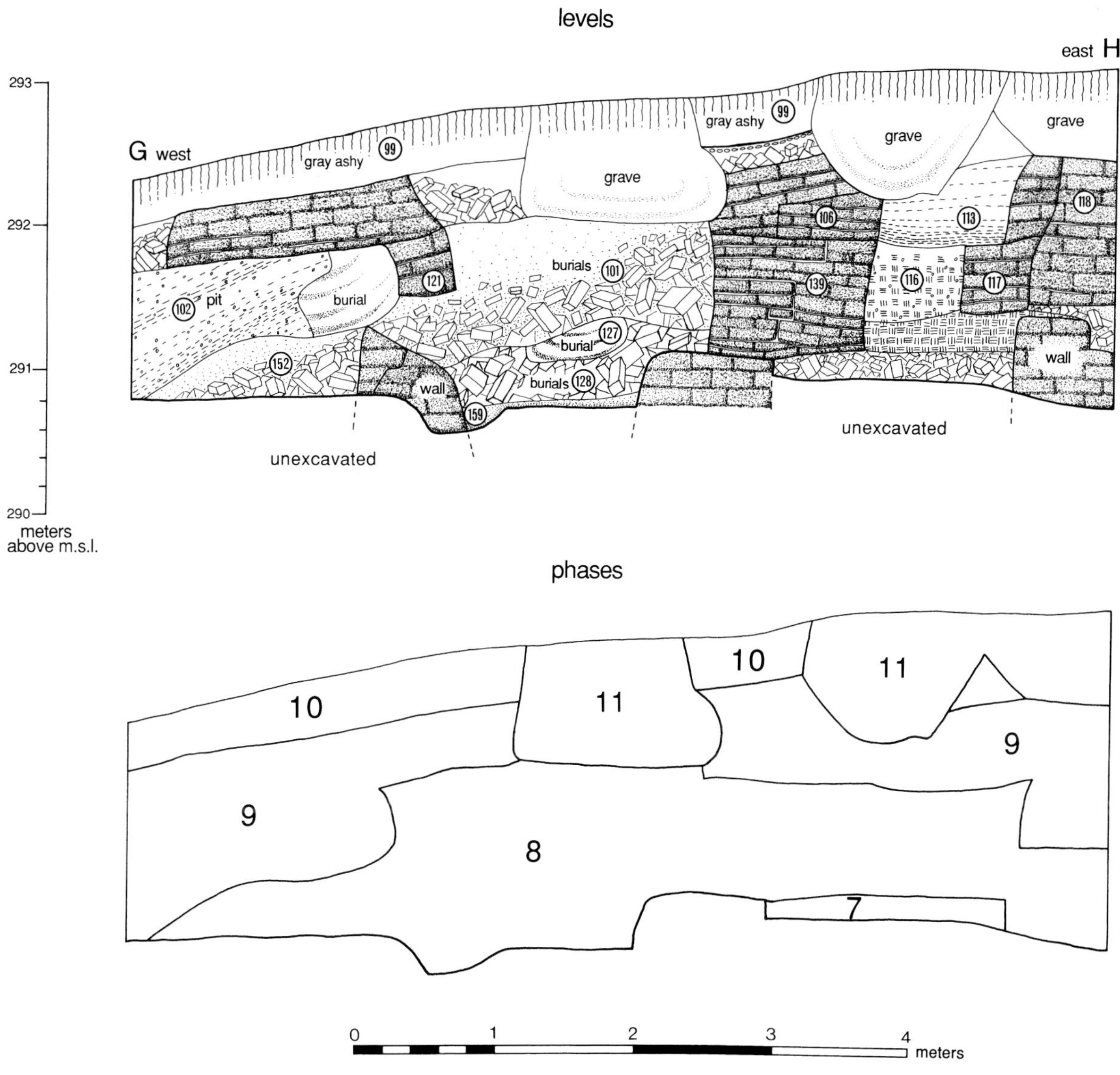

Figure 8.6 Trench B, Section G-H, levels and phases.

ner of the trench. The platform was raised 8 cm above the floor and was renewed twice. It may have served as a sitting and sleeping area.

Late in phase 5 a mudbrick wall was built on floor 193 across the northwest corner of the trench. The floor of this room was then covered with layers of red clay fill in which there were clay floors (192, 191,190).

The phase 5 occupation was covered with a further layer of red clay fill (187), and then another house was built above in phase 6. Part of one room of this house was exposed in the excavation (figure 8.9). A wall cut across the northwest corner of the trench, indicating that this house was built on the same alignment as the houses of earlier phases. The floor of the room was covered with black plaster. There was a hearth toward the center of the room (188, figure 8.10) while the plaster floor (187) ran up to another hearth (189) made of

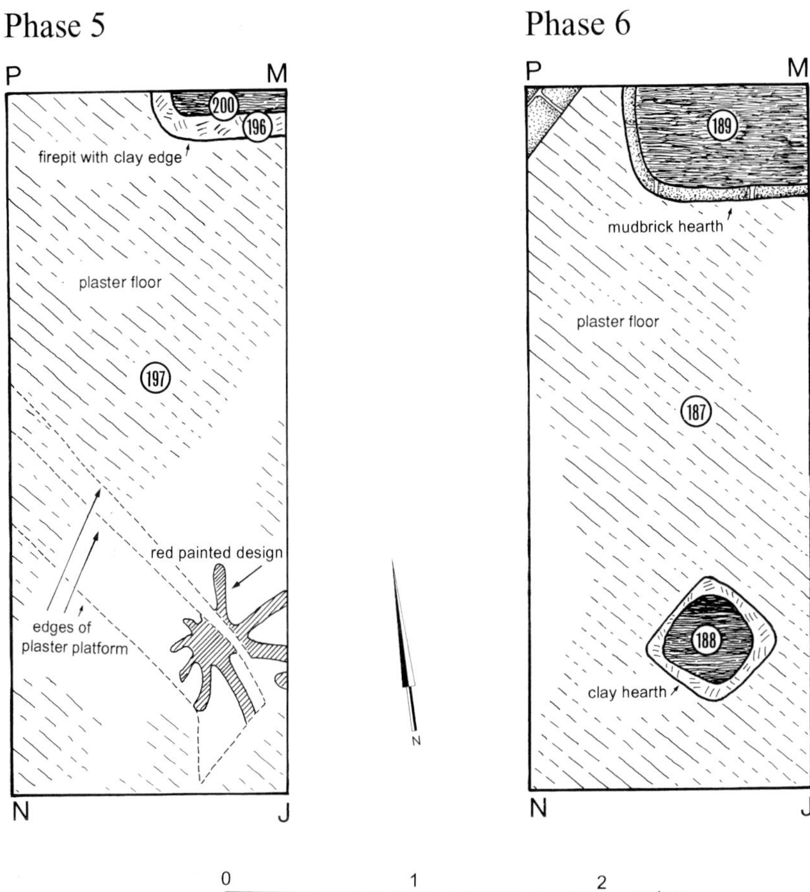

Figure 8.9 Trench B, plans of phases 5 and 6.

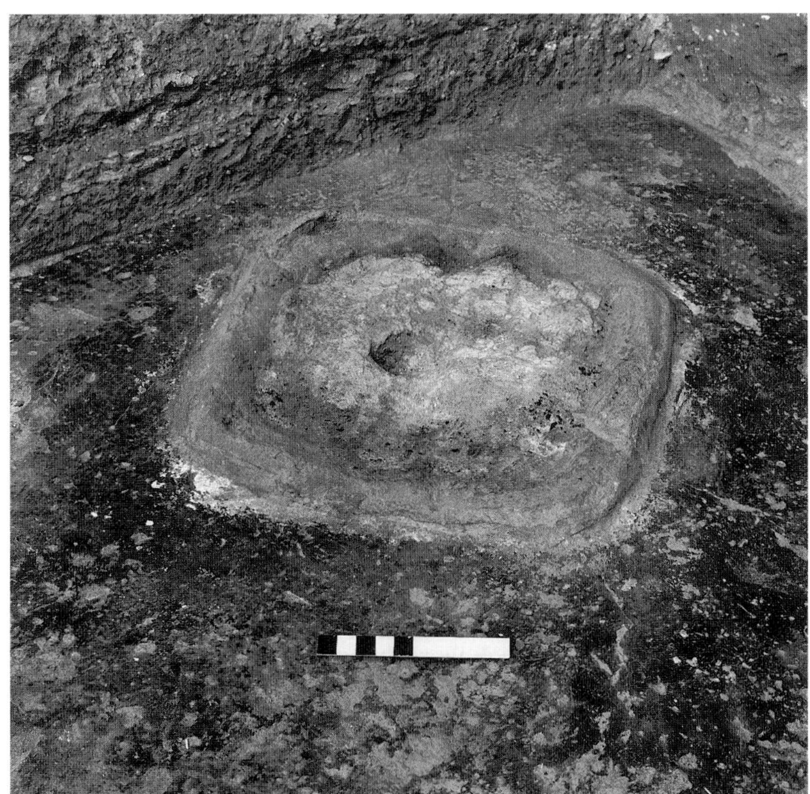

Figure 8.10 Trench B, hearth 188 set in a black plaster floor of the phase 6 house, from the northwest. Scale, 70 cm.

Trench B

Phase 7

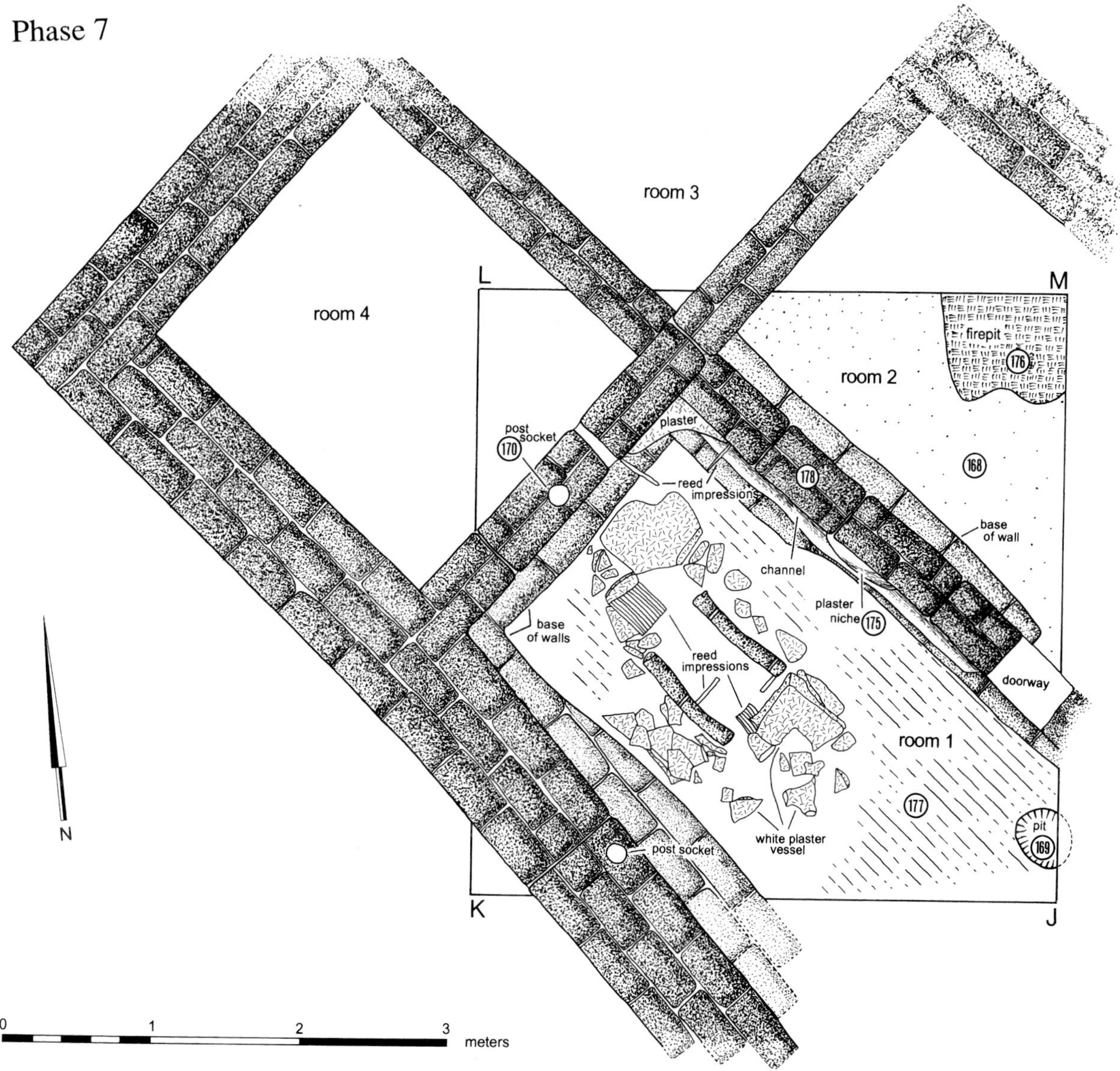

Figure 8.11 Trench B, plan of the phase 7 house.

have supported the roof, a second story, or some other superstructure. This suggests that the walls were preserved to about their original height.

The form of wall 178 was of particular interest. It butted directly against the crosswall in the northwest corner of the excavated area but was not bonded to it. The wall was built in at least two stages (figure 8.2). A plinth 80 cm wide and 40 cm high was constructed first. In room 1 the top of this plinth was molded in the form of a channel, of uncertain function. Next, a narrower (40 cm) dividing wall was constructed on top of the plinth. This was pierced by a small doorway (1.3 m high, 55 cm wide) at its eastern end (figure 8.13). The doorway had a sill 30 cm high. The mudbrick capping to the doorway was still intact, a testimony to the strength of the original construction. The interior of the doorway had probably been framed in timber to support this capping, al-

Figure 8.12 Trench B, rooms 1 and 2 in the phase 7 house, from the northeast. A plaster vessel lies broken on the floor of room 1. Scale, 50 cm.

Figure 8.13 Trench B, the doorway in wall 178 between rooms 1 and 2 of the phase 7 house, from the southwest. Scale, 1 m.

though no trace of such framing could be detected in the excavation. The southwest face of wall 178 incorporated one other remarkable feature, an oval niche 65 cm high, 55 cm wide, and 21 cm deep on the inside (175), made of plaster and recessed slightly into the wall (figure 8.14). This would have served as a receptacle at a convenient height above floor level. The niche was coated with whitewash within and without, as was the face of the entire wall on this side.

The floors in rooms 1 and 2 were repaired several times in phase 7. The original floor in room 1 was of black plaster; this was covered with layers of white plaster and clay, much of which later wore away. The floor in room 2 was so badly worn that little of the original plaster surface remained.

A large whiteware vessel sat in the center of the northwest end of room 1 on floor 177 (figure 8.12). It was built early in phase 7 and was obviously intended as a permanent feature of the room. The vessel was broken, but enough pieces of it lay on the floor to indicate its form (figure 8.15). Two parallel lines of mudbrick were laid 60 cm apart along the floor to define a rectangular space for the vessel. The openings between the ends of these lines of mudbrick were closed off with low vertical partitions of reeds set in white plaster. There was also a reed and plaster division toward the center of this space. Then the plaster vessel itself was constructed on top of this enclosure. The plaster vessel was rectangular in plan with rounded corners. It was about 1.1 m long, 70 cm wide, and at least 60 cm high. It sat on top of the mudbrick and plastered-reed box prepared for it, the floor of the room serving as the bottom of the vessel. The top of the vessel curved inwards toward a round hole in the center, and there was one other square hole in each end. This vessel seems to have served as a container, although there was nothing within it to indicate precisely what it

Figure 8.14 Trench B, the plaster niche 175 in wall 178, with channel below, from the southwest. Scale, 20 cm.

Figure 8.15 Trench B, the broken plaster vessel on the floor of room 1 in the phase 7 house, from the southwest. Scale, 50 cm.

may have once held. The nature of its construction meant that it must have been used to hold dry goods, perhaps foodstuffs.

Watson saw somewhat similar containers, which she termed chests, in houses in the village of Hasanabad in the Zagros (Watson 1979, figures 5.41–43). The chests were used to hold flour, grain, or other foodstuffs. They were freestanding, like two of those that we found, and made of chaff-tempered mud that had been dried in the sun. They were often rectangular in shape and stood up to 1.3 m high—a range of sizes similar to those from Abu Hureyra. The chests were filled through a hole in the top and emptied from the bottom. They thus provide a good analogy for our examples.

Rooms 1 and 2 were used from the beginning of phase 7 and were connected by the doorway in wall 178. Both rooms seem to have served domestic functions as living rooms and for storage of foodstuffs. The connecting doorway was later blocked with mudbrick and plaster on the room 2 side, creating a rectangular niche in room 1. Room 2 began to fill with occupation debris (168) in which traces of a later floor level were found. Both rooms were then abandoned and filled quite quickly with building debris and occupation material. The tip lines in level 165 in room 2 indicated that the material in this level was dumped in from the north. The relatively rapid filling of these rooms and, presumably, the others in the house, preserved it to an unusual height. Eventually the interior walls of the house were covered (163), leaving only the tops of the exterior walls visible.

The tops of the outer walls of the phase 7 house were used as foundations for a new building in phase 8. We excavated the entire 6 × 7 m area of Trench

B in this phase, revealing part of the plan of this structure and a little of an adjacent one in the southwest corner of the trench (figures 8.4–6, 8.16). The two buildings were separated by a 2-m-wide lane (147) choked with occupation refuse.

The deposits at the west end of the trench were attenuated because erosion had removed much of this side of the mound, leaving a steep slope down to the valley floor. In consequence, much of the house in the southwest corner of the trench (wall 107 and occupation level 136) had eroded away. The lane (147) once ran much farther in a northwesterly direction but it, too, had been truncated by erosion. This evidence, together with similar data from Trenches A and D, suggests that the mound had extended significantly farther to the west at the time the site was inhabited.

That part of the main phase 8 building found within the trench originally consisted of one large room, 7.25 m long and 5 m wide. There may have been other rooms to the northeast and southeast, as in later structures on this spot. The floor of the large room was leveled up with a mixture of red clay and pebbles, and a white plaster floor was laid down (142). Then a wall (139) was built across the northwest corner of the room, creating a small chamber at that end of the house, accessible from the main room through a doorway (figure 8.16). There were burials of children in that wall. The small chamber was used as a charnel room for bodies of the dead. We found numerous partial or complete human skeletons there, dug into the floor and in the fill of the room (159). The building itself looked like all the other houses we excavated in Trench B, and its primary function may have been as a dwelling, but the accumulation of burials within it was most unusual and gave it a special character (see chapter 10).

Later in phase 8 the two buildings in Trench B were remodeled (figure 8.17). The large room in the center of the trench was divided down the middle with a wall that had a wide base and narrower upper part (115, 97). This created two smaller, narrower rooms that had thin, heavily worn, white plaster floors (figure 8.18). Room 2 contained evidence of an episode of flint blade production in the form of a series of freshly struck blades with a double-ended core, all of the same kind of fine-grained flint. In the northwest corner of room 2, under the floor, there was a burial pit (144) 70 cm deep that contained a group of partial skeletons in poor condition (figure 8.19).

The doorway into the charnel room at the northwest end of the building was closed with mudbrick. This chamber was rebuilt and then continued to be used for depositing corpses throughout the remainder of the occupation of the building. There were two more levels there (128, 101) that contained partial or complete skeletons deposited over many years in at least three episodes. Access to the rebuilt chamber may have been from outside rather than from within the building. The upper level of burials (101) lay on a white plastered floor and had been burned. This accidental fire apparently occurred as the northwest end of the building collapsed, since pieces of reddened mudbrick were mixed with the other burned debris in the chamber. The burning in this area was quite intensive and was the reason why the chamber ceased to be used immediately afterward.

This building had a fourth room (room 4) beyond wall 117 in the northeast corner and a fifth (room 5) to the southeast. It was thus a structure of considerable size with at least five rooms, even if the individual rooms were small.

The lane separating this building from the house in the southwest corner of the trench continued in use. There were traces of several floor surfaces here

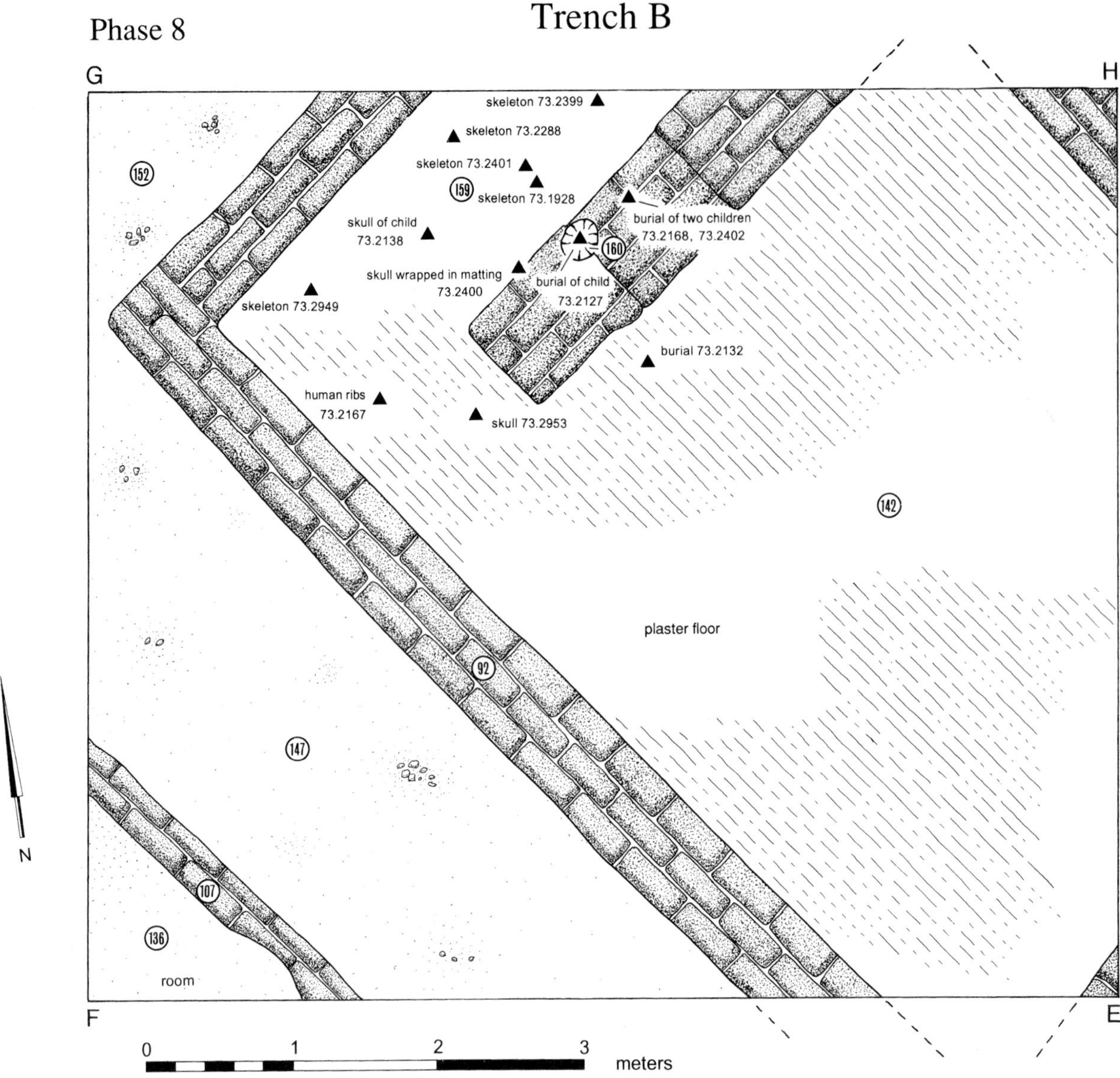

Figure 8.16 Trench B, plan of the phase 8 structures.

(70) as well as the remains of numerous small hearths. The lane had filled up with occupation debris, especially the bones of animals, mudbricks, and mud wash from the nearby walls. The outer wall of the house in the southwest corner was widened (wall 151), and late in the phase a small room was added on (wall 146) that projected into the lane, narrowing it still further.

These buildings then passed out of use. The walls were cut down until only stubs remained, presumably to provide material for construction elsewhere, and building debris accumulated in the structures and around them.

A new house was constructed in phase 9 on top of the main phase 8 building (figure 8.20). This closely followed the plan of its predecessor; indeed, several of the walls of the phase 9 house (111, 85, 106, 118) were built on or beside the stubs of walls of the phase 8 structure. This house, too, was a multiroomed, rectilinear building. We excavated two of its rooms (rooms 1 and 2) within the trench. These rooms had floors of trodden earth. The large amount of mudbrick

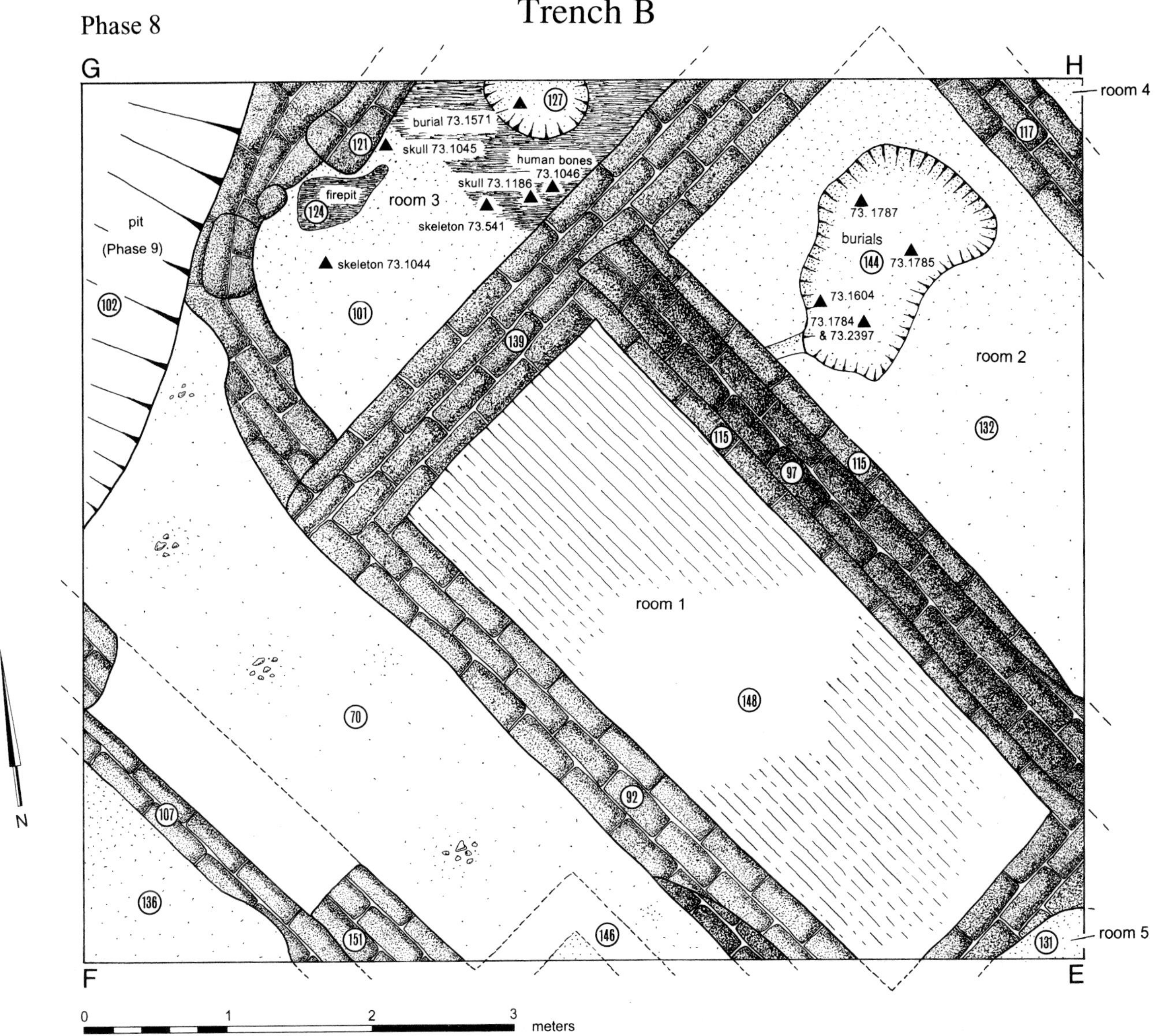

collapse found in and around this house suggested that there were more rooms in the unexcavated portion to the east.

A large pit (102) was dug in the northwest corner of the trench that penetrated deep into the underlying phase 8 levels. This pit was filled with ash, charcoal, stones, bones, and flint artifacts, all of them much affected by burning. The open space to the south of the pit also contained ashy occupation deposits that indicated the area had been intensively used for domestic activities by the inhabitants of nearby houses.

In time, the house fell into disrepair and was abandoned. Then its walls were rebuilt and habitation continued. Scraps of plaster floors were found associated with several of the rebuilt walls. Beyond the house, in the northwest corner of the trench and to the west, there were other mudbrick structures contemporary with this episode of reuse. The open area in the southwest corner continued to be used intensively. There were many superimposed floor sur-

Figure 8.17 Trench B, plan of the structures late in phase 8 after their remodeling.

Figure 8.18 Trench B, the phase 8 building, from the southeast. Scale, 1m.

Figure 8.19 Trench B, the phase 8 building, from the southeast. Note the doorway to the charnel room, and the burial pit in room 2. Scale 1 m.

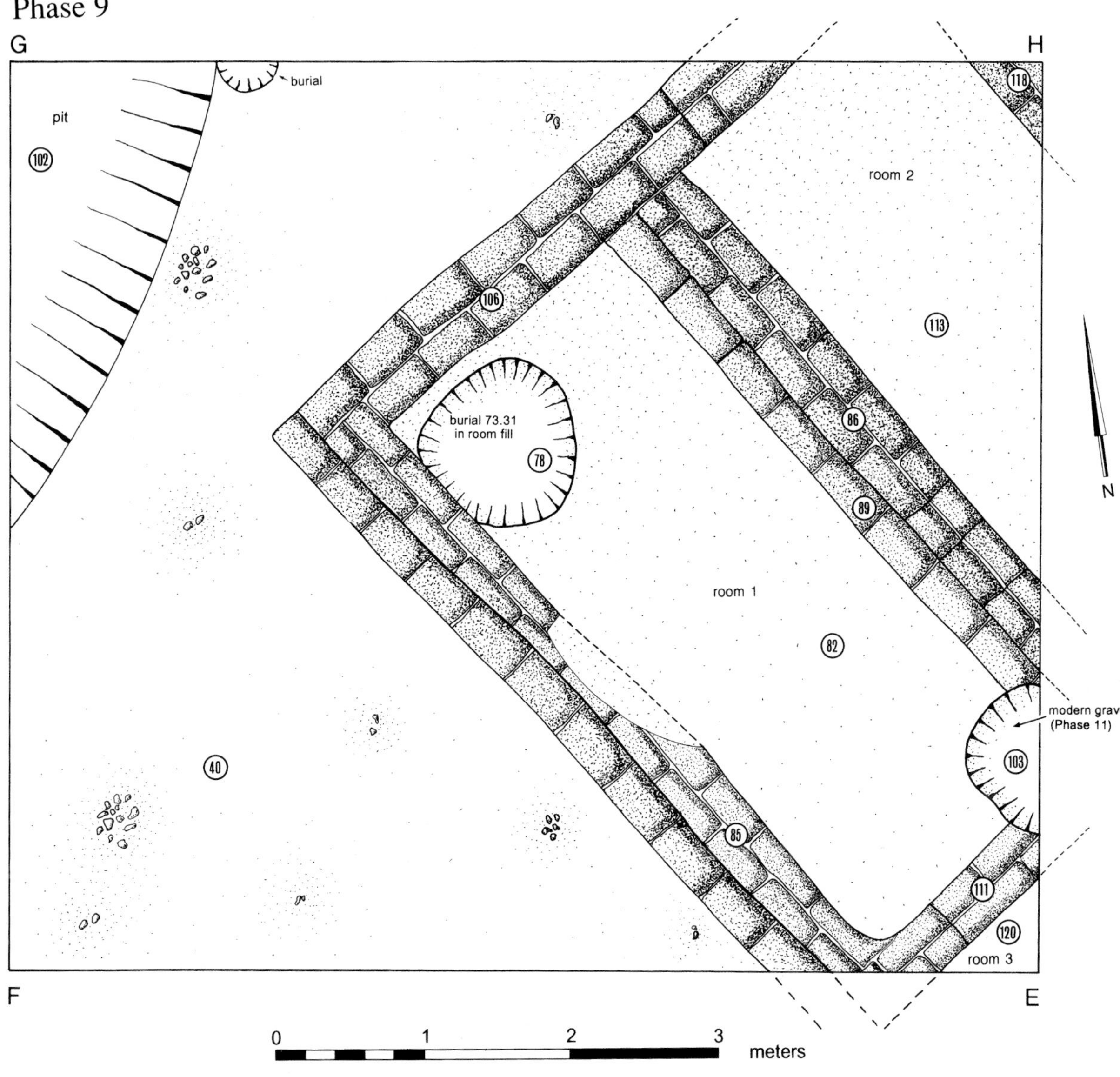

Figure 8.20 Trench B, plan of the phase 9 house.

faces here (40) that sloped up to the west. The evidence of these floors and the presence of buildings west of the trench indicated that the settlement extended much farther west on level, or even upwardly sloping, ground in this phase.

The phase 9 structures were eventually abandoned and allowed to collapse.

We examined the features characteristic of phase 10 in detail only in the 4 × 5 m trench excavated in 1972 (figure 8.21). During this phase a deposit of dark, ashy occupation debris accumulated all over the trench that survived to a depth of between 30 cm and 1 m. This deposit was originally dark in color but had weathered to gray because of its prolonged exposure on the surface of the mound. It was probably much deeper originally, but a great deal of this ashy material had washed off the mound into the Euphrates Valley. The phase 10 deposit was heavily disturbed by both the activities of the inhabitants themselves and people in recent times. The occupants dug at least three small, shal-

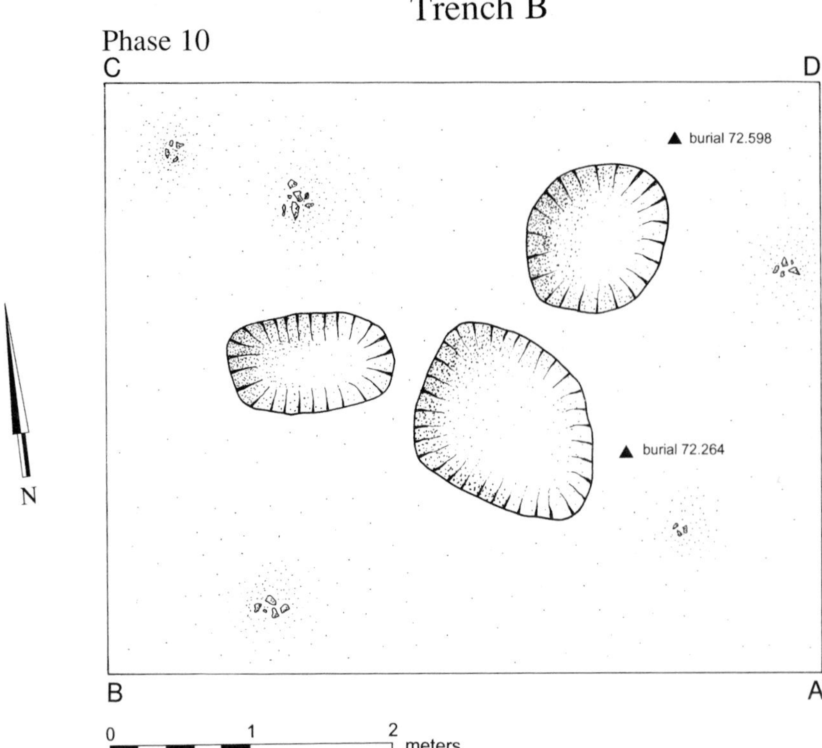

Figure 8.21 Trench B, plan of the features in phase 10.

low pits (32, 49, 55) into the mound that penetrated phase 9 levels. These pits were up to 1.45 m in diameter and 1 m deep. They were filled with ashy occupation debris, animal bones, charcoal, and flint artifacts. There were two shallow graves of humans beside these pits.

Prehistoric occupation in the vicinity of Trench B concluded at the end of phase 10.

Phase 11 encompassed all use of the Trench B area in historic times. The most conspicuous activity was the use of the soft, ashy soil of the surface of the mound for a cemetery. A series of graves was dug into the surface on an east-west alignment. They were usually oval in plan and large enough to accommodate an extended adult human burial. These graves were accompanied by very few artifacts, but the excellent condition of the bones suggested that they were dug in historic times. Beside the graves were pits that contained animal bones, scraps of iron, glass, and other modern artifacts.

Summary

The long sequence we found in Trench B apparently spanned almost the entire life of the Neolithic settlement at Abu Hureyra. It was matched only by the sequence from Trench C. Phases 1–9 consisted of a series of superimposed, rectilinear, mudbrick houses that were constructed on the same northwest-southeast alignment. The earliest house, built in phase 1, was constructed directly on the subsoil. Thereafter, in each phase a new house was constructed on the remains of its predecessor with no significant interval of erosion or soil deposition between.

We excavated several rooms in each of the house of phases 7, 8, and 9, enough to indicate that these structures were of similar plan. Some of the architectural details were precisely the same in each phase: one large room was built in the houses of phases 7 and 8, for example, that was later subdivided, a feature first noticed in the phase 3 house. A hearth was made in the same place, the northeast corner of the excavated area, in the houses of phases 3, 5, 6, and 7.

There was an abrupt change in use of the Trench B area in phase 10. Occupation of a domestic kind continued here, perhaps even more intensively than before, but the character of the structures changed markedly. The main feature was the digging of a series of pits of moderate size, themselves full of occupation refuse. One such pit was already present in the northwest corner of the trench in phase 9. There may have been mudbrick buildings nearby in phase 10, but none was definitely present in the trench. Clearly, such structures were spaced much more widely in this phase.

Abu Hureyra was abandoned at the end of phase 10 and not reinhabited until the twentieth century AD. A few centuries ago, the inhabitants of the region did, however, use the Trench B area for burying their dead.

TRENCH D

Excavation of the Trench

We excavated Trench D well down the western slope of the mound to ascertain the nature of the Abu Hureyra settlement toward its edge. We thought that this trench would provide information about the original extent of the settlement, and whether it had been surrounded by a wall at any time in its history, as contemporary Jericho had been (Kenyon 1981, figure 2). The trench was placed directly below Trench C so that the sequences of occupation in each of these trenches might be compared.

We excavated the 8 × 3 m rectangle of Trench D (figure 8.22) down to the natural surface in both seasons. We dug a test trench of 2.6 × 1 m into the subsoil at the bottom to establish the nature of the bedrock in this part of the mound. The sections of the trench and its level diagram are illustrated in figures 8.23–29.

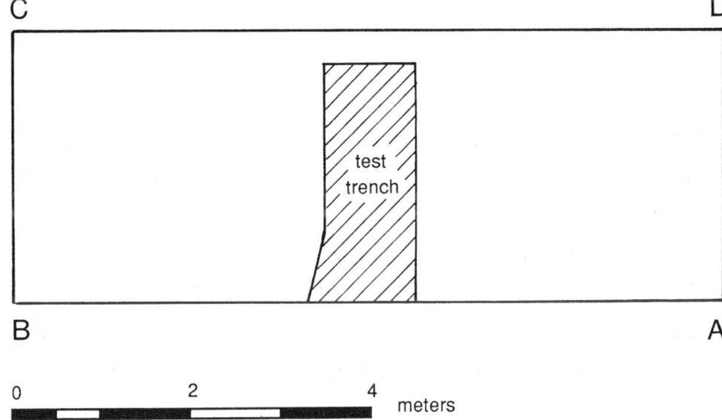

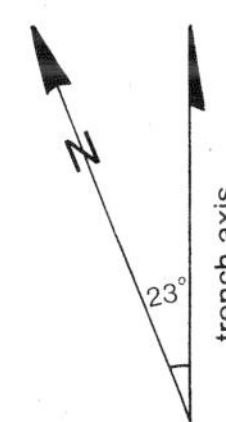

Figure 8.22 The excavation of Trench D.

Trench D Section A-B

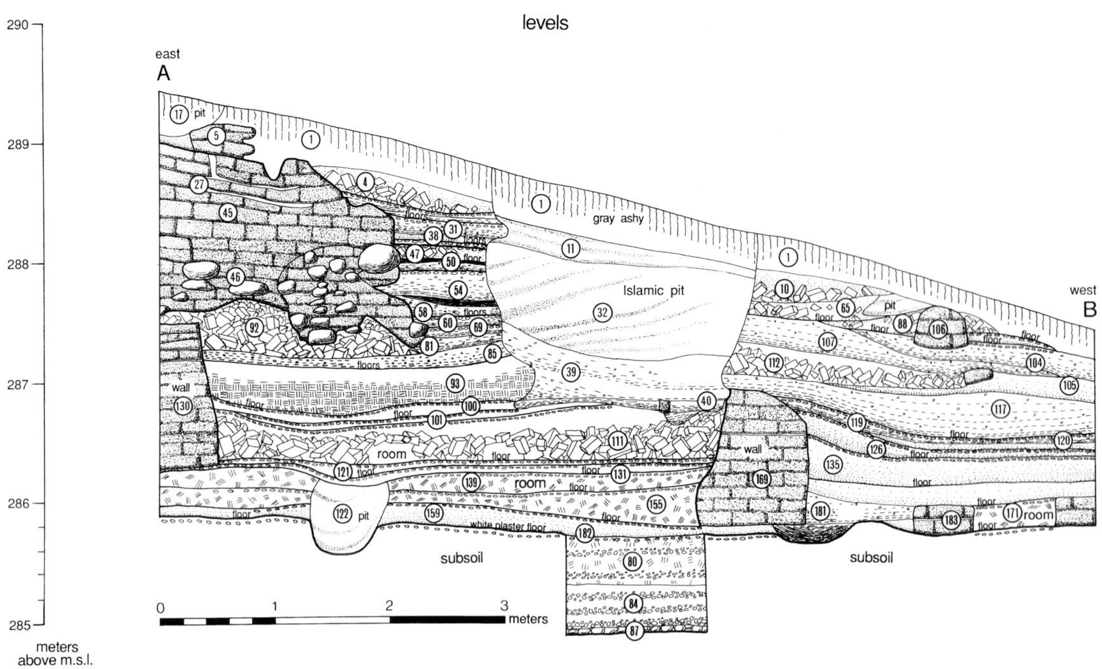

Figure 8.23 Trench D, Section A-B, levels.

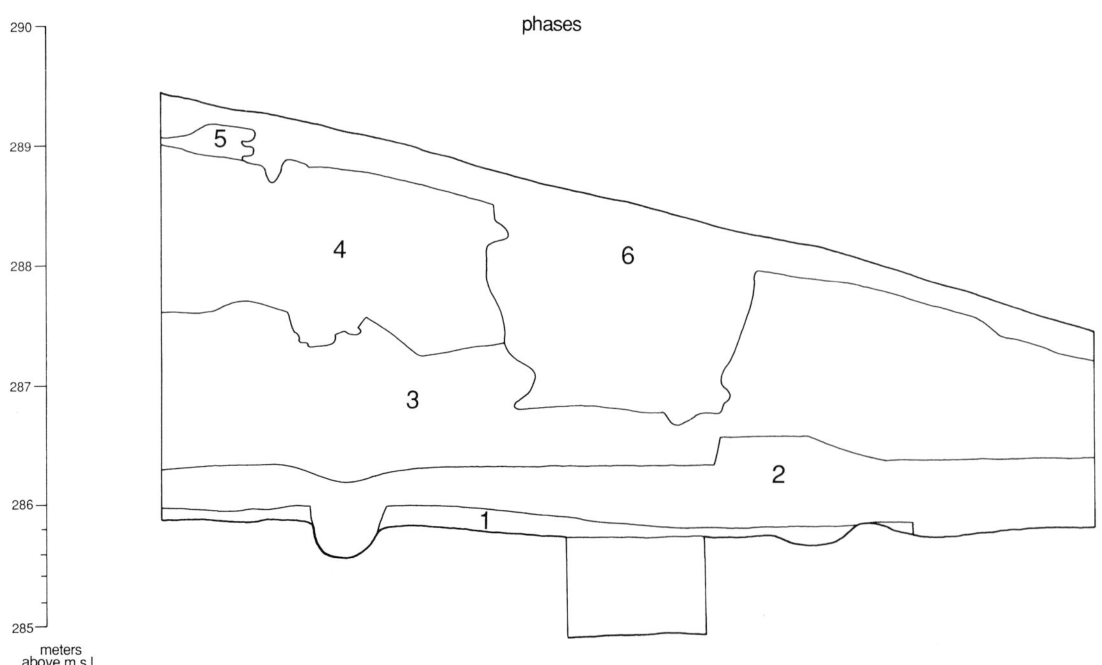

Figure 8.24 Trench D, Section A-B, phases.

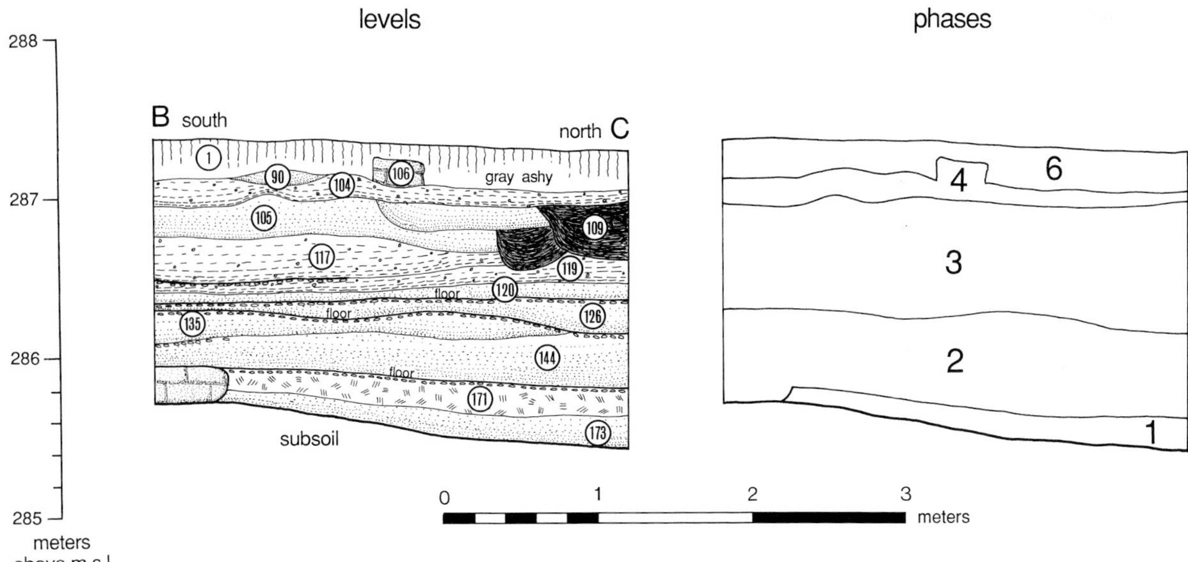

Figure 8.25 Trench D, Section B-C, levels and phases.

The Stratigraphic Sequence

The subsoil beneath the Trench D deposits consisted of hard, red clay with pebbles, overlying bedrock of concreted stones. In phase 1 the natural surface was leveled and a building was constructed on it. The only vestige of this building was a subrectangular, white plaster floor (182), but no trace remained of the walls that probably once enclosed it. This building was aligned approximately northwest-southeast (figures 8.30, 8.31), as were several later structures in Trench D.

North and east of the plaster floor the subsoil was covered by clay floors. In the northwest corner we found a pair of pits (176) filled with dark, ashy debris. They were covered by an extensive area of dark occupation soil.

A mudbrick building was constructed at the west end of the trench (wall 183) in phase 2. Then a more substantial structure, probably a house, was built to the east of it (walls 169, 170). These two buildings were separated by a narrow lane (figures 8.30, 8.32). The west building then passed out of use; its walls were cut down and a clay floor was laid over them, on which occupation debris accumulated.

The house to the east was a substantial, rectilinear structure, one room of which lay within the trench. The walls of this room were reconstructed several times. They were faced with white plaster on the inside. In its final form, wall 170 had a rectangular, plastered niche cut in its face. A succession of floors, one of them plastered, was laid down in the room.

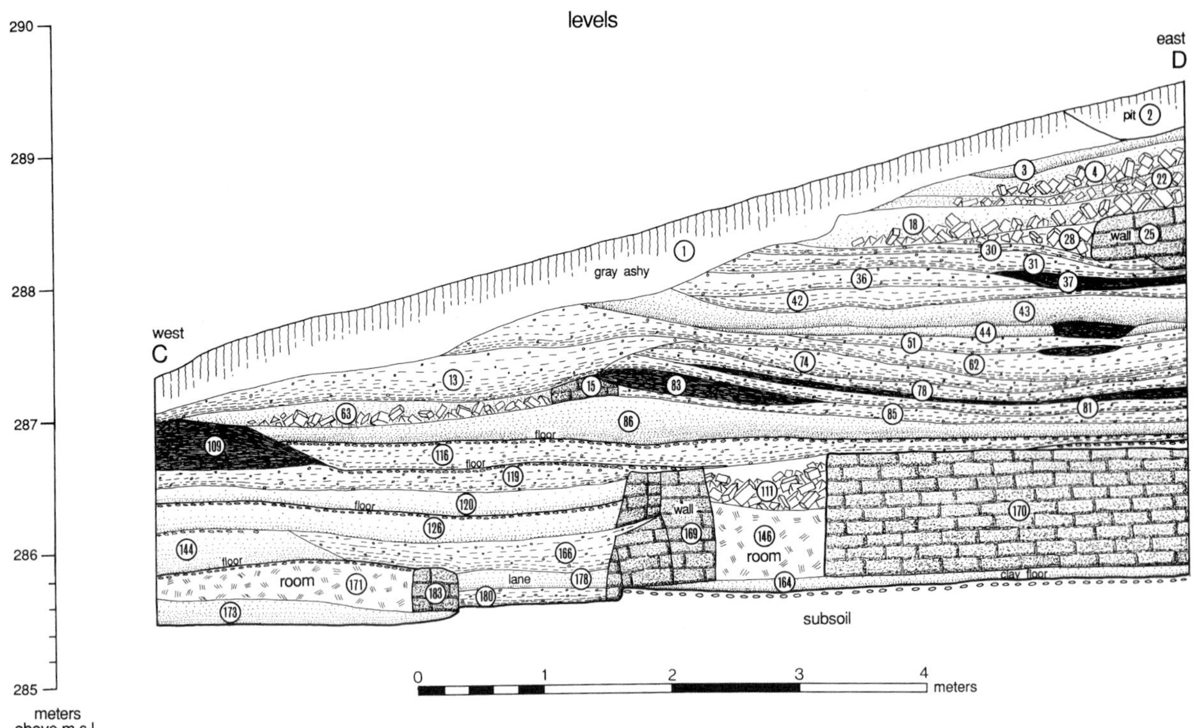

Figure 8.26 Trench D, Section C-D, levels.

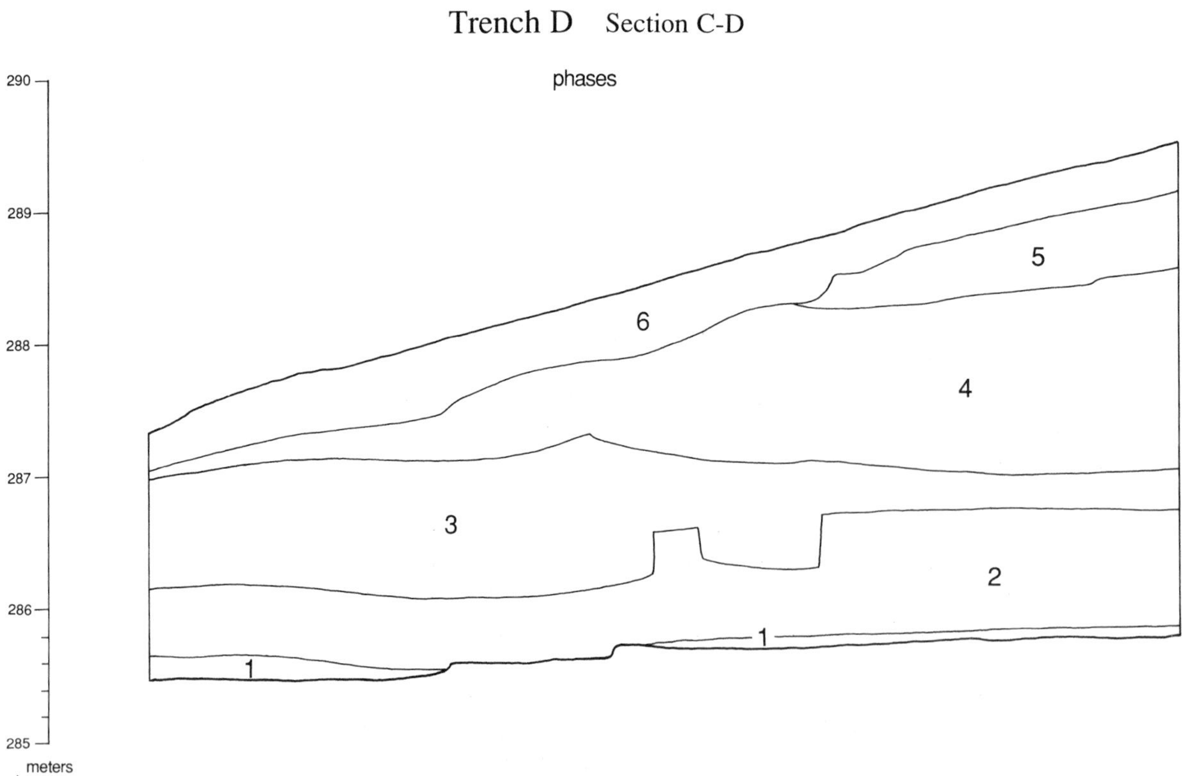

Figure 8.27 Trench D, Section C-D, phases.

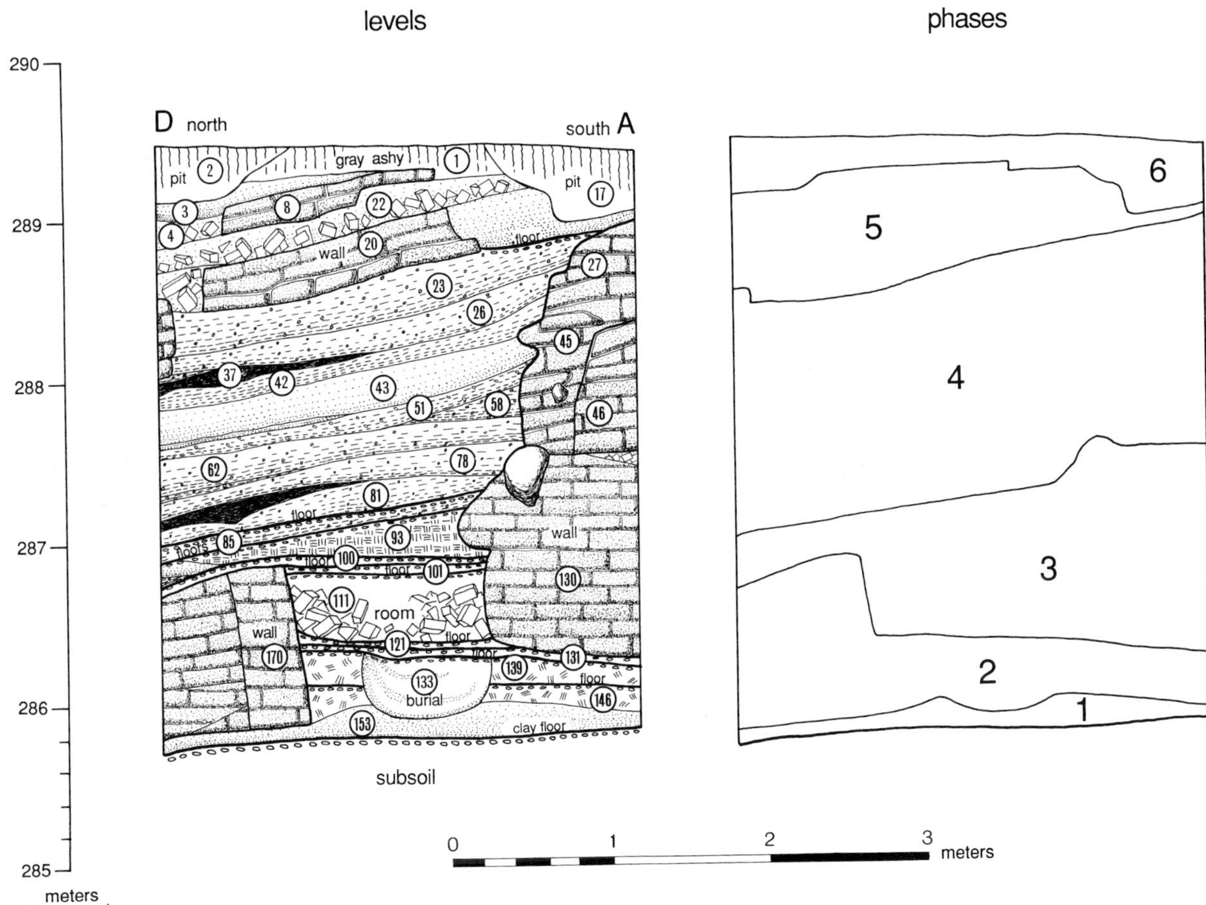

Figure 8.28 Trench D, Section D-A, levels and phases.

Beneath these floors were two pits (133, 146) that each contained an individual burial. Unusually, one of these burial pits (133) was rectangular in plan. There were also several other pits that contained no human remains.

The phase 2 house was substantially altered in phase 3. A new mudbrick wall (130) was built across the southeast corner of the trench, and walls 169 and 170 were reconstructed (figure 8.33). The phase 3 house probably had more rooms beyond the trench to the southeast.

Inside the room of the house, a clay floor (121) was laid, and two individuals were buried under it (123, 132). Then the room was filled to a depth of 50 cm with mudbrick debris (111), probably from the partial collapse of the walls. A fresh series of clay and plaster floors (101, 100) was laid on top of this mudbrick fill.

The area outside this house to the west was occupied intensively throughout phase 3. A substantial deposit of debris built up here, in which we could trace many floor surfaces and thin lines of mud wash from the house to the east. There were also several hearths with patches of heavily burned deposit.

Trench D levels

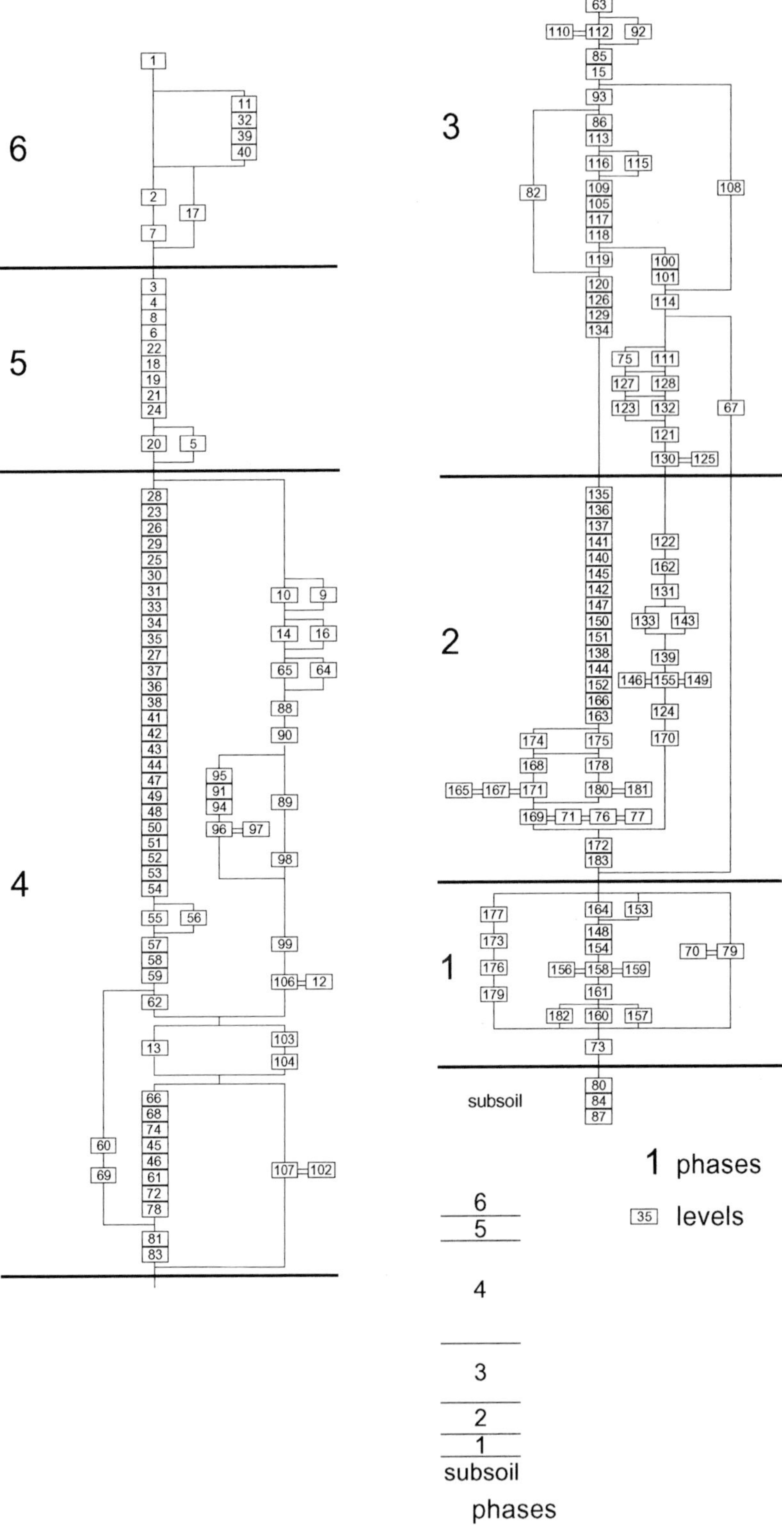

Figure 8.29 Trench D, level diagram.

Trench D

Phase 1

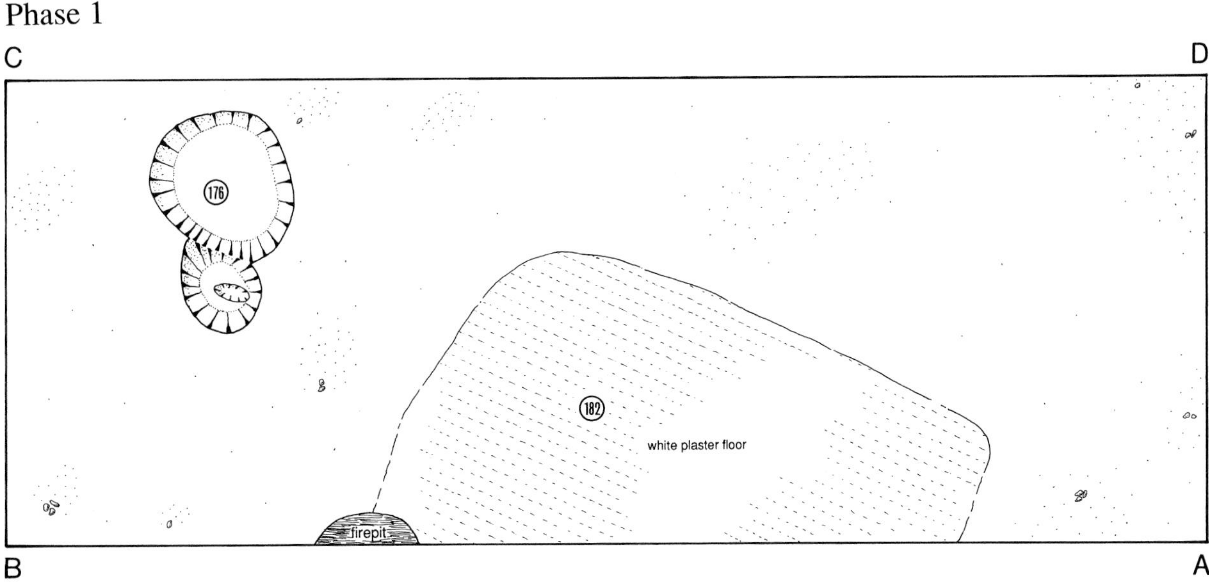

Phase 2

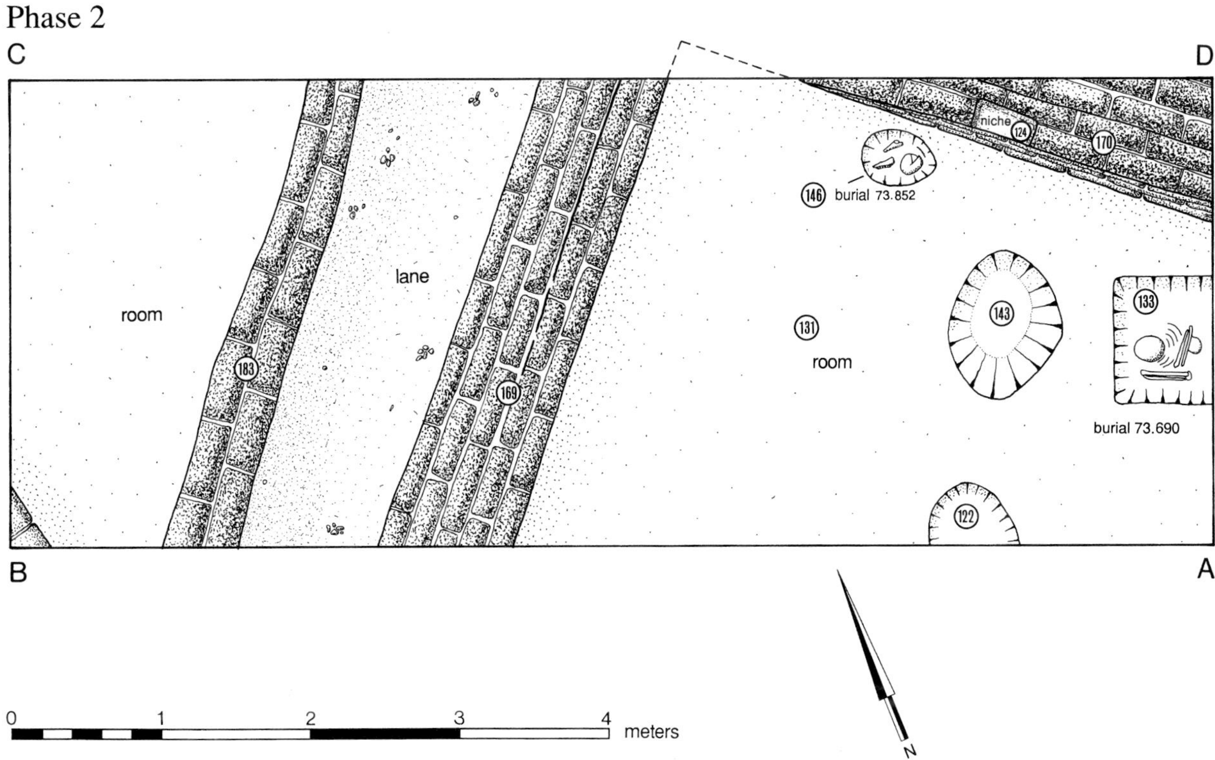

Figure 8.30 Trench D, plans of the structures in phases 1 and 2.

Figure 8.31 Trench D, the phase 1 and 2 structures, from the northeast. Scale, 1 m.

Figure 8.32 Trench D, the phase 2 buildings, from the west. Scales, 2 m.

Trench D

Phase 3

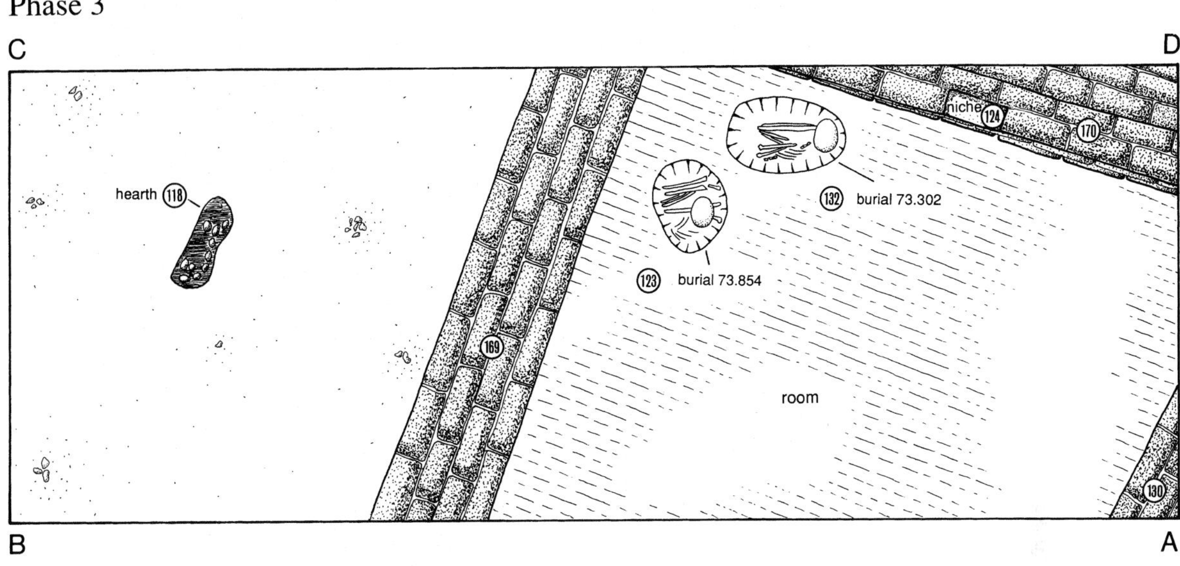

Phase 4

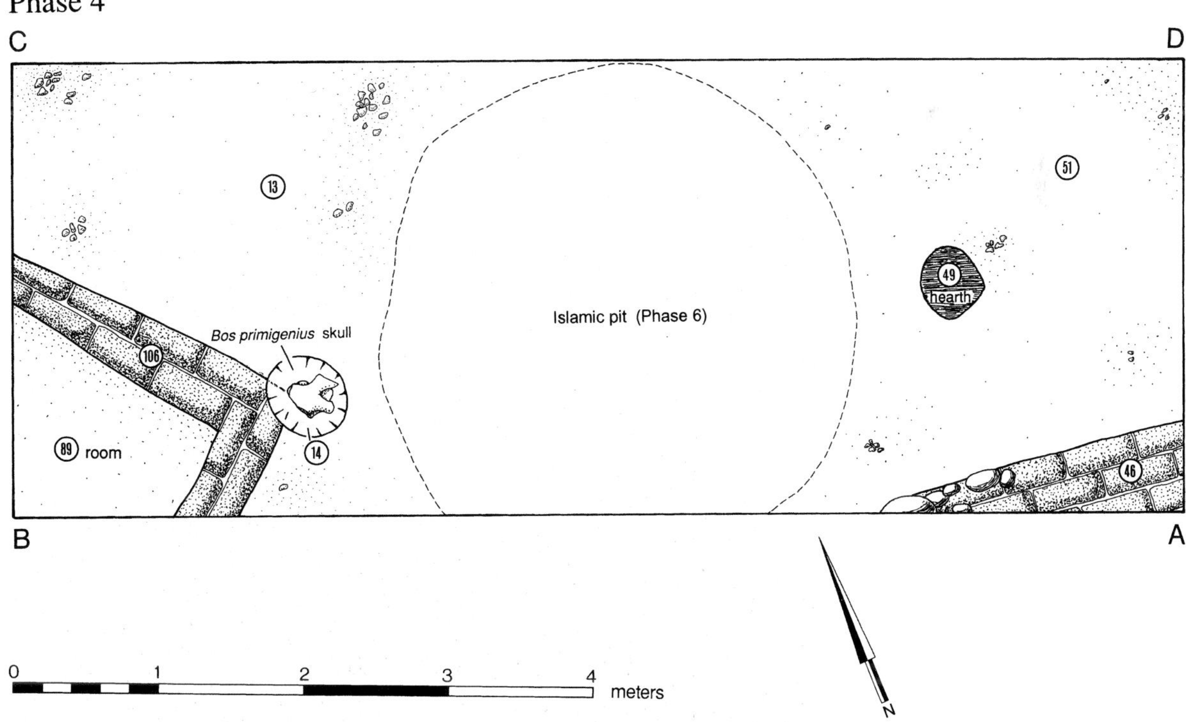

Figure 8.33 Trench D, plans of the structures of phases 3 and 4.

In time, the room of the phase 3 house passed out of use, and walls 169 and 170 were leveled off. Wall 130 was rebuilt, and several more clay floors were laid to the west of it, on top of the mudbrick fill (93) that had accumulated from the leveling. These floors were contained by other walls (112) that were subsequently removed almost entirely. Finally, wall 130 itself was allowed to decay.

In phase 4 a mudbrick wall (46) was built in the southeast corner of the trench, on top of the stub of wall 130. It ran approximately east-west and was apparently an exterior wall of a house that lay outside the trench (figure 8.33). Unusually, the wall rested on a rough foundation of several limestone and conglomerate blocks. This wall was reconstructed several times later in the phase.

A second building was constructed during phase 4, a corner of which was found in the southwest sector of the trench (wall 106). This building, probably another house, clearly extended well beyond the trench to the southwest, in a zone that subsequently eroded away completely. This house went out of use before the end of the phase. Late in phase 4 a pit (14) was dug into the decaying corner of this house. The skull of an aurochs (*Bos primigenius*) was deliberately placed upright in this pit and covered over (figure 8.34). Part of a *Bos* sp. horn core was also incorporated in the lower part of wall 46. The area between these two houses was open, but much of it was dug out when a large pit was excavated here in phase 6. The numerous hearths, patches of ash, and considerable quantities of flints and bones found here attest that this open area was used for domestic activities throughout phase 4. Mud continually washed out from nearby walls, and the inhabitants often added thin layers of clay to make

Figure 8.34 Trench D, phase 4. The skull of an aurochs (*Bos primigenius*) set upright in a pit. Scale, 20 cm.

patchy floors. These clay floors and ashy layers of occupation debris extended horizontally westward and continued well beyond the confines of the trench. Many of the phase 4 occupation levels seen in Section C-D (figure 8.26, levels 81–43) actually sloped upward because a stub of a phase 3 wall (15) provided a terrace-like support for them. The deposits that once existed west of the trench had all eroded away by the time of our excavation. The inference must be that the mound originally extended much farther to the west, and any supporting terraces or walls at the edge of the village would have lain a considerable distance beyond the trench.

Remains of phase 5 were found only in the eastern part of Trench D, because all its deposits farther to the west had eroded away. Intense occupation continued, and there are indications in Section D-A (figure 8.28) that at least two other mudbrick structures were erected here (walls 20 and 5, wall 8), one above another.

Building ceased in the area of Trench D in phase 6, and the surface of the mound began to erode. A few small pits (2, 17) were dug into the surface levels, but their contents could barely be distinguished from the surrounding deposits because of the effects of weathering. A large, almost circular pit was dug deep into the Trench D deposits during this phase (Section A-B, figures 8.23, 8.35, 8,36; levels 11, 32, 39, 40). The pit was 3.20 m in diameter, with almost vertical sides and a level bottom. Three rectangular mudbricks rested on the bottom. One of these bricks contained a small red-brown sherd. The functions of the pit and the mudbricks are unknown. The lowest layers in the pit consisted of silt and ashy deposits (39). The pit had then been filled up with ashy occupation debris, prob-

Figure 8.35 Trench D, the phase 6 circular pit dug in Islamic times, from the northeast. It had three mudbricks at the bottom. Scale, 2 m.

Trench D

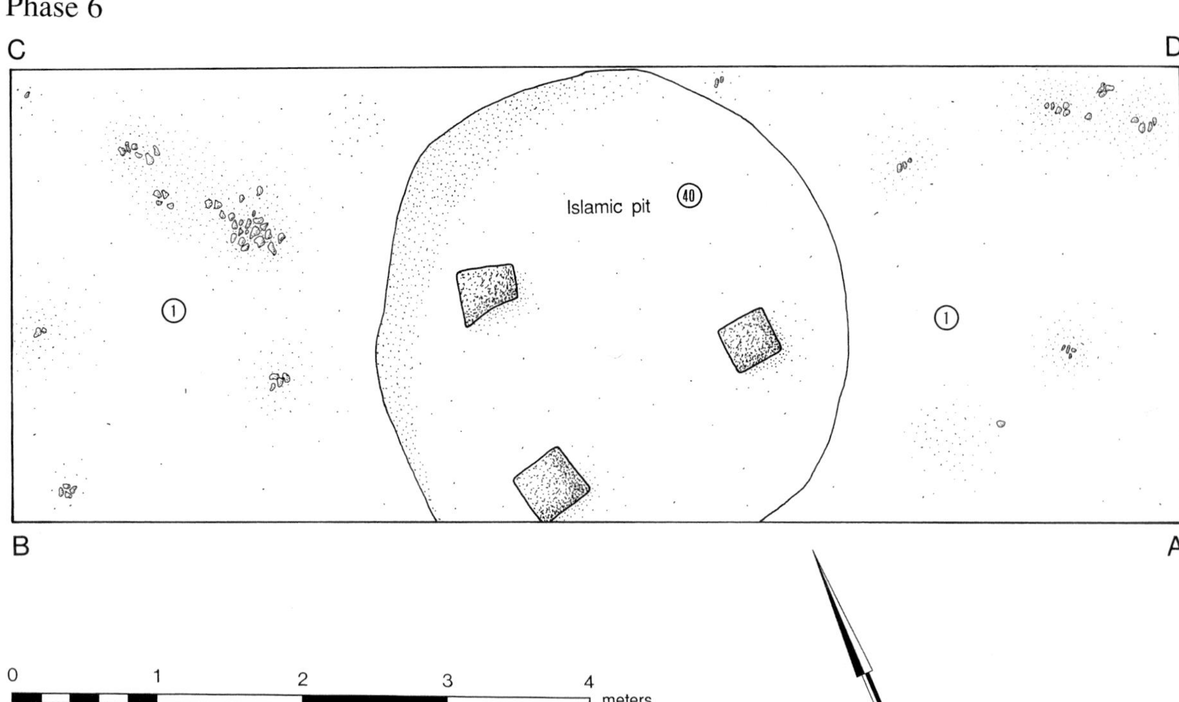

Figure 8.36 Trench D, plan of phase 6 showing the circular Islamic pit with three mudbricks at the bottom.

ably the same material that had been dug out of it. This fill contained one large sherd of pottery (72.363; figure 8.37) that Joan Huxtable of the Oxford Research Laboratory for Archaeology and the History of Art has since dated by thermoluminescence (see appendix 2). Her conclusion is that the sherd was made in the period from AD 600 to 1,000. The form of the sherd is consistent with this date, so we conclude that the pit was dug in early Islamic times.

Heavy erosion set in once occupation had ceased on the mound. The surface levels of Trench D began to wash downslope to the west, and the area started to grade off to a steep slope. Those upper levels that remained weathered to a uniform, gray, ashy deposit.

Summary

The occupation sequence in Trench D covered a period from the formation of the Neolithic village through its major phase of expansion. Because of the location of the trench, well down the western slope of the mound, the sequence here did not include the later phases of Neolithic occupation, found in Trenches A, B, C, and E.

The oldest evidence of occupation in Trench D was a plaster floor, probably belonging to a house, laid directly on the carefully leveled subsoil. Evidently, substantial preparation of the area took place before any buildings were erected. Thereafter, the settlement here, from phases 1 through 5, consisted of a series of mudbrick houses, almost all of which were constructed on the remains of their predecessors, with intensely utilized open spaces between

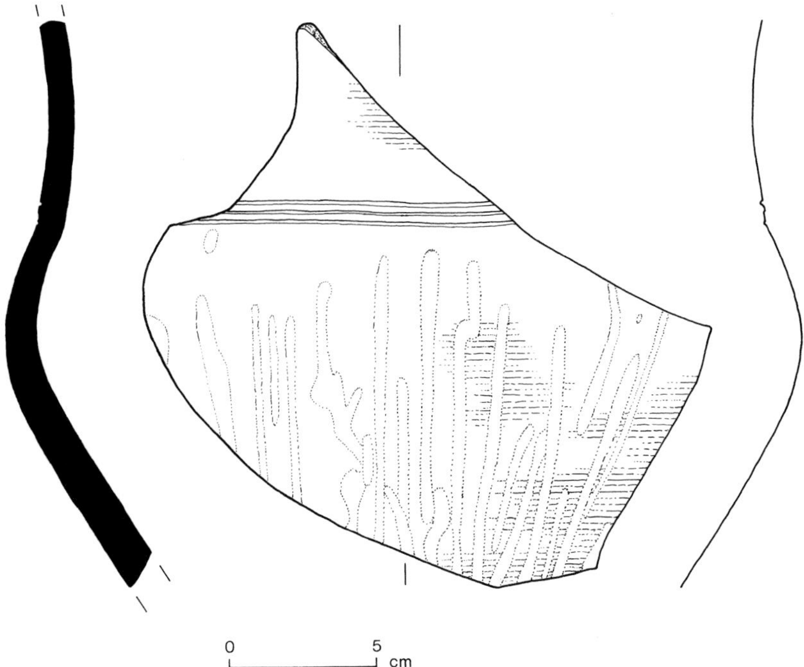

Figure 8.37 Trench D, the Islamic sherd, 72.363, found in the phase 6 pit. The sherd is hard fired with a gray-green fabric; its surface is burnished inside and out and decorated with three horizontal grooves at the base of the neck and vertical strokes of white paint on the body.

them. Most of these houses were aligned northwest-southeast, like other dwellings elsewhere at Abu Hureyra.

The levels associated with these buildings ran approximately horizontally westward. As the trench was located close to the modern edge of the mound, this strongly suggests that the settlement once extended much farther to the west, onto what is now the floodplain of the Euphrates.

A large pit was dug into the Trench D deposits in phase 6 during early Islamic times, but its purpose remains an enigma.

TRENCH E

Excavation of the Trench

We laid out Trench E on the long axis of the site approximately in line with the three other main soundings, Trenches A, B, and C, to determine the nature of settlement at the northern end of the mound. There was a low platform there that extended almost 150 m from west to east. Trench E was sited on this level ground, just south of a short, steep slope down to the floodplain.

We dug a 4 × 4 m trench, called E1, in 1972 (figure 8.38a) down to the natural subsoil 5 m below the surface of the mound. In the upper 4 m we found the corners of several superimposed, mudbrick houses. Beneath these was a 1-m-thick deposit of gray-black occupation soil lying on the natural surface. This contained a microlithic flint assemblage, different in character from that of the overlying village. We understood at once that we had evidence here for two superimposed settlements, Abu Hureyra 1 and 2, representing different ways of life. Deposits of the earlier settlement, Abu Hureyra 1, were found only in Trench E.

One of our principal aims in the 1973 season was to enlarge the trench in order to examine the Abu Hureyra 1 settlement over as large an area as pos-

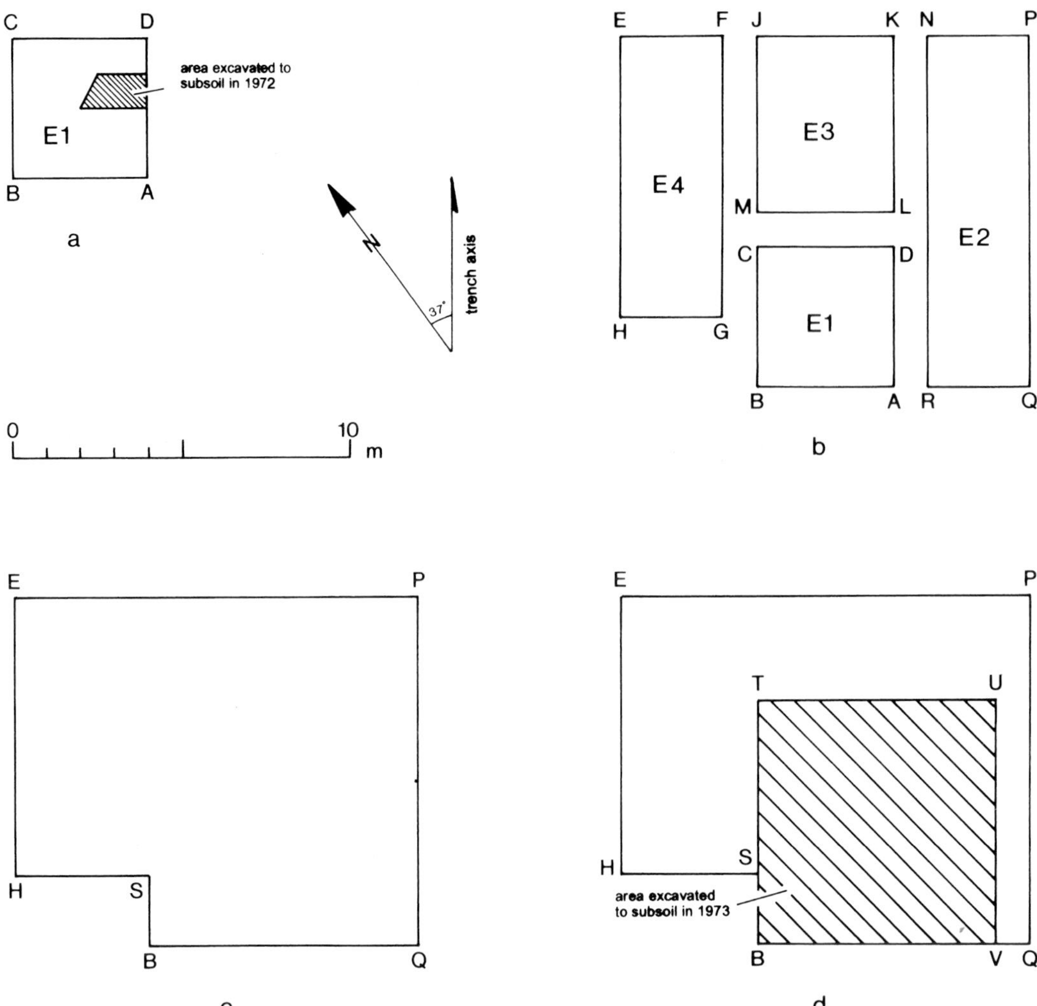

Figure 8.38 The excavation of Trench E in 1972(a) and in 1973, Trenches E 1–4(b), the trench after removal of the balks(c), and the area excavated to the natural subsoil (d).

sible. A second aim was to expose the complete plans of several of the Abu Hureyra 2 mudbrick houses. To achieve these ends we excavated three more trenches, designated E2, E3, and E4 (figure 8.38b). We estimated the likely size of the mudbrick houses discovered in Trench E1 in 1972, and then sited the new trenches to reveal their complete plans. The balks between trenches E1, E2, E3, and E4 were removed early in the 1973 season to form a single, large trench of 112 m^2 (figure 8.38c). The Abu Hureyra 2 deposits in Trench E were excavated over this entire area. Then we dug the underlying deposits of Abu Hureyra 1. The sections and level diagram for the enlarged Trench E are illustrated in figures 8.39–48.

The Stratigraphic Sequence

At the beginning of phase 4 the inhabitants of the Abu Hureyra 2 village removed the surface of the Abu Hureyra 1 settlement and any subsequent deposits to provide level ground on which to build their houses. They constructed

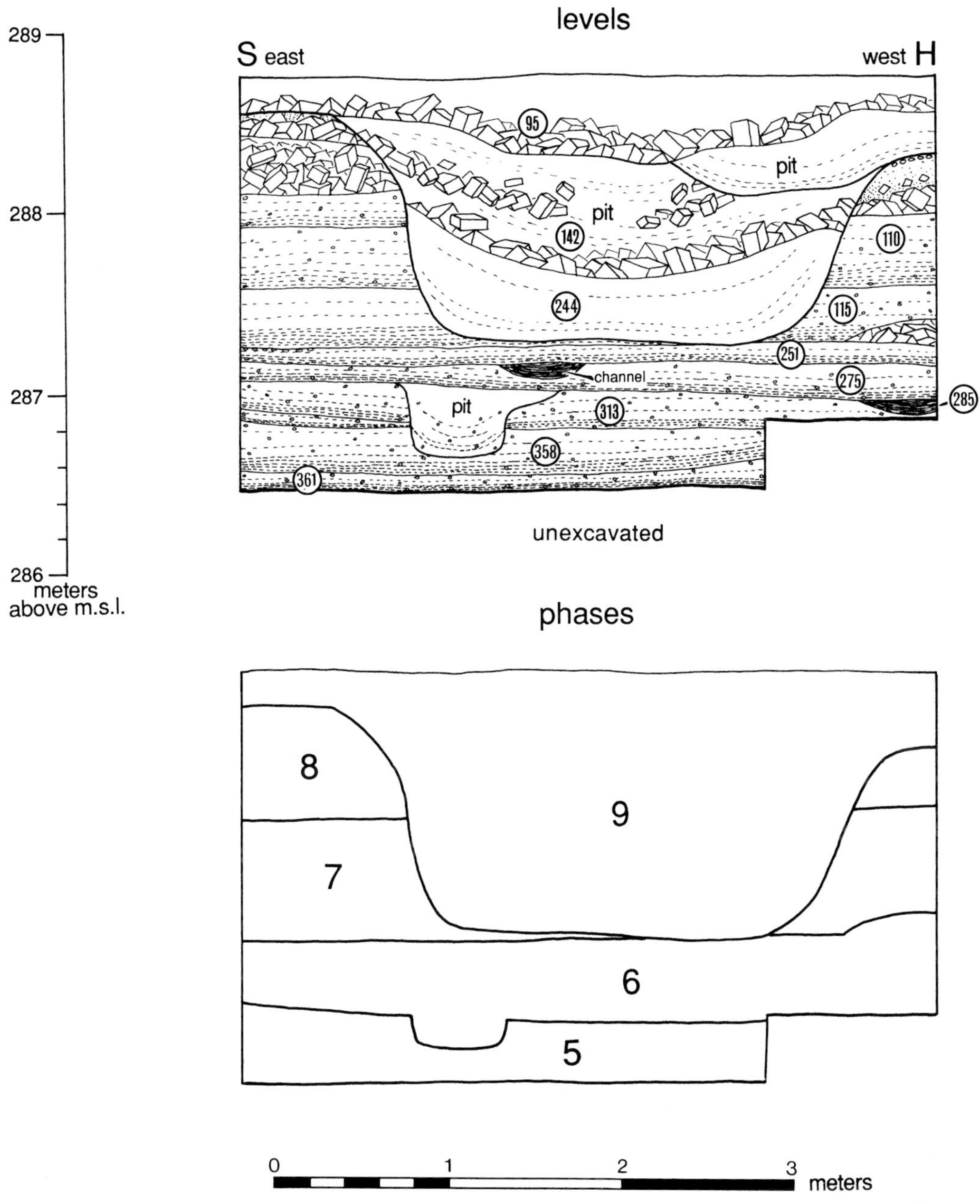

a rectangular, mudbrick building directly on the gray-brown, ashy soil of the underlying Abu Hureyra 1 settlement. The axis of this structure lay from north-northwest to south-southeast. It contained a number of rooms, all of which had floors of gray or black plaster that were renewed several times. There were indications that one room contained a plaster platform, raised 10 cm above the level of the plaster floor, and another a square hearth. In the yard just outside this house on its southeastern side there was a hollow that contained a red-colored skull (373, 73.3273), the earliest human burial in Trench E. A second

Figure 8.39 Trench E, Section S-H, levels and phases.

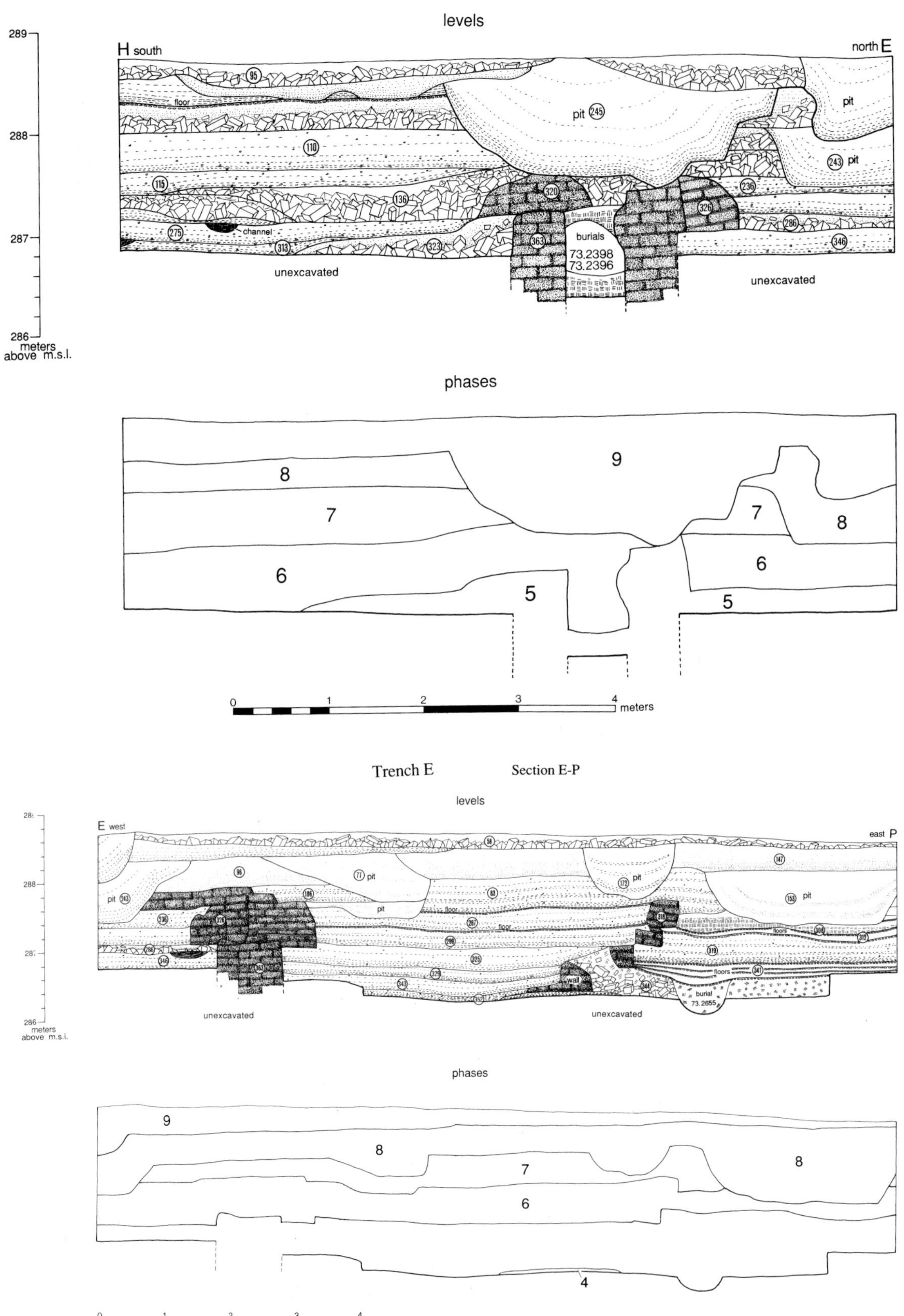

Figure 8.40 *(top)* Trench E, Section H-E, levels and phases.

Figure 8.41 *(bottom)* Trench E, Section E-P, levels and phases.

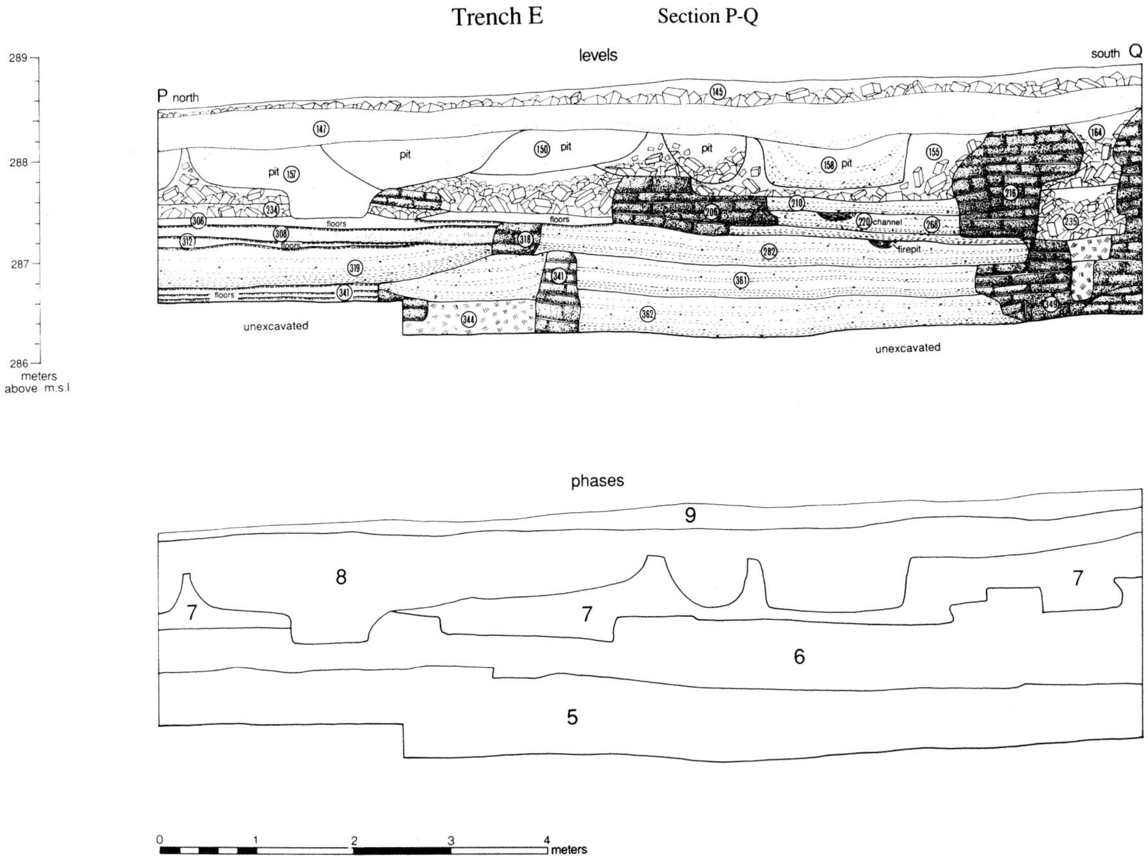

Figure 8.42 *(top)* Trench E, Section P-Q, levels and phases.

structure with a mudbrick exterior wall was built on the same alignment as this house in the northeast corner of the 7 × 7 m trench. These were the first buildings in a series to be built here, one on top of another, with similar plans, and on the same axis. Their form and contents suggest that they were all houses.

The first house in phase 4 was remodeled at least once. The stubs of a few of its walls were then incorporated in a new house, built directly on top of it. The construction of this second house obliterated most of the first one. The new house covered much of the 7 × 7 m trench and extended farther to the northwest (figure 8.49); it was probably the same size as the phase 5 house built over it. There were three rooms of this house in our trench; all were rectangular and had plaster floors, some of them colored black. Those in rooms 1 and 2 were renewed several times. Late in phase 4 an oval plaster vessel was installed on the floor of room 2 (371) for use as a container. At about the same time, a posthole was dug in the floor of room 1, presumably to provide additional support for the roof. Room 3 was different from the others: for much of the time it was open on its southwest side, then late in the phase it was turned into an L-shaped room with the addition of another wall in the southwest corner of the trench.

The mudbrick house in the northeast corner was rebuilt when the main house was reconstructed. A third house was built about this time, a corner of which projected into the southeast part of the trench. This, too, had a series of buildings on top of it. Thus, in phase 4 three houses were constructed in Trench E that set the plans for all later houses built there.

levels

289
288
287
286
285
284
meters
above m.s.l.
Q east
west B
grave
floor
floors
pit
unexcavated
firepit
gray weathered
subsoil
0 1 2 3 4 meters

Figure 8.43 *(bottom)* Trench E, Section Q-B, levels.

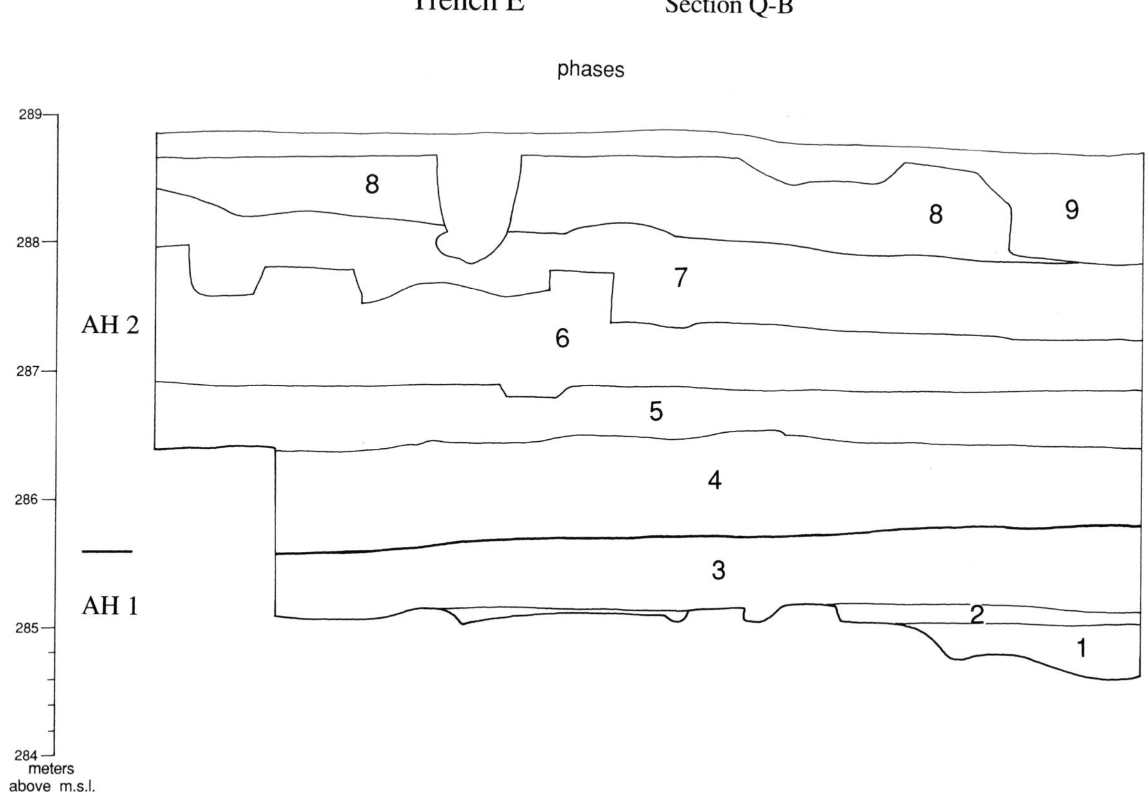

Figure 8.44 Trench E, Section Q-B, phases.

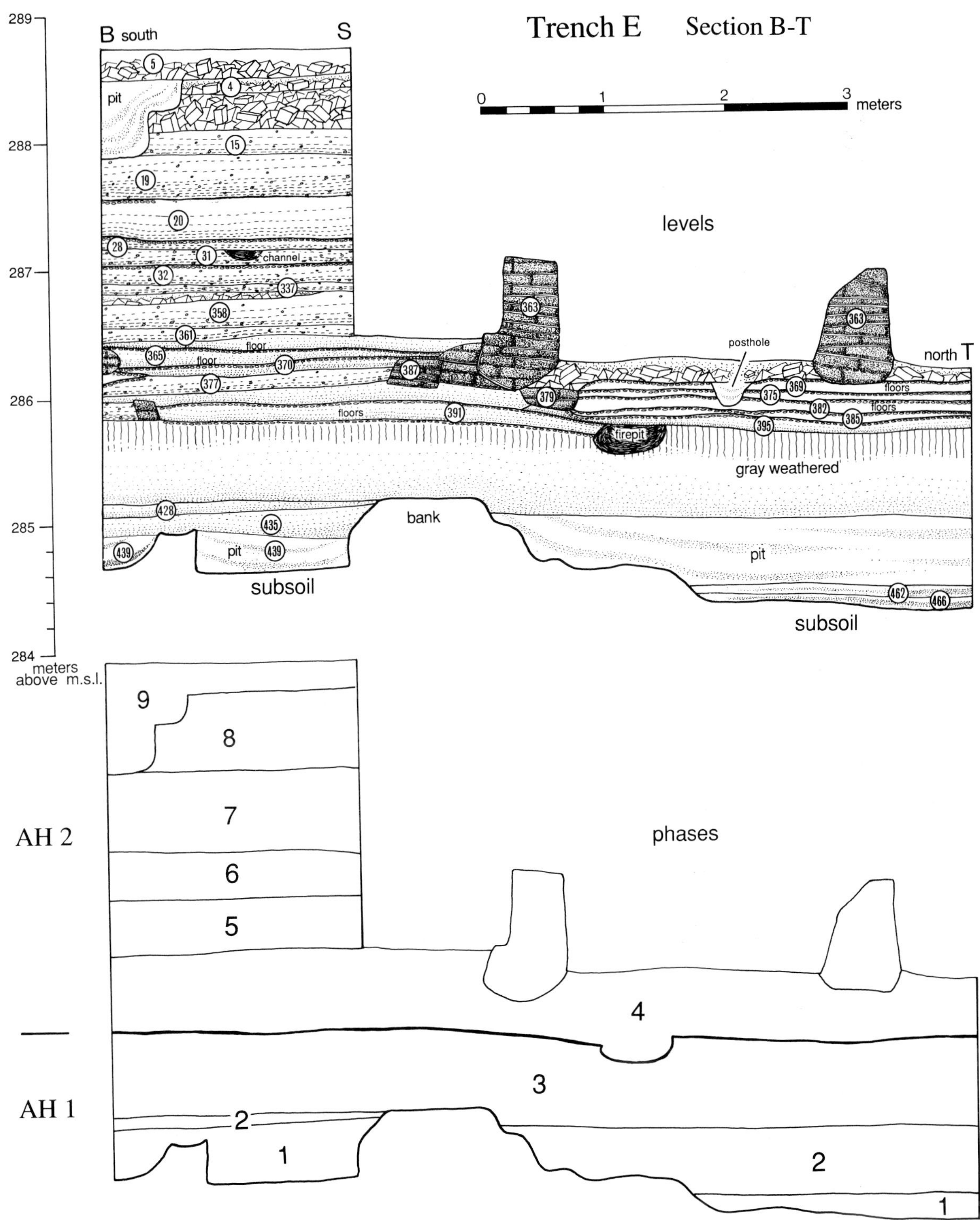

Figure 8.45 Trench E, Section B-T, levels and phases.

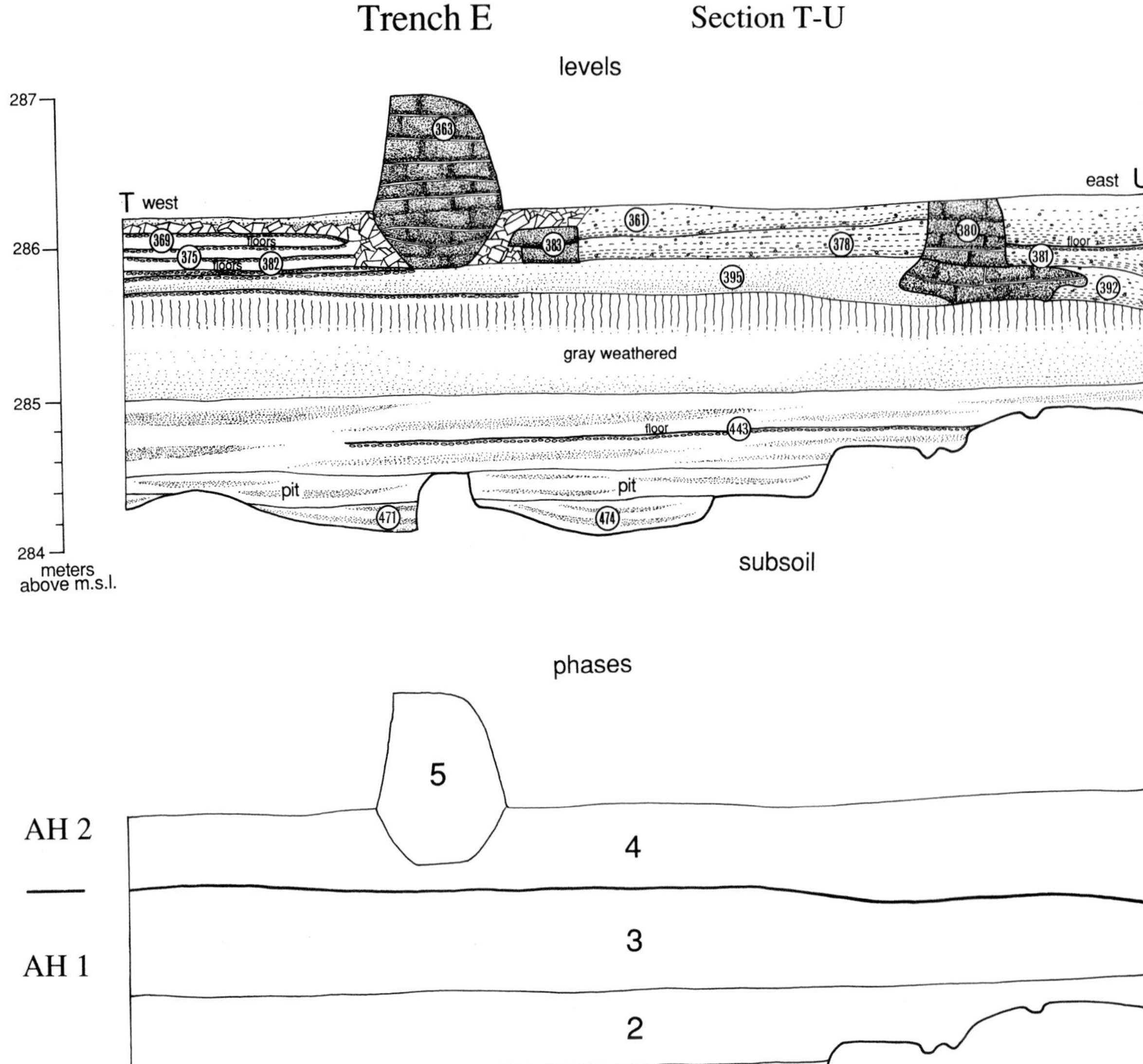

Figure 8.46 Trench E, Section T-U, levels and phases.

The main phase 4 house was replaced by a new mudbrick one, constructed over it at the beginning of phase 5. This house was excavated in its entirety in the enlarged 10 × 12 m trench. The phase 5 house closely followed the plan of its predecessor and used its walls as foundations (figure 8.50). The old walls were cut down, leaving only stubs protruding. These were then incorporated in the bases of the new walls, which were slightly offset from the stubs (figure 8.45). The walls of the new house were as much as 85 cm wide at the base, but only 40–50 cm wide from the floor level upward.

The phase 5 house was rectangular, 10.35 m long and 4.5 m wide (figures 8.51, 8.52), with walls that stood about 80 cm high when excavated. The walls were so narrow that the house probably had just one story. They were apparently reinforced with vertical posts in some places, as bases of postholes were found at intervals along them. Each of these was about 20 cm in diameter and

Section U-V

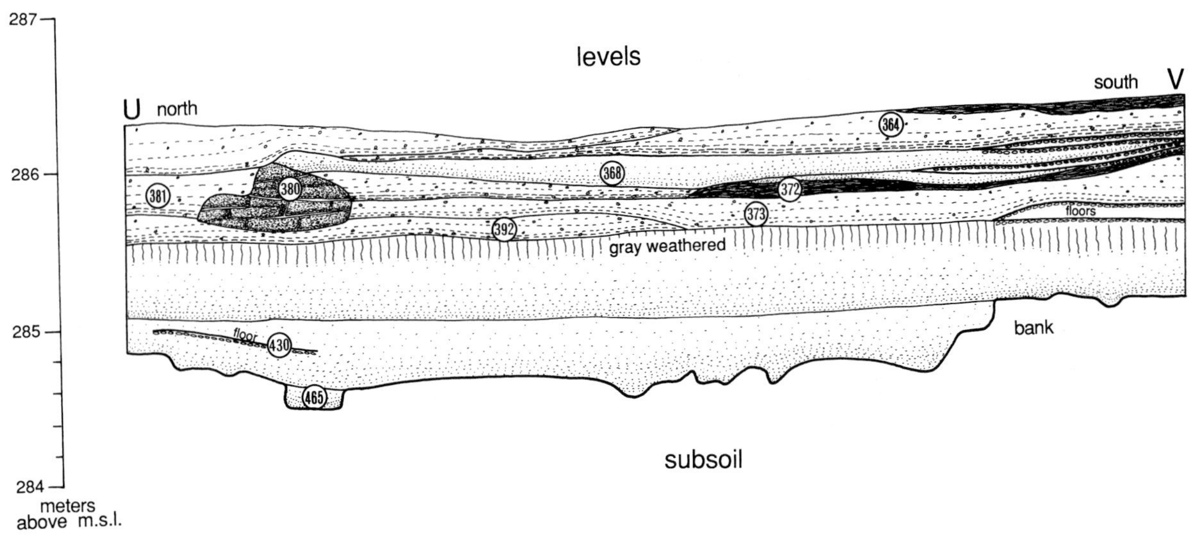

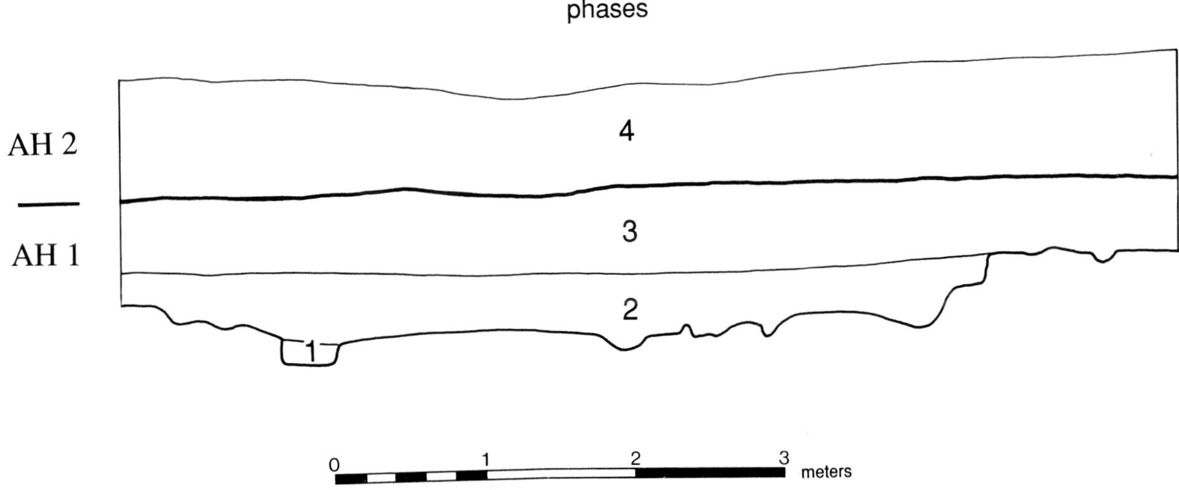

Figure 8.47 Trench E, Section U-V, levels and phases.

could be distinguished from the burrows of gerbils by its regular form. The house had five rooms, the three largest of which were 3.8 m long and 1.8 m wide. We found two superimposed plaster floors in room 5 and traces of another plaster floor in room 3; the other rooms had at least two floors of trodden earth. Room 5 also had a rectangular hearth with a plaster surround in its western corner (49). There was no entrance to the house at ground level, but inside there were low saddles between rooms 1 and 2, 2 and 4, and 3 and 4. We interpret these as the sills of porthole doors, similar to the complete door in the phase 7 house in Trench B. The house was used throughout the phase, and some reconstruction was carried out toward its end. The walls were repaired and some even rebuilt, while the floors were renewed.

We found another large mudbrick house in the northeast corner of the trench. This was the successor of the house built on the same spot in phase 4. The new house there had at least one large room, then was rebuilt on the same

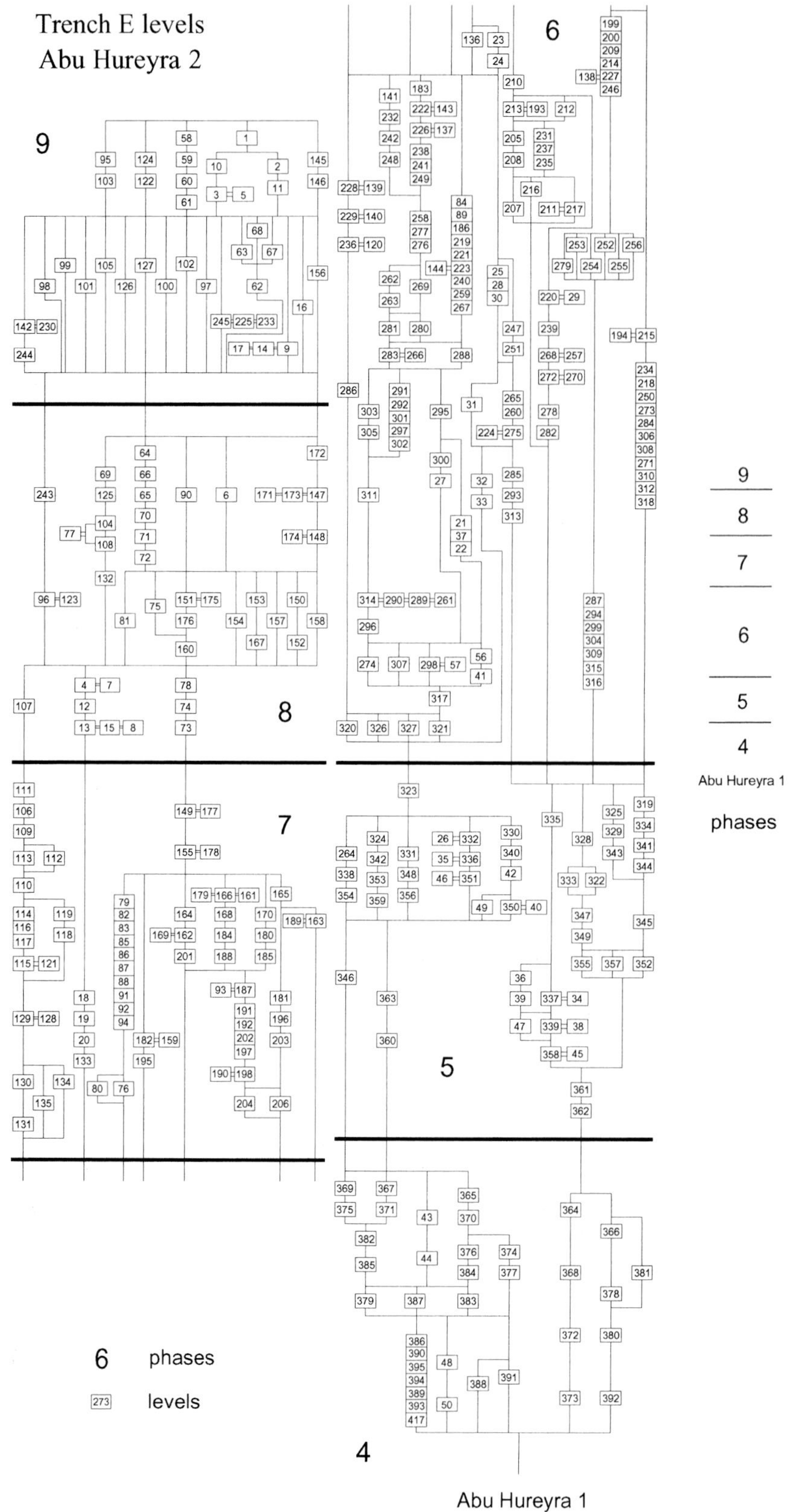

Figure 8.48 Trench E, level diagram.

Trench E

Phase 4

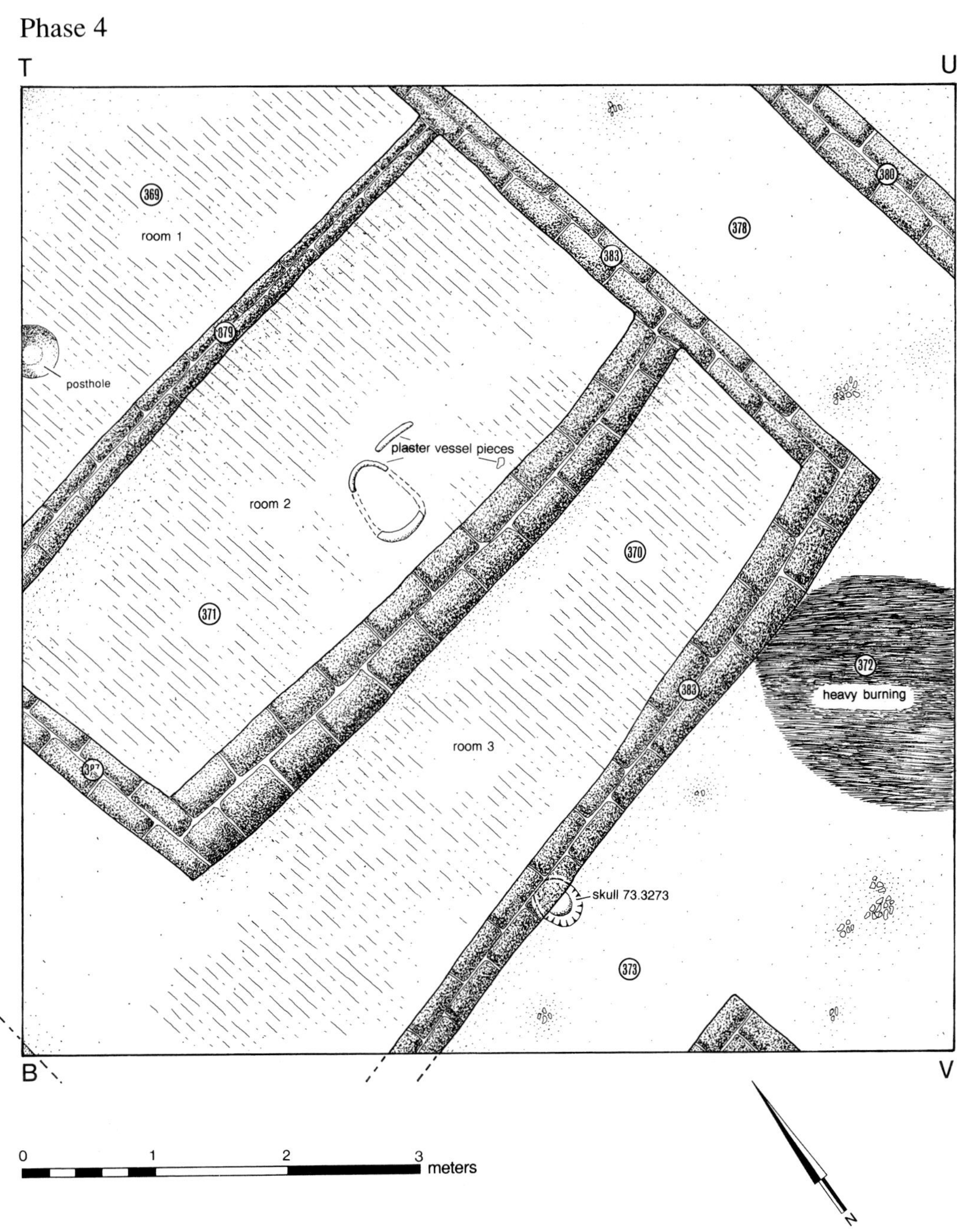

Figure 8.49 Trench E, plan of the phase 4 house.

Figure 8.50 Trench E, the phase 5 house superimposed on the phase 4 house beneath it. Scale, 1 m.

alignment but to a slightly different plan (figure 8.51). We excavated parts of two rooms of this second structure, the larger of which had a succession of four black plaster floors (341). In the southeast corner, too, a new rectilinear house was built on top of the cutdown walls of its phase 4 predecessor. A corner of this house (357) projected into the trench. It had unusually thick walls that were modified and rebuilt several times during phase 5. Late in the phase an extension was built on the west side of this house (339). Another mudbrick structure was built just outside rooms 1 and 2 of the main house at about the same time.

The arrangement of these phase 5 houses gives us a good indication of how the Abu Hureyra 2 settlement was laid out. The houses were built close to each other on similar alignments, with yards and lanes between them. These spaces were 2–3 m across, but subsequent building activities could reduce them to narrow passages no more than 1 m wide. A great deal of refuse had been thrown into the spaces between the houses, and there were also scatters of ash and charcoal from many fires. This suggests that food preparation and other activities of daily life were performed outdoors.

All the rooms of the main phase 5 house were filled with occupation and building debris that contained many artifacts. The inhabitants had apparently dropped some of them where they had been used. For example, in room 4 there was a quern with its rubbing stone in place in the south corner (72.555; figure 8.53). We excavated a number of burials, both in this house and in the one in the northeast corner, some of which are shown in figure 8.51. Several of the

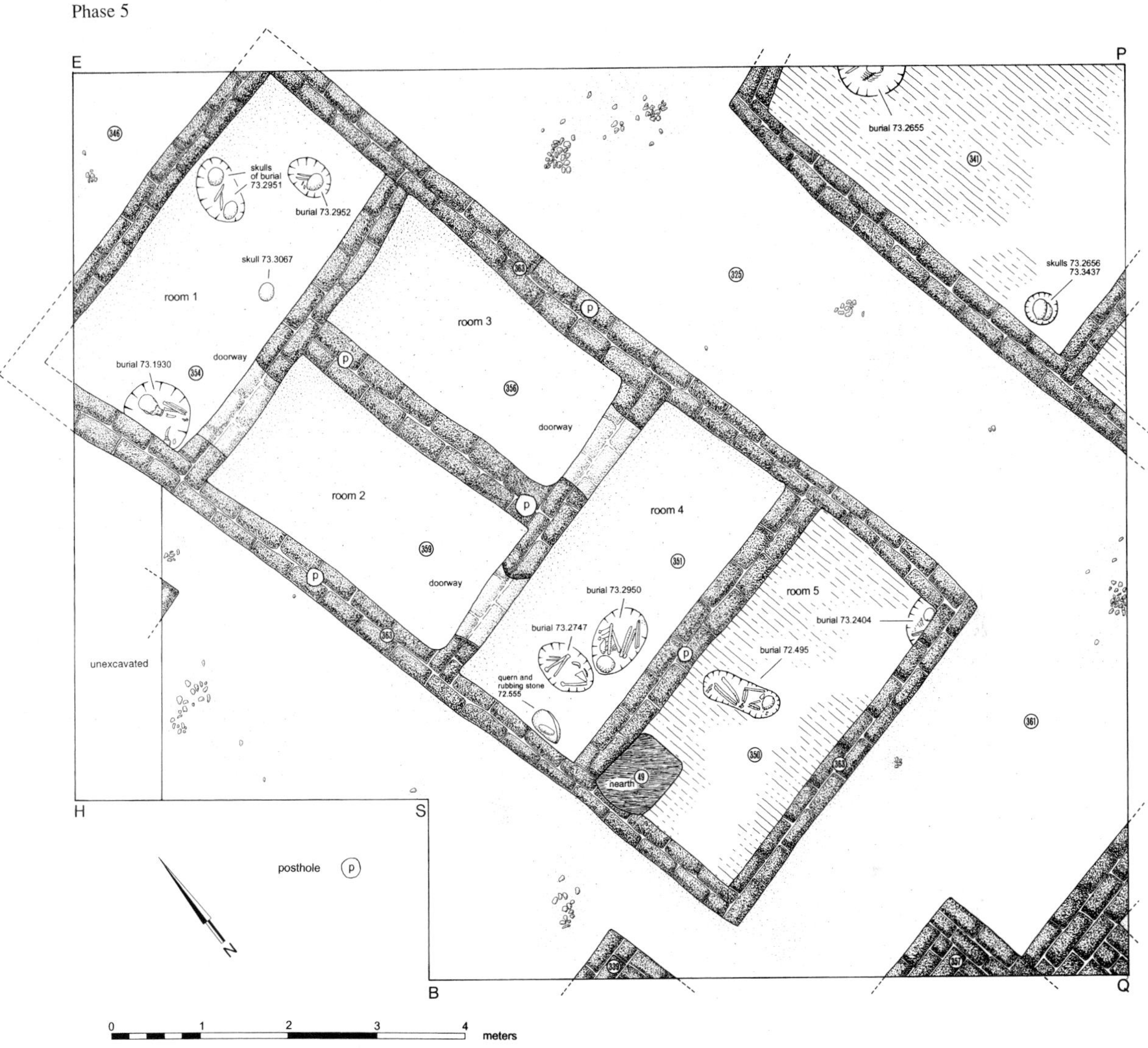

Figure 8.51 Trench E, plan of the phase 5 houses.

burials were in pits under the floors of the rooms, while others were in the deposits that filled them.

The phase 5 house then passed out of use and was immediately replaced by another one built on top of it. The walls of this later house were cut down to the same height to provide level foundations for its successor.

All three houses in Trench E were replaced in phase 6 by others built on the same alignment and to similar plans (figure 8.54). The two houses in the center and northeast corner of the trench had been damaged considerably by pits dug in succeeding phases, so many of their walls stood less than 50 cm high.

The house in the center of the trench was completely excavated. It was 4.5 m wide but only 8.8 m long because room 5 of the phase 5 house was not incorporated in the plan of the new structure. This enlarged the space between the main phase 6 house and the one in the southeast corner. The new house initially had one large room 5.8 m long and 3.6 m wide with a plaster floor. A

Figure 8.52 Trench E, the main phase 5 house, from the southeast. Scales, 2 m and 50 cm.

Figure 8.53 Trench E, the quern and rubbing stone (72.555) found in position in room 4 of the main phase 5 house. Scale, 20 cm.

Trench E

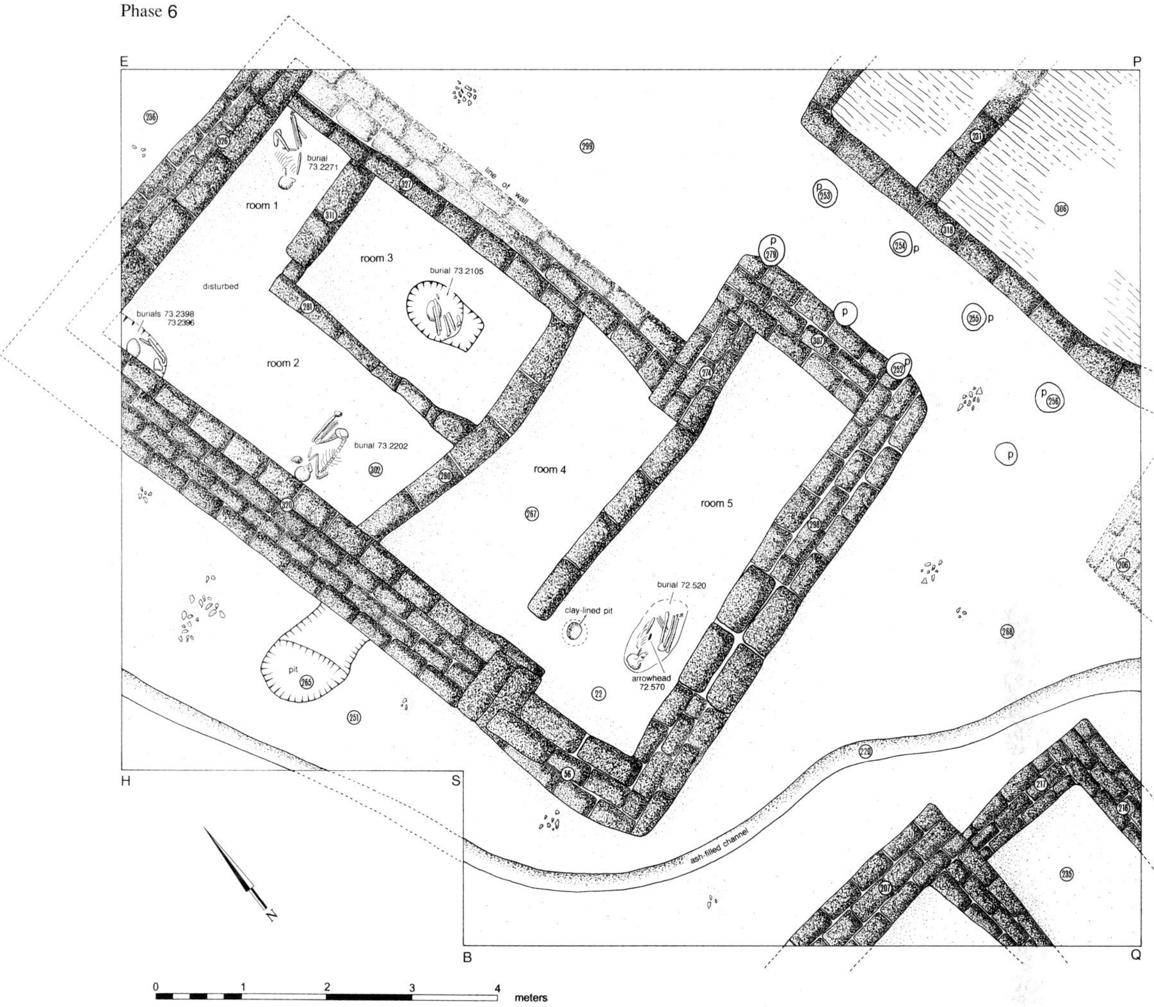

Figure 8.54 Trench E, Plan of the phase 6 houses and associated structures.

narrow doorway connected this with the only other room, a narrow one at the east end (room 5). The large room was subdivided later into four smaller rooms, 1, 2, 3, and 4, giving this house the same plan as the phase 5 house, though on a smaller scale.

Room 5 in the phase 6 house had a plaster floor, and set in it just to the left of the door was a circular pit with a clay lining. Originally the rim of the pit stood above the floor; then, as the floor was raised, it was covered over. The pit contained a grinding stone and was probably used for storage.

Late in phase 6 this house was substantially remodeled. The exterior was rebuilt by constructing new walls, considerably thicker than the originals, along its outer faces. Several of these walls were constructed of large mudbricks 80 cm long and 30–40 cm wide. The interior was also reconstructed with unusually thin mudbrick dividing walls, although the plan remained essentially the same. Later, some of the rooms were further subdivided. Several individuals were buried in rooms 1, 2, and 3 during this rebuilding. Room 5 was lengthened such that it projected as a wing on the northeast side. This narrowed the space between the main house and the one in the northeast corner. In this passage we found four pairs of postholes that evidently supported a roof (figure 8.55). This covering over the passage would also have provided a bridge between the roofs of the two houses. The two structures were thus linked and appear to have shared functions for a time. The area east of the main house was floored with plaster and served as an enclosed yard for both houses.

The house in the southeast corner of the trench was in use throughout phase 6. This was a substantial building with walls that were frequently rebuilt and, in consequence, rather thick at their bases. Later in the phase a channel (220), 30 cm wide and 10 cm deep, was cut between it and the main house (figures 8.54, 8.56). This curved around the corners of both houses and extended beyond the trench, both to the east and west. The channel was filled with ash that contained numerous large, charred seeds of the cultivated chickpea *Cicer arietinum*. There was no silt in it to suggest that it was used for drainage, only the evidence of burning. This channel was well defined, but there were traces of others in both earlier and later levels that followed the same line, indicating that this feature continued in use for some time. One likely explanation for the channel is that it was cut by the feet of flocks of sheep and goats as they passed through the settlement. Sheep and goats led by a shepherd often form single file and can create quite narrow channels when they pass repeatedly along a track, of precisely the cross section shown in figures 8.39, 8.40, 8.42, and 8.45. Their dung could easily have caught fire in the confined space between the buildings, leaving the ash that we saw in the channel. Domesticated sheep and goats were by this time important in the economy of the village and would frequently have been led through it. We may note also that the houses in Trench E built in phase 5 and after were spaced a little farther apart than be-

Figure 8.55 Trench E, phase 6. The four pairs of postholes that carried a roof over the passage between two houses, from the east. Scale, 1 m.

Figure 8.56 Trench E, the houses of phase 6, from the south. Note the channel (220) that ran across the open space in the foreground. Scale, 2 m.

fore, a trend that may be seen in the contemporary phases in Trench B. This may reflect the need to create space for the passage of flocks through the settlement as sheep and goats increased in numbers.

At the end of the phase the house in the center of the trench passed out of use, only to be rebuilt once more in phase 7.

The new buildings of phase 7 were damaged by pits dug into these levels during phases 8 and 9, and so survived only in fragmentary form. Enough remained to indicate that the house in the center of the trench was reconstructed on much the same plan as its phase 6 predecessor. The walls of the house in the south corner of the trench were rebuilt several times during phase 7, but its plan remained the same. The house in the east corner was replaced by another one on the same alignment, of which only a few scraps of walls survived. This house was displaced a little to the south, and its plan was somewhat different.

The passages and yards between these houses were used intensively by the inhabitants during this phase. In them were numerous trodden surfaces and lenses of ash, suggesting that many activities, including cooking, were carried on outdoors. The floors and ash were interleaved with thin layers of mud that had washed out from the walls of the surrounding buildings. The inhabitants continued to bury their dead in the houses, as in preceding phases.

Late in phase 7 all these structures, except the house in the south corner, were abandoned, and their walls allowed to collapse. Much of this building debris washed out into the open spaces surrounding the ruins.

The nature of the settlement in the vicinity of Trench E changed in phase 8. The inhabitants dug a series of large pits over much of the area (figures 8.57,

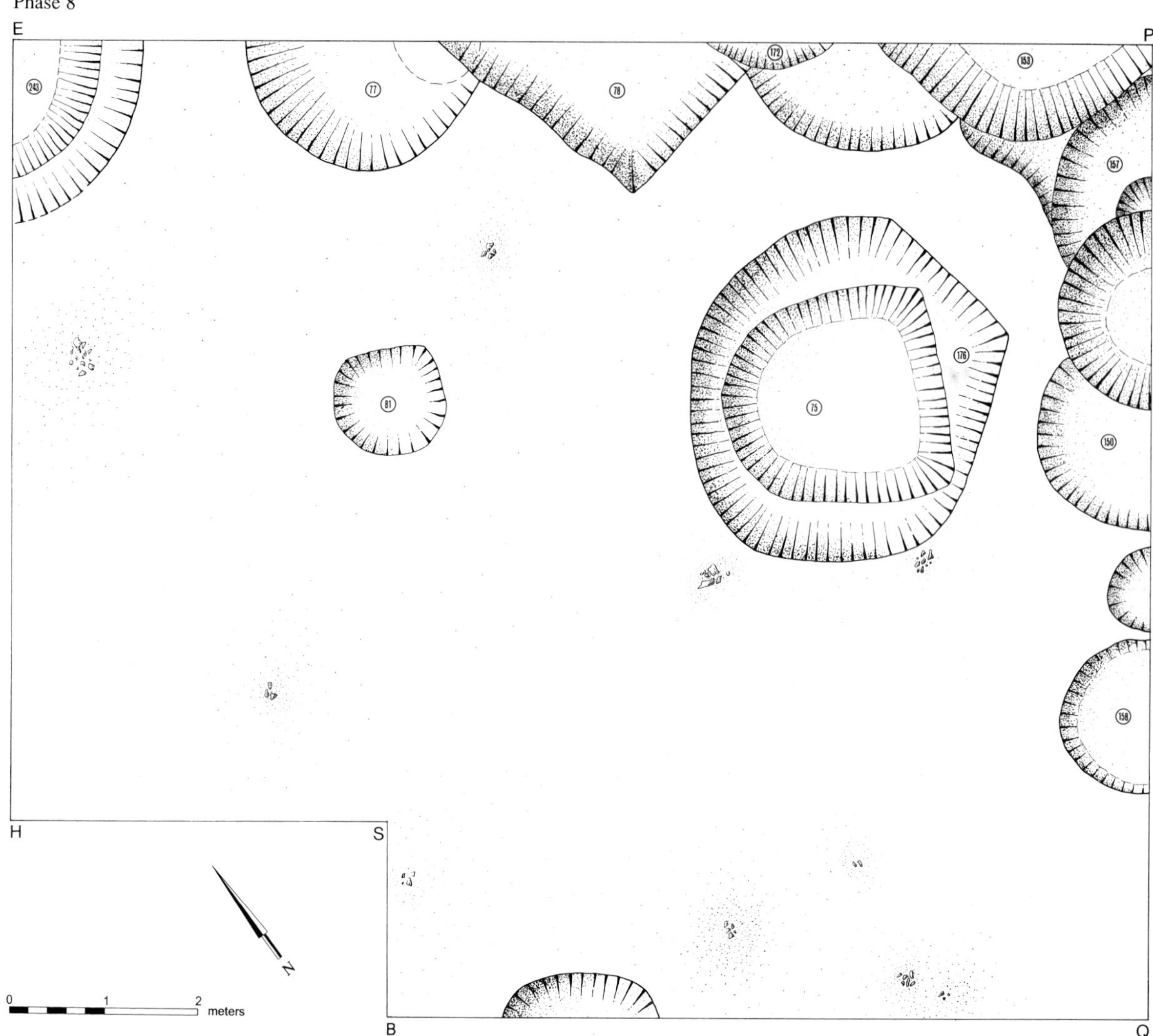

Figure 8.57 Trench E, plan of the phase 8 pits.

8.58). These were from 1 to 3 m across, up to 80 cm deep, and subcircular in plan, although a few (78, 176) had at least two straight sides. Several of them (75, 150, 157) were recut one or more times, indicating that they were used intensively. Most contained heavily burned material: ash, heat-fractured pebbles, burned animal bones, and flints, with some fragments of clay and brick. These pits often had flat bottoms (75, 153), and the burned pebbles were near the base of the fill. Their form and contents suggest that they were probably used as roasting pits for food, or perhaps as dwellings, rather than for making plaster and mudbricks. Several other pits containing silt and occupation debris may have served another function.

The pits were concentrated in the northern and eastern portions of Trench E. The central and southern parts of the excavated area were considerably disturbed by intrusive phase 9 pits but appear to have been open spaces during much of phase 8. These open areas were covered with levels of mud wash from the remains of the houses of the preceding phase. We found traces of a few mudbrick walls there, so one or two houses may have been built in this area of

Figure 8.58 Trench E2, the phase 8 pits 150, 153, 157, and 176, from the northeast. Scales, 2 m and 1m.

the site during phase 8. Eventually, the area was abandoned, and its surface weathered to a gray-brown ashy deposit, full of artifacts and organic remains.

The area around Trench E was used once more in historic times. The levels belonging to those episodes constitute phase 9. There was some activity in the Byzantine period, on the evidence of Byzantine sherds that we found in the surface levels. We also recovered some Islamic pottery and scraps of iron. The area was used for burials in the historic period, although none of those graves was visible on the surface. Some of them were probably Byzantine in date. Most recently, a mudbrick building was erected there and clay floors laid down in its vicinity. This structure then collapsed, and the material from it covered the entire area.

Summary

There appears to have been some activity in the vicinity of Trench E from the beginning of Abu Hureyra 2, but the area was not intensely occupied until much later. The radiocarbon dates, artifacts, fauna, and other remains indicate that the village expanded to cover the area around Trench E sometime before 8,300 BP. There was no obvious pause in human occupation of the area in the Trench E sequence, but there were periods when a building was allowed to decay for a long time before a new house was built on top of the ruins. The explanation for this difference may simply be that habitation was less intense away from the heart of the settlement, and, consequently, buildings were renewed less frequently.

In Trench E, as elsewhere, the inhabitants were careful to level the ground on which they built the first houses, in this case the surface of the Abu Hureyra 1 settlement and the deposits from the subsequent Intermediate Period episode of occupation there. They then constructed a group of houses, three of which projected into the excavated area. These were all similarly aligned from north-northwest to south-southeast. They give us the best indication of how houses were laid out in relation to one another at Abu Hureyra. The houses were rectangular or rectilinear, were built of mudbrick, and contained several rooms that were often floored with black, burnished plaster. They thus resembled other houses in the settlement. Each house was renewed in successive phases, usually by incorporating the stubs of the walls of its predecessor in its own foundations. One house was totally excavated in phase 5 and its successor in phase 6. They provide the best examples of complete houses that we found in Abu Hureyra 2.

The houses were separated from each other by narrow passages and small yards. The deposits in these open spaces had a character of their own: they contained many trodden floors, some of them reinforced with clay or plaster, and many ash lenses and patches of burning, indicating that fires were frequently lit outdoors, presumably for cooking and to dispose of waste. These areas yielded many artifacts and much organic material, so they must have been used intensely. As buildings went out of use and were replaced, mud from the decaying walls washed out into these spaces, adding considerably to the depth of deposit in them.

The last phase of prehistoric occupation in Trench E occurred in phase 8. The character of this quarter of the settlement altered, as elsewhere on the mound at the same time. Several large pits were dug across much of the excavated area; we interpret them as roasting pits for food since most contained material that was heavily burned. There were traces of walls in this phase that may represent the houses of the inhabitants. The phase 8 material from Trench E provides much the best evidence for the nature of the occupation at Abu Hureyra in this final stage of prehistoric habitation.

The settlement was then abandoned until the historic period. Some activity took place in Byzantine and again in Islamic times. Sometime during the historic period the area was also used as a cemetery. Then, more recently, a building was constructed here that collapsed, sealing much of the area with its debris.

TRENCH G

Excavation of the Trench

The eastern side of the mound of Abu Hureyra consisted of a platform 4–5 m lower in elevation than the western ridge. The platform rose slightly to the north where a permanent survey point was located, then dropped down to the valley floor (figure 2.14). We wanted to dig there to determine the sequence of occupation and the history of settlement in the northeast sector of the mound. Much of the area was covered by the cemetery of the modern village, precluding investigation of the center of the platform. We therefore decided to excavate a trench on the northern side of the cemetery at the crest of the slight rise. This was Trench G.

The trench was 4 × 5 m in size (figure 8.59), large enough we hoped to reveal a significant portion of the plan of any buildings we might encounter. The top 1.5 m of deposit was heavily weathered and revealed relatively little of interest, so the trench was reduced to a square of 4 × 4 m to speed progress toward the bottom. Once the building in phase 2 had been largely cleared, it became necessary to reduce the size of the trench further to a 2 × 4 m rectangle to reach the subsoil quickly. Finally, we made two cuts into the subsoil to determine its composition. The stratification, phasing, and sequence of the Trench G levels are shown in figures 8.60–64.

The Stratigraphic Sequence

The natural subsoil here consisted of compacted brown clay and pebbles. We found some occupation debris in the subsoil itself and in holes that penetrated it. The existence of this deposit and the date of 9,680 ± 90 BP (OxA-1228) that we have obtained for it indicate that some human activity took place around Trench G in the Intermediate Period between the end of Abu Hureyra 1 and Abu Hureyra 2.

Much later, the inhabitants cleared off the surface of the subsoil, thus removing virtually all the other deposits that would have been associated with the ini-

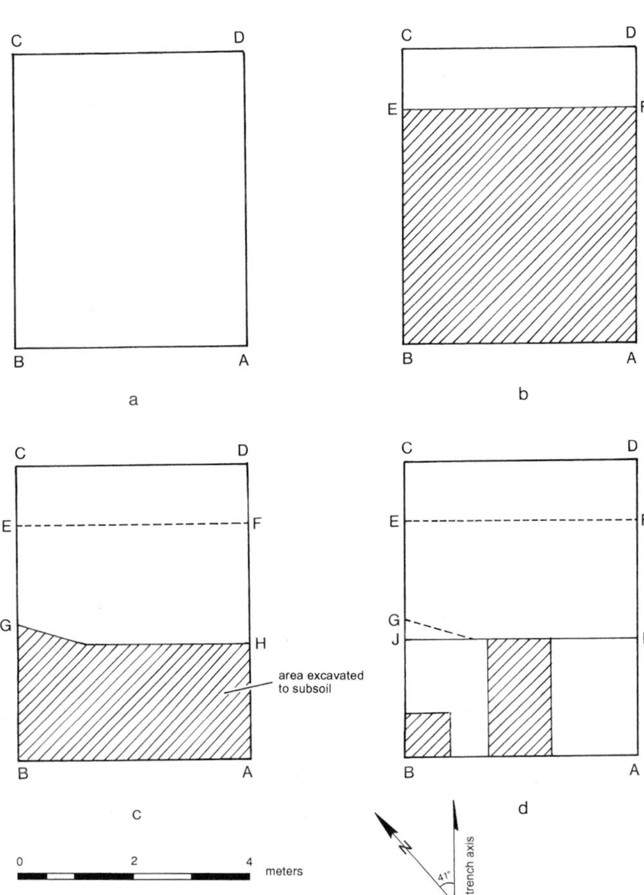

Figure 8.59 The excavation of Trench G, at the start of work (a), reduction of the excavation to a 4 × by 4 m square (b), excavation of a 2 × 4 m cut to the subsoil (c), and test cuts in the subsoil (d).

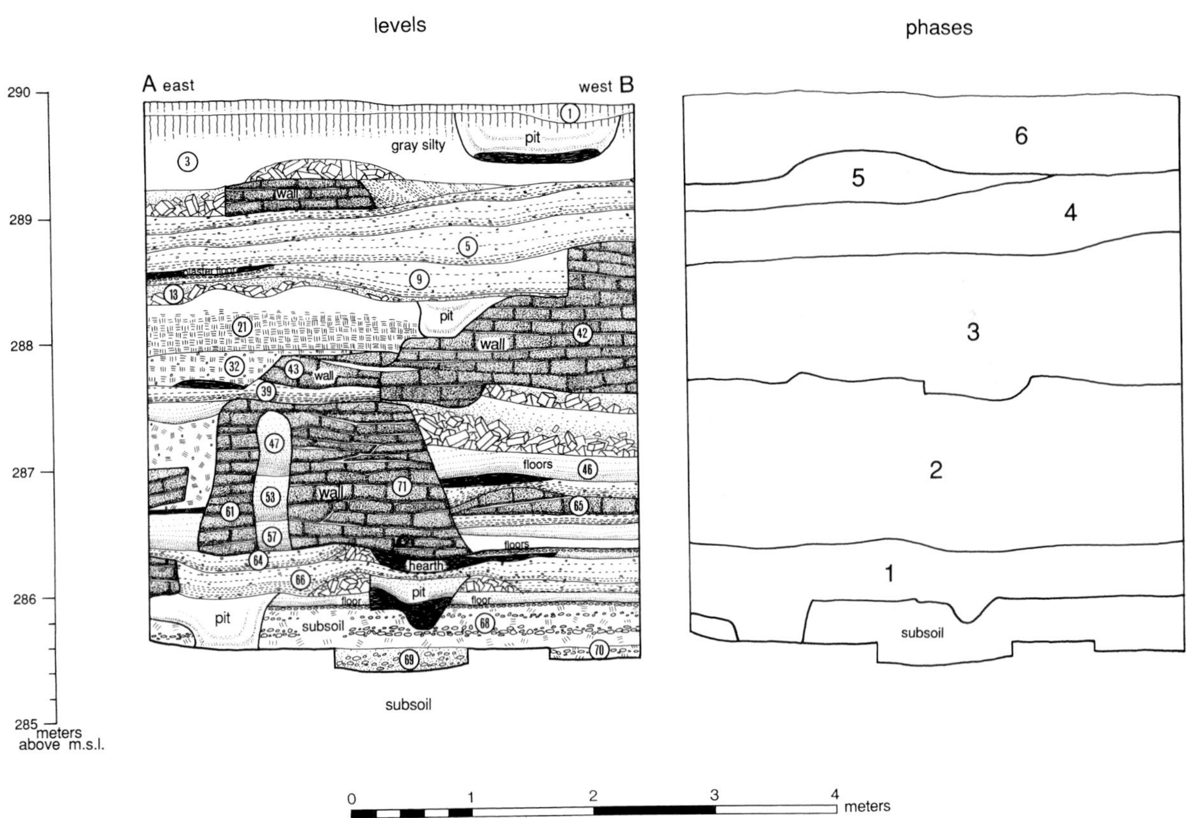

Figure 8.60 Trench G, Section A-B, levels and phases.

tial occupation of the area, and laid a clay floor on the level ground. This floor effectively sealed much of the surface of the subsoil, and was the first level of phase 1. The area was apparently an open space in which quite intense activity took place. A deposit of dark occupation soil accumulated, in which several trodden floors could be seen. The inhabitants dug a number of hearths and other pits into the deposits, a few of which penetrated the subsoil. Then they built a mudbrick structure at the east end of the trench. A human skull (73.3066) was buried in the occupation debris next to this structure. The building went out of use later on, but occupation debris and wash continued to build up.

A mudbrick building with at least four rooms that extended beyond the trench to the northwest and northeast was constructed here in phase 2 (figures 8.65, 8.66). This building was aligned from northwest to southeast like all the others in the Abu Hureyra 2 settlement. Its walls were only about 30 cm thick, too narrow to have supported a second story. Many of the mudbricks in these walls were quite small, about 30 cm square and from 5 to 15 cm thick. They were composed of various clays, often with a high proportion of pebbles, and were held together with mud mortar.

We excavated the southwest corner of this building, which consisted of two pairs of rectangular, parallel rooms, each at right angles to the other. This element of the plan was quite similar to parts of other Abu Hureyra 2 structures, such as the phase 5 house in Trench E. There was, however, a significant difference. Rooms 3 and 4 were unusually narrow, only 1 m and 70 cm wide,

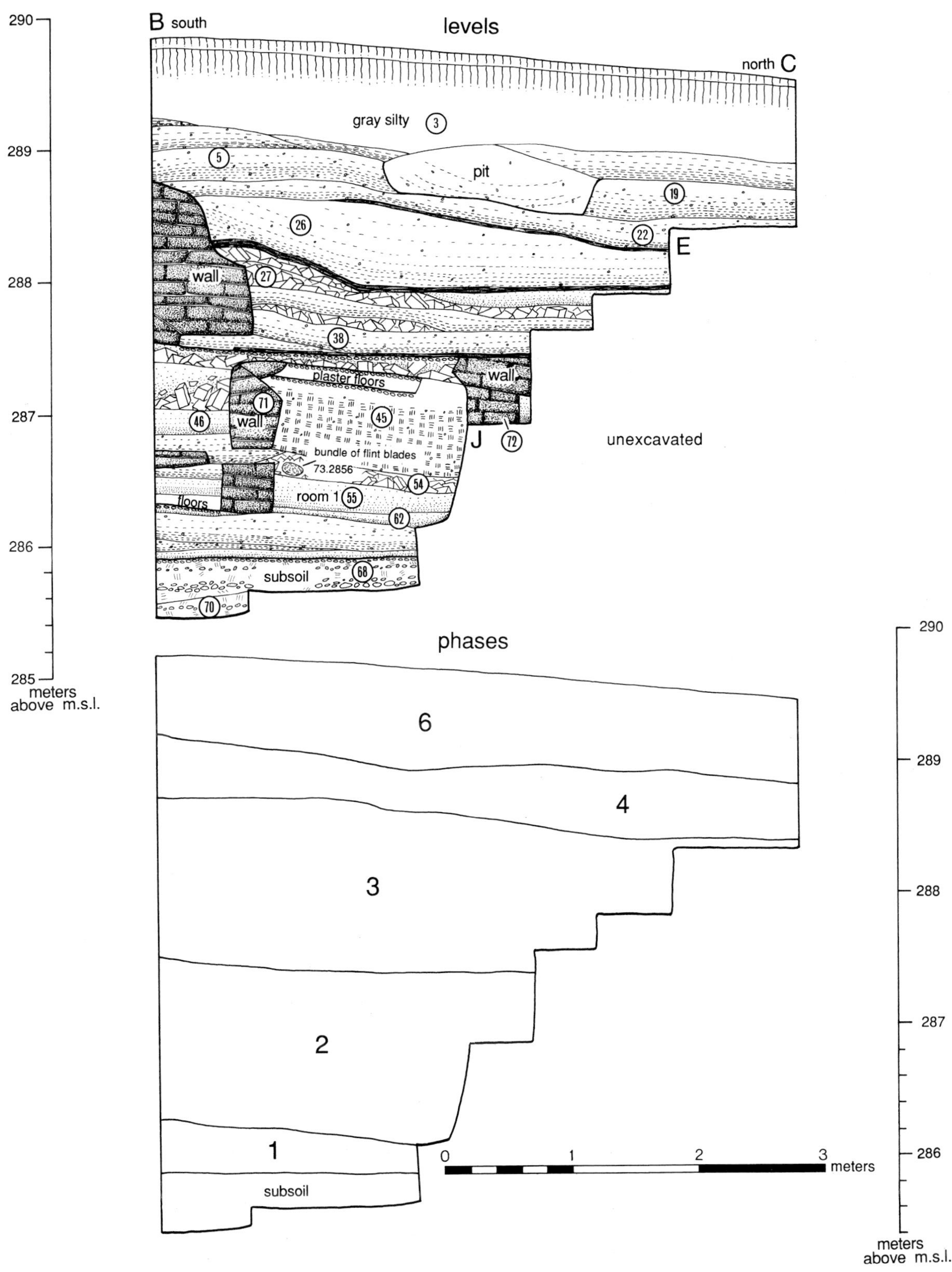

Figure 8.61 Trench G, Section B-C, levels and phases.

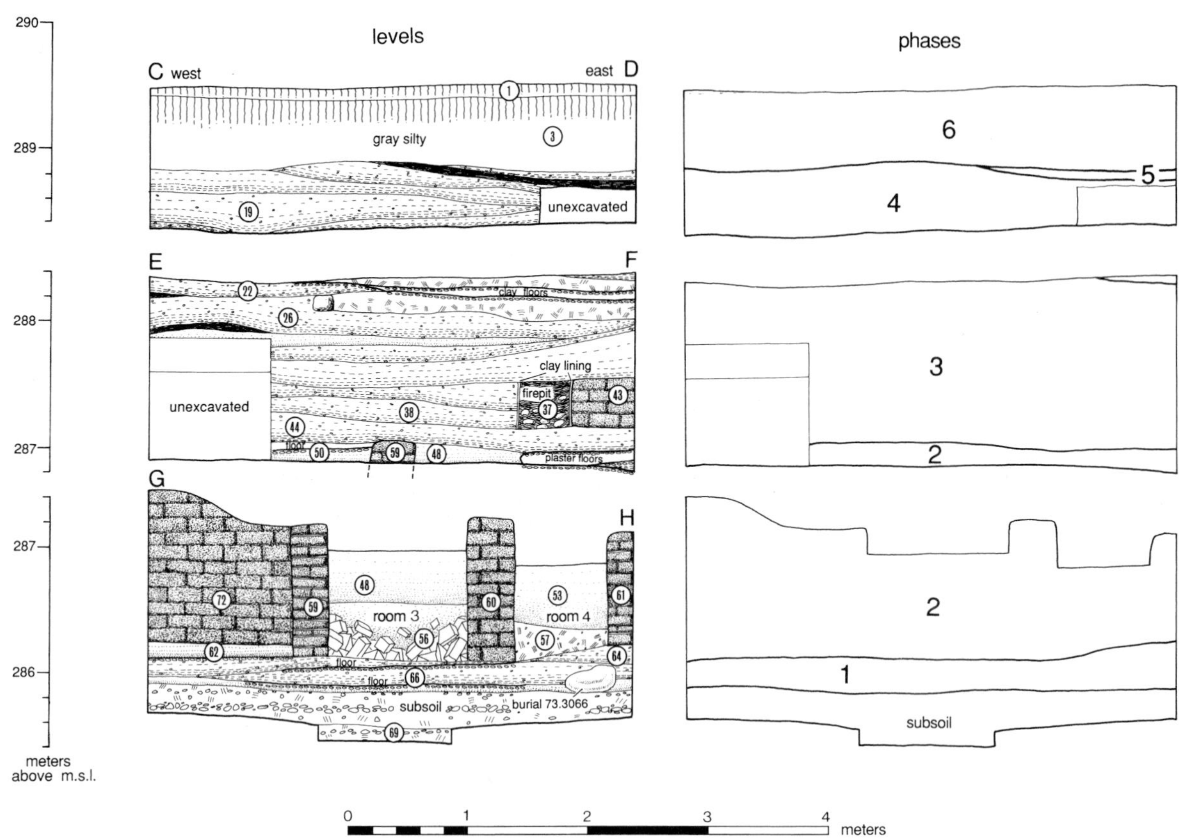

Figure 8.62 Trench G, Sections C-D, E-F, and G-H, levels and phases.

respectively, although both were over 4 m long. Their interiors were too restricted for people to move about and turn easily within them. It seems unlikely, therefore, that they were used by the inhabitants for preparing food, crafts, or repose, like the wider rooms of other houses. These two rooms had no solid floors, only a series of trodden surfaces that were renewed as they filled with debris. This, too, hints at a different function.

There was a large niche with a shelf in wall 60 of room 4, the wall separating it from room 3 (figure 8.67). The contents of rooms 3 and 4 were otherwise unremarkable, a few flint and other tools contained in a fill of building and occupation debris. Only the unusual dimensions of these two rooms, therefore, call for explanation. We suggest that they were probably used for storage, perhaps of foodstuffs; if kept dark, and so relatively free of flies, they could even have been used for drying meat. The rest of the building was probably a dwelling.

The walls of the phase 2 building were repaired later on. New walls were added on the south side of the structure, beyond wall 61, extending it in that direction. Wall 71 of room 1 collapsed and was rebuilt, but there was an interval during which this room must have been open to the west. We infer that some intense activity took place there then, because we recovered a large number of flint tools and other artifacts that dated from this episode. We found a collection of 230 fresh flint blades and lightly retouched blade knives (73.2856) clustered together in this level (54); they must once have been wrapped to-

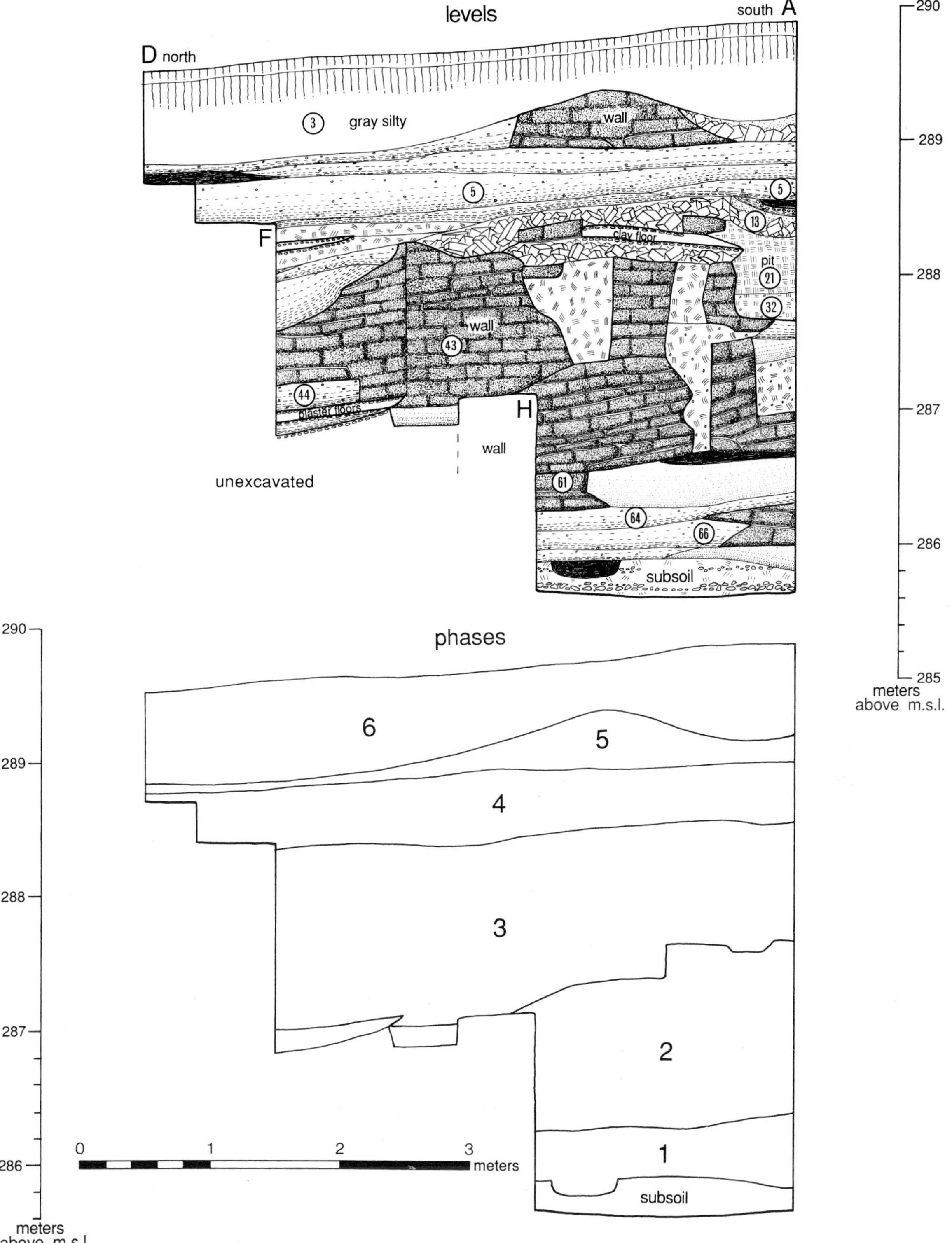

Figure 8.63 Trench G, Section D-A, levels and phases.

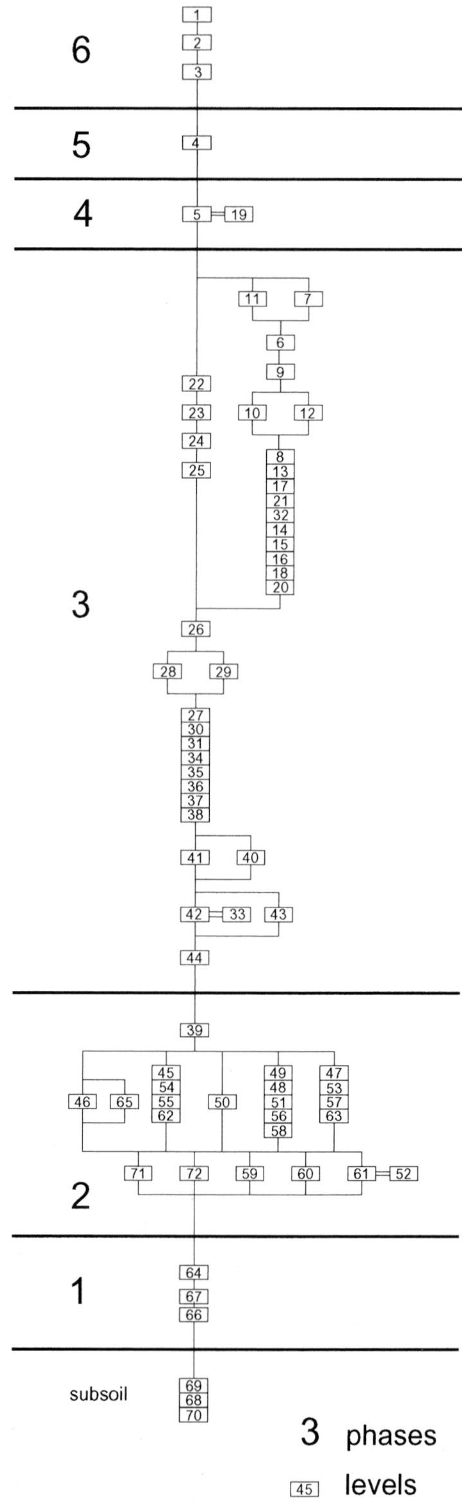

Figure 8.64 Trench G, level diagram.

Trench G

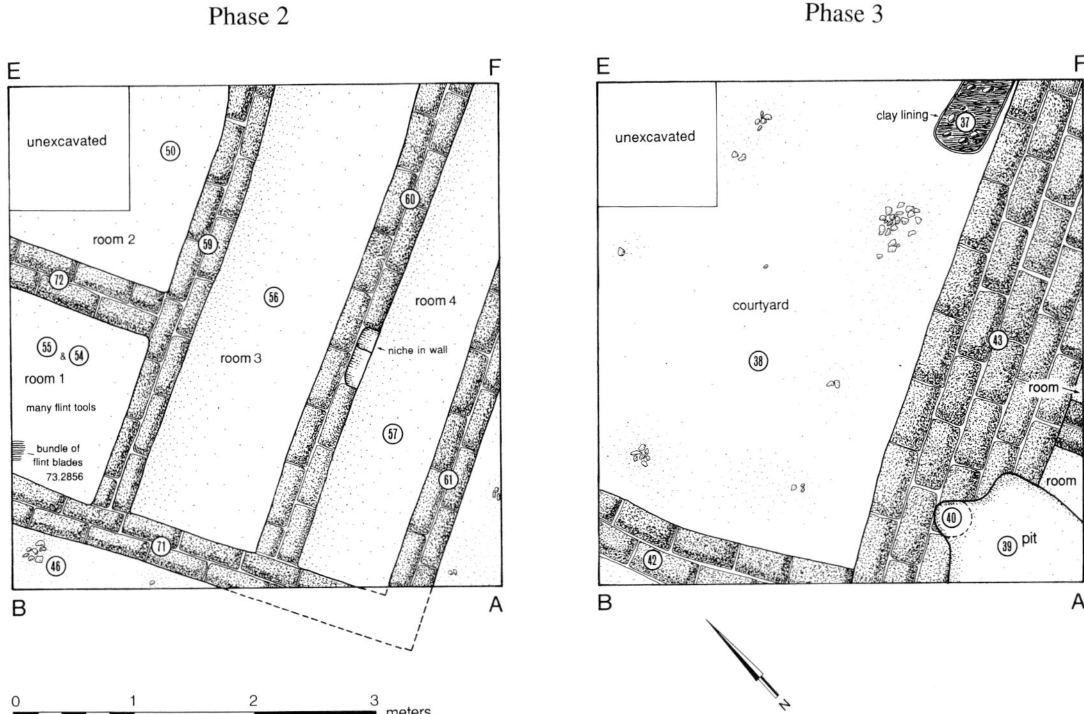

Figure 8.65 *(top)* Trench G, plans of the buildings in phases 2 and 3.

Figure 8.66 *(bottom)* Trench G, the phase 2 building, from the southwest. Scale, 50 cm.

Figure 8.67 Trench G, the large niche in wall 60 of room 4 in the phase 2 building. Scale, 20 cm.

gether in a bundle (figures 8.68, 8.69). Many of them were blanks for making retouched flint tools. The level contained a large number of other, apparently unused, flint tools that had been retouched on the spot (figure 8.70). There was, however, very little flint waste in this deposit, so it appears that the blades had been struck elsewhere.

The walls of the phase 2 building were modified slightly toward the end of its life, and a series of plaster floors was laid down in room 1. It then passed out of use. The area was open for a while, and it was during this episode that a pit (49) was dug in the ruins of room 3 and filled with animal bones.

In phase 3 the inhabitants leveled the walls of the phase 2 building and constructed a new mudbrick structure, similarly oriented, on top of it (figure 8.65). They built two exterior walls (42, 43) at right angles to enclose a courtyard that took up much of the excavated area. These walls were built on the stubs of walls 71 and 61. The two new walls were substantially thicker than their predecessors. Two rooms lay beyond wall 43 in the southeast corner of the trench.

Walls 42 and 43 were rebuilt several times during the life of the building. Thick levels of mudwash from these walls and occupation debris accumulated in the courtyard. Then the building began to decay, and a robber pit was dug into the walls in the southeast corner of the trench. Later, there was some new building in this corner, but only slight traces of this structure survived. Then all construction ceased and more mud washed out from the walls.

During phase 4 the area of Trench G was open, and no buildings were constructed in it. A deposit of mud wash mixed with some occupation soil accumulated here to a depth of 50 cm. Much of this material appears to have washed out from buildings in the vicinity of the trench.

Figure 8.68 Trench G, the bundle of fresh flint blades (73.2856) in room 1 of the phase 2 building, from the southwest. Scale, 50 cm.

Figure 8.69 Trench G, closeup of the bundle of flint blades (73.2856), from the east. Scale, 10 cm.

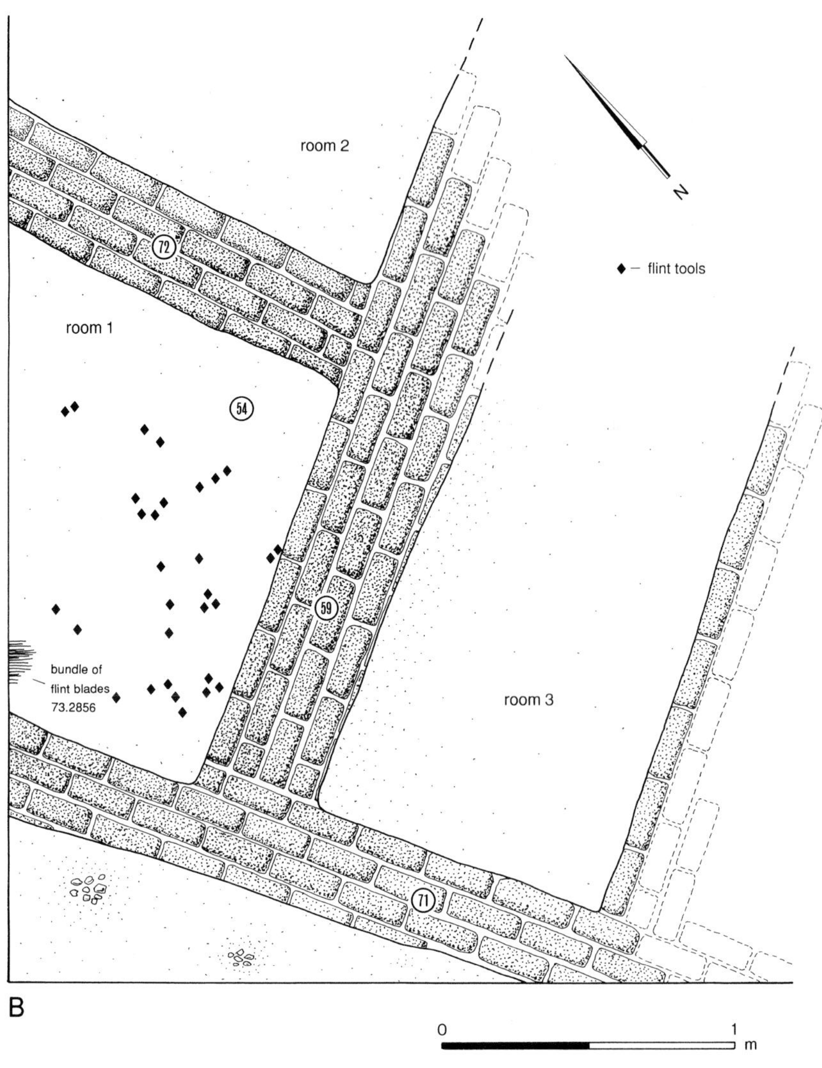

Figure 8.70 Trench G. The numerous flint tools in room 1, level 54, of the phase 2 building.

There was one more episode of building in phase 5. A building was constructed to the southeast of Trench G, one wall of which crossed corner A. This wall was built on the same line as wall 43 of phase 3, even though the two were separated by a considerable depth of wash. This illustrates again the extraordinary continuity of building locations and alignments in the Abu Hureyra 2 settlement. The building then passed out of use and fell into ruin, eventually eroding almost completely.

During the final phase of occupation in Trench G, phase 6, another thick level of debris built up that was composed of fine silt and occupation soil. Much of the silt came from the decay of mudbrick buildings beyond the limits of the trench. Here the inhabitants dug a pit at least 1.30 m in diameter and 40 cm deep, which filled up with ashy debris. The area was then abandoned; the surface began to erode away, and the remaining phase 6 deposits became heavily weathered.

Summary

The deposits in Trench G were 4.5 m deep, and the sequence of occupation represented by phases 1 to 6 was shorter than in the trenches along the main axis of the mound. This is demonstrated by the radiocarbon dates and the sequence of artifacts we found here. It also appears that there was less construction in this sector of the mound than elsewhere and that the space around Trench G was open for significant lengths of time. Thus less deposit accumulated there.

The initial settlement of this area took place shortly after the occupation of Abu Hureyra 1 and left some deposit in the subsoil. Whatever occupation debris may have accumulated on the surface of the ground was removed much later when the inhabitants of Abu Hureyra 2 expanded their village in this direction. They cleared off the subsoil and used the open ground for domestic activities. Then in phase 2 the first substantial building was constructed, a multiroomed dwelling with two rooms of unusually narrow dimensions that may have been used for storage or, perhaps, for penning animals. In phase 3 this was replaced by an L-shaped building with a courtyard.

The area around Trench G lay open for some time after the abandonment of this building, although activity continued there. Then another structure was built on the same alignment as the earlier ones. Finally, the area lay open once more, and a thick deposit of wash accumulated from the decay of neighboring buildings.

There were no obvious episodes of complete abandonment of the area around Trench G during the life of the settlement. Even during phases in which deep deposits of wash built up, there were traces of trodden floors, thin lenses of occupation soil, and ash in the wash, indicating that human activity continued. Furthermore, the buildings of phases 2, 3, and 5 were all similarly aligned. This suggests that there was not only remarkable continuity of building traditions, but also that the area around the trench was sufficiently restricted by other structures to dictate that new buildings should occupy space in similar ways to older ones on the same spot.

THE OCCUPATION SEQUENCE AND CHRONOLOGY OF ABU HUREYRA 2

The final part of the stratigraphic analysis is to correlate the phase sequences from the trenches to construct the occupation history of the settlement as a whole. This is a complicated task because the site was so large and its settlement history was complex. Several of the trenches were spaced far apart to find out how the history of occupation varied across the site, but this has made it difficult to correlate phase sequences between them. Nevertheless, it was obvious at the conclusion of the excavation that there were a few major changes in the nature of the structures and artifacts through time that could be seen over much of the site, so the general sequence of occupation was clear (Moore 1975, p. 58). The village of Abu Hureyra 2 was established early in the Pre-Pottery Neolithic. There followed a long initial period of occupation characterized by mudbrick buildings with plaster floors, and a typical flint assemblage with tanged arrowheads as a ubiquitous tool. Within this episode there was a gradual development from an earlier to a later period, the most conspicuous alteration being the greater variety of artifacts in the latter. Then, in the third and final period of occupation, there was a change in the form of the settlement: the inhabitants dug roasting pits between the buildings and began to use pottery. This third period we called the ceramic Neolithic. Within each of these periods of occupation there were many similarities in the remains of structures and artifacts from one part of the site to another.

Our task is to refine this general sequence to arrive at a precise history of occupation of the Abu Hureyra 2 settlement. The numerous radiocarbon and thermoluminescence dates for Abu Hureyra should then permit us to date the successive periods. We accomplish this by using all the sources of evidence that show changes in the nature of the settlement and the activities of its inhabitants through time. These are the stratigraphy of each trench, the evidence for changes in architecture and artifacts, the sequences of use of animals and plants, and the dates. Several of these categories have proved especially helpful in determining the sequence of occupation.

The stratified sequences of building phases within each trench are the core of the analysis, since it is from these that all the other sources of evidence are derived. It is not easy to correlate these sequences directly, however, because some areas of the site were occupied more intensively than others, and for different spans of time. We cannot assume, therefore, that building phases were always of the same duration across the site. Since the people of Abu Hureyra 2 built their houses in much the same way over long periods of time, there is little in the form of the buildings themselves that indicates change through time. The only major alteration in the organization of the settlement seems to have been the wider spacing of buildings and the digging of pits between them that occurred toward the end of the occupation. This provides us with a stratigraphic horizon that can be seen across much of the site.

The artifacts have proved less useful than we initially expected in refining the occupation sequence. This is because changes in the technology and typology of the major group, the flint tools, seem to have been slow. There are no distinctive types of artifacts that came into use suddenly, to be found in contemporary horizons across the site. The only class of artifacts of some help to us is the potsherds, since pottery began to be used late in the settlement's life, a little before the digging of the roasting pits. This innovation is quite useful, therefore, in providing an additional means of correlation, but otherwise the artifacts have given us only a general indication of changes in the occupation sequence. Further analysis may allow us to refine this view.

There is one major change in the faunal sequence, on the other hand, that has been of great importance in helping to determine the history of occupation. That is the rapid switch from intensive killing of gazelle to large-scale herding of sheep and goats that occurred late in the Pre-Pottery Neolithic. This has given us a means of subdividing this long period that close examination of the building sequences and artifacts has failed to do. It was evident early in the analysis of the faunal remains that many successive phases of occupation were characterized by high proportions of either gazelle or sheep and goat. The high proportions of gazelle always occurred early in the Abu Hureyra 2 stratigraphic sequence, as a continuation of the Abu Hureyra 1 pattern, and the dominance of sheep and goat was always late. We could observe the switch actually taking place in phase 8 in Trench B, where the event could be dated. Comparison with other trenches provided corroborating dating evidence. The switch thus gave us a well-dated faunal horizon that could be detected across the site.

The radiometric dates are of great importance in helping us to determine the sequence of occupation for the site and to place it in time. We have enough dates from each of the four trenches discussed here to make approximate correlations between their sequences of building phases. This information may then be combined to establish the chronology of the Abu Hureyra 2 settlement as a whole. The dates are so important for our chronological sequence that it is necessary to consider them in stratigraphic context within each trench first.

The Stratigraphic Context of the Radiometric Dates

There are seven radiocarbon and one thermoluminescence (TL) date for the Trench B sequence. They form a coherent sequence in rough chronological order from bottom to top (figure 8.71). Three of the dates in the cluster from phases 2, 3, and 4—OxA-2169, OxA-1190, and BM-1722R—are of similar magnitude. Another British Museum sample, BM-1122 from phase 3, suggests that occupation around Trench B began about 9,400 BP. The other dates from these phases confirm that the settlement was well underway in the early ninth millennium BP.

The two dates from the top of the Neolithic sequence, OxA-1232 and the TL date Ox TL 196a, indicate that occupation continued very late in the vicinity of Trench B. The potsherd used for the TL date had a Neolithic appearance, but, of course, simple, Neolithic-like wares continued to be used in north Syria into later times. The sherd was a good sample for TL dating, as the note by Joan Huxtable makes clear (appendix 2), so its date is reliable, especially as it is corroborated to some extent by another TL date from Trench E. TL dates are considered to give results close to the absolute age of the sample dated and so should be compared directly only with calibrated radiocarbon dates (Aitken 1985, p. 32). Most of the dates we have obtained are uncalibrated radiocarbon determinations that, in the time range concerned, are as much as 1,000 years younger than the absolute age of the samples dated (Kromer et al. 1986, table 1). This TL date of 7,250 ± 600 years ago suggests that occupation at Abu Hureyra may have continued, at least intermittently, until the late eighth millennium BP in absolute years.

We obtained eight radiocarbon dates for samples from Trench D, but two of these should be discounted in discussing Abu Hureyra 2. One of them, BM-1720R, has given a date that is far too early for any deposit we found at Abu

Trench B

Phase	14C date	TL and other 14C dates
11	170 ± 60 (OxA-2045)	
10		7,250 ± 600 (Ox TL 196a)
9	7,310 ± 120 (OxA-1232)	
8		
7	8,190 ± 77 (BM-1424)	
6		
5		
4	8,640 ± 100 (BM-1722R)	
3	9,374 ± 72 (BM-1122)	
2	8,500 ± 120 (OxA-1190)	
	8,640 ± 110 (OxA-2169)	
1		

Figure 8.71 Radiometric dates BP for Trench B in stratigraphic order.

Hureyra. It may hint at use of the place well before the foundation of the settlement, or may be aberrant. The other, OxA-880 on a charred bone of a wild ass from phase 4, gave a date of 14,920 ± 180 BP. This is significantly earlier than any date for even the Abu Hureyra 1 deposits and, anyway, is at odds with its stratigraphic context. The date, however, is not so improbable as to be discounted totally. The incorporation of a single ass bone of this age in Abu Hureyra 2 deposits might point to use of the site during the Epipalaeolithic prior to the establishment of Abu Hureyra 1. It should be noted that Trench D is the only part of the site that has yielded such early dates, both obtained by different radiocarbon methods. The possibility of earlier use of the site in the vicinity of Trench D cannot, therefore, be excluded.

The rest of the radiocarbon dates from Trench D (figure 8.72) form a tight cluster, most of which overlap at one standard deviation. They suggest that the occupation deposits here accumulated with extraordinary rapidity. The earliest date in the series, 8,870 ± 100 BP (OxA-881), on a charred caprine bone, actually comes from the latest phase, phase 6. It should be remembered that the sample came from a pit dug in later times that penetrated deep into the Abu Hureyra 2 levels and was filled almost entirely with material derived from these deposits. The sample thus gives us a date for the Abu Hureyra 2 settlement around Trench D, not the time when the pit was dug.

The six Trench D radiocarbon dates, taken together, suggest that the Abu Hureyra 2 occupation in this part of the mound began at or shortly after 9,000 BP, that is, about the same time as, or not long after, occupation in Trench B. It is clear from the location of the trench and its stratigraphy that the sequence of occupation here belongs in the earlier part of the Pre-Pottery period, an observation confirmed by the faunal data. The clustering of the dates provides additional evidence for this interpretation. They suggest that occupation continued until at least the mid ninth millennium BP and, if OxA-877 is correct, as late as 8,300 BP or so.

The TL date for the sherd from the phase 6 pit confirms that the pit was dug in early Islamic times.

We have fewer dates from the Abu Hureyra 2 deposits in Trench E than from Trenches B and D. One of the charcoal samples, BM-1723R (figure 8.73), gave a date appropriate for Abu Hureyra 1 but not Abu Hureyra 2, so the charcoal was

Trench D

Phase	14C date	TL and other 14C dates
6		AD 600-1,000 (TL)
		8,870 ± 100 (OxA-881)
5		
4		14,920 ± 180 (OxA-880)
	8,490 ± 110 (OxA-878)	
	8,570 ± 130 (OxA-879)	
3	8,490 ± 110 (BM-1721R)	
2		22,020 ± 200 (BM-1720R)
1	8,300 ± 150 (OxA-877)	
	8,500 ± 90 (OxA-876)	

Figure 8.72 Radiometric dates BP for Trench D in stratigraphic order.

Trench E

Phase	14C date	TL and other 14C dates
9		
8		5,350 ± 400 (Ox TL 196j)
7		
6	8,020 ± 100 (BM-1724R)	
		8,666 ± 66 (BM-1120)
		10,820 ± 510 (BM-1723R)
5	8,330 ± 100 (OxA-2168)	
4	8,270 ± 100 (OxA-2167)	

Figure 8.73 Radiometric dates BP for Trench E, Abu Hureyra 2, in stratigraphic order.

presumably derived from the settlement beneath. Samples of charcoal from several levels were combined to obtain another date, BM-1120; it should be regarded as giving no more than an approximate age for the deposits.

Four dates from phases 2 and 3 of the underlying Abu Hureyra 1 settlement span the intervening period between Abu Hureyra 1 and the large-scale development of settlement around Trench E in Abu Hureyra 2 times. Those dates are 9,860 ± 220 BP (OxA-6996), 9,100 ± 100 BP (BM-1719R), 9,060 ± 140 BP (OxA-475), and 8,700 ± 240 BP (OxA-6995). They suggest that there was continued human activity in the vicinity of Trench E during this long period of time. Any deposits that may have accumulated there as a result were subsequently removed as the Abu Hureyra 2 settlement expanded to this area.

The dates from stratified samples in the Abu Hureyra 2 deposits suggest that the main episode of Neolithic occupation around Trench E began sometime before 8,300 BP. This observation is strongly reinforced by the dates obtained from seven of the domesticated cereal grains found in phases 2 and 3 of the Abu Hureyra 1 deposits below that clustered between 8,290 and 8,115 BP.

Finally, there is a TL date of 5,350 ± 400 years ago (Ox TL 196j). This date may indicate that some activity took place around Trench E in the proto-historic period, long after Abu Hureyra 2 was abandoned.

One of the four dates from Trench G (figure 8.74) is very early, and the other three are late in the Abu Hureyra 2 sequence. The early date of 9,680 ± 90 BP (OxA-1228) was obtained from a sample of twig charcoal in an occupation deposit in the subsoil at the bottom of phase 1. It indicates that there was some occupation in the vicinity of this trench early in the tenth millennium BP.

Later, the area was inhabited once more, and the dates suggest that debris began to accumulate rapidly. We have two dates from near the bottom of phase 2, obtained for a level that contained an unusual mixture of wild and domesticated cereals. Grains of the wild cereals were dated to 8,180 ± 100 BP (OxA-1930), and of domesticated wheat to 7,890 ± 90 BP (OxA-1931). These dates suggest that the main period of occupation buildup around Trench G occurred quite late in the Abu Hureyra 2 sequence.

The dates and stratification suggest that, after an initial early episode of habitation, the Trench G area was intensively occupied only during the latter part of the Abu Hureyra 2 sequence.

Trench G

Phase	14C date
6	
5	
4	
3	8,320 ± 80 (OxA-1227)
2	7,890 ± 90 (OxA-1931)
	8,180 ± 100 (OxA-1930)
1	
subsoil	9,680 ± 90 (OxA-1228)

Figure 8.74 Radiometric dates BP for Trench G in stratigraphic order.

The Periods of Occupation

We must now combine the information from the stratigraphy, radiometric dates, faunal changes, and artifacts to determine the sequence of occupation for the site as a whole. We have seen that there is evidence that occupation continued at the site, especially at its northern end, from the end of Abu Hureyra 1 until the initial expansion of the Abu Hureyra 2 village. We call this episode the Intermediate Period. The strongest evidence comes from five radiocarbon dates of the ninth millennium BP from different trenches. The subsoil deposit in Trench G, itself with a radiocarbon date of 9,680 ± 90 BP (OxA-1228), provides further proof of this intermediate episode of occupation. Other occupation deposits that may have accumulated during this period were removed when the inhabitants of Abu Hureyra 2 scraped off the surface of the site to build their houses, at least in the areas we excavated. Of course, such deposits may still have existed in the intervening zones between our trenches.

The village of Abu Hureyra 2 was occupied continuously, but it is convenient to divide the sequence into three periods, 2A, 2B, and 2C. These periods correspond approximately to the three phases we described in our preliminary report of 1975, but their definitions have been modified, and they can now be dated. The final episodes of use of the site in the historic period, evidence for which was found in several trenches, we term Period 3. The duration of these periods, and the phases that should be attributed to them from each trench, are shown in figure 8.75.

Abu Hureyra 2A was the first period of substantial occupation in the Neolithic village that survived to be excavated by us. Throughout, the inhabitants constructed rectilinear dwellings of mudbrick, often floored with polished plaster. They used plaster, not only in building, but also to make containers; however, they did not yet have pottery. They made their flint artifacts on blades struck from bipolar cores, and their most numerous tools were tanged arrowheads. These people, like their predecessors, were farmers, but they still killed large quantities of gazelle. The continued hunting of gazelle is a distinguishing feature of this period of occupation.

The earliest radiocarbon date for this settlement from a level in the Abu Hureyra 2 village is c. 9,400 BP from Trench B, so we use this as the starting point for large-scale occupation at Abu Hureyra, recognizing that we cannot fix the time exactly. By 9,000 BP the village was growing rapidly around its cen-

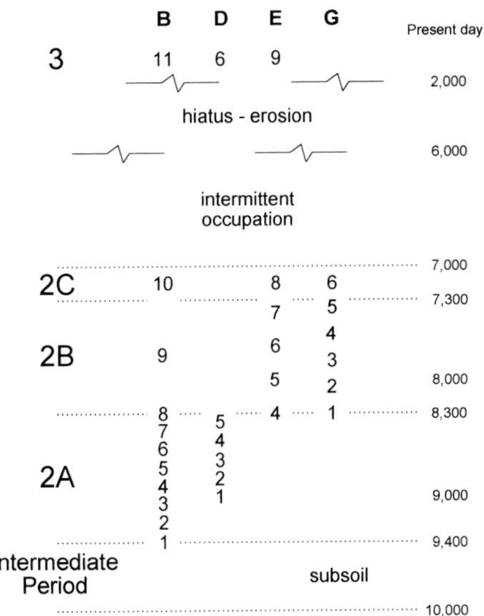

Figure 8.75 The chronology of the periods of Abu Hureyra 2 and correlation of the sequences of phases in each trench.

ter along the main axis of the mound in the area of Trenches B, C, D, and possibly A.

We have chosen the switch from the large-scale exploitation of gazelles to caprines as the key element that separates Period 2A from 2B, partly because it seems to have been an event of great moment in the history of the settlement, but also because it is the single major change that allows us readily to divide the long Pre-Pottery Neolithic stage of Abu Hureyra 2. The switch can be dated quite precisely using the dates from Trenches B, D, E, and G. The two earliest dates from Trench E of 8,330 ± 100 BP (OxA-2168) and 8,270 ± 100 BP (OxA-2167) actually mark the end of heavy gazelle exploitation and the transition to large-scale herding of sheep and goats in phases 4 and 5. In Trench B, where the actual switch is also well documented, there is a date on charcoal of 8,190 ± 77 BP (BM-1424) from phase 7, just prior to the event itself in phase 8. These dates suggest that the transition from gazelle to caprines occurred about 8,300 BP. There is confirmation of this date for the transition from other trenches. The dates from Trench D, with high proportions of gazelle throughout, are all earlier. On the other hand, phases 2–6 in Trench G all have high proportions of sheep and goat, and the two dates from phase 2 are 8,180 ± 100 BP (OxA-1930) and 7,890 ± 90 BP (OxA-1931). There is further corroboration from a date in Trench C of 8,393 ± 72 BP (BM-1425) before the event and from Trench A of 8,180 ± 200 BP (OxA-4660) after it. We propose, therefore, to date the switch from gazelles to sheep and goat, and thus the transition from Period 2A to 2B, at about 8,300 BP, recognizing that any such estimate must be subject to some latitude. Period 2A lasted, therefore, about 1,100 radiocarbon years.

The cultural characteristics of Abu Hureyra 2B are much the same as those of 2A. A wide range of artifacts was in use, though not yet pottery, but their diversity was already well established by the later centuries of 2A. The main change was the adoption of sheep and goats as the main source of meat and other animal products, and the first significant exploitation of cattle.

The beginning of this period may be fixed quite closely at c. 8,300 BP, as we have seen, but the date of the transition to Period 2C is uncertain. Phase 9 in

Trench B immediately preceded the transition to Period 2C and has a radiocarbon date of 7,310 ± 120 BP (OxA-1232). This, the only relevant date from the Abu Hureyra sequence, would imply that the transition occurred about 7,300 BP. A single determination is hardly sufficient to date such a major event, but there is some supporting evidence to indicate that it did indeed take place about the middle of the eighth millennium BP. The date itself is in the right stratigraphic order, both within Trench B and across the site. The date of 7,890 ± 90 BP (OxA-1931) from phase 2 in Trench G shows that Period 2B lasted well into the eighth millennium there, while the number of trench phases to be attributed to this period in both G and E would also suggest that Period 2B lasted for at least several centuries.

The nature of the settlement changed in Period 2C, and this can be detected across the site. Buildings were spaced farther apart and pits were dug between them; many of the pits were filled with burned debris that suggests they were used for roasting. Pottery was made now, and a few sherds were found in the upper levels of most of the excavated trenches. The inception of pottery, however, began late in Period 2B, since sherds have been found in phase 7 in Trench E and phase 5 in Trench G, the last phases of Period 2B in those trenches. The animal economy continued to be characterized by caprine exploitation, though cattle and pigs were increasingly important in this period.

The duration of this period can only be estimated because we have no radiocarbon dates from the top levels of the site. There is the further complication that the original surface of the mound has long since eroded away. We estimate that the deposits that remained to be excavated by us date to no later that c. 7,000 BP, but the actual abandonment of the Period 2C settlement probably occurred several centuries later than this. The TL date of 7,250 ± 600 years ago (OxA TL 196a) suggests that it may have occurred as late as the second half of the seventh millennium BP in radiocarbon years. Thereafter, Abu Hureyra was visited, and may even have been briefly inhabited, from time to time in later prehistory, events documented by another TL date, Ox TL 196j, and the find of an Ubaid sherd in a surface level of the site.

We have no evidence to indicate that such visits continued into the early historic period, although it is probable that they did. After all, this stretch of the Euphrates Valley served periodically as an important route between the Mediterranean lands and Mesopotamia. Intermittent use of the site resumed in Byzantine and again in Islamic times, then finally in the modern period. We found traces of Byzantine activities in Trenches E and G, while the large pit cut in Trench D and the numerous graves across the site dated by radiocarbon to Islamic times provide evidence for more recent use of the site. We assign these phases to a final period of occupation, Period 3.

Abu Hureyra 2 was occupied from c. 9,400 to at least 7,000 BP in uncalibrated radiocarbon years. When these dates are calibrated according to the recently published calibration curves (*Radiocarbon* 28, 2B, 1986; 35, 1, 1993), they become c. 10,400–7,800 Cal BP. Thus, the main effect of calibrating the dates is to extend them from 800 to 1,000 years back in time. Calibration also slightly lengthens the total span of occupation, but only by a couple of centuries.

The date of 7,800 Cal BP is, of course, simply an estimate of the age of the surviving surface deposits of Abu Hureyra 2. When this is compared directly with the TL date of 7,250 ± 600 years ago (Ox TL 196a), it appears even more likely that Abu Hureyra 2 continued to be inhabited for several more centuries, but the deposits associated with this episode have since eroded away.

Summary

The stratigraphic evidence, radiometric dates, and other data indicate that Abu Hureyra continued to be inhabited from the end of Abu Hureyra 1 until the establishment of the village of Abu Hureyra 2. This Intermediate Period occupation seems to have been concentrated at the northern end of the site around Trenches E and G.

Occupation of the Neolithic settlement of Abu Hureyra 2 began about 9,400 BP and continued without interruption until after 7,000 BP. The center of this village lay below the main western ridge of the mound in the vicinity of Trenches B, C, and D. The long occupation span of Abu Hureyra 2 may be divided into three periods, Abu Hureyra 2A, 2B, and 2C.

Period 2A lasted from c. 9,400 to 8,300 BP. The economy was based on farming and the continued hunting of gazelle. The culture of the inhabitants of the site falls squarely within the Pre-Pottery, or Archaic Neolithic, tradition of the Levant, especially its second stage, Neolithic 2. The transition from Period 2A to 2B was marked by a rapid shift from the exploitation of gazelle to that of sheep and goats. The culture of the site changed little in this period. Period 2B lasted from c. 8,300 to perhaps 7,300 BP. The last period of occupation, 2C, lasted from c. 7,300 to after 7,000 BP. The main changes in this period were cultural: buildings were spaced farther apart and pits were dug between them. Pottery was made in modest amounts, an innovation that began toward the end of Period 2B. The economy continued to be based on farming and herding of caprines, with the addition now of significant numbers of cattle and pigs. The cultural characteristics of Abu Hureyra 2C set it on the same horizon as Levantine sites of the Pottery Neolithic, or Neolithic 3.

Calibration of the radiocarbon dates for the Abu Hureyra 2 sequence of occupation extends the entire span about one thousand years back in time, but it has little effect on its duration.

Abu Hureyra was abandoned at the end of Period 2C, though it continued to be used intermittently in later prehistory. Then there was a hiatus in occupation. The site was used again in Byzantine and Islamic times as a cemetery and for other activities. The last phase of occupation occurred in the twentieth century AD. These various episodes of use in the historic period are designated Period 3.

9 The Buildings and Layout of Abu Hureyra 2

A. M. T. Moore

THE BUILDINGS

The village of Abu Hureyra 2 was composed of rectilinear, mudbrick buildings aligned approximately northwest-southeast and separated by narrow lanes and courts. When a building went out of use it was replaced by another built to much the same plan on the same alignment. Thus, the arrangement of many of the buildings and open spaces was maintained for long periods of time. The entire village seems to have been covered with these tightly packed buildings, although they were not all inhabited at the same time.

We excavated three buildings completely in Trench E and portions of many more in the other trenches. Hence, we can reconstruct the form of several of the buildings and discern some of the variations in their construction. We have already stated that their appearance, contents, and ubiquity suggest that most of them were houses. We suggest that they were family homes, that is, dwellings for parents with their children and perhaps a few other close relatives. The regularity of the plans of the houses and their separation from each other suggest that each family had clear ideas about building norms and its own place in the community. Families preferred to live in individual houses, and we may infer from this that notions of family tenure of property in the village were already strongly developed. The few buildings we excavated that might have been used for other purposes, like the Trench B phase 8 structure that appears to have had a special ritual function connected with burying the dead, were built in much the same way as the structures we call houses. It is possible, of course, that other kinds of buildings were constructed elsewhere in the settlement in areas we did not excavate.

Many of the houses were rectangular in plan, although some had additional rooms to make an L-shaped extension or some other rectilinear variant. The houses varied considerably in size. The complete examples we excavated in Trench E phases 5 and 6 were 46 and 50 m^2 in area, respectively, but these were quite small compared with some others. The phase 4 house in the same trench may have been about 58 m^2 when first built and was then expanded to perhaps 80 m^2. The phase 8 house in Trench B was also relatively large, covering at least 82 m^2.

The houses were usually composed of two or three parallel rooms built along the axis of the building, and one or two more rooms at right angles at each end. This was the form of the complete house in Trench E phase 5 (figure 8.51). It was repeated, not only in the other houses in the Trench E sequence, but in houses in Trenches B and G discussed here, as well as in Trench A and elsewhere on the site. This suggests that the community had well-defined ideas about what form a house should take. Sometimes the core of the house was built first as a single large room, as in Trench B phases 7 and 8, and then subdivided later into two or more rooms. In fact, the interior of a house was quite often divided into a series of smaller rooms during its life. This may have been done to accommodate an increase in the size of the family living there. The rooms were usually rectangular and about twice as long as they were wide. Many were from 3 to 5 m in length and from 1.5 to 2 m in width, about the measure of a person's outstretched arms. Most of the rooms were thus quite small. When the Trench B phase 8 building was first constructed its main room was much larger, measuring 7.55 × 5 m, but this was divided into three smaller rooms later on.

The plan of a house was decided at the outset, and much of the structure was apparently built in a single episode. Each house was usually constructed on the remains of an earlier one, and the form of that building largely determined the plan of its successor. The rooms of the ruined house were filled in and the stubs of its walls were cut down. The walls of the new house were often built alongside and over the stubs of the old, which served as foundations. Other walls were built directly on the leveled surface, not in a foundation trench. The walls of the houses were straight, and so were apparently laid out using string. The corners of many of the rooms were right angled originally, even if they subsequently became distorted. The dimensions of many of the rooms and of entire houses, such as the Trench E phase 5 example, were quite regular. This suggests that the plan of each building was measured out with care, and that its dimensions were adhered to during construction.

The exterior and interior walls of the houses ranged from 20 to 50 cm in width, with 40 cm being a common figure, although their thickness varied a good deal. These walls were too thin to have supported an upper floor, so we think that most of the houses were built with a single story and a light roof. One of the reasons the villagers made the rooms so small may have been the difficulty they had in supporting the span of the roof beams on such thin walls. This kind of rectilinear construction was still in the early stages of development, and some of the problems of design had not yet been resolved satisfactorily. Several of the houses in Trench B and a few elsewhere had thicker exterior walls about 80 cm in width. These were sturdy enough to have supported a substantial roof or other superstructure, perhaps even a second story.

All the buildings were constructed of mudbricks throughout the Abu Hureyra 2 sequence. Some of the bricks were large slabs as much as 80 × 40 × 20 cm in size. They were too large to transport far, since two men would have been needed to lift them. The slab bricks were presumably made where they were to be used, and some of them may actually have been formed on the wall itself. Other bricks were much smaller, in some cases 30 × 30 × 10 cm, although the bricks varied considerably in size, even within a single building. All the bricks were relatively thin for their size, and made of stiff clay tempered with straw and, sometimes, pebbles. The shape of each brick was sufficiently regular to suggest that it was made in a mold. None of them was baked deliberately, so we assume they were dried in the sun before use.

The mode of construction of the buildings was very simple. The walls were built of a single thickness of bricks secured with mud mortar. A wider wall was sometimes constructed of two parallel rows of bricks set lengthwise. Where two exterior walls met at a corner they might be bonded together, but walls were more often simply butted against each other with straight joins. Certain features that were an integral part of the structure, such as doors and niches in walls, were added as the building was constructed. The floors were laid down later. Buildings erected with these techniques were slight and vulnerable to collapse. On the other hand, the walls were quite flexible and, if they did fall down, would not bring the rest of the building with them. Our evidence suggests that local repairs were often made to parts of buildings, though they rarely collapsed completely before their normal span of use had passed.

None of the buildings survived to a sufficient height for us to determine with certainty how they were roofed. Indeed, it was rare to find roofing material within them because most had been leveled off and the associated building debris scattered so that another building could be built on top. We did find some lumps of clay and gypsum plaster with the impressions of wooden poles, perhaps of poplar, and reeds within some rooms that had apparently fallen from the roof overhead. The houses of the modern village of Abu Hureyra, and those of many villages up and down the Euphrates today, are built in much the same way as those of Abu Hureyra 2, that is, with mudbricks to a rectangular plan, and on a similar orientation. The principal differences are that the houses of the present day are larger, have thicker walls, and contain fewer rooms. They are roofed with poplar poles covered with reeds, or sometimes brush, made weatherproof with mud. It seems likely that the Abu Hureyra 2 houses were roofed in a similar manner.

The floors of the rooms of Abu Hureyra 2 houses were covered with hard plaster, or were more simply finished with a clay or trodden earth surface. The laying of a plaster floor required several steps. First, the original surface was carefully leveled. Then a thin bed of fine pebbles was spread over it and covered with red clay subsoil or *hamra*. Sometimes the *hamra* contained many pebbles itself, and this sufficed as a bed for the floor. Next, a layer of plaster was applied over the *hamra* bed and carefully smoothed. A floor of *hamra* and plaster together was usually about 5 cm thick. Analyses of floor plaster by Marie Le Mière (appendix 4) and Pamela Vandiver have shown that the plaster was made of gypsum. The plaster floors were usually colored black or, sometimes, red, although a few were left plain. The pigments, probably of soot and red ochre, were applied as a wash over the freshly laid floor. Finally, the surface of the floor was burnished to a shine with a polishing stone to seal it. The plaster floors were frequently renewed during the life of a room—at least two or three times, but sometimes as many as ten. At nearly every renewal the entire floor-laying process was repeated.

Room walls were often covered with a thin layer of mud plaster or whitewash. This, too, was refreshed with a new coat several times during the room's life. The surfaces of both walls and floors were decorated. We found a few designs intact on floors and scraps of many more among plaster fragments in building collapse, enough to suggest that the walls were frequently covered with paintings. Unfortunately, all the pieces of wall plaster were too small for us to make out the designs on them. We know that many were executed in red on a white background and that some consisted of patterns of lines, but that is all. One floor painting survived in good condition, the "sun" on the floor of the phase 5 house in Trench B (figure 8.9). Traces of several more were found on other floors, but they were all too worn to interpret. The evidence for internal decoration is thus frustratingly fragmentary, yet it is clear that many rooms had shiny black plaster floors and walls painted with red designs on white. The rooms would thus have presented a striking and rich appearance.

Some of the Abu Hureyra 2 houses had features built in the walls and floors. We found niches in the walls of the better-preserved houses (figure 8.14), and we conclude that these would have been a common convenience in most dwellings. Several houses had one room with a low plaster platform in a corner raised a few centimeters above the plaster floor (figure 9.1). These were often subrectangular in shape with a rounded edge. We infer that they were used for sleeping, in part on analogy with similar features in houses in the Euphrates Valley today. A few houses contained small bins at the side of a room. These had thin walls of mud or mudbrick that were plastered inside and out. The bins were probably used to store dry foodstuffs. In two other houses, one in Trench E phase 4 and the other in Trench B (figure 8.15), we found a large plaster vessel built in place toward the center of a room. Again, the most likely explanation of the function of these vessels is that they were used for storage.

We can say little about the movable artifacts with which the rooms might have been furnished because most such objects would have been made of organic materials that have not survived. It is likely that each house had reed

Figure 9.1 Trench A, a house room with a plastered floor. There is a plastered sleeping platform in the foreground and an oven in the opposite corner of the room. Scale, 1 m.

mats on some of the floors, bedding materials in a few rooms, some wooden containers, and racks to hold baskets, tools, and foodstuffs. A few heavy items such as grinding stones may have been pushed into a corner, as in the Trench E phase 5 house. Other items may have been suspended from the roof.

It was common to find a hearth within at least one of the rooms of a house. This might contain ash but had no food remains or other rubbish in its vicinity. We conclude that such interior hearths were used more for heating than for cooking. One room in a house in Trench A had a small oven in a corner that was presumably used for baking (figure 9.1). The hearths were often set in the same place in successive houses. A particularly striking example was the series of hearths in the houses of phases 2–7 in Trench B (figures 8.9–11). We conclude from this that the builders of a new house often remembered not only the plan but also the internal arrangements of its predecessor, and considered it appropriate to replicate both.

In some houses there were doors between the rooms so the inhabitants could move from one room to another without going outside. Thus, the houses at Abu Hureyra were characterized by an internal pattern of circulation. They are therefore among the earliest dwellings to exhibit what Aurenche (1981a, vol. I, p. 199) has called a "complex plan." Sometimes the doors were at floor level, as in the earlier version of the phase 8 house in Trench B (figure 8.16) and in a house in Trench A (figure 9.1). A second kind of door was like a porthole, that is, a rectangular opening in a wall with a high sill. The best example we found was the doorway with its lintel still intact in the phase 7 house in Trench B (figure 8.13). Porthole doorways were sufficiently small not to weaken the thin walls of the houses seriously. Their sills would have helped to prevent rubbish from the lanes outside getting indoors. We observed the sills of three porthole doors in the Trench E phase 5 house (figures 8.51, 8.52). The walls in many other houses did not survive to a sufficient height to preserve traces of porthole doors, but it seems probable that this was the usual means of passing from one room to the next because we found so few doors at floor level.

The low height of most surviving walls was the main reason why we found no windows in any building. Nonetheless, had windows been a common feature we would have expected to see them in houses that were reasonably well preserved, such as the Trench B phase 7 and Trench G phase 2 examples. We infer that most houses were windowless and thus had dim interiors. The houses needed some form of ventilation, especially during summer heat, so we assume they would have had small holes high up in their walls to allow for the circulation of air, as do many houses in the Euphrates Valley today. The houses in the village of Qirata beside the Sajur River, a tributary of the Euphrates in north Syria, illustrate this feature well (see figure 9.5). Houses with an interior hearth or oven may also have had a hole in the roof to allow smoke to escape.

We have enough information about the plans of the houses and many of the details of their construction and furnishings to illustrate what one of them would have looked like during its life. We have chosen the phase 5 house in Trench E because it was excavated in its entirety, its walls were preserved to a sufficient height for us to ascertain the internal pattern of circulation, and it yielded much information about how it had been used. Furthermore, enough of the area around the house was excavated for us to determine how the house was related to neighboring structures. The result is shown in the isometric drawing in figure 9.2. Almost all the details of the lower half of the house are attested in the plan of the excavated building (figure 8.51), while the upper part

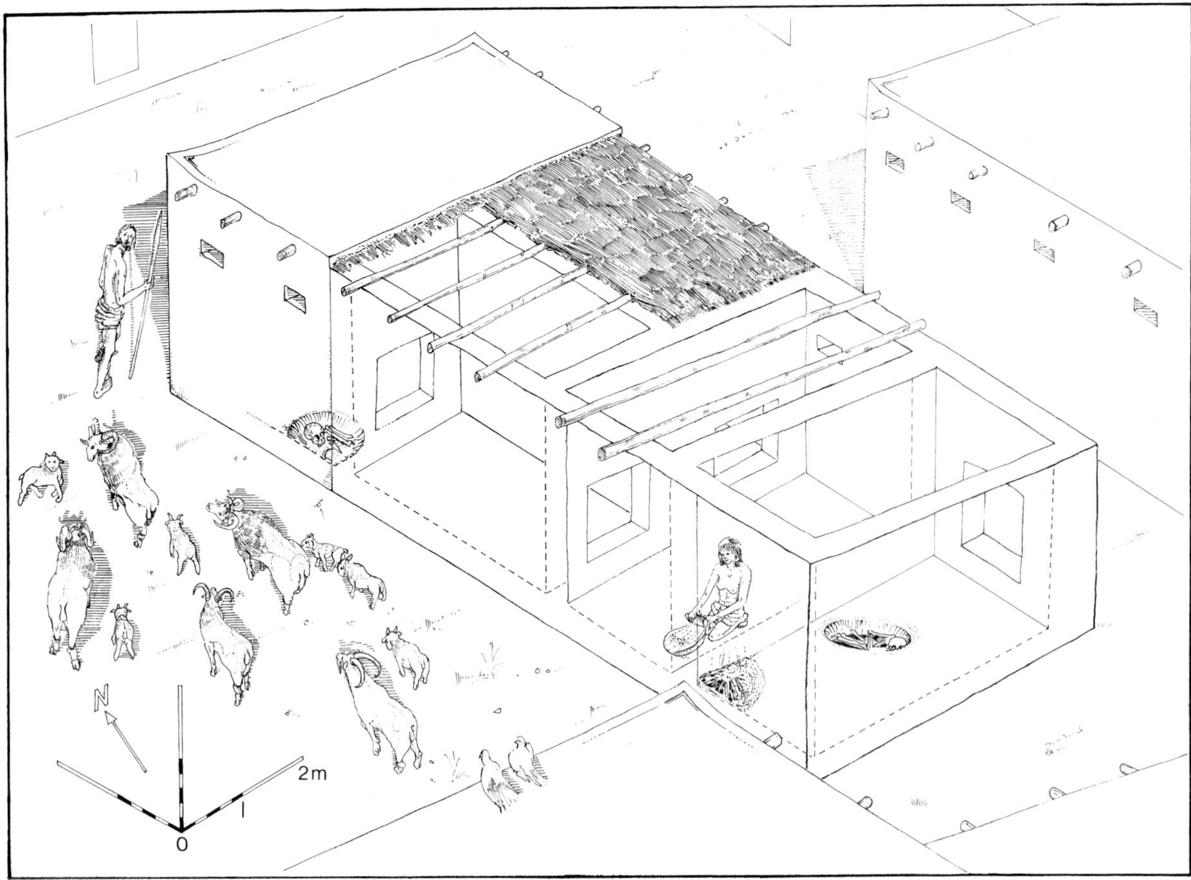

Figure 9.2 Isometric drawing of a reconstruction of the house in Trench E phase 5, from the southwest. The lower half of the house is drawn from the information about the plan of the building and its contents in figure 8.51. The upper part has been reconstructed to show how we think the houses of Abu Hureyra were roofed. The activities shown in the drawing are based on our interpretations of the human and animal skeletal remains.

has been reconstructed according to our observations, outlined above, on how the houses were built.

One of the most remarkable features of the Abu Hureyra 2 settlement was the long sequence of construction we found in each of the trenches we excavated. The houses in Trench E were rebuilt four, and the houses in Trench B no fewer than nine times. These houses were nearly always constructed in the same places and to approximately the same plan. The houses of Abu Hureyra 2 were so close together that there would have been severe constraints on the disposition of new buildings. A new house usually had to be built in the space occupied by its predecessor because the surrounding houses were often still occupied. Thus, many houses would be of approximately the same size and orientation as earlier houses on the same plot. This does not fully explain, however, why the plan of each new house followed that of the preceding dwelling so closely over several centuries. The builders probably knew the form of the old house and chose to match it. We know, too, that in some instances they themselves were the descendants of the inhabitants of the earlier structures (see chapter 11).

How long was a house occupied before it went out of use? It is difficult to answer this question precisely, but there are several kinds of evidence from which we may obtain an approximate figure. Most houses were lightly built, suggesting that even with repairs they would not have endured for much longer than a single human lifetime. In Trench D, five phases of buildings were constructed over perhaps 300–600 years, depending on how one interprets the radiocarbon dates. Allowing for some lapse of time between at least a few of the construction phases, it would seem that the structures here lasted for no more than a couple of generations. The same arguments may be applied to the sequence of buildings in Trench B, where eight houses were erected in succession over perhaps a millennium. Finally, there is the evidence of the burials under the floors discussed in chapter 10. This tends to reinforce the view that the houses lasted no more than two human lifetimes. We suggest, with due caution, that the lifespan of the houses was certainly less than a century, and perhaps of the order of 50 years.

The inhabitants of Abu Hureyra 1A had already built multiroomed dwellings in which one chamber communicated with another within the structure. Thus, it was relatively easy for them to enlarge their dwellings as their households grew. Yet the reincarnation of this principle in the mudbrick houses of Abu Hureyra 2 represented an architectural revolution. The materials used were new, as was the plan. The rectilinear houses of Abu Hureyra 2 were more durable and provided better protection from both winter chill and summer heat because of the insulating qualities of mudbrick. It was now easier to enlarge the house in any direction without weakening the existing structure. We should note, too, that the regularity of the plans of the Abu Hureyra 2 houses implies that the inhabitants had transformed their conception of how they should build their houses and what such structures symbolized.

The building of a settlement of the scale of Abu Hureyra 2 represented another kind of revolution. The vast quantities of mudbrick, plaster, timber, and reeds required to construct so many houses over so long a period of occupation were unprecedented. Mud, wood, and reeds were doubtless all obtained from the Euphrates floodplain adjacent to the site, but the nearest sources of workable gypsum for plaster were at least several kilometers distant from Abu Hureyra. Furthermore, two of the raw materials, mud and gypsum, had to be extensively processed before they could be used for building. Mud had to be mixed with straw and pressed into molds to make bricks. Pieces of gypsum rock had to be fired at temperatures of 200–400°C and then mixed with water to make plaster. This implies that the community had developed the means to organize labor on a large scale and to harness a novel technology, the manufacture of gypsum plaster. Most members of the community would have understood how to use these materials to build their houses, but it seems unlikely that all would have been engaged in their production to the same extent. We suggest, therefore, that the manufacture and use of plaster, and perhaps that of mudbrick, was in the hands of part-time specialists.

Considerable quantities of poplar poles and other timber would have been used to build the houses. Much more timber would have been needed, however, to heat gypsum rock to make plaster, and for domestic cooking and heating. The softwoods that would have been most readily available on the valley floor were quick-growing species that provided a renewable source of timber. Nevertheless, the inhabitants would have cleared some of the Euphrates floodplain and wadi bottoms of trees, and cut shrubs on the steppe, to obtain fuel.

LAYOUT OF THE VILLAGE

In all seven of the trenches we excavated we found the remains of houses, one superimposed upon another with only narrow spaces between them. It is possible that there were larger open areas between the houses in parts of the mound that we did not excavate, but we think it unlikely. Rather, we propose that the entire inhabited area of the village was covered with houses, packed tightly together. The open spaces for penning animals and other activities for which more room was required would have been at the edge of the settlement.

The houses in every trench were similarly aligned and built so close together that all the houses in the village probably shared the same orientation. There are good reasons for thinking that the inhabitants of Abu Hureyra 2 had an effective form of community organization to regulate the affairs of the settlement, but it does not necessarily follow that its layout was planned by a central body, despite its regular appearance. The houses in the modern village and in other settlements along the Euphrates Valley face southwest, apparently to catch the winter sun and to present the minimum surface area to the prevailing westerly wind that blows down the valley in winter. It is likely that the houses of Abu Hureyra 2 were built on the same alignment for similar reasons. Once this pattern was established, it would have been maintained over several generations because there was so little room between the houses to vary their axes. Thus, there were sound, practical reasons for aligning the houses northwest-southeast, although the tightly packed nature of the settlement and its nucleated form were probably the result of prevailing social ideas concerning the appropriate density at which to build.

The floors of the houses were usually clean, although the fill of ruined ones often contained domestic debris. The spaces around the outside of the houses, on the other hand, were choked with animal bones, charcoal and ashes from fires, charred plant remains, and other debris. Evidently, most of the preparation of food took place outdoors, and much domestic rubbish was deposited there. The smell of rotting organic matter and human waste would have been strong indeed. The contrast between interior cleanliness and exterior squalor was sharp—an enduring feature of settlements in Southwest Asia, as in Europe until recent times (Plumb 1965, p. 12).

The houses shared many similarities in form and construction, although their size varied. This suggests that even if there were differences in social status between households, they were not reflected in the form of these buildings. The differences between the smaller and larger houses were most probably a reflection of the variations in the size of the households that occupied them. Of course, these conclusions are based on the excavation of a tiny proportion of the settlement, although the evidence is similar from each of our widely spaced trenches. In recent excavations at Buqras a large area of the surface of the mound was cleared to reveal the plan of the settlement at a time broadly contemporary with Periods 2B and 2C at Abu Hureyra. The excavators found no significant differences among the buildings they examined (Akkermans, Fokkens, and Waterbolk 1981, p. 501), thus tending to confirm our observations at Abu Hureyra.

The layout of Abu Hureyra 2 changed in the last period of occupation, Period 2C. The inhabitants continued to construct rectilinear mudbrick buildings, but they spaced them much wider apart, leaving extensive open spaces between. In those spaces they dug large pits up to 1 m deep that contained considerable quantities of burned material and occupation debris. We interpret them as roasting pits. Thus, the form of the village changed in this final period, although there was some continuity in the building tradition.

Was Abu Hureyra enclosed by a wall? We had the precedent of Pre-Pottery Neolithic Jericho in mind when we excavated Abu Hureyra, and we dug Trench

D far down the western slope of the mound in part to answer this question. That trench demonstrated that the original western limit of the site had lain considerably farther out, and that the intervening deposits had since eroded away. We cannot, therefore, say for certain whether or not the site was bounded by a wall on its western side, but we think it unlikely. The gentle slope of the whole eastern side of the mound suggests that there was no wall on this, the landward, side either, although again subsequent erosion may have removed any traces of such a structure. There was a sharp drop of a little over 2 m just north of Trench E down to a low platform that marked the extreme northern end of the site. This steep slope was formed by the river that had cut into the terrace and the recent leveling of the fields beyond for irrigation cultivation.

GROWTH OF THE VILLAGE

When the occupation of Abu Hureyra 1 ended, some people continued to live at the site until the development of the village of Abu Hureyra 2. We infer that this Intermediate Period settlement consisted of structures built of perishable materials, between which occupation debris accumulated. It may have looked quite like its predecessor, the village of Abu Hureyra 1C. The occupied area stretched along the northern edge of the site from Trench G to the vicinity of Trench E, and it may have extended south toward the center of the mound. The settlement was apparently slight in nature and resulted in only a modest accumulation of debris, most of which was removed as Abu Hureyra 2 expanded.

The main settlement of the Neolithic period was established in Period 2A, about 9,400 BP, and soon became a substantial village. Along the central ridge of the mound in the area of Trenches B and D the inhabitants scraped off the bedrock and built houses with plaster floors directly on it. The configuration of the strata in the lower levels of Trench D indicates that the village extended farther out on the western side, beyond the present edge of the mound. A meter of occupation debris accumulated at the bottom of Trench C, and then mudbrick structures were built on top of it. The northern end of the site seems to have been only intermittently occupied until late in 2A, when the village expanded to around Trench E and, at the very end of the period, to Trench G. The eastern sector of the mound also seems to have been little used until the end of 2A, when occupation extended to Trench F and beyond during the same episode of growth. We assume that the village also extended toward the southern limits of the site around Trench A, because the deposits were apparently just as deep as at Trench B, but that has to remain a supposition since we did not excavate to the natural subsoil there.

It is important to note that the village grew considerably in the last few centuries of Period 2A, before the transition from gazelle hunting to large-scale sheep and goat herding. The total area covered by the village late in 2A was less than the entire surface of the mound, but it extended farther west than the present limits of the site. We estimate that the village had grown to at least 8 ha by late in Period 2A (figure 9.3). In this period and the next the intensity of occupation was such that building and occupation debris accumulated rapidly. Thus, in 2A over 5 m of deposit accumulated in Trench B, and 3.6 m of debris in Trench D.

The village expanded much more in Period 2B, after 8,300 BP, until it covered not only the entire area of the mound as we found it, 11.5 ha in all, but several additional hectares beyond. This observation is based on the strati-

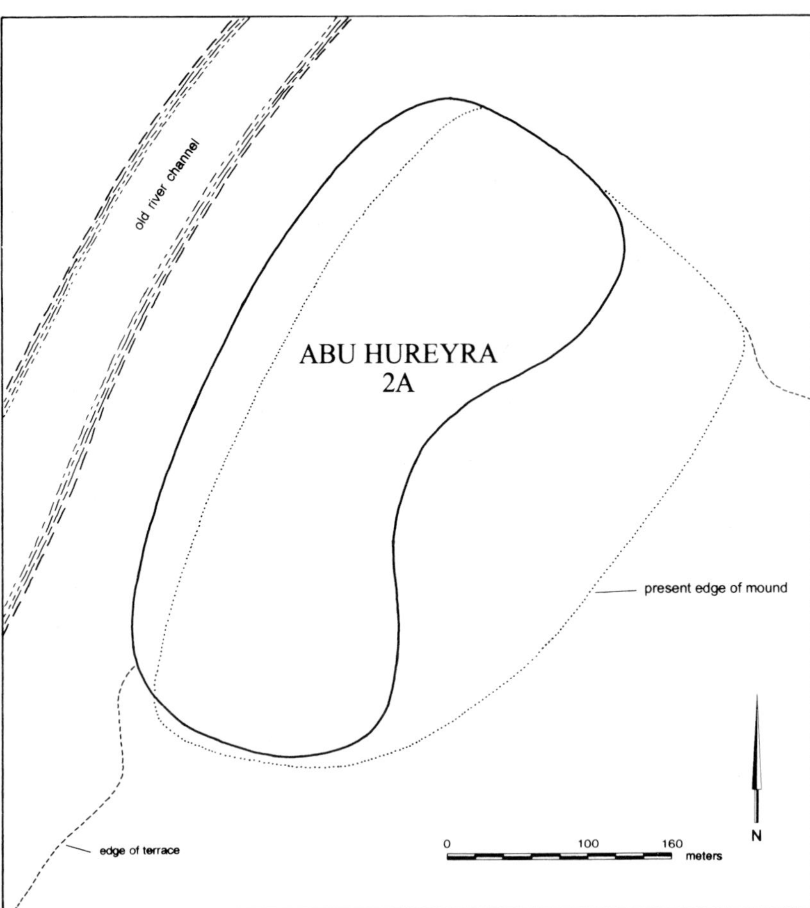

Figure 9.3 Estimated extent of the Abu Hureyra settlement late in Period 2A.

graphic evidence, faunal sequence, and similarities in culture across the site, and is confirmed by radiocarbon dates of essentially the same age from a series of widely spaced trenches. The site extended much farther west beyond Trenches A, B, and D, so the total area of the village during this period was probably more than 16 ha (figure 9.4). We emphasize that this is a conservative estimate for the maximum size of the village during Period 2B; it may well have been substantially larger. The Euphrates has cut deeply into the deposits on that side of the mound and has also removed material along the northern edge of the site, significantly reducing its size in the present day.

We illustrate the likely appearance of the village of Abu Hureyra early in this period of occupation in the frontispiece. It demonstrates the contrast between the concentration of occupation within this nucleated settlement and the emptiness of the surrounding landscape. The drawing shows the approximate density of houses determined from our excavations. Careful inspection of the picture will reveal the narrow passages and courts between the houses, and numerous other open spaces within the village that represent abandoned buildings and yards used for outdoor activities. The modern village of Qirata, though more spread out, provides an example of a settlement that looks quite similar to Abu Hureyra (figure 9.5); it attests to the extraordinary continuity of architectural traditions in north Syria.

In Period 2C, the last phase of significant prehistoric occupation on the site, the village contracted in size. Deposits of this period were found in Trenches

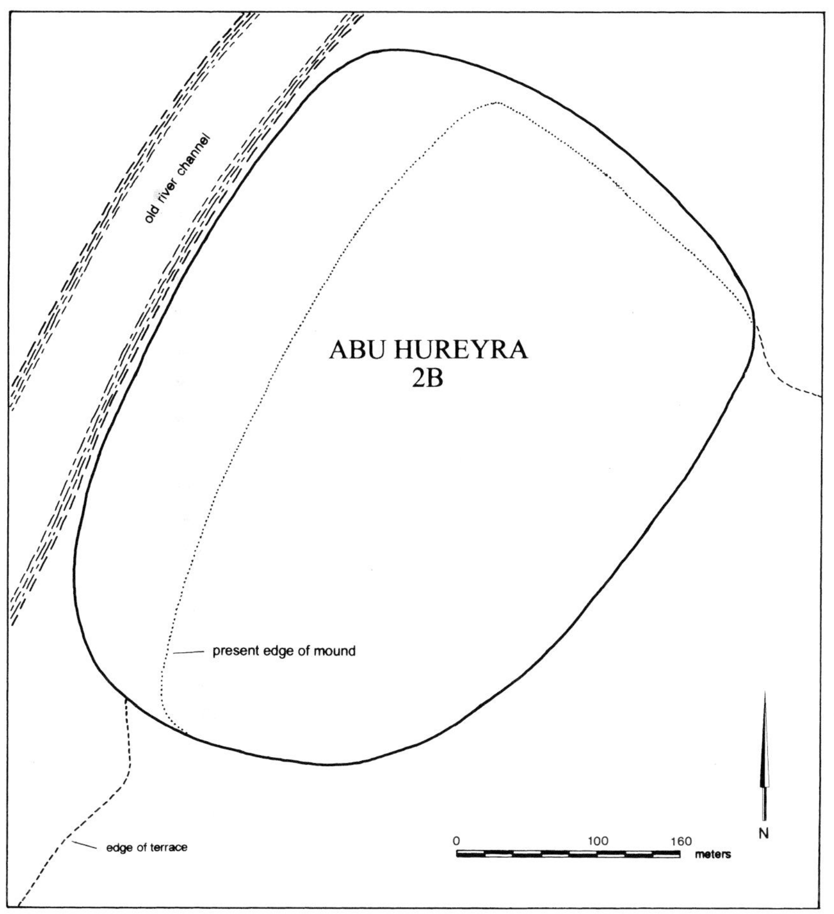

Figure 9.4 Estimated extent of the Abu Hureyra settlement in Period 2B.

Figure 9.5 The village of Qirata beside the Sajur river in north Syria, from the southwest. The Euphrates Valley is in the background. The photograph illustrates the houses of a village that share many of the features of dwellings in the Abu Hureyra 2 settlement. This view of the modern village is quite similar to our reconstruction of the appearance of Abu Hureyra 2 in the frontispiece.

A, B, C, E, and G, indicating that the village extended from south to north along the western ridge of the site, and from east to west along its northern side. It also extended farther to the west but those deposits have since eroded away. The area of lower ground on the southeast sector of the mound seems to have been given up for habitation. It is difficult to estimate precisely the area of the village during this period of occupation, but we suggest that it may have covered about 7 ha. We illustrate the changing size of the village during these periods of expansion and contraction in figure 9.6.

The Period 2C village lasted until at least 7,000 BP, and probably several centuries later, when it was abandoned. The site continued to be used occasionally for some time after that, occupation attested by the TL date for a potsherd of 5,350 ± 400 years ago, and the discovery of an Ubaid sherd in a surface level of Trench B. Dr. Thomas E. Davidson has determined through neutron activation analysis that the sherd was made locally.

Much later, there was some further activity on the site in Byzantine and Islamic times. Finally, some buildings were erected here early in the twentieth century AD, when Abu Hureyra was used as a police post on the road down the Euphrates Valley. These later activities in the historic period represent the Period 3 occupation on the mound.

Throughout this intermittent later occupation of the site the surface deposits were eroding away, a process that has continued down to the present. The top meter of deposit in all the trenches was heavily affected by weathering, and the surface of the mound was covered by a dense layer of flints derived from deflation. We thus presume that deposits of perhaps several meters in depth had been removed from the surface of the tell. Particularly severe erosion had taken place on the steep western side of the mound, where the migrating meanders of the Euphrates river have removed a wide strip of the settlement, cutting back the edge of the site. Subsequent weathering created three hollows on the western slope between Trenches A and B, B and C, and C and E. A considerable amount of debris washed out between Trenches A and B to form a fan at the foot of the mound (figures 2.7, 2.15).

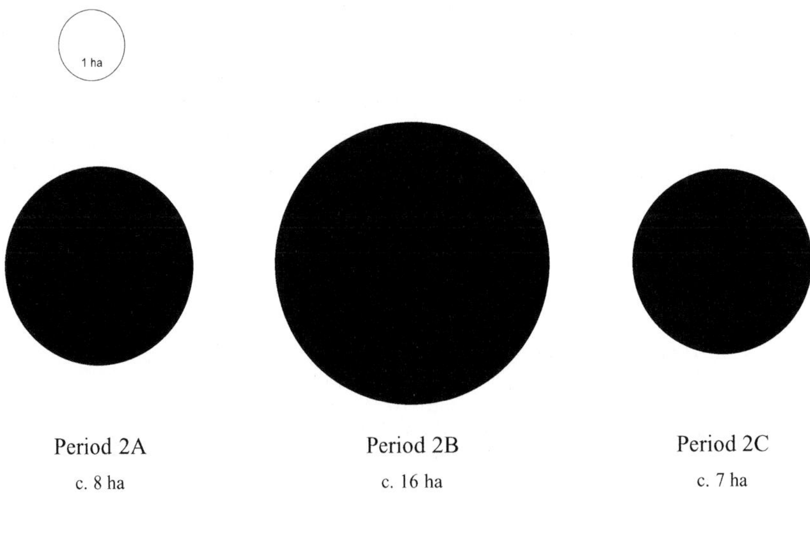

Figure 9.6 The changing size of the village of Abu Hureyra from Period 2A to 2C.

THE NUMBER OF INHABITANTS

Determining how many people may have inhabited an ancient settlement is a controversial task, but it is necessary if we are to understand how such a community lived and what its impact on its surroundings may have been. A number of archaeologists have investigated the composition of a variety of rural communities across Southwest Asia today in order to arrive at realistic estimates of the populations of some early villages (for example, Watson 1979; Kramer 1980; Aurenche 1981b). The problem with this ethnoarchaeological approach is that the houses and associated structures in many of the recent villages differ markedly from those of the ancient ones. This is certainly the case at Abu Hureyra. We prefer, therefore, to try to estimate the population of Abu Hureyra 2 from the archaeological evidence itself. We recognize that the figures we propose rest on a number of assumptions about the form of the village, and we suggest that they should be regarded as approximations only.

Our starting point is the observation made above that we encountered buildings packed tightly together wherever we excavated on the mound. We have determined the proportion of built-up to open space through measurement of the area taken up by mudbrick buildings in approximately contemporary deposits in each trench. The phases we have used all date from early in Period 2B: Trench B phase 8, E phase 6, G phase 2, and phases of similar age from Trenches A, C, and F. The proportions vary somewhat from trench to trench, but the average figures are 63% built-up space to 37% of open areas between the buildings. These figures seem reasonable to us because they reflect the reality of the density of buildings apparent in a visual inspection of the plans of almost all phases of occupation in each of the excavated trenches. We note that our figures are close to those given by Kramer (1980, p. 320) for the present-day village of Shahabad in western Iran, where 60% of the village was covered by houses.

The next step is to calculate the amount of built-up space for a given area of settlement, and the likely number of houses that it may have contained. Table 9.1 gives the figures of the built-up and open space in 1 ha of settlement, then for the 11.5 ha of Abu Hureyra that survived at the time of our excavation, and the 16 ha that we estimate was the likely area of the site in Period 2B. The houses we excavated ranged in size from less than 50 m^2 to more than 80 m^2, although most seem to have been nearer the higher figure. Thus, the average area taken up by each Abu Hureyra 2 house may have been about 70 m^2. The areas of built-up space given in table 9.1 can be divided by this figure to obtain an estimate of the total number of houses in the village. The results are given in table 9.2.

Table 9.1 The approximate areas of built-up and open space in the Abu Hureyra 2 settlement

Settlement area in ha	Area of mudbrick buildings in m^2	Open space in m^2
1	6,300	3,700
11.5	72,450	42,550
16	100,800	59,200

Table 9.2 The number of 70 m² houses in the Abu Hureyra 2 settlement

Settlement area in ha	Number of houses
1	90
11.5	1,035
16	1,440

The final step is to multiply the number of houses by the number of their inhabitants to arrive at figures for the population of the village as a whole. Here we have to decide how many people lived in each house. If these were family dwellings as we have suggested, then they may have housed an average of about six people. Obviously, this can be only an estimate, so we also give the figures for both five and seven inhabitants per house for purposes of comparison. These calculations yield figures for the total number of inhabitants in the village, assuming that all the houses were occupied simultaneously. The archaeological evidence indicates, however, that a proportion of the houses would have been in ruins or otherwise out of use, so only 70% of the houses may have been inhabited at any one time. It is possible that the rate might have fallen as low as 50% on occasion, so we give this figure, too. The range of estimates for the population of the village as a whole is given in tables 9.3–9.5.

In our view the most likely estimates for the population of Abu Hureyra 2 derived from these calculations are 378 people per hectare, 4,347 for the 11.5 ha of the settlement that survived to be investigated by us, and 6,048 for the 16 ha settlement of Abu Hureyra 2B. The population of the Abu Hureyra 2A and 2C settlements would have been about half the latter figure. Stated in round numbers, the population of Abu Hureyra in Periods 2A and 2C would thus seem to have been of the order of 2,500–3,000 people, rising to 5,000–6,000 in Period 2B, the time of maximum expansion of the village. Even if substantially more of the settlement had consisted of abandoned houses or open spaces than our evidence suggests, it would still appear that the population of the very large village of Abu Hureyra 2 consisted of several thousand people. That would have represented a ten- to twentyfold increase over the population of Abu Hureyra 1. It is a remarkable indication of the long-term consequences for the people of Abu Hureyra of adopting an agricultural way of life.

How reasonable are these figures? They are certainly larger than those Aurenche (1981b) and others have obtained from studies of present-day villages in Southwest Asia, although they are of the same order of magnitude as the presumed population of Buqras. This has been estimated at between 700 and 1,000 people based on the density of buildings in the settlement (Akkermans, Fokken,

Table 9.3 The number of inhabitants per hectare in Abu Hureyra 2

Inhabitants per house	Total estimated inhabitants per hectare		
	All houses occupied	70% of houses occupied	50% of houses occupied
5	450	315	225
6	540	378	270
7	630	441	315

Table 9.4 The number of inhabitants for the surviving 11.5 ha of Abu Hureyra 2

Inhabitants per house	Total estimated population		
	All houses occupied	70% of houses occupied	50% of houses occupied
5	5,175	3,623	2,588
6	6,210	4,347	3,105
7	7,245	5,072	3,623

Table 9.5 The number of inhabitants in the estimated 16 ha of Abu Hureyra 2B

Inhabitants per house	Total estimated population		
	All houses occupied	70% of houses occupied	50% of houses occupied
5	7,200	5,040	3,600
6	8,640	6,048	4,320
7	10,080	7,056	5,040

and Waterbolk 1981, p. 501). Abu Hureyra was between four and six times bigger than Buqras, and multiplying the Buqras estimates by these numbers yields population figures close to those we have calculated using other architectural criteria. How may we account for the differences between these figures derived from the archaeological evidence and those for present-day villages? Mudbrick houses in villages today are usually substantially bigger than those we excavated. They also have numerous appendages in the form of courtyards and outbuildings, and thus take up more space for a given number of inhabitants per dwelling. The houses at Abu Hureyra, on the other hand, were small and stood alone without additional structures. The density of human occupation in such early villages would thus seem to have been significantly greater.

10 Disposal of the Dead

A. M. T. Moore & T. I. Molleson

The large sample of human remains we found in the excavation consisted of numerous deliberate burials, both individual and collective, and scattered bones in habitation deposits. We recognized no deliberate burials for the levels of Abu Hureyra 1. The burials in Abu Hureyra 2 and the graves of historic age in the surface of the mound, on the other hand, contained many partial or complete skeletons. Those burials tell us much about how the inhabitants disposed of their dead and, by inference, something of the social significance of their burial rites, as well as their ideology. The human remains are of great value for the information they provide about the condition of the populations, especially their health, diet, and habits of work. The sample from Abu Hureyra 2 is one of the largest from an early agricultural site anywhere in Southwest Asia, and so is of special importance for understanding the impact of this new way of life on the people themselves. The historic burials are of considerable scientific worth for what they tell us about the life of recent peoples in the Euphrates Valley. When compared with the prehistoric human remains from Abu Hureyra they enable us to determine similarities and differences in the ways of life of those populations who lived in the same region but at widely separated times.

BURIAL PRACTICES IN ABU HUREYRA 1

The human remains in the Abu Hureyra 1 deposits consisted mainly of teeth, vertebrae, and bones from the extremities. We found these bones loose in occupation soil, and so they were not part of recognized burials. There were enough of them to suggest that some corpses had been buried in the settlement and then disturbed in subsequent reworking of the deposits.

We did find one skull of a mature adult with the distal condyle of a femur that had apparently been deliberately buried (72.501, level 53). The burial was deep in the phase 2 deposits and appeared to be well stratified, although it is possible that this unique find was intrusive from the overlying settlement of Abu Hureyra 2. Assuming that it did belong in the deposits in which it was found, it would indicate that the inhabitants of Abu Hureyra 1 were already separating skulls from the rest of the body and giving them special treatment. Perrot and his collaborators have found comparable evidence for the inception of this custom in the upper levels of Ain Mallaha in Palestine (Perrot and Ladiray 1988, p. 56), and the practice has also been attested at Hayonim (Belfer-Cohen 1988, p. 300).

We were able to excavate only a relatively small part of the Abu Hureyra 1 settlement, so our conclusions concerning the burial practices of the inhabitants must remain tentative. Nevertheless, it should be noted that human remains were scarce in the area excavated, despite the fact that it represented 1,500 years of occupation. The contemporary levels at Mugharet el Wad and Ain Mallaha, in contrast, contained a greater density of human remains in the form of deliberate burials (Garrod and Bate 1937, p. 13; Perrot and Ladiray 1988, figures 5–8); a 7 × 7 m trench dug in either site would have revealed more graves. We infer that most of the dead were buried elsewhere in the village or disposed of beyond the confines of the site.

THE BURIALS OF ABU HUREYRA 2

The inhabitants of Abu Hureyra 2 buried some of their dead within the settlement. The great majority of the burials we recovered were in houses, and the remainder were in shallow pits in the yards outside. In addition, we found human bones at random in the occupation deposits; these came from burials that had been disturbed by later interments, had accidentally dropped from exposed skeletons, or derived from other activities of the inhabitants. The indoor burials were usually in one of two places: under the floors of rooms, or in the fill of rooms that were being remodeled or had been abandoned. Occasionally we found burials in the mudbrick walls of buildings.

The burials were of two main kinds, single and collective. Graves for single individuals were dug just big enough to accept a tightly flexed body. The collective burials consisted of a number of individuals buried together, usually in a shallow pit dug for the purpose. Occasionally a pit was reopened later so that another body could be buried in it. Nearly 40% of the burials, both single and collective, were accompanied by small quantities of grave goods consisting of beads and tools of flint and bone. Both single and collective burials frequently contained the remains of incomplete rather than intact skeletons; the bones were placed tightly together and had often been secured in a bag or mat before final interment. This suggests that they represented a final stage of rites that involved exposure of the corpse until the flesh had decayed, then separation of some parts of the skeleton, followed by final burial of the bones. Some burials consisted of a skull or skulls, with few or no other human bones, while other burials, both single and collective, contained headless individuals. Separation of skulls seems therefore to have been a common practice in Abu Hureyra 2.

We must next examine the modes of burial, trench by trench, to determine in more detail how the dead were treated. Almost all the burials found in Trench B were from the later phases of occupation, although the remains of a child were recovered from phase 2 early in the sequence. This was probably because only the upper levels were excavated at all extensively. Most of the human remains in this trench came from burials in the phase 8 building. The building itself was comparable in its form and construction to the many others at Abu Hureyra that we have interpreted as houses, but the concentration of burials within it was unusual. There were two main burial deposits; one was a pit (144) under the floor of room 2, and the other was the charnel room, room 3, at the northwest end of the house.

Burial pit 144 lay across the northwest end of room 2 (figures 8.17, 8.19, 10.1), and was 1.6 m long, 1 m wide, and 70 cm deep. It had been dug through a solid white plaster floor laid down when the phase 8 house was first built, and it was covered by a thin white plaster floor. It seems, therefore, that the pit was dug and filled in a short period of time, perhaps as a single event. The pit contained the remains of 25–30 individuals, over 50% of whom were children and adolescents at about the onset of puberty, and the remainder mostly adults, several of whom were quite young (table 10.1). Both males and females were present. The presence of so many older children, adolescents, and young adults is unusual since we would expect those age classes to have had the lowest mortality rates in a family or community group in a premodern village. All the skeletons were poorly preserved, and several lacked their skulls or were otherwise incomplete. It is clear that these were not primary burials, but rather a deposit of human remains that had already decayed considerably before interment. They had apparently been exposed in air until decomposition of the flesh was complete. The skulls of most of the skeletons were then removed. It was probably at this stage that some of the other bones became separated from the parent skeletons. Finally, most of the remaining bones were gathered up and buried at the same time in pit 144, which was dug just large enough to contain the entire collection. Several of the skeletons were accompanied by four butterfly beads, a number of beads of baked clay, a turquoise bead, and bone points. Where the age and sex of those individuals could be determined, they were adult females.

Why were these people buried together, and how did they die? It is possible that they were members of a corporate group, and for this reason were buried in one grave. The quantity of skeletons and their unusual age distribution suggests that they may have been members of a cohort. We do know that several of them were members of the same family (see chapter 11). The few mature adults and infants—that is, children less than 6 months old—in the burial pit may not have been members of the core group of young people but simply associated with them in some way. We do not know whether all the people buried in the pit died at once, only that they were accorded similar treatment in death. The exceptional composition of the group may indicate, however, that the cause of their deaths was the same. There was no sign that any of them had died violently, although the poor preservation of the bones made it difficult to be certain on this point. This burial may represent the conclusion, intended or otherwise, of some ritual, such as a rite of passage involving cir-

Table 10.1 Trench B, phase 8. A classification of people buried in pit 144 by age group, where this can be determined

Perinatal	Infant	Child	Adolescent	Adult	TOTAL
2	0	6	5	8	21

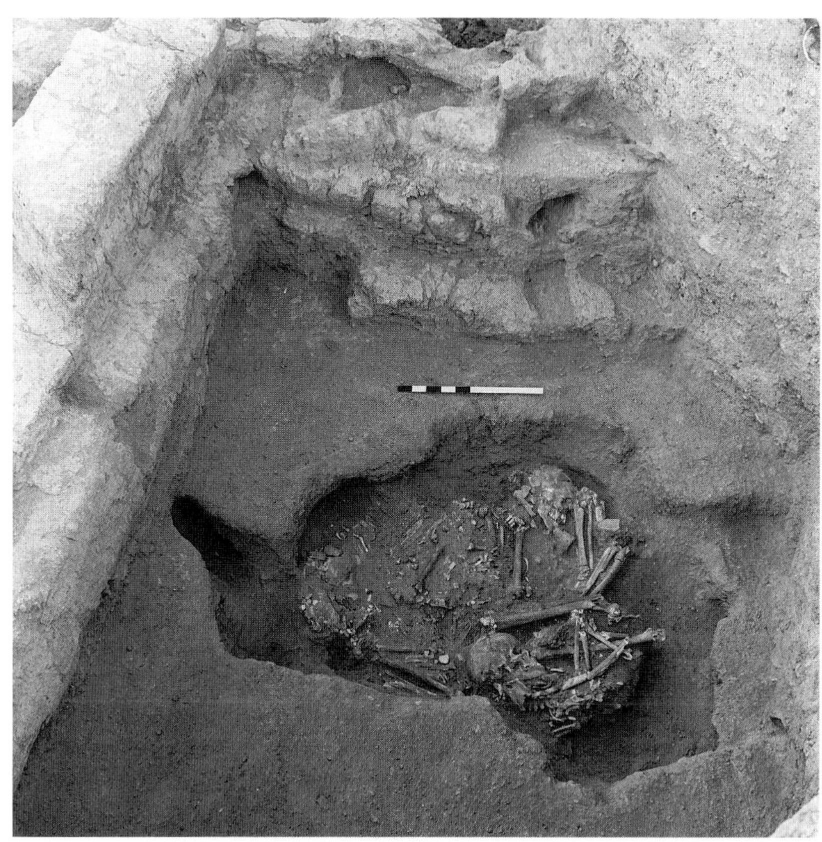

Figure 10.1 Trench B, phase 8: burial pit 144, from the east. Scale, 50 cm.

cumcision or scarification, in which the young played an essential part. Alternatively, they may have died from an infectious disease.

The charnel room at the northwest end of the phase 8 building was the only example of such an installation at Abu Hureyra. The fire that caused its abandonment and the subsequent partial collapse of the walls preserved its contents for us to study. This chamber apparently served as a repository for the dead during much of the life of the building, in contrast with the pit in room 2. There were at least three main episodes during which corpses were deposited there, while several additional bodies were carried in at other times. The human remains consisted of flexed corpses, often headless, and skulls deposited singly or in clusters (figures 8.16, 8.17; 10.2). The skulls had been separated from many of the bodies, apparently after the corpses had been allowed to decay. One skull in the chamber (73.2400) had been wrapped in matting coated with bitumen before it was deposited, and we found the impressions of the mat in the soil around it (figures 10.3, 10.4). This suggests that the skull was carried in from elsewhere. The fire charred some of the skulls and skeletons in the charnel room. Several of the skulls and other bones were burned on one side and not the other, confirming the contextual evidence that the fire was accidental rather than a deliberate incineration of the remains. We could also tell that many of these bodies had been laid directly on the floor or in hollows, exposing only the upper surfaces to the air, because the bones of several of the skeletons were distorted in a manner that suggested they still were still covered in flesh at the time of the fire.

The charnel room contained the remains of at least 24 individuals, of whom 80% were adults and the remainder children and adolescents (table 10.2). There

Figure 10.2 Trench B, phase 8: burials on the floor of room 3, from the north. Charred skulls can be seen in the left foreground. Scale, 50 cm.

Figure 10.3 Trench B, phase 8: skull 73.2400. Scale, 5 cm.

Figure 10.4 Trench B, phase 8: mat impression in soil behind skull 73.2400. Scale, 5 cm.

were conspicuously few infants, but otherwise the age structure of the group was close to what one would expect of the dead in a premodern village. Although some of the people in the charnel room and in pit 144 were apparently related (appendix 5), the number of corpses in the chamber and in the pit was considerable, far more than from the single family that may have inhabited the phase 8 house itself.

We must now try to determine what the remains that we found in the charnel room represent. There are two possibilities: first, that the corpses in room 3 were in an intermediate stage between death and burial, and second, that the treatment of their remains had been completed and this was their final place of interment. Exposure of the corpse for the flesh to decay followed by burial seems to have been a common practice at Abu Hureyra, and this would have required a place in which corpses could be reserved safe from scavengers. They could have been placed on the roofs of houses or on wooden platforms, but a closed room at the end of a house like room 3 would also have served the purpose well. None of the corpses was accompanied by grave goods, whereas

Table 10.2 Trench B, phase 8. A classification of people buried in room 3, the charnel room, by age group, where this can be determined

Perinatal	Infant	Child	Adolescent	Adult	TOTAL
0	1	3	1	19	24

nearly half the burials elsewhere in the settlement, both single and collective, had them. Furthermore, the bodies were placed on the floors toward the middle of the room, rather than at the sides of rooms and under the floors, as in completed burials elsewhere at Abu Hureyra. This suggests that room 3 was an intermediate place in which corpses could decay and in which the inhabitants could carry out other rites, such as separation of skulls. The skeletal remains could be extracted later for final burial under the floor of a house, a process that was interrupted by the accidental firing of the room shortly before the house was abandoned and rebuilt.

A difficulty with this interpretation is that the corpses were deposited in the room at intervals throughout the life of the house, and then the earlier ones were covered over and apparently forgotten. A white plaster floor was laid in the room between the second and third episodes of corpse placement, adding to the impression that this was the final place of burial for the earlier interments. These two possible interpretations, however, may represent different stages of the same series of rituals. Among the Berawan of Borneo, for example, secondary deposition of the dead is practiced, but not all the dead receive the full ritual treatment with final burial of the bones after the flesh has decayed (Huntington and Metcalf 1979, p. 78). Corpses may have been placed in room 3 for the flesh to decay and other intermediate rites to be observed, but only some of the skeletons may have been removed later for final burial inside another house.

There was one other group of burials in wall 139 of the phase 8 house. The remains of two children (73.2168, 73.2127) and the skeleton of a young adult female (73.2172) were found buried separately. These may have been foundation interments for which children were considered particularly suitable. One of the children, 73.2127, was a member of the family that apparently occupied the building.

The final question to consider is the function of the phase 8 building. We have noted that it looked like other houses at Abu Hureyra, yet it contained an extraordinarily large collective burial under the floor of room 2 and the remains of so many other people in the charnel room. The insertion of pit 144 under the floor of room 2 need not have interfered with domestic activities, and room 3 was built at one end and so would not have interrupted circulation patterns within the structure. Thus, it may have been a house, like the earlier and later structures on the same spot. On the other hand, no other house we excavated contained such numerous clusters of skeletons. There were simply too many corpses buried in pit 144 and deposited in the charnel room for the individuals to have been members of the household that might have occupied the building, although we do know that members of the same family were buried there (see chapter 11). Pit 144, too, seems to have been the final burial place of people from a social group distinct from that of a household. Thus, it seems that the dead we found there were assembled from other households in that quarter of the village and, therefore, that the building was used for ritual as well as domestic functions. It was an appropriate place in which, not only to bury the social group represented in pit 144, but also to place bodies during the process of excarnation.

We found another collective burial in a pit (78) in the fill of room 1 of the phase 9 house (figure 8.20) that replaced the building of phase 8. This pit contained the remains of six or seven individuals, both adults and juveniles, whose corpses had been exposed before their remains were finally buried. The incomplete skeletons of several other individuals not recognized as formal burials were found in levels of this phase. They were mainly elderly people. Most unusually for Abu Hureyra 2, a few bones from perhaps as many as five perinatal or young infants were also recovered. The remains of several more were found in phase 10.

The only formal burials in phase 10 were a few individual graves, a shift in burial pattern that may have been associated with evolving ideas about disposal of the dead and the change in the nature of the structures that took place in that phase. One of those burials (72.264B) was unusual; the body of a youth aged 12 had been tightly flexed, then the skeleton had been coated in gypsum plaster, and finally wrapped in matting before the plaster set hard. Traces of the mat-impressed plaster survived on the upper part of the trunk and on the drawn-up legs (figure 10.5), the sole example of the use of plaster on a burial that we found at Abu Hureyra. Part of the surface of the plaster had been stained red with cinnabar. The mineral does not occur in the vicinity of Abu Hureyra but may have been imported from Asia Minor. This was the only occurrence of cinnabar that we noted at Abu Hureyra. The corpse had been placed in a shallow grave, so the form of the burial was similar to that of others in the settlement.

In Trench D we found burials within the houses of phases 2 and 3 (figures 8.30, 8.33). Three out of five were single inhumations in shallow pits under the floors of rooms, although one was in fill. The corpses had first been exposed until much or all of the flesh had decayed, such that some bones were still articulated when buried. Then the bones were gathered up and inserted in oval pits that were just large enough to accommodate them. The long bones were always neatly arranged together with the detached skull, and some of the remains were tightly clustered as if buried in a bag.

Figure 10.5 Trench B, phase 10: the flexed skeleton of a youth, burial 72.264B, encased in gypsum plaster. Scale, 20 cm.

Burial 73.690 had some features that were a little different from other interments (figure 10.6). It contained the remains of two juveniles whose bones had been treated in the same manner as those of the other burials, but which were placed in a pit that was rectangular in plan, a unique instance of a grave of this shape. The pit was larger than usual and so may have been intended to hold more skeletons than were actually there. Furthermore, the remains were accompanied by a pair of fine greenstone peardrop beads and another pair of small stone beads. The presence of these grave goods and the unusual shape of the pit may indicate that the individuals in the grave had special status.

Burials were found in every Abu Hureyra 2 phase of occupation in Trench E. The graves contained the remains of one or, occasionally, two or three people, but there were no mass burials. Many of the skeletons were incomplete, and there were several deposits of skulls buried separately. Thus, most of the corpses were exposed after death, and skulls were frequently removed before final burial of the remains took place.

The oldest burial in the series (73.3273) came from phase 4. It was a single skull in a small pit just outside the east wall of the main house of this phase. The skull was colored red at the time of excavation, although the color has since faded, suggesting that it had been painted with a vegetable dye like madder.

Most of the phase 5 burials were within the house in the center of the trench, but a few additional ones came from the house in the northeast corner (figure 8.51). A few of the burials inside the central house were in graves beneath the room floors. There were two of these in room 5, the burial of a child in the east corner (73.2404) and that of an adult in the middle of the room (72.495).

Figure 10.6 Trench D, phase 2: closeup of burial 73.690, from the south. Scale, 10 cm.

Both skeletons were flexed, but that of the adult only slightly so, suggesting that this individual had been buried soon after death and before the flesh had decayed. The third burial beneath a floor was in the southwest corner of room 1. The skeleton of a woman (73.1930) was seated upright in the pit (figure 10.7), an unusual position for burials at Abu Hureyra. In phase 6 another indoor pit for burials was dug close by, and the uppermost of the two skeletons in it was in the same seated position (73.2398, figure 8.54). This suggests to us that a memory of both the location and the mode of the phase 5 burial was maintained and influenced those who carried out the burial of the succeeding phase.

The two skeletons buried one on top of the other in the phase 6 pit were unusual in other respects. The one underneath, 73.2396, was a female aged about 25 who was buried with an agate butterfly bead, another green butterfly bead, and a bone tube. Skeleton 73.2398 was a young male, aged about 18, who was buried with the finest dark green serpentine butterfly bead that we found at Abu Hureyra (figure 10.8).

The remaining burials in the center house were in the fills of rooms 1 and 4 and dated from slightly later in the phase when the house was still in use. These were burials of individuals whose corpses had first been exposed: one of them, 73.3067, consisted of a skull only. The burials were concentrated in three of the five rooms of the house, rooms 1, 4, and 5, leaving rooms 2 and 3 without graves. The reasons for this clustering are unclear. The successive burials in the house suggest that the building was in use for between one and two generations.

Figure 10.7 Trench E, phase 5: burial of a woman (73.1930) seated upright in its grave, from the southwest. A caprine horn core and other animal bones are with the skeleton in the grave. Scale, 10 cm.

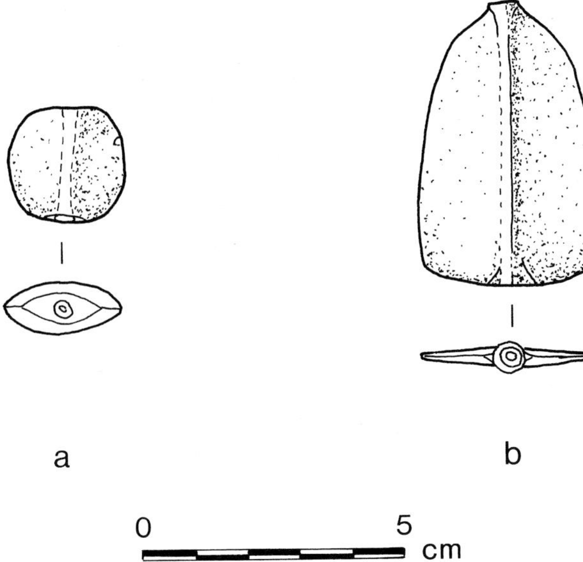

Figure 10.8 Trench E, phase 6: two butterfly beads buried with skeletons in a room of the phase 6 house. a, a translucent agate bead, 73.2635, buried with a female, 73.2396; b, a large serpentine bead, 73.2628, buried with a male, 73.2398.

The other burials of this phase were in two graves under the floor of a room in the house across the lane to the east. One of them contained a single skull (73.2655), and the other two skulls, of a child and an adult (73.3437, 73.2656).

The burials in phase 6 were similar in nature to those of phase 5. All except 73.1187, a piece of skull, were inside the central house (figure 8.54). There were several individuals buried under the floors of rooms 1, 3, and 5 and others in the fills of rooms 1, 2, and 4. Thus, almost the entire building was used for burials at some time during its life. Cut marks on the humerus of one skeleton (73.1996) in room 4 indicate that its flesh was cut off before burial (figure 10.9). The skeleton of the woman buried alone in room 2 (73.2202) was better preserved than many; it was in a flexed position on its left side, with the forefinger of its right hand in its mouth (figure 10.10). Neither this skeleton nor 72.520 in the same house seems

Figure 10.9 Trench E, phase 6: cut marks made with a flint tool on the mid-shaft of a humerus of skeleton 73.1996, indicating that the arm was defleshed.

Figure 10.10 Trench E, phase 6: burial of a woman (73.2202), from the east. Scale, 20 cm.

to have been exposed before burial, a rare occurrence at Abu Hureyra. The skeleton of a young man (72.520) in a pit under the floor of room 5 was also flexed and lying on its left side, but it was distinguished by one extraordinary feature: a tanged arrowhead was embedded in the chest cavity just beneath the ribs, with its tip pointing down toward the pelvis (figures 10.11, 10.12). We infer that the youth died from the injury he had sustained from the arrow. This is the only evidence that we have found for death by violence among the people of Abu Hureyra. The injury may have been caused accidentally, during a hunt, for example, or with the intention of inflicting a mortal wound.

There was no change in burial practice in phase 7. The three skeletons in the two graves recorded from that phase had all been exposed before final burial took place.

The form of the settlement changed in phase 8, and this was accompanied by a modification in burial practices. The excavated area in Trench E was open for much of the phase, the only features being a series of roasting pits. Several burials were found in this open area, suggesting that the inhabitants frequently chose to bury their dead outdoors. The same rites—exposure then burial of only a portion of the skeleton—still seem to have been practiced, however, since all the skeletons we recovered were incomplete. It also appears that the inhabitants separated some skulls from corpses, since in at least one instance (73.123), a skull was found alone.

We found one burial in Trench G (73.3066), toward the end of phase 1. This was a single skull placed in a shallow pit dug in occupation debris just outside a building.

Figure 10.11 Trench E, phase 6: burial of a young man (72.520), from the south. Scale, 20 cm.

Figure 10.12 Trench E, phase 6: burial of a young man (72.520), from the south. Removal of the skull and several of the ribs revealed an arrowhead embedded in the chest cavity. Scale, 20 cm.

Discussion

The salient features of the burials described above are these. Most corpses were exposed in air for the flesh to decay before final burial, perhaps in charnel rooms of the kind represented by room 3 in the phase 8 building in Trench B. Sometimes bodies were defleshed. Primary burial of fresh corpses was rare. Almost all burials took place indoors in houses that were apparently inhabited at the time of interment. Normally, the remains of an exposed body were placed in a shallow grave that had been dug just large enough to receive the often tightly flexed skeleton. Each person was usually buried alone or, occasionally, in a grave with several other individuals. Many people were buried lying on their sides, but there was no preferred side or orientation. Collective burials containing the remains of many individuals were rare in the Abu Hureyra 2 settlement and might have a distinctive composition, as in the example from room 2 of the phase 8 building in Trench B. The skull was often separated from the rest of the skeleton before final burial took place. It was sometimes given special treatment before being buried separately, either alone or with several other skulls. Many of the burials under floors seem to have been made after the house had been in use for some time because they often cut through earlier layers of floor plaster. Occasionally, the collective burials were reopened during the life of the house, since there was evidence that floors over them had been renewed and then cut through to open up the grave.

The location of the burials is also significant. Of the indoor burials whose position can be precisely pinpointed, 37% were in the corner of a room (table 10.3), while a similar percentage of the remainder were at one end or to the side of a room. Only two graves were found toward the center of any room of a building in the trenches described here. Thus, it seems the inhabitants preferred to bury their dead away from the center of their rooms near the outside walls. Sometimes a new grave in a room might be dug close to an earlier one, for example, in Trench D, phase 3 and Trench E, phase 5, but such graves did not overlap. This suggests that the inhabitants knew the precise location of the earlier grave and took care not to disturb it. The graves under floors were not marked, but many would have been easy to remember since plaster floors frequently sank somewhat into the softer fill of the pits.

The collective burials—that is, burials with remains of two or more individuals—were also set toward the margins of the living spaces. Of the five discussed here, three were in the corners of rooms and a fourth (Trench B, phase 8, room 2, 144) at one end of a room. The distribution of skeletons in the char-

Table 10.3 The locations of Abu Hureyra 2 burials within buildings and without, where this is known precisely

	In wall	Doorway	Corner of room	End of room	Side of room	Center of room
Single burials, indoors	4	1	10	3	7	2
Single burials, outside	5					
Collective burials, indoors			3	1	1	
Trench B, phase 8, room 3 (the charnel room)			2	1	8	4

nel room of the phase 8 building in Trench B was different: 80% were at the sides or center, and only 20% in the corners or at the ends of the room. This distribution strengthens the argument for interpreting the room as an intermediate place in which corpses were intended to be left for a while before final burial.

Some elements of the burial ritual seem to have persisted throughout the period of settlement while others changed. The customs of exposure of the corpse followed by a delayed burial and separation of skulls seem to have endured for the entire span of the Abu Hureyra 2 settlement; indeed, they may have already been observed by the inhabitants of Abu Hureyra 1. There was a marked shift, however, in the location of burials in the final stage of Neolithic occupation on the site, Period 2C, the period marked by the digging of numerous pits and a wider spacing of buildings. Until then most graves had been dug indoors, but now the majority were outside, as can clearly be seen in Trench B, phase 10, and Trench E, phase 8.

The largest number of burials of single, or at most two or three, individuals was in Trenches D and E. The ratio of women to men in these burials was 2:1. This suggests that women were usually buried under the floors of their houses, but that perhaps half the men were buried elsewhere on the site or away from Abu Hureyra altogether. The final place of burial may have been affected by lineage relationships or simply by where and how people spent their daily lives. Most women probably passed much of their days around their houses, while the men may have worked more in the fields or have spent time away from the settlement in hunting or herding. This would explain why many men were buried at some distance from the home.

There was a distinction between the treatment at death accorded perinatals and infants on the one hand, and older children, adolescents, and adults on the other. We recognized very few formal burials of perinatals and infants anywhere on the site. The remains of about ten perinatals were recovered from open spaces between buildings in phases 9 and 10 of Trench B. The bones were in quite good condition and had suffered neither from gnawing nor from insect attack. This suggests that they had actually been buried in shallow pits outdoors immediately after death. Others may have been disposed of away from the site. It appears that infants were deemed too young to be accorded the rites of burial appropriate for youths and adults, probably because, as Hertz pointed out (1907, p. 133), they had not yet become full members of society. We note, too, that these informal burials of infants were found only in the last two prehistoric phases of Trench B.

Older children, aged from about four to five years, and adults of both sexes were eligible for the full sequence of burial rites. That said, there were still fewer burials of children than of more mature individuals in the trenches we excavated, as though a higher proportion of their corpses were disposed of elsewhere. Furthermore, relatively few children seem to have had their skulls removed for separate burial; apparently, this practice was considered more appropriate for adults.

We found artifacts and other grave goods with many of the burials described here. They were usually beads of stone, shell, or occasionally, baked clay. The most conspicuous ornaments were the butterfly beads. Most of those were found in burials, suggesting that they had special funerary significance at Abu Hureyra. Flint and bone tools were the only other artifacts that might be included in burials at all regularly. Animal bones were deliberately deposited in a few graves, notably horn cores of cattle and caprines, and caprine jaws. The fill of most graves contained a few stray flints and animal bones, but these were ubiquitous in deposits across the site and so need not have been deliberately included.

Grave goods were found in 44% of burials throughout the Pre-Pottery Neolithic sequence of Abu Hureyra 2A and 2B, but in none of the burials of the pits episode, Period 2C. Nor were there any grave goods with the skeletons in the charnel house—that is, room 3 of the Trench B, phase 8 building—emphasizing its different character. Where the sex of the skeleton could be determined, we found that beads and bone tools were usually associated with females. Children and adolescents were less likely than adults to be buried with artifacts.

The butterfly beads, like the other ornaments, were usually found with women, a clear indication of distinction of gender in the burial rituals. The one intriguing exception was a burial of two people, a male and a female, both with unusually fine butterfly beads, in a room of the Trench E phase 6 house. The male (73.2398), a young man about 18 years old, was accompanied by the finest of the serpentine butterfly beads we excavated, and the women (73.2396), aged about 25, by a translucent, agate butterfly bead and another green one, as well as other grave goods (figure 10.8). This suggests that butterfly beads denoted more than just the gender of the deceased. They may also have indicated social status, or even devotion to a particular deity, as Kleppe (1986) has found among the Shilluk people of the Sudan.

What can we deduce of the ideology that found expression in these burial rites? We may begin with Hertz's observation (1907, p. 122) that the death of a human is more than just a biological event: it also abruptly terminates the social role of that individual. Funeral rites provide a means by which society mediates its loss and reaffirms its own continuity. In many societies death is a time of transition and of rebirth for the soul of the deceased and the community itself, processes that may take time (Hertz 1907, p. 81; Huntington and Metcalf 1979, p. 81). The institution of delayed or secondary burial provides a sequence of rites through which this may be accomplished. The process is the concern of society as a whole because it provides a means of perpetuating the community.

The practice of secondary burial is widespread in the ethnographic present (Huntington and Metcalf 1979, p. 15) in the Americas, in parts of Africa and Madagascar, among the Chinese, in early historic Japan, in island Southeast Asia, in Melanesia, and in other parts of the world. The most thorough anthropological treatment of the subject is still the essay by Hertz (1907), although his work has given rise to further studies in recent years. Hertz noted that secondary burial presupposes a belief in a soul and an afterlife (1907, p. 78). He saw such treatment of the corpse as a metaphor for the translation of the soul itself (Hertz 1907, p. 75), a point emphasized recently by Huntington and Metcalf (1979, p. 81). In societies that practice secondary burial, death is not considered to be an instantaneous event, but rather a slow process of transition for the soul and for the community remaining on earth. It is this that the rites themselves reflect.

The mode of secondary or delayed burial has a distinctive structure. First there is a ceremony at the time of physical death. Then the corpse is exposed or buried in order that the flesh can decay. There follows a period of months or years during which the corpse is reduced to a skeleton. Finally, the bones are reburied in a second ceremony that concludes the burial ritual. This basic three-stage framework is common to the burial rituals of most societies, as pointed out by van Gennep (1909, p. 275), although their beliefs concerning the soul and an afterlife may vary greatly. The initial treatment of the corpse and the often lengthy intermediate period that follows is the time during which the soul, and therefore the social aspect of the deceased, becomes separated from the physical remains (Hertz 1907, p. 57), a process that is represented materially by the decay of the flesh. This intermediate, or liminal, period can take on an importance of its own (van Gennep 1909, p. 209). It is often regarded as an uncertain and dangerous time, in which the soul has not yet reached its final destination and the community is adjusting to the loss of a member.

The final act is the burial of the remains of the deceased. According to Hertz (1907, p. 88), three things are accomplished in this ceremony: the disposal of the bones, the passage of the soul to the hereafter, and the conclusion of mourning for the living. For the community it is a time of reintegration and reaffirmation of its continuity, its triumph over death (Hertz 1907, p. 115; Bloch and Parry 1982, p. 4). The occasion is often one of celebration and feasting befitting its triumphant nature and the sense of release felt by many of the participants.

These elements of the ritual of secondary or delayed burial are common to most of the known examples in societies of the recent past, so we may, with caution, apply them to Abu Hureyra. Our evidence suggests that many corpses were given the same three-stage treatment that Hertz and van Gennep noted. There was probably an initial ceremony to mark the cessation of life, and then the bodies were set in a secure place for the flesh to decay. This and the period following during which the corpse was decomposing would have been a time of mourning. It may also have been a time of fear and uncertainty: fear of the polluting effects of the decaying corpse, and concern that the spirit of the recently deceased might exert a malevolent influence on the living before it arrived in the hereafter (Bloch 1982, p. 215; Huntington and Metcalf 1979, p. 81). The fear and distress would gradually have lessened as the community adjusted to its loss, and as the soul was believed to have reached its destination safely. This process was matched by the gradual decay of the corpse and drying of the skeleton. Then months later, when the corpse had decayed so that little more than the skeleton was left, the remains were recovered. The skeleton was tightly bundled and buried in a pit under the floor of a room, probably in the house it had once occupied and its descendants still inhabited. This last act marked the final translation of the spirit of the deceased, although in the concluding burial ceremony some part of the deceased's spirit may have returned to be near the living, and so have required propitiation. The occasion may have been a joyful one with feasting and other celebrations. The whole village may have participated to celebrate its own reintegration and affirm its continuity as a community.

This seems to have been the likely sequence of rites that followed the death of many of the adult inhabitants at Abu Hureyra. We have already noted that perinatals and infants were usually buried or otherwise disposed of with little ceremony, but most older children and adults seem to have been accorded the complex rites of delayed burial because they were regarded as participating members of society. The practice of burying people under the floors of their homes probably implied a cult of ancestors, as in Melanesia among the Tikopia and Gilbertese (Firth 1957, p. 77; Grimble 1972, p. 85). Sometimes this veneration was directed especially toward the skull of the deceased, which might receive special treatment. Here the idea seems to have been that the living should derive benefit from the powers believed to reside in the dead (Hertz 1909, p. 93). The Trobriand islanders, for example, used to preserve the skull and other bones of deceased relatives as a mark of piety (Malinowski 1931,

p. 133) and to perpetuate their social role for the benefit of the living (Weiner 1976, p. 84). In the Solomon Islands (Hocart 1922, p. 92) and elsewhere in Melanesia, skulls were frequently detached from corpses and preserved to propitiate the spirits of the dead and to invoke their aid. Ideas such as these seem to have found material expression in the particular forms of burial and treatment of skulls at Abu Hureyra. Among the Chinese, it is adults alone that are considered to be eligible for veneration as ancestors (Wolf 1974, p. 148), and this may be why the inhabitants of Abu Hureyra gave special attention to adult skulls.

Some Abu Hureyra 2 adults were buried in ways that departed from the standard pattern. Several were buried without prior exposure of the corpse, and one of these (72.520) had an arrowhead in its chest. The collective burial in pit 144 of Trench B phase 8 had distinctive features that marked it as different from every other burial described here. Another example of an unusual burial was the body of a 12–year-old (72.264B) encased in plaster colored with cinnabar. Many societies distinguish between "good" and "bad" deaths, that is, between deaths that occur in the approved manner and at the proper time and place, and other deaths that may, for example, happen away from home or be caused by accident or murder. Several of our unusual examples may represent these other kinds of deaths. The individual apparently killed by an arrowhead and the group in pit 144, all of whom appear to have died in an untimely manner, may be examples of "bad" deaths that merited different burial rites.

People of all ages and both sexes were represented in the burials, but our sample is not a true reflection of the original population. We have already noted that fewer children than we might have expected were found in the burials, and that more women than men were buried in the houses. Nevertheless, the burials enable us to form an impression of just how long the houses remained in use. The best evidence for this comes from Trench E, for here burials were associated with the three complete houses in phases 5, 6, and 7. Most of those burials were of adults. Nine individuals were buried in the phase 5 house, three under the floor and the rest in fill. Seven were buried in the phase 6 house, four under the floor and three on the floors or in fill. We found only three in the phase 7 house, all in fill, but this building had been badly damaged by later activities that may have destroyed all trace of any additional graves. The stratigraphic evidence suggests that the burials were made while the houses were occupied, or shortly after. Assuming that the people buried in the houses had lived in them during life, and that many of their inhabitants were buried indoors, it seems that the houses were used for only one or, at most, two generations. This relatively short span of use is supported by the radiocarbon dates from Trench D, which suggest that a sequence of five building phases may have spanned as little as 300 years.

The burial rites and associated ideology of the inhabitants of Abu Hureyra 2 were not unique to the settlement; evidence of similar practices has been recovered from some, though not all, contemporary sites throughout the Levant and in Asia Minor. This suggests that a system of beliefs and funerary customs was shared by societies in the two regions. Few of the excavators of these other sites have published detailed analyses of the burial practices they have found, but enough is known for some general comparisons to be made (Bienert 1991). These indicate that, while there are many similarities between the burial customs at these sites and at Abu Hureyra, there are also differences in detail.

The site nearest to Abu Hureyra at which burials have been found is Mureybit. The oldest were several burials from phase III (van Loon 1968, p. 275; J. Cauvin 1977, p. 36) dating to the earlier tenth millennium BP, during the intermediate period of occupation between the settlements of Abu Hureyra 1 and 2. The burials were secondary interments within houses; in several instances the skulls had been removed from the rest of the skeleton and buried separately. In a phase IV house, contemporary with early Abu Hureyra 2, there were two primary burials under the floor, and several skulls set on plinths on the floor itself (J. Cauvin 1977, p. 38). This evidence indicates that the inhabitants of Mureybit treated their dead in ways similar to those of the people of Abu Hureyra. It also confirms that these customs had a long history in the Middle Euphrates valley.

Indications of similar practices have been found farther afield in the Damascus Basin at the sites of Tell Aswad and Tell Ramad. The inhabitants of both sites buried their dead in individual and collective graves and practiced secondary burial (Contenson 1972, p. 79; 1977–1978, p. 208). Skulls were frequently detached from the rest of the skeleton and treated separately. At Tell Ramad some of the skulls were partly remodeled with plaster and painted with red ochre, giving them a lifelike appearance (Contenson 1967, pp. 20–21). These heads were associated with plaster human figures. Similar elaborate treatment of skulls with plaster has been found at three other sites in the southern Levant, Jericho, Beisamun, and Ain Ghazal, while several skulls from Nahal Hemar were coated with bitumen (Kenyon 1981, p. 77; Lechevallier 1978, p. 150; Rollefson 1983, p. 35; Yakar and Hershkovitz 1988). Such practices have not been attested farther north.

Jericho itself has yielded one of the largest samples of early Neolithic burials anywhere in Southwest Asia, representing some 500 individuals in all (Kurth and Röhrer-Ertl 1981, p. 408). Again, abundant evidence of a similar range of burial practices was found, spanning much of Neolithic 1 and 2. Elements of the same pattern of burials were found even farther south at Beidha in southern Transjordan (Kirkbride 1967, p. 9), although here it is thought that many of the inhabitants were buried beyond the confines of the site.

Evidence for burial practices has been found at sites on the Anatolian plateau, far to the northwest. In both the Aceramic Neolithic and the later settlements at Hacilar the inhabitants chose to dispose of most of their dead away from the settlement, but arrangements of a few human skulls were uncovered in the Aceramic settlement (Mellaart 1970, pp. 88, 6), contemporary with Abu Hureyra 2. Thus, while there was a preoccupation with skulls at this site, the prevailing rites of burial were different from those in the Levant. A great deal of evidence for burial practices was found at the site of Çatal Hüyük on the Konya Plain, and this accords in several respects with that from Abu Hureyra. Çatal Hüyük was occupied c. 8,000 BP, broadly contemporary with Abu Hureyra 2B. The inhabitants buried their dead indoors in single or collective graves under the floors of houses and "shrines" (Mellaart 1967, p. 204). The usual sequence of rites was initial exposure of the corpse followed by burial of the remains after the flesh had decayed. Skulls were detached in a few instances, but this seems to have been uncommon. Only a small proportion of the burials were accompanied by grave goods, but these were sometimes quite rich, perhaps indicating that the individuals concerned were people of high status (Mellaart 1975, p. 102). A few skeletons, mostly of females, were decorated with red ochre or cinnabar (Mellaart 1967, p. 207).

Farther to the east, the site of Çayönü near Diyarbakir was occupied for much of the Abu Hureyra 2 sequence, and the two settlements seem to have shared some similarities in burial rites. At Çayönü bodies were buried under the floors of buildings, usually in a flexed position, and clusters of skulls were buried separately (Braidwood and Braidwood 1982, p. 11). Over 70% of the human remains found at the site were recovered from one structure. This "skull building" consisted of a large room, across one end of which were small chambers in the floor that were filled with piles of skulls and other human bones (Schirmer 1990, p. 381). Nearby were some cattle bones. Most extraordinary of all, there were smears of blood from humans, wild cattle, and sheep on a stone slab in the room (Loy and Wood 1989). Traces of human and cattle blood were also found on a long flint knife in the building. We have here evidence of a particular kind of secondary burial in which the skull was separated from the rest of the corpse in rituals that involved the spilling of human and animal blood. A high proportion of the skeletal remains found in the skull building were those of adolescents and young adults (Özbek 1989), like burial pit 144 in Trench B, phase 8 at Abu Hureyra.

This, then, seems to have been the prevailing range of burial customs throughout the Levant and Asia Minor during the earlier Neolithic. People often buried many of their dead within their settlements and frequently engaged in rites of secondary burial. At many sites it was the custom to detach skulls and give them special treatment. Clearly, these people shared beliefs about the ideology of death and the appropriate treatment of the dead. The area over which customs most similar to those of Abu Hureyra prevailed is coterminous with the extent of Neolithic 2 culture in the Levant. Quite similar customs were also observed at some contemporary settlements in Asia Minor, a region that had certain elements of material culture in common with the Levant during the ninth and eighth millennia BP. These regions were linked, too, through long-distance exchange of obsidian and other prized stones and minerals. The prevailing cultural axis, therefore, was from north to south.

Some aspects of these burial customs were shared with the third major province of Neolithic culture in Southwest Asia, that of Mesopotamia and the Zagros. Some of the dead at Tell Maghzaliyeh on the southern flanks of the Jebel Sinjar were buried under the house floors (Bader 1989, p. 349), and evidence for special treatment of skulls has been found at Qermez Dere and Nemrik 9 in the same region (Watkins, Baird, and Betts 1989, p. 21; Szymczak 1990). Farther to the southeast at Ali Kosh and Ganj Dareh corpses were buried within the settlement in single or collective graves (Hole, Flannery, and Neely 1969, p. 248; Meiklejohn, Lambert, and Byrne 1980). Sometimes the burials were secondary. Nevertheless, there were significant differences, the principal one being that the corpses were buried intact with their skulls.

THE BURIALS OF HISTORIC AGE

A series of graves of historic age was found in the surface levels of Trenches B and E, and elsewhere on the mound. There was no trace of the graves on the surface, nor any memory of them among the inhabitants of the modern village. They obviously predated the recent settlement of the Euphrates Valley.

The graves usually contained a single individual lying in an extended position on the back or side, but they also included some prone burials. No artifacts accompanied the dead person. Most of the graves were oriented west-east or, occasionally, northwest-southeast. The body was usually laid in the grave with the head to the west. The graves held adults of both sexes, and also children. Their skeletons were usually complete and in a relatively good state of preservation compared with the Neolithic human remains.

We found ten burials of historic age in Trench B, phase 11—so many, in fact, that they were the most conspicuous features of the phase. The burials were concentrated in the eastern half of the trench. Most of them were in graves with curved ends and straight sides, dug large enough to receive a body at full length comfortably. At the time of excavation the bottom of these graves was from 60 cm to 1.3 m below the surface of the mound. Two of them were covered with stone slabs.

At least six of the burials were of children, an unusually high proportion, although we do not know whether they were buried in a single episode or over an extended period of time. One of the graves contained the skeleton of a mature adult female and two perinatal infants (72.162, 72.600), presumably her own children. This suggests that the deaths of all three occurred about the same time.

We found a total of 13 modern burials in Trench E, phase 9. The form and orientation of the graves were the same as in Trench B. The head of one individual lay toward the east, but all the others were to the west, for example, 73.300 (figure 10.13). Most of the bodies lay on their back or right side, such as 73.3438 (figure 10.14), but some were prone. Again, over half the burials were of children.

The salient features of the historic burials are clear enough: primary burial of both children and adults in individual graves oriented west-east, without

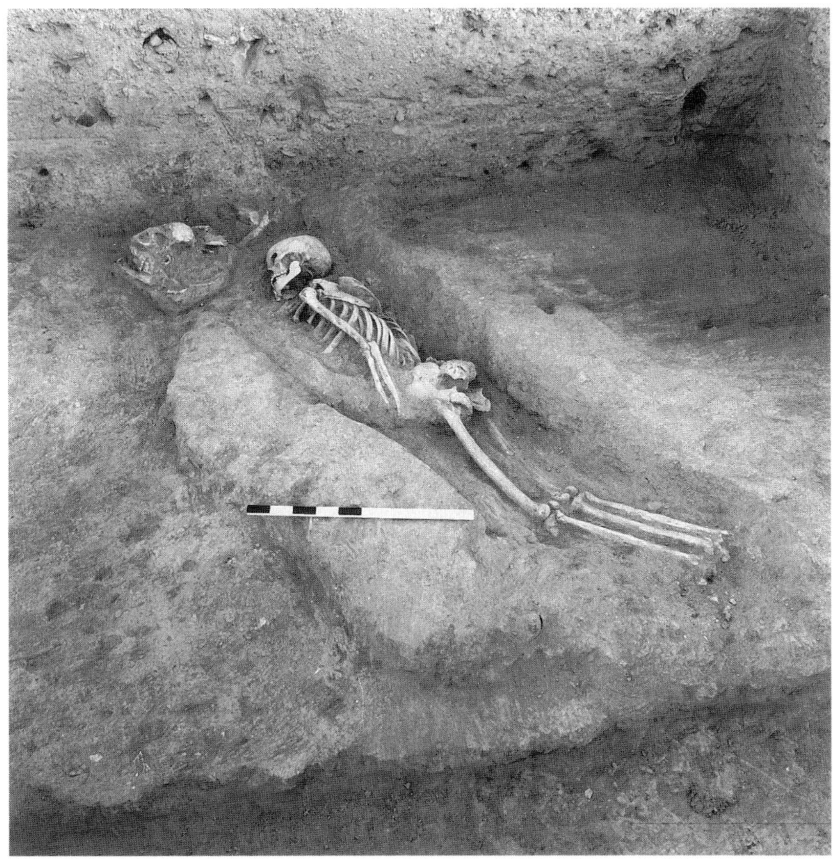

Figure 10.13 Trench E, phase 9: burial 73.300 of historic age, from the southeast. Burial 73.842 from the Abu Hureyra 2 settlement is just to the left of its head. Scale, 50 cm.

Figure 10.14 Trench E, phase 9: burial 73.3438 of historic age, from the northeast. Scale, 50 cm.

grave goods. The density of these burials was high where they occurred, suggesting intensive use of the prehistoric mound as a cemetery over many years. Graves of this kind were found in Trenches A and C, as well as B and E, that is, in all the trenches along the prominent north-south ridge of the site. There was only one in Trench G, and none in Trenches D and F. Thus, the burials seem to have been confined to those parts of the site that were most visible up and down the valley. There is reason to believe that at least some of the burials in Trench E were Byzantine in date; the heads of most of the skeletons were oriented to the west and Byzantine pottery was found in proximity. Several Byzantine burials were visible on the surface of the mound in the vicinity of Trench E. Contenson found a series of burials, similarly oriented and also lacking grave goods, in the surface levels at Buqras (Contenson 1985, p. 340, figure 9). The corpses had apparently been buried in wooden coffins, a feature lacking at Abu Hureyra. He, too, was inclined to attribute the burials to the Byzantine period because of their orientation.

In the absence of associated finds, the age of the other modern graves and the duration of use of the mound as a cemetery in the historic period could be determined only by accelerator mass spectometry (AMS) dating. We have obtained two dates for these burials, one from 72.85 in Trench A of 390 ± 60 BP (OxA-2044) and another from 73.70 in Trench B of 170 ± 60 BP (OxA-2045). The dates indicate that Abu Hureyra was used as a cemetery over several centuries in the recent past. The calibration curve for dates as young as these has several points of intercept (Stuiver and Pearson 1986, figure 1A). Thus, OxA-

2044 could be as old as the mid fifteenth century AD or as late as the earlier seventeenth century. The age of OxA-2045 ranges from the mid seventeenth to the twentieth century AD. It is unlikely that any burial we excavated dates from as late as the present century since there was no trace of those graves on the surface, all the bones in the graves were clean, and they had already suffered some deterioration in the soil. The likely range of ages is from the fifteenth to the early nineteenth century AD, that is, from the end of the Mameluke period through the middle years of the Ottoman Empire.

The only settlement in the vicinity of Abu Hureyra with traces of Byzantine occupation to which some of the people buried around Trench E could have belonged in life is Banat Abu Hureyra, or Old Abu Hureyra, 4 km to the east of the prehistoric mound, which was inhabited in Byzantine and early Islamic times (van Loon 1967, pp. 5–6). The people buried at Abu Hureyra in recent centuries may have lived in villages along the valley that have left no trace, or they may have been nomads.

11 The People of Abu Hureyra

T. I. Molleson

The study of a collection of human bones and teeth can achieve much more than just the description of the physical attributes of the individuals represented: it may provide insights into the social structure and cultural values of the society in which those individuals lived. Anthropologists are still inexperienced at interpreting such evidence, and my attempt here is intended to be a first step that will show something of the potential for analysis of the remarkable skeletal remains from Abu Hureyra.[1]

Moore and his team found human remains from deliberate inhumations associated with dwellings in six of the seven excavated trenches (A, B, C, D, E, G). I describe the skeletal remains from Trenches B, D, E, and G here; they provide evidence for the nature of the people who lived at Abu Hureyra during each of the major periods of the Neolithic, as well as a glimpse at those of the Epipalaeolithic. Analysis of the remains from Trenches A and C, together with an attempt to place all the skeletal remains in a wider geographic context, will be presented in a later publication.

We identified the skeletal remains of about 102 individuals, 52 juveniles and 50 adults, of whom 26 were female, from the Neolithic levels of the four trenches considered. They represented about 70% of the total sample of human remains and spanned more than 2,000 years of occupation. A small number of very significant bones were recovered from Abu Hureyra 1 levels in Trench E. The samples of remains attributed to Abu Hureyra Periods 2A, 2B (the largest group), and 2C, although individually quite small, have enabled us to form a good impression of the physique, habits, and persistence of the Neolithic population. The remainder of the skeletal material, dating to the historic period, has provided a rare opportunity for us to compare samples from prehistoric and recent times in one area.

Abu Hureyra was inhabited at a time when the skills of crop cultivation, cereal preparation, and domestication of animals were still quite new. We have deduced the effects on the skeleton of such momentous environmental, nutritional, and social innovations from a comparison of the developmental and pathological features presented by the remains.

Among the most important observations are the evidence for division of labor and role specialization in both the Epipalaeolithic and Neolithic, with the females carrying out most of the daily food preparation. We have detected a change in the hardness of the diet during the occupation of Abu Hureyra 2 that was related not only to the change in the foodstuffs but also to the method of food processing. At the social level there are very strong indications that particular families occupied individual houses for several generations. The importance of the family is underlined by their treatment of the dead, who were buried where they had lived under the floors of the houses, and who thus continued to be with the living. This suggests a sense of both permanence and continuity. The people must have been aware of the family concept in both space and time, and this would almost certainly imply that they had formed the construct of "lineage." Thus, it is probable that the lives of the people of Abu Hureyra were ordered by several of the fundamental principles of human society.

From the outset we realized that we could reconstruct the population and the society that supported it only by inductive methods. Finding out which part of the population was buried in the tell and which elsewhere would clearly bring us closer to the group of people who buried their dead there. We could derive some indication of the physique of those buried in the mound from the morphological features of their remains. A comparison of the frequencies of certain traits, both genetic and acquired, observed in remains from the different trenches and stratigraphic horizons would provide an indication of the homogeneity of the population and its persistence in the area.

The assemblage of human skeletal material from Abu Hureyra is a product of four main processes: excavation of the deposits, preservation of the skeletons, burial practices, and demography of the ancient population. Each had a profound effect on the collection and had to be taken into consideration before we could understand the nature of the people represented by the remains.

It is important to appreciate that the condition of most of the human bone recovered from Abu Hureyra limited the range of information that could be derived from the skeletons. The Neolithic material was in an extreme state of dehydration, had lost nearly all of its organic content, and was very friable.

The survival of bones and teeth depended not only on the original burial practices but also on the burial medium and the techniques of excavation. We had to eliminate any effects of selective recovery and differential preservation before we could attempt to interpret the burial practices. To our surprise, all parts of the skeleton were present in the sieved (bone bag) material, and in very much the same relative abundances as the excavated bones (figure 11.1). Thus, it is unlikely that the sieves recovered only those bones of the inhumations that had been missed by the excavators (in which case a preponderance of hand and foot bones would have been expected). The similarity of the two distributions implies, on the contrary, that additional skeletons were recovered by this method. All the bones of neonate infants were in bone bags, suggesting that the newborn dead were not in recognized graves.

There was a great deal of mixing of the bones, and burials were rarely if ever wholly discrete. In Abu Hureyra 2 new inhumations sometimes resulted in the disturbance of previous burials, suggesting that the inhabitants considered it important to be buried in a particular place. One of the more remarkable features of the bone assemblage from Trench B, where many of the buri-

TRENCH B

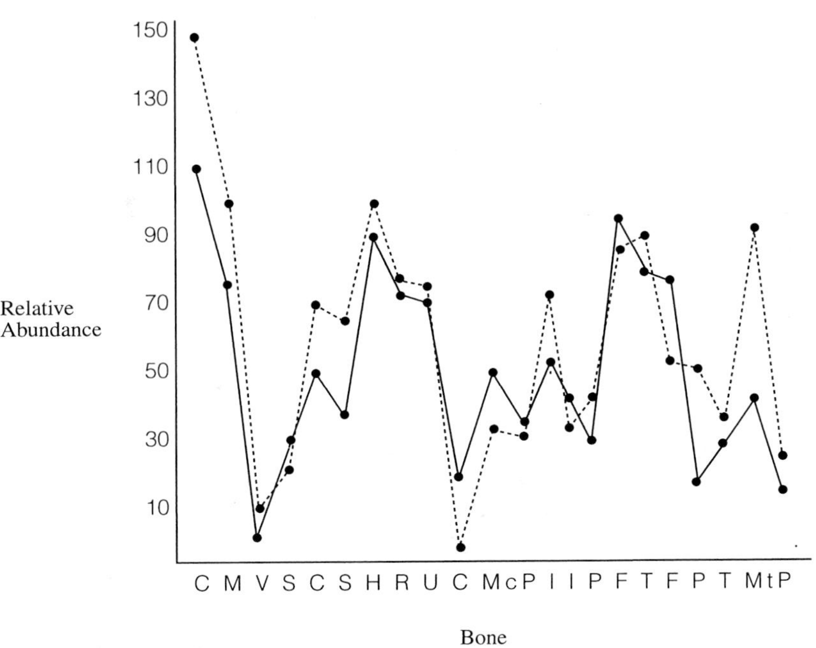

TRENCH D

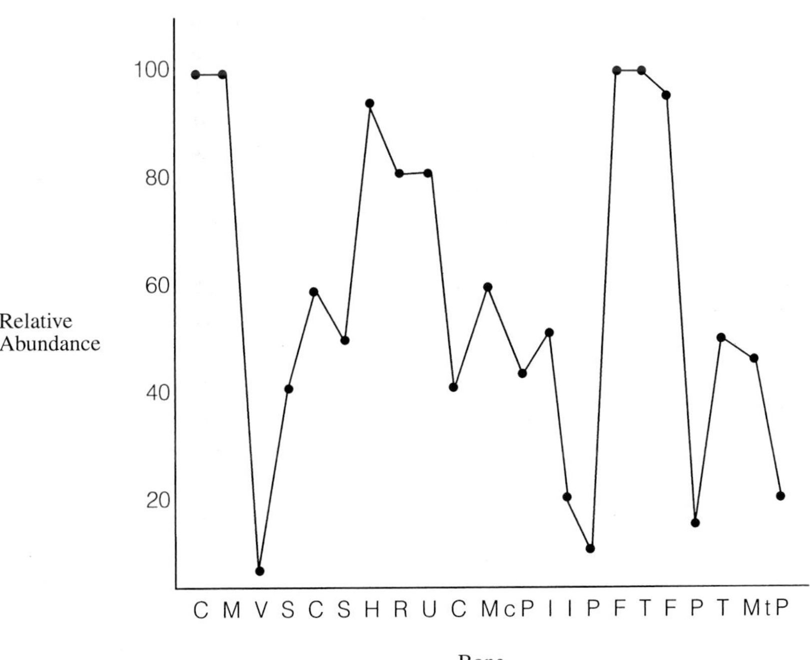

Figure 11.1 Relative abundance of human bone recovered from Trenches B, D, and E *(next page)*. Solid line: excavated skeletons; dashed line: bones from sieves. The relative abundance relates the number of bones of any type recovered to the number of those bones in the skeleton. It is clear that, while sieving increased the number of clavicles, patellae, tarsals, and metatarsals recovered, it did not complement the excavated bone; therefore, additional skeletons must have been located through this method of recovery.

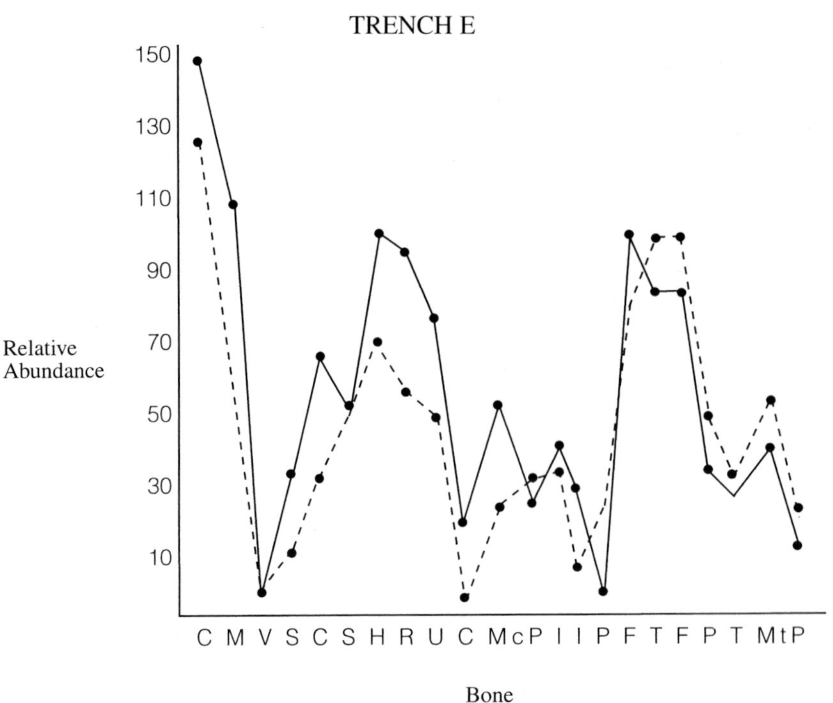

als were secondary with separation of head and postcranial parts, was that the relative abundances of the different bones recovered was about the same as that found in the other trenches (figure 11.1). Apparently, separation of the head from the rest of the body took place in the house, and the two parts were kept there, either displayed or interred.

Most of the numbered skeletons included the remains of more than one individual, but it was also clear from the distribution of bones that the remains of a single individual could be divided between two or more numbered inhumations. In some cases this had happened at the time of burial, for example, when the head had been buried separately. In other cases the division had occurred at the time of excavation. Therefore, before the number of individuals present was calculated, the remains of each skeleton were evaluated and those complementary parts that agreed as to age and sex were counted as one. Minimum numbers derived by this method differ from, and in many instances exceed, those derived from the relative abundance of parts. These figures are considered to be more realistic, however.[2]

THE PEOPLE OF ABU HUREYRA

Physically the adults were rather small and muscular, but wiry rather than especially robust. We noted a physical similarity between the Neolithic and historic remains that may underline the importance of the local environment in determining many aspects of appearance.

As work proceeded on the human remains it became clear that we had to find a method to assign sex to the incomplete skeletons. Accordingly, we devised additional measurements of certain bones. We used discriminant analysis[3] of five measurements to assign sex to 17 first metatarsals, taking as trainer samples known sex material from two British groups of quite different ages. T tests established that means for all the dimensions were significantly different in males and females (p value < .001) in both reference populations. All the dimensions recorded for the Abu Hureyra metatarsals approximated to the ranges of the two British samples, so we were justified in using these to assign sex to the Abu Hureyra foot bones (figure 11.2).

The discriminant function analysis using the combined reference samples selected 14 foot bones as female and three as male. This unequal representation of the sexes is taken to be a function of burial practices at the site.

The Abu Hureyra metatarsals proved to have a low dimorphism, with samples from females being as large or larger than those in the reference samples. They were also more robust, with the mediolateral shaft dimension being particularly stout—presumably a response to stress imposed on the bone by habitual exercise. In contrast, the dimensions of the proximal articulation were small in the females. If this dimension is related to weight transfer from ankle to toes then we can expect the women to have been rather light.

In their limb proportions the people of Abu Hureyra had a long shin (tibia) relative to the thigh (femur) and had long forearms. An indication of adult height can be derived from long bone lengths using standard formulas devised by Trotter and Gleser (1952).[4] Unfortunately, because of the fragmentary nature of many of the skeletons, we were able to make only a few determinations of stature.

Neither females nor males were tall, with female mean height about 155 cm (5 ft 1 in) and males about 162 cm (5 ft 4 in). Males were generally 7–10 cm taller than the females, a moderate degree of sexual dimorphism that is comparable to the observations recorded by Smith, Bar-Yosef, and Sillen (1984) for various Neolithic populations in the Levant. The people of Abu Hureyra were, however, considerably shorter than their more southern contemporaries. Average heights of females and males from Jericho Pre-Pottery Neolithic B were 158 and 171 cm, respectively (Smith, Bar-Yosef, and Sillen 1984). Statures and limb proportions of the historic sample from Abu Hureyra were comparable to those of the Neolithic.

The number of individuals for whom we could calculate the stature was too small for us to observe any change with time, but the two males and one

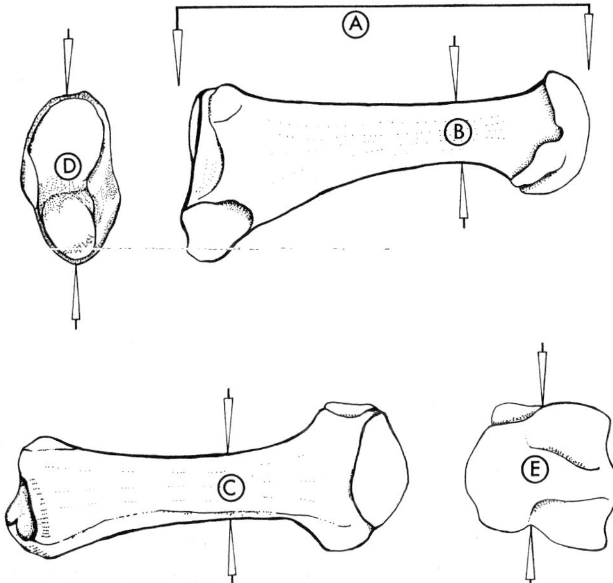

Figure 11.2 Dimensions taken on the first metatarsal. A: maximum length; B: minimum dorsoventral breadth; C: mediolateral breadth at right angles to B; D: maximum length of proximal articular surface; E: minimum mediolateral breadth of distal articular surface.

female from the earlier Neolithic period, 2A, were all above the mean height for their sex. Variation in height increased in 2B times, a factor that may be taken as a possible indication of the effects of change over time. The evidence for these trends is based on very small samples but has been observed elsewhere (Smith, Bar-Yosef, and Sillen 1984). The reduction in size may be attributed to a change in diet, with an increased reliance on cereal products at the expense of meat protein. The reduction in dimorphism between the sexes may reflect the increased workload of the women as well as the reduced nutritional quality of the diet.

THE JUVENILES

About half the individuals recovered from the Neolithic levels were immature, ranging in age from newborn to subadult. Although we identified 52 juveniles, their skeletons were very fragmentary and it proved impossible to establish growth patterns based on a correlation between dental development and bone length. Growth in the first two or three years appears to have been normal.

The neonates were usually recovered as isolated bones rather than as discrete skeletons, so it is difficult to assess how many individuals were represented. Our numbers were derived by assessing both the minimum number of individuals represented by the most common bone and the levels from which the bones came. Thus, for Trench B, bones from ten bone bags were taken to represent six individuals, two from the historic period, two from Period 2C, and two from 2B.

Most of the infants of newborn size were recovered from Trench E. We identified isolated bones of three or four babies among the bone bag material from phase 5 and a further three to five from phase 6 (2B). All came from rooms 2, 4, or 5 and were associated with the gray plaster floor in room 5, the pebble surface in room 2, or the mudbrick collapse and occupation debris in the rooms. It may have been the custom, therefore, to bury some of the newborns under the floors of the dwelling rooms; others seem to have been disposed of by placing them in disused buildings. Two or three neonates in phase 8 (2C) were recovered from deposits of occupation debris and mudbrick collapse and so appear to have been disposed of in a similar manner; one was found in a pit in the yard.

Two of the neonates recovered from Trench B were associated with the remains of adults, one (73.2060) an inhumation in room 2 of the phase 8 building. Others, from phase 9 (top of 2B) and 10 (2C) were associated with mudbrick collapse, the mudbrick wall deposits, or occupation debris in a large pit. They were like the Trench E phase 8 neonates, less clearly associated with living rooms, and it appears that by the end of 2B and in 2C times there was less concern to keep those who died near birth within the houses. This shift in burial practices correlates with the change in the layout of the settlement in Period 2C.

Another two of the Trench B neonates, B117A and B117B, from phase 10 (2C) were very small, equivalent to 35–36 weeks gestation according to the regressions of Scheuer, Musgrave, and Evans (1980), and may have been twins. The rest of the neonates were comparable in size to the neonates from the historic deposits on the tell. Generally, there was insufficient evidence to show whether a skeleton was of a stillborn fetus or of a live-born infant that had died shortly after birth. Two infants in which the annular ring of the auditory meatus had fused were at least full term.

A lack of suitable material has made it impossible to demonstrate clearly any effects of deficiencies in the weaning diet. Weanling children are especially vulnerable: the combination of a protein-deficient, cereal-rich diet and the effects of gastric infections can lead to a marked retardation in growth. Dental development is not usually severely affected, and a record of bone length against dental maturation can be an indicator of growth achievement. At Abu Hureyra the size of the long bones of the newborn infants compares with those of modern standards, implying that the mothers were reasonably well nourished. The few children for whom both dental age and bone length could be assessed, though small for their dental age, did not appear to show any sudden retardation, so we can probably assume that children were not weaned abruptly (Molleson 1989a).

The lack of wear on the teeth of two- and three-year-olds suggests that weaning was late. Scanning electron microscope studies of the wear on the teeth of a four- or five-year-old revealed striations characteristic of a soft, somewhat acid, diet. The wear patterns indicate that the food was of a coarseness similar to that of the adults from the same phase of the Neolithic (Period 2B) but required little mastication (Molleson and Jones 1991). It is possible that the child was given prechewed food as part of its weaning diet. It is common among both humans and nonhumans for an adult, usually the mother, to give food that has already been chewed to a young child directly from her mouth.

A few cases of enamel hypoplasia suggest that systemic stress, associated with high temperature, could affect the children. Hypoplastic defects were most frequent on the canines and central incisors. No clear trend could be detected between different periods of the Neolithic settlement, the frequency remaining low at about 2% throughout, with only a hint of a reduction in 2B. The frequency of hypoplastic defects was least in Trench E and highest in Trench B, possibly reflecting differences in living standards of the occupants of the houses exposed in those trenches.

We noted few other pathologies among the juveniles. An adolescent (73.851) from Trench D had a healing greenstick fracture with hematoma of the elbow. A few children (73.2168 and B189 from Trench B, and 73.1930 from Trench E) in whom the long bones were thickened by the growth of new bone along the shafts had presumably suffered from soft tissue infections.

DIET

Evidence for lifetime diet can occasionally be inferred from the morphology of the human remains, but such evidence is always indirect and must be interpreted with caution, since different causes may lead to similar symptoms. Several deficiency diseases produce recognizable bone pathologies in a majority of sufferers, particularly juveniles. The defects may be retained by the bones after healing and into adulthood. These diseases include rickets, scurvy, and anemia. We observed neither rickets nor scurvy, but we did find a few cases of suspected iron deficiency anemia. Cribra orbitalia of a child (73.1786) from Trench B, phase 8, suggested a chronic condition that may have been induced or exacerbated by a parasite infection or an infantile diarrheal condition.

Other mineral deficiencies such as those of calcium or zinc are less easy to detect from gross morphology. Smith has argued that reduction in tooth size observed in late Palaeolithic and early Neolithic material from the Levant can be attributed to dietary calcium depletion as cereals became an increasingly important part of the diet (Smith, Bar-Yosef, and Sillen 1984). We might have expected to see a similar secular trend in tooth size at Abu Hureyra as cereals became more important in the Neolithic, but we could not clearly demonstrate it. The lack of material from the Epipalaeolithic settlement of Abu Hureyra 1, when the reduction would have originated, and a high diversity of tooth size effectively obscured any trend, if there was one. It is even possible that tooth size actually increased in 2C times; mean buccolingual dimensions of both maxillary and mandibular teeth were larger than they had been in earlier periods of the Neolithic settlement. This, however, was as likely to be due to the presence of a few individuals with large teeth as to the effect of a change in diet.

The best indicators of the diet of the adults of Abu Hureyra were the macroscopic and microscopic condition of the jaws and teeth. We found evidence of changes that may be related to the adoption of cultivated cereal crops, and possibly to the switch from a reliance on gazelle meat to the products of domesticated sheep and goats.

The amount of wear on the teeth suggests that the diet in the Neolithic was extremely hard and coarse, and exceptionally so in 2A times. Teeth of quite young adults were often severely abraded, with wear on the chewing teeth being greatest on the palatal side of the upper teeth and on the buccal side of the lower teeth (figure 11.3). This type of wear was caused by powerful crushing movements to break up and masticate food particles. Associated with this was expansion of the articular surface of the mandibular condyles. All chewing teeth could be lost during life, even the anterior teeth; they too had to be

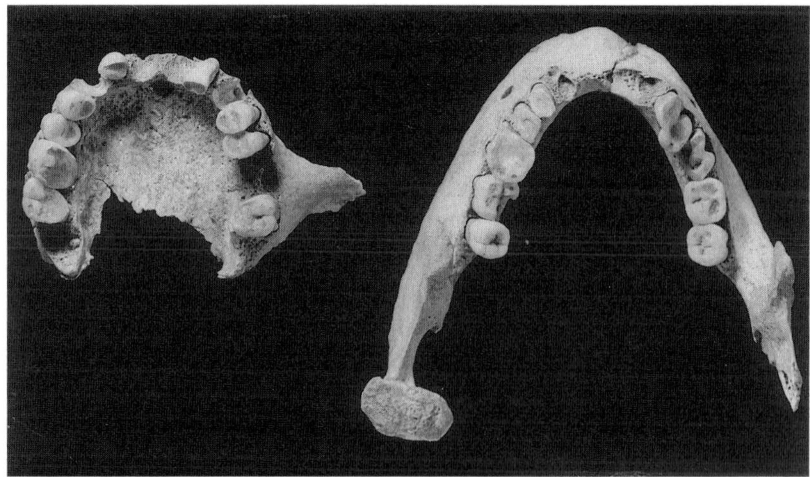

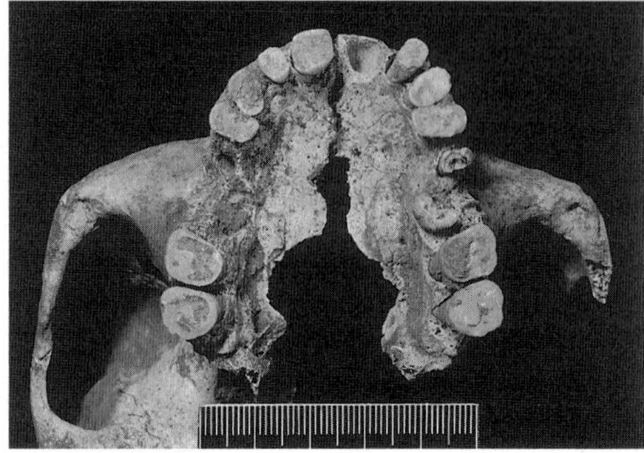

Figure 11.3 Jaws and dentitions of individuals from Abu Hureyra. *Top*, an adult, 73.3067, from Trench E, phase 5. The upper teeth are more worn on the palatal side, whereas the lower teeth are more worn on the cheek side. One mandibular tooth has been chipped, in another the pulp is exposed, and several of the anterior teeth were lost before death. The mandibular condyle is greatly enlarged. *Bottom*, the upper jaw of an adult female, 73.2949, from Trench B, phase 8. The teeth are very worn; two teeth on each side were damaged and two more lost before death.

used for mastication rather than biting if the molars had been lost (figure 11.3). We found a number of virtually edentulous (toothless) jaws with thickened alveolar crests. The people concerned must have sucked and masticated food with their hardened, toothless gums. The mylohyoid ridge, where the Mylohyoideus muscle originates, was particularly marked in those mandibles.

In a number of instances the crown of the tooth had been fractured, presumably by biting on hard particles in the food. Dental chipping was particularly noticeable in 2B material, yet there is some evidence that the food became less abrasive in 2B times. Photographic studies by scanning electron microscopy of the wear surfaces on chewing teeth revealed scratches and pitting of the enamel surface. The density of these features, together with the size of the pits, differed in teeth associated with Abu Hureyra 1 and 2A levels; they indicated that the food was both harder and coarser in Neolithic times, when much dried gazelle meat continued to be eaten and cereals were a mainstay of the diet (Molleson and Jones 1991). The wear patterns on the teeth show that the food consumed by the Epipalaeolithic inhabitants of the tell was soft and somewhat acidic. This is consistent with the evidence from the plant and animal remains described in chapters 12 and 13 by Hillman, Legge, and their colleagues. Teeth from 2B levels displayed a wide variation in wear features that may reflect an attempt by some of the people to control the damaging effects of the foods they were eating and their methods of preparing them. The introduction of pottery late in Abu Hureyra 2B had a marked impact on the diet. Cooking of foods in pottery vessels markedly reduced the wear on the teeth of the people of the village (Molleson, Jones, and Jones 1993). Mothers were able to wean their children earlier onto a diet of cooked cereal mush, a change that increased their fertility rates.

It was only from late 2B levels that we recorded instances of dental caries and healed dental abscesses, although some of the predisposing factors, including fractures, root exposure, and pulp exposure had been noted in 2A dentitions. About half of the abscesses were in the gums, of the kind that can result from local inflammation and subsequent infection of gingival tissue damaged by the trapping of foreign particles, such as sharp awns derived from plant seeds. Sample sizes were small, particularly for 2A levels, and frequencies were low, but it seems that the people altered their preparation and consumption of food in 2B times such that, though still coarse, it required less powerful mastication and was therefore less abrasive; the inclusion of hard particles, however, increased the risk of chipped and fractured teeth.

LABOR AND ROLE SPECIALIZATION

It is clear from the archaeological evidence that the inhabitants of Abu Hureyra engaged in a number of strenuous activities. Some, such as hunting, were of a seasonal nature and demanded intense activity over a relatively short period; others, such as the fabrication of mudbricks, the construction of houses, or the plastering of floors, would have been fairly arduous, but the burden on individuals could be regulated and the tasks varied. Several activities, in particular the preparation of grains, would have been both arduous and demanding. The grain had to be dehusked and ground daily, and sufficient amounts had to be prepared to feed the family. These are not tasks that could be regulated for convenience or comfort. After the introduction of cultivation there would have been the additional labor of preparing of the soil, planting the seed, harvesting the grain and pulses, and organizing their storage.

The extent to which any of these activities can be imprinted on the bones of the skeleton is difficult to ascertain. Individuals vary enormously in their reaction to activity, stress, or injury; different positions are taken up to perform similar tasks; or a variety of tasks may have a similar effect on the muscles and bones of the body. For example, rotation fractures of the tibia and fibula can result from catching the foot while plowing, horse riding, or skiing; in each case the foot is protected by a shoe. No such injuries were noted on the Abu Hureyra bones.

The people of Abu Hureyra 1 apparently lived there permanently and had adopted a sedentary way of life; that is, they went out to gather seeds, to search for game, or to tend the fields, and they returned to the same dwellings. They undertook activities within the confines of the settlement or in forays from it, and so had to carry products and necessities back to the village.

A considerable range of activities in Abu Hureyra 1 can be inferred from the archaeological evidence. The inhabitants constructed dwelling areas by artificially leveling the surface of the land and excavating large subcircular pits 2–2.5 m in diameter and up to 70 cm deep. They dug postholes and put wooden posts in place. They sometimes repaired floors with clay. Thus, the construction of a dwelling would have involved the digging out and removal of substantial quantities of earth and subsoil. This was time consuming and quite hard work. The inhabitants would have had to carry in clay, though not in large quantities, and fell and trim trees to make the posts. The demands of these activities were quite considerable, although the technology required was simple. The transport to the site of the heavy saddle querns would have required considerable effort, and we note that the querns were then left in place and not carried away.

There must have been a great increase in the amount of work required to sustain the population of the settlement in Neolithic times. They needed to clear, level, and work the soil; plant, protect, and harvest the crops; and carry, store, and prepare the grain and seeds. There were also some innovations in technology with the development of agricultural tools, although these would still have been simple. To manufacture mudbricks for the construction of the houses, whether on site or in a specialized area, they needed to transport the raw material or the finished bricks to the site. Similarly, they would have carried in plaster for the floors and walls. They would frequently have foraged for firewood and brought it back to the village.

We can identify the effects on the skeleton of the extra, and sometimes excessive, stresses involved in the carrying of loads, whether of game, crops, or building materials. These stresses can cause changes to the weight-bearing bones including the spine, shoulders, hips, and knees. We observed changes to the shape of the vertebral bodies, symptomatic of Scheuermann's disease, in the skeletons of subadults, especially adolescents, because they were required to labor in this way. The detached neural arch of a lumbar vertebra in a young adult (73.2255) from Trench B indicated spondylolisis arising from persistent and excessive load bearing, albeit in someone who was susceptible to develop this condition.

We think it likely that the inhabitants carried loads on their heads, as the people of the region still do today (figure 11.4). The vertebral bodies of the cervical spine were curved, providing a buttressing support for the neck, which otherwise might wobble under the weight of a heavy load. In some individuals we observed degenerative changes on the vertebral bodies and joint surfaces of the cervical vertebrae that may have developed as a result of injuries sustained during load bearing.

Figure 11.4 A woman from the modern village of Abu Hureyra carrying a full pot of liquid on her head.

It was the preparation of the daily meal that was the most demanding and labor-intensive activity of the settlement, as it still is today in so many places. The grain had to be prepared each day since, once dehusked, the seeds would not keep (Hillman 1984). The dehusking of the small grains in a mortar with a pestle and the subsequent grinding of the grain in a saddle quern would have taken many hours each day.

> Life in the oasis seemed to grind on at its own pace. For the women this was literally true, for they spent much of their time grinding grain on their hand mills. . . . I often watched Hawa as she placed a few grains at a time on the stoop of the base-stone and let them trickle down as she ground them, sweeping the flour into a bowl every few minutes. After an hour or so her little daughter, aged about nine, would take over and begin grinding furiously. It might take several hours to produce enough flour for one meal. (Asher 1988, p. 142)

The physical position in which the tasks of mortaring and grinding were performed was constrained by the fact that the activity had to be centered on the working area of the mortar or quern. In Abu Hureyra 2 both artifacts were usually small, and the operator must have had to kneel before them. It is significant that the two querns in Abu Hureyra 1A were found, apparently where they were used, placed directly on the ground and not raised on a plinth as was often done more recently (Richards 1939). Kneeling for many hours puts strain on the toes and knees, while the action of grinding causes additional strain on the hips and particularly the lower back as the body drives forward with the rubber and recoils at the end of the stroke, like scrubbing the floor with a scrubbing brush or using an exercise wheel (figure 11.5). When working with a saddle quern the arms are raised above the shoulders and the forearms are turned inward towards the body, actions that involve the deltoid and biceps muscles. The insertion areas of precisely these muscles on the humerus and radius were markedly developed in the otherwise gracile individuals from Abu Hureyra. The overdevelopment of the muscles was symmetrical, affecting both arms equally (figure 11.6a).

In grinding, the body pivots alternately around the knee and hip joints, and the femora are subject to considerable bending stresses, the effects of which can be seen in the curvature and buttressing of the shaft of the thigh bone of a female (73.2951) from Trench E, phase 5 (figure 11.6b). The articular surfaces of the knee in this individual were extended by the growth of osteophytes around the margins. Pressure was also exerted on the toes, which were curled under the foot so that purchase could be gained with the ground for pushing off at the beginning of a grinding stroke. The flattening of the heads of the first two metatarsals that we observed on foot bones from Abu Hureyra 1 and 2 levels can be attributed to pressure on the ball of the foot. Further, the articular surface of the heads of the first two metatarsals was extended onto the upper surface of the foot (figure 11.7). In older individuals growth of osteophytes around the margins of the articular surfaces of the interphalangeal joint of the big toe could be remarkably exuberant (figure 11.7c).

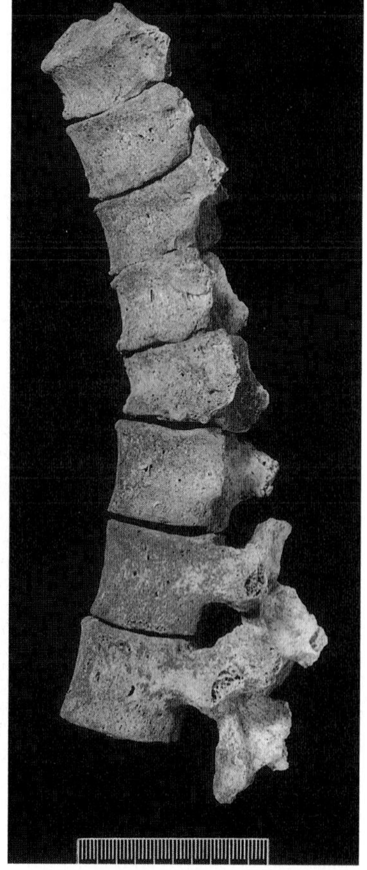

Figure 11.5 Degenerative changes to the thoracic vertebrae of the spine that may have been caused by injuries associated with the operation of a saddle quern to prepare grain. *Left,* the last thoracic vertebra, T12, of a female, 73.2271, from Trench B showing crushing of the vertebral body. *Right,* part of the spine of an adult female, 73.2963, showing similar compression of T12 vertebra.

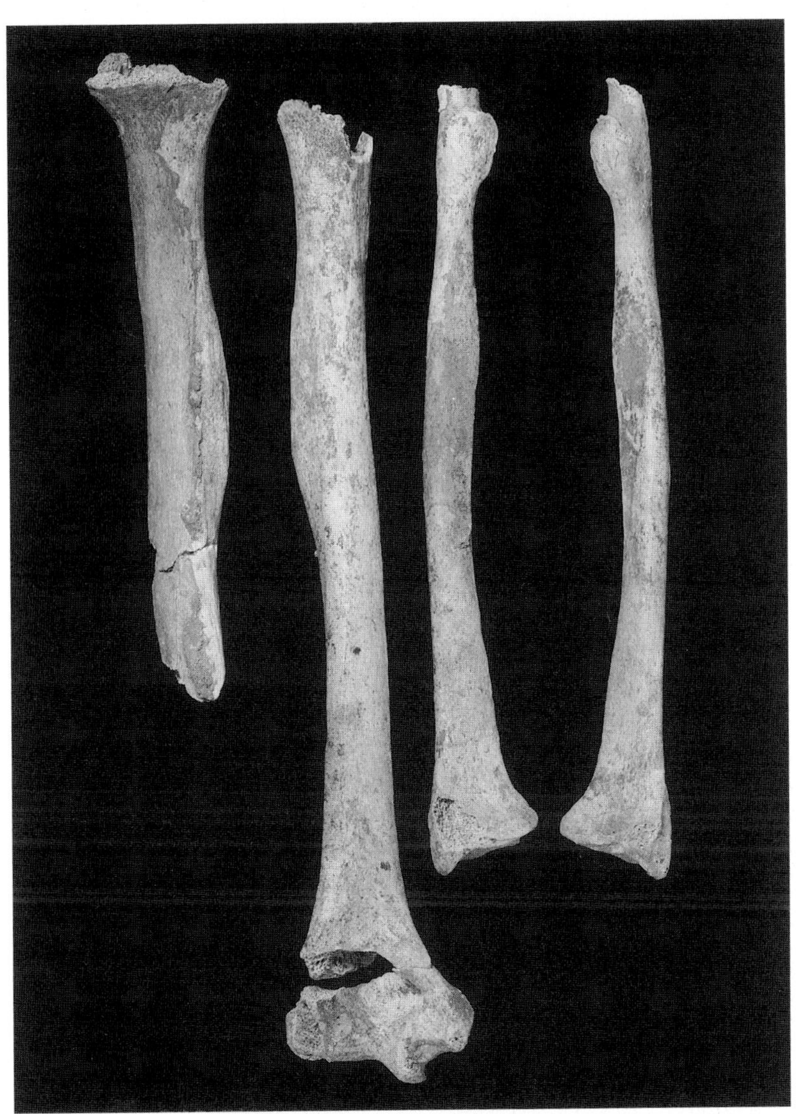

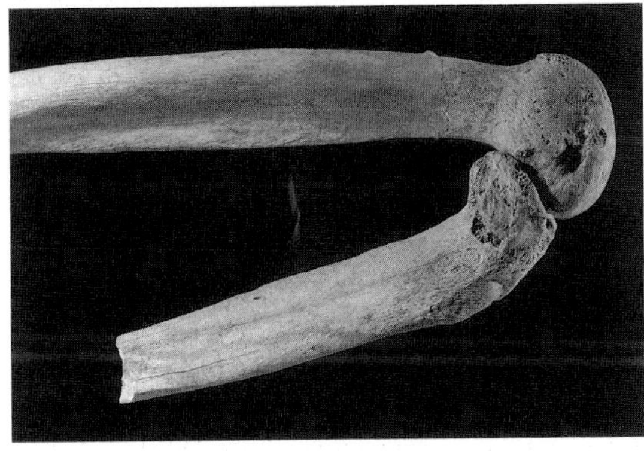

Figure 11.6 *Above* , arm bones of an adult female, 73.2949, from Trench B, phase 8, who had presumably spent much of her time preparing grain on a saddle quern. Left, the areas where the deltoid muscles insert on the humerus bones are particularly well developed. Right, the areas of insertion of the biceps muscles are very well developed on the radius bones. *Left,* the leg bones in the region of the knee of an adult female, 73.2951, from Trench E, phase 5, showing the tightly flexed position that would have been taken up when operating a saddle quern on the ground. The shaft of the thigh bone is more curved than is normal and has developed a buttress of bone to compensate. There are arthritic changes around the margins of the articular surfaces of the knee joint.

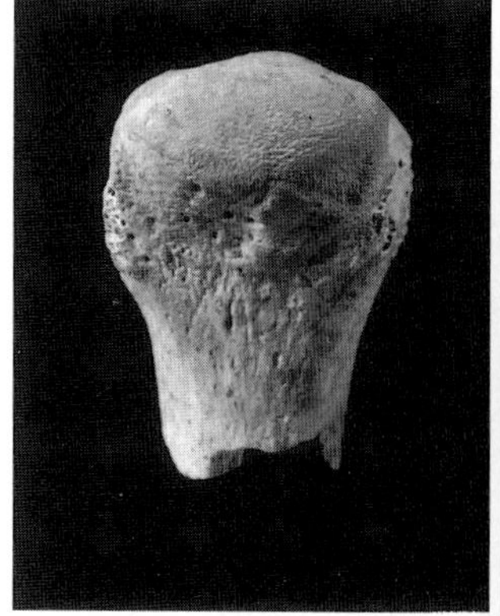
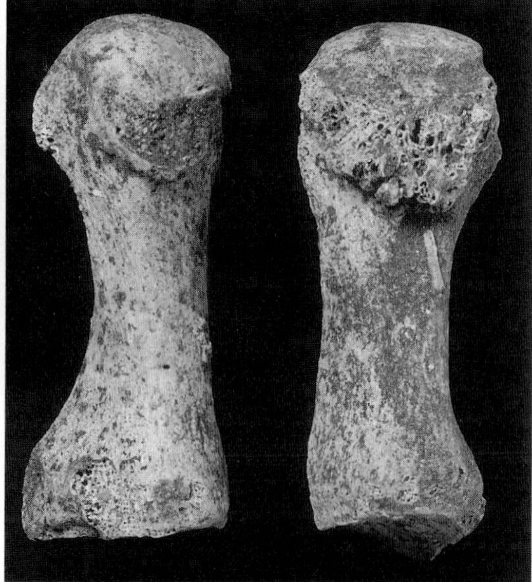
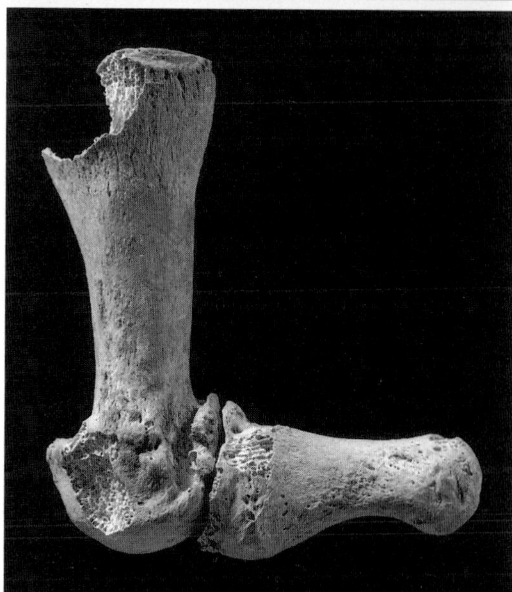

Figure 11.7 Deformation of the articular surface of the first metatarsal of the foot attributed to excessive pressure on the joint of the big toe exerted during kneeling to grind grain. *Top left,* the head of the first metatarsal of a young individual, 73.B502, from Trench E, phase 2 (Abu Hureyra 1B); the articular surface is extended onto the upper surface. *Top right,* the left and right first metatarsals of an adult female, 73.2949, showing progressive stages of osteoarthritis of the joint (Trench B, phase 8). *Bottom right,* the first metatarsal and proximal phalanx of the big toe in articulation showing the development of bony growths around the joint surface. Female, 73.2271, Trench E, phase 6.

We can best ascribe this complex of skeletal changes to the excessive demands of grain preparation and grinding. It provides a remarkable insight into the daily lives of so many of the people of Abu Hureyra from Epipalaeolithic times onward (Molleson 1989b) (figure 11.8).

By demonstrating that the first metatarsal was highly dimorphic between the sexes, we have been able to show that the majority of toe bones that displayed the articular changes associated with kneeling were from females, and therefore we can infer that most of the food preparation was carried out by women. From the number and distribution of querns it is probable that each household prepared its own cereal products. Thus, there was division of labor in the household. From this we may suppose that other role specializations would have followed, since the individuals not involved in food preparation would have been free to develop different skills. Well-made ornaments, such as the butterfly beads, may be examples of the craftsmanship that people de-

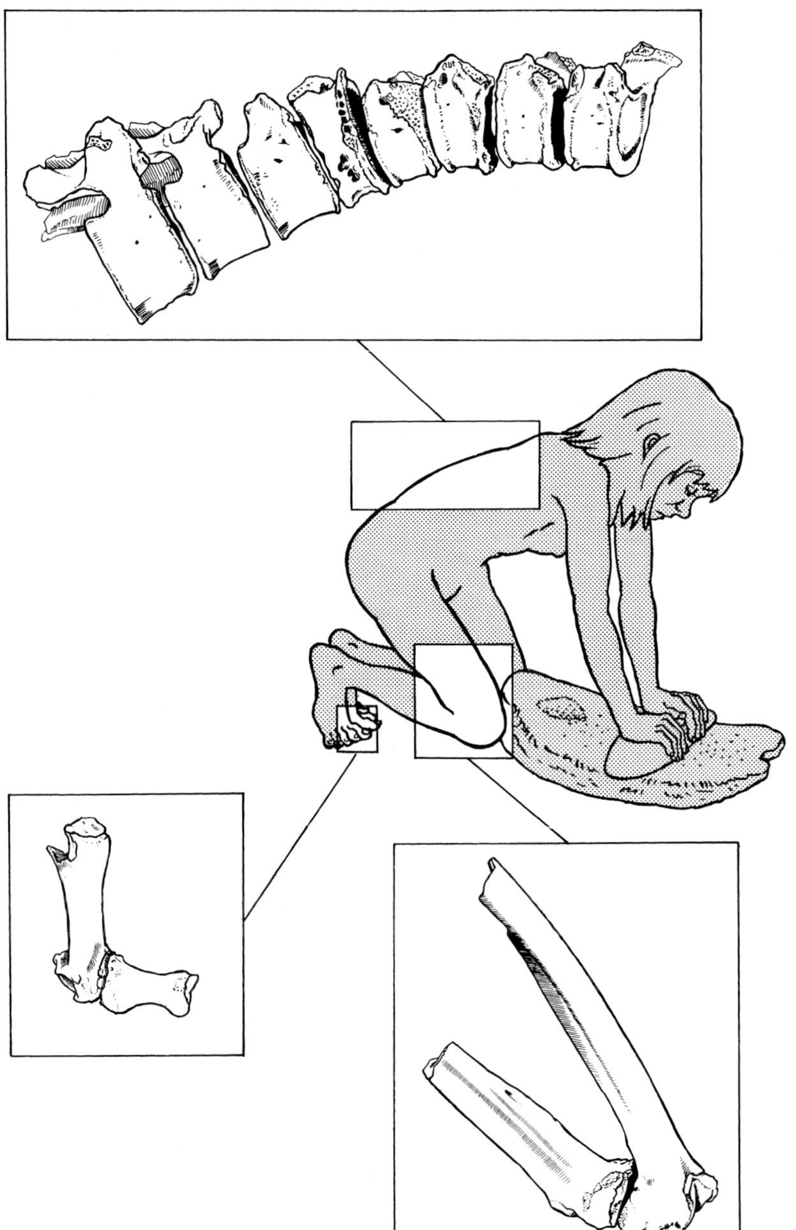

Figure 11.8 The areas of the skeleton that are most often affected by injuries associated with the use of the saddle quern.

veloped during this leisure time. Such activities were also a consequence of the permanence of the dwelling place.

Squatting, with the heels flat on the ground, appears to have been the habitual position of rest for males as well as females, at least from Period 2B times onward. In this position the ankle bone presses against the front of the shin and a squatting facet can be imprinted on the bone; the knee caps are notched where they press against the end of the thigh bone. We observed notched patellae and extended articular facets on the tali and distal ends of the tibiae, which have been identified with the squatting posture, in several individuals from 2B levels in Trench B. The extension of the articular surface at the ankle and knee allows the tibia to fold back on the femur, while the trunk remains vertical. The heels remain on the ground. Those who habitually sit on chairs, or perhaps wear shoes with a heel, cannot usually take up this position for any length of time. Not all individuals from Abu Hureyra possessed squatting facets, but it does not follow that they could not squat.

The habits of squatting and kneeling to prepare grain both exert pressure on the toes. They would have caused the plane of the proximal articulation of the toe phalanges to be more than usually inclined toward the upper surface of the foot. The epiphysis, which could still be discerned in the toe bone (73.B198) of an adolescent from Trench B, was wedge shaped.

HEALTH

Injuries, degenerative joint disease, and repetitive stress damage were the most common bone pathologies in the Abu Hureyra human remains. The conditions that caused them must, at times, have been painful and disabling. A number of individuals with degenerative joint disease and spinal injuries doubtless owed their condition to injuries incurred through operating a saddle quern. The most impressive case was that of a mature female (73.2949) from Trench B, phase 8. She bore the marks of a back injury that had been sustained many years before death. Determination of sex proved difficult; the skull and mandible were well developed, the limb bones were long but gracile, the sciatic notch was very narrow but was probably deformed as a result of injury, and the metatarsals were small. Metrically, the bones were those of a female. At 158.4 cm, using the formulas of Trotter and Gleser (1952) for a Negro female, she was tall. The molars were well worn despite her relatively young age. Although there was no evidence for dental caries, there was a possible healed root abscess of the upper right first molar, perhaps the result of inflammation caused by a sharp grass awn embedded between the gum and the tooth. The tooth and the one next to it had been shed some time before death.

Several of her cervical, thoracic, and lumbar vertebrae were preserved. There was degenerative damage to the body of C3 and C4; probably a healed compressed fracture of T11 and T12; and degenerative damage to the body of L5 and S1. The sciatic notch of the ilium was constricted, and the areas of ligament attachment on the preauricular sulcus were hypertrophied. The metatarsals of the big toes were severely deformed by the effects of gross degenerative disease. The right toe was particularly badly affected on both the dorsal and plantar surfaces (figure 11.7b).

There was pronounced spurring of the medial condyle of the humerus at the elbow. The deltoid tuberosity of both humeri and the biceps tuberosity of the radii were particularly well marked. The pattern of injury and degenerative change suggests a traumatic episode in which the lower back was damaged and the ligaments in the preauricular sulcus of the pelvis torn. It is likely that the woman was severely disabled, even crippled, as a result of her injuries. She remained mobile and active despite her disability. The symmetrical overdevelopment of the arm bones suggests habitual involvement in some activity that required the arms to be raised above the level of the shoulders and the forearms rotated. The combination of muscular development implies some strenuous activity such as the grinding of grain on a saddle quern. This would have put stress on the back and toes while developing the muscles of the arms (Molleson 1989b). The injuries, especially to the back and pelvis, were such that she would have had difficulty walking without the aid of a staff. She would have clutched the staff in front of her with both hands for support.

Another female (73.2271) from Trench E, phase 5, had severe osteoarthritis of the spine following an injury. There were exuberant fringe osteophytes around the body of T12 associated with spondylosis. The spinal canal was triangular with a medial osteophyte indentation causing spinal stenosis. The adjacent vertebra, L1, was wedge shaped, probably due to old vertebral collapse following trauma. Osteoarthritic changes in the first metatarsophalangeal joint were typical of hallux rigidus. The articular surfaces of the proximal phalanges of the toes were quite irregular. We attribute all these changes to injuries incurred through grinding grain on a saddle quern.

Osteoarthritic changes affecting both knee joints of another female (73.2951) from Trench E, phase 5, can be attributed to a meniscus injury. The articular surfaces appeared to have been eroded in the medial compartments and there were osteophytes projecting from the margins of the joints. The ebernation, following cartilage destruction, of the base of the proximal phalanx of the great toe of another specimen, B313, from the same phase indicated osteoarthritis, possibly resulting from repetitive stress injuries in operating a quern or mortar.

We diagnosed a few healed fractures from radiographs, in addition to the lumbar fractures described above (73.2271). A crushed cervical vertebral body from a mature adult male (73.852A) in Trench D was the result of an acute back injury. Degenerative spondylotic changes with osteophyte formation had developed as a consequence. Only the cranium and upper thorax were preserved, so we could not ascertain the extent of any subsequent disability.

An adolescent (73.851), also from Trench D, had a periosteal reaction at the lower end of the humerus on both sides, on a phalangeal shaft, and on the upper aspect of the left ulna. Just below the left coronoid process there seemed to be a buckle in the cortex reminiscent of a greenstick fracture. This, the bulging nature of the periosteal elevation, and the type of calcification, suggests a subperiosteal hematoma, with injury as a likely cause. Other causes of subperiosteal hemorrhage and even infection are virtually eliminated by the absence of cortical change and the normal texture of the bone.

We found no certain instances of nutritional disease, although the somewhat thickened parietal bones of two adults from Trench D may be indicative of childhood anemia, perhaps associated with infection. We did observe two further cases of porotic hyperostosis in young individuals from Trench B, phase 8 (73.2127, 73.2133), that may indicate a deterioration in living conditions in Period 2B. Quite severe cribra orbitalia was present in the orbits of an infant (73.1786) from that phase.

It is perhaps significant that the only case of suspected hemolitic anemia was from a modern level. The skull of a mature adult (73.3438) from Trench E, phase 9, had some thickening and altered cribriform pattern of the skull vault.

Congenital abnormalities were uncommon, as they are in most populations, and very rarely of a disabling nature. We noted three cases of detached neural arch of a lumbar vertebra (for example, 73.2255 from Trench B, phase 7), in one case associated with a cleft first sacral vertebra. There is often a genetic predisposition to this condition of the lower back (spondylolisis) that can then develop as a result undue load-bearing during adolescence (Wynne-Davis and Scott 1979).

We noted two cases of congenital fusion of two cervical vertebrae, one of an adult female (73.31) from Trench B, phase 9 (Period 2B, Neolithic), and another (73.300) from Trench E, phase 9 (Period 3, historic). These must, of course, be coincidences, given the great difference in age of the two skeletons.

The first signs of infections appeared in Abu Hureyra 2B times with the occurrence of both dental caries and osteitis. Two carious teeth of a female from Trench E, phase 5 (73.1930), were the first signs of a deterioration in oral health and the existence in the population of cariogens. Dental calculus, the product of plaque-forming bacteria, was never severe; a moderate amount was present on an incisor tooth (73.B198) from Trench B, phase 7, and in an old individual (B 61) from phase 9.

The earliest evidence for a soft tissue infection or ulceration leading to proliferative periostitis was observed on the shaft of a fibula (73.1930) from Trench E, phase 5. Nonspecific lamellar periosteal reactions on bones of two other individuals (73.1996 from Trench E and 73.2168/B189, a child from Trench B) probably resulted from soft tissue infections. In the latter case the changes were both marked and extensive, but the child was too old for cortical hyperostosis.

A localized proliferative periosteal reaction on a proximal phalanx (B14) from Trench E, phase 7, was due to an irritative process, possibly infective but also reminiscent of the early stages of a thorn osteoma, just the sort of foreign body inclusion that must always have been a hazard.

AFFINITIES

The sedentism and year-round occupation of the site from Epipalaeolithic times that has been demonstrated for Abu Hureyra must have reduced the range and limited the number of contacts with people from other areas, and so curtailed the gene flow between groups. The effects of this would have been to reduce genetic variation in later generations, especially if a minority of families contributed a disproportionate number of offspring to each succeeding generation. Given the size of Abu Hureyra, deleterious effects from inbreeding would be unlikely, however, even if no outgroup matings took place. The indications for genetic isolation and inbreeding at Abu Hureyra are difficult to examine, particularly given the lack of evidence concerning the genetic variability in contemporary populations in other parts of the Levant. Fluctuating frequencies of certain skeletal and dental traits provide the best source. Frequencies need to be above 10% for variations at the population level to be followed, and below this if the persistence of a family is to be observed.

Particularly small teeth of two individuals (73.854 and 73.302) who were buried in the same room in succeeding phases, 2 and 3, of Trench D provided evidence that members of the same family were buried in the one area, and that a house was already occupied by the same family in succeeding generations in 2A times.

Grooving of the lateral incisors was remarkably similar in three groups from Trench B, phase 8: 73.2127 from the wall (139), and 73.1604 and 73.1787 from the pit in room 2. This evidence may be taken to indicate the use of the house by members of one family. Similar teeth recovered from bone bag material probably reflect disturbance and scattering of burials.

The strongest evidence for family ties came from burials in Trench E, where agenesis of the third molar noted in three females from phase 5 and buried in room 1 must indicate that they were related to each other, to another female buried in the equivalent room in phase 6, and possibly to a mature adult in phase 4. Two males buried in rooms 1 and 5 of this house both had a detached lumbar arch (spondylolisis), and two other individuals had septate supra condylar fossas of the humerus. The frequency of Carabelli's cusp on molar teeth was low, with three examples in Trench B, from phases 2, 8 and 10; and two in Trench E, from phases 4 and 8. It is possible that some of those individuals, too, were related.

We noted rare enamel pearls on five maxillary molars and one mandibular molar: from two individuals in Trench B, 73.1787 from pit 144 in phase 8, and an 11- or 12-year-old child, B69, from phase 9; from one individual (73.851) in Trench D, phase 3; and from one individual (73.810) in Trench E, phase 8. Turner (1945) recorded frequencies for enamel pearls of 2.3% for maxillary teeth and 0.3% for mandibular teeth. The frequency at Abu Hureyra was 5.2%. The persistence of the trait may be an indication that direct descendants of the family that lived in the Trench D area of the tell in 2A times were living in the Trench B area in 2B times and in Trench E in 2C times. Enamel extensions were associated with the enamel pearls in two of the individuals.

A number of genetically determined traits commonly found in other populations were very rare. No case of metopism was noted and only two with extrasutural ossicles.

DEMOGRAPHIC TRENDS IN ABU HUREYRA 2

The burial practices that we described in chapter 10 give a general impression of the mortality patterns at Abu Hureyra. Our analysis of the sex ratios among adolescents and adults provides further, more detailed insights. There appeared to be a preponderance of females buried in 2B times, which, since the remains were recovered from the houses, suggests that burial practices were different for women than for men, not that there were more females in the population.

The mortality patterns for the earlier Neolithic periods 2A and 2B were broadly similar (figures 11.9, 11.10). Given the fact that neonates were recovered from the general fill of the houses, not from recognized graves, a number of them from families resident in the excavated areas would almost certainly have been disposed of elsewhere and so would not have been included in the excavated sample. It cannot be assumed, however, that their numbers were very great, since there did appear to have been a distinct preference for disposal of the dead within the houses at that time. There were, apparently, fewer newborn babies than infants aged under one year, an observation that we would have anticipated since we would not have expected a high perinatal mortality for that time if the mothers were adequately nourished and the babies suckled. It is unlikely that there was either the density of population or the cross contact for the spread of such killers as puerperal fever, supposing that the agent existed at the time. Nor would a high infant mortality have been expected. It is only after weaning when the young child starts to move about that it encounters infective organisms that can prove fatal.

About half the individuals recovered were subadults, although the figure was exaggerated by the underrepresentation of those adults, mostly males, who were not buried in the houses, at least in 2B times. This apparent proportion of 50% juveniles could have been caused by a high birth rate and a large number of children in the living population. An approximation of the mortality rate can be inferred by comparing the proportions of infants (0–1 year) and older juveniles (2–19 years) with the respective proportions for infants and juveniles, where the infant and juvenile mortality rate is known. With 20% infants and

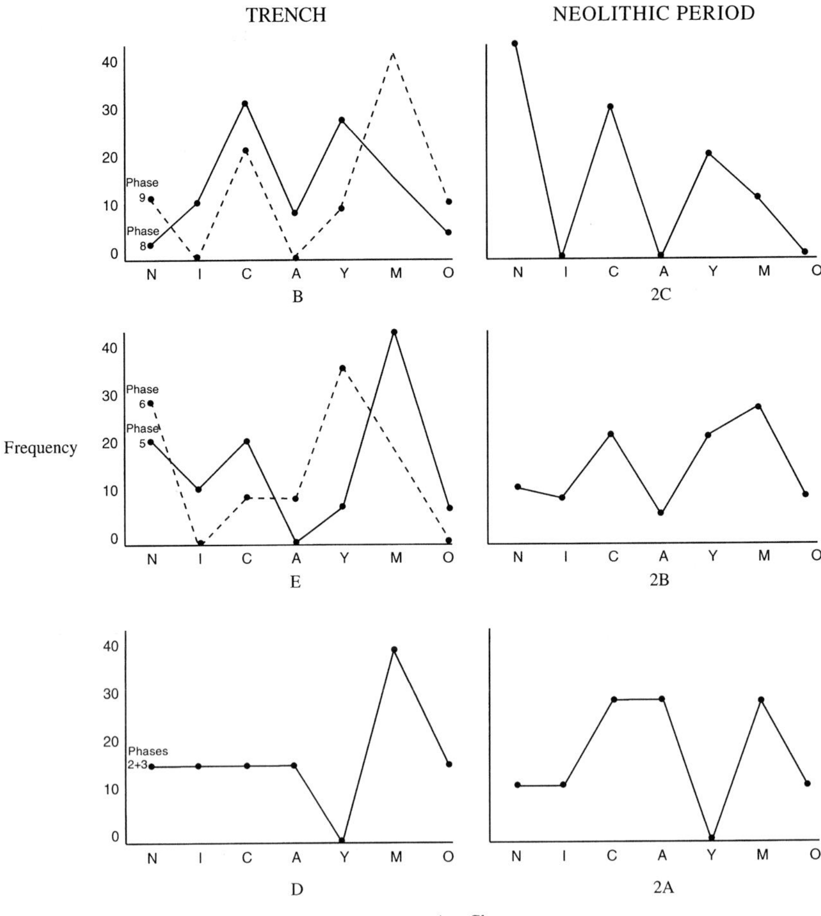

Figure 11.9 Relative frequencies, by age class, of human skeletons recovered from Abu Hureyra according to trench and Neolithic period. N: neonate; I: infant under 2 years; C: child 2–12 years; A: adolescent 13–19 years; Y: young adult 20–34 years; M: mature adult 35–49 years; O: old adult 50+.

31% juveniles, and without allowing for population increase, the neonate mortality rate would have been about 15% and the juvenile about 2% per annum. These figures imply higher mortality rates than are found among present-day hunter-gatherers but are comparable to those for some recent third world communities.

The number of adolescents recovered from 2A levels was unexpectedly high and might result from various causes. The burial of all those with as yet undifferentiated roles could have been within the domestic (female) zone; there could have been a large number of individuals of this age category in the population; or there could have been a higher mortality rate in this age group. In the first case burial in the domestic zone of those without a specific role in society would apply to all juveniles, but the number of adolescents was disproportionately high whether compared to younger juveniles or to adults. In most societies adolescents have the lowest mortality rate and are the least represented group in cemetery samples. In the last case a higher mortality of adolescents might been a consequence of an initiation ritual, such as circumcision, which had led to death.

We also identified a large number of adolescents in 2B from the phase 8 pit (144) of Trench B. Phase 9 of Trench B and the 2B levels of Trench E, as far as could be judged from the small numbers involved, did not contain an exceptional number of adolescents—in fact, only one was found.

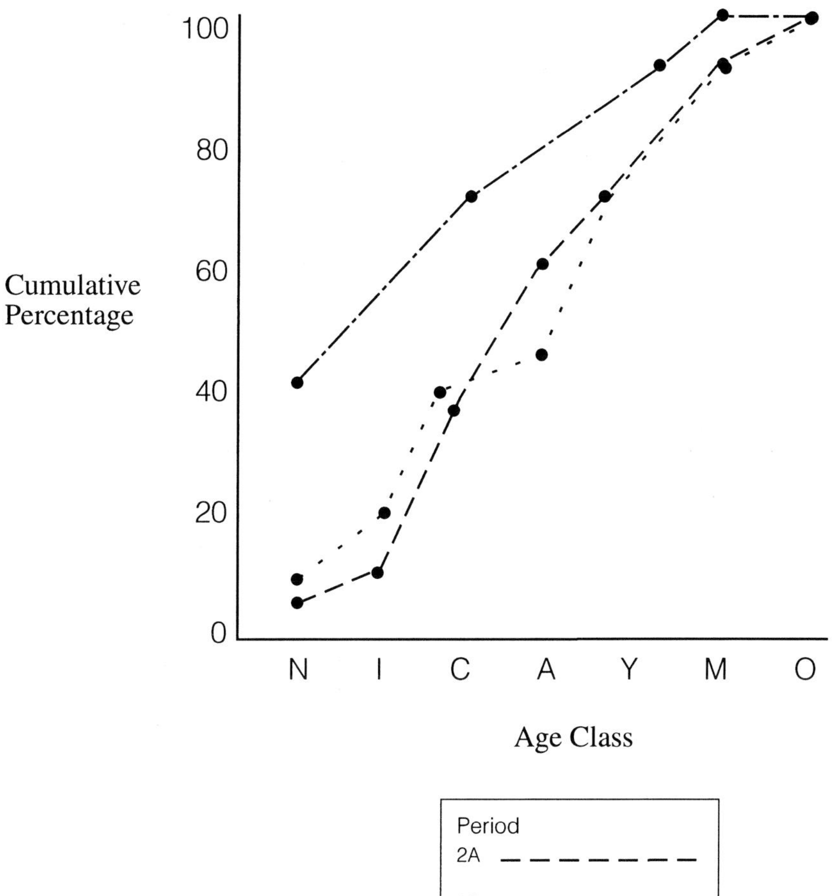

Figure 11.10 Cumulative frequencies, by age class, of human skeletons recovered from the Neolithic Periods 2A, 2B, and 2C at Abu Hureyra.

Period 2C, with four neonates and three children, had the highest proportion of subadults, but the sample size was very small and few burials were recovered from this period, although the area excavated in Trenches B and E was greater than for earlier periods. This may be a further indication that population size declined in 2C times.

SOCIAL ORGANIZATION AT ABU HUREYRA

The basic institutions of social organization can be readily identified in modern societies; many can still be recognized from the documents and artifacts of historic communities. The point at which hominids evolved to the stage when they could be said to have had a social organization is difficult to document in the archaeological record. Fundamental to human social organization is the existence of language, without which rules cannot be formulated and there can be no kinship systems or incest taboos—all essential to human society (Fortes 1983). Without language, furthermore, there can be no abstract thought or ritual; the evidence for this extends back into the Pleistocene, but whether any hominid community before the onset of agriculture had a *fully* human social organization must remain an open question; and whether human social organization emerged as part of a gradual or a sudden process depends on how the evidence is preserved, identified, and interpreted.

The challenge is to identify the hallmarks of human society in ever-older archaeological sites. The transition from hunting and gathering to agriculture and sedentism must have been salient in establishing the last characteristics of humanness in the repertoire of human social behavior.

The skeletal remains from Abu Hureyra have provided direct evidence for intensive labor activities among the people. They have provided clear indications of role specialization and division of responsibilities between the sexes. While males may have been more involved in hunting and procuring meat, the females especially were occupied in the preparation of food. Hunting was quite probably a cooperative activity, and the meat was presumably shared among the people according to certain rules.

Among the Hadza it is, significantly, the big game, cooperatively hunted, that must without fail be carried into the camp for sharing. Everyone has a share of the meat as a right, even men who have not taken part in the hunt or who have not contributed to the food supply for a long time. The vegetable and plant foods obtained by the women are not obligatorily shared (Woodburn 1968, p. 51; Fortes 1983, p. 27). Fortes describes this as prescriptive altruism and finds it among pastoralists and agriculturalists (Fortes 1970, pp. 242–249).

The burial of the dead under the floors of the houses, the presence of disproportionate numbers of females and juveniles, and the clustering of related individuals are strong indications that the dead were buried where they had lived. This inference suggests, further, that houses were occupied by a single family, and that the family was the domestic unit. The use of the same house by one family over several generations testifies to its sense of continuity in time and to the formulation of lineages.

The presence of domestic households implies a persistence of relationships, probably pair bonding in the form of marriage, and the existence of family life with all that it circumscribes. The presence of adolescents buried within the domestic area may be taken as evidence of extended rearing.

Division of roles, cooperative hunting and food sharing, family units, extended rearing, ancestors, and lineages have all been identified by Fortes (1983) as the basic parameters of human social organization. Fortes highlighted the importance of role division in the evolution of human society. He derived the idea of prescriptive altruism from the mothers who give life, love, and nurture freely, while offspring take freely. There is no element of contract or coercion or of binding reciprocity in this relationship. It is a model that, with cultural elaboration, becomes a moral principle (Fortes 1983, p. 24). In this context the role specialization in food preparation at Abu Hureyra can be seen as a natural and inevitable development of nurturing that provided for older children and fathers. And from this devolved all other aspects of the social organization of the village that was, indeed, fully human.

SUMMARY

The people of Abu Hureyra lived at the origins of not only agriculture and herding but also labor, craftsmanship, and the sort of family structure with which we are familiar today. Those who labor work more or less exclusively at a single task to produce food or objects in such quantities that the needs of others can be met; in turn they depend on the efforts of others to supply their wants. It was through this division of roles that specialists arose who could produce a surplus efficiently that could be exchanged for other commodities obtained in a similar way. In the realm of the household we envisage that the family would have preferred to spend time together, and those not involved in food preparation would have engaged in crafts. Thus, the men could have made a variety of tools while sitting round the hearth in the evening, while the women worked at spinning, weaving, and basket making after the day's grinding had been done.

The people were small of stature, females about 155 cm (5 ft 1 in) and males about 162 cm (5 ft 4 in) tall; relatively long-legged, presumably an adaptation to the hot climate; gracile and wiry rather than robust. They were generally healthy, and free from caries and nutritional or infective disease or injury. The heavy labor required to produce and process their new foods damaged their teeth and joints until they devised the means to avoid such pain and disability (Molleson 1994).

The advent of agriculture introduced a remarkably abrasive diet. Teeth were rapidly worn down to the roots, broken by hard particles in the food, and lost prematurely. The uneven wear on the teeth indicates that the people were eating hard, coarse foods that required crushing rather than grinding before being swallowed. They were probably foods like cracked wheat or bulgur, roasted grains or frikké, and unleavened bread or biscuit that needed to be chewed to moisten it so that it could be swallowed. The dried gazelle meat that was so important in the diet in Period 2A times would also have been very gritty to eat.

Scanning electron microscope photographs of the scratch marks and pitting on the surface of the teeth confirm that there was a change from a soft diet in Abu Hureyra 1 to a hard, crushing diet in Abu Hureyra 2A, and that there was some mitigation of the severe abrasiveness of the food in 2B times. This can be observed in the ratio of pit density to pit size or to feature density. The diet also appears to have been more acid in Abu Hureyra 1, suggesting that more meat was eaten then and, conversely, that cereals were a more important component of the diet in Abu Hureyra 2 times. The introduction of pottery late in Period 2B led to a revolution in cooking techniques. Henceforth, meat and vegetable foods could be thoroughly cooked, sharply reducing the wear on people's teeth.

Evidence for the nature of the diet of a four-year-old child implies that it had only recently been weaned and was eating food of the same type as its parents but much softer and more acidic, consistent with it being given particles of meat or cereal that had been prechewed. That was probably the only practical way of weaning a child in Pre-Pottery Neolithic cultures that lacked the facilities for cooking or containing a gruel.

The preparation of cereal grains to make the daily meal required considerable effort. Hillman has pointed out that the wild grains eaten in Abu Hureyra 1A had to be dehusked daily, probably using a pestle and mortar, because the naked grain rapidly deteriorates. The kernels were then ground to a flour using a grindstone. The domestic cereals eaten in Periods 1B through 2 also had to be ground each day. The very great effort that these processes demanded of the people of Abu Hureyra 1 and 2, and especially of the women, were strongly imprinted on the bones of the skeleton. The attachment areas for the muscles that raised and twisted the arms were unusually well developed on the left and right arms in equal measure. Several individuals had quite severe damage on the vertebral disks of the twelfth dorsal or thoracic vertebra. The knees, too, showed signs of osteoarthritis, and the thigh bone was buttressed in response to bending pressures exerted at the hip and knee.

We saw the most telling changes on the metatarsals of the big toes. These bore the marks of the head where the big toe had been pressed against the upper surface of the bone. The second metatarsal showed similar pressure marks, and when viewed from the side, the head was clearly flattened. We noted these changes first on bones from Abu Hureyra 1. We can best attribute the suite of anomalies in arms, back, knees, and toes to the effects of long hours spent operating a saddle quern of the kind found in place in some of the rooms of the houses. Our detailed analysis of the metatarsals determined that it was the women, for the most part, who undertook the labor of preparing the daily meal. The women, therefore, were tied to the house for several hours every day, while the men would have worked the fields and, in the appropriate season, trapped and processed game.

We found evidence that people transported loads by carrying them on their heads. Injuries to the neck associated with load-bearing resulted in disk damage and osteoarthritis of the joints of the neck vertebrae.

At home the habitual position of rest appears to have been squatting. Squatting is a position that most westerners find difficult to sustain for any length of time, but one which is comfortable for those who are adapted to it. The squatting posture taken up for many hours produces a stable, reassuring environment for the growing child who, assured that its protecting adults are likely to remain in position, has the confidence to extend the range of its environment by gradually exploring farther afield. On returning, the child finds the adults squatting near the ground at an approachable, intimate level. Psychologists working in communities where squatting is the habitual posture of rest have noted the greater confidence and ease of relationships between young children and adults.

The evidence for burial practices confirms that the house was the center of the family, and that successive houses on the same spot continued to be occupied by one family and its descendants for many generations. It seems that the dead were buried where they worked, so women were buried under the floors of the rooms.

Part IV THE ECONOMY OF THE TWO SETTLEMENTS AT ABU HUREYRA

12 The Plant Food Economy of Abu Hureyra 1 and 2

Abu Hureyra 1: the Epipalaeolithic

G. C. HILLMAN

VEGETATION AT THE START OF EPIPALAEOLITHIC OCCUPATION C. 11,500 BP

The wild plant foods available to the first Epipalaeolithic occupants of Abu Hureyra were more plentiful than at any time since the Glacial Maximum, and certainly much more prolific than those that would be provided by the modern potential vegetation summarized in figure 3.7. This was because the beginning of Epipalaeolithic occupation at Abu Hureyra coincided with peak moisture availability during the spring and summer growing period and the start of relatively high CO_2 levels, 33% above the very low levels that had probably limited growth for much of the preceding 50,000 years in all those trees and herbs that used the relatively inefficent C_3 form of photosynthesis (Sage 1995). The vast majority of the local trees and herbs were of this C_3 type, including most of the food plants. Consequently, this period represented the peak of the local spread of these trees and wild cereals.

However, remains of plant foods preserved by charring such as those recovered from Abu Hureyra provide only an incomplete picture of the ancient subsistence that was based on these rich resources; such are the vagaries of identifying charred remains. We can nevertheless begin to suggest the types and abundance of wild foods that were probably available, including foods missing from the remains, and to suggest their potential role in subsistence, by using "ethno-ecological modeling" (chapter 3, n.3). One of the first steps is to model the probable spatial limits of the major vegetal resource zones available to the local population (figure 12.1).

The map in figure 12.1 is based on four considerations. First, I have assumed that the charred remains of plant foods and twiggy wood identified from Abu

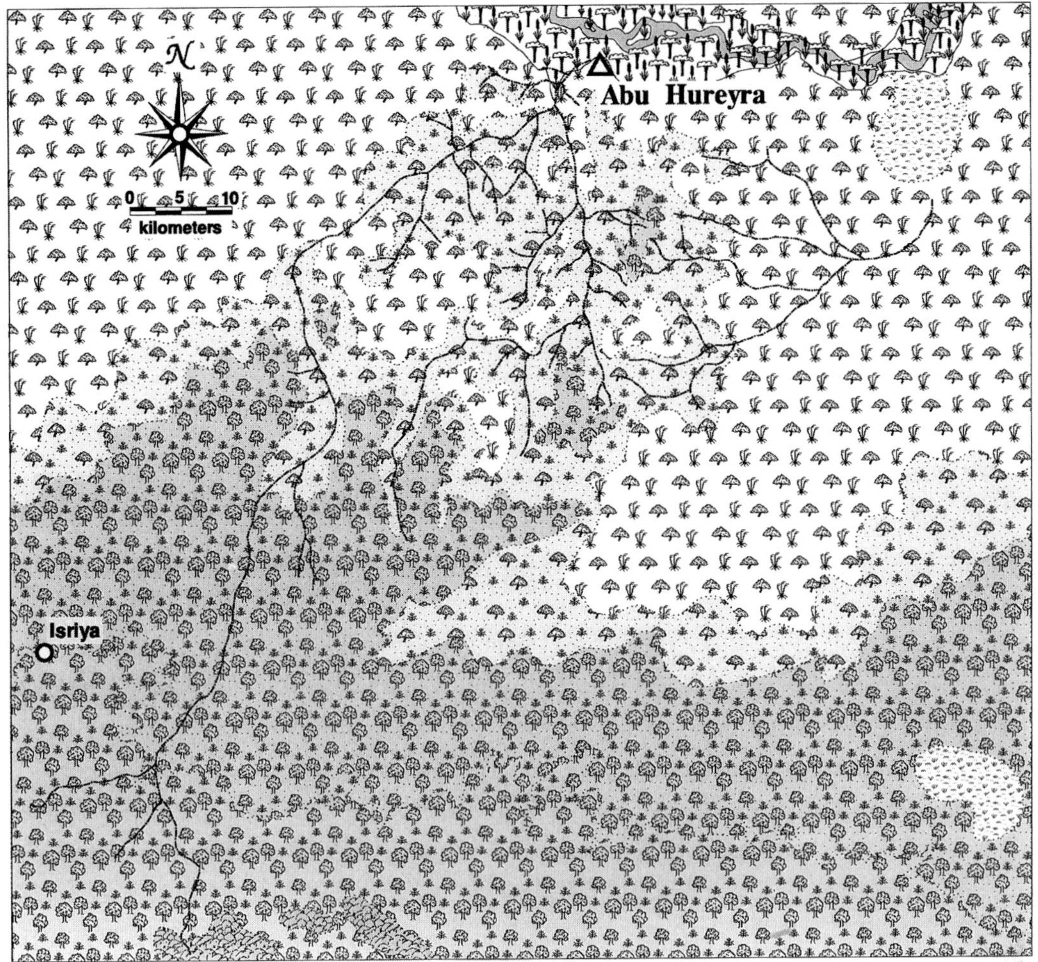

Figure 12.1 Map of distribution of major vegetation zones in the area south of Abu Hureyra c. 11,500 BP, at the start of the Epipalaeolithic occupation of Abu Hureyra 1, based on the ecological models discussed in the text, and using our models of potential present-day vegetation (see figure 3.7) as our starting point. At 11,500 BP the extent of woodland and wild cereals was apparently at its peak. Dense, broad stands of wild wheats and wild ryes would probably have occurred in the drier parts of oak-Rosaceae park-woodland (zone 3b) and throughout the moister subzone (4a) of woodland-steppe. By contrast, in the drier subzone (4b) of woodland-steppe, the dominant herbaceous plants were probably the feather-grasses whose grains also served as staple energy foods. Our ecological models suggest that the people of Abu Hureyra had equal access both to these major dryland resource zones and to the rich resources of the Euphrates Valley.

Key for Vegetation Map c. 11,500 BP

3. Xeric Woodland
    - 3a. Dense Deciduous Oak-Rosaceae Woodland
    - 3b. Oak-Rosaceae Park-Woodland
        - 3bi. Moister
        - 3bii. Drier, with dense stands of wild wheats and ryes
4. Terebinth-Almond Woodland-Steppe
    - 4a. Moister Woodland-Steppe with dense stands of wild wheats and ryes
    - 4b. Drier Woodland-Steppe
7. Riverine Forest
8. Salt-Flats with Scrub

Hureyra were gathered locally and that they therefore provide information about the proximity to the site of the different resource zones. Second, evidence from these remains indicates that by 11,500 BP all zones (high forest, park-woodland, woodland-steppe, and moist steppe) had spread almost one zone farther into drier areas than the equivalent zones of the potential present-day pattern summarized in figure 3.7. Third, despite spring and early-summer soil moisture having peaked at this point, seasonality was getting more extreme; that is, the winter was wetter and cooler than today, and high summer was hotter and drier. This trend peaked between 10,000 and 9,000 BP and favored large-seeded annuals such as wild cereals over most other vegetation (Blumler 1984; Byrne 1987, p. 28). Fourth, even though rapid plant migration during the Late Pleistocene dislocated many preexisting patterns of association, the vegetal spread into this area was already complete by 12,000 BP at least, giving some centuries of relative stability prior to the "turn of the tide" after 11,500 BP. During that time some associations were probably temporarily reestablished that bore some resemblance to plant communities that would occur in the present day in the absence of deforestation, cultivation, and heavy grazing by domestic animals.

In estimating the past proximity of oak-dominated park-woodland at 11,500 BP the existing pollen evidence for peak forest expansion at c. 11,500 BP tells us merely that the woodland-steppe and oak park-woodland zones would have been much closer to Abu Hureyra than in even the potential vegetation of the present day. However, in preparing the map we have had four further clues. Roitel and Willcox's identifications of occasional fragments of oak charcoal throughout Abu Hureyra 1 (appendix 6) indicate that oak trees were growing in areas accessible from the site. However, we have none of the remains of acorns that would be expected if oak trees grew close to the site in reasonable numbers, although this could be because the charred acorns had decayed in the archaeological deposits at Abu Hureyra (Mason 1992).[1] The small numbers of oak charcoal fragments could have come from small scatters of trees rather than full-blown park-woodland. Indeed, they might even have derived from dead branches washed kilometers down the wadis. Either possibility would accord with the absence of acorns. In this sort of terrain, such small scatters of trees routinely grow up to 10–15 km beyond the edge of the oak-dominated park-woodland proper. Assuming that wood came from the nearest available trees in such scatters, I have suggested on the map that the closest areas of full-blown oak-dominated park-woodland grew on hilltops about 15 km south of Abu Hureyra.

A few stones from fruits of dryland hackberry, *Celtis tournefortii*, tell a similar story. By 11,500 BP most hackberry trees were probably reassociated with some form of oak park-woodland, as they would potentially be today, but as with the oaks, there would be occasional trees growing well beyond the main edge of the park-woodland. The ripe, pale-brown fruits are very sweet and a great favorite with children. Consequently, on sites located in areas of potential park-woodland with lots of hackberries (for example, at ninth millennium BP Can Hasan III in Anatolia), the bone-white fruit stones occur in huge numbers because they are heavily silicified and can survive in archaeological deposits without need of charring (Hillman 1972, table 1). The presence of so few hackberry stones in the earliest levels of Abu Hureyra 1 therefore suggests that hackberry trees were *not* abundantly available close to the site, confirming that full-blown park-woodland grew at some distance, perhaps 15 km away, as suggested by the oak remains. The equally sparse remains of the edible seeds of the small-fruited asphodel, another plant of park-woodland, confirm this reconstruction. The most moist uplands within 15 km of the site are some hilltops a little below 400 m in height, and it is therefore roughly along this contour that we have drawn the limits of oak-dominated park-woodland on the map.

Present-day distributions lead me to suggest that the dominant oak species in the xeric woodlands south of Abu Hureyra would have been Boissier's oak, perhaps together with Brandt's oak. Brandt's oak was probably also present just north of the Euphrates. Although it is today limited largely to the Anti-Taurus and Zagros mountains (Browicz 1982, figure 52; M. Zohary 1973, figure 147), according to my model of potential present-day vegetation, it would be a codominant of the park-woodland extending south from the Anti-Taurus to within 70 km of Abu Hureyra. And at 11,500 BP, reasoning similar to that described above would bring it to within a few kilometers of the northern banks of the Euphrates opposite Abu Hureyra.

In contrast to the paucity of remains of trees and other plants of park-woodland, the relative abundance of charred remains of the fruitlets of the great terebinth suggests that these trees were available much closer to the site, and therefore that woodland-steppe grew right down to the Euphrates Valley. This fits with oak-dominated park-woodland extending down to the 400 m contour. By 11,500 BP the terebinths were doubtless also accompanied by at least some of the other trees typical of woodland-steppe such as wild almonds, hawthorn, and wild pear.

Estimating the past proximity of wild cereals is also critical. In view of the relative vegetal stability achieved in this area well before 11,500 BP, the general pattern of association between annual grasses and trees, as distinct from their overall distribution, may not have been very different from what we have proposed for potential vegetation of the present day in chapter 3. The wild wheats and ryes are part of the grassland mosaic among the patches of trees of the drier parts of oak-Rosaceae park-woodland (zone 3bii). They can grow beyond the lower altitudinal limits of the oaks wherever there are deep fine-grained soils not tolerated by the oaks, and they also extend into the adjacent, relatively moist parts of terebinth-almond woodland-steppe (zone 4a) in favorable habitats. Wild barley is much more drought resistant and can penetrate deep into the *drier* subzone of woodland-steppe (zone 4b)—again in favorable habitats.

Close to the limits of their occurrence in woodland-steppe, near the drier, outer edges of zone 4b, the wild wheats and ryes survive only where soils are better watered, as at breaks of slopes, on north-facing inclines, or on slopes fed with a network of small, barely incised wadis. In plotting the possible past distribution of dense stands of these cereals on slopes below and beyond the probable limits of park woodland, I have therefore taken account of not only altitude, but also aspect, breaks in slope, and any concentrations of small, nonincised wadis disgorging onto the slopes concerned.[2]

Aspect, breaks in slope, and wadi concentration all affect water availability and thus cereal distribution. The effect of aspect is today clearly apparent on the Jebel Abdul Aziz, where dry terebinth-almond woodland-steppe survives in quantity on only north-facing slopes, and where wild barley forms dense stands on only the upper parts of the steepest of these slopes (figures 3.9c, 3.10a). The effect of breaks in slope on water availability is most readily apparent out in the steppe during spring when the highest concentrations of color from spring-flowering annuals occur consistently where slopes, especially long slopes, abruptly become less steep (figure 12.2). In 1972 we saw the same consequences 10 km north of Risafe, where local farmers were able to cultivate cotton without any irrigation across an arc 1 km deep and perhaps 4 km wide on gently sloping alluvium, immediately below a clear break in a long, distinctly more angled, slope extending out all the way from the skirts of Jebel Bishri and the El Kum pass. Water draining onto slopes via shallow open channels allows moisture-demanding plants to penetrate far farther downslope. Figure 12.3 shows bleached annual grasses extending into gray *Artemisia*-Chenopodiaceae steppe east of Karapinar in the eastern Konya Basin, thanks to a small, barely incised wadi. Likewise, figure 3.13b shows the luxuriance of annual grasses, poppies, and other annuals in and around the shallow Wadi el-Adhib, in contrast to the relative paucity of these same annuals in the nevertheless still luxuriant steppe immediately outside this same wadi around the encampment of Sheik Zaharan (figure 3.13a).

On the map of figure 12.1 I therefore suggest that, in the dry areas north of Isriya where the soils are free-draining and where the wadis run for only a short distance, the wild wheats and ryes would not have reached even the 350 m contour, but that north of El Kum where there is a network of wadis flowing northward toward Abu Hureyra, these cereals and many other annual grasses would have extended much farther downslope—far below the 350 m contour. And in the still denser and more extensive wadi systems of the Wadi Shetnet es-Salmas and Wadi Hibna, which are fed by an even closer network of small, shallow side wadis throughout most of their length, I have correspondingly suggested that dense stands of wild wheats and ryes would have extended even closer to Abu Hureyra. Indeed, the effects of aspect together with the dense wadi networks and breaks in slope have led me to suggest that the east north-

Figure 12.2 Effect of break in slope in enhancing water availability and allowing a dense swathe of color from red poppies, blue grape hyacinths, deep yellow Hypecoums, and pink, white and pale yellow crucifers in the otherwise gray-green steppe near Isriya, central Syria, April 1983.

Figure 12.3 The effect of water draining onto slopes via shallow open channels in allowing moisture-loving plants to penetrate downslope. Here, bleached annual grasses have extended downslope into the gray absinthe-chenopod steppe on the foothills south of the volcano Hasan Dağ in central Turkey, thanks to water draining down a small, barely incised wadi. August 1977.

east-facing slopes of some of the wadi systems would have supported extensive stands of wild einkorn and probably wild rye, with an admixture of wild emmer in the einkorn stands, to within 2–3 km of Abu Hureyra itself. However, below the major break in slope in the northern Risafe Basin that recently supported fields of cotton without irrigation, I suggest that the far more moist conditions will have led to scrub outcompeting both annual and perennial grasses.

In many locations the two species of einkorn, *Triticum boeoticum* and *T. urartu*, would certainly have grown together in mixed stands. However, our review in 1983 of the records of accessions of both species of einkorn in the genebank at ICARDA near Aleppo led us to suggest that the less familiar of the two einkorn species, *T. urartu*, is able to survive in somewhat drier areas than *T. boeoticum* (Hillman et al. 1993), probably through having a shorter generation length that allows it to flower and seed before the soil dries out (Blumler 1996; Harlan 1972).[3] On this basis, I suggest that the einkorn stands closest to Abu Hureyra were probably dominated by *T. urartu*, albeit with the usual admixture of wild emmer. There was doubtless also some wild emmer in all the einkorn stands, just as we find throughout much of the Fertile Crescent today, together with the inevitable scattered plants of the tall, tussocked *perennial* wild rye, *Secale montanum*, especially toward the uphill edges of stands. Scattered plants of wild barley probably also grew with the wild wheats, but most barley was almost certainly concentrated in separate stands in somewhat drier locations, or in locations subject to natural disturbance, just as it is in most of Syria, Turkey, Iran, and Turkmenistan today. This suggestion is supported by the almost complete absence of wild barley among the remains of the other wild cereals in our charred remains from Abu Hureyra.

The big unknown is the probable past distribution of the wild annual rye, *Secale cereale* subsp. *vavilovii*. This wild cereal has been studied in relatively few locations today, so our knowledge of its ecology is slim. One of its last strongholds is on the lower slopes of Mount Ararat. Here we found it in very dense, remarkably pure stands that extended for many kilometers without a wild wheat anywhere to be found (see figures 3.9b, 12.4). Daniel Zohary has also found what seems to be the same rye growing with wild einkorn and wild emmer on the low volcanic massif of Karacadağ ("wild-goat mountain"), just west of Diyarbakir, not far from the border with Syria. It is therefore quite possible that at Abu Hureyra wild annual rye grew in mixed stands together with the two wild einkorns, accompanied by tussocks of its much taller cousin, wild perennial rye.

Today, areas dominated by either the wild wheats or wild ryes rarely seem to support many plants of the perennial species of feather-grass. Whether the occupants of Abu Hureyra had greater access to the cereals than to the feather-grasses would depend on the exact location of the key boundary of subzones 4a and 4b. Our ecological model suggests that the sinuous boundary of subzones 4a and 4b passed close by Abu Hureyra, and that the occupants therefore had instant access to both resources. This is supported by the plant remains themselves, which reveal that the grains of both wild cereals and feather-grass were heavily used. The merits of the location of Abu Hureyra for exploiting both of these key resources are clear.

Figure 12.4 A typically dense stand of wild annual rye, *Secale cereale* subsp. *vavilovii*, growing on Ararat and being examined by Patricia Anderson. Stands of this sort covered many miles of the flanks of this vast mountain. August 1992.

Treeless steppe is unlikely to have existed anywhere in the Abu Hureyra area shown on figure 12.1; the evidence suggests that by 11,500 BP woodland-steppe grew right up to the Middle Euphrates and extended far to the east of Abu Hureyra. This contrasts markedly with the distribution of primary steppe in the present day (figure 3.7). On the other hand, many plants typical of moist steppe today would potentially also grow as conspicuous components of terebinth-almond woodland-steppe, particularly in the drier parts of this zone, namely, subzone 4b. Such plants would have included several that we have identified in the charred remains, for example, the perennial tussock grasses, *Stipa* spp., cresses such as *Lepidium perfoliatum*, many of the clovers and medicks, several bulb plants such as grape hyacinths, and some of the chenopods, especially the spiny *Noaea spinosa*, the furry annual *Chenolea arabica*, the perennial camphor plant, and even the tall, furry *Krascheninnikovia ceratoides*. Our model is therefore reinforced by the fact that those steppe plants, for example, the large-grained feather-grass, that today grow prolifically in woodland-steppe are also relatively abundant in the charred remains, while those like *Krascheninnikovia ceratoides*, which are today much rarer in woodland-steppe, are also scarce in the charred remains.

The riverine forest would have been just as luxuriant as that potentially sustainable in the present day, albeit with more standing water and a much larger proportion of reed swamps. This is because, with the higher winter and growing-season rainfall at c. 11,500 BP, overbank flooding in the spring would have been more regular and would probably have extended to the limits of the valley-bottom alluvium, which was over 5 km across at Abu Hureyra. The valley would therefore have offered even greater yields of root foods and of seeds of wetland plants such as cattail, water lilies, bulrush, and club-rush.

The middle and lower reaches of all the major channels of the Wadi Shetnet es-Salmas and the Wadi Hibna would have been regularly flushed by strong water flows and so would have been more deeply incised than other parts of the extensive wadi network. Here, close to Abu Hureyra, the flushed wadi bottoms and flats doubtless supported the wild colocynth melon, small, pungently perfumed savory, and some annual saltworts, while the banks were probably dominated by tamarisk scrub, with occasional green-stemmed bushes of the Arab almond, spiny caper bushes, the knee-high oriental mesquite, and equally spiny, pink-flowered shrublets of the restharrows and camel-thorns, *Alhagi* spp.

Where several wadi systems fused in open flats, as in the lower, northern part of the Risafe Basin, we would have found the same tamarisk scrub with the Arab almond, chaste-plant bushes, stands of tall liquorice plants with their erect racemes of mauve flowers and flavorsome roots, and salty hollows with tangles of oriental mesquites, various shrubby seablites, saltworts, the finger-headed Bermuda grass, and prostrate mat-grasses such as the dwarf timothy and dwarf mud-grass. Finally, many raised areas would have supported stands of soft-headed lovegrasses and various members of the millet group. The same complex probably also existed at several points on the edge of the Euphrates Valley itself.

FOOD PLANTS AND FUELS IN THE ABU HUREYRA AREA C. 11,500 BP

Most of the examples that I cite are food plants and wood fuels that we have either identified in the charred remains or that our ecological models suggest would have been conspicuous components of the local vegetation. Other plants were favored by hunter-gatherers of various cultural affiliations who occupied environments with equivalent resources in recent times.

The people of Abu Hureyra in Period 1A could have obtained wood for fuel and construction in abundance locally from the river valley and from the woodland-steppe of the hinterland. The remains of wood charcoal that dominate every flotation sample from the Epipalaeolithic occupation reveal that most of their fuel came from valley-bottom species such as poplar, willow, ash, and tamarisk. Taking wood from these trees would have cleared no more than a very modest area of woodland adjacent to the site because the trees would have regenerated rapidly in the damp conditions of the valley bottom (Hillman, Rowley-Conwy, and Legge 1997). The inhabitants also gathered a little fuel from the terebinths of the woodland steppe and from the small scatters of oaks trees that were probably growing not far from Abu Hureyra.

The people of Abu Hureyra could obtain starch-rich root foods in bulk from cattail, bulrush, club-rush, and water lily, all plants of the valley wetlands that were at their prime between autumn and early spring. Apart from their ready digestibility, such foods also offered the advantage of automatic self-storage wherever they grew, which would have been of great value during the bleak months of winter when these foods carry their highest concentrations of starch (Hillman 1989; Hillman, Madeyska, and Hather 1989). Even more palatable root foods could be obtained, albeit in lower concentrations, from woodland-steppe in the form of the tubers and tap roots of the salsifys and pale cranesbill, and the bulbs of the Tartar lily, tulips, and grape hyacinths. Although these bulbs were usable throughout much of the year, they were at their starch-rich prime between autumn and early spring, albeit frustratingly difficult to locate after the tops had died back and blown away in summer and early autumn—as I have found many times when searching for them myself during those seasons. A type of truffle, the Arabic *kama*, would also have been available in great quantities throughout much of the woodland-steppe during the spring.

An especially favorable feature of the Abu Hureyra location was the huge stands of wild cereals that my model suggests would have dominated much of the dissected terrain to the south, and possibly have extended right up to the site. The proximity of such expanses of cereals so close to Abu Hureyra doubtless meant that the inhabitants rarely used the more distant stands, particularly those growing in open areas of the proximal, drier oak-Rosaceae park-woodland (zone 3bii in figure 12.1). Even on a single hillside close to Abu Hureyra, the cline in ripening times would have allowed the inhabitants to harvest progressively upslope as the stands ripened and thus to maximize yield (Harlan 1967; Hillman and Davies 1990a). Indeed, many farmers today adopt a similar strategy for harvesting *domestic* cereals in hilly terrain. Harvesting the wild cereals around Abu Hureyra would have started about May.

The people of Abu Hureyra successfully utilized a combination of wild annual rye, wild perennial rye, at least one of the wild einkorns—*T. urartu*—and some wild emmer, too (figures 12.5, 12.6). What they did *not* collect was wild barley, probably because it did not grow in dense stands within easy reach of the site.

A range of other wild grain and seed foods, rich in starch, and often in oils and protein, was probably also available in near-limitless supply. Dominating the ground flora for hundreds of kilometers across the drier zones of terebinth-almond woodland-steppe (subzone 4b in figure 12.1) were the perennial tussock-grasses, of which the larger feather-grasses, in particular, would probably have extended right up to the site, except in areas dominated by wild rye and

Figure 12.5 Charred remains of grains of a mixture of wild ryes and wheats from Abu Hureyra 1A (sample E 474).

wheat. They would have provided copious yields of awl-shaped, starch- and protein-rich grains that ripened in mid summer at Abu Hureyra, and progressively later upslope on the drier areas between those inclines supporting wild ryes and wheats. Equivalent species in the New World were apparently used extensively by hunter-gatherers of the Great Basin (Steward 1938).

Grain from several small-seeded grasses would also have been available in some abundance. The wall-barley and its relatives, the *Hordeum murinum* aggregate, grow widely but would have produced their densest stands in damp hollows in the driest areas of woodland-steppe. A second group in this category includes the small-grained wild millets and lovegrasses that would probably have formed occasional dense stands in areas of scrub in the Euphrates Valley but more especially in flushed areas at the wadi mouths, the flow from which probably determined their yield.

Wild peas, one of the potential pulse foods, would have grown best in proximal parts of the park-woodland zone (3b) and may therefore have been out of range for regular large-scale gathering. Certainly, there were none in the remains. One the other hand, lentils and large-seeded vetches were both present in the flotation samples. They also grow in park-woodland but, like the wild cereals, are more conspicuous a lot farther downslope in the moister parts of woodland-steppe (subzone 4a) and even into the drier zone of woodland-steppe (subzone 4b) in favored habitats where they often grow together with wild barley. But although these legumes are frequently found growing among the wild cereals, the two are unlikely to have been harvested together, because the legumes grow only a fraction of the height of the cereals and often ripen ahead of even the barley.

There was also a rich array of smaller seed foods that ripened from mid spring in the drier areas of woodland-steppe, through to mid summer in the glades of the higher zones of oak-Rosaceae park-woodland. Early in the year the inhabitants could have collected the potentially edible seeds of crucifers such as cress and some of its relatives, and followed the sequence of ripening upslope. By late spring they could have gathered a broad spectrum of small-seeded legumes and small-grained grasses, again ripening sequentially across the terrain. Later, in high summer, came the seeds of the lovegrasses and wild relatives of mil-

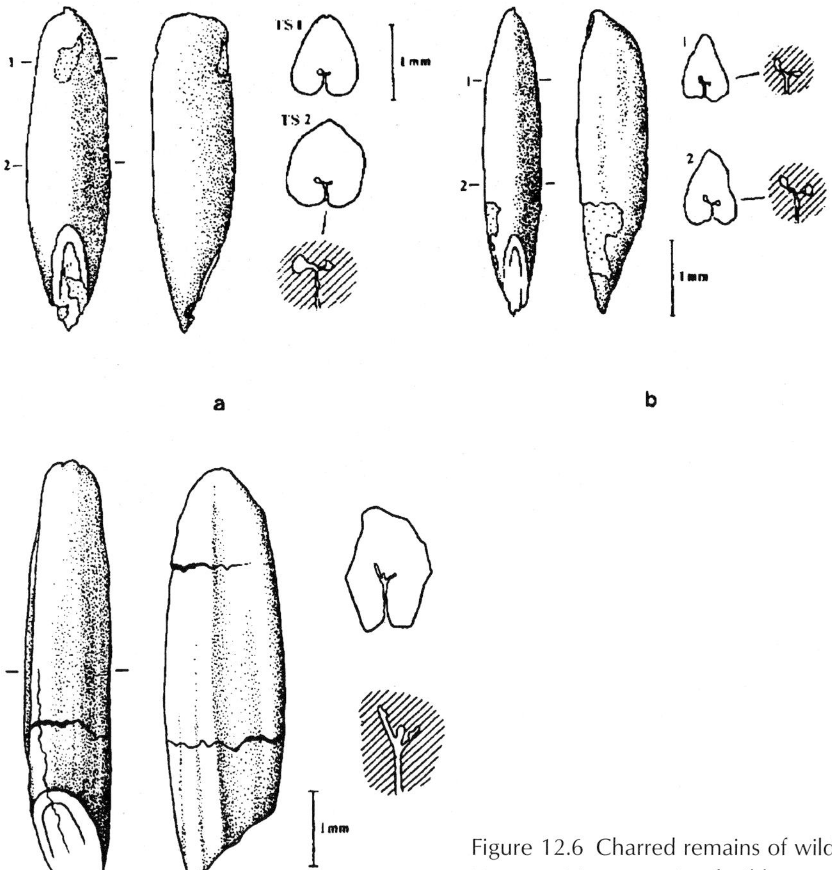

Figure 12.6 Charred remains of wild ryes and wheats from Abu Hureyra 1A. a, a grain of wild annual rye, *Secale cereale* subsp. *vavilovii*, sample E 430; b, a grain of wild perennial rye, *S. montanum*, sample E 470; c, a grain of one of the wild einkorn wheats, either *Triticum urartu* or *T. monococcum* subsp. *boeoticum*, sample E 449.

lets growing mainly on flushed areas of wadi mouths, and at the end of the summer, the minute, but nevertheless gatherable, grains of the prostrate mudgrass and the dwarf timothys that dominated the muddy fringes of shrinking backswamps and are present in the remains. In these same habitats during late summer the people of Abu Hureyra would have collected copious quantities of small nutlets from the low, dense, pink-tinged, glaucous-green carpets of Euphrates knotgrass. Charred remains of these nutlets are a conspicuous component of most of our flotation samples.

In late August and September nutlets of club-rush would also have been ready to harvest from the extensive stands which probably dominated many of the shallower areas of backswamps (figure 3.15). At about the same time, they could also have harvested the palatable, oil-rich seeds of the annual chenopod *Chenolea arabica* that is likely to have been available in many of the drier areas of the woodland-steppe, followed from November onward by equally oily seeds of *Krascheninnikovia ceratoides* and a progression of other perennial chenopods. Other seed foods available late in the year included those of the wild colocynth melon, which would have grown in flushed wadi bottoms close to the Euphrates Valley, where it may still be found today. Once the melons dry out, these rattling parcels of edible pips are bowled across the surface by the wind and flushed down to the wadi mouths, from where they could have been gathered well into the winter. All of these plants are present in the charred remains.

Of the local nut foods, the most obvious would have been the wild almonds of woodland-steppe. The species concerned are a wild, small-leaved, drought-resistant relative of the domestic almond, *Amygdalus communis* subsp. *microphylla*, which can grow as a shrub or small tree, and three shrub almonds: the sessile-leaved *A. trichamygdalus*, the furry-leaved oriental almond, *A. orientalis*, and the broom-like *A. scoparia*.[4] To these we can add the green-stemmed Arabian almond, which would have grown on low wadi banks. Kernels of most races of these almonds, particularly the oriental almond, could not have been eaten without detoxification to remove the cyanogenic glucocides. But this done, the oil-rich kernels from such an extensive and energy-rich food resource could have made a significant contribution to caloric needs.

Acorns could have offered even greater potential as a starch staple for the people of Abu Hureyra. Both Boissier's oak and Brandt's oak were probably codominants in the park-woodland that extended to within perhaps 15 km of the site, and ethnographic parallels suggest that the people of Abu Hureyra could have used them as one of their key caloric staples, although charred remains of acorns are currently lacking. That some of their foraging during Period 1A did, indeed, extend as far as the oak-dominated park-woodland is evidenced by the charred remains of edible seeds of the small-capsuled asphodel. They might also have gathered the edible root tubers of this plant since the tubers from a single large asphodel are certainly enough for an ample meal.[5]

Soft fruits would have been available from every vegetal zone. Wild grapes would have abounded in the liana-trellised canopy of the riverine forest and in the scrub at the edge of the valley. Although Roitel and Willcox have identified remains of vine wood, we have found no charred pips in the Abu Hureyra 1 plant remains; presumably either they were consumed off-site or else the pips were ingested with the rest of the fruit. At the valley edge and on the low cliffs, there would also have been wolf-berries, wild figs, and the sweet fruits of wild capers, precisely as we have described for the potential vegetation of the present-day. In addition, the terebinth-almond woodland-steppe would have offered the apple-flavored yellow hawthorn, the Syrian pear, the unripe fruits of wild almonds, and the sweet, red, mulberry-like fruits of the prostrate chenopod of rocky areas, *Chenopodium foliosum*. Closer to the oak-Rosaceae park-woodland the people of the village would also have found a rather sour wild plum, *Prunus ursina*; hackberries; a tasty red hawthorn, *Crataegus azarolus*, that has since spawned a domestic derivative; amelanchiers; mahaleb cherries; and sweet-resinous juniper berries, these in addition to the same fruits also found in the woodland-steppe. We may also include the dry, sweet, slightly liquorice-flavored fruits of the oriental mesquite, which are perfectly palatable when fresh, and which would have been available in scrub formations in the lower reaches of wadi systems and in some parts of the main valley.[6]

The range of green, leafy foods, together with leafy shoots and flower buds available in the area from all zones (Ertug-Yaras 1996; Guest 1933), especially in the spring, is much too diverse to itemize here.

Overall, the areas around Abu Hureyra at the time of its initial settlement c. 11,500 BP offered a remarkable diversity and abundance of plant foods. The potential caloric staples so important for survival would have been particularly well represented. Furthermore, with the exception of acorns, most of the key plant foods could have been gathered within a relatively short distance of the site. Indeed, two classes of these plants, the wild ryes and wheats of subzone

4a and the feather-grasses of subzone 4b, both probably extended virtually to the site, as did stands of the two food plants of the river valley that also seem to have served as staples, namely, club-rush and knotgrass.

PROBLEMS OF IDENTIFYING THE REMAINS OF SEEDS AND FRUITS

The systems of identification we developed for—and applied to—the charred seeds and fruits[7] at Abu Hureyra broke new ground and set new standards. This part of the Abu Hureyra project entailed assembling extensive reference collections of modern seeds and fruits to ensure that we could accurately identify all the critical types present in the ancient remains.

One of the most pervasive problems besetting archaeobotanical data is unreliable identifications, particularly in taxonomically critical groups such as the cereals where it is often necessary to distinguish between taxa that are not even biological species and therefore lack fertility barriers to restrict complications arising from unhindered introgression. Under these circumstances, poor understanding of the nature of variation in living, evolving populations, and the tendency to treat even infraspecific taxa as if they were watertight cubicles, has led to naive and erroneous identifications. These problems are compounded when confronting often poorly preserved charred remains from early sites such as Abu Hureyra. That is because detecting the beginnings of agriculture is often contingent on distinguishing between wild and domestic forms of the same species. In the Abu Hureyra project we have sought not only to apply biotaxonomically rigorous principles in all our identifications, but also to explore the potential of a wide range of novel anatomical, histological, and chemical criteria (Hillman et al. 1993).

Identifying the remains of cereals from Abu Hureyra presented me with enormous problems. First, Southwest Asia is the principal center of diversity, or gene center, of the wheats, ryes, and barleys, so the range of forms we had to consider was vast (Vavilov 1951; Zeven and Zhukovsky 1975). Second, it quickly became apparent that the Epipalaeolithic remains were dominated by a diverse array of wild forms that were taxonomically understudied, and extremely difficult to distinguish from each other and from their early domestic derivatives. Archaeologically, the most critical of these distinctions at Abu Hureyra was that between wild-type cereals on the one hand and their domestic derivatives on the other, particularly the very primitive domesticates that are likely to have dominated early crops.

Published studies were of little assistance as the standard of identification of charred remains of cereals throughout most of archaeobotany is, at best, very poor, not only as a result of the inadequate understanding of the nature of variation in dynamic populations noted above, but also because reference collections of modern specimens include far too narrow a range of forms of each species. These collections have been assembled from specimens obtained from botanic gardens that are all too often misidentified and/or heavily introgressed. This, in turn, has led to the long-standing use of inappropriate identification criteria, even of gross morphological features.

I sought to address this by devoting some years to assembling a very extensive reference collection of archaic cereals, as well as fruits and seeds of other species, from my own field research in many areas of Southwest Asia. I then reevaluated the full spectrum of criteria available for identifying the wheats and ryes, as well as other plants. The gross morphological criteria used in identifying the charred cereal remains from Abu Hureyra are all products of these cumulative reevaluations of specimens in our reference collections, including accessions of groups such as the wild einkorns and ryes which I collected specifically for the Abu Hureyra project.

In attempting to distinguish between wild and domestic forms, we investigated the use of bran histology—initially in collaboration with Üdelgard Körber-Grohne (1981), and later with Susan Colledge (1988); chemical markers studied via pyrolysis mass spectrometry; features of grain internal anatomy; and further chemical markers using both infrared spectrometry (IR) and gas chromatography mass spectrometry (GCMS) (McLaren, Evans, and Hillman 1991).

Our attempts to distinguish wild and cultivated forms of the various pulses from Abu Hureyra confronted us with problems similar to those outlined for the cereals. Ann Butler has explored a range of micromorphological criteria of the testa observable by a scanning electron microscope (SEM), and certain chemical criteria as well (Butler 1989, 1991; Hillman et al. 1993). Small-seeded legumes of the clover-medick-fenugreek tribe also posed formidable problems of identification, a particular frustration as their remains could potentially serve as invaluable ecological indicators.

Small-grained grasses are also a prominent feature of the Abu Hureyra remains, especially from the Epipalaeolithic, and, if identified to generic or species level, could again serve as potentially sensitive ecological indicators. However, these, too, presented us with serious problems of identification, not least because of the vast numbers of grass species native to Southwest Asia, and the absence of studies of any criteria for identifying their charred grains. Michelle Cave (1989) has recently explored the potential of chemical markers using Fourier transform infrared spectroscopy (FTIR) with the primary goal of distinguishing the grass grains from Abu Hureyra—at least at the level of tribe and genus, particularly the specimens where preservation is too poor to allow identification from morphology. Mark Nesbitt (1997) has launched a major project exploring the use of grain morphology and micromorphology to the same end. Both projects offer the prospect of identifying more precisely the many problematic remains of grass grains from both the Epipalaeolithic and Neolithic villages.

The Abu Hureyra 1 levels also produced charred remains of huge numbers of other seed types. However, most of them were too poorly preserved to allow identification using the conventional characteristics of seed shape and surface patterning. The surface layers were generally lost and most specimens survived only as fragments. The few intact grains had lost all semblance of their original shape. Clearly, we needed an entirely different approach to their identification.

A number of early systematists had made heavy use of the internal anatomy of fruiting structures and seeds (Gaertner 1788–1805; Le Maout and Descaine 1873; Martin 1946). However, their studies of fruits were insufficiently comprehensive and too little concerned with evolutionary webs to provide an effective predictive framework for identification of complete unknowns to the level of families, at which level one can turn to seed reference collections for identification to genus and species. I therefore developed a system of identification of Southwest Asian and European fruiting structures based on internal anatomy that allowed identification to the level of family. This I used to identify the many charred fragments of fruits from Abu Hureyra 1, listed in figure 12.7.

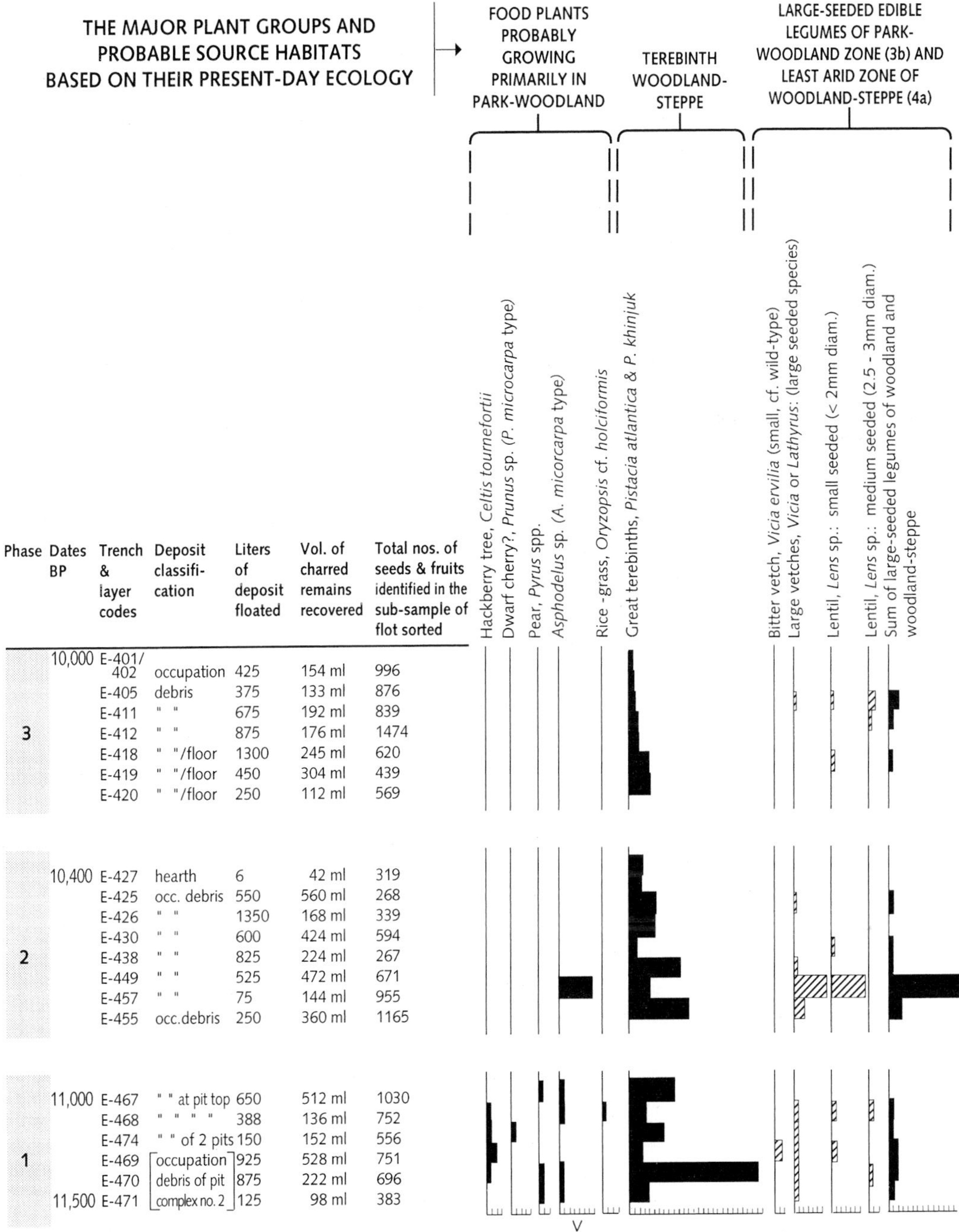

Phase	Dates BP	Trench & layer codes	Deposit classification	Liters of deposit floated	Vol. of charred remains recovered	Total nos. of seeds & fruits identified in the sub-sample of flot sorted
3	10,000	E-401/402	occupation	425	154 ml	996
		E-405	debris	375	133 ml	876
		E-411	" "	675	192 ml	839
		E-412	" "	875	176 ml	1474
		E-418	" "/floor	1300	245 ml	620
		E-419	" "/floor	450	304 ml	439
		E-420	" "/floor	250	112 ml	569
2	10,400	E-427	hearth	6	42 ml	319
		E-425	occ. debris	550	560 ml	268
		E-426	" "	1350	168 ml	339
		E-430	" "	600	424 ml	594
		E-438	" "	825	224 ml	267
		E-449	" "	525	472 ml	671
		E-457	" "	75	144 ml	955
		E-455	occ.debris	250	360 ml	1165
1	11,000	E-467	" " at pit top	650	512 ml	1030
		E-468	" " " "	388	136 ml	752
		E-474	" " of 2 pits	150	152 ml	556
		E-469	occupation	925	528 ml	751
		E-470	debris of pit	875	222 ml	696
	11,500	E-471	complex no. 2	125	98 ml	383

0 15 30 45 60 75 90 Numbers of charred seeds or fruits per 200 liters of deposit.

■ = edible (or potentially edible) seeds and fruits.
▨ = edible seeds or fruits whose histogram has also contributed to a solid-shaded summary histogram for the group as a whole.
∗ = seed types that are edible but which are unlikely to have been routinely gathered as food in Abu Hureyra 1, phases 2 and 3.
□ = seeds or fruits which are generally difficult to detoxify or make palatable for bulk consumption and which were possibly used medicinally, as hallucinogens, as dyes, for thatching, or for bedding.
V = species whose vegetative parts (roots or bulbs, leaves, shoots, flower buds, or immature green fruits) were probably gathered as food.

Figure 12.7 Numbers of seeds and fruits identified in flotation samples from Abu Hureyra 1A. Each bar indicates the numbers of specimens identified per 200 liters of deposit. I have excluded 42 seed types that were present as only single occurrences. Most of the specimens were preserved as a result of charring.

(*continued*)

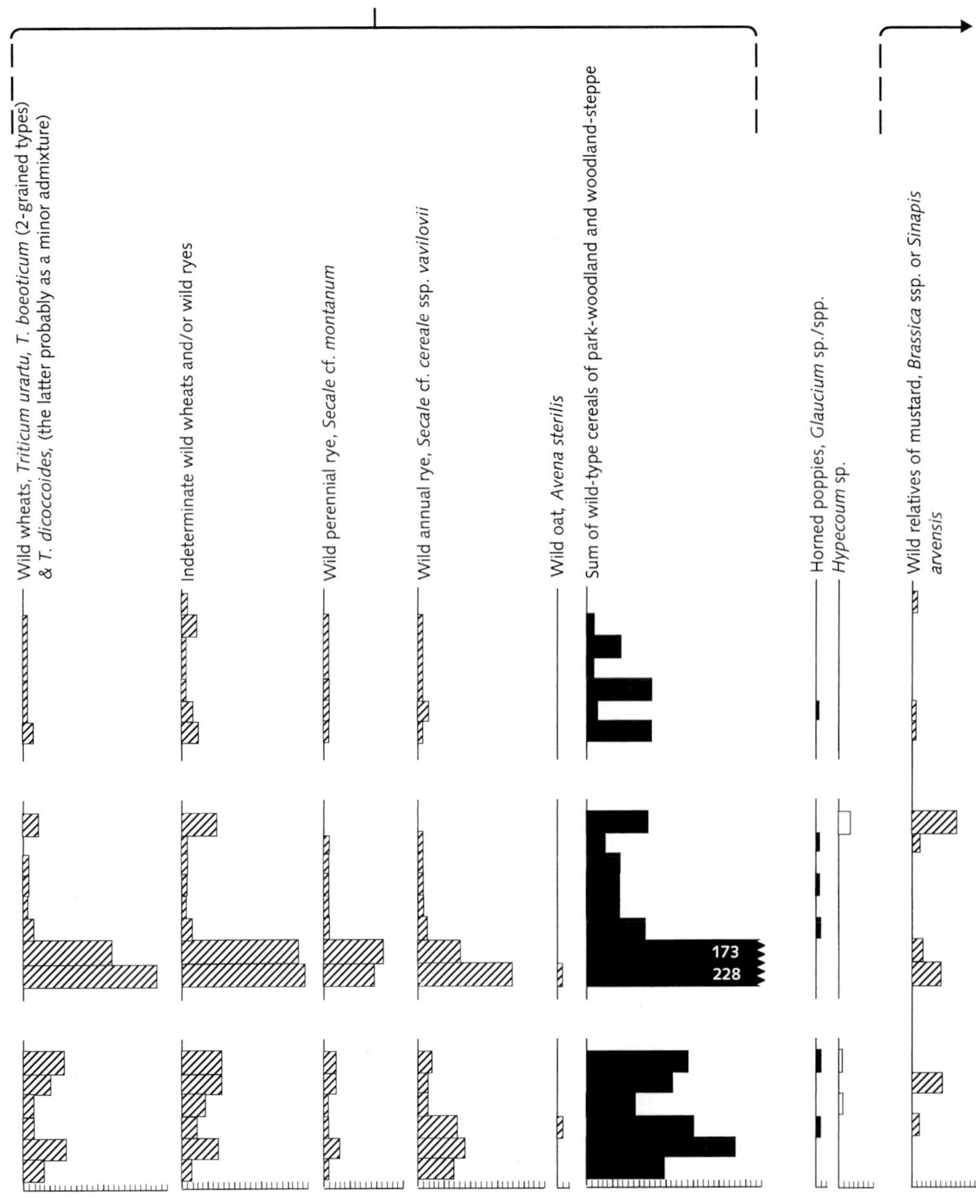

Figure 12.7 (*continued*)

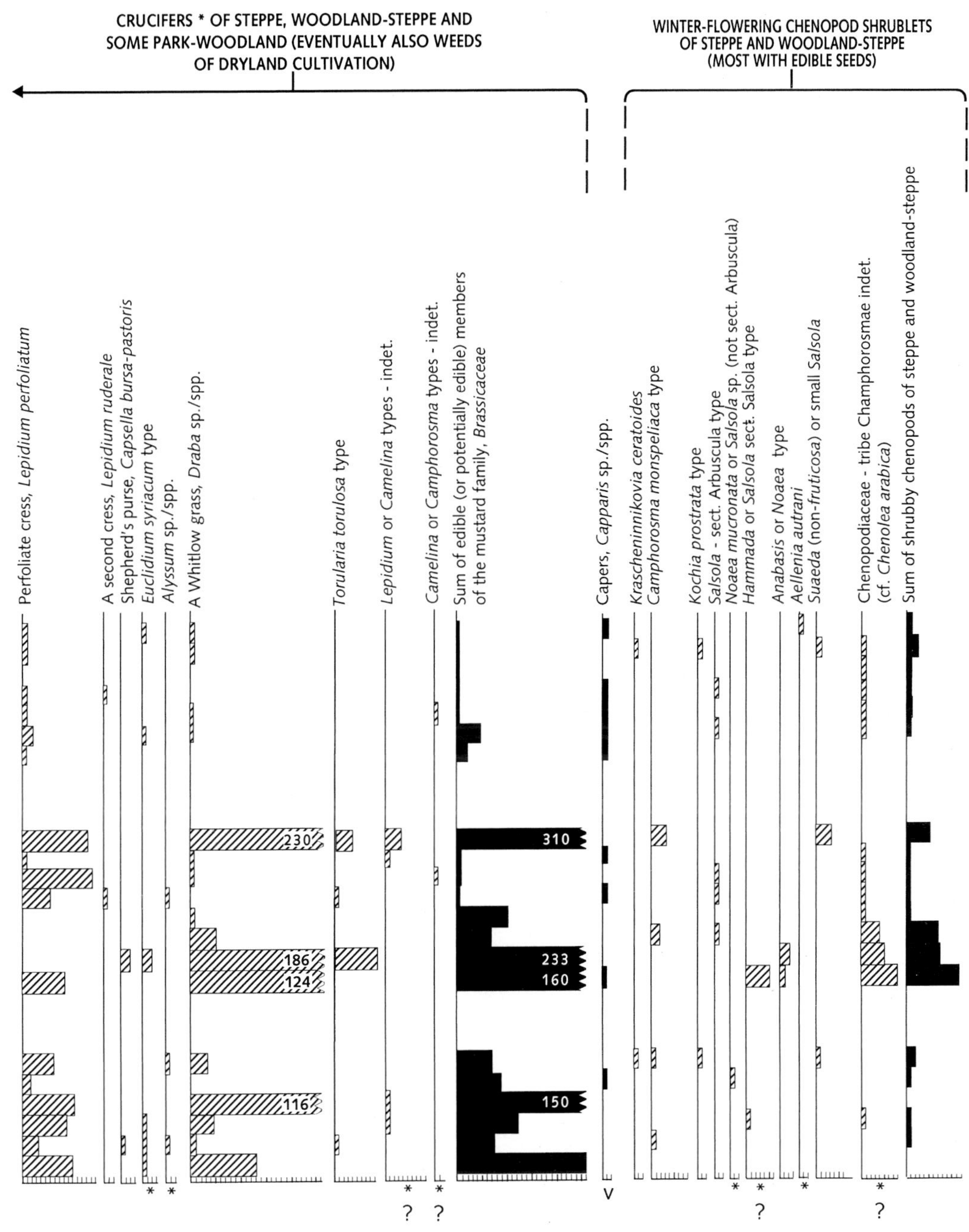

* "Crucifers" are members of the mustard famliy Brassicaceae (formerly Cruciferae)

(*continued*)

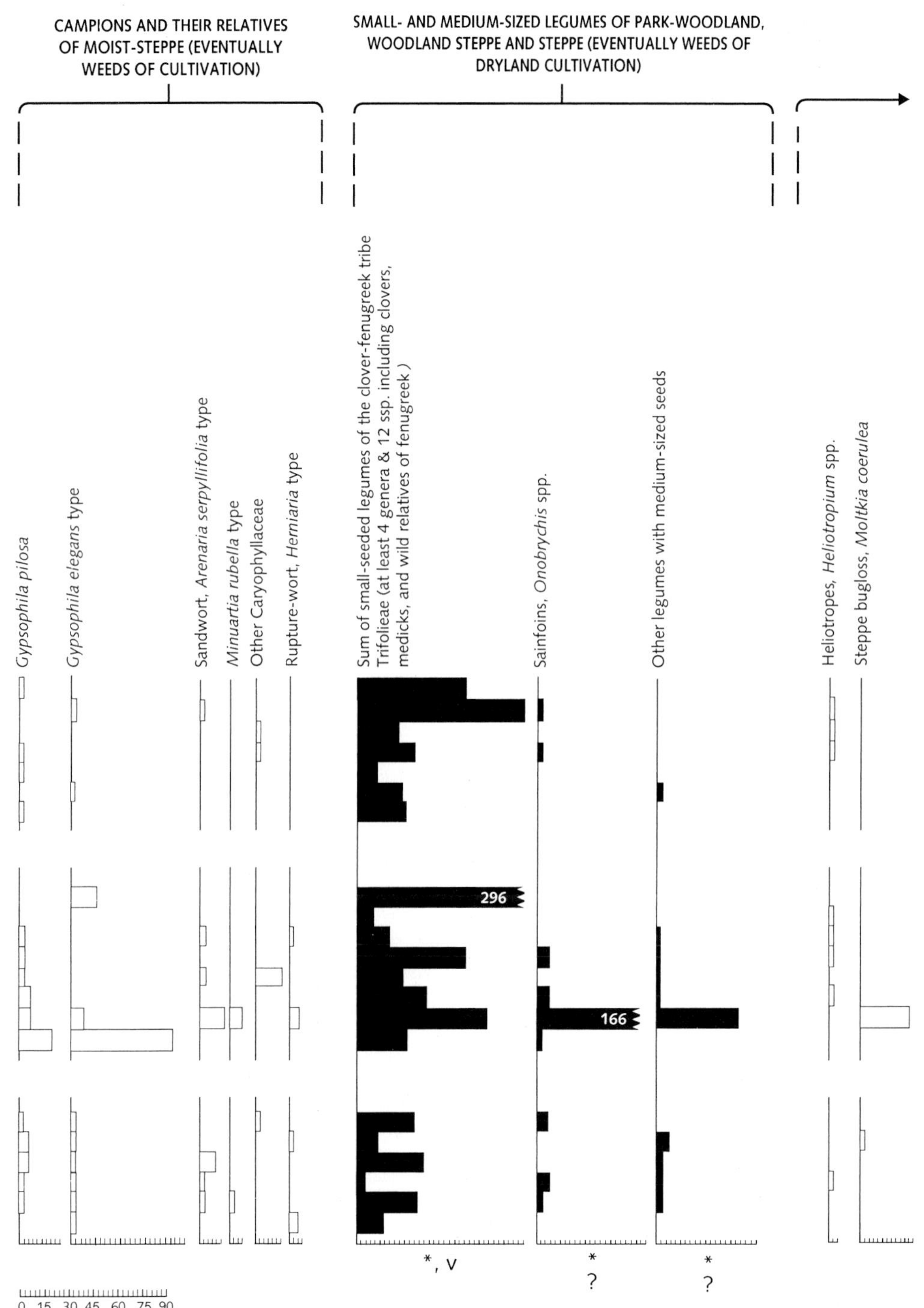

Figure 12.7 *(continued)*

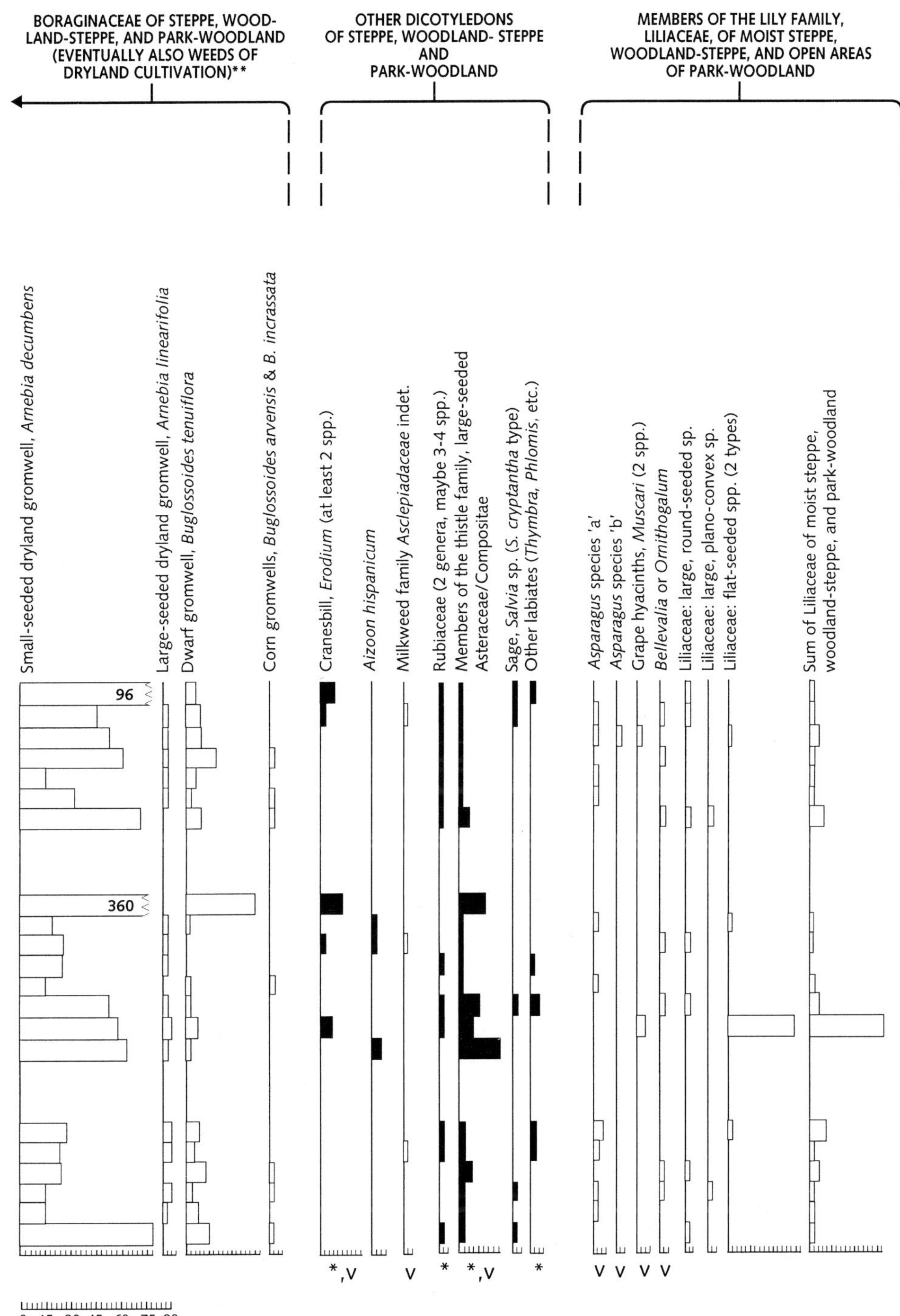

** The family Boraginaceae includes borage, bugloss and the gromwells. Most members are represented by silicified nutlets which survive without charring and are relatively over-represented.

(*continued*)

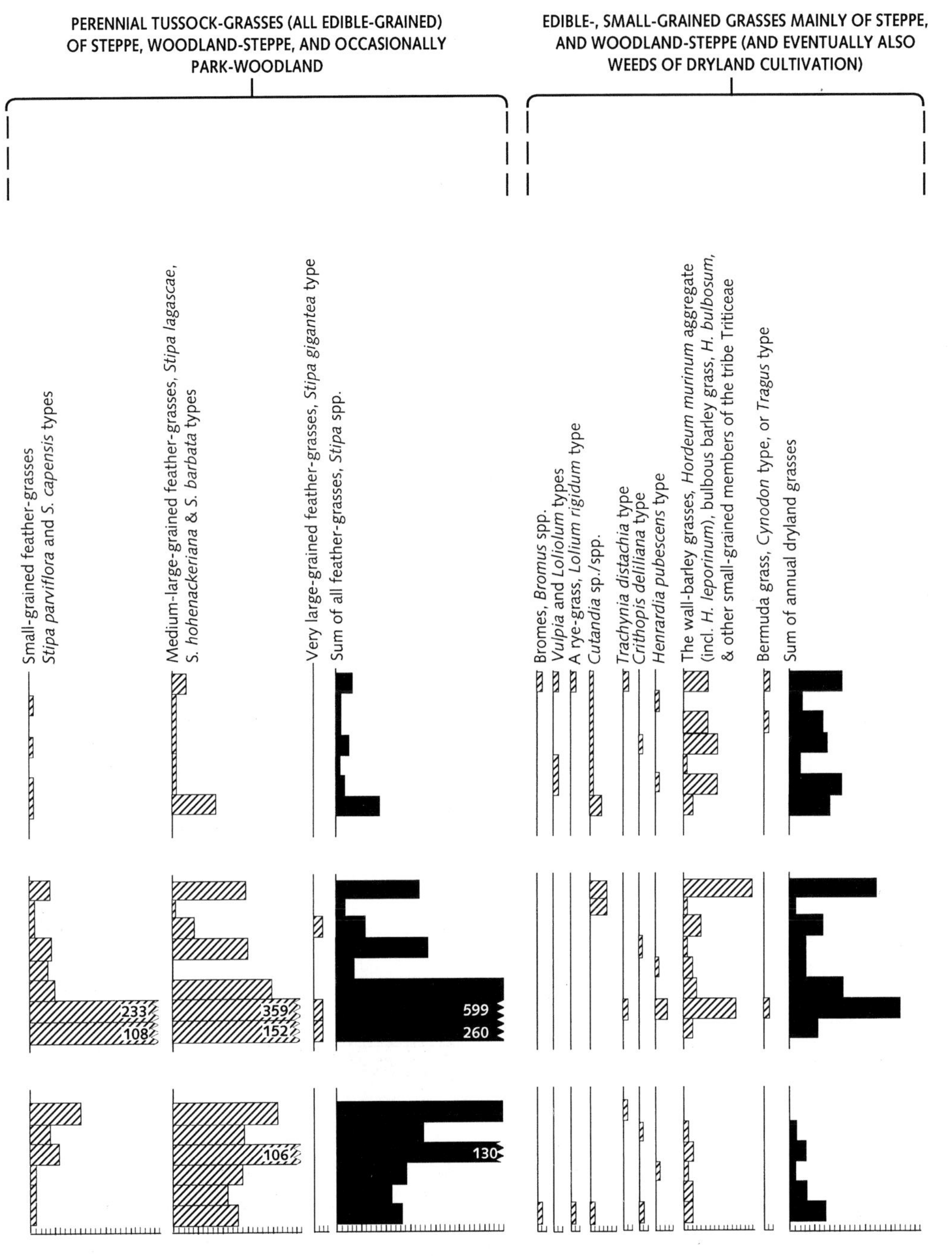

Figure 12.7 (*continued*)

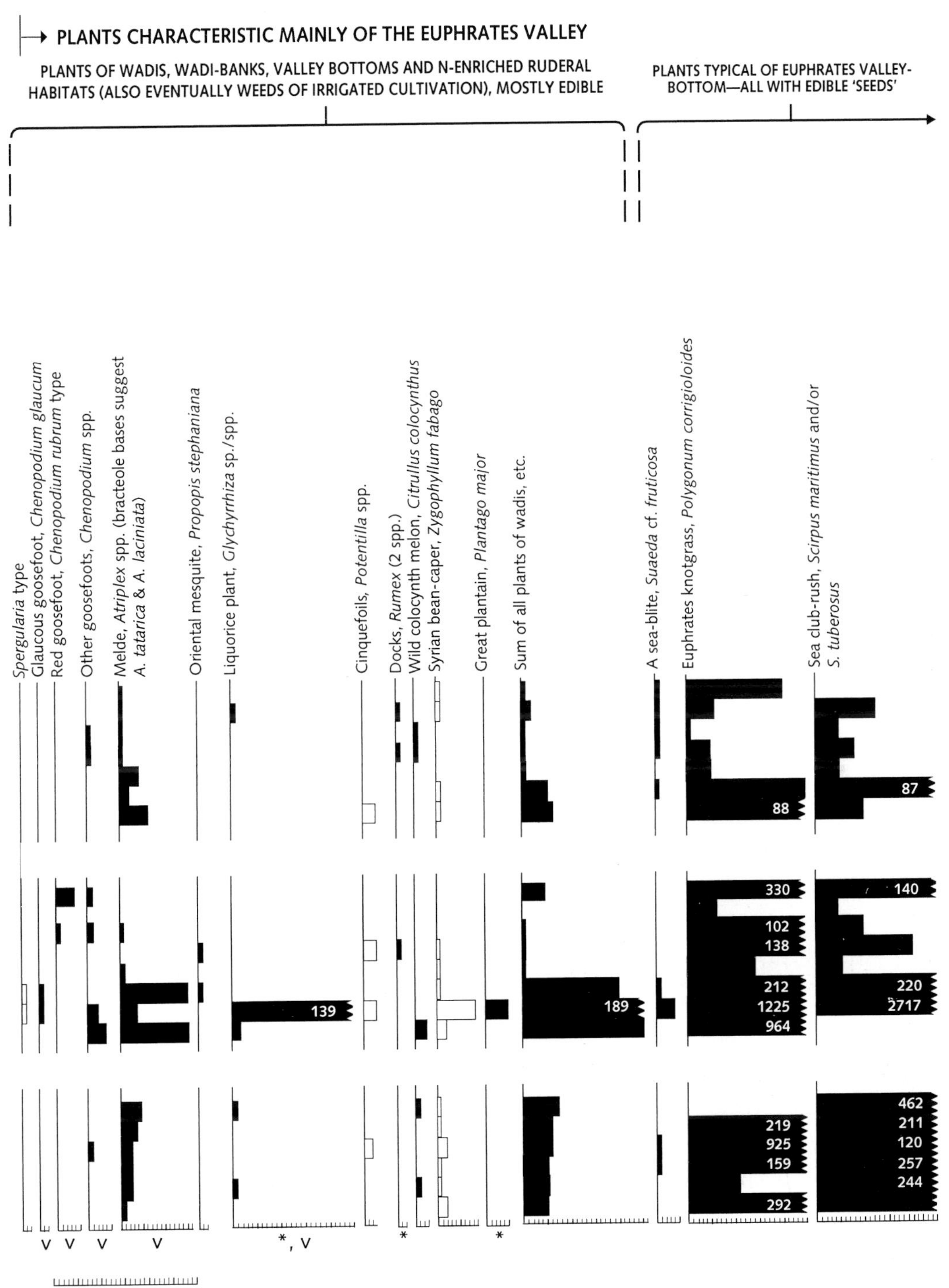

PLANTS CHARACTERISTIC MAINLY OF THE EUPHRATES VALLEY
PLANTS OF WADIS, WADI-BANKS, VALLEY BOTTOMS AND N-ENRICHED RUDERAL HABITATS (ALSO EVENTUALLY WEEDS OF IRRIGATED CULTIVATION), MOSTLY EDIBLE
PLANTS TYPICAL OF EUPHRATES VALLEY-BOTTOM—ALL WITH EDIBLE 'SEEDS'
Spergularia type
Glaucous goosefoot, Chenopodium glaucum
Red goosefoot, Chenopodium rubrum type
Other goosefoots, Chenopodium spp.
Melde, Atriplex spp. (bracteole bases suggest A. tatarica & A. laciniata)
Oriental mesquite, Propopis stephaniana
Liquorice plant, Glychyrrhiza sp./spp.
Cinquefoils, Potentilla spp.
Docks, Rumex (2 spp.)
Wild colocynth melon, Citrullus colocynthus
Syrian bean-caper, Zygophyllum fabago
Great plantain, Plantago major
Sum of all plants of wadis, etc.
A sea-blite, Suaeda cf. fruticosa
Euphrates knotgrass, Polygonum corrigioloides
Sea club-rush, Scirpus maritimus and/or S. tuberosus
88
87
330
140
102
138
139
189
212
1225
964
220
2717
219
925
159
292
462
211
120
257
244
V
V
V
V
*, V
*
*
0 15 30 45 60 75 90

(*continued*)

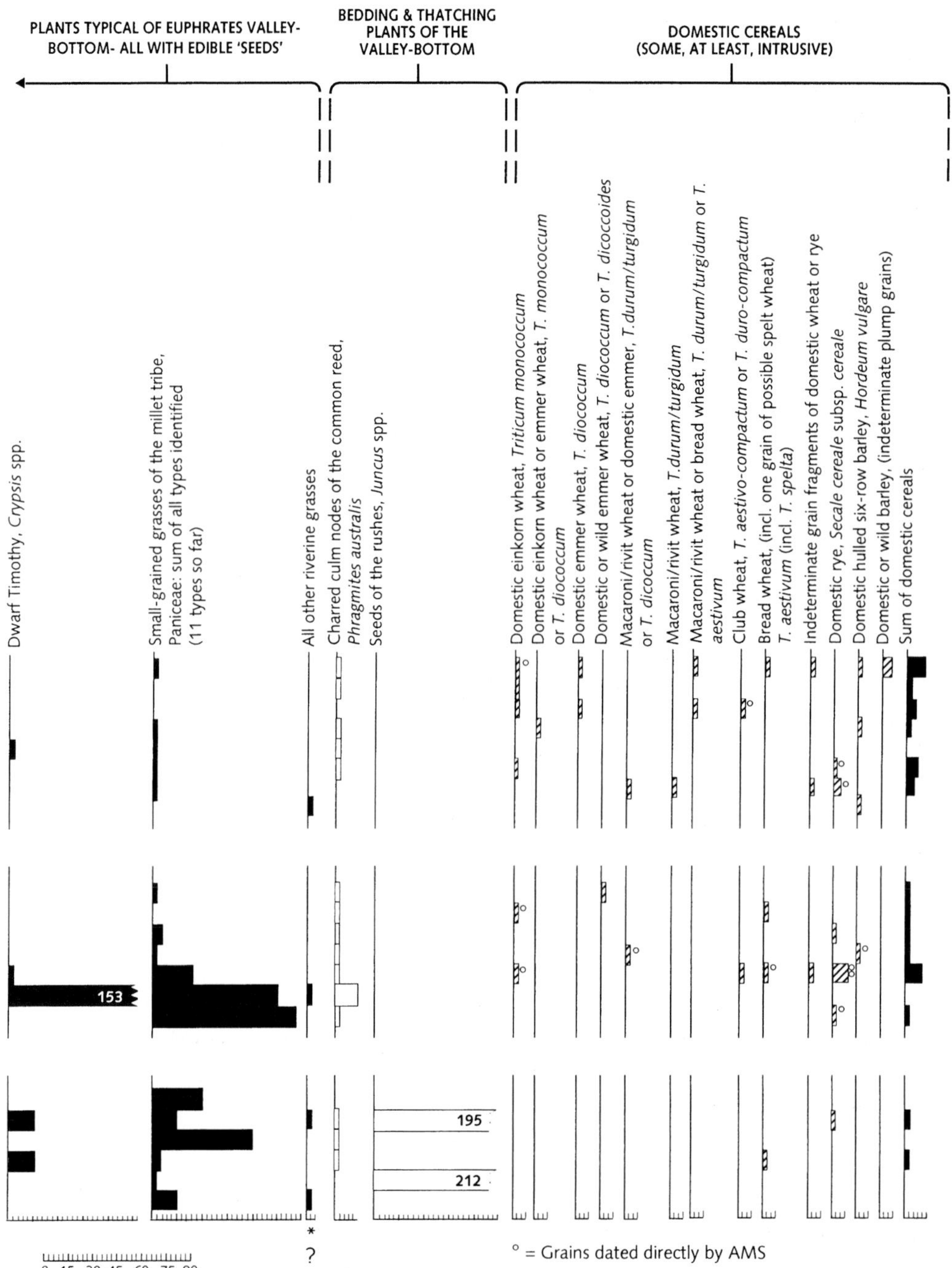

Figure 12.7 (*continued*)

Studies of seed internal anatomy such as that of Martin (1946) reveal its potential to facilitate identification to the level of natural order and family. But, although Martin's is a superb study of arrangements of embryo and endosperm, it omits any details of the relationship of these structures to overlying tissues such as those of the testa, pericarp, and hypanthium. I therefore assembled details of these anatomical relationships from dissections of modern seeds for all the taxa that had to be considered in the Abu Hureyra study, and it is these that have provided the basis for identifications of most of the fragmentary remains of seeds from Abu Hureyra 1 levels.

The results of all these identifications of the Epipalaeolithic remains[8] are presented in figure 12.7. However, even with the novel systems mentioned above, there were large numbers of specimens surviving only as poorly preserved fragments that could not even be identified to family. These do not appear in the figure.

NUTRITIONAL QUALITIES OF MAJOR WILD FOOD PLANTS AND HOW THEY WERE HARVESTED, PROCESSED, AND PREPARED

The choice of location for the Abu Hureyra village was influenced not only by the availability of water but also by the fact that two major resource zones met at this point, namely, riverine forest, and woodland-steppe, and that a third zone, the park-woodland, was not far away. Furthermore, within the woodland-steppe zone, Abu Hureyra was probably also the meeting point between two subzones: 4a with its wild ryes and wheats, and 4b with its billowing sea of feather-grasses. Both these subzones would have supported a myriad of other plant and animal food resources.

We next consider the role in subsistence and diet of a few of the major plant foods, explore the ways in which they might have been harvested and processed, and suggest the sort of technology and tools that the inhabitants of Abu Hureyra 1 are likely to have employed. For each of the examples there is a broad range of ethnographic records of their use as food by hunter-gatherers in recent times, as with all the other plants that we suggest contributed to the Abu Hureyra diet.[9]

The Wild Cereals

The vast populations of wild ryes and wheats that probably extended right up to the site from the south would have provided a plentiful supply of starch and protein, some essential fatty acids, the B vitamins, and vitamin E. They were also very palatable, were easily gathered, required no detoxification, and the grains or, better still, the intact spikelets were eminently storable.

Harris (1984) has noted that the methods used by traditional farmers to process their domestic cereals appear to have been inherited in relatively unaltered form from those used by hunter-gatherers to process their wild grasses. Clues to the methods used to process the wild wheats and ryes at Abu Hureyra can therefore be gleaned from the traditional processing of the domestic derivatives of these wild wheats and ryes (Hillman 1984a, 1984b).

All the wild cereals could have been harvested as soon as an economically worthwhile proportion of the ears had started to ripen (figure 12.8). If the people of Abu Hureyra had little use for wild cereal straw, then the most efficient way of harvesting the grain would have been by beating rather than by uprooting

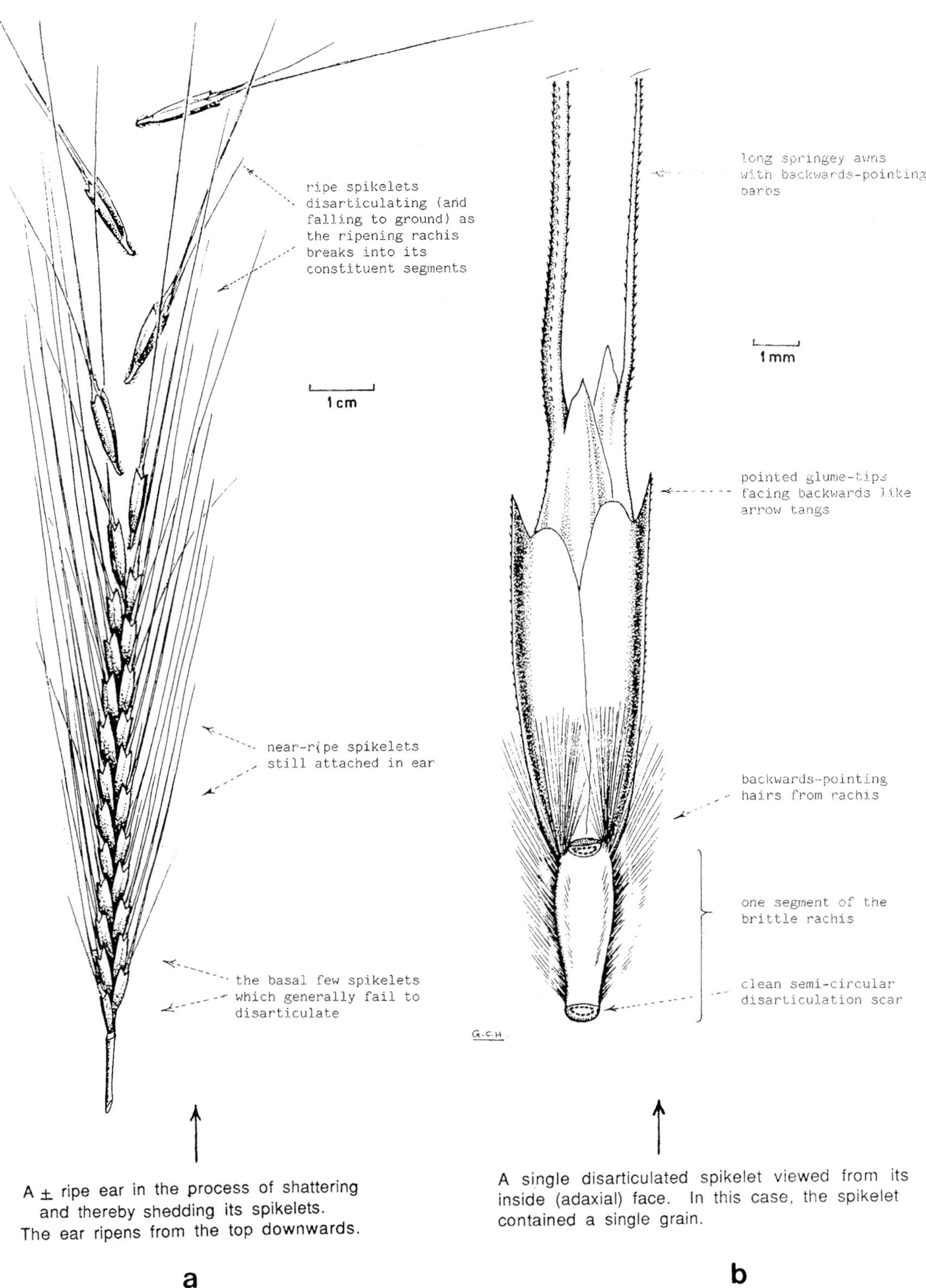

Figure 12.8 Wild einkorn wheat, *Triticum monococcum* subsp. *boeoticum*. a, an ear in the process of shattering and shedding its arrow-like spikelets, which then bury themselves in cracks in the ground; b, a single spikelet containing one (or sometimes two) grains; the ear shatters when the rachis (the central axis of the ear) disarticulates, that is, breaks into a series of segments (each with a spikelet attached) by abscissing at a series of special nodes.

or by reaping with a sickle. Although any one round of beating leaves behind all those ears, and parts of ears, that have yet to fully ripen and disarticulate and thus gives a relatively poor return *per unit area*, our experiments have revealed that it gives a better return *per unit of time* (Hillman and Davies 1990a, 1992). Given extensive wild resources, it is more important to maximize yield per unit of time or energy expended, so beating would probably have been the preferred method. Beating would also have avoided the preliminary stages of processing required when cereals are harvested by uprooting or reaping (figure 12.9).

If two or more of the five different cereals, that is, the two ryes, the two einkorns, and emmer, grew in mixed stands, the advantages of harvesting by beating would have been increased. This is because the ears of different species mature at different rates, so reaping or uprooting would have harvested a mass of unripe ears with the ripe ones, and this would have slowed subsequent stages of processing. Beating, by contrast, would have harvested only the ripe spikelets. However, if the cereal straw was a valued secondary product, the plants might have harvested by uprooting, even though this would have involved much more effort.

Because they are unlikely to have harvested the wild cereals with sickles, it might be expected that sickle blades would be rare on the site. However, such a conclusion overlooks the fact that, in most nonagrarian societies of recent times, the principal role of sickles was the cutting of reeds and rushes, neither of which can be gathered without some sort of blade. The relative abundance of sickle blades at Abu Hureyra is therefore unlikely to bear any relationship to cereal harvesting—until they started to cultivate. From that point, even with morphologically wild-type cereals, it would have made good sense to start harvesting by sickle reaping or by uprooting (Hillman and Davies 1990a, pp. 195–198; 1992, pp. 142–144).

If the inhabitants had harvested the wild cereals by uprooting or sickle reaping, then the sheaves or heaps of loose plants would first have been dried out, whereupon unripe ears would have started to disarticulate, even if they were so unripe that they lacked usable grain. The harvesters would then have "lashed" the heads of the sheaves against the ground to shake out all the remaining spikelets. Winnowing was probably unnecessary unless there were large quantities of straw still mixed with the spikelets. If the cereals had been harvested by beating, then lashing and winnowing would clearly have been unnecessary.

Freeing the grains from the enveloping husks of the spikelets would have necessitated dehusking with either a pestle and mortar made of stone or wood, or with a saddle quern, although my experiments with the latter reveal it to be very inefficient in this role. We have found that the grain of the ryes, especially wild annual rye, was quickly and easily freed from the spikelets with a pestle and mortar as long as the ears were bone dry. However, the wild wheats have much tougher, tighter husks, and it was almost impossible to fragment them with a pestle and mortar to release the grain unless they were first parched to render the woody husks more brittle.[10] The simplest way of doing this was to burn the sheaves, rather as farmers in Western Asia do today in producing the Turkish *firig* and the Arabic *frikké* (Hillman 1984b, 1985), and as the Bagundji of Australia do in processing their wild millets (Allen 1974). We found that the burning usefully eliminated the straw and awns, and also rendered the husks brittle enough to be more easily fragmented in the wooden pestle and mortar.[11] Pounding in the pestle and mortar then quickly freed the grain from the

Figure 12.9 Gathering and processing wild ryes and wheats in Period 1A when such resources abounded. a, harvesting wild cereal growing in the moister zone of terebinth-almond woodland-steppe (sub-zone 4a) by beating the disarticulating spikelets into a basket; b, singeing a heap of harvested spikelets to eliminate the awns and make the glumes brittle (the latter is essential with wild einkorn but much less important with rye). The spikelets adhere in tangled masses through the interlocking of their barbed awns, but as soon as the awns start to ignite the smoking mass must quickly be dropped into the open basket before it disintegrates; c, pounding the spikelets to free the grain from the husks with a wooden mortar and mallets; d, winnowing out fragments of light chaff freed by pounding using a tail wind; e, sifting out heavy bits of chaff with a sieve designed to retain the grain but eliminate small contaminants; f, grinding the grain using a quern of the type found in the pit dwellings of Period 1A (the last operation is clearly unnecessary for preparing groats or whole-grain products such as porridge). (By Ivan Crowe).

spikelet chaff. In wild rye the chaff is very light and can easily be eliminated by simple winnowing. In the wild wheats, by contrast, much of the chaff is heavy and can be separated from the grain only by sieving or by agitating the mixture on a wooden tray or dish.[12]

The clean grain could then be prepared as food: as roasted whole grain, boiled whole grain, boiled crushed grain eaten as a porridge, boiled cracked grain eaten as the Turkish bulgur or Arabic burghul, or as ground grain eaten as a paste, as a pancake perhaps prepared as the Alyawara of Australia cook a damper, or as some sort of bread. None of these cereal products will, of themselves, induce tooth wear. However, whole-grain or cracked-grain products generally contain grain-sized stones, and these regularly cause coarse pitting and tooth fracture. Ground grain products, although containing far fewer stones, do contain quantities of abrasive rock powder that greatly accelerates tooth wear.

The wild ryes offered a number of conspicuous advantages compared to the two wild einkorns and wild emmer. Wild annual rye, but not mountain rye, tends to grow in exceptionally dense stands, making it much easier to harvest efficiently (figure 12.4). This contrasts particularly with wild emmer.[13] Freeing wild rye grains from their spikelets using a wooden pestle and mortar is very quick and easy compared to the wild wheats; even without any prior parching, they are much easier to dehusk than even the most thoroughly preparched wild einkorn or emmer. Eliminating the resulting spikelet chaff from the grain is also much simpler in rye; the chaff of wild rye is very light and can be simply be winnowed out, while elimination of the heavy chaff of wild wheats requires the much more tedious operations of sieving or tray agitation. Because the grains of wild rye are more floury than the glassy-grained wild wheats, rye grains are less gritty if eaten roasted, are more quickly and easily crushed for preparation as a porridge, mush more quickly when boiled in water so porridge cooks more rapidly, and are more readily ground to flour for making pastes, pancakes, and bread. The mushability would also have made them ideal for preparing weaning foods for the little ones.

Finally, once eaten, the low glycemic index of rye-based foods makes them much more sustaining than those of wheats. Following a meal, therefore, the starch of rye is hydrolyzed much more slowly than that of the wheats, and the resulting sugars are absorbed through the gut wall and into the bloodstream over a much longer period. This avoids the surge of blood sugars, the ensuing rush of insulin, and the consequent plummeting of blood sugar levels that quickly leave people feeling hungry again after a wheat-based meal. Rye-based foods therefore offer high satiety. Certainly, if I were a hunter-gatherer at Epipalaeolithic Abu Hureyra wanting a sustaining breakfast, I would opt for rye foods over wheat foods. But of course, they had a plethora of other foods available to them, too, most of which are unfamiliar to us in the present day.

Grain of Feather-Grass

Charred remains of feather-grasses, *Stipa* and *Stipagrostis* spp., are a conspicuous feature of almost every deposit, although they start to decline in phase 2 (Period 1B). This seems to suggest a significant role in subsistence, and this, in turn, accords with the heavy use of feather-grass grains as food by foragers in the arid zones of North America (Bohrer 1975; Steward 1933, 1941; Strike 1994),

Australia (Johnston and Cleland 1943, p. 95; Lawrence 1968), and North Africa (Harlan 1989, p. 83). It also accords with our ecological model, which suggests that at 11,500 BP the expanses of feather-grasses are likely to have dominated vast tracts of the drier subzone of woodland-steppe to the southeast of Abu Hureyra, right up to the settlement itself.

Each feather-grass spikelet contains a single floret with a single grain. The husks of each floret extend into a robust awn, silvery with hairs, and 20–30 cm long in some species. At the base of each floret, at the point of disarticulation, there is a needle-sharp tip, the callus, that readily penetrates the skin of the hands, and the delicate mucosae of the mouths of hapless herbivores attempting to graze it. In field experiments I have found that the most efficient method of gathering the grain is to grab handfuls of the long awns and to tug on them with a loose grip. All the florets with grains nearing maturity readily detach, while a loose grip allows the completely unripe spikelets to be left on the plant for a subsequent round of gathering, if required. These completely unripe florets are best left behind in any case, as they are very difficult to dehusk, and end up contaminating the otherwise clean grain. The gathering is made more efficient by the fact that, when fully mature florets disarticulate spontaneously, their awns often start to twist around each other, and the whole mass becomes attached to the awns of the unripe florets that are still fixed to the plant. The harvester is thus able to gather not only the near-ripe florets still on the plant, but also the fully ripe, disarticulated florets that would otherwise have dropped to the ground (figure 12.10).

With some grasses, the grains can be freed from their enveloping husks by rubbing them between the hands or, on a larger scale, by treading them with a twisting movement of motion of the feet.[14] With the feather-grasses, this is impossible because the sharp tips of the florets immediately penetrate the skin and underlying flesh. (I tried it . . . once!). I therefore attempted to dehusk them by rubbing the grains with stone grinders, with and without prior parching. The parching made dehusking much easier, but either way, the grain ended up contaminated with thousands of fragments of awns that were tedious to eliminate from the grain. The most efficient solution was to singe the tangled heap of florets by holding them over a small straw fire, in a way similar to the traditional Spanish singeing of emmer and spelt spikelets described by Peña-Chocarro (1996, p. 140). With feather-grasses, the singeing burns off the awns and callus tips and makes the tight husks start to unfurl and become brittle. The grains can then be freed from the husks by simple rubbing, and the chaff eliminated by winnowing. The singing also serves to roast the grain ready for preparation as food. However, even the most careful singeing results in some charring, and this is probably the origin of the charred grains from Abu Hureyra (figure 12.11).

Nutlets of Club-Rush

Charred remains of the small nutlets of club-rush are abundant in every deposit, although slightly less so after phase 1 (see figure 12.22). The probability that they arrived in the hearths having been gathered as food and roasted is reinforced by the prominent role of club-rush nutlets as a starch-rich food among a range of recent hunter-gatherers. It is further reinforced by archaeological finds of the nutlets in contexts where their consumption as food is not in doubt, for example, in a human coprolite from Late Palaeolithic Wadi Kubbaniya in Egypt (Hillman, Madeyska, and Hather 1989, pp. 196–198), in

Figure 12.10 Gathering grains of feather-grass. *Top,* disarticulating florets of one of the feather-grasses, *Stipa holosericea,* retained in the grass-head through their awns becoming intertwined with those of florets that have not yet spontaneously disarticulated; *middle,* a few florets pulled from a head and showing their needle-sharp callus points that are exposed when the rachilla disarticulates (the rachilla is the tiny axis within a spikelet, whereas the rachis is the axis that connects spikelets within an ear of grasses such as barley, rye, and wheat); *bottom,* gathering florets of feather grass by pulling on the awns. (By Ivan Crowe).

Figure 12.11 Charred fragments of the awl-like grains of two or more species of feather-grass from level E 469 of Abu Hureyra 1. They possibly became charred during singeing to remove the callus and awns and make the husks brittle enough to be removed by rubbing.

almost all the 300 coprolites analyzed from Lovelock Cave in Nevada (Napton and Heizer 1970), and as a large cache in an Archaic Indian food store in Hidden Cave in Nevada (Thomas 1984). It might perhaps be argued that the Abu Hureyra seeds arrived with plants cut as thatching, matting, or loose floor covering, as I suggest below for certain reed and rush remains. Certainly, Aylan Erkal tells me that she has observed club-rush being used to make matting in central Asia Minor. However, unlike the stems of some other reeds and rushes used for matting, those of club-rush have to be cut well before they set seed, as thereafter they become too brittle. The presence of mature nutlets in such large numbers is explicable, therefore, only on the basis that they were gathered for food.

The inflorescences of club-rush are borne on the top of the sharply trigonous 50 cm to 1 m tall culms (figure 12.12). These can be plucked or stripped off in late summer and, once thoroughly dry, threshed by rubbing the bunches of spikelets together between the hands. The chaff can then be eliminated by winnowing.

The fresh nutlets are almost impossible to masticate if ingested raw, and presumably pass through the gut undigested. They are also almost impossible to grind as the rubbing stones simply slip on the hard shiny seeds. However, I found that, when roasted, the nutlets explode like popcorn and become very friable. In this state, although somewhat gritty, they can be eaten or can readily be reduced to flour for consumption as a paste, as pancakes, or as griddle cakes. This accords with the ethnographic record: the Lakota Sioux ate them "parched and ground to flour" and cooked as griddle cakes (Rogers 1980, p. 23), and the Cahuilla of southern California ate the nutlets after parching and grinding them "into a mush" (Bean and Saubel 1972, p. 139). It is appropriate, therefore, that the ancient nutlets from a Kubbaniya coprolite showed clear signs of having been roasted prior to ingestion. Roasting could have been done on flat stones heated by the hearths or, on a larger scale, by rolling hot stones around in baskets containing the nutlets.[15]

How club-rush nutlets were eaten at Abu Hureyra we shall never know, but once roasted and ground or pounded, the flour could have been eaten as a moist paste, fried as a damper (on hot stones or on hot earth beneath a cleared fire), or pressed into cakes for further roasting. Our experiments with all three methods reveal the nutlets to be perfectly palatable, albeit a trifle bland unless other wild foods or flavorings are added. The abundant charred remains of intact nutlets, then, presumably represent occasional accidents during over-zealous roasting (figure 12.12).

Nutlets of the Euphrates Knotgrass

The nutlets of a wide range of knotgrass and other *Polygonum* species have been used as food by hunter-gatherers on four continents. It is therefore not unreasonable to suggest that the very large number of charred nutlets present

Figure 12.12 *Top*, plants of club-rush, *Scirpus maritimus*, growing on the Pevensey Marshes in southern England—each lanceolate spikelet generally contains large numbers of chestnut-brown seeds; *bottom*, charred seeds of club-rush from level E 470 at Abu Hureyra 1—eaten as griddle cakes these starchy seeds are quite palatable, albeit gritty if insufficiently ground.

in every level arrived at Abu Hureyra as gathered food (see figure 12.22). The glossy, three-angled nutlets of the common knotgrass, *Polygonum aviculare*, a close relative of the Euphrates knotgrass, *P. corrigioloides*, were eaten by several groups in California (Chestnut 1902, p. 345); those of the near relative wild buckwheat, *Eriogonum*, were a major summer food of the Cahuilla (Bean and Sauble 1972, p. 72); the nutlets of *P. douglasii* were eaten by groups in Montana and Oregon (Coville 1897, p. 95; Blankinship 1905, p.18); and those of *P. plebejum* by the Ngamini in southern Australia (Johnston and Cleland 1943, p. 153); and so the list continues. Nutlets of the common knotgrass were also grown as a cereal substitute by Icelandic farmers in Viking times (Maurizio 1927, p. 24), and used as a famine food throughout Medieval Europe. That this usage has some time depth is further suggested by finds of club-rush nutlets from Mesolithic sites in Europe (Schwantes 1939, p. 146) and from a wide range of Archaic sites in North America reviewed by Murray and Sheehan (1984). The latter include finds in human feces where their consumption as food is indisputable.

In almost all cases, the ethnographic records describe the nutlets being roasted and then ground to flour, which was used to produce mush or griddle cakes. Our own experiments show that the nutlets cannot be rubbed free of the enveloping floral parts, that is, the persistent perianth, unless these have first been made brittle by parching; otherwise the perianth and nutlet merely form resilient little balls. Furthermore, the hard, shiny little nutlets cannot be ground to flour unless they, too, have been parched to a brittle state. We found that the only quick and effective way of achieving both these aims was to singe the inflorescences over a fire, but this had to stop short of the point at which a significant portion of the flowers started to ignite. Even with well-controlled singeing, however, occasional nutlets and flowers ignited and fell into the fire. Equivalent events were perhaps the source of the charred remains we found at Abu Hureyra (figure 12.13).

Once flowers and nutlets had been singed and parched or roasted to brittleness (figure 12.14), we found that rubbing the flowers quickly fragmented them and released the nutlets. These were readily ground to flour that could be eaten as a wet paste, as pancakes, as dampers, or as roasted griddle cakes. All three proved to be extremely palatable with a slightly sweet, nutty flavor and with no hint of bitterness. We also found that using slightly immature nutlets offered two advantages: first, the damp nutlets popped when singed, which subsequently made them easier to grind, and second, they tasted still sweeter.

Grains of Small-Seeded Grasses

Grains from small-grained grasses are prominent throughout the Abu Hureyra 1 deposits. During phases 2 and 3 the majority of the charred remains of these grasses probably came from plants growing as weeds of early crops and were sieved out of the cereal grain during grain cleaning, together with the many other weed seeds we find in these phases. But during phase 1 where we have no evidence of cultivation it is probable that they were gathered as food. This accords with the prominent role of small grass grains in the subsistence of a vast range of nonagrarian populations in the arid zones of four continents.[16] Although studies rooted in optimal foraging theory invariably note that small-seed foods such as grass grains serve as staples only in areas where other foods are scarce (Russell 1988, pp. 147–148), grass seeds do offer advantages over root foods such as easy storage, relatively predictable yields, and higher protein and

Figure 12.13 The nutlets of the Euphrates knotgrass, *Polygonum corrigioloides*, that produce very palatable griddle cakes when roasted and ground. *Top*, modern seeds from plants growing on the edge of backswamps in the Euphrates Valley just below Abu Hureyra; *bottom*, charred remains of seeds from level E 470 of Abu Hureyra 1.

oils contents (Simms 1987). Nevertheless, with the rich pickings available at Abu Hureyra, it is possible that they represented only secondary foods rather than primary staples.

The most common small-grained grass in the charred remains are members of the wall-barley group. Present-day stands dominated by this group invariably contain smaller numbers of other grasses, and several of these are found in the remains. Gathering these grains therefore probably involved a "lawn mower" approach to the harvesting of just such stands in the past, rather as in figure 12.15 (Hillman 1989). In this way very large quantities of plants bearing edible grain can be harvested in minutes, ready for bulk processing. The presence of small amounts of other grass genera is thus fortuitous; they would not have been targeted deliberately.

a

b

Figure 12.14 Processing knotgrass to free the edible seeds and roast them ready for grinding or pounding. For these experiments, we used the common knotgrass, *Polygonum aviculare*, a close relative of Euphrates knotgrass. a, Seona Anderson spreading plants with slightly immature nutlets on a drying frame; b, Suzie Hilmi singeing the dried plants over a fire—this rendered the floral parts sufficiently brittle to be rubbed free and readied the seeds to be ground to flour; c, Claire Rhodes separating the seeds from the freed husks by agitating them on a tray, and winnowing away the husks by blowing; d, pounding the seeds to flour in a pestle and mortar.

Seeds of Winter Flowering Shrub Chenopods

If abundance in the remains is any measure of importance, and this is questionable, then the combined finds of seeds of the shrubby saltbushes, *Atriplex* spp., the sea-blite, and the various other, mainly perennial, shrub chenopods may suggest that they made a significant contribution, especially during phase 2. Certainly, the dietary potential of the seeds of these shrub chenopods is enhanced by the fact that they often grow in great abundance (figure 12.16), each bush can produce huge quantities of seed (a point repeatedly emphasized in the ethnobotanical record), most of them produce their seed in winter when other seed foods are scarce, and they are easy to gather and process. Compared with other wild chenopods such as fat-hen, they have much thinner seed coats

c

d

and a correspondingly higher-energy yield (figure 12.17). Most of them are also rich in protein, the seeds of those few taxa such as *Anabasis* that contain toxins are easily detoxified, and the resulting foods keep better than those of many other seeds (Hillman 1996, p. 179).

Seeds of the shrubby chenopods have served as caloric staples in several hunter-gatherer societies, especially during the autumn and winter. Examples from North America include the Cahuilla use of the seeds of soapweed, *Suaeda suffruticosa*, and at least two species of saltbush (Bean and Saubel 1972, pp. 45, 141); the Seri consumption of the seeds of iodine bush, *Allenrolfea*, and several other shrub chenopods (Felger and Moser 1985, p. 275); and the Lakota use of seeds of saltbush and Mexican fireweed, *Kochia scoparia* (Rogers 1980, p. 66). However, whether the shrub chenopods found at Abu Hureyra also served as major winter staples remains uncertain.

Figure 12.15 *Top,* Dominique de Moulins harvesting a sward of small-seeded grasses dominated by wall-barley with a flint-bladed sickle north of El Kum in April 1988, using the lawn mower approach; *bottom,* Jane Reed harvesting swards dominated by a closely related form of wall-barley in Britain in 1990—in this case, we found it was quickest to harvest by uprooting, as the plants were tall and many culmed, and the soil was damp and friable.

Fruitlets of the Great Terebinths

The various species of terebinth range from small shrubs of 1–3 m in the lesser terebinths, *P. terebinthus* and *P. palaestina,* to large trees in the great terebinth, *Pistacia atlantica* (figure 3.10). The fruitlets are mostly reddish, or occasionally turquoise-blue, in color with a fleshy outer skin overlying a thin shell and an oily little kernel (figure 12.18). They are best eaten while still unripe because, at maturity, shell tissue predominates.

Figure 12.16 The shrubby chenopods commonly offer remarkably high returns of edible seeds. *Top*, two perennial taxa, a *Hammada* species and *Anabasis syriaca*, are growing prolifically in the Wadi Jilat in eastern Transjordan, in the outer fringes of the steppe zone, in late November 1988; *bottom*, closeup of one of the *Hammada* bushes with the usual mass of pale winged seeds. Our measurements of yields revealed that each bush produced tens of thousands of edible seeds. However, the *Anabasis* seeds required detoxification by leaching prior to being prepared as food.

Figure 12.17 Another perennial chenopod, the furry *Krasheninnikovia ceratoides*. *Top*, meter-high bushes growing in the moist steppe zone close to Can Hasan in Central Anatolia; *bottom*, closeup of a single bush, November 1970.

I include terebinth fruitlets here because they were prominent in the remains and used extensively in our ecological modeling. Ethnographic records suggest they were used primarily as a flavoring and preservative—always after roasting. Certainly, the aftereffects of eating large quantities on occasions when I had exhausted other foods convinced me that they are unlikely to have served as a staple. The villagers of Maden Sehir on Karadağ in central Asia Minor, like our friends in many other Anatolian villages, always added a sprinkling of terebinth fruits when they roasted wheat grain to make the crunchy snack called *kavurmaç*,

Figure 12.18 A fruiting branch of the southeast Anatolian variety of one of the great terebinths, *Pistacia atlantica* var. *kurdica*, growing near Cemisgezek in the Munzur Mountains in September 1971. This particular tree was 7 m tall and the fruits were about 7 mm across.

while shepherds near Karaman in central Anatolia informed me that their wives crushed the roasted fruits of the lesser terebinth, *P. palaestina*, and mixed them into meatballs and bulgur cakes to prevent the food going bad during the two or more days the shepherds were out on the steppe with their flocks. Today, they roast the fruitlets in an upturned sheet-iron container (Turkish: *saç*, Arabic *saj*), but in premetal and preceramic times they could have used flat stones beside the hearth or rolled hot round stones around in a basket containing the fruitlets.

Reeds and Rushes

Charred culm nodes of the common reed, *Phragmites australis*, are present in almost all deposits and were probably gathered as thatching and to provide loose floor coverings, just as they are today. The tiny seeds of one of the soft rushes, *Juncus* sp., found in considerable quantities in just two deposits in phase 1 almost certainly represent the collection of the soft stems for small-scale weaving, loose floor covering, or possibly even to provide the soft pith usable as wicks for rushlight lamps. Certainly, all three uses continued until recent times in Europe (Pierpoint Johnson 1862, p. 273). The true bulrush, *Schoenoplectus tabernaemontani*, was only represented by a few charred seeds and was probably gathered primarily for basketry and matting for which its long, soft, pliable, but tough stems were the preferred raw material until the present day.

The harvesting of all three of these reeds and rushes would have necessitated the use of some sort of blade and was doubtless a function of the sickle blades found in the deposits. Today, the standard harvesting tool is a reed hook, which resembles a small sickle with a strongly recurved blade. An almost identical tool has recently been recovered from the Bronze Age reed-swamp settlement of Shinewater in southern England.

Other plants are likely to have been gathered as flavorings, medicines, dyes, and hallucinogens.

THE ROLE OF PLANT FOODS NOT FOUND IN THE REMAINS BUT LIKELY TO HAVE BEEN USED BY THE PEOPLE OF ABU HUREYRA 1A

The uneven preservation of charred remains of many plant foods makes it unsafe to assume that their apparent absence is an automatic indication that they were not used. This is particularly true of soft fruits like wild grapes and figs that are likely to have been consumed off-site, and soft root and leaf foods that have a relatively poor chance of being preserved by charring in identifiable form.

There are a number of such food plants that are absent from the remains but that our ecological models and, in a few cases, charcoal remains indicate were present in the vicinity of Abu Hureyra, and which ethnographic parallels from recent hunter-gatherers occupying analogous resource environments in recent times indicate were likely to have been favored as starch staples. Preeminent among such staples are nut foods like almonds and acorns and the roots of wetland plants. Inevitably, in a botanically rich area such as the Abu Hureyra catchment there are many other plants that were likely to have been used as food, but just a few examples must suffice here.

Four or so species of almond would have grown in the woodland-steppe with the great terebinth, and would probably have included the small-leaved almond, the sessile-leaved almond, the furry-leaved oriental almond, and the broom almond. The endless vistas of woodland-steppe would therefore have offered the people of Abu Hureyra a vast supply of wild almonds, and if eaten in the mature state, the oil-rich kernels could have made a massive contribution to caloric needs. After all, they are about 35% fat by weight, and fats yield about four times as much energy as the same weight of starch. However, kernels of most races of these almonds, particularly the oriental almond, could not have been eaten without detoxification to remove the dangerous prussic acid, present as a cyanogenic glucocide. Detoxification could have been achieved by fermentation, or by roasting, followed by grinding and leaching. Without this, Daniel Zohary has told us, just 20–25 kernels of the oriental almond could have proved fatal.

Despite the local availability of almonds at the start of the Epipalaeolithic occupation, we have not found a single fragment of charred almond shell in the remains. Their absence can be explained in two ways. First, the people of Abu Hureyra may have reduced transport costs by removing the shells as they gathered the nuts, for example, at collection points where there were rocks with flat surfaces on which to crack the nuts with handstones. This would have made good sense because the thick shells of wild almonds make up at least half the weight and two thirds of the bulk of the whole nut. This was standard practice among many hunter-gatherers using nut foods such as the piñon and acorn in recent times. Under such conditions, the nut shells would never have arrived back in the village to end up charred on the fires.

A second explanation for the absence of shell remains is that they might have been consumed as entire fruits in the green, unripe state, well before the stone, botanically the endocarp, had started to harden. The green almonds would have been complete with the fleshy outer layers, the mesocarp and epicarp, which those of us in the European tradition normally discard. Today, the domestic forms of green almonds are sold on the streets of Turkey as *can bademi* ("soul of almond") and eaten with a pinch of salt. No detoxification is needed, as the plant produces prussic acid purely to protect the kernel, which at this stage is no more than a small sack of liquid. However, in the absence of a mature kernel, eating these green fruits would have provided only a minimal caloric return, although the fruits doubtless contained useful amounts of vitamins C and E and a range of trace nutrients.

Both Boissier's and Brandt's oak were probably present in the Abu Hureyra catchment, allowing small-scale collection of the acorns. However, their use as a caloric staple would almost certainly have entailed gathering them from extensive oak-dominated park-woodland that was perhaps 15 km away (figure 12.1). Although the energy costs of schlepping bulky harvests 15 km would clearly have been considerable, ethnographic parallels exist for just such an investment by groups like the Cahuilla and Chumash of California, who depended heavily on acorns (Bean and Saubel 1972; Grant 1978, pp. 516–517), and the Owens Valley Paiute in their harvesting of nuts of the piñon pine (Steward 1933, 1941; Thomas 1979). To limit energy costs in travel, the Cahuilla and Chumash adopted forms of collecting in which most of the band migrated up to 15 miles to the oak woods for one to three weeks of acorn harvesting and processing, and then returned to their base camps with the large quantities of acorn products needed to see them through the winter and spring. In harvesting their piñon nuts, the Owens Valley Paiute adopted a similar strategy, except that, when the harvests were good, the heavy transportation costs led them to set up their winter villages in the piñon woods.[17]

Our ecological model suggests that, at 11,500 BP, the people of Abu Hureyra had access to a set of resource zones surprisingly similar to a hybrid between those available to the Owens Valley Paiute and those enjoyed by the Cahuilla and Chumash (barring the lowest, desertic zone of most Cahuilla catchments). The choice of zone in which to locate the site was also strikingly similar. As at Abu Hureyra, the base camps of these modern groups were located close to the broadest spectrum of resources well downslope from the oak or piñon park-woodland, so these nut groves were 5–15 miles away—despite their central role in subsistence (Bean and Saubel 1972, p. 123). The rationale here is that, while the gathering seasons of the diverse resources of the lower zones were spread though much of the year and required these groups to live nearby, the autumn acorn harvest was concentrated into one to three weeks, allowing everyone to relocate and camp out for this brief period, whereafter acorn products "were hauled back to the village by the ton."[18]

For these recent gatherers, the 15 miles involved a two-day journey when carrying young children and equipment, and this was generally the maximum they were prepared to travel for these nut foods. The 15 km distance we suggest separated oak park-woodland from Abu Hureyra clearly falls within this maximum.[19] It was therefore presumably feasible for the people of Abu Hureyra to have used the acorn resources growing 15 km away in just the same way as the Cahuilla, Chumash, and Owens Valley Paiute. On the other hand, the Paiute practice of overwintering in the park-woodland in good nut years was almost certainly *not* applied at Abu Hureyra. Here, the plant and animal remains indicate year-round occupation of the site. Acorn harvests would therefore probably have been brought back to the permanent settlement.

The complete absence of acorn remains from Abu Hureyra does not necessarily preclude such a scenario. Most recent groups who gathered their acorns from this sort of distance processed the acorns at the harvesting camps, and most of the harvest arrived back at the settlement as ground flour or mush, ready to cook or eat as it was. We should therefore not necessarily expect to find tell-tale traces of charred acorn cups and shells discarded on the hearths, and in any case, Mason (1992) has found that the thin shells rarely survive exposure to fire. In addition, any wooden pestles and mortars used in the processing will not have survived, and heavy stone ones are likely to have been left every autumn at the processing sites, so we would not necessarily find these either.[20]

In recent times tannin-rich species of acorn were typically cracked open by using a pebble against a boulder, dried in the sun, deshelled, ground into a flour with a grinder or pounded in a pestle and mortar, and then leached. One way of doing this was by putting the flour in a basket and running water through it until most of the bitter tannins were flushed out. Alternatives included either leaving the intact acorns in sacks in running water, or soaking them in hot springs, in both cases to remove the tannins prior to drying and grinding (Bean and Saubel 1972, pp. 126–129; Mason 1992).

However, the acorns of the two species of oak likely to have grown near Abu Hureyra, Boissier's oak and Brandt's oak, are today consumed without leaching. I saw acorns of Boissier's oak being sold for human consumption in Karaman in south-central Anatolia in 1971, and Sarah Mason and Mark Nesbitt have told us that, among Syriac Christian communities on the Tur Abdin Plateau near Mardin in Southeast Asia Minor, they were eaten after simple roasting. The same communities preferred the acorns of Brandt's oak, which they ate roasted after cutting off the tannin-rich embryo end. Nevertheless, as with all nut and seed foods, grinding or pounding them with pestles and mortars, generally after roasting, offers the only means of ensuring adequate digestion, so either of these two operations is likely to have formed part of acorn processing at Abu Hureyra, regardless of tannin content.

A second class of potential staples is the root foods of riverine plants such as the cattail or reedmace and club-rush. Both grow in and around backswamps in the Euphrates Valley today, and the abundance of charred remains of nutlets of club-rush in all levels indicates not only that they were probably a major food, but also that club-rush grew locally. The thick rhizomes of cattail are rich in starch, especially between autumn and spring, and in our field studies of yields, we have regularly been able to gather 3–4 kg of cleaned, usable rhizome per square meter of typical stands—this within half an hour. Suitably prepared, they make a very palatable food, and in recent times they were correspondingly the preferred starch staple of a broad spectrum of hunter-gatherers occupying lacustrine or riverine environments across four continents (Casey 1990; Hillman, Madeyska, and Hather 1989, pp. 193–196).

A third class of potential caloric staple would have been the fleshy roots of dryland herbaceous perennials such as the mauve and yellow-flowered wild salsifys (figure 12.19), the fleshy stem bases of the giant yellow steppic broomrapes, and lily bulbs such as those of the purple Tartar lily, the blue and mauve grape hyacinths, and many others. The highest concentrations of this broad spectrum of palatable root foods occur in woodland-steppe and moist steppe, where they are gathered by the beduin today. Some such as the salsify and Tartar lily are delicious and can be eaten even without cooking, and I find it inconceivable that they and the many other root foods of herbaceous perennials were not also eaten in quantity by the people of Epipalaeolithic Abu Hureyra, in much the same way that the bulbs of the camas lily served as a starch staple for so many groups of indigenous peoples of North America. Certainly, most root

Figure 12.19 The common mauve-flowered salsify, *Scorzonera,* with its fleshy edible root tubers gathered near El Kum in central Syria, April 1988.

foods offer the advantage over seed foods of requiring relatively little processing, although some need prolonged cooking to ensure complete digestibility.[21] Indeed, it is for this reason that the Alyawara of northwestern Australia are prepared to travel twice as far to gather root foods than they are to travel to gather small seeds that require extensive processing (Cane 1989).

DIETARY DIVERSITY AND NUTRITION AT 11,500 BP: THE PLANT COMPONENTS

In recent times, the diet enjoyed by most hunter-gatherers was much more diverse than that of the vast majority of farming societies. This is reflected in the archaeological record. Although the original transition from foraging to farming involved different dietary changes in different areas, the one common feature was the collapse of this dietary diversity. In Southwest Asia, this collapse appears to have been complete by the end of Neolithic 2, c. 8,000 BP. By this point, agrarian systems were almost fully developed and the dietary contribution of plant gathering had dwindled to a low plateau.

The remains of food plants from Abu Hureyra at 11,500 BP appear to reflect just such a diverse hunter-gatherer diet. In the charred remains from the Epipalaeolithic occupations we identified 142 species of plant (figure 12.7) and isolated at least another 50 types that were too poorly preserved and too fragmentary to determine precisely. Of the 142 identified species, 118 of them were plants known to have served regularly as food among recent hunter-gatherers. Furthermore, all these potential foods were seeds and hard fruits that are rich in starch or oils, and several of them have correspondingly served recent hunter-gatherers as caloric staples. And like many seed foods, most of them also contain useful quantities of proteins.

These 118 species represent only part of the probable spectrum of plant foods. The absence in the charred remains of recognizable remains of root foods, green shoots, leaves, flower buds, or soft fruits does not mean that they did not eat such foods, merely that these soft tissues rarely get preserved by charring in readily identifiable form. In reality, the people of Abu Hureyra probably consumed such foods in the same sort of quantities and diversity as hunter-gatherers who occupied equivalent resource environments in recent times. Even today some traditional farming communities in Western Asia eat up to 100 species of wild greens gathered from the weeds of fallow fields and field margins, and hunter-gatherers in equivalent but less degraded environments consume an even broader range. With these green foods, roots, and other soft foods added, the total number of plant foods probably consumed at Abu Hureyra around 11,500 years ago was probably well over 250. Such diversity contrasts dramatically with the narrow diets typical of groups practicing fully developed agriculture, and even more starkly with the yet-narrower diets of town dwellers.

Today we encounter higher levels of dietary diversity among hunter-gatherers occupying resource environments that are ecologically more varied. Our evidence from Abu Hureyra seems to accord with this pattern in indicating both a diverse diet and an exceptionally varied environment. By contrast, recent hunter-gatherers such as the various San peoples of the Kalahari, the Eastern Hadza of Tanzania, and the Bagundji, Alyawara, and Gidjingale of Australia enjoyed diets that, although vastly more diverse than those of farming peoples in similar environments, were seemingly less diverse than that at Abu Hureyra.[22] It is therefore significant that, although they sometimes obtained huge caloric yields from individual food plants, as the !Kung San did from mongongo nuts, their environments had seemingly fewer edible species available than indicated at Abu Hureyra 11,500 years ago.

Even more significant is the fact that some of the key examples of recent hunter-gatherers with exceptionally diverse diets occupied resource catchments that embraced some of the same ecological zones as those at Abu Hureyra. Indeed, many of their food-plant genera were the same. For example, the remarkably diverse diet of the Maidu of the Sacramento Valley in California derived from a catchment that embraced open oak-dominated park-woodland, grading below into a chaparral-grassland mosaic, the equivalent of the woodland-steppe in Western Asia, with marshlands, rivers, and lakes below that (Duncan 1963). This is very reminiscent of the ecological zonation at Abu Hureyra 11,500 years ago. A second example comes from the Cahuilla of southern California who enjoyed a very broad-spectrum plant diet that, for most Cahuilla groups, was gathered from five ecological zones. Three of these zones were equivalent to those at Abu Hureyra (Bean and Saubel 1972).[23]

A third example comes from the Owens Valley Paiute of the southwestern Great Basin. They had access to what Steward (1933, pp. 233–236) described as "an unusually fertile environment" with "extreme geographical diversity." The major zones included piñon-juniper park-woodland. Below this was a grassland zone that, in Southwest Asia, would pass as woodland-steppe and that, as in the Abu Hureyra catchment, yielded an abundance of wild grass grain. Lower still were valley-bottom wetlands, again as at Abu Hureyra. Each zone provided a diverse array of food plants that allowed a broad-spectrum diet, albeit with yields that were sometimes unpredictable (Steward 1933, 1941; Thomas 1979).

From these and many other examples of recent hunter-gatherers, we can conclude that in areas where they had access to ecologically diverse resource environments, and particularly where the pattern of resource zones was similar to that indicated for the period of initial settlement at Abu Hureyra, they generally enjoyed especially high levels of dietary diversity. We should therefore not be surprised by the great variety of food plants identified in the Abu Hureyra remains.

Despite the dietary diversity typical of recent hunter-gatherers, ethnobotanical studies reveal that the range of caloric staples consumed at any one season of the year is limited. Examples include the Dobe !Kung, who used "over 100 species" of plants as food during the course of a year, but a mere 23 of them "made up about 90% of the vegetable diet by weight, and one species, the mongongo nut, accounted for at least half the total" (Yellen and Lee 1976, p. 38). Similarly, Tanaka (1976, p. 115) reports that the Kade San ate 79 food-plant species in the year, but that the bulk of the diet was provided by just 13 of them. And for the Eastern Hadza, Woodburn (1968, p. 51) notes that "although a large number of species of food plant are eaten, . . . the bulk of the food . . . is obtained from only ten" of them. Analogous patterns are reported from Australia. For example, Jones and Meehan (1989) note that the Gidjingale use a narrow range of staples in any one season but draw on a very wide range of supplementary foods.

The Abu Hureyra record, for all its inevitable incompleteness, may well reflect this phenomenon. We can usefully compare the abundance of the charred remains of only those taxa exposed to processing practices conferring similar probabilities of preservation by charring, and where the remains were equally resilient to the ensuing depredations of time. Of the more resilient seeds and fruits requiring parching or roasting prior to dehusking or grinding, those most abundant in phase 1 and the most likely to have served as caloric staples at 11,500 BP were grains of three or four of the five species of wild wheat and rye, grains from probably two of the five species of feather-grass, club-rush nutlets, knotgrass nutlets, grain from wild millets of the Euphrates Valley (the bulk probably provided by just two of the eleven species identified), and then, less certainly, the seeds of shrubby chenopods from perhaps two of the twelve taxa, including melde or saltbush and *Chenolea*, and suitably detoxified seeds of two of the ten crucifers, perfoliate cress (figure 12.20) and Whitlow-grass. There are also categories of plant food totally absent from the remains but that were likely to have included further caloric staples. The most likely candidates are two species of acorns, wetland root foods such as the rhizomes of cattail and the tubers of club-rush, and dryland root foods such as the tubers of two species of wild salsify and the bulbs of the Tartar lily.

These 20 or so species probably met most of the caloric needs of the people of Abu Hureyra. The vast array of other plants that seem to have served as secondary or minor foods ensured that their overall diet was remarkably diverse.

The nutritional status of this diverse diet is impressive, and its impact on health probably far-reaching. Imbalances and deficiencies abound in the diet of modern affluent societies, often resulting from an insufficiency of, for example, green foods or fiber, and we even have to resort to dietary supplements such as seed oils rich in gamma- and alpha-linolenic acid (GCL and ALA). The positive effects of such supplements on blood pressure, circulation, and the alleviation of certain inflammatory diseases clearly indicate that even these privileged modern diets entail major deficiencies.

Hunter-gatherer diets based on a rich variety of food resources suffer from few of these deficiencies and imbalances. For example, the Abu Hureyra diet was rich in small seed foods and so would not have been lacking in essential

Figure 12.20 Perfoliate cress, *Lepidium perfoliatum*, growing near Anau in southern Turkmenistan in April 1989. The small, charred seeds of this plant were abundant in almost all levels of Abu Hureyra 1, but declined after Period 1A. *Top*, the 10–20-cm-high plants commonly form extensive, densely packed swards, and this makes the seeds very easy to gather in quantity; *bottom*, a closeup of the same plants nearing maturity. Although recent hunter-gatherers used ground cress seeds only as a condiment (albeit a condiment sometimes consumed in considerable quantities, as the Bavarians consume mild, whole-grain mustard), crucifers with less pungent seeds provided flour that was consumed as a major, calorie-rich food (Bean and Saubel 1972; Rogers 1980).

fatty acids such as GLA. The amount of green foods and fruits consumed by recent hunter-gatherers in rich resource environments would also have preempted deficiencies in most of the key minerals and in vitamins A, C, and E. Indeed, a handful of wild fruits such as those of the sea buckthorn provide very high levels of vitamins C and E. And the amounts of soluble and insoluble fiber in the Abu Hureyra diet would certainly have ensured that the bacterial flora of the lower gut had sufficient substrate needed to generate the short-chain fatty acids that, as Anthony Leeds has informed me, are becoming recognized as important for healthy liver function.

More generally, diverse diets help us avoid eating too much of anything potentially detrimental, for example, phytates from cereal bran in quantities capable of limiting calcium uptake (Harland and Oberleas 1987). They ensure that we get the broad spectrum of carbohydrates, essential fatty acids, amino acids, vitamins, and minerals that we need. But diverse diets provide a further tier of nutrition; many plants contain a string of secondary compounds that, while sometimes toxic or medicinal in large quantities, have an important role in maintaining health when consumed in small quantities (Fellows 1993). Diverse hunter-gatherer diets such as those at Abu Hureyra in Period 1A would have provided a galaxy of such secondary compounds, especially if we include the great variety of plants that were probably consumed in small quantities as supplementary greens and that contained secondary compounds that were able to survive cooking and the usual hunter-gatherer detoxification procedures.

Humankind evolved as hunter-gatherers, and this dietary diversity can probably be traced back at least to the point in the Palaeolithic when our ancestors mastered the use of fire for preparing food and could begin eating the many plant foods requiring heat treatment to make them palatable, digestible, and safe (Stahl 1984, 1989).[24] It is therefore inevitable that our physiology became evolutionarily adapted to require this diversity of nutrients, including the galaxy of secondary compounds. But with the transition to agriculture this diverse diet was narrowed dramatically. Farming diets typically exhibited gross dietary imbalances and lacked a range of the nutrients and secondary compounds seemingly essential for complete health.

For most of us a mere 200 human generations have elapsed since the last of our hunter-gatherer ancestors walked the planet, and it can be argued that 200 generations is simply too few to have allowed selection for a physiology perfectly adapted to the new, aberrant, agrarian diet. Genetically, then, we are still evolutionarily adapted to a hunter-gatherer diet, and to a number of those more subtle aspects of hunter-gatherer life where adaptive physiology or psychology is to some degree genetically determined. Put crudely, we still have hunter-gatherer guts. The diet of the late preagrarian hunter-gatherers such as those from Abu Hureyra, therefore, can provide some clues to our nutritional requirements in the present day.

We do not yet understand with certainty the role of the many rubbing stones, querns, grinding dishes, mortars, and pestles recovered from Abu Hureyra 1. Furthermore, we will never know what use they made of wooden pestles and mortars and other perishable processing equipment inevitably absent from the archaeological record (figure 12.21). In recent times, many hunter-gatherers have been almost obsessive about pounding or grinding seed and other foods to pulp or powder prior to eating them. The same may have been true at Abu Hureyra.

Pounding and grinding have far-reaching effects on nutrition (Stahl 1989). Reducing food to small particles ensures more complete digestion and the

Figure 12.21 Pounding with wooden mallets and a concrete mortar in the village of Sulusaray in north-central Asia Minor, July 1976. The mortar was made of concrete because it was "easier than carving one out of wood, or chipping one out of stone."

proper absorption of nutrients that might otherwise be deficient, and thereby reduces the amount of food that needs to be consumed. In other words, if you digest twice as much of your food, you need eat only half as much. Not having to gather so much food allows further savings in energy expended on travel, in transport of food, and in all stages of its processing, other than the pounding and grinding operations themselves in which *extra* energy is spent. For most foods, the result is a net saving of energy.

The degree to which seed and nut foods are incompletely digested became apparent from exhaustive experiments by Timothy Holden on a range of healthy male and female postgraduates (Holden 1990, chapter 3). His research revealed that when roasted seed or nut foods were consumed the only cells whose starch, oils, and protein were digested were the broken cells on the surface of each food particle. The contents of the remaining cells passed through the gut unscathed. With unground or unpounded foods and despite normal mastication, the particles were so large that the contents of over 90% of the cells remained undigested. This was particularly true of seeds and nuts rich in oil. The advantages of reducing such foods to small particles prior to consumption are therefore clear.

Our experiments in the processing of wild seeds and nuts indicate that nut foods such as acorns, hazel nuts, and almonds could be efficiently reduced to an acceptable flour with large pestles and mortars made of wood or stone. However, fine-grinding hard little seeds such as those of plantains, knotgrasses, docks, and wild crucifers presented a bigger problem, even after they had been thoroughly roasted or singed to make them brittle. We found that, with a wooden pestle and mortar, reducing such seeds to a digestible, fine-ground flour was very slow, and sometimes almost impossible. It was faster with a stone pestle and mortar and fastest of all with a grinder and rubbing stone—in the form of a classic saddle quern of the kind found in Abu Hureyra 1. We therefore concluded that *bulk* processing of such seeds to a fine flour really required the use of grinding tools but that, for small-scale processing, stone mortars with stone or hardwood pestles would probably have been sufficient.[25] Flourier seeds such as those of club-rush, once popped by roasting, could be efficiently ground in a wooden pestle and mortar, although a grinder was arguably still more efficient.

The concentration of remains of grinding tools in the first two phases of Abu Hureyra 1, with very few grinders in phase 3 and the ensuing Neolithic, may reflect these limitations. Certainly, it is in the first two phases of the Epipalaeolithic that we encounter evidence of the heaviest use of those seed foods such as knotgrass, crucifers, and chenopods that, by virtue of their small size and hardness, would have required the use of stone grinding tools to produce a fully digestible flour. Phase 3 sees not only the decline in the apparent use of such seed foods, but the start of their replacement by domestic cereals, and this is when the grinders almost disappear.

Another central aspect of food preparation is, of course, cooking, that is, exposure to heat. Heating is important because it makes available many wild foods that would otherwise be inedible (Stahl 1984). The roots, tubers, and bulbs of many members of the dandelion and lily families, for example salsify roots and grape hyacinth bulbs, store their carbohydrates as inulin rather than starch. However, humans lack the enzymes needed to break the inulin into sugars. Having passed through the anterior gut undigested, the inulin is attacked by the bacteria of the colon to yield useful short-chain fatty acids, and quantities of less useful methane gas. The latter product will not be unfamiliar to eaters of Jerusalem artichokes, another member of the dandelion family! Although these short-chain fatty acids yield some energy, this falls far short of that which would have come from hydrolyzing inulin to sugars in the anterior gut.

If, however, the roots or bulbs are cooked for a day or so, the inulin is converted to instantly assimilable fructose sugar. The three-day pit-roasting of camas bulbs by the Nez Perce Indians of Idaho observed by Chestnut at the turn of the century will thus have maximized energy yield from this food, one of their key staples (Konlade and Robson 1972). Similar strategies were almost certainly applied at Abu Hureyra, not only to inulin-rich roots but also to the many other foods that required heat treatment to make them palatable and digestible.

A broad spectrum of foods gathered from a range of closely packed ecological zones not only allows dietary diversity but can also enhance subsistence stability by providing a series of fallback foods when preferred ones fail. It also minimizes the need for residential mobility in which the population moves its village to gather and consume different staple foods at different times of the year. Instead, it allows more logistical strategies in which gathered foods are brought back to a permanent base camp for consumption. It further tends to allow higher population densities. Examples among recent hunter-gatherers include the Owens Valley Paiute, whose rich and diverse resource environment allowed them to minimize residential mobility, that is, to be more sedentary, as well as allowing higher population densities (Steward 1933; Thomas 1979, pp. 33–40). At Abu Hureyra in Period 1A, the resource environment appears to have been at least as rich and diverse at that of the Owens Valley Paiute, and probably more predictable. The evidence for year-round occupation of the village, and a relatively large population, should therefore come as no surprise.

CHANGES IN AVAILABILITY OF PLANT FOOD RESOURCES AND DIET DURING THE EPIPALAEOLITHIC

We have considered the patterns of vegetal resources available 11,500 years ago and have concluded that the plant components of the diet of the people of Abu Hureyra 1 were remarkably diverse. This in turn would have had a positive effect on their nutrition and health. Our charred remains of food plants suggest that this favorable pattern persisted right through phase 1 of the Epipalaeolithic occupation. However, the climate was already becoming more arid, coinciding with the start of the Younger Dryas. The continued availability of seemingly rich resources at Abu Hureyra probably reflects the fact that the peak of increased moisture at 11,500 BP seems to have been extreme, and the initial decline reduced it to a level that was still moister than at any time since the Glacial Maximum. However, at the end of phase 1, around 11,000 BP, we see a systematic change in the use of plant foods, indicating reduced local access to, or reduced productivity of, all the more moisture-demanding of the food plants represented in the remains. This, in turn, presumably reflects a progressive reduction in soil water during the spring and summer growing season with the beginning of the Younger Dryas.

First, foods of park-woodland were seemingly no longer gathered, although, appropriately, the gathering of seeds and, perhaps, the edible roots from the slightly more drought-tolerant asphodel continued for a fraction longer than those from the trees (figure 12.7).

Second, there was a dramatic slump in the use of the wild cereals just after the start of phase 2, around 10,900 BP (figures 12.7, 12.22). This suggests that the inhabitants were losing their nearest stands, with the concomitant increases in transport costs eroding net caloric returns. A similar decline also seems to have afflicted the use of wild relatives of the moisture-demanding millets that, because they were probably gathered primarily from open scrub formations of the lower wadi systems and fans, would have been hit by reduced wadi discharge.

The use of the grain of feather-grasses peaked at about this point and then held steady before finally starting to decline later in phase 2. This decline suggests that, after woodland-steppe was replaced by moist steppe, it in turn was rapidly replaced by dry steppe in which the combined species of feather-grasses grew at significantly lower densities.

EVIDENCE FOR CEREAL CULTIVATION DURING THE EPIPALAEOLITHIC

We have exhaustively explored the evidence for and against the occupants of Epipalaeolithic Abu Hureyra having practiced some form of cultivation since the conclusion of the excavation 25 years ago. We can now report that the balance of evidence suggests that rye was not only under cultivation from the beginning of Period 1B, but was also morphologically domesticated. The impetus for the adoption of cultivation probably involved declining yields from wild staples such the wild cereals, wild feather-grasses, and possibly even acorns. Any cultivation was doubtless initially on a small scale, and for a while much of the hunting and gathering continued as before. However, the increasingly drier conditions of the intensifying Younger Dryas continued to reduce the availability of the wild starch staples and a range of other food plants, and this would have further reinforced the need to cultivate alternative sources of starch.

The evidence for rye cultivation having started during the occupation of Abu Hureyra 1 comes in four forms. First, we have morphologically domestic-type grains from phases 2 and 3 (Periods 1B and 1C). Of those grains dated so far, the earliest are all ryes, AMS-dated as follows: 11,140 ± 100 BP

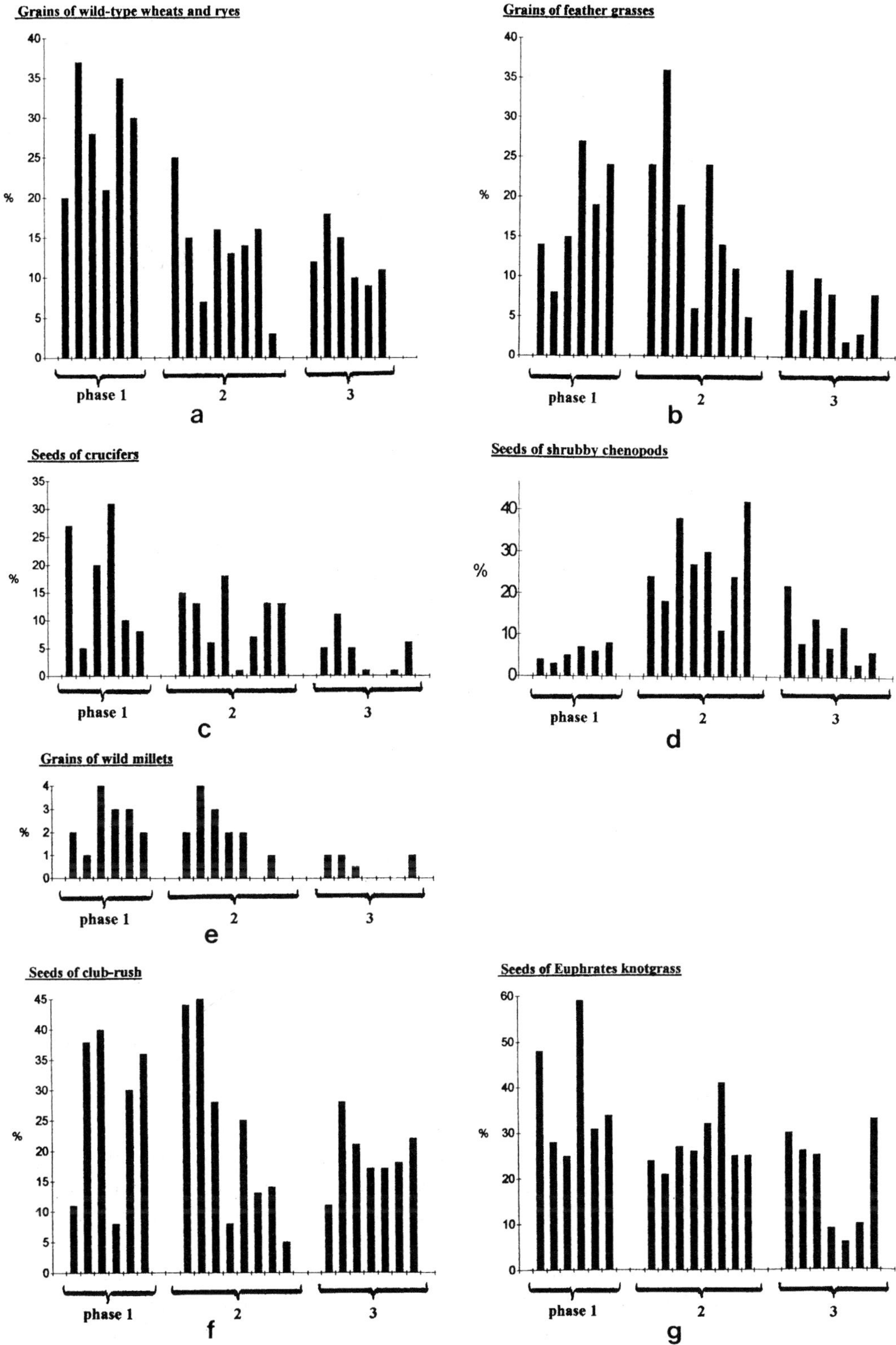

Figure 12.22 Histograms showing the pattern of change in the relative abundance of seven major groups of wild foods from Abu Hureyra 1. a, wild wheats and ryes; b, feather-grasses; c, members of the cress family ("crucifers"), combined; d, shrubby chenopods; e, the wild millets; f, club-rush; g, knotgrass. In histograms a–d the frequencies are expressed as percentages of the total number of charred seeds of dryland species from that level, and in e–g as percentages of all charred seeds.

(OxA-8718), 10,930 ± 120 BP (Ox-6685), and 10,610 ± 100 BP (OxA-8719). Second, changes during the Epipalaeolithic in the relative frequencies of seeds of wild plants reveal the emergence of a distinctive flora of weeds of cultivation—again from the start of phase 2. Third, the steep rise in the relative frequency of large-seeded legumes in the final phase of Abu Hureyra 1, following their earlier decline and disappearance as a gathered food, seems to indicate that they, too, were taken into cultivation toward the end of theEpipalaeolithic. Fourth, we have been able to reconstruct a detailed model of vegetal change that allows us to identify pressures on carrying capacity, starting at the end of phase 1, that would have favored cultivation of starch staples such as cereals.

The evidence from Abu Hureyra does not stand alone. Similar data have been recovered from Mureybit, a site dating from perhaps 10,500 BP, where, as at Abu Hureyra 1, almost all the cereals and other food plants are of the wild type. Colledge's (1994) multivariate analyses of wild seed assemblages from a range of early sites in Southwestern Asia indicate that, at Mureybit, the seed assemblages of even the earliest levels are typical of cultivation. This suggests that the morphologically wild-type einkorns, ryes, and barley were already under predomestication cultivation. Indeed, the inhabitants of Mureybit might also have been cultivating crops of domesticated plants. Van Zeist and Bakker-Heeres (1984, pp. 186–187) identified several specimens of morphologically domestic-type wheats and barley in phases I, II, and III at Mureybit. But although they suggest that these specimens may have been intrusive, there is no record of domestic-type grains from overlying levels. It clearly would be worthwhile dating some of these early domestic grains by accelerator mass spectrometry (AMS).

Cultivation by 11,000 BP is, in any case, of no great surprise. We have already argued that environmental pressures arising from the start of the Younger Dryas are inherently likely to have triggered the adoption of cereal cultivation (Moore and Hillman 1992). I have since explored the ecological mechanisms for this shift in some detail (Hillman 1996), proposing that we should also expect a few even earlier attempts at cultivation from c. 14,500 BP in favored locations in the eastern fringe of the Levant and in adjacent western areas of the northern Fertile Crescent.[26] The subsequent and more widespread adoption of cultivation at the start of the Younger Dryas would then have represented a second set of shifts. However, if the earliest postulated cultivators of the fifteenth millennium BP built structures of the standard Epipalaeolithic type rather than using mound-forming mudbrick and adobe, then finding these earliest farming sites will present a formidable problem.

The First Line of Evidence for Cultivation: Remains of Domestic-type Cereals

I had already found a couple of domesticates in the early stages of research and had dismissed them as intrusives from the overlying Neolithic (Hillman 1975). Susan Colledge and I then identified more domesticates but we decided against publishing any of this information until we had examined enough of the remains to see if there was any pattern to the occurrence of domesticates. We also needed to obtain AMS dates for key specimens. We had to carry out further ecological studies to understand better the pattern of changes in resource base that might have triggered early attempts at cultivation. Finally, we needed to complete our mathematical models of domestication rates, so that we would have a clear idea of the date by which the process of cultivation must have started (Hillman and Davies 1990b, 1992).

In the final stages of research, Susan Colledge undertook the formidable task of screening all the remaining unsorted samples for cereal grain—whether wild or domestic. From these, I have now identified a total of 40 definite domestic-type cereals, and a further five that are almost certainly domesticated. The latter group consisted of four nontwisted barley grains, and one grain of domestic or wild emmer. All the domestic-type specimens were grains, barring one spikelet fork of domestic einkorn. I am confident of the domesticated status of all of the main group of 40 specimens. However, in selecting specimens for AMS dating, I have chosen only those where the diagnostic features are sufficiently well preserved for their identity to be instantly obvious to any archaeobotanist. In all 40 cases they stood out like a sore thumb from the mass of wild types present in the same samples, a point that struck Susan Colledge when she initially sorted the cereal grains from the source samples. The validity of the criteria I have used to identify these specimens as domestic is substantiated by the fact that several of them eventually proved to be intrusive from the overlying Neolithic levels in Trench E, in which Dominique de Moulins identified very few wild types but many indisputable domesticates (see figures 12.28–12.31). Thus, if other archaeobotanists wish to contest the identification of the domestic-type cereal grains dated to the Epipalaeolithic, they will also have to contest the identification of all the other domestic grains dated to the later periods of occupation at Abu Hureyra.

I submitted twelve specimens of the most unequivocal of the domesticates for AMS dating.[27] Three grains of domestic rye, *Secale cereale* subsp. *cereale*, have produced dates of 11,140 ± 100 BP (OxA-8718), 10,930 ± 120 BP (OxA-6685), and 10,610 ± 100 BP (OxA-8719). A fourth grain of domestic rye was dated to 9,860 ± 220 BP (OxA-6996), early in the Intermediate Period at Abu Hureyra. The other eight specimens produced a tight set of dates that coincided with those already obtained for the basal levels of the overlying Neolithic in the same trench (appendix 1). Clearly, these grains were intrusive from those levels.

The Grains of Domestic Rye Dated to the Epipalaeolithic

I applied several criteria in identifying the grains of domestic rye from the Epipalaeolithic (figure 12.23a). The grains were large without the truncation of the embryo tip—4.9 mm long, 2 mm wide, and 1.8 mm high. In size and overall shape they closely resembled the forms of domestic rye grown on the Anatolian Plateau in recent times, both the greenish-grained forms that Sheibe (1934) regarded as typical of acid soils, and the brown-grained forms that he associated with base-rich soils. These Anatolian ryes are more compact than the northern European ryes and are of just the same morphology as most of the tough-rachised weed ryes that also grow on the Anatolian Plateau. The absence of any large scale splitting apart of the hilum groove suggests that the grains were barely distorted by charring, if at all.

The grains were typical of all ryes in being strongly attenuated at the embryo end in both dorsal and side views, and in the presence of a symmetrical ridge running all the way up from just above the embryo. The apical ends were rounded in dorsal view and rounded-truncate in side view, a typical feature of the Anatolian domestic ryes. Certainly, the grains were too broad and thick to be mistaken for any of the wild ryes: wild mountain rye, *Secale monta-*

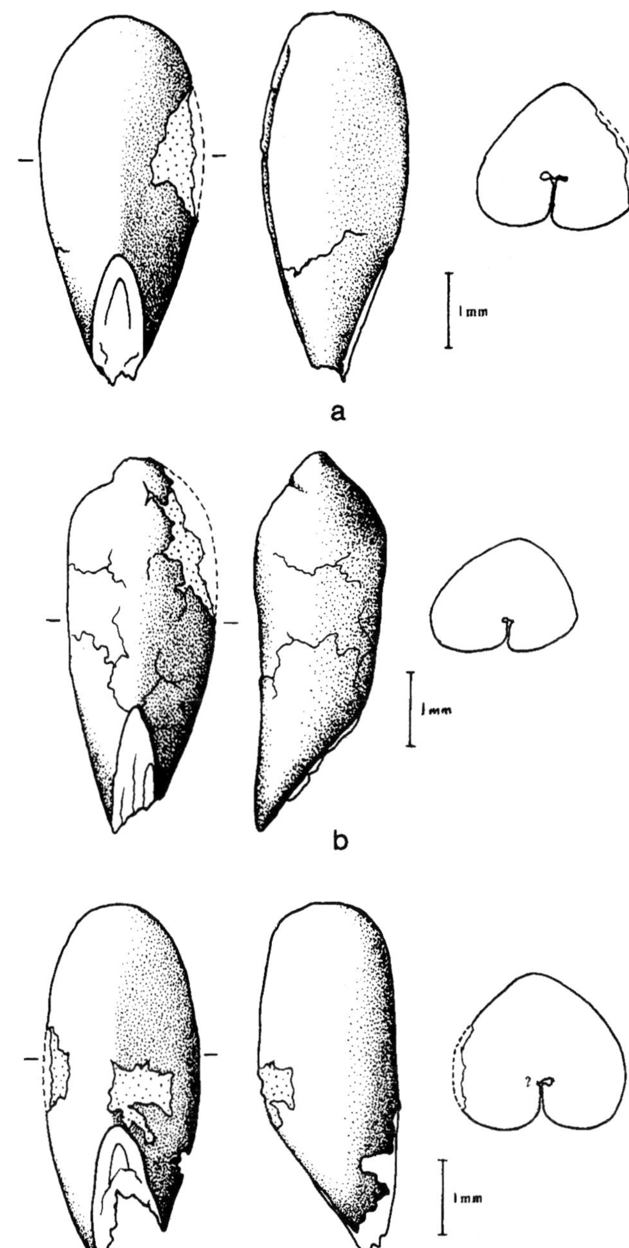

Figure 12.23 Some of the grains of domestic rye recovered from Abu Hureyra 1. a, the grain from E 455 AMS dated to 10,930 ± 120 BP; b, the grain from E 418 AMS-dated to 11,140 ± 100 BP; c, the grain from E 419 AMS-dated to 10,610 ± 100 BP; d and e, two grains from E 449 that have not so far been dated because they were contaminated with silver dag used in SEM examination (Colledge 1988), and therefore require a modified form of pretreatment before being dated; f, the diagnostic embryo end of a grain of domestic rye, *Secale cereale* subsp. *cereale*, also from E 499 but AMS-dated to 9,860 ± 220 BP; g, the tip of a grain of domestic rye complete with diagnostic embryo and scutellum, again from E 449 but AMS-dated to 8,275 ± 65 BP. Note that these domestic rye grains are not only much plumper but also very much larger than the grains of the wild types (compare figure 12.6).

num, wild annual rye, *Secale cereale* subsp. *vavilovii*, or even the seemingly feral *Secale cereale* subsp. *ancestrale*.[28] Like all ryes, but unlike the wheats, the hilum grooves were a partially lacunate T shape, the scutellum and coleoptile scars were strongly attenuated, and the coleoptile scars terminated in a point.

It should be stressed that there is no obvious difference in size or morphology between the domestic-type rye grains that produced the Epipalaeolithic dates, the rye grain dated to the Intermediate Period, the rye grain dated to Neolithic 2, and other domestic-type rye grains found in situ in Abu Hureyra 2 levels.

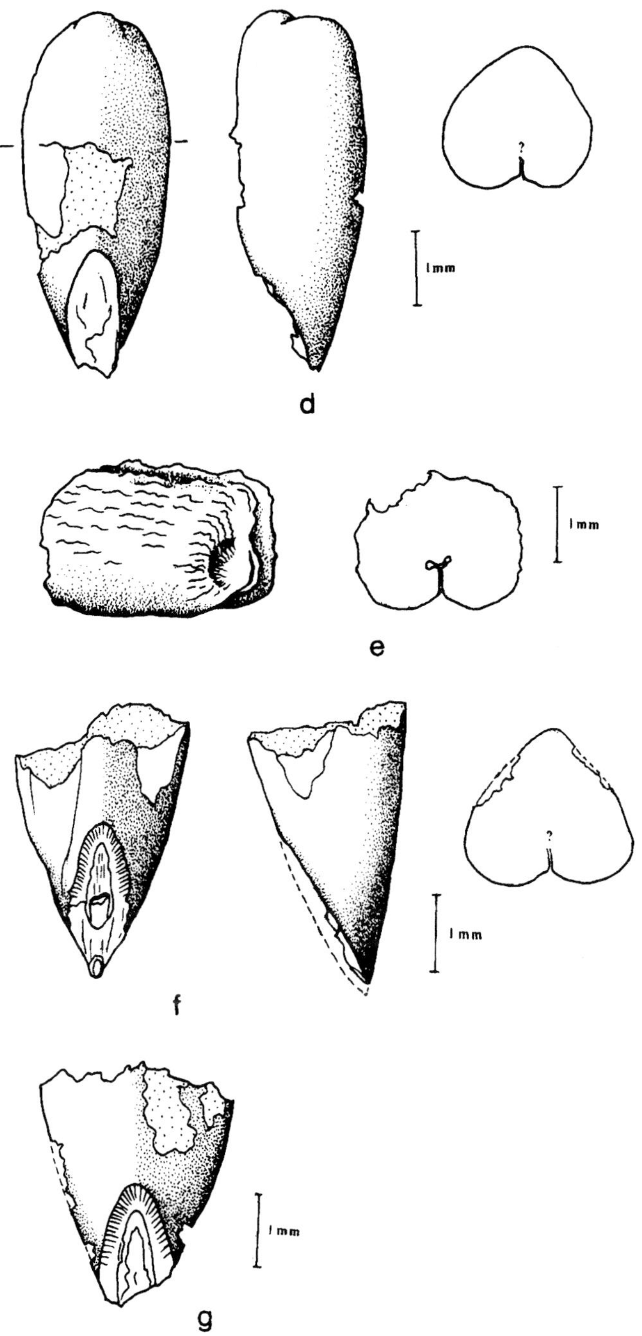

There is another, theoretical, explanation for the presence of grains with domestic-type morphology that does not entail their actually being domesticated, and that therefore does not imply Epipalaeolithic cultivation. Domestic traits, whether a tough rachis or a fat grain, are not created by cultivation; they are produced within populations of otherwise wild-type plants as a result of mutations. The earliest crops of wild-type cereals were originally sown from seeds gathered from wild stands. All that cultivation did was to impose selective pressures on those plants that advantaged the rare domestic-type mutants relative to the normal wild-types, such that, eventually, the mutant domestic types came to dominate the crop (Hillman and Davies 1990a, 1990b, 1992).

Thus, all wild populations throw up occasional domestic-type mutants. However, they do so at a more or less predictable rate. Genes at most chromosomal loci mutate approximately once every million plant generations, so a mutated form of any particular gene will be carried by roughly one plant in a million. However, such genes are generally recessive and will express themselves and become apparent only when they are present in a double dose, that is, as a homozygous recessive. For near-inbreeders like the wheats, one plant in every two to four million will carry this double dose and thus manifest the mutation. But for many traits more than one pair of genes is involved. For example, in diploid wheats such as wild einkorn, rachis fragility is controlled by genes at two positions (loci) on the chromosomes, although, as it happens, a double dose of mutant genes at just one of these positions is enough to make the resulting plant semi-tough-rachised and behave more or less like a domesticate. In stands of wild einkorn, therefore, one plant in every two to four million will have a semi-tough rachis. Rye is also diploid but is relatively understudied, and it remains uncertain whether the first, wild-type crops would have been inbreeders or outbreeders. If it was essentially inbreeding, it is probable that tough-rachised mutants would have occurred at roughly the same low frequency as those cited above for einkorn. If, however, it was outbreeding, these frequencies would have been *extremely* low.

What about other domestic traits such as fat grains? Such a feature is determined by more genes than rachis toughness. Precisely how many would need to be present in a single plant of rye or einkorn in mutated form and at a double dose to ensure that the grains were of the fat, domestic type remains uncertain. However, the chances are that even in inbreeders such plants would occur at considerably lower frequencies than one in four million. And in outbreeders, the frequencies would be even more miniscule.

To summarize, then, in naturally occurring wild stands of rye and einkorn wheat, mutant plants with nonshattering, domestic-type rachises will be *extremely* rare, and those with fat, domestic-type grains will be even rarer. And in outbreeders, which wild rye might have been, these frequencies become infinitesimally small. Given the few domestic grains from Abu Hureyra 1, the changes of encountering such a fat, domestic-type grain as a component of seeds gathered entirely from wild stands therefore tends to zero. The domestic-type rye grain dated to the Epipalaeolithic was therefore almost certainly the product of domestication under cultivation, as, no doubt, were grains of essentially the same type dated to the Intermediate Period and to Abu Hureyra 2.

Why are there so few grains of Epipalaeolithic domestic cereals? On many archaeological sites, cereal grains of the typical, fat, domestic type tend to be underrepresented compared to seeds or wild or weedy species. There are three reasons for this. The first concerns the lack of robustness of these grains when they are preserved by charring. The fat grains of domestic cereals have the same number of cells as their skinny wild progenitors, but the cells are larger. This makes the component tissues less dense and therefore more vulnerable. During the process of charring, soft tissues such as those of mealy grained domestic cereals become vesicular and thence more brittle and susceptible to mechanical damage.

Second, once the grains are charred, repeated wetting and drying reduces the spongy, brittle grains of domesticates to unidentifiable particles much faster than it does the dense-tissued weed seeds and wild-type cereal grains. This is especially so if high-temperature charring had already made the domestic grains differentially more vesicular. We would expect, therefore, that the domestic-type rye grains at Abu Hureyra are underrepresented relative to the wild-type grains, the seeds of other wild foods, and the possible weeds.

There is also a cultural factor. Even today, cultivators go to a lot of trouble not to waste grain raised at the expense of so much time and effort. Their concern was probably even stronger during the earliest stages of cultivation when domestic grains were still a rarity. Once again, therefore, in any remains resulting from normal domestic activities, there will be fewer cultivated grains than waste products such as weed seeds and chaff.

Archaeological examples of underrepresentation of domestic cereal grains abound. For example, although we know that wheat and barley provided the caloric staples at farmstead sites such as Cefn Greanog and Wilderspool in Roman-occupied Britain, in the charred remains from these sites prime grains of both crops were very rare compared with the vast numbers of weed seeds and chaff fragments (Hillman 1981, 1984a). Rowley-Conwy (1982–1983) cites similar examples from sites in Bronze Age Denmark, where an abundance of charred weed seeds is often accompanied by relatively few of the domestic grains. We must therefore exercise extreme caution in attributing any great significance to the relative rarity of domesticates in remains preserved by charring.

If the inhabitants of Abu Hureyra 1 were cultivating rye from early in phase 2, then why do we continue to get wild-type cereal grains throughout phases 2 and 3? Wild-type grains found in levels postdating the first appearance of domestic-type grains probably derived from three sources. First, it is likely that a significant percentage of the small, wild-type grains from phases 2 and 3 derive from tough-rachised, domesticated plants that continued to produce predominantly skinny grains indistinguishable from those of wild types. Even when domestication is largely complete, modifier genes and other factors often ensure that a fluctuating admixture of wild-type characteristics continues for centuries or even millennia in otherwise domestic crops (Hillman and Davies 1990b, figure 11; 1992, figure 13). This occurs with rachis fragility and even more with grain fatness.

The effects of both conscious and unconscious selection will have ensured that ryes with skinny grains persisted in the crop population much longer than those with brittle rachises. Let us consider conscious selection first. For the cultivators, any plants with brittle rachises would have been a nuisance because their ears would have tended to shatter before or during harvest and transport and, as a result, would not only have failed to contribute to overall yield but, worse still, also sowed themselves and then competed with the domesticates of next year's crop. The cultivators would therefore have done their utmost to eliminate them. However, plants whose only wild-type feature was their skinny grains would have been much less deleterious to overall yield and were probably tolerated.

Unconscious selection against plants manifesting a brittle rachis will likewise have continued to be intense, as it resulted automatically from the crop being harvested with sickles or by uprooting. By contrast, any unconscious selection against plants producing small, wild-type grains is likely to have been much less intense, as it would have depended on the quality of their sieves and on just how assiduously they used them in sieving the grain to separate the seed corn for sowing the next year's crop. As a result, ryes with predominantly small, wild-type grains are likely to have persisted in otherwise domesticated crops for many centuries, and certainly much longer than any plants with brittle rachises. Skinny grains resembling those of the wild types were therefore almost certainly part of the very broad distribution of grain sizes that characterized early, tough-rachised, domestic crops.

A proportion of the wild-type grains probably came from brittle-rachised wild-type plants growing in the crop as weeds. Wild cereals regularly infest crops of domesticated cereals throughout Western Asia today. Thus, wild einkorn is a persistent weed of domestic wheats across the Anatolian Plateau, and in Syria, wild barley is a pernicious weed of domestic barley, particularly the two-rowed form that it so closely resembles.

During the early years of cultivation at the start of phase 2, a proportion of the small, wild-type grains could well have arrived on-site from parallel utilization of cultivated domestic rye and wild ryes gathered from wild stands. Continued gathering of wild cereals alongside cultivation would clearly have been encouraged by any social structure in which different families pursued different subsistence strategies. Thus, if the Abu Hureyra population included family groupings that each had different patterns of access to the territory in which they obtained their foods, then groups with rights to wild cereals exclusively in the low-lying areas closest to Abu Hureyra would have been the first to find their wild cereal harvests reduced by increasing aridity. At this point, they could well have been driven to cultivate some rye, while other families whose rights were to the wild cereals in more distant areas at higher elevation could have continued to gather them for much longer. Certainly, just such patterns of differential access to specific wild resources are widely reported among recent hunter-gatherers.

Even in the absence of such groupings within the Abu Hureyra population, rye cultivation could still have been accompanied by the continued gathering of wild grain from ever more distant wild stands. While the wild stands were still available relatively close to the site and were still productive, this might have seemed a sensible option, especially in view of the high net energy costs involved in cultivation. But as the wild stands became more distant, such an option would clearly have become less attractive.

However, by the height of the Younger Dryas in the middle of phase 2, there would have been no stands of wild ryes or wheats growing anywhere within gathering range of Abu Hureyra. The wild-type grains of rye and einkorn present after this point must therefore have originated from the cultivated crops. The wild-type einkorn grains must have come from plants growing as weeds, while the wild-type rye grains could have come either from domestic plants still producing predominantly skinny grains or from brittle-rachised wild-type weeds infesting the crop.

The Second Line of Evidence for Cultivation: The Emergence of Segetal Weed Floras

Of all the plant taxa identified from Epipalaeolithic Abu Hureyra, there are just three major groups that follow a pattern of changes that is different from everything else. Interestingly, it is precisely these same three groups that were eventually to become the dominant weeds of the driest zones of Southwest Asian rain-fed cereal cultivation. Their abrupt increase during phases 2 and 3 probably therefore represents the advent of cultivation. The three groups of plants are the small-seeded legumes comprising the clovers, medicks, and wild relatives of the fenugreek; small-seeded grasses, particularly the wall-barley grasses of the *Hordeum murinum* aggregate and their close relatives, the dwarf twitches, *Eremopyron* spp.; and the stony-seeded gromwells of the bugloss family.

In preparing figure 12.7 we could see that these three groups followed a trend that was the reverse of that followed by almost all other plants. Thus, whereas major food plants such as the wild cereals, feather-grasses, Euphrates knotgrass, club-rush, wild millets, and terebinths were declining during the occupation of Abu Hureyra 1, particularly in phases 2 and 3, these three groups were doing the opposite. Our initial interpretation was that during phase 1 the small-seeded grasses and small-seeded legumes had been gathered as secondary foods but that during phases 2 and 3, as the primary starch staples slowly declined in availability, these other seed foods were gathered in increasing quantities as fallback foods to make up the deficit.

I was not satisfied with this explanation because several of the species of clovers, medicks, wall-barleys, and the dwarf twitches that appeared to be represented in the remains would themselves have eventually been adversely affected by the drier conditions. Also, it did not account for the parallel changes in the Boraginaceae, the stony seeds of which could surely not have served as fallback starch staples. I therefore recalculated the frequencies of occurrence of all the more abundant taxa as percentages to eliminate any distortions due to the effects of context-related variation, and to see if any clearer trends became apparent.

From the new histograms, it was immediately clear that, compared to all other dryland taxa, each of these three groups had initially declined to very low levels during phase 1 but that, at the start of phase 2, they began to increase synchronously and systematically—far more dramatically than had previously been apparent (figure 12.24).

So, what do these histograms tell us? For phase 1, the earlier hypothesis remains the most plausible, namely, that small-seeded grasses and legumes were gathered as secondary foods and that this usage declined slightly during the phase 1 occupation. This accords with the use of these seeds as secondary foods by recent hunter-gatherers who, like the people of Abu Hureyra, had access to a wealth of other plant food resources, for example, the consumption by the Cahuilla of medick and clover seed (Bean and Saubel 1972, pp. 88, 141), by the Maidu of brome and poa-grass grains (Duncan 1963, p. 54), and by the Seri of the small grains of ziizil grass, *Muhlenbergia* (Felger and Moser 1985, p. 309).

The use of the seeds of the gromwells during phase 1 was evidently even more modest. Because the silicified seeds survive without charring, the frequencies in the histogram represent a gross overrepresentation relative to the other seed types. This seemingly modest level of use accords with their possible utilization as a source of an oil that required the investment of considerable effort—both in the gathering of the seeds and in the process of extraction. The oil's value probably lay not only in its good flavor but also in its health-giving properties. Like the oil from the closely related star-flower, it is rich in gamma-linolenic acid (GLA) and would perhaps have been recognized as relieving inflammatory disease and high blood pressure.[29]

For phases 2 and 3, the percentage-based histograms suggest that, although the fallback food interpretation remains a possibility for a few of the species present in the legume and grass groups, this explanation does not otherwise fit the evidence. All three of these groups, the small-seeded legumes, small-

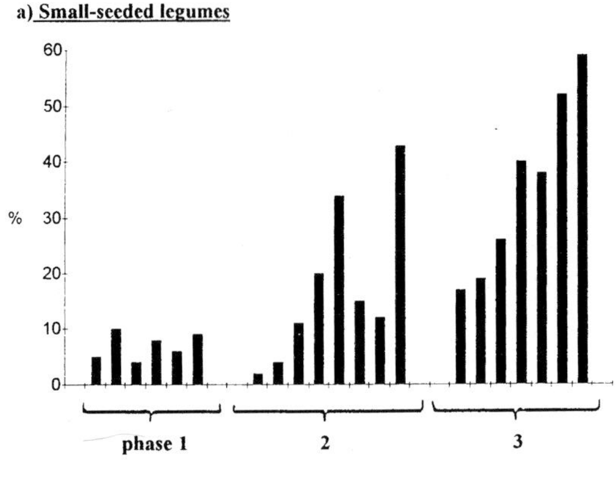

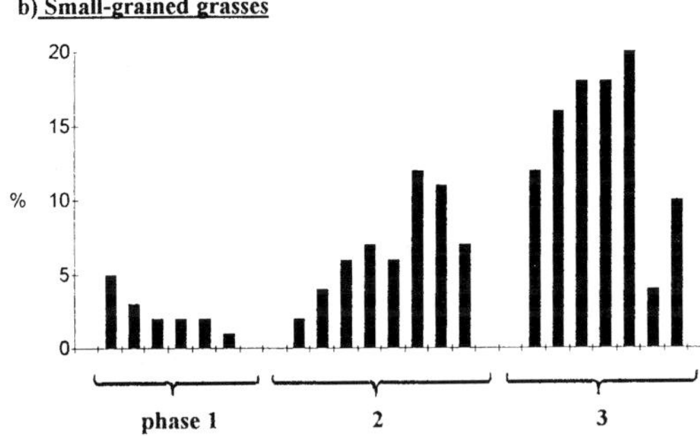

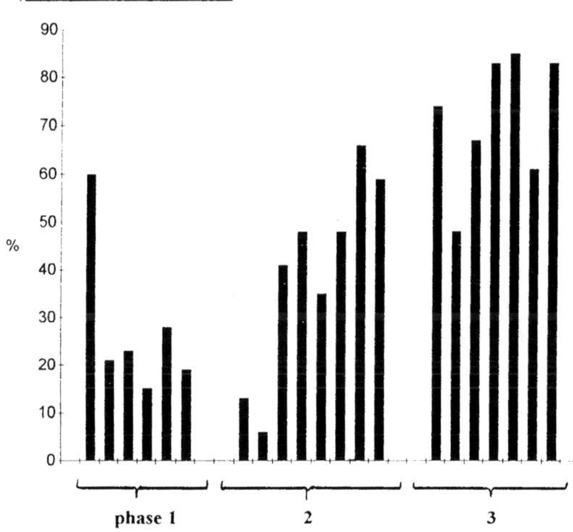

Figure 12.24 Histograms showing pattern of changes in the relative abundance of three groups of plants during Abu Hureyra 1. a, small-seeded legumes; b, small-grained grasses; c, stony-seeded gromwells. Today, all three groups are classic weeds of dryland cultivation in areas potentially capable of supporting woodland-steppe, steppe, and dry steppe. Their steep rise from the start of Period 1B (phase 2) reflects the start of dryland cultivation in steppe habitats that were becoming increasingly arid.

seeded grasses, and stony-seeded gromwells, are classic weeds that today dominate the segetal and ruderal weed floras of dryland cultivation, and it is therefore probable that the dramatic and synchronous increase of all three groups reflects the start of some new form of soil disturbance. As there were no large flocks or herds of domestic animals at this time, and the wild herds of gazelle and onagers passed through swiftly, cultivation is the obvious candidate. We therefore seem to be confronted by a pattern reflecting the rise of a weed flora under arable cultivation.

As weeds, these three groups are today characteristic specifically of dryland, rainfed cultivation, rather than either irrigation agriculture or cultivation of the valley bottom in areas with high water tables. Had there been any irrigation or valley-bottom cultivation during phases 2 and 3, we would have expected a systematic rise in seeds from those plants that eventually became weeds of such areas, namely, the wild millets, dwarf timothys, knotgrasses, and club-rush. In fact, we find no such pattern.

The dryland weed flora could also have come from the cultivation of elevated dry areas of the valley bottom such as old levee systems, as proposed for Neolithic Thessaly (van Andel and Runnels 1995). Compared to Thessaly, however, old levee systems would have been far less important for early cultivators at Abu Hureyra because they had the extended network of shallow wadi systems nearby, each with narrow strips of land offering enhanced soil water (figure 2.12). Van Andel tells me that there were no equivalent resources on the Plains of Thessaly because of the hard bedrock there.

We next need to identify precisely what forms of dryland, rain-fed cultivation are characterized by these three groups of weeds. In the present day, they grow as the dominant weeds of dryland cultivation only in the more arid zones of Western Asia, that is, in areas potentially capable of supporting woodland-steppe, moist steppe, and dry steppe. These are the very zones that would have dominated the Abu Hureyra area during phases 2 and 3. In slightly moister zones of rain-fed cultivation in Western Asia today, these same three weed groups, although still abundant, are outnumbered by other groups of weeds. For example, at the village of Asvan in Southeast Asia Minor in an area of potential park-woodland my analyses of the weed contaminants of granaries revealed that our three weed groups were outnumbered by the weed ryes, by large-seeded weed vetches, by members of the chervil family (Umbelliferae) such as the bur-parsleys, by crucifers such as charlock, and by members of the campion family (Caryophyllaceae) such as the winged soapwort. A further difference in these moister areas is that the most numerous small-seeded grasses are the rye grasses such as darnel, which was seemingly absent from Abu Hureyra, while the bugloss family is dominated by the corn gromwell, itself relatively uncommon at Abu Hureyra, and borage and bugloss genera such as *Anchusa*, *Echium*, and *Alkanna*.

So, just what weed floras do we find today in the driest zones of rain-fed cultivation? In fields cultivated in areas ranging from woodland-steppe, for example, near Jebel Abyad, through moist steppe to dry steppe south of Raqqa, we have invariably found that the present-day weed flora is dominated, first, by members of the bugloss family such as the small dryland gromwell, *Arnebia decumbens*, the dwarf gromwell, *Buglossoides tenuiflora*, and the large dryland gromwell, *A. linearifolia*; second, small-seeded legumes including a wide range of the wild relatives of fenugreek, for example, *Trigonella astroites* and *T. monantha*, a number of medicks such as *Medicago minima* and *M. polymorpha*, and a few clovers such as *Trifolium scabrum* and *T. tomentosum*; and third, small-seeded grasses such as drought-tolerant members of the wall-barley complex, dwarf twitches, tail-grass, *Lepturus pubescens*, and spiked tail-grass, *Loliolum* sp. It is seed remains from these very plants that we find increasing so rapidly and systematically in Abu Hureyra 1 during phases 2 and 3. We therefore conclude that, during these two phases, such plants were indeed growing as weeds of dryland, arable cultivation.[30]

The continued increase in the seeds of these plants throughout phases 2 and 3 probably represents the progressive expansion of the areas under cultivation, rather than an increasing density of weed infestation in any one area. The latter would reflect either a response to increasing aridity or the evolution of forms better adapted to the disturbed conditions of cultivation. However, neither is likely to have played a role here. First, even in their totally wild state in remote steppe, these plants are already preadapted to multiply with any form of disturbance, whether natural or artificial, without needing centuries of selection under cultivation. Second, because all three of the weed groups thrive under cultivation in woodland-steppe at least as prolifically as they do in moist steppe, and even more than in dry steppe, their increase during phases 2 and 3 is unlikely to be attributable to the increasing desiccation.

We are left, therefore, with expanding cultivation as the simplest explanation for the increase in these three groups of plants during phases 2 and 3 of the Epipalaeolithic occupation of Abu Hureyra.

The Third Line of Evidence for Cultivation: The Possibility that Pulses Were Adopted as a Second Batch of Cultigens in Phase 3 of Abu Hureyra 1

The frequency distribution for the large-seeded legumes shows lentils and the large-seeded vetches to have followed a pattern that was entirely different from that seen in all the other wild plant foods, and also different from that found in the three groups that seemingly become weeds of cultivation during phases 2 and 3. Lentils and the large-seeded vetches seem to have been a component of Epipalaeolithic subsistence from the outset (figure 12.25). Their role in diet might well have been greater than the small number of seeds recovered implies, as the large-seeded legumes tend to be underrepresented in charred remains. As wild plants in phase 1, these pulses would have thrived primarily in the moister parts of the same zones as the wild wheats and ryes. Advancing desiccation would therefore have eliminated them somewhat sooner than it eliminated these cereals. The early, rapid decline of these legumes in phase 1, and their complete disappearance in phase 2, may reflect this greater susceptibility to drought, although the effects of mere chance when dealing with such low numbers cannot be disregarded.

However, the subsequent steep rise of these legume seeds in the middle of phase 3 is anomalous. It fails to fit the pattern of continued steady decline that we see in almost all the other wild food plants, and the rise happens much too late to coincide with the dramatic emergence of what seem to have been arable weed floras. It also cannot be explained as a response to moister conditions starting during phase 3 and marking the end of the Younger Dryas, as this would certainly have been insufficient to allow wild lentils to reestablish anywhere within gathering range of Abu Hureyra.

The only simple explanation is that their reappearance and steep rise in the middle of phase 3 represents the point at which they were taken into cultivation. If this was so, the cultivators must have obtained their seed stocks from wild stands that by this time would have grown only at some distance to the west, from the south in the Jebel Abu Rujmein, or from other groups who had

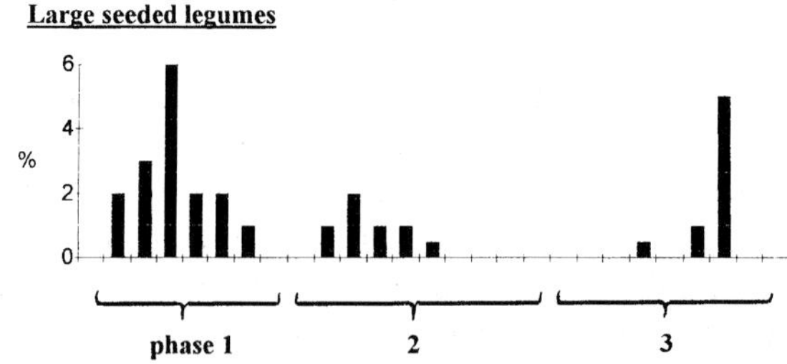

Figure 12.25 Histogram showing changes in the relative abundance of seeds of the large-seeded legumes during Abu Hureyra 1. They include lentils and large-seeded vetches, and the frequencies represent percentages of the number of charred seeds of dryland species present in each level. Again, their sudden reappearance after a period of absence, and at a point when wild stands would have been locally unavailable, probably reflects the start of their cultivation.

perhaps already domesticated and begun to cultivate them. The possibility that cultivation started as early as c. 14,500 BP at a few favorable locations farther to the west (Hillman 1996) clearly favors this scenario.

However, the remains of the seeds themselves provide, as yet, no means of independently testing whether they were under cultivation, or even whether they were domesticated. Although modern domestic pulses are distinguished by their indehiscent pods, loss of dormancy, generally larger seeds, and, in some cases, smoother and/or thinner testas (D. Zohary 1989; Ladizinsky 1989), none of these criteria is useful in determining the cultivated or domestic status of lentil and vetch remains preserved by charring (Butler 1989, 1991). First, the pods themselves do not survive in charred remains. Second, we have yet to isolate chemical or histological markers of dormancy that survive charring—except in pea, which is not involved here. Third, seed size is unreliable for distinguishing domesticates; for example, Vavilov and Bukinich (1929, p. 331) found domestic lentils in Afghanistan with seeds of 3 mm diameter, which is smaller than those of many surviving populations of their wild progenitor.

The early cultivation of lentils and large-seeded vetches suggested by their anomalous increase in frequency during phase 3 cannot be tested, therefore, from the seed remains themselves using currently available criteria. In the meantime, their cultivation from midway through phase 3 of the Epipalaeolithic currently offers the only simple explanation.

Where Did the Domestic Rye Come From, and How Long Would the Domestication Process Have Taken?

As with the apparently cultivated legumes, the domesticated rye must either have arrived at Abu Hureyra from elsewhere or have been domesticated locally. Wherever it happened, the domestic forms first emerged in wild-type crops initially sown from seed gathered from wild stands during a period of predomestication cultivation (Hillman and Davies 1990a). As yet, there are no sites with evidence of cereal cultivation predating phase 2 of Abu Hureyra 1, though some may eventually be found. In the meantime, we must explore the arguments for local initiation of cultivation with on-the-spot domestication, and for the adoption of agriculture and domestic seed stocks from elsewhere, perhaps accompanied by some of the farmers themselves.

The first scenario would be the import of seeds from other groups already cultivating domestic cereals. It is quite possible that the first Abu Hureyra cultivators obtained their seeds stocks of domesticates from other groups in the region who were already cultivating them. Certainly the web of long-distance contacts typical of ancient and recent hunter-gatherers, and documented by imported artifacts, shells, and raw materials, makes it probable that the inhabitants of Abu Hureyra 1 were well aware of the subsistence strategies and food plants of groups as distant as the Levantine coast.

The second scenario would be on-the-spot domestication. The rye could, alternatively, have been domesticated locally at Abu Hureyra. In this case, some of the wild-type rye grains in levels predating the emergence of the dated domesticates probably derive from cultivated wild-type crops that were not yet domesticated. And in this case, we need to consider how far back in the Epipalaeolithic this predomestication cultivation of wild-types started.

Our studies of domestication rates (Hillman and Davies 1990a, 1990b, 1992) suggest that, as soon as early farmers began harvesting essentially inbreeding, wild-type crops such as wheats and barleys with sickles or by uprooting, then the crop would have become largely domesticated within 200 years, possibly much faster. Such a brief phase of predomestication cultivation of wild-type cereals would often be archaeologically undetectable. At Abu Hureyra, we need to consider two issues.

The first is protracted predomestication cultivation. What if the first farmers initially harvested their wild-type crops by *different* methods such as beating?[31] In that case, there could be a long period during which the crops would have remained indefinitely in their wild-type state. We have called this nondomestication cultivation because it does not, of itself, lead inexorably to the crop becoming domesticated. Is this, perhaps, what was happening in phase 1 of Abu Hureyra 1, and was the eventual appearance of domesticates in phase 2 the result of having changed to harvesting with sickles or by uprooting after a long period of nondomestication cultivation spanning much of phase 1?

The answer is almost certainly—No! If the rapid emergence of what we now interpret as segetal weed floras is, indeed, linked with the cultivation of cereals, as we suggest above, then the absence of any trace of such a trend in phase 1 seems, for the moment, to preclude any possibility of either a protracted period of predomestication cultivation or an extended prior period of nondomestication cultivation. If, therefore, there was an independent, local initiation of cultivation of these cereals, followed by their domestication, then it must have happened quite rapidly, toward the faster end of the range of possibilities proposed in our model.[32]

The second is the problem of outbreeders. Our mathematical model of domestication rates in wild cereals indicates that domestication occurs within 200 years only if the level of inbreeding is around 90%, as it is in the wild wheats and barley. Indeed, our model suggests that, with a wild-type crop that is almost totally outbreeding, even the most intense selective pressure favoring domestic, tough-rachised mutants would fail to establish them as a significant component of the crop population after as much as 8,000 years, which was the upper limit we set for our mathematical simulation. This poses us a problem in explaining the early domestic rye from Abu Hureyra, not only because present-day domestic rye is generally accepted to be an outbreeder, albeit admittedly often less then 60% outbreeding, but also because current evidence suggests that its immediate wild ancestor, *Secale cereale* subsp. *vavilovii*, is also an outbreeder. How, then, do we explain how crops of wild-type rye ever became domesticated? In seeking an explanation we must address three questions.

First, could the first farmers have accelerated the domestication process by consciously picking out and separately propagating the rare, tough-rachised mutants? Our mathematical model of domestication rates assumed *unconscious* selection arising primarily from harvesting with sickles or by uprooting. We specifically dismissed any possibility of conscious selection because the first farmers could never be expected to detect tough-rachised mutant ears occurring at a frequency of just one per two to four million brittle, wild-type ears, especially when the ears were all ripening at different rates. We also dismissed the argument that, in gathering their seed from wild stands for sowing the first crops, they needed only to wait until all the wild-type ears had shattered so they could then have collected the isolated ears of the rare tough-rachised mutants. It seemed to us unlikely that such solitary upstanding ears would survive bird predation for more than a few hours, and in any case, this scenario required a remarkable measure of foreknowledge of the advantages of these mutants under a yet-to-be-developed agrarian system. Hunter-gatherers already had to be expert naturalists at every level, but requiring them to have mastered precognition seemed unreasonable.

Nevertheless, we were perhaps too dismissive; maybe bird predation would not have been so immediate, and perhaps the proto-farmers could have picked the rare tough-rachised ears, say, after a summer storm, and then sown the seed to multiply the stock, and thus had a fully tough-rachised crop within just a few years.

Second, is *Secale cereale* subsp. *vavilovii* really an outbreeder in any case? The literature is confused on this point; although Kobyljanskij (1989) describes it as an outbreeder, Hammer, Skolimowska, and Knüpffer (1987) describe it as an inbreeder. Our own studies of what appears to be *Secale cereale* subsp. *vavilovii* on Mount Ararat show it to be unequivocally an outbreeder. For the moment, we suspect that Hammer's description probably applies to another species, *Secale iranicum* (Kobyl.), that is unlikely to be involved in the evolution of the domesticate but that had mistakenly been accessed in the Gartersleben genebank as *vavilovii*.

But are we right to assume that the Ararat rye, which we have provisionally referred to *vavilovii*, really is the ancestor of domestic rye? Terence Miller of the John Innes Cambridge Laboratories in Norwich has found that it is clearly capable of being the ancestor; certainly it crosses readily with the domesticate to give a fertile F1 hybrid producing seven chromosomal bivalents at metaphase 1 of meiosis. However, even in the present day, there are several forms of rye reported from Iran, for example, that have never been studied, and in the 11,000 or more years since the domestication of the rye at Abu Hureyra, there have doubtless been hundreds of other races that have disappeared without trace. Some of these will inevitably have been much closer to the race or races of wild rye that were first taken into cultivation and domesticated than any wild population surviving today. All that we can realistically say of the Ararat rye is that it is the nearest presently known surviving relative of the original ancestor of domestic rye.

One of the many, now extinct forms could have been an *inbreeding* equivalent of the Ararat rye. Such a form need carry different genes at only a few chromosomal loci, and this would not necessarily prevent it from being interfertile with domestic rye (and, indeed, with the present-day Ararat *vavilovii*). As such, it would be just as fitting a candidate for the immediate wild ancestor. If taken into cultivation 11,000 or more years ago, such an inbreeding rye crop could have become domesticated as rapidly as crops of inbreeding wild wheats, even with entirely unconscious selection. Thereafter, this domesticated crop of inbreeding rye could have been introgressed by genes from related, outbreeding forms, with the result that the crop eventually changed from an inbreeder to an outbreeder.

It is also relevant to recall that present-day domestic rye is, itself, not uniformly outbreeding anyway. Terence Miller informs me that outbreeding within the cultivated subspecies varies from 90% down to 20% and is phenotypically quite plastic. Its wild ancestor need not, therefore, have been so strongly outbreeding after all.

We can therefore dismiss neither the possibility of very rapid conscious selection of a domestic crop population regardless of its breeding behavior, nor the possibility that the immediate wild ancestor of domestic rye was to some degree inbreeding and could therefore have been relatively rapidly domesticated—even with entirely unconscious selection. The period required for crops of wild-type rye to become domesticated may therefore not pose such an insurmountable problem after all—whether for local domestication at Abu Hureyra or for earlier domestication elsewhere. For the moment, however, the matter must remain open.

In summary, then, domestic seeds stocks could have been either obtained from other groups or domesticated on the spot, although in the latter case domestication must have occurred relatively rapidly. My personal view is that cereal and pulse cultivation at Abu Hureyra probably arrived fully fledged from elsewhere, albeit possibly in stages. At the moment, our scanty evidence from Abu Hureyra suggests that domestic rye arrived first, followed by some pulses, and then, in the Intermediate Period, the wheats and barleys, followed later by chickpeas and horsebean. However, this view could quickly be changed by new evidence, and it is not impossible that the rye will eventually prove to have been domesticated locally, with the other crops arriving later, in stages, from elsewhere.

Why did they choose to cultivate rye? Whether domestic rye arrived from elsewhere or was domesticated locally, it offered a number of advantages over other cereals. Even while still gathering rye grain from wild stands, the foragers of Abu Hureyra would have been aware that wild rye had advantages over the wild wheats and barleys. But domesticated rye offered the additional advantages of having a fully tough rachis, and the already flimsy chaff was also very loose. Together, these features would have ensured that the grains could be freed from the ears by a single threshing, and that the straw and chaff could then be eliminated from the grain by a single round of winnowing. Such a cereal is termed "free-threshing." Equivalent advanced forms of wheat such as bread wheat and macaroni wheat evolved later.

By contrast, the first domesticated wheats to emerge were glume wheats such as domestic einkorn and domestic emmer. These required not only vigorous threshing to break the ears into their component spikelets and free them from the straw, but also after the first winnowings to eliminate the straw, they then required pounding in a pestle and mortar to fragment the spikelets and thereby release the grain. A further round of winnowings was required to eliminate the light chaff from the grains, followed by sieving to eliminate the heavier chaff components. Clearly, therefore, it was much easier to process rye.[33]

There were other advantages, too. As with wild rye, the grains of most domestic ryes were much easier to mush for porridge and to grind for bread than the grains of any glume wheats. And, again like wild rye, foods from domestic rye would have been much more sustaining than equivalent foods from wheats and barleys.

Domestic rye continued to be cultivated at Abu Hureyra during the Intermediate Period and in Period 2. It turns up next in the archaeological record at Neolithic Can Hasan III in Anatolia and Bronze Age Alaca Höyük (Hillman 1978). Elsewhere, however, it appears to have been supplanted by the wheats. In view of its many advantages, this might seem surprising. An explanation probably lies in one or more of its disadvantages. For many people, the most obvious drawback is the sour taste that rapidly develops in rye products kept after cooking; even today, most populations prefer the flavor and rapid digestibility of wheat products. As an outbreeder, it is susceptible to infection by the ergot fungus, *Claviceps purpurea*, that replaces the grain with a purple-black sclerotium that, if present in grain products, renders them poisonous. Small quantities are abortifacient and hallucinogenic; slightly larger quantities are lethal (Forsyth 1979). Rye tends to grow taller than wheat and is therefore more prone to lodging in high winds or rain. Because most forms of cultivated rye mature somewhat later than most wheats, it is more susceptible to the soil drying out in the spring.

Wild perennial rye was unlikely to have been cultivated. After many generations of gathering the grain of perennial rye from wild stands as foragers, the first cultivator's intimate knowledge of its ecology and life cycle would have told them it was pointless trying to grow it, as it produces very little yield for at least two years after sowing.

Where would the people of Abu Hureyra have grown their rye crops? Contrary to popular perceptions among many palaeoecologists and archaeobotanists (but not farmers!), the various forms of domestic rye are tolerant of a wide range of edaphic conditions ranging from base-poor sands to base-rich marls, and from well-drained gravels to sticky clays (Hillman 1978; Sheibe 1934). However, in view of rye's susceptibility to the soil drying out in the spring, the ever-drier conditions of the Younger Dryas in phase 2 would have obliged the first cultivators at Abu Hureyra to sow their crops in locations where there was enhanced soil moisture that was likely to last right into April. The most obvious locations would have been the moistest of those where, in recent times, local farmers sowed their modern wheats and barleys, namely, at breaks in slope, particularly on wadi sides, and even on the floors of dry wadis, albeit only in patches where the near-mature crops would not be flushed away by a spring spate in wet years (figures 12.26, 12.27). Certainly, the plots must have been in locations that were moister than those where the wild ryes and wheats had already been experiencing water stress.

The plant remains suggest that the people of Abu Hureyra were cultivating neither low-lying areas of the main Euphrates Valley nor the lower parts of the fan of the merged Wadis Shetnet es-Salmas and Hibna. First, the three classes of weed flora that increased so dramatically from the start of phase 2 are all typical of *dryland* cultivation. Had they cultivated moist areas of the valley bottom at this time, we would expect to see a similarly steep rise in the seeds of, for example, the wild relatives of millet and the dwarf timothys, whereas we see relatively few such seeds after the middle of phase 2 (figure 12.22). Second, although the steady decrease in the use of club-rush during phase 2 indicates reduced overbank flooding—presumably as a result of the Younger Dryas—the continued availability of reasonable quantities of club-rush and Euphrates knotgrass indicates that some overbank flooding continued, even during the trough of the Younger Dryas around the middle of phase 2. Any such flooding would probably have posed too great a risk for valley-bottom cultivation, particularly as flooding occurred in the spring at just the point when the autumn-sown crops would have been ripening.[34]

The Pressures to Start Cultivating Cereals and Pulses at Abu Hureyra

No hunter-gatherers occupying a productive locality with a range of wild foods able to provide for all seasons are likely to have started cultivating their caloric staples willingly. Energy investment per unit of energy return would have been too high, and the act of cultivation would probably have required them to overturn ecological, ethical, and spiritual perceptions concerning their relationship to their environment and the Creator (MacLuhan 1972). However, cultivation offered one major advantage: it allowed more calories to be extracted per unit area of land, albeit at the expense of much hard work and ecological damage.

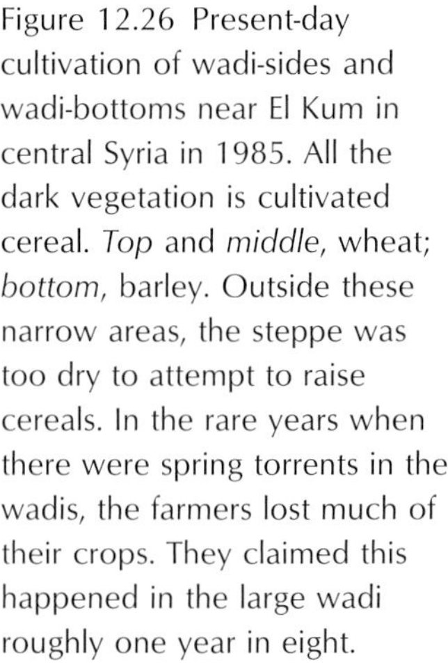

Figure 12.26 Present-day cultivation of wadi-sides and wadi-bottoms near El Kum in central Syria in 1985. All the dark vegetation is cultivated cereal. *Top* and *middle*, wheat; *bottom*, barley. Outside these narrow areas, the steppe was too dry to attempt to raise cereals. In the rare years when there were spring torrents in the wadis, the farmers lost much of their crops. They claimed this happened in the large wadi roughly one year in eight.

Figure 12.27 An impression of the early cultivation of rye c. 10,500 BP when the dry conditions of the Younger Dryas had resulted in wholesale die-back of trees of the local woodland-steppe (note the dead terebinth trees), and had eliminated local stands of wild wheats, ryes, and pulses. a, tilling a patch of ground with a wood- or stone-headed mattock in early autumn at a relatively moist break-of-slope beside the Wadi Shetnet es-Salmas just above Abu Hureyra, and sowing it with domestic rye; b, harvesting the same crop in early summer using a short, curved flint-bladed sickle of the type found at Mugharet el Wad. The ears of the crop are not shattering because they are either already tough-rachised or are being harvested while still slightly unripe. (By Ivan Crowe).

It was probably acute pressure on the carrying capacity of the land that drove hunter-gatherers to start cultivating some of their caloric staples. At Abu Hureyra, this stress on carrying capacity seems to have resulted from the dry conditions of the Younger Dryas causing reductions in the yields of their major wild plant energy sources. The people of Abu Hureyra were already occupying the location with the richest wild foods of the region, so there was nowhere better to go, except far to the west where the prime locations were probably already getting crowded. Migration was therefore unlikely to have offered an alternative to staying put and starting to cultivate.

Of the starch staples probably available to the people of Abu Hureyra 1, the first to decline would have been acorns. Even at the start of phase 1, acorn gathering from the nearest park-woodlands would have involved the foragers in 15 km translocations in late summer (figure 12.1). Fifteen kilometers is two thirds of the maximum distance that was traditionally acceptable for large-scale acorn gathering by recent hunter-gatherers occupying similar environments. Once the Younger Dryas began later in phase 1 and the oaks in park-woodland at lower elevations ceased to bear acorns, their use must eventually have tailed away. This would have made the people of Abu Hureyra much more heavily dependent on wild cereals, pulses, and other energy foods.

The next significant resource to start to die out in areas close to Abu Hureyra was probably the large-seeded legumes, usage of which began to decline around the middle of phase 1 (figure 12.25). This was followed at the start of phase 2 by a sharp decline in the use of wild cereals such as annual rye, einkorn, and emmer (see figure 12.22). However, with all these wild foods, the decline in their availability probably started well before the eventual decline in their use. This is because the people of Abu Hureyra would doubtless have attempted to maintain gross returns from the retreating resources by traveling greater distances, until it became uneconomic.

It was the loss of stands of wild cereals in areas reasonably close to Abu Hureyra around the start of phase 2 that probably stimulated some families to try to maintain grain yields from wild-type cereals. They would have selected nearby areas of land that were moister than those where the stands of wild cereals were now failing, but where wild cereals were normally outcompeted by other vegetation that did not provide staple foods. Then they would have cleared this vegetation and broken or tilled the ground.[35] After obtaining either domestic grain from groups already cultivating crops elsewhere or wild-type grain from local stands of wild rye, they would have sowed it on the tilled plots; harrowed it into the soil to limit predation by rodents, birds, and ants; and protected the plots against predation by wild boar and hare. They would have undertaken the tilling and sowing immediately after the start of the autumn rains, because moistening the hard, gypsiferous soil makes it much easier to till, and sown seeds are not safe from seed-eating predators until they have become wet and germinated.

The progressive increase in the weed seeds suggests that not all families adopted cultivation straight away. Some families were probably able to continue using stands of wild cereals growing farther from Abu Hureyra for a while until these, too, retreated out of range. The greater drought resistance of the various feather-grasses would have allowed them to replace the wild ryes and wheats as the latter retreated, so some families will have used the feather-grasses as a nutritious alternative to the wild cereals. The first feather-grass to fill the gap would have been the least drought-resistant species, *Stipa holosericea* (*S. lagascae*), followed by *S. barbata*, *S. hohenackeriana*, *S. parviflora*, and finally *S. capensis*. Significantly, the use of feather-grass grain appears to have peaked just after the start of phase 2, simultaneously with a decline in the use of wild cereal grain. A third reason for some families possibly delaying starting cultivation might have been fundamental ecological, ethical, and spiritual misgivings over "playing God" by destroying entire areas of natural vegetation, disturbing the ground on a scale well beyond that ever involved in obtaining edible tubers (MacLuhan 1972, pp. 15, 56), and replacing the natural vegetation with one alien to that habitat.

The ever-increasing abundance of the weed flora suggests that cultivated crops became an increasingly major component of their subsistence through phases 2 and 3, and the use of wild feather-grass grains finally started to decrease.

SUMMARY: THE PLANT COMPONENTS OF SUBSISTENCE DURING THE EPIPALAEOLITHIC

The start of occupation at Abu Hureyra 1 coincided with optimal growing conditions across Southwest Asia, and our ecological models indicate that the inhabitants had access to an exceptionally diverse plant-food resource base that included a range of productive caloric staples. The remains of food plants from phase 1 correspondingly reveal the plant components of diet to have been diverse and nutritious. The staples apparently included the grain or seeds of wild ryes and wheats, wild feather-grasses, club-rush, Euphrates knotgrass, wild millets, and wild shrubby chenopods. Ethno-ecological modeling also suggests that acorns, almonds, and a range of wild root foods almost certainly served as additional staples. Altogether, seed foods appear to have included over 120 types, and the total number of plant-food species consumed probably exceeded 250.

However, even during phase 1 we start to see a decline in the use of wild foods characteristic of the most moist of the nonriverine vegetal zones, namely, oak-dominated park-woodland. The Younger Dryas was taking hold. Among the first foods to decline were asphodel seeds, wild lentils, and some woodland fruits. However, much more dramatic in its effect on subsistence would have been the rapid loss of acorns, which had almost certainly served as a caloric staple. These probably ceased to be available by the middle of phase 1. By phase 2, even less moisture-demanding foods were being affected; we soon see a decline in the use of wild ryes and wheats, followed by the feather-grasses, club-rushes, and crucifers. The decline in the use of club-rush seeds probably reflects the effect of the Younger Dryas in reducing discharge from the upstream catchment of the Euphrates, thereby reducing the frequency and extent of overbank flooding.[36]

But as soon as the use of key starch staples such as wild cereals, feather-grasses, and club-rush seeds declines, we see the start of a dramatic *increase* in the seeds of three groups of classic weeds: small-seeded legumes, small-seeded grasses, and stony-seeded gromwells. These are the self-same three groups of plants that today classically dominate the weed flora of dryland cultivation in the woodland-steppe, moist steppe, and dry steppe zones. The rise in these three weed groups thus strongly suggests the start of cultivation within these same vegetal zones at Abu Hureyra.

Coinciding with the start of the rise of this classic weed flora is the appearance of the first charred grains of domesticated rye, the earliest of which are AMS-dated to 11,140 ± 100 BP, 10,930 ± 120 BP, and 10,610 ± 100 BP. After exploring other explanations for the presence of rye grains of domestic morphology, we concluded that they must have been the product of cultivation and domestication. Such a conclusion is supported by the fact that the beginning of rye cultivation coincides with a sharp decline in the apparent availability and use of the very starch staples that domestic cereals eventually replaced, namely, the grains of wild cereals and other large-seeded grasses.

The progressive increase in the abundance of the three groups of weeds throughout phases 2 and 3 further suggests that the area of land under cultivation at Abu Hureyra steadily expanded, and that the contribution of domestic rye to the Abu Hureyra diet increased accordingly. This increase seems to have paralleled, and perhaps compensated for, the progressive decrease in seed-based starch staples gathered from the wild. It is significant that this decline in the use of wild seed foods such as feather-grass grain continued throughout phase

3. This was despite an increase in moisture toward the end of the phase that would probably have been sufficient to have allowed the feather-grasses to increase in abundance and to reestablish themselves as zonal dominants close to Abu Hureyra, along with several other food plants. This suggests that the continuing increase in the use of domestic rye was sufficient to obviate any need to return to gathering the grains of these wild alternatives.

The fact that the rise in weed floras was not accompanied by an equivalent increase in the abundance of remains of the domesticates themselves comes as no great surprise. Fat-grained domesticates tend to be underrepresented, and in any case, most of the grains from the early rye crops are likely to have continued to be of the skinny wild-type even after the crop was domesticated with respect to tough rachis. In any case, by the middle of phase 2 these skinny grains could not have come from stands of wild rye because no such stands would have survived within gathering distance of Abu Hureyra. Equally, the increase in moisture during phase 3 would have been insufficient to allow any stands to reestablish later on. All the wild-type rye grains in the latter part of phase 2 and in phase 3 (figure 12.22) must therefore have come from the cultivated crop. It remains uncertain, however, whether rye was taken into cultivation as an already domesticated import from elsewhere, or whether its cultivation was initiated independently at Abu Hureyra using grain taken from local wild stands to give wild-type crops that eventually became domesticated on the spot.

Phase 3 saw a slight resurgence in the use of club-rush seeds. This possibly reflects its increased availability with the return of moister conditions and increased overbank flooding, although it is surprising to encounter such an effect so early in phase 3. It is also in this phase that we see what appears to have been the start of the cultivation of large-seeded legumes, lentils in particular, probably representing the introduction of cultigens from elsewhere. Certainly, their sudden reappearance at Abu Hureyra cannot be explained by the return of slightly moister conditions allowing the local reestablishment of wild lentils, as the climatic amelioration at the end of the Younger Dryas would have been insufficient to allow wild lentils to grow anywhere within gathering range of Abu Hureyra.

By the end of the Epipalaeolithic occupation, therefore, cultivation appears to have already become a significant component of the subsistence of the people of Abu Hureyra 1, with cultigens replacing wild cereals hitherto gathered from wild stands, together with most of the feather-grasses, and a wide range of other wild food plants. Of the major wild seed foods, only club-rush and Euphrates knotgrass appear to have continued to make a significant contribution right up to the end of the Epipalaeolithic, albeit in somewhat lower amounts than in phase 1.

Overall, therefore, from the time the Younger Dryas began, the pattern of decline in the apparent use of edible seeds from the many different wild food plants follows exactly the sequence that we would expect from differences in their tolerance of drought observable in the present day. Likewise, the appearance of domestic rye, for all its rarity in the remains, and the immediate, steep, and systematic rise in the classic weed flora coincide precisely with the decline in use of just those key caloric staples that one would expect eventually to have been replaced by cultivated cereals. The overall picture is therefore remarkably consistent.

PLANT REMAINS FROM THE INTERMEDIATE PERIOD

One of the several grains of domestic rye recovered from the upper levels of the Epipalaeolithic deposits has been dated by AMS to 9,860 ± 220 BP (OxA-

6996). This falls within the timeframe of the Intermediate Period at Abu Hureyra (c. 10,000–9,400 BP). Slightly later in date is a small group of specimens from the subsoil of Trench G (level G 68) that includes grains of domestic einkorn, a bread wheat, a second domestic wheat, and a couple of lentils (see figure 12.33). The level also contained the usual weeds of cultivation (see figure 12.31). These seeds are all associated with twig charcoal from this level that has been dated to 9,680 ± 90 BP (OxA-1228). They suggest that the people of Abu Hureyra were not only continuing to cultivate the ryes and lentils already indicated for Abu Hureyra 1 but had now added additional crops to their repertoire, including a free-threshing hexaploid that implies earlier cultivation somewhere in the region of a domestic tetraploid such as domestic emmer.

The finds of domestic cereals in these early levels are particularly significant in view of the fact that, at other contemporary sites dated to Neolithic 1 such as Netiv Hagdud and Jerf el Ahmar, the remains suggest that the cereals under cultivation were still in the morphologically wild state (Kislev 1997; Willcox 1996).

Abu Hureyra 2: plant remains from the Neolithic

D. DE MOULINS

By about 10,000 BP, the region was emerging from the dry, cold conditions of the Younger Dryas and the vegetation in the Abu Hureyra area would have started to reexpand to close to its potential present-day limits (figure 3.7). Despite this reexpansion, however, the vegetation around Abu Hureyra did not achieve the richness of the period of initial settlement at c. 11,500 BP, and wild cereal species including the wild ryes and wheats never again grew within gathering distance of the site. Steppe species, however, such as the feather-grasses would have continued to grow close to Abu Hureyra.

COMPOSITION OF THE PLANT REMAINS

Over 650 flotation samples were recovered from Abu Hureyra 2 levels. From these I selected 94 samples for analysis from four trenches, B, D, E, and G, that represented each phase of occupation within each trench, and comprised a variety of contexts.[37] My aim was to investigate the diet and activities of the people of Abu Hureyra. The samples of charred plant remains were commonly between 100 and 200 ml in size, but a few from Trench B that were particularly rich in charcoal measured as much as 2,000 ml. The results of the analysis are shown in the level diagrams for each trench (figures 12.28–12.31).

Plant Remains from Abu Hureyra 2A

The Period 2A flotation samples that I studied included phases 1–5 in Trench D and phases 1–7 in Trench B (figures 12.28, 12.29). The composition of the plant remains from these phases was relatively uniform. The samples were dominated by weed seeds, particularly small-seeded legumes, with cereal grains accounting for about 10% of the total in most samples. There was little chaff in these samples.

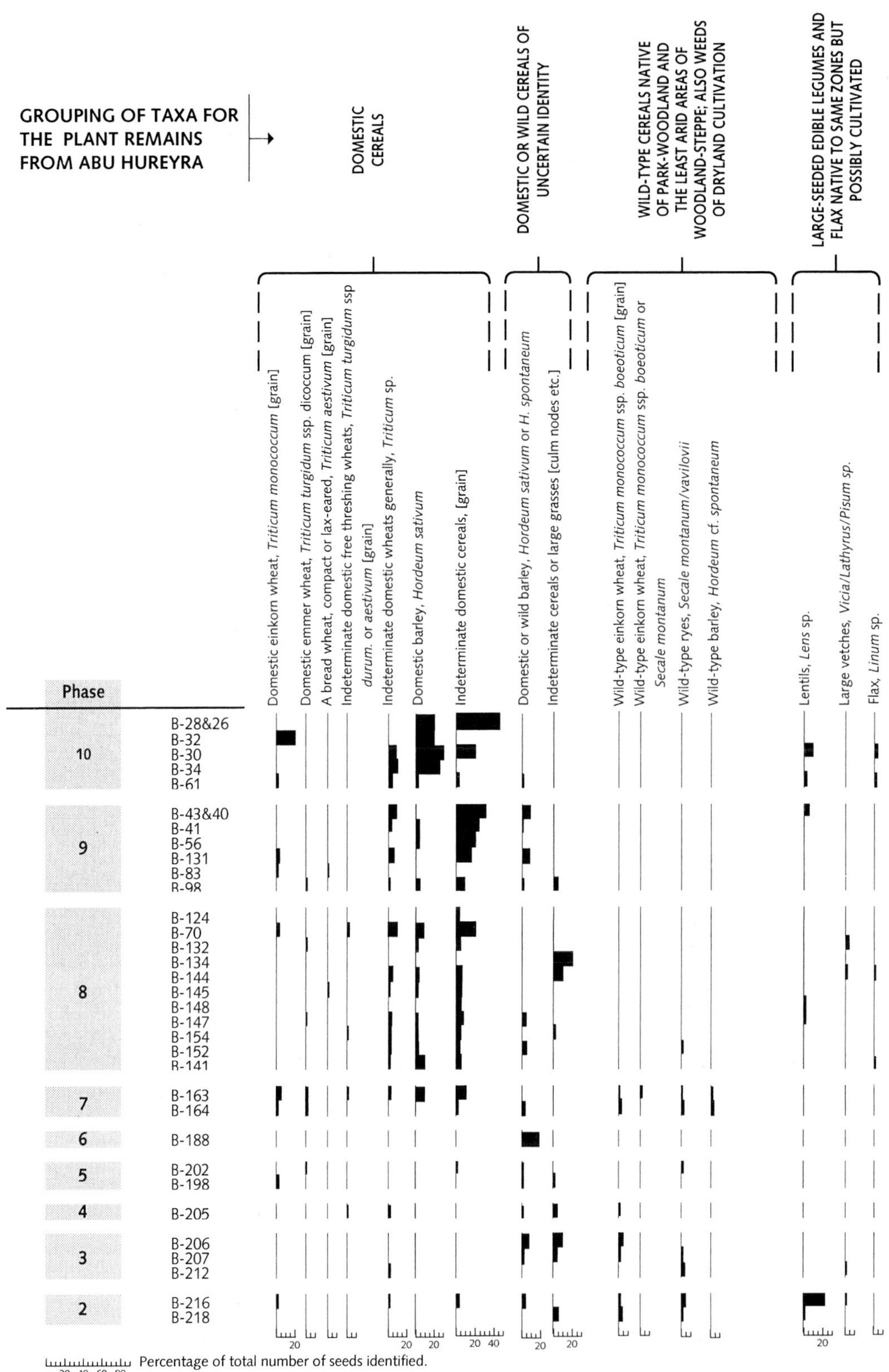

Figure 12.28 Plant remains from Trench B by chronological phase, expressed as a percentage of the total identifications in each sample.

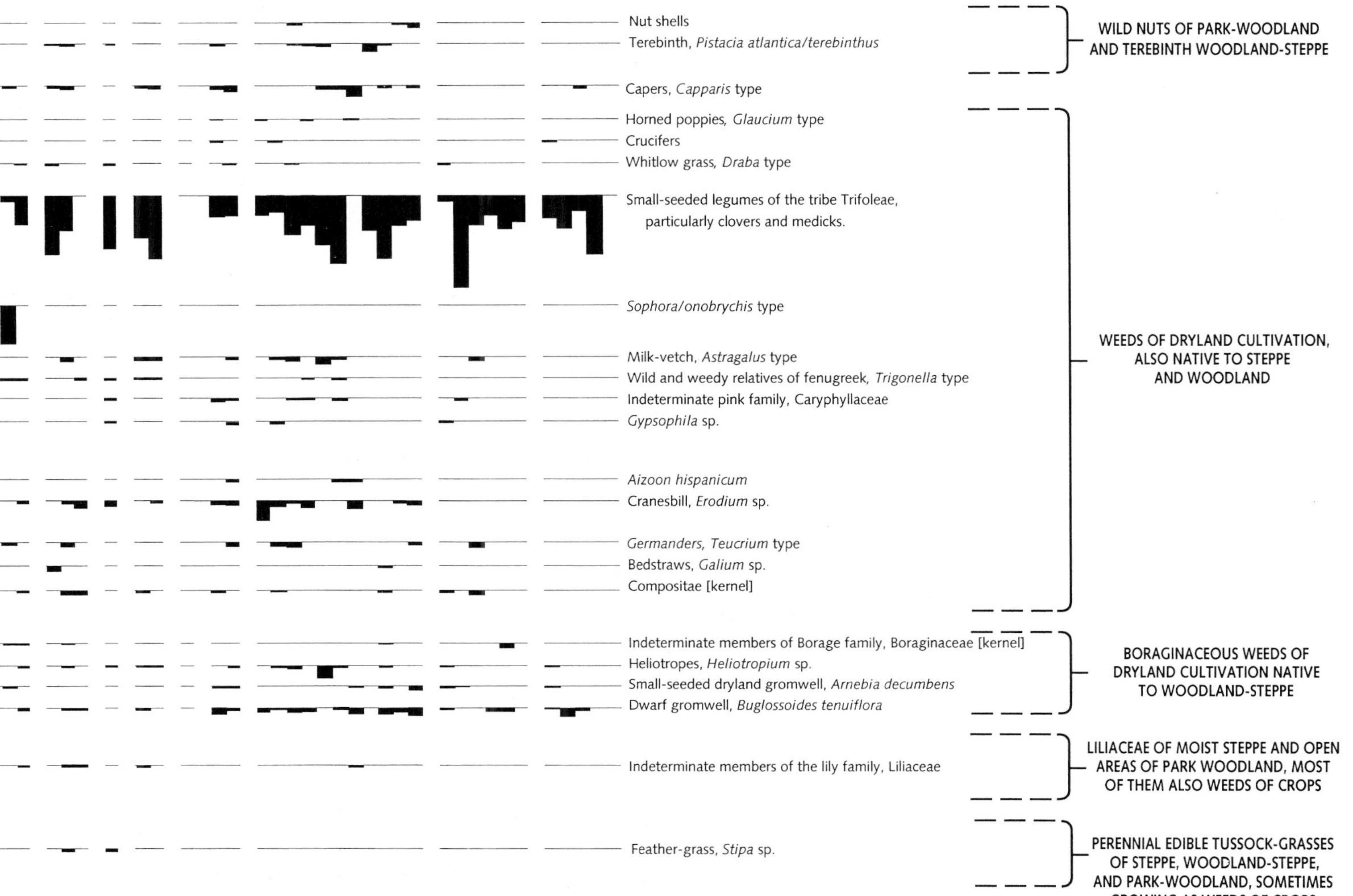

Nut shells
Terebinth, *Pistacia atlantica/terebinthus*
Capers, *Capparis* type
Horned poppies, *Glaucium* type
Crucifers
Whitlow grass, *Draba* type
Small-seeded legumes of the tribe Trifoleae, particularly clovers and medicks.
Sophora/onobrychis type
Milk-vetch, *Astragalus* type
Wild and weedy relatives of fenugreek, *Trigonella* type
Indeterminate pink family, Caryphyllaceae
Gypsophila sp.
Aizoon hispanicum
Cranesbill, *Erodium* sp.
Germanders, *Teucrium* type
Bedstraws, *Galium* sp.
Compositae [kernel]
Indeterminate members of Borage family, Boraginaceae [kernel]
Heliotropes, *Heliotropium* sp.
Small-seeded dryland gromwell, *Arnebia decumbens*
Dwarf gromwell, *Buglossoides tenuiflora*
Indeterminate members of the lily family, Liliaceae
Feather-grass, *Stipa* sp.
20 40 60 80
20 40 60 80 100
20 40
20
20
WILD NUTS OF PARK-WOODLAND AND TEREBINTH WOODLAND-STEPPE
WEEDS OF DRYLAND CULTIVATION, ALSO NATIVE TO STEPPE AND WOODLAND
BORAGINACEOUS WEEDS OF DRYLAND CULTIVATION NATIVE TO WOODLAND-STEPPE
LILIACEAE OF MOIST STEPPE AND OPEN AREAS OF PARK WOODLAND, MOST OF THEM ALSO WEEDS OF CROPS
PERENNIAL EDIBLE TUSSOCK-GRASSES OF STEPPE, WOODLAND-STEPPE, AND PARK-WOODLAND, SOMETIMES GROWING AS WEEDS OF CROPS

(continued)

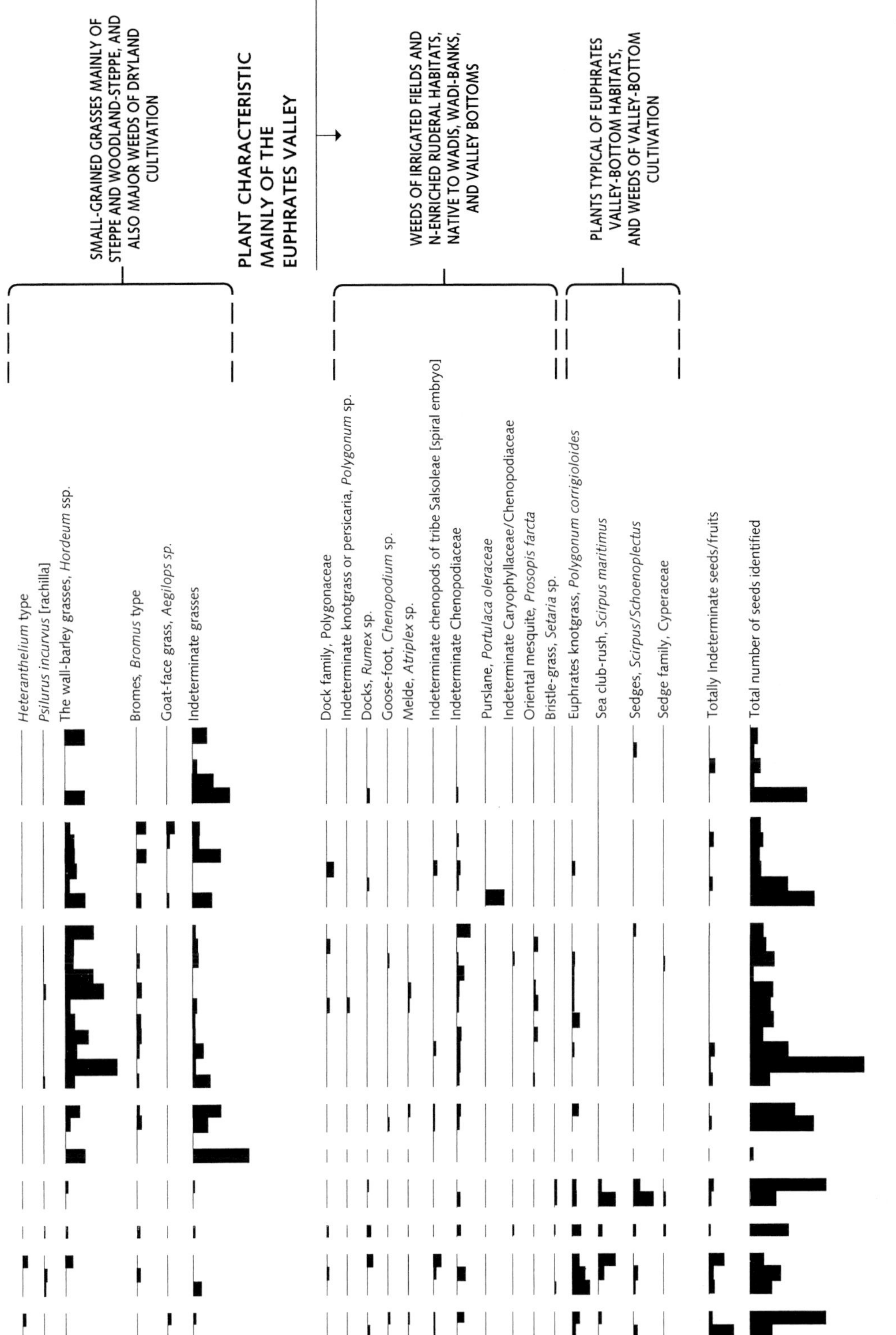

Figure 12.28 (continued)

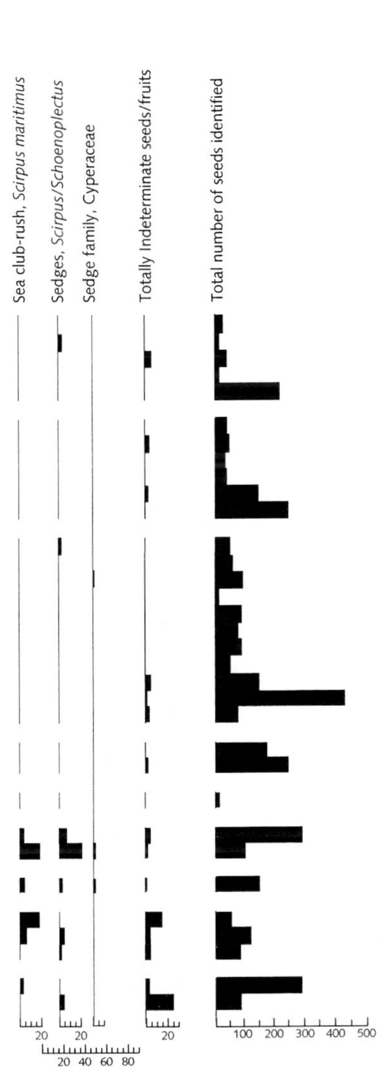
Sea club-rush, *Scirpus maritimus*
Sedges, *Scirpus/Schoenoplectus*
Sedge family, Cyperaceae
Totally Indeterminate seeds/fruits
Total number of seeds identified
20
20
20 40 60 80
20
100 200 300 400 500

(*continued*)

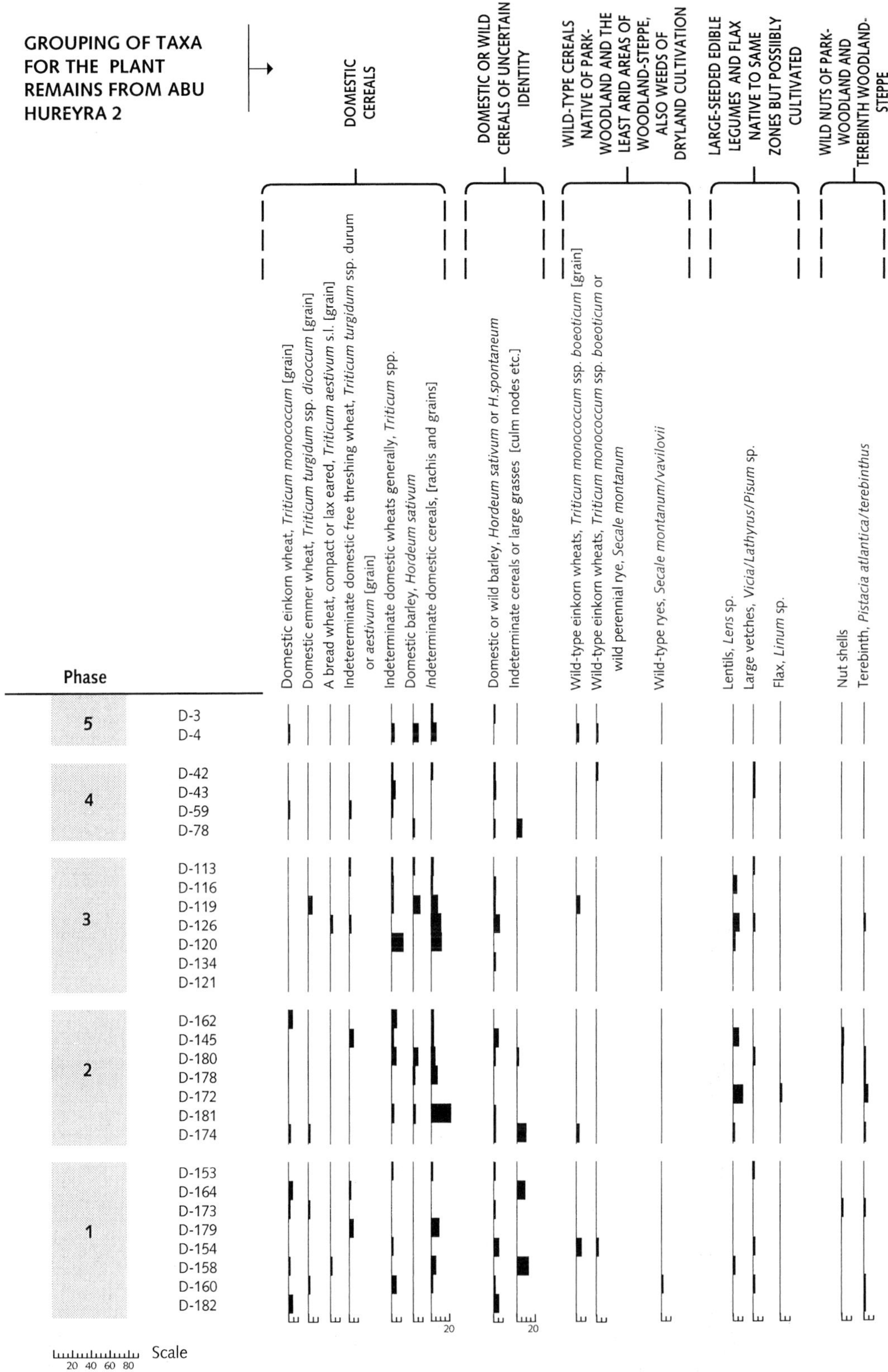

Figure 12.29 Plant remains from Trench D by chronological phase, expressed as a percentage of the total identifications in each sample.

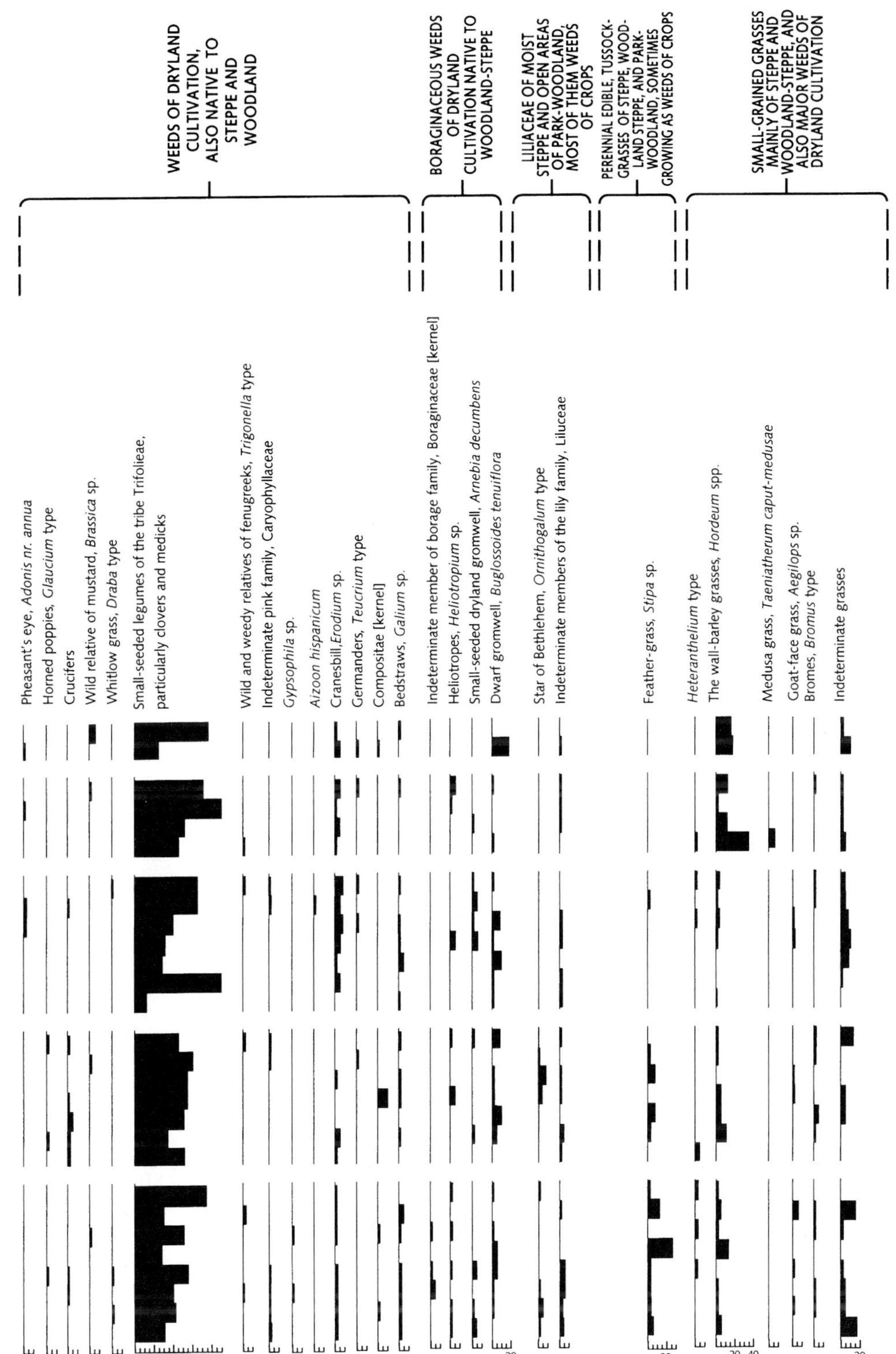

Capers, *Capparis* type
Pheasant's eye, *Adonis nr. annua*
Horned poppies, *Glaucium* type
Crucifers
Wild relative of mustard, *Brassica* sp.
Whitlow grass, *Draba* type
Small-seeded legumes of the tribe Trifolieae, particularly clovers and medicks
Wild and weedy relatives of fenugreeks, *Trigonella* type
Indeterminate pink family, Caryophyllaceae
Gypsophila sp.
Aizoon hispanicum
Cranesbill, *Erodium* sp.
Germanders, *Teucrium* type
Compositae [kernel]
Bedstraws, *Galium* sp.
Indeterminate member of borage family, Boraginaceae [kernel]
Heliotropes, *Heliotropium* sp.
Small-seeded dryland gromwell, *Arnebia decumbens*
Dwarf gromwell, *Buglossoides tenuiflora*
Star of Bethlehem, *Ornithogalum* type
Indeterminate members of the lily family, Liliuceae
Feather-grass, *Stipa* sp.
Heteranthelium type
The wall-barley grasses, *Hordeum* spp.
Medusa grass, *Taeniatherum caput-medusae*
Goat-face grass, *Aegilops* sp.
Bromes, *Bromus* type
Indeterminate grasses
WEEDS OF DRYLAND CULTIVATION, ALSO NATIVE TO STEPPE AND WOODLAND
BORAGINACEOUS WEEDS OF DRYLAND CULTIVATION NATIVE TO WOODLAND-STEPPE
LILIACEAE OF MOIST STEPPE AND OPEN AREAS OF PARK-WOODLAND, MOST OF THEM WEEDS OF CROPS
PERENNIAL EDIBLE, TUSSOCK-GRASSES OF STEPPE, WOOD-LAND STEPPE, AND PARK-WOODLAND, SOMETIMES GROWING AS WEEDS OF CROPS
SMALL-GRAINED GRASSES MAINLY OF STEPPE AND WOODLAND-STEPPE, AND ALSO MAJOR WEEDS OF DRYLAND CULTIVATION
20 40 60 80
20
40
Scale

(continued)

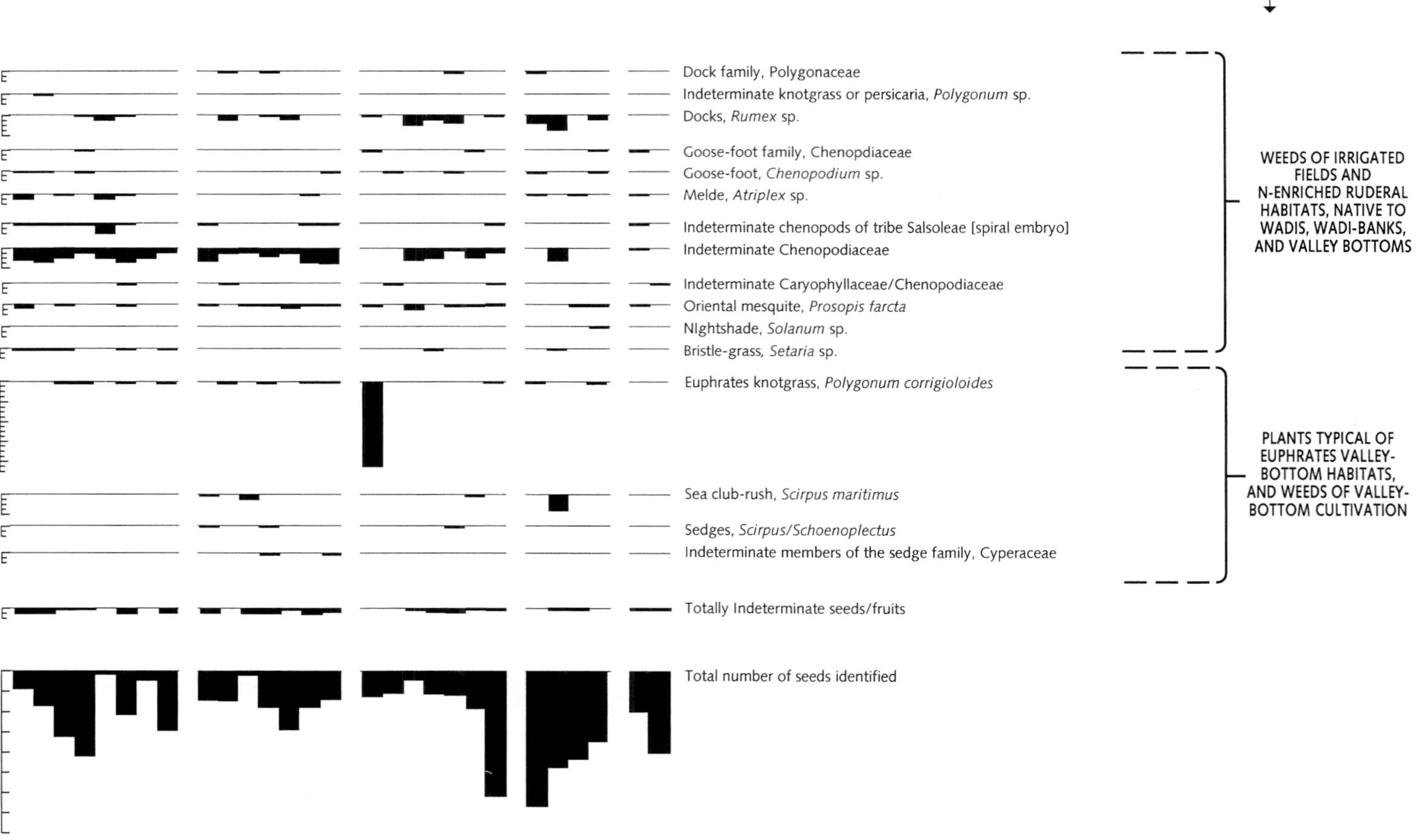

Figure 12.29 (*continued*)

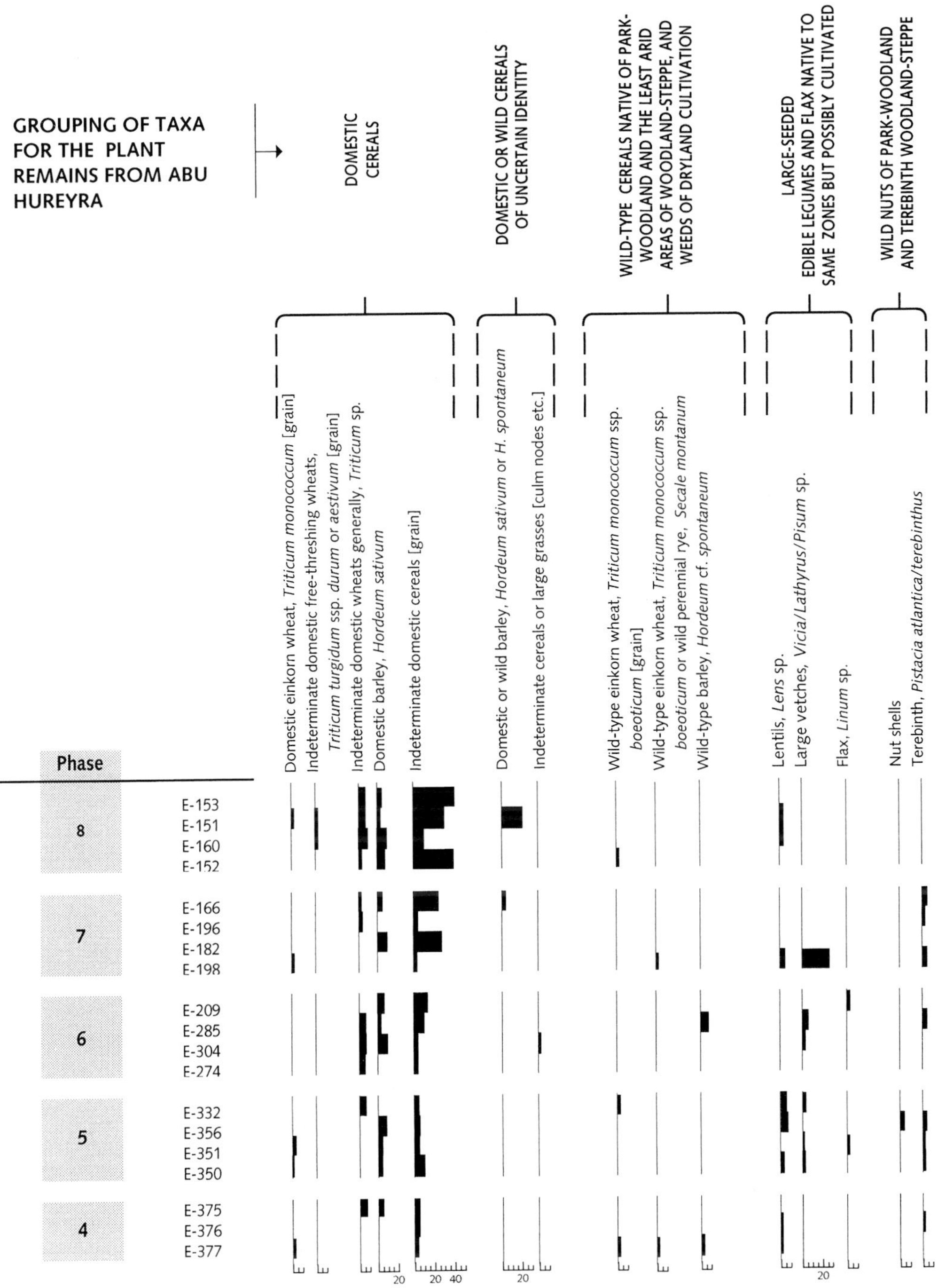

Figure 12.30 Plant remains from Trench E by chronological phase, expressed as a percentage of the total identifications in each sample.

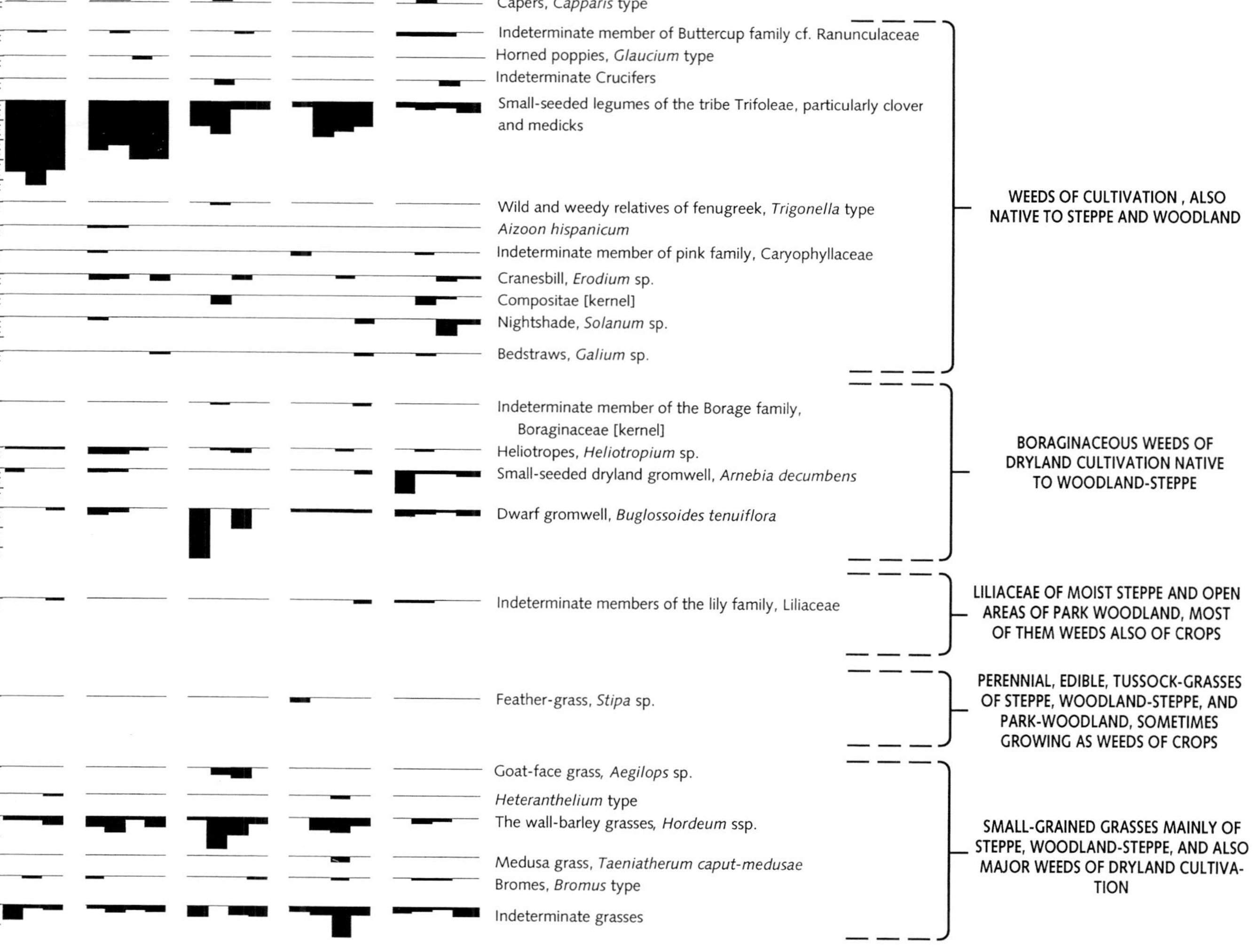

Figure 12.30 *(continued)*

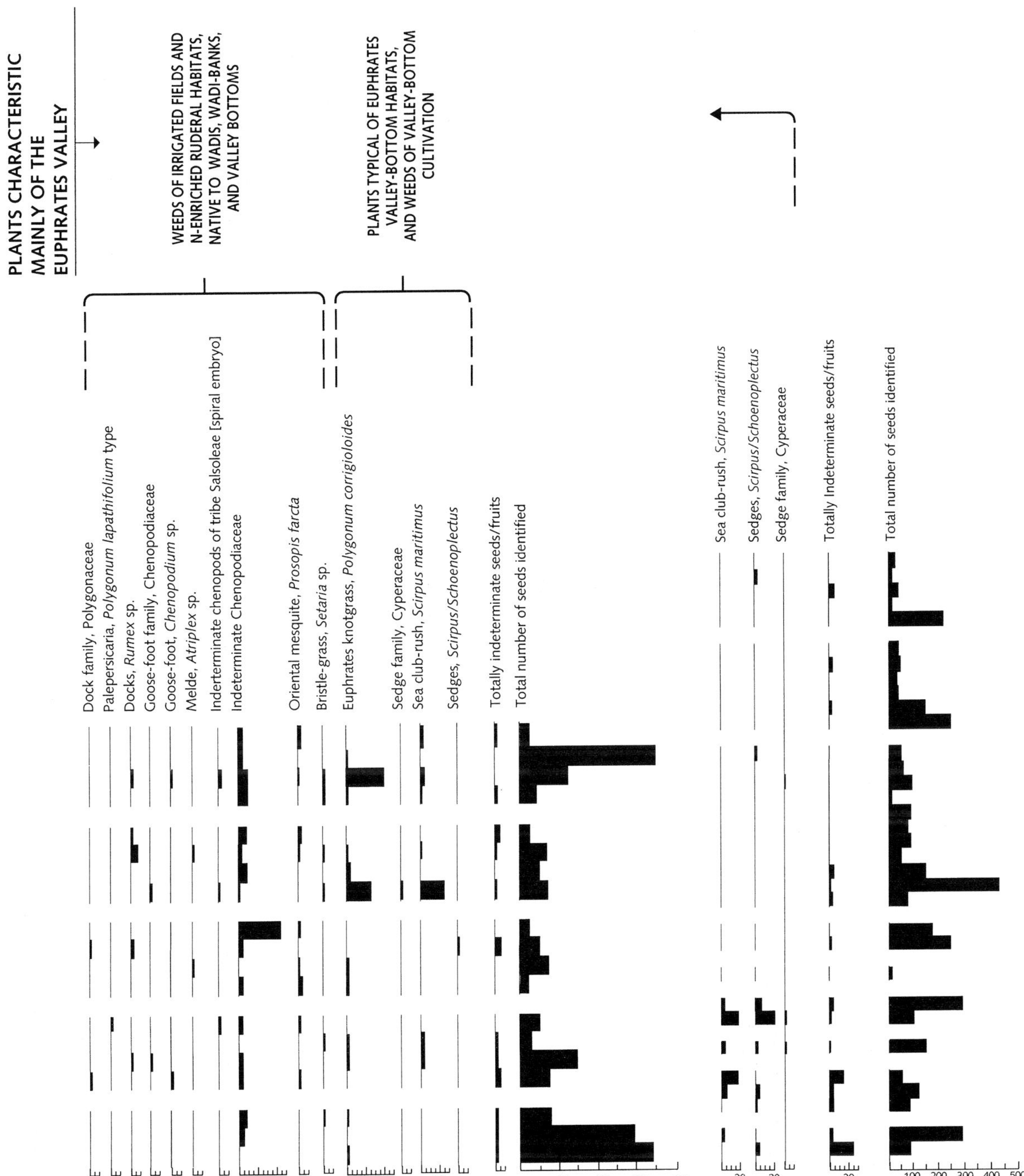

PLANTS CHARACTERISTIC MAINLY OF THE EUPHRATES VALLEY
WEEDS OF IRRIGATED FIELDS AND N-ENRICHED RUDERAL HABITATS, NATIVE TO WADIS, WADI-BANKS, AND VALLEY BOTTOMS
PLANTS TYPICAL OF EUPHRATES VALLEY-BOTTOM HABITATS, AND WEEDS OF VALLEY-BOTTOM CULTIVATION
Dock family, Polygonaceae
Palepersicaria, Polygonum lapathifolium type
Docks, Rumex sp.
Goose-foot family, Chenopodiaceae
Goose-foot, Chenopodium sp.
Melde, Atriplex sp.
Inderterminate chenopods of tribe Salsoleae [spiral embryo]
Indeterminate Chenopodiaceae
Oriental mesquite, Prosopis farcta
Bristle-grass, Setaria sp.
Euphrates knotgrass, Polygonum corrigioloides
Sedge family, Cyperaceae
Sea club-rush, Scirpus maritimus
Sedges, Scirpus/Schoenoplectus
Totally indeterminate seeds/fruits
Total number of seeds identified
20 40
20 40
20
200 400 600 800
Sea club-rush, Scirpus maritimus
Sedges, Scirpus/Schoenoplectus
Sedge family, Cyperaceae
Totally Indeterminate seeds/fruits
Total number of seeds identified
20
20
20 40 60 80
20
100 200 300 400 500

In the final phases of Abu Hureyra 1, Hillman found that the morphologically wild-type cereal grains declined in abundance, and there was evidence for increasing amounts of cultivation. This trend continued into the early phases of Abu Hureyra 2, with the cereal grains in Trench D, at least, comprising more domesticates than wild types. Of the cereals identifiable with certainty, the most conspicuous were domestic einkorn and domestic barley, with a slightly thinner scatter of domestic emmer and free-threshing wheats—including bread wheat. The wild-type cereals comprised both ryes and einkorns, as in the Epipalaeolithic.

The seeds of weeds and wild plants commonly accounted for over 85% of the samples, and occasionally reached 98%. About 50% of the weed and wild seeds consist of small-seeded legumes of the clover and medick tribe, with a modest contribution from small-grained grasses, particularly members of the wall-barley group. These legumes and, to a lesser degree, the small-grained grasses continued, therefore, at the same high levels they reached by the end of the Epipalaeolithic, with about 100 weed species present. One obvious interpretation is that they represent similar patterns of weed infestation of dry-land cultivation. This indicates a major element of continuity from the end of phase 3 of the Epipalaeolithic through the Intermediate Period into the early phases of the Neolithic.

Plant Remains from the Transition between Periods 2A and 2B, and from Period 2B

In phase 7 of Trench B we see a slight change in the plant remains immediately preceding the switch from gazelle to sheep and goat, c. 8,300 BP. The proportion of domestic cereals in the charred remains increased, including much more barley, domestic einkorn, and the rachis fragment of a free-threshing wheat. The two principal groups of weed seeds from the small-seeded legumes and small-seeded grasses increased even further. The seeds included some gypsophila and purslane, *Portulaca olearacea*.

The large quantities of charred material, mostly wood charcoal, indicate that a fire had occurred, and the density of seeds was particularly high for this site. Samples 163 and 164, the two samples I examined from Trench B phase 7, contained approximately 3,056 and 2,720 specimens, respectively, together with roughly 672 cereal grains and chaff fragments. Nevertheless, the proportion of weed seeds remained as high as in the earlier phases (92% and 75%, respectively). It may be that partially cleaned cereal grain was stored in the phase 7 buildings, with a major admixture of weed seeds, and that the difference between these samples and those from earlier levels is attributable to context-related variation.

The next samples in the sequence come from deposits during and after the switch to sheep and goat, from Trench B phases 8 and 9, Trench G phases 1–5, and Trench E phases 4–7. In Trench B phases 8 and 9, cereals were better represented than in phases 1–6, with three samples comprising 20%, 22%, and 42% cereal grains but still little chaff. In all samples, the weed seeds continued to include large numbers of small-seeded legumes, together with many grains of wall-barley. Half the samples also included grains of brome grass. However, by phase 9 other weed seeds were present in proportionately fewer samples than in phase 8, and several were now absent altogether. For example, there were very few docks and pale persicaria, the previously frequent cranesbill seeds were present in only one sample, and there were no weeds of the lily family, wild rye, and club-rush. Wild shrubs such as capers and the oriental mesquite

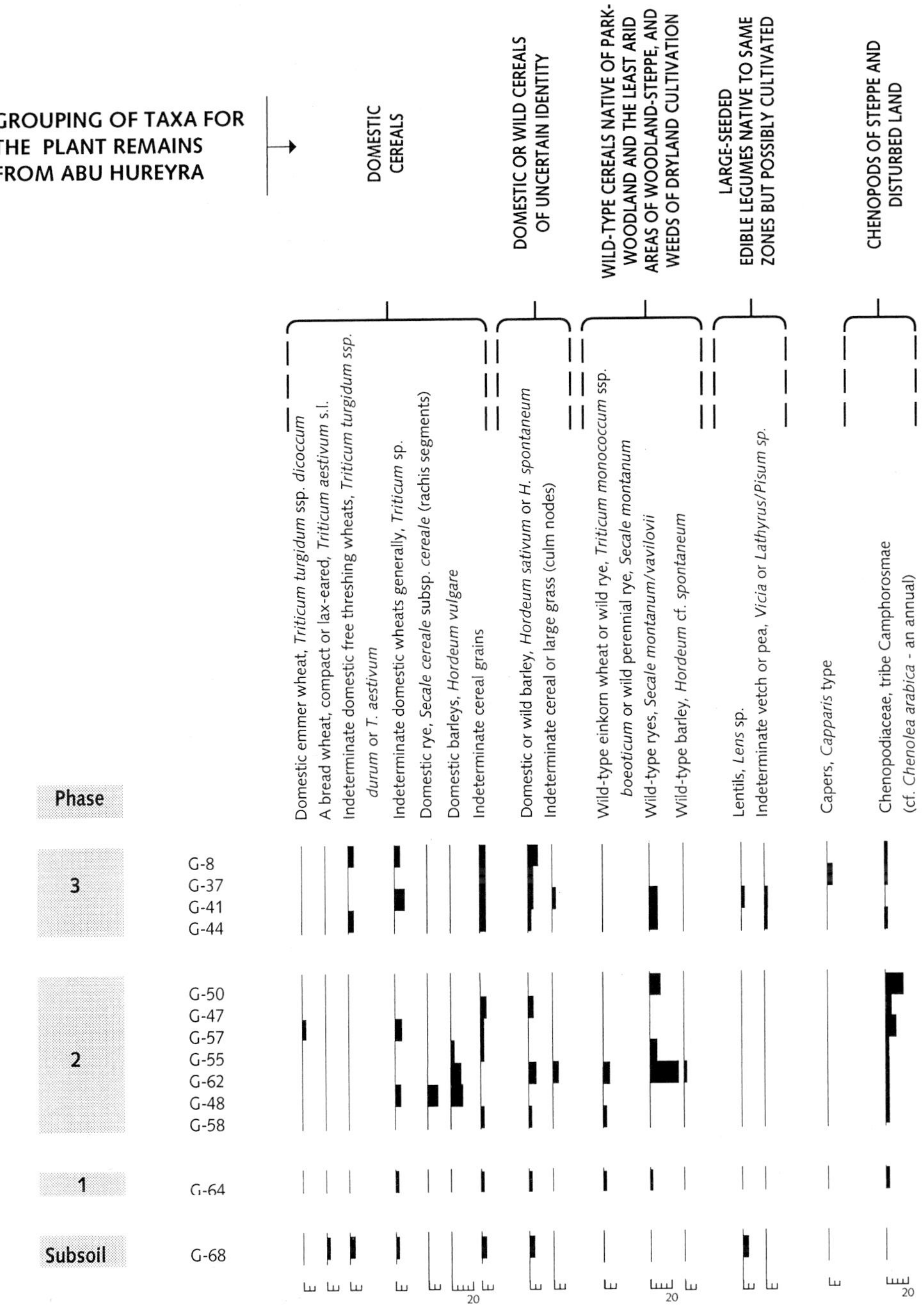

Figure 12.31 Plant remains from Trench G by chronological phase, expressed as a percentage of the total identifications in each sample.

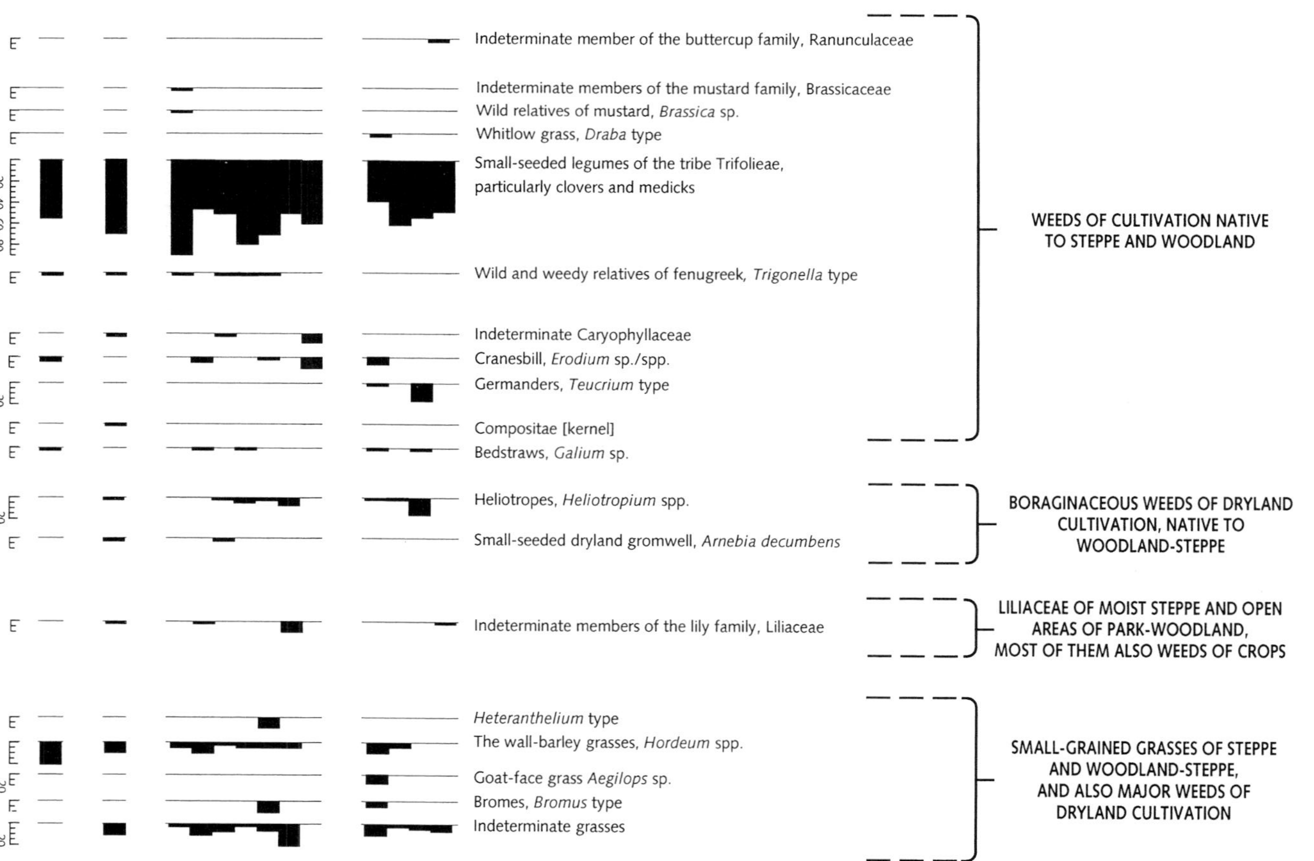

Figure 12.31 (*continued*)

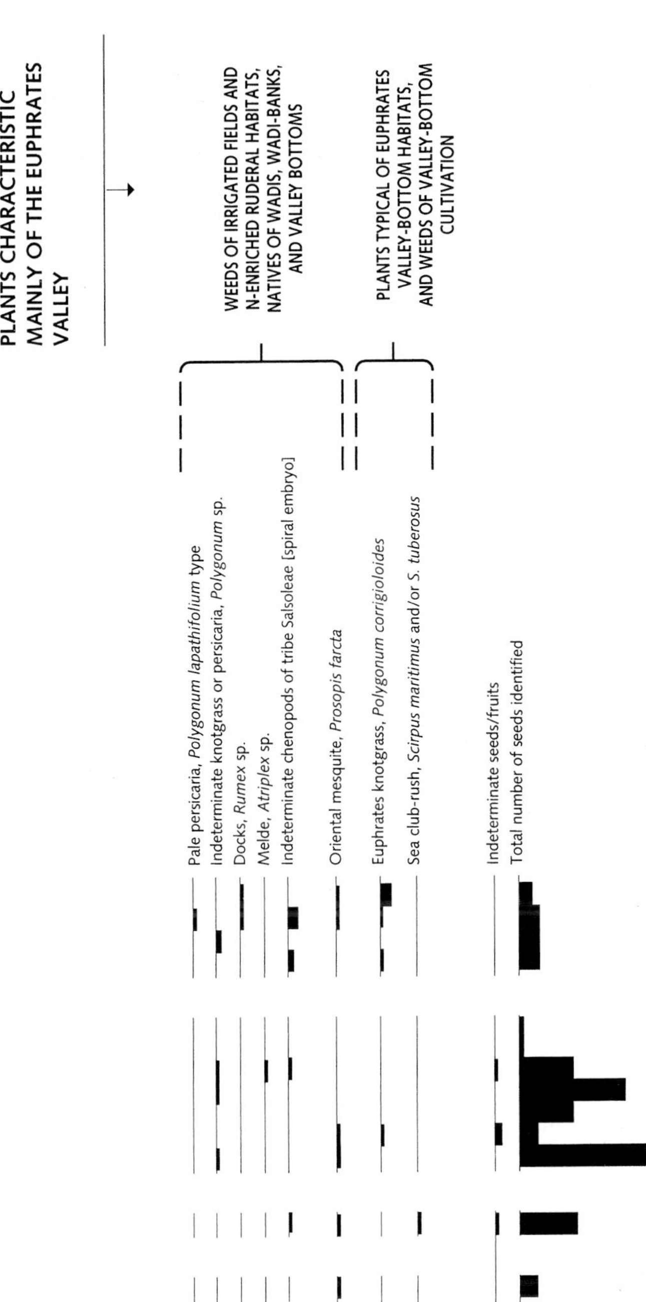

PLANTS CHARACTERISTIC MAINLY OF THE EUPHRATES VALLEY
WEEDS OF IRRIGATED FIELDS AND N-ENRICHED RUDERAL HABITATS, NATIVES OF WADIS, WADI-BANKS, AND VALLEY BOTTOMS
PLANTS TYPICAL OF EUPHRATES VALLEY-BOTTOM HABITATS, AND WEEDS OF VALLEY-BOTTOM CULTIVATION
Pale persicaria, Polygonum lapathifolium type
Indeterminate knotgrass or persicaria, Polygonum sp.
Docks, Rumex sp.
Melde, Atriplex sp.
Indeterminate chenopods of tribe Salsoleae [spiral embryo]
Oriental mesquite, Prosopis farcta
Euphrates knotgrass, Polygonum corrigioloides
Sea club-rush, Scirpus maritimus and/or S. tuberosus
Indeterminate seeds/fruits
Total number of seeds identified
20
200
400
600

were also absent. Overall, almost all the surviving plants were likely to have arrived as weeds of crops.

By contrast, the large numbers of weed seeds in the assemblages from phases 4–6 of Trench E were accompanied by relatively few cereals, and some of the einkorn grains were morphologically close to the wild-type, possibly representing "tail grains"[38] sieved out of the prime grain together with the weed seeds. Throughout the sequence in Trench E there is a gradual reduction in small-seeded legumes, especially from phase 6 onward (average of 75% in phase 4, 50% in phase 5, 21% in phase 6).

A number of samples of these later phases produced unique occurrences. The sample from Trench E phase 6, level 220, from a small gully just outside one of the houses (figure 8.54) was the only one studied from the site that produced a concentration of charred chickpeas, probably of the domestic species, *Cicer arietinum*. This phase has been dated to 8,020 ± 100 BP (BM-1724R), and so the find represents one of the earliest examples of the probable cultivation of chickpeas (Zohary and Hopf 1993, p. 103). Both samples 198 and 160 from Trench E had fairly large numbers of seeds of club-rush and Euphrates knotgrass. Although these would have flourished in moist areas on the valley floor, they could also have grown as weeds of crops sown in these same areas. Sample 198 also contained large-seeded legumes of the vetch type. Finally, in sample 62 in Trench G phase 2, there were a few grains and several rachis segments of domestic rye (figure 12.32).

Period 2C

In Trench B phase 10 and Trench E phase 8, cultivated barley and other cereals were more prominent in the assemblages. This may be due to the fact that there were many pits between the buildings that contained burned material in

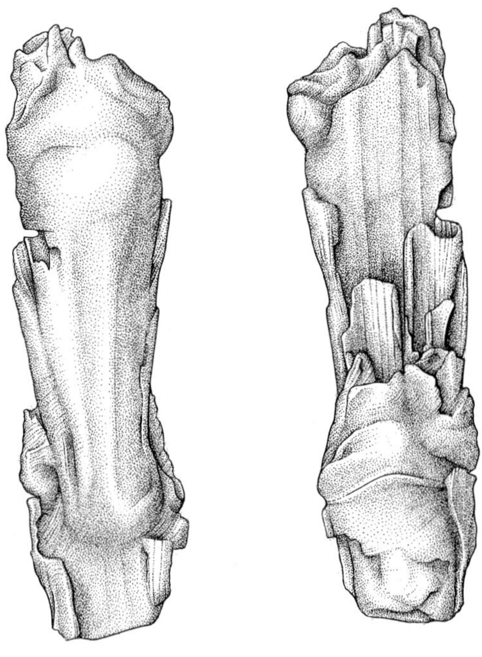

Figure 12.32 Domesticated rye rachis segment from Trench G, level 62.

these phases. Thus, the contexts were different from those of earlier levels. The high proportion of cereals also meant there were fewer weed seeds. In addition, in Trench B phase 10 the assemblages included many fragments of soft plant tissue. They probably came from roots or tubers, but unfortunately, the state of preservation of these fragments was such that they were not identifiable.

Imprints in Mudbricks

There are certain classes of information obtainable from impressions in mudbrick or adobe that are rarely available from plant remains preserved by charring. The samples of unbaked mudbrick that I studied were all from Period 2B in Trench E. A few samples had very large imprints thought to be from reeds. I examined two other samples for chaff imprints. First, I looked at the surfaces of the mudbrick fragments and then I broke these open to see nonabraded surfaces. Most of the imprints were from straw; these were either striations on the surfaces of the bricks or small holes in the brick material representing the shaft of the straw. The bigger imprints and holes appeared to be from large cereal stems, but other much thinner ones could have come from either narrow-stemmed cereals such as einkorn or from weeds or wild grasses such as the wall-barleys. A few larger cavities may have been made by whole spikelets. I could see no imprints from individual grains or identifiable chaff fragments in the few samples I examined.

COMPARISON WITH THE PLANT REMAINS FROM ABU HUREYRA 1

There was considerable continuity in the assemblages of plant remains from the later stages of Abu Hureyra 1 through the Intermediate Period into the early phases of Abu Hureyra 2. Many of the same species were present, and certain major trends in overall composition continued almost unbroken from the Epipalaeolithic into the Neolithic. An obvious example of continuity is found in the small-seeded legumes and small-grained grasses. By the end of Abu Hureyra 1 these two groups had come to dominate the remains. The high proportion of small seeded legumes and grasses not only continued into the Neolithic but also was maintained well into Period 2B. The gromwells were abundant in both periods, although they appear more plentiful in the Epipalaeolithic in the histograms because of the different method Hillman used to record them.[39]

We see continuity in two plants—domestic rye and large-seeded legumes, particularly lentils—that were probably under cultivation by the end of the Epipalaeolithic. Domestic rye grains have been directly dated to the Intermediate Period (9,860 ± 220 BP) and Period 2B (8,275 ± 65 BP), while lentils continued right through the Neolithic. Morphologically wild-type einkorn and wild-type rye were present in both periods. By the end of Abu Hureyra 1 these two wild-type cereal grains had declined significantly. They continued to be the only securely identified wild-type cereals present right through Period 2A—apart from a very rare occurrence of definite wild barley. Their low numbers at the beginning of Abu Hureyra 2, and their eventual disappearance by the end of Period 2A, probably represented a continuation of their decline during the later stages of the Epipalaeolithic.

The indications are, therefore, that there was continuity in the exploitation of plants from Abu Hureyra 1 into Abu Hureyra 2. The only significant change was that there were more domesticated cereals from the beginning of the Neolithic, and therefore that the extent of cultivation may have been greater than before. This corresponds to the evidence for continuity in the exploitation of animals, as we know that the inhabitants obtained much of their meat from hunting gazelle throughout Abu Hureyra 1 well into Abu Hureyra 2 times.

The Neolithic witnessed some new additions to the seed flora including water purslane, pale persicaria, bedstraws, and pheasant eye. There was also a marked increase in the bromes and docks. Most of these are likely to have grown as weeds of crops.

Overview: the plant-based components of subsistence in Abu Hureyra 1 and 2

G. C. HILLMAN

Our research on the seed and fruit remains from Abu Hureyra has continued for 25 years. At each step we have reevaluated the implications of our results and have often fundamentally revised of our perceptions. We have had the privilege of establishing certain aspects of the subsistence of preagrarian hunter-gatherers; we have learned that local cultivation of cereals and probably legumes began in the Epipalaeolithic; de Moulins has demonstrated that some wild caloric staples continued to be used until c. 8,500 BP, when the people of Abu Hureyra came to depend fully on cultigens, although this still preceded the advent of full-scale mixed farming by several centuries.

Identifying the wide range of poorly preserved seeds and fruits has posed many problems and has taken years of exploring novel morphological, anatomical, histological, and chemical criteria, particularly for distinguishing taxa within critical groups such as the wild wheats and ryes, small-grained grasses, and shrubby chenopods. Plant-ecological field studies, combined with analyses of published ecological, climatic, and agricultural data, have enabled us to model the potential distribution of present-day vegetation in some detail. This has revealed that, even with the climate of the present day, major vegetal resource zones could potentially exist much closer to Abu Hureyra than we had hitherto assumed (figure 3.7). Our research has also provided the basis for modeling the distribution of *ancient* vegetation. This indicated that, at the start of the Epipalaeolithic occupation of Abu Hureyra 1, the occupants had access to an unexpectedly rich array of wild plant food resources, including abundant supplies of several plants that could have served as caloric staples. This conclusion finally made sense of the presence in our charred remains of food plants such as the wild ryes and einkorns that we had previously thought could not have grown locally.

Correspondingly, the plant remains indicate that, at the start of the Epipalaeolithic occupation, the people of Abu Hureyra used a great variety of wild foods. As always, deciding which of the identified plants were likely to have been used as food, and the quantities in which they could have been gathered, not only depended on their pattern of abundance in the remains and an understanding of their taphonomy, but also depended heavily on our ecological models of past patterns of resource availability, and our knowledge of the ecology of the individual plants. We also took into account ethnobotanical data on wild food preferences and patterns of seasonal resource scheduling among recent hunter-gatherers, particularly those who utilized a range of resource environments similar to those at Abu Hureyra 1, and who thus had a similar choice of plant foods, season by season. In fact, the use of wild plant foods indicated for Abu Hureyra at the start of the Epipalaeolithic has proved to be remarkably similar to major patterns of use recorded for some recent hunter-gatherers of North America such as the Chumash, Maidu, Cahuilla, and Owens Valley Paiute.

Among the numerous wild plant foods indicated for Period 1A, those that served as caloric staples appear to have included the grains of wild ryes and wheats, the grains of feather-grasses, and the seeds of club-rush and Euphrates knotgrass. They also may have included the grains of wild grasses of the millet group, and the seeds of saltbushes (melde) and the other shrubby chenopods. Our ecological models suggest that acorns and almonds probably served as caloric staples, and seeds of wild crucifers appear to have also played a prominent role.

Thereafter, toward the end of Period 1A and into Period 1B, we see a decline in the use of key wild seed foods: first the most drought-sensitive such as wild lentils, then the slightly less drought-sensitive wild wheats and ryes, thereafter the more drought-resistant feather-grasses, and finally the even more drought-resistant shrubby chenopods. The dry conditions of the Younger Dryas episode clearly had a sharp effect. But when the use of wild cereal grain dropped, we see the start of a dramatic rise of the classic weeds of arid-zone cultivation. At the same point, we also see the first appearance of domestic rye grains.

Contrary to my own expectations, this three-way juxtaposition suggests that it was specifically the reduction in availability of wild cereals that prompted their cultivation, not the reduced availability of *other* starch staples such as the grain of feather-grasses. It also suggests that the start of cultivation at Abu Hureyra was triggered specifically by environmental change. *If* the crops were taken into cultivation as wild types, rather than being adopted as already domesticated seed stocks from elsewhere, then the conjunction of the start of cultivation as indicated by the weed flora and the appearance of a domesticate suggests that the process of domestication had occurred very rapidly. This has profound implications for either the breeding behavior of the wild ancestor of rye or the nature of early selection.

The systematic increase in weed floras throughout the remainder of Abu Hureyra 1 suggests that the area under cultivation probably increased progressively. This expansion in cultivation, combined with the parallel decline in the use of wild plant foods such as feather-grass grain, further suggests there was a steady increase in overall dependence on the cultivated staples. The early stages of the expansion in cultivation probably represented additional families adopting cultivation as wild cereal yields declined in the areas available to them. In the later stages, individual families probably expanded the areas under cultivation as food yields from other wild starch staples such as the feather-grasses continued to decline.

The start of the cultivation of large-seeded vetches and lentils in Period 1C would have augmented this process. That the sudden resurgence in their use represents their cultivation is supported by the fact that wild stands of both lentils and large-seeded vetches would have long ceased to exist within gathering range of Abu Hureyra. This also suggests that the seed stocks necessary for their initial cultivation were probably obtained from other settlements already growing them as crops.

Wild stands of wheats and ryes would also have ceased to have been available during the first half of Period 1B. From that point, therefore, all the morphologically wild-type cereal grains found in the remains must have originated from the crops. We are left with three wild starch staples that continued to be gathered in some quantity right up to the end of the Epipalaeolithic and beyond. The first two were club-rush and Euphrates knotgrass, both slightly reduced by this point; the third was feather-grass, whose use, although still significant, was now less intense. The inhabitants apparently continued to collect several wild supplementary foods.

While the find of domestic rye tells us that crops were already under cultivation, it provides no information on the *composition* of these crops. The domestic grain was found with many skinny, wild-type grains, and these could have come from plants that were fully domesticated with respect to tough rachis, from brittle-rachised wild-type plants growing as weeds of the crop, or from both. Any brittle-rachised plants could either have dominated the crop (which could have been at some stage of predomestication cultivation or, less probably, nondomestication cultivation), or might have been a minority component. The skinny, wild-type grains are likely to have dominated any grain present in the waste fractions from sieve cleaning. The huge numbers of arable weed seeds present from the latter part of the Epipalaeolithic suggest that the charred remains are dominated by precisely these cleanings from grain sieving. Thus, most of the grain from these later levels could well be mere tail grain from the same grain-cleaning operations that eliminated the huge numbers of weed seeds. The rarity of plump-grained domesticates in the charred remains is, therefore, to be expected. Farmers today avoid wasting their prime grain, and this was perhaps even more the case when plump-grained domesticates were still sufficient a novelty to be treated with some reverence.

In the Intermediate Period (c. 10,000–9,400 BP), AMS-dated remains of a domestic rye grain indicate that rye continued to be cultivated at the site. The occupants had also started to cultivate einkorn and a free-threshing hexaploid wheat. The latter indicates prior cultivation somewhere in the region of a tetraploid wheat such as domestic emmer (figure 12.33). Their seed stocks are quite likely to have originated from farming sites farther to the west or north.

The results from de Moulins's analyses of the remains from the main Neolithic sequence reveal the continuation of several trends from the end of Abu Hureyra 1 through the Intermediate Period into Abu Hureyra 2. First, we see the continued use of the same three wild caloric staples: feather-grass, club-rush, and Euphrates knotgrass.[40] Their use steadily declined during the early stages of Period 2A, and they finally disappeared around 8,500 BP, by which point there appears to have been almost complete dependence on domesticates for plant-based energy foods. At Abu Hureyra, therefore, this process of transfer of dependency from caloric staples gathered from the wild to those raised under cultivation took 2,500 years, from the start of crop cultivation shortly before 11,000 BP to the final abandonment of the wild caloric staples abound 8,500 BP.

Following the apparent cultivation of domestic rye, einkorn, bread wheat, and lentils in the Intermediate Period, additional domesticated crops were added in Period 2A, including domestic emmer and barley. We also find that these domesticates now included a much smaller admixture of morphologically wild-type grains; for example, the domesticates from Trench D outnum-

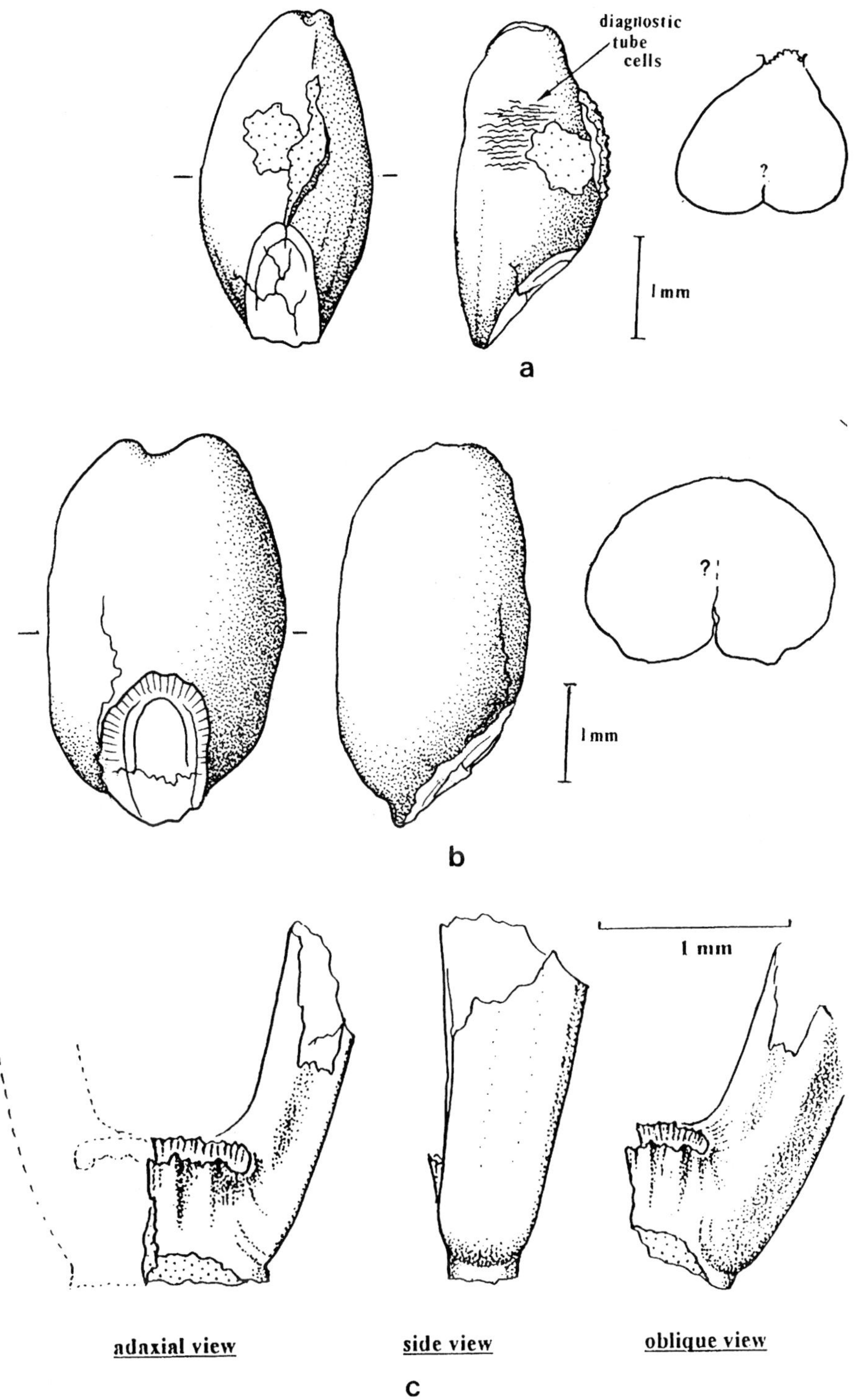

Figure 12.33 Domestic cereals from the Intermediate Period and Period 2B. a, domestic einkorn, *Triticum monococcum* subsp. *monococcum*, from level G 68; b, a grain of club-eared bread wheat, *Triticum aestivo-compactum*, from level G 68; c, half a spikelet fork of domestic einkorn, *Triticum monococcum*, subsp. *monococcum*, from E 401 but AMS-dated to 8,140 ± 90 BP (OxA-6336).

bered wild types by 8 to 1. This suggests that the effects of modifier genes were waning, and/or that the effects of long-term selection against wild-type weeds and against small-seededness in domesticates were nearing fixation. These processes were, it seems, largely complete by the start of Period 2B. Lentils and large-seeded vetches continued to be cultivated, although whether the seeds of flax in Trenches B, D, and E represented cultigens or weeds remains uncertain. In Period 2B, these crops were joined by chickpeas and field bean, and there were two brief reappearances of cultivated rye.

The classic arid zone weed floras continued to maintain the levels of abundance they had achieved by the end of the Epipalaeolithic. Small-seeded legumes dominated the remains, accompanied by large quantities of small-grained grasses such as the wall-barleys, and the gromwells. These major weed groups were also accompanied by small numbers of a range of other classic weeds of cultivation such as the docks.

Barring the continued presence of three wild plant-food staples in the early stages of Period 2A, the composition of these seed assemblages from the Neolithic accords with that of "fine-cleanings" sieved out of harvested grain once it has been threshed and winnowed. This waste fraction is typically dominated by weed seeds, small skinny tail grain, and dense fragments of chaff such as glume bases. The relative paucity of chaff in the remains probably reflects either the effect of high-temperature charring (Boardman and Jones 1990), or else poor conditions of preservation preventing the survival of these more delicate tissues, just as in the equivalent Epipalaeolithic assemblages.

By the end of Period 2A, therefore, the people of Abu Hureyra were dependent primarily on cultivated cereals and pulses to provide their plant-based energy needs (figure 12.33c). Relative to the broad spectrum of seed foods used in Period 1A of the Epipalaeolithic, dependence on these few cultigens represented a significant reduction in dietary diversity. However, it will have been offset by two factors. First, even agrarian populations continue to gather wild greens, shoots, and soft fruits, although the range available will have narrowed. Second, many weed seeds, including some species formerly gathered as food, contaminate the grain of domesticates used as food and thus contribute to diet, this despite the best endeavors of the farmers to eliminate them. Nevertheless, the narrowing of dietary diversity may well have been sufficient to have had an effect on human health.

CONCLUSIONS

Twenty five years of laboratory analyses of the plant remains and ecological studies in the field have enabled us to trace changes in the plant-based components of subsistence at Abu Hureyra from 1,500 years before the end of the Pleistocene well into the Holocene. Our core conclusions are as follows:

1. The initial occupants of Abu Hureyra were primarily hunter-gatherers.
2. They used a very wide range of wild plant foods and enjoyed considerable dietary diversity. These wild foods included several that served as caloric staples.
3. The use of these staples and several other wild foods declined rapidly from late in Period 1A through Period 1B. The timing coincided

with the early stages of the cool, dry Younger Dryas climatic episode, and the sequence of the species manifesting this decline is commensurate with advancing desiccation.

4. The decline in wild cereals was immediately followed by a rapid rise in a weed flora typical of arid-zone cultivation involving substantial tillage.
5. This conjunction of events suggests that cultivation was precipitated by the decline in wild cereals, and that environmental change was the trigger.
6. At the same moment we find the first grains of domestic rye, indicating that rye was among the first crops to be cultivated at Abu Hureyra.
7. The rye could either have been taken into cultivation locally and thereafter domesticated, or have arrived in an already domesticated state from preexisting, but as yet unknown, farming settlements elsewhere. In the former case, rye domestication must have occurred very rapidly, and this has profound implications for either the breeding behavior of the wild ancestor of rye or the nature of early selection under cultivation.
8. Although later stages of the Epipalaeolithic saw a systematic decline in the use of plant food staples gathered from the wild, the inhabitants continued to gather significant amounts of feather-grasses, club-rush, and Euphrates knotgrass to the end of the period and beyond.
9. A domestic rye grain AMS-dated to 9,860 BP indicates that rye cultivation continued into the Intermediate Period. Domestic einkorn, bread wheat, and lentils were also under cultivation by this point.
10. A number of trends in plant use from the latter stages of Abu Hureyra 1 continued through the Intermediate Period into early Abu Hureyra 2, and many of the species remained the same.
11. The classic weed flora of dryland cultivation continued at the same high levels it had reached by the end of the Epipalaeolithic, and the principal weed taxa remained the same. This pattern continued through much of the Neolithic. The clear association of this classic weed flora with cultivation in Abu Hureyra 2 reaffirms the use of these same taxa as indicators of cultivation when they suddenly started to increase in Period 1B of Abu Hureyra 1.
12. Cultivation of lentils and other large-seeded legumes also continued from Period 1C of the Epipalaeolithic right through the Neolithic.
13. But even by the start of Abu Hureyra 2, they were also cultivating at least three domestic wheats, including bread wheat, and these were soon joined by domestic barley. Later, in Period 2B, these crops were joined by chickpeas and field bean. Whether the seeds of flax represent a cultigen remains uncertain.
14. In the early Neolithic we also see continued use of the three caloric staples that had been used right up to the end of the Epipalaeolithic: feather-grass grain, and the seeds of club-rush and Euphrates knotgrass. Their use steadily declined during the early stages of Period

2A and ceased about 8,500 BP. At this point, there was apparently almost complete dependence on domesticates for plant-based energy foods.

15. At Abu Hureyra, therefore, transfer of dependency from caloric staples gathered from the wild to those raised under cultivation took 2,500 years, from the start of crop cultivation shortly before 11,000 BP to the final abandonment of the wild caloric staples abound 8,500 BP.

16. Relative to the great variety of seed foods used in Period 1A of Abu Hureyra 1, the range of cultivated grains used by 8,500 BP represents a significant narrowing of dietary diversity that could well have impacted on human health.

13 The Exploitation of Animals

A. J. Legge & P. A. Rowley-Conwy

The large quantity of well-preserved animal bones recovered systematically from Abu Hureyra has provided a rich source of evidence for the changing patterns of animal exploitation at the site. In common with many sites in the region, the bones had lost almost all of their organic content, so only charred bones could be used for direct accelerator mass spectrometry (AMS) dating (Legge and Rowley-Conwy 1986b). The complete loss of the organic part of the bone structure caused the bones and teeth to become very brittle. Consequently, there was some degree of damage to specimens in excavation.

This chapter concentrates on the first essentials: the species found, the long faunal sequence, the hunting methods employed, and the evidence for the earliest domestic species. We shall discuss other aspects of the site fauna more fully in future publications.

MAMMAL SPECIES FOUND AT ABU HUREYRA

Gazelles

The common gazelle species at Abu Hureyra was the Persian or goitred gazelle, *Gazella subgutturosa*, as shown by the horn cores. In the two other gazelle species, the Palestine (*Gazella gazella*) and the Dorcas (*Gazella dorcas*) gazelle, the horn cores are relatively straight when viewed from the front and are swept backward in an even curve. The tips of the horns in the Palestine gazelle may be turned forward, but this is not manifest on the bony horn core. The horns of males in the Persian gazelle show a marked divergence, and this is reflected in the form of the horn core at the base. At the point where the horn arises from the skull, the surface of the horn core is smooth. A little above the base the surface becomes rough and porous, and it is channeled with longitudinal grooves. This is the part of the horn covered with the horn sheath. At that point where the surface texture changes there is a slight outward kink in the plane of the horn core, and the upper part of the core then continues to curve outward, reflecting the lyrate form of the horns in this species (Compagnoni 1978, figure 1, specimen A2).

In the Palestine and Dorcas gazelles the females carry horns, with a form similar to that of the males, but more slender. The females of the Persian gazelle are commonly hornless, although small horns may develop in some. The extent to which this feature varied in recent populations in Syria cannot now be known. Among the horn cores at the site were a few very small (20–30 mm), straight horn cores with a dense and even surface. This feature precludes the possibility that these cores came from juvenile males. Among the collection of Persian gazelle skulls from Turkmenia that Legge has studied in the Lomonsov Museum of Zoology, University of Moscow, three adult females exhibited small horn cores, or had horn sheaths that covered such horn cores, while fourteen individuals had only low bony protrusions on the skull. Some of these had a roughened pad on their surface, indicating the point where a very short horn sheath was supported. A further two adult females exhibited only unilateral horn development with a single horn core or sheath, with a low bony protrusion at the site of the other horn core.

The Abu Hureyra gazelles also appear to have had a rather infrequent horn development in the females, as these small horn cores were rather few. Their morphology was very similar to that of the modern Turkmenian collection of Persian gazelles. It is possible that the Abu Hureyra collection contains some specimens of other gazelle species. The evidence from early Abu Hureyra 1 shows that plants characteristic of xeric woodland grew near the site, although these declined later on. Such indicators of relatively moist conditions suggest that the site may have been within the distribution of the Palestine gazelle at that period, and possibly for some time after. Occasional gazelle bones were found that were noticeably small. However, it is evident that almost all of the gazelle bones came from the Persian gazelle.

Sheep and Goat

Wild sheep, *Ovis orientalis*, and the wild goat, *Capra aegagrus*, were historically distributed from Asia Minor through the upland regions of Mesopotamia, Iran, and Transcaspia (figure 13.1). The preferred habitats of the two species are somewhat different: goats, because of their climbing abilities, are able to occupy steep and rocky terrain, while sheep by preference avoid such landforms and are usually found in hilly rather than mountainous areas. Recent archaeological evidence

Figure 13.1 Wild sheep.

has shown that the distribution of sheep was wider in the late Pleistocene than is the case now, although the species is uncommon or rare among the bones from archaeological sites of that period. The distribution of sheep in late Pleistocene and Holocene archaeological sites has been summarized by Uerpmann (1979) and Legge and Rowley-Conwy (1986b). The presence of pre-Neolithic sheep at archaeological sites in northern Mesopotamia and Iran has been known for some time, although the range has been extended considerably to the southwest by recent discoveries at Douara Cave near Palmyra (Payne 1983, p. 60), at Hatula (Davis 1985), and even as far south as the Negev Desert in the Epipalaeolithic (Davis, Goring-Morris, and Gopher 1982). The origin of modern domestic sheep is now attributed to the Asiatic mouflon, *Ovis orientalis* (Nadler, Hoffmann, and Wolf 1973; Nadler et al. 1972; Nadler, Lay, and Hassinger 1971), on the evidence from chromosome studies. The mouflon sheep of Anatolia, northern Mesopotamia, and northwest Iran has a chromosome number of 2n = 54, while the Urial sheep, *Ovis vignei*, has the number 2n = 58. Where these species intergrade, a zone of hybridization occurs, with sheep showing intermediate chromosome numbers and morphological characteristics.

In their recent study of the mammal remains from the Belt Cave (Gar-e Khamarband) and Ali Tappeh, Uerpmann and Frey have showed that the *Ovis* horn cores had the characteristic cross section of the Urial sheep. In this species the horn core cross section tends to be flattened on its anterior surface, with distinct angles at the outer margin of that surface (Uerpmann and Frey 1981, figure 2). West Asian ibex also have a horn core with a broad frontal surface, but Davis (1987, figure 6.4) has shown these to be of somewhat elliptical form and without the conspicuous sharp angles at the margins of the anterior surface. Early sheep from Abu Hureyra had a horn section that was much closer to that of the mouflon, *Ovis orientalis* (figure 13.2).

The goat, *Capra aegagrus* (figure 13.3), has been found at later Pleistocene sites in the Levant (Uerpmann 1979) from the Ksar Akil rockshelter in Lebanon (Hooijer 1961) to sites such as En Gev I in the Jordan Valley (Davis 1974), El Khiam in Judea (Vaufrey 1951) and, near Petra in Transjordan, the Epipalaeolithic Wadi Madamagh shelter and the Natufian levels at the nearby site of Beidha (Hecker 1982). Besides its Levantine area of distribution, the species has also been found to the east of the Tigris-Euphrates Basin at sites in the Zagros Mountains such as the Palegawra Cave (Turnbull and Reed 1974) and the Warwasi rock shelter near Kermanshah (Turnbull 1975).

The wild goat, too, had a wider distribution in the late Pleistocene than in recent times, although this is more problematic because the two species, *Capra aegagrus* and *Capra ibex*, can be difficult to distinguish other than by horn core form. Thus, the discovery of a single horn core type does not preclude the presence of the second species in an archaeological site. In a recent study Evins (1982) has suggested that, at the Shanidar Cave, the wild goats were all ibex. The distribution of goats must have been substantially greater in the late Pleistocene than is suggested by records from the recent past. This inference is strengthened by the recent discovery of an isolated living population of *Capra aegagrus* in the south of the Arabian peninsula (Harrison 1968). Wild and domestic goats and the ibex exhibit the same chromosome number (Gray 1972) and are fully interfertile. On the evidence of horn form, the origin of modern domestic goats, *Capra hircus aegagrus*, is attributed to the wild Bezoar goat, *Capra aegagrus*. The horn cores of goats from early Neolithic sites show the characteristic section of *Capra aegagrus*, and this form was characteristic of the goats from Abu Hureyra 2A and 2B (figure 13.2B).

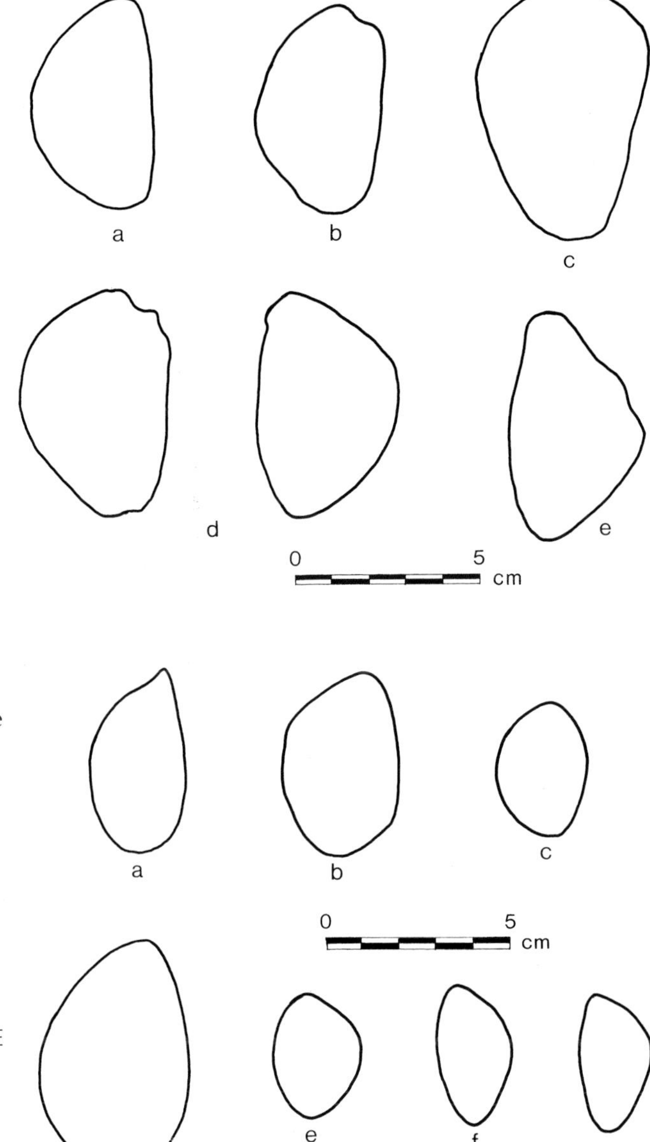

Figure 13.2 Cross sections of caprine horn cores from Abu Hureyra. All cross sections are taken near to the base of the horn core. *Top,* sheep horn cores. a, Trench E 73, B314 left. b, Trench E 73, B181 left. c, Trench E 73, B183 left. d, Right and left horn cores of same specimen but skull broken, Trench B 73, B95. e, Trench E 73, B281. *Bottom,* goat horn cores. a, Trench E 73, B311, left. b, Trench E 73, B182, left. c, Trench E 73, B329, left. d, Trench E 73, B314, left. e, Trench E 73, B314, right. f and g, Trench E73, B338, both right.

Equid Species

Equid bones were not common at Abu Hureyra and were very fragmented. The species fell from 14% during early Abu Hureyra 1, to between 1% and 5% in Abu Hureyra 2 levels, though always in variable frequency. It is striking that the species was markedly less abundant among the mammal remains at Abu Hureyra on the west bank of the Euphrates River than at Mureybit on the east bank (Ducos 1978) or at the later site of Umm Dabaghiyah (Bökönyi 1973, 1978), farther east near the Tigris River. At neither Mureybit nor Umm Dabaghiyah were gazelles very common, and although there was some possibility of retrieval bias against the smaller bones in those excavations, equids were apparently considerably more abundant in sites to the east of the Euphrates.

Bökönyi (1986) has shown that the Umm Dabaghiyah equids were substantially larger than those from Mureybit. The few measurable specimens from

Figure 13.3 Wild goat.

Abu Hureyra fall within the dimensions of the Mureybit population and are in consequence also smaller than those from Umm Dabaghiyah (figure 13.4). Bökönyi saw the separation between the two populations as a difference at the subspecies level, although this proposal needs to be considered in relation to the geographical proximity of the two sites, since they were no more than 250 km apart and were otherwise separated only by the catchment of the Khabur River. The equids from Mureybit and Abu Hureyra were substantially larger than the few recent specimens of the supposed Syrian onager, *Equus hemionus hemippus* (Ducos 1978, Uerpmann 1987) and cannot therefore be equated with that uncertain species.

The measurements of equid bones from Abu Hureyra indicate a population of the same size as that from Mureybit (figure 13.4). While the populations from Abu Hureyra and Mureybit appear to be morphologically similar, this alone says little about the species to which they belonged. The identity of Western Asian equids from archaeological sites remains the source of some contention; specimens are identified either as the onager, *Equus hemionus*, or as an ass, either *Equus asinus* or *Equus africanus*.

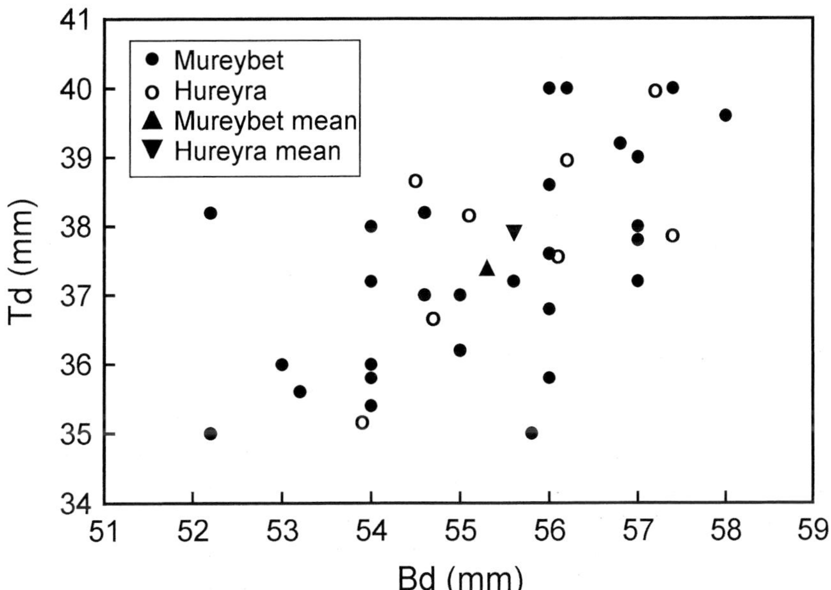

Figure 13.4 Measurements of equid distal tibiae from Abu Hureyra compared with those from Tell Mureybit (conventions follow von den Dreisch 1976).

In his original study, Ducos (1970) identified the Mureybit equids as belonging to the *asinus* group, rather than that of *hemionus*—that is, as an ass rather than as an onager. This identification was later reinforced (Ducos 1975) on the basis of the slenderness index of a complete metatarsal from that site. In support of his contention, Ducos (1986) has shown the uncertainties that attend the provenance of the few recent skeletons of *E. hemionus hemippus* that have survived, suggesting that these remains cannot be used to judge the taxonomy of prehistoric specimens. Using a ratio diagram to compare measurements, Ducos (1986, figure 1) has argued that the Mureybit specimens were closer in morphology to the recent African wild ass, *E. africanus*, than any known recent specimen of the onager, *E. hemionus*. However, to suggest that the Mureybit specimens were more like modern African asses than recent onagers of doubtful provenance is at best an uncertain method by which to show population affinities. In the light of the evident morphological variation in prehistoric equids found between the Euphrates and Tigris rivers, it seems doubtful that this problem can be resolved by purely metrical tests.

The distinction between species of equids is commonly made on the form of the folding in the tooth enamel (Eisenmann 1980, 1981, 1986). The equid teeth from Abu Hureyra were exceedingly brittle and did not withstand the process of excavation well. Besides loose teeth, the more complete specimens consisted of an entire right mandibular tooth row, a partial right mandibular tooth row, and a complete left maxillary tooth row (figure 13.5). The enamel folding on the teeth conformed with that described by Eisenmann (1980, 1986) and Meadow (1986) as characteristic for the onager. The metaconids and

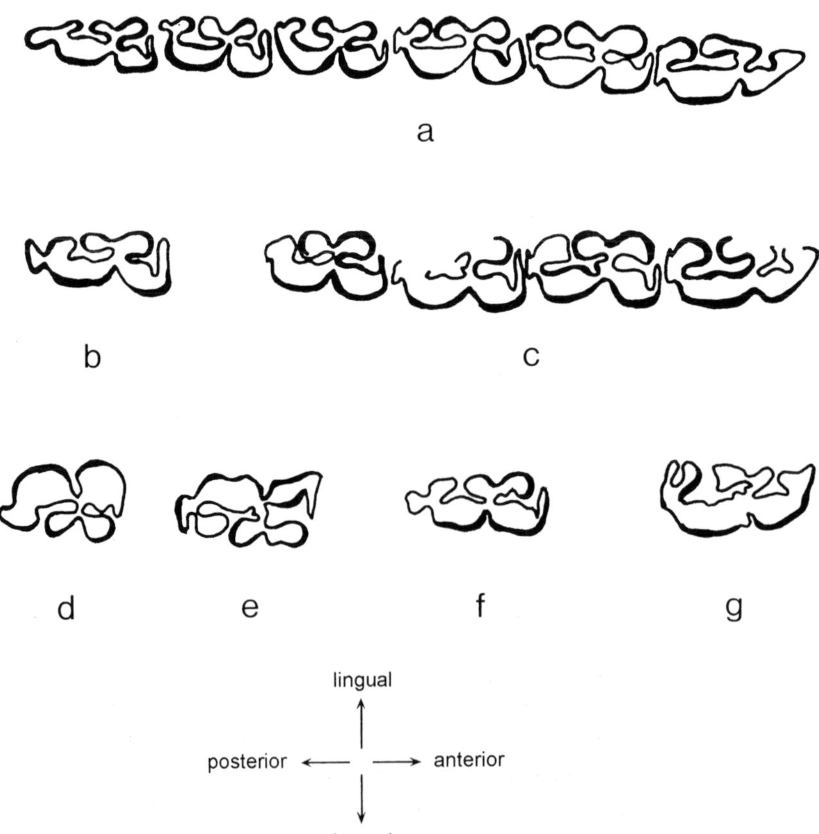

Figure 13.5 Patterns of tooth enamel in adult equids at Abu Hureyra. a, right mandible, P_2–M_3, Trench D, B153; b, right M_3, Trench E73, B291; c, right mandible, P_2–M_1, Trench E73, B252; d, left P_4, Trench D, B86; e, left P_3, Trench D, B86; f, right M_3, Trench D, B86; g, right P_2, Trench D, B86.

metastylids were rounded, and of about equal size, while the postflexids were long. The buccal sulcus was relatively short in the premolars and longer in the molars, but only in the M_2 of specimen D153 did it enter the gap between the pre- and postflexids (figure 13.5). In no case did the buccal sulcus approach closely to the lingual sulcus in the manner described for *E. hydruntinus* (Davis 1981), identified from Upper Palaeolithic sites in the Levant, or seen by Sebastian Payne in examples from Neolithic Can Hasan III in Anatolia.

On the relatively small sample available for study from Abu Hureyra, it was only possible to confirm that the population appeared to conform to the criteria commonly used for the identification of the onager, *Equus hemionus*. There seems no reason to anticipate any other equid species at the site, other than as a rare find.

A single, unfused, distal humerus from Abu Hureyra was so large that it could not have been from *Equus hemionus*. The specimen came from a deep and secure context within Abu Hureyra 2 levels, so there was little reason to suspect that it was intrusive. As the specimen was not charred, we have not attempted to date it directly as we have for other species (Legge and Rowley-Conwy 1986b). Recently, Davis (1980b) has identified the extinct *Equus hydruntinus* from sites near the Mediterranean coast, and Payne also attributes the equids from Can Hasan in Turkey to this species. Such as is known of the postcranial skeleton of this species suggests that it was at most only a little more robust than that of *Equus hemionus* (Eisenmann and Beckouche 1986). The distal humerus from Abu Hureyra was an unfused condyle, and it was also badly damaged. However, it is obviously well outside the size of contemporary onagers. It is probable that this bone did come from one of the rare examples of a caballine horse, *Equus caballus*, that are occasionally found in the late Pleistocene sites of Southwest Asia (Garrod and Bate 1937; Davis 1980b).

THE FAUNAL SEQUENCE AT ABU HUREYRA

This investigation is based on the animal bones from Trenches B, D, and E. The stratigraphic relationship of these trenches is shown in figure 8.75.

Abu Hureyra 1

In our preliminary accounts we reported on the fauna from Abu Hureyra 1 as one unit and did the same for the fauna from Abu Hureyra 2 (Legge 1975, 1977). Since those reports were written, Moore has divided the stratification into phases and periods, making it possible to examine the faunal sequence in more detail.

The faunas of the three periods of Abu Hureyra 1 are shown in figure 13.6. Each period had abundant Persian gazelles at about 80% of the identified bones. The onager, *Equus hemionus*, comprised an average of 11% of the fauna, but division by periods shows that the species declined from 1A to 1C from 14% to 8%. Cattle, *Bos primigenius*, and sheep, *Ovis musimon*, were also certainly part of the Abu Hureyra 1 fauna, and the latter species has been directly dated by accelerator mass spectrometry, using charred bones that could confidently be identified as *Ovis* (Legge and Rowley-Conwy 1986b; appendix 1). The position of the goat as part of the Epipalaeolithic fauna is less clear. The final stratigraphic division of the site has shown that, in the original study of the Abu Hureyra 1 fauna (Legge 1975), some material from the Abu Hureyra 2 levels above had

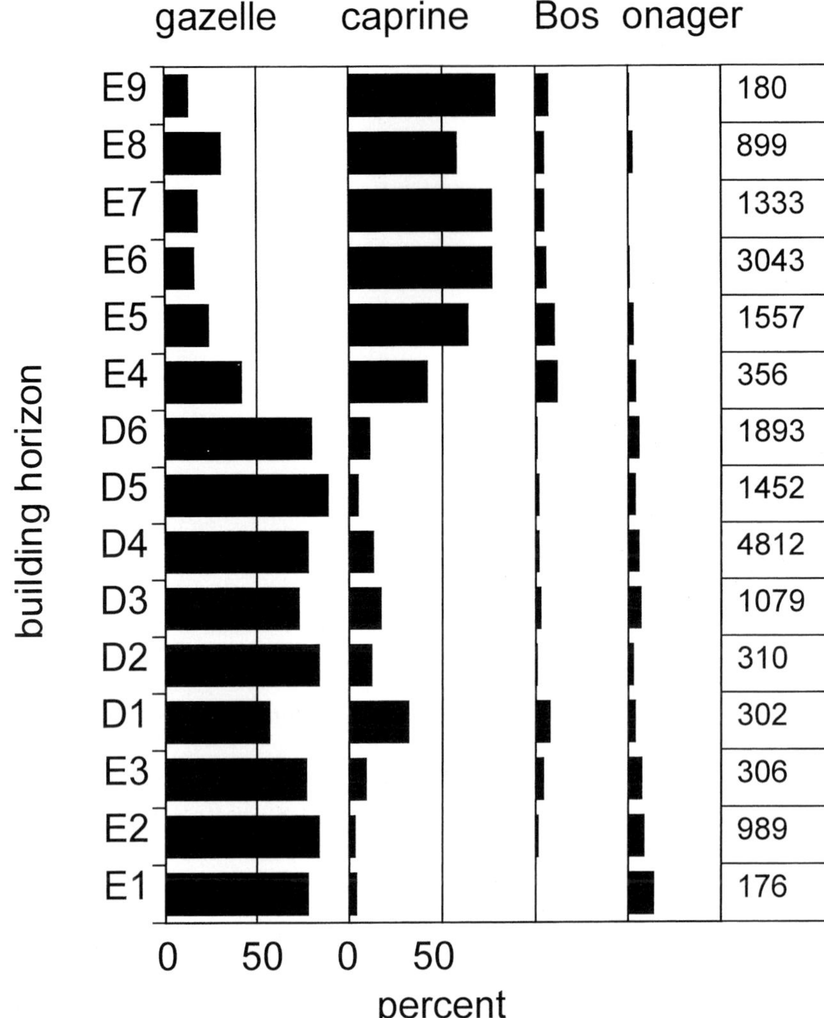

Figure 13.6 The faunal sequence of Abu Hureyra based on Trenches D and E. Trench E phases (building horizons) 1–3 are Abu Hureyra 1; Trench D phases 1–5/6 are Abu Hureyra 2A, and Trench E phases 4–8/9 are Abu Hureyra 2B and 2C. Right-hand column: total number of bones in each phase.

been included. No bones in the Abu Hureyra 1 levels can now be certainly identified as those of goats. Indeed, we would not have anticipated their presence during the Epipalaeolithic period at Abu Hureyra on environmental grounds. The site was located where rolling steppe abutted the river valley, and this did not provide the type of habitat with which wild goats are commonly associated. A few fallow deer bones, *Dama dama mesopotamica*, were found throughout the Abu Hureyra 1 layers, but the pig, *Sus scrofa*, was rare and was found only in Period 1B.

The hare, *Lepus capensis*, was common during the Epipalaeolithic period at Abu Hureyra. We showed in chapter 3 that hares were most commonly taken in recent times by the use of a throwing stick. If this same method was used by the people of Abu Hureyra 1, they did so to some effect; of all identified mammal remains from those levels, the bones of hare comprised some 10%. When these are divided by period, it can be seen that the species showed a marked abundance in Period 1A (phase 1) at 12.4% (figure 13.7), but declined quite sharply to about 6% in Period 1C (phase 3). An even faster decline is seen in the fox, *Vulpes vulpes*, which was moderately abundant only in Period 1A at 4.3%, falling to 1.3% in Period 1B and 1.0% in Period 1C. Bird bones, *Aves* spp., were found in a consistent proportion of about 3% through the three periods.

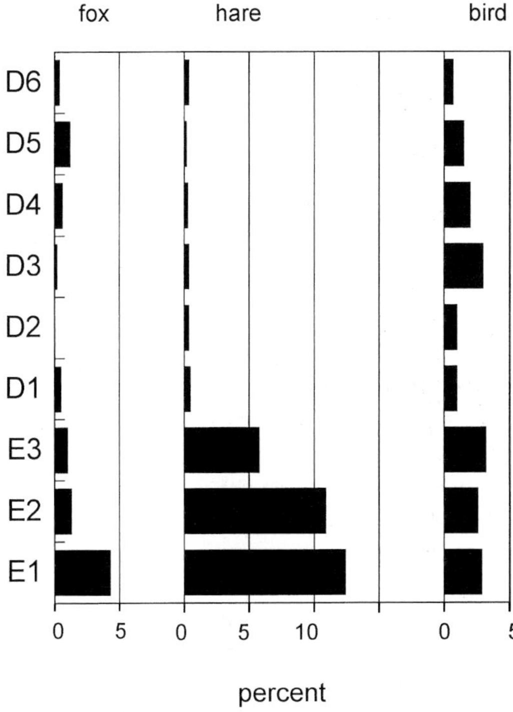

Figure 13.7 Frequency of fox, hare, and bird bones from Abu Hureyra 1 and Abu Hureyra 2A. Proportions are shown as percentages of total bone identifications.

The Abu Hureyra 1 fauna is thus marked by the abundance of gazelles and by the decline in onager, hare, and fox during the three periods. It is probable that this was the result of hunting pressure, and this raises the question as to why these species should have been the most vulnerable. The onager is a large animal with slow maturity and prolonged maternal dependence of the young. We argue that the onager, like the gazelle, was a migratory species and that it was hunted seasonally at Abu Hureyra. The gazelle breeds annually and, in the case of the Persian gazelle, twin births are common (Tsapluyk 1972), while the onager has a two-year spacing between births (Groves 1974) and twins are rare. The species would thus be more vulnerable in the type of hunting based on herd interception that is evident at Abu Hureyra (see below). It can thus be argued that hunting pressure alone could be responsible for the decline of the onager.

The same argument can be advanced for both the hare and fox. These are largely nonmigratory species that would have been vulnerable to year-round predation and could have been taken by means of a simple technology. It can, of course, be suggested that the apparent decline of hare and fox is the product of a proportional diagram (figure 13.7), in other words, an apparent decline in reality caused by a relative increase in the abundance of other species through more intensive predation. However, we note that bird bones did not decline in the same way, and even in the Abu Hureyra 2A deposits of Trench D, birds were as common in some levels as in Abu Hureyra 1. The bird remains thus provide a valuable baseline against which to measure changes in the proportions of small mammals.

Birds, inherently highly mobile, could more readily sustain high levels of local predation, as recruitment from outside areas was not restricted by the aridity of the steppe. The number of birds would therefore reflect the time that people were willing to spend in pursuit of them, perhaps during times of seasonal abundance, rather than the predation of a fixed local biomass as with the hare and fox.

After dry sieving, the sediments selected for flotation were water sieved with finer meshes. Figure 13.7 shows the recovery of hare bones from those Abu Hureyra 1 levels where both methods of sieving were used. A significant proportion of hare bones passed through the dry sieves but were caught in the fine-mesh wet sieves. However, it is notable that the bones passing through the dry sieves included a high proportion of the very small phalanges and metapodial fragments. A similar proportion of fox bones were also recovered only by wet sieving, although in this case almost all were the small phalanges and metapodial fragments. Nearly all of the identifiable bird bones were found in the dry sieve, mainly because they were less broken that those of the small mammals. The wet sieve sample consisted largely of shaft fragments that are in any case difficult to identify to species. The proportions of hare, fox, and bird bones shown in figure 13.7 are therefore based on the dry sieved samples, as these adequately reflect the proportions of the three species.

Figure 13.7 shows that bird bones remained a constant proportion of all bones identified, while hare and fox declined. If the proportion of birds taken was approximately constant in relation to the human population, then the decline of the other species can be seen as a function of more intense exploitation. As such, we suggest that their decline during Abu Hureyra 1 was caused by an increase in the size of the site; the virtual absence of the hare in Abu Hureyra 2, when the occupation of the site was on a far larger scale, further supports this interpretation.

The Fauna of Abu Hureyra 2A

The animal bones of Period 2A that we discuss here came from Trench D, phases 1–6 (figure 13.6) and Trench B, phases 1–7 (figure 13.8). The number of identified bones from phases 2–6 in Trench B was quite small, and phase 1 had only unidentifiable bone fragments. In phases 7–11 of Trench B the sample

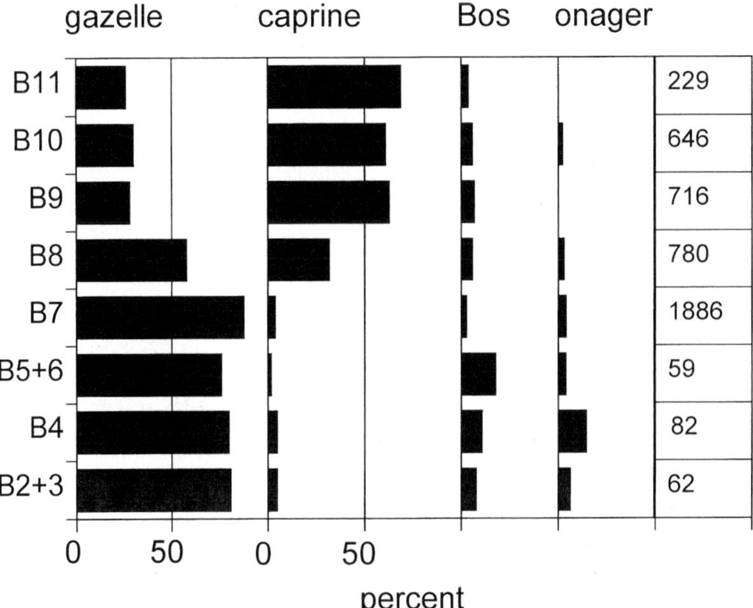

Figure 13.8 Identified large mammal bones from Trench B.

numbers were large, though in phases 10 and 11 the bones were again more fragmented. The samples from Period 2A in Trench D were larger. In general, the bones nearer the surface of the mound were brittle, more fragmented, and encrusted with crystalline salts.

The Abu Hureyra 2A fauna from Trench D and lower Trench B shows only minor changes from that of Abu Hureyra 1. Caprines, from their low frequency in Abu Hureyra 1, had the most significant increase. The Abu Hureyra 2A sequence began with an apparent peak of caprines (30%) in phase 1 of Trench D, but this fell back to about 12% in phases 4–6. The proportion of caprines in phases 2–7 of Trench B was lower than in levels of the same age in Trench D, but lower Trench B was a narrow sounding, and only 202 identifiable bones were recovered from phases 1–6 together. Apart from this, the two trenches had a very similar faunal composition through the several phases in each. Gazelles were abundant throughout Abu Hureyra 2A, and both trenches showed low frequencies of onager and cattle. The latter were more abundant in phases 2–6 in Trench B, though again, the number of identified bones from lower Trench B was small. We found bones of fallow deer and pigs only sporadically in the samples from both trenches.

The most marked change in species abundance is shown by the hare and the fox. From the rather high proportions of Abu Hureyra 1 the hare declined to the point where, in Abu Hureyra 2A levels in both Trenches B and D, it was less than 1% of the identified bones. The fox was found only sporadically in Abu Hureyra 2A. As the inhabitants were cultivating cereals, it might seem that the change in the abundance of hares was a reflection of habitat disturbance. Yet in many countries, and from our observations in Syria, too, the hare is common among cultivated fields. A more likely explanation for the low proportion of hares lies in the greatly increased size of the village of Abu Hureyra 2A. The increased number of inhabitants would have exerted even more hunting pressure than that which had caused the species to decline during Abu Hureyra 1. The biomass of hares within the area routinely exploited by the inhabitants of Abu Hureyra would have been finite, and under sustained exploitation the population could have been maintained only by immigration from the less exploited periphery of the territory of the village. The fox, as a burrowing mammal, is even more vulnerable once its earth is located. It could be dug out, especially with the assistance of dogs, or taken in traps or snares.

The Fauna of Abu Hureyra 2B and 2C

The faunal sample for Periods 2B and 2C[1] came from Trench E, phases 4–9 (figure 13.6), and Trench B, phases 8–10 and 11 (figure 13.8). In both trenches the fauna shows marked changes from earlier times. From the abundant gazelles and less common caprines of Abu Hureyra 1 and 2A there was a marked reversal as caprines became common, rapidly increasing to become 65–80% of the identified bones of large mammals, while gazelles fell to 15–30%. At the same time other wild species also declined. The 2B and 2C fauna in both Trenches B and E showed a declining proportion of onager, and the remains of pig and deer became very rare.

The rise in caprines was paralleled by a fairly marked increase in cattle (figure 13.9), from 2–3% in Period 2A in Trench D to 5–7% in Periods 2B and 2C in Trench E. This frequency was also found in the 2B and 2C levels in Trench B, where cattle were also some 6–7% of the identified bones, though this was

Figure 13.9 The aurochs, *Bos primigenius.*

partly masked by the high cattle values in the small samples from the lower levels of Trench B (Abu Hureyra 2A).

The most important aspect of the faunal sequence is the nature of the reversal in relative importance of gazelles and caprines. Although the transition is clearly evident when we compare the faunas of Trench D, Period 2A, and Trench E, Period 2B, these samples are from different parts of the settlement and so do not represent continuous buildup of deposit at one point on the mound.

Trench B offers a continuous record of this transition, and the sequence also shows the pronounced rise in caprines that was seen in phase 4 of Trench E. This highlights the importance of the Trench B sequence. Here we could follow the faunal sequence through 11 building phases (figure 13.8) that spanned the whole of the Abu Hureyra 2 occupation. The large sample of identified bones from phase 7 in Trench B (1,886 bones) confirmed the high proportion of gazelles and the lower proportion of caprines found in phases 1–5 of Trench D, as did the small samples from the earlier phases 1–6 in Trench B. The decline in gazelles began with phase 8 (780 bones) in Trench B, and by phase 9 (716 bones) the reversal in the importance of these species was complete. The relative proportions then remained constant through the upper phases 10 (646 bones) and 11 (229 bones). A further sample from level 99 in Trench B (340 bones) also conformed to this pattern, as it contained a high proportion of caprines; the level consisted of a mixture of sediments from phases 10 and 11.

Yet closer examination shows that the transition occurred within phase 8 of Trench B. Consequently, we have subdivided the fauna of phase 8 on stratigraphic grounds into three sequential units (figure 13.10). The lower unit (8/I) of the phase contained predominantly the bones of gazelles, while in the middle unit (8/II) gazelle and caprine bones were of equal abundance. In the upper unit (8/III) caprine bones were the most abundant. Radiocarbon dates would suggest a duration of about 50–100 years per building phase (see chapter 9). From such an estimate, the gazelle-to-caprine transition was remarkably rapid and took place in about 50 years, in other words, within a human lifetime.

This of course raises the question of the status of the caprines at the time when they first exceeded gazelles in number. Their marked increase could be taken alone to show domestication, which we discuss in detail below. However, this was not the first time that caprines showed an increase during the

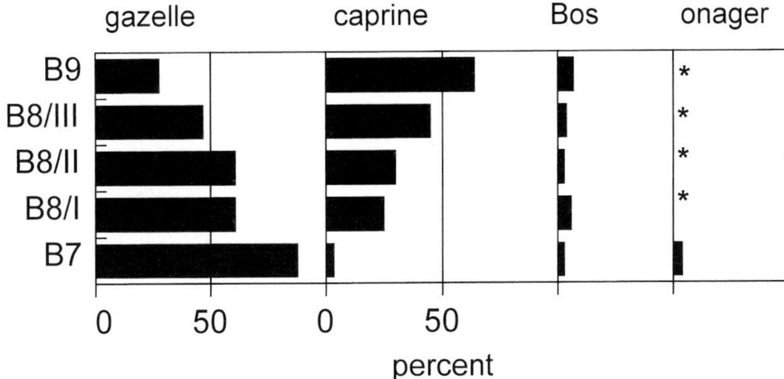

Figure 13.10 Identified large mammal bones from Trench B showing the faunal transition in phase 8.

Abu Hureyra sequence: between the upper phase of Abu Hureyra 1 and the earliest phases of Abu Hureyra 2A the abundance of caprines doubled. This raises the possibility that the caprines of Abu Hureyra 2A were domesticated, even though they were less abundant than the gazelles. We shall examine that possibility later in this chapter.

Overall, the fauna of Abu Hureyra shows continuity in the exploitation of the gazelle, with a decline in other wild species (cattle, onager, pig, deer, hare, and fox), probably due to local overexploitation. The numbers of these species quickly declined during Abu Hureyra 1 times, and this conflicts with Flannery's hypothesis (1969, p. 77) that the intensification of hunting and gathering could be recognized as a precursor to agriculture by a "broad spectrum revolution" in which such minor food resources would become more abundant in the face of dietary stress. That hypothesis has also been recently criticized by Edwards (1989a) on the grounds that such intensification is largely the product of more careful retrieval methods with a concomitant increase in diversity of the smaller species that are identified.

The fauna of early Abu Hureyra 2A shows a continued decline of these minor food resources, associated with a significant increase in the abundance of caprines. The major change within the Abu Hureyra faunal sequence is manifest in the transition between Abu Hureyra 2A and 2B with the massive reversal in the relative abundance of gazelle and caprines.

GAZELLE AND ONAGER HUNTING AT ABU HUREYRA: THE EVIDENCE FOR THE TECHNIQUE EMPLOYED

In recent work on animal bones more attention has been given to the determination of the season of death of the animals killed at archaeological sites. For mammals, the season of death can best be determined using the patterns of tooth eruption, tooth wear, and bone growth in the young. We have published a preliminary account of the application of these methods to the gazelle remains from Abu Hureyra (Legge and Rowley-Conwy 1987). The animal bones included a substantial proportion of infantile and juvenile gazelles, and we examined them closely in order to determine the season of death.

Evidence from the Dentition

The mandibular third milk molar (dp_4) of gazelles comes into wear shortly after birth and is later replaced by the fourth permanent premolar (P_4). Davis (1980a) has shown that in modern specimens of the Palestine gazelle the dp_4 is replaced at about 14 months of age. A recent collection of skulls of Persian gazelles from the Badghyz Reserve in Turkmenia is housed in the Lomonsov Museum of Zoology of the University of Moscow, and many of these have their death date recorded. Legge studied their dentition to help understand dental development and wear in the gazelle teeth from Abu Hureyra.

Some of the modern skulls were from young animals killed in the early summer of their second year, that is, at an age of about 13–14 months. The dp_4 in these specimens showed heavy wear, and this tooth was close to replacement by the permanent P_4. This shows that the age for the replacement of dp_4 in the Persian gazelle cannot be significantly different from that found in the Palestine gazelle. We took crown height measurements from the dp_4, measuring from the cementum-enamel margin just above the roots to the occlusal surface of the middle cusp (see Legge and Rowley-Conwy 1987). From these measurements it was possible to determine the season in which an individual animal was killed and thus whether the cull was intermittent or continued throughout the year. In the former case, crown heights would be found to group into few stages, while in the latter case the milk teeth would show all degrees of wear and the full range of crown heights from unworn to heavily worn.

We used the dental crown height measurements from the museum specimens to test the Abu Hureyra data (figure 13.11). The modern specimens had a steady rate of crown loss from birth to the replacement of these teeth at rather more than one year of age. The archaeological specimens of the dp_4 from Abu Hureyra showed that gazelle killing was markedly seasonal. Unworn milk teeth indicated that neonatal animals, with recently erupted milk molars, were killed in their birth season. These teeth had an enamel crown height of about 9.6 mm, similar to the recent Turkmenian specimens. A second group, with heavily worn milk molars, were killed at about 12 months of age, by which time the crown height of dp_4 was reduced by rather more than 5 mm, to a mean height of 4.3 mm.[2] We found no specimens intermediate between the unworn and heavily worn states.

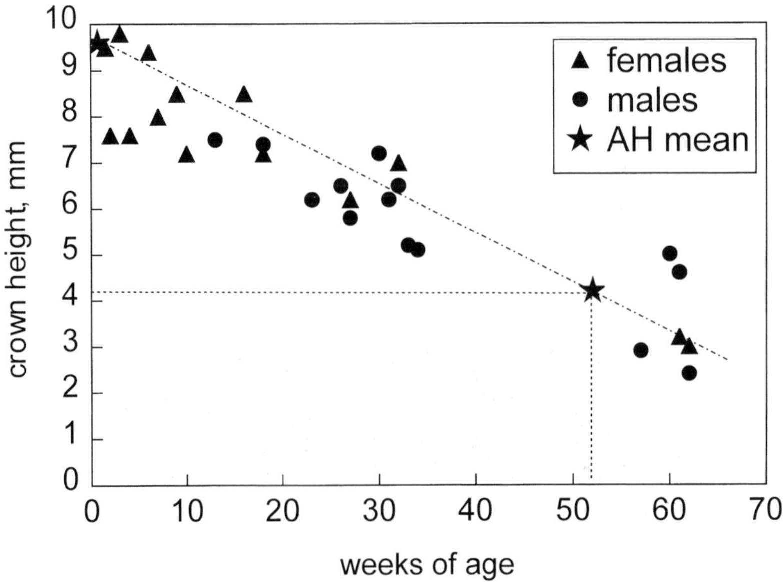

Figure 13.11 Crown heights of dp_4 in early and recent gazelles. The recent gazelles (given as females and males) are modern Turkmenian specimens of known death date. The stars represent the mean heights of the unworn and heavily worn samples of dp_4 from Abu Hureyra, at 9.5 and 4.2 mm, respectively. The birth season was May, and the older group was also killed in May.

Crown height measurements on the second permanent mandibular molar (M_2) showed further that adult animals were killed in all age classes from early maturity to old age (figure 13.12). As this tooth remains in wear throughout the adult life of the animal, wear is much slower and the annual reduction in crown height is small. Natural differences in tooth size, eruption time, and wear rate will inevitably blur the seasonal decrement where this is present. Consequently, the mature teeth cannot be used to determine season of death, although there is some evidence of seasonal groupings in crown height measurements during the first year or two of wear on this tooth.

Our observations on tooth wear were supplemented by measurements of the growing bones. Measurements of the corpus of the calcaneum and measurements of the juvenile humerus confirmed the intermittent cull (figures 13.13, 13.14), though the pattern observed when using measurements of growing bone will be blurred by differences in birthdate, body size, and growth rate among the young animals. Despite this, the calcaneum in particular showed three distinct groups of animals in the cull (figure 13.13):

1. infantile gazelles with very small, unfused calcanea,
2. immature gazelles, nearly of adult size, but with calcanea still unfused, and
3. fully adult gazelles with fused calcanea.

These groups represented, respectively, newborn gazelles, one-year-old gazelles, and fully adult gazelles of more than 14 months of age. This pattern of intermittent cull was identical to that shown by the crown heights of dp_4.

The onager teeth suggested that this species, too, was killed in seasonal episodes, though the sample of deciduous teeth was smaller than that of the gazelles. Onager milk teeth were also found either unworn or heavily worn, indicating that the onagers were killed in the same manner as the gazelles, and also in the birth season.

Our measurements of bone growth, tooth eruption, and tooth wear on the gazelles and onagers therefore demonstrate two principal features. First, tooth

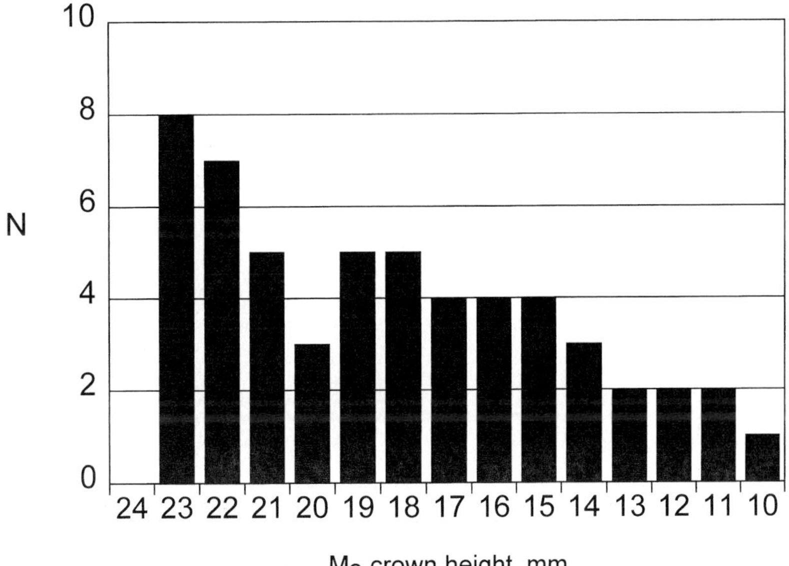

Figure 13.12 Crown heights of the permanent lower M_2 of gazelles. This tooth erupts before maturity and wears throughout adult life. The declining frequency in each height class shows the increasing adult mortality with age and reflects the population structure of the adult herd.

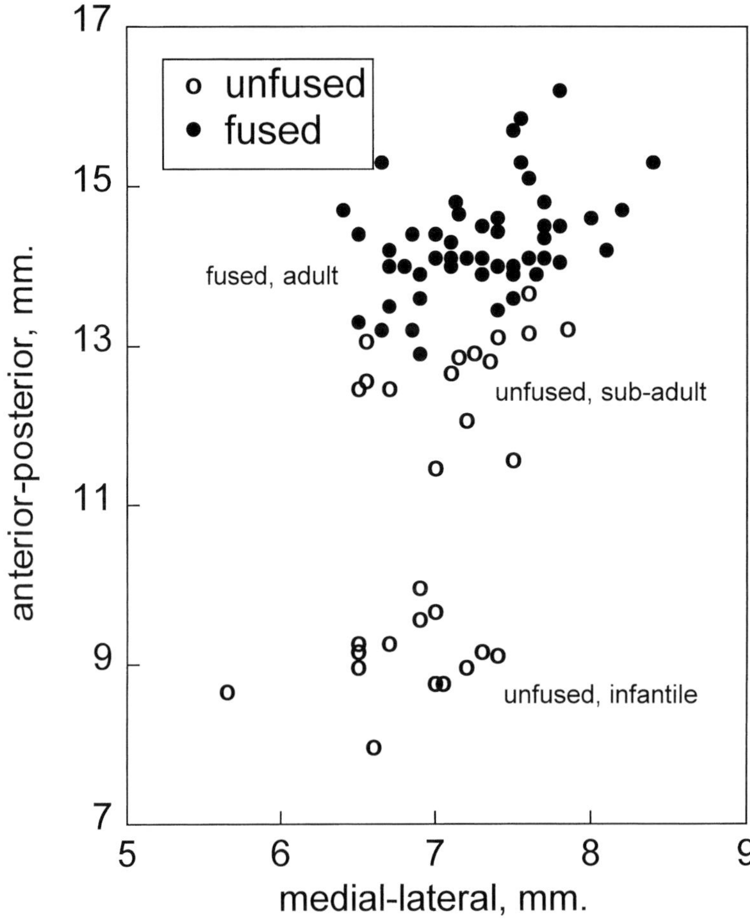

Figure 13.13 Measurements of the corpus of the gazelle calcaneum. We give an interpretation of the three clusters.

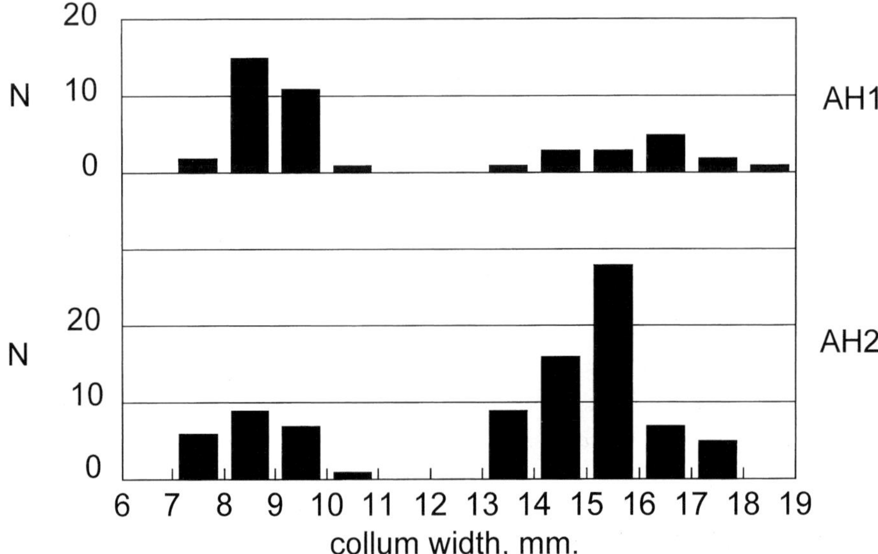

Figure 13.14 Measurements of the collum (neck) width of the scapula from Abu Hureyra 1 and Abu Hureyra 2 compared. The smaller specimens are unfused and newborn, while the larger are subadult and adult. Note the discontinuity of size distribution.

eruption and tooth wear patterns—especially in the case of the milk dentition—showed that the cull was intermittent and occurred at about the birth season of both species. Second, the degree of wear on the permanent dentition showed that all age classes of adult gazelles and onagers were killed. This pattern is typical of catastrophic mortality in which whole herds are exterminated.

Evidence for the Migrations of Gazelles

We have shown above that there is good evidence for a seasonal gazelle cull at Abu Hureyra. Gazelles were killed in all age classes, and only in the early summer. The seasonality of the cull, and the population structure exhibited, support two main conclusions. First, the gazelles were killed in seasonal episodes of mass slaughter. Second, the absence of age classes in the young other than newborn and one year old implies that the gazelles were absent at other times of the year; in other words, the people of Abu Hureyra were exploiting a seasonal migration of gazelle (Legge and Rowley-Conwy 1987).

The accounts of several early travelers in this region provide evidence for the former abundance of gazelles in this region and their pattern of migration. Aharoni stated that the objective of his travels was the observation of the migration of the gazelles (Mendelssohn 1974; Meshel 1974). This suggests that the phenomenon was well known. The record is explicit that the migration he saw was from north to south, and although the time of year is not given, other accounts suggest that this would have been at some time during mid or late summer. Bearing in mind that our evidence is for a gazelle cull in the birth season (late April to early May in the Abu Hureyra region), the weight of evidence is for the northward migration to have taken place in the spring. The gazelles seen by Aharoni were migrating in large herds, and because he was an informed observer, his estimate of their numbers is probably reliable. Support for this pattern of migration can be found in the journals of other travelers.

Musil (1928a, p. 149) found that gazelles were absent from the Palmyra region in winter, although his guide assured him that the area "swarmed with gazelles in summer, which go south for the winter and the spring to the Hamad" (the rock desert of Jordan). Burton and Tyrwhitt Drake (1872) were near Ma'arret en Nu'man, some 70 km southwest of Aleppo and now on the main Aleppo to Damascus road, during late October and they recorded that "gazelles, which are said to abound in summer, had already migrated eastwards."

Lady Anne Blunt saw abundant gazelles migrating north in late March near Deir ez-Zor, although she was traveling on the east bank of the Euphrates at the time: we "passed through an immense herd of gazelles, many thousands of them, all moving in the same direction—northwards, and we drove one or two before us for a mile or two" (Blunt 1879, I, p. 239).

It is evident that the gazelles formed very large herds when on migration. Blunt also described the herds as being "packed together" when on the move, which is obviously relevant to the type of hunting that could be employed to take them. A little later (3 April) she saw gazelles near Palmyra and met a family of the "Sleb" hunters (more usually given as Sleyb) who were hunting gazelle. According to Blunt the Sleyb hunters "follow the herds of gazelles as they migrate north and south. On these they live, making their food, their clothing and their tents out of the creatures that they catch and kill" (Blunt 1879, II, p. 109). Blunt recorded that the Sleyb family that she saw moved in a regular cycle with the gazelles from the Palmyra region in summer, and as far south as the Nejd in northern Saudi Arabia in winter.

Barker (1876, pp. 267–268) has given a similar account, reporting from journals kept by his father. He described the gazelles as migrating northwards in summer in "numerous herds—many thousands together," and further went on to describe the hunting of gazelles with stone-built kites. Lanoy (1678, published 1707) and Drummond (1754) both recorded gazelles near Aleppo during July. Lanoy saw them being hunted again by the Sleyb at this time, while Drummond saw them at Sfira, about 20 km southeast of the city. Skinner (1836) traveled from Damascus in the direction of the Euphrates River on the 3rd of April; on the 16th, when within a few days' travel of the river, he recorded that "a great number of gazelles are about us. I found a young thing a week old, and gave it to an Arab boy to nurse." The following day he found more young gazelle, and also recorded the abundance of hares and "hybarra," which must be the Houbara bustard, *Chlamydotis undulata*.

Yet, in the winter gazelles appear to have been uncommon in the region north of Palmyra and the Jebel Abu Rujmein. Teonge (1679, published 1928) wrote of the European traders living in Aleppo that their "main occupation from September to March" was coursing hares with greyhounds, and hunting wild boar. In this and other accounts of winter hunting southeast of Aleppo, gazelles were not mentioned. Irby and Mangles (1844) recorded the presence of a few gazelles a little to the south of Aleppo in winter. However, they were traveling south toward Hama and were a little north of "Khan Shekune" (Khan Sheikhun); they were thus well to the west of the "little desert" of central Syria and in a different environment from that of the Abu Hureyra region. Because of this it is probable that they were seeing occasional specimens of the Palestine gazelle rather than the more arid land adapted Persian gazelle that was found at Abu Hureyra.

In general, the pattern that emerges is of few gazelles being seen in traveler's accounts of the desert of north Syria between September and April, the time of year when most journeys were made due to lower temperatures and more available water. While such accounts of journeys made during the winter months did not record gazelles in northern Syria, some were quite explicit as to why this was so; the absence of gazelles was attributed to a seasonal migration. Other travelers saw gazelles actually on migration and mentioned encountering very large associations of gazelles in their published accounts.

We have good evidence that the cull of gazelles at Abu Hureyra was in the birth season, which was historically in late April or early May. Gazelles are adapted to very dry lands, and they can survive for much of the year with little or no water intake. However, the lactating female must have access to water or green food at the time of birth. The pattern of migration reconstructed here, therefore, reflects this need. The northward migration to the vicinity of Abu Hureyra brought the herds to a region of higher rainfall, arriving at the time of maximum growth in the herbaceous vegetation of this region, Hillman's woodland-steppe of zone 4. The southward migration, probably as far as northern Transjordan, took the herds beyond the range of the harsh winter on the Syrian plateau, and to an area of milder climate and good grazing in the winter.

Herd Interception Strategies

The mortality pattern at Abu Hureyra is characteristic of a "catastrophic" system of hunting that involved the use of cooperative drives and the slaughter of whole herds, employing either natural topographic features or artificial structures that allowed the herds to be enclosed or stampeded to their death. Such techniques are described widely in the literature of the recent past. Perhaps the best known examples come from North America, where the mass hunting of the buffalo, *Bison occidentalis*, the pronghorn antelope, *Antilocapra americana*, and the caribou, *Rangifer tarandus*, are recorded historically and are also known from archaeological examples.

Hunters in North America used either natural features such as steep gullies into which the herds were stampeded, or specially constructed enclosures, usually with long training walls or wings, or rows of artificial human silhouettes that served to guide the stampede into a small killing enclosure (Egan 1917; Frison 1971, 1978; Osgood 1936). Once trapped, the animals were killed either by being driven over a small precipice into specially dug pits at the termination of the training walls, or being speared or shot with arrows. The sole aim of the hunters was to destroy the herd; all animals, regardless of sex or age, were killed.

While examples of such mass kills are well known from North America, the same technique was widely used in other parts of the world. Satterthwaite (1986) has reviewed Aboriginal net hunting in Australia and has noted examples where brushwood wings were added to net enclosures for the hunting of large game. Galton (1853, p. 106) described massive wooden fences built to guide herd animals into pitfalls constructed by hunters in southern Africa. Such structures were not restricted to arid or semi-arid areas; besides the example of mass interception of caribou, the elk, *Alces alces*, was trapped by such means in Norway, and in Scotland, stone-built enclosures with diverging training walls known as "tainchells" were used in the trapping of red deer, *Cervus elaphus*.

It is important here to distinguish between active hunting by means of enclosure traps and passive hunting by the use of pitfall traps. Among many peoples static traps are used to take animals in an opportunistic fashion. Such traps were usually unattended and visited only at intervals, and even the larger types could be constructed by only a few hunters. Contemporary illustrations show that such traps were used in medieval Europe (for example, Gaston Phoebus [1331–1391], published by Bise in 1984). This work depicted unattended pitfall traps for the capture of wolves or wild boar (Bise 1984, pp. 84–87), while other types were shown used in organized drives. The unattended pitfall was commonly used for the capture of species that lived in woodland or other cover. In such environments, large mammals are usually found in small groups or are even solitary for most of the year. Because of this, the hunting of woodland mammals by driving required very large numbers of participants as well as the use of extensive fencing or netting to control the direction of movement of the game, as was the practice in medieval hunting in Britain. In the case of the red deer, we have been informed by Phillip Ratcliffe that attempted driving of this species in woodland for the purpose of a research census resulted in most deer breaking back through the line of beaters, who usually remained unaware that this had happened.

On the other hand, mass drives in which large numbers of animals are killed show quite different characteristics. First, such methods are most often found in open landscapes. Under such conditions grazing mammals commonly form large herds, which in some seasons can number many thousands. Such local concentrations of large-bodied animals and their dependence upon seasonally variable pasture and climate will tend to foster a regular pattern of migration. Second, such herds in open land are less easily taken by the use of unattended traps, as there are few predictable trails on which they regularly move. In such a situation, mass drives into specially constructed enclosures will secure the best return. This, in turn, imposes particular requirements of labor on the hunters. The work required in the construction of a substantial timber or stone enclosure, on pitfalls, and on the training walls would be considerable, and a large number of hunters may be needed to surround a sufficient area of land for the herd to be successfully intercepted and driven to the enclosure. It is obvious that a certain level of return will be anticipated by each hunter for the expenditure of effort and cooperation in driving. It is also necessary for the hunters to use a method of meat storage where the operation of mass killing structures contributes a major part of the annual protein supply.

Only in recent years has it become apparent that such methods of mass interception were widely used in Southwest Asia, and that structures built for this purpose survive extensively in the steppes and deserts of that region. The use of mass drives for the killing of gazelles was known to European travelers and was recorded on several occasions between the seventeenth and twentieth centuries. However, their records of this activity were overlooked or misinterpreted, even when these structures had been widely recorded and photographed from the air.

The Discovery of "Desert Kites" and Their Historical Use

While editor of the journal *Antiquity*, O. G. S. Crawford did much to encourage the early use of aerial photography in Western Asia. Maitland (1927) and Rees (1929) published accounts in *Antiquity* in which they described extensive chains of stone-walled structures that they had seen across the deserts of northern Transjordan in the region of the Wadi Rajil. Rees coined the name "kites" for these structures, for when seeing them from the air "one is reminded of a small boy's kite." In his paper, Rees illustrated the general form of kites that he had observed. The killing enclosure was commonly star-shaped, and from this enclosure the training walls diverged, often extending more than a kilometer across the desert surface. As Rees noted, the training walls frequently terminated in a cairn, which must have served as markers for the hunters who may have been driving some distance from the ends of the walls. In some of the kites the training walls continued for some distance into the killing enclosure, after the manner of the funnel entrance of a modern cage trap; Rees called these extensions the "barbs."

Rees interpreted these structures as military installations and suggested that herders with their livestock would retreat into the enclosure when danger threatened. On the other hand, Crawford (1929, pp. 400–401) inserted an editorial note at the end of Rees's paper quoting a passage from Burckhardt (1830) in which the structure of a kite and its use in the killing of gazelles was described. Crawford stopped short of making an exact correlation between Burkhardt's description and Rees's photographs, but the note contained the implication that Crawford had seen this connection.

At about the same time that Maitland and Rees were photographing kites in Transjordan, similar work was done in Syria by Poidebard (1934), and again among his published photographs are examples of kites. Poidebard also chose to give a military explanation for these structures, despite information given to him by a local beduin that they were used for the killing of gazelles. This was shown by Poidebard's descriptions; plate CXLVII illustrated a small kite near Jebel Cembe and was entitled "mur et ouvrage de défense indigène," while on his distribution map of the sites discovered during aerial surveys the kites were recorded as "enceinte de partisans nomades."

The first definite recognition of the purpose for which the kites were intended came from Field (1954) following his extensive survey of the region; he attributed to these structures the purpose of hunting "gazelles, oryx, ostrich, etc." Since that time further work by Meshel (1974), Parr and colleagues (1977), and Betts (1983, 1984, 1985) has done much to elucidate the distribution of the kites, which are now known to occur widely in Syria, Transjordan, the northern Arabian peninsula, and in the Sinai Desert.

Before the construction of the Suez Canal, European traders and others going to India would commonly go by the overland route (Grant 1937), traveling by caravan from Aleppo in northern Syria to Basra at the head of the Persian Gulf. Others made extensive journeys in Western Asia from the desire to observe and document the cultures and ways of life of its peoples. Several of their journals contain accounts of the kites and are quite specific about the use to which they were put. Some travelers doubtless saw the kites in action, while others appear to have based their accounts on explanations provided by Arab companions or guides. Among the descriptions are those that were clearly derived from other published sources; for example, Tristram (1889, p. 130) recorded that "a more wholesale mode [of hunting gazelles] is practiced in the Hauran, by driving a herd into a decoy enclosure, with a pitfall on either side, where they are easily taken." Such observations were clearly secondary and are not further considered below.

An early record of kites, that of Pedro Teixeira in 1604, is in many ways the most interesting. First, the location of the kite was a little to the north of the village of Taibe (38°56' E, 35°05' N), about 60 km south southeast of Abu Hureyra. Second, the form of the kite was quite different from those used farther to the west and south. In Transjordan, most kites stand on rock desert (Betts 1983, 1984, 1985), an area of volcanic outflows that have carpeted the land with basaltic lavas. The boulders resulting from the weathering of the lava provided material from which the kites were constructed. In Syria, the lava carpets only the southernmost part of the desert, in an area contiguous with that in northern Transjordan. Elsewhere, ready supplies of boulders were not available, and Teixeira's (1604) account shows the interception of gazelle herds was also possible using a simpler form of kite:

> On these plains, the people of Taybe catch many gazelles in this wise: they set up over a wide space, amidst the plain, two rows of wands, about a cubit high, each with a rag pennant, forming a long and wide avenue. In this they make many and great pitfalls. Then, scouring the hill and plains in bands, they rouse the game and drive them to the rods. These, in terror alike of their pursuers and of the pennants fluttering on either hand, fall headlong into the pits and are taken alive or dead. (p. 99)

Burckhardt (1830) described kites just to the northeast of Damascus, in the region of the modern town of Qaryatein:

> *Gazelles*. These are seen in considerable numbers all over the Syrian Desert. On the eastern frontiers of Syria are several places allotted for the hunting of gazelles; these places are called *masiade*. An open space on the plain, of about one mile and a half square, is enclosed on three sides by a wall of loose stones, too high for the gazelles to leap over. In

> different parts of the wall gaps are purposefully left, and near each gap a deep ditch is made on the outside. The enclosed space is situated near some rivulet or spring to which in summer the gazelles resort. When the hunting is to begin, many peasants assemble and watch until they see a herd of gazelles advancing from a distance towards the enclosure, into which they drive them; the gazelles, frightened by the shouts of these people and the discharge of firearms, endeavour to leap over the wall, but can only effect this at the gaps, where they fall into the ditch outside, and are easily taken, sometimes by hundreds. The Chief of the herd always leaps first, and the others follow one by one. The gazelles thus taken are immediately killed, and their flesh sold to the Arabs and neighbouring fellahs. Several villages share in the profits of each *mesiade*, or hunting party, the principal of which are near Kariatein, Hassia and Homs. (pp. 220–222)

From this account, it appears that Burckhardt did not look closely at the kites, as his account is very general, and there are few "rivulet or spring" in that region near which kites could be located.

A similar general account was given by Musil; his observations were made in 1908–1909.

> Conspicuous in the lowlands were numerous enclosures, fenced around by rough stone walls. Many of these measured several hundred meters in circumference, and the walls were up to two meters in height. The *fellahin* from Dmejr and the northern settlements catch gazelles in them. These enclosures, called *mesajid* or *mesajed*, are triangular with a single narrow entrance at the sharpest angle. The walls do not end at the entrance, but extend to a distance of several hundred meters, widening out gradually and becoming lower all the time. If a herd of gazelles is grazing somewhere near, the hunters begin to drive the animals cautiously towards the enclosure to get them into the widest opening of the walls first. When they succeed in this, the usual method is to frighten the beasts from behind, this making the frenzied game run right into the narrow opening, which the hunters quickly close. Then the hunters begin to throw missiles of all kinds at the trapped animals. The wall enclosing the base of the triangle is purposely made lower in some places, with deep pits dug outside. Frightened as the gazelles are, they invariably jump over the walls into the pits, where they break their necks or legs and become easy prey to the hunters. In this cruel manner from fifty to sixty gazelles are often captured in half a day. (Musil 1928a, pp. 3–4)

Musil (1928a, p. 4) also recorded that the entrance of the kites were marked by stone cairns which were "visible from a great distance and therefore well suited to our purpose—i.e. a base line for survey and star sight." It seems likely that these cairns were intended to serve as a means by which the drivers of the game could themselves orient their progress.

Musil (1928b) made a similar record of kites to the southern border of "Palmyrena," that is, south of the ancient city of Palmyra. His description of the plan of the kites was similar to that above; low places in the walls, and pitfalls 2–3 m deep were again the means by which the gazelles were taken. The main difference in practice when compared to those sites near Dumayr was the use of a dog (given as *Sluke*), which was released into the killing enclosure to terrify the gazelles further and encourage them to leap over the wall and into the pitfalls.

An even more vivid, and certainly eye-witness, account of this hunting was made by the zoologist Aharoni about 1915. The account has been somewhat abbreviated here from Mendelssohn's translation; the same quotation is also given with a slightly different wording by Meshel (1974):

> Once I made a four-day excursion into the desert with Baron von Wirtenau in order to observe the migration of gazelles. We saw them with binoculars and saw innumerable flocks, one after the other. Our estimate is that we saw more than 10,000, all of which were returning from north to south. They start their migration in herds of thousands, and the Bedouin know this time well and hunt them during this migration.
>
> I and Y. Hankin, my hunter and reliable companion in my desert travels, witnessed once a shocking spectacle, when 500–600 gazelles were trapped in a corral not far from Racheimah (East Jordan). . . . In order to trap several hundred gazelles at once, the Bedouin enclose a large triangular area which extends over many km. In the wall, which is higher than a man, are places which are lower, and before each one a deep trench is dug. When the Bedouin saw a migrating flock of gazelles, they drove them from all directions into the broad opening of the corral. The gazelles were not afraid, as the walls, built from desert stone, were similar to their surroundings. When several hundred gazelles had entered the corral, the Bedouin closed in on them, running from left to right, shouting ferociously. The frightened gazelles tried to escape, jumping over the wall at the lower parts of it, and fell into the trenches outside of them. We saw how many of them were pulled out of the trenches with broken limbs and their bleating in agony was heart-rending. (Mendelssohn 1974, pp. 726–727)

Aharoni further wrote that the gazelles were carried to the beduin camp by camel, and there were skinned and preserved by drying and salting.

Wright (1895) has given a description of kites near Qaryatein that conforms essentially to the pattern in those given above. Wright confirms that the boundary wall of the killing enclosure contained gaps, and that deep pits were dug outside these. His account gives "forty or fifty" gazelles taken at one time. Barker (1876) has also transcribed a description of this hunting method.

Although the above accounts refer to gazelles, the tooth wear patterns on the deciduous teeth of the onagers from Abu Hureyra also suggest that these, too, were killed seasonally. We know of no witness accounts of onager hunting by means of mass drives; the species was already rare in Syria by the eighteenth century AD. Yet a depiction of this activity does survive at the Umayyad hunting palace of Qusayr ʿAmra east of Amman in Transjordan (eighth century AD). There a large mural depicts just such a hunting scene (Creswell 1989, p. 110). Onagers are being stampeded by dogs between lines of rope and into a netting enclosure, where they are killed by men with spears. Other men stand with burning torches along the rope guides, although this is probably a further means of frightening the animals rather than evidence that the activity took place at night. Scenes of skinning and butchery of the onagers are also shown.

It can be seen that the above accounts of gazelle and onager hunting differ in detail, but conform to a general pattern. Although some of the later accounts may have been enhanced by familiarity with the earlier examples, there is little doubt that each traveler did see the kites, and knew their real purpose, even if the observation was at a time of year when they were probably not in use. Three of the travelers described kites in the vicinity of Qaryatein (Burckhardt, Musil, and Wright), and Musil further noted the presence of these structures to the south of Palmyra. Teixeira was clearly quite close to Abu Hureyra and described a kite of otherwise unknown form in Southwest Asia, although very similar structures of poles and pitfalls were used in North America for the capture of the pronghorn antelope (Grinnell 1923).

Certainly the most vivid record is that of Aharoni; he no doubt saw the kite actually at work, and recorded his location as "Rachiemeh" or "Rachiemah." Z. Meshel has informed us that Aharoni was probably somewhere to the east of the ancient city of Palmyra at the time the record was made; this is much farther to the north than might be implied by "East Jordan" in Mendelssohn's translation. It is tempting to place Aharoni's "Racheimeh" as the Wadi Rcheme, near the site of El Kum, a little to the north of Taibe; there is a concentration of kites there that was recorded by Poidebard (1934), and Teixeira also saw his peculiar form of kite to the north of that place.

The village of Taibe is at a very significant point in the local landscape. Immediately to the west of the village rise the hills of Jebel Qal'at Mqebrah, which is a spur extending from the extensive Jebel Hawitat er-Ras. To the east rises the Jebel Bishri. The gap between these ranges is about 15 km wide, and in it are situated the village of Taibe and, a little to the north, the late Palaeolithic-Epipalaeolithic archaeological sites at El Kum, and also a cluster of kites. The caravan route from Aleppo to Baghdad also passed through Taibe (Grant 1937), and it was people from this village who were seen by Teixeira (1604) to use the form of kite made up of pennants and pitfalls. This pass separates the "little desert" of northern Syria (Grant 1937) from the much larger area of open country to the south. It seems probable that this gap in the hills would have funneled the migration at this point, as shown in our reconstructed route for this migration (Legge and Rowley-Conwy 1987, p. 91).

Blunt and Aharoni estimated that they saw gazelle herds numbering many thousands migrating at one time; Blunt also described them as traveling "packed together" when on a northward migration in early summer, while Aharoni saw large and dense herds moving south, which must have been later in the year. The northward migration would have passed through the gap in the Jebel Bishri where Taibe and El Kum are situated and have reached the vicinity of Abu Hureyra 100 km farther on. The large westward bend of the Euphrates where Abu Hureyra stands would have deflected the herds to the immediate vicinity of the settlement, before they turned west and dispersed over the plains for the birth season. It is difficult to estimate the length of time that the gazelles would have remained on their birth grounds. Drummond (1754) saw "great numbers of antelopes sporting on the plains" in early July near "Spheree" (Sfira), which stands at the northern end of the Sabkhat al Jabbul, the seasonal salt lake to the southeast of Aleppo, about 80 km northwest of Abu Hureyra. Yet the tooth wear evidence shows that gazelles were not killed through the later summer. It seems likely that the gazelle herds were by then more dispersed, rendering the method of mass drives inoperable, or that the animals had moved too far away from the vicinity of the site for hunting to be a worthwhile activity. Nor does it seem that the southwards movement in the autumn could be intercepted. The migration probably began with a general southward drift of small herds, which gradually coalesced into the large herds as seen by Aharoni when moving south through the pass at Taibe.

Besides the historical evidence for the use of mass interception of gazelle herds, other methods of hunting were commonly employed in which animals were taken singly. We consider these next as possible alternatives to the use of mass trapping.

Other Methods of Hunting Gazelles

An alternative method by which gazelles could be taken would be by stalking and then shooting with arrows. Arrowheads are abundant among the flint tools of the Neolithic of Southwest Asia, and were especially common in the village of Abu Hureyra 2. Many European travelers in Southwest Asia were struck by the presence of a desert hunting tribe who were known as the Sleyb, or Solubah; many variants of such spellings exist. This people lived among the beduin but were not part of beduin society, although they were commonly employed as hunters, as well as for their manual skills and knowledge of veterinary and human medicine (Palgrave 1865; Dickson 1949). The Sleyb owned donkeys, and sometimes a few goats. Their services as desert guides were also much used by European travelers.

The Sleyb were briefly described by Glubb (1943) and Field (1951), who included photographs of individuals in his publication. Doughty (1888) noted that they lived throughout the Arabian peninsula, and they were mentioned in travelers' journals from almost every part of Arabia. Their encampments were usually small: Chesney (1868) saw a group of small tents which he recorded as being 7 feet (a little over 2 m) long and 3 feet (1 m) high.

An early reference is that of Lanoy (1678, published 1707), who in mid July encountered two Sleyb hunters (given as Selebee) a little to the south of Aleppo when he was traveling to Palmyra. Even at such an early time the hunters possessed a gun. Lanoy described the skin pads bound to the hands, elbows, and knees of the Sleyb to facilitate crawling on rough ground during the stalk for their prey. Burckhardt (1830) noted that the Sleyb (given as El Szoleyb) wore gazelle skin clothing, and that "the dried flesh of gazelles is their food during the whole year." Lady Anne Blunt also saw Sleyb (given as Sleb) near Palmyra during April, and she further noted that their clothing was made entirely from gazelle skins. Sleyb were also seen south of Taibe during May (A Gentleman 1784), and also by Wright (1895), as he traveled from Damascus to Palmyra during late May and early June. It is notable that the Sleyb were in this area during spring and summer when seen by Wright, Blunt, an anonymous writer, and Lanoy, especially in the light of Blunt's observations that the Sleyb migrated north-south as they followed the seasonal movements of the gazelles.

The method by which the Sleyb hunted was stalking or concealment. Musil (1928b) said that they could catch 20 or 30 gazelles in one day of such hunting, with the hunters working in pairs. Bushes and twigs were used as camouflage, and even ostriches and the ibex could be taken by stalking in this manner. Lanoy (1707) also described the use of an ass as a stalking horse, offering concealment to the hunter until he was close enough to shoot.

Stalking of individual animals is comparatively time consuming. This hunting method also offers the opportunity to practice some degree of selection in terms of the preferred age and sex of the prey, and would be likely to introduce some degree of age or sex bias into the cull. Animals in a particular age group may be easier to take, or be more desirable. At Abu Hureyra, the finding of all age classes from newborn to very old, and the equal representation of males and females, does not argue for a selective technique of cull.

A different method of gazelle hunting that was often described by travelers was the use of a trained hawk, usually in conjunction with a fast-running dog (Layard 1853; Dickson 1949). The hawks were specially trained to attack the heads of gazelle by regularly feeding them from meat secured between the horns of a captive specimen. Such a method allows gazelles to be taken only singly, and there is no evidence that this was other than an occasional diversion practiced for sport by the more wealthy people.

Parsons (1808) traveled the desert route from Aleppo to India and saw the coursing of gazelles by a tame leopard at the end of his journey in northern India. This again was a very specialized activity for the aristocracy and cannot be regarded as a means of obtaining regular meat supplies.

Gazelles and other similar species may also be taken using different forms of tread traps (see, for example, Clark 1952, pp. 52–53). We have not encountered references to such traps in the journals of travelers in Southwest Asia, but Asher (1986, pp. 141–142) has described them more recently among the Kababish nomads of Sudan. These traps had spikes projecting inward from a stout circular rim, leaving a small space through which the animal's leg could pass, but from which it could not be withdrawn. The mode of use generally depended upon the trap being set on a known game trail. The advantage of the method lay in the fact that the trap did not need to be supervised, although it had to be visited often for the game to be secured in a worthwhile condition. The overall success rate of this type of trapping is rather low, and it seems improbable that a settlement as large as Abu Hureyra could have supplied itself with gazelle meat by this means.

Newborn gazelles commonly remain in concealment for a few days until ready to follow their mother. During this time the young can be captured, and this was often done by the desert people who raised the fawns as pets (Parsons 1808; Blunt 1879, II). Burton (1879) recorded the remarkable tameness that such animals might develop:

> The Bedawin bring them in, and so succeed in taming the timid things that they will follow their owner like dogs, and amuse themselves by hopping on his shoulders. . . . The wild ones can be bought at almost every fort. (p. 293)

While it was obviously possible to capture and raise young gazelles in a wholly tame state, this again cannot be considered as a means of securing the meat at Abu Hureyra. If the captured infantile gazelles were killed at once, there would be evidence of a seasonal cull, but only of a single immature age class. Were the gazelles to be tamed, kept for longer, and periodically slaughtered, then no seasonal cull would be evident.

The strategy of mass interception resulted in the killing of large numbers of gazelle without regard for age or sex, but this does not appear to have diminished the ability of the herds to sustain their numbers throughout the periods of the Abu Hureyra 1 and 2A settlements. The Persian gazelle is an animal that grows rapidly, reaching breeding age by its second year (Tsapluyk 1972). Breeding is annual, and the period of maternal dependence is correspondingly short. The incidence of twinning is quite high, exceeding 50% of births in a good year (Gorelov 1972; information from V. V. Zhevnerov communicated in 1984). The factors combine to give the herds a high reproductive potential that, together with the evident lack of competing settlements in the area, was able to sustain this form of mass predation by the people of Abu Hureyra through some thousands of years. The lack of competing contemporary settlements was a further important reason for the long-term viability of this mode of exploitation by the people of Abu Hureyra throughout the duration of the settlement.

On the other hand, the frequency of onagers in the faunal remains of Abu Hureyra declined through the Abu Hureyra 1 settlement (figure 13.6), probably because the species was more vulnerable to human predation. First, the period of gestation is about one year and births are two years apart (Groves 1974). Second, there is also a prolonged period of maternal dependence, with lactation also continuing for more than a year. Consequently, the herds had a lower reproductive potential and were less able to sustain high levels of predation, which inevitably resulted in the killing of many young.

Summary of Hunting Methods

Evidence from Abu Hureyra, based upon the crown heights of the permanent teeth (figure 13.12), shows that gazelles of all ages from the very young to the old were taken and, although bone measurements of gazelles do not exhibit a high degree of sexual dimorphism, the range of each dimension in the adults indicates that both sexes were taken in about equal proportions. The wear pattern shown by the deciduous dentition and measurements of bone growth in the young all demonstrate that the cull was highly seasonal. These data together can be best explained by the slaughter of entire herds, and the historical evidence shows that this was regularly accomplished by the use of some form of "kite" structure, an established practice even into this century. Estimates for the number of gazelle killed vary from about 50 to over 500 in a single episode, and the contemporary descriptions show that large numbers of people combined to conduct each hunt. This was especially notable in the case of the kites near Qaryatein where the hunting was done by otherwise sedentary farmers.

It seems likely that, in more recent times, the use of kites would have caused marked fluctuations in the numbers of gazelle, with their use being temporarily abandoned as uneconomic if the herds were too small. For this reason it is possible to see that, while hunting with the kites could rapidly diminish the numbers of gazelle where predation was sustained, it is equally obvious that the method did not result in their extinction; only the modern rifle has accomplished that.

The data from Abu Hureyra, the known distribution of kites in Syria and northern Transjordan, and the historical evidence for herd interception and migration all combine to show that this form of exploitation was of long standing, and was used from the beginning of settlement at Abu Hureyra. The location of late Palaeolithic sites near Taibe, close to our reconstructed migration route, argues for an even earlier beginning. In the relatively stoneless steppe south of Abu Hureyra it is likely that the pole and pitfall form of kite described by Teixeira was routinely used to supply the greater part of the meat eaten by the early inhabitants of the site (figure 13.15). Indeed, so successful was this that the practice continued after the first appearance of domestic mammals at Abu Hureyra, and even the smaller percentage of gazelles in the fauna of Periods 2B and 2C still showed the same grouping of size classes among both immature bones and milk teeth.

Figure 13.15 Reconstruction of a gazelle hunt at Abu Hureyra, illustrating the use of a pole and pitfall animal trap or "desert kite".

THE PRESERVATION OF MEAT

Given that the gazelles at Abu Hureyra were obtained by means of mass kills, and only in the early summer season, some form of preservation must have been employed to make full advantage of the meat supply from these wild mammals. The use of dried gazelle meat by the Sleyb is commonly described in historical accounts, although some later writers appear to have taken this observation from Burckhardt (1830, p. 14), who said of them that "the dried flesh of the gazelle is their food during the whole year." Carré (1672–1674, published 1948) was given dried gazelle meat near Taibe during June. Chesney (1868) crossed the desert by camel on a compass bearing from the Euphrates to Damascus. At a desert well he encountered Sleyb hunters, and again a little farther on his journey, where a "salted gazelle" was provided for him to eat.

The widespread practice of drying gazelle meat was best recorded by Dickson (1949). This work was written from 1929 to 1936 and was based on his experiences early in this century. He described the beduin hunting of gazelles from camel back with the assistance of a Saluki hunting dog, and gave a detailed account of the method of preparing gazelle meat:

> The young hunters go far from their tents, and if they find that the gazelle meat will not keep, they spread the carcase out in the shape of a mat, having removed the ribs and larger bones, and prepare the venison with salt into what they call *yellah*, a sort of biltong, slashing it into long slices to allow the salt to penetrate and to enable ribbon-like strips to be easily removed at home for food. (pp. 33–34)

Dickson's account suggests that the main limb bones were removed besides the ribs, and it is probable, too, that the head would be detached at the same time. This would result in a bone accumulation at the place of kill, high in limb bones but probably lacking in vertebrae and pelvises, as these would be difficult to remove without complete meat stripping from the carcass, which seems to have been kept whole. Chesney's record of a "salted gazelle" suggests that the usual practice was to retain the carcass whole after the removal of most limb bones.

A similar pattern was seen by Asher (1986). His observations were among the Kababish nomads of the Sudan, who hunted gazelles with rifles and Saluki dogs and also prepared gazelle meat by drying. Hunting involved extensive trips by small parties using camels. He described[3] the method of processing the gazelle meat thus:

> After the gazelle has been shot or slaughtered, the carcass is carefully skinned, on the ground or hanging from a tree if one is available. If on the ground, the skin acts as a sort of "dust sheet." It is generally kept intact to use as a waterskin or other vessel. The meat is cut into long, thin strips. There is a particular way of cutting, in which the "butcher" tries to make the strips continuous, rather like peeling an apple in one go. The bones, including the ribs, are generally removed and roasted on the embers of the fire. The nomads prize the marrowbone jelly very highly, and will often smash open the larger bones and suck it out, after which the bones are discarded. The vertebrae and parts of the pelvis are often left amongst the dried meats. The long strips are then left to dry in the sun (but not in direct sunlight if possible) for about 24 hours after which they have begun to turn hard. . . . I have never seen salt being used to preserve meat in the Sahara, as the meat is fairly sterile once it's dry. . . . Once the meat has become hard, maggots will no longer breed in it. The above points apply equally to goats and sheep, though gazelle meat is preferred. (pp. 260–261)

It can be seen from the above that the vertebrae and pelvis were commonly left with the dried meat. Meat from the heads of the gazelles was eaten at the point of kill:

> The meat of the head of gazelles, goats and sheep is considered a great delicacy. The head is always baked in the sand under the embers of a fire. This process takes some hours, which is why the head is always the last part of the carcass to be eaten. The head is broken open with a stick and everything—eyes, nasal membrane, tongue and brain—is eaten with great relish.[4]

The eyewitness accounts of Dickson and Asher describing the processing of gazelle meat are thus very similar. Both involved the use of camels for long-distance hunting trips, and in both cases the meat was dried as a means of preservation. The use of camels also means that it was possible to bring back large numbers of gazelles, especially when the meat was dried and deboned, to the encampment. In Syria salt was used to assist preservation, and the carcass perhaps needed less cutting because of this. Both methods resulted in most limb bones and the head being cooked and discarded at the point of kill. In the instance where meat was preserved as a carcass, the vertebrae and parts of the pelvis seem most likely to have been transported with the dried meat, as these bones are difficult to remove. When the meat was cut and dried in strips, few if any bones would have been transported with the finished product.

Gazelles were thus taken at the northern end of a possibly lengthy migration, the precise extent of which remains to be determined, and this was during the birth season in May. It might be thought that the meat would be of low quality at that time, with the animals lean and the meat in consequence low in fat. However some evidence suggests that the converse is likely. Russell (1756, p. 54) described the gazelles found east of Aleppo in some detail, both from his interest in natural history and in their consumption: "In the sporting season they are lean, but have a good flavour. In the summer, when fat, they may vie even with our venison in England." This agrees well with information that herders in this region provided us in April 1983; they described the grazing as at its worst during December and January, and at its best from the end of February to the end of May. This was the reason why gazelles traveled to this region to breed, and it is probable that the animals arrived near the site in their best physical condition.

BONE REPRESENTATION IN HUNTED AND DOMESTIC MAMMALS

The observations on bone representation we give here are necessarily of a preliminary nature.[5] We have shown that the gazelles, and probably the onagers too, were killed only in the early summer. The technique used was almost certainly cooperative drives into nets or fixed traps. This process commonly involved the processing of the carcasses at the point of kill, and so the transport of meat back to the living site would have resulted in a marked deficiency of certain bones. At Abu Hureyra it is also improbable that any domestic mammals were used for transportation.

Gazelles

The gracile skeleton of the gazelle is vulnerable to attack by dogs and other scavengers, and many of the gazelle bones from Abu Hureyra showed the characteristic surface erosion that comes from partial digestion. We noted this mainly on bones that were adult or nearly so, as it is doubtful that the bones of the infantile gazelle would have survived such attack. The bones of canids were few, and when found they were very fragmented, making precise identification problematic. The presence of the dog in contemporary sites in Southwest Asia is well known (Davis and Valla 1978), and from the incidence of part-digested bones at Abu Hureyra we think it probable that dogs were present from the time of the first settlement.

In Abu Hureyra 1, infantile gazelle comprised 20–28% of all the gazelle bones that were identified (figure 13.16). Because of their form and very small size, we could attribute these bones with some confidence, and even separate them from the much less common infantile bones of sheep and goat. At the same time, the incidence of partial digestion that could be seen on the fused or nearly fused gazelle bones was low, at about 5–8%. In Abu Hureyra 2A (Trench D, phases 1–5 and 6) the proportion of newborn gazelle bones fell to 5–11%, while the incidence of partially digested bones rose significantly. The occupation of Abu Hureyra 2 was on a much larger scale than that of Abu Hureyra 1, and our evidence indicates the continuity of predation by herd interception. We therefore argue that the low proportion of newborn gazelle bones in Abu Hureyra 2A is not a reflection of different hunting practice or of a different age profile in the gazelle herds, but rather comes from a higher degree of dog destruction of the infantile bone. The inverse relationship between the survival of immature bone and the incidence of dog gnawing is clear from figure 13.16.

We think it likely, therefore, that the incidence of partial digestion of the gazelle and other bones in Abu Hureyra 1 was due to the presence of the dog, rather than the activities of jackals and other wild canids. We have shown that dogs were commonly used in gazelle drives to increase the panic of the trapped animals, and it is notable that dogs, as evidenced by the higher proportion of

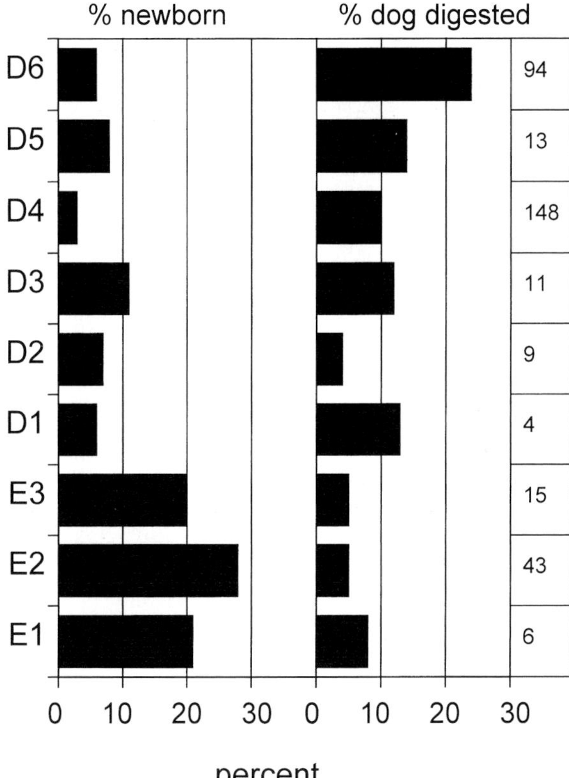

Figure 13.16 Proportion of infantile gazelle bones in Abu Hureyra 1 and 2 compared with the incidence of canid-digested bones.

partly digested bones and occasional coprolites of crushed bone, were apparently much more common in the settlement of Abu Hureyra 2. Because of the very low utility of infantile gazelles as food and the variable proportions in which their bones survived through the Abu Hureyra sequence, all the calculations of bone representation below are based only on bones of adult or near adult development and size, and on mandibles of one year old or more.

The pattern of bone survival of gazelles at Abu Hureyra gives no indication that any form of selection was practiced in the body parts that were brought to the site. We chose two samples of gazelle bones from individual archaeological contexts where they were especially abundant to test this observation, and the bone representation within these is shown in figure 13.17. Both samples came from deposits with much ash, and it is possible that they were associated with some particular processing activity.

In the bone samples, there was no deficiency of limb bones or mandibles beyond the variability that could be associated with the different density of the various bones, and their consequent different ability to withstand the processes of attrition from dogs and other agencies. The sample from D68 was better preserved than that from B95. This showed best in the survival of the more fragile proximal articulations of the limb bones, notably the ulna, radius, metacarpal, and metatarsal. The proximal ulna and scapula were common, as were distal humerus, tibia, and the metapodials. The samples taken together argue that the gazelles were processed at the site, after being brought there as whole carcasses. This in turn indicates, in the complete absence of evidence for animal transport from this period, that the kites were situated within a short distance of the site. It seems likely that the major wadi system to the south of Abu Hureyra was associated with the interception of the gazelle herds.

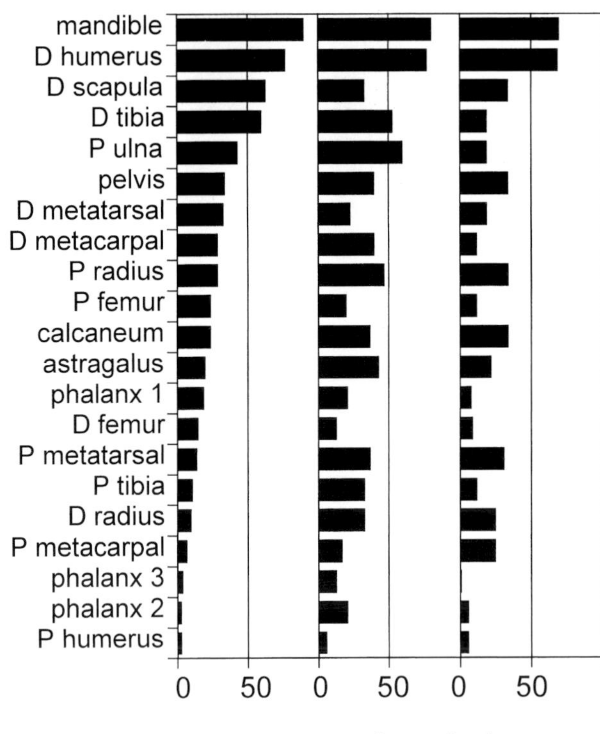

Figure 13.17 Bone survival in gazelles and caprines from Abu Hureyra. The samples of gazelle consist of 469 bones from Trench B level 95 and 265 bones from Trench D level 68. The sample of caprines consists of 200 bones from Trench E level 73.55/199.

Caprines

As a comparison with the gazelle bone survival, we give the same data for sheep and goat bones in figure 13.17. The overall pattern of bone survival is not very different from that of the gazelles in Trench B level 95. Again, certain bones, vulnerable to destruction because of their shape, low density, or later fusion show rather higher survival percentages in the caprines, notably the proximal radius, metatarsal, calcaneum, and metacarpal, although the differences between the species are not great. There is little doubt that the sheep and goat were fully under human control in the 2B levels of Trench E, and it is reasonable to conclude that the animals would have been killed at or very near the site, so differential transportation would have been unlikely to bias the bone representation.

Equids

In the case of the onager, the inhabitants were hunting a considerably larger mammal; certainly several people would have been required to carry a butchered specimen back to the site even if it was killed nearby. However, equids were not abundant in the fauna of Abu Hureyra, so bone representation studies can only be based upon a combined sample of identified onager bones from each of the main cultural episodes at the site (figure 13.18). Survival was generally good, as we might anticipate for the robust bones of equids. The Abu Hureyra sample shows low values for some distal limb bones, and possibly some degree of differential transportation is in evidence here, though not to the extent that the representation of the onager bones is marked by a heavy bias. Again, we would suggest that the interception of onagers was organized in such a

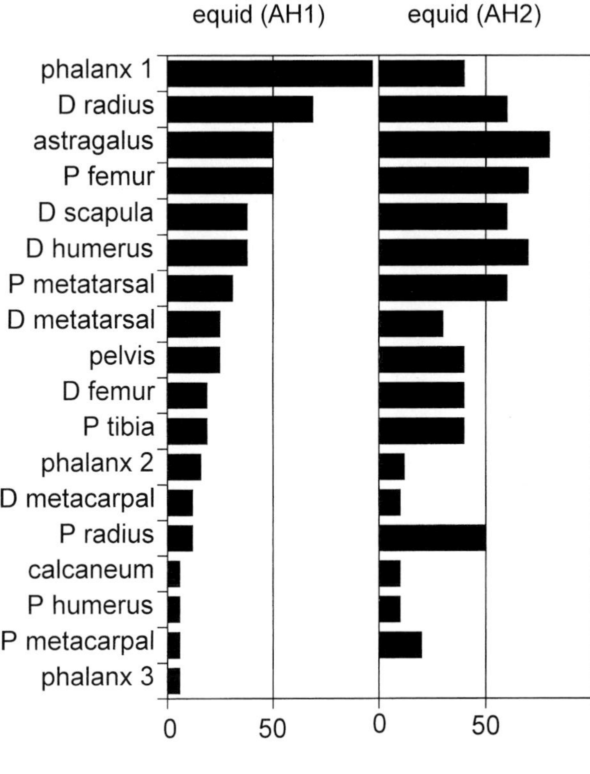

Figure 13.18 Bone survival in equid bones from Abu Hureyra.

manner that the killing took place near the site to minimize transportation problems.

The bones of cattle are too few in number for a consideration of bone representation to be made at this stage of the analysis. This will be done, with a more detailed and context-related study of the gazelle and caprine remains, when the stratigraphic analysis and bone identification is complete for the remaining trenches.

THE EVIDENCE FOR EARLY MAMMAL DOMESTICATION IN SOUTHWEST ASIA

Methods of Study

The criteria by which mammal domestication are identified have been widely reviewed in the archaeological literature (for example, Bökönyi 1969, 1989; Davis 1987; Meadow 1989). We discuss here the four that bear most directly on the recognition of early mammal domestication: introduction of new species, change in species abundance, morphological and size change, and population structure.

Introduction of New Species

When a new species enters the Holocene archaeological record there are grounds for considering that it may have been introduced as a domestic mammal. This is obvious where the species is alien to its new home, but it is less clear when the new species appears in a region that is adjacent to its natural range. This test is normally applied to species that are domestic now.

Change in Species Abundance

The marked increase in the abundance of a species within the archaeological sequence of one site, or in the sites of one region, can be taken as evidence for domestication, especially for those species that are domestic now.

Morphological and Size Change

Morphological and size changes have been applied to sheep, goat, cattle, and pig. The implication is that the process of domestication results in a visible morphological change in either body size or, among those species with horns, changes in the form of the horn core, or even in the loss of horns.

Population Structure

Archaeozoologists have commonly argued that the logical consequence of domestication is the purposeful manipulation of the age and sex proportions of a herd. This is evident in the study of the bone remains when a large proportion of subadults has been culled and when the surviving adults are largely females. While hunting will show a variety of culling patterns that would, for example, change with the season of the year and other variables, the age and sex distribution of the cull is unlikely to mimic the structured cull in a domestic flock at a site that was occupied year-round. Other possible criteria, such as the findings of artifacts associated with the use of domestic animals or of artistic representations that clearly depict domestication (Zeuner 1963; Bökönyi 1969), are not relevant to this investigation.

In recent studies of early mammal domestication, the most useful evidence has been obtained by methods involving the investigation of change in body size through time (Uerpmann 1979; Meadow 1984) and of population structure (Hesse 1984). Where size change is employed as evidence for early domestication, it is obviously essential to have a predomestic population of the same species against which size change can be measured. These will be late Palaeolithic and Epipalaeolithic specimens that may then be compared with the possibly domestic species from the early Neolithic. However, sheep and goat bones are rare in Southwest Asia before the later aceramic Neolithic of the ninth millennium BP. In consequence, bone samples of predomestic caprines are few and usually consist of low numbers of identified specimens at any site. It is therefore problematic to compare ancient wild and early domestic caprines using bone measurements; for example, the number of measured distal metacarpals or other bones in any sample is very small and, in consequence, the full range of size will not be adequately shown.

A number of scholars have therefore applied to archaeological specimens a method that allows the comparison of measurements from different bones in one histogram (Simpson and Roe 1939; Uerpmann 1979; Meadow 1984). In this method the measurements of different bones of a modern wild mammal—for example, the articular widths of humerus, metacarpal, or metatarsal—are used as "standard" dimensions against which archaeological specimens of the same species are compared. Each archaeological bone measurement is expressed as the proportion by which it differs from the standard measurement using these as a common baseline. This method thus increases the number of specimens available for comparison within a sample.

By this means Uerpmann (1979, figures 2, 3) has shown that, within the limitations of the technique and the small sample sizes, the size of Epipalaeolithic sheep and goats in Western Asia cannot be separated from those of the late Palaeolithic. It would therefore appear either that the slight size reduction found in gazelles at c. 14,000 BP (Davis 1981) did not affect caprines or, more likely, that the samples of caprine bones are not adequate for this level of analysis.

For the study of size change in goats, Uerpmann (1979) combined material from two sites from the Epipalaeolithic period (Palegawra Cave in the Zagros, and Jiita in Lebanon; 34 bones), four sites of "Proto-Neolithic" date (early Jericho, Zawi-Chemi Shanidar, and Karim Shahir in the Zagros, and Tepe Asiab; 49 bones), and four sites covering both early and late phases of the aceramic, or early, Neolithic period (Çayönü, Aşikli Hüyük, and Can Hasan III in Anatolia; Ganj Dareh in the Zagros; 67 bones). Although there are some chronological uncertainties in these groupings, the goat bones showed no size change through the late Palaeolithic, Epipalaeolithic, and "Proto-Neolithic" periods, while those of the aceramic Neolithic and later times were significantly smaller.

Uerpmann (1979) has demonstrated a similar pattern for the sheep bones. He drew the Epipalaeolithic samples from Palegawra (47 bones), the "Proto-Neolithic" specimens from four sites (Mureybit, Zawi-Chemi Shanidar, Karim Shahir, Tepe Asiab; 98 bones), and the aceramic Neolithic specimens also from four sites (Çayönü, Aşikli Hüyük, Can Hasan III, Buqras; 284 bones). Again, he observed a reduction in size between the "Proto-Neolithic" and aceramic Neolithic periods.

However, the problem remains that Uerpmann did not separate the early and late phases of the aceramic Neolithic; in consequence, the earlier aceramic Neolithic, when caprines were rare, was grouped with the later aceramic Neolithic, when they became abundant. The geographical distribution of the samples was also less than ideal; for both species, the earlier material (putative wild) was drawn from sites in the Zagros and from the Levantine coast, while the later samples (putative domestic) come from Anatolian sites. Thus, while Uerpmann found a significant size reduction in both caprine species, the precise significance of this observation is difficult to interpret.

In addition to the analysis using combined bone measurements, Uerpmann (1978, figure 1) gave dimensions of the sheep astragalus from various sites in Southwest Asia. Among these, 32 specimens came from late Palaeolithic and early Holocene sites mainly in the Zagros region. Though small, the sample showed a size distribution and range that would correspond to a wild population with an equal number of both sexes. The bones in a more numerous sample from three Neolithic sites (Çayönü, Jarmo, Pre-Pottery Neolithic B Jericho) were of smaller size, although the wide distribution of dimensions showed that some larger wild sheep were also present.

More recently, Helmer (1989) has investigated size change in early caprines, cattle, and pig using the same method but treating the specimens from different sites separately. He has shown that the size reduction in caprines took place *during* the aceramic Neolithic, with large sheep at early aceramic Neolithic sites (Period 2 and early Period 3 in the Lyon chronological classification) and smaller sheep in later aceramic Neolithic sites (late Period 3). He has found that goats showed a very similar pattern, with large specimens in the earlier sites and smaller specimens in the later ones.

While one can express reservations about the results discussed above, one must recognize that the limited material available for study has obliged archaeozoologists to adopt a generalized approach to the use of size reduction as a means for detecting early domestication. As we shall apply this method in the discussion that follows, we need to set out the attendant uncertainties in the application of this and other techniques.

Problems in the Recognition of Early Domestication

The effect of local environment on the size and morphology of sheep and goats was probably marked, as it is now in species such as the red deer (Legge and Rowley-Conwy 1988). It is unlikely that the two species were of uniform type and size over a range that extended from Anatolia to the southern Zagros Mountains. Where size change is used to suggest domestication, it is obviously desirable that bone samples should be drawn from a restricted region and, as far as this can be judged, from similar environments. As Uerpmann (1978) has noted, modern wild sheep vary in size according to the environment in which they are found, and in the wetter uplands of Asia Minor and Mesopotamia they are larger than in more arid regions. Archaeological specimens from the upland setting of the Palegawra Cave in the Zagros and those from sites on the steppes to the west of the Tigris-Euphrates Basin came from dissimilar environments.

Both sheep and goats exhibit sexual dimorphism, to a moderate degree in the former species, and a very marked degree in the latter. Even the dimensions of subadult, unfused, male goat bones will commonly be larger than those of adult females. The proportion of adult males and females in a given bone sample will thus be reflected in both the mean and median points of the distribution of measurements, as Meadow (1984) has noted, although this will not affect the range of population size as long as both sexes are represented and specimens are sufficient in number. In both sheep and goat the sexes spend much of the year apart, so seasonal hunting might result in a bias to one sex; Hesse (1984) argued this in his interpretation of the caprine bones from level E at Ganj Dareh. Ideally, the sex and age structure of a bone sample, when used to test for evidence for early domestication, should be supported by evidence for the seasonal or permanent occupation of the site in question.

There is a third problem that has yet to be fully explored in studies of animal bones, that of postfusion bone growth. It has been widely assumed, despite occasional cautionary notes (von den Dreisch 1976, p. 4), that the articular ends of mammalian limb bones undergo little or no growth after fusion of the diaphysis and the epiphysis. Recent investigation of the skeletons of modern mammals suggests that this is far from being so. In a sample of 29 modern red deer that had been tagged at birth, we found substantial postfusion growth in early-fusing bones such as the scapula glenoid and the distal humerus, although such growth was less in the later fusing metapodials (Legge and Rowley-Conwy 1988). We have obtained much the same result from the study of a larger sample of sheep of the Soay breed.

Not only do early-fusing bones show the most growth, but the early fusion ages also confer a survival advantage on these bones, so the distal humerus and scapula are common in almost all bone assemblages, as we found at Abu Hureyra. This raises the probability that the measurements of even fused bones will depend to some degree upon the age of animals at death, as the most commonly measured bones will be those that fuse earliest in the mammal's life.

Thus, a number of factors may influence the results obtained from combining samples of bones from different sites. The limitations imposed by small sample size, varying proportions of males and females, and postfusion bone growth all need to be recognized. It is further evident that no single test for mammal domestication can provide an unequivocal answer when used alone. Where we can combine several such lines of inquiry, we can advance a stronger case.

Although sheep and goat are abundant species in the more recent archaeological record of Southwest Asia, evidence for the early domestication of caprines still comes from few sites (Legge and Rowley-Conwy 1986b; Uerpmann 1987). We review some of these sites next, concentrating on those where sheep or goat appear in an early Neolithic cultural setting. We consider Epipalaeolithic faunas only from sites with extensive later Neolithic levels that provide a basis for comparison within the same vicinity.

The Archaeological Evidence

One of the most important sites to have yielded evidence for early domestication west of the Tigris-Euphrates Basin is Tell es-Sultan, ancient Jericho (Zeuner 1955; Clutton-Brock 1971; Clutton-Brock and Uerpmann 1974). At Jericho there were only four bones from the Epipalaeolithic levels, and none of these was caprine. Two sheep bones are known from the early aceramic Neolithic, or Pre-Pottery Neolithic A, in a fauna that was otherwise largely composed of gazelle and fox. In the Pre-Pottery Neolithic B, or later aceramic, levels caprines constituted some 70% of the large mammals; of these, seven bones have been identified as sheep, with a further five specimens attributed to that species (Clutton-Brock and Uerpmann 1974). The evidence for the domestication of caprines comes from an increase in their importance from 5% in the Pre-Pottery Neolithic A to 55% in the Pre-Pottery Neolithic B, with a corresponding decline in the importance of the wild fauna.

Radiocarbon dates place the early Neolithic settlement at Tell Aswad in the Damascus Basin between 9,800 and 8,800 BP—that is, from the end of Neolithic 1 (Pre-Pottery Neolithic A) through the earlier part of Neolithic 2 (Pre-Pottery Neolithic B). In this sequence goat bones were more common than those of sheep (Ducos 1993), which were found only in the final part of the occupation. The goats were small bodied, and the population distribution shows a bias toward the smaller females (Ducos 1993, figures 4, 5). Ducos has identified a significant peak of killing between one and two years of age. He interprets the goats as domestic throughout the early Neolithic of Tell Aswad.

In the same area the later site of Ghoraife (middle Neolithic 2) had a fauna in which the goat was more abundant in phase I but was exceeded by sheep in phase II (Ducos 1993). The predominance of sheep bones has also been found at Tell Ramad.

The site of Hatoula (Davis 1985) near Latrun in Palestine has a fauna from the Natufian period in which gazelle bones made up more than 97% of those identified from the larger mammals. Besides these, there were a few bones from cattle, pig, possibly the hartebeeste, and several that were referred to sheep. The Neolithic 1 (Pre-Pottery Neolithic A) fauna had the same very high proportion of gazelles, again with only rare cattle, pig, and possibly hartebeest and sheep. Goat bones were absent from both the Natufian and Pre-Pottery Neolithic A levels.

Other sites in the region having only later aceramic Neolithic occupations (Neolithic 2 or Pre-Pottery Neolithic B), confirm the sequence seen at Jericho.

At Abu Gosh and Beisamun (Davis 1978) near the Levantine coast sheep and goat predominated, as they did at the sites of Buqras and Tell es-Sinn (Clason 1979) in the Euphrates Valley.

The Neolithic 2 sites of Ain Ghazal (Köhler-Rollefson 1989), Beidha (Hecker 1975, 1982), and Basta (Becker 1987, 1991) in Transjordan have faunas with a marked predominance of goats. In each case the goats were small bodied and were probably domestic (Legge 1996). At Basta the proportion of sheep is rather higher, and these too were of small size.

East of the Tigris-Euphrates Basin the Epipalaeolithic is less well known. The early Neolithic open settlements excavated in Mesopotamia and Iran, apart from a few sites in caves or rock shelters, do not have the extensive Epipalaeolithic settlements that were found at Jericho and Abu Hureyra, so no record is available, as at Abu Hureyra, of the pre-Neolithic fauna at the site in question.

The early Neolithic site of Ganj Dareh (Hesse 1984) has been divided into five levels, from the uppermost level A down to level E. New dates suggest that the site was occupied during the early ninth millennium BP (Hedges et al. 1990, p. 231). The site contained abundant remains of both sheep and goat, though from those caprine bones identified to species level, goats outnumbered sheep by almost nine to one (Hesse 1984, table 1, p. 249).

In his study of the goat bones Hesse paid particular attention to the proportion of the sexes culled in relation to their age classes at death. Goats present the ideal opportunity for this type of analysis because the species shows a high degree of sexual dimorphism, so measurements from even the unfused bones of relatively juvenile males are substantially larger than those of mature females with fused limb bones. Davis (1987, figure 1.9) has shown that among modern goats this discrimination is possible after the age of 12 months; male goats killed before that time, with unfused metacarpals, have bone dimensions that fall within the female range. This means that only young male goats killed after the age of one year will be sufficiently large to be discriminated by measurement from the females with either unfused or fused limb bones.

Hesse (1984, figure 1, p. 252) was able to demonstrate that the goat cull at Ganj Dareh was highly selective. Measurements of the fused bones showed that the adult herd was made up of numerous females and few males, while the unfused bones indicated that many more young males than young females were culled. Dimensions from other bones have been published by Hesse (1984, figure 2, p. 253); all show the adult herd was mostly female. Helmer (1989) has drawn attention to the fact that the goat bones at Ganj Dareh showed no size change through the archaeological sequence, and that those from the earliest level E were no larger than those from the four later levels. While Hesse (1984, 315) was cautious in his interpretations, regarding the goats as "husbanded, though morphologically wild," this understates the evidence for the small size of the goat bones (Helmer 1989; Legge 1996). Together with the evidence for a controlled and purposeful cull, it supports the interpretation that the goats were domestic throughout the archaeological sequence at Ganj Dareh.

The low degree of sexual dimorphism in sheep means that the same methods of investigation do not work well with that species; a plot of sheep bone measurements seldom shows a clear distinction between the sexes. Although the bone sample for sheep was small, there were sufficient measurements to show that the sheep at Ganj Dareh were large (Helmer 1989). While we would expect that where goats were domestic so too would be the sheep, there is no evidence to challenge Hesse's interpretation (1984, p. 314) that the sheep were wild.

At Ali Kosh (Hole, Flannery, and Neely 1969) sheep and goat were the most common species. The evidence advanced that both species were domesticated rested on the proportion of fused and unfused epiphyses, which showed that a substantial proportion were killed as juveniles. The excavators also suggested that the presence of a hornless individual among the sheep indicated that the population was domestic. Recent evidence suggests that the Ali Kosh sequence may be somewhat later than was originally proposed (Hedges et al. 1990, p. 231). While it seems probable that both sheep and goat were domesticated at the site, further analysis of the population structure of the caprines would be valuable.

Tepe Asiab near Kermanshah in Iran was inhabited from c. 9,755 to 8,700 BP, and thus dates to the earliest Neolithic. The fauna of Tepe Asiab showed considerable diversity (Bökönyi 1977); the larger species identified were cattle, sheep, goat, pig, onager, gazelle, and red, roe, and fallow deer. Sheep and goat together amounted to 36% of the identified bones, and red deer were unusually common (38%) for a site in Southwest Asia. Pigs, which Bökönyi thought were wild, made up a further 18.6%, and cattle 6.5%. Gazelles and the other large mammals were uncommon or rare.

According to Bökönyi the evidence for domestic mammals at Tepe Asiab was slight. The cattle, sheep, and pigs were either regarded as wild or, because of the small bone sample, their status could not be determined. Bökönyi (1977, pp. 20–22) regarded the Asiab goats as a mixture of wild and "transitional" forms. He thought that the latter reflected the first stage of morphological change under domestication. Three horn cores showed slight twisting that is often associated with early domestication (Bökönyi 1977, pp. 17–19). The goats were mainly adult, with only 18% killed before maturity. Although the number of sheep and goat bones from Tepe Asiab is small, it appears that both species were of large body size and can be regarded as wild.

The evidence for early sheep and goat domestication is thus limited both by the few published bone samples and chronological uncertainties. Most sites of the later Palaeolithic and Epipalaeolithic had faunas in which gazelles were common, with some fallow deer, wild pig, and cattle. Wild sheep or goats were rare, except in better-watered or more mountainous regions. In the early aceramic Neolithic period sites still had a large proportion of wild mammal bones, usually with a small proportion of caprine bones, while in the later aceramic Neolithic almost all sites had abundant caprines. During this period the number of sites inhabited increased significantly and people occupied more marginal zones (Moore 1983, p. 98).

The Evidence from Abu Hureyra

We shall consider the evidence for mammal domestication at Abu Hureyra in relation to the criteria that we have discussed above, beginning with the changes in species abundance.

We have shown that sheep were present in Abu Hureyra 1 (Legge and Rowley-Conwy 1987), at some 6% of the identified large mammal bones (figure 13.6). The bones are too few for body size to be established. From their association with an Epipalaeolithic settlement, we assume that the sheep were wild.

In Abu Hureyra 2A caprine bones increased to about 12% of those identified (figure 13.6). As an indication of the first domestication of caprines at Abu Hureyra this fact alone is of some value. There is no doubt that the majority of mammals were wild (gazelle, onager, and probably pig and cattle). This increase in the percentage of caprines could be explained by natural variation in the local abundance or an increase in hunting intensity. Yet there are two reasons why both possibilities are unlikely. First, Abu Hureyra 2 was a settlement of much greater size than Abu Hureyra 1, and it is improbable that rather rare species could sustain higher hunting pressure. Second, the fauna can be divided into two sorts, that of migratory (gazelle, onager) and nonmigratory (wild cattle, pig, fox, hare) species. The nonmigratory species declined markedly through Abu Hureyra 1 into Abu Hureyra 2A. Caprines, on the other hand, showed a sustained increase over the same period.

The continued importance of the migratory species, especially gazelle, at a time when the human population of Abu Hureyra had increased greatly can be understood in relation to the lack of other human competition for the same resources, since no contemporary settlements have been found on the steppe to the south of the village. We have demonstrated that the gazelles were migratory (Legge and Rowley-Conwy 1987) based on a study of the third milk molars (dp_4), which show only two closely grouped wear states. The same teeth of sheep and goat were also found at all stages of wear between the extremes of unworn and heavily worn, but did not show the conspicuous seasonal groupings of the gazelle molars (figure 13.19). This tooth is replaced in sheep and goats nearer the age of two years than the 14 months of the gazelle, so we would expect that the annual reduction in crown height would be smaller. However, this method has been shown to detect seasonal killing in domestic sheep (Legge, Williams, and Williams 1992), and as the crown height is greater in the larger-bodied caprines, the average rate of tooth wear is comparable between the species. The crown heights of caprines certainly indicate a wider range of seasons in the cull than we found for the gazelle, reflecting their more sedentary nature. The increase in caprines in Abu Hureyra is therefore unlikely to have been the result of greater hunting activity. The settlement and population size of the village had grown to the point where the other sedentary species were much reduced by hunting pressure.

Our second criterion is the appearance of new species. All the caprine bones from Abu Hureyra 1 that could be attributed to species level were from sheep.

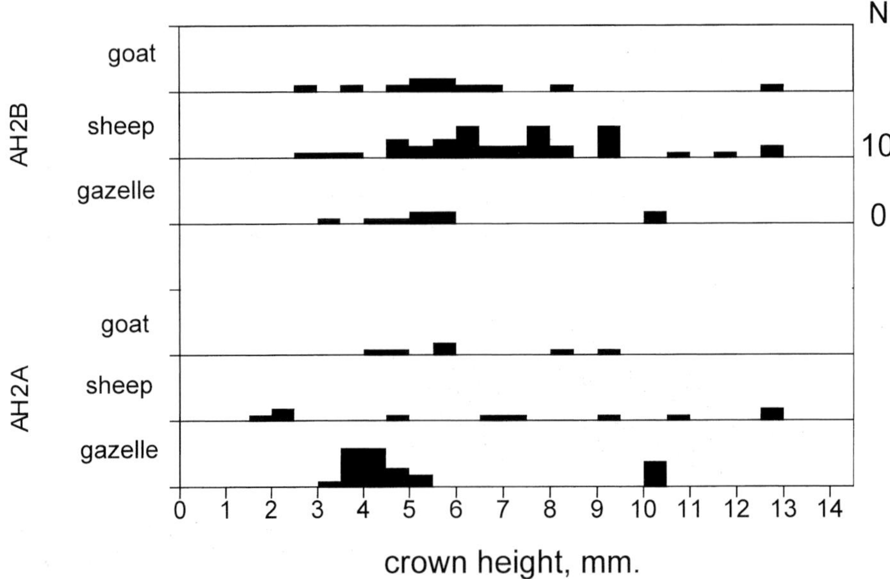

Figure 13.19 Crown heights of the lower deciduous molar dp_4 from sheep, goat, and gazelle, comparing Abu Hureyra 2A and 2B. In both instances the gazelle teeth show two groups, either unworn or heavily worn. The dp_4 of sheep and goat are found at all heights between unworn and heavily worn.

However, in Abu Hureyra 2A goats outnumbered sheep by about five to one. From then on there was a consistent trend in which sheep became more common (figure 13.20). Thus, the caprine bones found early in Abu Hureyra 2A were mainly from the goat, which was absent from Abu Hureyra 1.

The presence of goats in Abu Hureyra 2A and the fact that they outnumbered sheep are therefore very significant; it seems improbable that this could arise from any cause other than the species being fully domesticated. By the later phases of Abu Hureyra 2A the proportions of sheep and goat were more nearly equal, and by Abu Hureyra 2B sheep steadily increased to a level where they greatly outnumbered goats. This pattern is confirmed at other sites within the locality. Three small late aceramic Neolithic sites in inland Syria show the same high proportion of sheep among the caprine bones; at Tell es-Sinn and Bouqras sheep outnumbered goats, respectively, by about two to one and four to one (Clason 1979). Legge has examined the animal bones from the late Neolithic site of Tell Kashkashok northwest of Hasseke excavated by Matsutani (1991) and has found that sheep outnumbered goats there by six to one.

A significant feature of the Abu Hureyra faunal sequence lies in the presence of Epipalaeolithic levels at the base of the mound. This provides an important opportunity to monitor not only change in faunal composition, but also body size, and thus morphological change, in the common species such

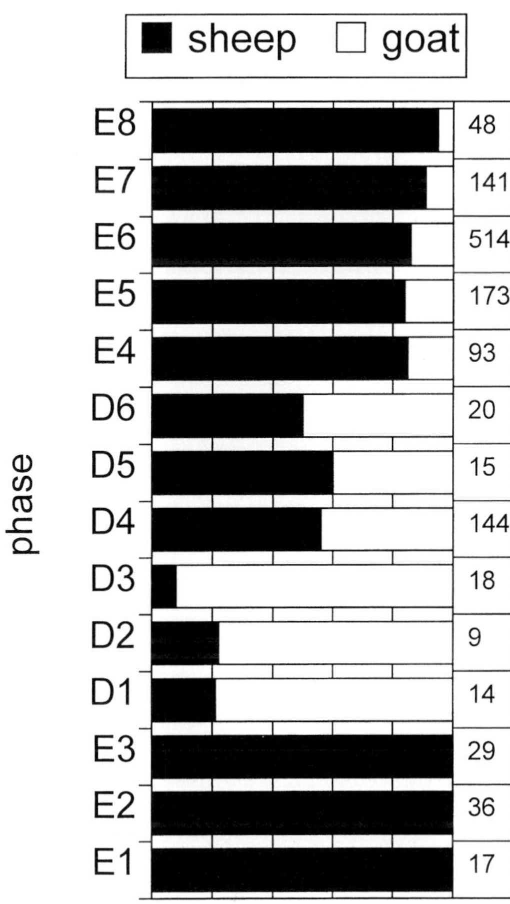

Figure 13.20 Proportions of identified sheep and goat bones through the Abu Hureyra sequence.

as gazelles. We can thus establish a background against which to assess body size among the caprines.

Kurtén (1965) has demonstrated a Late Glacial size reduction in a range of carnivore species from the eastern Mediterranean. Davis (1981; 1987, p. 136) has also found evidence for a size decrease among archaeological populations of *Gazella gazella* from northern Palestine at about the same time. Abu Hureyra 1 was established about 11,500 BP, broadly contemporary with the Natufian culture of Palestine. The gazelle bones from Abu Hureyra are sufficiently abundant for their size to be determined from almost all building phases, with an adequate sample of a later fusing bone such as the distal metacarpal or distal metatarsal. The gazelles at Abu Hureyra exhibit no evidence for size change throughout the archaeological sequence (figure 13.21); evidently the reduction in size observed by Kurtén and Davis antedated the first settlement at the site.

We established the distinction between sheep and goat among the bone remains from Abu Hureyra by means of the published criteria (Boessneck, Müller, and Tiechart 1964; Boessneck 1969; Prummel and Frisch 1986). The distal humerus is the best-represented element among the measurable caprine bone in Abu Hureyra 2A and 2B, as is commonly the case in archaeological faunal collections of all periods. This is due to the relatively high density of that bone, and also the early age at which it fuses. The distal humeri are also quite readily separated into sheep and goat on the basis of the form of the epicondyles.

However, while the early fusion of the distal humerus secures a high level of survival among the identifiable bones, this bone also has a high potential for postfusion growth. The effect of this is to give the population a greater range of size than would be determined from later fusing bones such as the metapodials, as the sample will contain both newly fused humeri from young animals and those of fully adult size. The distal humerus dimensions will therefore be influenced not only by the body size of the adult population, but also by the age at death of the specimens that are measured. Even when two populations of the same adult size are compared, a sample with more adult individuals would show a larger mean size than one in which there were more young sheep. Thus, distal humerus measurements will be influenced by the pattern of cull as well as by changes in adult body size.

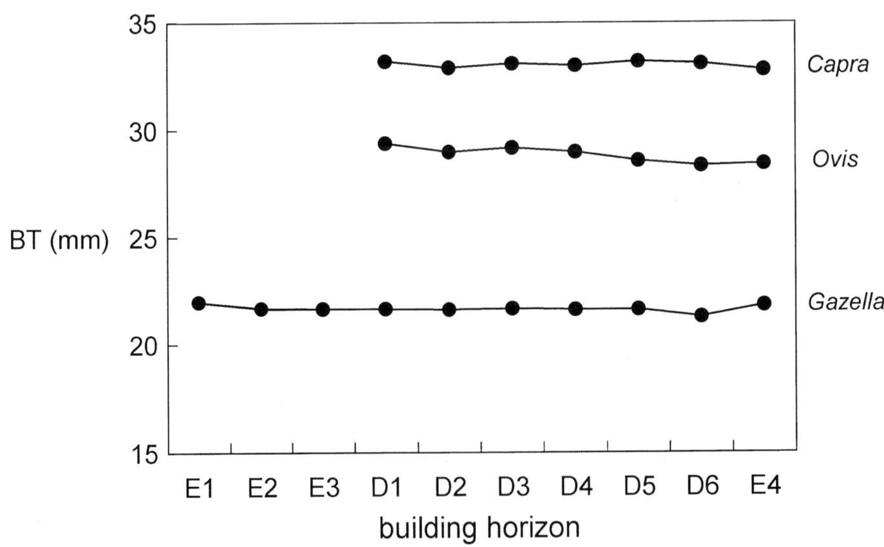

Figure 13.21 Distal humerus measurements of gazelle, sheep, and goat through the Abu Hureyra sequence (conventions follow von den Dreisch 1976). In Abu Hureyra 1 goats are absent, and there are too few sheep bones to provide sufficient measurements.

Bearing these points in mind, we have compared the dimensions of the distal humerus for all specimens from Abu Hureyra 2A with those from 2B (figure 13.22). Two points are evident from the distribution: first, the mean dimensions are practically identical for both populations, and second, the ranges of the two populations also show no significant difference. In modern sheep the distal humerus can grow significantly after bone fusion, and the distribution of the distal humerus measurements further indicates that the age structure of the two populations was essentially the same.

The number of sheep bones from Abu Hureyra is limited. We need to use a method, therefore, in which the different bone measurements can be combined using the difference of logarithms (Meadow 1984). The mean dimension and range of these combined samples are again identical (figure 13.23). Thus, we can determine no size change between the sheep populations of Abu Hureyra 2A and 2B. Because of the relatively low degree of sexual dimorphism shown in the sheep skeleton, a detailed analysis of the proportions of the sexes in the cull is problematic. The sheep of Abu Hureyra 2B do show a slight bias toward the smaller end of the range (figure 13.22, AH2B). It is tempting to see this as a bias toward an adult herd composed mainly of females, but bone growth occurs after bone fusion, and the smaller individuals may include young of both sexes as well as more adult females. This approach is more revealing where the goat is concerned.

The marked degree of sexual dimorphism among the bones of goats allows us to approach the problem of identifying early domestication by means of body size and the sex ratio in the cull. First, we plotted a combined sample of the measured goat bones by difference of logarithm. The result is shown in figure 13.24, again comparing the specimens from Period 2A with those from 2B. As with the sheep bones, both the mean and range of dimensions are indistinguishable for the two samples. In both there is a marked bias toward the smaller end of the size range, indicating that the majority of goat bones came from females.

Because of the high degree of sexual dimorphism exhibited by goat bones, we can examine the population structure in more detail than is possible with the sheep. The sample of measured goat distal metacarpals, both fused and unfused, from Period 2B is shown in figure 13.25. The fused specimens form

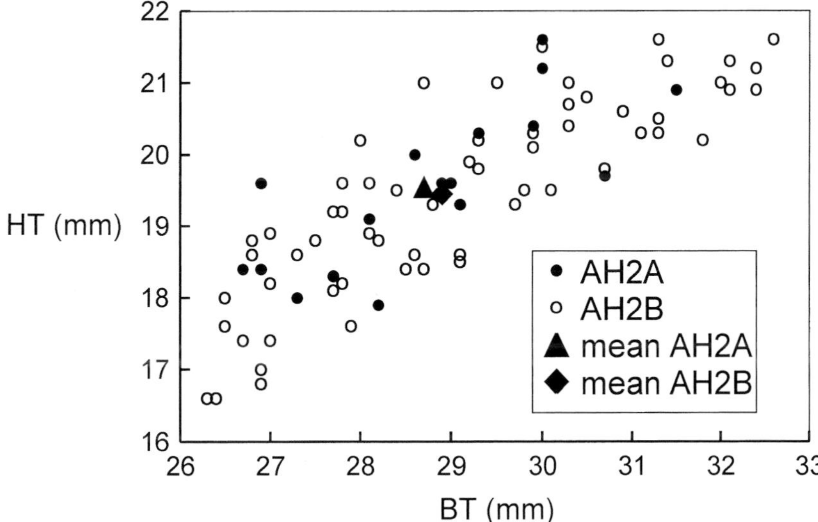

Figure 13.22 Distal humerus measurements of sheep from Abu Hureyra 2A and 2B (conventions follow von den Dreisch 1976).

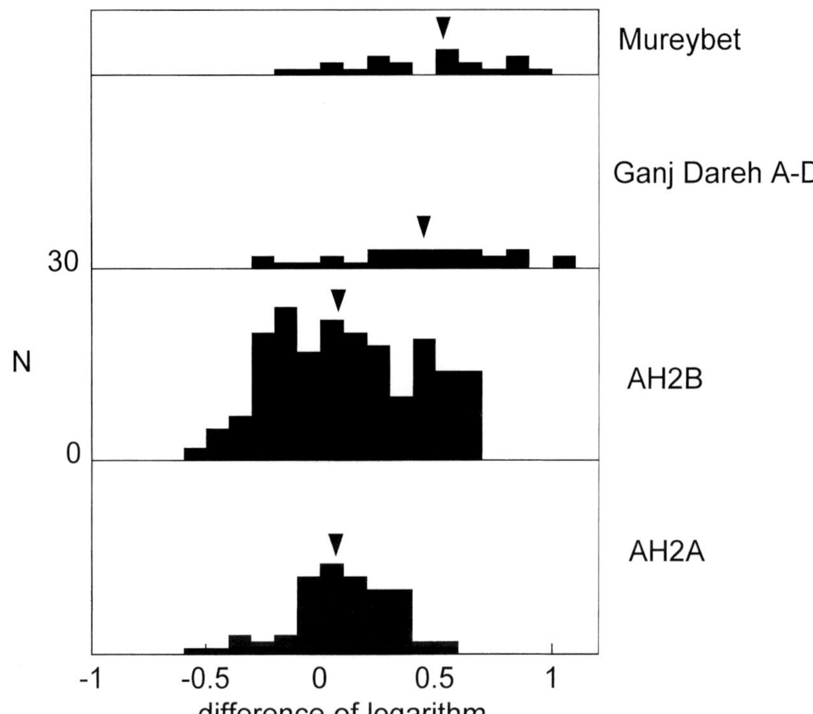

Figure 13.23 Combined measurements of sheep bones from Abu Hureyra 2A and 2B shown by the difference of logarithm method, and compared with samples from Ganj Dareh and Tell Mureybit.

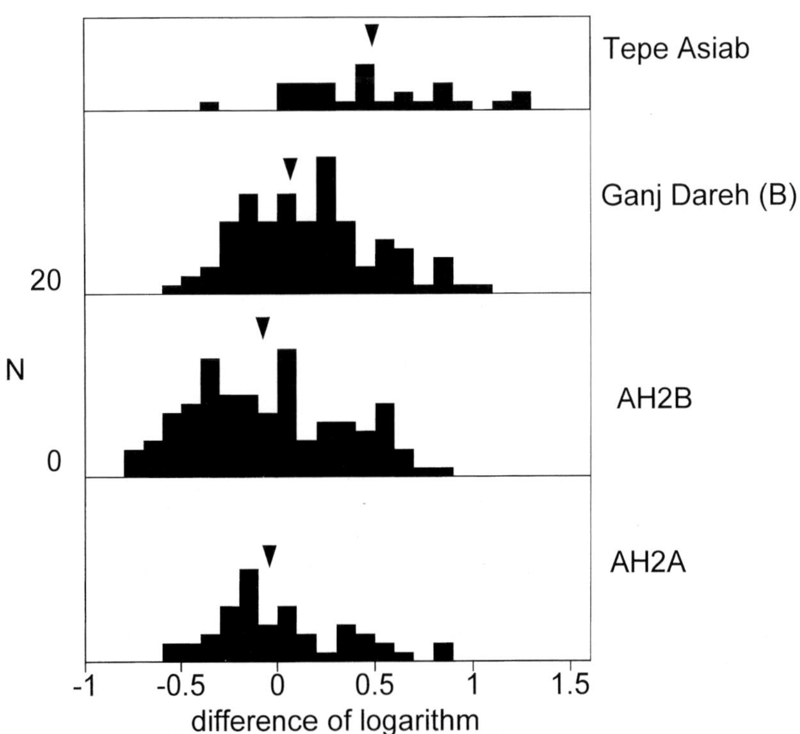

Figure 13.24 Combined measurements of goat bones from Abu Hureyra 2A and 2B shown by the difference of logarithm method, and compared with samples from Ganj Dareh level B and Tepe Asiab.

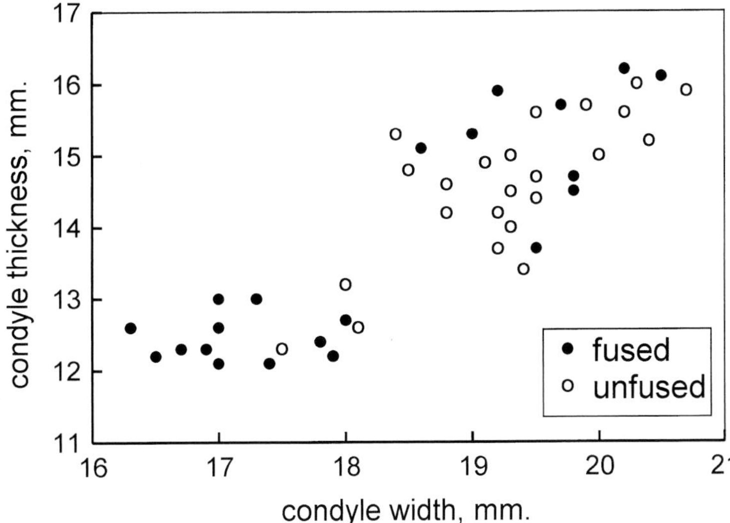

Figure 13.25 Measurements of goat distal metacarpals from Abu Hureyra 2B.

two groups that can be interpreted as representing males (larger) and females (smaller). Most unfused specimens fall within or near the scatter of fused male metacarpals, and only a few fall among the fused female bones. This diagram shows a distribution very similar to that produced by Hesse (1984) from the site of Ganj Dareh, and as he did at that site, we interpret this as the result of a purposeful cull. We can see that the young males with unfused distal metacarpals were killed late enough toward maturity for most growth to have been completed. Bearing in mind that this sample is from Abu Hureyra 2B, in which caprines were abundant, this evidence for a purposeful cull further supports our interpretation that the goat population was domesticated at that time.

Inevitably, there are considerably fewer measurable goat bones from Abu Hureyra 2A, when caprines were much less common. However, sufficient Period 2A specimens of goat metacarpals exist to indicate that the pattern of cull, within the limits of a small sample, was the same as that found from Period 2B.

Figure 13.26 shows the measurements of four different goat bones from Period 2A in Trench D. Given that the goat is a species with marked sexual dimorphism, the distributions can in each case be interpreted as comprising more numerous females and few males. The distribution of measurements corresponds closely with those of the same goat bones from Period 2B in Trench E. Although the samples of any one goat bone from Period 2A are rather small, the results are consistent across a range of bones, each set of measurements showing a pattern that is commonly associated with purposeful husbandry.

One final test can be applied, that of the proportion of fused limb bones found in the assemblage. Coon (1951) argued that the high incidence of unfused metapodia among Neolithic caprines at Belt Cave indicated they were domesticated. This approach was formalized by Hole, Flannery, and Neely (1969) in the study of caprine bones from Ali Kosh. They used different bones that fuse in sequence, and the proportion of fused versus unfused bones at each point in the Ali Kosh sequence was drawn as a "survivorship curve," sometimes more pessimistically known as a slaughter pattern. The earlier-fusing bones showed a high proportion of fused specimens, and the later-fusing bones showed a high proportion of unfused bones. In other words, most caprines survived long enough for early-fusing bones such as the scapula, distal humerus, and phalanges to fuse, but most were killed before the late fusing bones such as the

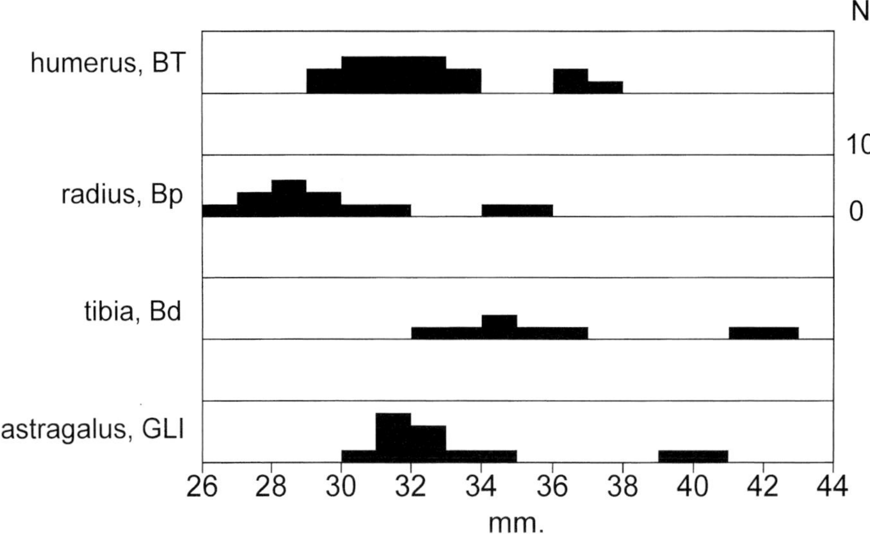

Figure 13.26 Measurements of four goat bones from Abu Hureyra 2A, Trench D (conventions follow von den Dreisch 1976).

metapodia and tibia were fused. This was seen as evidence for a purposeful cull because it showed selective killing of those animals that were approaching the most efficient meat weights.

While the caprines at Ali Kosh were quite probably domestic, it has been widely recognized that the interpretation of age structure in isolation from other evidence can be misleading, as patterns thought characteristic of domestic flocks or herds can be replicated by certain hunting methods applied to wild species (Legge 1977). The survival of unfused bones in relation to those which have fused by the time of death is also questionable. Despite these limitations, the method does have some utility where the same species from two sequential cultural episodes at one site are being compared, and where other lines of evidence that bear on the status of the mammal population are also available.

We present the data in figure 13.27. The diagram shows a decline in the proportion of unfused bones with increasing age. Bones thought to fuse in the 18–28-month period (distal metapodials, distal tibia) show 55–65% fusion, falling to 30–40% fusion with the 36–42-month-fusing bones, the distal radius and femur. The pattern thus provides some indication of the manner of cull, with relatively few young being killed at less than 18–28 months of age, and rather more between 28 and 42 months of age. This pattern is intermediate between those found in the Bus Mordeh phase at Ali Kosh and at Tepe Guran (Hole, Flannery, and Neely 1969). However, the relevant point here is not a comparison among sites by this method, but rather between the patterns of caprine mortality in Abu Hureyra 2A and 2B; the two cannot readily be distinguished. Although it might be suggested that such an age profile could be the product of hunting, this argument becomes implausible if the earlier, Period 2A, population is seen as wild and the later, Period 2B, as domesticated.

We have also compared the Abu Hureyra data relating to body size with those published by Uerpmann (1979). Figures 13.28 and 13.29 show the results from the Abu Hureyra sheep and goat bones. The vertical bars indicate the range of measurements for each population, and the data points are the mean values. Uerpmann's Upper Palaeolithic, Mesolithic, and "Protoneolithic" samples are all of large size for both species. The Abu Hureyra 2A and 2B samples are of significantly smaller body size, and both show the same mean and range. They agree well with Uerpmann's generalized aceramic Neolithic

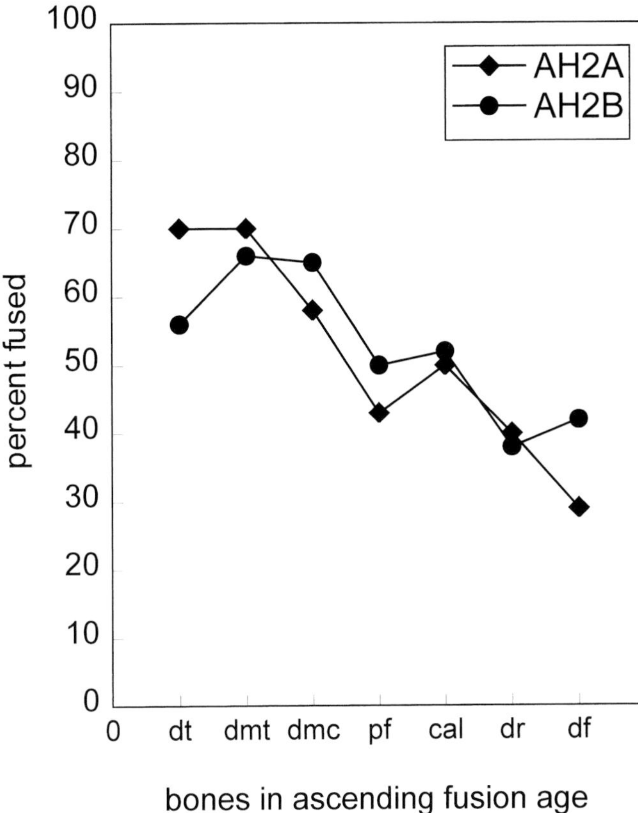

Figure 13.27 Proportions of unfused and fused bones for all caprines from Abu Hureyra 2A and 2B.

samples, shown in figures 13.28 and 13.29 as AN. In Uerpmann's sample the upper end of the range includes some specimens of large size that he interpreted as wild animals. The smaller range of the Abu Hureyra sample shows that wild caprines were absent from the steppe.

In summary, the evidence from Abu Hureyra indicates that, when the sheep and goats from Abu Hureyra 2A and 2B are compared, no significant differences can be seen. The populations of both species show

1. the same mean bone dimensions and the same, or very similar, size ranges;
2. a distribution of measurements from the goat bones showing, in both cultural episodes, an adult population with a bias toward females;
3. evidence for a controlled cull from the measurements from both fused and unfused goat bones; and
4. the same pattern of cull shown by unfused/fused proportions across a range of bones that fuse sequentially through the animal's early life.

The number of sheep and goat bones from Abu Hureyra 1 is too small to provide a baseline for the study of size change for these species in Abu Hureyra 2. Within Periods 2A and 2B no change in size or in population structure is evident. These observations lead to a number of possible hypotheses:

(a) The sheep and goat were wild during both Period 2A and 2B and were hunted by the same method. They were hunted with greater intensity in 2B, when caprines were abundant and the village had reached its greatest extent.

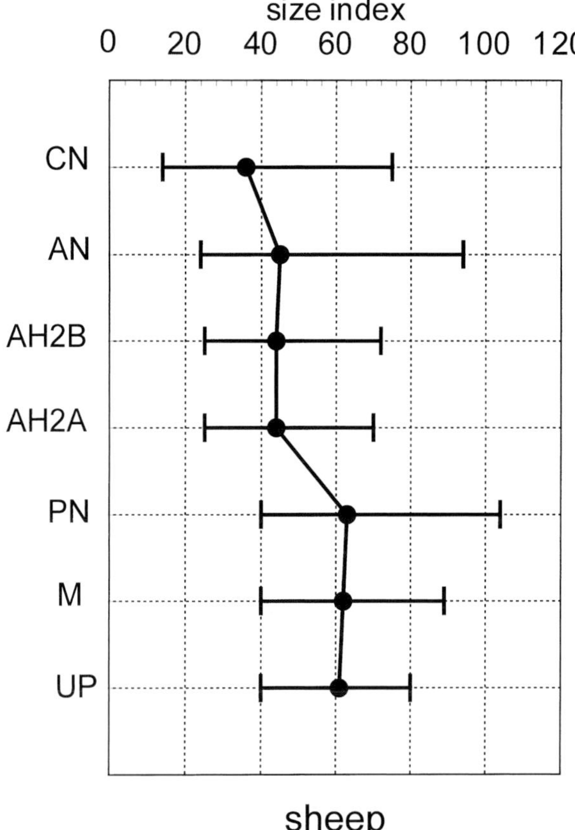

Figure 13.28 Sheep bones from Abu Hureyra 2A and 2B compared with other sites by means of Uerpmann's index (comparative data from Uerpmann 1979). UP: Upper Palaeolithic; M: Mesolithic; PN: "Protoneolithic"; AN: combined Aceramic Neolithic; CN: Ceramic Neolithic. The data points indicate the population means, and the vertical bars show the range of measurements.

(b) The sheep and goat at Abu Hureyra were domesticated only by Period 2B, when caprines became abundant, but this had no effect on their body size or on the observable population structure.

(c) The sheep and goats were domesticated from the beginning of Period 2A. In other words, caprine domestication was accomplished at the same time as the large-scale development of agriculture and initial expansion of the Neolithic settlement but remained a small-scale activity while wild protein was abundant.

It seems inherently improbable that hypothesis (a) is the correct interpretation. The abundance of sheep and goat in Period 2B and the very large scale of the village makes the hunting of both sheep and goat implausible as an explanation for the frequency of their bones. This is especially so in relation to the goat, as the terrain around Abu Hureyra would have been unsuited to that species in the wild. Other evidence from Abu Hureyra 2B that shows a clear age- and sex-related bias in the cull, argues that goats were fully domestic by that time.

Hypothesis (b) seems unlikely on the grounds that the village persisted for over 2,000 years after the beginning of Abu Hureyra 2, and it is unlikely that no size change in sheep and goat would have been manifest during this period if the animals had been wild. In the archaeological sequences at Tepe Asiab and Tepe Sarab (Bökönyi 1977), and at Mehrgarh (Meadow 1984), a marked and rapid size reduction was manifest in the caprines. In both instances the time scale for this change was less than that of Period 2 at Abu Hureyra.

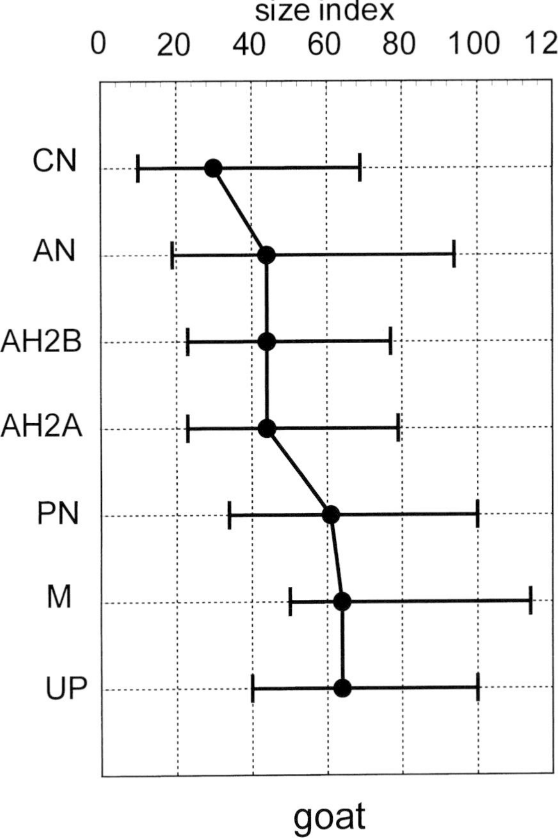

Figure 13.29 Goat bones from Abu Hureyra 2A and 2B compared with other sites by means of Uerpmann's index (comparative data from Uerpmann 1979). UP: Upper Palaeolithic; M: Mesolithic; PN: "Protoneolithic"; AN: combined Aceramic Neolithic; CN: Ceramic Neolithic. The data points indicate the population means, and the vertical bars show the range of measurements.

Hypothesis (c) is best supported by the evidence available, and we argue here that the domestication of both sheep and goat was accomplished at the time of the establishment of the Abu Hureyra 2A village. The evidence we have set out above shows that at the start of Period 2A there was a significant increase in abundance of both sheep and goat compared to the fauna of Abu Hureyra 1, at a time when the settlement was substantially larger. There is no evidence for size change between Periods 2A and 2B in either sheep or goat, nor is there any apparent change in population structure and slaughter ages. It is probable that domestic goats were introduced to the site from elsewhere, as perhaps were some of the cultivated plants. The sheep may have had a local origin, or these too could have come from elsewhere.

The evidence for the domestication of sheep and goats during Abu Hureyra 2A shows that mammalian domestication proceeded in two main episodes. First, there was an initial stage, represented in Abu Hureyra 2A, when the inhabitants kept small numbers of domestic sheep and goat. At that time the wild fauna of the region was still abundant, and the migratory animals were hunted on a large scale. The expansion of settlements during Neolithic 2 (Moore 1983, p. 98) increased the pressure on the wild herds, which soon resulted in their decline. Larger-scale herding of sheep and goats then replaced the missing wild protein. The marked increase in the abundance of caprines in the later aceramic Neolithic sites of Western Asia, therefore, marks not the first mammal domestication, but rather its effective extension to replace the inevitable failure of hunting in the face of human population pressure.

Part V THE SIGNIFICANCE OF ABU HUREYRA

14 The Development of Abu Hureyra

THE FAVORABLE SETTING

Abu Hureyra was sited to take advantage of a particularly favorable set of ecological circumstances. Its location on the ecotone between the Euphrates Valley and the steppe gave the inhabitants easy access to the resources of both zones. The Euphrates was a fast-flowing river with numerous meanders and backswamps rich in riparian species of plants and animals. The river had laid down a thick layer of alluvium on the valley floor on which grew a dense forest of trees and moisture-loving plants that offered cover for animals such as cattle, pigs, and fallow deer. The woodland-steppe (zone 4) was well drained with light but quite fertile soils and a rich cover of annual plants, shrubs, and scattered trees. It had a high carrying capacity and supported a considerable variety of herbivores and other animals. Beyond it to the west and north lay the open park-woodland (zone 3b) that was close enough, at least during Abu Hureyra 1A times, to have been an important source of plant foods for the inhabitants of the site.

These general conditions were obviously attractive to the people of Abu Hureyra, but there were additional factors that drew them there, characteristics that made the place unique among potential locations for settlement along the Middle Euphrates. The first of these was the proximity of the Wadi Shetnet es-Salmas, because it offered a supply of surface water close to the site that was often more accessible than the Euphrates itself. It also served as a corridor along which terebinths and other trees characteristic of the xeric woodland could extend as far as Abu Hureyra. Second, Abu Hureyra was on a natural highway along the river valley that linked the steppe to the south with the forested hills to the north, and that afforded potential access to minerals and other raw materials not available locally. Most of the right bank of the Euphrates for many kilometers east and west of Abu Hureyra consisted of cliffs or steep hills. But the land to the south sloped gently up the plateau, so it was easy to reach the open steppe at that point, while the central Levant lay a few day's walk away through the El Kum pass.

Each spring herds of Persian gazelle moved northward from their wintering grounds in southern Syria, past Palmyra, through the El Kum pass, and on to the Euphrates. They were attracted by the exceptionally rich grazing of the open steppe south of Abu Hureyra. Their most likely route took them northwest to the river valley at Abu Hureyra, where they turned westward to fan out across the steppe. It was the proximity of the site to the gazelle migration route that made Abu Hureyra such a compellingly attractive place in which to establish a settlement.

The location thus combined several elements that favored it uniquely, since they were not found together anywhere else along the Middle Euphrates. That provides part of the explanation for the longevity of the site, and its extraordinary growth and development under four successive economic systems: hunting and gathering in Abu Hureyra 1A; hunting, gathering, and farming in Abu Hureyra 1B, 1C, and the Intermediate Period; hunting and farming in Abu Hureyra 2A; and herding and farming in Abu Hureyra 2B and 2C. The attractions of the spot for people intending to live by hunting and gathering are obvious. The abundant plant foods and game from the steppe and valley bottom could supply much of their food for most of the year. Furthermore, the dense herds of gazelle that passed by each spring were open to mass slaughter. Their meat could be preserved and stored in quantity for later consumption. These factors remained of fundamental importance to the economy during much of the life of the site. But Abu Hureyra was also extraordinarily well endowed with the resources needed by early farmers and herders: extensive open land with light, easily tilled soils on the steppe, and adequate natural rainfall for dry farming; the damper bottom lands in the Wadi Shetnet es-Salmas and the heavier, moister alluvium of the Euphrates floodplain; ample grazing on the steppe from winter to early summer, and in the valley at other seasons; and plentiful surface water. No other location in the Middle Euphrates Valley or anywhere else in the region offered such a combination.

Abu Hureyra 1 and 2, with the short Intermediate Period between, endured an extraordinarily long time, well over four thousand years (figure 14.1). Later in prehistory and during the historic period the site was used on occasion as a cemetery and for other purposes. The great size of Abu Hureyra and the unusual length of its sequence of occupation set it apart from all other sites of the late Pleistocene and early Holocene, not only in the Euphrates Valley but in the whole of Southwest Asia. In these respects it is unique. Of special significance is the superimposition of the two settlements: one inhabited by foragers who adopted farming, and the second built by their farmer successors. This is important because it has enabled us to explore the similarities and contrasts between the foraging and farming ways of life at a location where the resources available to both groups were, for the most part, comparable. Of the few other sites in Southwest Asia that have afforded the same opportunity, among which Mureybit and Jericho are the best known, none has yielded the combination of a lengthy and well-documented sequence of occupation with the recovery during excavation of abundant economic and environmental data. At Abu Hureyra we have been able to examine in an integrated manner the cultural, economic, and environmental changes that took place during the crucial period of time when the people of the Levant ceased to be hunters and gatherers alone and adopted farming and herding. We have found that all three elements were connected, such that change in one affected the other two.

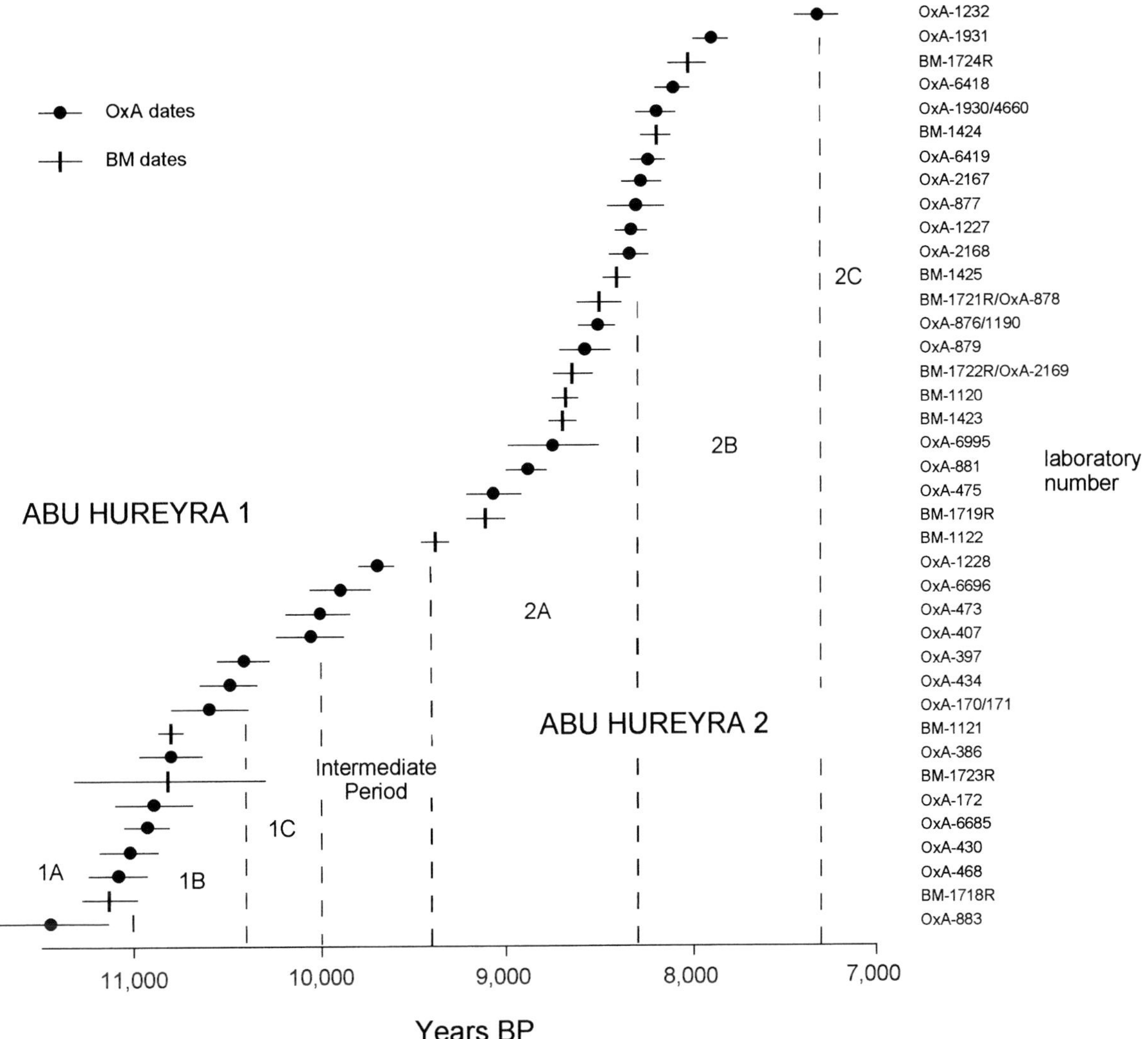

Figure 14.1 Radiocarbon dates in chronological order and the sequence of periods for the villages of Abu Hureyra 1 and 2.

ABU HUREYRA 1, C. 11,500–10,000 BP

The initial settlement of Period 1A consisted of a series of pit dwellings. By Period 1B these had filled with occupation debris, and the form of the settlement changed to a village of huts built on level ground. This settlement endured, with minor modifications, until the end of Period 1C (figure 14.2). Thus, there was one major change in the form of the settlement during its life, but no apparent break in occupation. Indeed, certain features, notably the use of the hearth area, were maintained from Period 1A to 1B in the same place, strongly suggesting that the same group of people continued to inhabit the village without interruption. The reasons why the inhabitants chose to alter the form of their dwellings are uncertain, but may simply have been a response to the accumulating occupation debris. When the site was first inhabited, the uneven surface of the subsoil may have lent itself to the construction of partly subterranean dwellings to take advantage of the shelter offered by natural hollows in the ground. Once the hollows had filled up with occupation debris, the surface of the settlement became quite even. At that point it would have been easier to construct huts above ground.

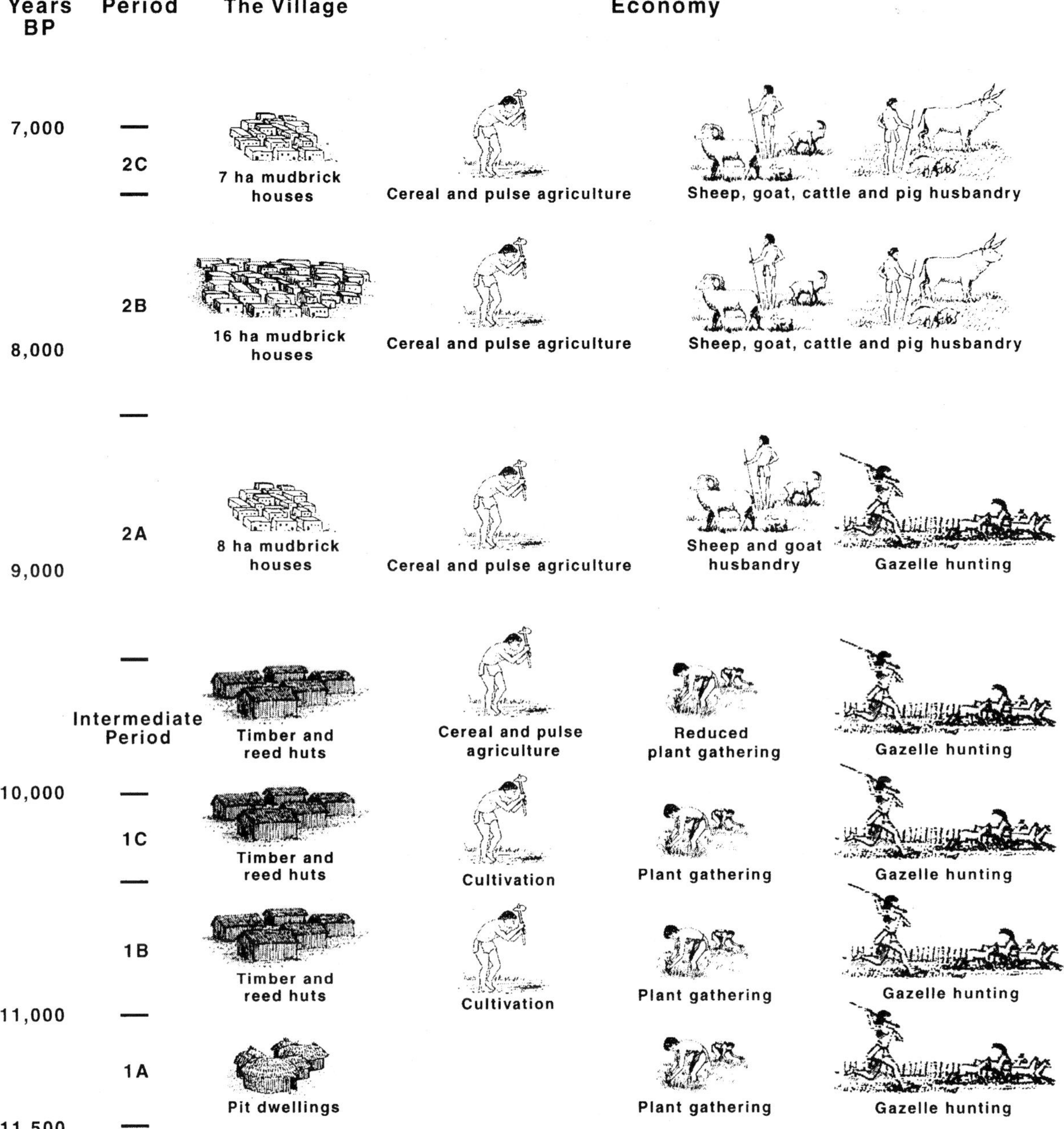

Figure 14.2 The main chronological periods with their cultural and economic characteristics.

The technology and typology of the flint and bone artifacts changed little over the duration of the settlement. Olszewski has detected a few alterations in the proportions of certain flint tools, and suggests that these may, in part, be linked to changes in processing of animal hides, increased clearance of the valley bottom, and more woodworking over time. The continuity in tool design and the overall stability of their relative proportions indicate, however, that many of the activities of daily life in which flint and bone tools were used continued to be pursued in much the same manner over 1,500 years.

Many of the stone tools we recovered, especially the grinding dishes, rubbing stones, and pestles, seem to have been used to process foods. Their total number was not large considering the duration of the settlement. We infer from this that much of the collection and preparation of plant foods, in particular, was done with tools made of perishable materials, for example, wooden dishes, pestles, and mortars, and also baskets that have not survived. Most of the stone tools were made in Periods 1A and 1B, while their manufacture sharply declined in 1C, in contrast with the relative stability in the flint and bone tools. The drop was most marked among the grinding tools, beginning during 1B. This was just when nuts and the seeds of wild cereals and valley-bottom plants ceased to be a major constituent of the diet, and we infer that the two trends were connected. In other words, when the inhabitants adopted farming, they no longer needed many of the processing tools they had previously used.

This change had other consequences since it meant that much less basalt was needed in Period 1C. There would have been fewer trips to obtain basalt from the sources a couple of days' walk away, and thus less contact with groups in those regions. The slight increase in obsidian use through time hints at a strengthening of other ties in a quite different direction, up the Euphrates. The presence of exotic materials throughout the Abu Hureyra 1 sequence indicates that the inhabitants were in touch, at least occasionally and perhaps through intermediaries, with other people, sometimes at a considerable distance. This is important because it reminds us that exchanges of ideas as well as goods could take place between the people of Abu Hureyra and other communities.

The most conspicuous feature of the exploitation of plants is the enormous variety of species that the inhabitants of Abu Hureyra 1 collected. The diversity of plants that they obtained from the vicinity of the site attests to a highly varied vegetable intake. It also helps to explain how the villagers were able to become sedentary. On the other hand, it seems that relatively few individual plant species were actually major components of the diet.

The major shift in plant exploitation occurred quite rapidly at the beginning of Period 1B. The inhabitants collected far fewer grains of wild einkorn, other wild cereals, and the fruits of terebinth and other trees, all species of the park-woodland and woodland-steppe. This was an immediate result of the onset of the cooler, more arid climate of the Younger Dryas that caused the woodland zone to retreat westward away from Abu Hureyra. The inhabitants compensated for the decline in availability of these species by adopting farming. We have direct evidence from charred grains dated to 11,140 ± 100 BP, 10,930 ± 120 BP, and 10,610 ± 100 BP, that they started to grow domestic rye from the beginning of Period 1B. There are indications from finds of other domestic grains in 1B and 1C levels that they may also have cultivated several more species of cereals during these periods and have grown some legumes. In addition, we have indirect evidence of the inception of cultivation from a steady increase in the incidence of field weeds through Periods 1B and 1C. These data, taken together, indicate that beginning about 11,000 BP the people of Abu Hureyra 1 started to farm. They were thus among the first to do so anywhere in Southwest Asia and, perhaps, the world.

During Period 1C, their use of several species of valley bottom plants, among them club-rush and reeds, declined. One possible explanation for this is that the plants became less abundant because of reduced river flow due to increased aridity, but as the Euphrates receives most of its water from the mountains of eastern Asia Minor, this may not be a sufficient cause. Another reason why the people of Abu Hureyra collected fewer of these species may be because they were overexploiting the plants of the valley bottom for food, partly in response to the withdrawal of the woodland species but also because of their own increasing numbers.

The most striking feature about the animal economy of Abu Hureyra 1 is its continuity, in marked contrast to the plants. The annual, late spring slaughter of migrating gazelle and of onager was a constant feature of life there and, later, in Abu Hureyra 2. Evidently the gazelle migration was so regular and so abundant that it could supply meat in whatever amounts were needed over a very long period. As with most migratory species, there would have been considerable fluctuations in the size of the herds over decades, but the overall abundance seems to have been more than sufficient for the long-term needs of the inhabitants of Abu Hureyra 1. At the time the site was founded the park-woodland came quite close to Abu Hureyra, so the area of steppe available for the gazelle to graze was somewhat restricted. Later, as the woodland receded, the steppe expanded, and with it the area of spring grazing. Thus, more gazelle may have come to Abu Hureyra 1 in the later periods of occupation, counteracting the increasing hunting pressures.

The only significant change in the fauna over time was the decline in the proportions of onagers, hares, and foxes that were killed. We have already explained that this probably reflects an increase in the population of the site. The prolonged maternal dependence of their young made the onagers especially vulnerable to overhunting. Some of the animal bones had passed through the digestive tracts of canids, and one bone tool had been chewed by a dog. From this we infer that the inhabitants kept domesticated dogs at the settlement.

The exploitation of animals was tightly focused on those few species that offered the highest return of meat and other products for the labor expended in killing them. The converse of this observation is that the inhabitants of Abu Hureyra 1 neglected other species that had less food value or were, perhaps, undesirable for cultural reasons. Our large-scale wet sieving of the flotation samples yielded very few fish or bird bones, and shellfish were uncommon on the site. This implies that the inhabitants ate very few such minor food resources, even though the Euphrates was so close. Pigs were certainly present in the vicinity but were direct competitors with the people of Abu Hureyra for many of the plant foods in the river valley and thus may have been killed simply to reduce their numbers. The pigs lived in the confines of the valley bottom through the lengthy dry summer and autumn and so may never have been abundant.

The hunting and gathering way of life pursued by the people who founded the village of Abu Hureyra 1 had a number of distinctive characteristics. It was strongly seasonal in nature because the main species of plants and animals used for food were available in abundance only during a few weeks or months of the year. The mass slaughter of gazelle and the selective gathering of small-seeded plants indicate that the inhabitants practiced a particularly intensive kind of hunting and gathering. That called for investment in fixed structures to aid in securing and keeping food, the best example being the kites or their local equivalent at Abu Hureyra. The efforts of the inhabitants were carefully focused on a narrow range of animals, and although they collected a wide range of plant species for food and other purposes, the bulk of their vegetable food actually came from relatively few of those plants.

The adoption of agriculture reinforced the strongly seasonal pattern of the economy. In a sequence that extended from the autumn to the following summer, the inhabitants had to prepare the soil, sow their crops, weed them, then harvest and process the mature plants. They also had to develop a new set of techniques and tools for farming. This added a further set of activities to an already complex annual cycle.

The climate changes of the Younger Dryas had consequent effects on the locations of the zones of vegetation exploited by the inhabitants in Period 1A. Their successors in Periods 1B and 1C found it necessary to adjust their pattern of plant exploitation to compensate for diminished access to the woodland. They adopted cereal, and perhaps legume, farming to provide alternative supplies of plant foods. Thus, climatic change was an important factor in the adjustments the people made in their economy. It follows that environmental, economic, and cultural change were closely linked.

The evidence of the plant and animal remains suggests that the people of Abu Hureyra 1B adjusted quite successfully to the environmental changes induced by the onset of the Younger Dryas, because the site continued to be occupied. Indeed, it was the adoption of agriculture that enabled the population of Abu Hureyra 1 to remain there for so long.

Seasonality and Sedentism

Did the inhabitants of Abu Hureyra 1 occupy the site for just part of the year then leave to exploit wild foods that were available elsewhere, or did they remain there year-round? The answer to this question is of fundamental importance because, in Southwest Asia, the inception of sedentism is often associated with the development of village life based on agriculture. The transition to sedentary life is usually accompanied by changes in social organization and can have important demographic consequences. We need to know, therefore, when sedentism began and how it was related to the shift from foraging to farming.

The Levant is a region of strong seasonal contrasts in climate, and thus variations in seasonal availability of plants and animals in any given locality. It is likely that many Levantine late Pleistocene hunters and gatherers maintained a mobile existence, moving from one location of preferred plant and animal foods to another, in a cycle determined by the seasonal occurrence of these resources. This way of life is familiar to us from the ethnographic record and fits the archaeological evidence. Most late Epipalaeolithic sites were small and were apparently inhabited for no more than a few weeks or months at a time. In contrast, Abu Hureyra 1 was inhabited over a long span of years. The structures and the numerous heavy tools we recovered indicate that the inhabitants spent considerable time there maintaining their settlement and manufacturing the equipment they needed. This evidence implies that the site was occupied year-round. Such inferences from the cultural remains, while suggestive, can never be conclusive, however. We know from the ethnographic record that some mobile groups may spend at least part of the year in settlements of solid houses furnished with bulky equipment. The beduin of present-day north Syria provide an excellent example from our region. On the other hand, subsistence farmers like the Azande of central Africa who live in permanent villages may move away for several weeks of the year to engage in hunting (Reining 1970).

The question of whether the inhabitants of Abu Hureyra 1 were mobile or sedentary can be satisfactorily resolved only by determining the times of the year when they were present at the settlement. The way to do this is to examine materials brought onto the site that were available in specific seasons. The best sources of such information are the remains of plants and animals used for food and other purposes, and fortunately we have ample samples of both.

We have already discussed in detail in preceding chapters the evidence for the successive seasons of occupation derived from the plant and animal remains, but we combine the information here. There were two periods of heavy plant collection, from May to July, and from August to November. The harvest seasons are likely to have been longer than this botanically sanctioned minimum because many of the patches of wild plants would have been visited several times as they matured. Once agriculture got under way in Period 1B, this pattern of essentially sedentary life would have been reinforced. The inhabitants would have planted their crops in the autumn and stayed to protect them during the growing season. Wild pigs, especially, would have been an ever-present menace to the growing crops during the spring. The crops would have been harvested in May and processed in June. This means that the plant remains provide positive evidence that the site was occupied for at least ten months of the year, with the slight possibility of a gap in the sequence in late July and early August.

Roots, tubers, corms, and other soft vegetable plants would have provided an important additional source of food, although the remains of such species are sparsely represented at Abu Hureyra 1 because they decay rapidly, and few were preserved through charring. Many of these plants would have been available during periods when seeds were not. The rhizomes of cattails, reeds, and bulrushes would have been at their best during the winter months, and the tubers of club-rushes and sedges in the summer. We believe that these foods made a significant contribution to the plant diet and that the inhabitants exploited them during the winter and midsummer when few other plant foods were available. This would indicate that the site was, in fact, inhabited year-round.

The most striking example of seasonal exploitation of animals is the killing of gazelle and onager that took place in April and May. This evidence also confirms that the late spring and early summer were the times of most concentrated labor for the inhabitants of Abu Hureyra. But there are indications of hunting at other times of the year. Legge's analysis of the bones of the fallow deer and pigs has shown that they were killed during the winter from November to January, thus providing meat when other supplies were scarce; the few sheep seem to have been hunted at all seasons. Thus, the evidence of the animal bones reinforces that of the plant remains and confirms the hypothesis that the village was inhabited year-round.

The wild cereals, legumes, nuts, and other forest-edge plants, as well as the small seeds of the grasses and other plants favored in the later periods of occupation of Abu Hureyra 1, can all be stored for many months. That is also true of many of the roots and tubers. The crops of domestic rye and other plants could have been stored for use until the next year's harvest. The smaller pits found next to the pit complexes in Period 1A may have been used for storage, together with baskets and containers made of wood and other perishable materials. We think that significant quantities of foodstuffs were stored after the spring and late summer harvests, as well as at other seasons of the year. This practice would have prolonged the periods of consumption of the main plant foods, both wild and domestic, from the summer through the autumn and winter, when few fresh food plants were available. Similarly, there was little point in killing such vast quantities of gazelle every spring in such an elaborate manner unless much of the prodigious meat yield was preserved to be eaten later. Its preservation would have extended the season of consumption of gazelle meat through the rest of the year.

What of the possibility that people moved away from Abu Hureyra during certain seasons of the year? The steppe would have been at its most inhospitable climatically in winter, cold, wet, and with little shelter from biting winds. The Euphrates Valley tempered the cold and wind, as the beduin of today know, since some of them move there in the autumn for three to four months to avoid such unpleasant weather. Neither would the steppe have offered much in the way of sustenance during the winter. With the advent of the autumn rains there would have been some new growth of annuals and tubers, although most would have been of little value as food until the spring. Likewise, game would have dispersed and been difficult to hunt. The Euphrates Valley, on the other hand, offered plentiful vegetable foods and some game during the winter. The steppe was even less inviting during the summer because of the lack of surface water and the drying up of the vegetation, while the valley floor and backswamps offered plentiful plant foods. So in midsummer, too, the most concentrated resources of food were in the Euphrates Valley.

We argue from the plant and animal evidence that the inhabitants of Abu Hureyra 1 were present at the settlement the whole year round. The only period for which our evidence is less than conclusive is a few weeks in midsummer, a season in which the most advantageous place to live would have been the Euphrates Valley. We conclude, therefore, that the inhabitants of Abu Hureyra 1 lived there year-round and so should be considered a sedentary population.

We have seen that the archaeological evidence suggests that Abu Hureyra 1 was inhabited over the very long period of a millennium and a half. This does not necessarily mean that people were present at Abu Hureyra 1 for every one of those 1,500 years, something that would be impossible to demonstrate archaeologically. The inhabitants may have left the site from time to time, but such absences, if they occurred, were sufficiently brief to leave no indication in the stratification of the site, nor to show up in the sequence of radiocarbon dates.

Does our conclusion that the population was sedentary mean that all the inhabitants remained at Abu Hureyra throughout the year? The region in which Abu Hureyra is situated is one of broad expanses of generally similar terrain stretching away for considerable distances. This is in sharp contrast with the Mediterranean coast of the Levant from Mt. Carmel north to the Gulf of Alexandretta, for example, or the Jordan Valley, where there are great changes in altitude over short horizontal stretches. Thus the inhabitants of sites in those regions were within a day's walk of several environmental zones. This means that, unlike in some other regions of the Levant, one would have had to travel far away from Abu Hureyra to find a different range of wild foods, as part of a seasonal cycle of movement lasting many weeks. The plant and animal remains offer no indication that this happened and, anyway, our evidence that Abu Hureyra was inhabited year-round contradicts this hypothesis.

On the other hand, the very openness of the steppe and the relatively even distribution of plants and animals across it would have encouraged quite wide-ranging local patterns of movement in search of vegetable foods and game. Thus, at certain times of the year some people may have left the site for trips lasting perhaps several days to hunt and to collect seeds, roots, tubers, and terebinth nutlets. The early spring and autumn may have been particularly appropriate times for these longer foraging and hunting trips. To back up these inferences, we can point to the solid evidence of the artifacts indicating that materials were reaching the site regularly from up to 80 km away, and occasionally from much farther afield. This evidence would suggest that the inhabitants were accustomed to going a few day's walk away from the site to obtain raw materials, even if some of the exotic stones reached them through intermediaries.

Sedentism at Abu Hureyra meant, therefore, that the site remained occupied for most, if not all, of the 1,500 years indicated by the radiocarbon dates. The majority of the inhabitants probably stayed on or close to the site throughout the year, although some of them may have left for trips lasting perhaps a few days in search of food, game, and raw materials.

The Annual Cycle

We can use the evidence of the plant and animal remains to reconstruct the seasonal round of foraging, hunting, and farming followed by the inhabitants of the village. For the hunter-gatherers of Period 1A, the year was divided into three seasons, determined by the availability of the main plants and animals they used for food (figure 14.3): late spring and early summer from April to June, the summer and autumn from July to November, and the winter and early spring from December to March. The environment of Abu Hureyra was sufficiently rich in wild plants and animals for ample food to be available at almost all seasons. Nonetheless, it does look as though the greatest variety and abundance of foods were to be found in the early summer.

The cycle began with the onset of the first season in April, as the leading gazelle herds reached Abu Hureyra from the south. This event was probably preceded by weeks of increasing activity as the kites or their equivalent were prepared, the appropriate tools for the ensuing slaughter and butchery of the gazelle were made, and scouts were dispatched to warn of the arrival of the first herds. As soon as the animals reached the vicinity of Abu Hureyra, a period of intense work ensued. The herds of gazelle had to be driven into the traps set for them, then slaughtered and butchered and their carcasses taken back to the settlement to be dried and probably salted. Once the meat had dried, it could be stored away in aerated shelters protected from scavengers. The skins, too, needed to be cleaned and prepared for later use. The scale of the work was considerable, since it is likely that hundreds of gazelle carcasses were processed during the few weeks of April and May when the animals were passing by. Herds of onager were approaching about the same time, perhaps from the south like the gazelle, or from the east around the northeastern end of the Jebel Bishri. We know the inhabitants of Abu Hureyra 1 slaughtered some of them as well, so adding to the intensity of the work.

Meanwhile, many of the important park-woodland and woodland-steppe food plants were ripening nearby. Among these were the wild einkorn, rye, lentils, and vetches. On the steppe were patches of grasses and clovers awaiting harvesting. All these plants were to be found within an hour or two's walk from the village, while other stands were situated a few hours away. Their successful harvesting would have required several visits to each patch during the ripening season. Again, a sustained effort was called for if the villagers were to obtain enough seeds from these plants to provide a good yield, to extend the period of immediate consumption, and to store for use over many weeks to come.

Nearly all these activities were performed close to the site since the gazelle were coming to the inhabitants, and most of the plants were available in the vicinity. It would have been essential for the villagers to protect their access to the gazelle migration route at the point where it approached close to their settlement. They would also have needed to preserve the best sweeps of plant

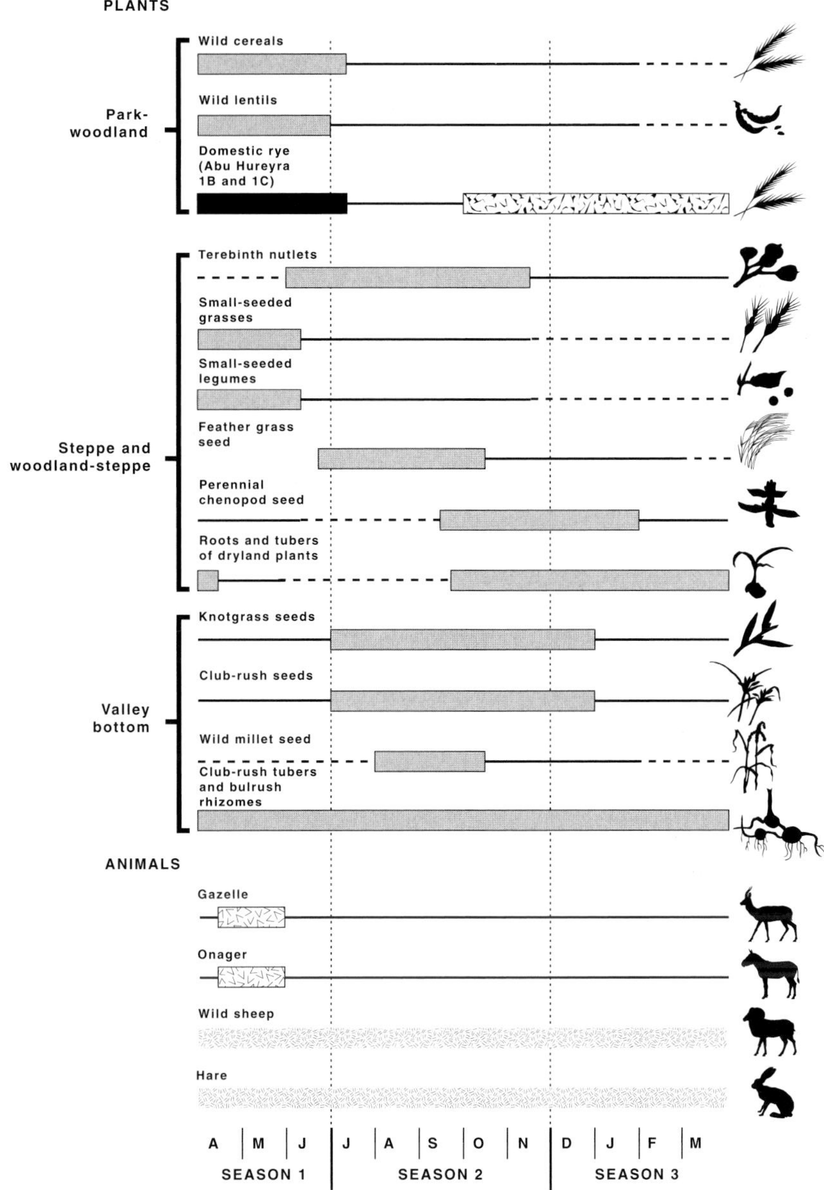

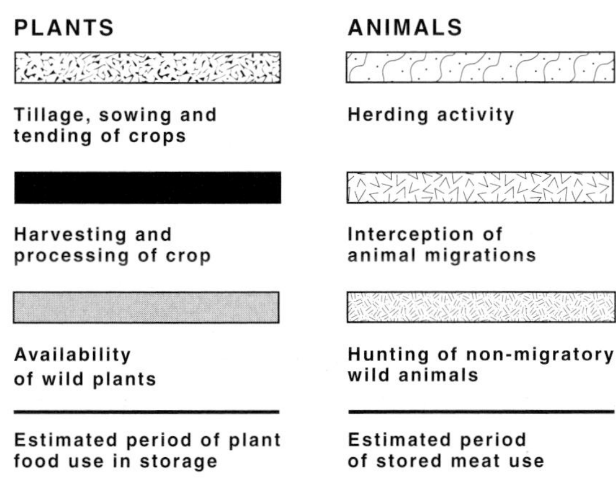

Figure 14.3 Abu Hureyra 1: the seasons of availability and use of the main wild plant and animal foods, and crops used by the inhabitants.

growth on the steppe and in the park-woodland for themselves. This unique concentration of plant and animal foods in a single season of exploitation would have inspired a strong sense of territoriality, as is the case among similarly placed recent hunter and gatherers (Forde 1956, pp. 92, 375; Netting 1986, p. 25).

The first season of the annual cycle was certainly the period of most concentrated work, but also of greatest abundance, when the widest variety of foods became available. It was the time when most of the meat and much of the plant food could be obtained and stored away for consumption later. The gazelle were so important to the inhabitants of Abu Hureyra that their arrival would have been eagerly anticipated, and the gazelle slaughter would also have been the most exciting event in the seasonal round. The combination of ample food, the most important hunt of the year, and the presence of all able-bodied villagers is likely to have occasioned a burst of ceremonial activity, as in many recent hunting and gathering societies (Oliver 1962, p. 54; Drucker 1965, p. 120; Lee 1979, p. 365). This may have been the most appropriate time to conduct marriage or betrothal ceremonies, initiation exercises, important village business, and other social and community events. There may have been some brief celebrations associated with the arrival of the gazelle (see Drucker 1965, p. 94), but much of this presumed activity is likely to have awaited the quieter time in June or July, after the gazelle had passed and most of the seeds had been harvested.

The second season began with the onset of high summer and lasted through the autumn. The villagers could find some plant foods on the steppe during this season, in particular feather-grass, and from September onward roots and tubers. Otherwise, they turned their attention to the Euphrates Valley, where most of the plants harvested during this season were to be found. They gathered seeds in abundance from knotgrass, club-rush, and the millets, and probably also collected the rhizomes of club-rush and sedge. Some of this harvest would have been stored to be eaten later. The water in the river and the grazing on the valley floor would have attracted game during the summer and well into the autumn, so the few animals hunted in this season are likely to have been killed close to the village. The most probable species taken were wild sheep, a few wild cattle, pigs, and fish, while hares were hunted on the steppe.

The villagers would have gathered terebinth nutlets in this season for immediate consumption and to be stored for later use. The trees were to be found in the wadi system to the west of the site, in patches across the steppe, and in the park-woodland. Their fruits would have been valued as flavorings for food, for their resins, and as tanning agents. Thus, terebinth nutlets may have been used to process gazelle and onager skins. Terebinth nutlets and fenugreek seeds may also have been added to meat as a preservative.

With much meat and plant food already safely in storage, this second season from July to November would have been a period of relative leisure for the villagers. Assuming that the same division of labor held in this season as in the first, the men would have had little hunting to do, although they may have visited the terebinth stands. This would have been a good time, therefore, in which to manufacture some of the articles needed during the rest of the year such as baskets, wooden containers, nets, and mats; to repair dwellings; and to continue processing gazelle skins.

The third season began in December, soon after the onset of winter. Once again most of the available wild foods were to be found in the valley, especially the rhizomes of reeds and bulrushes. There, too, were several of the species of game available at that time of the year: wild sheep, cattle, pigs, and deer. As winter turned into early spring, fresh grazing and surface water would have appeared on the steppe, tempting some of the animals to range more widely. The pattern of hunting during this season is likely, therefore, to have oscillated between the valley and the steppe; even so, hunting does not seem to have contributed much to the diet. Some of the steppe plants with edible roots and tubers would have been at their most nutritious during this season, and could have been dug up quite easily because the ground was moist.

There would always have been a variety of wild plants and animals to eat during this season, although the choice was more restricted and it may have been difficult to find much game. It is also likely that many of the foods stored earlier in the year would have been eaten by late in the winter, so this was probably a relatively lean period. By March people would have started preparing for the arrival of the gazelle. So, late in the season, there would have been a growing sense of anticipation of the plentiful supplies of animals and plants about to become available, but also a need for more work. The arrival of the gazelle would have signaled the renewal of the seasonal cycle.

The adoption of agriculture in Periods 1B and 1C would have blurred this three season cycle but not supplanted it. The villagers would have begun to prepare the soil and to plant their crops of rye during October, in season 2. They would have cared for the growing crop throughout the spring in season 3, and then harvested and processed it in May and June, that is, in season 1. If, as seems likely, they were also cultivating legumes, they would have prepared the soil and planted those seeds in the late winter, and harvested and processed the crop from April through June. The effect of these novel activities would have been to increase the work load during the winter, and to augment the press of tasks that had to be accomplished during season 1 from April to June, with some carryover into July. The greater pressure of work in season 1 would have increased tension in the system, for in some years it might not have been possible to kill an abundance of gazelle, harvest the rye and other crops, and still collect large quantities of wild plant foods within the same few weeks. The evidence suggests that the villagers maintained a rough balance among these activities at first, but eventually they came to devote more time to their crops and less to gathering wild plant foods.

How satisfactory was the diet of the villagers of Abu Hureyra 1? They seem to have eaten large quantities of plant foods, dried meat, and some fresh game during much of the year. To these they probably added leafy foods, undetectable in the plant remains from the site. They should, therefore, have consumed enough carbohydrate, protein, and vitamins to ensure a well-balanced diet. In the first season there would have been unlimited supplies of fresh meat available to boost their protein intake. Storage of gazelle meat, seeds, their cereal crops, and other plant foods would have helped to maintain good nutrition throughout the year.

The one potential dietary problem concerns the state of the gazelle on their arrival at Abu Hureyra. Speth and Spielmann (1983) have pointed out that most hunters and gatherers in temperate and Arctic environments find it difficult to maintain a balanced diet in the late winter and early spring, because they are obliged to consume unhealthy quantities of lean meat at a time when there are few fat-rich animals or plants rich in carbohydrates available. In northern Syria, the grazing would have been at its best from March to May, providing a rich source of food for the gazelle. Furthermore, this was the season in which the female gazelles were giving birth, so they would have been in good physical condition. This suggests that the meat of the gazelles would not have been unduly lean during the season in which the inhabitants of Abu Hureyra killed them.

There were plenty of other sources of fat and carbohydrate available during the late winter and spring. Some fat could have been obtained from bone marrow, so it is significant that most of the bones of gazelle and other animals we recovered had been highly processed to extract it. Another good source of fatty meat at all times of the year in the Euphrates region would have been the sheep. Eating a few waterfowl would also have boosted people's fat intake during the winter. Roots and tubers would have provided an important source of carbohydrates at times when other plants were scarce.

Our direct evidence for storage of food is limited, partly because we excavated only a small part of the site but also because the storage facilities used by the inhabitants would have been constructed mainly of perishable materials. Yet, as we have seen, it is probable that food storage was an important part of the subsistence arrangements, reinforcing the sedentary life of the inhabitants. It would have permitted the villagers to even out their supplies from one season to the next, assuring them of a sufficiency during the times of the year when food was more difficult to obtain.

The cereals, both wild and domestic, could have been stored through one annual cycle, although supplies may often have run out before the next harvest was ripe. The seeds of the weedy plants of the steppe and the terebinth nutlets would have kept well, but it seems doubtful that enough of them could have been gathered to last more than a few months. The rhizomes and tubers of the rushes and sedges could be dried and preserved for much of the year. The roots and tubers of the steppe plants would have kept for only a month or two. The gazelle, and to a lesser extent the onager, seem to have been so important that we assume large quantities of their meat were preserved for eating over the rest of the annual cycle. The main limiting factor would have been the wet winters, which would have accelerated the decay of the meat, so making it difficult to keep enough to last through the third season. These assumptions are incorporated in figure 14.3.

Social Organization

Interpretation of the social organization of the inhabitants is difficult because we were able to excavate only a modest area of the settlement. Nevertheless, we can derive certain inferences from the nature of the site, its contents, and its setting, that enable us to form a general impression of the society that inhabited it. Abu Hureyra 1 represented a new kind of settlement that appeared in the Levant for the first time during the later Epipalaeolithic, one that was unusually large, long-lived, and inhabited by a sedentary community. It was founded to take advantage of the rich concentration of resources of interest to hunters and gatherers in the Middle Euphrates Valley. The social arrangements of its inhabitants would have been conditioned in part by these novel circumstances.

Mobile hunters and gatherers are known to have quite low birth rates, so their populations remain relatively stable or increase quite slowly over time (Netting 1986, p. 19). Births are often spaced several years apart for a variety of physiological and physical reasons (Lee 1979, pp. 318, 326; Konner and Worthman 1980). Once they settle down, these constraints are relaxed and their diet may change, so the birth rate increases and the population of the group grows more rapidly (Binford and Chasko 1973, pp. 134–135; Lee 1979, p. 442). The size of the group will continue to increase unless steps are taken to limit its rise, or the supply of food is insufficient to support it. There are indications that something like this pattern of growth happened at Abu Hureyra. Whatever the size of the initial settlement of Period 1A, it probably extended over 2,000–6,000 m^2 in Periods 1B and 1C. This would have made it one of the largest known late Epipalaeolithic settlements in the Levant, and far larger than almost all early Epipalaeolithic sites.

The increase in the number of inhabitants provided an incentive for developing agriculture to support the growing population of the village. The decision to grow rye as the first cereal crop had an additional advantage beyond its ease of processing and inherent food value: it could readily be cooked as a mush. Rye mush would have made a good weaning food, thus reducing the health risk in the transition from infancy to childhood. This would have contributed to sustaining the increase in population.

Can we propose a figure for the likely number of inhabitants of Abu Hureyra 1? We do not have the evidence to determine the population with accuracy, but can suggest with due caution that, based on our estimates of the size of the village, perhaps 100–300 people may have lived there during its period of maximum extent.

We have suggested that the pit complexes of Period 1A may have been family dwellings, although our evidence is obviously too limited to confirm this. We can say a little more about how the inhabitants distributed their principal activities among themselves. Molleson's analysis of the burials of Abu Hureyra 2 indicates quite clearly that, in this later village, all the women but only some of the men engaged in the severe labor of grinding foodstuffs, leading to deformation of their toes. The discovery of a few similarly deformed toe bones in the Abu Hureyra 1 settlement may mean that the same division of labor already operated among the first inhabitants of the site. In most hunter-gatherer societies it is the men who hunt and the women who do much of the gathering. It is quite likely, therefore, that the same arrangement was followed at Abu Hureyra. The annual gazelle hunts were probably organized by the men, even if women may have participated in processing the carcasses at the site, as ethnographic accounts of antelope hunting on the Great Plains suggest (Grinnell 1923, p. 282). Similarly, the stalking of game at other seasons was probably a male prerogative.

The slaughter of gazelle was concentrated in a period of a few weeks in April and May. That was the same season during which the wild einkorn, other cereals, the legumes, and small-seeded plants all ripened, and also when the crops had to be harvested. This put severe pressure on the available labor force, since it was during those weeks that a substantial portion of the annual food supply had to be garnered and stored. One likely way the inhabitants dealt with this problem was by maintaining a division of responsibilities by sex. Thus, while the men were preoccupied with the gazelle, it is probable that many of the women were out on the steppe collecting the plant foods. Children, too, may have been pressed to assist in this important activity. But, beginning in Period 1B, the men would also have needed to harvest the crops, probably with the aid of the women. Many of the gazelle would have arrived before the rye crop was fully ripe, allowing for sequential scheduling of gazelle killing and crop harvesting, but there must often have been some overlap of these activities, with consequent pressure on the entire adult population of the village.

Abu Hureyra is the first site in Southwest Asia at which such an intensive mode of concentrated seasonal killing of migratory animals has been documented. Thus, the mass slaughter of gazelle and onager seems to have been an innovation in hunting technique. The method required the cooperation of relatively large numbers of people and, conversely, there was little point in undertaking such an elaborate exercise unless there were many people in the vicinity to eat the resulting meat. Enough surveys have been carried out along the Middle Euphrates to indicate that there were no other contemporary sites that could have supplied substantial numbers of people to help in the hunt. The nearest known one is Dibsi Faraj East (Wilkinson and Moore 1978), and that was quite small. We know less about the potential distribution of sites on the steppe, but present indications are that they, too, would have been small and ephemeral. Thus, the only place that could have supplied enough hunters was Abu Hureyra itself, and the evidence for the gazelle hunt supports our view that its population was substantial.

Abu Hureyra 1 seems to have been inhabited by a community of several hundred people who lived together in permanent dwellings all the year round, and whose descendants occupied the site for many centuries. These characteristics entitle us to describe their settlement as a village. This was an innovation of the foragers who founded the village in Period 1A, and it contrasts in important ways with the mode of existence described, for example, by Lee (1979) for the !Kung San. They, and many other hunters and gatherers known to us ethnographically, might come together and form a large community during one season of the year. Such gatherings provided an opportunity for intense social activity, as well as opportunities for exchange. Then, after a few weeks, heightened social tensions and the increasing costs of obtaining food from the wild would lead one group after another to break away. The inhabitants of Abu Hureyra evidently developed a different mode of life, first as hunter-gatherers and later as forager-farmers. They resolved the problems of maintaining the cohesion of a large group, and so were able to remain together indefinitely.

This novel way of life required a new form of organization. We cannot define its precise form but we can state what some of its necessary characteristics were. There was a need for a person or group to exercise authority on behalf of the community to regulate the affairs of the village. This would have called for qualities of leadership and skill in mediation, as well as the cooperation of the inhabitants. Mechanisms were needed to resolve disputes between individuals and groups for the community to remain intact and act together when necessary. The resources of most interest to the inhabitants of Abu Hureyra were to be found seasonally at specific places in the valley and on the plateau, so it would have been necessary to regulate access to them and their exploitation. The gazelle hunt would have required a communitywide exercise of authority (Grinnell 1923, p. 263) and the cooperation of the entire village to repair the kites and organize the mass drives. In later years it would have fallen to the leaders of the community to allocate land for farming, and perhaps to arrange activities such as communal clearance of weeds from ground that had been left fallow in preparation for sowing.

Our evidence suggests that Abu Hureyra was self-sufficient in foodstuffs, and almost so in raw materials. Nonetheless, some exotic materials were reaching the site, suggesting that communications were maintained with other people. That would have provided a means of obtaining marriage partners from outside the community.

Summary

The first inhabitants were hunters and gatherers who were attracted to Abu Hureyra by its favorable location. The village they founded about 11,500 BP, Abu Hureyra 1, lay on the edge of the terrace at the junction of the valley floor and the steppe, and within easy reach of the park-woodland beyond. Every spring gazelle migrated northward to the Euphrates Valley at Abu Hureyra, providing an abundant source of meat for the inhabitants. The environs of the site were so rich in plants and animals in all seasons that the inhabitants were able to live there year-round. In consequence the population of the settlement grew. Climatic fluctuations, especially the onset of the cooler, drier conditions of the Younger Dryas, brought about significant changes in the vegetation around the site. This obliged the villagers to modify their plant gathering and was one of the reasons why they adopted agriculture. Those adjustments were successful because they enabled the villagers to remain there for about 1,500 years. The formation of such a substantial and long-lived sedentary settlement was an unprecedented event in Levantine prehistory.

In Period 1A, from c. 11,500 to 11,000 BP, the settlement consisted of pit dwellings built close together, each composed of several connected subcircular chambers. Their superstructure consisted of a framework of poles roofed with branches and reeds or, perhaps, gazelle skins. These appeared to be family dwellings. As debris accumulated, the form of the settlement changed; in Periods 1B (c. 11,000–10,400 BP) and 1C (c. 10,400–10,000 BP) the dwellings were built on the surface of the ground. They were still roofed with perishable materials and had floors of trodden earth or clay.

The surviving artifacts consisted of flint, stone, and bone tools. The flint assemblage was characterized by microliths, principally lunates, and flake tools. The stone artifacts were dominated by grinding tools, especially dishes and rubbing stones. Abu Hureyra 1 yielded an unusual variety of artifacts compared with most contemporary sites. Many of the grinding dishes, ornaments, and other artifacts were made with great care, a reflection of the sedentary way of life of their makers, their artistic sense, and symbolic concerns. The range of objects and their typology is consonant with the assemblages from other late Epipalaeolithic Levantine sites.

The villagers of Period 1A depended on hunting and gathering for their livelihood. Their year was divided into three seasons. In the first, from April to June, they were out on the steppe killing gazelle in mass drives using kites or similar devices. They also harvested wild cereals, small-seeded plants, and legumes from the steppe and park-woodland. Much of the gazelle meat and many of the cereals, legumes, and other seeds were stored for later consumption. The second season, from July to November, was mainly spent in the valley collecting the seeds and rhizomes of rushes, sedges, and other valley-bottom plants, and hunting sheep and other game. Some people collected roots and tubers on the steppe, and terebinth nutlets in the wadis and from the park-woodland a little distance away. In the third season, from December to March, the villagers again obtained much of their food from the valley, gathering rhizomes of reeds and other plants, and hunting sheep, cattle, deer, and other animals. They collected the roots and tubers of some plants on the steppe. Stored produce helped the villagers maintain their sedentary way of life by evening out the supply of plant and animal foods from season to season.

The way of life of the inhabitants changed to accommodate the increase in their numbers and the rapid reversal in climate marked by the Younger Dryas episode from c. 11,000 to 10,000 BP. The climatic changes caused the park-woodland to recede from Abu Hureyra during Period 1B, and obliged the inhabitants to adopt agriculture immediately to remain together. They were among the first people to do so anywhere in the world. Their principal cereal crop was rye, but they may also have grown some legumes. More animals were killed over time, but the gazelle herds seem to have been unaffected by the increase in hunting.

The village was inhabited by several hundred people who devised novel social arrangements that enabled them to maintain their community over many centuries. Authority was probably vested in a person or group who, with community approval, regulated access to resources such as agricultural land, organized the gazelle drives and other large-scale enterprises, and mediated in disputes. The community divided into working bands, probably according to sex, to carry out major subsistence tasks such as the gazelle drives and harvesting of wild plants. The same was probably true of food processing, including the harvesting and processing of crops of domestic cereals and legumes. Thus, division of responsibilities along gender lines was probably an important organizing principle from the beginning. In establishing a permanent settlement based initially on hunting and gathering with, in time, the addition of farming, and in developing the social system that enabled them to maintain it, the people of Abu Hureyra 1 effected a social and economic revolution that anticipated the Neolithic world of settled farming villages by a millennium and a half.

THE INTERMEDIATE PERIOD, C. 10,000–9,400 BP

The occupation of Abu Hureyra 1 waned sometime after 10,000 BP and the focus of settlement shifted; the precise date of this change is uncertain because the crucial top levels of the Abu Hureyra 1 village were removed by the later inhabitants. The main area of habitation in the succeeding Intermediate Period (c. 10,000–9,400 BP) was along the northern side of the site in the vicinity of Trenches E and G, overlooking the Euphrates floodplain. The shift in settlement coincided with the end of the Younger Dryas and the return of warmer, moister climatic conditions. It is likely that these environmental fluctuations were one reason why settlement at Abu Hureyra underwent some adjustment.

It is important to note that the shift in occupation we have found at Abu Hureyra is matched at several of the other sites occupied in both the late Epipalaeolithic and early Neolithic, elsewhere in the Levant. It thus coincides with a reordering of the settlement pattern over a much wider region that suggests there may have been other factors at work of a more general nature that cannot be comprehended fully on the evidence from Abu Hureyra alone. This is a matter which we consider further in chapter 15.

The indications are that the settlement of the Intermediate Period was an open village of structures built of organic materials, not unlike those of Abu Hureyra 1B and 1C. Much of the deposit that accumulated during this period was removed by the inhabitants of Abu Hureyra 2 as they expanded their village. From the modest amount of evidence we recovered for this episode, especially the radiocarbon dates (figure 14.1), we conclude that occupation was continuous.

The plant remains from level 68 in Trench G, the one deposit we can ascribe to this period, indicate that a second phase of agricultural development was underway. The charred remains included grains of free-threshing wheats and bread wheat, as well as domestic einkorn, barley grains, lentils, and a variety of weed seeds. The few animal bones suggest that gazelle were still of primary importance to the inhabitants.

ABU HUREYRA 2, C. 9,400–7,000 BP

Toward the end of the Intermediate Period the moister steppe would have expanded to the vicinity of Abu Hureyra. Thus, the environment of Abu Hureyra during the second half of the tenth millennium BP would have been distinctly more favorable for human settlement, although it never completely recovered its Late Glacial richness. It was in this setting that the village of Abu Hureyra 2 took shape and began to expand at or soon after 9,400 BP (figure 14.2). Two important additional ecological factors that sustained the village were the continuation of the gazelle migration, and the potential of the environs for more intensive agriculture.

The culture and economy of the inhabitants of Abu Hureyra 2 changed significantly from the patterns that had obtained in Abu Hureyra 1 and through the Intermediate Period. The village of Abu Hureyra 2 consisted of rectilinear mudbrick houses, and grew to great size on the basis of a farming economy. The inhabitants developed new crafts that attest to skilled artisanship and a rich aesthetic sense. The village represented, therefore, the maturing of a new mode of existence. Nonetheless, there were some similarities in stone artifacts and bone tools in the assemblages from Abu Hureyra 1 and 2. The inhabitants of Abu Hureyra 2A largely depended for their subsistence on the cultivation of crops, a way of life that was already over a millennium and a half old at Abu Hureyra. They no longer gathered many wild plants for food, but continued to obtain much of their meat from the annual slaughter of gazelle. Thus, there was significant continuity in culture and economy from Abu Hureyra 1 through the Intermediate Period to Abu Hureyra 2.

The village of Abu Hureyra 2A grew until it covered eight hectares. The second major phase of expansion occurred after the transition from Period 2A to 2B, and the concomitant switch from dependence on gazelle to large-scale herding of sheep and goats. The settlement expanded over the entire area of the mound that survived into modern times, and farther out on the western side until it probably covered 16 ha or more. The inhabitants expanded their crafts and, before the end of the period, began to make pottery. Long-distance contacts seem to have quickened, since increasing quantities of obsidian reached the site from Anatolia. The Period 2B settlement lasted about a millennium (c. 8,300 to perhaps 7,300 BP), before further changes took place that marked the transition to the final episode of extensive prehistoric occupation, Period 2C (c. 7,300 to at least 7,000 BP). During this period the settlement contracted considerably, and its appearance also changed because the houses were built with more space between them. These open areas were often taken up with pits used for roasting and other activities. The economy, as far as we can tell, remained the same. The village was then abandoned, to be used occasionally thereafter in later prehistory. Some activities took place on the site in historic times, that is, in Period 3.

This, then, is the outline of the development of the Abu Hureyra 2 village, but it means little on its own. It needs to be considered in conjunction with the alterations in the form of the settlement, the exploitation of plants and animals, and the associated activities of the people themselves reflected in the morphology of their skeletons. Only when the connections between these have been established can we expect to comprehend why Abu Hureyra 2 developed in the way it did, and so perceive its significance.

The Abu Hureyra 2 Village

The most striking characteristics of the village of Abu Hureyra 2 are its longevity—it lasted, after all, for two and a half millennia—and great size. In Period 2B, when it reached its greatest extent, it was one of the largest contemporary settlements in Southwest Asia, and several times bigger than nearly all other Neolithic sites in the Levant. The village probably supported a population of 2,500–3,000 people in Period 2A, growing to 5,000–6,000 in 2B, a ten- to twentyfold increase over the estimated population of Abu Hureyra 1. The formation of a community on that scale represented a new order of settlement in Southwest Asia that was a direct result of, and a striking testimony to, the success of the agricultural economy that sustained it. The number of inhabitants was so large that the impact on their surroundings would have been heavy, especially over such a long period of time. The ecosystem of the steppe, in particular, was fragile and vulnerable to human exploitation. The economy, too, was delicately balanced. The fact that the village lasted so long indicates that its inhabitants were able to adjust their way of life to cope with fluctuations in the ecology of the surrounding region, but any marked deterioration in the environment would have threatened its continuation.

Abu Hureyra 2 was the dominant village in the middle reaches of the Euphrates Valley because of its great size. The few hamlets we found nearby, along the terrace at the edge of the valley, were probably dependent on Abu Hureyra itself. The only other known Euphrates sites partially contemporary with Abu Hureyra, Mureybit, Buqras, and Tell es-Sinn (Roodenberg 1979–1980) were spaced far apart and were much smaller. This was probably because their environs did not have the extraordinary concentration of resources that occurred at Abu Hureyra. All four sites seem to have been largely self-sufficient and do not appear to have been in regular contact with each other.

Abu Hureyra represented an extreme form of nucleated settlement. Its multiroomed houses, with floors often made of colored gypsum plaster, were set close together with only narrow passages and courts between them. The construction of large numbers of such dwellings constituted an architectural revolution. The houses were of the same kind from one end of the settlement to the other, and seem to have filled up much of the inhabited area of the site. Abu Hureyra 2 was thus a type of settlement for which there is no close, present-day parallel. The alignment, layout, and mode of construction of the houses were established in the early years of occupation and hardly altered throughout the two millennia of Periods 2A and 2B. Only toward the end, in Period 2C, was the basic layout of the settlement modified. Thus, there was extraordinary stability over a long period of time in both the arrangement of the settlement and the architectural principles embodied in its construction, even though the houses themselves were frequently replaced after no more than a couple of generations, or about every 50 years.

We found no large open spaces between the houses, no substantial storage buildings, and no workshops in the areas we excavated. We did find small storage bins within some of the houses, and there were abundant indications of artisan activities close by. Some of the rooms in the houses could have been used for larger-scale storage, but it is likely that the inhabitants constructed granaries on the edge of the settlement. It is there, too, that they probably kept their livestock, since we found no pens for animals beside the houses.

The scale and sophistication of the village, the range and quality of the artifacts produced by its inhabitants, and the evidence from the burials of some ideological complexity might be taken to indicate that there was a qualitative difference not only between Abu Hureyra 2 and earlier sites, but also between it and many contemporary settlements. That Abu Hureyra 2 represented a precocious development is undoubted, yet we note that while the buildings of Abu Hureyra 2 represented a new kind of architecture, their similarity in all parts of the site suggests that the inhabitants were on the same level in material terms. There was no indication from the burials that they had developed a social system based on a hierarchy of classes that was maintained from one generation to the next. Abu Hureyra, then, was an unusually large, early Neolithic village. It had not developed all the characteristics, for example, substantial public buildings, a social hierarchy, and large-scale trade, that we associate with the towns of early historic times in Southwest Asia.

The Economy

The economy of Abu Hureyra 2 developed in two stages: first farming, the raising of some domestic animals, hunting, and a continued interest in wild plant foods in Period 2A, and then farming and herding in Periods 2B and 2C. Thus, it was not until quite late in the sequence of occupation that the full Neolithic economy was adopted at Abu Hureyra. This was because the location of the site continued to favor a way of life that was based in part on a continuation of hunting, and a little gathering.

The people of Abu Hureyra 2A cultivated five domesticated cereals: rye, einkorn, emmer, bread wheat, two- and six-row hulled barley; and at least three pulses: lentils, peas, and vetches. Field beans and chickpeas were certainly cultivated by 2B times, if not before. The presence of rye and einkorn in the cereal remains is a clear indication of the importance of these crops in the early agricultural economies of sites in the northern Levant and southern Anatolia. De Moulins's discovery that bread wheat occurred in the Intermediate Period, and throughout the Abu Hureyra 2 sequence, is significant because it indicates that free-threshing wheat was a constituent of the farming economy from the earliest Neolithic at Abu Hureyra. It also demonstrates that this plant, a cross between emmer and goat-faced grass (*Aegilops squarrosa*), was hybridized much earlier than had been supposed hitherto, and probably in the northern Levant. Some samples of plant remains from levels in the early phases of Trench B, and even as late as phase 2 in Trench G, contained specimens of wild-type cereals; these plants continued to grow as an admixture in the fields of domestic cereals until early in Period 2B. Some other plants of the valley bottom and steppe also continued to be gathered for food and other purposes.

The ubiquity of the remains of domesticated cereals and pulses across the site is itself a clear indication that the economy of Abu Hureyra 2 was based on agriculture. The economy thus represented a development of the pattern established in Periods 1B and 1C of the preceding Epipalaeolithic village. The small quantities of such seeds in each flotation sample, compared with the more numerous seeds of weeds and other plants, especially in 2A levels, is a reflection of the methods by which the inhabitants processed their crops. The threshing floors were probably outside the settlement, as is so often the case in villages across Western Asia today. The tight clustering of dwellings would have precluded carrying out any threshing within the village itself. Thus, the crops would already have been partly processed when they were carried into the heart of the village where our trenches were located. Then, as now, great care would have been taken to conserve the grains and pulse seeds for food in subsequent cleaning and sieving. It is not surprising, then, that so few seeds of crops were swept into fires and charred. The fate of the weed seeds would have been different. Many of these would have been burnt in domestic hearths after they had been separated out through sieving.

The great size of the site and the large number of its inhabitants provide further indirect evidence of the importance of agriculture in the economy. People living at the subsistence level consume about 2,500 calories a day, and need the equivalent of about 250–300 kg of wheat a year for sustenance (Clark and Haswell 1967, pp. 18–19, 60). A single hectare of reasonably fertile land can readily yield 1,000 kg of wheat a year using simple agricultural techniques, thus supplying the needs of three to four people. The inhabitants of Abu Hureyra probably conducted much of their farming on land within a radius of 2–3 km from the site (Chisholm 1968, pp. 66, 131; Hillman 1973, p. 236), which had a potential cultivable area of between 1,000 and 2,500 ha. Thus, the number of people that we estimate were living at Abu Hureyra during Period 2 could have supported themselves by simple farming. Molleson's discovery that the inhabitants systematically ground grain lends further weight to this observation. On the other hand, it is quite clear that the people of Abu Hureyra 2 could not have existed on the much lower returns per hectare available from foraging.

The most remarkable feature of the animal economy was the strong continuity of the seasonal gazelle killing established in Abu Hureyra 1. The gazelle hunt was carried out on a much larger scale than before in order to provide enough meat for the greatly increased population of Abu Hureyra 2, but evidently the herds were numerous enough to sustain the inhabitants over many centuries. They probably used domesticated dogs to aid in the hunts. Certainly, the great increase in dog-digested bones in Abu Hureyra 2 levels suggests that these animals were kept in much greater numbers than before.

The most significant innovation was the appearance of domesticated sheep and goats in Abu Hureyra 2A, because this marked the inception of animal herding on the Middle Euphrates. The quantities of feather-grass in the deposits declined from the beginning of Abu Hureyra 2, an apparent early indication of increased grazing pressure on the steppe caused by the introduction of domesticated caprines. The contribution of these animals to the meat diet was modest. It seems that relatively few of them were kept, perhaps in individual households, and that they were maintained as much for their dairy products, skins, and sinews as for meat. The increased role of caprines in the economy would have helped even out the supply of protein and fat during the year. The milk from these animals would have been most abundant from the early spring, before the arrival of the gazelle, providing food during that relatively lean season.

The economy of Abu Hureyra 2A was thus based on the cultivation of domestic plants and the herding of some domestic caprines, with the continuation of large-scale gazelle hunting and the gathering of some wild plants. This combination enabled the population to live there year-round. The economy was sufficiently productive to support the first major expansion of the settlement during Period 2A, so that by the mid ninth millennium BP Abu Hureyra was one of the largest villages in Southwest Asia.

The transition to the second economic stage of Periods 2B and 2C was accomplished with extraordinary speed about 8,300 BP, when gazelle hunting abruptly declined and the flocks of sheep and goats expanded. We suggest that the gazelle herds diminished in size because the growing populations of Abu Hureyra itself, and of other communities along the migration route, were all increasing their predation. This followed the expansion of population that took place throughout the Levant after the introduction of agriculture (Moore 1983, p. 98). At Abu Hureyra, the inhabitants responded to the crisis by expanding their existing flocks of caprines. It is probable that the switch from gazelle to caprines was accomplished in less than a century, and perhaps in 50 years or fewer, that is, in a single generation. The main reason the villagers could so readily replace the gazelle with sheep and goats was, of course, because they had long maintained small numbers of them as domestic animals.

The economy in 2B and 2C was based on flocks of domesticated caprines, with some domestic cattle and pigs. Some gazelle continued to be killed each year, though on a much smaller scale than in the past. The expansion of the flocks of sheep and goats not only ensured that meat would continue to be available, but also provided much more dairy food, something that could not be obtained from the gazelle. The other indication of increased human interaction with domestic animals was the greater amount of chewing and ingestion of bones by dogs over time. Agriculture provided almost all the plant foods that were eaten. The switch from gazelle to caprines is reflected in the gradual impoverishment of the steppe flora, a process that was accentuated later by an increase in aridity as the temperature approached its Holocene maximum.

We have used the switch from gazelle to caprines across the site as the indicator of the transition from Period 2A to 2B because it was such a major event in the history of Abu Hureyra 2. The expansion of the site to its greatest size occurred in Period 2B, following this transition, and was linked to the adoption of a full farming and herding economy. The location of the site was favorable enough to support a flourishing agricultural village of unprecedented size, and the climate was still sufficiently moist for the inhabitants to cultivate the fertile soils of the steppe. This zone supported a varied flora and offered abundant grazing for their flocks and herds. There was more arable land in the damp bottom of the wadis to the west, and extensive cultivation was carried out on the Euphrates floodplain. The valley would have provided grazing in the summer months for sheep and goats, and year-round forage for domestic cattle. The vegetation of the floodplain supplied not only wild foods but also abundant timber, reeds, and other materials for building and crafts.

Mixed farming was the essence of the agricultural system of Abu Hureyra in Periods 2B and 2C. Because the village was nucleated and its population sedentary, the fields would have been close by and worked intensively. The greatest pressure would have been on land within a radius of 2 km of the village, and the village was located at a point where 50% of it would have been steppe and the other 50% floodplain (figure 2.13). It is likely that there would have been a mix of private and communal control over land and other resources (Netting 1986, pp. 78–79). The community probably controlled such matters as the allocation of arable land, water rights, grazing rights, and the pasturing of flocks.

We found no heavy agricultural tools on the site, and so presume that cultivation was carried out with wooden implements. The inhabitants may have prepared and sown the land with digging sticks or hoes, since it is possible to conduct quite intensive farming with this simple technology. We note, however, that domestic cattle were present in some numbers from 2B times on, and it is difficult to account for their presence simply as providers of meat, milk, and hides. Cattle are heavy feeders, and their need to drink frequently would have confined them to the Euphrates Valley for much of the year. We suggest, therefore, that one reason they were kept was for use as draft animals, and in that role they may have tilled the soil with a wooden ard. That would have raised agricultural productivity significantly. The need to farm the land quite intensively may have been met through a short fallow system, and care was probably taken to maintain the fertility of the soil. Both cereals and pulses were major crops, so it is likely that some rotation was practiced. The flocks of sheep and goats were probably pastured on the stubble after the harvest, as in Syria today and widely elsewhere, thus manuring the land.

A few tiny, short-lived sites, perhaps contemporary with the later periods of occupation at Abu Hureyra, were located from 1.5 to 6 km eastward along the terrace and up the wadis Shetnet es-Salmas and Hibna. This raises the possibility that some people lived away from the village. They may have farmed land that was too far to be reached conveniently from Abu Hureyra because the village was so large that it needed additional land several kilometers from the site in order to support itself. There would have been a good deal of grazing within a day's walk of the village on the steppe and in the valley, but shepherds may have left the settlement for several days at a time to graze the community's flocks on more distant pastures, especially on the steppe during the spring.

Abu Hureyra 2 and its contemporary sites in the Euphrates Valley, with El Kum to the southeast, seem to have functioned independently as far as subsistence was concerned. Yet our evidence indicates that the people of Abu Hureyra regularly obtained basalt, limestone, and alabaster from sources up to 130 km away, as well as obsidian from Anatolia, and other materials from more distant regions. The modest quantities of cowrie shells and exotic stones—a few pieces of turquoise among them—are hardly sufficient to demonstrate more than occasional contacts with the rest of the Levant and the Taurus and Anti-Taurus mountains. The presence of obsidian on the site in regular amounts that increased through time testifies to more formal exchange arrangements. Abu Hureyra would have absorbed much greater quantities of exotic materials than other sites simply because of its size, so it would have served as a regional focus for such exchanges.

The Cycle of the Seasons

The farming and hunting economy of Abu Hureyra 2A was based on a modified version of the annual cycle followed by the people of Abu Hureyra 1B and 1C. The year was now divided into four seasons, beginning with the onset of cooler, damper weather in October. Once the soil had absorbed enough moisture to be workable, the fields could be cleared of vegetation and prepared for sowing. The cereals were probably sown in the autumn to ensure the best yield (figure 14.4). After the seeds had germinated, the young plants would have needed some weeding, but the work in the fields would have eased in the middle of winter as the colder weather slowed growth. Thus, there would have been a short season of leisure in midwinter during which the villagers could pursue crafts. The small flocks of sheep and goats would have required attention throughout the year. In the autumn they probably grazed close to the village because the forage farther afield would have been sparse.

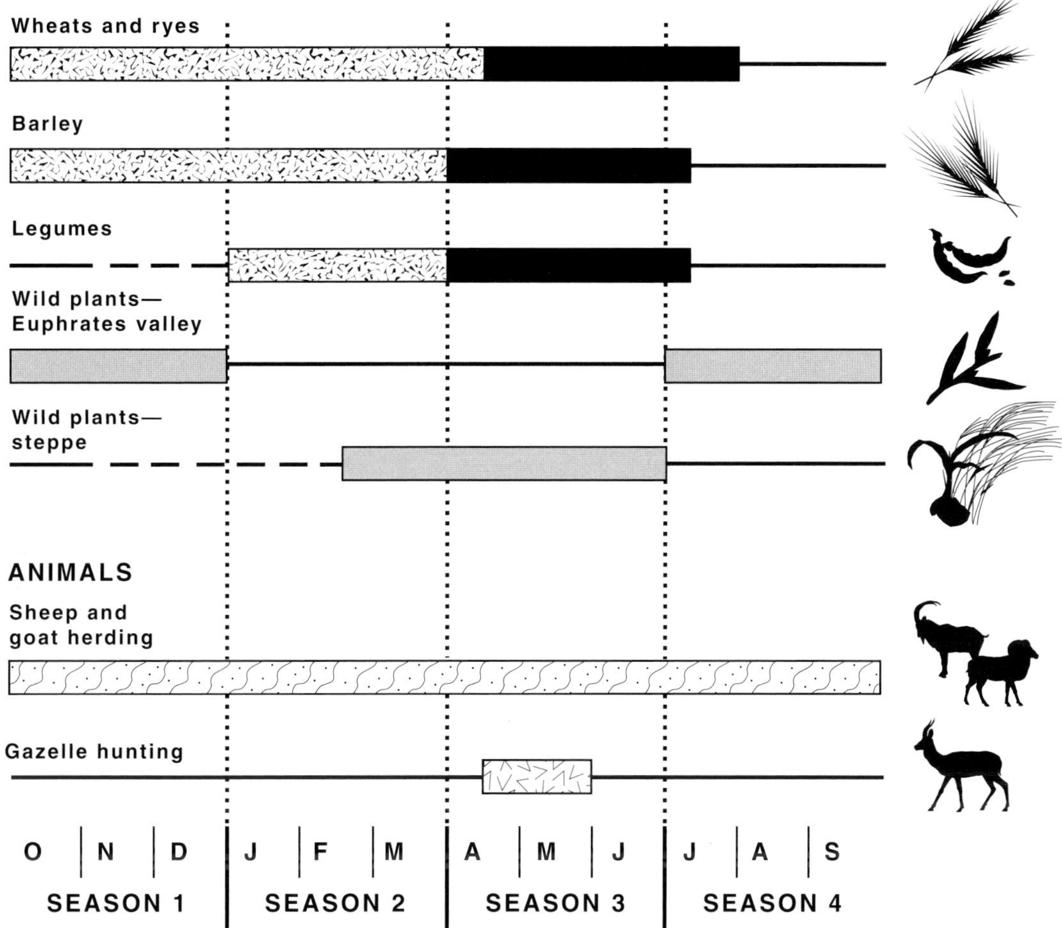

ABU HUREYRA 2A

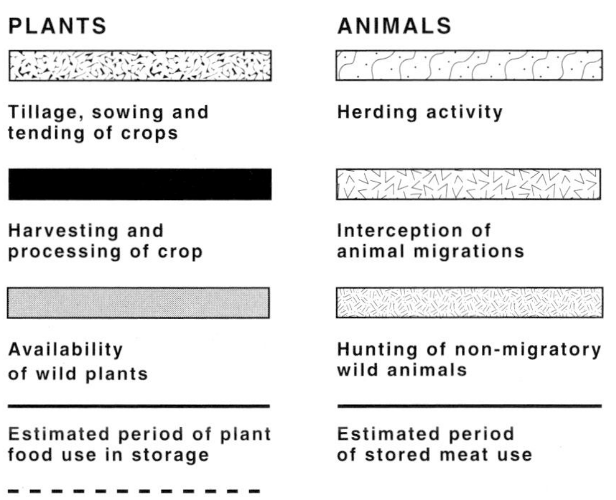

Figure 14.4 Abu Hureyra 2A: the seasons of availability and use of the main crops, plants, and animals used by the inhabitants.

The second season began with the turn of the year. As the risk of frost decreased and the soil began to warm up, the villagers prepared more land for sowing legumes. Both the newly germinated legumes and the cereals would have required weeding and protection from animals as the season advanced. Later on, they may have taken the sheep and goats onto the steppe to profit from the renewal of the grazing there.

The gazelle arrived in April, ushering in the period of most concentrated work in the entire cycle—that of the third season. The villagers had to secure, process, and store much of the meat they needed for the year during the few weeks in which the gazelle herds passed by. The crops would have started to ripen in April, too, and the harvest would have begun soon after. The cereals and the legumes had to be harvested in May and early June and then processed. Some wild plants had to be collected from the steppe as they ripened. All these concurrent tasks obliged the villagers to make the best use of the available labor. We suppose that the men concentrated on the gazelle hunt while the women devoted some time to gathering, but it is likely that all participated in bringing in the crops as the season advanced and more of them ripened. The effort to obtain food was spread over so many activities during this third season that, as the population of the village increased, people would have been obliged to invest only in those that gave the best returns in a given year.

The onset of high summer in July brought a slackening of the pace. The villagers had to process and put into store the rest of the crops; they still had seeds to collect from the valley bottom, but an extended period of reduced labor would have set in. This would have allowed them time, not only for building and other dry-season activities, but also for the pursuit of crafts and the manufacture of new tools in preparation for the beginning of the next agricultural year. The conclusion of the harvest probably stimulated the villagers to celebrate not only its achievement and the end of the seasonal cycle, but also other social events. It may have been the best time, too, to have exchanged goods with other communities.

The pattern of activities changed once more in Periods 2B and 2C. The year continued to be divided into four seasons, but there was more emphasis on farming and herding, less on hunting, and little on gathering (figure 14.5). This marked the emergence not only of a mature Neolithic way of life at Abu Hureyra, but also of one that was recognizably "modern." Thus, many aspects of the seasonal round will be familiar to us from recent peasant practice in Southwest Asia.

The village reached its maximum extent during Period 2B, so the autumn tilling and planting season would have been more intense because enough land had to be sown to keep every household in grain for a year. After a brief period of reduced activity in midwinter, the pace of work in the second season would have increased with the advance of spring. The villagers needed to plant a much larger crop of legumes, and had to do a great deal more work to tend their fields.

In the flocks kept by the beduin of the region today, the lambing season begins in December and continues through January. The lambs are ready to be weaned in March just as the spring grazing is at its best. It is likely that lambing at Abu Hureyra, too, began at the end of the first season, or a little later, and continued into season 2. The shepherds probably led their flocks to graze out on the steppe in the second season to benefit from the fresh growth of spring pasture. The milk yield would have been at its highest then, so it would have been the best time to prepare yoghurt, butter, cheese, and other dairy prod-

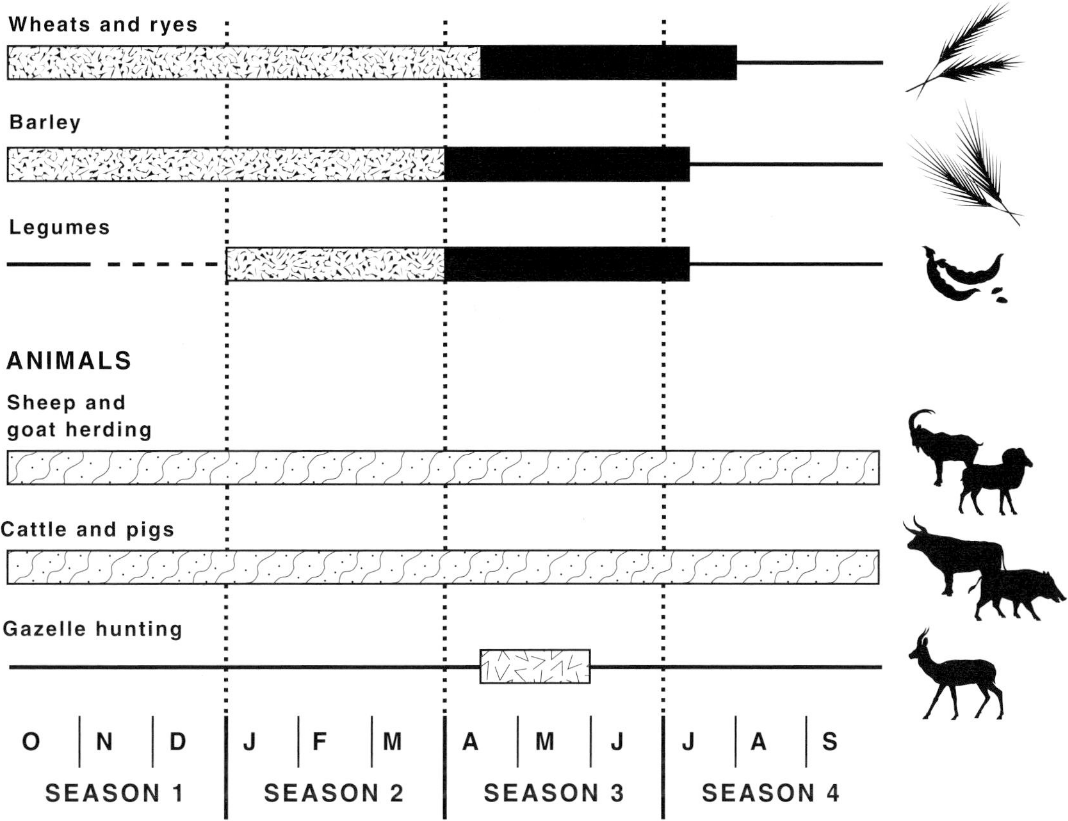

ABU HUREYRA 2B and 2C

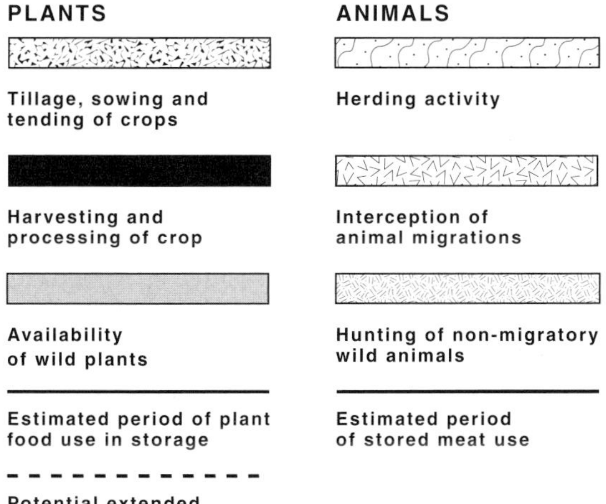

Figure 14.5 Abu Hureyra 2B and 2C: the seasons of availability and use of the main crops and animals used by the inhabitants.

ucts. Some of the butter and cheese was probably preserved for consumption later in the year. In Western Asia cheese from sheep's milk is traditionally valued more highly than that of goats because it keeps better from one season to the next.

Once again, the intensity of work was greatest in the third season. It is probable that the entire community went into the fields to bring in the crops, and to begin threshing and winnowing them for storage. The flocks had to be tended, and dairying would have continued throughout the season. Some gazelle were still killed each spring to provide meat and skins. The arrival of the herds would have added to the demand for labor, just as the inhabitants were preparing to harvest their crops. Thus, the people of Abu Hureyra probably killed fewer gazelles than the herds could sustain, simply because not enough people could be spared to engage in the hunt. It is probable, however, that this survival from an earlier way of life was important symbolically to the villagers because it represented their last major hunting pursuit.

The fourth season was a time of relative calm, although there was still much crop processing to be done. On analogy with recent agricultural practice among traditional peasant farmers in the region, some of the fields were probably hoed during this season to control weeds. As the steppe dried up the village flocks and herds would have been pastured in the valley. These activities still left time for crafts and building activities, and also leisure for communitywide festivities as the cycle of the agricultural year was completed.

We illustrate what Abu Hureyra 2B may have looked like during the third season, and on into the fourth, in the frontispiece. Almost all the information contained in the drawing can be demonstrated from the archaeological evidence. The village is located where the steppe and the floodplain meet, and dominates the Euphrates Valley. A stream from the Wadi Shetnet es-Salmas flows across the scene on its way to join the Euphrates, away in the jungle to the northeast. Crops of cereals and legumes have been planted extensively on the steppe and on the valley floor. The harvest is at its height, and the reaped plants are being carried back to the village. Some people are threshing and winnowing grain on the edge of the settlement. The villagers carry heavy loads on their heads, and habitually squat, at work and at rest. The work is hard and puts much strain on their backs. All of this is attested, of course, by the skeletal evidence. Several crops need to be dried before they are stored, while gazelle skins from the hunt that has just concluded have to be stretched; we have shown some of the house roofs being used for these activities.

The Euphrates floodplain is still forested, although much of the jungle near the settlement is secondary growth. There has been some clearance around the village, and this has opened up land for grazing. As summer advances, the flocks are brought in from the steppe and pastured there. Once the harvest is over, there is more time to engage in other activities, one of the most important of which is construction. The drawing shows a house being built on the west side of the village. Reeds are being cut in the foreground for use as roofing material, and also for baskets and mats.

The People of the Village

Our evidence suggests that division of labor was an important principle of life in the village of Abu Hureyra 2. Women spent more time at home preparing food, running their households, and looking after their children, while the men would have been more involved in agriculture and the care of livestock. Children may have played a significant role in the production of food, for example, by weeding and helping to look after the animals. The burial evidence certainly supports this interpretation of role specialization by sex, since more women than men were buried beneath the house floors. All women, but few men, suffered from the distinctive deformation of the toes and other parts of the body associated with grinding grain, affirming that such a division of tasks was a regular part of daily life at Abu Hureyra.

Molleson's analysis of the skeletal remains indicates that the adoption of an agricultural mode of life and the associated cultural changes had a great impact on the people themselves. From an early age most of them worked sufficiently hard to affect their skeletal morphology. The tasks requiring the heaviest labor were nearly all connected with farming: preparation of the soil, tending and harvesting the crops, and processing them for storage and consumption. The other heavy work they had to undertake was house construction. It seems that from the beginning of Abu Hureyra 2, agriculture required sustained labor from the villagers throughout their lives, as it has in peasant communities across the world down to the present day.

The most striking evidence for the relentless demands of such work is Molleson's observation that so many women devoted several hours of their day to the grinding of grain, and that they began this as adolescents. The few men who also ground grain habitually may have lived in households without women, or have been unable to participate fully, perhaps through disability, in regular male work outside the home. We recall that some of the inhabitants of Abu Hureyra 1 spent a sufficiently long time grinding grain for their own feet to be deformed in a manner similar to those of the women of Abu Hureyra 2, so this practice was already under way in the late Epipalaeolithic at Abu Hureyra.

The hard work that everybody had to perform, and the pain the women endured, are fierce indications of the heavy price the inhabitants of Abu Hureyra paid for adopting an agricultural way of life. But they found time to care for their own, too. The woman crippled with a severe back injury who was buried in the phase 8 building in Trench B (73.2949) was unable to do much to obtain food through her own labor except grind grain, yet she survived well into adulthood. Apparently the community was prepared to support her throughout her adult life, but they did expect her to help prepare food to the extent that she was able to do so.

Craft activities left distinctive traces in several skeletons. Molleson (1994, p. 74) has observed that a few individuals had grooves in their front teeth. She believes that these people were basket makers who held a cane between their teeth while weaving. The traces of baskets and matting that we found in the soil confirm this striking observation from the skeletal remains themselves. Baskets and mats were probably ubiquitous artifacts in every household.

The evidence of the skeletons provides more vivid insights on aspects of daily life. The unusually well-developed chewing muscles of most of the villagers suggests that their diet included a high proportion of tough foods, one of which would have been dried gazelle meat. Among the other foods may have been coarse, dry bread, cracked wheat, and roasted grains—inferences supported by the evidence of heavy wear and chipping on teeth. The cereals were ground on stone querns and so became mixed with grit, or pounded in mortars in dusty conditions. The dusty environment and dirt around the village ensured that the other foods were also heavily contaminated with gritty particles. Despite the wear this caused, the inhabitants had little dental caries, a testimony to their relatively good state of health. The change in cooking techniques that followed the introduction of pottery later in 2B times lessened the heavy wear on people's teeth.

The diet of the villagers was apparently both well-balanced and sufficient. The main crops provided ample carbohydrates and plenty of vegetable protein. There were enough gazelle and caprines available most of the time to ensure a satisfactory intake of meat, and people probably also consumed dairy products. Doubtless, the diet was supplemented by leafy foods, tubers, and small game from the wild.

The skeletal evidence indicates that, like many people in Southwest Asia today, the villagers habitually assumed a squatting posture for many activities, and while at rest. This suggests that they had no seats or other furniture in their houses, artifacts for which there was little space in the tiny rooms.

There are indications that children were weaned relatively late, perhaps between three and four years of age or even older. This was about the same weaning age as among the hunting and gathering !Kung San, the beduin of Arabia (Lee 1979, p. 329; Dickson 1949, p. 506), and, as we have observed, some Syrian villagers today. This may be partly because many of the foods consumed at Abu Hureyra were tough to chew and digest.

Once people reached adulthood, they could live to an advanced age of at least 60–70 years, although some older individuals did suffer from degenerative diseases. Thus, potential life expectancy was about the same as for people of the region in recent times. There seems to have been an increase in the incidence of infectious disease over time that was probably related to the growth of the settlement during Periods 2A and 2B.

The villagers of Abu Hureyra 2 engaged in both medium- and long-distance trade on a greater scale than the inhabitants of Abu Hureyra 1. Such traffic would have brought them into contact with other contemporary groups in north Syria and farther afield. Yet the surveys that have been carried out suggest that there were not many other Neolithic 2 sites along the Middle Euphrates or elsewhere in north Syria (Moore 1981, figure 1; Sanlaville 1985). If the present distribution of sites is any indication of their density in prehistory, then contacts between the people of Abu Hureyra and other groups would have been few. This accords with the evidence for inbreeding found in the skeletons. It seems that the inhabitants of Abu Hureyra were always relatively isolated.

Social Organization and Beliefs

Our inferences concerning the nature of social and community organization are derived from the form of the settlement and the buildings within it, the economy, evidence for the activities of the villagers obtained from the artifacts, and burial customs. Families consisted of children, adults, and often older relations—that is, two or three generations. Occasionally, a household might include a member who was unable to provide fully for his or her own sustenance. The nature of the settlement and its economy implies that the family spent part of their time working for themselves and cultivating their own plots, but also participated in larger-scale economic activities organized by the community, such as gazelle drives. The burials indicate that the children had a recognized place in society, yet this was achieved only after several years of life. Children would have been able to contribute significantly to the production of food through weeding, herding animals, and other activities. Adolescents participated in food processing, as the evidence of toe deformation among young females shows. It was customary for adult women to be adorned with jewelry when they were buried, while the graves of some of the men contained a few flint tools—a clear affirmation of the different ways in which the villagers perceived the sexes.

Molleson has detected evidence for family descent in burials within and between trenches. Members of one family were buried in houses in two successive phases in Trench D, and of a second family in three successive phases in Trench E. Moreover, descendants of a third family that had lived in Trench D in 2A times were living in houses in Trench B in 2B, and in Trench E in 2C, a clear indication of the persistence of families over generations. This extraordinary evidence provides strong confirmation for our view that the houses were family dwellings. It also indicates that a family could lay claim to the space its house occupied in the village, and its descendants could build a new house on the same spot in which to live. In other words, family rights to property were firmly established in Abu Hureyra 2.

The similarity in the houses across the site and the lack of differentiation between the burials of each sex suggest that in material terms the villagers were of similar status. Notwithstanding, there is reason to believe that some individuals were skilled in making baskets, mats, plaster, in building, and in fashioning fine stone objects, and so were at least part-time specialists. Thus, Abu Hureyra 2 seems to have been an egalitarian community, yet some of its members were distinguished by their special skills.

The village was so large that authority to take decisions affecting the whole community had to be vested in an individual or small group. The size of the community alone would have required that such political arrangements be organized on a relatively formal basis. Such a group, acting with community consent, would have dealt with such matters as settling disputes between the villagers, mediating access to resources of importance to all, and organizing collective activities. It was the community leaders who probably arranged the distribution of land of varying quality within the territory of the village, and who controlled the use of surface water. They, too, might have organized the gazelle and onager hunts.

Much of what we have learned of the beliefs of the villagers we have deduced from their burials. With the exception of the unusual building in Trench B phase 8, we found no structures that need have been anything other than houses. Almost all the artifacts, a few clay and stone figurines excepted, seem to have had a mainly utilitarian purpose. Thus, there is little in the evidence we recovered to suggest that the villagers had a system of beliefs that required the construction of special buildings or the manufacture of artifacts with a mainly symbolic function, although we must always bear in mind how little of the mound we were able to excavate.

There are a few hints in the record of an interest in the natural world, and beliefs about it. Much of the meat eaten in Abu Hureyra 2A was obtained from hunting gazelle, an activity that still played a role in the life of the settlement long after the animals ceased to be an important part of the diet. Thus, both hunting and the gazelle probably had a symbolic, as well as practical, importance for the inhabitants throughout the existence of Abu Hureyra 2. This is reflected in the exquisite head of a female Persian gazelle made from a granite pebble that we recovered from Trench B (figure 14.6). The head is a work of art of high quality with a distinctly stylized appearance, and is carved with great skill. It had been broken off the sculpture of the animal in antiquity. The head was found in a phase that postdated the switch from gazelle to caprines. The

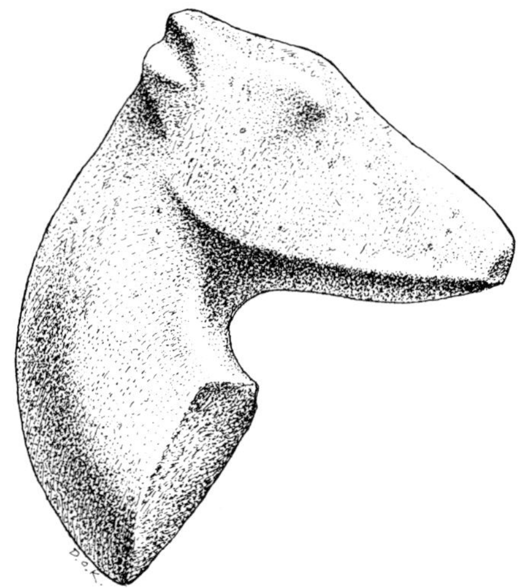

Figure 14.6 Head of a female Persian gazelle (*Gazella subgutturosa*), 73.359, from Trench B, phase 10, level 99. The head is worked on a granite pebble, probably from the Euphrates. It is very small (3.7 × 3.7 cm) and carved with great delicacy.

sculpture could have derived from an earlier context, but if not, we may reasonably infer that the gazelle remained of compelling symbolic interest to the inhabitants long after it ceased to be essential to their diet. One enigmatic find may also attest to the symbolic importance of wild animals to the people of Abu Hureyra 2—the skull of an aurochs deliberately buried upright in a pit in Trench D, phase 4 (figure 8.34).

The burials provide eloquent testimony of the villagers' beliefs about society and the place of the individual in it, and relations between the living and the dead. Ancestor worship seems to have been an important part of the ideology. Thus, the system of beliefs is likely to have been conservative in nature, holding the cohesion of the community and its perpetuation as important aims. The practice of delayed burial and the elaborate and lengthy procedures that were followed in carrying it out suggest that there was a belief in souls and their translation to an afterlife. The special attention given to skulls implies that the living hoped to derive benefit from contact with the dead, and reinforces our sense of the conservative philosophy of the villagers, in keeping with their peasant way of life. It is significant that so many people were buried under the floors of their houses, since it suggests that the ties to the household were very strong, and maintained over several generations.

In Period 2C the emphasis on ancestor reverence and collective burial rites diminished. This may have marked a decrease of communal food production, and an increase in the importance of farming by individual households.

The End of Abu Hureyra 2

Why, after two and a half millennia of sustained occupation, did the inhabitants of Abu Hureyra 2 leave? It is possible that problems developed with their water supply or that they suffered an outbreak of infectious disease, but we think it unlikely that such events, if they occurred, would have led to the permanent abandonment of the village. The erosion of the surface levels of the site makes it impossible to offer a full explanation, but there were changes taking place in the ecology of Abu Hureyra that allow us to propose a general hypothesis. Abu Hureyra itself had grown so large during Period 2B that its people were having a considerable impact on the landscape. Cultivation and grazing were causing degradation of the steppe vegetation, and may have led to loss of soil fertility. This was happening during a period when the temperature was continuing to rise and the interior of Syria was becoming more arid. This combination would have caused increasing difficulties for the inhabitants, making it harder for them to sustain their farming way of life. The indications are that some of them left during Period 2C, and the rest soon after. The difficulties that the population of Abu Hureyra experienced affected other communities over a wide area, as discussed in chapter 15.

The population of Abu Hureyra apparently left the area, since no other large settlement came into existence nearby to replace it. A village was founded in Halaf times at Kreyn, 4 km downstream, but this was small and short-lived. Thereafter, the region was abandoned until the Bronze Age, when the construction of massive canals made it possible for farmers to reoccupy this semiarid segment of the Euphrates Valley.

ABU HUREYRA 3

Abu Hureyra was never extensively occupied again. It was visited occasionally in later prehistory, during the Ubaid period, and perhaps at other times. People used the site in the Byzantine period when some graves were dug at the north end, and the mound again served as a cemetery in the Islamic period down to a century or two ago. Then, in the twentieth century AD, the prominent location of the site on the valley road encouraged Ottoman and, later, French officials to establish police posts on the site. These episodes of activity constitute Period 3.

AN INTEGRATED INTERPRETATION

Our research has shown that the changes in climate and environment, in the nature of the village and the number of its inhabitants, in the artifacts, in the economy, in social organization, and even, we believe, in ideology, were all connected. Change in one element led to change in the others, so it is only by considering them together that we can understand how Abu Hureyra developed, and how the transition from foraging to farming happened there.

The Late Glacial improvement in climate and expansion of woodland vegetation, combined with the proximity of Abu Hureyra to the path of the gazelle migration, made the site a most attractive location for the group of hunters and gatherers who settled there eleven and a half thousand years ago. They took full advantage of the resources of the place, and so were able to live there year-round. In consequence, their numbers grew and their settlement took on the attributes of a village. That, in turn, helped them to extract higher returns from their hunting and gathering through collective organization.

The abrupt change to the cooler, drier conditions of the Younger Dryas c. 11,000 BP, and their own increasing numbers, obliged the inhabitants to modify their way of life. They adopted agriculture, taking up the cultivation of domestic rye and probably other cereals and legumes. They were thus among the first people anywhere to develop a farming economy, so initiating a revolution with the most profound consequences for human society. They continued to gather plants but, because of vegetation change, shifted their attention to species that had been of less interest in the past. Over time, the importance of gathering diminished as the villagers obtained more food from their crops.

Meanwhile, their own population growth increased hunting pressures. This mode of life proved so successful that it enabled the people of Abu Hureyra 1 to stay there for a millennium and a half.

The return of a warmer, moister climate at the beginning of the Holocene provided the ecological conditions for continuation of settled life at Abu Hureyra. The economy of the village during the Intermediate Period was based on agriculture, with the cultivation of a wider range of cereals and legumes, hunting, and some plant gathering. The spread of woodland-steppe and moist steppe set the stage for an expansion of settlement at Abu Hureyra late in the tenth millennium BP.

The economy of the village of Abu Hureyra 2 was based on the cultivation of crops, herding of domestic sheep and goats, and continued hunting of gazelle, with some gathering of wild plants. This combination of farming and foraging with sedentary life stimulated the growth of the village to an unprecedented size. The culture of the inhabitants, though exhibiting some elements of continuity with the past, was largely new. So was the social organization of the village and its ideology, even if they, too, had roots in Abu Hureyra 1.

The new way of life was extraordinarily productive. Together with a reorganization of the seasonal cycle that provided some extended periods of leisure time, it led to a flowering of crafts and increased exchange of exotic goods. The villagers developed a rich ideology, illuminated most vividly in their burial customs. Yet farming also imposed heavy costs on the people themselves. They had to work much harder than before to produce their food, and women, in particular, spent hours each day grinding grain to eat. Their diet, though nutritious, caused severe dental wear. Their dependence on agriculture, its benefits notwithstanding, bound them to a life of toil.

The basic social unit in the village was the family. Families had rights to property, notably their houses, and those rights passed from one generation to the next through inheritance. Our evidence has enabled us to reconstruct the lives of the villagers from birth to death, and to establish the outlines of their system of beliefs. Their ideology seems to have governed the main events of the life cycle, and to have extended into the world beyond. Reverence for ancestors provided support for their claims to ownership of property within the village.

The increase in the population of Abu Hureyra, and elsewhere in the Levant, was a delayed consequence of the development of farming. It led to more intense predation of the gazelle and, consequently, a sharp drop in their numbers. This event necessitated a rapid adjustment of the economy. The people of Abu Hureyra decided to increase the size of their flocks and the productivity of their crops. This response had a deleterious impact on the vegetation around the village. The sudden switch to full mixed farming, with the addition of cattle and pigs as domesticates, stimulated further growth of the settlement until it reached its maximum extent. Continued hunting of modest numbers of gazelle preserved one traditional element of the economy that was to endure until the end.

The villagers had to work as hard as ever to sustain their way of life, but they found a way to diminish the wear on their teeth by cooking their food in pots. In Period 2C the configuration of the village altered, and there were some changes in burial practices and ideology. These were linked to other factors, for instance, the need to create space for more domestic animals within the settlement, and the increased importance of the household in food production.

During Abu Hureyra 2C times the village began to decrease in size—the beginning of a trend that led to its abandonment. The causes were, in part, a deterioration in the environment brought about by grazing and cultivation pressures, themselves exacerbated by the large population of the village. The environs of the site were always semi-arid and thus vulnerable to vegetation and soil damage. A climatic shift to warmer, drier conditions further undermined the way of life of the villagers.

THE IMPORT OF THE RECORD

The material remains of the successive villages at Abu Hureyra were well stratified and their preservation was relatively good. This has enabled us to reconstruct the history of the settlement from the trenches we dug across the mound. Our systematic recovery of large quantities of animal bones and plant remains, as well as artifacts, has provided the evidence for us to determine the sequence of cultural and economic developments at Abu Hureyra, and to discern the relationships between them. We have been able to form a series of hypotheses about the changes that took place there, and then to test them against the ample record of artifacts and organic material. From the stratification and detailed radiometric chronology we have built up an unusually tight sequence of occupation. Finally, we have combined the different sources of information about the site and its inhabitants to construct an integrated interpretation of the development of Abu Hureyra. The location of the site was so special that we have often interpreted the record in strictly local terms, yet to achieve fuller understanding we have had to take the wider Levantine context into account. This is because, even if the people of Abu Hureyra were essentially self-sufficient, they were always part of regional economic and cultural systems.

We have already stated many of the more important observations to be made about life at Abu Hureyra over 4,500 years, but there are other general lessons to be derived from the record as a whole. It is our considered view that sedentary life based on hunting and gathering preceded the adoption of agriculture at Abu Hureyra, though only by a few centuries. The main changes in the way of life of the people of Abu Hureyra took place step by step. First, they were hunters and gatherers. Then, later in Abu Hureyra 1, they adopted agriculture while continuing to forage and hunt gazelle. By Abu Hureyra 2 times, they were shepherds as well as farmers, but still obtained much of their meat from the gazelle herds. Large-scale caprine herding began, not when domesticated sheep and goats were first brought to the village, but much later after the supply of gazelle diminished. These changes often took place with extraordinary rapidity, followed by periods of consolidation. This was the case with the switch from gazelle to caprines, and the final expansion of the village in Period 2B. Despite their apparently conservative ideology, the people of Abu Hureyra were capable of making swift adjustments to their way of life in order to cope with change.

We can see now that it was the hunter-gatherer inhabitants of Abu Hureyra 1 who first adopted agriculture. Their successors went on to develop a mixed farming way of life that has endured to the present and, in one variant or another, has spread across the world. Abu Hureyra is the only site in Western Asia where it has been possible to trace a sequence of development from the initial stages of farming by a community of hunter-gatherers to a fully agricultural way of life. We note that cultivation of domestic grains began a full thousand years earlier at Abu Hureyra than has so far been demonstrated at any other site in Western Asia.

It should be clear by now that economic and cultural adjustments at Abu Hureyra came about through the interaction of a series of factors. The length of the occupation sequence, and the fact that it spanned the Pleistocene-Holocene transition, have helped us to see how important the impact of environmental change was. Climatic change was largely responsible for the shift from foraging to agriculture at the beginning of Abu Hureyra 1B, and environmental deterioration, partly caused by the inhabitants themselves, was an important influence on the decision to abandon the village at the end of Abu Hureyra 2C.

The diet of the hunters and gatherers of Abu Hureyra 1A was apparently well balanced and adequate for their needs. That remained the case following the adoption of farming in Periods 1B and 1C. Although the range of plants eaten was reduced later in Abu Hureyra 2, the quantity of food consumed and its variety nevertheless remained satisfactory until near the end. Thus, the advent of agriculture and herding at Abu Hureyra did not immediately result in poorer nutrition. Our understanding of what life was like for the hunter-gatherers of Abu Hureyra 1A provides a plausible precursor for the development of agricultural village life in 1B and 1C, and helps us to understand how and why such people adopted farming. It is most unlikely, however, that they foresaw some of the other implications of their decision to take up the new way of life. They could hardly have expected it to bind them so tightly to such a strenuous existence. Nor could they have foreseen that by Abu Hureyra 2B, if not before, their choice had become effectively irreversible.

15 Abu Hureyra and the Beginning of Agriculture

The aim of our final chapter is to determine the place of Abu Hureyra in the Levant and the rest of Southwest Asia during the late Epipalaeolithic and early Neolithic, to understand its role in the transition from hunting and gathering to farming and herding. The setting of the site, its pattern of growth, and many aspects of the way of life of its inhabitants were unique. This makes it difficult to generalize from the archaeological record at Abu Hureyra about contemporary prehistoric life in the Levant as a whole. The problem is a universal one, since the major sites from which we derive most of our insights about late hunter-gatherer and early farming societies—Ain Mallaha, Jericho, and Çatal Hüyük, for example—each had unique characteristics. Yet elements of the culture and economy of the successive settlements at Abu Hureyra were shared with wider regional cultures. They need to be distinguished so that we may discern the more important patterns of change of which Abu Hureyra was a part.

THE WORLD OF ABU HUREYRA 1

Abu Hureyra 1 was a new kind of settlement, a permanently inhabited village with perhaps several hundred occupants. It was one of several that appeared for the first time in the Levant during Epipalaeolithic 2. Abu Hureyra 1 belongs firmly within the late Epipalaeolithic tradition in the Levant because it shared many cultural elements with contemporary sites, stretching south from the Middle Euphrates to Transjordan and Sinai. That established, it is also clear that there were significant differences between the material remains of Abu Hureyra 1 and those of other late Epipalaeolithic sites in the Natufian heartland (for example, Mugharet el Wad, Ain Mallaha, and Wadi Hammeh 27) and in Transjordan (Azraq 18, Beidha, and Wadi Judayid). The pit dwellings of Abu Hureyra 1A, the preference for flint flakes as blanks for tools, variations in chipped stone typology, and the predominance of grinding dishes and rubbing stones, all distinguish the site from others to the south. It seems that there were several distinct cultural regions within the Levant during the late Epipalaeolithic: the Middle Euphrates; Transjordan and southern Syria; and the Natufian heartland in Palestine, extending north into the Beqa'a Valley.

There was also significant cultural variation between the few known late Epipalaeolithic sites along the Middle Euphrates. The three main ones, Abu Hureyra 1, Dibsi Faraj East, and Mureybit IA, were located in similar positions in the river valley and shared some cultural characteristics, yet there were marked differences between the two excavated sites, Abu Hureyra and Mureybit, in structures, chipped stone assemblages, and other stone tools. At Abu Hureyra, of course, we have evidence for the inception of agriculture in Periods 1B and 1C, but as yet, there is uncertainty over when the inhabitants of Mureybit adopted farming. Mureybit was situated 36 km farther upriver in a slightly moister zone and in a different physical setting, which accounts in part for these differences, but it also seems that the Euphrates acted as a barrier to intercourse between the two sites.

It is difficult to compare the economy of Abu Hureyra 1 with other contemporary excavated sites because none has yielded the quantity of plant and animal remains that we recovered. Thus, it is not possible to evaluate in detail the various ways in which late Epipalaeolithic peoples in the Levant obtained their food. Abu Hureyra is, for the moment, the only site in Western Asia for which there is clear evidence for the adoption of agriculture in the late Epipalaeolithic, c. 11,000 BP. While we would expect that similar evidence would eventually be recovered from at least a few other late Epipalaeolithic sites, at present the earliest evidence for farming elsewhere in the region dates from the beginning of the Neolithic, a thousand years later. On present evidence, therefore, we conclude that most late Epipaleolithic people in Western Asia were hunters and gatherers.

The inhabitants of most excavated Epipalaeolithic sites practiced a selective form of hunting, killing large quantities of the main species of mammals that lived in the vicinity of their sites. The most common game was usually one of the three subspecies of gazelle. At sites in Palestine such as Mugharet el Wad, Hayonim, and Nahal Oren, the proportion of gazelle bones to those of other species was often more than 80% (Garrod and Bate 1937, p. 141, figure 1; Bar-Yosef and Tchernov 1966, p. 129; Noy, Legge, and Higgs 1973, p. 90), and at Hatula over 90% (Davis 1985, p. 79). Bones of cattle, pigs, deer, and a very few caprines have also been found at these sites. The proportion of gazelles was lower at Rosh Horesha in the Negev (c. 60%), where nearly 40% of the bones came from wild goats (Butler et al. 1977, table 13–1). Wild goats were the main quarry of the inhabitants of Beidha during this period (Hecker 1989, table 30). Evidently goats were plentiful in the broken country around both sites. Gazelle, equids, and cattle were killed in about equal amounts at Azraq 18 in Transjordan, suggesting that the inhabitants found their game on the steppe and in the dense vegetation around the Azraq pools (Garrard et al. 1988, p. 331). The occupants of these and other sites killed a range of small mammals, carnivores, and birds, although these creatures seem to have contributed little additional food to the meat diet.

Cope (1991, p. 346) has found that the inhabitants of Hayonim and several other Palestinian sites killed off more male than female gazelles. Bouchud (1987, pp. 61, 97) has identified a similar pattern at Ain Mallaha, where the inhabitants killed mature, usually male, animals aged over two years in preference to younger ones. Thus, the evidence indicates that one or two species, usually gazelle, were hunted almost exclusively, and that sometimes animals of a particular sex were specially selected; in other words, people were exercising a degree of control over the herds of these animals. Legge has found evidence for seasonal mass slaughter of onager at Mureybit, but so far this method of killing has not been recognized at the few other excavated steppic sites. The existence of Epipalaeolithic sites in the steppe, at Azraq and elsewhere in Transjordan, for example (Garrard et al. 1988; Betts 1988), implies that their inhabitants pursued a distinct steppic variant of the hunting and gathering economy. The gazelle herds would have been quite widely spread in this region, their presumed winter feeding grounds. This may account for the extensive spread of kites (Helms and Betts 1987) and the dispersed nature of Epipalaeolithic sites. This is in contrast with the concentration of kites near Taibe, at the entrance to the pass leading northward to El Kum and the Euphrates, revealed in Poidebard's air photographs (see chapter 13). The annual massing of the gazelle herds at this constriction would have afforded an excellent opportunity to kill large quantities of the animals in several hunting episodes.

Archaeologists and archaeobotanists have recovered plant remains from a few late Epipalaeolithic sites. Van Zeist and Bakker-Heeres (1984, table 2) have identified quite a wide range of legumes, cereals, and other wild plants from phase I at Mureybit. Among the cereals were grains of wild barley, a species absent from Abu Hureyra. The wild plants were collected from all three zones within reach of the site—the Euphrates floodplain, steppe, and park-woodland. Mureybit is the one other known site at which agriculture may have begun during the late Epipalaeolithic, as described in chapter 12. A few fragments of lentils, other legumes, barley, grasses, lilies, and almond shells have also been recovered from the Natufian sites of Wadi Hammeh 27, Nahal Oren, and Hayonim (Edwards et al. 1988, p. 552; Noy, Legge, and Higgs 1973, table 6; Hopf and Bar-Yosef 1987). This slight evidence suggests that the inhabitants of Epipalaeolithic 2 sites in the steppe and forest fringe zones collected a range of plants for food and other purposes.

The coastline of the Levant would have lain several kilometers farther west during Epipalaeolithic 2 times than today, which explains why no sites have been found whose inhabitants depended on marine resources for subsistence. At the few inland riverine sites, especially Abu Hureyra and Mureybit, people ate relatively few fish, shellfish, and waterfowl. Only at Ain Mallaha beside Lake Huleh did fish and wildfowl contribute significantly to the diet (Pichon 1987, p. 144; Desse 1987, p. 156).

The contrast between the numerous animal bones but few plant remains recovered from most excavated Epipalaeolithic 2 sites makes comparison between these two elements in the economy difficult. It is clear that Epipalaeolithic 2 people were gatherers as well as hunters, and they seem to have been well nourished (Smith, Bar-Yosef, and Sillen 1984, p. 129). Furthermore, there are indications that humans took numerous species of animals as far back as the early Upper Pleistocene (Edwards 1989a, figure 1). Hunter-gatherers certainly used a diverse range of plant species in earlier times, as Hillman (1989) found at the late Palaeolithic site of Wadi Kubbaniya in Egypt. An Epipalaeolithic 1 site of Kebaran affinities on the shores of the Sea of Galilee, Ohalo II, has also yielded remains of a variety of edible plants (Kislev, Nadel, and Carmi 1992). We agree with Edwards (1989a, p. 225), therefore, that Flannery's (1969) "broad spectrum revolution" of c. 20,000 BP (p. 77) may not have occurred, because people had in fact been exploiting a considerable variety of animals and plants since at least the Middle Palaeolithic.

On the other hand, the foraging patterns of these other Epipalaeolithic 2 groups seem to have been more intensive, and often more closely focused, than anything seen earlier (Moore 1982b, p. 227). Their hunting was highly specialized and concentrated on a very few species of ungulates. Consequently, several other potentially useful sources of meat, notably pigs and fish, were hardly exploited. The dog alone was kept as a domestic animal on Epipalaeolithic 2 sites, on the evidence from Mugharet el Wad, Ain Mallaha (Garrod and Bate 1937, p. 153; Valla 1975–1977), and, of course, Abu Hureyra itself, perhaps because of its social qualities and usefulness in the hunt.

It is also apparent from the location of sites, artifacts, and organic remains that the pattern of hunting and gathering varied from one locality to another, depending on the terrain and the animals and plants available. There seems to have been a significant contrast between the foraging way of life of people in the steppe and woodland zones. In the woodland zone, especially, there were some differences in adaptation between the highlands and lowlands. The few lacustrine and riverine sites also had special characteristics. A number of sites, like Abu Hureyra itself, were situated adjacent to two environmental zones that offered abundant, diverse, and often complementary, wild resources. Yet the evidence for exchange of marine shells and other items indicates that the inhabitants of many sites were participating in larger economic systems. This was certainly the case at Abu Hureyra, since the reliance of its inhabitants on gazelle placed them in an indirect relationship with the people of El Kum, and of other sites farther south, that may have been exploiting the same resource along the migration route.

Sedentism

About 100 Epipalaeolithic 2 sites have been found in the Levant, in every environmental zone from the Mediterranean coast eastward to the edge of the desert (figure 15.1). Most of them were situated at relatively low elevations along the present coastal plain, in valleys emerging from the hills, or beside springs and ancient lakes. Some, however, were found at higher elevations, in the hill country of Judea, for example, or the Anti-Lebanon Mountains. Most of them were very small, less than 500 m^2 in area, and thus about the same size as many Epipalaeolithic 1 sites. A dozen or so were substantially larger than this, covering up to 2,000 m^2 or occasionally even more. Seven of these (Abu Hureyra, Ain Mallaha, Hayonim, Mugharet el Wad, Shukbah, Wadi Hammeh 27, and Jericho) yielded a variety of artifacts, often had traces of structures, and also relatively deep occupation deposits, indicating that they were used over an extended period of time of, perhaps, several centuries or more. A few very large Epipalaeolithic 1 or Kebaran sites have recently been identified in Transjordan (Garrard et al. 1988, p. 320; Muheisen 1988) that indicate some people were inhabiting substantial sites several thousand years earlier. Most of the larger Epipalaeolithic 2 sites were in the Natufian heartland of northern Palestine, and discussions have usually focused on them because they were one of the most distinctive features of the period, yet we must remember that they actually represent just 7% of the total number known.

It is often claimed, but rarely demonstrated, that the inhabitants of the larger Epipalaeolithic 2 sites were sedentary (J. Cauvin 1978, p. 20; Bar-Yosef and Belfer-Cohen 1989, p. 490; Henry 1989, p. 38). The usual assumption is that because these sites were relatively substantial, and contained a variety of artifacts and structures, they were inhabited year-round. Such evidence can never

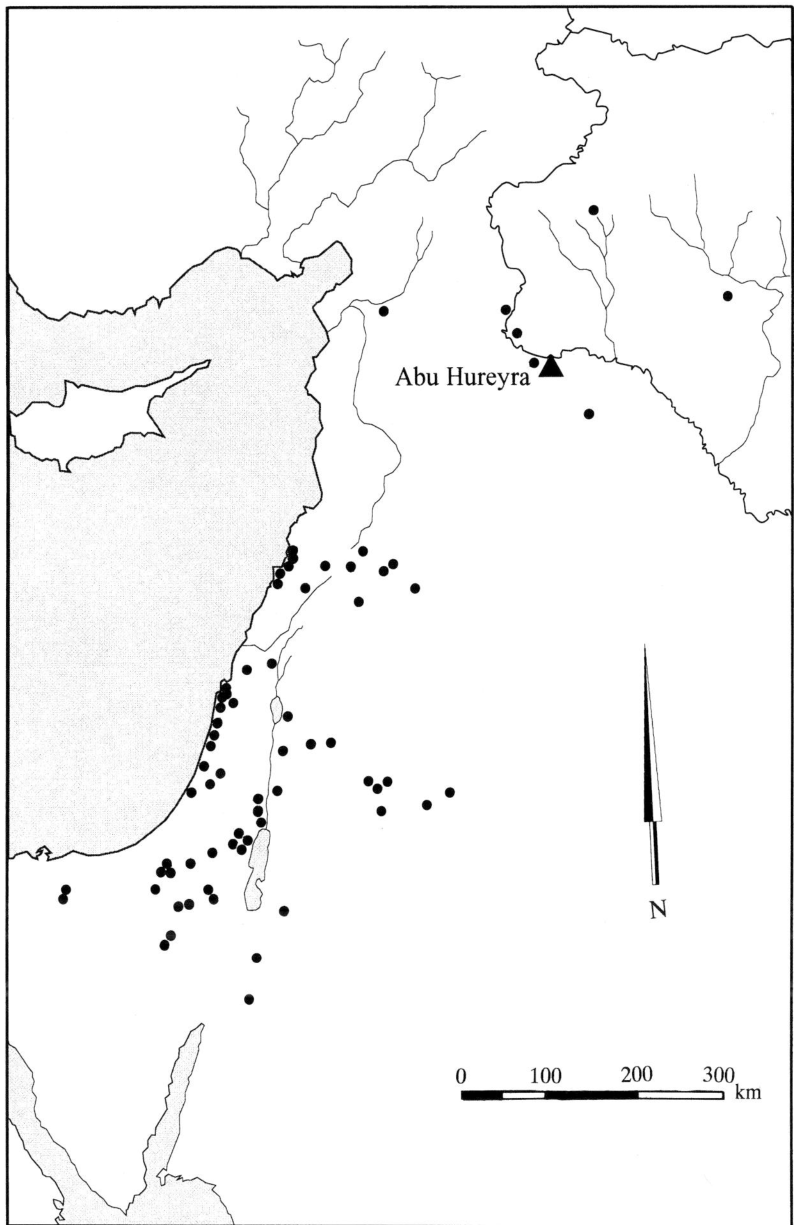

Figure 15.1 Distribution of Epipalaeolithic 2 sites in the Levant.

be more than circumstantial and is open to other interpretations (Edwards 1989b). Pichon's (1991, p. 379) recent analysis of bird bones to determine their seasons of availability suggests that Hayonim and Ain Mallaha were occupied for extended periods during the year, but the number of sites for which this may be claimed is still very small. Abu Hureyra is the only site in Southwest Asia at which a thorough study of the seasonal occurrence of both plants and animals has been made to determine whether its inhabitants were sedentary or not. Our conclusion that the settlement was occupied year-round holds for Abu Hureyra alone, and cannot readily be applied to other large Epipalaeolithic 2 sites, many of which were in the forest and woodland zones.

The few substantial and long-lived Epipalaeolithic 2 settlements were all in areas that were particularly favorable for human settlement: on the southern flanks of Mt. Carmel, in valleys on the western side of Galilee and Judea, beside lakes and springs in the Jordan Valley, and on the Middle Euphrates. These places apparently afforded a sufficient abundance of wild plants and animals to permit long-term residence. More people seem to have inhabited these sites than the smaller camps, and their numbers may have increased over time simply because they were less mobile. That would have intensified their need for wild foods and so may have led to excess pressure on the plants and animals available in the vicinity of their sites. Thus, a paradox may have been created in which the greatest pressure on resources was exerted by the inhabitants of sites in the most favorable locations.

Outside these core areas, in southern Palestine, the Negev and northern Sinai, in Transjordan, along the coast of Lebanon, in the Anti-Lebanon Mountains, and in central Syria, sites were much smaller and occupied for probably no more than a few weeks at a time. Thus, most people were still mobile hunters and gatherers who moved several times in the course of a year, probably in a regular pattern determined by the seasonal availability of wild foods. The nature of these patterns is still unknown. Where there were marked local differences in altitude, people may have moved up and down the hill slopes; in the more open landscapes of Transjordan and central Syria, they may have traveled longer distances. In the seasons when wild plants and animals were readily available they may have gathered in larger numbers, then broken up into smaller groups and dispersed across the landscape during the leaner seasons (Byrd 1989, p. 187). Such patterns of aggregation and dispersal are common among hunters and gatherers known to us ethnographically (Netting 1986, p. 14).

The number of known Epipalaeolithic 2 sites is about the same as for Epipalaeolithic 1, yet the period was much shorter. That alone would suggest that the total population of the Levant was higher in Epipalaeolithic 2 than in Epipalaeolithic 1, a trend that Moore (1983, p. 94) has linked to the improvement in the environment that occurred during the Late Glacial. There are indications that the population began to increase toward the end of Epipalaeolithic 1 during the Geometric Kebaran period (Bar-Yosef 1981, p. 396). Thus, in Epipalaeolithic 2 people were living closer together than in earlier times. That would have reduced the extent of their annual foraging territories, so even the mobile Epipalaeolithic 2 groups may have experienced some restrictions on their patterns of movement.

Those pressures would have been exacerbated by the climatic changes that took place during the Younger Dryas. Occupation at the larger villages in the Natufian heartland was disrupted in the later centuries of Epipalaeolithic 2, coinciding with the reversion to cooler, drier conditions. In the eleventh millennium BP there was a return to a more mobile pattern of life throughout the Levant (Moore and Hillman 1992, p. 491). During the next period, there was a noticeable reduction in the area inhabited—localities previously occupied far out in the steppe, around El Kum and northeast of Azraq, for example, were abandoned. This strengthens our argument that increasing aridity played a role in the retraction of settlement, and thus in the economic changes that were taking place.

Well to the northeast, on a tributary of the Tigris in southeast Asia Minor, during the later eleventh millennium BP the village of Hallan Çemi was inhabited by a sedentary population of hunters and gatherers (Rosenberg 1994, p. 131). Hallan Çemi was situated in a zone with higher rainfall and seems to have flourished throughout this period. Yet it, too, was abandoned c. 10,000 BP. Only at Abu Hureyra did occupation continue, but there it was the adoption of agriculture that enabled the inhabitants to sustain settled village life. Elsewhere in Southwest Asia, the environmental fluctuations and the disruption in settlement combined with the new, higher densities of population increased the stresses on prevailing modes of foraging. Together, these factors would have provided powerful incentives for people to take up farming over a wide area.

THE TRANSITION FROM EPIPALAEOLITHIC TO NEOLITHIC

The cultural transition from Epipalaeolithic to Neolithic throughout the Levant was abrupt. It took place swiftly, though at slightly different times from one area to another, and was accompanied by a reordering of the pattern of settlement (Moore 1983, p. 97). Most Epipalaeolithic 2 sites were abandoned. At the few sites like Jericho and Nahal Oren with both Epipalaeolithic 2 and early Neolithic deposits, occupation was disrupted and then resumed in other parts of the settlement. At Abu Hureyra, there was an adjustment in settlement with the inception of the Intermediate Period. At Mureybit, habitation apparently continued uninterrupted from Epipalaeolithic 2 into the Neolithic (J. Cauvin 1977, p. 26). The change in artifacts seems to have been almost as sharp. Although indications of cultural continuity have been found at sites such as Abu Hureyra, Jericho, and Mureybit (Moore 1982a, p. 4), the inhabitants of these and other early Neolithic sites soon developed distinctive buildings and flint assemblages, and new kinds of other artifacts. Relatively few Neolithic sites have been found dating to the earlier tenth millennium BP, but several of them were villages that were much bigger than sites of the preceding Epipalaeolithic 2 period.

Nearly all early Neolithic sites were established in locations that were suitable for farming, and the remains of domesticated plants have been recovered from three of them in addition to Abu Hureyra: Jericho, Tell Aswad, and Mureybit (Hopf 1983, p. 607; van Zeist and Bakker-Heeres 1979, p. 164; van Zeist and Bakker-Heeres 1984, p. 186). It appears, therefore, that from its beginnings in the late Epipalaeolithic, agriculture spread widely in the early Neolithic. Furthermore, though not yet established rigorously at any site other than Abu Hureyra, it is likely that these villages were occupied year-round. Thus, many of the earliest Neolithic settlements throughout the Levant were permanently inhabited villages of farmers.

A similar cultural and economic transition was taking place to the northeast, in southern Asia Minor and northern Mesopotamia, that is in the central portion of the Fertile Crescent. The Neolithic village of Çayönü, on a tributary of the upper Tigris, was inhabited by people who developed an original architectural tradition of buildings with stone foundations. In the early stages of settlement, from about 9,300 to 8,700 BP, they were cultivating wheat and pulses but still hunting a variety of wild animals (van Zeist 1972; Lawrence 1982). An even earlier stage of the Neolithic is represented at Qermez Dere, a small village in the foothills of the Jebel Sinjar, west of Mosul (Watkins 1995). The flint industry at Qermez Dere had similarities with the Neolithic 1 stage in the Levant. The inhabitants apparently subsisted on hunting and gathering, but this conclusion remains provisional pending further study. The village of Nemrik 9, on the Tigris north of Mosul, was inhabited from about 10,000 to the mid ninth millennium BP. Its inhabitants were gazelle hunters, but soon after the foundation of the settlement they started to keep a few domesticated sheep and goats (Lasota-Moskalewska 1994, p. 26). This evidence for early caprine domestication is similar to Legge and Rowley-Conwy's findings at Abu Hureyra. Lasota-Moskalewska claims that by 9,000 BP the people of Nemrik were also raising domesticated cattle and pigs.

The transition from Epipalaeolithic to Neolithic c. 10,000 BP marked the spread of a way of life based on permanent settlement in larger villages supported by agriculture. The near-simultaneous appearance of domesticated plants on several early Neolithic sites indicates that the spread of farming was rapid, and thus that this new form of plant exploitation answered a pressing need felt by groups not only throughout the Levant, but across a broad swathe of Southwest Asia.

The Question of Domestication

Research on the beginning of farming and herding in Southwest Asia has concentrated on defining the locations and dates of plant and animal domestication (Renfrew 1973, p. 2; Bökönyi 1976). Our research has shown that another question was quite as important, namely, when and in what circumstances did people decide to adopt agriculture and herding as major sources of food once the plants and animals had been domesticated. It is clear that these two questions should be distinguished, for widespread adoption of farming and herding did not necessarily follow domestication immediately. A third question concerns the possible connection between the domestication of plants and animals. Were plants and animals domesticated in separate localities and at different times, or did the two processes take place together? The issue is important because it bears on the question of how the two systems, with their different requirements, were combined.

The distributions of the wild ancestors of the cereals, legumes, and caprines in the late Pleistocene are still not known precisely. This makes it difficult to determine just where they may have been domesticated. Today, wild rye is found across Asia Minor eastward to Transcaspia. Wild emmer, einkorn, and barley occur in clearly defined zones within the hill country around the fringe of the Fertile Crescent (Zohary and Hopf 1993, maps 1, 3, 5); the distribution of wild einkorn extends northward into Anatolia and that of barley eastward to Afghanistan. The core area of distribution of peas and lentils is broadly similar, with an extension northward into Anatolia in both cases (Ladizinsky 1989), although wild chickpea occurs in a more restricted zone in southeast Asia Minor. The distribution of these wild plants 11,000 years ago would have been significantly different, yet the earliest finds of domesticated cereals and pulses have all been made on sites in the hills and on the steppic plains around the Fertile Crescent. The dates for the earliest domesticated plants are higher in the west than in the east, beginning with the date of c. 11,140 BP for rye at Abu Hureyra with, perhaps, several other cereals and pulses. At Abu Hureyra grains of bread wheat, other free-threshing wheats, barley, and lentils have been found in levels dated c. 9,700 BP. Seeds of domesticated emmer, einkorn, barley, lentils, and chickpeas have been recovered from levels at Jericho and Tell Aswad dating to c. 10,000 BP or shortly after (Hopf 1983; van Zeist and Bakker-Heeres 1979). The inhabitants of Cafer Hüyük and Çayönü in Asia Minor were apparently growing emmer, einkorn, lentils, peas, and vetches in the second half of the tenth millennium (de Moulins 1994, p. 173; van Zeist 1972). The domesticated barley in level E at Ganj Dareh may also date from late in the tenth millennium BP (van Zeist et al. 1984, p. 219). This suggests that the cereals and legumes were domesticated beginning about 11,000 BP, in a zone stretching from the central Levant northeastward to the Anti-Taurus, and were then adopted as crops in villages over much of Southwest Asia. Why did groups over such a wide area adopt farming once the domesticated plants became available? The answer must be that agriculture offered an appropriate solution to a compelling need. We suggest that it provided a means of supporting the relatively numerous groups of people who could no longer be sustained by late Epipalaeolithic patterns of hunting and gathering following the disruptions in climate and vegetation caused by the Younger Dryas episode. Agriculture also provided the only viable, long-term support for sedentary village life.

We now know that during the late Pleistocene and early Holocene the wild ancestors of domestic sheep and goats inhabited a much larger area than they do today, from Asia Minor eastward to Afghanistan, and south to the Arabian peninsula. It is likely, therefore, that sheep and goats were domesticated over a wide area of western Asia, on perhaps several occasions. How does the timing of ovicaprine domestication compare with that for the cereals and legumes? We have stated that bones of domesticated sheep and goats were present in the early levels of Abu Hureyra 2A. Our evidence suggests, therefore, that these animals were domesticated well after rye, the other cereals, and legumes. If the people of Abu Hureyra 2A had domestic sheep and goats, then the inhabitants of other early Neolithic sites in the Levant were probably raising them as well, even though the fauna on those sites has hitherto been interpreted as entirely wild. Certainly, it now seems that domestic caprines were being kept by the inhabitants of early Neolithic sites farther east, among them Nemrik 9, Ganj Dareh, and other sites in the Zagros (Hesse 1982, pp. 412–413).

One of the most important deductions we have made from the Abu Hureyra evidence is that the adoption of domesticated plants and animals as major sources of food was a step-by-step process. There are indications that the transition from hunting and gathering to farming and herding took place in several steps elsewhere in the Levant. That was certainly the case at Jericho, where presumed hunting and gathering during the Natufian was followed by an early stage of agriculture with continued hunting of gazelle in the Proto-Neolithic and Pre-Pottery Neolithic A periods (Clutton-Brock 1979, pp. 154–155; Hopf 1983, p. 607). Only in Pre-Pottery Neolithic B did domesticated goats and sheep replace gazelle as the main source of meat. At Nahal Oren there was a contemporary increase in ovicaprines (Legge 1977, p. 58), while they dominated faunal assemblages at other Neolithic 2 and later sites from the Euphrates to Palestine, for example, at Buqras, Munhatta, and Beidha (Clason 1983; Ducos 1969, table 1; Hecker 1982).

The switch from gazelle to domesticated sheep and goats took place swiftly at Abu Hureyra. We might expect that the occupants of other sites in the steppe, who had participated in the same pattern of gazelle exploitation, would have adopted domesticated sheep and goats about the same time. This expectation has recently been fulfilled in the Azraq Basin. Gazelle were usually the most common game animals found on Epipalaeolithic and earlier Neolithic sites there. Then, late in Neolithic 2, the inhabitants of the site of Azraq 31 adopted the first sheep and goats (Garrard et al. 1988, pp. 332–333). The radiocarbon date for this event is 8,350 ± 120 BP (OxA-870). This date is about the same as we have determined for the change from gazelle to sheep and goats at Abu Hureyra. More caprine bones have been found at the site of Jilat 13, dated to the very beginning of the eighth millennium BP (7,920 ± 100 BP, OxA-1800; 7,870 ± 100 BP, OxA-1801) and Jilat 25 (Garrard et al. 1994, p. 106). The dates, like most of those from Abu Hureyra, were obtained from the Oxford laboratory. They strongly suggest that a similar replacement was taking place about the same time at both ends of the gazelle migration route, and presumably for the same reason: excessive hunting of the gazelle herds to feed growing numbers of humans following the spread of farming.

It cannot be a coincidence that the village of Buqras, well down the Euphrates from Abu Hureyra, was founded during this period of population expansion, at about 8,400 BP (Contenson 1985, p. 341). The deposits on the site postdated the switch from gazelle to ovicaprines; accordingly, the fauna of Buqras was dominated by domestic sheep and goats (Clason 1983, p. 361).

THE CONSEQUENCES OF THE ADOPTION OF AGRICULTURE

The spread of agriculture throughout the Levant was accompanied by a new pattern of settlement, and coincided with a transformation in culture that marked the inception of the Neolithic. This strongly implies that the processes of economic and cultural change were connected. The Neolithic villages of the tenth millennium BP and later were founded on land suitable for tillage, close to sources of surface water. Thus the needs of agriculture dictated their location. These villages, of which Jericho and Tell Aswad are good examples, were often substantially larger than settlements of the later Epipalaeolithic—another important consequence of the spread of farming. Later, during Neolithic 2, the population of the Levant grew substantially (figure 15.2). This is reflected in an increase in the number and extent of sites, many of which were inhabited for longer than before (Moore 1983, p. 98).

One of the most remarkable features of the earlier Neolithic in the Levant was the growth of several extraordinarily large settlements, of which Abu Hureyra (11.5 ha) is a prime example. Jericho (4 ha) was already a substantial settlement in the tenth millennium BP, but several sites that flourished in the ninth millennium exceeded it in area, among them Ras Shamra VC (c. 8 ha), Ain Ghazal, Basta, and Beisamun (c. 10 ha each) (Rollefson and Simmons 1988, p. 393; Gebel, Muheisen, and Nissen 1988, p. 107; Lechevallier 1978, p. 127). The trend may also be observed in Asia Minor, where Çayönü (3 ha) and, later, Çatal Hüyük (12.5 ha) grew very large indeed. Several of the very large sites had populations of a few thousand people, and were occupied for many centuries. Such great concentrations of people in a single settlement were a new phenomenon, not only in western Asia but across the inhabited world.

Most sites were smaller than these, just villages ranging in size from a few thousand square meters to a hectare, and also campsites of no more than a few hundred square meters. The smallest sites were occupied by two or three families, and the villages by scores or, at most, a few hundred persons. Thus, a hierarchy of settlements was developing throughout the Levant. What were the implications of such a pattern? The evidence from Abu Hureyra and elsewhere suggests that the larger sites had a greater range of crafts, and that they attracted a wider range of imported objects. Otherwise, the culture of both the larger and smaller sites was similar, despite the enormous differences in scale. The exchange of obsidian and other scarce materials shows that these communities were in touch with each other, yet each village appears to have been self-sufficient in foodstuffs and most raw materials. Thus, the emergence of a hierarchy of sites does not seem to have brought these settlements together politically, as far as we can infer from the material remains. Indeed, the skel-

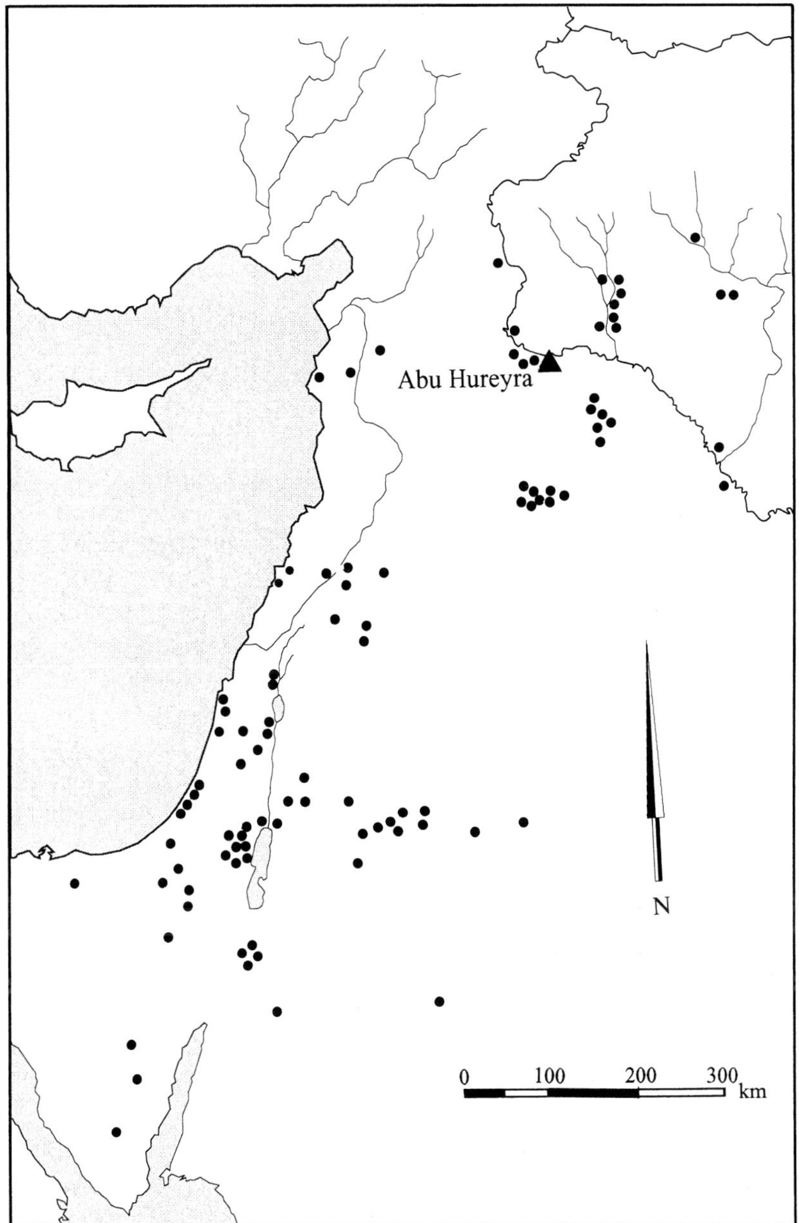

Figure 15.2 Distribution of sites in the Levant during the ninth millennium BP.

etal evidence from Abu Hureyra suggests that the inhabitants of these settlements remained somewhat isolated from each other. The increase in long-distance exchange that followed the adoption of farming may have been undertaken in part to counteract this.

Nevertheless, the fact that so many more people were living together in a settlement for centuries at a time testifies to the emergence of new forms of social organization within each village, not only at Abu Hureyra but throughout Southwest Asia. The members of these new communities needed to make appropriate arrangements to regulate their affairs. Their numbers were so great that they would have been obliged to cede authority in such matters to a smaller group within their village. This constituted a social revolution that was quite as important as the economic one. It was an essential step in the development of more complex patterns of organization during the succeeding Chalcolithic period.

The villages themselves consisted of densely packed, multiroomed houses, apparently the dwellings of individual families. They were so large that prodigious quantities of materials were required to construct the houses and other structures. People used mudbrick and plaster for their dwellings in much of the Levant, but stone for walling in southern Transjordan and in Asia Minor. The series of stone walls around the village at Jericho, the rock-cut ditch, and the stone tower within were the earliest monumental structures built anywhere in the world. Construction on this scale required organization of the necessary labor and demanded a considerable effort on the part of the builders. We have argued in the previous chapter that specialized artisans carried out some of the work, an inference that is strengthened by the evidence for the development of crafts. All of this was new.

The rich evidence from the graves at Abu Hureyra for delayed burial and special treatment of skulls, with its implications of reverence for ancestors, represented a considerable elaboration of religion and its practice. A complex ideology was developing concerned with tenets about death and an afterlife. Many of these beliefs seem to have been shared by communities throughout the Levant and in Asia Minor. The elaborate form of their expression was also novel, but basic aspects of the ritual derived from earlier times. Burial of the dead within the settlement was a common practice in the southern Levant during Epipalaeolithic 2 at sites like Mugharet el Wad, Ain Mallaha, Hayonim, and even Azraq 18. Certain innovations, particularly collective secondary burial and the separation of skulls, may be traced as far back as the graves in the late Natufian levels at Ain Mallaha (Perrot and Ladiray 1988, p. 63). Thus, there was continuity in beliefs from Epipalaeolithic to Neolithic.

The extraordinary cultural changes that accompanied the inception of the Neolithic were a direct result of the spread of farming and, later, of large-scale herding. Much greater quantities of food could be raised in the immediate vicinity of well-placed agricultural villages than had been available under the older hunting and gathering regime. Such produce, when stored, would supply an increasing amount of food for the burgeoning populations of the villages. Many of the early farming villages were apparently continuously inhabited for several centuries. We infer from this that the agricultural system reinforced stable settlement. The fertility of the surrounding fields was maintained over long periods, presumably by rotation of crops, the application of organic waste and manure as fertilizer, and fallowing. Yet, in this semi-arid environment, the agricultural system was always delicately balanced, so a modest intensification of farming and herding could have deleterious consequences for the soil and vegetation cover. The ecosystems of the Levant, especially of the steppe, had little capacity to absorb increased human exploitation before degradation set in. The effects would have been felt first around individual sites, but later could affect whole regions.

The increase in human numbers that took place during the ninth millennium BP seems to have had just this result. Degradation of the steppe around Abu Hureyra was already evident early in Period 2, and continued thereafter. The switch from gazelle hunting to large-scale sheep and goat herding seems to have been the direct result of population growth within and among settlements, and it would have increased the pressure on vulnerable grazing lands. The excavators of Ain Ghazal, situated in the park-woodland zone of Transjordan, have invoked just such environmental degradation to explain the changes they have observed in their sequence of occupation (Köhler-Rollefson 1988). Climatic change, too, had an effect. The postglacial rise in temperature resumed at the beginning of the Holocene. It was accompanied by a decline in effective rainfall in the southern Levant, on the evidence of pollen cores from Lake Huleh (Bottema and van Zeist 1981, p. 116; Baruch and Bottema 1991, figure 3). A similar reduction set in a millennium or two later in the northern Levant (van Zeist and Woldring 1980, figure 2). The rise in temperature and diminution of effective rainfall tended to increase aridity throughout the Levant, but their effects were most marked in the steppe.

These trends had important long-term consequences, leading the inhabitants of many sites in the steppe to abandon their settlements. Mureybit was already deserted in the first half of the ninth millennium BP (J. Cauvin 1977, p. 48). Buqras and Tell es-Sinn, well down the Euphrates, were abandoned about 8,000 BP (Contenson 1985, p. 341; Roodenberg 1979–1980, p. 26). Occupation continued on the tell at El Kum until a little before 7,000 BP (Dornemann 1986, p. 54), and for several centuries longer at Abu Hureyra; then the inhabitants of these sites, too, departed. A similar hiatus seems to have occurred farther to the south in the Azraq Basin, and in the vicinity of Beidha in southern Transjordan. People apparently moved west and north where, in Neolithic 3, new settlements were established throughout the woodland zone; their inhabitants were by now making pottery (Moore 1983, p. 99). In Syria, the areas with the greatest density of new sites were along the coast, in the Amuq Basin, in the woodland zone that is today bisected by the frontier between Syria and Turkey, and in the Al Matah Basin south of Aleppo.

This large-scale adjustment in the pattern of settlement appears to have brought into existence one of the principal elements of the way of life of people in the region in historic times—the dichotomy between the desert and the sown. Most of the new farming villages were situated in the woodland zone, which, with its rich Mediterranean soils, had considerable potential for agriculture but was less suitable for extensive stockraising. Some people continued to live in the steppe, leaving traces of occupation on modest campsites (Betts 1988, p. 376). They hunted gazelle and other game, but seem also to have kept flocks of sheep and goats. Specialized pastoralism could develop only after herding of sheep and goats became widespread, so the opportunity to pursue this way of life did not arise until the eighth millennium BP. The two ways of life, settled farming and mobile pastoralism, may have been pursued largely independently, but in historic times they were complementary, with the pastoral nomads of Arabia exchanging camels, sheep, goats, and their products for grain and manufactured items from the farmers.

THE SIGNIFICANCE OF THE RESEARCH

Abu Hureyra was occupied for over four and a half thousand years, from the late Epipalaeolithic through much of the Neolithic. That has enabled us to fulfill one of the main goals of the excavation: to confirm the archaeological sequence for those periods in northern Syria. The excavations at Mureybit and other sites in the region have provided valuable additional evidence to complete the record. The two superimposed settlements at Abu Hureyra represented a succession of ways of life that flourished in the same location: hunting, gathering, and farming in Period 1, and farming, hunting, and herding in Period 2. By comparing them we have learned how each system functioned, and so have come to understand how the transition from foraging to farming happened at Abu Hureyra. The extraordinary size of Abu Hureyra, its unique history of development, and the record it has revealed of the rich elaboration of culture that followed the adoption of farming were unsuspected in northern Syria when we started to excavate. These discoveries are a remarkable outcome of the salvage campaign in the Euphrates Valley initiated by the Syrian authorities, and demonstrate just how important a part this region played in the development of agriculture, herding, and settled life.

The inception of farming at Abu Hureyra was preceded by a brief period during which the inhabitants pursued an intensive and specialized form of hunting and gathering. We have evidence that the inhabitants of other sites in the region also engaged in intensive foraging. It was but a minor step for some of these people to domesticate a few of the plants and animals they were exploiting; the widespread adoption of the domesticates as major sources of food, however, would transform the lives of people throughout Southwest Asia and beyond.

The evidence from Abu Hureyra indicates that environmental fluctuations during the late Pleistocene and early Holocene were a vital factor in the changes that took place there. Environmental change was the main reason why the inhabitants of Abu Hureyra 1 became farmers 11,000 years ago, and an important reason why other communities across Southwest Asia adopted farming centuries later. Furthermore, environmental deterioration after 8,000 BP, combined with other factors, influenced the desertion of not only Abu Hureyra but other villages in the steppe zone. A second major influence throughout was the growth of population at Abu Hureyra itself, and in the region as a whole. The increasing population of the site and its effects on the economy and local environment were factors in the change in the settlement and its economy at the end of Abu Hureyra 1, and in the shift from gazelle hunting to large-scale herding in Abu Hureyra 2. Regional population growth also contributed to the latter shift.

The evidence recovered from Abu Hureyra and elsewhere has enabled us to state that plants were first domesticated beginning at approximately 11,000 BP, even if the location of these events has not yet been precisely determined. It now seems likely that sheep and goats were also domesticated in the same region sometime after 10,000 BP, and not just in the Zagros, as hitherto supposed. Thus, plants and animals were domesticated very early in the western Fertile Crescent.

The large-scale adoption of agriculture and herding across Southwest Asia did not follow the domestication of plants and animals immediately. On the contrary, our evidence and indications from other sites suggest that the change to farming and herding was strongly influenced by local and regional circumstances. At Abu Hureyra and elsewhere, it proceeded in a series of steps, first hunting and gathering, then farming with foraging, next farming with continued hunting, and finally farming and stockraising. The progression from one step to the next in the economic sequence and in other aspects of culture was often rapid. We emphasize that each of these events was conditioned by a set of related factors: the economy itself, population densities, technological adjustments, social patterns, and the environment.

The impact of the adoption of agriculture in the Levant was far-reaching. The pattern of settlement, the form of the villages, the activities and beliefs of their inhabitants, and population levels all changed. The transformation spread widely, since its effects were seen not only throughout the Levant but in Asia

Minor, northern Mesopotamia, the Zagros, and beyond to the Oxus and Indus. The new way of life also passed to Africa and Europe.

What are the implications of these observations for the general models of agricultural development we discussed in chapter 1? The models have proved useful inasmuch as they have highlighted a number of general factors that influenced the development of agriculture on a regional scale. However, none of those proposed so far accounts for what happened at Abu Hureyra, or in other important localities such as the Damascus Basin, the Jordan Valley, and the upper Tigris. Our research has demonstrated that the unique settings of individual sites in part conditioned the transition from hunting and gathering to farming and herding, while the sequence of events was often regulated by a complex set of factors. Thus, the pattern of change varied from one place to another. It is essential, therefore, to build up a mosaic of understanding of the processes of agricultural transformation with all its consequences, locality by locality. Only then is it possible to distinguish between the unique local factors and the important general trends in the regional systems to which each site belonged.

We chose deliberately, in the excavation of Abu Hureyra and in our subsequent analysis, to give equal weight to the cultural and economic evidence. That approach has enabled us to propose an integrated account of the development of the settlement and the way of life of its inhabitants. We have learned that the changing ecology of the site was of crucial importance throughout its existence. The first inhabitants organized themselves to secure ample supplies of food from their surroundings, and in so doing established one of the first sedentary villages in the world. That proved to be a catalyst for much that followed. We have discovered that farming began very early at Abu Hureyra, earlier, indeed, than anywhere else in Western Asia. It is clear that the steppe country stretching eastward from the edge of the park-woodland zone was of crucial importance in the development of farming, in contrast to earlier views that sought to locate the phenomenon in the hills. The consequences of the adoption of farming at Abu Hureyra are strikingly clear, from the enormous growth of the village to the impact of farming on the people themselves. We have been able to reconstruct the cycle of the seasons at Abu Hureyra, and have been privileged to study the habitual activities of the inhabitants themselves, thus revealing aspects of their daily lives. The extraordinary record from Abu Hureyra has illuminated the adoption of settled life, the development of farming, and their consequences in unprecedented detail, and has led us to a new understanding of how they came about. That is the ultimate significance of the site.

Appendices

Appendix 1: Radiocarbon and thermoluminescence dates

Table A.1 Radiocarbon and thermoluminescence dates from Abu Hureyra

Trench	Phase	Level	Material	Laboratory number	Date BP
Abu Hureyra 1: Conventional and AMS radiocarbon dates in stratigraphic order					
E	2 and 3	451, 425, 411, 410, 409, 408	charcoal	BM-1121	10,792 ± 82
E	2	447	charcoal	BM-1718R	11,140 ± 140
E	3	398	charcoal	BM-1719R	9,100 ± 100
E	1	470	carbonized grain fragments of wild einkorn	OxA-172	10,900 ± 200
E	1	470	charred *Bos* sp. bone	OxA-387	11,070 ± 160
E	1	470	charred *Bos* sp. bone, repeat of OxA-387	OxA-468	11,090 ± 150
E	1	470	humic fraction of OxA-468	OxA-469	10,920 ± 140
E	1	470	humic fraction of OxA-468	OxA-470	10,820 ± 160
E	1	470	carbonized grain fragments of wild einkorn	OxA-883	11,450 ± 300
E	1	468	carbonized grain fragments of wild einkorn	OxA-882	6,100 ± 120
E	2	460	charred gazelle bone	OxA-430	11,020 ± 150
E	2	460	humic fraction of OxA-430	OxA-431	10,680 ± 150
E	2	457	carbonized grain fragments of wild einkorn	OxA-171	10,600 ± 200
E	2	455	carbonized grain of domestic rye	OxA-6685	10,930 ± 120
E	2	449	carbonized grain fragment of domestic rye	OxA-6996	9,860 ± 220

(continued)

Table A.1 (*continued*)

Trench	Phase	Level	Material	Laboratory number	Date BP
E	2	449	carbonized grain fragment of domestic einkorn	OxA-6995	8,700 ± 240
E	2	449	carbonized grain fragment of domestic rye	OxA-5843	8,275 ± 65
E	2	449	carbonized grain fragment of spelt or bread wheat	OxA-5842	8,260 ± 75
E	2	438	carbonized grain of macaroni wheat or of domestic emmer	OxA-6419	8,230 ± 80
E	2	438	carbonized grain of domestic six-rowed hulled barley	OxA-6418	8,115 ± 80
E	2	430	carbonized grain fragments of wild einkorn	OxA-397	10,420 ± 140
E	2	430	charred gazelle bone	OxA-434	10,490 ± 150
E	2	430	humic fraction of OxA-434	OxA-435	10,450 ± 180
E	2	430	fulvic fraction of OxA-434	OxA-476	9,600 ± 200
E	2	429	humic fraction of charred wild sheep bone	OxA-474	10,930 ± 150
E	2	426	charred grain fragment of domestic einkorn	OxA-7122	8,290 ± 75
E	2	425	charred wild sheep bone	OxA-473	10,000 ± 170
E	2	425	humic fraction of OxA-473	OxA-472	10,750 ± 170
E	3	420	carbonized grain fragments of wild einkorn	OxA-386	10,800 ± 160
E	3	419	carbonized grain fragment of domestic rye	OxA-8719	10,610 ± 100
E	3	419	charred wild sheep bone	OxA-407	10,050 ± 180
E	3	419	humic fraction of OxA-407	OxA-408	10,250 ± 160
E	3	419	humic fraction of OxA-407 (repeat)	OxA-471	10,620 ± 150
E	3	418	carbonized grain fragment of domestic rye	OxA-8718	11,140 ± 100
E	3	411	carbonized grain fragment of domestic free-threshing wheat	OxA-6417	8,170 ± 90
E	3	405	carbonized grain fragments of wild einkorn	OxA-170	10,600 ± 200
E	3	401	carbonized glume-base of domestic einkorn	OxA-6336	8,140 ± 90
E	3	396	charred gazelle bone	OxA-475	9,060 ± 140
Abu Hureyra 2 and Abu Hureyra 3: Conventional and AMS radiocarbon dates in stratigraphic order					
A		1972/13	human bone	OxA-2044	390 ± 60
A		1973/167	human bone	OxA-4660	8,180 ± 200
B	3, 10	206, 39	charcoal	BM-1122	9,374 ± 72
B	4	205	charcoal	BM-1722R	8,640 ± 100
B	7	164	charcoal	BM-1424	8,190 ± 77
B	2	218	carbonized grain fragments of einkorn and barley	OxA-2169	8,640 ± 110

(*continued*)

Table A.1 (*continued*)

Trench	Phase	Level	Material	Laboratory number	Date BP
B	2	216	carbonized grain fragments of emmer and einkorn	OxA-1190	8,500 ± 120
B	9	72	charred bone	OxA-1232	7,310 ± 120
B	11	87	human bone	OxA-2045	170 ± 60
C		73/131, 73/130	charcoal	BM-1423	8,676 ± 72
C		73/62, 73/31	charcoal	BM-1425	8,393 ± 72
D	2	155	charcoal	BM-1720R	22,020 ± 200
D	3	129	charcoal	BM-1721R	8,490 ± 110
D	1	73	charred wild onager bone	OxA-876	8,500 ± 90
D	1	70	charred sheep/goat bone	OxA-877	8,300 ± 150
D	4	68	charred wild onager bone	OxA-878	8,490 ± 110
D	4	41	charred wild onager bone	OxA-879	8,570 ± 130
D	4	10	charred wild onager bone	OxA-880	14,920 ± 180
D	6	32	charred sheep/goat bone	OxA-881	8,870 ± 100
E	3, 4, 6, 7	396, 377, 309, 115	charcoal	BM-1120	8,666 ± 66
E	6	199	charcoal	BM-1724R	8,020 ± 100
E	6	22	charcoal	BM-1723R	10,820 ± 510
E	4	375	carbonized grain fragments of six-row barley, emmer, and grass seeds	OxA-2167	8,270 ± 100
E	5	340	twig charcoal	OxA-2168	8,330 ± 100
G	subsoil	68	twig charcoal	OxA-1228	9,680 ± 90
G	2	62	carbonized grain fragments of wild cereals of *Secale montanum/Secale vavilovii/Triticum boeoticum* group	OxA-1930	8,180 ± 100
G	2	62	carbonized grain fragments of domesticated wheat *Triticum* sp.	OxA-1931	7,890 ± 90
G	3	8	twig charcoal	OxA-1227	8,320 ± 80
Abu Hureyra 2 and Abu Hureyra 3: Thermoluminescence dates					
B	10	49	potsherd	Ox TL 196a	7,250 ± 600 BP
D	6	39	potsherd		AD 600-1,000
E	8	123	3 potsherds	Ox TL 196j	5,350 ± 400 BP

Sources: Bowman, Ambers, and Leese 1990; Burleigh, Ambers, and Matthews 1982; Burleigh, Matthews, and Ambers 1982; Gowlett et al. 1987; Hedges et al. 1990; Hedges et al. 1996.

Appendix 2: Thermoluminescence Dating of Sherds from Abu Hureyra 2

J. HUXTABLE

Sherds excavated in 1972 and 1973 from several areas in the Neolithic settlement of Abu Hureyra 2 were submitted for dating to the Research Laboratory for Archaeology and the History of Art, University of Oxford, by Andrew Moore. All relevant burial soils were included in the sample. I measured the material from two areas, Trench B, level 49, and Trench E, level 123, and calculated dates in 1977.

The sherds studied did not contain sufficiently large amounts of quartz for this to be dated separately. The dating was done using the fine grains of mixed mineralogy extracted from the pottery by gentle crushing. This fine-grain method of dating is described in detail in Zimmerman (1971), and a general introductory review of the thermoluminescence (TL) dating method is given in Seeley (1975).

There was only one sherd from Trench B, level 49, but it had excellent TL characteristics. There were more sherds from E, level 123, but some had poor TL characteristics. I investigated eight sherds but dated only three of them. All the dated sherds were free from anomalous fading (Wintle 1973). The TL ages for these two levels are as follows:

Trench B, level 49: 7,250 ± 600 BP (laboratory reference number 196a)

Trench E, level 123: 5,350 ± 400 BP (laboratory reference number 196j)

The error limit quoted is the total error, both random and systematic, at the 68% confidence level, calculated according to the method of Aitken and Alldred (1972).

Moore submited one more sherd for testing by TL in 1987. This sherd (Trench D, level 39) was one of two excavated in 1972 from the base of a pit that cut into the Abu Hureyra 2 levels. The fill of the pit was Neolithic but the two sherds were not. The fabric of the sherds was unremarkable from a stylistic point of view, the two most likely periods suggested by Moore being the Bronze Age or Medieval.

Unfortunately, the fill of the pit was not available for radioactivity measurements, but several soils had been analyzed in 1977 and the spread of the two most likely dates was such that an average value based on the previous measurements was sufficient to resolve which of the two suggested periods was most likely. The estimated TL age of the sherd was found to be within the period AD 600–1,000. It cannot be attributed to the Bronze Age, so this possibility is eliminated.

Appendix 3: Key to Sections and Plans

The figure presented here (figure A3.1) provides a key to understanding the conventions used in preparing all the section drawings and plans in chapters 5 and 8. Readers should consult it when interpreting the drawings that illustrate those chapters.

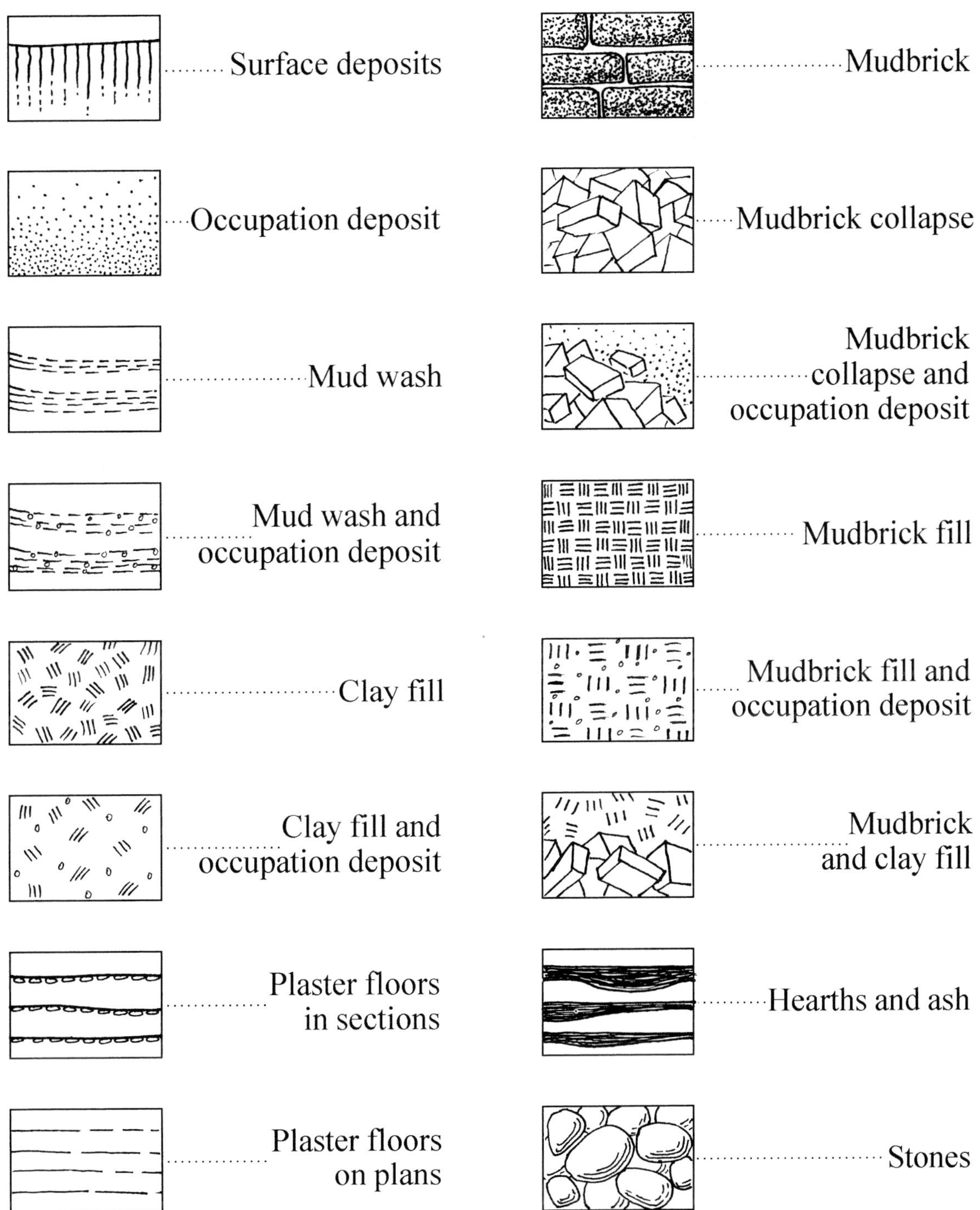

Figure A3.1 Key to sections and plans

Appendix 4: Pottery and Plaster Analysis

M. LE MIÈRE

POTTERY

The samples I analyzed consisted of seven potsherds and one fragment of pisé or cob.

I used the x-ray fluorescence technique for the chemical analysis. I measured eight main elements (table A4.1) and present a cluster analysis of the results here in a dendrogram (Figure A4.1). They show that the assemblage is homogeneous with the exception of one sample, AHR 13, which had a composition different from most of the elements. The homogeneity of this assemblage, including as it does a sample of pisé that serves as a reference for the clay that was used, indicates that the pottery was made locally.

Sample AHR 13 could perhaps be regarded as an import, for not only did it have a distinctive composition, but also its appearance distinguished it from the other potsherds, particularly its thickness (6 mm instead of 9–12 mm) and its surface color (gray instead of beige). Its color and surface polish suggest a relationship with the dark-faced burnished ware of northern Syria and Cilicia. Determining the provenance of a unique sample, especially when there is practically no information about the composition of the pottery of this period, is a hopeless task. However, for dark-faced burnished ware it happens that the geological background of Cilicia and northern Syria is distinctive. This gives the numerous clays of the region their characteristic compositions with significant traces of chrome, nickel, and often magnesium (Le Mière 1986, p. 229; Le Mière and Picon 1987). That is why I analyzed the trace elements in sample AHR 13, but the results did not allow me to ascribe it with certainty to a particular source of pottery manufacture in northern Syria or Cilicia.

THE PLASTER

I analyzed a fragment of a plaster vessel from Trench G using x-ray diffraction and was able to confirm that it was made of gypsum plaster or plaster of paris. There were traces of calcite in the sample, but they amounted to no more than 1.5% of the matrix and so were present simply as impurities in the gypsum used to make the plaster.

Table A4.1 Chemical analysis of the potsherds and fragments of pisé

Sample numbers	Ca	Fe	Ti	K	Si	Al	Mg	Mn
AHR 2	15.00	9.40	0.83	2.40	49.49	14.90	7.85	0.1500
AHR 6	21.26	7.33	0.81	1.70	48.92	13.31	6.55	0.1073
AHR 8	12.09	9.07	0.88	3.28	52.44	14.80	7.30	0.1439
AHR 10	12.99	9.26	0.86	2.66	52.05	14.83	7.21	0.1473
AHR 11	19.10	7.90	0.78	2.36	49.62	13.28	6.81	0.1405
AHR 13	3.85	4.95	0.70	2.62	74.30	12.12	1.41	0.0511
AHR 14	11.03	9.19	0.88	3.06	53.52	14.91	7.25	0.1522
AHR 17	17.17	7.02	0.89	1.86	52.94	13.01	6.98	0.1398

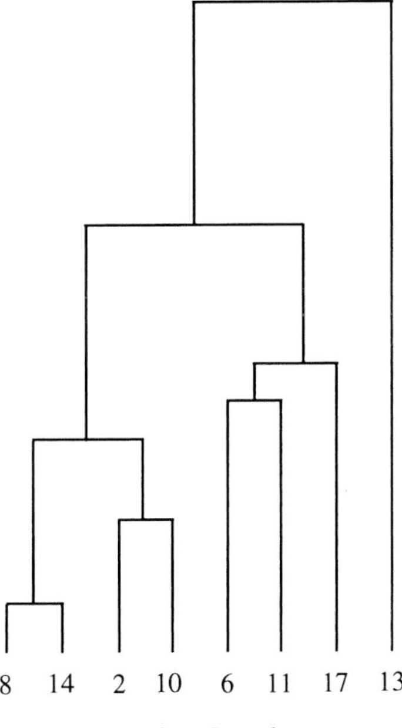

Figure A4.1 Dendrogram of a cluster analysis of samples of pottery and pisé from Abu Hureyra 2C.

I examined one other sample, a piece of a plaster floor from Trench B. A sulfuric acid test of this sample and of the vessel fragment indicated that both were composed of the same material, that is, gypsum plaster.

It should be noted that the immediate environs of Abu Hureyra are calcareous, consisting of a chalk substrate, but there are sources of gypsum not far away.

Appendix 5: The Human Remains

T. I. MOLLESON

THE PRESERVATION AND ANALYSIS OF THE HUMAN BONE

The excavators recovered only a small number of intact human bones,[1] so we were able to take very few measurements of them (see chapter 4). Post-mortem distortion of even the better-preserved skulls further limited the number of measurements that we could obtain. In fact, only one Neolithic skull was sufficiently well preserved to be measured in the detail that allowed comparison with material from other populations. It had been burnt.

Some of the Neolithic bones, notably from Trench B, phase 8, room 3, had been charred by fire, but the color and condition of most of them indicated accidental fires rather than intentional cremation. The effect of the charring was to harden the bones, and the skeletons concerned were among the better preserved. Immature bones were frequently in a better state of preservation than adult ones, probably because these bones have a relatively high organic content. This was particularly noticeable for the skeletons of newborn and perinatal infants. The bones of historic age were usually more complete and did not fragment as readily because a portion of the organic material remained in the bone. The cancellous bone of the epiphyses had often been destroyed as a result of insect activity. The bore holes and channels of insects were evident in some of the bones from Trench A where even skull bones had been attacked.

Repeated wetting by rain water and evaporation had resulted in the deposition of salts in some bones. The salts corroded and destroyed the bone in patches as they crystallized. On some skulls this destroyed the vault while the face and base were left intact and well preserved. The same process caused long bones to break in half lengthwise. The fragmented edges of the bones looked burnt, the result of corrosion and the deposition of salts along the edge.

We identified small crystals adhering to many of the bones from Trench D as gypsum, a hydrous calcium sulfate ($CaSO_4 \cdot 2H_2O$) that forms as an evaporite mineral. Trench D cut through the part of the tell nearest to the river, an area where surface evaporation induced by the direct heat of the sun would tend to draw ground waters to the surface by capillary action, a sort of rising damp. As the fluid evaporated, dissolved salts crystallized out to form small (1–2 mm), clear crystals of gypsum embedded in the sandy matrix around the bones, which became somewhat indurated. The source of sulfate may have been decomposition products of the decaying body that, with calcium derived from the bone mineral, would have been an ideal environment for the formation of gypsum.

Superficial black staining by manganese of a few bones was presumably the consequence of secondary mobilization of the salts in the deposits by oxygenated ground waters.

Percentage recovery of the individual bones of the skeleton was variable (figure 11.1). We compared the recovery of skeletal parts between trenches by deriving the relative abundance (RA) of each element from the expected number (EN), given the minimum number of individuals (MNI) in the sample and the number (N) of each element recovered, where RA = EN/MNI. It was necessary to follow this procedure, which Andrews (1990) describes in detail, to take into account the fact that in the skeleton there are many more bones like vertebrae and phalanges than there are long bones.

The patterns of relative abundance showed that, in general, the levels of recovery were very high. For the numbered skeletons, the femur, humerus, and other long bones were best represented. The apparent overrepresentation of the skull was due to the fragmentation of the bones and to the difficulty of assessing numbers. Recovery of the patellae and small bones of the hands and feet was only moderately good; these are bones that preserve quite well but are not always noticed by excavators. Underrepresentation of the vertebrae, sternum, and bones of the shoulder and pelvic girdles reflects the fragility of these bones; relatively few were preserved and recovered for study. The difference in the numbers of single-rooted and multiple-rooted teeth most likely reflects recovery methods; sieves with centimeter diameter holes probably did not retain the smaller teeth.

A group of advanced students in the Extra-Mural Department of Birkbeck College sorted the human skeletal material and conducted the preliminary analysis of it. The bags containing bones received from the excavators included considerable amounts of fine alluvial sand that they removed by sieving. They identified the bones, determined age and sex wherever possible, and noted anomalies or pathologies. Where there was evidence for the remains of more than one individual, as was generally the case, the secondary material was treated as derived unless there was clear indication from the number of bones present that there was a second or third burial. The students attempted to match fragments of skeletons that had been bagged separately.

We repaired breaks in bones if this allowed a measurement to be made, but otherwise we did not undertake extensive reconstruction. It was not generally necessary to clean the bones.

We did restore one skull. We hardened friable areas of the bone using dilute polyvinyl acetate (PVA) emulsion. Then we carefully removed matrix using a pin and spatula and coated newly exposed bone with dilute PVA. We filled large holes and cracks using plaster of paris, which was colored to distinguish it from the bone. The mandible was more difficult to treat, as half was missing and the other half was attached to bandage. Since the consolidants used for the bone and for applying the bandage were identical, attempts to remove the bandage with solvent resulted in any consolidant in the bone being dissolved and the bone fragmenting further. We eventually coated the bone with Formvar and allowed it to dry. This resin is insoluble in acetone, and therefore when acetone was applied to the bandage to remove it, the bone remained consolidated. We photographed the skull before, during, and after treatment.

We x-rayed pathological specimens and submitted the radiographs to a practicing radiologist for an opinion. We photographed significant cases of bone pathology and drew an interpretive reconstruction (figure 11.8). We invite the reader to examine the evidence for our interpretation presented in chapter 11 and to form an independent view. This approach is particularly important because some of the lifetime changes observed on the bones suggest a degree of sophistication for the Epipalaeolithic and Neolithic populations that has not hitherto been claimed for people of those periods.

It often proved impossible to identify the bone fragments to bone type or side of the body, although we noted cross-section shape and direction of the nutrient foramen on a long bone fragment whenever possible. Identified bones of small dimensions or with evidence of an unfused epiphysis were classed as juvenile, while larger fragments were classed as adult.

It proved difficult to identify teeth, because they were either fragmented or extremely worn. We relied on cross-sectional shape of the root and position of the root fossa to ascertain tooth type and side. We recorded standard buccolingual and mesiodistal dimensions of the teeth using digital calipers accurate to .1 mm. We measured both buccal and lingual or palatal crown height of the premolars and molars.

We took the standard cranial and long bone measurements wherever possible, following definitions in Bass (1987) or Brothwell (1981). Because of the fragmented nature of the material, the position for measurement of the midshaft dimensions of the clavicle, humerus, and femur could not in every case be determined accurately but had to be estimated. We felt that this procedure was justified in order to build up a reasonable data base. We measured the bones of juveniles, including neonates, and adults.

We determined the sex of skeletons or individual bones as far as possible by reference to the secondary sex characters of the pelvis and skull (Brothwell 1981; Acsadi and Nemeskeri 1970). Many of the bones could not be sexed in this way, but we could assign a proportion to female or male by the comparison of certain tooth and bone dimensions with those of the sexed group, although in general we felt that size should not be used for sexing. We devised a few additional measurements to establish the sex of the first metatarsal, since this could not always be achieved by reference to other parts of the skeleton. There were too many missing data to perform a useful discriminant function analysis, with the exception of the information derived from the first metatarsal.

We tried to assign the skeletal remains to an age class at death. We did not generally attempt more precise aging, given the present lack of confidence in most of the standard methods. Neonates were aged on bone size and skeletal maturity, following the recommendations of Scheuer, Musgrave, and Evans (1980) and Fazekas and Kosa (1978; see also Molleson 1989a). Age at death of older juveniles was estimated wherever possible by reference to stage of development of the teeth using charts of Schour and Massler (1941). Bone lengths of those children with teeth were then used as the basis from which the age of other children could be inferred.

We decided that the best method for estimating age at death of adults would be by reference to the amount of attrition on the teeth. In many individuals the wear patterns were so extreme that it was only by evaluating crown height on both buccal and lingual (or palatal) sides that some indication of the rate of wear could be obtained. We determined the rate of wear in young individuals by reference to stage of dental development. It was then possible to extrapolate the wear gradients to older individuals. This method could give only a guide to age at death, since any tooth pathology or change in the abrasive nature of the diet would have altered the rate of wear. Further, there were many adults who had lost several teeth in life. Other skeletal indicators of age were assessed, in particular cranial suture closure and pubic symphysis change (Acsadi and Nemeskeri 1970). Finally, we categorized adults as young (20–34), mature (35–49), or old (over 50).

A number of skeletal and dental characters are known to run in families and have a genetic basis; others are determined by occupation or health. We recorded variations in tooth form and number and, if necessary, took radiographs of the jaws to check for unerrupted or undeveloped teeth. We noted palatogingival grooves on the anterior teeth of two different individuals from Trench B, and fused roots of the second lower molars in several individuals from Trench E. Agenesis of the third molars was quite frequent. Sutural ossicles, metopism, and variants in foramina were recorded.

We scored the number and situation of dental caries, and abscesses, and recorded evidence for enamel hypoplasia and periodontal disease. We did not observe growth displasias, or rickets; even cribra orbitalia was rare. Degenerative disease of the joints was common, with the spine, temporomandibular joints, knees, and big toes in particular being affected.

SKELETAL REMAINS FROM THE TRENCHES

Trench B

The human bone recovered from Trench B comprised inhumations and isolated bones that were associated with the more complete skeletons or were mixed with animal bones. There was a concentration of remains in phases 8 and 9 but very little material from the earlier levels.

All the human bones from phase 2 were recovered from level 216, associated with red clay fill, and levels 219 and 220, associated with the black plaster floor. The bones were fragmented but represented a young child (73.B273) and perhaps part of an older child. One of the lateral incisor teeth showed a moderate degree of shoveling.

The remains of two adolescents were recovered from phase 7. At the time of excavation, 73.2255 was recognized as a burial in a shallow grave cut into occupation soil in level 163. The lower back and pelvic region of an adolescent were recovered. The neural arch of the fifth lumbar vertebra had failed to unite to the body of the vertebra, a congenital condition known as spondylolisis. The neural arch of the first sacral vertebra was cleft. There is often a genetic predisposition for this weakness of the lower back, which can then develop as a result of excessive load-bearing during adolescence. The size of the upper canine suggested that the skeleton was male.

The feet and pelvic fragments of the other adolescent (73.B99) were recovered from level 162. The crests of the ilium and ischium were unfused; the epiphyses of the metatarsals and phalanges of the feet were fusing, indicating a pubescent individual of much the same age as 73.2255. The plane of the proximal articulation of the toe phalanges was more than usually inclined toward the upper surface of the foot. The epiphysis, which can still be discerned in the adolescent toe, 73.B198, was noticeably wedged, thinning toward the upper surface of the foot. Such a condition implies pressure and might have developed as a result of prolonged kneeling with the toes curled under (Molleson 1989b).

We noted a moderate amount of calculus on an incisor tooth, 73.B198. This may be associated with the change in diet toward the inclusion of more grain products.

The human remains associated with deposits of phase 8 were excavated from three main areas: room 2, room 3, and the vicinity of the mudbrick wall 139. Additional human skeletal parts were recovered from among the animal bones.

A child (73.2127) with a dental age of about ten years that still had its deciduous molars was found in wall 139. Wear on its deciduous teeth was considerable, indicating that it had consumed hard, coarse food. There was some cribra parietalia, a porotic condition of the skull bones that is associated with iron deficiency anemia. This may have been caused by dietary deficiencies or infection. Another skeleton (73.2133) a young adult from the area of the wall also showed evidence of cribra parietalia. Carabelli's cusps were present on both the upper molars, and the lateral incisors were shovel-shaped in a way that is reminiscent of a child (73.B273) from phase 2.

The fragmented remains of two children, or possibly one child (73.2168 and B189) less than six years old, had extensive periosteal new bone growth on the shafts of the long bones, radius, ulna, femur, tibia, and fibula. It is difficult to attribute a cause to this sort of new bone growth. It may have resulted from a fall or some long-standing inflammatory condition, or it may have been due simply to normal rapid growth processes.

Other human bones from the area of the wall represented two adults and an infant. They were recovered from the plaster floor under wall 139.

There were a large number of burials in the main phase 8 house (levels 142, 148, 154, 159). One of the more complete skeletons (73.2132) of an adult female lacked the skull but was accompanied by the left mandibular ramus of a child aged about 12 years. The patella had a squatting facet.

An important series of burials was recovered from the charnel room, room 3, at the northern end of the house. They provide an impressive insight into the Neolithic way of life. Females, males (in greater numbers than usual), and juveniles were represented. Two of the skulls in level 159, one that of a male (73.2400), the other presumably female (73.2401), had been wrapped in matting—an early instance of weaving on the site. The female skull was not examined but when excavated was associated with postcranial bones of a young adult female (73.2399). Postcranial bones of a male included with remains of a juvenile and a female in 73.2167 could have been those of 73.2400.

Much of the skeletal material recovered from the charnel room had been exposed to fire, so the bones were more or less burnt. Some were merely charred, the discoloration from black to brown being indicative of the amount of burning; others were calcined and distorted in such a way as to suggest that the body was fleshed when exposed to the fire. The remains of 73.1571 from level 127 illustrates the variable degree of charring that could be sustained by different bones of the skeletons. Three individuals were identified, at least two adults and an adolescent. The skulls and postcranial bones were present, and this may distinguish the nature of the emplacement of this group from the burials in the levels below, in which the head was usually separate from the rest of the body. The bodies were also less tightly contracted than usual for this site. The main skeleton was that of a young male in whom the fusion line of the epiphyses of the femur head and distal condyle could still be distinguished. There were signs of burning on some of the bones. The pelvis was very blackened and fragmented, and the bones had an open, porous appearance. The right leg, most of which showed signs of charring, was much more solid in texture. The remains of the second adult were very fragmented, only part of the right arm and leg being recovered. The bones were much lighter in color and weight than those of the first adult. The adolescent consisted of parts of the skull, spine, left arm, and both legs. The bones were partially charred, especially the cranium, spine, left humerus, and right clavicle. Neither the mandible and maxillae nor the left radius and ulna were blackened. Broken ends of the long bones showed the black discoloration to be superficial. The distribution of charring on the bones of this group can best be explained if the adolescent had been lying on its right side and the adult male on his left so that the left and right sides respectively were exposed to the fire.

The fragmented skeleton of a gracile young adult male (73.541) was recovered from within the burnt zone. The skull and the postcranial bones including both hands were represented. The bones, especially those of the head and neck, were burnt. The skull was relatively complete.

The skeleton of a mature male (73.B66) probably also came from this part of room 3. The bones, which represented both skull and postcranial parts of the skeleton, had been exposed to severe heat, probably while they were still fleshed. All the bones were calcined and distorted, particularly the axis, ulna, radius, and leg bones. The skeleton was that of an older individual who had developed osteoarthritis of the axis and atlas vertebrae of the neck and of the lumbar vertebrae. The phalanges of the toes showed the everted angle of articulation seen in other individuals from this phase. Medial and lateral exostosis on the phalanges linked this individual to another group (73.B71) from the same level. We noted peculiar pits on the dorsal surface of the phalanges of the thumb.

Burnt bones were mixed with the remains of 73.1570 from level 128, a collection of at least three individuals including an adult female and two children aged about six and ten years. Some of the bones of the younger child had been eaten by insects, implying that they had not been interred at the same time.

The fragments of 73.1928, also from level 128, were not burnt. This sample consisted of the skeleton of a young adult male and the mandible of an older individual in which the canine was slightly rotated. This burial was to the southwest of the area of burning. Similar rotation of the canine in 73.1044, an adult female from level 126 of room 3, suggests that the two were related.

The degree of dental abrasion on the teeth of even quite young individuals was considerable, indicating that the diet was hard and coarse. The presence of healed dental abscesses in at least three individuals, and the extreme rarity of carious lesions, may be related to the way the cereal grains were prepared.

The foot bones of one individual, 73.B71, from this area showed, in addition to the upwardly inclined angle of articulation of the proximal phalanges already noted for other people, unusual exostoses along the medial and lateral borders of the proximal phalanges and the terminal phalanges of the big toes.

There was quite strong evidence that some of the individuals buried in room 3 were related. Both the supposed cripple (73.2949) and the nearby child (73.2133) had cervical ribs associated with the neck vertebrae; this child, the nearby male (73.2400) and the adolescent with 73.1571 from the pit in room 3 all had wurmian bones in the skull. Agenesis of the third molar was shared by three individuals from this area, including the adolescent (73.1571, 73.2949) and the juvenile (73.2127) interred seated in a pit (160) in wall 139. The relationships may have extended to those buried in room 2, with segmented sternums occurring both with 73.2399 (159) and with 73.1785 from the pit (144) in room 2.

Pit 144 dug into the floor of room 2 during the later part of phase 8 contained the fragmented remains of many individuals, including an unusual number of adolescents, some of whom appear to have been genetically related. A bone point, a butterfly bead, and a number of other beads were found with the skeleton of a mature or old adult female (73.1785A). Both skull and post-cranial bones were present. The third molar was reduced. She had degenerative joint disease, mild osteoarthritis of the spine, scapula, and hand, and some asymmetry of the thoracic vertebrae (mild Scheuermann's disease). Two other individuals, a juvenile and an adolescent, were associated with this find number.

There were two adolescents in the group (73.1787). Both had Carabelli's pits on the crown of the second molar and one had an enamel pearl on the cervical margin of the tooth. The skeletal maturity suggested an individual, possibly male, about the age of puberty. The other individual was slightly older, as the epiphyses of the phalanges and calcaneus were fusing. A mild degree of periostitis on the tibia may have related to an inflammatory condition.

Two further adolescents comprised 73.2397 and 73.1604B. The skeletal maturation of the latter was irregular; the dental age was between 12 and 15, although the second molars had not erupted. The acetabulum, scapula, and epiphyses of the long bones were not united, but the epiphyses of the medial phalanges had fused.

At the bottom of the pit was a group of five individuals (73.1786), an adult, three juveniles aged about six, eight, and twelve, and an infant. The cranium of one of the infants was preserved—most unusual in this pit. We noted quite severe cribra orbitalia in the orbits.

The pit contained the remains of 25–30 individuals, all fragmented and incomplete. The state of the bones and the lack of crania suggest that the pit was used for the secondary burial of bodies that had been exposed and from which the head had then been removed. Most of the individuals were immature, with a striking preponderance of adolescents approaching the age of puberty. Both males and females were present. This age distribution cannot represent the deaths from natural causes of any family or small community group. Part of the collection could reflect greatly increased mortality in some loosely defined age cohort.

The fragmented remains of a number of adults (73.2748, B60, B163, B172) were recovered from the debris filling the lane that existed between the two buildings during the later part of phase 8. Squatting facets were noted on the patellae. Marked osteoarthritis of the cervical vertebrae of one older adult, B60, was perhaps evidence that this person carried loads on the head.

There was one substantial assemblage (73.31) from phase 9. It comprised the remains of six or seven individuals, including the skulls of one adult and a juvenile. It was not possible to associate the postcranial bones with either, although parts of a juvenile were present. The adult, probably a female, had periodontal resorption around the first upper molar, which may have been due to a palatal abscess. The palate was also very pitted. The mandible of another adult showed signs of osteitis following an abscess involving the second molar. In another adult the skull bones were thickened, perhaps a consequence of anemia.

Among the postcranial bones were two congenitally fused cervical vertebrae. A number of vertebrae and hand bones had degenerative lipping. The angle of articulation of the toe phalanges was everted.

Peculiar pits on the dorsal side of the proximal phalange of the thumb of an adult, B111, recalled similar pits on the three phalanges from two (or possibly one) individuals in phase 8. These pits may have been congenital, or they may have developed as a result of persistently holding the fingers clenched.

An old man (B64) with very worn teeth, three abscesses, and a number of molars lost before death provided early evidence of caries at Abu Hureyra. The ante-mortem loss of teeth and the degree of degenerative joint change of the mandibular condyle and vertebrae suggest that he was well over 40 when he died. The condition of the spine was probably exacerbated by an old injury involving the lower back. The first lumbar vertebra had probably been fractured. In contrast to the spine, there was little degenerative joint disease, and persistent load bearing was probably not a contributory factor to the spinal arthritis.

We observed dental caries in another old individual (B61) who also had considerable calculus deposits on the teeth. Enamel hypoplasia indicated a severe systemic illness at about four years.

Squatting facets were noted on isolated tibiae, patellae, and femora from presumed males as well as females.

We identified few juveniles. The skeleton of one child (B60) aged about two or three years was relatively complete. The deciduous teeth of this child were largely missing but in another (B189) of about the same age, the lack of wear on the deciduous molars would appear to indicate that it had not been weaned. This child had periosteal new bone growth on the shaft of the ulna.

The isolated bones of newborn-sized infants became prevalent for the first time in phase 9. Five infants were possibly represented, although no complete skeleton was found. The presence of neonates may be evidence of a change in burial practice, but no discrete inhumation was found. The neonate bones were usually well preserved compared to the bones of older children or of adults.

In phase 9 there was evidence for an increase in the incidence of stress and trauma with osteoarthritis of the neck, back, and joints. There was also evidence for an increase in infection, and indirectly for an increase in the density of the population, since this was a factor that would enhance the spread of infective organisms. The number of old people is as likely to be a consequence of a larger population as of any change in longevity. The appearance of neonates in the death assemblage may also derive from the change in population size.

A very few human bones were recovered from phase 10, among them a number of babies, both newborn and infant. We identified the remains of two babies (72.B117) of similar size, both small for neonates. They may have been twins that died at birth. In the past twins rarely survived, partly because of their small birth size; these equated with 35-week fetuses (Fazekas and Kosa 1978). One infant, with cribra parietalia, showed signs of an anemic condition at a very early age. Since it is most unlikely that an unweaned baby would already have developed an iron deficiency, the possibility of a hemolytic condition should be considered.

The burial of a 12-year-old youth (72.264B) had been undertaken with unusual care (figure 10.5). The head had been encased in gypsum plaster stained red with cinnabar (mercury sulfide), a naturally occurring mineral. Apart from the skull and jaw bones, only fragments of the skeleton were preserved. We determined the child's sex from the large size of the upper canine. There was surprisingly little wear on the occlusal surface of the first molar for a child of this age if he ate the normal coarse diet, and thus it is possible that he had been eating cooked food. A Carabelli's cusp on the molar provides a possible genetic link with 73.2127 from phase 8.

The remains of infants (babies under two years of age) and young children (aged two to four years) predominated among the burials of phase 11 in the historic period. One group (72.162) consisted of a mature adult female and a newborn infant and was conceivably a mother and child. The baby was full size and full term to judge from the skeletal maturity. The adult had a cleft first sacral vertebra and slight scoliosis of the lower spine with degenerative arthritis of the thoracic (Th 4, 5, 6) and lumbar (L 3, 4, 5) vertebrae. These changes may have been the consequence of a back injury or of excessive load-bearing from adolescence. There was considerable wear on the teeth, and the cranial vault bones were somewhat thickened. Two other mature adult females had extensive degenerative changes affecting, in particular, the vertebrae and shoulder joints. A male (B75) showed signs of strained ligaments (enthesopathy) of the knee.

The prevalence of arthritic change, back injury, and joint strain, together with well-marked muscle insertions on the arms, are indications that the people of phase 11 were exposed to considerable and sometimes excessive physical exercise during their lifetimes. Loads were carried on the head, at least by the women; when at rest some were in the habit of squatting.

There was apparently a high mortality among the infants, many of whom would not have been weaned. Cribra parietalia of one baby, B53, could be a sign of hemolytic anemia associated with malaria, since it is unlikely that so young a child would have become severely iron deficient. There were no other signs of nutritional deficiency, although the cortical thickness of the shafts of the bones of the adults was noticeably thinner than were the bones of the Neolithic people.

Skeletal maturation of the children in this group appeared to be advanced. The mandibular rami of a four-month baby (72.161) had fused. The crowns of the first permanent molars were already complete in a child (72.588) aged about nine months according to its deciduous dentition.

Physically the adults were rather small and muscular. Their limb proportions were non-European with a long tibia relative to the femur.

Trench D

The remains of ten skeletons were recovered from Trench D, including two adult females, two males, and four juveniles. They came from near the middle of the excavated sequence. Six individuals were identified from five inhumations; the grave (73.852) of an adult male also contained the remains of an infant of about six months. In addition a single tooth (phase 1), two metacarpals, a metatarsal (phase 4), and a hand phalanx (phase 6) were recovered from the bone bag material.

The bodies were in tightly flexed bundles, and some were disarticulated (suggesting secondary burial) but heads were not separated from the rest of the body. All ages except infants were accorded this treatment. The bones were generally in a fragmented and dehydrated state and proved more difficult to clean than the bones from the other trenches, because the enclosing silt deposit was quite often indurated by the formation of a gypsum crystalline matrix. We observed small crystals of the mineral adhering to the bone surface.

The age and sex distribution of the human remains had the characteristics of a domestic group, and as elsewhere it seems probable that individuals were buried where they had lived.

The skeletons bore the marks of some of the stresses to which they had been exposed during life. The dentitions of the adults showed the extreme and uneven wear that was brought about by chewing hard, coarse (though not necessarily abrasive) food. Wear must have been rapid and could exceed the formation of secondary dentine such that the pulp cavities were exposed. No associated abscesses were noted, implying that infection rates were low, but teeth were eventually lost through overeruption and alveolar resorption. One adult male (73.852) had lost 8 of 14 tooth positions that could be examined. The fracturing and chipping that we observed on some of the teeth could be attributed to the inclusion of hard particles in the food. The excessive forces imposed on the teeth and jaws led to massive development of the mandibular condyles.

Degenerative changes of the spinal vertebrae in one female (73.854) affected four cervical and the first three lumbar vertebrae, including the joints. This woman also had arthritic hips and feet. We suppose that she had spent a considerable part of her life in the preparation of cereals for food.

We noted traumatic lesions in a deformed wrist bone of an adult male (73.302) resulting from an injured thumb. We also observed a greenstick fracture of the ulna with associated hematoma causing periosteal new bone growth on the left elbow of the adolescent 73.851. The nine-year-old child (73.690) had enamel hypoplasia of the canine and must have survived an earlier infection. The somewhat thickened parietal bones of two of the adults (73.B16+18 and 73.B101) may be indicative of childhood anemia, perhaps associated with infection.

Trench E

No burials as such were recognized in phases 1–3 of Abu Hureyra 1, but a number of isolated human bones, primarily hand and foot bones, from individuals of all ages were recovered. A fragment of the first metatarsal of a young adult (B 502/512) showed the extension of the articular surface of the distal end that we have identified with the excessive pressure on the toe imposed by the position taken up during the preparation of seeds in a mortar or on a saddle quern.

The earliest Abu Hureyra 2 human remains in Trench E were found in phase 4. They consisted of the fragmented skeleton of a child (73.3273) recovered from a hollow in the yard just outside a rectangular mudbrick house. The skull had been coated with plaster stained red. Shoveling of the incisors in this individual recalled those of 73.851 from Trench D as well as several others from later levels in both Trench E and B.

There were a number of burials in pits under the floors and in deposits filling the rooms of the main phase 5 house, and in the contemporary house in the northeast corner of the trench. In addition to the remains of about ten juveniles, there were several newborn infants buried in the fill of the rooms. Some were represented by skull bones only. Of the six or seven individuals buried in pits, three were young or mature females and two were juveniles. Bones of juveniles were included with most of the female burials. It may not be coincidence that a saddle quern was found in the south corner of the room in which the female (73.3436) was buried. She bore the characteristic signs on metatarsal I of having used a saddle quern.

Most of the other females also showed changes associated with grinding: three had buttressed femora and one had changes to the first metatarsal. Four females also had squatting facets on the tibia or patella, and presumably squatting was the posture habitually taken up for other tasks, such as sorting and picking over grain.

A female (73.2271) from phase 5 had severe osteoarthritis of the spine following an injury. Exuberant fringe osteophytes around the body of T12 were associated with spondylosis. The spinal canal was triangular with a medial osteophyte indentation causing spinal stenosis. The adjacent vertebra, L1, was wedge shaped, probably due to old vertebral collapse following trauma. Osteoarthritic changes in the first metatarsophalangeal joint were typical of hallux rigidus. The articular surfaces of the proximal phalanges of the toes were quite irregular. We attribute these changes to injuries associated with the use of a saddle quern for grinding grain.

The only male (73.2952) a mature adult from this phase was buried in room 1. The postcranial skeleton was incomplete, but no evidence of changes associated with grinding was found. He did have a chipped tooth and extensive ante-mortem loss of teeth and so ate the same hard, coarse foods as other villagers.

Two carious teeth of 73.1930 were among the first signs of the deterioration in oral health and the existence in the population of cariogens. The female also had a pathological fibula. Other burials from the fill showed a high rate of dental chipping and ante-mortem loss.

Pits dug into the floors of the rooms in the main house in phase 6 contained the remains of about nine individuals. Heads were not separated from bodies. Skeletal evidence for continuity with the previous phase was provided by a mature adult female (73.2271) buried in room 1 who had agenesis of a third molar, as did three of the females from the equivalent room in phase 5. A male (73.2398) and a female (73.2396) buried together in the corner of the room appeared to have genetic links with individuals buried in other rooms of the house. The female, a juvenile (73.1996) in room 4, and a youth (72.520) in room 5 all had septate supra condylar fossas on the humerus; both males had a detached lumbar arch (spondylolisis).

The females had kneeling modifications to the first metatarsal (not displayed by the males), and two had suffered injuries to the lower back. In 73.2271 these were severe, were associated with stenosis of the spine, and may have impaired movement. Wear on the teeth continued to be heavy, with abrasion, fracturing, and ante-mortem loss common in older individuals.

The youth (72.520) was found with an arrowhead in the region of the thorax (figure 10.12). However, we noted no bone lesions.

There were a number of markers for the presence of pathogens, including dental hypoplasia in two individuals and vertebral collapse with signs of healing pyogenic infection in another two. Thickened skull bones and cribra orbitalia were present in two cases. Neither dental caries nor abscesses were recorded.

The skeletal material from phase 7 was recovered from the area of the main house that had been rebuilt. A male (73.1316) was associated with an arrowhead but no injuries to the bones were noted. There were more males in this group than usual, and several, for example, 73.1315A, had modifications of the metatarsals associated with kneeling. One juvenile (B51) had a septate humerus, which recalls those of the previous phase.

Skeletal material from phase 8 was very fragmented, and most was recovered from the sieves; none could be attributed to the fill of the large pits that often contained burnt animal bone. Only one human bone, a tibia (B101), was charred. Adults and juveniles of all ages were represented.

Enamel pearls and a Carabelli's cusp on molars of one youth (73.810) provided evidence of a possible link with individuals from earlier levels in other trenches. Squatting facets on the tibia of three individuals (B25, B35, B101) indicate that squatting was the habitual posture. Unfortunately, we could not establish from the remains whether the saddle quern continued to be used extensively for preparing grain, although one adult (73.B86) had a buttressed femur. Wear on the teeth appeared to be less severe, and it is possible that people were eating cooked food more often.

Females, males, and numerous children were buried in the area of Trench E during phase 9 in historic times. Arthritic changes and degenerative joint disease were common among the adults. Periosteal new bone growth on a juvenile femur and severe osteitis of the skull of an infant (73.95) indicated the presence of infective disease. Three individuals had noticeably thickened skull bones that could be indicative of hemolytic condition or malaria.

Trench G

Fragments of the skull of a juvenile (73.3066) were recovered from the occupation debris next to a mudbrick structure in phase 1. The dental age assessed from the stage of development of the permanent dentition was about 9.5 years; the deciduous dentition appeared to be delayed—a characteristic noted elsewhere in the material.

Appendix 6: Analysis of Charcoal from Abu Hureyra 1

V. ROITEL AND G. WILLCOX

We analyzed 3,118 fragments of charcoal dispersed through 15 levels in the Abu Hureyra 1 deposits. Most of the charcoal probably came from multiple firings of hearths over an extended period. The inhabitants of Abu Hureyra 1 collected fuel for their fires nearby, so the charcoal represents species of trees and shrubs that would have been present in the local vegetation.

We examined the charcoal using standard laboratory techniques (Vernet 1992). Our identifications were based on comparisons with reference material we have collected in the field from a large number of locations in Southwest Asia, and we also consulted three atlases of wood anatomy (Greguss 1959; Schweingrüber 1990; Fahn, Werker, and Bass 1986). The diversity of species in Southwest Asia made specific identifications difficult in most cases. For example, about 30 species of oak, 28 of buckthorn, and 17 of almond grow in the region today (Zohary 1973, pp. 353, 357).

The charcoal from Abu Hureyra 1 was finer and more fragmented compared to charcoal from other sites on the Middle Euphrates that we have analyzed. Oak was broken along the rays and at right angles along the growth rings, producing very small fragments. We sorted the fine fraction of the charcoal from levels 470, 473, 455, and 405 using a low-power microscope, and this may account for the higher frequencies of oak compared to the other samples. Because of the bias introduced by fragmentation, the small differences in frequencies between woodland-steppe species are probably not significant.

It is clear from the results (figure A6.1) that the inhabitants of Abu Hureyra 1 obtained most of their fuel from the gallery forest in the Euphrates Valley. The valley contained an abundance of trees with soft wood that were easy to cut down and that regenerated rapidly. Woodland-steppe trees such as the great terebinth, oak, and almond have very hard wood and would have been preserved for their fruits (Hillman, Colledge, and Harris 1989, p. 224). The wood charcoal and fruits of woodland-steppe species found at Abu Hureyra indicate that these trees grew in the area during the occupation of the site, although they are no longer found there today. While one might argue that some wood could have floated down the Euphrates from farther north, there are several reasons to suppose that this is not the case. First, species such as conifers characteristic of moister vegetation zones upstream have not been found at Abu Hureyra; second, oak charcoal has been recovered from five sites along the Middle Euphrates, one of which (Halula) is about 5 km from the river; third, most of the charcoal has very narrow growth rings, indicating that the trees grew on drier soils well away from the river.

The woodland-steppe association of Abu Hureyra 1 resembles vegetation found occasionally in the central part of Syria today, though it is now highly degraded. This association occurs in upland areas above 700 m where annual rainfall exceeds 300 mm. Relicts of what were once more extensive stands occur on the Jebels Abdul Aziz, Bishri, and Abu Rujmein. The Jebel Abdul Aziz has species such as oriental almond (*Amygdalus orientalis*), great terebinth, red haw-

Figure A6.1 The wood charcoals from Abu Hureyra 1: the frequencies of charcoal fragments of each taxon, calculated as the percentage of the total number of fragments identified from that sample.

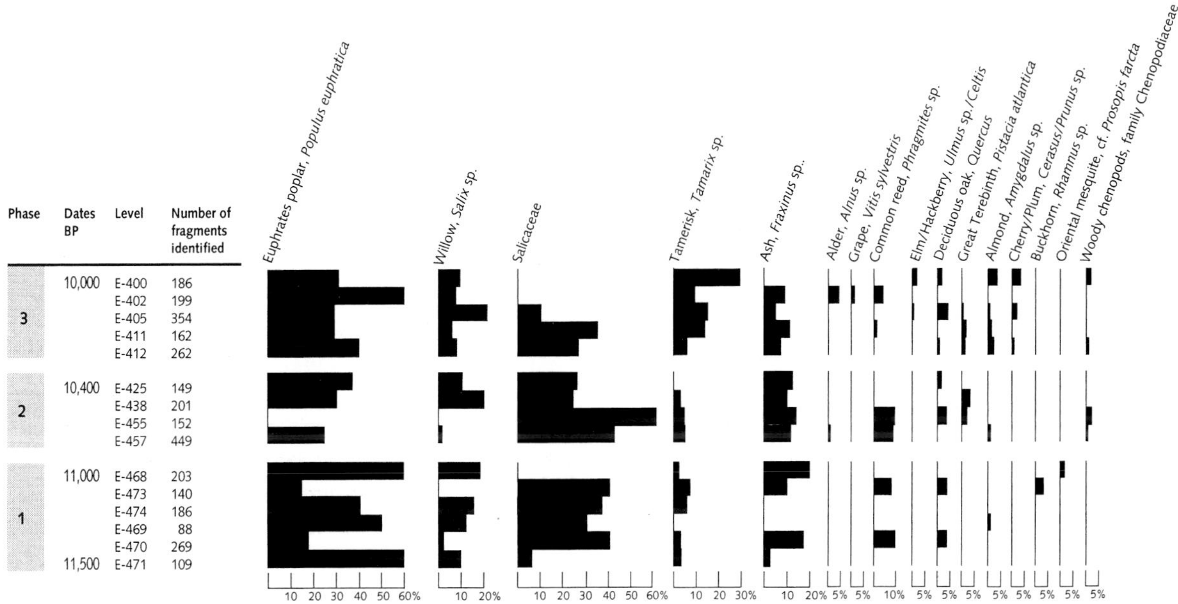

thorn (*Craetagus azarolus*), and miniature cherry (*Cerasus microcarpa*), but it lacks oak that was present at Abu Hureyra. These species also form part of the deciduous oak forest in areas above 800 m with over 500 mm of annual rainfall. The Jebel Sinjar is a good example. In Transjordan and Asia Minor, Tabor oak and Brandt's oak occur as dominants of the woodland-steppe vegetation that fringes the steppe.

The gallery forest was much richer in species during the Epipalaeolithic, but today it is very degraded. The only species that remain and are still exploited are Euphrates poplar, tamarisk, willow, and common reed. The diversity of species may have been partly due to the moister, cooler conditions that prevailed early in Abu Hureyra 1 times, but it is also likely that several species have simply died out because their habitat has been greatly reduced by human exploitation of shade-providing trees such as Euphrates poplar and clearance for valley-bottom agriculture. Species such as alder, vine, and ash are found today in gallery forest farther north at higher altitudes in Anatolia and the Zagros. In northern Mesopotamia, Syrian ash (*Fraxinus syriaca*) forms pure stands in the mountain gallery forest (Guest and al-Rawi 1966, p. 84). Common reed, which is well represented in the charcoal, could have been used as a building material.

We identified relatively small quantities of charcoal of steppe plants, such as the chenopods. They may be underrepresented because the occupants preferred woodland species that were more effective as fuel and much easier to gather.

Our results do not show any major changes in the exploitation of woody species during the occupation of Abu Hureyra 1. The climatic changes that were taking place may not have affected the availability of woody species in the same way as they influenced fruit and seed collecting or pollen production. It is possible that during periods of climatic deterioration the woodland-steppe species may have been limited to only the most favorable habitats. Oaks may have been restricted to deep soils that retained moisture such as in the side valleys leading down from the steppe plateau to the Euphrates.

The woodland-steppe species that we have identified at Abu Hureyra 1 were also represented in charcoal from the sites of Jerf el Ahmar, Dja'de, and Halula, situated 50 km upstream and dating from the tenth and ninth millennia BP, but there is no direct local evidence as to when these species first colonized the Syrian steppe. High-altitude pollen sites such as Lake Zeribar and Lake Van indicate that conditions during the last Ice Age did not permit woodland vegetation to grow in the Zagros and in eastern Anatolia. Low-altitude pollen sites such as Lake Huleh and the Ghab are in areas where there was a strong Mediterranean influence. Oak was insignificant at lakes Zeribar and Van during the Late Glacial and did not expand there until well into the Holocene, although it was definitely present in the Mediterranean zone during the glacial maximum (Baruch and Bottema 1991, p. 11; Kislev, Nadel, and Carmi 1992, p. 162). In the Syrian steppe, the earliest data come from Abu Hureyra 1. Given the evidence for lower temperatures, it is possible that depressions from the Mediterranean penetrated farther east into the Syrian steppe, making it more favorable to tree species at a relatively early date during the cooler periods that preceded the occupation of the site (Hillman 1996). In the steppe of southern Transjordan pollen analyses of aerobic archaeological sediments from sites on the Jebel Mishraq indicate the sporadic presence of deciduous oak pollen during the Epipalaeolithic (c. 16,000–12,500 BP; Emery-Barbier 1995, p. 380).

The evidence of the charcoal suggests that conditions were cooler and perhaps moister during the occupation of Abu Hureyra 1. Today's 200 mm annual rainfall at Abu Hureyra could not have sustained the woodland-steppe vegetation that occurred there in the twelfth and eleventh millennia BP. The climate in areas of higher altitude where we find this kind of vegetation today is cooler and moister, so it would appear that the wooded zones occurred at lower altitudes during the Epipalaeolithic. However, estimating the annual rainfall from the charcoal evidence is problematic. The present-day woodland-steppe vegetation requires a minimum of 300–350 mm of annual rainfall, but given the cooler temperatures that prevailed during the occupation of the site, this figure may have been somewhat lower.

Appendix 7 Location of the Material Recovered from the Excavation

The Directorate General of Antiquities and Museums in Syria divided the artifacts from the excavation in Aleppo in 1977; it retained half for deposit in the Aleppo Museum and duly allocated the other half to the expedition under the terms of the excavation agreement. That material has been further divided among the ten museums that contributed to the project and sent on to them as study of it has been completed. All artifacts from any one stratigraphic sequence have been kept together so that the collections now held by the institutions that supported the project are as complete and representative as possible. We have also attempted to group subdivisions of the material in museums that are situated close to each other geographically. They thus retain the maximum possible value for students who may wish to conduct their own studies of the artifacts. The details of these dispositions are given in table A7.1.

The Syrian authorities graciously allowed us to export all the organic remains for study and curation. They are now in London. The human remains have been presented to the British Natural History Museum. The animal bones and other faunal remains are presently housed at the Centre for Extra-Mural Studies, Birkbeck College, University of London, while study of them continues; we anticipate that they will eventually be transferred to the Natural History Museum. The flotation samples are currently in the Archaeobotany Laboratory of the Institute of Archaeology, University College, London, where they, too, continue to be analyzed. They will be presented to another institution for long-term curation in due course.

Appendix 8: Data Tables

We take seriously our obligation to publish all the data recovered from the excavation. Other scholars need to be able to examine in detail the information from which we have derived our conclusions. They should also be able to conduct their own analyses, perhaps using new approaches that will illuminate further the extraordinary record from the site. The data are so abundant that it has seemed best to make them available as an electronic archive. They may thus be stored cheaply and yet readily be examined by scholars anywhere in the world who have access to the Internet. Furthermore, we can add new data to the archive as our own studies continue, thus increasing its value to other scholars in the years to come.

Table A7.1 Location of material excavated from Abu Hureyra

Trench	Excavation season	Levels and periods	Disposition
A	1972 and 1973	all: 72/1–72/51, 73/1–73/245. AH 2	Aleppo Museum
B	1972	1–23. AH 2	Liverpool Museum
B	1972	24–68. AH 2	Bolton Museum
B	1973	all: 69–221. AH 2	Aleppo Museum
C	1972 1973	all: 72/1–72/60, 73/1–73/134. AH 2	Ashmolean Museum, University of Oxford
D	1972	1, 4. AH 2	British Museum
D	1972	2, 3, 5–87. AH 2	Oriental Institute, Chicago
D	1973	all: 88–183. AH 2	Oriental Institute, Chicago
E	1972	all: 1–57. AH 1 and 2	Oriental Institute, Chicago
E	1973	58–94. AH 2	Pitt Rivers Museum, University of Oxford
E	1973	95–144. AH 2	Royal Ontario Museum, Toronto
E	1973	145–153. AH 2	Manchester University Museum
E	1973	154–214, 216. AH 2	Birmingham Museum
E	1973	215, 217–395. AH 2. 396–423. AH 1	Aleppo Museum
E	1973	424–441. AH 1	Royal Ontario Museum, Toronto
E	1973	442–454. AH 1	Oriental Institute, Chicago
E	1973	455–475. AH 1	British Museum
F	1973	all: 1–32. AH 2	Aleppo Museum
G	1973	all: 1–72. AH 2	Aleppo Museum
Collection from surface of site, plus samples of floor and wall plaster	1973	AH 2	Warrington Museum, Lancashire, England
Collection from surface of site	1971	AH 2	Pitt Rivers Museum, University of Oxford

You may obtain access to the Abu Hureyra electronic data archive by typing the electronic address (http://www.rit.edu/abuhureyra) into a computer linked to the Internet through a modem. Once you have opened the archive you should follow the instructions given there on how to proceed. You may transfer the data to your computer and may print out copies to aid in perusal and analysis.

A list follows of the information currently stored in the electronic archive.

Level tables. A detailed description and classification of each level dug in the trenches described in this book, that is, for Abu Hureyra 1, Trench E, and for Abu Hureyra 2, Trenches B, D, E, and G.

Phase lists. A list of every level in each phase determined stratigraphically for Trenches B, D, E, and G.

Burial tables. A complete inventory of burials for Trenches B, D, E, and G. The tables contain full information about the location, nature, and contents of each burial.

Human remains. Tables of the detailed analyses of all the human remains from Trenches B, D, E, and G.

Abu Hureyra 1 chipped stone industry. A complete inventory of the chipped stone, both tools and debitage, recovered from each level in Abu Hureyra 1.

Abu Hureyra 1 stone artifacts. A complete inventory of all the stone artifacts recovered from Abu Hureyra 1, with the stratigraphic location, dimensions, and a description of each object.

Notes

Chapter 3

1. The vegetation map (figure 3.7) draws on information from Michael Zohary (1973) and Pabot (1957) in particular, and also on ideas and information culled from Birand (1970), Bor and Guest (1968), Browicz (1982), Davis (1965–1988), Frey and Kürschner (1989), Gökmen (1962), Guest and al-Rawi (1966), Louis (1939), Mouterde (1966), Sankary (1977, 1982), UNESCO-FAO (1969), Walter (1956), van Zeist and Bakker-Heeres (1982), and van Zeist and Bottema (1991). One of the problems in using these sources is the dramatic lack of unanimity on the potential limits of the different zones and the potential "climax" vegetation of each, particularly in the zones we here refer to as steppe, woodland-steppe, and xeric woodland.

2. See Hillman (1996) for an example of this modeling as applied to the Late Pleistocene migration of wild einkorn.

3. For an account of this "ethno-ecological modeling," see Hillman (1989), Hillman, Madeyska, and Hather (1989), and Wetterstrom (1986).

4. The probable intensity of early deforestation to meet the burgeoning need for timber, domestic fires, and industrial operations such as plaster production in the vicinity of individual sites, is discussed by Moore (1979, p. 58; 1981, p. 452; 1983, p. 99), Rollefson and Simmons (1988), and van Zeist and Bottema (1991, 7.3–7.6).

5. The types of montane forest are not subdivided here but are described in detail in Zohary (1973), and in Frey and Kürschner (1989), and more briefly outlined in van Zeist and Bottema (1991).

6. "Rosaceae" is the rose family that includes not only the roses but also blackberries, amelanchiers, apples, pears, hawthorns, and plums.

7. Different combinations of dwarf shrubs characterize each of Zohary's subzones of this "steppe-maquis" in the region as a whole (Zohary 1973, pp. 541–543), but none of the combinations relates specifically to the northern Levant.

8. When the great terebinths do successfully establish themselves in well-watered valley bottoms, they often grow to a huge size. One remarkable specimen we observed in a valley at Yaprakli near Çankiri was about 30 m tall.

9. Van Zeist and Bakker-Heeres (1982, p. 169) likewise suggest that this zone could extend down to the 200 mm isohyet. The same conclusion is reached by McCorriston (1992), who notes that "generally lands with less than 200 mm annually support no trees" (p. 34).

10. The meaning of the Arabic word "butum" is great terebinth, *Pistacia atlantica*.

11. See figure 12.3 for photographs of annual grasses penetrating down wadi systems into, in this case, full-blown steppe.

12. The grass family "Gramineae" is now technically known as "Poaceae."

13. From his poem "The steppe" recently translated into English by Richard McKane (1998).

14. The evidence we use here has been drawn principally from wetland pollen cores, notably from Lake Huleh, the Ghab, Karamik-Batakliği and Söğüt Gölü in Southwest Turkey, and Lake Zeribar (Baruch 1994; Baruch and Bottema 1991; Bottema and van Zeist 1981; Niklewski and van Zeist 1970; van Zeist and Bottema 1977, 1982, 1991; van Zeist, Woldring, and Stapert 1975; and information from Yasouda about a new pollen core from the Ghab). This evidence is reinforced by studies of pollen preserved without waterlogging in archaeological deposits on sites such as Hayonim and Ain Mallaha (Leroi-Gourhan 1984; Leroi-Gourhan and Darmon 1991; van Zeist and Bottema 1991); by studies of food plants from the Late Palaeolithic site of

Ohalo II on the Sea of Galilee (Kislev, Nadel, and Carmi 1992); and most recently by studies of wood charcoals from Abu Hureyra 1 by Roitel and Willcox (appendix 6).

All these lines of evidence suggest broadly the same trends, with the exception of one of the two independent pollen sequences from the Ghab. And even this accords with the general trends if we adjust the single, suspect, mollusk-based radiocarbon date for the upper part of the sequence and, more importantly, if we alter the interpolated dates published for the preceding phases, as recommended by Moore and Hillman (1992, p. 489), Baruch (1994, p. 111), and Hillman (1996, pp. 166–175).

15. This problem has been discussed in depth by M. Davis (1983), Huntley (1991), Huntley and Birks (1983), Huntley and Webb (1989), and Webb (1986).

16. The more important primary and secondary sources for these data are Bottema (1986), Bottema and van Zeist (1981), van Zeist and Bottema (1977, 1982, and 1991), and van Zeist and Woldring (1978).

17. In assembling this model of migration, Hillman (1996) used figures based on isopoll data from Huntley (1988, 1991), Huntley and Birks (1983), Huntley and Webb (1989), and Webb (1988) to suggest that, if oak migration across the Fertile Crescent started from the north of the Levantine refuge around 15,000 BP, and then the oaks should have reached Lake Zeribar a millennium or so either side of 9,000 BP, and the terebinths and wild cereals several centuries earlier. The Lake Zeribar pollen diagram (van Zeist and Bottema 1977, diagram Zeribar Ib) supports just such a scenario, with the first oaks arriving in the area around 10,000 BP, a dramatic rise in grass pollen a millennium earlier at c. 11,000 BP, and terebinth arriving a little before that. Hillman (1996, pp. 166–175) argues that this rise in "other gramineae" is attributable primarily to wild annuals migrating together with the largely cleistogamous cereals.

18. CO_2 levels had already reached a plateau by this point (Sage 1995, figure 1) and are not implicated in these changes.

Chapter 4

1. Correlations between the field level numbers and those used here are presented in the electronic archive.

2. The level tables and accompanying phase lists may be consulted in the electronic archive.

3. Early in our accelerator dating program the Oxford laboratory dated one sample twice, and also dated different chemical fractions of several samples for experimental purposes. The laboratory considers the dates on the chemical fractions to be less accurate than those on the original samples. Those dates are all listed in appendix 1 but have not been used in our chronological analyses.

Chapter 6

1. My research was conducted over several years and involved the assistance of many individuals and institutions. Accordingly, I thank the following: earlier portions of this study benefited from the comments of A. J. Jelinek, P. R. Fish, and R. H. Thompson. I am responsible, however, for the final expressed opinions. I examined a number of collections of chipped stone assemblages during the course of my research, and this was facilitated by the aid of several people. I thank A. Bahnassi (National Museum, Damascus), A. Bounni (National Museum, Damascus), K. Toueir (National Museum, Damascus), W. Khayata (National Museum, Aleppo), H. Hammade (National Museum, Aleppo), N. Jabri (National Museum, Aleppo), R. Inskeep (Pitt Rivers Museum), D. Roe (Donald Baden Powell Quaternary Research Centre, Oxford), P. R. S. Moorey (Ashmolean Museum), P. L. Carter (Museum of Archaeology and Anthropology, Cambridge), G. de G. Sieveking (British Museum), P. Robinson (British Museum), M. Newcomer (Institute of Archaeology, London), J. and M.-C. Cauvin (Maison de l'Orient, Lyon), A. E. Marks (Southern Methodist University, Dallas), and D. Kaufman (Southern Methodist University, Dallas).

This study was made possible by a variety of grants. These include the Graduate College Development Fund of the University of Arizona, the Educational Fund of the Department of Anthropology at the University of Arizona, Sigma Xi Grants-in-Aid-of-Research, and a research fellowship from the Fulbright Program for study in the Syrian Arab Republic.

Chapter 7

1. There are numerous examples in the collections of the Museum of the American Indian, Heye Foundation, New York City. Most of those artifacts will be transferred to the new National Museum of the American Indian in Washington, D.C. Some are displayed in the George Gustav Heye Center of the National Museum of the American Indian in New York.

Chapter 11

1. I thank the students of the Post Diploma Osteology Course at the University of London for their assistance; Philip Crabb, Photo Studio, Natural History Museum, London; Colin Threadgall and Robert Kruszynski, Natural History Museum, for illustrations; Lorraine Cornish, Laboratory of the Department of Palaeontology, Natural History Museum; Terry Williams, Gary Jones, and Vic Din, Department of Minerals, Natural History Museum; and Dawn Hodgson, Percy Cohen, Tim Crompton, Karen Jones, Barbara Adams, and Professor John Price for reading the radiographs.

2. The data supporting many of the statements and conclusions in this chapter are presented in a series of tables in the electronic archive (see appendix 8).

3. The analysis was conducted with SPSS-X, release 3.01.

4. The agreement between the stature estimates derived from the individual bones of a single skeleton is closest when Trotter and Gleser's formulas for Negroes rather than people of European descent are used. This does not imply that the people were Negroes; formulas for present-day western Asian populations are not available.

Chapter 12

1. Certainly, there was a long tradition of acorns being eaten by at least some groups in Southwest Asia, as evidenced at early Epipalaeolithic Ohalo II in the Jordan Valley, c. 19,000 BP (Kislev, Nadel, and Carmi 1992), and this continues into the present day.

2. The limited surface water flow of the Middle and Upper Pleistocene has allowed weathered sediments to accumulate in all the myriad small branches of the wadi systems to the south of Abu Hureyra, and to generally soften the wadi sections, making them far less incised. The consequent tendency of this close network of now very shallow and open palaeo-wadis of all the finer side branches of the wadi system, not only to gather water from higher upslope, but also to retain much of it in these sediments, encourages extensive colonization by annual grasses, including the wild cereals, in and around them. Figure 12.3 shows a small-scale example of precisely this effect.

However, where wadis were regularly flushed by strong flows of water, then the actual wadi bottoms and banks would have supported an entirely different flora. With the relatively moist spring–early summer seasons that characterized the period around 11,500 BP, I suggest that this regular flushing occurred in the middle and lower reaches of the main course of both the Wadi Shetnet es-Salmas and Wadi Hibna.

3. George Willcox informs us that ICARDA has now accessed a large number of additional collections of both of the wild einkorns, and the distribution of their source locations reinforces our earlier observation that *T. urartu* is better able to survive in locations where the soil dries out early than is *T. boeoticum*.

4. For details of the ecology of these wild almonds, see Browicz and Zohary (1996).

5. Polunin and Huxley (1967) cite Atchley's account of the roots being eaten in Greece as recently as the First World War, as well as Theophrastus' report of the roots, "stalk," and seeds being eaten in his day. By "stalk," I guess he means the young flowering shoot just at its emerging. I personally find this (once boiled) even more tasty than the related asparagus shoots. The seeds are tasty when roasted, ground, and cooked as a "damper" (the aboriginal Australian equivalent of a pancake; see Cane 1989), while the roots are good either boiled or, better, roasted in the embers of a fire.

6. It is not impossible that the same habitats would also have supported thickets of spiny, gray-leaved bushes of the sea buckthorn (*Hippophaë rhamnoides*), even though its present-day distribution remains north of the present-day border with Turkey (Browicz 1982, p. 54). If so, their sharp-flavored, oily, orange fruits would have provided an exceptionally rich source of essential fatty acids, vitamin C (a remarkable 2 g per 100 g), vitamin E (160 mg per 100 g; i.e., many thousands of times the US RDA), and vitamin A (10 mg per 100 g; i.e., 100 times the US RDA) (Lánská 1992, p. 110).

7. The term "fruits" is here used in its botanical sense, namely, any structure resulting from the fertilization of a flower, for example, the dry capsules of poppies, the achenes of buttercups, the nuts of hazel, and the tiny nutlets of knotgrass, as well as the soft, fleshy fruits of cherries and apples.

8. My decision to express the absolute frequencies (as represented by the bars) as the numbers of specimens of any one type identified per *200 liters* of excavated deposit was somewhat arbitrary. I needed to choose a volume of excavated deposit that was less than that actually floated in most of the more typical levels, as this both avoided giving an inflated impression of the numbers of items actually identified and usefully reduced the length of bars, making the diagram more compact. But this device still left a few levels where the volume of deposit floated was less then 200 liters and where, therefore, the numbers of items actually identified had to be multiplied up. However, I felt that, for the majority of levels, a denominator of even less than 200 liters would produce understated frequencies that were too remote from the actual numbers of items identified. Overall, then, in using the patterns of abundance represented in the multihistogram, it must be remembered that absolute numbers indicated by most of the bars are an understatement of the numbers of seeds or fruits that were actually identified in the remains.

I chose to use absolute rather than relative (for example, percentage) frequencies for the multihistogram for three reasons. The first concerned the perennial problem of relative frequencies. Given that a few taxa such as club-rush, knotgrass, feather-grass, and the bugloss family are present in very large numbers, calculation of the frequency of each seed type as a percentage of the total numbers of specimens identified from that same deposit would mean that apparent changes in abundance through time in any one seed type would not necessarily reflect any change in how often that plant arrived on site and got preserved. Rather, it would reflect merely the changing pattern of adundance of everything else, particularly the few really abundant types. Second, a large number of the seed types are present in quite small numbers, and percentage frequencies in such cases are especially meaningless.

Third, compared to the Neolithic deposits with their obvious mudbrick structures, the Epipalaeolithic deposits were relatively uniform and were seemingly dominated by ashes raked out of the hearths and scattered over the occupation surfaces. Correspondingly, initial results seemed to suggest that, across any one time horizon, context-related variation in both the composition and overall abundance of plant remains was minimal. Furthermore, rates of accumulation of these ashy deposits seemed to be fairly uniform, and this situation paralleled the primary requirement for palynologists using absolute rather than relative pollen diagrams, namely, that the pollen matrix (for example, lake-bottom silts) should have accumulated at a uniform rate.

Nevertheless, further work revealed that there was, after all, some context-related variation in both composition and overall abundance across any one time horizon. Correspondingly, there was a clear need to calculate percentage-based frequency distributions for all the more abundant seed types that were particularly important in subsistence reconstruction, However, we still needed to avoid the first of the drawbacks of relative diagrams noted above. As the most abundant of all the *charred* seed/fruit remains were the riverine species, and the most abundant of the plant remains overall were those seeds that survived largely without charring (thanks to their heavily silicified fruit walls), I excluded both these categories from the seed totals used as denominators in the calculation of percentages of each of the dryland foods, and excluded the silicified seed totals from calculations of the percentages of charred remains of riverine foods. The frequency distributions of charred remains of nonriverine plant such as wild cereals and feather-grass were therefore calculated as percentages of all dryland plant foods (with all other classes excluded); those of riverine food types as percentages of all charred remains (with all silicified remains excluded); and those of the silicified borage family as a percentage of *all* plant remains.

9. It must be stressed that I have suggested that particular plants were gathered as food only in cases where (a) they have served as food among a broad spectrum of recent hunter-gatherers, or as a famine food among a range of agrarian populations; (b) our ecological model suggests that the plant would have been abundantly available in the Abu Hureyra area, at least at the start of the Epipalaeolithic occupation, and worth the effort of gathering it; and (c) there are no more plausible alternative explanations for the plants seeds/fruits arriving on site and getting preserved by charring.

10. In this, the wild wheats seem to differ somewhat from the domesticated glume wheats. Although I have described (Hillman 1981, 1984a, 1984b) traditional processing of domestic emmer as sometimes including parching, there were few villages where I actually observed parching in practice, and in retrospect, I suspect that the heating/singeing of the spikelets prior to bulk storage and/or dehusking repeatedly described to me by villagers in very wet areas of northeast Asia Minor may simply have been undertaken to ensure they were completely dry, and not so much to render them brittle. Certainly, villagers farming in drier areas with whom I raised the matter described it as unnecessary, which is why (in Hillman 1981, figure 5) I described parching as occurring only in wet areas. This view is supported by the findings of Peña-Chocarro (1996).

11. The work of Peña-Chocarro (1996) indicates that this singeing is also achievable without much straw, so it can still be applied to awned spikelets harvested by beating (which leaves behind the straw).

12. The separation of materials of different density by agitating them on a flat tray is found not only among Australian aboriginal peoples as recorded by Cane (1989), but also among some traditional farmers in Southwest Asia (for example, al Azm 1986; Dalman 1964; Neil 1913).

13. Although certain forms of wild emmer today grow in dense stands, for example, in the hills overlooking Galilee, these gregarious forms have several characteristics suggesting that they are the product of introgression of genes of locally cultivated macaroni wheat (*T. durum*) into earlier forms of wild emmer (Blumler 1996; information from T. Miller and D. Zohary). This is the conclusion we had also reached from our own analyses of spikelet morphology. All the forms of wild emmer that are unequivocally free of this introgression grow as isolated plants in generally more rocky terrain.

14. Just such a system of dehusking wild grass florets by treading is described by Garar Gumundsson (1996) for the traditional processing of wild lyme-grass, *Elymus arenarius*, in Iceland.

15. Fenton (1978) records equivalent procedures applied to domestic grain by traditional farmers in the Shetland Isles, together with the same charred by-products of accidents (termed "ministers" in Scots English).

16. A few examples of sources outlining the use of small-grained grasses must suffice: from arid-zone North and Central America, Bean and Saubel (1972), Felger and Moser (1985), Rogers (1980), Simms (1987), and Steward (1933, 1941); from arid-zone North Africa, Harlan (1989); from Asia, Cable and French (1950), Maurizio (1927), and Przchewalski (1884); from Australia, Allen (1974), Cane (1989), Harris (1984), Lawrence (1968), and Tindale (1977). A very useful tabulation of many of the wild grass taxa used by recent nonagrarian peoples appears in Nesbitt (1997, table 3.1).

17. Despite the current debate, there seems little doubt that acorns were the principal caloric staple in not only these hunter-gatherer societies, but also many others in entirely different parts of the world (Mason 1992; McCorriston 1994; Olszewski 1993; Petruso and Wickens 1994).

18. Although Bean and Saubel (1972, p. 20) note that "no village was located more than 16 miles from all its food-gathering ranges, and approximately 80% of all food resources used by a village could be found within 5 miles," they also note that most groups were prepared to travel two days from their village (leaving behind only the very old) to harvest acorns. (It is clear from other passages of this book that the "80% of all food resources used" refers to 80% of the *different species* used, rather than 80% of the total quantity gathered or consumed.)

19. That some of their foraging during phase 1 did, indeed, extend as far as the oak-dominated park-woodland is evidenced by the charred remains of edible seeds of the small-capsuled asphodel, *Asphodelus microcarpus* (figure 12.7).

20. The practice of leaving heavy stone grinders and pestles and mortars at seasonal processing camps is reported for the Cahuilla by Bean and Saubel (1972, p. 124) and for various Aboriginal peoples of Australia by Smith (1989) and Levitt (1981).

21. Roots such as the cyanogenic forms of manioc that require long, complex processing are rare exceptions in this regard.

22. For details see Lee (1979), Tanaka (1976), Woodburn (1968), Allen (1974), Cane (1989), and Jones and Meehan (1989).

23. The details of the ecological zonation of a typical Cahuilla catchment reinforce some of the similarities with Abu Hureyra. First, near the top end of the catchment was a zone dominated by open yellow pine park-woodland with scattered oak groves. Although this zone provided about

15% of the food species used, one of them (acorns) met a major part of caloric needs. Below this was an open pinõn-juniper zone with scattered oaks and, lower down, areas of chaparral/woodland-steppe, together providing 60% of the food species used. The base camps were generally located toward the lower part of this zone. Then, below this, was a desert zone with creosote bushes and washes dominated by various mesquites, and finally, within the desert zone, wet areas with reed swamps, palms, and other species. The last two zones provided 25% of the species used.

24. The roots of extreme dietary diversity could well go back beyond the mastery of fire, which has recently been pushed back to c. 450,000 years ago by John Gowlett's find of what seem to be hearths at Beecham's Pit in Britain. Without cooking, many potential wild plant foods are toxic or contain antidigestive compounds and so cannot be consumed in quantity. Prior to the use of fire, therefore, these potential foods could have contributed to hominid diet only if eaten in mixtures in which each of the problem species made a relatively small contribution. Early dietary diversity would therefore have offered not only an adaptive advantage, but possibly the only means of allowing people to eat the plant foods they required. That is why we argued that dietary diversity probably had its roots in the Lower Palaeolithic (Hillman, Madeyska, and Hather 1989, pp. 228–230).

25. Mortars, generally made of wood, were used almost worldwide by hunter-gatherer and agrarian groups until recent times (although it seems that Australia is an exception). For example, for the !Kung San, Lee (1979, p. 153) notes that wooden mortars (and nut-cracking stones) featured in the preparation of every meal. Examples from traditional agrarian societies are mostly of the "stand-up" kind and can be found from the Shetland Isles to Africa, and from Spain to Japan (Hillman 1984b, 1985; Maurizio 1927, pp. 276–285).

26. Examples of such favored locations likely to have witnessed any such early attempts at cultivation include parts of the Damascus Basin, and the catchment of the Quweiq River, south of Aleppo.

27. Three of the specimens of domestic-type rye with distinctively domestic morphology were chemically contaminated, and Robert Hedges informs us that they will require a modified form of chemical pretreatment before being AMS dated. The contamination comes from silver dag used in SEM examination to attach them to the SEM stub (Colledge 1988) and, in one of the three, also from solvents used in infrared analysis (Hillman et al. 1993).

28. The last type, *Secale cereale* subsp. *ancestrale*, is not likely to have existed at this time, because its ecology as a weed of disturbed ground in orchards near Aydin and other parts of the Büyük Menderes Valley in western Asia Minor (Zhukovskii 1951, pp. 303–305) suggests, according to Daniel Zohary, that it is a feral offshoot of domestic rye, rather than a true wild form. As such, it was clearly not the ancestor of domestic rye that its species name implies.

29. Use of oil from a wide range of members of the borage family, Boraginaceae, can probably be traced back well into the Middle Palaeolithic, for example, at Douara Cave near Palmyra in Syria.

30. The expanding weed flora would inevitably have included a scatter of other plants not belonging to these three major groups. The most obvious examples include poppies, annual chenopods such as *Chenolea arabica*, and probably some crucifers. The tiny seeds of classic segetals such as the poppies are absent from the remains, perhaps because they were winnowed out of the harvested grain or failed to survive charring. Other classic weeds such as the rockets, *Sisymbrium* spp., were present only as ones and twos and have therefore been excluded from figure 12.7. Yet others—such as some of the annual chenopods and the heliotropes—are present in slightly higher numbers, but these are still insufficient to reveal any trend through time. Certainly, in each of these cases (and many others), studies of areas of steppe newly opened up to cultivation in recent times indicate that they are likely to have invaded any tilled areas within the first year or two of the inception of cultivation. However, even combined, these additional weeds are unlikely to have been as important as any one of the three main weed groups discussed above.

31. In reality, there would have been good reasons for harvesting by beating only as long as they were targetting extensive stands of wild cereals. As soon as they started cultivating, there would have been equally good reasons to change to harvesting with a sickle or by uprooting. This is explained in detail in Hillman and Davies (1990b, 1992).

32. It should be noted that one of the reasons for previously excluding the possibility that the wild cereals in the Epipalaeolithic were under pre- (or non-) domestication cultivation (Hillman, Colledge, and Harris 1989) now has to be qualified. Our argument was based on the fact that the charred grains of wild annual rye and wild einkorn (which are both annual and potentially cultivable) appear to have been harvested together with those of wild perennial rye, *Secale montanum*, and that, because wild perennial rye cannot tolerate cultivation, the annual wild einkorn and annual rye were probably not cultivated either.

Now, however, I have found a remarkably robust race of *Secale montanum* growing as a weed of bread wheat on the Uzun Yayla Plateau in central Turkey. The few huge tussocks were scattered through the crop, together with the usual even spread of tough-rachised annual weed rye, *Secale cereale* subsp. *segetale*, and occasional plants of brittle- and semi-brittle-rachised forms (resembling *Secale cereale* subsp. *vavilovii*). And on rocky ground around the edges of the field, I found thick stands of typical tussocks of the more usual form of wild perennial rye and a mass of wild einkorn invading the edges of the crop. (Similar robust forms of *S. montanum* were found independantly on the same plateau by Daniel Zohary and Frances McLaren.) It is not impossible that the form of perennial rye growing near Abu Hureyra in the Epipalaeolithic was of this same, robust, cultivation-tolerant type, and therefore that its grain could possibly have been harvested as part of a cultivated crop of wild-type annual rye.

33. For details of systems of processing these crops among traditional farmers of Western Asia, see al-Azm (1986), Dalman (1964), and Hillman (1981, 1984a, 1984b, 1985).

34. The genetically predetermined photoperiodic triggering mechanism of cereals will have ensured that the cultivators would have been unable to significantly alter ripening dates by merely changing the dates of sowing. In this mechanism the point at which the growing plant initiates the formation of the flowering head (ear) primordium is triggered only when the hours of daylight have increased to a particular level. However, the plant can respond to the trigger in this way only if, by that point, it has reached a sufficiently advanced state of vegetative development. Eventual changes in this response mechanism to the critical photoperiod as found in, for example, modern spring-sown cereals required prolonged periods of selection under cultivation. For this reason, Miller (1987) has rightly stressed that all the early cereal cultigens would have had to have been autumn sown.

35. Although George Willcox found that, in sowing cleared pastureland around the Jalès research station in southern France, he obtained good (and sometimes superior) yields from wild-type cereals sown without prior tilling, the thin, compacted gypsiferous soils around Abu Hureyra would have offered a far less penetrable surface, as well as higher predation rates from Southwest Asian seed-eating ants. In wild stands on such soils, high levels of seed wastage are the norm; after all, maintenance of the population requires only one spikelet in about forty to self-sow, germinate, and establish itself (Hillman and Davies 1990b, 1992). However, with the food stress resulting from increasing desiccation, the people of Abu Hureyra would have tried to avoid wasting cereal seed, and they will certainly have noticed how wild cereals thrived under conditions of any natural disturbance (as did other native plants that would soon become arable weeds). It is therefore almost certain that they would have opted to break up the soil surface prior to sowing—doubtless using the same digging sticks that they used to gather their wild root foods.

36. The reason club-rush was more adversely affected than the Euphrates knotgrass probably reflects its greater need of standing water.

37. I have already published in full my methods of study, and analyses of the detailed counts of seeds for each sample from Abu Hureyra (Moulins 1994, 1997). Interested readers should consult those works for more information about these matters.

38. Tail grain is small grain eliminated from the rest of the grain during sieve-cleaning in the latter stages of crop processing. The purpose of the sieving is to remove weed seeds and small pieces of chaff from the grain, but a sieve size that allows most of the weed seeds to pass through (while retaining most of the grain) inevitably also allows the smallest of the grain (the tail grain) to pass through as well. Such grain often resembles the wild types or can be somewhat malformed. These particular groups of waste products (called "fine cleanings") are often swept into the nearest fire and are the most common crop by-product regularly preserved by charring on the majority of farming sites in western Eurasia.

39. The siliceous seedcoats of the gromwells and most other members of the bugloss family survive without need of charring, and this has prompted different approaches to their scoring. Hillman scored all such seeds as predominantly ancient and dated to their source deposit unless the seeds had small holes in their seed coat bored by seed-eating insects. In the latter case, he assumed that seed-eating species of ants had carried them down into the subterranean nests and fed them to their larvae, hence the holes. He believed that this could have taken place at any time since the source deposit was laid down. He had studied such behavior by seed-eating ants in the Ergani area of Turkey and had traced seed transport by ants down to a depth of 2 m. But he also found that the entirety of the seeds were fed to the larvae and that they were left with a tell-tale hole. Although most of the empty seed coats were taken to the surface and discarded by the ants, many were left underground.

On the other hand, I myself assumed that only the charred (dark gray) and semi-charred (light gray) seeds could be guaranteed to date to the deposit where they were found, and that many of the large numbers of noncharred specimens (admixed with the charred and semi-charred specimens) could have been blown into rodent burrows and have worked their way underground subsequent to the deposit being laid down. Therefore, the frequency of the gromwells appears to be different in the two periods on the histograms (figures 12.7, 12.28–12.31), and this is due to the difference in methodology. The uncharred gromwells of the Neolithic have been fully recorded (Moulins 1994, 1997) but have not been calculated in the histograms.

40. There were significant quantities of club-rush and Euphrates knotgrass in Trench B phases 2–5 and throughout the Trench D sequence (Period 2A). Feather-grass was also present in small amounts in these phases.

Chapter 13

1. Phase 9 in Trench E and phase 11 in Trench B have been assigned to the historic period, Period 3, but most of the bones in those deposits were from the Abu Hureyra 2 occupation. The same is true of Phase 6 in Trench D.

2. Sample = 23, range 3.0–5.4 mm.

3. Letter from M. Asher to AJL, 27 March 1988.

4. Letter from M. Asher to AJL, 30 December 1988.

5. We intend to present a more extensive discussion of bone representation, especially in relation to the range of archaeological contexts that have been defined at Abu Hureyra, at a future date following further analyses.

Appendix 5

1. I have presented the detailed information about all the human bones that we have analyzed in a series of tables. These are in the electronic data archive.

References

Acsadi, G., and Nemeskeri, J. 1970. *History of Human Lifespan and Mortality*. Budapest: Akademiai Kiado.

Ainsworth, W.F. 1888. *A Personal Narrative of the Euphrates Expedition*. 2 vols. London: Kegan Paul, Trench.

Aitken, M.J. 1985. *Thermoluminescence Dating*. London: Academic Press.

Aitken, M.J., and Alldred, J.C. 1972. The assessment of error limits in thermoluminescent dating. *Archaeometry* 14, 2, 257–267.

Akkermans, P.A., Fokkens, H., and Waterbolk, H.T. 1981. Stratigraphy, architecture and lay-out of Bouqras. In *Préhistoire du Levant*, ed. J. Cauvin and P. Sanlaville. Actes du Colloque International 598. Paris: Centre National de la Recherche Scientifique. Pp. 485–501.

Al-Azm, A.N.M. 1986. *An Ethno-Agricultural Study of Certain Sieving Systems at the Village of El-Findara in the Alawite Mountains*. MSc thesis, University College, London.

Albrecht, G. 1977. Testing of materials as used for bone points of the Upper Paleolithic. In *Méthodologie Appliquée à l'Industrie de l'Os Préhistorique*, ed. H. Camps-Fabrer. Paris: Centre National de la Recherche Scientifique. Pp. 119–123.

Allen, H. 1974. The Bagundji of the Darling Basin: cereal gatherers in an uncertain environment. *World Archaeology* 5, 309–322.

Andel, T.H. van, and Runnels, C.N. 1995. The earliest farmers in Europe. *Antiquity* 69, 481–500.

Anderson-Gerfaud, P. 1983. A consideration of the uses of certain backed and "lustred" stone tools from late Mesolithic and Natufian levels of Abu Hureyra and Mureybet (Syria). In *Traces d'Utilisation sur les Outils Néolithiques du Proche Orient*, ed. M.-C. Cauvin. Travaux de la Maison de l'Orient 5. Lyon: Maison de l'Orient. Pp. 77–105.

Andrews, P. 1990. *Owls, Caves and Fossils*. London: British Museum (Natural History).

Arndt, S.L., and Newcomer, M.H. 1986. Breakage patterns on prehistoric bone points: an experimental study. In *Studies in the Upper Palaeolithic of Britain and Northwest Europe*, ed. D.A. Roe. Oxford: British Archaeological Reports International Series 296. Pp. 165–173.

Asher, M. 1986. *A Desert Dies*. London: Penguin.

Aurenche, O. 1980. Un exemple de l'architecture domestique en Syrie au VIIIe millénaire: la maison XLVII de Tell Mureybet. In *Le Moyen Euphrate*, ed. J.C. Margueron. Leiden: Brill. Pp. 35–53.

Aurenche, O. 1981a. *La Maison Orientale*. 2 vols. Bibliothèque Archéologique et Historique 109. Paris: Geuthner.

Aurenche, O. 1981b. Essai de démographie archéologique. L'exemple des villages du Proche Orient ancien. *Paléorient* 7, 1, 93–105.

Bader, N.O. 1989. *Earliest Cultivators in Northern Mesopotamia* (in Russian). Moscow: Nauka.

Bard, E., Arnold, M., Fairbanks, R.G., and Hamelin, B. 1993. ^{230}Th-^{234}U and ^{14}C ages obtained by mass spectrometry on corals. *Radiocarbon* 35, 1, 191–199.

Bard, E., Hamelin, B., Fairbanks, R.G., and Zindler, A. 1990. Calibration of the ^{14}C timescale over the past 30,000 years using mass spectrometric U-Th ages from Barbados corals. *Nature* 345, 405–410.

Barker, E.B.B., ed. 1876. *Syria and Egypt Under the Last Five Sultans of Turkey*. London: Tinsley.

Baruch, U. 1994. The Late Quaternary pollen record of the Near East. In *Late Quaternary Chronology and Paleoclimates of the Eastern Mediterranean*, ed. O. Bar-Yosef and R.S. Kra. Tucson: Radiocarbon. Pp. 103–119.

Baruch, U., and Bottema, S. 1991. Palynological evidence for climatic changes in the Levant ca. 17,000–9,000 B.P. In *The Natufian Culture in the Levant*, ed. O. Bar-Yosef and F.R. Valla. Ann Arbor: International Monographs in Prehistory. Pp. 11–20.

Bar-Yosef, O. 1970. *The Epi-palaeolithic Cultures of Palestine*. Doctoral thesis, Hebrew University, Jerusalem.

Bar-Yosef, O. 1981. The Epi-Palaeolithic complexes in the southern Levant. In *Préhistoire du Levant*, ed. J. Cauvin and P. Sanlaville. Actes du Colloque International 598. Paris: Centre National de la Recherche Scientifique. Pp. 389–408.

Bar-Yosef, O., and Belfer-Cohen, A. 1989. The origins of sedentism and farming communities in the Levant. *Journal of World Prehistory* 3, 4, 447–498.

Bar-Yosef, O., and Goren, N. 1973. Natufian remains in Hayonim Cave. *Paléorient* 1, 49–68.

Bar-Yosef, O., and Tchernov, E. 1966. Archaeological finds and the fossil faunas of the Natufian and microlithic industries at Hayonim cave (western Galilee, Israel). *Israel Journal of Zoology* 15, 104–140.

Bar-Yosef, O., and Tchernov, E. 1970. The Natufian bone industry of ha-Yonim Cave. *Israel Exploration Society* 20, 141–150.

Bar-Yosef, O., and Valla, F.R. 1979. L'évolution du Natoufien. Nouvelles suggestions. *Paléorient* 5, 145–152.

Bass, W.M. 1987. *Human Osteology*, 3rd ed. Columbia: Missouri Archaeological Society.

Bate, D.M.A. 1937.Palaeontology. In *The Stone Age of Mount Carmel* I, by D.A. Garrod and D.M.A. Bate. Oxford: Clarendon Press. Pp. 135–122.

Bean, L.J., and Saubel, K.S. 1972. *Temalpakh: Cahuilla Indian Knowledge and Usage of Plants*. Banning, Calif.: Malki Museum.

Beawes, W. 1929. Remarks and occurrences in a journey from Aleppo to Basra, by way of the desert. In *The Desert Route to India*, ed. D. Carruthers. London, Hakluyt Society, II, 63.

Becker, C. 1987. Faunal remains. In Report of the first two seasons of excavation at Basta, ed. H.J. Nissen, M. Mcleisen, and H.G. Gebel. *Report of the Department of the Department of Antiquities of Jordan* 31, 115–117.

Becker, C. 1991. The analysis of bones from Basta, a pre-pottery Neolithic site in Jordan: problems and potential. *Paléorient* 17, 59–75.

Belfer-Cohen, A. 1988. The Natufian graveyard in Hayonim Cave. *Paléorient* 14, 2, 297–308.

Bender, B. 1978. Gatherer-hunter to farmer: a social perspective. *World Archaeology* 10, 204–222.

Berger, W.H. 1990. The Younger Dryas cold spell—a quest for causes. *Palaeogeography, Palaeoclimatology, Palaeoecology (Global and Planetary Change Section)* 89, 219–237.

Bergman, C.A., and Newcomer, M.H. 1983. Flint arrowhead breakage: examples from Ksar Akil, Lebanon. *Journal of Field Archaeology* 10, 238–243.

Besançon, J., Copeland, L., and Hours, F. 1975–1977. Tableaux de préhistoire libanaise. *Paléorient* 3, 5–46.

Betts, A.V.G. 1982. A Natufian site in the Black Desert, eastern Jordan. *Paléorient* 8, 2, 79–82.

Betts, A.V.G. 1983. Black Desert survey, Jordan; first preliminary report. *Levant* 15, 1–10.

Betts, A.V.G. 1984. Black Desert survey: second preliminary report. *Levant* 16, 25–34.

Betts, A.V.G. 1985. Black Desert survey, Jordan: third preliminary report. *Levant* 17, 29–52.

Betts, A.V.G. 1988. The Black Desert survey. Prehistoric sites and subsistence strategies in eastern Jordan. In *The Prehistory of Jordan*, ed. A.N. Garrard and H.G. Gebel. British Archaeological Reports International Series 396. 2 vols. Pp. 369–391.

Bienert, H.-D. 1991. Skull cult in the prehistoric Near East. *Journal of Prehistoric Religion* 5, 9–23.

Binford, L.R. 1968. Post-Pleistocene adaptations. In *New Perspectives in Archaeology*, ed. S.R. Binford and L.R. Binford. Chicago: Aldine. Pp. 313–341.

Binford, L.R., and Chasko, W.J. 1973. Nunamiut demographic history: a provocative case. In *Demographic Archaeology*, ed. E. Zubrow. Albuquerque: School of American Research. Pp. 63–143.

Bintliffe, J.L., and van Zeist, W. 1982. *Palaeoclimates, Palaeoenvironments and Human Communities in the Eastern Mediterranean Region in Later Prehistory*. Oxford: British Archaeological Reports International Series 133.

Birand, H. 1970. Die Verwüstung der Artemisia-Steppe bei Karapinar in Zentralanatolien. *Vegetatio* 20, 21–47.

Bise, G. 1984. *The Hunting Book* (Gaston Phoebus). London: Regent Books.

Blankinship, J.W. 1905. Native economic plants of Montana. *Montana College Experimental Station Bulletin* 56.

Bleek, D.F. 1936. Beliefs and customs of the /Xam Bushmen. *Bantu Studies* 10, 2, 131–162.

Bloch, M. 1982. Death, women and power. In *Death and the Regeneration of Life*, ed. M. Bloch and J. Parry. Cambridge: Cambridge University Press. Pp. 211–230.

Bloch, M., and Parry, J. 1982. Introduction: death and the regeneration of life. In *Death and the Regeneration of Life*, ed. M. Bloch and J. Parry. Cambridge: Cambridge University Press. Pp. 1–44.

Blumler, M.A. 1984. *Climate and Annual Habit*. MA thesis, Department of Geography, University of California, Berkeley.

Blumler, M.A. 1991. Winter-deciduous *versus* evergreen habit in Mediterranean regions: a model. In *Proceedings of the Symposium on California's Oak Woodlands and Hardwood Rangeland Management, Davis, California*. Berkeley: United States Department of Agriculture, Pacific Southwest Forestry and Range Experimental Station.

Blumler, M.A. 1993. Successional patterns and landscape sensitivity in the Mediterranean and Near East. In *Landscape Sensitivity*, ed. D.S.G. Thomas and R.J. Allison. Chichester: Wiley. Pp. 287–305.

Blumler, M.A. 1996. Ecology, evolutionary theory and agricultural origins. In *The Origins and Spread of Agriculture and Pastoralism in Eurasia*, ed. D.R. Harris. London: UCL Press. Pp. 25–50.

Blunt, A. 1879. *Beduin Tribes of the Euphrates*. 2 vols. London: Murray.

Boardman, S., and Jones, G.E.M. 1990. Experiments on the effects of charring on cereal plant components. *Journal of Archaeological Science* 17, 1–11.

Boerma, J.A.K., and Roodenberg, J.J. 1977. Une deuxième industrie épipaléolithique sur le Nahr el Homr. *Palaeohistoria* 19, 7–17.

Boessneck, J. 1969. Osteological differences between sheep (*Ovis aries* L.) and goats (*Capra hircus* L.) In *Science in Archaeology*, ed. D.R. Brothwell and E.S. Higgs, 2nd ed. London: Thames and Hudson. Pp. 331–358.

Boessneck, J., Müller, H.-H., and Tiechert, M. 1964. Osteologishe Unterscheidungsmerkmale zwischen Schaf (*Ovis aries* L.) und Zeige (*Capra hircus* L.) *Kuhn-Archiv* 78, 1–129.

Bohrer, V.L. 1975. The prehistoric and historic role of the cool-season grasses in the Southwest. *Economic Botany* 29, 199–207.

Bökönyi, S. 1969. Archaeological problems and methods of recognizing animal domestication. In *The Domestication and Exploitation of Plants and Animals*, ed. P.J. Ucko and G.W. Dimbleby. London: Duckworth. Pp. 219–229.

Bökönyi, S. 1973. The fauna of Umm Dabaghiya: a preliminary report. *Iraq* 35, 9–11.

Bökönyi, S. 1976. Development of early stock rearing in the Near East. *Nature* 264, 19–23.

Bökönyi, S. 1977. *Animal Remains from the Kermanshah Valley, Iran*. Oxford: British Archaeological Reports Supplementary Series 34.

Bökönyi, S. 1978. Environmental and cultural differences as reflected in the animal bone samples from five early Neolithic sites in southwest Asia. In Approaches to Faunal Analysis in the Middle East, ed. R.H. Meadow and M.A. Zeder. *Peabody Museum Bulletin* 2, 57–62.

Bökönyi, S. 1986. The equids of Umm Dabaghiyah, Iraq. In *Equids of the Ancient World*, ed. R.H. Meadow and H.-P. Uerpmann. Beihefte zum Tubinger Atlas des Vorderen Orients. Reihe A (Naturwissenschaften) 19, 1. Weisbaden: Reichert. Pp. 309–313.

Bökönyi, S. 1989. Definitions of animal domestication. In *The Walking Larder,* ed. J. Clutton-Brock. London: Unwin Hyman. Pp. 22–27.

Bond, G., Broecker, W., Johnsen, S., McManus, J., Labeyrie, L., Jouzel, J., and Bonani, G. 1993. Correlations between climate records from North Atlantic sediments and Greenland ice. *Nature* 365, 143–147.

Bor, N.L., and Guest, E. 1968. *Flora of Iraq*, Vol. 9: *Gramineae*. Baghdad: Ministry of Agriculture of the Republic of Iraq.

Bordaz, J. 1973. Current research in the Neolithic of south central Turkey: Suberde, Erbaba and their chronological implications. *American Journal of Archaeology* 77, 282–288.

Boserup, E. 1965. *The Conditions of Agricultural Growth*. London: Allen and Unwin.

Bostanci, E.Y. 1959. Researches on the Mediterranean coast of Anatolia, a new Palaeolithic site at Beldibi near Antalya. Preliminary report. *Anatolia* 4, 129–178.

Bostanci, E.Y. 1962. A new Upper Palaeolithic and Mesolithic facies at Belbasi rock shelter on the Mediterranean coast of Anatolia. *Belleten* 26, 101–104, 252–292.

Bottema, S. 1986. A Late Quaternary pollen diagram from Lake Urmia (northwestern Iran). *Review of Palaeobotany and Palynology* 47, 241–261.

Bottema, S., and van Zeist, W. 1981. Palynological evidence for the climatic history of the Near East, 50,000–6,000 BP. In *Préhistoire du Levant*, ed. J. Cauvin and P. Sanlaville. Actes du Colloque International 598. Paris: Centre National de la Recherche Scientifique. Pp. 111–132.

Bottéro, J. 1971. Syria before 2200 B.C. In *The Cambridge Ancient History* 1, part 2, ed. I.E.S. Edwards, C.J. Gadd, and N.G.L. Hammond, 3rd ed. Cambridge: Cambridge University Press. Section 2, pp. 321–327.

Bouchud, J. 1987. *La Faune du Gisement Natoufien de Mallaha (Eynan) Israël*. Mémoires et Travaux du Centre de Recherche Français du Jérusalem 4. Paris: Association Paléorient.

Bounni, A. 1973. *Sauvegarde des Antiquités du Lac du Barrage de l'Euphrate*. Damascus: Direction Générale des Antiquités et des Musées.

Bowman, S.G.E., Ambers, J.C., and Leese, M.N. 1990. Reevaluation of British Museum Radiocarbon dates issued between 1980 and 1984. *Radiocarbon* 32, 59–79.

Braidwood, L.S., and Braidwood, R.J. 1982. *Prehistoric Village Archaeology in South-Eastern Turkey*. Oxford: British Archaeological Reports International Series 138.

Braidwood, R.J. 1940. Report of two sondages on the coast of Syria, south of Tartous. *Syria* 21, 183–221.

Braidwood, R.J., and Braidwood, L.S. 1960. *Excavations in the Plain of Antioch* I. University of Chicago Oriental Institute Publications 61. Chicago: University of Chicago Press.

Braidwood, R.J., and Howe, B. 1960. *Prehistoric Investigations in Iraqi Kurdistan*. Studies in Ancient Oriental Civilization 31. Chicago: University of Chicago Press.

Brice, W.C., ed. 1982. *The Environmental History of the Near and Middle East Since the Last Ice Age*. London: Academic Press.

Brothwell, D.R. 1981. *Digging Up Bones*, 3rd ed. London: British Museum (Natural History).

Browicz, K. 1982. *The Chorology of Trees and Shrubs in Southwest Asia and Adjacent Regions* 1. Warsaw: Polish Scientific Publications.

Browicz, K., and Zohary, D. 1966. The genus *Amygdalus* L. (Rosaceae): species relationships, distribution and evolution under domestication. *Genetic Resources and Crop Evolution* 43, 229–247.

Büller, J. 1983. Methodological problems in the microwear analysis of tools selected from the Natufian sites of el

Wad and Aïn Mallaha. In *Traces d'Utilisation sur les Outils Néolithiques du Proche Orient*, ed. M.-C. Cauvin. Travaux de la Maison de l'Orient 5. Lyon: Maison de l'Orient. Pp. 107–126.

Burckhardt, J.L. 1830. *Notes on the Bedouin and Wahabys*. London: Colburn and Bentley.

Burleigh, R., Ambers, J., and Matthews, K. 1982. British Museum Natural Radiocarbon Measurements XV. *Radiocarbon* 24, 3, 262–290.

Burleigh, R., Matthews, K., and Ambers, J. 1982. British Museum Natural Radiocarbon Measurements XIV. *Radiocarbon* 24, 3, 229–261.

Burton, R.F. 1879. *The Land of Midian*. London: Kegan Paul.

Burton, R.F., and Tyrwhitt Drake, C.F. 1872. *Unexplored Syria*. London: Tinsley.

Butler, A. 1989. Cryptic anatomical characters as evidence of early cultivation in the grain legumes (pulses). In *Foraging and Farming: The Evolution of Plant Exploitation*, ed. D.R. Harris and G.C. Hillman. London: Unwin and Hyman. Pp. 390–407.

Butler, A. 1991. The Vicieae: problems of identification. In *New Light on Early Farming. Recent Developments in Palaeoethnobotany*, ed. J.M. Renfrew. Edinburgh: Edinburgh University Press. Pp. 61–73.

Butler, B.H., Tchernov, E., Hietala, H., and Davis, S. 1977. Faunal exploitation during the late Epipaleolithic in the Har Harif. In *Prehistory and Paleoenvironments in the Central Negev, Israel*, Vol. 2, ed. A.E. Marks. Dallas: Southern Methodist University. Pp. 327–345.

Byrd, B.F. 1987. *Beidha and the Natufian: Variability in Levantine Settlement and Subsistence*. Doctoral dissertation, University of Arizona, Tucson. Ann Arbor: University Microfilms.

Byrd, B.F. 1988. The Natufian of Beidha: report on renewed field research. In *The Prehistory of Jordan 1986*, ed. A.N. Garrard and H.G. Gebel. Oxford: British Archaeological Reports International Series 396. Pp. 175–197.

Byrd, B.F. 1989. The Natufian: settlement variability and economic adaptations in the Levant at the end of the Pleistocene. *Journal of World Prehistory* 3, 2, 159–197.

Byrne, R. 1987. Climatic change and the origins of agriculture. In *Studies in the Neolithic and Urban Revolutions*, ed. L. Manzanilla. Oxford: British Archaeological Reports International Series 349. Pp. 21–34.

Cable, M., and French, F. 1950. *The Gobi Desert*. London: Hodder and Stoughton.

Calley, S. 1984. Le débitage natoufien de Mureybet: étude préliminaire. *Paléorient* 10, 2, 35–48.

Calley, S. 1986. *Technologie du Débitage—Mureybet, Syrie. 9e–8e Millénaire*. Oxford: British Archaeological Reports International Series 312.

Campana, D. 1979. A Natufian shaft-straightener from Mugharet El Wad, Israel: an example of wear-pattern analysis. *Journal of Field Archaeology* 6, 237–242.

Campbell, J. 1907. The travels of Richard Bell and John Campbell in the East Indies, Persia and Palestine. *Indian Antiquary* 36, 130–133.

Cane, S. 1989. Australian Aboriginal seed grinding and the archaeological record: a case study from the Western Desert. In *Foraging and Farming: The Evolution of Plant Exploitation*, ed. D.R. Harris and G.C. Hillman. London: Unwin and Hyman. Pp. 99–119.

Carre, Abbé. 1948. *The Travels of the Abbe Carré in India and the Near East, 1672–74*. London: Hakluyt Society, II, 97.

Cartwright, J. 1611. *The Preacher's Travels Through Syria, Persia etc*. London.

Casey, U. 1990. *Ethnographic Evidence for Patterns of Dietary Preference for the Use of 'Root' Foods From Reeds and Rushes*. BSc thesis, University College, London.

Cauvin, J. 1972. Nouvelles fouilles à Tell Mureybet (Syrie) 1971–1972. Rapport préliminaire. *Annales Archéologiques Arabes Syriennes* 22, 105–115.

Cauvin, J. 1974. Troisième campagne de fouilles à Tell Mureybet (Syrie) en 1973. Rapport préliminaire. *Annales Archéologiques Arabes Syriennes* 24, 47–58.

Cauvin, J. 1977. Les fouilles de Mureybet (1971–1974) et leur signification pour les origines de la sédentarisation au Proche-Orient. *Annual of the American Schools of Oriental Research* 44, 19–48.

Cauvin, J. 1978. *Les Premiers Villages de Syrie-Palestine du IXème au VIIème millénaire avant J.C.* Collection de la maison de l'orient méditerranéen ancien 4, série archéologique 3. Lyon: Maison de l'Orient.

Cauvin, J. 1994. *Naissance des Divinités Naissance de l'Agriculture*. Paris: CNRS Editions.

Cauvin, J., Cauvin, M.-C., and Stordeur, D. 1979. Recherches préhistoriques à El Kowm (Syrie). Première campagne 1978. *Cahiers de l'Euphrate* 2, 80–117.

Cauvin, M.-C. 1973. Une station de tradition natoufienne dans le Hauran (Syrie): Taibe, près de Deraa. *Annales Archéologiques Arabes Syriennes* 23, 105–110.

Cauvin, M.-C. 1974. Note préliminaire sur l'outillage lithique de la Phase IV de Tell Mureybet (Syrie). *Annales Archéologiques Arabes Syriennes* 24, 59–63.

Cauvin, M.-C. 1980. Du Natoufien sur l'Euphrate? In *Le Moyen Euphrate*, ed. J.C. Margueron. Leiden: Brill. Pp. 11–20.

Cauvin, M.-C. 1981a. L'Epipaléolithique de Syrie d'après les premières recherches dans la cuvette d'El Kowm (1978–1979). In *Préhistoire du Levant*, ed. J. Cauvin and P. Sanlaville. Actes du Colloque International 598. Paris: Centre National de la Recherche Scientifique. Pp. 375–388.

Cauvin, M.-C. 1981b. L'Epipaléolithique du Levant. In *Préhistoire du Levant*, ed. J. Cauvin and P. Sanlaville. Actes du Colloque International 598. Paris: Centre National de la Recherche Scientifique. Pp. 439–441.

Cauvin, M.-C., Coqueugniot, E., Le Mière, M., Muhesen, S., and Nierlé, M.-C. 1982. Prospection préhistorique à Mallaha-Jayroud (Qalamoun, Syrie). *Les Annales Archéologiques Arabes Syriennes* 32, 273–281.

Cave, M. 1989. *Chemical Criteria for Identifying Charred Remains of Wild Barleys from Epipalaeolithic Sites*. BSc thesis, University College, London.

Chesney, F.R. 1833. *Reports on the Navigation of the Euphrates*. London: His Majesty's Government.

Chesney, F.R. 1868. *Narrative of the Euphrates Expedition*. London: Longmans, Green.

Chestnut, V.K. 1902. *Plants Used by the Indians of Mendocino County, California*. Contributions from the United States National Herbarium 7. Washington, D.C.: U.S. Department of Agriculture.

Childe, V.G. 1928. *The Most Ancient East*. London: Kegan Paul, Trench, Trubner.

Chisholm, M. 1968. *Rural Settlement and Land Use*, 2nd ed. London: Hutchinson.

Clark, C., and Haswell, M. 1967. *The Economics of Subsistence Agriculture*, 3rd ed. London: Macmillan.

Clark, J.G.D. 1952. *Prehistoric Europe: The Economic Basis*. London: Methuen.

Clason, A.T. 1979. The animal remains from Tell es-Sinn compared with those from Bouqras. *Anatolica* 7, 35–53.

Clason, A.T. 1983. Faunal remains. In Bouqras revisited: preliminary report on a project in eastern Syria, by. P.A. Akkermans, J.A.K. Boerma, A.T. Clason, S.G. Hill, E. Lohof, C. Meiklejohn, M. le Mière, G.M.F. Molgat, J.J. Roodenberg, W. Waterbolk-van Rooyen, and W. van Zeist. *Proceedings of the Prehistoric Society* 49, 359–362.

Clason, A.T., and Buitenhuis, H. 1978. A preliminary report on the faunal remains of Nahr el-Homr, Hadidi and Ta'as in the Tabqua Dam region in Syria. *Journal of Archaeological Science* 5, 1, 75–84.

Clutton-Brock, J. 1971. The primary food animals of the Jericho Tell from the Proto-Neolithic to the Byzantine period. *Levant* 3, 41–55.

Clutton-Brock, J. 1979. The mammalian remains from the Jericho Tell. *Proceedings of the Prehistoric Society* 45, 135–157.

Clutton-Brock, J., and Uerpmann, H.-P. 1974. The sheep of early Jericho. *Journal of Archaeological Science* 1, 3, 261–274.

COHMAP Members. 1988. Climatic change of the last 18,000 years: observations and model simulations. *Science* 241, 1043–1052.

Colledge, S.M. 1988. Scanning-electron microscope studies of the pericarp layers of some wild wheats and ryes. Methods and problems. In *Scanning-Electron Microscopy in Archaeology*, ed. S.L. Olsen. Oxford: British Archaeological Reports International Series 452. Pp. 225–236

Colledge, S.M. 1994. *Plant Exploitation on Epipalaeolithic and Early Neolithic Sites in the Levant*. PhD thesis, University of Sheffield.

Compagnoni, B. 1978. The bone remains of *Gazella subgutturosa* from Shahr-I Sokhta. In *Approaches to Faunal Analysis in the Middle East*, ed. R.H. Meadow and M.A. Zeder. Peabody Museum Bulletin 2. Pp. 57–62.

Conkey, L.E., Boissevain, E., and Goddard, I. 1978. Indians of southern New England and Long Island: late period. In *Handbook of North American Indians*, Vol. 15: *Northeast*, ed. B.G. Trigger. Washington, D.C.: Smithsonian Institution. Pp. 177–189.

Contenson, H. de. 1966. La station préhistorique de Qornet Rharra, près de Seidnaya. *Annales Archéologiques Arabes Syriennes* 16, 2, 197–200.

Contenson, H. de. 1967. Troisième campagne à Tell Ramad, 1966. Rapport préliminaire. *Annales Archéologiques Arabes Syriennes* 17, 17–24.

Contenson, H. de. 1971. Tell Ramad, a village of Syria of the 7th and 6th millennia B.C. *Archaeology* 24, 278–285.

Contenson, H. de. 1972. Tell Aswad. Fouilles de 1971. *Les Annales Archéologiques Arabes Syriennes* 22, 75–84.

Contenson, H. de. 1977–1978. Tell Aswad. Fouilles de 1972. *Les Annales Archéologiques Arabes Syriennes* 27–28, 207–215.

Contenson, H. de. 1985. La campagne de 1965 à Bouqras. *Cahiers de l'Euphrate* 4, 335–350.

Contenson, H. de., and van Liere, W.J. 1966. Premier sondage à Bouqras en 1965, rapport préliminaire. *Les Annales Archéologiques Arabes Syriennes* 16, 181–192.

Coon, C.S. 1951. *Cave Explorations in Iran, 1949*. Philadelphia: University Museum.

Coote, E. 1860. Diary of a journey from Bassora to Aleppo in 1780. *Journal of the Royal Geographical Society* 30, 198–211.

Cope, C. 1991. Gazelle hunting strategies in the southern Levant. In *The Natufian Culture*, ed. O. Bar-Yosef and F. Valla. Ann Arbor: International Monographs in Prehistory. Pp. 341–358.

Copeland, L., and Hours, F. 1977. Engraved and plain bone tools from Jiita (Lebanon) and their early Kebaran context. *Proceedings of the Prehistoric Society* 43, 295–301.

Coville, F.V. 1897. *The Plants Used by the Klamath Indians of Oregon*. Contributions from the United States National Herbarium 5. Washington, D.C.: U.S. Department of Agriculture.

Crawford, O.G.S. 1929. Note by editor. *Antiquity* 3, 400–401.

Creswell, K.A.C. 1989. *A Short Account of Early Muslim Architecture*. Aldershot: Scolar Press.

Crowley, T.J., and North, G.R. 1991. *Paleoclimatology*. New York: Oxford University Press.

Culin, S. 1907. *Games of the North American Indians*. Twenty-Fourth Annual Report of the Bureau of American Ethnology to the Secretary of the Smithsonian Institution 1902–1903.

Dalman, G. 1964. *Arbeit und Sitte in Palästina*, 2nd ed. Hildesheim: Georg Olms.

Dansgaard, W., and Oeschger, H. 1989. Past environmental long-term records from the Arctic. In *The Environmental Record in Glaciers and Ice Sheets*, ed. H. Oeschger and C.C. Langway, Jr. Chichester: Wiley. Pp. 287–317.

Davis, M. 1983. Climatic instability, time lags and community ecology. In *Community Ecology*, ed. J. Diamond and T.J. Chase. New York: Harper and Row. Pp. 269–284.

Davis, P.H. 1965–1988. *Flora of Turkey and the East Aegean Islands*. 10 vols. Edinburgh: Edinburgh University Press.

Davis, S.J.M. 1974. Animal remains from the Kebaran site of Ein Gev I, Jordan Valley. *Paléorient* 2, 453–462.

Davis, S.J.M. 1978. Etude de la faune. In *Abou Gosh et Beisamoun: Deux Gisements du VIIe Millénaire avant l'ère*

Chrétienne en Israël, by Monique Lechevallier. Mémoires et Travaux du Centre de Recherches Préhistoriques Français de Jérusalem 2. Pp. 195–197.

Davis, S.J.M. 1980a. A note on the dental and skeletal ontogeny of *Gazella*. *Israel Journal of Zoology* 29, 129–134.

Davis, S.J.M. 1980b. Late Pleistocene and Holocene equid remains from Israel. *Journal of the Linnaean Society* 70, 289–312.

Davis, S.J.M. 1981. The effects of temperature change and domestication on the body size of late Pleistocene to Holocene mammals of Israel. *Palaeobiology* 7, 101–114.

Davis, S.J.M. 1983. The age profiles of gazelles predated by ancient man in Israel: possible evidence for a shift from seasonality to sedentism in the Natufian. *Paléorient* 9, 55–62.

Davis, S.J.M. 1985. A preliminary report of the fauna from Hatoula: a Natufian-Khiamian (PPNA) site near Latroun, Israel. In *Le Site Natoufien-Khiamien de Hatoula, prés de Latroun, Israël*, by M. Lechevallier and A. Ronen. Centre de Recherche Français de Jérusalem. Pp. 71–98.

Davis, S.J.M. 1987. *The Archaeology of Animals*. London: Batsford.

Davis, S.J.M., Goring-Morris, N., and Gopher, A. 1982. Sheep bones from the Negev Epipalaeolithic. *Paléorient* 8, 1, 87–93.

Davis, S.J.M., and Valla, F.R. 1978. Evidence for domestication of the dog 12,000 years ago in the Natufian of Israel. *Nature* 276, 608–610.

Denton, G.H., and Hendy, C.H. 1994. Younger Dryas age advance of Franz Josef Glacier in the Southern Alps of New Zealand. *Science* 264, 1434–1437.

Desse, J. 1987. Mallaha: l'ichthyfaune. In *La Faune du Gisement Natoufien de Mallaha (Eynan) Israël*, by J. Bouchud. Mémoires et Travaux du Centre de Recherche Français du Jérusalem 4. Paris: Association Paléorient. Pp. 151–156.

Dickson, H.R.P. 1949. *The Arab of the Desert*. London: Allen and Unwin.

Dornemann, R.H. 1986. *A Neolithic Village at Tell el Kowm in the Syrian Desert*. Studies in Ancient Oriental Civilization 43. Chicago: University of Chicago Press.

Doughty, C.M. 1888. *Travels in Arabia Deserta*. Cambridge: Cambridge University Press.

Dreisch, A. von den. 1976. *A Guide to the Measurement of Animal Bones from Archaeological Sites*. Peabody Museum of Archaeology and Ethnology Bulletin 1. Cambridge, Mass.: Harvard University.

Drucker, P. 1965. *Cultures of the North Pacific Coast*. San Francisco: Chandler.

Drummond, A. 1754. *Travels Through Different Cities and Several Parts of Asia, as Far as the Banks of the Euphrates*. London.

Ducos, P. 1968. *L'Origine des Animaux Domestiques en Palestine*. Publication de l'Institut de Préhistoire de l'Université de Bordeaux, Mémoire 9.

Ducos, P. 1969. Methodology and results of the study of the earliest domesticated animals in the Near East (Palestine). In *The Domestication and Exploitation of Plants and Animals*, ed. P.J. Ucko and G.W. Dimbleby. London: Duckworth. Pp. 265–275.

Ducos, P. 1970. The Oriental Institute excavations at Mureybit, Syria, preliminary report on the 1965 campaign. Part IV: Les restes d'equidés. *Journal of Near Eastern Studies* 29, 273–289.

Ducos, P. 1975. A new find of an equid metatarsal bone from Tell Mureibet in Syria and its relevance to the identification of equids from the early Holocene of the Levant. *Journal of Archaeological Science* 2, 71–73.

Ducos, P. 1978. *Tell Mureybit; étude archéozoologique et problèmes d'écologie humaine*. Paris: Editions du Centre National de Recherche Scientifique.

Ducos, P. 1986. The equid of Tell Muraibit, Syria. In: *Equids of the Ancient World*, ed. R.H. Meadow and H.-P. Uerpmann. *Beihefte zum Tübinger Atlas des Vorderen Orients*, Reihe A (Naturwissenschaften) 19, 1. Weisbaden: Reichert. Pp. 238–240.

Ducos, P. 1993. Proto-élevage et élevage au Levant sud au VIIe millénaire B.C. Les données de la Damascène. *Paléorient* 19, 153–173.

Duncan, J.W. 1963. *Maidu Ethnobotany*. MA dissertation, Sacramento State College, California.

Edwards, P.C. 1988. Natufian settlement in the Wadi al-Hammeh. *Paléorient* 14, 2, 309–315.

Edwards, P.C. 1989a. Revising the Broad Spectrum Revolution, and its rôle in the origins of Southwest Asian food production. *Antiquity* 63, 239, 225–246.

Edwards, P.C. 1989b. Problems of recognizing earliest sedentism: the Natufian example. *Journal of Mediterranean Archaeology* 2, 1, 5–48.

Edwards, P.C. 1991. Wadi Hammeh 27: an early Natufian site at Pella, Jordan. In *The Natufian Culture in the Levant*, ed. O. Bar-Yosef and F.R. Valla. Ann Arbor: International Monographs in Prehistory. Pp. 123–148.

Edwards, P.C., Bourke, S.J., Colledge, S.M., Head, J., and Macumber, P.G. 1988. Late Pleistocene prehistory in the Wadi al-Hammeh, Jordan Valley. In *The Prehistory of Jordan*, ed. A.N. Garrard and H.G. Gebel. British Archaeological Reports International Series 396. 2 vols. Pp. 525–565.

Egan, W.M. 1917. *Pioneering the West 1846–1878*. Salt Lake City: Major Howard Egan.

Eisenmann, V. 1980. *Les chevaux (Equus sensu lato) fossiles et actuels; crânes et dents jugales supérieures*. Paris: Editions du Centre National de la Recherche Scientifique.

Eisenmann, V. 1981. Etude des dents jugales inférieures des *Equus* (Mammalia, Perissodactyla) actuels et fossiles. *Palaeovertebrata* 10, 127–226.

Eisenmann, V. 1986. Comparative osteology of modern and fossil horses, half-asses, and asses. In *Beihefte zum Tübinger Atlas des Vorderen Orients*, ed. R.H. Meadow and H.-P. Uerpmann. Reihe A (Naturwissenschaften) 19, 1. Weisbaden: Reichert. P. 125.

Eisenmann, V., and Beckouche, S. 1986. Identification and discrimination of metapodials from Pleistocene and modern *Equus*. In *Beihefte zum Tübinger Atlas des*

Vorderen Orients, ed. R.H. Meadow and H.-P. Uerpmann. Reihe A (Naturwissenschaften), 19, 1. Weisbaden: Reichert. Pp. 302–318.

Eldred, J. 1927. The voyage of Mr. John Eldred to Trypolis in Syria by sea, and from thence by land and river to Babylon and Basora: anno 1583. In *The Principal Navigations, Voyages, Traffiques and Discoveries of the English Nation*, Vol. III, ed. R. Hackluyt. London: Dent. Pp. 321–328.

El-Moslimany, A.P. 1990. Ecological significance of common nonarboreal pollen: examples from drylands of the Middle East. *Review of Palaeobotany and Palynology* 64, 343–350.

El-Moslimany, A.P. 1994. Evidence of early Holocene summer precipitation in the continental Middle East. In *Late Quaternary Chronology and Paleoclimates of the Eastern Mediterranean*, ed. O. Bar-Yosef and R.S. Kra. Tucson: Radiocarbon. Pp. 121–130.

Emery-Barbier, A. 1995. Pollen analysis: environmental and climatic implications. In *Prehistoric Cultural Ecology and Evolution*, ed. D.O. Henry. New York: Plenum Press. Pp. 375–384.

Emiliani, C. 1978. The cause of the Ice Ages. *Earth and Planetary Science Letters* 37, 349–352.

English Merchants. 1707. An extract of the journals of two several voyages of the English merchants of the factory of Aleppo to Tadmor, anciently call'd Palmyra, 1678. In *A Relation of a Voyage from Aleppo to Palmyra in Syria: Miscellanea Curiosa Containing a Collection of Curious Travels, Voyages and Natural Histories of Countries, as They Have Been Delivered to the Royal Society, 1707*, 3. London: Royal Society.

Erol, O. 1978. The Quaternary history of the lake basins of central and southern Anatolia. In *The Environmental History of the Near and Middle East Since the Last Ice Age*, ed. W.C. Brice. London: Academic Press. Pp. 111–139.

Ertug-Yaras, F. 1996. Contemporary plant gathering in central Anatolia: an ethnoarchaeological and ethnobotanical study. In *Plant Life in Southwest Asia*. Proceedings of the IVth Symposium. Izmir: Ege Üniversitesi Matbaasi.

Evins, M.A. 1982. The fauna from Shanidar Cave: Mousterian wild goat exploitation in northeastern Iraq. *Paléorient* 8, 37–58.

Fahn, A., Werker, E., and Bass, P. 1986. *Wood Anatomy and Identification of Trees and Shrubs from Israel and Adjacent Regions*. Jerusalem: Israel Academy of Sciences and Humanities.

Fazekas, I.G., and Kosa, F. 1978. *Forensic Fetal Osteology*. Budapest: Akadémia Kiadò.

Felger, R.S., and Moser, M.B. 1985. *People of the Desert and Sea: Ethnobotany of the Seri Indians*. Tuscon: University of Arizona Press.

Fellows, L.E. 1993. What can higher plants offer the industry? *Pharmaceutical Journal*, May, 658–660.

Fenton, A. 1978. *The Northern Isles: Orkney and Shetland*. Edinburgh: John Donald.

Field, H. 1951. Anthropology of Iraq: the northern Jezira. *Papers of the Peabody Museum* 46, 1.

Field, H. 1954. North Arabian desert survey 1925–50. *Papers of the Peabody Museum* 47, 129–131.

Firth, R. 1957. *We, the Tikopia*, 2nd ed. London: Allen and Unwin.

Fisher, W.B. 1978. *The Middle East*, 7th ed. London: Methuen.

Flannery, K.V. 1969. Origins and ecological effects of early domestication in Iran and the Near East. In *The Domestication and Exploitation of Plants and Animals*, ed. P.J. Ucko and G.W. Dimbleby. London: Duckworth. Pp. 73–100.

Forde, C.D. 1956. *Habitat, Economy and Society*, 5th ed. London: Methuen.

Forsyth, A.A. 1979. *British Poisonous Plants*. London: Ministry of Agriculture, Fisheries and Food.

Fortes, M. 1970. *Kinship and the Social Order*. London: Routledge.

Fortes, M. 1983. Rules and the emergence of society. *Royal Anthropological Institute of Great Britain Occasional Papers* 39. P. 52.

Fowler, C.S., and Liljeblad, S. 1986. Northern Paiute. In *Handbook of North American Indians*, Vol. 11: *Great Basin*, ed. W.L. D'Azevedo. Washington, D.C.: Smithsonian Institution. Pp. 435–465.

Frey, W., and Kürschner, H. 1989. *Vorderer Orient. Vegetation 1: 8,000,000 Karte A VII*. Tübinger Atlas des Vorderen Orients. Weisbaden: Reichert.

Frison, G.C. 1971. Shoshonean antelope procurement in the Upper Green River Basin, Wyoming. *Plains Anthropologist* 16, 258–284.

Frison, G.C. 1978. *Prehistoric Hunters of the High Plains*. New York: Academic Press.

Gaertner, J. 1788–1805. *De Fructibus et Seminibus Plantarum*. 3 vols. Stuttgart, Tübingen, and Leipzig.

Galton, F. 1853. *Narrative of an Explorer in Tropical South Africa being an Account of a Visit to Damaraland in 1851*. London: John Murray.

Garrard, A.N., Baird, D., Colledge, S., Martin, L., and Wright, K. 1994. Prehistoric environment and settlement in the Azraq Basin: an interim report on the 1987 and 1988 excavation seasons. *Levant* 26, 73–109.

Garrard, A.N., Betts, A., Byrd, B., and Hunt, C. 1988. Summary of palaeoenvironmental and prehistoric investigations in the Azraq Basin. In *The Prehistory of Jordan*, ed. A.N. Garrard and H.G. Gebel. British Archaeological Reports International Series 396. 2 vols. Pp. 311–337.

Garrard, A.N., and Payne, S. 1983. *Camelus* from the Upper Pleistocene of Mount Carmel, Israel. *Journal of Archaeological Science* 10, 243–247.

Garrod, D.A.E. 1932. A new Mesolithic industry: the Natufian of Palestine. *Journal of the Royal Anthropological Institute* 62, 257–269.

Garrod, D.A.E. 1942. Excavations at the Cave of Shukbah, Palestine, 1928. *Proceedings of the Prehistoric Society* 8, 1–20.

Garrod, D.A.E. 1957. The Natufian culture: the life and economy of a Mesolithic people in the Near East. *Proceedings of the British Academy* 43, 211–227.

Garrod, D.A.E., and Bate, D.M.A. 1937. *The Stone Age of Mount Carmel* 1. Oxford: Clarendon Press.

Gasse, F., Arnold, M., Fontes, J.C., Fort, M., Gibert, E., Huc, A., Bingyan, L., Yuanfang, L., Qing, L., Mélières, F., Van Campo, E., Fubao, W., Qingsong, Z. 1991. A 13,000-year climate record from western Tibet. *Nature* 353, 742–745.

Gebel, H.G., Muheisen, M.S., and Nissen, H.J. 1988. Preliminary report on the first season of excavations at Basta. In *The Prehistory of Jordan*, ed. A.N. Garrard and H.G. Gebel. British Archaeological Reports International Series 396. 2 vols. Pp. 101–134.

Gennep, A. van 1909. *Les Rites de Passage*. Paris: Emile Nourry.

A Gentleman. 1784. *A Journal Kept on a Journey from Bassora to Bagdad Over the Little Desert to Aleppo, Cyprus, Etc. in the Year 1779*. London.

Glubb, J.B. 1943. The Sulubba and other ignoble tribes of Southwestern Asia. *General Series in Anthropology* 10, 14–17.

Gökmen, H. 1962. *Distribution of Forest Trees and Shrubs in Turkey*. (A map of the scale of 1: 2,500,000). Ankara: Orman Genel Müdürlügü.

Gonzalez-Echegaray, J. 1966. *Excavaciones en la Terraza de "el Khiam" (Jordania)*. Madrid: Bibliotheca Praehistorica Hispana 15, 1.

Goodyear, A. 1707. A relation of a voyage from Aleppo to Palmyra in Syria. *Miscellanea Curiosa; containing a Collection of Curious Travels, Voyages and Natural Histories of Countries as the have been Delivered to the Royal Society, London* III.

Gorelov, Y.O. 1972. Breeding of gazelles (*Gazella subgutturosa* Gueld) in Badghys (in Russian). *Teriologia* I, 420–424.

Gould, R.A. 1969. *Yiwara*. New York: Scribner's.

Gowlett, J.A.J., Hedges, R.E.M., Law, I.A., and Perry, C. 1987. Radiocarbon dates from the Oxford AMS system: archaeometry datelist 5. *Archaeometry* 29, 1, 125–155.

Grant, C. 1978. Eastern coastal Chumash. In *Handbook of North American Indians*, Vol. 8: *California*, ed. R.F. Heizer. Washington, D.C.: Smithsonian Institution.

Grant, C.P. 1937. *The Syrian Desert*. London: A. and C. Black.

Gray, A.P. 1972. *Mammalian Hybrids*, 2nd ed. Farnham Royal: Commonwealth Agricultural Bureaux.

Grayson, A.K. 1982. Assyria: Ashur-dan III to Ashur-Nirari V (934–745 B.C.). In *The Cambridge Ancient History*, Vol. 3, ed. J. Boardman, I.E.S. Edwards, N.G.L. Hammond, and E. Sollberger, 2nd ed. Cambridge: Cambridge University Press. Pp. 238–281.

Greguss, P. 1959. *Holzanatomie der Europäischen und Bäume Sträucher*. Budapest: Akadémia Kiadò.

Griffiths, J. 1805. *Travels in Europe, Asia Minor and Arabia*. London.

Grigson, C. 1983. A very large camel from the Upper Pleistocene of the Negev Desert. *Journal of Archaeological Science* 10, 311–316.

Grimble, R. 1972. *Migrations, Myths and Magic from the Gilbert Islands*. London: Routledge and Kegan Paul.

Grinnell, G.B. 1923. *The Cheyenne Indians*. 2 vols. New Haven: Yale University Press.

Groves, C. 1969. On the smaller gazelles of the genus *Gazella* de Blainville, 1916. *Sonderdruck aus Z. f. Säugetierkunde* 34, 1, 38–60.

Groves, C. 1974. *Horses, Asses and Zebras in the Wild*. Newton Abbot: David and Charles.

Groves, C. 1983. Notes on the gazelles IV. The Arabian gazelles collected by Hemprich and Ehrenberg. *Sonderdruck aus Z. f. Säugetierkunde* 48, 6, 371–381.

Groves, C., and Harrison, D.L. 1967. Taxonomy of the gazelles (genus *Gazella*) of Arabia. *Journal of Zoology* 152, 381–387.

Guest, E. 1933. *Notes on Plants and Plant Products, with Their Colloquial Names in Iraq*. Bulletin 27. Baghdad: Agricultural Directorate.

Guest, E., and al-Rawi, A., eds. 1966. *Flora of Iraq*, Vol. 1: *Introduction to the Flora*. Baghdad: Ministry of Agriculture of the Republic of Iraq.

Gumundsson, G. 1996. Gathering and processing of lymegrass (*Elymus arenarius*) in Iceland: an ethnohistorical account. *Vegetation History and Archaeobotany* 5, 13–23.

Hallam, S.J. 1979. *Fire and Hearth*. Canberra: Australian Institute of Aboriginal Studies.

Hammer, K., Skolimowska, E., and Knüpffer, H. 1987. Vorarbeiten zur monographischen Darstellung von Wildpflanzensortimenten: *Secale* L. *Die Kulturpflanze* 35, 135–177.

Harlan, J.R. 1967. A wild wheat harvest in Turkey. *Archaeology* 20, 197–201.

Harlan, J.R. 1972. Crops that extend the range of agricultural settlement. In *Man, Settlement and Urbanism*, ed. P.J. Ucko, G.W. Dimbleby, and R. Tringham. London: Duckworth. Pp. 239–243.

Harlan, J.R. 1989. Wild-grass seed harvesting in the Sahara and Sub-Sahara of Africa. In *Foraging and Farming: The Evolution of Plant Exploitation*, ed. D.R.Harris and G.C.Hillman. London: Unwin and Hyman. Pp. 79–98.

Harland, B.F., and Oberleas, D. 1987. Phytate in foods. *World Revue of Nutrition and Diet* 52, 235–59.

Harris, D.R. 1977. Alternative pathways toward agriculture. In *Origins of Agriculture*, ed. C.A. Reed. The Hague: Mouton. Pp. 179–243.

Harris, D.R. 1984. Ethnohistorical evidence of the exploitation of wild grasses and forbs: its scope and archaeological implications. In *Plants and Ancient Man: Studies in Palaeoethnobotany*, ed. W. van Zeist and W.C. Casparie. Rotterdam: Balkema. Pp. 63–69.

Harris, E.C. 1975. The stratigraphic sequence: a question of time. *World Archaeology* 7, 1, 109–121.

Harrison, D.L. 1968. *Mammals of Arabia* 1. London: Ernest Benn.

Harrison, D.L., and Bates, P.J.J. 1991. *Mammals of Arabia*, 2nd ed. Sevenoaks: Harrison Zoological Museum.

Haude, W. 1963. Über vieljährige Schwankungen des Niederschlages im Vorderen Orient und nordöstlichen Afrika und ihre Auswirkung auf die Ausbreitung von Tier und Mensch. *Die Erde* 94, 3–4, 281–312.

Hecker, H. 1975. *The Faunal Analysis of the Primary Food Animals from Beidha (Jordan)*. Ann Arbor: University Microfilms.

Hecker, H.M. 1982. Domestication revisited; its implications for faunal analysis. *Journal of Field Archaeology* 9, 217–236.

Hecker, H.M. 1989. Beidha Natufian: faunal report. In *The Natufian Encampment at Beidha*, by B.F. Byrd. Jutland Archaeology Society Publications 23, 1. Aarhus: Aarhus University Press. Appendix C, pp. 97–101.

Hedges, R.E.M., Housley, R.A., Bronk, C.R., and Van Klinken, G.J. 1990. Radiocarbon dates from the Oxford AMS system: *Archaeometry* datelist 11. *Archaeometry* 32, 2, 211–237.

Hedges, R.E.M., Housley, R.A., Pettitt, P.B., Bronk Ramsey, C., and Van Klinken, G.J. 1996. Radiocarbon dates from the Oxford AMS system: *Archaeometry* datelist 21. *Archaeometry* 38, 1, 181–207.

Heinzelin, J. de 1967. Investigations on the terraces of the Middle Euphrates. In *The Tabqa Reservoir Survey 1964*, by M.N. van Loon. Damascus: Direction Générale des Antiquités et des Musées. Supplement A, pp. 22–26.

Helfer, Mme. 1878. *Travels of Dr. and Madame Helfer in Syria, Mesopotamia, Burmah and Other Lands*. London: Bentley.

Helmer, D. 1989. Le développement de la domestication au Proche-orient de 9500 à 7500 BP: les nouvelles données d'El Kowm et de Ras Shamra. *Paléorient* 15, 111–121.

Helms, S., and Betts, A. 1987. The desert "kites" of the Badiyat esh-Sham and north Arabia. *Paléorient* 13, 41–67.

Henry, D.O. 1973. *The Natufian of Palestine: Its Material Culture and Ecology*. Doctoral dissertation, Southern Methodist University, Dallas. Ann Arbor: University Microfilms.

Henry, D.O. 1976. Rosh Zin: a Natufian settlement near Ein Avdat. In *Prehistory and Paleoenvironments in the Central Negev, Israel*, Vol. 1, ed. A.E. Marks. Dallas: Southern Methodist University. Pp. 317–347.

Henry, D.O. 1977. An examination of the artifactual variability in the Natufian of Palestine. *Eretz-Israel Moshe Stekelis Memorial* 13, 229–240.

Henry, D.O. 1981. An analysis of settlement patterns and adaptive strategies of the Natufian. In *Préhistoire du Levant*, ed. J. Cauvin and P. Sanlaville. Actes du Colloque International 598. Paris: Centre National de la Recherche Scientifique. Pp. 421–432.

Henry, D.O. 1983. Adaptive evolution within the Epipaleolithic of the Near East. *Advances in World Archaeology* 2, 99–160.

Henry, D.O. 1989. *From Foraging to Agriculture*. Philadelphia: University of Pennsylvania Press.

Henry, D.O., and Leroi-Gourhan, A. 1976. The excavation of Hayonim terrace: an interim report. *Journal of Field Archaeology* 3, 4, 391–405.

Hertz, R. 1907. Contribution à une étude sur la répresentation collective de la mort. *L'Année Sociologique* 10, 1905–1906, 48–137.

Hesse, B. 1979. Rodent remains and sedentism in the Neolithic: evidence from Tepe Ganj Dareh, western Iran. *Journal of Mammalogy* 60, 856–857.

Hesse, B. 1982. Slaughter patterns and domestication: the beginnings of pastoralism in western Iran. *Man* 17, 3, 403–417.

Hesse, B. 1984. These are our goats: the origins of herding in West Central Iran. In *Animals and Archaeology*, Vol. 3: *Early Herders and Their Flocks*, ed. J. Clutton-Brock and C. Grigson. Oxford: British Archaeological Reports International Series 202. Pp. 243–264.

Higgs, E.S., and Jarman, M.R. 1969. The origins of agriculture: a reconsideration. *Antiquity* 43, 169, 31–41.

Higgs, E.S., and Vita-Finzi, C. 1972. Prehistoric economies: a territorial approach. In *Papers in Economic Prehistory*, ed. E.S. Higgs. Cambridge: Cambridge University Press. Pp. 27–36.

Hill, G. 1901. *With the Bedouins; a Narrative of Journeys and Adventures in Unfrequented Parts of Syria*. London: T. Fisher Unwin.

Hillman, G.C. 1972. Plant remains. In Excavations at Can Hasan III 1969–1970 by D.H. French. *Papers in Economic Prehistory*, ed. E.S. Higgs. Cambridge: Cambridge University Press. Pp. 182–188.

Hillman, G.C. 1973. Agricultural resources and settlement in the Asvan region. *Anatolian Studies* 23, 217–240.

Hillman, G.C. 1975. The plant remains from Tell Abu Hureyra: a preliminary report. In The excavation of Tell Abu Hureyra in Syria: a preliminary report, by A.M.T. Moore. *Proceedings of the Prehistoric Society* 41, 70–73.

Hillman, G.C. 1978. On the origins of domestic rye—*Secale cereale*: the finds from Aceramic Can Hasan III in Turkey. *Anatolian Studies* 28, 157–174.

Hillman, G.C. 1981. Reconstructing crop husbandry practices from charred remains of crops. In *Farming Practice in British Prehistory*, ed. R. Mercer. Edinburgh: Edinburgh University Press. Pp. 123–162.

Hillman, G.C. 1984a. Interpretation of archaeological plant remains: the application of ethnographic models from Turkey. In *Plants and Ancient Man: Studies in Palaeoethnobotany*, ed. W. van Zeist and W.C. Casparie. Rotterdam: Balkema. Pp. 1–42.

Hillman, G.C. 1984b Traditional husbandry and processing of archaic cereals in recent times: the operations, products and equipment which might feature in Sumerian texts. *Bulletin on Sumerian Agriculture* 1, 114–152.

Hillman, G.C. 1985. Traditional husbandry and processing of archaic cereals in recent times: the operations, products and equipment which might feature in Sumerian texts. Part II: free threshing cereals. *Bulletin on Sumerian Agriculture* 2, 1–31.

Hillman, G.C. 1989. Late Palaeolithic plant foods from Wadi Kubbaniya in Upper Egypt: dietary diversity, infant weaning, and seasonality in a riverine environment. In *Foraging and Farming*, ed. D.R. Harris and G.C. Hillman. London: Unwin Hyman. Pp. 207–239.

Hillman, G.C. 1996. Late Pleistocene changes in wild plant-foods available to hunter-gatherers of the northern Fertile Crescent: possible preludes to cereal cultivation. In *The Origins and Spread of Agriculture and Pastoralism in Eurasia*, ed. D.R. Harris. London: UCL Press. Pp. 159–203.

Hillman G.C., Colledge S.M., and Harris, D.R. 1989. Plant-food economy during the Epipalaeolithic period at Tell Abu Hureyra, Syria: dietary diversity, seasonality, and modes of exploitation. In *Foraging and Farming*, ed. D.R. Harris and G.C. Hillman. London: Unwin Hyman. Pp. 240–268.

Hillman, G.C., and Davies, M.S. 1990a. Measured domestication rates in wild wheats and barley under primitive cultivation, and their archaeological implications. *Journal of World Prehistory* 4, 157–222.

Hillman, G.C., and Davies, M.S. 1990b. Domestication rates in wild wheats and barley under primitive cultivation. *Biological Journal of the Linnean Society* 39, 39–78.

Hillman, G.C., and Davies, M.S. 1992. Domestication rates in wild wheats and barley under primitive cultivation: preliminary results and archaeological implications of field measurements of selection coefficient. In *Préhistoire de l'Agriculture: Nouvelle Approches Expérimentales et Ethnographiques*, ed. P.C. Anderson. Paris: Éditions du CNRS. Pp. 113–158.

Hillman, G.C., Madeyska, E., and Hather, J.G. 1989. Wild plant foods and diet at Late Palaeolithic Wadi Kubbaniya: the evidence from charred remains. In *The Prehistory of Wadi Kubbaniya*, Vol. 2: *Palaeoeconomy, Environment and Stratigraphy*, ed. F. Wendorf, R. Schild, and A. Close. Dallas: Southern Methodist University Press. Pp. 162–242.

Hillman, G.C., Rowley-Conwy, P., and Legge, A.J. 1997. On the charred seeds from Epipalaeolithic Abu Hureyra: food or fuel ? *Current Anthropology* 38, 651–655.

Hillman, G.C., Wales, S., McLaren, F., Evans, J., and. Butler, A. 1993. Identifying problematic remains of ancient plant foods: a comparison of the role of chemical, histological and morphological criteria. *World Archaeology* 25, 1, 94–121.

Hocart, A.M. 1922. The cult of the dead in Eddystone of the Solomons. Part 1. *The Journal of the Royal Anthropological Institute* 52, 71–112.

Holden, T. 1990. *Taphonomic and Methodological Problems in Reconstructing Diet from Ancient Human Gut and Faecal Remains*. PhD thesis, University College, London.

Hole, F. 1977. *Studies in the Archeological History of the Deh Luran Plain. The Excavation of Chagha Sefid*. Memoirs of the Museum of Anthropology, University of Michigan 9. Ann Arbor: University of Michigan.

Hole, F., and Flannery, K.V. 1967. The prehistory of southwestern Iran: a preliminary report. *Proceedings of the Prehistoric Society* 33, 147–206.

Hole, F., Flannery, K.V., and Neely, J.A. 1969. *Prehistory and Human Ecology of the Deh Luran Plain*. Memoirs of the Museum of Anthropology, University of Michigan 1. Ann Arbor: University of Michigan.

Hooijer, D.A. 1961. The fossil vertebrates of Ksâr'Akil, a Palaeolithic rock shelter in the Lebanon. *Zoologische Verhandelingen Leiden* 49, 1–67.

Hopf, M. 1983. Jericho plant remains. In *Excavations at Jericho*, Vol. 5, by K.M. Kenyon and T.A. Holland. London: British School of Archaeology in Jerusalem. Appendix B, pp. 576–621.

Hopf, M., and Bar-Yosef, O. 1987. Plant remains from Hayonim Cave, western Galilee. *Paléorient* 13, 1, 117–120.

Huntington, R., and Metcalf, P. 1979. *Celebrations of Death*. Cambridge: Cambridge University Press.

Huntley, B. 1988. Glacial and Holocene vegetation history: Europe. In *Vegetation History*, ed. B. Huntley and T. Webb III, Dordrecht: Kluwer. Pp. 341–383.

Huntley, B. 1991. How plants respond to climate change: migration rates, individualism and the consequences for plant communities. *Annals of Botany* 67 (supplement), 15–22.

Huntley, B., and Birks, H.J.B. 1983. *An Atlas of Past and Present Pollen Maps for Europe: 0–13000* BP. Cambridge: Cambridge University Press.

Huntley, B., and Webb, T. III 1989. Migration species' response to climatic variations caused by changes in the earth's orbit. *Journal of Biogeography* 16, 5–19.

Ionides, M.G. 1937. *The Régime of the Rivers Euphrates and Tigris*. London: Spon.

Irby, C.L., and Mangles, J. 1844. *Travels in Egypt and Nubia, Syria and the Holy Land*. London: Murray.

Irwin, E. 1780. *A Series of Adventures in the Course of a Voyage Up the Red Sea, on the Coasts of Arabia and Egypt; and of a Route Through the Deserts of Thebais, Hitherto Unknown to the European Traveller. In the Year MDCCLXXVII*. London.

Iversen, J. 1954. The Late-Glacial flora of Denmark and its relation to climate and soil. *Dansmarks Geologiske Undersøgelse* II, 80, 87–119.

Jarman, H.N., Legge, A.J., and Charles, J.A. 1972. Retrieval of plant remains from archaeological sites by froth flotation. In *Papers in Economic Prehistory*, ed. E.S. Higgs. Cambridge: Cambridge University Press. Pp. 39–48.

Johnston, T.H., and Cleland, J.B. 1943. Native names and uses of plants in the Northeastern corner of South Australia. *Transactions of the Royal Society of South Australia* 67, 96–162.

Jones, R., and Meehan, B. 1989. Plant foods of the Gidjingali: ethnographic and archaeological perspectives from northern Australia on tuber and seed exploitation. In *Foraging and Farming: The Evolution of Plant Exploitation*, ed. D.R. Harris and G.C. Hillman. London: Unwin and Hyman. Pp. 120–135.

Kaiser, K. 1961. Die Ausdehnung der Vergletscherungen und "periglazialen" Erscheinungen während der Kaltzeiten des quärtären Eiszeitalters innerhalb der

Syrisch-Libanesischen Gebirge und die Lage der klimatischen Schneegrenze zur Würmeiszeit in östlichen Mittelmeergebiet. *International Association for Quaternary Research: Report of the VIth International Congress on the Quaternary (Geomorphological Section)* 3, 127–148. Warsaw.

Kaiser, K., Kempf, E.K., Leroi-Gourhan, A., and Schütt, H. 1973. Quartarstratigraphische Untersuchungen aus dem Damaskus-Becken und seiner Umgebung. *Zeitschrift für Geormorphologie* 17, 263–353.

Keeley, L.H. 1983. Neolithic novelties: the view from ethnography and microwear analysis. In *Traces d'Utilisation sur les Outils Néolithiques du Proche Orient*, ed. M.-C. Cauvin. Travaux de la Maison de l'Orient 5. Lyon: Maison de l'Orient. Pp. 251–256.

Kenyon, K.M. 1979. *Archaeology in the Holy Land*, 4th ed. London: Benn.

Kenyon, K.M. 1981. *Excavations at Jericho*, Vol. 3. London: British School of Archaeology in Jerusalem.

Kinglake, A.W. 1898. *Eothen*. London: G. Bell.

Kirkbride, D. 1966. Five seasons at the Pre-Pottery Neolithic village of Beidha in Jordan. *Palestine Exploration Quarterly* 98, 8–72.

Kirkbride, D. 1967. Beidha 1965: an interim report. *Palestine Exploration Quarterly*, 5–13.

Kislev, M. 1997. Early agriculture and palaeoecology of Netiv Hagdud. In *An Early Neolithic Village in the Jordan Valley*, part 1: *The Archaeology of Netiv Hagdud*, ed. O. Bar-Yosef and A. Gopher. American School of Prehistoric Research Bulletin 43. Cambridge, Mass.: Peabody Museum of Archaeology and Ethnology, Harvard University. Pp. 209–236.

Kislev, M.E., Nadel, D., and Carmi, I. 1992. Epipalaeolithic (19,000 BP) cereal and fruit diet at Ohalo II, Sea of Galilee, Israel. *Review of Palaeobotany and Palynology* 73, 161–166.

Kleppe, E.J. 1986. Religion expressed through bead use: an ethnoarchaeological study of the Shilluk, southern Sudan. In *Words and Objects*, ed. G. Steinsland. Oslo: Norwegian University Press. Pp. 78–90.

Kobyljanskij, V.D. 1989. *Flora of Cultivated Plants of the USSR* 2, part 1. Rye (in Russian). Leningrad: Agropromizdat.

Köhler-Rollefson, I. 1988. The aftermath of the Levantine Neolithic revolution in the light of ecological and ethnographic evidence. *Paléorient* 14, 1, 87–93.

Köhler-Rollefson, I. 1989. Changes in goat exploitation at ʾAin Ghazal between the early and late Neolithic; a metrical analysis. *Paléorient* 15, 141–146.

Konlade, J.E., and Robson, J.R.K. 1972. The nutritive value of cooked camas as consumed by Flathead Indians. *Ecology of Food and Nutrition* 2, 193–195.

Konner, M., and Worthman, C. 1980. Nursing frequency, gonadal function, and birth spacing among !Kung hunter-gatherers. *Science* 207, 788–791.

Körber-Grohne, Ü. 1981. Distinguishing prehistoric grains of *Triticum* and *Secale* on the basis of their surface patterns using scanning electron microscopy. *Journal of Archaeological Science* 8, 197–204.

Kovacs, M.G. 1989. *The Epic of Gilgamesh*. Stanford: Stanford University Press.

Kramer, C. 1980. Estimating prehistoric populations: an ethnoarchaeological approach. In *L'Archéologie de l'Iraq du Début de l'Epoque Néolithique à 333 avant Notre Ere*, ed. M.-T. Barrelet. Actes du Colloque International 580. Paris: Centre National de la Recherche Scientifique. Pp. 315–334.

Kromer, B., Rhein, M., Bruns, M., Schoch-Fischer, H., and Münnich, K.O. 1986. Radiocarbon calibration data for the 6th to the 8th millennia BC. *Radiocarbon* 28, 2B, 954–960.

Kudrass, H.R., Erienkeuser, H., Vollbrecht, R., and Weiss, W. 1991. Global nature of the Younger Dryas cooling event inferred from oxygen isotope data from Sulu Sea cores. *Nature* 349, 406–409.

Kukla, G.J. 1977. Pleistocene land-sea correlations. 1. Europe. *Earth-Science Reviews* 13, 307–374.

Kumerloeve, H. 1967. Zur verbreitung kleinasiatischer raub- und huftiere sowie einiger grossnager. *Saugetierkundliche Mitteilungen* 4, 337–409.

Kurtén, B. 1965. Carnivora of the Palestine caves. *Acta Zoologica Fennica* 107, 1–74.

Kurth, G., and Röhrer-Ertl, O. 1981. On the anthropology of the Mesolithic to Chalcolithic human remains from the Tell es-Sultan in Jericho, Jordan. In *Excavations at Jericho*, Vol. 3, by K.M. Kenyon. London: British School of Archaeology in Jerusalem. Pp. 407–499.

Kutzbach, J.E., Guetter, P.J., Behling, P.J., and Selin, R. 1993. Simulated climatic changes: results of the COHMAP climate-model experiments. In *Global Climates Since the Last Glacial Maximum*, ed. H.E. Wright, Jr., J.E. Kutzbach, T. Webb III, W.F. Ruddiman, F.A. Street-Perrott, and P.J. Bartlein. Minneapolis: University of Minnesota Press. Pp. 24–93.

Ladizinsky, G. 1989. Origin and domestication of the Southwest Asian grain legumes. In *Foraging and Farming*, ed. D.R. Harris and G.C. Hillman. London: Unwin Hyman. Pp. 374–389.

Lamb, H.H., and Woodroffe, A. 1970. Atmospheric circulation during the last Ice Age. *Quaternary Research* 1, 29–58.

Lanoy, T. 1707. A relation of a voyage from Aleppo to Palmyra in Syria. *Miscellanea Curiosa; containing a Collection of Curious Travels, Voyages and Natural Histories of Countries as they have been Delivered to the Royal Society, London*, III.

Lánská, D. 1992. *The Illustrated Guide to Edible Plants*. London: Chancellor Press.

Lasota-Moskalewska, A. 1994. Animal remains from Nemrik, a Pre-Pottery Neolithic site in Iraq. In *Nemrik 9*, 4, ed. S.K. Kozlowski. Warsaw: Wydawnictwa Uniwersytetu Warszawskiego. Pp. 5–52.

Lawrence, B. 1982. Principal food animals at Çayönü. In *Prehistoric Village Archaeology in South-Eastern Turkey*, ed, L.S. Braidwood and R.J. Braidwood. Oxford: British Archaeological Reports International Series 138. Pp. 175–199.

Lawrence, R. 1968. *Aboriginal Habitat and Economy.* Canberra: Australian National University, Department of Geography.

Layard, A.H. 1849. *Nineveh and Its Remains.* 2 vols. London: Murray.

Layard, A.H. 1853. *Discoveries in the Ruins of Niniveh and Babylon.* London: Murray.

Lechevallier, M. 1978. *Abou Gosh et Beisamoun.* Mémoires et Travaux du Centre de Recherches Préhistoriques Français de Jérusalem 2. Paris: Association Paléorient.

Lee, R.B. 1979. *The !Kung San.* Cambridge: Cambridge University Press.

Legge, A.J. 1975. The fauna of Tell Abu Hureyra: preliminary analysis. In The excavation of Tell Abu Hureyra in Syria: a preliminary report, by A.M.T. Moore. *Proceedings of the Prehistoric Society* 41, 74–76.

Legge, A.J. 1977. The origins of agriculture in the Near East. In *Hunters, Gatherers and First Farmers Beyond Europe,* ed. J.V.S. Megaw. Leicester: Leicester University Press. Pp. 51–67.

Legge, A.J. 1986. Seeds of discontent: accelerator dates on some charred plant remains from the Kebaran and Natufian cultures. In *Archaeological Results from Accelerator Dating,* ed. J.A.J. Gowlett and R.E.M. Hedges. Oxford: Oxford University Committee for Archaeology. Pp. 13–21.

Legge, A.J. 1996. The beginning of caprine domestication in Southwest Asia. In *The Origins and Spread of Agriculture and Pastoralism in Eurasia,* ed. D.R. Harris. London: UCL Press. Pp. 238–262.

Legge, A.J., and Rowley-Conwy, P.A. 1986a. The beaver (*Castor fiber* L.) in the Tigris-Euphrates basin. *Journal of Archaeological Science* 13, 469–476.

Legge, A.J., and Rowley-Conwy, P.A. 1986b. New radiocarbon dates for early sheep at Tell Abu Hureyra. In *Archaeological Results from Accelerator Dating,* ed. J.A.J. Gowlett and R.E.M. Hedges. Oxford: Oxford University Committee for Archaeology. Pp. 23–35.

Legge, A.J., and Rowley-Conwy, P.A. 1987. Gazelle killing in Stone Age Syria. *Scientific American* 255, 8, 88–95.

Legge, A.J., and Rowley-Conwy, P.A. 1988. *Star Carr Revisited: A Re-analysis of the Large Mammals.* London: Centre for Extra-Mural Studies, Birkbeck College.

Legge, A.J., Williams, J., and Williams, P. 1992. The determination of season of death from the mandible and bones of the domestic sheep (*Ovis aries*). In *Archeologia della Pastorizia nell 'Europa Meridionale.* Revista di Studi Liguri 57, 1–4.

Le Maout, E., and Descaine, J. 1873. *A General System of Botany: Descriptive and Analytical.* Translated from the French by Hooker.

Le Mière, M. 1986. *Les premières céramiques du Moyen-Euphrate.* 2 vols. Doctoral thesis, University of Lyon II.

Le Mière, M., and Picon, M. 1987. Production locales et circulation des céramiques au VIe millénaire, au Proche-Orient. *Paléorient* 13, 2, 133–147.

Leroi-Gourhan, A. 1984. L'environement de Mallaha (Eynan) au natoufien. *Paléorient* 10, 2, 103–106.

Leroi-Gourhan, A., and Darmon, F. 1991. Analyses polliniques de stations natoufiennes au Proche Orient. In *The Natufian Culture in the Levant,* ed. O. Bar-Yosef and F.R. Valla. Ann Arbor: International Monographs in Prehistory. Pp. 21–26.

Levitt, D. 1981. *Plants and People: Aboriginal Uses of Plants on Groote Eylandt.* Canberra: Australian Institute of Aboriginal Studies.

Lewis, H.T. 1973. *Patterns of Indian Burning in California: Ecology and Ethnohistory.* Ramona: Ballena Press Anthropological Papers 1.

Liere, W.J. van. 1960–1961. Observations on the Quaternary of Syria. *Berichten van de Rijksdienst voor het Oudhuidkundig Bodemonderzoek* 10–11, 7–69.

Loon, M.N. van. 1967. *The Tabqa Reservoir Survey 1964.* Damascus: Direction Générale des Antiquités et des Musées.

Loon, M.N. van. 1968. The Oriental Institute excavations at Mureybit, Syria: preliminary report on the 1965 campaign. Part 1: architecture and general finds. *Journal of Near Eastern Studies* 27, 265–282.

Louis, H. 1939. *Das natürliche Pflanzenkleid Anatoliens.* Geographische Abhandlungen 3, 12. Stuttgart: Pencke.

Loy, T.H., and Wood, A.R. 1989. Blood residue analysis at Çayönü Tepesi, Turkey. *Journal of Field Archaeology* 16, 451–460.

MacGregor, A.G., and Currey, J.D. 1983. Mechanical properties as conditioning factors in the bone and antler industry of the third to the 13th century A.D. *Journal of Archaeological Science* 10, 71–77.

MacLuhan, T.C. 1972. *Touch the Earth: A Self-Portrait of Indian Existence.* London: Abacus.

Maitland, R.A. 1927. Works of the "Old Men" in Arabia. *Antiquity* 1, 197.

Malinowski, B. 1931. *The Sexual Life of Savages.* London: Routledge.

Marks, A.E., and Larson, P.A., Jr. 1977. Test excavations at the Natufian site of Rosh Horesha. In *Prehistory and Paleoenvironments in the Central Negev, Israel,* Vol. 2, ed. A.E. Marks. Dallas: Southern Methodist University Press. Pp. 191–232.

Marshall, D.N. 1982. Jericho bone tools and objects. In *Excavations at Jericho,* Vol. 4, by K.M. Kenyon and T.A. Holland. London: British School of Archaeology in Jerusalem. Appendix E, pp. 570–622.

Martin, A.C. 1946. The comparative internal morphology of seeds. *The American Midland Naturalist* 36, 513–660.

Mason, S.L.R. 1992. *Acorns in Human Subsistence.* Doctoral thesis, University College, London.

Matsutani, T., ed. 1991. *Tell Kaskashok: The Excavations at Tell No. II.* Tokyo: University of Tokyo, Institute of Oriental Culture.

Maurizio, A. 1927. *Die Geschichte unserer Pflanzennahrung.* Berlin: Parey.

McCorriston, J. 1992. *The Early Development of Agriculture in the Ancient Near East: An Ecological and Evolutionary*

Study. Doctoral dissertation, Yale University. Ann Arbor: University Microfilms 92-35550.

McCorriston, J. 1994. Acorn eating and agricultural origins: California ethnographies as analogies for the ancient Near East. *Antiquity* 68, 258, 97–107.

McKane, R. 1998. *Poets for Poets*. London: Hearing Eye.

McLaren, F.S., Evans, J., and Hillman, G.C. 1991. Identification of charred seeds from Epipalaeolithic sites of S.W. Asia. In *Archaeometry '90: Proceedings of the 26th International Symposium on Archaeometry, Heidelberg, 1990*, ed. E. Pernick and G.A. Wagner. Basel: Birkhaüser Verlag. Pp. 797–806.

Meadow, R.H. 1984. Animal domestication in the Near East: a view from the eastern margin. In *Animals and Archaeology*, Vol. 3: *Early Herders and Their Flocks*, ed. J. Clutton-Brock and C. Grigson. Oxford: British Archaeological Reports International Series 202. Pp. 309–337.

Meadow, R.H. 1986. Some equid remains from Çayönü, Southeastern Turkey. *Beihefte zum Tübinger Atlas des Vorderen Orients*, Reihe A (Naturwissenschaften) 19, 1. Weisbaden: Reichert. Pp. 266–301.

Meadow, R.H. 1989. Osteological evidence for the process of animal domestication. In *The Walking Larder*, ed. J. Clutton-Brock. London: Unwin Hyman. Pp. 80–90.

Meiklejohn, C., Lambert, P., and Byrne, C. 1980. Demography and pathology of the Ganj Dareh population: early Neolithic of Iran. Abstract of paper given at the 49th annual meeting of the American Asociation of Physical Anthropologists. *American Journal of Physical Anthropology* 52, 255.

Mellaart, J. 1967. *Çatal Hüyük*. London: Thames and Hudson.

Mellaart, J. 1970. *Excavations at Hacilar*. 2 vols. Edinburgh: Edinburgh University Press.

Mellaart, J. 1975. *The Neolithic of the Near East*. London: Thames and Hudson.

Mendelssohn, H. 1974. The development of the populations of gazelles in Israel and their behavioural adaptations. In *The Behaviour of Ungulates and Its Relation to Management*, ed. V. Geist and F. Walther. Switzerland: Morges.

Meshel, Z. 1974. New data about "desert kites." *Tel Aviv* 1, 4, 129–173.

Messerli, B. 1966. Das problem der eiszeitlichen Vergletscherung am Libanon und Hermon. *Zeitschrift für Geomorphologie* 10, 37–68.

Messerli, B. 1967. Die eiszeitliche und die gegenwärtige Vergletscherung in Mittelmeerraum. *Geographica Helvetica* 22, 105–228.

Miller, T.E. 1987. Systematics and evolution. In *Wheat Breeding: Its Scientific Basis*, ed. F.G.H. Lupton. London: Chapman and Hall. Pp. 1–30.

Molist Montaña, M. 1996. *Tell Halula (Siria) un Yacimiento Neolítico del Valle Medio del Éufrates Campañas de 1991 y 1992*. Madrid: Ministerio de Educación y Cultura.

Molleson, T.I. 1989a. Social implications of mortality patterns of juveniles from Poundbury Camp, Romano-British Cemetery. *Anthropologie Anzeiger* 47, 27–38.

Molleson, T.I. 1989b. Seed preparation in the Mesolithic: the osteological evidence. *Antiquity* 63, 239, 356–362.

Molleson, T. 1994. The eloquent bones of Abu Hureyra. *Scientific American* 271, 2, 70–75.

Molleson, T., and Jones, K. 1991. Dental evidence for dietary change at Abu Hureyra. *Journal of Archaeological Science* 18, 525–539.

Molleson, T., Jones, K., and Jones, S. 1993. Dietary change and the effects of food preparation on microwear patterns in the Late Neolithic of abu Hureyra, northern Syria. *Journal of Human Evolution* 24, 455–468.

Mook, W.G. 1986. Recommendations/resolutions adopted by the Twelfth International Radiocarbon Conference. *Radiocarbon* 28, 2A, 799.

Moore, A.M.T. 1975. The excavation of Tell Abu Hureyra in Syria: a preliminary report. *Proceedings of the Prehistoric Society* 41, 50–77.

Moore, A.M.T. 1979. A pre-Neolithic farmer's village on the Euphrates. *Scientific American* 241, 2, 50–58.

Moore, A.M.T. 1981. North Syria in Neolithic 2. In *Préhistoire du Levant*, ed. J. Cauvin and P. Sanlaville. Actes du Colloque International 598. Paris: Centre National de la Recherche Scientifique. Pp. 445–456.

Moore, A.M.T. 1982a. A four-stage sequence for the Levantine Neolithic, ca. 8500–3750 B.C. *Bulletin of the American Schools of Oriental Research* 246, 1–34.

Moore, A.M.T. 1982b. Agricultural origins in the Near East: a model for the 1980s. *World Archaeology* 14, 2, 224–236.

Moore, A.M.T. 1983. The first farmers in the Levant. In *The Hilly Flanks and Beyond*, ed. T.C. Young, Jr., P.E.L. Smith, and P. Mortensen. Studies in Ancient Oriental Civilization 36. Chicago: University of Chicago Press. Pp. 91–111.

Moore, A.M.T. 1985. The development of Neolithic societies in the Near East. *Advances in World Archaeology* 4, 1–69.

Moore, A.M.T. 1991. Abu Hureyra 1 and the antecedents of agriculture on the Middle Euphrates. In *The Natufian Culture in the Levant*, ed. O. Bar-Yosef and F. R. Valla. Ann Arbor: International Monographs in Prehistory. Pp. 277–294.

Moore, A.M.T. 1992. The impact of accelerator dating at the early village of Abu Hureyra on the Euphrates. *Radiocarbon* 34, 3, 850–858.

Moore, A.M.T., Gowlett, J.A.J., Hedges, R.E.M., Hillman, G.C., Legge, A.J., and Rowley-Conwy, P.A. 1986. Radiocarbon accelerator (AMS) dates for the Epipaleolithic settlement at Abu Hureyra, Syria. *Radiocarbon* 28, 3, 1068–1076.

Moore, A.M.T., and Hillman, G.C. 1992. The Pleistocene to Holocene transition and human economy in Southwest Asia: the impact of the Younger Dryas. *American Antiquity* 57, 3, 482–494.

Moss, E. 1983. The functions of burins and tanged points from Tell Abu Hureyra (Syria). In *Traces d'Utilisation sur les Outils Néolithiques du Proche Orient*, ed. M.-C. Cauvin. Travaux de la Maison de l'Orient 5. Lyon: Maison de l'Orient. Pp. 143–155.

Moulins, D. de. 1994. *Agricultural Changes at Euphrates and Steppe Sites in the Mid-8th to the 6th Millennium B.C.* Doctoral thesis, University of London.

Moulins, D. de. 1997. *Agricultural Changes at Euphrates and Steppe Sites in Mid-8th to The 6th Millennium B.C.* Oxford, British Archaeological Reports International Series 683.

Mouterde, P. 1966. *Nouvelle Flore du Liban et de la Syrie.* Beirut: Imprimerie Catholique.

Muheisen, M. 1988. The Epipalaeolithic phases of Kharaneh IV. In *The Prehistory of Jordan,* ed. A.N. Garrard and H.G. Gebel. Oxford: British Archaeological Reports International Series 396. 2 vols. Pp. 353–367.

Muir, A. 1951. Notes on the soils of Syria. *Journal of Soil Science* 2, 2, 163–182.

Murray, P.M., and Sheehan, M.C. 1984. Prehistoric *Polygonum* use in the Midwestern United States. In *Experiments and Observations on Aboriginal Plant Food Utilization in Eastern North America,* ed. P.J. Munson. Indianapolis: Indiana Historical Society. Pp. 282–298.

Musil, A. 1928a. *Palmyrena.* Oriental Explorations and Studies 4, New York: American Geographical Society.

Musil, A. 1928b. *The Manners and Customs of the Rwala Bedouins.* Oriental Explorations and Studies 6. New York: American Geographical Society.

Nadler, C.F., Hoffmann, R.S., and Wolf, A. 1973. G-band patterns as chromosome markers and the interpretation of chromosome evolution in wild sheep (*Ovis*). *Experientia* 29, 117–179.

Nadler, C.F., Korobitsina, K.V., Hoffman, R.S., and Vorontsov, N.N. 1972. Cytogenetic differentiation, geographical distribution and domestication in palearctic sheep (*Ovis*). *Zeitschrift für Säugetierkunde* 38, 2, 109–125.

Nadler, C.F., Lay, D.M., and Hassinger, J.D. 1971. Cytogenetic analyses of wild sheep populations in north Iran. *Cytogenetics* 10, 137–152.

Napton, L.K., and Heizer, R.F. 1970. *Archaeology and the Prehistoric Great Basin Lacustrine Subsistence Regime as Seen from Lovelock Cave, Nevada.* Contributions of the University of California Archaeological Research Facility 10. Berkeley: University of California Archaeological Research Facility.

Naveh, Z. 1967. Mediterranean ecosystems and vegetation types in California and Israel. *Ecology* 48, 445–459.

Neale, F.A. 1851. *Eight Years in Syria, Palestine and Asia Minor.* 2 vols. London: Colburn.

Neev, D., and Emery, K.O. 1967. The Dead Sea. *Bulletin of the Geological Survey of Israel* 41, 1–147.

Neil, J. 1913. *Everyday Life in the Holy Land.* London: Church Mission to the Jews.

Nesbitt, R.M.A. 1997. *Archaeobotanical Identification of Near Eastern Grass Caryopses.* PhD thesis, University College, London.

Netting, R.M. 1986. *Cultural Ecology,* 2nd ed. Prospect Heights: Waveland Press.

Neuville, R. 1951. *Le Paléolithique et le Mésolithique du Désert de Judée.* Archives de l'Institut de Paléontologie Humaine Mémoire 24. Paris: Institut de Paléontologie Humaine.

Newcomer, M.H. 1974. Study and replication of bone tools from Ksar Akil (Lebanon). *World Archaeology* 6, 138–153.

Nierlé, M.C. 1982. Mureybet et Cheikh Hassan (Syrie): outillage de mouture et de broyage (9ème et 8ème millénaires). *Cahiers de l'Euphrate* 3, 177–216.

Niklewski, J., and van Zeist, W. 1970. A late Quaternary pollen diagram from northwestern Syria. *Acta Botanica Neerlandica* 19, 5, 737–754.

Noy, T., Legge, A.J., and Higgs, E.S. 1973. Recent excavations at Nahal Oren, Israel. *Proceedings of the Prehistoric Society* 39, 75–99.

Noy-Meir, I. 1973. Desert ecosystems: environment and producers. *Annual Review of Ecology and Systematics* 4, 25–52.

Oliver, S.C. 1962. Ecology and cultural continuity as contributing factors in the social organization of the Plains Indians. *University of California Publications in American Archaeology and Ethnology* 48, 1–90.

Olivier, G.A. 1809. *Travels in the Ottoman Empire, Egypt and Persia.* 2 vols. London.

Olsen, S.L. 1984. *Analytical Approaches to the Manufacture and Use of Bone Artifacts in Prehistory.* Doctoral thesis, University of London.

Olszewski, D.I. 1984. *The Early Occupation at Tell Abu Hureyra in the Context of the Late Epipaleolithic of the Levant.* Doctoral dissertation, University of Arizona, Tucson. Ann Arbor: University Microfilms.

Olszewski, D.I. 1986a. *The North Syrian Late Epipaleolithic: The Earliest Occupation at Tell Abu Hureyra in the Context of the Levantine Late Epipaleolithic.* Oxford: British Archaeological Reports International Series 309.

Olszewski, D.I. 1986b. A reassessment of average lunate length as a chronological marker. *Paléorient* 12, 1, 39–44.

Olszewski, D.I. 1988. The north Syrian Late Epipaleolithic and its relationship to the Natufian complex. *Levant* 20, 127–137.

Olszewski, D.I. 1993. Subsistence ecology in the Mediterranean forest: implications for the origins of cultivation in the Epipaleolithic southern Levant. *American Anthropologist* 95, 2, 420–435.

Olszewski, D.I., and Barton, C.M. 1990. A note on biases in early excavations at Mugharet el-Wad and Nahal Oren. *Levant* 22, 43–46.

Osgood, C. 1936. *Contributions to the Ethnography of the Kutchin.* Yale University Publications in Anthropology 14.

Özbek, M. 1989. Son buluntularin isiginda Çayönü Neolitik insanlari. *Arkeometri Sonuçlari Toplantisi* 5, 161–172.

Palgrave, W.G. 1865. *Narrative of a Years Journey Through Central and Eastern Arabia.* London: Macmillan.

Pabot, H. 1957. *Rapport au Gouvernement de Syrie sur l'Ecologie Végétale et ses Applications.* FAO/57/7/4125. Rome: United Nations Food and Agriculture Organization.

Parr, P., Zarins, J., Ibrahim, M., Waechter, J., Garrard, A., Clarke, C., Bidmead, M., and al-Badr, H. 1978. Preliminary report on the second phase of the Northern Province survey 1397/1977. *ATLAL* 2, 29–50.

Parsons, A. 1808. *Travels in Asia and Africa, etc.* London: Longman, Hurst, Rees, and Orme.

Passemard, E. 1926. Les terraces alluviales de l'Euphrate et les industries qu'elles contiennent. *Comptes rendus hebdomadaires des séances de l'Academie des Sciences* 183, juillet-décembre, 365–368.

Payne, S. 1983. The animal bones from the 1974 excavations at Douara Cave. In Paleolithic Site of Douara Cave and Paleogeography of Palmyra Basin in Syria, Part III: Animal bones and further analysis of archeological materials. *The University Museum, The University of Tokyo, Bulletin* 21, 1–108.

Peña-Chocarro, L. 1996. In-situ conservation of hulled wheats. In *Hulled Wheats*, ed. S. Paulos, K. Hammer, and J. Heller. Proceedings of the First International Workshop on Hulled Wheats, 21–22 July 1995, Castelvecchiopascoli, Italy. Rome: International Plant Genetic Resources Institute. Pp. 129–146.

Perkins, D. 1966. The fauna from Madamagh and Beidha. In Five seasons at the Pre-Pottery Neolithic village of Beidha in Jordan, by D. Kirkbride. *Palestine Exploration Quarterly*, 66–67.

Perrot, J. 1966. Le gisement natoufien de Mallaha (Eynan), Israël. *L'Anthropologie* 70, 437–484.

Perrot, J. 1968. La préhistoire palestinienne. In *Supplément au Dictionnaire de la Bible* 8, ed. Letouzey and Ané. Paris. Cols. 286–446.

Perrot, J. 1974. Mallaha (Eynan), 1975. *Paléorient* 2, 2, 485–486.

Perrot, J., and Ladiray, D. 1988. Les sépultures. In *Les Hommes de Mallaha (Eynan) Israël*, ed. J. Perrot. Mémoires et Travaux du Centre de Recherche Français du Jérusalem 7. Paris: Association Paléorient.

Pervès, M. 1946–1948. La préhistoire de la Syrie et du Liban. *Syria* 25, 109–129.

Peters, J.P. 1897. *Nippur, or Explorations and Adventures on the Euphrates*, 2. New York: Putnam.

Petruso, K.M., and Wickens, J.M. 1994. The acorn in aboriginal subsistence in Eastern North America: a report on miscellaneous experiments. In *Experiments and Observations on Aboriginal Wild Plant Food Utilization in Eastern North America*, ed. P. Munson. Indianapolis: Indiana Historical Society. Pp. 360–378.

Phillips, J.L., and Mintz, E. 1977. The Mushabian. In *Prehistoric Investigations in Gebel Maghara, Northern Sinai*. *Qedem* 7. Jerusalem: Institute of Archaeology Press. Pp. 149–183.

Pichon, J. 1987. L'avifaune de Mallaha. In *La Faune du Gisement Natoufien de Mallaha (Eynan) Israël*, by J. Bouchud. Mémoires et Travaux du Centre de Recherche Français du Jérusalem 4. Paris: Association Paléorient. Pp. 115–150.

Pichon, J. 1991. Les oiseaux au Natoufien, avifaune et sédentarité. In *The Natufian Culture in the Levant*, ed. O. Bar-Yosef and F.R. Valla. Ann Arbor: International Monographs in Prehistory. Pp. 371–380.

Pierpoint Johnson, C. 1862. *The Useful Plants of Great Britain: A Treatise*. London: William Kent.

Plaisted, B. 1929. Narrative of a Journey from Busserah to Aleppo in 1750. In Journals of Four Travellers Aleppo-Basra, 1745–*1751*, ed. D. Carruthers. *Hakluyt Society*, II, 63, 49–129.

Plumb, J.H. 1965. *England in the Eighteenth Century (1714–1815)*. Harmondsworth: Penguin.

Poidebard, A. 1934. *La Trace du Rome dans le Désert du Syrie*. Paris: Geuthner.

Polunin, O., and Huxley, A. 1967. *Flowers of the Mediterranean*. London: Chatto and Windus.

Polunin, O., and Walters, M. 1985. *A Guide to the Vegetation of Britain and Europe*. Oxford: Oxford University Press.

Ponafidine, P. 1911. *Life in the Moslem East*. London: Hodder and Stoughton.

Porter, J.L. 1855. *Five Years in Damascus Including an Account of the History, Topography and Antiquities of that City; with Travels and Researches in Palmyra, Lebanon and the Hauran*. 2 vols. London: Murray.

Prummel, W., and Frisch, H.-J. 1986. A guide for the distinction of species, sex and body size in bones of sheep and goat. *Journal of Archaeological Science* 13, 567–577.

Przchewalski, N. von. 1884. *Reisen in Tibet und am Oberen Lauf des Gelben Flusses, 1879–1880*. Jena: Hermann Costenoble.

Rau, C. 1884. *Prehistoric Fishing in Europe and North America*. Smithsonian Contributions to Knowledge 509. Washington, D.C.: Smithsonian Institution.

Redman, C.L. 1978. *The Rise of Civilization*. San Francisco: Freeman.

Rees, L.W.B. 1929. The Transjordan Desert. *Antiquity* 3, 389–407.

Reifenberg, A. 1952. The soils of Syria and the Lebanon. *Journal of Soil Science* 3, 1, 68–88.

Reining, C.C. 1970. Zande subsistence and food production. In *African Food Production Systems*, ed. P.F.M. McLoughlin. Baltimore: Johns Hopkins Press. Pp. 125–163.

Renfrew, C., Dixon, J.E., and Cann, J.R. 1966. Obsidian and early cultural contact in the Near East. *Proceedings of the Prehistoric Society* 32, 30–72.

Renfrew, J.M. 1973. *Palaeoethnobotany*. London: Methuen.

Richards, A. 1939. *Land, Labour and Diet in Northern Rhodesia*. London: Oxford University Press.

Rihaoui, A.K. 1965. Etude préliminaire sur la sauvegards des monuments dans la région du barrage de l'Euphrate. *Les Annales Archéologique de Syrie* 15, 1, 99–111.

Rindos, D. 1984. *The Origins of Agriculture*. Orlando: Academic Press.

Rogers, D.J. 1980. *Edible, Medicinal, Useful and Poisonous Wild Plants of the Northern Great Plains, South Dakota Region*. Sioux Falls: Augustana College.

Rollefson, G.O. 1983. Ritual and ceremony at Neolithic Ain Ghazal (Jordan). *Paléorient* 9, 2, 29–38.

Rollefson, G.O., and Simmons, A.H. 1988. The Neolithic settlement at 'Ain Ghazal. In *The Prehistory of Jordan*, ed. A.N. Garrard and H.G. Gebel. British Archaeological Reports International Series 396. 2 vols. Pp. 393–430.

Roodenberg, J.J. 1979–1980. Sondage des niveaux néolithiques de Tell es Sinn, Syrie. *Anatolica* 7, 21–33.

Rosenberg, M. 1994. Hallan Çemi Tepesi: some further observations concerning stratigraphy and material culture. *Anatolica* 20, 121–140.

Rowley-Conwy, P. 1982–1983. A new sample of carbonized grain from Voldtofte (Bronzealderkorn fra Voldtofte). *Kuml* 1982–1983, 139–152.

Russell, A. 1756. *The Natural History of Aleppo and Parts Adjacent*. London: Millar.

Russell, K.W. 1988. *After Eden: The Behavioural Ecology of Early Food Production in the Near East and North Africa*. Oxford: British Archaeological Reports International Series 391.

Rust, A. 1950. *Die Höhlenfunde von Jabrud (Syrien)*. Neumünster: Karl Wachholtz.

Sage, R.F. 1995. Was low atmospheric CO_2 during the Pleistocene a limiting factor for the origin of agriculture? *Global Change Biology* 1, 93–106.

Sankary, M.N. 1977. *Ecology, Flora and Range Management of Arid and Very Arid Zones of Syria: Conservation and Management*. Aleppo: University of Aleppo.

Sankary, M.N. 1982. *Potential Natural Vegetation Map in the Semi-arid, Arid and Very Arid Areas in Syria*. Aleppo: University of Aleppo.

Sanlaville, P., ed. 1985. *Holocene Settlement in North Syria*. Oxford: British Archaeological Reports International Series 238.

Satterthwaite, L.D. 1986. Aboriginal Australian net hunting. *Mankind* 16, 1, 31–48.

Schaeffer, C.F.A. 1962. Les fondements préhistoriques d'Ugarit. In *Ugaritica* IV, by C.F.A. Schaeffer. Mission de Ras Shamra 15. Paris: Imprimerie Nationale. Pp. 151–250.

Scheuer, J.L., Musgrave, J.H., and Evans, S.P. 1980. The estimation of late fetal and perinatal age from limb bone length by linear and logarithmic regression. *Annals of Human Biology* 7, 257–265.

Schirmer, W. 1990. Some aspects of building at the 'aceramic-neolithic' settlement of Çayönü Tepesi. *World Archaeology* 21, 363–387.

Schour, I., and Massler, M. 1941. The development of the human dentition. *Journal of the American Dental Association* 28, 1153–1160.

Schwantes, G. 1939. *Die Vorgeschichte Schleswig-Holsteins (Stein und Bronzezeit)* 1. Neumünster: Karl Wachholz.

Schweingrüber, F. 1990. *Anatomy of European Woods*. Berne: Haupt.

Sease, C. 1987. *A Conservation Manual for the Field Archaeologist*. Archaeological Research Tools 4. Los Angeles: Institute of Archaeology, University of California, Los Angeles.

Seeley, M.-A. 1975. Thermoluminescent dating in its application to archaeology: a review. *Journal of Archaeological Science* 2, 17–43.

Shackleton, N.J., and Opdyke, N.D. 1973. Oxygen isotope and palaeomagnetic stratigraphy of Equatorial Pacific core V28-238: oxygen isotope temperature and ice volumes on a 10^5 and 10^6 year scale. *Quaternary Research* 3, 39–55.

Shackleton, N.J., and Opdyke, N.D. 1976. Oxygen-isotope and paleomagnetic stratigraphy of Pacific core V28–239. Late Pliocene to latest Pleistocene. In *Investigations of Late Quaternary Paleoceanography and Paleoclimatology*, ed. R.M. Cline and J.D. Hays. Washington, D.C.: Geological Society of America. Pp. 449–464.

Sheibe, A. 1934. Die Verbreitung von Unkrautsroggen und Taumellolch in Anatolien (mit Benerkungen zun Roggen-abstammungsproblem). *Angewandte Botanik* 17, 1–22.

Shipek, F.C. 1989. An example of intensive plant husbandry: the Kumeyaay of southern California. In *Foraging and Farming*, ed. D.R. Harris and G.C. Hillman. London: Unwin Hyman. Pp. 159–170.

Simms, S. 1987. *Behavioural Ecology and Hunter-Gatherer Foraging: An Example from the Great Basin*. Oxford: British Archaeological Reports International Series 381.

Simpson, G.G., and Roe, A. 1939. *Quantitative Zoology*. New York: McGraw-Hill.

Skinner, T. 1836. *Adventures During a Journey Overland to India*. 2 vols. London: Bentley.

Smith, M.A. 1989. Seed gathering in Australia: current evidence from seed grinders on the antiquity of the ethnohistorical pattern of exploitation. In *Foraging and Farming: The Evolution of Plant Exploitation*, ed. D.R. Harris and G.C. Hillman. London: Unwin and Hyman. Pp. 302–317.

Smith, P., Bar-Yosef, O., and Sillen, A. 1984. Archaeological and skeletal evidence for dietary change during the late Pleistocene/early Holocene in the Levant. In *Paleopathology at the Origins of Agriculture*, ed. M.N. Cohen and G.J. Armelagos. Orlando: Academic Press. Pp. 101–136.

Smith, P.E.L., and Young, T.C., Jr. 1972. The evolution of early agriculture and culture in Greater Mesopotamia: a trial model. In *Population Growth: Anthropological Implications*, ed. B. Spooner. Cambridge, Mass.: MIT Press. Pp. 1–59.

Smith, P.E.L., and Young, T.C., Jr. 1983. The force of numbers: population pressure in the central western Zagros 12,000–4500 B.C. In *The Hilly Flanks and Beyond*, ed. T.C. Young, Jr., P.E.L. Smith, and P. Mortensen. Studies in Ancient Oriental Civilization 36. Chicago: University of Chicago Press. Pp. 141–161.

Speth, J.D., and Spielmann, K.A. 1983. Energy source, protein metabolism, and hunter-gatherer subsistence strategies. *Journal of Anthropological Archaeology* 2, 1–31.

Stahl, A.B. 1984. Hominid dietary selection before fire. *Current Anthropology* 25, 151–168.

Stahl, A.B. 1989. Plant food processing: implications for dietary quality. In *Foraging and Farming: The Evolution of Plant Exploitation*, ed. D.R. Harris and G.C. Hillman. London: Unwin and Hyman. Pp. 171–194.

Stekelis, M., and Yizraely, T. 1963. Excavations at Nahal Oren—preliminary report. *Israel Exploration Journal* 13, 1–12.

Steward, J.H. 1933. Ethnography of the Owens Valley Paiute. *University of California Publications in American Archaeology and Ethnology* 33, 233–350.

Steward, J.H. 1938. Basin-plateau aboriginal sociopolitical groups. *Bulletin of the Bureau of American Ethnology* 120, 1–346.

Steward, J.H. 1941. Culture element distributions: XIII Nevada Shoshoni. *Anthropological Records, University of California* 4, 209–359.

Stordeur, D. 1979. Quelques remarques préliminaires sur l'industrie de l'os du Proche-Orient du Xème au VIème millénaire. In *L'Industrie en Os et Bois de Cervidé durant le Néolithique et l'Age des Metaux*, ed. H. Camps-Fabrer. Paris: Centre National de la Recherche Scientifique. Pp. 37–46.

Stordeur, D. 1982. L'industrie osseuse de la Damascène du VIIIe au VIe millénaire. In *L'Industrie en Os et Bois de Cervidé durant le Néolithique et l'Age des Metaux* 2, ed. H. Camps-Fabrer. Paris: Centre National de la Recherche Scientifique. Pp. 9–25.

Strike, S.S. 1994. *Ethnobotany of the California Indians*, Vol. 2: *Aboriginal Uses of California's Indigenous Plants*. Champaign, Ill.: Koeltz.

Stuiver, M., ed. 1993. Calibration 1993. *Radiocarbon* 35, 1.

Stuiver, M., and Kra, R., eds. 1986. Proceedings of the12th International Radiocarbon Conference—Trondheim, Norway. *Radiocarbon* 28, 2B.

Stuiver, M., Kromer, B., Becker, B., and Ferguson, C.W. 1986. Radiocarbon age calibration back to 13,300 years BP and the ^{14}C age matching of the German oak and US bristlecone pine chronologies. *Radiocarbon* 28, 2B, 969–979.

Stuiver, M., and Pearson, G.W. 1986. High-precision calibration of the radiocarbon time scale, AD 1950–500 BC. *Radiocarbon* 28, 2B, 805–838.

Syrian Arab Republic, Central Bureau of Statistics. 1947–1997. *Statistical Abstract*. Damascus: Government Printing Press.

Szymczak, K. 1990. Human remains. In *Nemrik 9*, ed. S.K. Kozlowski. Warsaw: Wydawnictwa Uniwersytetu Warszawskiego. Pp. 55–57.

Tanaka, J. 1976. Subsistence ecology of the central Kalahari San. In *Kalahari Hunter-Gatherers: Studies of the !Kung San and Their Neighbors*, ed. R.B. Lee and I. DeVore. Cambridge, Mass.: Harvard University Press. Pp. 89–119.

Taylor, J. 1789. *Travels from England to India in the Year 1789, with Instructions for Travellers etc.* London.

Teixeira, P. 1604. *Travels of Pedro Teixeira*, trans. W.F. Sinclair. London: Hakluyt Society, Series II, 9.

Teonge, H. 1928. *The Diary of Henry Teonge*, ed. G.E. Mainwaring. London: Broadway Travellers Series.

Thomas, D.H. 1979. Complexity among Great Basin Shoshoneans: the world's least affluent hunter-gatherers? In *Affluent Foragers: Pacific Coasts East and West*, ed. S. Koyama and D.H. Thomas. Senri Ethnological Studies 9. Osaka: National Museum of Ethnology. Pp. 19–52.

Thomas, D.H. 1984. Three generations of archaeology at Hidden Cave, Nevada. *Archaeology* 37, 40–47.

Thuesen, I. 1988. The pre- and protohistoric periods. *Hama Fouilles et Recherches 1931–1938* I. Nationalmuseets Skrifter, Større Beretninger XI. Copenhagen: Nationalmuseet.

Thunell, R.C. 1979. Eastern Mediterranean Sea during the last glacial maximum: an 18,000 years B.P., reconstruction. *Quaternary Research* 11, 353–372.

Thureau-Dangin, F., and Dunand, M. 1936. *Til-Barsib*. Haut-commissariat de la République Française en Syrie et au Liban, Service des Antiquités. Bibliothèque archéologique et historique 23. Paris: Geuthner.

Tindale, N.B. 1977. Adaptive significance of the grass-seed culture of Australia. In *Stone Tools as Cultural Markers*, ed. R.V.S. Wright. Canberra: Australian Institute of Aboriginal Studies. Pp. 345–349.

Tixier, J. 1974. Poinçon decoré du Paléolithique Supérieur à Ksar ʿAqil (Liban). *Paléorient* 2, 187–192.

Tristram, H.B. 1889. *The Natural History of the Bible*. London: Society for Promoting Christian Knowledge.

Trotter, M., and Gleser, G.C. 1952. Estimation of stature from long-bones of American Whites and Negroes. *American Journal of Physical Anthropology* 10, 463–514.

Tsapluyk, O.E. 1972. Growth and seasonal dynamics of sexual activity in *Gazella subgutturosa* Guld (in Russian). *Izv. Akad. Nauk. Kaz. SSR*, Biological Series 3, 39–46.

Turnbull, P.F. 1975. The mammalian fauna of Warwasi Rock Shelter, West-central Iran. *Fieldiana Geology* 33, 8, 141–155.

Turnbull, P.F., and Reed, C.A. 1974. Fauna from the terminal Pleistocene of Palegawra Cave, a Zarzian occupation site in northeastern Iraq. *Fieldiana Anthropology*, 63, 3, 81–146.

Turner, C. 1945. A note on enamel pearls. *British Dental Journal* 78, 39.

Uerpmann, H.-P. 1978. Metrical analysis of faunal remains from the Middle East. In *Approaches to Faunal Analysis in the Near East*, ed. R.H. Meadow and M.A. Zeder. Cambridge, Mass.: Peabody Museum, Harvard University. Pp. 41–45.

Uerpmann, H.-P. 1979. *Probleme der Neolithisierung des Mittelmeerraums*. Beihefte zum Tübinger Atlas des Vorderen Orients, Reihe B, 28. Weisbaden: Reichert.

Uerpmann, H.-P. 1987. *The Ancient Distribution of Ungulate Mammals in the Near East*. Beihefte zum Tübinger Atlas des Vorderen Orients, Reihe A, 27. Weisbaden: Reichert.

Uerpmann, H.-P, and Frey, W. 1981. Die Umgebung von Gar-e Kamarband (Belt Cave) und Gar-e ʿAli Tappe (Beh-Sahr, Mazandaran, N-Iran) heute und im Spätpleistozän. In *Beitrage zur Umweltgeschichte des Vorderen Orients*, by W. Frey and H.-P. Uerpmann. Beihefte Zum Tübinger Atlas Des Vorderen Orients,

Reihe A (Naturwissenschaften) 8. Weisbaden: Reichert.

UNESCO-FAO. 1969. *Vegetation Map of the Mediterranean Zone*. Arid Zone Research 30. Paris: UNESCO.

Upton, R.D. 1881. *Gleanings from the Desert of Arabia*. London: Kegan Paul.

U.S. Department of Commerce. 1966. *World Weather Records 1951–1960*, Vol. 2: *Europe*. Washington, D.C.: U.S. Department of Commerce.

Valla, F.R. 1975a. *Le Natoufien. Une culture Préhistorique en Palestine*. Cahiers de la Revue Biblique 15. Paris: Gabalda.

Valla, F.R. 1975b. Note sur l'Industrie lithique de Mallaha ('Eynan). *Israel Exploration Journal* 25, 1, 1–7.

Valla, F.R. 1975–1977. La sépulture H.104 de Mallaha (Eynan) et le problème de la domestication du chien en Palestine. *Paléorient* 3, 287–292.

Valla, F.R. 1981a. Les établissements natoufiens dans le nord d'Israël. In *Préhistoire du Levant*, ed. J. Cauvin and P. Sanlaville. Actes du Colloque International 598. Paris: Centre National de la Recherche Scientifique. Pp. 409–419.

Valla, F.R. 1981b. Les industries de silex de Nahal Oren et les stades du natoufien. *Union Internacional de Ciencias Prehistoricas y Protohistoricas X Congreso Comision V: Terminología de la Prehistoria del Cercano Oriente*. Mexico City: UNESCO. Pp. 71–100.

Valla, F.R. 1984. *Les Industries des Silex de Mallaha (Eynan) et du Natoufien dans le Levant*. Memoires et Travaux du Centre de Recherche Française de Jérusalem 3. Paris: Association Paléorient.

Valla, F.R., Bar-Yosef, O., Smith, P., Tchernov, E., and Desse, J. 1986. Un nouveau sondage sur la terrasse d'El-Ouad, Israel. *Paléorient* 12, 1, 21–38.

Vaufrey, R. 1951. Etude Paléontologique. In *Le Paléolithique et le Mésolithique du Désert de Judée*, by R. Neuville. Archives de l'Institut de Paléontologie Humaine, Mémoire 24. Paris. Pp. 198–217.

Vaux, R. de, O.P. 1966. Palestine during the Neolithic and Chalcolithic periods. *Cambridge Ancient History* 1, revised ed., fascicle 47. Cambridge: Cambridge University Press.

Vavilov, N.I. 1951. *The Origin, Variation, Immunity and Breeding of Cultivated Plants*. New York: Chronica Botanica.

Vavilov, N.I., and Bukinich, D.D. 1929. *Agricultural Afghanistan* (in Russian). Leningrad: Instituta Prikladnoi Botaniki i Novykh Kultur.

Vernet, J.L., ed. 1992. Les charbons de bois, les anciens écosystèmes et le rôle de l'homme. *Bulletin Société Botanique Française* 139, 157–725.

Vesey-Fitzgerald. L.D.E.F. 1952. Wild life in Arabia. *Oryx* 1, 5, 232–235.

Walter, H. 1956. Das Problem der zentralanatolischen Steppe. *Naturwissenschaften* 43, 97–102.

Watkins, T., ed. 1995. Qermez Dere, Tell Afar: interim report no. 3. *Department of Archaeology Project Paper* 14. Edinburgh: University of Edinburgh.

Watkins, T., Baird, D., and Betts, A. 1989. Qermez Dere and the early aceramic Neolithic of N. Iraq. *Paléorient* 15, 1, 19–24.

Watson, P.J. 1979. *Archaeological Ethnography in Western Iran*. Viking Fund Publications in Anthropology 57. Tucson: University of Arizona Press.

Watson, P.J. 1983. Jarmo worked bone. In *Prehistoric Archaeology Along the Zagros Flanks*, ed. L.S. Braidwood, R.J. Braidwood, B. Howe, C.A. Reed, and P.J. Watson. Oriental Institute Publications 105. Chicago: Oriental Institute, University of Chicago. Pp. 347–367.

Webb, T. III. 1986. Is vegetation in equilibrium with climate? How to interpret Late Quaternary pollen data. *Vegetatio* 67, 75–91.

Webb, T. 1988. Glacial and Holocene vegetation history: eastern North America. In *Vegetation History*, ed. B. Huntley and T. Webb III. Dordrecht: Kluwer. Pp. 385–414.

Weiner, A.B. 1976. *Women of Value, Men of Renown*. Austin: University of Texas Press.

Wetterstrom, W. 1986. *Food, Diet and Population at Prehistoric Arroyo Hondo Pueblo, New Mexico*. Santa Fe: School of American Research, Archaeological Series, 6.

Wijmstra, T.A. 1969. Palynology of the first 30 metres of a 120 m deep section in northern Greece. *Acta Botanica Neerlandica* 18, 4, 511–527.

Wilkinson, T.J. 1978. Erosion and sedimentation along the Euphrates valley in northern Syria. In *The Environmental History of the Near and Middle East Since the Last Ice Age*, ed. W.C. Brice. London: Academic Press. Pp. 215–226.

Wilkinson, T.J., and Moore, A.M.T. 1978. A prehistoric site near Dibsi Faraj in Syria. *Levant* 10, 26–36.

Willcox, G.W. 1996. Evidence for domestic cereal exploitation and vegetation history from three early Neolithic Pre-Pottery sites on the Euphrates (Syria). *Vegetation History and Archaeobotany* 5, 143–155.

Wintle, A.G. 1973. Anomalous fading of thermoluminescence in mineral samples. *Nature* 245, 143–144.

Woillard, G.M., and Mook, W.G. 1982. Carbon-14 dates at Grande Pile: correlation of land and sea chronologies. *Science* 215, 159–161.

Wolf, A.P. 1974. Gods, ghosts, and ancestors. In *Religion and Ritual in Chinese Society*, ed. A.P. Wolf. Stanford: Stanford University Press. Pp. 131–182.

Wolfert, R. 1967. *Geologie von Syrien und dem Libanon*. Berlin: Borntraeger.

Woodburn, J. 1968. An introduction to Hadza Ecology. In *Man the Hunter*, ed. R.B. Lee and I. DeVore. Chicago: Aldine. Pp. 49–55.

Woolley, C.L. 1921. *Carchemish*, part 2. London: British Museum.

Woolley, C.L., and Barnett, R.D. 1952. *Carchemish*, part 3. London: British Museum.

Wright, W. 1895. *An Account of Palmyra and Zenobia, with Travels and Adventures in the Bashan and the Desert*. New York: Nelson.

Wynne-Davis, R., and Scott, J.H.S. 1979. Inheritance and spondylolithesis. *Journal of Bone and Joint Surgery* 61B, 301–305.

Xenophon. 1972. *The Persian Expedition*. London: Penguin Classics.

Yakar, R., and Hershkovitz, I. 1988. The modelled skulls. *ʿAtiqot* 18, 59–63.
Yechieli, Y., Magaritz, M., Levy, Y., Weber, U., Kafri, U., Woelfli, W., and Bonani, G. 1993. Late Quaternary geological history of the Dead Sea area, Israel. *Quaternary Research* 39, 59–67.
Yellen, J.E., and Lee, R.B. 1976. The Dobe-/Du/da environment: background to a hunting and gathering way of life. In *Kalahari Hunter-Gatherers: Studies of the !Kung San and Their Neighbors*, ed. R.B. Lee and I. DeVore. Cambridge, Mass.: Harvard University Press. Pp. 28–46.
Yohe, R.M., II, Newman, M.E., and Schneider, J.S. 1991. Immunological identification of small-mammal proteins on aboriginal milling equipment. *American Antiquity* 56, 659–666.
Zeist, W. van. 1972. Palaeobotanical results of the 1970 season at Çayönü, Turkey. *Helinium* 12, 3–19.
Zeist, W. van, and Bakker-Heeres, J.A.H. 1979. Some economic and ecological aspects of the plant husbandry of Tell Aswad. *Paléorient* 5, 161–169.
Zeist, W. van, and Bakker-Heeres, J.A.H. 1982. Archaeobotanical studies in the Levant 1. Neolithic sites in the Damascus Basin: Aswad, Ghoraifé, Ramad. *Palaeohistoria* 24, 165–256.
Zeist, W. van, and Bakker-Heeres, J.A.H. 1984. Archaeobotanical studies in the Levant 3. Late-Palaeolithic Mureybit. *Palaeohistoria* 26, 171–199.
Zeist, W. van, and Bottema, S. 1977. Palynological investigations in Western Iran. *Palaeohistoria* 19, 19–85.
Zeist, W. van, and Bottema, S. 1982. Vegetational history of the eastern Mediterranean and the Near East during the last 20,000 years. In *Palaeoclimates, Palaeoenvironments and Human Communities in the Eastern Mediterranean Region in Later Prehistory*, ed. J.L. Bintliffe and W. van Zeist. Oxford: British Archaeological Reports International Series 133 (ii). 2 vols. Pp. 277–321.
Zeist, W. van, and Bottema, S. 1991. *Late Quaternary Vegetation of the Near East*. Beihefte zum Tübinger Atlas des Vorderen Orients, Reihe A (Naturwissenschafter) 18. Weisbaden: Reichert.
Zeist, W. van, Smith, P.E.L., Palfenier-Vegter, R.M., Suwijn, M., and Casparie, W.A. 1984. An archaeobotanical study of Ganj Dareh Tepe, Iran. *Palaeohistoria* 26, 201–224.
Zeist, W. van, and Woldring, H. 1978. A postglacial pollen diagram from Lake Van in East Anatolia. *Review of Palaeobotany and Palynology* 26, 249–276.
Zeist, W. van, and Woldring, H. 1980. Holocene vegetation and climate of northwestern Syria. *Palaeohistoria* 22, 111–125.
Zeist, W. van, Woldring, H., and Stapert, D. 1975. Late Quaternary vegetation and climate of southwestern Turkey. *Palaeohistoria* 17, 53–143.
Zeuner, F.E. 1955. The goats of early Jericho. *Palestine Exploration Quarterly*, 70–86.
Zeuner, F.E. 1963. *A History of Domesticated Animals*. London: Hutchinson.
Zeven, A.C., and Zhukovsky, P.M. 1975. *Dictionary of Cultivated Plants and Their Centres of Diversity*. Wageningen: PUDOC.
Zhukovskii, P.M. 1951. *Türkiyenin Ziraî Bünyesi*. Ankara: Türkiye Seker Fabrikalari A.S. (Turkish Translation of the Russian original: *Zemeledelcheskaya Tutsiya*. Leningrad, 1933).
Zimmerman, D.W. 1971. Thermoluminescent dating using fine grains from pottery. *Archaeometry* 13, 1, 29–52.
Zohary, D. 1989. Domestication of the Southwest Asian Neolithic crop assemblage of cereals, pulses and flax: the evidence from the living plants. In *Foraging and Farming*, ed. D.R. Harris and G.C. Hillman. London: Unwin Hyman. Pp. 358–373.
Zohary, D., and Hopf, M. 1993. *Domestication of Plants in the Old World*, 2nd ed. Oxford: Clarendon Press.
Zohary, M. 1973. *Geobotanical Foundations of the Middle East*. Stuttgart: Fischer.
Zohary, M. 1985. Vegetation of Israel and the Near East. In *Atlas of Israel*. Jerusalem: Survey of Israel, Ministry of Labour. Amsterdam: Elsevier. Section VI, I.

Index